GUIDE TO AMERICAN INDIAN DOCUMENTS IN THE CONGRESSIONAL SERIAL SET: 1817–1899

The Library of American Indian Affairs

From the Indian Claims Commission Series

Microfiche Publications

Decisions of the Indian Claims Commission
Expert Testimony before the Indian Claims Commission
Transcripts of Oral Expert Testimony before the Indian Claims Commission
Legal Briefs before the Indian Claims Commission
General Accounting Office Reports on Offsets
Legislative History of the Indian Claims Commission Act

Books

Index to the Decisions of the Indian Claims Commission
Index to the Expert Testimony before the Indian Claims Commission
Index to the Oral Expert Testimony, Briefs and GAO Reports (in preparation)

Other Publications

The Office of Indian Affairs, 1824-1880: Historical Sketches by Edward E. Hill

Indian Land Tenure: Bibliographical Essays and a Guide to the Literature by Imre Sutton

Guide to the Annual Reports of the Lake Mohonk Conference of Friends of the Indian; Introductions by Dr. Larry E. Burgess and Dr. Laurence Hauptman and Foreword by A. Keith Smiley

Guide to American Indian Documents in the Congressional Serial Set: 1817-1899, by Steven L. Johnson

Annual Reports of the Lake Mohonk Conference of Friends of the Indian (microfiche)

Indian Committee of the Society of Friends: 1696-1974 (microfilm)

The American Indian Oral History Collection (audio tape), Dr. Joseph H. Cash, General Editor

Editorial Advisory Board

Guide To American Indian Documents In The Congressional Serial Set: 1817 - 1899

Steven L. Johnson

A Project of the Institute
for the Development of Indian Law

Clearwater Publishing Company, Inc.
New York and Paris

This project was supported by contributions from the Lilly Endowment, Inc., the IBM Corporation and the Center for the History of the American Indian of the Newberry Library.

Library of Congress Cataloging in Publication Data

Johnson, Steven L 1949–
Guide to American Indian documents in the Congressional Serial Set, 1817-1899.

(The Library of American Indian affairs)
Includes bibliographical references and index.
1. Indians of North America–Legal status, laws, etc.–Indexes. 2. Indians of North America–Government relations–Indexes. I. Institute for the Development of Indian Law. II. Title. III. Series.
KF8201.A1J63 016.3405'2 75-45321
ISBN 0-88354-107-6

Clearwater Publishing Company, Inc.
75 Rockefeller Plaza, New York, N.Y. 10019
Manufactured in the United States of America

Contents

Foreword

A complete Serial Set, with its 14,000 volumes, stretches aisle after aisle and presents an imposing sight to the researcher. Lacking adequate indexes and organized in a complex system of mutually exclusive numerical classifications, the wealth of information it contains is often inaccessible. Many scholars have found that the only successful approach is to browse from volume to volume within a particular time period in hopes of finding wanted information. If the particular Serial Set is incomplete (and most seem to be), the browsing researcher is at a further disadvantage that is hard to overcome. Such a search, besides being time-consuming, can rarely claim to be exhaustive.

Despite these difficulties, historians and other students of the American Indian *have* used the Serial Set. The more available documents, such as the Annual Reports of the Commissioner of Indian Affairs and of the Secretary of War, have been much used, as have most of the major reports on Indian wars. But in addition to these there are thousands of other documents referring to American Indians which have been only infrequently used for Indian studies. References to the Serial Set have also frequently suffered from incomplete or incorrect citations, making them difficult or even impossible to find again. It was to remedy this problem–to make these inaccessible documents much more available to all students of American Indian affairs–that the present work was undertaken.

The title *Guide* is very appropriate. As the work progressed it became clear that no mechanical index could be prepared, and that even a page-by-page search through the Serial Set required a great deal of critical judgment to decide which documents to include. It is likely that someone else preparing this *Guide* would have omitted some of the documents listed here or added others. Johnson, however, has defined his subject area broadly and the result is a nearly comprehensive listing of documents in the Serial Set prior to 1900 relating to the American Indian.

It is of the greatest importance that the user understand that this *Guide* is intended as an aid to research in helping to locate potential sources of data. It is not intended as a comprehensive index to where material will be found on any particular tribe or subject. The greatest value of the *Guide* is not that it leads mechanically to *all* the material on any subject, but that it leads to thousands of the less immediately obvious documents on American Indians.

It is also important that the nature of the documents printed in the Serial Set be well understood. With regard to Indians, the documents deal primarily with Indian relations with the United States Government. Most deal with "Indian affairs" rather than with descriptions of Indians or Indian life. The primary relations of Indians to the federal government were legal and fiscal; the documents therefore relate mostly to the Indians' legal rights and to the cost to the government of Indian administration. The largest categories of documents are concerned with claims prosecuted against the government for losses caused by Indian depredations and for service in Indian wars.

Scanning the Chronological Section for any period of time is functionally equivalent to browsing through a portion of the Serial Set itself. For many users this will be the most effective method of using this book. For those looking for documents on specific tribes, events or regions, the Subject Index will provide a starting place. Either way, the reader with an understanding of the *Guide* will not only save time, but also will discover many documents in the Serial Set that otherwise might be overlooked. This volume is an important work because it opens up the Serial Set to Indians themselves and to lawyers, anthropologists, students, and general users. It will also be a valuable aid to professional historians.

Raymond J. DeMallie
Project Director
Institute for the Development of Indian Law

December, 1976
Bloomington, Indiana

Acknowledgements

This project was developed and supervised by Raymond J. DeMallie, Assistant Professor of Anthropology, Indiana University, and its completion has been due in large part to his continued assistance. It was Ray, in fact, who proposed the project to Vine Deloria, Jr. and the Institute for the Development of Indian Law. The support of Vine and the Institute is gratefully acknowledged.

Special thanks are due to Ronald R. Royce for preparing the Subject Index. I wish also to express my thanks to Jan L. Richardson, Alan Goldberg, Margaret A. Rhoades and Malcolm R. Peek for their time and help.

Finally, I wish to express my great appreciation to the Lilly Endowment, Inc., the IBM Corporation and the Center for the History of the American Indian of the Newberry Library, whose contributions to the Institute for the Development of Indian Law helped make this work possible.

Steven L. Johnson
Research Associate
Institute for the Development of Indian Law

December, 1975
Bloomington, Indiana

Acknowledgements

Introduction

THE GUIDE IN CONTEXT

Congressional Publications

The term "Congressional publications" is generally taken to mean anything published under the authority of the Congress as a whole, of either house, or of any committee of either house. Virtually all of these publications fall into one of four categories: (1) the debates of Congress; (2) bills and resolutions; (3) documents and reports; and (4) miscellaneous publications.

The published *debates* of Congress represent a chronicle of the proceedings on the floor of each house, though very often speeches and articles from other sources are incorporated into them by members of Congress. The debates have been published in the *Annals of Congress,* the *Register of Debates*, the *Congressional Globe* and the *Congressional Record.*

Bills and *resolutions* (i.e., formally proposed legislation) are printed by each house and can be found in the Library of Congress, the National Archives, the Office of the Clerk of the House of Representatives and the Office of the Secretary of State. In addition, some of these are also printed in the *Congressional Record*, in the journals of each house and in the Congressional Serial Set. Should a bill or resolution become law, it is then also printed in *Statutes at Large.*

Documents and *reports* are published in a series variously known as the "Congressional Set," "Serial Set" or "Congressional Serial Set." *Documents* printed in this series are received by Congress from a number of sources, though they come primarily from the various executive departments. *Reports* published in this collection are those received from committees of each house. These reports are most often concerned with proposed legislation or with the results of Congressional investigations.

This volume concerns itself only with *documents* and *reports* which have been published in the Congressional Serial Set. More specifically, it is confined to those documents and reports which were ordered to be printed by the 15th through the 55th Congresses, or during the period 1 December 1817 to 3 March 1899. The *Guide* thus deals with information (i.e., documents and reports) *received* by Congress, rather than with the legislative process or with the end products of that process (laws, resolutions, etc.).

It must be understood, therefore, that the *Guide* is concerned with only *one* of the major classes of Congressional publications. No attempt has been made to incorporate materials into this work which have been published outside of the Serial Set.

The Congressional Serial Set

As noted above, the Congressional Serial Set contains documents and reports received by Congress from executive departments, Congressional committees and various other sources. Beginning with the 15th Congress, documents and reports published in the Serial Set were organized into named series according to their original source and according to which house ordered the material printed. Originally there were only two series of publications:

House Documents (HD)
Senate Documents (SD)

All documents published during the 15th Congress (1817-1819) were in one or the other of these two series depending upon whether they were ordered printed by the House or Senate.

From the 16th Congress (1819) through the 29th Congress (1847) there were three series of documents:

Senate Documents (SD)
House Documents (HD)
House Reports (HR)

Under this system the Senate published reports and documents together, while the House separated documents from committee reports.

At the beginning of the 30th Congress (1847) a new classification system was created which remained in effect through the 53rd Congress (1895). This system was comprised of the following series:

Senate Executive Documents (SED)
Senate Miscellaneous Documents (SMD)
Senate Reports (SR)
House Executive Documents (HED)
House Miscellaneous Documents (HMD)
House Reports (HR)

Under this classification scheme executive documents consisted of all materials received from the executive departments of government, reports were materials received from Congressional committees, and miscellaneous documents were all other materials received by Congress and ordered to be printed.

The next change in series designations occurred at the beginning of the 54th Congress (1895). The new system was in effect through the 55th Congress (1899) and consisted of the following series:

Senate Documents (SD)
Senate Reports (SR)
House Documents (HD)
House Reports (HR)

During these Congresses, executive and miscellaneous documents were again bound together, while committee reports remained a separate series.

In addition to the series of publications mentioned above, House and Senate Journals were published along with the Serial Set, but they are not generally considered to be a part of it. For this reason the *Guide* does not deal with materials located in these Journals. Similarly, some volumes from the Court of Claims have been bound in the Serial Set, but they are considered to be no more than adjuncts to the House Reports.

Serial Numbers

During the last decade of the 19th century all volumes in the Congressional Set were arranged into one sequence according to date of publication (Congress and session) and according to which series of documents they contained. The volumes were then numbered consecutively. These numbers, applied to every volume in the Congressional Set, were called the "serial numbers," and the Congressional Set became alternatively known as the Serial Set and the Congressional Serial Set.

The existence of serial numbers greatly simplified use of the Congressional Set. Previously it had been necessary to know the Congress and session, document series, document number and volume number in order to find a document. Using the serial number system to locate a particular document one need know only the Serial Set number and document number. (Since some government depositories have not applied serial numbers to their Sets, the *Guide* employs both systems of reference in the Chronological Section.)

Other Catalogs and Indexes Concerning Serial Set Publications

Most volumes published in the Serial Set–beginning with the 15th and continuing through the 53rd Congresses–contain an index to the documents in that volume. These volume indexes are often little more than tables of contents (this is particularly true for volumes of Senate and House Reports) and they are often compiled only from information contained in the titles of documents. Consequently, they do not always reveal a document's relevance to Indian affairs.

With the 54th Congress the volume indexes were replaced by an annual *Document Index*, which lists all documents and reports printed during a given session. This *Document Index* is published at the end of each Congressional session as a volume of the Serial Set.

In addition, several general catalogs and indexes have been published which are concerned with a much wider range of documents. These purport to list and index all government publications for particular time periods, though they tend to be primarily compilations of Congressional publications.

First among these is Ben. Perley Poore's *A Descriptive Catalogue of the Government Publications of the United States, September 5, 1774-March 4, 1881* (Washington, DC: 1885). Entries in Poore's *Catalogue* are arranged chronologically and are accompanied by an alphabetical index. Unfortunately, the entries are indexed only acccording to information contained in their titles, and thus many documents concerned with Indian affairs have been overlooked. The volume also suffers from inaccuracies in both the index and document listings.

John G. Ames' *Comprehensive Index to the Publications of the United States Government, 1881-1893* (Washington, DC: 1905) is another general index which contains numerous entries from the Serial Set. Unlike Poore's *Catalogue*, the Ames *Index* does not have a chronological listing of documents.

Following the publication of Ames' *Index*, the government began printing a biennial *Document Catalog* in the Serial Set. This publication is similar to both Poore's *Catalogue* and Ames' *Index* in that it is not restricted to Congressional publications, but is concerned with all government publications. However, the *Document Catalog* is organized as an index and contains no listing of documents.

In addition to the volume indexes and subsequent annual indexes of Serial Set documents and the general catalogs and indexes, there exist various more specialized indexes concerned with particular classes of documents in the Serial Set. These include indexes to the Annual Reports of the Bureau of American Ethnology, the Records of the War of the Rebellion, the publications of the Smithsonian Institution, the Annual Reports of the American Historical Association, etc.

USE OF THE GUIDE

The Chronological Section

The 10,649 documents on Indian affairs which were located in the Serial Set volumes from 1817 through 1899 are listed sequentially in the Chronological Section. Each entry in the listing consists of: (1) document title and date, (2) document citation and (3) description of the contents of the document.

Document titles in the listing generally repeat the original printed titles found in the Serial Set, however in many cases titles have either been rewritten to better reflect the contents of the documents or they have been abbreviated to a more convenient length.

Each document title is followed either by the date the document was ordered to be printed by Congress or the date of the covering or transmittal letter printed in the document itself. In some cases a document was actually printed long after the Congressional session in which it was ordered printed. In such cases the document has been listed following all of the documents from the Congress and session in which it was to have appeared, and "no date" is put in parentheses following the title.

The document citations used in the listing provide, in abbreviated form, *all* the information required to find a particular document in the Serial Set. A standardized format is used that gives: (1) the document series, (2) the document number, (3) the Congress and session, (4) the volume in which the document is printed, (5) the number of pages in the document and (6) the serial number of the volume in which the document is to be found. For example, a typical entry reads:

> HED 50, 45-2, v1, 2p. [2111]

This, in non-abbreviated form, is to be read:

> House Executive Document number 50, 45th Congress, 2nd session, volume 1, 2 pages. Serial Set volume number 2111.

Each entry in the listing includes a brief abstract of the particular document. These descriptions vary in length from a single word to ten lines or more, depending on the nature of the document. The abstracts are not intended to be exhaustive, only to specify the tribes mentioned and the main subjects covered. As a general rule, abstracts of private claims or petitions give little more than the name of the Indian tribe involved, whereas reports from Congressional committees tend to have longer abstracts.

All of the documents have been kept in chronological order and are numbered sequentially within each year. Documents in the listing can therefore be referred to by the year and the sequential number. For example, the first document listed for 1842 is referred to as 1842:1. These numbers have been used in the Subject Index and Appendix II.

The Subject Index

The Subject Index was prepared from the titles and abstracts of documents as they appear in the Chronological Section. Thus it is an index to the listings and not to the contents of the documents.

Furthermore, the index is organized primarily by tribal headings, with items indexed only residually under geographical and topical designations. For example document 1830:7, titled and abstracted "Report on Indian Depredations–Creek Indians; Georgia," would be entered in the index under "CREEK INDIANS–depredations and hostilities" only. Normally no entries would be made in the index under other possible headings such as "Georgia" or "depredations." A similar document described as "Report on Indian Depredations–Georgia" would be entered under "GEORGIA–depredations and hostilities" because no specific tribe is mentioned in the listing. Only if a document were described merely as "Report on Indian Depredations" would it be entered under the heading "DEPREDATIONS AND HOSTILITIES."

This means that the reader interested in a particular Indian group will find it rather easy to locate specifically relevant documents in the Chronological Section. For example, all of the documents whose titles or abstracts mention the Creek Indians can be found in the index under "CREEK INDIANS." To aid the reader in locating documents on specific subjects, subheadings (e.g. "lands," "populations," "reservations") have been provided where appropriate. The reader should keep in mind, however, that much material concerning particular tribes is also likely to be found in documents of a very general or comprehensive nature, as in reports of agencies, commissions, expeditions and so forth. These documents may be located by referring to the appropriate major headings. Also relevant would be documents entered under geographical headings for areas (regions, states, reservations, etc.) occupied by the group, or entered under other Indian groups, individuals, military posts, or whatever, prominent in the history of the group.

The reader interested in the history of a particular geographical area or in a specific topic will not be able to proceed quite so directly. If one is interested, for example, in some aspect of Indian affairs in Georgia, one must look not only under "GEORGIA," but also under the headings for each of the tribal groups known to have lived in Georgia. Similarly, if one is interested in a particular topic, such as the conduct of Indian removal, one must look under the appropriate tribal and geographical headings, as well as under "REMOVAL," and also under related headings, e.g. "APPROPRIATIONS," or "WAR, SECRETARY OF–Annual Reports." Here, the subheadings provided should prove useful in leading the reader to appropriate items.

What should be kept in mind is that in order to keep the index to a useful length, items have been indexed under the most specific headings appropriate, with preference given to tribal headings over geographical headings and to geographical areas over topics. As the reader uses the index he will discover priorities for entries among subheadings as well. These further serve to reduce the number of entries so as to keep the index within useful and practical limits. As the reader will also discover, however, certain topics, considered to be of special interest to students of Indian affairs, have been cross-indexed so as to be especially accessible.

Appendixes

Three appendixes have been provided following the Subject Index. The first lists those documents on Indian Affairs from the period 1817-1881 which were included in Poore's *Catalogue* but which were not published in the Serial Set. The second appendix is divided into two sections. The first lists documents on Indian Affairs that were published in both the *American State Papers* and the Serial Set, while the second lists those documents which were published only in *American State Papers.* Items published only in the Serial Set are of course listed in this volume under the appropriate years.

The third appendix provides a brief guide to the Records of the War of the Rebellion, which were printed in the Serial Set during the years 1882 to 1899. Although many documents in these volumes pertain to Indian Affairs, the volumes have not been examined for, nor have records from them been included in, the present volume, since a guide to these volumes already exists. The appendix merely provides cross-references from the Rebellion Records series to the Serial Set designations.

None of the documents referred to in any of the three apendixes is indexed in the Subject Index, with the exception of those items listed in part 1 of Appendix II. Fuller descriptions of the appendixes are provided in that section of the book.

NOTE: The spellings of tribal names in the *Chronological Section* conform to the spellings used in the documents cited, and some variations will therefore be encountered. In the *Subject Index* the most commonly accepted spellings have been used.

ABBREVIATIONS

ASPIA	American State Papers on Indian Affairs
BIA	Bureau of Indian Affairs
C	Congress
Capt.	Captain
CIA	Commissioner of Indian Affairs
co.	company
Col.	Colonel
comm.	committee
com'r	commissioner
dept.	department
Gen.	General
HD	House Document
HED	House Executive Document
HMD	House Miscellaneous Document
HR	House Report
HRCC	House Report: court of claims
L-C	Letter on the claim
Legis.	Legislature
L-M	Letter on the Memorial
Maj.	Major
Mem.	Memorial
no.	number
p.	page(s)
Pres.	President
pt.	part
R-C	Report on the claim
Rep.	Representative
Resol.	Resolution
R-M	Report on the memorial
R-P	Report on the petition
SD	Senate Document
Sec.	Secretary
SED	Senate Executive Document
Sen.	Senator
Sess.	Session
SMD	Senate Miscellaneous Document
SR	Senate Report
Suppl.	Supplement
U.S.	United States
vol.	volume

Chronological Section

1817

1. Inaugural Message; Pres. Monroe. 3 Mar.
   Senate Journal, 15-1, pp. 9-20 [1]
   Relations with the Indians.
2. Annual Message to Congress; Pres. Monroe. 2 Dec.
   SD 1, 15-1, v1, 11p. [2] *or* HD 1, 15-1, v1, 11p. [5]
   Indian affairs.
3. Resol. of Sen. Campbell. 12 Dec.
   SD 10, 15-1, v1, 1p. [2]
   Land in Tennessee to which Indian claim has not been extinguished.
4. Resol. of Sen. Morrow. 16 Dec.
   SD 15, 15-1, v1, 1p. [2]
   On lands in the Virginia military tract to which Indian title has not been extinguished.
5. Report Giving Estimates of Appropriations. 16 Dec.
   HD 13, 15-1, v2, 57p. [6]
   For the year 1818.
6. Mem. of the Mississippi Convention. 17 Dec.
   HD 15, 15-1, v2, 8p. [6]
   Creek, Choctaw, and Chickasaw Indian land titles.
7. Letter on Appropriations for Military Service. 18 Dec.
   HD 50, 15-1, v3, 8p. [7]
   Observations on each item of appropriation.
8. R-C of Georgia Militia. 22 Dec.
   HD 16, 15-1, v2, 3p. [6]
   Creek Indian hostilities; 1793-1794.
9. Mem. of the Tennessee Legis. 29 Dec.
   SD 28, 15-1, v1, 6p. [2]
   Involving North Carolina, Tennessee, and the Cherokee Indians on title to land.
10. Petition of J. Cowan. 29 Dec.
    HD 140, 15-1, v6, 14p. [10]
    War with the Creek Indians; 1814-1815.
11. R-P of W. Edwards and J. Stubbs. 30 Dec.
    SD 31, 15-1, v1, 1p. [2]
    Surveys in Illinois; Indian land near the Illinois River.

1818

1. Report on Expenditures in the War Dept. 1 Jan.
   HD 32, 15-1, v2, 3p. [6]
   From 1 Oct. 1816 to 30 Sept. 1817.
2. R-C of Georgia Militia. 2 Jan.
   HD 27, 15-1, v2, 43p. [6]
   Reports of 14 Mar. 1800 and 4 Feb. 1813; Creek, Cherokee, and Chickasaw Indian wars of 1793-1794.
3. Resol. of Sen. Campbell. 7 Jan.
   SD 45, 15-1, v1, 1p. [2]
   On the expediency of having the nominations of Indian agents confirmed by the Senate.
4. Report on the Case of Col. Earle. 9 Jan.
   HD 43, 15-1, v3, 7p. [7]
   Special agent of the government to enlist the aid of southern Indians in defense of the U.S.
5. Resol. of Sen. Williams. 21 Jan.
   SD 69, 15-1, v1, 1p. [2]
   Seminole Indian war.
6. Report on Indian Affairs. 22 Jan.
   HD 59, 15-1, v3, 4p. [7]
   Indian trade; trading posts; foreign traders; missionary societies.
7. R-P of Maj. Austin. 23 Jan.
   HD 60, 15-1, v3, 4p. [7]
   Service against hostile Indians and their British allies; 1813.
8. R-P of A. Jackson et al. 25 Jan.
   HD 86, 15-1, v4, 36p. [8]
   Georgia; Indian hostilities.

9. Message Relating to the Subsistence of Troops. 28 Jan.
SD 87, 15-1, v1, 5p. [2]
Transmitting report of the Sec. of War showing the manner in which the troops engaged in the war with the Seminole Indians were subsisted.

10. Resol. of Sen. Campbell. 3 Feb.
SD 93, 15-1, v1, 1p. [2]
On establishing a law concerning salaries for Indian agents.

11. Resol. of Sen. Williams. 4 Feb.
SD 96, 15-1, v1, 1p. [2]
Requests list of Indian agents and pay from Pres.

12. Message on Surveys of Northern Mississippi. 13 Feb.
SD 117, 15-1, v1, 11p. [2]
Report from the Sec. of Treasury; Creek Indian village.

13. Resol. of Sen. Talbott. 3 Mar.
SD 123, 15-1, v1, 1p. [2]
On extinguishing Indian title to land in Kentucky.

14. Message on Contracts for Provisions. 11 Mar.
SD 136 (no. 2), 15-1, v2, 26p. [3]
To supply troops on the Georgia frontier; Creek Indian lands.

15. Resol. of Sen. Dickerson. 24 Mar.
SD 156, 15-1, v2, 1p. [3]
Services against British and Indian forces; 1813.

16. R-P of J. Loomis and J. Bassett. 24 Mar.
HD 172, 15-1, v7, 2p. [11]
Florida war.

17. Message on Seminole Indian War. 25 Mar.
HD 173, 15-1, v7, 29p. [11]
Transmits correspondence.

18. Message on Indian Affairs. 9 Apr.
SD 183, 15-1, v2, 8p. [3]
Report from the Sec. of War listing Indian agents, etc.

19. Letter on Additional Appropriations. 11 Apr.
HD 192, 15-1, v7, 5p. [11]
For treaties with the Cherokee, Creek, Illinois, Kickapoo, Pottawatomie, Wyandot, Delaware, Quapaw, Miami, and Chickasaw Indians.

20. Annual Message to Congress with Documents; Pres. Monroe. 17 Nov.
SD 1, 15-2, v1, 11p. [14] *or* HD 2, 15-2, v1, 167p. [17]
Indian affairs (House version includes documents).

21. Annual Report of the Sec. of the Treasury. 23 Nov.
HD 4, 15-2, v1, 39p. [17]
Indian expenses.

22. Report on Choctaw Indian Boundaries. 1 Dec.
HD 10, 15-2, v1, 3p. [17]
Confining said Indians to their present boundaries; prohibiting their settlement west of the Mississippi River.

23. Estimate of Appropriations. 1 Dec.
HD 12, 15-2, v1, 61p. [17]
For 1819; includes War Dept., etc.

24. Message on the Seminole Indian War. 2 Dec.
SD 35, 15-2, v1, 165p. [14] *or* HD 14, 15-2, v1, 165p. [17]
A full view of the manner in which the war was conducted; court-martial of Arbuthnot and Ambrister; etc.

25. Resol. of Sen. Lacock. 4 Dec.
SD 28, 15-2, v1, 1p. [14]
Refers message of the Pres. to a select com.

26. Report on Trade with the Indians. 5 Dec.
HD 25, 15-2, v1, 14p. [17]
Recommending the abolition of the existing Indian trade establishments of the U.S., and providing for the opening of trade between the Indians and individuals.

27. Resol. of Sen. Johnson. 7 Dec.
SD 33, 15-2, v1, 1p. [14]
On the Pres. taking possession of East Florida to protect U.S. citizens from Indian hostilities.

28. Report on the Military Peace Establishment. 11 Dec.
HD 36, 15-2, v2, 56p. [18]
Organization of the Army, etc.

29. Report on the Case of T. Carr et al. 14 Dec.
HD 31, 15-2, v2, 5p. [18]
Indian hostilities in Georgia.

30. Message on the Arrest of Capt. Wright. 14 Dec.
HD 34, 15-2, v2, 21p. [18]
Correspondence between the Governor of Georgia and Gen. Jackson on the arrest of Capt. Wright who was in command of a detachment of the Georgia militia that attacked Chehaw, a Creek Indian village.

31. R-C of H. Wakefield. 16 Dec.
HD 40, 15-2, v2, 1p. [18]
Captured in 1814 by Indians in service of the British.
32. Letter on Appropriations for 1819. 22 Dec.
HD 56, 15-2, v4, 10p. [20]
Indian expenses such as treaties, etc.
33. Petition of the Society of Friends. 23 Dec.
SD 47, 15-2, v1, 4p. [14]
For Indian education and farming (civilization).
34. Message on the Seminole Indian War. 28 Dec.
SD 88, 15-2, v2, 16p. [15]
Transmitting copies of the correspondence between U.S. and Spain relative to the Seminole war and the execution of Arbuthnot and Ambrister; Gen. Jackson on the subject of the destruction of Chehaw, a Creek Indian village, etc.
35. Message and Documents on Indian troubles in Florida. 28 Dec.
HD 65, 15-2, v4, 215p. [20]
Letter from J. Q. Adams, Sec. of State, to G. W. Erving, Minister to Spain and 72 other letters on said troubles.

1819

1. Message on Certain Correspondence. 4 Jan.
HD 68, 15-2, v4, 7p. [20]
Between the Governor of Georgia and Gen. Jackson on the arrest of Capt. Wright for leading an attack on Chehaw, a Creek Indian village.
2. Message on a Convention with Spain. 5 Jan.
HD 75, 15-2, v4, 16p. [20]
Includes information on the Seminole war in Florida.
3. Message on the Army. 11 Jan.
SD 58, 15-2, v1, 13p. [14]
Report on Sec. Calhoun.
4. Report on the Conduct of the War Against the Seminoles. 12 Jan.
HD 82, 15-2, v4, 4p. [20]
Gen. Jackson censured; the trial and execution of Arbuthnot and Ambrister disapproved.
5. Report on the Execution of Arbuthnot and Ambrister. 12 Jan.
HD 86, 15-2, v6, 12p. [22]
Gen. Jackson in the right; Creek Indian treaty of 1814.
6. Report on Roads and Canals. 14 Jan.
HD 87, 15-2, v6, 13p. [22]
Military transportation on the frontiers; Indian hostilities.
7. Report on the Civilization of Indian Tribes. 15 Jan.
HD 91, 15-2, v6, 3p. [22]
On improvement in the educational system, etc.
8. Letter on the Friendly Creek Indians. 16 Jan.
HD 98, 15-2, v6, 8p. [22]
On payment of claims under the treaty of 1814.
9. Documents on Expenses of the War Dept. 22 Jan.
SD 65, 15-2, v2, 92p. [15]
Expenses of the Seminole war.
10. Message on the Occupation of Amelia Island. 30 Jan.
HD 117, 15-2, v6, 17p. [22]
Supplies furnished hostile Indians by the Spaniards.
11. Letter on the Negro Fort in East Florida. 1 Feb.
HD 119, 15-2, v6, 21p. [22]
Creek Indian hostilities.
12. Letter on the Destruction of the Negro Fort in East Florida. 2 Feb.
HD 122, 15-2, v6, 26p. [22]
Destroyed in 1816; Seminole, Cherokee, and Creek Indians.
13. Letter on Treaties with Indian Tribes. 3 Feb.
SD 85, 15-2, v2, 3p. [15]
On appropriations to carry treaties into effect.
14. Message on Military Operations in Florida. 6 Feb.
HD 128, 15-2, v7, 6p. [23]
Letter from the Governor of Florida to Gen. Jackson.
15. Report on the Sale of Public Lands. 9 Feb.
SD 91, 15-2, v2, 92p. [15]
On altering laws for sale of lands; procedures to off-set the high cost of extinguishing Indian title to lands.
16. Statements on Sale of Public Lands. 16 Feb.
SD 95, 15-2, v2, 3p. [15]

On land under Indian title; land Indians can occupy.

17. Report on the Seminole War. 24 Feb.
SD 100, 15-2, v2, 50p. [15]
History of the war; Gen. Jackson censured; the trial of Arbuthnot and Ambrister.

18. Report on the Seminole War. 3 Mar.
SD 102, 15-2, v2, 5p. [15]
Additional testimony on the conduct of the war.

19. Annual Message to Congress with Documents; Pres. Monroe. 7 Dec.
SD 1, 16-1, v1, 96p. [26] *or* HD 2, 16-1, v1, 96p. [31]
Indian affairs; reports of Sec. of War, etc.

20. Resol. of the Missouri Legis. 8 Dec.
HD 4, 16-1, v1, 6p. [31]
Frontier defenses against Indian depredations, etc.

21. R-C of T. Carr et al. 14 Dec.
HR 2, 16-1, v1, 6p. [40]
Georgia land settlements; Indian hostilities.

22. Estimates of Appropriations. 23 Dec.
HD 13, 16-1, v2, 51p. [32]
For the year 1820.

23. Letter on Topographical Reports. 28 Dec.
HD 17, 16-1, v2, 10p. [32]
Includes a canal constructed between the Chicago and Desplaines Rivers by the French and Indians.

24. Appropriations of the War Dept. 28 Dec.
HD 19, 16-1, v2, 13p. [32]
For the year 1819.

1820

1. Report on the Expedition up the Missouri River. 3 Jan.
HR 24, 16-1, v1, 10p. [40]
Reasons for the expedition; Indian hostilities; British and Indian trade.

2. Letter on Expenditures of the War Dept. 4 Jan.
HD 31, 16-1, v2, 5p. [32]
From 1 Oct. 1818 to 30 Sept. 1819.

3. R-P of S. Dale. 10 Jan.
HR 36, 16-1, v1, 1p. [40]
Creek Indians; 1812; trading license.

4. On the Relief of C. Miller. 12 Jan.
HR 37, 16-1, v1, 2p. [40]
Taken prisoner by the Indians in Kentucky in 1783.

5. Report on the Expenditures of the Army. 13 Jan.
HD 53, 16-1, v3, 4p. [33]
Estimates for 1820.

6. Report on Indian Affairs. 15 Jan.
HD 46, 16-1, v3, 3p. [33]
General.

7. Report on the Transportation of Troops. 18 Jan.
HD 50, 16-1, v3, 5p. [33]
To the Mandan villages on the Missouri River.

8. Report on Unexpended Funds. 20 Jan.
HD 52, 16-1, v3, 13p. [33]
Funds for Cherokee and Delaware treaties; negotiations; Indian boundaries in Missouri Territory; etc.

9. R-P of J. Nichols. 26 Jan.
SD 35, 16-1, v1, 16p. [26]
Creek Indians; supplies.

10. Letter on Money Owed to Col. Johnson. 3 Feb.
HD 65, 16-1, v5, 11p. [35]
Expedition up the Missouri River to the Mandan villages; frontier protection and breaking up the British-Indian trade.

11. Statement of Receipts and Expenditures. 7 Feb.
HD 75, 16-1, v5, 23p. [35]
From the commencement of the government to 31 Dec. 1819; includes Indian Dept.

12. R-P of J. McGrew et al. 8 Feb.
HR 64, 16-1, v1, 1p. [40]
Mississippi Territory, 1793; land titles within Indian boundaries granted by the Spaniards.

13. Report on Indian Trade and Intercourse. 16 Feb.
SD 47, 16-1, v1, 9p. [26]
Present system of trade has retarded the civilization of Indians; it has proved injurious to them.

14. Accounts of the War Dept. 22 Feb.
HD 123, 16-1, v9, 91p. [39]
From 1 Oct. 1818 to 1 Oct. 1819.

15. R-P of R. Purdy. 23 Feb.
SD 58, 16-1, v1, 2p. [26]
Liquor sold in Indian country; Tennessee jurisdiction.

16. R-P of the Stockbridge Indians. 24 Feb.
HR 70, 16-1, v1, 12p. [40]
On land granted by the Miami Indians in Indiana to the Delaware, Mohican or Stockbridge, and Munsee Indians of New York; treaty of 1818 at St. Mary's; treaty of 1805 near Vincennes; treaty of 1809 at Fort Wayne; etc.

17. Report on Subsistence for the Army. 28 Feb.
HR 72, 16-1, v1, 95p. [40]
On troops raised without authority; Creek Indians in the Seminole war; etc.

18. R-P of J. Shields. 3 Mar.
HR 73, 16-1, v1, 1p. [40]
Delaware Indians in Indiana; trading post.

19. Mem. of Gen. Jackson. 6 Mar.
SD 73, 16-1, v1, 61p. [26]
Defending his conduct in the Seminole war.

20. Report on East and West Florida. 9 Mar.
HR 76, 16-1, v1, 2p. [40]
Indian hostilities in Spanish territory.

21. R-P of W. Conner. 13 Mar.
SD 84, 16-1, v2, 1p. [27]
On Delaware Indian lands in Indiana; treaty of 1818 at St. Mary's.

22. Message on the Indian Title to Lands in Georgia. 17 Mar.
House Journal, 16-1, p. 315. [30]
To extinguish Creek and Cherokee lands in Georgia.

23. R-P of G. Mayfield. 21 Mar.
SD 91, 16-1, v2, 1p. [27]
Creek Indians; negotiation of the treaty of 1814 at Fort Jackson.

24. Documents Accompanying the Amendments to the Military Appropriations Bill. 22 Mar.
SD 92, 16-1, v2, 6p. [27]
Transportation costs up the Missouri River to the Mandan villages.

25. Mem. of the Georgia Legis. 27 Mar.
House Journal, 16-1, p. 338. [30]
Treaty of 1817 with the Cherokee Indians; Creek Indians.

26. On the Reiief of those Engaged in the Seminole War. 29 Mar.
HR 84, 16-1, v1, 4p. [40]
Officers and volunteers.

27. R-C of J. Piatt. 5 Apr.
SD 102, 16-1, v2, 6p. [27]
Supplies furnished Indians near Detroit.

28. Report on Indian Lands in Georgia. 5 Apr.
SD 103, 16-1, v2, 1p. [27]
Extinguishing Cherokee and Creek title to land.

29. Report on Indian Trade. 5 Apr.
SD 105, 16-1, v2, 4p. [27]
Inexpedient to abolish the system of Indian trade established by the law of the 2d of March, 1811.

30. Report on the Indian Trade. 12 Apr.
HD 110, 16-1, v8, 5p. [38]
Report on T. L. McKenney showing amount and cost of goods sent to Indian houses since 1815.

31. R-P of J. Konkopot et al. 13 Apr.
SD 113, 16-1, v2, 2p. [27]
Members of the Stockbridge Indians of New York.

32. Report on the Revenue of the U.S. 14 Apr.
HR 91, 16-1, v1, 10p. [40]
Includes Indian annuities, civilization funds, etc.

33. Report on the Remonstrance of S. Blackburn et al. 8 May.
SD 132, 16-1, v2, 1p. [27]
Concerning the act to regulate trade with the Indians; Creek Indians.

34. Report on the Brownstown Treaty. 12 May.
HR 98, 16-1, v1, 14p. [40]
Michigan Territory, 1808; lands ceded to the U.S. by Indians for a road in order that they might receive their annuities; problems in carrying out the treaty.

35. Annual Message to Congress; Pres. Monroe. 15 Nov.
SD 2, 16-2, v1, 8p. [42] *or* HD 1, 16-2, v1, 8p. [48]
Includes Indian affairs.

36. Letter on Lands Purchased from the Indians. 16 Nov.
SD 5, 16-2, v1, 26p. [42] *or* HD 8, 16-2, v1, 26p. [48]
Since the Declaration of Independence; acres purchased, etc.

37. Report on Balances. 27 Nov.
HD 10, 16-2, v3, 86p. [50]
Includes accounts of Indian agents, etc.

38. Annual Report of the Sec. of the Treasury. 1 Dec.
SD 12, 16-2, v1, 41p. [42] *or* HD 9, 16-2, v1, 41p. [48]
Includes the Indian Dept., etc.

39. Report on Indian Annuities. 4 Dec.
SD 14, 16-2, v1, 11p. [42]
Of all annuities payable by the U.S. to Indians.

40. Report on Indian Expenses. 5 Dec.
SD 15, 16-2, v1, 18p. [42]
Money expended since the Declaration of Independence on treaties and their negotiations, annuities, trade, salaries of employees, etc.

41. Report on the Expenses of the War and Navy Depts. 6 Dec.
HD 18, 16-2, v1, 14p. [48]
From Nov. 1818 to Nov. 1819.

42. R-C of J. Holmes. 7 Dec.
SD 13, 16-2, v1, 1p. [42]
Battle of Emuckfaw, with the Creeks; 22 Jan. 1814.

43. R-C of M. Brown. 8 Dec.
SD 16, 16-2, v1, 1p. [42]
Creek Indians.

44. Report on the Indian Trade. 13 Dec.
SD 19, 16-2, v1, 8p. [42]
On the state of the trade with the Indians.

45. R-P of J. McCartney. 15 Dec.
HR 14, 16-2, v1, 2p. [57]
Cattle confiscated by the Army on Indian lands in Alabama.

46. Report on the Seminole War. 16 Dec.
HD 29, 16-2, v1, 4p. [48]
On horses furnished the troops, etc.

47. Supplement to the Annual Report of the Sec. of the Treasury. 21 Dec.
HD 32, 16-2, v1, 10p. [48]
Includes the Indian Dept.

48. Estimate of the Appropriations. 21 Dec.
HD 33, 16-2, v1, 54p. [48]
Includes Indian treaties, civilization funds, etc.

1821

1. Letter on Military Affairs. 2 Jan.
HD 41, 16-2, v2, 6p. [49]
U.S. military posts and their personnel.

2. Message on the Indian Dept. 4 Jan.
HD 47, 16-2, v4, 10p. [51]
Expenditures and receipts from 1811.

3. R-P of N. Perkins. 9 Jan.
SD 42, 16-2, v2, 1p. [43]
Mississippi Territory; land to which Indian title was extinguished.

4. On the Relief of Citizens of Peoria, Illinois. 10 Jan.
SD 76, 16-2, v2, 45p. [43]
Indian trade; Indian hostilities, etc.

5. R-C of Those Engaged in the Seminole War. 10 Jan.
HR 26, 16-2, v1, 1p. [57]
Postpones settlements indefinitely.

6. R-C of J. Jerome et al. 10 Jan.
HR 33, 16-2, v1, 13p. [57]
Indian and British troops; 1813; Michigan.

7. Report on a Choctaw Land Grant. 18 Jan.
SD 51, 16-2, v2, 1p. [43]
Chiefs request that land be granted to S. Dinsmore; treaty of 1805.

8. Message on the Six Nations of Indians. 18 Jan.
HD 70, 16-2, v5, 8p. [52]
Report of negotiations with the New York tribes since 1 Jan. 1816.

9. Letter on Indian Trade. 18 Jan.
HD 71, 16-2, v5, 8p. [52]
Merchandise on hand at trading houses, and in the hands of the Supt. of Indian Trade.

10. Letter on Money in the Treasury. 22 Jan.
HD 73, 16-2, v5, 10p. [52]
Includes funds for Indian annuities, treaties, etc.

11. Mem. of the Tennessee Field Officers. 24 Jan.
HD 74, 16-2, v5, 5p. [52]
For the loss of horses in the Seminole war.

12. R-P of J. May. 24 Jan.
HR 44, 16-2, v1, 6p. [57]
Near Detroit; 1813; Indians in the Army.

13. Report on Settling the Pacific Coast and Columbia River. 25 Jan.
HR 45, 16-2, v1, 15p. [57]
Includes trade with the Indians, etc.

14. Report on Appropriations for the War Dept. 2 Feb.
HD 91, 16-2, v6, 5p. [53]
For the year 1820.

15. R-P of T. Boyles. 5 Feb.
SD 80, 16-2, v2, 1p. [43]
Creek Indian treaty; Mississippi Territory.

16. Report on the Revenue. 6 Feb.
HR 57, 16-2, v1, 8p. [57]

Expenditures for Indian civilization, etc.

17. Report on Balances. 8 Feb.
HD 108, 16-2, v7, 10p. [54]
Accounts on Indian affairs, etc.

18. Report on Land Grants for Education. 9 Feb.
SD 85, 16-2, v2, 4p. [43]
Requires extinguishment of Indian title to land.

19. L-C of J. Piatt. 15 Feb.
SD 104, 16-2, v3, 29p. [44]
Supplies furnished to Indians near Detroit.

20. R-P of Konaloolaskee. 19 Feb.
SD 102, 16-2, v3, 1p. [44]
Cherokee treaty of 1817 in Alabama; treaty of 1818 in Washington, D.C.

21. R-P of W. Doak. 21 Feb.
SD 98, 16-2, v3, 1p. [44]
Choctaw Indian land ceded to U.S. in Mississippi.

22. General, War, and Navy,Accounts. 22 Feb.
SD 120, 16-2, v5, 207p. [46]
From 1 Oct. 1819 to 9 Sept. 1820.

23. Documents on the Claim of J. Johnson. 27 Feb.
HD 110, 16-2, v8, 299p. [55]
For transport of expedition up the Missouri River to the Mandan villages.

24. Report on Finances. 28 Feb.
HR 66, 16-2, v1, 4p. [57]
Indian annuities, trading houses, etc.

25. Report on the Transportation of Troops. 1 Mar.
HR 70, 16-2, v1, 5p. [57]
On the claim of J. Johnson; expedition up the Missouri River to the Mandan villages.

26. Annual Message to Congress with Documents; Pres. Monroe. 5 Dec.
SD 1, 17-1, v1, 70p. [59] *or* HD 1, 17-1, v1, 70 p. [63]
Indian hostilities in Florida; reports; etc.

27. Resol. of Rep. Wood. 6 Dec.
HR, Resol. 2, 17-1, v2, 1p. [71]
Matter in Indian trade should be referred to a special com.

28. Annual Report of the Sec. of the Treasury. 10 Dec.
SD 2, 17-1, v1, 31p. [59] *or* HD 3, 17-1, v1, 31p. [63]
Indian Dept., etc.

29. Partial Appropriation for 1822. 27 Dec.
HD 7, 17-1, v1, 5p. [63]
Indian Dept. funds.

1822

1. R-P of J. May. 2 Jan.
HR 7, 17-1, v1, 6p. [70]
Supplies for Indians in U.S. Army; near Detroit; 1813.

2. Report on Roads and Canals. 2 Jan.
HR 8, 17-1, v1, 100p. [70]
Report on Sec. of War on frontier defense against Indians, etc.

3. Report on the Treaties with the Creek and Cherokee Indians. 7 Jan.
HR 10, 17-1, v1, 12p. [70]
Conflict between the agreements of the U.S. with the state of Georgia and with the Indians; Indian treaties violate the sovereign rights of Georgia.

4. Report on the Indian Trade. 14 Jan.
SD 10, 17-1, v1, 10p. [59]
Number and location of trading posts; accounts.

5. R-C of Tennessee Volunteers. 14 Jan.
HR 13, 17-1, v1, 23p. [70]
Seminole war.

6. Expenditures of the Indian Dept. 15 Jan.
HD 24, 17-1, v2, 15p. [64]
For the years 1820-1821.

7. Report on the Settlement of the Columbia River Region. 18 Jan.
HR 18, 17-1, v1, 15p. [70]
Indian trade.

8. Documents on the Indian Trade. 19 Jan.
SD 60, 17-1, v1, 62p. [59]
Statements showing the amount of trade, etc.

9. Estimate of Appropriations. 19 Jan.
HD 30, 17-1, v2, 61p. [64]
For the year 1822; Indian Dept., etc.

10. Message on the Civilization of the Indians. 20 Jan.
HD 34, 17-1, v3 (pt. 1), 9p. [65]
Expenditures made on said service.

11. Letter on Indian Appropriations. 21 Jan.
HD 33, 17-1, v2, 5p. [64]

For treaties with the Creek and Cherokee Indians.

12. R-P of J. Jerome et al. 25 Jan.
HR 34, 17-1, v1, 30p. [70]
British and Indian forces; 1813.

13. Contracts of the War Dept. 26 Jan.
HD 41, 17-1, v3 (pt. 2), 8p. [65]
Transportation on the Missouri River expedition, etc.

14. R-P of N. Osborne and W. Doake. 28 Jan.
SD 19, 17-1, v1, 1p. [59]
Cession of Indian lands near Natchez and New Orleans for taverns; 1804.

15. R-P of M. Brown. 30 Jan.
HR 30, 17-1, v1, 2p. [70]
Creek war; Georgia.

16. R-P of the Executors of T. Carr. 28 Jan.
SD 29, 17-1, v1, 2p. [59]
Indian hostilities on the Georgia frontier; 1784-1785.

17. R-P of S. Walker. 7 Feb.
SD 44, 17-1, v1, 1p. [59]
Indian hostilities in Indiana during the war with Britain.

18. Letter on the Indian Settlements in Florida. 7 Feb.
HD 55, 17-1, v2 (pt. 3), 5p. [65]
Listing all Creek, Seminole, etc., villages; populations.

19. Letter on Indian Affairs. 9 Feb.
HD 60, 17-1, v4, 132p. [66]
Affairs in Michigan Territory during 1820-1821, etc.

20. Appropriations for the War Dept. 12 Feb.
HD 62, 17-1, v4, 6p. [66]
For the year 1821; Indian expenses.

21. Message on the Civilization of the Indians. 15 Feb.
HD 59, 17-1, v4, 23p. [66]
Report of the Sec. of War.

22. Military Appropriations for 1822. 19 Feb.
HD 85, 17-1, v5, 10p. [67]
Treaties with the Creeks, Ottawas, Pottawatomies, Kickapoos, etc.

23. General, War, and Navy Accounts. 22 Feb.
SD 95, 17-1, v3, 215p. [61]
From 1 Oct. 1820 to 30 Sept. 1821.

24. Message on the Civilization of the Indians. 23 Feb.
SD 50, 17-1, v1, 7p. [59]
On the annual disposition of the sum of $15,000 which was appropriated by an act of Congress in 1802 to promote civilization among friendly Indian tribes.

25. Message on Land Titles. 23 Feb.
HD 74, 17-1, v5, 12p. [67]
On Indian title to land extinguished by the U.S. and claimed by any state; treaties with the Six Nations, Creeks, Cherokees, Chickasaws, Oneidas, Mohawks, and Senecas.

26. R-P of H. Prout. 25 Feb.
SD 49, 17-1, v1, 1p. [59]
Creek Indians; 1815-1816.

27. Message on the Indian Title to Land in Georgia. 25 Feb.
HD 80, 17-1, v5, 2p. [67]
Appropriation requested to negotiate with the Cherokee and Creek Indians for their land in Georgia.

28. Expenses of the Army. 1 Mar.
HD 83, 17-1, v5, 7p. [67]
Seminole Indian war, etc.

29. Report on an Indian Treaty. 8 Mar.
HR 61, 17-1, v2, 14p. [71]
Treaty of Brownstown, for the construction of a road; with the Chippewa, Ottawa, Pottawatomie, Wyandot, and Shawnee Indians.

30. Report on Land Offices. 13 Mar.
HD 94, 17-1, v6, 4p. [68]
Lands acquired from Choctaw Indians in Mississippi, etc.

31. R-C of the Georgia Militia. 26 Mar.
HR 91, 17-1, v2, 24p. [71]
Cherokee and Creek Indian wars; 1792-1794.

32. Message on the Florida Campaign. 8 Apr.
HD 108, 17-1, v6, 6p. [68]
Report from the Sec. of War.

33. Report on the Indian Dept. 11 Apr.
HD 110, 17-1, v6, 19p. [68]
Accounts from 1 Jan. 1820.

34. R-C of the Georgia Militia. 15 Apr.
SD 84, 17-1, v2, 7p. [60]
Creek and Cherokee wars; 1792-1794.

35. Message on Florida. 18 Apr.
HD 113, 17-1, v6, 46p. [68]
On concentrating the Creek Indians in one area, etc.

36. Report on Balances. 23 Apr.
HD 116, 17-1, v7, 24p. [69]
Items on Indian expenses, etc.

37. Message on J. Carver's Claim. 23 Apr.
HD 117, 17-1, v7, 9p. [69]
Granted land along the Mississippi River near the falls of St. Anthony in 1767 by the Nandowessie Indians.
38. Message on Army Subsistence. 30 Apr.
SD 92, 17-1, v2, 13p. [60]
Includes provisions for Indians.
39. Report on Finances. 30 Apr.
HR 103, 17-1, v2, 12p. [71]
Indian annuities, etc.
40. Message on Lead Mines in Missouri. 7 May.
SD 94, 17-1, v2, 19p. [60] *or* HD 129, 17-1, v7, 19p. [69]
Land cessions in 1816 by the Chippewa, Ottawa, and Pottawatomie Indians.
41. Annual Message to Congress with Documents; Pres. Monroe. 3 Dec.
SD 1, 17-2, v1, 91p. [73] *or* HD 2, 17-2, v1, 91p. [76]
Indian trade; reports of the War Dept., etc.
42. Message on Copper Mines. 7 Dec.
SD 5, 17-2, v1, 33p. [73]
On Indian tribes who claim title to the copper regions surrounding Lake Superior; Chippewas, Ojibwas, Sioux, Menomonees, Winnebagoes, Pottawatomies, Crees, etc.
43. Resol. of Mr. Tattnall. 7 Dec.
HR, Resol. 4, 17-2, v2, 1p. [87]
Reserving land for the Creek and Cherokee Indians within the state of Georgia is against its sovereign rights.
44. Message on the Christian Indians. 9 Dec.
SD 3, 17-2, v1, 58p. [73]
On the condition and land in Ohio of said Indians; from the Society of United Brethren.
45. Report on Indian Treaties. 10 Dec.
HR 1, 17-2, v1, 12p. [86]
Cherokee treaties of 1817 and 1819; Creek treaty of 1814; within Georgia.
46. R-P of M. Brown. 12 Dec.
HR 8, 17-2, v1, 2p. [86]
Creek Indians; Georgia.
47. R-P of J. Jerome et al. 12 Dec.
HR 26, 17-2, v1, 27p. [86]
British and Indian forces; 1813.
48. Report on the Browntown Treaty. 19 Dec.
HR 50, 17-2, v1, 14p. [86]
Treaty of 1808 with the Chippewa, Ottawa, Pottawatomie, Wyandot, and Shawnee Indians.
49. R-C of the Georgia Militia. 20 Dec.
HR 52, 17-2, v1, 23p. [86]
Cherokee and Creek wars; 1792-1794.
50. On the Case of Gen. Glascock. 20 Dec.
HR 53, 17-2, v1, 1p. [86]
Seminole war; battle of Mickasooke.
51. R-P of R. Purdy. 23 Dec.
SD 7, 17-2, v1, 1p. [73]
Peddler selling liquor to the Indians in Tennessee during the year 1809.
52. Annual Report of the Sec. of the Treasury. 23 Dec.
SD 8, 17-2, v1, 37p. [73] *or* HD 12, 17-2, v1, 37p. [76]
Indian Dept. and Indian expenses.

1823

1. L-C of J. Piatt. 3 Jan.
HD 15, 17-2, v1, 30p. [76]
Supplies furnished to Indians near Detroit; 1813.
2. Report on Public Lands in Georgia. 6 Jan.
HR 57, 17-2, v2, 2p. [87]
For the extinguishment of Indian title to said land.
3. R-C of Georgia Militia. 7 Jan.
SD 13, 17-2, v2, 7p. [74]
Cherokee and Creek wars; 1792-1794.
4. Mem. of Citizens of St. Augustine. 8 Jan.
HD 19, 17-2, v1, 5p. [76]
Seminole Indians.
5. Estimate of Appropriations. 16 Jan.
HD 28, 17-2, v3, 55p. [78]
For the year 1823; Indian Dept., etc.
6. R-C of S. Harrison. 23 Jan.
SD 20, 17-2, v2, 2p. [74]
Land near the falls of St. Anthony on the Mississippi River granted by the Nandowessie Indians in 1766.
7. Message on a Columbia River Establishment. 25 Jan.
HD 45, 17-2, v3, 65p. [78]
Indian trade.
8. Letter on the Florida Indians. 28 Jan.
HD 51, 17-2, v3, 19p. [78]
Transmits documents and correspondence.

9. R-P of W. Wilson et al. 28 Jan.
HR 72, 17-2, v2, 2p. [87]
Cherokee Indians from Alabama ask for reserves of land.
10. Expenditures of the War Dept. 1 Feb.
HD 55, 17-2, v4, 10p. [79]
For the year 1822.
11. Message on the Mem. of the Florida Legis. 3 Feb.
SD 27, 17-2, v2, 11p. [74] *or* HD 53, 17-2, v3, 11p. [78]
Indian hostilities.
12. Message on Indian Title to Lands. 3 Feb.
HD 57, 17-2, v4, 8p. [79]
In Georgia and Missouri.
13. R-P of H. Prout. 3 Feb.
HR 79, 17-2, v2, 1p. [87]
Creek Indian war soldiers; 1815-1816.
14. Report on the Civilization of the Indians. 7 Feb.
SD 29, 17-2, v2, 2p. [74]
Work of the Society of United Brethren among the Christian Indians in Ohio.
15. General, War, and Navy Accounts. 14 Feb.
HD 109, 17-2, v8, 175p. [83]
From 1 July 1821 to 30 June 1822.
16. Message on Indian Land Titles in Georgia. 14 Feb.
SD 35, 17-2, v2, 17p. [74]
Lands ceded by the Indians; Indian title remaining to be extinguished; treaties; Creek, Cherokee, etc., land.
17. Report on Indian Expenses. 18 Feb.
HD 80, 17-2, v5, 8p. [80]
Accounts of agents and supts.
18. Report on Indians in Florida. 21 Feb.
HR 97, 17-2, v2, 8p. [87]
On authorizing the Pres. to look to their civilization.
19. Abolishing Indian Trading Establishments. 1 Mar.
HR 104, 17-2, v2, 29p. [87]
The advisability of such a move.
20. R-P of the Reps. of J. Piatt. 3 Mar.
HR 102, 17-2, v2, 34p. [87]
Supplies furnished to Indians near Detroit in 1813.
21. Annual Message to Congress with Documents; Pres. Monroe. 2 Dec.
SD 1, 18-1, v1, 267p. [89] *or* HD 2, 18-1, v1, 267p. [93]
Includes a statement on the "Rickaree" hostilities on the Missouri River; reports of the Sec. of War, and the Indian Dept., etc.
22. Report on Indian Trading Licenses. 15 Dec.
HD 7, 18-1, v1, 12p. [93]
Licenses granted, by whom, where, etc.

1824

1. Annual Report of the Sec. of the Treasury. 2 Jan.
SD 16, 18-1, v1, 35p. [89] *or* HD 16, 18-1, v1, 35p. [93]
Indian Dept., Indian annuities, etc.
2. Estimate of Appropriations. 9 Jan.
HD 17, 18-1, v2, 55p. [94]
For the year 1824; Indian service.
3. R-M of Reps. of J. Piatt. 9 Jan.
HR 21, 18-1, v1, 34p. [105]
Supplies furnished to Indians near Detroit in 1813.
4. R-P of T. Williamson et al. 12 Jan.
SD 14, 18-1, v1, 2p. [89]
Seminole war, 1818.
5. Report on Indian Agencies. 12 Jan.
HD 56, 18-1, v4, 6p. [96]
List of agents, tribes, etc.
6. R-P of the Executors of D. Rawlings. 22 Jan.
SD 24, 18-1, v1, 1p. [89]
Supplied Army on the Tennessee River during the Creek Indian war; 1813-1814.
7. Mem. of Officers of the Seminole War. 22 Jan.
HD 42, 18-1, v2, 10p. [94]
During the year 1818.
8. Report on Indian Expenses. 24 Jan.
HD 47, 18-1, v2, 3p. [94]
Disbursements for civilization in 1823.
9. Report on the Georgia Militia Claims. 28 Jan.
HR 45, 18-1, v1, 17p. [105]
Creek and Cherokee wars; 1792-1794.
10. Report on War Dept. Contracts. 2 Feb.
HD 59, 18-1, v4, 13p. [96]
For the year 1823; Indian expenses.
11. R-M of the Arkansas Legis. 4 Feb.
HR 56, 18-1, v1, 2p. [105]
Cherokee Indian treaty of 1817.
12. R-P of C. Bradford. 11 Feb.
HR 59, 18-1, v1, 2p. [105]
Prisoner of the Indians near Detroit in 1813.

13. R-P of A. Moore and S. Orgain. 12 Feb.
SD 34, 18-1, v2, 4p. [90]
Services for the Tennessee volunteers during the Seminole war.
14. R-C of J. Holliday. 13 Feb.
HR 62, 18-1, v1, 2p. [105]
Indian hostilities in 1812.
15. R-P of G. Harlin. 13 Feb.
HR 70, 18-1, v1, 2p. [105]
A Cherokee Indian delegate to Washington, D.C. in the 1819 treaty negotiations.
16. Message on the Arkansas Boundary. 23 Feb.
HD 84, 18-1, v5, 5p. [97]
Choctaw Indian treaty.
17. Message on the Transport of Troops. 23 Feb.
HD 85, 18-1, v5, 8p. [97]
From Council Bluffs to the Columbia River; purchase of horses from the Pawnee or Mandan Indians.
18. On the Case of W. Blount. 24 Feb.
HR 76, 18-1, v1, 2p. [105]
Tennessee volunteers in British-Indian war, etc.; governor of the territory.
19. Mem. of the American Board of Com'rs. for Foreign Missions. 3 Mar.
HD 102, 18-1, v5, 8p. [97]
Seeks money from the government to provide educational services for the Indians.
20. Mem. of the Mississippi Legis. 4 Mar.
SD 49, 18-1, v3, 2p. [91]
Chickasaw Indian territory should be purchased.
21. Resol. and Mem. of the Ohio Legis. 10 Mar.
HD 113, 18-1, v6, 8p. [98]
Extinguishment of Indian title to lands.
22. Report on the Civilization of the Indians. 23 Mar.
HR 92, 18-1, v2, 7p. [106]
On establishments in the Indian country for the purpose of civilizing the Indians, etc.
23. Message on Salt Springs, and Lead and Copper Mines. 30 Mar.
HD 128, 18-1, v6, 111p. [98]
On Chippewa, Ottawa, and Pottawatomie Indian lands.
24. Message on Compact with Georgia. 2 Apr.
SD 63, 18-1, v3, 82p. [91] *or* HD 127, 18-1, v6, 82p. [98]
Regarding extinguishment of Cherokee and Creek Indian title to lands in Georgia.
25. Report on Lands in Ohio. 2 Apr.
HR 99, 18-1, v2, 7p. [106]
Christian Indians of Ohio; Society of the United Brethren.
26. Mem. of the Georgia Legis. 5 Apr.
HD 125, 18-1, v6, 5p. [98]
On extinguishing Indian land titles.
27. Report on Creek Indian Claims. 5 Apr.
HR 101, 18-1, v2, 10p. [106]
Compensation of friendly Creeks for losses incurred during the Creek war.
28. R-P of Col. Cocke. 9 Apr.
HR 105, 18-1, v2, 2p. [106]
Creek Indian war.
29. Report on the Compact with Georgia. 15 Apr.
HR 109, 18-1, v2, 18p. [106]
Recommends appropriation to rectify the situation existing as regards Creek and Cherokee land titles in Georgia; agreement between the state and the U.S. government in 1802.
30. Report on Settlement of the Columbia River. 15 Apr.
HR 110, 18-1, v2, 5p. [106]
Indian trade with foreigners must be controlled; Mandan, Minnataree, Assiniboin, Blackfoot, Arikara, and other Missouri River Indians.
31. Indian Reservation in Georgia. 16 Apr.
HD 133, 18-1, v10, 4p. [102]
Cherokee delegates protesting any action towards dispossessing them of their land.
32. Message on Cession of Cherokee Indian Lands. 16 Apr.
HD 136, 18-1, v10, 16p. [102]
Report on the Sec. of War on the Cherokee proposals.
33. Report on Pre-Emption Rights to Settlers. 23 Apr.
HR 115, 18-1, v2, 5p. [106]
Settlers neighboring the Indians.
34. Documents on Indian Depredations. 27 Apr.
SD 71, 18-1, v3, 6p. [91]
On the Upper Missouri River; Arikara, etc.
35. Report on Indian Affairs. 14 May.
SD 79, 18-1, v3, 3p. [91]
On removal of Indians from Missouri Territory; Shawnee, Delaware, Osage, Peoria, Kickapoo, and Piankeshaw Indians.

36. Abolition of Indian Trading Establishments. 25 May.
HR 129, 18-1, v2, 32p. [106]
Views on the subject; leave the matter before Congress.
37. Annual Message to Congress with Documents; Pres. Monroe. 7 Dec.
SD 1, 18-2, v1, 367p. [108] *or* HD 2, 18-2, v1, 367p. [113]
Includes plan to civilize the Indians; reports of the Sec. of War, Chief Clerk of the Indian Dept.
38. Petition on a Wagon Road. 13 Dec.
SD 2, 18-2, v1, 12p. [108]
From the Missouri River to the Columbia River for frontier defense, control of Indian trade, etc.
39. Documents on the Claim of the Georgia Militia. 21 Dec.
HD 16, 18-2, v2, 41p. [114]
Creek and Cherokee wars; 1792-1794.
40. Instructions for a Treaty with the Cherokee Indians. 23 Dec.
HD 19, 18-2, v2, 17p. [114]
Instructions under which the treaty with the Cherokees of 1804 was negotiated.
41. R-C of W. Hambly. 27 Dec.
HR 7, 18-2, v1, 1p. [122]
Florida Indian treaty of 1823.

1825

1. On Trade Between Missouri and Mexico. 3 Jan.
SD 7, 18-2, v1, 14p. [108]
Pawnee and Comanche hostilities in 1822, etc.
2. Annual Report of the Sec. of the Treasury. 3 Jan.
SD 8, 18-2, v1, 40p. [108] *or* HD 26, 18-2, v2, 40p. [114]
Indian Dept., etc.
3. Mem. of the Ohio Legis. 7 Jan.
HD 37, 18-2, v2, 8p. [114]
Extinguishing Indian title to land.
4. R-C of R. Bedford. 7 Jan.
HR 15, 18-2, v1, 1p. [122]
Seminole war; 1818; Tennessee volunteers.
5. Report on Cherokee Land Claims. 10 Jan.
HD 43, 18-2, v3, 12p. [115]
Proposed plan of extinguishment of Cherokee claim to land.
6. Estimates of Appropriations. 11 Jan.
HD 41, 18-2, v3, 56p. [115]
Indian agencies, treaties, civilization funds, etc.
7. Report on Indian Trading Licenses. 15 Jan.
HD 54, 18-2, v3, 7p. [115]
For the year ending 1 Sept. 1824.
8. Message on Indian Trading Establishments. 20 Jan.
HD 61, 18-2, v4, 36p. [116]
Progress in abolishing these.
9. On the Purchase of Copper Lands. 21 Jan.
SD 19, 18-2, v2, 2p. [109]
On obtaining cessions of land bordering Lake Superior from the Chippewa Indians.
10. R-M of the Arkansas General Assembly. 25 Jan.
HR 39, 18-2, v1, 2p. [122]
Cession of land by the U.S. to the Cherokee Indians.
11. Petition of A. Eccles and T. and R. Pettigrew. 26 Jan.
SD 20, 18-2, v2, 2p. [109]
Cherokee Indians; prior to 1798.
12. Message on the Government of the Indians. 27 Jan.
SD 21, 18-2, v2, 27p. [109] *or* HD 64, 18-2, v4, 27p. [116]
On the future location and government of the Indians; their removal westwards; reports of the Sec. of War and Supt. of Indian Affairs.
13. R-P of Dr. Peters. 28 Jan.
HR 44, 18-2, v1, 19p. [122]
"Carver's Grant," made by the Nandowessie Indians; near the falls of St. Anthony on the Mississippi River.
14. R-C of W. Little. 31 Jan.
HR 49, 18-2, v1, 1p. [122]
Seminole war; 1818.
15. Appropriations for the War Dept. 1 Feb.
HD 67, 18-2, v4, 5p. [116]
For the year 1824; Indian treaties, etc.
16. R-M of the Michigan Legis. 2 Feb.
SD 23, 18-2, v2, 4p. [109]
On a road through the territory; Indian hostilities.
17. Report on a Post Road in Indian Country. 4 Feb.

SD 28, 18-2, v2, 3p. [109]
Between Columbus and Jackson, Mississippi.

18. Report on Treaties with the Indians. 8 Feb.
HR 77, 18-2, v1, 1p. [122]
On an appropriation to extinguish Creek and Cherokee title to land in Georgia.

19. Petition of Citizens of Missouri. 14 Feb.
HD 79, 18-2, v4, 8p. [116]
On the need to protect trade routes to Mexico from Indian depredations.

20. Address from the Choctaw Delegation. 18 Feb.
SD 35, 18-2, v3, 3p. [110]
Ask improvement of their condition.

21. On the Case of S. Dale. 18 Feb.
HR 75, 18-2, v1, 1p. [122]
Creek and Seminole wars.

22. Disbursements to Indians. 24 Feb.
HD 109, 18-2, v7, 95p. [119]
From 1 Sept. 1823 to 1 Sept. 1824.

23. Report on Creek Indian Treaty Negotiations. 25 Feb.
HD 72, 18-2, v4, 41p. [116]
Report and proceedings of Com'rs appointed to extinguish Indian title to land in Georgia.

24. Message on Indian Treaties. 25 Feb.
HD 95, 18-2, v6, 11p. [118]
Copies of treaties with the Quapaw and Choctaw Indians.

25. Report on the Comanche Indians. 25 Feb.
HR 82, 18-2, v2, 1p. [123]
Against taking any measures against said Indians.

26. Annual Message to Congress with Documents; Pres. Adams. 6 Dec.
SD 2, 19-1, v1, 210p. [125] *or* HD 1, 19-1, v1, 210p. [131]
Relations with Indian tribes; report of the Sec. of War, Indian Affairs office, etc.

27. Mem. of the Ohio Legis. 9 Dec.
HD 8, 19-1, v1, 8p. [131]
Indian land titles not yet extinguished.

28. Annual Report of the Sec. of the Treasury. 22 Dec.
SD 6, 19-1, v1, 40p. [125] *or* HD 13, 19-1, v1, 40p. [131]
Indian Dept., etc.

29. Message on the Creek Indian Treaty. 27 Dec.
HD 17, 19-1, v1, 11p. [131]
Instructions given relating to the treaty with Creek Indians at Fort Jackson in Alabama; cession of lands; roads through country; navigation; establishment of military posts; etc.

1826

1. Message on the Treaty with the Cherokee Indians. 3 Jan.
HD 21, 19-1, v3, 8p. [133]
On concluding the treaty which was ratified in 1819; cession of land in North Carolina, etc.

2. R-P of D. Deming. 5 Jan.
SD 13, 19-1, v1, 6p. [125]
Supplies for the Indians near Fort Harrison, Indiana.

3. Estimate of Appropriations. 5 Jan.
HD 24, 19-1, v3, 59p. [133]
Indian agencies, annuities, etc.

4. R-P of J. and M. Wolcott. 6 Jan.
HR 26, 19-1, v1, 3p. [141]
Treaty of 1818 with the Miami Indians of Indiana.

5. Report on the Relief of W. Hambly and E. Doyle. 10 Jan.
HR 27, 19-1, v1, 2p. [141]
Creek Indians in Florida.

6. Report on Land Register and Receiver in Louisiana. 13 Jan.
HR 33, 19-1, v1, 6p. [141]
Includes land owned by Indians.

7. Report on Exploration of the Northwest Coast. 16 Jan.
HR 35, 19-1, v1, 26p. [141]
Indian trade, population, etc.

8. Report on the Defense of the Northwestern Frontier. 16 Jan.
HR 42, 19-1, v1, 18p. [141]
Protection from Indian hostilities; prevention of trade between foreigners and Indians; etc.

9. Message on the Northwestern Boundary of the U.S. 31 Jan.
HD 65, 19-1, v4, 26p. [134]
Indian trade, etc.

10. Report on a Proposed Road from Detroit to Chicago. 1 Feb.
HD 68, 19-1, v4, 6p. [134]
Will cross land to which Indian title has not been extinguished.

11. Statement of Appropriations. 1 Feb.
HD 69, 19-1, v4, 7p. [134]
For the Treasury, War, and Navy Depts. in 1825.
12. Report on Indian Treaties. 1 Feb.
HD 74, 19-1, v4, 109p. [134]
Instructions given Com'rs for negotiations with the Florida Indians, etc.
13. Report on the Civilization of the Indian Tribes. 3 Feb.
HD 102, 19-1, v5, 22p. [135]
Evaluation of present system; removal of Indians west of the Mississippi River; cession of lands; etc.
14. Report on Land Claims. 6 Feb.
HD 80, 19-1, v4, 74p. [134]
Claims of the Chetimache Indians.
15. Resol. of the Alabama Legis. 7 Feb.
SD 32, 19-1, v2, 7p. [126]
On lands acquired by treaty with the Creek Indians.
16. Report on a Road in Louisiana. 8 Feb.
HR 67, 19-1, v1, 2p. [141]
Frontier defenses against the Indians.
17. Report on Lands in Tennessee. 9 Feb.
HR 68, 19-1, v1, 5p. [141]
Chickasaw Indian lands.
18. R-M of J. McCartney. 15 Feb.
HR 74, 19-1, v1, 1p. [141]
For cattle taken by the U.S. Army on Cherokee Indian lands in 1817.
19. R-P of J. Pratte et al. 15 Feb.
HR 75, 19-1, v1, 17p. [141]
Chickasaw Indians, 1769.
20. Report on Compensation to Government Employees. 17 Feb.
HR 77, 19-1, v1, 1p. [141]
An Indian agent in Michigan.
21. Report on a Canal in Indiana. 21 Feb.
SD 47, 19-1, v2, 3p. [126]
Indian land titles need be extinguished.
22. Report on Leases of Lead Mines and Salt Springs. 22 Feb.
SD 45, 19-1, v2, 19p. [126]
Mines originally wrought by the Sac and Fox Indians.
23. Mem. of the Illinois General Assembly. 23 Feb.
SD 49, 19-1, v2, 4p. [126]
A canal would be advantageous in the event of Indian hostilities.
24. Report on Trade with the Indians. 28 Feb.
HD 112, 19-1, v7, 115p. [137]
On agents, agencies, annuities, provisions, etc.
25. Message on the Florida Indians. 1 Mar.
HD 111, 19-1, v6, 6p. [136]
On the suffering condition of the Indians.
26. Petition of W. Hollinger. 1 Mar.
HR 91, 19-1, v1, 1p. [141]
Creek Indian treaty at Fort Jackson in Alabama.
27. Report on the Expedition up the Missouri River. 4 Mar.
HD 117, 19-1, v6, 16p. [136]
Movements of the Atkinson expedition; situation, number, and strength of the Indian tribes, etc.
28. Report on Indian Trading Licenses. 4 Mar.
HD 118, 19-1, v6, 7p. [136]
Licenses granted, by whom, date granted, place, etc.
29. Mem. of the Missouri Legis. 6 Mar.
SD 55, 19-1, v2, 106p. [126]
Sac, Fox, Kickapoo, Piankeshaw, Pottawatomie, and Iowa depredations.
30. Mem. of Citizens of Kentucky. 6 Mar.
HD 116, 19-1, v6, 5p. [136]
Indian hostilities in Kentucky; British and Indian war, 1813.
31. Report on Civilization of the Indians. 7 Mar.
HD 124, 19-1, v8, 7p. [138]
Removal, west, of the Indians; education; annuities; habits of the Indians; etc.
32. Bill for Regulation of the Fur Trade. 8 Mar.
SD 58, 19-1, v3, 12p. [127]
To repeal the 1824 act making it the duty of Indian agents to designate places for trade with Indians, and requiring all traders to transact business at places thus designated; Upper Missouri and Northern Indiáns mainly.
33. Message on the Florida-Georgia Boundary Line. 17 Mar.
HD 133, 19-1, v8, 6p. [138]
Creek Indians; treaty of Indian Springs.
34. Letter on the Superintendency of Indian Affairs. 20 Mar.
HD 146, 19-1, v8, 12p. [138]
On the law establishing the office, number of employees, compensation, etc.
35. R-C of W. Morrison. 21 Mar.
HR 130, 19-1, v1, 10p. [141]

Cattle stolen in 1816 near Prairie du Chien (Fort Crawford), by the Sac, Fox, Sioux, and Winnebago Indians.

36. Report on a Road in Michigan. 28 Mar.
HR 144, 19-1, v2, 4p. [142]
Frontier defense against the Indians.

37. Report on Lands in Ohio. 28 Mar.
HR 145, 19-1, v2, 31p. [142]
Indian boundary lines.

38. Petition of S. Chitwood. 4 Apr.
HR 152, 19-1, v2, 3p. [142]
Creek Indian campaign; Tennessee volunteers.

39. Report on Florida Indians. 17 Apr.
HD 161, 19-1, v9, 7p. [139]
Location, country, soil, etc.

40. Accounts of the Treasury Dept. 20 Apr.
HD 184, 19-1, v10, 208p. [140]
Individual accounts; expenses for Indian services.

41. On the Compensation of Indian Agents. 21 Apr.
SD 82, 19-1, v4, 1p. [128]
Equalizing the compensation of the Supt. and agents of Indian affairs according to responsibility and labor.

42. Message on the Treaty with the Creek Indians. 25 Apr.
HD 165, 19-1, v9, 13p. [139]
On their removal west of the Mississippi River; treaty of 1825.

43. R-C of B. and A. Smith. 12 May.
HR 208, 19-1, v2, 1p. [142]
Cattle taken by Arapaho Indians near Santa Fe.

44. Report on Treaty with the Six Nations. 13 May.
HR 209, 19-1, v2, 2p. [142]
On appointment of a Com'r to hold a treaty with the independent tribes of the Six Nations.

45. R-P of G. Perpall. 15 May.
HR 210, 19-1, v2, 2p. [142]
Creek Indians of East Florida.

46. Report on the Northwest Coast. 15 May.
HR 213, 19-1, v2, 22p. [142]
Expedition of S. Ruddock from Council Bluffs to the Columbia River; Mandan villages on the Upper Missouri River.

47. Appropriation for the Creek Indians. 17 May.
SD 97, 19-1, v4, 6p. [128]
Related to the treaty concluded with said Indians; Cherokee Delegates.

48. Message on Treaties with Indians. 17 May.
HD 178, 19-1, v10, 3p. [140]
Treaties ratified during the first session of the 19th Congress; Osage, Sioux, Cheyenne, Arikara, Mandan, Crow, Pawnee, and other Indian tribes.

49. Report on a Road in New York. 17 May.
HR 223, 19-1, v2, 1p. [142]
Would pass through an Indian reservation.

50. Report on Trade with the Indians. 20 May.
HR 226, 19-1, v2, 11p. [142]
On education, and trade with the Indians.

51. Statement of Appropriations. 22 May.
HD 183, 19-1, v10, 27p. [140]
Indian treaties, etc.

52. Report on Reorganization of Executive Depts. 22 May.
HR 232, 19-1, v2, 11p. [142]
Removing the Indian Office from the War Dept.

53. Annual Message to Congress with Documents; Pres. Adams. 5 Dec.
SD 1, 19-2, v1, 516p. [144] *or* HD 2, 19-2, v1, 516p. [148]
Indian affairs; reports of Sec. of War and Indian Office.

54. Message on Land Donations by the Indians. 8 Dec.
HD 5, 19-2, v2, 14p. [149]
Land cessions made by treaty; Creek, Cherokee, Choctaw, and Chickasaw Indians; Florida Indians.

55. R-P of W. Wing. 8 Dec.
HR 2, 19-2, v1, 1p. [159]
Indian agent appointed in Michigan Territory.

56. Message on Indian Affairs. 11 Dec.
HD 9, 19-2, v2, 13p. [149]
On education; treaty made between the Osage and Delaware Indians in 1826; removal of Delawares west of the Missouri state line.

57. R-P of the Heirs of F. Valle. 11 Dec.
HR 4, 19-2, v1, 17p. [159]
Chickasaw Indians; 1769.

58. Petition of D. and S. Hale. 11 Dec.
HR 24, 19-2, v1, 3p. [159]
Creek Indian half-breeds; Fort Jackson treaty; 1814 in Alabama.

59. Annual Report of the Sec. of the Treasury. 13 Dec.
SD 3, 19-2, v2, 40p. [145] *or* HD 11, 19-2, v2, 40p. [149]
Indian Dept., etc.
60. Report on the Executive Depts. 15 Dec.
HR 10, 19-2, v1, 15p. [159]
Transfer of the Indian Office from the War Dept. to a new dept. to be organized.
61. Resol. of Rep. McLean. 15 Dec.
HR, Resol. 2, 19-2, v2, 2p. [160]
Removal of Indians west of the Mississippi River; obstacles to removal; how to overcome these obstacles; etc.
62. Letter on the Florida Indians. 16 Dec.
HD 17, 19-2, v2, 39p. [149]
On the condition of the Indians, etc.
63. On the Relief of J. McCartney. 26 Dec.
SD 8, 19-2, v2, 7p. [145]
Cattle confiscated on Cherokee lands in Alabama by the U.S. Army; 1817.
64. R-P of J. Winton. 26 Dec.
HR 17, 19-2, v1, 2p. [159]
For land belonging to the Cherokee Nation.
65. Resol. of Rep. Rivers. 29 Dec.
HR, Resol. 3, 19-2, v2, 1p. [160]
Indian expenditures should be referred to the Com. on Indian Affairs.

1827

1. Report on Removal of the Indians. 2 Jan.
HD 28, 19-2, v2, 13p. [149]
The costs of removal; disposition of the Indians towards removal; obstacles to removal.
2. Estimate of Appropriations. 4 Jan.
HD 36, 19-2, v3, 57p. [150]
For the year 1827; Indian expenses.
3. Letter on the Stockbridge Indians. 5 Jan.
HD 38, 19-2, v3, 3p. [150]
Present condition; effect of liquor on their lives.
4. Report on Encroachments on Choctaw Lands. 5 Jan.
HD 39, 19-2, v3, 8p. [150]
In Arkansas Territory; resistance by the Indians, and removal of the settlers.
5. Report on the Differences Between the U.S. and Georgia. 23 Jan.
HD 59, 19-2, v4, 404p. [151]
On treaties with the Creek Indians; claim of government to control the Indians.
6. Report on the Quapaw Indians. 9 Jan.
HD 43, 19-2, v3, 15p. [150]
On their condition and removal; claims to land extinguished.
7. Report on a Proposed Detroit-Chicago Road. 10 Jan.
HR 39, 19-2, v1, 4p. [159]
Frontier defense against the Indians; British and Indian war.
8. R-P of J. Overall. 10 Jan.
HR 42, 19-2, v1, 11p. [159]
Indian hostilities in western Georgia in 1785.
9. Resol. of the Georgia Legis. 11 Jan.
SD 16, 19-2, v2, 5p. [145]
Frontier defense against the Indians; militia claims.
10. Report of Indian Com'rs. 15 Jan.
SD 21, 19-2, v2, 51p. [145]
Treaty with the Choctaw and Chickasaw Indians for the purpose of extinguishing their claims to land in Mississippi; would not accede to the terms offered.
11. Report on Land Claims at Opelousas, Louisiana. 17 Jan.
HR 49, 19-2, v1, 32p. [159]
Claims of the Chetimache Indians.
12. Resol. of Sen. Reed. 23 Jan.
SD 28, 19-2, v2, 1p. [145]
To remove the whites encroaching on Chickasaw and Choctaw lands; to fulfill the treaty between the U.S. and said Indians.
13. Report on a Canal in Indiana. 23 Jan.
SD 29, 19-2, v2, 6p. [145]
Indian reservations involved.
14. Report on Indian Depredations in Missouri. 23 Jan.
HR 51, 19-2, v1, 3p. [159]
Sac, Fox, Osage and Iowa Indians in 1815.
15. Report on a Road from Lake Michigan to the Ohio River. 25 Jan.
SD 31, 19-2, v2, 2p. [145]
Cession of land to the U.S. by the Pottawatomie Indians for said road.
16. R-P of J. Scull et al. 27 Jan.
HR 60, 19-2, v1, 4p. [159]
Treaty of 15 Nov. 1824 with the Quapaw Indians in Arkansas.

17. Report on the Florida Indians. 30 Jan.
HD 82, 19-2, v5, 7p. [152]
Their condition.

18. R-P of the Widow of W. Hull. 31 Jan.
HR 63, 19-2, v1, 2p. [159]
Husband in the Indian service.

19. Mem. of Georgia Citizens. 1 Feb.
SD 38, 19-2, v2, 5p. [145]
Depredations committed by the Creek Indians prior to 1802.

20. Letter on Chickasaw and Choctaw Lands. 1 Feb.
SD 39, 19-2, v2, 5p. [145]
On encroachments of the whites.

21. Message on the Treaty with the Choctaws. 2 Feb.
SD 42, 19-2, v2, 4p. [145]
On execution of the treaty of 18 Oct. 1820.

22. Letter on the Friendly Creek Indians. 2 Feb.
HD 79, 19-2, v5, 4p. [152]
Transmitting a resol. of the Georgia Legis.

23. Statement of Military Appropriations. 3 Feb.
HD 132, 19-2, v7 (pt. 1), 10 p. [154]
For the year 1826.

24. Message on the Survey of Creek Lands. 5 Feb.
HD 76, 19-2, v5, 9p. [152]
In the state of Georgia; their rights to this land are founded on treaties; etc.

25. Licenses to Indian Traders. 7 Feb.
SD 58, 19-2, v3, 9p. [146] *or* HD 86, 19-2, v5, 10p. [152]
By whom issued, to whom, when, place of trade, etc.

26. Message on Indian Depredations in Georgia. 8 Feb.
SD 47, 19-2, v2, 7p. [145]
Creek Indians.

27. Message on the Survey of Creek Lands. 8 Feb.
HD 87, 19-2, v5, 7p. [152]
Interruption of surveys in Georgia by an Indian protest.

28. Report on Georgia Military Claims. 10 Feb.
HR 77, 19-2, v1, 8p. [159]
Indian hostilities on the state's frontier.

29. Message on the Public Lands. 16 Feb.
SD 63, 19-2, v3, 38p. [146]
Sums paid for purchase of land from the Indians, and expenses of holding treaties since 1776.

30. Accounts of the Treasury. 19 Feb.
HD 145, 19-2, v7 (pt. 1), 182p. [154]
Indian expenses.

31. Report on Indian Appropriations. 22 Feb.
HR 86, 19-2, v2, 1p. [160]
Estimates for the Indian service, including removal, Creek Indian Agency, Delaware claims, etc.

32. Disbursements to Indians. 23 Feb.
HD 112, 19-2, v8, 146p. [156]
From 1 Sept. 1825 to 1 Sept. 1826.

33. R-M of the Arkansas Legis. 27 Feb.
HR 93, 19-2, v2, 4p. [160]
Quapaw treaty of 1818; Choctaw lands by treaty of 1820.

34. Report on the Georgia Question. 1 Mar.
SD 69, 19-2, v3, 9p. [146]
Grounds on which the Executive has interfered with the proceedings of Georgia relative to Creek Indian lands.

35. Message on the Georgia Indian Treaties. 2 Mar.
HD 127, 19-2, v6, 9p. [153]
Creek Indians, etc.

36. Statement of Appropriations. 3 Mar.
HD 126, 19-2, v6, 23p. [153]
Indian treaties, annuities, etc.

37. Report on the Georgia Indian Controversy. 3 Mar.
HR 98, 19-2, v3, 846p. [161]
Creek and Cherokee Indians.

38. Annual Message to Congress with Documents; Pres. Adams. 4 Dec.
SD 1, 20-1, v1, 265p. [163] *or* HD 2, 20-1, v1, 265p. [169]
Indian treaties; Atkinson expedition up the Missouri River; reports of the Sec. of War, Indian Dept., etc.

39. Annual Report of the Sec. of the Treasury. 10 Dec.
SD 4, 20-1, v1, 50p. [163] *or* HD 4, 20-1, v1, 50p. [169]
Indian Dept., etc.

40. R-P of G. Perpall. 10 Dec.
HD 6, 20-1, v1, 12p. [169]
Creek Indians in Florida.

41. R-P of R. Davis. 18 Dec.
HR 10, 20-1, v1, 5p. [176]
Seminole war in 1818.

42. R-P of the Widow of Gen. Hull. 19 Dec.

HR 18, 20-1, v1, 3p. [176]
Indian Dept. accounts outstanding.

43. R-P of W. and J. Pierce. 20 Dec.
HR 25, 20-1, v1, 1p. [176]
Creek Indian depredations.

44. R-M of the Tennessee Legis. 24 Dec.
HR 32, 20-1, v1, 6p. [176]
Chickasaw Indian land.

1828

1. Estimate of Appropriations. 2 Jan.
HD 40, 20-1, v2, 57p. [170]
For 1828; Indian appropriations.

2. Report on Land Claims in Michigan. 2 Jan.
HR 42, 20-1, v1, 515p. [176]
British-Indian forces; Indian council, 1812; etc.

3. Report on the Creek Indian Fund. 7 Jan.
HD 44, 20-1, v2, 11p. [170]
Fund inadequate for defraying the expenses attending their removal; amount of appropriation.

4. Report on Lead Mines. 7 Jan.
HD 45, 20-1, v2, 10p. [170]
Chippewa, Ottawa, Pottawatomie, and Winnebago Indian lands.

5. Report on the Troops. 7 Jan.
HD 46, 20-1, v2, 7p. [170]
Winnebago Indian hostilities.

6. Report on the Removal of Indians. 7 Jan.
HR 56, 20-1, v1, 4p. [176]
Appropriation for removing Indians westward.

7. Report on the Creek Indians. 8 Jan.
HD 74, 20-1, v3, 2p. [171]
Number who have removed west of the Mississippi; expense.

8. R-P of J. Winton. 11 Jan.
HR 66, 20-1, v2, 2p. [177]
Cherokee Indian treaty of 1819.

9. Report on the Cherokee Government. 14 Jan.
HR 67, 20-1, v2, 2p. [177]
Reports that the Government of the U.S. has no right to interfere with the form of government adopted by the Cherokee Indians so far as relates to the government of their own people.

10. R-M on the Proposed Territory of Huron. 15 Jan.
HR 79, 20-1, v2, 13p. [177]
Potential Indian hostilities; Chippewa, Ottawa, Pottawatomie and Winnebago Indians; traders; etc.

11. Report on a Proposed Road in Ohio. 21 Jan.
HD 73, 20-1, v3, 3p. [171]
Through the Wyandot reservation.

12. Report on Emigrant Indians. 21 Jan.
HD 283, 20-1, v7, 3p. [175]
On the suffering condition of emigrant Indians; removal.

13. Report on Road in New York and Pennsylvania. 21 Jan.
HR 91, 20-1, v2, 43p. [177]
Frontier defense against Indians, etc.

14. Report on Cherokee Indian Lands. 22 Jan.
HR 92, 20-1, v2, 8p. [177]
Recommends refunding to North Carolina the sum paid to Indians for reservations of land granted to them by treaty of 1819.

15. Report on the Treaty with the Cherokee Indians. 23 Jan.
HD 104, 20-1, v3, 6p. [171]
List of persons entitled to reservations under treaty of 27 Feb. 1819; returns of com'rs appointed to survey reservations.

16. R-P of F. Felix. 23 Jan.
HR 93, 20-1, v2, 1p. [177]
Indians under British command; 1813; Detroit.

17. Report on the Winnebago Indian Lands. 26 Jan.
HD 117, 20-1, v3, 5p. [171]
Complaints of Indians respecting intrusion upon their lands; purchase of lands recommended; reports of Gov. Cass and Col. McKenney.

18. An Act of the British Parliament. 28 Jan.
SD 67, 20-1, v2, 7p. [164]
On fur trade with the Indians.

19. Report on the Public Lands. 28 Jan.
HR 102, 20-1, v2, 5p. [177]
Choctaw district of Mississippi; Indian title extinguished in 1820.

20. Report on the Cherokee Indian Lands. 29 Jan.
HD 106, 20-1, v3, 39p. [171]
Report of com'rs appointed to negotiate with Indians for a portion of their country; Indians unwilling to dispose of land within the limits of their nation.

21. Report on School Lands in Ohio. 30 Jan.
HR 109, 20-1, v2, 1p. [177]
Indian title to land.

22. Statement of Appropriations for War Dept. 31 Jan.
HD 129, 20-1, v3, 10p. [171]
For the year 1827; Indian expenses.

23. R-P of S. Chitwood. 31 Jan.
HR 117, 20-1, v2, 1p. [177]
Creek Indians.

24. Resol. of the Georgia Legis. 4 Feb.
SD 80, 20-1, v3, 13p. [165] *or* HD 102, 20-1, v3, 13p. [171]
On extinguishing Cherokee title to land.

25. Petition of Col. Tennille. 4 Feb.
HD 115, 20-1, v3, 5p. [171]
Creek Indian war; Georgia.

26. Report on Public Lands. 5 Feb.
HR 125, 20-1, v2, 8p. [177]
Amount of land to which Indian title has been extinguished.

27. R-P of Chippewa Indians. 5 Feb.
HR 127, 20-1, v2, 2p. [177]
Recommends that petition for a section of land be granted.

28. Report on Creek Indian Claims. 5 Feb.
HR 128, 20-1, v2, 23p. [177]
It would be inexpedient to legislate upon the subject of claims against the Creek Indians.

29. Report on Emigration of the Creek Indians. 6 Feb.
HR 130, 20-1, v2, 2p. [177]
Recommends appropriation for the aid of Creek Indians in removing westward, and also to enable the president to extinguish the title of the Cherokee Indians to lands in the state of Georgia.

30. Report on Expenditures of the War Dept. 7 Feb.
SD 93, 20-1, v3, 8p. [165]
For year 1827.

31. R-M of Arkansas Legis. 8 Feb.
SD 95, 20-1, v3, 4p. [165]
Payment due J. Scull; Quapaw treaty of 19 Feb. 1824.

32. Report on Trade with the Indians. 8 Feb.
SD 96, 20-1, v3, 7p. [165] *or* HD 140, 20-1, v4, 6p. [172]
Licenses to trade with Indians; by whom granted; to whom; date; term; etc.

33. Report on the Chickasaw Country. 11 Feb.
HR 135, 20-1, v2, 1p. [177]
Inexpedient to make appropriation to obtain part of Chickasaw country to be attached to the county of Monroe, Mississippi.

34. Report on Court Martial of Tennessee Militiamen. 11 Feb.
HR 140, 20-1, v2, 63p. [177]
Creek Indian campaign.

35. Mem. of the Georgia Legis. 12 Feb.
HD 135, 20-1, v4, 8p. [172]
Against the Creek Indians under the 1821 treaty at Indian Springs.

36. R-C of R. Irvin. 13 Feb.
HR 144, 20-1, v3, 2p. [178]
Creek Indians.

37. Report on Selling Spirits to the Indian Tribes. 16 Feb.
HD 148, 20-1, v4, 2p. [172]
Regulations.

38. Statement on the Bill for the Relief of Thomas L. McKenney. 18 Feb.
SD 109, 20-1, v3, 1p. [165]
Supt. of Indian Affairs.

39. Correspondence of Gen. Jackson. 18 Feb.
HD 146, 20-1, v4, 22p. [172]
On the Creek Indian war.

40. R-M of W. Blount. 19 Feb.
SD 110, 20-1, v4, 63p. [166]
Former Governor of Tennessee; Tennessee militia; Creek Indian war; British-Indian war; etc.

41. R-P of Michigan Citizens. 29 Feb.
HR 167, 20-1, v3, 1p. [178]
Indian title extinguished; settlers near Lake Michigan.

42. R-M of the Alabama Legis. 3 Mar.
HR 171, 20-1, v3, 1p. [178]
Creek Indian war.

43. Report on a Road to the Illinois Lead Mines. 4 Mar.
HR 177, 20-1, v3, 3p. [178]
Would pass through Indian territory; their title to land must be extinguished.

44. Report on the Finances. 12 Mar.
HR 185, 20-1, v3, 36p. [178]
Expenditures and receipts for 1827; Indian expenses.

45. Report on the Creek Indians. 15 Mar.
HD 200, 20-1, v5, 34p. [173]
Indemnity for damages by Creek Indians.

46. R-M of R. Taylor. 18 Mar.
SD 142, 20-1, v4, 7p. [166]
Indian wars in Kentucky; 1791-2.

47. Report on a Judge for Michigan. 18 Mar.
HR 197, 20-1, v3, 1p. [178]
Would not have jurisdiction over cases growing out of intercourse with Indian tribes.

48. Message on the Treaty with the Creek Nation. 21 Mar.
HD 210, 20-1, v5, 7p. [173]
Transmitting copy of the treaty.

49. Message on the Cherokee Indians. 22 Mar.
HD 211, 20-1, v5, 17p. [173]
On the formation of a new government by the Cherokee Indians of North Carolina, Georgia, Tennessee, and Alabama.

50. R-P of J. Russel. 22 Mar.
HR 206, 20-1, v3, 2p. [178]
Cherokee Indian treaty of 1817.

51. Letter on Indian Chiefs. 27 Mar.
HD 219, 20-1, v5, 18p. [173]
In the territory of Michigan in 1827, and the Creek Nation.

52. Information relative to Indian Tribes. 29 Mar.
HD 233, 20-1, v6, 4p. [174]
On Indians removed to the west of the Mississippi; location; tribes removed; number.

53. R-M of Baptist Missionary Convention. 1 Apr.
HR 219, 20-1, v3, 1p. [177]
Ask permission to form a settlement west of the Mississippi for the remnant tribes of Indians.

54. Estimates of Appropriations. 5 Apr.
HD 241, 20-1, v6, 33p. [174]
For the first quarter of 1829.

55. Message on the Treaty with the Creek Indians. 8 Apr.
HD 238, 20-1, v6, 24p. [174]
On the treaty concluded 15 Nov. 1827.

56. Report on Indian Agent. 15 Apr.
HD 248, 20-1, v6, 28p. [174]
On charges against the agent for the Creek Indians since 1 Jan. 1826; intrusion of agent on Indian improvements; erection of stores and public houses.

57. Report on Land Grant for Roads. 15 Apr.
HR 234, 20-1, v4, 3p. [179]
St. Mary's treaty of 1818.

58. R-P of W. Tipton. 21 Apr.
HR 235, 20-1, v4, 2p. [179]
Indian war; 1783; south of the Ohio River.

59. Message on Removal of an Indian Agency. 1 May.
SD 189, 20-1, v5, 26p. [167]
From Fort Wayne, Indiana.

60. Message on Payments to Citizens of Georgia. 9 May.
HD 268, 20-1, v7, 68p. [175]
On payments under the 4th article of the treaty of 8 Feb. 1821 with the Creek Indians.

61. Report on Road in Alabama and Tennessee. 13 May.
HR 256, 20-1, v4, 1p. [179]
Passing through the Chickasaw territory.

62. Report on Reduced Expenses. 15 May.
HR 259, 20-1, v4, 199p. [179]
In the Indian Dept., etc.

63. Report on Indian Hostilities. 19 May.
HD 277, 20-1, v7, 17p. [175]
On the northwestern frontier; causes; Winnebagoes, Chippewas, Sioux, etc.

64. Message on Indian Treaty. 22 May.
HD 279, 20-1, v7, 5p. [175]
Copy of treaty with Eel River band of Miami Indians.

65. Statement of Appropriations. 30 May.
HD 288, 20-1, v7, 34p. [175]
During the 1st session of the 20th Congress; amount and object of each.

66. Annual Message to Congress, with Documents; Pres. Adams. 2 Dec.
SD 1, 20-2, v1, 188p. [181] *or* HD 2, 20-2, v1, 188p. [184]
Legal status of Indians; reports of Sec. of War, Indian Bureau, and Land Office, etc.

67. Message on Estimate of Appropriations, and Expenditures. 8 Dec.
SD 4, 20-2, v1, 15p. [181]
Report of Sec. Rush; for the year 1828; Indian treaties, etc.

68. Message on the Cherokee Council. 8 Dec.
HD 6, 20-2, v1, 13p. [184]
On the survey for a canal through the Cherokee country.

69. Report on Civilization of the Indians. 8 Dec.
HD 11, 20-2, v1, 8p. [184]

On appropriations for the promotion of Indian civilization; Indian schools; increase of appropriation required.

70. Annual Report of the Sec. of the Treasury. 9 Dec.
SD 7, 20-2, v1, 38p. [181] *or* HD 9, 20-2, v1, 40p. [184]
Indian Dept., etc.

71. Mem. of J. Bradford. 10 Dec.
HD 13, 20-2, v1, 6p. [184]
Asks government protection of settlement on Oregon River for the purpose of hunting, trapping, and trading with the Indians.

72. Report on Michigan-Ohio Boundary. 10 Dec.
HR 2, 20-2, v1, 3p. [190]
Indian land at the south end of Lake Michigan.

73. Resol. of the Florida Legis. 15 Dec.
HD 17, 20-2, v1, 1p. [184]
Removal of Florida Indians.

74. Report on Indian Lands. 16 Dec.
HD 22, 20-2, v2, 2p. [185]
On sale of Indian reservations in the state of Indiana; Miami Indians.

75. R-P of J. Scull. 16 Dec.
HR 5, 20-2, v1, 1p. [190]
Quapaw Indian treaty.

76. Report on Florida Indians. 19 Dec.
HD 31, 20-2, v2, 3p. [185]
From the agent in Florida on the wish of the Seminole Indians to remove to the country west of the Mississippi.

77. Report on Lands in Florida. 19 Dec.
HR 9, 20-2, v1, 1p. [190]
Land granted to an Indian chief in treaty of 18 Sept. 1823.

78. Report on a Road from Columbus to New Orleans. 22 Dec.
HD 23, 20-2, v2, 4p. [185]
Through Choctaw Indian lands.

79. Report on Military Road in Michigan. 23 Dec.
HD 29, 20-2, v2, 3p. [185]
Protection of northwestern boundary, and control of Indian trade.

80. Message on Lead Mines in Illinois and Missouri. 23 Dec.
HD 30, 20-2, v2, 8p. [185]
Treaties with Chippewa, Pottawatomie, Sac, Fox, Ottawa, Winnebago, and Choctaw Indians.

81. On the Relief of T. Wheatley. 24 Dec.
HR 15, 20-2, v1, 3p. [190]
Expedition on Wabash River against Indians, 1812.

82. R-P of T. Cooksey. 24 Dec.
HR 16, 20-2, v1, 1p. [190]
Expedition against British and Indians in 1813.

83. On the Case of H. Bernard. 29 Dec.
HR 22, 20-2, v1, 2p. [190]
Chetimache Indians in Louisiana; 1804.

1829

1. Statement of Contingent Expenditures. 2 Jan.
HD 53, 20-2, v2, 5p. [185]
For 1828; Indian interpreters.

2. Report on Indian Tribes. 3 Jan.
SD 27, 20-2, v1, 7p. [181]
Indian tribes within the U.S.; extent and location of lands to which the Indian title has been extinguished.

3. Estimates of Appropriations. 3 Jan.
HD 49, 20-2, v2, 56p. [185]
Year 1829; Indian Dept., etc.

4. Report on Florida Military Road. 3 Jan.
HD 52, 20-2, v2, 7p. [185]
Florida Indians.

5. Report on the Indians. 6 Jan.
HD 57, 20-2, v2, 6p. [185]
On the wishes of the Seneca Indians residing in Ohio as to their removal.

6. R-P of I. Moore. 7 Jan.
SD 30, 20-2, v1, 1p. [181]
Shawnee Indians, Missouri.

7. Resol. of Sen. Prince. 8 Jan.
SD 31, 20-2, v1, 1p. [181]
Relative to provisions of law required for the removal of Indians.

8. R-P of J. Elliott et al. 12 Jan.
HR 42, 20-2, v1, 2p. [190]
Land cessions by the Cherokee Indians; treaty of 8 July 1817.

9. Letter on a New Territory. 13 Jan.
HD 66, 20-2, v2, 5p. [185]
Indian trade and land titles in the proposed Huron territory.

10. R-P of H. La Croix et al. 14 Jan.
HR 46, 20-2, v1, 2p. [190]
British and Indian forces; 23 Jan. 1813.

11. Report on Publishing Costs. 16 Jan.
HR 47, 20-2, v1, 17p. [190]
Indian treaties, etc.
12. Message on the Creek Indians. 17 Jan.
HD 80, 20-2, v2, 9p. [185]
Claims of Georgia and of the Creek Indians under the treaty of 1821.
13. R-P of M. Couture. 19 Jan.
HR 51, 20-2, v1, 6p. [190]
British and Indians; Michigan; 1813.
14. Report on the Trade with Indians. 20 Jan.
SD 47, 20-2, v1, 2p. [181]
Licenses issued from 1 Sept. 1827 to 1 Sept. 1828; etc.
15. Letter of Indian Trade Licenses. 21 Jan.
HD 84, 20-2, v2, 5p. [185]
Those granted for the year ending 30 Sept. 1828.
16. Message Transmitting Copies of Indian Treaties. 21 Jan.
HD 88, 20-2, v2, 8p. [185]
Copies of treaties with the Winnebago Indians and United Tribes at Green Bay on 25 Aug. 1828; treaty with Pottawatomie Indians concluded 20 Sept. 1828.
17. Mem. of the Missouri Legis. 26 Jan.
SD 52, 20-2, v1, 3p. [181]
Missouri to Mexico trade route; Pawnee depredations; British fur trade on the Upper Missouri River; etc.
18. Mem. of the New York Indian Tribes. 26 Jan.
SD 55, 20-2, v1, 2p. [181]
Ask that treaty with the Winnebagoes and Menomonees for land in Michigan territory not be confirmed.
19. Message on Indian Com'rs. 26 Jan.
HD 91, 20-2, v3, 11p. [186]
Copies of instructions to the Com'rs who concluded the treaty at Indian Springs in 1821 with the Creek Indians.
20. Message on the Cherokee Indians. 30 Jan.
HD 95, 20-2, v3, 14p. [186]
Treaty of May 1828; Georgia.
21. Correspondence on the Treaty of San Lorenzo El Real. 30 Jan.
HD 96, 20-2, v3, 18p. [186]
Seminole Indians.
22. Report on the Indians. 3 Feb.
HD 108, 20-2, v3, 9p. [186]
On agreement between the Creek and Cherokee Indians relative to boundary lines; 1815.
23. Military Appropriations for 1828. 7 Feb.
HD 115, 20-2, v3, 11p. [186]
Indian annuities, treaty stipulations, education, etc.
24. Report on the Fur Trade. 9 Feb.
SD 67, 20-2, v1, 19p. [181]
Control of Upper Missouri River trade; exclusion of British.
25. Report on Indian Affairs. 9 Feb.
SD 72, 20-2, v1, 118p. [181] *or*
HD 117, 20-2, v3, 120p. [186]
On a revised system of laws and regulations; general regulation of intercourse with Indians; payment of annuities; code of regulations for the government of the Indian Dept.; Indian tribes in the U.S.; situation and number.
26. Mem. of the Indiana Legis. 11 Feb.
SD 74, 20-2, v1, 2p. [181]
Asks extinguishment of Miami Indian land titles.
27. Mem. of Cherokee Indians. 17 Feb.
HD 124, 20-2, v3, 15p. [186]
Asks passage of bill allowing interest on money withheld under treaty with the U.S.; made in 1804, ratified in 1824.
28. Report on Removal of Indians Westward. 18 Feb.
HR 87, 20-2, v1, 48p. [190]
Recommends that lands upon which Indians may be located shall be so secured that they be not dispossessed of them in the future; that they be paid a just compensation for improvements which they abandon; protection afforded them in their new homes; recommends appropriation to aid in their removal; Chickasaw, Cherokee, Creek, Choctaw, and other Indians.
29. Report on Lands Between the Ludlow and Roberts' Lines in Ohio. 18 Feb.
HR 88, 20-2, v1, 19p. [190]
Indian land titles.
30. On the Case of J. Royal. 18 Feb.
HR 89, 20-2, v1, 1p. [190]
Creek Indians; 1814.
31. Mem. of the Missouri Legis. 19 Feb.
SD 88, 20-2, v2, 2p. [182]
Asks certain Indian lands be purchased by the U.S.
32. Abstract of Expenditures on Account of Indians. 25 Feb.
HD 129, 20-2, v3, 6p. [186]

On account of the deputation of Winnebago Indians; estimated expense of concluding treaty with the Indians for the purchase of the lead district in Illinois.

33. Report on Public Lands. 25 Feb.
HR 95, 20-2, v1, 22p. [190]
Land to which Indian title has been extinguished.

34. Message on Army. 26 Feb.
SD 101, 20-2, v2, 79p. [182]
Correspondence on Indians and Indian Department.

35. R-C of Florida Citizens. 26 Feb.
HR 99, 20-2, v1, 34p. [190]
Indian hostilities.

36. Mem. of J. Ross et al. 27 Feb.
HD 145, 20-2, v4, 3p. [187]
Protest against the act of the Georgia Legis. adding a portion of the Cherokee territory to the state.

37. Message Transmitting Indian Treaties. 28 Feb.
HD 131, 20-2, v3, 7p. [186]
Copies of treaties with the Chippewa, Menomonee, Winnebago, and Pottawatomie Indians.

38. Letter on Florida-Georgia Boundary. 3 Mar.
HD 140, 20-2, v4, 84p. [187]
Indian hostilities.

39. Statement of Appropriations. 3 Mar.
HD 142, 20-2, v4, 30p. [187]
During the 2d session of the 20th Congress.

40. Annual Message to Congress with Documents; Pres. Jackson. 8 Dec.
SD 1, 21-1, v1, 328p. [192] *or* HD 2, 21-1, v1, 328p. [195]
Condition of Indians; proposed Indian territory; reports of Sec. of War, Indian Office, Land Office, etc.

41. Annual Report of the Sec. of the Treasury. 15 Dec.
SD 3, 21-1, v1, 82p. [192] *or* HD 6, 21-1, v1, 82p. [195]
Indian affairs, etc.

42. Mem. of the Indiana Legis. 24 Dec.
SD 6, 21-1, v1, 2p. [192]
Asks that title of Miami Indians to lands in Indiana be extinguished.

43. Estimate of Appropriations. 28 Dec.
HD 14, 21-1, v1, 49p. [195]
For 1830.

44. R-P of G. Godfroy. 30 Dec.
HR 35, 21-1, v1, 2p. [199]
British and Indians; 1813.

45. R-P of H. La Croix. 30 Dec.
HR 36, 21-1, v1, 3p. [199]
British and Indians; 1813.

46. R-P of W. Tipton. 30 Dec.
HR 37, 21-1, v1, 2p. [199]
Indian war south of the Ohio River in 1783.

47. R-P of F. Comparet. 30 Dec.
HR 38, 21-1, v1, 1p. [199]
Pottawatomie treaty of Sept. 1828.

1830

1. R-M of J. Edgar. 5 Jan.
SD 10, 21-1, v1, 4p. [192]
Loss of land to the Indians.

2. Report on the Defence of Arkansas. 5 Jan.
HD 17, 21-1, v1, 1p. [195]
For the defence and protection of its frontiers from Indians.

3. Report on the Territory of Huron. 6 Jan.
HR 56, 21-1, v1, 12p. [199]
Tribes which will be within the boundaries of the proposed territory; west of Lake Michigan.

4. R-M of Indiana Legis. 7 Jan.
SD 14, 21-1, v1, 2p. [192]
Recommends extinguishment of Miami and Pottawatomie titles to land in Indiana.

5. On the Case of P. Gasney. 8 Jan.
HR 65, 21-1, v1, 1p. [199]
British and Indians in Canada in 1813.

6. Mem. of J. Kennedy. 9 Jan.
SD 94, 21-1, v2, 4p. [193]
Asks indemnification for losses; in Creek war of 1810.

7. Report on Indian Depredations. 9 Jan.
HD 25, 21-1, v2, 102p. [196]
Creek Indians; Georgia.

8. R-P of Cherokee Indians. 11 Jan.
HR 69, 21-1, v1, 2p. [199]
Wish to remove west, from lands granted to them by the treaty of 8 July 1817.

9. Message Transmitting Indian Treaties. 14 Jan.
HD 24, 21-1, v2, 13p. [196]
Copies of treaties with the Winnebago, Chippewa, Ottawa, and Pottawatomie Indians; estimate of ap-

propriations to carry the treaties into effect.

10. On the Case of Capt. Wood. 15 Jan.
HR 82, 21-1, v1, 1p. [199]
Cherokee Indian treaty of 1817.

11. Message Transmitting Information on the Indians. 20 Jan.
HD 34, 21-1, v2, 3p. [196]
On the appropriation to pay the annuity due from the U.S. to the Society of Christian Indians.

12. Report on Ludlow's and Roberts' Lines. 20 Jan.
HR 103, 21-1, v1, 19p. [199]
Indian land titles in Ohio.

13. On the Case of H. Williams. 25 Jan.
HR 108, 21-1, v1, 1p. [199]
Creek Indian war; 1813.

14. On the Case of L. Rouse. 25 Jan.
HR 110, 21-1, v1, 4p. [199]
Supplies for troops *en route* to an Indian council near St. Anthony Falls; 1818.

15. R-C of Citizens of Georgia. 26 Jan.
HR 115, 21-1, v1, 2p. [199]
For property destroyed by the Creek Indians.

16. Resol. of the Indiana Legis. 29 Jan.
SD 97, 21-1, v2, 2p. [193]
Land in Miami Indian reservation.

17. Unexpended Balances. 30 Jan.
HD 42, 21-1, v2, 11p. [196]
Indian expenses.

18. Mem. of Citizens of Ohio. 1 Feb.
HR 265, 21-1, v2, 2p. [200]
Ask that Cherokee and other Indians be protected in the possession of their lands.

19. Mem. of the Citizens of Wilmington, Delaware. 2 Feb.
SD 56, 21-1, v2, 3p. [193]
Asks Congress to carry out stipulations of treaties made with the Cherokee Indians.

20. Mem. of the Pennsylvania Baptist Association. 2 Feb.
SD 64, 21-1, v2, 2p. [193]
Approve plan of settling Indians west of the Mississippi; removal.

21. Report on Indians. 2 Feb.
HD 47, 21-1, v2, 3p. [196]
On the wish of the Seneca tribe to sell its reservation in Ohio.

22. Mem. of the Creek Nation. 3 Feb.
SD 53, 21-1, v2, 5p. [193]
Protests acts of the Alabama Legis. in relation to annuities.

23. Mem. of the Chiefs of Creek Nation. 3 Feb.
HR 169, 21-1, v1, 5p. [199]
Ask fulfillment of treaties between the U.S. and the Creek Nation.

24. On the Case of A. Reynolds. 4 Feb.
HR 153, 21-1, v1, 1p. [199]
Indian wars in Kentucky.

25. Pre-Emption to Persons in Florida. 5 Feb.
HR 162, 21-1, v1, 1p. [199]
Lands ceded to Indians by treaty of 18 Sept. 1823.

26. Message on Trade Between Missouri and Mexico. 8 Feb.
SD 46, 21-1, v1, 9p. [192]
Protection from Pawnee, Shawnee, Kansa, and Iowa Indian raids.

27. Mem. of Citizens of Boston, Massachusetts. 8 Feb.
HR 245, 21-1, v2, 7p. [200]
Ask act to enforce the provisions of treaties with the Cherokee and other Indians.

28. Mem. of the Board of Emigration. 9 Feb.
HR 233, 21-1, v2, 3p. [200]
Ask provisions be made for the removal, preservation, and improvement of the aborigines of America.

29. R-P of J. Webb. 10 Feb.
HR 183, 21-1, v2, 2p. [200]
Creek Indian lands in Georgia; U.S. mail carrier shot.

30. Report on Florida-Georgia Boundary. 13 Feb.
HR 191, 21-1, v2, 8p. [200]
Indian hostilities.

31. Mem. of the Alabama Legis. 15 Feb.
HR 204, 21-1, v2, 4p. [200]
Consideration by the government given the Creeks and Cherokees.

32. Mem. of the Ladies of Steubenville. 15 Feb.
HR 209, 21-1, v2, 2p. [200]
Protest the forcible removal of the Indians.

33. Mem. of the New York Missionary Society. 16 Feb.
SD 59, 21-1, v2, 1p. [193]
Ask colonization of Indians east of the Rocky Mountains; removal.

34. Petition of the Society of Friends. 16 Feb.
HR 246, 21-1, v2, 3p. [200]
Asks Congress to provide for removal and settlement of Indians west of the Mississippi River.

35. Mem. of the Baptist Missionary Society. 16 Feb.
HR 247, 21-1, v2, 2p. [200]
Asks Congress to provide Indians with a permanent home west of the Mississippi River.

36. Report on President's Message on Indian Affairs. 22 Feb.
SD 61, 21-1, v2, 9p. [193]
For the removal west of the Indians.

37. Mem. of Citizens of Pennsylvania. 22 Feb.
HR 261, 21-1, v2, 2p. [200]
Ask that Cherokees and other Indians be protected on their lands.

38. Mem. of Citizens of Ohio. 22 Feb.
HR 263, 21-1, v2, 2p. [200]
Ask that Cherokees and other Indians be protected on their lands.

39. Mem. of Pennsylvania Citizens. 22 Feb.
HR 264, 21-1, v2, 7p. [200]
Cherokee and other Indians.

40. Mem. of the Ladies of Burlington. 23 Feb.
SD 66, 21-1, v2, 2p. [193]
Ask Congress to protect the Indians in the enjoyment of their rights and possession of their lands.

41. Report of Disbursements to Indians. 23 Feb.
HD 87, 21-1, v3, 139p. [197]
Accounts for year ending 30 Sept. 1829.

42. Report on Removal of the Indians. 24 Feb.
HR 227, 21-1, v2, 32p. [200]
Recommends appropriation to aid in removing the Indians west of the Mississippi River.

43. Mem. of Citizens of New Jersey. 26 Feb.
SD 73, 21-1, v2, 2p. [193]
Ask Congress to extend its protection to the Cherokee Indians.

44. Mem. of Citizens of Connecticut. 27 Feb.
SD 74, 21-1, v2, 4p. [193]
Ask Indians may be protected in their rights and the possession of their lands.

45. Mem. of Citizens of New Jersey. 28 Feb.
SD 77, 21-1, v2, 1p. [193]
Ask Indians may be protected in the enjoyment of their rights and the possession of their lands.

46. Mem. of Pennsylvania Citizens. 1 Mar.
HR 254, 21-1, v2, 2p. [200]
For protection of the Cherokee and other Indians.

47. Mem. of Citizens of Pennsylvania. 1 Mar.
HR 255, 21-1, v2, 2p. [200]
Ask that the Cherokees and other Indians be protected in the possession of their lands and the enjoyment of their laws and customs.

48. Mem. of New Jersey Citizens. 1 Mar.
HR 256, 21-1, v2, 2p. [200]
To protect Cherokee and other Indians.

49. R-P of W. King et al. 2 Mar.
HR 249, 21-1, v2, 1p. [200]
For travelling expenses incurred in examining site for location of Indians; Chickasaw Indian talks of 9 Oct. 1827; removal.

50. Mem. of the Pennsylvania Legis. 3 Mar.
SD 76, 21-1, v2, 2p. [193]
Ask that Indians be protected in the enjoyment of their rights and the possession of their lands.

51. Mem. of the Pennsylvania Baptist Association. 3 Mar.
HR 253, 21-1, v2, 2p. [200]
Ask Congress to grant a permanent home to the Indians.

52. Mem. of the Indiana Legis. 4 Mar.
SD 79, 21-1, v2, 1p. [193]
Ask that Miami and Pottawatomie Indian title to lands in Indiana be extinguished.

53. Mem. of Citizens of Maine. 6 Mar.
SD 92, 21-1, v2, 1p. [193]
Ask that Georgia, Alabama, and Mississippi Indians not be removed from their present places of abode without their free consent.

54. Documents of Georgia's Jurisdiction Over Indians. 8 Mar.
SD 98, 21-1, v2, 11p. [193]
Jurisdiction of states over Indians within their borders; Creeks, Cherokees.

55. Mem. of the Indiana General Assembly. 8 Mar.
HR 291, 21-1, v2, 1p. [200]
Ask appropriation to extinguish Miami and Pottawatomie Indian title to certain lands in Indiana.

56. Mem. of Citizens of Maine. 20 Mar.
SD 96, 21-1, v2, 1p. [193]
Ask Indians be protected in their rights and possession of their lands.

57. R-C of R. Forsythe. 10 Mar.
HR 285, 21-1, v2, 2p. [200]
General Indian council in Ohio, 1814.
58. Report on War Dept. 12 Mar.
HD 78, 21-1, v3, 17p. [197]
Appropriations for 1829; militia claims for Indian campaigns.
59. Report on a Road in Alabama. 15 Mar.
HR 293, 21-1, v2, 1p. [200]
Chickasaw Indian land to be crossed.
60. Mem. of Cherokee Indians. 15 Mar.
HR 311, 21-1, v3, 9p. [201]
Indians wish to remain on their present land; against removal.
61. Report on Salaries of Judges in Michigan. 17 Mar.
HR 304, 21-1, v3, 3p. [201]
Act of Congress on 11 Jan. 1805 to divide Indian territory.
62. Mem. of Citizens of Massachusetts. 17 Mar.
HR 310, 21-1, v3, 2p. [201]
Ask Indians be protected in their right of self-government and in the possession of their lands.
63. Report on Lands for Education. 18 Mar.
HR 312, 21-1, v3, 3p. [201]
Expenditures on purchases of Indian lands.
64. Laws relating to Indians. 19 Mar.
HR 319, 21-1, v3, 52p. [201]
Compilation of state and Colonial laws relative to Indians.
65. Mem. of the Yearly Meeting of Friends. 22 Mar.
SD 100, 21-1, v2, 1p. [193]
Ask government to extend its protection to the Cherokee and Southwestern Indian tribes.
66. Mem. of Citizens of Connecticut. 22 Mar.
SD 101, 21-1, v2, 3p. [193]
Ask Cherokee and Southwestern Indians be protected in their rights and possession of their lands.
67. Report on the Indians. 25 Mar.
SD 110, 21-1, v2, 22p. [193]
Statement of progress made in the civilization of the Indians during the last eight years; present condition of Indians; number of Indian children at school.
68. R-M of J. Kennedy. 29 Mar.
SD 105, 21-1, v2, 2p. [193]
For property destroyed by Creek Indians.
69. Protest of the North Carolina Legis. 29 Mar.
SD 108, 21-1, v2, 6p. [193]
Against treaties with Cherokee and Chickasaw Indians.
70. Report on Creating a Home Dept. 29 Mar.
SD 109, 21-1, v2, 13p. [193]
Recommends the establishment of an Executive Dept. to be called the Home Dept., and that it be given jurisdiction over Indian affairs.
71. R-C of R. Crittenden. 31 Mar.
HR 339, 21-1, v3, 1p. [201]
Seminole war; 1818.
72. Message on Cherokee Lands. 2 Apr.
HD 89, 21-1, v3, 49p. [197]
On intrusions on land claimed by the Cherokee Indians.
73. Report on a Mounted Force. 8 Apr.
HR 350, 21-1, v3, 1p. [201]
To be positioned south of the Missouri River to control Indian hostilities.
74. Expenditures for 1828 and 1829. 13 Apr.
SD 122, 21-1, v2, 25p. [193]
Indian expenses.
75. Expenditures and Appropriations from 1789 to 1829. 13 Apr.
SD 123, 21-1, v2, 7p. [193] *or* HD 90, 21-1, v4, 7p. [198]
Indian Dept.
76. Message on Removal of Indians. 13 Apr.
HD 91, 21-1, v4, 9p. [198]
Statement on the expenses incident to removal of Indians west of the Mississippi and their support; military force necessary for their protection.
77. R-C of W. Blount. 14 Apr.
HR 362, 21-1, v3, 12p. [201]
Raised funds and troops for Creek war, etc., while governor of Tennessee.
78. R-P of J. McIver. 14 Apr.
HR 363, 21-1, v3, 2p. [201]
Cherokee Indians; treaty of 27 Feb. 1819.
79. Report on Cherokee Claim. 16 Apr.
HR 367, 21-1, v3, 3p. [201]
Whites in Indian country taking Indian property.
80. R-M of J. and J. Pettigrew. 16 Apr.
HR 368, 21-1, v3, 3p. [201]
Cherokees; 1794.

81. Mem. of Citizens of Ohio. 3 May.
HR 302, 21-1, v3, 1p. [201]
Ask Government aid for removal and colonization of Indians.

82. Mem. of the Cherokee Delegation. 3 May.
HR 397, 21-1, v3, 3p. [201]
Protest against alteration of established boundaries.

83. R-C of J. Cassedy. 7 May.
HR 394, 21-1, v3, 1p. [201]
Creek Indian boundary-lines.

84. R-C of B. Reeves, et al. 26 May.
HR 416, 21-1, v3, 14p. [201]
On a road from Missouri to Mexico; expenses for Indian negotiations.

85. Report on Expenses of Foreign Missions. 29 May.
SD 146, 21-1, v2, 11p. [193]
For treaties with Indians.

86. Report on Army Expenditures. 29 May.
HD 120, 21-1, v4, 11p. [198]
Transportation cost rise partially due to posts being located in Creek and Cherokee Country.

87. Statement of Appropriations. 31 May.
HD 122, 21-1, v4, 23p. [198]
During the 1st session of the 21st Congress.

88. Annual Message to Congress with Documents; Pres. Jackson. 6 Dec.
SD 1, 21-2, v1, 251p. [203] *or* HD 2, 21-2, v1, 251p. [206]
Indian policy; report of Sec.of War, Indian Bureau, Land Office, etc.

89. Annual Report of the Sec. of the Treasury. 16 Dec.
SD 6, 21-2, v1, 143p. [203] *or* HD 7, 21-2, v1, 143p. [206]
Indian expenses.

90. Mem. of Citizens of Maine. 18 Dec.
SD 18, 21-2, v1, 4p. [203]
Ask that Cherokees be protected in their rights.

91. Estimate of Appropriations for 1831. 21 Dec.
HD 10, 21-2, v1, 56p. [206]
Indian expenses.

92. R-C of L. Anderson. 22 Dec.
HR 8, 21-2, v1, 1p. [210]
Seminole war, 1818.

93. R-P of J. Rodgers. 28 Dec.
HR 12, 21-2, v1, 1p. [210]
Married to a Cherokee woman; Cherokee-Creek boundary.

94. Mem. of Citizens of Pennsylvania. 31 Dec.
SD 16, 21-1, v1, 2p. [203]
Ask for repeal of act removing the Indians west of the Mississippi.

1831

1. Mem. of Citizens of New Jersey. 1 Jan.
SD 31, 21-2, v1, 1p. [203]
Ask repeal of removal act, and protection of Indian rights.

2. R-M of F. Raymer. 3 Jan.
HR 17, 21-2, v1, 2p. [210]
Prisoner of Indians in 1777.

3. R-C of G. Mayfield. 3 Jan.
HR 18, 21-2, v1, 1p. [210]
Treaty of 1814 at Fort Jackson with the Creek Indians.

4. R-M of the Indiana Legis. 4 Jan.
SD 22, 21-2, v1, 4p. [203]
Recommends extinguishment of Miami and Pottawatomie title to lands in Indiana.

5. Statement of Creek Indian Chiefs. 4 Jan.
HD 24, 21-2, v1, 2p. [206]
Group desirous of emigrating.

6. Mem. of Citizens of Pennsylvania. 7 Jan.
SD 25, 21-2, v1, 4p. [203]
Ask that Cherokee and other Indians be protected in their rights.

7. Report on Indian Trade Licenses. 7 Jan.
HD 41, 21-2, v2, 9p. [207]
Licenses granted to 30 Sept. 1830.

8. R-P of G. Godfroy and J. Beaugrand. 12 Jan.
HR 35, 21-2, v1, 1p. [210]
British and Indians in Michigan in 1813.

9. R-P of D. Hull. 13 Jan.
HR 37, 21-2, v1, 2p. [210]
British and Indians in Michigan in 1812.

10. Mem. of Cherokee Indians. 15 Jan.
HD 57, 21-2, v3, 9p. [208]
Protest the claim of Georgia to Cherokee lands; treaty of 1828 at Indian Springs.

11. Mem. of Citizens of Maine. 17 Jan.
HD 89, 21-2, v3, 1p. [208]
Approve of the act providing for the removal of the Georgia Indians.

12. Mem. of Citizens of Pennsylvania. 19 Jan.

SD 33, 21-2, v1, 3p. [203]
Ask that Cherokee and other Indians be protected in their rights.

13. Mem. of Citizens of Massachusetts. 21 Jan.
SD 34, 21-2, v1, 3p. [203]
Ask that Cherokee, Choctaw, and other Indians be protected in their rights.

14. Message on Protection of the Western Frontiers. 24 Jan.
SD 39, 21-1, v1, 36p. [203]
On military force for protection of the frontier; fur trade; trade with the Mexican colonies.

15. Resol. of the Indiana Legis. 24 Jan.
HD 68, 21-2, v3, 1p. [208]
On total extinguishment of Indian title to land in the state.

16. R-P of J. Torrey. 25 Jan.
HR 44, 21-2, v1, 2p. [210]
Assigned as counsel for the defense of Osh-Rosh, a chief, and two other principal men of the Menomonee Indians; charged with murder in 1830.

17. Mem. of the American Board Foreign Missions. 26 Jan.
SD 50, 21-2, v2, 10p. [204]
Ask that all treaty stipulations with the Cherokee, Choctaw, Chickasaw, and other Indians be observed.

18. Letter on Trade with the Indians. 27 Jan.
SD 43, 21-2, v2, 3p. [204]
On reduction of duty on certain articles of goods furnished the Indians; American Fur Company; British trade competition.

19. Documents on the Indian Trade. 3 Feb.
SD 44, 21-2, v2, 2p. [204]
British trade competition.

20. Message on Indian Lands. 3 Feb.
HD 85, 21-2, v3, 12p. [208]
Correspondence on the location of lands ceded by the Pottawatomie Indians for the benefit of Indiana.

21. Mem. of Citizens of Massachusetts. 3 Feb.
HD 106, 21-2, v4, 5p. [209]
Ask for repeal of law providing for removal west of the Cherokee and other Indians.

22. Mem. of Citizens of Pennsylvania. 8 Feb.
HD 90, 21-2, v3, 3p. [208]
Ask protection for Cherokee Indians from intrusion on their lands.

23. Report on Indian Annuities. 8 Feb.
HD 102, 21-2, v3, 2p. [208]
Paid to Cherokee Indians.

24. Report on Indian Accounts. 9 Feb.
HD 101, 21-2, v3, 112p. [208]
For the year ending 31 Aug. 1830.

25. R-P of W. Duval and P. Carnes. 9 Feb.
HR 74, 21-2, v1, 1p. [210]
Violation of Indian trade act; goods seized by Col. Arbuckle near Fort Gibson in Arkansas in 1829.

26. Mem. of Citizens of Pennsylvania. 14 Feb.
SD 53, 21-2, v2, 5p. [204]
Ask that Cherokee and other treaties be preserved inviolate.

27. Petition of Citizens of Massachusetts. 14 Feb.
HD 105, 21-2, v4, 1p. [209]
Ask protection of Indian rights guaranteed them by treaty.

28. Mem. of Citizens of Maine. 21 Feb.
HD 138, 21-2, v4, 2p. [209]
Approve the law for removal west of the southern Indians.

29. Petition of Citizens of Virginia. 21 Feb.
HD 139, 21-2, v4, 2p. [209]
Ask protection of Cherokee and other Indian rights.

30. Message on Trade with the Indians. 22 Feb.
SD 65, 21-2, v2, 10p. [204]
Evaluation of regulatory Act of 30 March 1802; state laws, etc.

31. R-M of J. Campbell. 23 Feb.
HR 96, 21-2, v1, 1p. [210]
Family taken captive by Indians and Tories in 1778; New York State.

32. Mem. of the Missouri Gen. Assembly. 28 Feb.
SD 71, 21-2, v2, 5p. [204]
Express fear of Indian hostilities as a direct result of the policy of removal; Delaware, Sac, and Fox Indians.

33. Message on Indian Treaties. 1 Mar.
HD 123, 21-2, v4, 20p. [209]
Copies of treaties with the Cherokee Indians, and with the Sac, Fox, Sioux, Omaha, Ottoe, Iowa, and Missouri Indians.

34. R-M of Creek Indians. 2 Mar.
HR 109, 21-2, v1, 3p. [210]
Indemnification for property alleged to have been taken by citizens of Georgia.

35. List of Appropriations. 3 Mar.
HD 128, 21-2, v4, 26p. [209]
During 2d session, 21st Congress; Indian expenses.

36. Statement of War Dept. Appropriations. 3 Mar.
HD 136, 21-2, v4, 16p. [209]
For 1830; Indian expenses.

37. Annual Message to Congress with Documents; Pres. Jackson. 6 Dec.
HD 2, 22-1, v1, 274p. [216]
Indian affairs; reports of Sec. of War, Indian Dept., Land Office, etc.

38. Annual Report of the Sec. of the Treasury. 7 Dec.
HD 3, 22-1, v1, 72p. [216]
Indian expenses.

39. Estimates of Appropriations. 8 Dec.
HD 10, 22-1, v1, 54p. [216]
For 1832; Indian expenses.

40. R-P of J. Rodgers. 20 Dec.
HR 10, 22-1, v1, 1p. [224]
Married to a Cherokee woman; Cherokee/Creek boundary line; treaty with Cherokees of 8 July 1817.

41. R-P of J. Torrey. 23 Dec.
HR 49, 22-1, v1, 1p. [224]
Attorney defending a Menomonee chief and two headmen on charges of murder; 1830.

42. Report on Indian Depredation Claims. 27 Dec.
HR 65, 22-1, v1, 4p. [224]
Recommends claims of citizens of Georgia on account of depredations by the Creek Indians be paid; treaty of 8 Jan. 1821.

43. R-P of W. King. 30 Dec.
HR 85, 22-1, v1, 2p. [224]
Cherokee treaties of 1817 and 1819.

1832

1. On the Case of M. Daws et al. 3 Jan.
HR 94, 22-1, v1, 1p. [224]
Treaty of 18 Sept. 1823 with the Florida Indians.

2. Report on Indian Depredation Claims. 4 Jan.
HD 38, 22-1, v2, 117p. [217] *or* HD 26, 23-1, v1, 117p. [254]
List of claims.

3. R-C of Godfroy and Beaugrand. 4 Jan.
HR 128, 22-1, v1, 2p. [224]
British and Indians; Michigan; 23 Jan. 1813.

4. Mem. from Cherokee Indians. 5 Jan.
HD 45, 22-1, v2, 5p. [217]
Refer Congress to former memorials on their removal west, and to the spoliation of their land.

5. Report on a Road from Green Bay to Prairie du Chien. 6 Jan.
HD 42, 22-1, v2, 4p. [217]
Frontier defense against Indians.

6. Report on Wisconsin Territory. 6 Jan.
HR 145, 22-1, v1, 9p. [224]
Indian land titles in the proposed territory.

7. Mem. from Creek Indians. 9 Jan.
HD 56, 22-1, v2, 8p. [217]
Oppose passage of the act to carry into effect the 4th article of the treaty of 8 Jan. 1821 between the U.S. and the Creeks.

8. Mem. of the Mississippi Legis. 10 Jan.
HD 75, 22-1, v2, 2p. [217]
Treaty of 27 Sept. 1830 with the Choctaw Indians.

9. R-P of J. Thomas. 10 Jan.
HR 148, 22-1, v1, 1p. [224]
Indian hostilities in Michigan.

10. On the Case of G. Mayfield. 13 Jan.
HR 182, 22-1, v1, 2p. [224]
Taken prisoner by Creek Indians in 1789; later a spy and interpreter for U.S.

11. R-P of W. Tennille. 13 Jan.
HR 185, 22-1, v1, 1p. [224]
Creek war in 1813; Georgia.

12. R-M of W. and J. Hardrige. 16 Jan.
HR 192, 22-1, v1, 1p. [224]
Creek Indians; Alabama.

13. R-P of F. Arredondo. 20 Jan.
HR 223, 22-1, v1, 31p. [224]
On property claims from the Florida Indian war.

14. Message on Indian Lands. 24 Jan.
HD 76, 22-1, v2, 7p. [217]
On Choctaw reservations.

15. Mem. of the Creek Indians. 24 Jan.
HD 102, 22-1, v3, 5p. [218]
Against their removal west of the Mississippi.

16. Report on Salary of Judges and the Governor. 30 Jan.
HR 242, 22-1, v2, 2p. [225]
Pay of Governors in Arkansas,

Florida, and Michigan as Supts. of Indian Affairs.

17. R-C of R. Wilkinson. 30 Jan.
HR 243, 22-1, v2, 5p. [225]
Creek Indians; treaty of 16 June 1802.

18. R-P of Chiefs of Choctaw Nation. 30 Jan.
HR 246, 22-1, v2, 2p. [225]
Recommends grant of land to J. Dukes, teacher at the Indian School.

19. R-C of G. Turnbull. 30 Jan.
HR 247, 22-1, v2, 2p. [225]
Choctaw Indians.

20. Resol. of Sen. Frelinghuysen. 2 Feb.
SD 43, 22-1, v1, 1p. [212]
That the U.S. is bound by treaty stipulations to protect the Cherokee Nation from all intrusion upon their territory.

21. Message on the Fur Trade and Trade to Mexico. 8 Feb.
SD 90, 22-1, v2, 86p. [213]
Indian trade at U.S. borders; Indian hostilities on the Missouri-Mexico trade route.

22. Mem. of Citizens of Pennsylvania. 14 Feb.
SD 61, 22-1, v2, 2p. [213]
Ask that Cherokee Indians have their rights and lands protected.

23. Mem. of the Alabama Legis. 15 Feb.
SD 65, 22-1, v2, 4p. [213]
Attack on friendly Creeks by hostile Indians.

24. Message on Removal of the Indians. 15 Feb.
HD 116, 22-1, v4, 17p. [219]
Report from the Sec. of War on the removal west of the Indians.

25. On the Case of J. Trimble. 15 Feb.
HR 292, 22-1, v2, 1p. [225]
British and Indians; 1814; near Prairie du Chien.

26. R-C of J. Brown. 17 Feb.
HR 311, 22-1, v2, 2p. [225]
Cherokee Indians; Tennessee; 1785-1798.

27. Report on Indian Trading Licenses. 20 Feb.
HD 121, 22-1, v4, 6p. [219]
List of licenses granted to 30 Sept. 1831.

28. Report on Indian Depredations in Georgia. 20 Feb.
HR 317, 22-1, v2, 2p. [225]
Authorize settlement of claims against Creek Indians; from 1826 to 1830.

29. R-M of Arkansas Legis. 21 Feb.
HR 321, 22-1, v2, 2p. [225]
Cherokee treaty of 1817.

30. R-M of Choctaw Indians. 24 Feb.
HR 328, 22-1, v3, 2p. [226]
Recommends grant of land to J. Harlan.

31. Statement on Indian Annuities. 27 Feb.
HD 127, 22-1, v4, 7p. [219]
Shows number and amount of annuities now payable under treaty articles.

32. Report on Expenditures of War Dept. 27 Feb.
HD 134, 22-1, v4, 17p. [219]
For 1831.

33. Mem. of C. Clark. 27 Feb.
HD 143, 22-1, v4, 18p. [219]
Creek Indian depredations.

34. R-P of J. Caulfield. 28 Feb.
HR 336, 22-1, v3, 1p. [226]
Land purchased from Creek Indians in Mississippi.

35. On the Case of G. Field. 2 Mar.
HR 346, 22-1, v3, 1p. [226]
Cherokee Indian; Creek war in 1813.

36. Mem. of Citizens of New York. 5 Mar.
HD 175, 22-1, v4, 2p. [219]
Ask Congress to preserve inviolate the treaties with the Cherokees.

37. Report of Expedition to the Indian Country. 7 Mar.
HD 152, 22-1, v4, 20p. [219]
Account of an expedition to Indian country by H. R. Schoolcraft; Sioux, Chippewa, and other Indians; Huron Territory.

38. R-C of J. Kennedy. 9 Mar.
HR 357, 22-1, v3, 3p. [226]
Creek Indians; 1813; Alabama.

39. Message on Indian Agents. 12 Mar.
SD 101, 22-1, v2, 20p. [213]
Shows names and compensation of agents employed in the removal of the Choctaw and Cherokee Indians; time employed; money disbursed.

40. Message on Indian Annuities. 12 Mar.
HD 161, 22-1, v4, 1p. [219]
Report of the Sec. of War on Indians who joined the enemy during the late war and are drawing annuities from the U.S.

41. Mem. of Citizens of Tennessee. 12 Mar.
HD 162, 22-1, v4, 3p. [219]
Ask that Cherokee Indians be protected against the usurpation of Georgia.

42. Message on Removal of the Indians. 12 Mar.
HD 171, 22-1, v4, 91p. [219]
Shows money expended in the removal of the Indians to the West.
43. R-P of P. Ducharme. 12 Mar.
HR 363, 22-1, v3, 2p. [226]
Cession of Indian lands near Green Bay in 1793.
44. Report on Indian Lands. 16 Mar.
HD 172, 22-1, v4, 15p. [219]
On the country west of the Mississippi reserved for the Indians.
45. R-P of the Reps. of W. Young. 17 Mar.
HR 389, 22-1, v3, 1p. [226]
Cherokee treaty of 1817.
46. Report on a Land Office in Mississippi. 17 Mar.
HR 392, 22-1, v3, 2p. [226]
Choctaw treaty of Dancing Rabbit Creek.
47. R-C for Property Destroyed at Detroit. 17 Mar.
HR 393, 22-1, v3, 3p. [226]
British and Indians; 1813.
48. Report on Indian Expenditures. 22 Mar.
HD 180, 22-1, v4, 128p. [219]
From 1 Aug. 1830 to 21 Oct. 1831.
49. R-P of Heirs of J. and T. Pettigrew. 22 Mar.
HR 406, 22-1, v3, 24p. [226]
Creek Indians.
50. Report on Expenses of Indian Treaty. 24 Mar.
HD 181, 22-1, v4, 4p. [219]
Report of the 2d Auditor on the expenses of holding a treaty with the Cherokee Indians during the months of Aug. and Sept. 1830.
51. Mem. of American Board of Foreign Missions. 24 Mar.
HD 194, 22-1, v5, 17p. [220]
Ask Congress to take measures to ascertain the value of the buildings and improvements belonging to the board on the territory of the Choctaw Indians.
52. R-M of J. Navarre. 28 Mar.
HR 418, 22-1, v3, 8p. [226]
Indians near Detroit in 1813.
53. Report on Small-Pox among the Indians. 29 Mar.
HD 190, 22-1, v5, 9p. [220]
Transmitting information.
54. R-M on the Louisville-St. Louis Mail Road. 3 Apr.
SD 117, 22-1, v3, 4p. [214]
Strategic value of road on the whole northwestern Indian frontier.
55. Letter on Public Lands. 6 Apr.
HD 196, 22-1, v5, 4p. [220]
Indian land titles.
56. Report on Case of S. Betton. 6 Apr.
HR 430, 22-1, v3, 2p. [226]
As Com'r in charge of cession of land to the Creek Indians; treaty of 24 Jan. 1826.
57. On the Case of S. Graham and A. Llewellyn. 6 Apr.
HR 432, 22-1, v3, 2p. [226]
Choctaw Indians; Mississippi.
58. On the Relief of Maj. Twiggs et al. 9 Apr.
HR 437, 22-1, v3, 7p. [226]
Illegal timber cutting on Indian lands in Michigan.
59. Report on Cherokee Claims. 11 Apr.
HD 233, 22-1, v5, 3p. [220]
On account of spoliation of stock and destruction of buildings.
60. Message on Indian Treaties. 19 Apr.
HD 210, 22-1, v5, 25p. [220]
Transmits copies.
61. Message on Public Lands. 23 Apr.
SD 133, 22-1, v3, 6p. [214]
Indian lands to which title has or has not been extinguished.
62. R-C of I. Shannon. 28 Apr.
HR 455, 22-1, v3, 1p. [226]
Osage Indians.
63. R-P of J. Rodgers. 5 May.
HR 464, 22-1, v5, 2p. [228]
Cherokee Indian treaty of 6 May 1828.
64. Report on a Canal in Indiana. 14 May.
SD 143, 22-1, v3, 19p. [214]
Proposed southern route is within Indian boundary lines.
65. Report on Indian Annuities. 22 May.
HD 242, 22-1, v6, 19p. [221]
Payments during the years 1830 and 1831.
66. Letter on a Canal in Illinois. 25 May.
HD 245, 22-1, v6, 7p. [221]
Indian trade.
67. Report on Indian Reservation. 6 June.
HR 488, 22-1, v5, 49p. [228]
Is of opinion that the title to a certain Chickasaw Indian reservation has reverted to the U.S.; treaty of 19 Oct. 1818.
68. R-P of J. Anderson. 25 June.
HR 492, 22-1, v5, 2p. [228]
British and Indians; 1812; Michigan.

69. Report on Contract with S. Houston. 5 July.
HR 502, 22-1, v5, 75p. [228]
Charge against Sec. Eaton of having corruptly given to S. Houston a contract to supply emigrant Indians with rations.

70. On the Relief of S. Pleasanton. 5 July.
HR 511, 22-1, v5, 4p. [228]
Indian accounts in the 5th Auditor's office.

71. Report on Expenditures of the War Dept. 10 July.
HR 507, 22-1, v5, 2p. [228]
Indian Dept.

72. Statement of Appropriations. 14 July.
HD 305, 22-1, v6, 32p. [221]
During the 1st session of the 22d Congress.

73. Report on the Boundaries of Missouri. 14 July.
HR 512, 22-1, v5, 1p. [228]
Inroads of Indians upon white settlements.

74. Annual Message to Congress with Documents; Pres. Jackson. 4 Dec.
HD 2, 22-2, v1, 240p. [122]
Includes removal and preservation of Indians; reports of Sec. of War, Com'r of the General Land Office, Indian Dept., etc.

75. Annual Report of the Secretary of the Treasury. 5 Dec.
HD 3, 22-2, v1, 56p. [233]
Indian expenses; 1832.

76. Resol. of the Comm. of Whole. 10 Dec.
HR, Resol. 1, 22-2, v1, 2p. [236]
Refers portion of the Annual Message of the Pres. dealing with Indians to the Com. on Indian Affairs.

77. Estimate of Appropriations. 12 Dec.
HD 10, 22-2, v1, 57p. [233]
For 1833.

78. Report on Indian Annuities. 20 Dec.
SD 39, 22-2, v1, 7p. [230]
For 1833.

79. Report on Receipts and Expenditures. 21 Dec.
SD 15, 22-2, v1, 23p. [230]
Since 1789; Indian Affairs.

80. Report on Mounted Rangers. 28 Dec.
HR 17, 22-2, v1, 2p. [236]
On the Sec. of War's recommendations as to the formation of a regiment of dragoons; mounted troops necessary for frontier contact with Indians.

1833

1. R-P of R. Bullard. 4 Jan.
HR 24, 22-2, v1, 2p. [236]
Creek Indian expedition.

2. R-P of D. Fletcher. 4 Jan.
HR 26, 22-2, v1, 2p. [236]
Horse taken by Indians in Upper Canada; 1814.

3. R-P of A. Robison. 9 Jan.
HR 30, 22-2, v1, 1p. [236]
Creek Indian removal.

4. R-P of J. McClenahan. 9 Jan.
HR 31, 22-2, v1, 2p. [236]
Sale of a certain Indian improvement in 1818 by the governor of Tennessee.

5. On the Case of S. Fisher. 10 Jan.
HR 37, 22-2, v1, 4p. [236]
Choctaw treaty at Dancing Rabbit Creek on 27 Sept. 1830.

6. R-P of the Reps. of J. Thompson. 10 Jan.
HR 40, 22-2, v1, 1p. [236]
Choctaw treaty at Dancing Rabbit Creek on 27 Sept. 1830.

7. On the Case of the Heirs of Doctor Reynolds. 16 Jan.
HR 44, 22-2, v1, 3p. [236]
Indian depredations near Detroit in 1812.

8. R-P of N. Agnew et al. 18 Jan.
HR 49, 22-2, v1, 1p. [236]
British and Indians; 1812; on the Raisin River.

9. Report on the General Land Office. 24 Jan.
SD 50, 22-2, v1, 47p. [230]
Indian claims; Choctaw treaty of 1832.

10. Report on the Survey and Sale of Public Lands. 24 Jan.
HD 62, 22-2, v2, 5p. [234]
Land to which Indian title has been extinguished.

11. R-P of J. and J. Brown. 28 Jan.
HR 73, 22-2, v1, 2p. [236]
Cherokee Indians.

12. R-P of J. Moore. 29 Jan.
HR 76, 22-2, v1, 2p. [236]
Shawnee Indian country.

13. Letter on the Indians. 1 Feb.
HD 82, 22-2, v2, 6p. [234]
Report of the CIA on the subject of vaccination of Indians.

14. Report on Trade with Indians. 1 Feb.
HD 137, 22-2, v3, 138p. [235]
Disbursements of money and goods for year ending 30 Sept. 1832.

15. Report on Bill to Pay for Horses Lost in Service. 6 Feb.
HR 83, 22-2, v1, 2p. [236]
Against the Sac and Fox Indians on the frontiers of Illinois; and in other Indian campaigns.

16. Letter on Indian Trade. 12 Feb.
HD 104, 22-2, v2, 4p. [234]
Licenses granted for year ending 30 Sept. 1832.

17. R-C of T. Triplett. 26 Feb.
HR 116, 22-2, v1, 1p. [236]
Improvements of the emigrating Creek Indians.

18. Letter on Indian Country. 2 Mar.
HD 125, 22-2, v3, 16p. [235]
Copy of an account of an expedition to the country of the northwestern Indians; Sioux, Chippewa, Menomonee, Winnebago, and other Indians.

19. Report on Appropriations for War Dept. 2 Mar.
HD 128, 22-2, v3, 16p. [235]
For the year 1832.

20. Statement of Appropriations. 2 Mar.
HD 131, 22-2, v3, 27p. [235]
During the 2d session of the 22d Congress.

21. R-P of D. Brearley. 2 Mar.
HR 125, 22-2, v1, 4p. [236]
Creek Indians; removal; blacks in Indian country.

22. R-M of the Alabama Legis. 2 Mar.
HR 127, 22-2, v1, 3p. [236]
Recommends indemnification of certain friendly Creek Indians for property destroyed by hostile Indians.

23. Annual Message to Congress with Documents; Pres. Jackson. 3 Dec.
SD 1, 23-1, v1, 273p. [238] *or* HD 1, 23-1, v1, 273p. [254]
Indian Affairs; report of Sec. of War. Indian Bureau, Land Office, etc.

24, Message on Proceeds from the Sale of Public Lands. 5 Dec.
SD 3, 23-1, v1, 15p. [238]
Amounts paid to extinguish Indian titles to land.

25. Annual Report of the Sec. of the Treasury. 17 Dec.
SD 9, 23-1, v1, 69p. [238] *or* HD 15, 23-1, v1, 69p. [254]
Indian expenses.

26. R-P of J. Moore. 20 Dec.
HR 58, 23-1, v1, 2p. [260]
Shawnee Indians; 1797.

27. Estimate of Appropriations. 23 Dec.
HD 21, 23-1, v1, 67p. [254]
For 1834; Indian expenses.

28. Report on Invalid Pensioners. 23 Dec.
HR 69, 23-1, v1, 5p. [260]
British and Indians; 1814; Prairie du Chien.

29. R-P of J. McClenahan. 24 Dec.
HR 78, 23-1, v1, 2p. [260]
Sale of an Indian improvement in Tennessee.

30. Report on School Lands in Ohio. 24 Dec.
HR 84, 23-1, v1, 1p. [260]
Indian land title.

31. R-C of G. Elliott. 27 Dec.
HR 88, 23-1, v1, 2p. [260]
Expenses incurred in securing privileges of citizenship as a Cherokee Indian.

32. R-P of H. Northup. 30 Dec.
HR 95, 23-1, v1, 3p. [260]
British and Indians in Michigan; 1812.

33. R-P of D. Bradley. 31 Dec.
SD 18, 23-1, v1, 2p. [238]
Intruders of Cherokee lands.

34. R-P of J. Kimberlin. 31 Dec.
SD 19, 23-1, v1, 1p. [238]
Indian attack at Pigeon Roost, Indiana, in 1812.

1834

1. Report on Invalid Pensioners. 3 Jan.
HR 122, 23-1, v1, 3p. [260]
Creek Indians; 1790.

2. R-P of S. Edmondson. 7 Jan.
HR 132, 23-1, v1, 3p. [260]
Choctaw and Chickasaw lands.

3. Report on Indian Depredation Claims. 7 Jan.
HR 140, 23-1, v1, 4p. [260]
Creek Indians; Georgia; treaty of 8 Jan. 1821.

4. R-C of M. Mead. 7 Jan.
HR 144, 23-1, v1, 2p. [260]
Cherokee lands; Creek treaty at Fort Jackson.

5. R-P of J. Robinson. 8 Jan.
HR 146, 23-1, v1, 2p. [260]
British and Indians in 1813 in Ohio.
6. R-P of J. Bennett et al. 10 Jan.
SD 32, 23-1, v1, 1p. [238]
Treaty with the Miamis at St. Mary's in Ohio on 6 Oct. 1818.
7. R-P of H. Hunter. 14 Jan.
SD 33, 23-1, v1, 1p. [238]
Horse lost in Seminole Indian war.
8. R-C of J. McCarty. 14 Jan.
HR 168, 23-1, v1, 1p. [260]
Horse lost in engagement with Indians; 1812.
9. Report on Senate Bill for Relief of P. Spencer. 14 Jan.
HR 169, 23-1, v1, 2p. [260]
Hostile Indians on Illinois frontier; 1832.
10. R-P of A. Robison. 14 Jan.
HR 172, 23-1, v1, 1p. [260]
Medical services for emigrating Creek Indians; removal.
11. R-P of J. Brown. 14 Jan.
HR 175, 23-1, v1, 3p. [260]
Cherokee Indians.
12. Report on Indian Licenses. 15 Jan.
HD 45, 23-1, v1, 7p. [254]
Licenses granted to trade with Indians since 10 Sept. 1832.
13. Report on Relief of J. McCartney. 17 Jan.
SD 46, 23-1, v2, 6p. [239]
Cattle seized on Cherokee lands in Mississippi; 1817.
14. R-P of S. Fisher. 17 Jan.
HR 191, 23-1, v1, 5p. [260]
Choctaw treaty of 27 Sept. 1830 at Dancing Rabbit Creek.
15. Mem. of the North Carolina Legis. 20 Jan.
HD 71, 23-1, v2, 4p. [255]
On extinguishment of Indian title to land in state.
16. R-C of Col. Clark. 21 Jan.
SD 50, 23-1, v2, 1p. [239]
Hostile Indians in Arkansas in 1830.
17. Report on Employees of the Indian Dept. 21 Jan.
HD 60, 23-1, v2, 12p. [255]
During the year 1833.
18. R-P of S. Harford. 23 Jan.
HR 207, 23-1, v2, 3p. [261]
British and Indians; 1812.
19. Letter on Creek Indian Treaty. 27 Jan.
SD 59, 23-1, v2, 3p. [239]
Estimate of funds required to carry into effect the treaty with the Creek Indians of 24 Mar. 1832.
20. R-C of N. McPherson. 7 Feb.
HR 382, 23-1, v3, 2p. [262]
Property taken by Indians near Detroit.
21. R-M of Arkansas Legis. 10 Feb.
HR 255, 23-1, v2, 2p. [261]
Recommends removal of troops at Fort Gibson to the frontiers of Arkansas; Cherokee Indians.
22. Report on Survey of Public Lands. 13 Feb.
SD 91, 23-1, v2, 2p. [239]
Progress made in the survey of lands acquired from the Pottawatomies.
23. R-P of J. Cullins. 14 Feb.
HR 268, 23-1, v2, 2p. [261]
Indian attack in Pennsylvania; 1777.
24. R-P of J. Taylor. 22 Feb.
SD 107, 23-1, v2, 2p. [239]
Black Hawk war.
25. R-P of J. Cooper. 25 Feb.
HR 280, 23-1, v2, 4p. [261]
Creek Indians in Georgia; removal.
26. Report on Extension of Pension Laws. 25 Feb.
HR 284, 23-1, v2, 4p. [261]
To those engaged in wars with the Indians prior to 1795.
27. R-C of A. Stewart. 25 Feb.
HR 369, 23-1, v3, 3p. [262]
For the value of five slaves taken by the Cherokee Indians in 1780.
28. Estimates of Indian Annuities. 27 Feb.
HD 133, 23-1, v3, 12p. [256]
Annuities now payable under treaty stipulations; date of treaties; tribes.
29. Report on Death of H. Owens. 3 Mar.
HD 149, 23-1, v3, 30p. [256]
Soldier employed in removing intruders from the lands of the Creek Indians in Alabama.
30. R-P of P. Gamblins. 4 Mar.
HR 300, 23-1, v2, 2p. [261]
Hostile Indians near Vincennes in 1813.
31. R-P of P. Adams. 11 Mar.
HR 328, 23-1, v3, 3p. [262]
Black Hawk war; 1832; Sac Indians.
32. R-P of H. Stoddard. 11 Mar.
HR 330, 23-1, v3, 2p. [262]
Shawanoese Indians; Ohio; 1821.
33. Mem. of the Michigan Legis. 14 Mar.
SD 176, 23-1, v3, 3p. [240] *or* HD 244, 23-1, v4, 3p. [257]
Indian depredations in 1812.

34. R-P of W. Purcell. 22 Mar.
SD 206, 23-1, v3, 1p. [240]
Campaign against the Indians on the Wabash River in 1811.

35. Mem. of the Com. on Territories. 25 Mar.
HD 245, 23-1, v4, 3p. [257]
Sac and Fox land cessions; settlers in Missouri.

36. Report on Properties Lost. 3 Apr.
HR 383, 23-1, v3, 8p. [262]
Seminole and Black Hawk wars; Sac Indians.

37. R-C of J. Harding. 4 Apr.
HR 390, 23-1, v3, 6p. [262]
Boat sunk while transporting grain for emigrating Indians; removal.

38. Report on Boundary Line of Missouri. 8 Apr.
SD 263, 23-1, v3, 2p. [240]
Indian removal.

39. Message on Sale of Public Lands. 8 Apr.
SD 264, 23-1, v3, 6p. [240]
From the Com'r of the General Land Office on the sale of lands acquired from the Choctaw Indians by the 12 Aug. 1833 treaty at Dancing Rabbit Creek.

40. Report on Indian Reservations. 8 Apr.
SD 266, 23-1, v3, 195p. [240]
From the CIA on location of reservations under the Choctaw treaty of 27 Sept. 1830.

41. R-C of J. Manley. 9 Apr.
HR 402, 23-1, v3, 2p. [262]
Property destroyed by Indians; 1812; Tennessee.

42. Report on Indian Expeditions. 11 Apr.
HD 323, 23-1, v4, 68p. [257]
Transmitting report of Allen and Schoolcraft's expedition to the country of the Northwestern Indians in 1832.

43. R-P of L. Voorhise. 11 Apr.
HR 407, 23-1, v3, 2p. [262]
Indian attack near Fort St. Clair in 1792.

44. R-P of J. Caulfield. 11 Apr.
HR 408, 23-1, v3, 2p. [262]
Improvements made by half-breed in Alabama.

45. R-C of Col. Morgan. 11 Apr.
HR 409, 23-1, v3, 1p. [262]
Cherokee Indians.

46. Report on the Chesapeake and Ohio Canal. 17 Apr.
HR 414, 23-1, v3, 378p. [262]
Purchase of Indian lands.

47. On the Relief of J. McCartney. 30 Apr.
HR 433, 23-1, v3, 2p. [262]
Property seized on Cherokee land.

48. R-C of J. Bezior. 30 Apr.
HR 437, 23-1, v3, 3p. [262]
Holding a treaty with the Indians in 1806.

49. On the Case of W. Baden. 1 May.
HR 438, 23-1, v3, 1p. [262]
Indian engagement in Ohio; 1794.

50. R-C of J. Elder. 2 May.
HR 441, 23-1, v3, 1p. [262]
Transporting baggage for emigrating Cherokee Indians; removal.

51. Expenditures of the War Dept. 5 May.
SD 341, 23-1, v4, 22p. [241]
For the year 1833.

52. Appropriations of the War Dept. 6 May.
HD 390, 23-1, v5, 31p. [258]
For the year 1833.

53. Report on the Southern Boundary of Tennessee. 6 May.
HR 445, 23-1, v3, 13p; [262]
Chickasaw Indian land cessions.

54. Mem. of Cherokee Indians. 17 May.
SD 386, 23-1, v5, 31p. [342]
Complain of certain acts of the state of Georgia, and ask protection of their rights.

55. Report on Indian Affairs. 20 May.
HR 474, 23-1, v4, 132p. [263]
Bills for the organization of the OIA, for regulating trade with the Indians, etc.

56. R-C of E. Davis, Jr. 22 May.
HR 476, 23-1, v4, 2p. [263]
Black Hawk war; Sac Indians.

57. R-P of B. Stickney. 27 May.
HR 487, 23-1, v4, 1p. [263]
Indian agent at Fort Wayne.

58. R-P of T. Morton. 31 May.
HR 499, 23-1, v4, 1p. [263]
Creek Indians; 1813.

59. On the Relief of C. Hand. 31 May.
HR 502, 23-1, v4, 2p. [263]
Horses lost by the Indiana militia in an expedition against the Indians in Illinois; 1832.

60. Disbursements to Indians. 14 June.
HD 490, 23-1, v6, 174p. [259]
For the year ending 30 Sept. 1833.

61. On the Case of Maj. Croghan et al. 18 June.
SD 447, 23-1, v6, 3p. [243]
Defending Fort Sandusky against British and Indians; 1813.

62. R-M of Delegates of Cherokee Nation. 20 June.

SD 465, 23-1, v6, 1p. [243]
Recommends the Pres. be requested to ascertain on what terms the claims of the Cherokee Nation to lands in Georgia might be extinguished.

63. R-M of Z. McGirth and S. Bradford. 24 June.
HR 540, 23-1, v4, 1p. [263]
Creek and Seminole wars.

64. Mem. of Delegation of Cherokee Indians. 25 June.
SD 486, 23-1, v6, 2p. [243]
Ask Congress to protect them in their rights.

65. R-C of the Reps. of J. Piatt. 27 June.
SD 488, 23-1, v6, 28p. [243]
Supplies furnished troops and Indians in the northwest frontier from 1814 to 1815; Wyandot Indians.

66. On the Relief of W. Purcell. 27 June.
HR 558, 23-1, v4, 2p. [263]
Indian attack on the Wabash River in 1811.

67. R-M of W. Blount. 28 June.
HR 559, 23-1, v4, 2p. [263]
Creek war.

68. Statement of Appropriations. 30 June.
HD 522, 23-1, v6, 39p. [259]
During the 1st session of the 23rd Congress.

69. Documents on Emigration of Indians. 31 Oct.
SD 512, 23-1, vols. 7-11, 4271p. [244-248]
Correspondence from 30 Nov. 1831 to 27 Dec. 1833 on the subject of the emigration of the Indians; abstract of expenditures incurred in the removal and subsistence of the Indians.

70. Mem. of J. and J. Armstrong. 8 Nov.
HD 23, 23-2, v2, 1p. [272]
Indian hostilities in Virginia; 1794; Wyandot Indians.

71. Annual Message to Congress with Documents; Pres. Jackson. 1 Dec.
SD 1, 23-2, v1, 543p. [266] *or* HD 2, 23-2, v1, 543p. [271]
Indian Affairs; reports of Sec. of War, Indian Office; General Land Office, etc.; Col. Dodge's journal of the 1834 campaign.

72. Annual Report of the Sec. of the Treasury. 3 Dec.
SD 2, 23-2, v1, 95p. [266] *or* HD 3, 23-2, v1, 95p. [271]
Year ending 30 June 1834; Indian expenses.

73. Estimate of Appropriations. 3 Dec.
HD 5, 23-2, v1, 64p. [271]
For 1835; Indian expenses.

74. Report on Public Lands. 10 Dec.
HR 1, 23-2, v1, 13p. [276]
Land to which Indian titles has been extinguished.

75. Mem. of the Michigan Legis. 23 Dec.
SD 24, 23-2, v2, 12p. [267] *or* HD 34, 23-2, v2, 12p. [272]
Much of the land between Lake Superior and the Mississippi River must remain the hunting grounds of Indian tribes for many years.

76. R-P of J. Wellborn, Jr. 23 Dec.
HR 10, 23-2, v1, 1p. [276]
Cherokee treaties of 1817 and 1819.

1835

1. Resol. of Sen. Poindexter. 1 Jan.
SD 33, 23-2, v2, 1p. [267]
For the preparation of maps of the states and territories on the northwestern frontier, indicated lands to which Indian title has not yet been extinguished.

2. R-P of T. Reddick. 6 Jan.
HR 31, 23-2, v1, 2p. [276]
Indian land and trade; 1799; Louisiana.

3. Mem. of the Chiefs and Warriors of the Fox Tribe. 7 Jan.
HD 63, 23-2, v2, 4p. [272]
Sac and Fox Nation; annuities to individuals and families rather than tribes.

4. Mem. of the Chiefs and Warriors of the Sac and Fox Tribes. 7 Jan.
HD 64, 23-2, v2, 5p. [272]
Annuities to individuals and families rather than tribes.

5. R-P of C. Juzan. 13 Jan.
SD 53, 23-2, v3, 2p. [268]
Choctaw Indian treaty of 27 Sept. 1830; land grant.

6. R-M of Col. Newnan. 15 Jan.
HR 50, 23-2, v1, 1p. [276]
Creek Indians.

7. R-P of Capt. Cole. 16 Jan.
HR 52, 23-2, v1, 1p. [276]
Onondaga Indians.

8. Mem. of Delegates of Cherokee Nation. 19 Jan.
SD 71, 23-2, v3, 54p. [268]
Asking protection from the U.S., and protesting against certain articles of agreement between the agent of the U.S. and a certain part of the Cherokee Nation.

9. Mem. of the Cherokee Indians. 19 Jan.
HD 91, 23-2, v3, 19p. [273]
Council of 28 Nov. 1834 in Georgia; ask aid in removal west.

10. Report on Trade with Indians. 21 Jan.
SD 69, 23-2, v3, 11p. [268] *or* HD 97, 23-2, v3, 11p. [273]
Licenses granted to trade with Indians for year ending 10 Mar. 1834.

11. R-C of H. Hunter. 22 Jan.
HD 100, 23-2, v3, 3p. [273]
Seminole campaign.

12. Mem. of the Indiana Legis. 22 Jan.
HD 129, 23-2, v3, 1p. [273]
Asking that the title of the Miami and Pottawatomie Indians to certain lands in Indiana be extinguished.

13. R-P of H. Morgan. 26 Jan.
SD 82, 23-2, v3, 4p. [268]
Indian wars around 1774; western Virginia.

14. Mem. of the Missouri Legis. 28 Jan.
HD 107, 23-2, v3, 10p. [273]
Asking that certain Indian lands west of the Missouri River be added to the state; Ioways, Sac, Fox, and Pottawatomie Indians.

15. Report on War Dept. Appropriations. 29 Jan.
HD 112, 23-2, v3, 16p. [273]
For the year 1834.

16. R-P of W. Burkler. 31 Jan.
HR 71, 23-2, v1, 2p. [276]
Indian war; 1812; Missouri.

17. R-P of Citizens of Michilimackinac. 3 Feb.
SD 99, 23-2, v3, 1p. [268]
On granting public land for the maintenance of an academy for Indian youth.

18. Report on Trade. 3 Feb.
HD 116, 23-2, v3, 4p. [273]
Indian trade west of the Rocky Mountains.

19. Petition of A. Parker et al. 3 Feb.
HD 124, 23-2, v3, 7p. [273]
Creek Indian reserve land purchased.

20. Documents Accompanying House Bill No. 696. 3 Feb.
HR 79, 23-2, v1, 28p. [276]
On land pre-emption rights; Choctaw treaty of 1830; Mississippi.

21. Message on Indian Land Reservations. 5 Feb.
HD 138, 23-2, v4, 48p. [274]
Treaty of 1830 with the Choctaw Indians.

22. On the Case of T. Simpson. 5 Feb.
HR 88, 23-2, v1, 1p. [276]
British and Indians.

23. Report on a Road in Michigan Territory. 6 Feb.
HD 132, 23-2, v3, 4p. [273]
Menomonee, Winnebago, and New York Indians.

24. Mem. of the Indiana Legis. 7 Feb.
SD 128, 23-2, v3, 1p. [268] *or* HD 168, 23-2, v4, 1p. [274]
Ask pension laws be extended to persons serving in Indian wars prior to 1794.

25. R-P of J. Calvin. 7 Feb.
HR 93, 23-2, v1, 2p. [276]
British and Indians; 1813; Lower Canada.

26. R-P of S. Eskridge. 10 Feb.
HR 100, 23-2, v1, 1p. [276]
Money loaned to R. Meigs, late Cherokee Indian agent.

27. Mem. of Delegates of Cherokee Nation. 13 Feb.
SD 120, 23-2, v3, 6p. [268]
Ask payment for land in Alabama and Tennessee under the treaty of 27 Feb. 1819.

28. Report on Indian Accounts. 17 Feb.
HD 150, 23-2, v4, 163p. [274]
During the year ending 30 Sept. 1834.

29. R-P of A. Stelson. 21 Feb.
HR 120, 23-2, v1, 2p. [276]
Indian wars; Indiana; 1832.

30. Mem. of the Indiana Legis. 24 Feb.
SD 136, 23-2, v3, 1p. [268]
Land to which Indian title has been extinguished.

31. Mem. of the Indiana Legis. 25 Feb.
SD 141, 23-2, v4, 1p. [269]
On the western frontier when depredations were continued by the Indians after the conclusion of peace with Britain, until June, 1815.

32. Report of Persons Employed in Indian Dept. 2 Mar.
HD 181, 23-2, v5, 3p. [275]
For the year 1834.

33. Report of Featherstonhaugh's Geological Investigations. 3 Mar.
SD 153, 23-2, v4, 43p. [269] *or* HD 151, 23-2, v4, 97p. [274]
Between the Missouri and Red Rivers in Arkansas Territory; Indian mounds and artifacts on the ancient river beds; country possessed by Quapaws when settled by whites.
34. Report on Indian Annuities. 3 Mar.
HD 186, 23-2, v5, 16p. [275]
For the years 1833, and 1834.
35. Statement of Appropriations. 3 Mar.
HD 196, 23-2, v5, 41p. [275]
During the 2d session of the 23rd Congress.
36. Annual Message to Congress with Documents; Pres. Jackson. 7 Dec.
SD 1, 24-1, v1, 428p. [279] *or* HD 2, 24-1, v1, 428p. [286]
Removal of Indians; reports of Sec. of War, Indian Office, etc.
37. Annual Report of the Sec. of the Treasury. 8 Dec.
SD 2, 24-1, v1, 54p. [279] *or* HD 3, 24-1, v1, 54p. [286]
1835, and estimates for 1836.
38. Annual Report of the Com'r of the General Land Office. 8 Dec.
SD 3, 24-1, v1, 37p. [279] *or* HD 5, 24-1, v1, 39p. [286]
Indian treaties where land title has been extinguished.
39. Report of Receipts and Expenditures. 8 Dec.
SD 4, 24-1, v1, 12p. [279]
For the first three quarters of 1835; Indian expenses.
40. Petition of J. Bogy. 8 Dec.
SD 23, 24-1, v2, 14p. [280]
Spoliations on his property by Choctaw Indians while on a trading expedition up the Arkansas River.
41. Estimate of Appropriations. 8 Dec.
HD 4, 24-1, v1, 53p. [286]
For 1836.
42. Message on Transfer of Appropriations. 10 Dec.
HD 6, 24-1, v1, 2p. [286]
Survey of Choctaw cession in Mississippi.
43. R-P of J. Cooper. 21 Dec.
HR 3, 24-1, v1, 4p. [293]
Supplies for removal of Creek Indians.
44. R-P of B. Stickney. 21 Dec.
HR 18, 24-1, v1, 1p. [293]
Indian agent at Fort Wayne.
45. R-C of the Reps. of W. Blount. 21 Dec.
HR 27, 24-1, v1, 3p. [293]
Creek Indian war of 1813.
46. R-P of A. Stelson. 21 Dec.
HR 39, 24-1, v1, 2p. [293]
Indian war; 1832; Indiana.
47. Mem. of Citizens of Missouri. 24 Dec.
SD 22, 24-1, v2, 5p. [280]
For protection from Indians removed to that area.
48. R-P of S. Cozad. 29 Dec.
HR 54, 24-1, v1, 1p. [293]
Captured by Shawnee Indians in 1794.
49. R-P of H. Hunter. 31 Dec.
SD 37, 24-1, v2, 9p. [280]
Seminole war.

1836

1. Letter on Indian Hostilities. 4 Jan.
HD 38, 24-1, v2, 1p. [287]
Hostilities have been commenced by the Seminole Indians.
2. Report on Public Expenditures. 4 Jan.
HD 39, 24-1, v2, 51p. [287]
From 1816 to 1834.
3. Report on Tennessee Vacant Lands. 5 Jan.
HR 57, 24-1, v1, 25p. [293]
Cherokee and Chickasaw land cessions; road through Creek nation.
4. R-P of J. Caulfield. 5 Jan.
HR 77, 24-1, v1, 2p. [293]
Half-breed in Alabama.
5. R-P of R. Bullard. 6 Jan.
HR 88, 24-1, v1, 3p. [293]
Creek Indian war.
6. Petition of S. Johnston. 7 Jan.
HD 47, 24-1, v2, 11p. [287]
Daughter of a Chippewa Chief; married a fur trader.
7. R-P of the Heirs of J. Smith. 12 Jan.
HR 101, 24-1, v1, 1p. [293]
Trader among the Chippewas; treaty of 1819.
8. R-P of H. Stoddard. 12 Jan.
HR 114, 24-1, v1, 2p. [293]
Land granted by the Shawanese Indians of Ohio in 1821; treaty of 8 Aug. 1831.
9. R-P of the Heirs of T. Reddeck. 12 Jan.
HR 117, 24-1, v1, 2p. [293]
Indian trade; 1799; upper Louisiana.

10. R-P of J. and J. Brown. 12 Jan.
HR 122, 24-1, v1, 1p. [293]
Cherokee treaty; 1819.

11. Proceedings of a Meeting of Citizens of Florida. 13 Jan.
HD 80, 24-1, v3, 8p. [288]
On aspects of the Indian hostilities; Creeks and Seminoles.

12. R-P of J. Collier. 13 Jan.
HR 127, 24-1, v1, 1p. [293]
Spy for expedition against the Indians in 1794; Alabama.

13. R-C of Col. Morgan. 13 Jan.
HR 130, 24-1, v1, 1p. [293]
Battle of the "Horse Shoe" against the Cherokees.

14. R-P of J. Alexander and T. Nash. 13 Jan.
HR 131, 24-1, v1, 1p. [293]
Removal of Sac and Fox Indians to Missouri in 1813.

15. Report on Senate Bill for Relief of B. Murphy. 13 Jan.
HR 162, 24-1, v1, 10p. [293]
Property taken by the Cherokee Nation in 1830; treaty of May, 1828.

16. Report on Land Claims. 20 Jan.
SD 69, 24-1, v2, 20p. [280]
Treaty with the Choctaw Indians on 27 Sept. 1830 at Dancing Rabbit Creek.

17. Petition of the Heirs of A. Chouteau and J. Mullanphy. 20 Jan.
SD 73, 24-1, v2, 3p. [280]
"Dubuque Claim"; Fox Indians in 1788; Sac and Fox treaty of 3 Nov. 1804; etc.

18. R-P of S. Evans. 20 Jan.
HR 186, 24-1, v1, 2p. [293]
Hostile Indians in Illinois; 1832.

19. R-P of J. McPherson. 20 Jan.
HR 194, 24-1, v1, 3p. [293]
Late Indian sub-agent to the Seneca and Shawanese Indians.

20. Documents on a Military Road. 21 Jan.
SD 77, 24-1, v2, 7p. [280]
From Fort Des Moines, via Fort Leavenworth, to Fort Gibson; Indian hostilities on the frontier; Sac, Fox, Pottawatomie, and emigrating Indians.

21. R-M of the Arkansas Legis. 23 Jan.
HR 208, 24-1, v1, 16p. [293]
Cession of a portion of that territory to the Choctaw Indians in 1821.

22. Report on the Purchase of Public Land. 25 Jan.
SD 80, 24-1, v2, 4p. [280]
By the Indian Dept., etc.

23. R-P of A. Bronson. 27 Jan.
SD 91, 24-1, v2, 2p. [280]
Ottawa, Chippewa, and Pottawatomie treaty of 29 Aug. 1821.

24. Report on War Dept. Appropriations. 27 Jan.
HD 83, 24-1, v3, 13p. [288]
For the year 1835.

25. R-P of J. Wellborn, Jr. 27 Jan.
HR 227, 24-1, v1, 2p. [293]
Cherokee treaties of 1817 and 1819.

26. R-P of J. Pitcher. 27 Jan.
HR 230, 24-1, v1, 1p. [293]
Late Indian sub-agent for the Sioux of the Missouri River.

27. On the Case of B. Curry. 28 Jan.
SD 97, 24-1, v2, 2p. [280]
Agent for the removal of the Cherokee Indians.

28. R-P of A. Anderson. 29 Jan.
HR 252, 24-1, v1, 1p. [293]
Cherokee Indians.

29. Mem. of the Illinois Legis. 1 Feb.
HD 88, 24-1, v3, 1p. [288]
For granting pensions to persons engaged in Indian wars before the treaty of Greenville; 1795.

30. Petition of Citizens of Mississippi. 1 Feb.
HD 89, 24-1, v3, 3p. [288]
Choctaw treaty of 1830; Dancing Rabbit Creek.

31. Report of Employees of Indian Dept. 1 Feb.
HD 95, 24-1, v3, 7p. [288]
Names and compensation.

32. Mem. of Choctaw Indians. 1 Feb.
HD 119, 24-1, v4, 3p. [289]
Ask for lands in lieu of land of which they have been unjustly deprived under the treaty of 27 Sept. 1830.

33. Report of Persons Employed in the Indian Dept. 2 Feb.
SD 109, 24-1, v2, 8p. [280]
For the year 1835.

34. Mem. of Citizens of East Florida. 2 Feb.
HD 92, 24-1, v3, 3p. [288]
Seminole Indians.

35. R-P of R. Matson. 4 Feb.
SD 122, 24-1, v2, 2p. [280]
Indian war in Illinois; 1832.

36. Report on Indian Depredation Claims. 4 Feb.

HR 266, 24-1, v1, 5p. [293]
Sac and Fox removal in 1813.

37. R-P of W. Christy. 4 Feb.
HR 271, 24-1, v1, 3p. [293]
British and Indians.

38. R-P of L. Voorhise. 4 Feb.
HR 278, 24-1, v1, 2p. [293]
Indian attack in 1792.

39. Mem. of the Indiana Legis. 5 Feb.
SD 127, 24-1, v2, 4p. [280]
Choctaw and Chickasaw lands.

40. R-P of J. and J. Brown. 5 Feb.
HR 288, 24-1, v1, 3p. [293]
Cherokee treaty; 1819.

41. Mem. of the Alabama Legis. 8 Feb.
SD 132, 24-1, v2, 3p. [280]
Opposed to granting reservations to Cherokee and Creek Indians; removal.

42. Mem. of the Alabama Legis. 8 Feb.
SD 133, 24-1, v2, 2p. [280]
Ask public land for each township in which the sixteenth section is valueless or has been taken up by Creek and Choctaw Indian reservations.

43. R-C of Missouri Militia. 8 Feb.
SD 147, 24-1, v2, 2p. [280]
Black Hawk war; 1832; Sac and Ioway Indians.

44. R-P of J. Beaubien. 8 Feb.
SD 148, 24-1, v2, 1p. [280]
Treaty of 1832 at Tippecanoe.

45. Message on Indian Hostilities in Florida. 10 Feb.
SD 152, 24-1, v3, 52p. [281]
Shows measures taken by the Administration to suppress the hostilities; information as to the causes of said hostilities; proceedings of treaty council with Seminoles; treaty of 9 May 1832 at Payne's Landing.

46. Message on Indian Lands. 10 Feb.
HD 107, 24-1, v3, 4p. [288]
Correspondence with agents and persons connected with the sale and transfer of Indian reserves of land east of the Mississippi since 1825.

47. R-P of J. Bogardus. 10 Feb.
HR 312, 24-1, v1, 2p. [293]
Winnebago Indians; 1828; Pottawatomie territory; Winnebago treaty of 1 Aug. 1829.

48. Report on Camp Equipage for Militia. 13 Feb.
HD 113, 24-1, v3, 1p. [288]
Seminole war.

49. Report on Extension of Pension Laws. 16 Feb.
HR 338, 24-1, v1, 12p. [293] *or* HR 96, 24-2, v1, 12p. [305]
Recommends that pensions be extended to persons engaged in Indian wars between 1783 and 1795.

50. Resol. of Sen. Linn. 18 Feb.
SD 182, 24-1, v3, 4p. [281]
On the Mississippi River; Indian hostilities.

51. Letter on Indian Hostilities. 18 Feb.
HD 115, 24-1, v4, 2p. [289]
On Indian hostilities in Florida and the removal west of the Creeks.

52. R-P of S. Tillet. 19 Feb.
HR 362, 24-1, v2, 3p. [294]
School teacher among the emigrating Choctaws; treaty of 27 Sept. 1830.

53. R-P of Tennessee Settlers. 19 Feb.
HR 369, 24-1, v2, 2p. [294]
Chickasaw treaty of 19 Oct. 1818.

54. R-P of P. Knaggs. 23 Feb.
SD 194, 24-1, v3, 1p. [281]
Chippewa treaty of 24 Sept. 1819.

55. Journal of Col. Dodge's Expedition. 23 Feb.
SD 209, 24-1, v3, 38p. [281] *or* HD 181, 24-1, v4, 38p. [289]
To the Rocky Mountains in 1835; talks with the Ottoe, Omaha, Pawnee, Arikara, Cheyenne, Arapaho, Gros Ventre, and Blackfoot Indians; maps.

56. Mem. of Citizens of Mississippi. 24 Feb.
SD 200, 24-1, v3, 7p. [281]
On disadvantages growing out of the treaty of Dancing Rabbit Creek in 1830 with the Choctaws.

57. Resol. of the Mississippi Legis. 25 Feb.
SD 202, 24-1, v3, 8p. [281]
Disadvantages of treaty of Dancing Rabbit Creek in 1830 with the Choctaws.

58. Documents on Extending the Northern Boundary of Missouri. 26 Feb.
SD 206, 24-1, v3, 8p. [281]
Indian removal; Chicago treaty with Pottawatomies; council with Ioways, Sacs, and Foxes.

59. Report on Indian Lands. 26 Feb.
HR 379, 24-1, v2, 6p. [294]
Recommends that Indian title to certain lands on the Missouri River

be extinguished; Sac, Fox, Sioux, and other Indians.

60. Report on Winnebago Indians. 1 Mar.
SD 215, 24-1, v3, 11p. [281]
Showing the condition of said Indians occupying the country ceded to the U.S. between Lake Michigan and the Mississippi River; treaty of 15 July 1830 with the Sacs, Foxes, Sioux, Iowas, Missouris, Omahas, and Ottoes.

61. Mem. of the Alabama Legis. 1 Mar.
HD 149, 24-1, v4, 2p. [289]
Those who lost land because of treaties.

62. Resol. of the Indiana Legis. 1 Mar.
HD 151, 24-1, v4, 1p. [289]
British and Indians.

63. Letter on Horse Claims. 2 Mar.
HD 135, 24-1, v4, 16p. [289]
For horses lost in Indian wars; 1831-32 on the frontiers of Illinois and Michigan.

64. R-P of N. Leamaster. 3 Mar.
SD 217, 24-1, v3, 1p. [281]
Indian hostilities in 1812; Indiana.

65. Report on the Western Frontier. 3 Mar.
HR 401, 24-1, v2, 14p. [294]
Tribes bordering the frontier settlements; number of Indians who have been removed west; number emigrated; etc.

66. R-P of J. Baker. 3 Mar.
HR 414, 24-1, v2, 2p. [294]
Indian war of 1832 in Illinois; Sac Indians.

67. Report on Petitions for Pensions. 3 Mar.
HR 415, 24-1, v2, 4p. [294]
Recommends extension of pension laws to widows and children of troops killed in wars with the Indians.

68. Petition of R. and J. Heath. 4 Mar.
HD 253, 24-1, v6, 2p. [291]
Lands in Missouri; Osages; Chouteau claim.

69. R-P of T. Mullens. 7 Mar.
SD 224, 24-1, v3, 2p. [281]
Creek Indians; 1814.

70. Report on Indian Lands. 7 Mar.
SD 229, 24-1, v3, 5p. [281]
On extinguishment of Indian title to lands in the vicinity of Green Bay and north of the Wisconsin and Iowa Rivers; Chippewas, Sioux, Menomonees, and other tribes.

71. Report on the Indians, Army, etc. 8 Mar.
SD 228, 24-1, v3, 25p. [281]
On the situation and number of Indians on the frontiers of the U.S., with a plan for an increase of the Army; removal.

72. Report on Exchange of Indian Lands. 15 Mar.
SD 246, 24-1, v3, 8p. [281]
Recommends passage of bill providing for the exchange of lands belonging to the Indians in any state or territory, and for their removal west of the Mississippi River.

73. R-P of J. Bogy. 15 Mar.
SD 247, 24-1, v3, 2p. [281]
Attacked by Choctaws while trading with the Osages in 1807; Arkansas River.

74. Report on Indian Land Titles. 16 Mar.
SD 251, 24-1, v3, 8p. [281]
Recommends that efforts be made to extinguish the remaining Indian titles to certain lands on the Missouri River; Sac, Fox, Sioux, Omaha, Ottoe, Ioway, and Missouri Indians.

75. Report on Winnebago Indians. 17 Mar.
SD 252, 24-1, v3, 2p. [281]
Recommends exchange of land occupied by the Winnebago Indians and their removal west of the Missouri River.

76. Report on Indian Lands. 21 Mar.
SD 260, 24-1, v3, 1p. [281]
Recommends that Indian titles to lands in any state or territory be extinguished wherever the Indians can be persuaded to move west.

77. R-P of J. Leframbois. 21 Mar.
SD 261, 24-1, v3, 1p. [281]
Pottawatomie Indian whose house was set afire by whites; Chicago; 1833.

78. R-P of T. McCanless. 21 Mar.
HR 427, 24-1, v2, 1p. [294]
Creek war; 1814.

79. R-P of J. Hancock. 21 Mar.
HR 430, 24-1, v2, 7p. [294]
Choctaw treaty; 1830; Dancing Rabbit Creek.

80. R-P of L. Leonard. 21 Mar.
HR 439, 24-1, v2, 2p. [294]
Indian hostilities in 1777; Capt. of Indian spies.

81. Report on Defence of Arkansas Frontier. 21 Mar.
HR 442, 24-1, v2, 8p. [294]
Recommends moving troops from Fort Gibson to the Arkansas Frontier.

82. R-P of M. Yates. 21 Mar.
HR 447, 24-1, v2, 2p. [294]

Choctaw treaty; 27 Sept. 1830; Dancing Rabbit Creek.

83. Report on Claims to Choctaw Reservations. 22 Mar.
SD 265, 24-1, v3, 6p. [281]
Under Choctaw treaty of 1830; Dancing Rabbit Creek.

84. Report on Case of J. Clyman. 24 Mar.
HR 468, 24-1, v2, 1p. [294]
Attacked by Menomonee Indians near Green Bay.

85. R-P of D. Sherwood. 24 Mar.
HR 469, 24-1, v2, 3p. [294]
Indian disturbances in Illinois; 1832.

86. Report on a Surveyor's Office West of Lake Michigan. 24 Mar.
HR 476, 24-1, v2, 4p. [294]
Indian lands which have been ceded to the U.S.

87. Report on Choctaw Claims. 24 Mar.
HR 479, 24-1, v2, 2p. [294]
Choctaw treaty; 27 Sept. 1830; Dancing Rabbit Creek.

88. R-P of P. Hadgo. 25 Mar.
HR 488, 24-1, v2, 2p. [294]
Creek treaty; 9 Aug. 1814.

89. R-P of A. Crow. 25 Mar.
HR 491, 24-1, v2, 2p. [294]
Black Hawk war; 1832; Illinois.

90. R-P of S. Johnston. 25 Mar.
HR 515, 24-1, v2, 4p. [294]
Indian fur trade.

91. Abstract of Florida War Claims. 26 Mar.
HD 231, 24-1, v6, 8p. [291]
In connection with the Seminole Indian hostilities.

92. R-P of C. Grignon. 31 Mar.
HR 523, 24-1, v2, 4p. [294]
Land in Michigan claimed under a Menomonee Indian grant of 1831; Green Bay.

93. Report on Case of J. McCartney. 5 Apr.
HR 530, 24-1, v2, 6p. [294]
Payment for cattle straying on Cherokee Indian lands and driven off by U.S. troops.

94. R-P of G. Willard. 5 Apr.
HR 533, 24-1, v2, 1p. [294]
Indian war of 1832; Michigan territory.

95. R-P of S. Pleasanton. 5 Apr.
HR 541, 24-1, v3, 9p. [295]
Indian accounts; fifth auditor.

96. R-P of W. Spiller. 6 Apr.
HR 544, 24-1, v3, 1p. [295]
Indian disturbances in 1832; Illinois.

97. Message on Military Defenses. 8 Apr.
SD 293, 24-1, v4, 88p. [282] *or* HD 243, 24-1, v6, 88p. [291]
Indian frontier.

98. Petition of J. Janis, Sr., 11 Apr.
SD 299, 24-1, v4, 2p. [282]
Indian war in 1778.

99. R-P of G. Cubbage. 12 Apr.
HR 569, 24-1, v3, 1p. [295]
Property destroyed by Indians in 1832; Black Hawk war.

100. R-P of Citizens of LaSalle County, Illinois. 15 Apr.
HR 579, 24-1, v3, 1p. [295]
For property destroyed during the Black Hawk war.

101. R-C for Property Destroyed. 15 Apr.
HR 580, 24-1, v3, 2p. [295]
Claims of settlers on the frontiers of Illinois and Michigan for property destroyed by the Indians in 1832; Sac and Fox Indians.

102. Report on Choctaw Indians. 16 Apr.
HD 229, 24-1, v6, 2p. [291]
Expenditures incurred in the removal and subsistence of the Choctaws.

103. On the Case of L. Combs. 18 Apr.
SD 315, 24-1, v4, 3p. [282]
British and Indians; 1813.

104. Petition of the Choctaw Indians. 18 Apr.
HD 220, 24-1, v6, 2p. [291]
Ask Congress to define the line between the territory of the Choctaw Nation and Arkansas.

105. R-P of T. Triplet. 20 Apr.
HR 587, 24-1, v3, 2p. [295]
Services in carrying into effect the treaty of 1826 with the Creek Indians; emigration.

106. R-P of Us-se-yo-ho-lo. 20 Apr.
HR 588, 24-1, v3, 2p. [295]
Land in Alabama; Creek treaty of 24 Mar. 1832.

107. R-M of the Indiana and Illinois Legis. 20 Apr.
HR 589, 24-1, v3, 10p. [295]
Frontier defense against the Indian hostilities, etc.

108. R-P of B. Brown. 22 Apr.
HR 605, 24-1, v3, 1p. [295]
Miami Indians; negotiation of treaty in Oct. 1834.

109. Report on Pre-emption Rights in Alabama. 22 Apr.
HR 606, 24-1, v3, 2p. [295]
Concerns settlers on lands ceded to the Indians in 1834; Creeks and Choctaws.

110. Mem. of the Indiana Legis. 23 Apr.
SD 328, 24-1, v4, 1p. [282]
To extinguish Miami and Pottawatomie title to land, and to remove them from the state.

111. R-P of F. Gardiner. 27 Apr.
HR 611, 24-1, v3, 2p. [295]
Indian engagement; 1835.

112. Mem. of the Cherokee Delegation. 30 Apr.
SD 340, 24-1, v5, 12p. [283]
Treaty of 24 Oct. 1804; annuities.

113. Report on Land Exchanges. 4 May.
SD 348, 24-1, v5, 7p. [283]
With the Pottawatomie Indians; treaty of 1833 in Chicago; removal; Sioux, Chippewas, Kickapoos, Ottawas, Pawnees, Miamies, Shawnees, and other tribes.

114. Report on Exchange of Indian Lands. 4 May.
SD 349, 24-1, v5, 1p. [283]
Recommends an exchange of lands southwest of the Missouri River for lands in Indiana now held by the Miami and other Indians.

115. Letter on Frontier Defences. 4 May.
HD 249, 24-1, v6, 2p. [291]
Recommends appropriation for defense of western frontier against Indians.

116. R-P of J. Slough. 5 May.
SD 352, 24-1, v5, 2p. [283]
Indian battle in 1794.

117. R-C of D. Madrazo. 6 May.
HR 629, 24-1, v3, 6p. [295]
Slaves taken to the Creek Agency in Georgia in 1817.

118. R-M of Clerks in Executive Depts. 10 May.
HR 641, 24-1, v3, 10p. [295]
Indian Office.

119. Report on Choctaw Land Claims. 11 May.
HR 663, 24-1, v3, 54p. [295]
Under the Choctaw treaty of 27 Sept. 1830; Dancing Rabbit Creek.

120. R-P of Z. Copeland. 11 May.
HR 664, 24-1, v3, 2p. [295]
Cherokee Indian hostilities; 1793-4.

121. On the Case of J. Perkins. 11 May.
HR 668, 24-1, v3, 1p. [295]
Seminole war; 1818.

122. Report on Removal of Creek Indians. 12 May.
SD 373, 24-1, v5, 2p. [283]
On the contract made by the War Dept. for the Creek removal west.

123. R-M of Cherokee Indians. 14 May.
SD 371, 24-1, v5, 2p. [283]
Interest on annuities withheld from the Cherokees; treaty of 1804.

124. R-P of Administrator of E. Duval. 17 May.
HR 685, 24-1, v3, 3p. [295]
Treaty of 6 May 1828 with the Cherokees.

125. R-P of M. Ricketts. 19 May.
HR 692, 24-1, v3, 1p. [295]
Seminole war; 1817.

126. Report on the Seminole Hostilities. 26 May.
HD 267, 24-1, v6, 22p. [291]
Causes of, and measures to repress the hostilities; Creek Indians.

127. R-P of G. Priest. 28 May.
HR 699, 24-1, v3, 2p. [295]
Florida Indians; 1835.

128. Letter on the Creek Indians. 31 May.
HD 268, 24-1, v6, 3p. [291]
Extracts of instructions to Gen. Jessup and of letter from Governor Schley on the removal of the Creek Indians.

129. R-C of A. Morgan. 31 May.
HR 701, 24-1, v3, 3p. [295]
Indian war; 1832; Sac and Fox Indians.

130. R-P of J. Wilson. 31 May.
HR 703, 24-1, v3, 2p. [295]
Missouri militia in the Black Hawk war.

131. On the Case of W. Warden. 1 June.
HR 721, 24-1, v3, 1p. [295]
British and Indians.

132. Report on Seminole Hostilities. 3 June.
HD 271, 24-1, v7, 272p. [292]
Reports and correspondence on the causes and repression of the hostilities.

133. Letter on Indian Treaties. 3 June.
HD 282, 24-1, v7, 36p. [292]
Estimates of appropriations to carry into effect the treaties with the Cherokees, Chippewas, Ottawas, and Pottawatomies; copies of treaties.

134. Report of Purchase of Negroes from Indians. 6 June.
HD 275, 24-1, v7, 2p. [292]
Shows the action of the War Dept. relative to the sale of negroes by the Seminole Indians.

135. Report on Indian Hostilities. 6 June.
HD 276, 24-1, v7, 413p. [292]
Of the Creek Indians.

136. R-P of H. Heiskell. 8 June.
HR 746, 24-1, v3, 1p. [295]
Seminole war.

137. R-P of R. McBride. 9 June.
HR 749, 24-1, v3, 1p. [295]
Creek war; 1816.

138. R-P of F. Durey. 9 June.
HR 755, 24-1, v3, 1p. [295]
Caddo Indians; 1816.

139. R-C of A. Pierce. 9 June.
HR 756, 24-1, v3, 1p. [295]
Horses killed by Indians in 1832.

140. R-P of Doctor Maxwell. 9 June.
HR 759, 24-1, v3, 2p. [295]
Indian hostilities; Wabash River; 1814; Indiana.

141. R-C of Heirs of G. Galphin. 13 June.
SD 396, 24-1, v5, 1p. [283]
Cherokee Indians; treaty of 29 Dec. 1835 at New Echota.

142. R-P of W. Beckwith. 15 June.
HR 766, 24-1, v3, 2p. [295]
Indian engagement; 1813; Michigan.

143. Report on Lost-Horse Claims. 15 June.
HR 768, 24-1, v3, 1p. [295]
In campaign against the Kickapoo Indians; 1832; Illinois River.

144. On the Case of J. Baker. 15 June.
HR 769, 24-1, v3, 4p. [295]
Sac Indian hostilities; 1832; Illinois militia.

145. Report on Cherokee Indians. 16 June.
SD 403, 24-1, v5, 376p. [283]
On enrollments, emigration, and improvements of the Cherokees residing east of the Mississippi.

146. R-P of R. Doughty. 17 June.
HR 784, 24-1, v3, 1p. [295]
Indian attack.

147. R-P of J. Morrisson. 18 June.
HR 787, 24-1, v3, 1p. [295]
Indian war; 1832; Sac and Fox Indians.

148. R-P of E. Wise. 21 June.
HR 793, 24-1, v3, 2p. [295]
Indian war; 1832; Illinois.

149. Mem. of the Cherokee Nation. 22 June.
HD 286, 24-1, v7, 167p. [292]
Assenting that the treaty purporting to be made with the Cherokee Nation at New Echota in Dec. of 1835 is false and fraudulent, and made without the sanction of the Cherokee people; protesting against its ratification or enforcement.

150. Letter on Indian Hostilities. 27 June.
HD 291, 24-1, v7, 6p. [292]
Appropriations needed to suppress the hostilities of the Seminoles and the Creeks.

151. Report on the Cherokee Treaty. 28 June.
HD 290, 24-1, v7, 1p. [292]
Copies of documents related to the Cherokee treaty lately ratified.

152. Message on Sales of Indian Reservations. 1 July.
SD 425, 24-1, v6, 388p. [284]
On frauds in the sales of public lands on Indian reservations under any of the treaties recently made.

153. R-P of R. Frazier. 1 July.
HR 840, 24-1, v3, 1p. [295]
Attack on a Kickapoo town; 1812.

154. Report on Surplus Revenue. 1 July.
HR 851, 24-1, v3, 8p. [295]
Expenditures for Indian treaties and hostilities; Chippewas, Ottawas, Creeks, and Seminoles.

155. Report on Horses Lost. 2 July.
HR 843, 24-1, v3, 2p. [295]
In Indian wars; Black Hawk war, 1832; present war.

156. Report on Abuses in the Indian Dept. 2 July.
HR 853, 24-1, v3, 1p. [295]
Progress of investigation, and that there are sufficient grounds for its continuance.

157. Report on Appropriations. 8 July.
SD 426, 24-1, v6, 6p. [284]
Indian expenses.

158. Annual Message to Congress with Documents; Pres. Jackson. 5 Dec.
SD 1, 24-2, v1, 554p. [297] *or* HD 2, 24-2, v1, 554p. [301]
Indian affairs; reports of Sec. of War, Indian Office, etc.

159. Annual Report of the Sec. of the Treasury. 6 Dec.
SD 2, 24-2, v1, 96p. [297] *or* HD 4, 24-2, v1, 96p. [301]
Indian expenses.

160. Annual Report of the Com'r of the General Land Office. 6 Dec.
SD 3, 24-2, v1, 41p. [297] *or* HD 6, 24-2, v1, 41p. [301]
Treaties with the Pottawatomie, Chippewa, Wyandot, Sac, and Fox Indians which include land cessions; etc.

161. Estimate of Appropriations. 6 Dec.
HD 5, 24-2, v1, 48p. [301]
For 1837; Indian expenses.

162. Report on Disbursements. 7 Dec.
SD 4, 24-2, v1, 8p. [297]
Emigrating Indian bureau; CIA; etc.

163. Report on Investment of Indian Funds. 7 Dec.
SD 6, 24-2, v1, 4p. [297] *or* HD 11, 24-2, v1, 4p. [301]
Chickasaw funds; treaties of 20 Oct. 1832 and 24 May 1834.

164. Report of Disbursements of War Dept. 7 Dec.
SD 11, 24-2, v1, 9p. [297]
For last session of Congress; Indian expenses.

165. Mem. of Citizens of Pennsylvania. 12 Dec.
HD 23, 24-2, v2, 1p. [302]
Ask pensions be extended to persons who served against the northwestern Indians in 1794.

166. Resol. on the Annual Message to Congress by Pres. Jackson. 13 Dec.
HR, Resol. 1, 24-2, v2, 2p. [306]
Refers part of message dealing with Indian affairs to the Com. on Indian Affairs; refers parts of message dealing with Indian depredations in Florida, Alabama, and Georgia to the Com. on Claims.

167. Letter on Indian Hostilities. 19 Dec.
HD 29, 24-2, v1, 3p. [302]
Appropriations needed to suppress hostilities in Florida and elsewhere.

168. R-P of S. Miller. 21 Dec.
SD 17, 24-2, v1, 1p. [297]
Reward for arrest of a Cherokee Indian charged with murder.

169. Army Estimates for the Year 1837. 21 Dec.
HD 32, 24-2, v2, 27p. [302]
Creek and Seminole campaigns.

170. Estimates for Indian Dept. for 1837. 21 Dec.
HD 34, 24-2, v2, 14p. [302]
For annuities, and other objects provided for by Indian treaties; list of treaties.

171. R-P of J. Kenner. 22 Dec.
HR 3, 24-2, v1, 1p. [305]
Seminole war; 1836.

172. R-P of J. Willson. 26 Dec.
HR 20, 24-2, v1, 2p. [305]
Indian battle in 1791 at Fort Recovery.

173. Message on Unexpended Balances. 27 Dec.
SD 31, 24-2, v1, 11p. [297]
Indian accounts.

174. R-P of J. Reilly. 28 Dec.
HR 32, 24-2, v1, 2p. [305]
Attacked by Creek Indians in Georgia.

175. R-C on Land Between the Rio Hondo and Sabine Rivers. 30 Dec.
HR 50, 24-2, v1, 2p. [305]
Caddo Indians.

1837

1. R-P of G. Brand. 3 Jan.
SD 47, 24-2, v1, 2p. [297]
Cherokee traders; Creek agency; Arkansas.

2. Mem. of the Tennessee Legis. 9 Jan.
SD 57, 24-2, v1, 2p. [297]
Indian war; 1836; Tennessee volunteers.

3. Report on Exchange of Lands with Indians. 9 Jan.
HD 82, 24-2, v2, 12p. [303]
The expediency of holding treaties with, and purchasing lands belonging to, the Sac, Fox, Sioux, and Winnebago Indians in Wisconsin Territory, and to provide for their removal west of the Mississippi River.

4. R-P of Certain Creek Indians. 12 Jan.
SD 62, 24-2, v1, 1p. [298]
Treaty with the Creek Indians at Fort Jackson in 1814.

5. R-C of H. Russel. 13 Jan.
HR 87, 24-2, v1, 2p. [305]
Creek hostilities in Alabama; 1836.

6. R-P of S. Tiffany. 13 Jan.
HR 88, 24-2, v1, 1p. [305]
British and Indians in North Carolina.

7. R-M of L. Malone. 14 Jan.
HR 105, 24-2, v1, 1p. [305]
Seneca Indians; 1779.
8. Report on Undrawn Accounts. 16 Jan.
SD 71, 24-2, v2, 18p. [298]
Indian accounts.
9. R-M of Choctaw Indians. 18 Jan.
SD 81, 24-2, v2, 2p. [298]
The Choctaw treaty of 27 Sept. 1830.
10. Message on the Claim of J. Galphin. 18 Jan.
SD 83, 24-2, v2, 12p. [298]
Correspondence on the claim of the heirs of Galphin against the Cherokee and Creek Indians in Georgia.
11. R-P of J. McCormick. 19 Jan.
HR 127, 24-2, v1, 2p. [305]
Indian hostilities; 1778.
12. Report on Indian Campaign in Florida. 20 Jan.
SD 100, 24-2, v2, 24p. [298]
Correspondence between the War Dept. and the Governor of Florida.
13. R-P of W. Bowman. 20 Jan.
HR 130, 24-2, v1, 1p. [305]
Indians on the frontier of Missouri in 1832.
14. Petition of Citizens of Mississippi. 21 Jan.
SD 91, 24-2, v2, 3p. [298]
Ask inquiry into the claims of the Choctaws to lands under the treaty of Dancing Rabbit Creek on 27 Sept. 1830.
15. Letter on Indian Dept. 23 Jan.
HD 108, 24-2, v3, 10p. [303]
Estimates of additional appropriations required for the year 1837; removal, subsistence, and treaties.
16. R-P of Citizens of Alabama. 23 Jan.
HR 137, 24-2, v1, 3p. [305]
Cherokee treaties of 1817 and 1819; land in Alabama.
17. On the Case of S. Miller. 25 Jan.
HR 155, 24-2, v1, 1p. [305]
For apprehension of an Indian charged with murder; Alabama.
18. Documents on Blankets for Indian Trade. 26 Jan.
SD 106, 24-2, v2, 5p. [298]
Letters from J. J. Astor and other documents on supply of blankets for the Indian trade; competition with British traders.
19. R-C of J. Bulow, Jr., 27 Jan.
SD 109, 24-2, v2, 2p. [298]
Buildings destroyed by Indians in 1836; Florida.
20. Mem. of the Michigan Legis. 27 Jan.
SD 112, 24-2, v2, 4p. [298]
To negotiate treaties with the tribes at the headwaters of the Mississippi River for lands upon which the tribes of the lake region might be located.
21. R-M of Executive Clerks. 27 Jan.
HR 161, 24-2, v1, 35p. [305]
Indian Dept.; Chickasaw and Cherokee treaties.
22. R-P of G. Johnston. 31 Jan.
SD 120, 24-2, v2, 1p. [298]
Shawnee Indian trader.
23. Letter on War Dept. Appropriations. 31 Jan.
HD 119, 24-2, v3, 17p. [303]
Appropriations and expenditures for the year 1836; Indian expenses.
24. R-M of Econchattanico. 2 Feb.
SD 131, 24-2, v2, 1p. [298]
Trespass on the land of this Seminole Indian.
25. Report on Disbursements to the Indians. 6 Feb.
HD 137, 24-2, v3, 126p. [303]
From 1 Oct. 1835 to 30 Sept. 1836.
26. R-P of J. McIntosh. 7 Feb.
SD 158, 24-2, v2, 2p. [298]
Seminole war; 1835-6.
27. R-P of G. Humphreys. 7 Feb.
SD 162, 24-2, v2, 1p. [298]
Seminole war; 1836.
28. Letter on the Militia. 7 Feb.
HD 140, 24-2, v3, 89p. [303]
Orders issued by the War Dept. on calls for volunteers for service in the Florida war; Seminole and Creek Indians.
29. Report on Persons Employed in Indian Dept. 7 Feb.
HD 141, 24-2, v3, 14p. [303]
For the year 1836.
30. R-C of Tennessee Volunteers. 8 Feb.
HR 196, 24-2, v1, 8p. [305]
Not mustered into service; Indian wars of 1836.
31. R-C of Indiana Militiamen. 8 Feb.
HR 197, 24-2, v1, 4p. [305]

For expenses incurred in protecting the Pottawatomie Indians on the Tippecanoe River in 1836 while receiving annuities.

32. Report on Disbursements in Indian Dept. 10 Feb.
SD 165, 24-2, v2, 8p. [298]
Relative to commissions on disbursements of money in the Indian Dept.

33. Letter on Indian Reservations. 11 Feb.
SD 180, 24-2, v2, 8p. [298]
Sale of Creek reservations under the treaty of 24 Mar. 1832.

34. Letter on Indian Hostilities. 11 Feb.
HD 152, 24-2, v4, 3p. [304]
Florida, Georgia, and Alabama; Cherokee country.

35. Message on Indian Hostilities. 14 Feb.
HD 154, 24-2, v4, 61p. [304]
Report of the Com'rs appointed to investigate the causes of the late hostilities of the Creek Indians.

36. On the Case of C. Widrig. 14 Feb.
HR 211, 24-2, v2, 2p. [305]
Battle of Fort Mike with British and Indians.

37. R-P of J. Houseman. 14 Feb.
HR 215, 24-2, v1, 2p. [305]
Indian hostilities in Florida in 1836.

38. R-P of Duncan and Taylor. 14 Feb.
HR 217, 24-2, v1, 2p. [305]
For goods seized in Indian country while engaged in Indian trade without license; Missouri.

39. R-P of Citizens of St. Augustine, Florida. 14 Feb.
HR 218, 24-2, v1, 1p. [305]
Seminole war; 1836.

40. R-M of A. Heileman. 14 Feb.
HR 225, 24-2, v2, 2p. [306]
Florida Indian war; 1836.

41. Report on a Road from Memphis to Fort Gibson. 22 Feb.
HR 251, 24-2, v2, 2p. [306]
Indian hostilities.

42. Report on Payment of Alabama Troops. 22 Feb.
HR 258, 24-2, v2, 1p. [306]
For services in 1836; Creek Indian war.

43. R-P of J. McPherson. 22 Feb.
HR 267, 24-2, v2, 2p. [306]
Subsistence of Indians; 1812.

44. R-P of W. Purcell. 22 Feb.
HR 268, 24-2, v2, 3p. [306]
Indian attack in 1811 on the Wabash River.

45. R-P of A. Hall. 22 Feb.
HR 269, 24-2, v2, 1p. [306]
Creek war.

46. R-P of Avery, Saltmarsh, and Co. 23 Feb.
HR 280, 24-2, v2, 9p. [306]
Attacked by Creek Indians while transporting the mail in Alabama; Creek war.

47. R-P of Capt. Thistle. 25 Feb.
SD 204, 24-2, v2, 2p. [298]
Invented saddle for carrying wounded; especially fit for Indian wars; now being used in Florida.

48. Report on Land Surveys in Illinois and Missouri. 28 Feb.
HD 178, 24-2, v4, 19p. [304]
Land cessions by Pottawatomies under the treaty of 20 Oct. 1832; etc.

49. Report on Resignations of Army Officers. 1 Mar.
HD 183, 24-2, v4, 9p. [304]
Includes number of companies operating during the past year against the Creeks and Seminoles.

50. Report on Impressment of Property and Indian Depredations. 1 Mar.
HR 301, 24-2, v2, 7p. [306]
Com. asks to be discharged from further consideration of relief of sufferers by Indian depredations or by the operations of our own troops in Florida, Alabama, and Georgia; Creeks and Seminoles.

51. R-C of City of Mobile. 1 Mar.
HR 304, 24-2, v2, 3p. [306]
Expenses of Creek war; 1836.

52. R-C of Augusta, Georgia. 3 Mar.
HR 319, 24-2, v2, 1p. [306]
Expenses of raising troops for the Florida Indian war; 1836.

53. R-C of Citizens of Georgia. 3 Mar.
HR 322, 24-2, v2, 2p. [306]
For the suppression of Florida Indian hostilities.

54. Appropriations in 1837. 13 Mar.
HD 189, 24-2, v4, 41p. [304]
Indian expenses.

55. Report of Court of Inquiry. 29 Mar.
SD 224, 24-2, v3, 734p. [299]
Case of Major-Gen. Scott (failure of the Florida campaign in 1836); Case of Major-Gen. Scott (delay in opening and prosecuting the

Creek campaign); Case of Major-Gen. Gaines; etc.

56. Mem. of the Mississippi Legis. 7 Sept. SD 3, 25-1, v1, 2p. [309]
Land ceded by the Chickasaw Indians.

57. Letter on Indian Hostilities. 14 Sept. SD 18, 25-1, v1, 2p. [309] *or* HD 19, 25-1, v1, 2p. [311]
Seminole war.

58. Report on Indians in the Military Service. 21 Sept.
HD 27, 25-1, v1, 13p. [311]
Creeks, Delawares, Shawnees, Sac and Foxes, Kickapoos, and Choctaws serving in the Seminole war.

59. Report on Unexpended Appropriations. 22 Sept.
HD 17, 25-1, v1, 101p. [311]
Indian accounts.

60. State of the Treasury. 30 Sept.
HD 37, 25-1, v1, 1p. [311]
Florida war.

61. Message on the U.S.-Mexico Boundary. 3 Oct.
HD 42, 25-1, v1, 94p. [311]
Indian hostilities.

62. Message on the Case of Gen. Wool. 9 Oct.
HD 46, 25-1, v1, 85p. [311]
Conduct in the Cherokee country.

63. Statement of Appropriations. 17 Oct. SD 37, 25-1, v1, 2p. [309]
During the 1st session of the 25th Congress; for suppressing Indian hostilities.

64. Annual Message to Congress with Documents; Pres. Van Buren. 4 Dec. SD 1, 25-2, v1, 808p. [314] *or* HD 3, 25-2, v1, 870p. [321]
Indian hostilities in Florida; Indian removal; annual report of the Sec. of War; annual report of the CIA.

65. Annual Report of the Sec. of the Treasury. 6 Dec.
SD 2, 25-2, v1, 41p. [314] *or* HD 4, 25-2, v1, 41p. [321]
Indian Dept.

66. Resol. of Rep. Haynes. 7 Dec.
HR, Resol. 1, 25-2, v4, 2p. [336]
Refers portion of the Annual Message of the Pres. dealing with Indian hostilities to the Com. on Military Affairs; portion dealing with Indian affairs sent to the Com. on Indian Affairs.

67. Report on Chickasaw Fund. 8 Dec. HD 17, 25-2, v2, 2p. [322]
Investment and disbursement of funds received under treaties with the Chickasaw Indians from sales of land.

68. Estimate of Appropriations. 11 Dec. HD 20, 25-2, v2, 43p. [322]
For the year 1838.

69. On the Case of J. Bulow, Jr., 12 Dec. SD 10, 25-2, v1, 2p. [314]
Florida Indians; 1836.

70. Annual Report of the Com'r of the General Land Office. 13 Dec.
SD 11, 25-2, v1, 74p. [314] *or* HD 23, 25-2, v2, 88p. [322]
Indian treaties and land cessions.

71. R-P of J. Baker. 14 Dec.
HR 16, 25-2, v1, 2p. [333]
Indian depredations in Illinois in 1832; Sac Indians.

72. R-P of T. McCanless. 14 Dec.
HR 18, 25-2, v1, 1p. [333]
Creek war; 1814.

73. R-P of A. Crow. 14 Dec.
HR 22, 25-2, v1, 2p. [333]
Black Hawk war in 1832; Illinois militia.

74. R-P of F. Gardner. 14 Dec.
HR 35, 25-2, v1, 2p. [333]
Florida Indian engagement in 1836.

75. R-C of J. Perkins. 14 Dec.
HR 43, 25-2, v1, 1p. [333]
Seminole war; 1818.

76. R-P of Administrator of E. Duval. 14 Dec.
HR 47, 25-2, v1, 3p. [333]
Cherokee treaty of 6 May 1828; Arkansas.

77. R-C of A. Morgan. 14 Dec.
HR 50, 25-2, v1, 3p. [333]
Sac and Fox Indians; 1832.

78. R-P of J. Wilson. 14 Dec.
HR 52, 25-2, v1, 2p. [333]
Black Hawk war.

79. R-P of Doctor Maxwell. 14 Dec.
HR 55, 25-2, v1, 2p. [333]
Indian campaign of 1814 in Indiana.

80. R-P of J. Kenner. 14 Dec.
HR 59, 25-2, v1, 2p. [333]
Seminole war; 1836.

81. On the Case of H. Russel. 14 Dec.
HR 61, 25-2, v1, 2p. [333]
Creek hostilities of 1836 in Alabama.

82. Documents on the Claim of Executor of J. Bulow, Jr., 16 Dec.
SD 36, 25-2, v1, 12p. [314]
For property destroyed by the Seminole Indians in Florida; Creek Indians.

83. Mem. of W. Slacum. 18 Dec.
SD 24, 25-2, v1, 31p. [314]
Survey of the inhabitants of the Columbia River; Chinook and other Indians; fur trade.

84. Message on Claims to Indian Reservations. 19 Dec.
SD 25, 25-2, v1, 29p. [314]
Choctaw treaty of 1830.

85. R-P of S. Miller. 19 Dec.
SD 27, 25-2, v1, 1p. [314]
Captured escaped Indians in Alabama.

86. Mem. of J. Roby. 19 Dec.
SD 29, 25-2, v1, 8p. [314]
Asks to locate a floating Indian reservation of land on any unappropriated lands of the U.S. in Illinois or Wisconsin Territory; Pottawatomie treaty of 20 Oct. 1832, etc.

87. On the Relief of S. Ferguson. 21 Dec.
SD 34, 25-2, v1, 2p. [314]
Indian war in Illinois; 1832.

88. Letter on Indian Hostilities. 21 Dec.
HD 65, 25-2, v2, 3p. [322]
Ask additional appropriation for the suppression of said hostilities.

89. R-P of J. Wellborn, jr. 22 Dec.
HR 91, 25-2, v1, 3p. [333]
Cherokee treaties of July, 1817 and Feb., 1819.

90. R-M of the Arkansas Legis. 22 Dec.
HR 99, 25-2, v1, 16p. [333]
Ask indemnity for loss of improvements ceded to Choctaw Indians; treaty of 1820.

91. R-M of Col. Vigo. 22 Dec.
HR 118, 25-2, v1, 33p. [333]
Illinois campaign of 1778; captured by Indians.

92. R-P of A. and M. Yates. 22 Dec.
HR 146, 25-2, v1, 2p. [333]
Choctaw treaty of 27 Sept. 1830 at Dancing Rabbit Creek.

93. R-P of C. Dennison. 22 Dec.
HR 171, 25-2, v1, 1p. [333]
British and Indians; 1775-81.

94. Mem. of Arkansas Legis. 27 Dec.
SD 53, 25-2, v1, 3p. [314]
On the location of Indian reservations in the state; Osage treaty of 2 June 1825.

95. Documents on the Claim of Dubuque and Chouteau. 28 Dec.
SD 51, 25-2, v1, 4p. [314]
To a tract of land on the Mississippi River; Sac and Fox Indians.

96. Letter on the Osage Indians. 28 Dec.
SD 59, 25-2, v1, 10p. [314]
On the distressed and starving condition of the Osage Indians, and recommending measures for their relief.

97. R-P of G. Willard. 28 Dec.
HR 203, 25-2, v1, 1p. [333]
Indian war of 1832 in Michigan Territory.

98. R-P of W. Stephans. 28 Dec.
HR 210, 25-2, v1, 2p. [333]
Cherokee reservation in Alabama.

99. R-P of T. Triplett. 28 Dec.
HR 211, 25-2, v1, 3p. [333]
For services in carrying into effect the treaty of 24 Jan. 1826 with the Creek Indians.

100. R-P of R. Gentry. 28 Dec.
HR 212, 25-2, v1, 5p. [333]
Sac and Fox Indian removal in 1813.

101. R-P of W. Bowman. 28 Dec.
HR 223, 25-2, v1, 1p. [333]
Indian campaign of 1832 on the Missouri frontier.

102. R-P of R. Carter. 28 Dec.
HR 229, 25-2, v1, 2p. [333]
Indian engagements in 1795 and 1799 in Indiana.

103. Mem. of Citizens of Pennsylvania. 29 Dec.
HD 52, 25-2, v2, 8p. [322]
British and Indians; Wyoming claims.

104. Estimate of Funds for the Indian Dept. 29 Dec.
HD 57, 25-2, v2, 31p. [322]
For the year 1838.

105. Report on Execution of Osage Treaty. 30 Dec.
SD 64, 25-2, v1, 12p. [314]
Progress made in survey of lands to be granted to the Osage Indians under the treaty of 2 June 1825; Delaware treaty of 24 Sept. 1829.

106. Letter on the Protection of the Western Frontier. 30 Dec.

HD 59, 25-2, v2, 20p. [322]
Aggressions of the Indians; force of the Indians beyond the frontier; etc.

1838

1. Report on Protection of the Western Frontier. 3 Jan.
SD 65, 25-2, v1, 19p. [314]
Against Indian aggressions: list of tribes east of the Mississippi River, of Indians who have emigrated west, and of indigenous tribes within striking distance of the frontier.
2. Report on Surveyor General's Office in Wisconsin. 4 Jan.
HR 238, 25-2, v1, 4p. [333]
Indian land cessions and emigration; Winnebago, Sac, and Fox Indians.
3. Petition of S. Gregory. 5 Jan.
HD 66, 25-2, v2, 1p. [322]
Asks justice for the aborigines of this country.
4. Letter on Military Operations in Florida. 6 Jan.
HD 78, 25-2, v3, 1038p. [323]
Campaigns against the Creek and Seminole Indians; proceedings of a court of inquiry on said operations.
5. Report on Land Offices. 6 Jan.
HR 237, 25-2, v1, 1p. [333]
Sac and Fox lands; Wisconsin.
6. Letter on the Cherokee Indians. 8 Jan.
HD 82, 25-2, v5, 13p. [325]
On their emigration west of the Mississippi.
7. Report on Unexpended Appropriations. 9 Jan.
HR 303, 25-2, v1, 7p. [333]
Indian expenses.
8. R-P of R. Frazier. 9 Jan.
HR 320, 25-2, v1, 1p. [333]
Attack on a Kickapoo town in 1812-13.
9. R-P of S. Tiffany. 9 Jan.
HR 321, 25-2, v1, 1p. [333]
British and Indians.
10. R-P of D. McKinney. 9 Jan.
HR 325, 25-2, v1, 2p. [333]
Indian engagement of 1779 in Pennsylvania.
11. Report on Pensions to Indian Fighters. 9 Jan.
HR 327, 25-2, v1, 3p. [333]
Recommends extension of laws to the period 1783 to 1795.
12. R-P of A. Kingsley. 9 Jan.
HR 329, 25-2, v1, 1p. [333]
Indian hostilities of 1812 in Florida.
13. R-P of the Heirs of T. Johnson. 9 Jan.
HR 331, 25-2, v2, 2p. [334]
Indian campaign of 1783 in Illinois.
14. R-P of T. Walker. 9 Jan.
HR 333, 25-2, v2, 2p. [334]
Cherokee agency.
15. R-P of A. Hunter. 10 Jan.
HR 341, 25-2, v2, 2p. [334]
Cherokee nation in 1836.
16. R-P of G. Hollenbeck et al. 10 Jan.
HR 351, 25-2, v2, 2p. [334]
Sac and Fox depredations of 1832 in Illinois.
17. Report on War Dept. Appropriations. 11 Jan.
SD 95, 25-2, v2, 16p. [315] *or* HD 92, 25-2, v5, 17p. [325]
For the year 1837; Indian expenses.
18. Report on the Pottawatomie Indians. 11 Jan.
SD 96, 25-2, v2, 2p. [315]
Occurrences at the payment of the annuity to said Indians in 1836.
19. R-P of T. Hall. 11 Jan.
HR 371, 25-2, v2, 1p. [334]
Indian wars in 1775-77.
20. Letter on Clerks in Indian Office. 12 Jan.
SD 101, 25-2, v2, 6p. [315]
From the CIA on the need for more clerks.
21. Report on the Cherokee Indians. 12 Jan.
SD 120, 25-2, v2, 1090p. [315]
Cherokee treaty of 1835.
22. R-P of W. Lewis. 12 Jan.
HR 373, 25-2, v2, 3p. [334]
Indian hostilities of 1836 in Florida.
23. R-P of E. Neale. 12 Jan.
HR 391, 25-2, v2, 1p. [334]
Indian hostilities of 1814 on the Mississippi River.
24. Letter on Alleged Indian Frauds. 13 Jan.

HD 97, 25-2, v5, 3p. [325]
Frauds allegedly committed against the Indians; Creek treaty of 24 Mar. 1832.

25. Letter on Indian Hostilities. 13 Jan.
HD 113, 25-2, v5, 2p. [325]
Indian war in Florida.

26. Mem. of the Cherokee Delegation. 15 Jan.
HD 99, 25-2, v5, 49p. [325]
Against the treaty of 1835 at New Echota.

27. Report on Location of Indian Reservations. 16 Jan.
SD 104, 25-2, v2, 2p. [315]
Purchase of the Osage reservations of land under the treaty of 2 June 1825; Arkansas.

28. Report on Payment of Indian Annuities. 16 Jan.
SD 106, 25-2, v2, 2p. [315]
Tribes receiving annuities for the past year; amount; etc.

29. R-P of Tennessee Settlers. 17 Jan.
HR 407, 25-2, v2, 3p. [334]
Chickasaw treaty of 19 Oct. 1818 at Old Town.

30. Documents on the Western Frontier. 18 Jan.
HD 114, 25-2, v5, 5p. [325]
Expense of establishing posts against Indian hostilities.

31. R-M of the Alabama Legis. 18 Jan.
HR 434, 25-2, v2, 2p. [334]
Location of Creek and Choctaw reservations on settler's improvements.

32. Documents on the Cherokee Indians. 22 Jan.
SD 121, 25-2, v2, 43p. [315]
On the validity of the Cherokee treaty of 1835.

33. R-C of G. Duval. 23 Jan.
SD 125, 25-2, v2, 19p. [315]
On spoliations of the property of this Cherokee Indian by U.S. citizens.

34. R-P of J. Knipe. 25 Jan.
HR 459, 25-2, v2, 1p. [334]
Indian attack of 1814 on the Canadian frontier.

35. R-P of A. Ross. 25 Jan.
HR 462, 25-2, v2, 1p. [334]
Seminole war.

36. R-P of the Indiana Militia. 25 Jan.
HR 465, 25-2, v2, 5p. [334]
Protection of Pottawatomies collecting their annuities in 1836.

37. R-P of the Heirs of J. Caller. 25 Jan.
HR 475, 25-2, v2, 2p. [334]
Land in Mississippi to which Indian title has been extinguished.

38. R-P of G. Fisher. 25 Jan.
HR 484, 25-2, v2, 1p. [334]
Indian hostilities of 1813 in Mississippi.

39. R-P of Heirs of G. Moffit. 27 Jan.
HR 493, 25-2, v2, 2p. [334]
Shawnee treaties and removal.

40. R-C of M. Armbrister. 29 Jan.
SD 143, 25-2, v3, 2p. [316]
Creek treaty of 24 Mar. 1832.

41. Message on Indian Depredations. 29 Jan.
HD 127, 25-2, v6, 69p. [326]
Seminole and Creek Indians.

42. Report on Florida War. 29 Jan.
HD 133, 25-2, v6, 11p. [326]
Number of troops; enlisted Indians; Seminole campaign.

43. Report on Persons Employed in Indian Dept. 29 Jan.
HD 135, 25-2, v6, 19p. [326]
For the year 1837.

44. R-P of A. Heileman. 30 Jan.
HR 501, 25-2, v2, 4p. [334]
Florida Indian campaign; 1836.

45. R-C of T. Ledwith. 30 Jan.
HR 506, 25-2, v2, 2p. [334]
Indian depredations of 1836 in Florida.

46. R-P of J. Naurse. 31 Jan.
HR 510, 25-2, v2, 4p. [334]
Seminole war of 1836 in Florida.

47. Report on Grants of Land on the Frontier. 1 Feb.
SD 152, 25-2, v3, 5p. [316]
Recommends grant of quarter-section of land to each settler who shall occupy land bordering the country to which Indians have been removed.

48. Resol. of Indiana Legis. 1 Feb.
SD 191, 25-2, v3, 2p. [316]
Asks to be able to purchase the Miami Indian lands recently ceded to the U.S.

49. R-P of L. Evans. 1 Feb.
HR 519, 25-2, v2, 2p. [334]
Trader in Cherokee country.

50. R-P of B. Brown. 2 Feb.
HR 524, 25-2, v2, 1p. [334]
Miami Indian treaty of Oct., 1834 in Indiana.

51. Mem. of Citizens of Mississippi. 5 Feb.
SD 165, 25-2, v3, 10p. [316]
Choctaw purchase.

52. Letter on Indian Hostilities. 6 Feb.
SD 173, 25-2, v3, 8p. [316]
Number of Creeks engaged in the war during 1836 and 1837.

53. On Relief for B. Murphy. 6 Feb.
HR 549, 25-2, v2, 10p. [334]
Cherokee treaty of May, 1828.

54. R-P of J. Milligan and P. Meroney. 7 Feb.
HR 547, 25-2, v2, 4p. [334]
Trading house established under a Cherokee treaty.

55. Letter on the Missouri-Indian Boundary. 8 Feb.
HD 148, 25-2, v7, 2p. [327]
Iowa, Kansa, Sac, and Fox treaties.

56. R-P of H. Turk. 9 Feb.
HR 555, 25-2, v3, 2p. [335]
Agent for the removal of the Cherokees when shot in 1835.

57. R-P of D. Robb. 13 Feb.
SD 192, 25-2, v3, 2p. [316]
Indian services in Indiana; emigration and treaties.

58. Letter on Indian Annuities. 13 Feb.
SD 198, 25-2, v3, 67p. [316]
On the payment of annuities and restrictions on Indian traders.

59. Mem. of the Wisconsin Legis. 14 Feb.
HD 173, 25-2, v7, 1p. [327]
Asking that citizenship be granted to the Stockbridge Indians residing on the east shore of Lake Winnebago.

60. Letter on Defense of Western Frontier. 14 Feb.
HD 276, 25-2, v8, 21p. [328]
Against the native and emigrant Indians.

61. R-P of Avery, Saltmarsh and Co. 17 Feb.
HR 561, 25-2, v3, 10p. [335]
Creek Indian war disrupts mail service.

62. R-P of J. Vroman. 17 Feb.
HR 578, 25-2, v3, 1p. [335]
Indian hostilities of 1780 in Lower Canada.

63. R-P of B. Vroman. 17 Feb.
HR 579, 25-2, v3, 1p. [335]
Indian hostilities in 1780 in New York.

64. Petition of Citizens of Mississippi. 19 Feb.
SD 212, 25-2, v3, 4p. [316]
Choctaw purchase.

65. Resol. of the Indiana Legis. 19 Feb.
HD 185, 25-2, v7, 2p. [327]
Miami lands purchased by the U.S.

66. On the Case of C. Atwater. 20 Feb.
SD 219, 25-2, v3, 3p. [316]
Treaty negotiations in 1829; from Ohio.

67. Report on Seminole War. 20 Feb.
SD 226, 25-2, v3, 12p. [316]
U.S. forces employed; number of Seminole warriors; cost; etc.

68. Report on Action with the Seminoles. 20 Feb.
SD 227, 25-2, v3, 13p. [316]
Action of 25 Dec. 1837.

69. Report on a Fort for Western Arkansas. 21 Feb.
SD 224, 25-2, v3, 24p. [316]
Defense against the Indians; Cherokees, Choctaws, Creeks, and Osages.

70. Documents on an Armory in the West. 21 Feb.
SD 231, 25-2, v3, 14p. [316]
Indian hostilities.

71. R-P of S. Phillips. 21 Feb.
HR 597, 25-2, v3, 1p. [335]
Creek Indians; 1836.

72. R-P of J. Becker. 23 Feb.
HR 607, 25-2, v3, 1p. [335]
British and Indians in 1778.

73. R-P of Capt. Hunter. 23 Feb.
HR 611, 25-2, v3, 2p. [335]
Indian engagement of 1811 at Tippecanoe.

74. Report on Sales of Shawnee Lands. 24 Feb.
HD 188, 25-2, v7, 3p. [327]
Information on amount realized, how invested, etc.

75. R-P of the Heirs of A. Tipton. 1 Mar.
HR 618, 25-2, v3, 1p. [335]
Killed by Indians in 1781 near the falls of the Ohio River.

76. R-P of N. Hooe. 2 Mar.
HR 626, 25-2, v3, 2p. [335]
Choctaw land in Alabama; 1833.

77. Report on Improvements Lost. 2 Mar.
HR 629, 25-2, v3, 2p. [335]
Under the Choctaw treaty of 1825; Choctaw and Cherokee treaty of 1828.

78. R-P of Executor of T. Galphin. 5 Mar.
SD 260, 25-2, v3, 2p. [316]
Creek and Cherokee debts prior to 1773.

79. Mem. of the Indiana Legis. 5 Mar.
HD 214, 25-2, v8, 1p. [328]
Land purchased by the U.S.; Miami Indians.

80. Message on the Florida War. 6 Mar.
HD 219, 25-2, v8, 8p. [328]
Present state of the campaign; disposition of the Indians to treat for peace.

81. Report on Land in Indiana. 10 Mar.
SD 285, 25-2, v4, 2p. [317]
Pottawatomie treaty of 16 Oct. 1826.

82. Mem. of the Mississippi Legis. 10 Mar.
SD 289, 25-2, v4, 2p. [317]
Choctaw treaty of 1835; Dancing Rabbit Creek.

83. R-P of D. Newman. 13 Mar.
HR 674, 25-2, v3, 1p. [335]
Creek Indian campaign during war of 1812.

84. R-P of M. Francis. 13 Mar.
HR 677, 25-2, v3, 1p. [335]
Creek war of 1813 in Tennessee.

85. R-P of Lieut. Allison. 13 Mar.
HR 678, 25-2, v3, 1p. [335]
Campaign against the western Indians in 1791.

86. R-P of Reps. of J. Brown. 13 Mar.
HR 685, 25-2, v3, 1p. [335]
Interest on claim; Indian Affairs Com.

87. R-M of Tennessee Volunteers. 13 Mar.
GR 686, 25-2, v3, 1p. [335]
Cherokee service.

88. R-P of J. Dougherty. 14 Mar.
HR 687, 25-2, v3, 1p. [335]
Winnebago treaty of 1829; land concerns.

89. Letter on the Creek Indians. 15 Mar.
SD 306, 25-2, v4, 7p. [317]
Correspondence between the War Dept. and the Governor of Alabama on Creek hostilities.

90. Letter on Indian Hostilities. 17 Mar.
HD 265, 25-2, v8, 15p. [328]
Estimates of appropriations necessary for 1838.

91. Report on Issue of Certain Land Patents. 19 Mar.
SD 311, 25-2, v4, 2p. [317]
Authorize patents for land reservations to O-ca-chee and Be-si-ah, Pottawatomie Indians; treaty of 20 Oct. 1832.

92. R-P of M. Murray. 20 Mar.
HR 696, 25-2, v3, 1p. [335]
Cherokee treaty of 6 May 1828.

93. Report on Volunteer and Regular Troops. 21 Mar.
HD 271, 25-2, v8, 19p. [328]
Numbers engaged by the U.S. for the past 6 years; Black Hawk war, Florida war, Creek war, Cherokee disturbances, and southwestern frontier.

94. Letter on Indian Hostilities. 21 Mar.
HD 272, 25-2, v8, 2p. [328]
Hostilities in Florida; removal west of the Seminole Indians.

95. Mem. of a Deputation of the Cherokee Nation. 21 Mar.
HD 285, 25-2, v8, 24p. [328]
To mediate for peace with the Seminoles in Florida.

96. R-P of E. Bently. 21 Mar.
HR 707, 25-2, v3, 2p. [335]
Tories and Indians in 1777.

97. R-P of Heirs of W. Young. 21 Mar.
HR 709, 25-2, v3, 1p. [335]
Com'r to take the census of the Cherokee Indians west of the Mississippi River.

98. R-C of J. Hanks. 22 Mar.
SD 320, 25-2, v4, 5p. [317]
Black Hawk war; Sac and Fox Indians; 1832; Illinois.

99. R-C of A. Westfall. 22 Mar.
SD 321, 25-2, v4, 5p. [317]
Black Hawk war; Sacs and Foxes; 1832; Illinois.

100. R-P of Heirs of F. Contraman. 22 Mar.
SD 323, 25-2, v4, 1p. [317]
Pottawatomie treaty of 20 Oct. 1832.

101. Letter on the Creek Indians. 22 Mar.
HD 274, 25-2, v8, 173p. [328]
Contract between Gen. Jessup, certain Creek chiefs, and J. Watson in relation to sale of certain lands belonging to Creek Indians, and documents connected therewith.

102. Letter on Road on Western Frontier. 23 Mar.
HD 278, 25-2, v8, 25p. [328]
A military road; construction of posts thereon; Indians near Arkansas.

103. Report on the State of the Treasury. 23 Mar.
HR 716, 25-2, v3, 6p. [335]
Indian accounts.

104. R-P of Choctaw Indians. 23 Mar.
HR 719, 25-2, v3, 2p. [335]
Treaty of 27 Sept. 1830 at Dancing Rabbit Creek.

105. R-P of Inhabitants of St. Augustine, Florida. 23 Mar.

HR 724, 25-2, v3, 2p. [335]
Seminole hostilities in 1836.

106. Letter on the Indiana Militia. 26 Mar.
SD 341, 25-2, v4, 10p. [317]
For services during the payment of annuities to the Pottawatomies in 1836.

107. R-P of J. Brown. 27 Mar.
HR 729, 25-2, v3, 2p. [335]
Seminole war; 1836.

108. R-M of G. Johnson. 30 Mar.
HR 744, 25-2, v3, 4p. [335]
Trader in the Shawnee Nation of Ohio.

109. Letter on Military Forces in Florida. 3 Apr.
HD 299, 25-2, v9, 8p. [329]
During 1837; including Creek, Shawnee, and Delaware Indians.

110. Documents on the Battle of Lake Okeechobee. 5 Apr.
SD 356, 25-2, v4, 9p. [317]
Missouri volunteer officers on the action of 25 Dec. 1837, in Florida.

111. Mem. of Arkansas Citizens. 5 Apr.
SD 357, 25-2, v4, 2p. [317]
Protection from Indians; fort on the frontier.

112. Resol. of Citizens of Arkansas. 5 Apr.
SD 358, 25-2, v4, 2p. [317]
Indian hostilities; frontier defense.

113. Plan for Defense of Western Frontier. 6 Apr.
HD 311, 25-2, v9, 59p. [329]
Necessary to afford protection to the inhabitants from Indian hostilities.

114. Reports on Lands to Militiamen. 6 Apr.
HR 756, 25-2, v3, 6p. [335]
Indian hostilities on the western frontier; lands to which Indian title has been extinguished.

115. R-P of J. Allen. 6 Apr.
HR 760, 25-2, v3, 2p. [335]
Violation of the Chickasaw treaty of 20 Sept. 1816 regarding trade.

116. R-M of R. Bush. 6 Apr.
HR 761, 25-2, v3, 2p. [335]
Indian campaign of 1778-9 in Pennsylvania.

117. Report on the Northern Boundary of Missouri. 6 Apr.
HR 768, 25-2, v3, 2p. [335]
Purchase of lands from half-breeds.

118. Mem. of the Cherokee Nation. 9 Apr.
HD 316, 25-2, v9, 7p. [329]
Denying the validity of the treaty of Dec. 1835 made at New Echota.

119. Mem. of New Jersey Citizens. 9 Apr.
HD 324, 25-2, v9, 2p. [329]
Opposed to enforcement of treaty of 1835; Cherokees.

120. Letter on Seminole Prisoners. 10 Apr.
HD 327, 25-2, v9, 14p. [329]
Those captured under a flag of truce, or with Cherokee Indians acting as mediators.

121. Mem. of Pennsylvania Citizens. 11 Apr.
SD 374, 25-2, v4, 2p. [317]
Questions legitimacy of 1835 treaty; New Echota; Cherokees.

122. Petition of G. Davenport. 13 Apr.
HD 331, 25-2, v10, 11p. [330]
Campaign against the Indians of Illinois in 1813; Sac and Fox Indians in 1816; Pottawatomie Indian chiefs in 1831.

123. R-M of D. Snider. 13 Apr.
HR 788, 25-2, v3, 2p. [335]
Horses running loose in Indian country.

124. R-P of W. Hallowes. 13 Apr.
HR 790, 25-2, v3, 4p. [335]
Indian war of 1835 in Florida; removal.

125. On the Relief of S. Ferguson. 17 Apr.
HR 800, 25-2, v3, 2p. [335]
Sac and Fox campaign of 1832 in Illinois.

126. Mem. of S. Fansher. 18 Apr.
SD 385, 25-2, v4, 12p. [317]
Establishment of vaccination institution for Indian Dept., etc.

127. Message on the Claim of Econchatta Nico. 18 Apr.
SD 393, 25-2, v5, 15p. [318]
Chief of the Appalachicola Indians; Florida.

128. Mem. of New Jersey Citizens. 19 Apr.
SD 388, 25-2, v5, 2p. [318]
Ask annulment of 1835 treaty; Cherokees.

129. Mem. of New Jersey Citizens. 19 Apr.
SD'389, 25-2, v5, 2p. [318]
Annulment of 1835 treaty at New Echota between Cherokees and U.S.

130. Mem. of Pennsylvania Citizens. 19 Apr.
SD 390, 25-2, v5, 3p. [318]
Question legality of 1835 treaty; Cherokees.

131. Letter on Emigrated Indians. 19 Apr.
SD 395, 25-2, v5, 5p. [318]
On survey and assignment of lands to Indians who have emigrated beyond the Mississippi River.

132. R-P of M. Duncan. 19 Apr.
HR 804, 25-2, v3, 3p. [335]
Expedition to the Osage villages in 1836.

133. Report on School Lands. 20 Apr.
HR 812, 25-2, v3, 4p. [335]
School lands in Indian reservations in Ohio; Ottawa, Seneca, Shawnee, Wyandot, and Choctaw treaties.

134. Mem. of the Yearly Meeting of Friends. 24 Apr.
SD 402, 25-2, v5, 2p. [318]
Florida war; Cherokee removal.

135. Mem. of Creek and Choctaw Delegations. 26 Apr.
SD 407, 25-2, v5, 1p. [318]
Oppose bill to provide for the security and protection of Indians west of Missouri and Arkansas.

136. Documents on the Claims of Missouri Volunteers. 26 Apr.
SD 409, 25-2, v5, 19p. [318]
Years 1829 to 1836; Indian encounters.

137. Letter on Sites for Military Posts. 28 Apr.
HD 357, 25-2, v10, 4p. [330]
On the western frontier of Arkansas and Missouri.

138. Report on Indian Disbursements. 1 May.
HD 362, 25-2, v10, 165p. [330]
Year ending 30 Sept. 1837.

139. Mem. of Vermont Citizens. 3 May.
SD 416, 25-2, v5, 2p. [318]
Asks 1835 treaty not be enforced; Cherokees.

140. Mem. of New Jersey Citizens. 3 May.
SD 417, 25-2, v5, 2p. [318]
Pray annulment of 1835 treaty with Cherokees.

141. Report on Indian Annuity. 4 May.
HD 367, 25-2, v10, 11p. [330]
Due the Seneca Indians for 1837.

142. Report on Survey of Indian Lands. 7 May.
SD 425, 25-2, v5, 2p. [318]
Survey and partition by the U.S. of the lands assigned to emigrated Indian tribes west of the Mississippi River.

143. Report on Investment of Indian Funds. 8 May.
SD 426, 25-2, v5, 9p. [318]
Detailed accounts.

144. Letter on the Creek Indians. 10 May.
HD 381, 25-2, v10, 2p. [330]
Copy of the agreement made with the Creek warriors serving in the Seminole war.

145. Report on Bill of Relief for G. Duval et al. 10 May.
HR 824, 25-2, v4, 32p. [336]
Cherokee Indians; Arkansas; treaty of 6 May 1828.

146. R-M of J. Paxton. 11 May.
SD 433, 25-2, v5, 7p. [318]
British and Indians; 1813.

147. R-C of C. Atwater. 11 May.
HR 832, 25-2, v4, 3p. [336]
Treaties negotiated with the Winnebago, Chippewa, Ottawa, and Pottawatomie Indians in 1829.

148. R-P of W. West. 11 May.
HR 836, 25-2, v4, 2p. [336]
Seminole campaign in Florida.

149. R-C of W. Paulett. 11 May.
HR 841, 25-2, v4, 1p. [336]
Creek hostilities.

150. R-P of J. Pomar. 11 May.
HR 842, 25-2, v4, 1p. [336]
Seminole war of 1836 in Florida.

151. R-P of the Heirs of J. Motlow. 11 May.
HR 845, 25-2, v4, 2p. [336]
Cherokee treaty of 1798.

152. R-P of E. Higley. 11 May.
HR 877, 25-2, v4, 1p. [336]
British and Indians in 1813.

153. Report on Bill of Relief for M. Armbrister. 11 May.
HR 888, 25-2, v4, 1p. [336]
Creek Indian land patent.

154. Report on Indian Trust Funds. 15 May.
HR 892, 25-2, v4, 6p. [336]
Shows present disposition and condition of said funds.

155. R-P of F. Jones. 15 May.
HR 893, 25-2, v4, 1p. [336]
Indian spy in 1778.

156. R-M of Alabama Legis. 15 May.
HR 932, 25-2, v4, 6p. [336]
Creek Indian war.

157. R-C of A. Pickett and G. Gayle. 17 May.
HR 894, 25-2, v4, 2p. [336]
Creek war of 1836 in Alabama.

158. R-C of G. and J. Anderson. 17 May.
HR 896, 25-2, v4, 3p. [336]
Seminole war in Florida; 1835.

159. Letter on Indian Hostilities. 19 May.
HD 371, 25-2, v10, 3p. [330]
Shows necessity of immediate appropriations; Seminole war.

160. R-P of Colonel Lowry. 19 May.
HR 916, 25-2, v4, 2p. [336]
Attorney for the Cherokee Indians; treaties of 8 July 1817 and 27 Feb. 1819.

161. Mem. of Citizens of Ohio. 21 May.
HD 374, 25-2, v10, 3p. [330]
Opposed to enforcement of 1835 treaty; Cherokees.

162. Message on the Cherokee Indians. 21 May.
HD 376, 25-2, v10, 4p. [330]
Communication from the Sec. of War to the Cherokee delegation on the removal west of the Cherokee Nation.

163. Mem. of Pennsylvania Citizens. 21 May.
HD 384, 25-2, v10, 2p. [330]
Opposed to enforcement of 1835 treaty; Cherokees.

164. Mem. of the Yearly Meeting of Friends. 21 May.
HD 385, 25-2, v10, 2p. [330]
Pray Indians will be able to enjoy their rights.

165. Resol. of the Massachusetts Legis. 21 May.
HD 404, 25-2, v10, 2p. [330]
Against 1835 Cherokee Indian treaty and Indian wars aimed at extermination.

166. R-C of G. Humphreys. 22 May.
SD 449, 25-2, v5, 1p. [318]
Seminole war; 1836.

167. Report on Lands Between the Rio Hondo and Sabine Rivers. 22 May.
SD 450, 25-2, v5, 1p. [318]
Caddo Indians.

168. Report on Horses and Property Lost in the Military Service. 23 May.
HR 921, 25-2, v4, 7p. [336]
Indian campaigns.

169. R-C of Z. Philips. 23 May.
HR 1027, 25-2, v4, 2p. [336]
Creek Indian depredations in 1817-18.

170. Letter on the Removal of Cherokees. 25 May.
SD 461, 25-2, v5, 1p. [318]
Stating that the Cherokee delegation has declared its willingness to cooperate with the U.S. in the peaceable removal of the Cherokee Nation.

171. Letter on the Cherokee Indians. 25 May.
HD 401, 25-2, v10, 1p. [330]
Additional allowances propsoed to be made to the emigrating Cherokees.

172. On the Case of the Reps. of Doctor Cheears. 25 May.
HR 928, 25-2, v4, 7p. [336]
Cherokee and Creek nations; 1837.

173. R-P of R. Banks. 28 May.
SD 459, 25-2, v5, 2p. [318]
Losses sustained on contract to furnish rations to emigrant Indians.

174. Report on Cherokee Treaty. 31 May.
HD 410, 25-2, v10, 3p. [330]
On the valuation of improvements under the treaty of 1835, and the amounts paid thereon, payments to Cherokees for spoliations, etc.

175. On the Relief for Missouri Volunteers. 31 May.
HR 948, 25-2, v4, 3p. [336]
Florida campaign; 1837.

176. Report on the Cherokee Indians. 5 June.
SD 446, 25-2, v5, 2p. [318]
Recommends appropriation be made for the benefit of the Cherokee Indians and to hasten their removal west; treaty of 1835.

177. Report on Occupying Oregon Territory. 6 June.
SD 470, 25-2, v5, 23p. [318]
Indian trade.

178. Documents on the Claim of E. Sprague. 6 June.
SD 486, 25-2, v6, 3p. [319]
Sac and Fox war; 1832; Illinois.

179. Message on the Cherokee Treaty. 6 June.
HD 421, 25-2, v10, 3p. [330]
Correspondence with the Governor of Georgia in relation to a modification of the Cherokee treaty of 1835.

180. R-C of E. Park. 6 June.
HR 958, 25-2, v4, 2p. [336]
Creek Indian war of 1837 in Alabama.

181. R-P of W. Dickson. 7 June.
HR 959, 25-2, v4, 2p. [336]
Florida army in 1836; Creek nation.

182. R-P of A. Rembert. 9 June.
HR 966, 25-2, v4, 2p. [336]
Creek war; 1836 in Alabama.

183. R-P of D. Collins. 9 June.
HR 967, 25-2, v4, 1p. [336]
Indian hostilities of 1837 in Florida.

184. R-P of J. Piggott. 9 June.
HR 970, 25-2, v4, 1p. [336]
Indian campaign on the western frontier in 1780-82.

185. On the Relief for J. McCartney. 12 June.
HR 976, 25-2, v4, 1p. [336]
Action of Indian Affairs Com., etc.

186. Report on Indian Disturbances. 15 June.
SD 487, 25-2, v6, 4p. [319]
On the Arkansas frontier; Delawares, Quapaws, Creeks, Choctaws, and Chickasaws.

187. Letter on Indian Hostilities. 16 June.
HD 434, 25-2, v11, 10p. [331]
On the Western frontier; Delawares, Quapaws, Creeks, Choctaws, Chickasaws, Osages, Sacs, Foxes, Ottoes, Sioux, and other tribes.

188. Report on Exchange of Indian Lands. 23 June.
SD 492, 25-2, v6, 2p. [319]
An exchange of lands southwest of the Missouri River for the land of the Pottawatomies and other Indians.

189. R-P of Jemison and Williamson. 27 June.
HR 991, 25-2, v4, 5p. [336]
Creek war of 1836-37 in Alabama disrupts mail service.

190. R-P of C. Taylor. 27 June.
HR 992, 25-2, v4, 2p. [336]
Loss of mail service related to Indian hostilities in Florida.

191. R-P of A. Watson. 27 June.
HR 1001, 25-2, v4, 6p. [336]
Seminole Indian war in 1836.

192. R-P of Doctor Morrow. 27 June.
HR 1024, 25-2, v4, 2p. [336]
Cherokee country in 1836.

193. Letter on Indian Treaties. 28 June.
HD 456, 25-2, v11, 7p. [331]
Estimates of additional sums required for carrying into effect new treaties with the Indians, and for other objects.

194. Documents on Public Expenditures. 29 June.
SD 497, 25-2, v6, 22p. [319]
From 1823 to 1837 inclusive; Indian Dept.

195. Report on Indian Depredations. 2 July.
HR 1028, 25-2, v4, 11p. [336]
By the Seminole and Creek Indians in Florida, Georgia, and Alabama.

196. Report on Wyoming Claims. 2 July.
HR 1032, 25-2, v4, 2p. [336]
Indian depredations.

197. Message on the Creek Indians. 3 July.
HD 452, 25-2, v11, 102p. [331]
Report from the War Dept. in relation to the investigation of frauds alleged to have been committed on the Creeks in the sales of their reservations.

198. Letter on the Cherokee Indians. 3 July.
HD 453, 25-2, v11, 26p. [331]
Correspondence between the War Dept. and Major-Gen. Scott on the westward removal of the Cherokees.

199. Report on Military Operations in Florida. 6 July.
SD 507, 25-2, v6, 12p. [319]
Operations against the Seminole Indians.

200. R-P of J. Hernandez. 6 July.
HR 1043, 25-2, v4, 3p. [336]
Seminole war in Florida; 1835-36.

201. R-C of J. McCarty. 6 July.
HR 1045, 25-2, v4, 1p. [336]
Entries on Cherokee land.

202. Report on Horses Lost in the Military Service. 6 July.
HR 1060, 25-2, v4, 4p. [336]
Indian campaigns.

203. R-P of Administrators of H. Gratiot. 7 July.
HR 1053, 25-2, v4, 2p. [336]
Sac and Fox Indian war in 1831-32; sub-agent for the Winnebago Indians.

204. On the Relief of J. Hanks. 7 July.
HR 1061, 25-2, v4, 2p. [336]
Sac and Fox war of 1832 in Illinois.

205. On the Relief of A. Westfall. 7 July.
HR 1062, 25-2, v4, 1p. [336]
Sac and Fox war of 1832.

206. R-P of S. and P. Douthet. 7 July.
HR 1067, 25-2, v4, 1p. [336]
Cherokee Indians; treaty of New Echota.
207. R-C of the City of Augusta, Georgia. 7 July.
HR 1068, 25-2, v4, 4p. [336]
Supplies for volunteers in the Florida war of 1836.
208. Report on Appropriations. 18 July.
HD 464, 25-2, v11, 36p. [331]
During the 2d session of the 25th Congress; Indian expenses.
209. Statements of Appropriations. 13 Aug.
SD 509, 25-2, v6, 47p. [319]
During 2d session of the 25th Congress; Indian expenses.
210. Annual Message to Congress with Documents; Pres. Van Buren. 4 Dec.
SD 1, 25-3, v1, 669p. [338] *or* HD 2, 25-3, v1, 619p. [344]
Indian affairs; annual reports of the Sec. of War, CIA, etc.
211. Estimate of Appropriations for 1839. 4 Dec.
HD 5, 25-3, v1, 55p. [344]
Indian expenses.
212. Annual Report of the Sec. of the Treasury. 5 Dec.
SD 2, 25-3, v1, 54p. [338] *or* HD 4, 25-3, v1, 111p. [344]
Indian expenses (House version includes estimates for 1839).
213. Letter on the Indian Dept. 17 Dec.
HD 36, 25-3, v3, 16p. [346]
Estimate of appropriations for 1839.
214. Annual Report of the Com'r of the General Land Office. 18 Dec.
SD 17, 25-3, v1, 21p. [338]
Indian treaties and land cessions.
215. Documents on the Claim of E. Sprague. 19 Dec.
SD 18, 25-3, v2, 3p. [339]
Sac and Fox campaign of 1832 in Illinois.
216. R-M of J. Paxton. 19 Dec.
SD 20, 25-3, v2, 7p. [339]
British and Indian forces on the Maumee River near Fort Meigs in 1813; captured by Indians.
217. Letter on Chickasaw Treaty. 20 Dec.
HD 33, 25-3, v3, 5p. [346]
Statement of lands sold under the treaty of 20 April 1836.
218. R-P of Capt. Hunter. 21 Dec.
HR 33, 25-3, v1, 2p. [351]
Indian battle of 1811 at Tippecanoe.
219. R-P of A. Lecroix. 21 Dec.
HR 37, 25-3, v1, 1p. [351]
British and Indians; 1813 at the river Raisin.
220. Report on Sales of Chickasaw Lands. 26 Dec.
SD 29, 25-3, v2, 2p. [339]
Cession of 1832.
221. Letter on Ceded Lands. 26 Dec.
HD 46, 25-3, v3, 10p. [346]
Lands ceded to the U.S. in each state and territory and to which the Indian title has been extinguished.
222. Resol. of Rep. Haynes. 26 Dec.
HR, Resol. 2, 25-3, v2, 2p. [352]
Distribution of Annual Message of Pres.; Indian Affairs to Indian Affairs Com.; Indian hostilities to Military Com.
223. Letter on Indians in Florida. 30 Dec.
SD 42, 25-3, v2, 3p. [339]
On settlement of that part of Florida now occupied by hostile Seminole Indians.
224. Resol. of Rep. Cushing. 31 Dec.
HR, Resol. 7, 25-3, v2, 2p. [352]
U.S. and Great Britain relations; war subsidies by Britain to Indians in the U.S.

1839

1. Report on the Indians. 2 Jan.
HD 51, 25-3, v3, 2p. [346]
Smallpox among the Indians.
2. R-P of R. Davis. 2 Jan.
HR 43, 25-3, v1, 1p. [351]
Seminole Indians; 1818.
3. R-P of J. Robinson. 2 Jan.
HR 61, 25-3, v1, 3p. [351]
Indian depredations of 1813 in Ohio.
4. R-P of N. Taylor. 2 Jan.
HR 92, 25-3, v1, 2p. [351]
Chickasaw Indians; 1813.
5. Resol. of Rep. Everett. 2 Jan.
HR, Resol. 8, 25-3, v2, 1p. [352]

That the Pres. indicate the number of troops employed, and moneys expended in the Seminole war.

6. Report on Unappropriated Land in Tennessee. 4 Jan.
SD 43, 25-3, v2, 26p. [339]
Cherokee treaty of 7 Jan. 1806; Chickasaw treaty of 19 Oct. 1818.

7. R-C of J. Richey. 4 Jan.
SD 44, 25-3, v2, 1p. [339]
Sac and Fox campaign of 1832.

8. R-C of J. Scott. 4 Jan.
SD 45, 25-3, v2, 1p. [339]
Sac and Fox campaign of 1832.

9. R-C of R. Robertson. 4 Jan.
SD 47, 25-3, v2, 2p. [339]
Supplied Army in Indian country; Alabama in 1814.

10. R-P of W. Whitehead. 4 Jan.
HR 100, 25-3, v1, 2p. [351]
Seminole war in Florida; 1835-36.

11. Report on Oregon Territory. 4 Jan.
HR 101, 25-3, v1, 112p. [351]
Indian trade.

12. R-C of D. Powers. 4 Jan.
HR 107, 25-3, v1, 2p. [351]
Black Hawk war of 1832.

13. Letter on Horse Claims of Alabama Volunteers. 7 Jan.
SD 58, 25-3, v2, 3p. [339]
Seminole war.

14. Petition of Alabama Citizens. 8 Jan.
SD 61, 25-3, v2, 3p. [339]
Creek treaty of 1832.

15. Report on Emigrating Indians. 8 Jan.
HD 61, 25-3, v3, 2p. [346]
To guard emigrating Cherokees in Alabama.

16. R-C of G. Allen. 8 Jan.
HR 113, 25-3, v1, 2p. [351]
Under the treaty of 24 May 1834 with the Chickasaw Indians.

17. Report on Lands in Tennessee. 8 Jan.
HR 119, 25-3, v1, 26p. [351]
Cherokee cession of 1806; Chickasaw cession of 1818.

18. Report on Choctaw Lands. 9 Jan.
SD 69, 25-3, v2, 3p. [339]
Quantity of land ceded in the treaty with the Choctaw Indians at Dancing Rabbit Creek.

19. R-P of W. Cuddeback. 9 Jan.
HR 125, 25-3, v1, 1p. [351]
Indian hostilities of 1777 in New York.

20. R-P of M. Kershaw. 9 Jan.
HR 127, 25-3, v1, 1p. [351]
Indian depredations of 1836 in Georgia.

21. R-P of W. Stout. 9 Jan.
HR 128, 25-3, v1, 1p. [351]
Indian depredations of 1813 in Illinois.

22. R-P of H. Grady. 9 Jan.
HR 141, 25-3, v1, 4p. [351]
Fort Butler; Cherokee Nation; 1837.

23. Report on Mississippi Lands. 9 Jan.
HR 173, 25-3, v1, 5p. [351]
Treaty of Dancing Rabbit Creek in 1830 with the Choctaws.

24. Mem. of the Alabama Gen. Assembly. 10 Jan.
SD 72, 25-3, v2, 4p. [339]
Creek depredations of 1836; treaty of 24 Mar. 1832.

25. R-C of G. Humphreys. 10 Jan.
SD 75, 25-3, v2, 1p. [339]
Seminole war in 1836.

26. On the Relief of F. Laventure et al. 10 Jan.
SD 76, 25-3, v2, 6p. [339]
Indian treaty of 27 Sept. 1833 at Chicago.

27. R-P of A. Deblieux. 10 Jan.
HR 150, 25-3, v1, 1p. [351]
Rio Hondo claim; Caddo Indians; 1835; Louisiana.

28. R-P of D. Denham et al. 11 Jan.
HR 162, 25-3, v1, 1p. [351]
Indian depredations of 1836 in Florida.

29. Petition of Illinois Citizens. 14 Jan.
SD 83, 25-3, v2, 3p. [339]
Lands occupied by Indians at the close of the Black Hawk war in 1833.

30. R-P of E. Moreland et al. 15 Jan.
HR 175, 25-3, v1, 2p. [351]
Cherokee Indian treaties of 1817 and 1819.

31. Message on the Seminole Indians. 16 Jan.
SD 88, 25-3, v2, 3p. [339] *or* HD 93, 25-3, v3, 3p. [346]
On the condition of the Seminoles who have emigrated; should be separate from the Creeks.

32. R-P of M. Hagan. 16 Jan.
SD 91, 25-3, v2, 1p. [339]
Seminole war; 1835.

33. Letter on the Settlement of Florida. 17 Jan.
SD 93, 25-3, v2, 4p. [339]

In that part of Florida occupied by hostile Indians.

34. On the Case of C. Widrig. 16 Jan.
HR 180, 25-3, v1, 2p. [351]
British and Indians in New York.

35. R-P of Administrator of L. Roy. 16 Jan.
HR 184, 25-3, v1, 1p. [351]
Sac, Fox, and Pottawatomie depredations of 1815 in Missouri.

36. R-P of J. Kennedy. 17 Jan.
SD 92, 25-3, v2, 2p. [339]
Creek Indians; 1813.

37. Report on War Dept. Appropriations. 17 Jan.
SD 94, 25-3, v2, 19p. [339] *or* HD 104, 25-3, v3, 19p. [346]
For 1838; Indian expenses.

38. Report on Persons Employed in the Indian Dept. 17 Jan.
SD 95, 25-3, v2, 14p. [339] *or* HD 103, 25-3, v3, 20p. [346]
For the year 1838.

39. Letter on Indian Disbursements. 18 Jan.
SD 106, 25-3, v2, 3p. [339] *or* HD 49, 25-3, v3, 3p. [346]
To defray the expenses of said disbursements.

40. Letter on Additional Clerks. 18 Jan.
SD 107, 25-3, v2, 2p. [339] *or* HD 50, 25-3, v3, 2p. [346]
For the Office of Indian Affairs.

41. Mem. of H. Thistle. 18 Jan.
SD 108, 25-3, v2, 8p. [339]
Submits communications on the expelling of the hostile Indians from Florida.

42. R-P of W. Smith. 21 Jan.
SD 117, 25-3, v2, 1p. [339]
Creek depredations of 1793 in Georgia; treaty of 1821.

43. R-C of J. Bulow, jr. 22 Jan.
SD 129, 25-3, v2, 13p. [339]
Seminole depredations in Florida.

44. R-P of J. Hernandez. 22 Jan.
SD 130, 25-3, v2, 2p. [339]
Seminole war.

45. Report on Indians. 22 Jan.
HD 107, 25-3, v3, 9p. [346]
On the intermeddling of any foreign government with Indians within the limits of the U.S.

46. Letter on Indian Refugees. 22 Jan.
HD 109, 25-3, v3, 5p. [346]
On the pursuit, capture, etc., of Indian refugees and murderers within the limits of the U.S.; on land relinquished by the Cherokees.

47. Letter on Indian Hostilities. 22 Jan.
HD 123, 25-3, v4, 2p. [347]
Estimate of funds necessary for suppression of hostilities in Florida.

48. R-P of J. White. 22 Jan.
HR 199, 25-3, v1, 1p. [351]
Chickasaw nation in Mississippi.

49. R-P of T. Puerifoy. 22 Jan.
HR 203, 25-3, v1, 1p. [351]
Indian depredations of 1838 in Florida.

50. R-P of R. Brannin et al. 22 Jan.
HR 207, 25-3, v1, 1p. [351]
Black Hawk war of 1832 on the Missouri frontier.

51. Report on Accounts of L. Cass. 23 Jan.
HD 112, 25-3, v3, 17p. [346]
Statement of the final settlement of accounts of the late Supt. of Indian Affairs.

52. R-C of Officers of the Florida Militia. 23 Jan.
HR 209, 25-3, v1, 2p. [351]
Seminole war of 1835 in Florida.

53. Report on the State of the Treasury and Expenditures. 24 Jan.
HR 218, 25-3, v1, 27p. [351]
Indian expenses.

54. Extracts from the Message of Governor Call, Florida. 25 Jan.
SD 139, 25-3, v2, 4p. [339]
On the Seminole Indian hostilities in Florida.

55. R-P of J. McClenahan. 25 Jan.
HR 222, 25-3, v1, 2p. [351]
Cherokee depredations of 1820; treaty of 8 July 1807.

56. R-P of F. Rivar. 25 Jan.
HR 225, 25-3, v1, 2p. [351]
Sac, Fox, and Pottawatomie depredations of 1851 in Missouri.

57. R-P of M. Levy. 26 Jan.
HR 236, 25-3, v1, 2p. [351]
Indian hostilities of 1835 in Florida.

58. Mem. of the Wisconsin Legis. 28 Jan.
SD 148, 25-3, v3, 2p. [340]
On extinguishment of Menomonie title to land near Green Bay.

59. Letter on Indian in Michigan. 28 Jan.
SD 155, 25-3, v3, 3p. [340]
From the CIA on the removal of the

Swan Creek and Black River bands of Chippewa Indians residing in Michigan; treaty of 9 May 1836.

60. Documents on the Settlement of a Portion of Florida. 28 Jan.
SD 163, 25-3, v3, 4p. [340]
That portion occupied by hostile Seminole Indians.

61. Mem. of the Wisconsin Legis. 28 Jan.
HD 125, 25-3, v4, 5p. [347]
Indian wars on the western frontier.

62. Letter on Purchase of Supplies. 30 Jan.
HD 127, 25-3, v4, 22p. [347]
Creek Indians west of the Mississippi River.

63. Boundary Between Missouri and Iowa. 30 Jan.
HD 128, 25-3, v4, 24p. [347]
Indian boundary line; Black Hawk war in 1832.

64. R-P of R. Banks. 31 Jan.
SD 167, 25-3, v3, 2p. [340]
Supplies for emigrant Indians.

65. R-C of A. Johnson and S. Love. 1 Feb.
SD 171, 25-3, v3, 5p. [340]
Seminole war.

66. Report on Payment of State Troops. 1 Feb.
HD 137, 25-3, v4, 2p. [347]
Cherokee Indian country.

67. Report on Annuities to Seneca Indians. 1 Feb.
HD 138, 25-3, v4, 38p. [347]
On payments due them in 1837 and 1838, and the expenditure of the appropriations for the expenses of the Seneca treaty.

68. Mem. of R. Currin. 2 Feb.
HD 139, 25-3, v4, 5p. [347]
Chickasaw treaty of 1818.

69. Letter on Removal of Indians. 4 Feb.
HD 147, 25-3, v4, 9p. [347]
Number of Indians annually removed from the eastern to the western side of the Mississippi River from 1798 to 1838, and the lands purchased from them, together with an exhibit of the quantity of land granted to each of the states and territories.

70. Report on Payment of North Carolina Volunteers. 5 Feb.
HD 148, 25-3, v4, 2p. [347]
Cherokee Indian country.

71. Report on Public Lands. 5 Feb.
HD 164, 25-3, v4, 14p. [347]
Lands to which Indian title has been extinguished; cost of said lands; expenses of Indian wars; etc.

72. Letter on Indians in Florida. 6 Feb.
SD 185, 25-3, v3, 2p. [340]
Plan for the subjugation and expulsion of the hostile Indians.

73. Resol. of Sen. Wright. 6 Feb.
SD 186, 25-3, v3, 1p. [340]
On the claims of sufferers in the late Indian wars in the South.

74. R-P of the Heirs of C. DeVillemont. 6 Feb.
HR 243, 25-3, v1, 4p. [351]
Indian hostilities of 1802 on the Mississippi River.

75. R-P of Brothertown Indians. 6 Feb.
HR 244, 25-3, v1, 5p. [351]
Remnants of New England tribes settled in Wisconsin; Menomonie treaty of 27 Oct. 1832; Oneida Indian lands.

76. R-P of S. Tiffany. 6 Feb.
HR 258, 25-3, v1, 1p. [351]
British and Indians in Upper Canada.

77. R-C of J. Baldridge. 7 Feb.
SD 188, 25-3, v3, 2p. [340]
Cherokee treaty of 8 July 1817.

78. R-C of P. Hadgo. 7 Feb.
SD 189, 25-3, v3, 2p. [340]
Creek Indian removal; treaty of 9 Aug. 1814 at Fort Jackson.

79. R-C of J. Dukes. 7 Feb.
SD 190, 25-3, v3, 1p. [34o]
Choctaw Indian half-breed.

80. Report on Indian Depredation Claims. 9 Feb.
SD 195, 25-3, v3, 4p. [340]
Indian wars in the South; Seminole and Creek Indians.

81. Documents on the Claim of J. Bulow, jr. 9 Feb.
SD 196, 25-3, v3, 3p. [340]
Florida Indian war.

82. Letter on the Cherokee Claims Commission. 9 Feb.
SD 198, 25-3, v3, 5p. [340]
On termination of the commission for the adjudication of claims arising under the treaty of 29 Dec. 1835.

83. Letter on the Cherokee Treaty. 9 Feb.
SD 199, 25-3, v3, 4p. [340]
Statement of expenses incurred in the negotiation and conclusion of the Cherokee treaty of 29 Dec. 1835.

84. Report on Disbursements to Indians. 9 Feb.
HD 174, 25-3, v4, 118p. [347]
Year ending 30 Sept. 1838.

85. Report on Judges in Iowa. 9 Feb.
HR 270, 25-3, v1, 2p. [351]
Indian land title extinguished in 1833.

86. Report on a Road in Florida. 9 Feb.
HR 271, 25-3, v1, 1p. [351]
Indian hostilities; militia movement.

87. Report on Public Receipts and Expenditures. 11 Feb.
SD 212, 25-3, v3, 3p. [340]
Since the year 1817; Indian Dept.

88. R-C of T. Taylor. 13 Feb.
HR 275, 25-3, v2, 3p. [352]
Black Hawk war of 1832 in Illinois.

89. R-P of C. Sumption. 13 Feb.
HR 281, 25-3, v2, 1p. [352]
Treaty of Greenville, Ohio, in 1814, with the Wyandot and Seneca Indians.

90. R-P of J. McCartney. 14 Feb.
SD 218, 25-3, v3, 1p. [340]
Cattle driven off Cherokee lands.

91. Documents on the Claim of Col. Morgan. 16 Feb.
SD 228, 25-3, v3, 6p. [340]
Florida war; commanded Delawares and Shawnees.

92. R-P of A. Anderson. 16 Feb.
HR 284, 25-3, v2, 3p. [352]
Cherokee Indians in 1787; treaties of 1791, 1794, and 1798.

93. R-P of T. Wilson. 16 Feb.
HR 291, 25-3, v2, 1p. [352]
Indian engagement in 1791.

94. R-P of R. Carter. 16 Feb.
HR 292, 25-3, v2, 2p. [352]
Indian engagements of 1795-1799.

95. Mem. of the Florida Legis. 18 Feb.
SD 233, 25-3, v3, 2p. [340]
Seminole war.

96. Petition of Citizens of Wyoming. 18 Feb.
HD 203, 25-3, v4, 40p. [347]
Attack of the Mohawk Indians on the town of Wyoming during the Revolutionary War.

97. R-C of Choctaw Indians. 19 Feb.
SD 238, 25-3, v3, 2p. [340]
Depredations committed by the Choctaws on J. Bogy, trader to the Osages, in 1807.

98. Report on Sales of Indian Reservations. 20 Feb.
HD 209, 25-3, v4, 48p. [347]
Reports of com'rs in Alabama; sale of Creek lands.

99. Report on Land Reservations. 22 Feb.
HR 294, 25-3, v2, 4p. [352]
Under the Choctaw treaty of 1830.

100. R-P of E. Bently. 25 Feb.
HR 302, 25-3, v2, 2p. [352]
British and Indians in 1777.

101. R-P of J. Pounds. 25 Feb.
HR 316, 25-3, v2, 1p. [352]
Black Hawk war in 1832.

102. R-P of W. Spiller. 25 Feb.
HR 317, 25-3, v2, 1p. [352]
Indian campaign in Illinois during 1832.

103. R-P of J. Camparu. 26 Feb.
SD 268, 25-3, v4, 7p. [341]
Chippewa treaty of 24 Sept. 1819 in Michigan.

104. Report on Mode of Furnishing Indian Supplies. 26 Feb.
SD 273, 25-3, v4, 75p. [341]
Proposals for furnishing supplies to the Indian Dept.; contracts entered into since 1 May 1838; correspondence on the subject; etc.

105. Report on Cherokee Indians. 27 Feb.
HD 224, 25-3, v5, 2p. [348]
Number and condition of Cherokees residing in North Carolina; removal.

106. Blacks Captured from Hostile Indians. 27 Feb.
HD 225, 25-3, v5, 126p. [348]
Seminoles of Florida.

107. Report on Execution of Cherokee Treaty of 1835. 28 Feb.
SD 277, 25-3, v5, 100p. [342]
Names of persons employed to aid in carrying into effect said treaty, their duties and compensatión, etc.

108. Report on Indian Treaties. 1 Mar.
HD 228, 25-3, v6, 7p. [350]
Progress made in the execution of the treaties of 1824 and 1825 with the Chickasaws, and the treaty of 1830 with the Choctaws.

109. Letter on the Winnebago Indians. 1 Mar.
HD 229, 25-3, v6, 112p. [350]
Information and documents on the execution of the treaty of 1 Nov. 1837 with said Indians.

110. Letter on the Pottawatomie Indians. 1 Mar.
HD 231, 25-3, v6, 13p. [350]
Documents on the treaties of the 20th, 26th, and 27th of Oct., 1832.

111. Letter on Claims against Miami Indians. 2 Mar.
SD 302, 25-3, v5, 56p. [342]
Report of com'rs sent to investigate; treaty of 24 Oct. 1834.

112. Message on Indian Treaties. 2 Mar.
HD 238, 25-3, v6, 14p. [350]
Reports of the Secs. of State, Treasury, War, and Navy respecting the amounts paid to persons concerned in negotiating treaties with the Indians since 1829.

113. Report on Indian Affairs. 3 Mar.
HD 244, 25-3, v6, 8p. [350]
Compensation to Supts. of Indian Affairs in the territories.

114. Report on Appropriations. 18 Mar.
HD 249, 25-3, v6, 26p. [350]
During 3rd session of the 25th Congress; Indian accounts.

115. Statements of Appropriations. 1 May.
SD 305, 25-3, v5, 37p. [342]
During 3rd session of the 25th Congress; Indian expenses.

116. Annual Message to Congress with Documents; Pres. Van Buren. 24 Dec.
SD 1, 26-1, v1, 622p. [354] *or* HD 2, 26-1, v1, 893p. [363]
Florida war and Indian Affairs; Annual Report of the Sec. of War; Annual Report of the CIA, including emigration, education, condition of tribes, Cherokee disturbances, and fiscal statements; etc.

117. Annual Report of the Sec. of the Treasury. 24 Dec.
SD 2, 26-1, v1, 65p. [354] *or* HD 3, 26-1, v1, 113p. [363]
Indian accounts (House version includes estimates for 1840).

118. Message on the Disputed Iowa-Missouri Boundary. 24 Dec.
SD 4, 26-1, v1, 17p. [354] *or* HD 5, 26-1, v1, 17p. [363]
Old Indian boundary line.

119. Report on Chickasaw Fund. 24 Dec.
SD 9, 26-1, v1, 5p. [354] *or* HD 15, 26-1, v2, 5p. [364]
Expenditures and investments of funds received from sale of land; treaty of 20 Oct. 1832.

120. Estimate of Appropriations. 24 Dec.
HD 4, 26-1, v1, 48p. [363]
For the year 1840; Indian expenses.

121. Annual Report of the Com'r of the General Land Office. 30 Dec.
SD 21, 26-1, v2, 112p. [355]
Indian treaties and land cessions.

122. Resol. of Sen. Linn. 30 Dec.
SD 25, 26-1, v2, 1p. [355]
Overawing Indian tribes in Oregon by a show of force.

123. Public Expenditures, 1835-1838. 30 Dec.
HD 17, 26-1, v2, 9p. [364]
Indian expenses.

124. Mem. of Chiefs of Seneca and Six Nations. 31 Dec.
SD 33, 26-1, v2, 2p. [355]
Protest treaty negotiated by R. Gillet, and ask that action be deferred until a delegation shall appear before Congress.

1840

1. Message on the Disputed Iowa-Missouri Boundary. 3 Jan.
SD 35, 26-1, v2, 20p. [355] *or* HD 36, 26-1, v2, 20p. [364]
Old Indian boundary line; Indian treaties.

2. R-M of J. Paxton. 7 Jan.
SD 41, 26-1, v2, 7p. [355]
Indian engagement; 1813.

3. Removal of Stockbridge and Munsee Indians. 7 Jan.
SD 42, 26-1, v2, 3p. [355]
Appropriation to pay cost of removal.

4. Report on Operations of the Topographical Bureau. 9 Jan.
SD 58, 26-1, v2, 271p. [355]
Boundaries between Indian tribes west of the Mississippi River.

5. Message on the Proceedings of a Court of Inquiry. 10 Jan.
SD 59, 26-1, v3, 432p. [356]

The case of Lieut.-Col. Brant; Winnebago disturbances of 1828; Black Hawk war of 1832; Creek campaign of 1836 in Alabama; Florida war in 1837-38.

6. Estimate of Appropriations for the Indian Dept. 13 Jan.
SD 73, 26-1, v3, 11p. [356] *or* HD 44, 26-1, v2, 14p. [364]
For 1840 (House version includes explanatory statement).

7. R-P of Reps. of J. Piatt. 14 Jan.
SD 87, 26-1, v3, 5p. [356]
Supplies furnished Indians in Michigan in 1814.

8. Expenditures of the War Dept. 21 Jan.
SD 99, 26-1, v3, 19p. [356] *or* HD 107, 26-1, v3, 19p. [365]
Indian expenses.

9. R-P of J. Hancock. 21 Jan.
SD 105, 26-1, v3, 1p. [356]
Head of a Choctaw Indian family; treaty of 1830 at Dancing Rabbit Creek.

10. Documents on the Claim of Missouri Volunteers. 22 Jan.
SD 106, 26-1, v3, 19p. [356]
Indian engagements, 1829-36; Iowa and Sac Indians.

11. Mem. of the Alabama Legis. 24 Jan.
SD 113, 26-1, v3, 1p. [356]
Land district in Cherokee Nation.

12. R-M of G. Whitman. 24 Jan.
SD 114, 26-1, v3, 2p. [356]
Creek Indian war; Alabama; 1836.

13. R-P of J. McIntosh. 24 Jan.
SD 116, 26-1, v3, 2p. [356]
Seminole war of 1835 in Florida.

14. Report on Employees in the Indian Dept. 28 Jan.
SD 126, 26-1, v4, 8p. [357] *or* HD 109, 26-1, v3, 8p. [365]
For 1839.

15. R-P of Lieut. Paschal. 28 Jan.
SD 127, 26-1, v4, 3p. [357]
Cherokee Indian treaty of 1835 in Georgia.

16. R-C of J. Reynolds. 28 Jan.
SD 128, 26-1, v4, 9p. [357]
Disbursing agent of Indian Dept.; Winnebagoes at Fort Crawford in 1838.

17. Report on Massacres by Indians in Florida. 29 Jan.
SD 130, 26-1, v4, 3p. [357]
Creek and Seminole Indians.

18. R-M of Authorities of Mobile. 29 Jan.
SD 132, 26-1, v4, 3p. [357]
Creek and Seminole Indians; Florida.

19. R-P of R. Grignon. 30 Jan.
SD 134, 26-1, v4, 3p. [357]
Menomonie treaty of 3 Sept. 1836.

20. R-P of L. Rivard. 30 Jan.
SD 137, 26-1, v4, 1p. [357]
Black Hawk war of 1832.

21. R-C of General Clinch. 3 Feb.
SD 145, 26-1, v4, 1p. [357]
Florida Indian depredations in 1835-36.

22. Report on the Iowa-Missouri Boundary. 4 Feb.
HR 2, 26-1, v1, 11p. [370]
Osage treaty of 1808; Iowa, Sac, and Fox Indian claims to land.

23. Mem. of S. Riggs et al. 5 Feb.
HR 60, 26-1, v3, 2p. [365]
On ending warfare in the northwest; Sioux, Chippewa, Sac, and Fox Indians.

24. Petition of Wisconsin Citizens. 6 Feb.
HD 69, 26-1, v3, 2p. [365]
Ask separation of offices of territorial governor and Supt. of Indian Affairs.

25. Mem. of the Alabama Legis. 6 Feb.
HD 113, 26-1, v3, 4p. [365]
Creek depredations; treaty of 24 Mar. 1832.

26. Petition of the Stockbridge Indians of Wisconsin. 6 Feb.
HD 127, 26-1, v3, 11p. [365]
Miami treaty of 30 Sept. 1809 granting land to the Stockbridge or Mohecan Nation; Menomonie and Winnebago treaty of 1832 granting land near Green Bay to the Stockbridges; treaty of 18 Aug. 1821 with the Menomonies and Winnebagoes; etc.

27. R-C Against Miami Indians. 10 Feb.
SD 164, 26-1, v4, 10p. [357]
Report of Com'r to investigate claims for the year 1839.

28. Petition of Kentucky Citizens. 10 Feb.
SD 172, 26-1, v4, 2p. [357]
Indian hostilities.

29. Memoir on the Northwest Coast of America. 10 Feb.
SD 174, 26-1, v4, 228p. [357]
History, Indian trade, etc.

30. Letter on Purchase of an Island. 12 Feb.
HD 82, 26-1, v3, 20p. [365]
Based upon treaty with certain Sioux Indians on 9 Aug. 1820; records do not show Col. Leavenworth authorized to conclude such a treaty; title to the island already claimed by the U.S.

31. Letter on the Reorganization of the Indian Dept. 12 Feb.
HD 103, 26-1, v3, 11p. [365]
Prepared by the CIA; recommends formation of a Southern superintendency to embrace the country west of the Mississippi River and South of the northern line of the Osage reservation.

32. Employment of Bloodhounds Against Indians. 17 Feb.
SD 187, 26-1, v4, 5p. [357]
Defends use of dogs in Florida.

33. R-P of F. Wood. 18 Feb.
SD 198, 26-1, v5, 9p. [358]
Violation of laws regulating trade with Indian tribes; trade west of the Mississippi River.

34. Documents on "Carver's Claim." 18 Feb.
SD 204, 26-1, v5, 2p. [358]
Land grant from the Nadoweisa Indians in 1767 on the upper Mississippi River.

35. R-P of J. Johnston. 21 Feb.
SD 215, 26-1, v5, 1p. [358]
Indian agent at Pequa in Ohio in 1839.

36. R-C of A. Hall. 21 Feb.
SD 217, 26-1, v5, 1p. [358]
Creek war of 1814.

37. On the Relief of F. Laventure et al. 25 Feb.
SD 223, 26-1, v5, 25p. [358]
Indian treaty of 27 Sept. 1833 at Chicago; Indian land titles; trade of the Menomonies, Winnebagoes, Pottawatomies, Chippewas, and Ottawas; other treaties.

38. Letter on Public Lands. 25 Feb.
HD 120, 26-1, v3, 14p. [365]
Land to which Indian title has been extinguished.

39. Report on Military Posts in the Territories. 26 Feb.
SD 231, 26-1, v5, 3p. [358]
On establishment of a line of posts from Missouri to the Oregon or Columbia River; control of trade and Indian hostilities; Sioux, Blackfeet, Pawnee and other tribes.

40. R-P of T. Taylor. 29 Feb.
HR 15, 26-1, v1, 3p. [370]
Black Hawk war of 1832 in Illinois.

41. R-P of W. Nicholas. 29 Feb.
HR 36, 26-1, v1, 1p. [370]
Indian depredations in 1814.

42. R-P of R. Hathaway et al. 29 Feb.
HR 40, 26-1, v1, 2p. [370]
Kickapoo campaign of 1812 on the Illinois River.

43. R-P of R. Henderson. 29 Feb.
HR 45, 26-1, v1, 2p. [370]
Seminole war; 1835.

44. R-P of W. Randall. 29 Feb.
HR 51, 26-1, v1, 1p. [370]
Florida war; 1836.

45. R-P of P. Frazier. 29 Feb.
HR 61, 26-1, v1, 2p. [370]
Florida war in 1836.

46. Report on the Dade Institute. 5 Mar.
HR 93, 26-1, v1, 4p. [370]
Seminole war.

47. R-P of H. Lassel. 5 Mar.
HR 101, 26-1, v1, 1p. [370]
Pottawatomie treaty of 16 Oct. 1826 in Indiana.

48. R-P of W. Cuddeback. 5 Mar.
HR 124, 26-1, v1, 1p. [370]
Indian hostilities of 1777-78 in New York.

49. On the Case of D. Sleeth. 5 Mar.
HR 145, 26-1, v1, 2p. [370]
Indian hostilities of 1778 in Virginia.

50. On the Case of C. Widrig. 5 Mar.
HR 147, 26-1, v1, 2p. [370]
British and Indians.

51. On the Case of J. Lybrook. 5 Mar.
HR 151, 26-1, v1, 1p. [370]
Indian incursions in 1776.

52. R-M of H. Bush. 5 Mar.
HR 154, 26-1, v1, 1p. [370]
Indian hostilities in 1778.

53. R-P of H. Miller. 5 Mar.
HR 161, 26-1, v1, 2p. [370]
Indian hostilities in 1780.

54. R-P of Captain Hunter. 5 Mar.
HR 172, 26-1, v1, 2p. [370]
Battle of Tippecanoe with the Indians; 1811 in Indiana.

55. R-P of W. Hughes. 5 Mar.
HR 187, 26-1, v1, 1p. [370]
Creek war of 1814.

56. R-P of T. Wilson. 5 Mar.
HR 190, 26-1, v1, 1p. [370]
Indian war; 1791.

57. R-P of R. Frazier. 5 Mar.
HR 196, 26-1, v1, 1p. [370]
Attack on Kickapoo town in 1812.

58. R-P of S. Tiffany. 5 Mar.
HR 202, 26-1, v1, 1p. [370]
British and Indians in Upper Canada.

59. R-P of J. Knipe. 5 Mar.
HR 206, 26-1, v1, 1p. [370]
Indian hostilities of 1814 in Canada.

60. R-P of W. Bowman. 5 Mar.
HR 216, 26-1, v1, 1p. [370]
Indian fighting; Missouri frontier in 1832.

61. R-P of Lieut. Allison. 5 Mar.
HR 219, 26-1, v1, 1p. [370]
Indian fighting; western campaign of 1791.

62. Report on Land to Soldiers of the Old 4th Regiment. 5 Mar.
HR 232, 26-1, v1, 7p. [370]
Indian campaigns; 1812; Indiana.

63. Mem. of the Mississippi Legis. 10 Mar.
SD 268, 26-1, v5, 2p. [358]
Chickasaw cession.

64. R-P of J. Campau. 10 Mar.
SD 271, 26-1, v5, 2p. [358]
Chippewa treaties of 17 Nov. 1807, and 9 May 1836.

65. Message Concerning the War in Florida. 12 Mar.
SD 278, 26-1, v5, 246p. [358]
Report of Army officers, giving details of the campaign against the Seminoles.

66. Mem. of a Delegation of Cherokees. 12 Mar.
HD 129, 26-1, v3, 117p. [365]
Removal of Cherokee Indians from their native country east of the Mississippi River to the wilderness of the west.

67. Letter on Payment of Indian Annuities. 13 Mar.
HD 147, 26-1, v3, 3p. [365]
Troops at the Des Moines River guarding the annuity payment; Sac and Fox Indians.

68. Mem. of the Wisconsin Legis. 16 Mar.
HD 135, 26-1, v3, 2p. [365]
Military road from Fort Howard to Fort Snelling; Indian hostilities.

69. Mem. of Ex-Governor Call. 16 Mar.
HD 136, 26-1, v3, 16p. [365]
On his removal from office; Seminole war; etc.

70. Resol. of the Ala. Legis. 16 Mar.
HD 137, 26-1, v3, 2p. [365]
Creek and Seminole hostilities during 1836-37.

71. Mem. of the Wisconsin Assembly. 16 Mar.
HD 144, 26-1, v3, 5p. [365]
Fort Snelling reservation; Sioux treaty of 1837.

72. R-P of Z. and R. Williams. 17 Mar.
SD 288, 26-1, v6, 2p. [359]
Creek war of 1836 in Georgia.

73. R-P of Clements, Bryan and Co. 17 Mar.
SD 289, 26-1, v6, 2p. [359]
For furnishing supplies to emigrating Cherokee Indians.

74. Letter on Claims Growing out of the Florida War. 18 Mar.
HD 142, 26-1, v3, 4p. [365]
Seminole depredations.

75. Letter on Horses Lost in Indian Wars. 19 Mar.
HD 146, 26-1, v3, 3p. [365]
Creek and Seminole wars in Florida and Alabama.

76. Report on Removal of Winnebago Indians. 20 Mar.
SD 297, 26-1, v6, 3p. [359]
Treaty of 1 Nov. 1837.

77. Removal of Cherokee Indians. 26 Mar.
SD 320, 26-1, v6, 1p. [359]
Removal of Indians near Fort Wayne, Arkansas; treaty of 29 Dec. 1835.

78. Report on Land Claims in Michigan. 31 Mar.
SD 344, 26-1, v6, 5p. [359]
Land to which Indian title has been extinguished.

79. Differences between the Government and Cherokees. 1 Apr.
SD 247, 26-1, v6, 62p. [359]
A statement of the difficulties which exist and arrangements being made with reference thereto.

80. Mem. of the Cherokees of the West. 1 Apr.
HD 162, 26-1, v4, 15p. [366]
Condition of the tribe; treaties; etc.

81. Report on Pay to Guard Company. 4 Apr.
HD 165, 26-1, v4, 2p. [366]
Guarding emigrating Cherokees.

82. R-P of D. Clinch. 4 Apr.
HR 303, 26-1, v2, 7p. [371]
Seminole Indian war; 1835 in Florida.

83. R-P of General Cooke. 4 Apr.
HR 304, 26-1, v2, 2p. [371]
Com'r to treat with Cherokee Indians.

84. R-P of the Trustees of Dublin Township, Ohio. 4 Apr.
HR 320, 26-1, v2, 7p. [371]
Indian land title.

85. Report on School Lands in Indian Reservations. 4 Apr.
HR 321, 26-1, v2, 5p. [371]
Other land selected; Ohio; Seneca and Wyandot reserves.

86. R-P of J. Haas. 4 Apr.
HR 335, 26-1, v2, 1p. [371]
Pottawatomie treaty of 20 Oct. 1832 at Tippecanoe.

87. R-M of S. Norris. 4 Apr.
HR 338, 26-1, v2, 4p. [371]
Caddo Indians in Louisiana.

88. R-M of the Iowa Legis. 4 Apr.
HR 344, 26-1, v2, 2p. [371]
Sac and Fox treaty of 1824; school lands in Iowa for half-breeds.

89. R-P of G. Mayfield. 4 Apr.
HR 360, 26-1, v2, 1p. [371]
Creek Indians; captive for ten years; Creek war; Seminole war of 1818.

90. R-P of J. Baugh. 4 Apr.
HR 362, 26-1, v2, 1p. [371]
Cherokee campaign of 1776; Shawnee expedition of 1778.

91. R-C of B. Murphy. 4 Apr.
HR 364, 26-1, v2, 3p. [371]
Cherokee Indian treaty of 16 May 1828; Arkansas.

92. R-M of C. Sumption. 4 Apr.
HR 373, 26-1, v2, 1p. [371]
Treaty with Wyandot and Seneca Indians in 1814 at Greenville.

93. R-P of A. Gentry. 4 Apr.
HR 376, 26-1, v2, 1p. [371]
Creek and Seminole wars of 1836.

94. R-P of J. Robinson and R. Pearce. 4 Apr.
HR 378, 26-1, v2, 1p. [371]
Cherokee cession in Alabama.

95. R-P of E. Moorehead et al. 4 Apr.
HR 379, 26-1, v2, 1p. [371]
Indian reservation in Alabama.

96. Report on Irwinton Academy in Alabama. 4 Apr.
HR 381, 26-1, v2, 2p. [371]
Creek war.

97. R-P of S. Mayfield. 4 Apr.
HR 409, 26-1, v2, 1p. [371]
Indian depredations in 1813.

98. R-P of W. Baker. 4 Apr.
HR 411, 26-1, v2, 1p. [371]
Creek war.

99. R-P of J. and G. Johnson. 4 Apr.
HR 431, 26-1, v2, 1p. [371]
Creek war of 1836.

100. R-P of J. Hancock. 9 Apr.
SD 361, 26-1, v6, 3p. [359]
Choctaw treaty of 27 Sept. 1830 at Dancing Rabbit Creek.

101. Disbursements to the Indians. 9 Apr.
HD 173, 26-1, v4, 176p. [366]
Year ending 30 Sept. 1839.

102. Message on Indians on the Northwest Frontier. 10 Apr.
HD 178, 26-1, v4, 18p. [366]
Trade; foreign interference; emigration of Indians to Canada officially recommended in 1836; tribes who have emigrated north; etc.

103. Plan for Defense of Western Frontier. 13 Apr.
SD 379, 26-1, v6, 14p. [359] *or* HD 161, 26-1, v4, 14p. [366]
Name of Indian tribes and number of warriors west of Missouri and Kansas, and within striking distance of frontier, etc.

104. Letter on Horses Lost. 14 Apr.
HD 184, 26-1, v4, 2p. [366]
In the Florida war.

105. Report on the Cherokee Indians. 15 Apr.
HD 188, 26-1, v4, 48p. [366]
Interference of agents with the internal government of said Indians.

106. R-M of D. Gardiner. 17 Apr.
SD 395, 26-1, v6, 5p. [359]
Supplied troops in Florida campaign; 1836-37.

107. Inland trade with Mexico. 17 Apr.
HD 191, 26-1, v4, 8p. [366]
Trade with Indians.

108. Petition of the Missouri Volunteers. 18 Ap.

SD 405, 26-1, v6, 2p. [359]
Florida campaign of 1837-38.

109. On Claim of G. Johnston. 21 Apr.
SD 413, 26-1, v6, 7p. [359]
Shawnee Indian debts.

110. R-P of J. Schoolcraft. 23 Apr.
SD 415, 26-1, v6, 3p. [359]
Losses in trade with Ottawa and Chippewa Indians at Michilimackinack; treaty with said Indians of 28 Mar. 1836.

111. R-P of Langtry and Jenkins. 24 Apr.
SD 420, 26-1, v6, 1p. [359]
Cherokee emigration; 1838.

112. R-P of M. Keith. 24 Apr.
HR 427, 26-1, v2, 2p. [371]
Indian spoliations in Florida.

113. R-P of J. Anderson. 24 Apr.
HR 428, 26-1, v2, 2p. [371]
Indian campaign of 1832 in Illinois.

114. R-P of B. Evans. 24 Apr.
HR 430, 26-1, v2, 1p. [371]
Indian campaign in Florida; 1837.

115. Report on the Burlington and Des Moines Transportation Co. 24 Apr.
HR 435, 26-1, v2, 2p. [371]
Land in Iowa belonging to the Indians.

116. On the Relief of G. Paschall. 24 Apr.
HR 448, 26-1, v2, 2p. [371]
Destruction of whiskey intended for Cherokee Indians; treaty negotiations of 1835 at New Echota, Georgia.

117. R-P of J. Shields. 25 Apr.
HR 451, 26-1, v2, 1p. [371]
Choctaw treaty of 1830 at Dancing Rabbit Creek.

118. R-P of G. Bedinger. 25 Apr.
HR 464, 26-1, v2, 1p. [371]
Indian spy in Revolutionary War; 1779 near Boonsborough.

119. Report on Pensions to Officers and Soldiers. 25 Apr.
HR 470, 26-1, v2, 6p. [371]
For the Indian wars in the west from 1783 to 1795.

120. R-P of I. McHenry. 25 Apr.
HR 483, 26-1, v2, 10p. [371]
Indian spy in Revolutionary war.

121. R-M of Citizens of Iowa. 25 Apr.
HR 489, 26-1, v2, 2p. [371]
On request for arms to protect themselves from Indian attack.

122. R-P of L. Clarke. 25 Apr.
HR 503, 26-1, v2, 10p. [371]
Contracted to furnish supplies to emigrating Creek, Seminole, and Choctaw Indians bound for Arkansas.

123. Report on Expenditures of Government. 7 May.
SD 450, 26-1, v7, 6p. [360]
From 1824 to 1839, inclusive; Indian removal and wars.

124. Report on Military and Naval Defenses. 8 May.
SD 451, 26-1, v7, 115p. [360]
Defense of the western frontier.

125. R-M of W. Smith. 10 May.
HR 589, 26-1, v4, 1p. [373]
Cherokee Indian emigration.

126. Letter on the Georgia Military Claim. 12 May.
HD 202, 26-1, v4, 25p. [366]
Seminole, Cherokee, and Creek campaigns in 1835-36.

127. Report on Inland Trade to Mexico. 12 May.
HR 540, 26-1, v3, 17p. [372]
Indian trade.

128. R-P of S. Cozard. 14 May.
SD 466, 26-1, v7, 1p. [360]
Shawnee Indian captive in 1794.

129. Letter on the Wyandot Indians. 15 May.
HD 205, 26-1, v4, 4p. [366]
On the progress of effecting a treaty for the purchase of land in Ohio from said Indians, and for their removal west.

130. Message on Negotiations of Indian Treaties. 18 May.
HD 210, 26-1, v6, 7p. [268]
Statement of amounts paid to persons concerned with negotiating Indian treaties since 1829; list of treaty Com'rs.

131. On the Relief of E. Griddle. 22 May.
SD 486, 26-1, v7, 3p. [360]
Creek Indian campaign; 1813.

132. On the Relief of J. Paxton. 25 May.
HR 516, 26-1, v3, 6p. [372]
Campaign against the Mississiniway towns on the Wabash River (Indiana) in 1812.

133. R-P of N. Coats. 25 May.
HR 575, 26-1, v3, 1p. [372]
Creek Indian war of 1837 in Alabama.

134. Mem. of the Cherokee Indians. 26 May.
HD 222, 26-1, v6, 23p. [368]
On discussions between the Eastern and Western Cherokees.

135. On the Relief of W. Cuddeback. 3 June.
SD 510, 26-1, v7, 1p. [360]
Indian incursions in New York; Revolutionary war.

136. On the Relief of W. Davis. 5 June.
SD 522, 26-1, v7, 1p. [360]
Pottawatomie Indian annuity payment in 1836; Indiana; protection of Indians.

137. Message on Indian Lands. 9 June.
HD 240, 26-1, v7, 9p. [369]
Land within the Chickasaw cession; treaties of 1832 and 1834.

138. Report on Cherokee Land Grants. 19 June.
HR 591, 26-1, v4, 3p. [373]
On lands acquired by treaty; settler difficulties; treaties of 1817 and 1819.

139. R-P of D. Mitchell. 19 June.
HR 593, 26-1, v4, 2p. [373]
Debt due from an Indian chief to citizens of Tennessee.

140. R-M of G. Mayfield. 23 June.
HR 597, 26-1, v4, 14p. [373]
Creek Indian captive.

141. Documents on the Claims of Wallis, Arthur et al. 26 June.
SD 579, 26-1, v8, 7p. [361]
Sac and Fox Indians; 1836; rations to Missouri volunteers.

142. On Roads in Iowa. 7 July.
SD 598, 26-1, v8, 8p. [361]
From Burlington to the Indian agency.

143. R-P of J. Calhoun. 10 July.
HR 654, 26-1, v4, 8p. [373]
Seminole and Creek wars of 1836.

144. On the Relief of J. Richey. 10 July.
HR 656, 26-1, v4, 1p. [373]
Sac and Fox war of 1832 in Illinois.

145. On the Relief of J. Scott. 10 July.
HR 658, 26-1, v4, 2p. [373]
Sac and Fox war of 1832 in Illinois.

146. On the Relief of S. Mackay. 10 July.
HR 659, 26-1, v4, 2p. [373]
Agent for the Creek Indian removal in 1836.

147. R-P of A. Dade. 10 July.
HR 667, 26-1, v4, 1p. [373]
Florida Indian hostilities of 1835.

148. R-P of M. Collins. 10 July.
HR 675, 26-1, v4, 1p. [373]
Attacked by Indians; 1815 in Indiana.

149. R-P of J. Bibb. 10 July.
HR 679, 26-1, v4, 3p. [373]
Florida campaign of 1836.

150. R-C of S. Allen. 10 July.
HR 680, 26-1, v4, 1p. [373]
Cherokee Indian country; 1838.

151. R-P of T. Stone. 10 July.
HR 681, 26-1, v4, 1p. [373]
Choctaw Indians; 1814-1815.

152. R-C of S. Carter. 10 July.
HR 682, 26-1, v4, 1p. [373]
Creek Indians in West Florida; 1837.

153. R-P of W. and R. Ewing. 10 July.
HR 685, 26-1, v4, 1p. [373]
Campaign of 1812 against the northwestern Indians.

154. R-C of W. Fleming. 10 July.
HR 690, 26-1, v4, 1p. [373]
Cherokee depredations of 1792-93 in Georgia.

155. R-P of A. Watson. 10 July.
HR 694, 26-1, v4, 1p. [373]
Seminole Indian war of 1836.

156. R-C of W. Cooley. 10 July.
HR 695, 26-1, v4, 1p. [373]
Florida Indian hostilities in 1836.

157. R-C of S. Enocks. 10 July.
HR 697, 26-1, v4, 1p. [373]
Sac and Fox (Black Hawk) war of 1832.

158. R-P of J. Baldwin. 10 July.
HR 698, 26-1, v4, 2p. [373]
Indian hostilities in Florida; 1836.

159. R-M of A. Gandy. 10 July.
HR 699, 26-1, v4, 2p. [373]
Creek war of 1836 in Alabama.

160. R-C of T. Chamblin. 10 July.
HR 702, 26-1, v4, 1p. [373]
Florida campaign of 1836.

161. R-P of A. Owens. 10 July.
HR 703, 26-1, v4, 1p. [373]
Removal of Creek Indians from Cherokee lands.

162. R-C of A. Hall. 10 July.
HR 704, 26-1, v4, 1p. [373]
Creek war of 1814.

163. On the Case of J. Brown. 10 July.
HR 705, 26-1, v4, 1p. [373]
Removal of the Pottawatomie Indians from Indiana to the west.

164. R-C of Shropshire and Ross. 10 July.
HR 711, 26-1, v4, 2p. [373]
Black Hawk war of 1832.

165. R-P of R. McGuire. 10 July.
HR 712, 26-1, v4, 1p. [373]
Attacked by Indians; 1813; Pennsylvania.

166. R-C of Alabama Volunteers. 13 July.
SD 605, 26-1, v8, 2p. [361]
Seminole Indian campaign of 1836-37 in Florida.

167. Message Concerning Indian Lands. 20 July.
SD 616, 26-1, v8, 13p. [361]
Purchases of Indian lands since establishment of Government.

168. Statement of Appropriations. 4 Aug.
SD 620, 26-1, v8, 29p. [361] *or* HD 265, 26-1, v7, 31p. [369]
During the 1st session, 26th Congress; Indian expenses.

169. Annual Message to Congress with Documents; Pres. Van Buren. 9 Dec.
SD 1, 26-2, v1, 541p. [375] *or* HD 2, 26-2, v1, 541p. [382]
Indian emigration; annual report of the Sec. of War; annual report of the CIA; etc.

170. Annual Report of the Sec. of the Treasury. 9 Dec.
SD 2, 26-2, v1, 35p. [375] *or* HD 3, 26-2, v1, 80p. [382]
Receipts and expenditures; Indian expenses (House version includes estimates for 1841).

171. Estimates for Indian Dept. 9 Dec.
HD 28, 26-2, v2, 9p. [383]
To meet current expenses, pay annuities, etc., for 1841.

172. Letter on Indian Hostilities. 15 Dec.
HD 8, 26-2, v1, 16p. [382]
Stating expenditures in Florida.

173. Report on the Chickasaw Trust Fund. 17 Dec.
SD 15, 26-2, v2, 3p. [376] *or* HD 19, 26-2, v1, 3p. [382]
Treaties of 20 Oct. 1832, and 1 July 1834.

174. Resol. of Rep. Barnard. 17 Dec.
HR, Resol. 1, 26-2, v1, 2p. [388]
On revenue and expenses for 1841; requests statements concerning Indian treaties and hostilities.

175. R-P of J. Paxton. 30 Dec.
SD 33, 26-2, v2, 7p. [376]
Indian campaign in Ohio; 1811-13.

1841

1. R-P of J. Cline. 4 Jan.
HR 36, 26-2, v1, 1p. [388]
Cherokee Nation; 1838; treaty of 1835.

2. R-P of T. Wilson. 4 Jan.
HR 48, 26-2, v1, 1p. [388]
Indian engagement in 1791.

3. R-P of R. Perry. 4 Jan.
HR 55, 26-2, v1, 1p. [388]
Indian engagement of 1815 at Tippecanoe.

4. Letter on the Iowa-Missouri Boundary. 5 Jan.
SD 40, 26-2, v2, 13p. [376]
Indian boundary line.

5. Report on Private Claims. 5 Jan.
SD 236, 26-2, v5 (pt. 1), 643p. [379]
List of claims from the 14th Congress, to date; includes claims related to Indian affairs.

6. Annual Report of the Com'r of the General Land Office. 6 Jan.
SD 61, 26-2, v3, 137p. [377] *or* HD 38, 26-2, v2, 137p. [383]
Indian land cessions and treaties.

7. Estimates for the Army in 1841. 6 Jan.
HD 47, 26-2, v2, 22p. [383]
For barracks at Turkey River as a consequence of the removal of the Winnebagoes.

8. Mem. of the Iowa Legis. 7 Jan.
HD 53, 26-2, v2, 1p. [383]
Military road; Indian hostilities.

9. On the Case of J. Lybrook. 7 Jan.
HR 75, 26-2, v1, 1p. [388]
Indian hostilities in 1776.

10. R-P of P. Sky. 7 Jan.
HR 86, 26-2, v1, 1p. [388]
An Onondaga chief injured in the Revolutionary War.

11. Mem. of B. Ferris. 8 Jan.
HD 66, 26-2, v2, 3p. [383]
Against carrying out the Seneca treaty; treaty of 1794 with the Six Nations; treaty of 17 Mar. 1802 with the Senecas and Onondagas; removal.

12. R-C of Tennessee Volunteers. 9 Jan.
HR 93, 26-2, v1, 2p. [388]
Florida war of 1836.

13. R-P of R. Carter. 9 Jan.
HR 94, 26-2, v1, 2p. [388]
Indian battle at Big Hill on the Great Miami River in 1799.

14. Report on Navigation of Rivers in Wisconsin. 9 Jan.
HR 96, 26-2, v1, 5p. [388]
Prevention of Indian disturbances.

15. R-C of W. Dickinson. 12 Jan.
SD 65, 26-2, v3, 1p. [377]
Fox River Agency; Winnebago Indians of Wisconsin; 1833.
16. R-C of G. Hinant. 12 Jan.
SD 67, 26-2, v3, 2p. [377]
Creek Indian removal in 1836.
17. R-C of D. Skinner. 15 Jan.
SD 86, 26-2, v3, 3p. [377]
Alabama militia supplies; Indian war of 1836.
18. R-M of G. Fisher. 16 Jan.
HR 102, 26-2, v1, 2p. [388]
Indian depredations of 1813-14 in Mississippi.
19. R-C of G. Walton. 16 Jan.
HR 108, 26-2, v1, 1p. [388]
Indian depredations of 1840 in Florida.
20. R-C of Dallam and Hamburgh. 16 Jan.
HR 111, 26-2, v1, 1p. [388]
Indian traders in Florida, in 1840.
21. Appropriations for the Continuance of the Florida War. 21 Jan.
HD 70, 26-2, v2, 8p. [383]
Estimates for 1841; Indian hostilities.
22. Report on Expenditures in War Dept. 22 Jan.
SD 103, 26-2, v3, 18p. [377] *or* HD 74, 26-2, v2, 18p. [383]
For 1840; Indian expenses.
23. Report on Troops on Frontiers. 22 Jan.
SD 104, 26-2, v3, 3p. [377]
From Fort Snelling to Fort Jesup; protection from Indian hostilities.
24. Message on the Michigan-Wisconsin Boundary. 3 Feb.
SD 151, 26-2, v4, 16p. [378]
Encroachments by surveyors on Chippewa lands; interview had with Ca-sha-o-sha, one of the principal chiefs of the Chippewas.
25. Letter on Indian Disbursements. 5 Feb.
SD 161, 26-2, v4, 116p. [378] *or* HD 108, 26-2, v3, 116p. [384]
For year ending 30 Sept. 1840.
26. R-C of J. Johnston. 12 Feb.
HR 114, 26-2, v1, 3p. [388]
Agent to the Shawnee Indians from 1812 to 1829.
27. R-C of O. Lacey. 12 Feb.
HR 120, 26-2, v1, 1p. [388]
Pottawatomie treaty of 20 Sept. 1828.
28. Report on Damages by Troops in Florida. 12 Feb.
HR 131, 26-2, v1, 6p. [388]
Florida war of 1814; refugee Creeks.
29. R-C of Clements, Bryan and Co. 12 Feb.
HR 137, 26-2, v1, 66p. [388]
For provisioning the Cherokee Indians while emigrating.
30. R-C of B. Murphy. 12 Feb.
HR 186, 26-2, v1, 3p. [388]
Cherokee Indians; treaty of 16 May 1828.
31. On the Relief of J. Reynolds. 12 Feb.
HR 188, 26-2, v1, 11p. [388]
Disbursing agent for the Indian Dept. among the Winnebagoes in 1838.
32. R-P of F. Gardner. 12 Feb.
HR 194, 26-2, v1, 1p. [388]
Seminole Indians; 1836.
33. R-P of J. Johnson. 12 Feb.
HR 226, 26-2, v1, 1p. [388]
Service with General Wayne against Indians.
34. R-P of J. Spears. 12 Feb.
HR 228, 26-2, v1, 1p. [388]
Service with General Wayne against Indians; 1792-95.
35. R-P of W. Parker. 12 Feb.
HR 239, 26-1, v1, 1p. [388]
An Indian of the Seneca tribe.
36. Report on Indiana Lands. 15 Feb.
SD 190, 26-2, v4, 20p. [378]
Treaties of 1837 and 1839 with the Miami Indians.
37. Survey by Nicollet of the Upper Mississippi River. 16 Feb.
SD 237, 26-2, v5 (pt. 2), 170p. [380]
Sioux and Chippewa country; wars with Sac and Fox; etc.
38. Report on Payment of Indian Claims. 20 Feb.
SD 205, 26-2, v4, 5p. [378]
Under the treaty with the Stockbridge and Munsee Indians of 3 Sept. 1839.
39. Petition of Citizens of New York. 22 Feb.
SD 210, 26-2, v4, 3p. [378]
Ask that treaty may not be enforced against the Senecas averse to emigration.
40. Petition of Citizens of New York. 23 Feb.
SD 213, 26-2, v4, 2p. [378]
Ask that treaty may not be enforced against the Senecas averse to emigration.
41. Mem. of Citizens of New York. 23 Feb.
SD 214, 26-2, v4, 2p. [378]

Many Seneca are averse to emigration, and did not ratify amendments to their treaty with the U.S.

42. Report on Excess Appropriations for the Years 1837-39. 2 Mar.
SD 226, 26-2, v4, 7p. [378]
Indian Dept.

43. Letter on Fulfillment of Treaty Stipulations. 3 Mar.
HD 109, 26-2, v3, 179p. [384]
Treaties of 1820, 1825, etc., with the Choctaws; founding and operations of the Choctaw Academy in Kentucky.

44. Report on Horses Lost. 3 Mar.
HD 119, 26-2, v5, 21p. [386]
Claims arising from Black Hawk and Seminole wars.

45. Statement of Appropriations. 31 Mar.
SD 235, 26-2, v4, 25p. [378] *or* HD 124, 26-2, v5, 26p. [386]
For 2d session, 26 Congress; Indian expenses.

46. Message to Congress with Documents; Pres. Tyler. 1 June.
SD 1, 27-1, v1, 75p. [390] *or* HD 1, 27-1, v1, 75p. [392]
Abuses in the Indian Dept. with respect to expenditures earmarked for treaties, subsistence, and removal; Report of the Sec. of War; etc.

47. Report of the Sec. of the Treasury. 3 June.
SD 10, 27-1, v1, 23p. [390] *or* HD 2, 27-1, v1, 23p. [392]
For the year 1840; Indian expenses.

48. Resol. of Sen. Sevier. 12 June.
SD 18, 27-1, v1, 1p. [390]
Calling for names of contractors and officers who have been guilty of bribery and fraud with respect to emigration and subsistence in the southwest.

49. Estimate of Additional Appropriations for the War Dept. 21 June.
HD 19, 27-1, v1, 7p. [392]
For 1841; Indian hostilities in Florida.

50. Explanations of Appropriations for Fortifications and Surveys. 7 July.
HD 30, 27-1, v1, 15p. [392]
Preventing Indian hostilities; surveys of land of each Indian tribe friendly with the U.S.

51. Appropriations and Expenditures. 9 July.
HD 31, 27-1, v1, 65p. [392]
Indian Dept. from 1829 to 1840.

52. Report on Sales of Public Lands. 10 July.
SD 62, 27-1, v1, 22p. [390]
Includes Indian titles extinguished; amount set apart for Indian tribes; etc.

53. Resol. of Rep. Levy. 29 July.
HR, Resol. 1, 27-1, v1, 1p. [393]
Requests information on the Seminole Indians; treaties of 9 May 1832 and 28 Mar. 1833, annuities, expenditures to curb hostilities of said Indians, emigration, etc.

54. Letter on Miami Indians. 3 Aug.
HD 43, 27-1, v1, 7p. [392]
Estimates of funds needed to execute the treaty of 28 Nov. 1840 between Com'rs Milroy and Hamilton and the Miami tribe; copy of the treaty.

55. Document on Fortifications on Kansas Frontier. 4 Aug.
SD 86, 27-1, v1, 1p. [390]
Forts Smith, Gibson, Wayne, and Towson; smaller posts in Indian country.

56. Petition of J. Naill. 17 Aug.
SD 96, 27-1, v1, 2p. [390]
Asks outstanding claims to a reservation under the treaty of Dancing Rabbit Creek be satisfied; Choctaw Indians.

57. Report on Surveys and Sales of Public Land. 23 Aug.
SD 104, 27-1, v1, 3p. [390]
Miami, Cherokee, and Choctaw land cessions.

58. Letter on Troops on the Frontier. 31 Aug.
HD 59, 27-1, v1, 4p. [392]
At Forts Gibson, Towson, Smith, and Wayne; Arkansas frontier; Indian depredations.

59. Report on Investment of Indian Moneys. 9 Sept.
SD 116, 27-1, v1, 3p. [390]
Chickasaw fund, etc.

60. Statement of Appropriations. 13 Sept.
HD 62, 27-1, v1, 6p. [392]
During the 1st session, 27th Congress; Indian expenses.

61. Annual Message to Congress with Documents; Pres. Tyler. 7 Dec.
SD 1, 27-2, v1, 494 p. [395] *or* HD 2,

27-2, v1, 472p. [401]
Indian war in Florida; annual report of the Sec. of War; annual report of the CIA, including emigration, treaty negotiations, condition of tribes, Indian disturbances, and subsistence; etc.

62. Message on Military Defenses. 13 Dec.
SD 2, 27-2, v1, 45p. [395]
On the western frontier, etc.

63. Mem. of Choctaw Indians. 15 Dec.
HD 15, 27-2, v1, 5p. [401]
Treaty for lands; proposed removal west of the Mississippi; demand that U.S. carry out the treaty and do them justice; Dancing Rabbit Creek, 1830.

64. Caddo Indian Treaty. 15 Dec.
HD 25, 27-2, v1, 51p. [401]
Testimony taken under a commission of the Indian Affairs Com.

65. R-P of J. Thomas et al. 20 Dec.
SD 13, 27-2, v2, 1p. [396]
Miami Indian treaty.

66. Annual Report of the Sec. of the Treasury. 20 Dec.
SD 17, 27-2, v2, 20p. [396] *or* HD 18, 27-2, v1, 20p. [401]
Indian expenses.

67. Estimate of Appropriations for 1842. 20 Dec.
HD 19, 27-2, v1, 50p. [401]
Indian expenses.

68. Annual Report of the Com'r of the General Land Office. 28 Dec.
SD 22, 27-2, v2, 116p. [396] *or* HD 24, 27-2, v1, 113p. [401]
Indian treaties and land cessions.

69. R-P of Lieut. Cline. 29 Dec.
HR 1, 27-2, v1, 2p. [407]
Cherokee country east of the Mississippi River in 1838.

70. R-P of P. Sky. 29 Dec.
HR 18, 27-2, v1, 1p. [407]
An Onandaga Indian on the Niagara frontier.

1842

1. Letter on Land Claims at Opelousas, Louisiana. 6 Jan.
HD 33, 27-2, v2, 97p. [402]
Some claims (those labelled "class 2") fall under the Caddo treaty.

2. Letter on Indian Dept. 13 Jan.
HD 41, 27-2, v2, 12p. [402]
Persons employed; compensation.

3. R-P of J. Paxton. 25 Jan.
SD 68, 27-2, v2, 7p. [396]
Indian campaign; 1812; Indiana.

4. Report on Appropriations for 1842. 25 Jan.
HR 44, 27-2, v1, 44p. [407]
From various Depts., including War.

5. R-M of W. Waller. 26 Jan.
SD 73, 27-2, v2, 1p. [396]
Title to an Indian reservation; Creek lands in Alabama.

6. Report on Funds of Chickasaw Indians. 27 Jan.
SD 74, 27-2, v2, 5p. [396] *or* HD 56, 27-2, v2, 4p. [402]
Statement carrying into effect the Chickasaw treaty of 20 Oct. 1832; sales of lands; stocks held.

7. R-P of H. Andrews. 28 Jan.
SD 81, 27-2, v2, 5p. [396]
Florida; 1835; Seminole war.

8. Message on the Seminole War. 29 Jan.
HD 55, 27-2, v2, 9p. [402]
From the Sec. of War as to the origin of the war; slaves captured by U.S. troops; etc.

9. Statement of Expenditures of the War Dept. 31 Jan.
HD 62, 27-2, v2, 19p. [402]
Indian expenses.

10. R-P of J. Hunt et al. 9 Feb.
HR 51, 27-2, v1, 3p. [407]
Authorizing the Chiefs, head men, and warriors of the Ottawa Indians to appropriate money due their tribe from the U.S. to payment of debts due by them to Petitioners.

11. Report on an Additional Land Office in Iowa. 9 Feb.
HR 68, 27-2, v1, 1p. [407]
Indian boundary line.

12. R-P of Citizens of Perrysburg, Ohio. 9 Feb.
HR 70, 27-2, v1, 3p. [407]
Land cessions by Indians at the treaty of Greenville in 1795.

13. Report on School Lands in Ohio. 9 Feb.
HR 73, 27-2, v1, 5p. [407]
Lands in Indian reservations; Ottawa treaty of 30 Aug. 1831; Seneca/Shawnee treaty of 20 July 1831; Shawnee treaty of 8 Aug. 1831;

Wyandot treaty of 19 Jan. 1832;
Seneca treaty of 28 Feb. 1831;
Wyandot treaty of 23 Ap. 1836.

14. Report on Indian Appropriations for 1842. 9 Feb.
HR 75 (a), 27-2, v1, 24p. [407]
Current and contingent expenses; treaty stipulations; list of treaties.

15. R-P of R. Carter. 9 Feb.
HR 131, 27-2, v1, 2p. [407]
Indian battle at Fort Recovery; campaign of 1795-99.

16. R-P of J. Martin. 9 Feb.
HR 144, 27-2, v1, 1p. [407]
Creek campaign of 1836.

17. R-P of G. Mayfield. 9 Feb.
HR 147, 27-2, v1, 1p. [407]
Creek Indian war; Seminole war of 1818.

18. R-P of G. Bedinger. 9 Feb.
HR 154, 27-2, v1, 1p. [407]
Indian spy in 1779.

19. R-P of A. Brightwell. 9 Feb.
HR 162, 27-2, v1, 1p. [407]
Indian battle at Talleshatchie in 1813.

20. R-P of C. Howe. 9 Feb.
HR 171, 27-2, v1, 1p. [407]
Florida Indian hostilities in 1840.

21. R-P of W. Rowlett. 9 Feb.
HR 172, 27-2, v1, 1p. [407]
Seminole depredations in 1840.

22. R-P of J. Monroe. 9 Feb.
HR 173, 27-2, v1, 1p. [407]
Indian depredations of 1839 in Florida.

23. R-P of W. Garrard. 9 Feb.
HR 180, 27-2, v1, 2p. [407]
Creek Indians; Alabama; 1836.

24. R-P of C. Wallace. 9 Feb.
HR 189, 27-2, v1, 7p. [407]
Virginia reservation in Ohio; Indian boundary line.

25. R-P of J. Houseman. 9 Feb.
HR 207, 27-2, v1, 2p. [407]
Florida Indian war; 1836.

26. Report on Huntsville Land District. 9 Feb.
HR 248, 27-2, v1, 2p. [407]
Cherokee country; Alabama; treaty of 29 Dec. 1835 at New Echota.

27. Resol. of the Iowa Legis. 12 Feb.
HD 85, 27-2, v2, 2p. [402]
Ask donation of lands for school purposes in half-breed Sac and Fox reservation.

28. Resol. of the Iowa Legis. 12 Feb.
HD 86, 27-2, v2, 2p. [402]
To purchase lands of the Sac and Fox Indians.

29. Resol. of the Iowa Legis. 23 Feb.
HD 107, 27-2, v2, 2p. [402]
Licensing Indian traders.

30. R-P of J. Johnston. 23 Feb.
HR 252, 27-2, v1, 3p. [407]
Shawnee Indians.

31. Resol. of the Iowa Legis. 2 Mar.
HD 117, 27-2, v2, 2p. [402]
Ask resurvey of boundary lines of the Sac and Fox reservation.

32. Extra Pay to General Scott. 4 Mar.
HD 121, 27-2, v3, 12p. [403]
For services in removing Cherokee Indians in 1838.

33. R-C of B. Murphy. 8 Mar.
SD 166, 27-2, v3, 2p. [397]
Cherokee Indians; 1828; Arkansas.

34. R-P of Administrator of J. Hickman. 8 Mar.
HR 265, 27-2, v1, 1p. [407]
Florida war of 1836.

35. R-P of D. Hughes et al. 8 Mar.
HR 267, 27-2, v1, 2p. [407]
Creek Indian emigration from Florida to Arkansas in 1837.

36. R-P of J. Morrow and J. Tipton. 8 Mar.
HR 272, 27-2, v1, 1p. [407]
Cherokee treaty of 1835.

37. R-P of L. Trickel. 8 Mar.
HR 280, 27-2, v1, 2p. [407]
Caddo Indians in Louisiana.

38. R-P of G. Collier and W. Pettis. 8 Mar.
HR 334, 27-2, v2, 2p. [408]
Indian Dept.; Indian treaty of 15 June 1838.

39. R-P of J. Clayton et al. 8 Mar.
HR 342, 27-2, v2, 3p. [408]
Florida Indian campaign of 1836.

40. R-P of Mrs. Murry. 8 Mar.
HR 344, 27-2, v2, 2p. [408]
Cherokee treaty negotiations in Washington; 1828.

41. R-C of W. Graham. 8 Mar.
HR 347, 27-2, v2, 1p. [408]
Agent of Seminole Indians while commanding officer at Fort King.

42. R-P of J. Dabney. 8 Mar.
HR 351, 27-2, v2, 1p. [408]
Seminole Indians; 1837.

43. Report on Pensions to Soldiers in Indian Wars Prior to 1795. 8 Mar.
HR 361, 27-2, v2, 6p. [408]

Ask pensions be given to said soldiers.

44. R-C of the Louisiana Militia. 8 Mar.
HR 364, 27-2, v2, 4p. [408]
Seminole war; 1836; Florida.

45. R-P of J. Haas. 8 Mar.
HR 407, 27-2, v2, 1p. [408]
Bought lands reserved to the Pottawatomies; treaty of 20 Oct. 1832.

46. On the Relief of G. and R. Allen. 8 Mar.
HR 408, 27-2, v2, 1p. [408]
Pottawatomie treaty of 20 Oct. 1832.

47. R-P of W. Parker. 8 Mar.
HR 445, 27-2, v2, 1p. [408]
A Seneca Indian.

48. Treaty with the Choctaw Indians. 16 Mar.
SD 188, 27-2, v3, 13p. [397]
14th and 19th articles of Dancing Rabbit Creek treaty of 27 Sept. 1830 remain unexecuted; negligence of U.S. agent; claims arising.

49. Mem. of the Stockbridge Indians of Wisconsin. 16 Mar.
SD 189, 27-2, v3, 26p. [397]
Title to land; Miami treaty of 30 Sept. 1809; Menomonie treaties of 23 Sept. 1822 and 8 Feb. 1831; etc.

50. Report on Public Expenditures. 17 Mar.
SD 190, 27-2, v3, 13p. [397]
From 1 Oct. to 31 Dec. 1841; Indian expenses.

51. R-P of Capt. Collins. 17 Mar.
HR 453, 27-2, v2, 16p. [408]
Disbursing agent in Arkansas for the Indian Dept.; emigrated Chickasaw Indians.

52. Report on Removal of Chickasaw Indians. 17 Mar.
HR 454, 27-2, v2, 12p. [408]
On contracts and expenditures.

53. Letter on the Iowa-Missouri Boundary. 19 Mar.
HD 141, 27-2, v3, 37p. [403]
Indian boundary line; Sac and Fox treaty of 4 Aug. 1834; Otoe and Missouria treaty of 15 Oct. 1836; Kanza treaty of 3 June 1825; etc.

54. Claims Against Pottawatomie Indians. 19 Mar.
HD 143, 27-2, v3, 151p. [403]
Report of commission on claims against Pottawatomie, Ottawa, and Chippewa Indians; "Chicago treaty" of 26 Nov. 2833; etc.

55. Report on Public Expenditures. 21 Mar.
HR 458, 27-2, v2, 37p. [408]
For Indian removal, etc.

56. Report on Cherokee Claims. 24 Mar.
SD 200, 27-2, v3, 1p. [397]
Arising from the treaty of 1835-36.

57. R-M of R. Currin. 28 Mar.
SD 206, 27-2, v3, 6p. [397]
Chickasaw Indians; Tennessee; treaty of 1818.

58. R-P of A. Thompson. 29 Mar.
SD 209, 27-2, v3, 1p. [397]
Indians and Tories in the Revolutionary War.

59. Disbursements to Indians. 31 Mar.
HD 164, 27-2, v3, 146p. [403]
From 1 Oct. 1840 to 30 Sept. 1841.

60. R-P of R. Davis. 1 Apr.
HR 467, 27-2, v2, 2p. [408]
Seminole Indians; 1818.

61. R-C of J. McIntosh. 1 Apr.
HR 470, 27-2, v2, 6p. [408]
Seminole war; 1836.

62. R-P of J. Elzaurdi. 1 Apr.
HR 472, 27-2, v2, 5p. [408]
Seminole war; 1835.

63. R-P of Trustees of Dublin Township, Ohio. 1 Apr.
HR 483, 27-2, v2, 7p. [408]
Indian land titles.

64. R-P of R. Lapetter. 1 Apr.
HR 491, 27-2, v2, 1p. [408]
Black man shot as hostile Indian by South Carolina volunteers.

65. R-P of T. Linton. 1 Apr.
HR 492, 27-2, v2, 1p. [408]
Slaves killed by Seminole Indians; 1838.

66. R-P of T. Sailors et al. 1 Apr.
HR 513, 27-2, v2, 1p. [408]
Miami reservations in Ohio.

67. Message on Public Land Sales. 11 Apr.
SD 227, 27-2, v3, 5p. [397]
Miami, Cherokee, and Choctaw land cessions.

68. Report on Lead Mines. 12 Apr.
SD 228, 27-2, v3, 3p. [397]
Indian land title in Wisconsin.

69. Report on Indian Lands. 12 Apr.
HR 557, 27-2, v3, 2p. [409]
Pottawatomie treaty of 20 Oct. 1832.

70. R-P of General Watson. 12 Apr.
HR 558, 27-2, v3, 3p. [409]
Bought slaves from Creek warriors who had captured them in war against Seminoles; 1836.

71. Report on Paying the Georgia Militia. 12 Apr
HR 584, 27-2, v3, 2p. [409]
Called out in 1840 to meet the Indians of Florida.

72. R-P of W. Sanders. 12 Apr.
HR 590, 27-2, v3, 6p. [409]
Indian hostilities of 1836 in Florida.

73. On the Relief of Arkansas Citizens. 12 Apr.
HR 601, 27-2, v3, 1p. [409]
Creek Indian treaty.

74. On the Relief of Missouri Volunteers. 12 Apr.
HR 602, 27-2, v3, 3p. [409]
Called out to suppress Indian hostilities; Sac and Fox Indians.

75. Report on Indian Depots in Arkansas. 12 Apr.
HR 604, 27-2, v3, 13p. [409]
Misapplication of funds; subsistence for Chickasaws and other emigrating Indians.

76. R-P of G. Catlin. 12 Apr.
HR 636, 27-2, v3, 3p. [409]
Asks exemption from duty for his book on Indians being published in Britain.

77. R-P of C. Howe. 12 Apr.
HR 368, 27-2, v3, 1p. [409]
Florida Indian hostilities in 1840.

78. On the Relief of E. Sprague. 12 Apr.
HR 642, 27-2, v3, 3p. [409]
Sac and Fox campaign of 1832 (Black Hawk war); Illinois.

79. R-P of S. Cross. 12 Apr.
HR 654, 27-2, v3, 1p. [409]
Indian campaign of 1779 in Pennsylvania.

80. R-P of the Heirs of M. Cryder. 12 Apr.
HR 656, 27-2, v3, 1p. [409]
Indian campaign of 1777-80 in Pennsylvania.

81. Letter on the Iowa-Missouri Boundary. 14 Apr.
SD 241, 27-2, v4, 11p. [398] *or* HD 48, 27-2, v2, 11p. [402]
Indian boundary line.

82. Report on Expenditures of War Dept. 20 Apr.
SD 248, 27-2, v4, 10p. [398]
On retrenching said expenditures, and abolishing offices.

83. Report on Depredations in Florida. 20 Apr.
HR 668, 27-2, v3, 7p. [409]
By the U.S. Army; Gen. Jackson pursues the Creeks to Florida in 1814; etc.

84. On the Treaty with Choctaw Indians; 21 Apr.
SD 252, 27-2, v4, 1p. [398]
Claims under treaty of Dancing Rabbit Creek; 1830.

85. Depredations by Indians and Troops in Georgia. 22 Apr.
HD 200, 27-2, v4, 74p. [404]
Correspondence between Governor of Georgia and the War Dept. since 4 Mar. 1841; Seminole depredations.

86. R-P of M. Thompson. 26 Apr.
SD 264, 27-2, v4, 2p. [398]
Agent for settling claims on Indian reservations.

87. Mem. of the Mississippi Legis. 29 Apr.
SD 280, 27-2, v4, 2p. [398]
Chickasaw land cession.

88. Resol. of the Mississippi Legis. 29 Apr.
SD 281, 27-2, v4, 1p. [398]
Urges adjustment of claims and removal of Indians under the treaty of Dancing Rabbit Creek; Choctaws; 1830.

89. Report on Resol. to Pension W. Bilsland 3 May.
SD 288, 27-2, v4, 1p. [398]
Defense of frontier against Indians; 1832; Illinois.

90. Report on Removal of the Winnebago Indians. 9 May.
HR 680, 27-2, v3, 7p. [409]
Recommends appropriation to aid in removing said Indians to Iowa; the Sac, Fox, and Sioux Indians complain of the present location of the Winnebagoes as a violation of treaty stipulations, and threaten to remove them by force; correspondence.

91. Message on Hostilities in Florida. 11 May.
SD 295, 27-2, v4, 2p. [398] *or* HD 223, 27-2, v4, 2p. [404]
It is too expensive to follow the few Indians under arms; has author-

ized the commanding officer to announce cessation of hostilities and invite Indians to go west; etc.

92. Murders on Neutral Ground. 12 May.
HD 222, 27-2, v4, 2p. [404]
On murders of U.S. citizens by Indians in Iowa Territory.

93. Report on Militia Claims of Georgia. 16 May.
HR 684, 27-2, v3, 16p. [409]
For repressing Indian hostilities in 1836; Creeks and Seminoles.

94. Documents on the Defense of Georgia. 18 May.
HD 229, 27-2, v4, 4p. [404]
Against Indians; Seminole war.

95. Letter on the Choctaw Academy. 20 May.
HD 231, 27-2, v4, 37p. [404]
On expenses of the academy for education of Indian youth at Great Crossings, Kentucky; expenditures; number educated.

96. R-P of W. Barnes. 20 May.
HR 694, 27-2, v3, 1p. [409]
Indian war of 1792.

97. R-M of J. Baldwin. 20 May.
HR 695, 27-2, v3, 2p. [409]
Indians in Florida; 1836.

98. R-P of P. Garcias. 20 May.
HR 712, 27-2, v3, 1p. [409]
Florida Indians; 1840.

99. R-P of Heirs of C. Gooch. 20 May.
HR 713, 27-2, v3, 1p. [409]
Sioux and Fox Indians in Missouri; 1810.

100. R-P of Heirs of J. Ormond. 20 May.
HR 723, 27-2, v3, 6p. [409]
Suwanu Indians; 1818; Florida.

101. R-P of S. Shipman. 20 May.
HR 727, 27-2, v3, 2p. [409]
Indian campaigns in 1778 and 1791.

102. R-P of Executor of W. Jones. 20 May.
HR 731, 27-2, v3, 1p. [409]
Destruction of houses by Indians in 1840.

103. R-P of S. Rockwell et al. 20 May.
HR 733, 27-2, v3, 3p. [409]
Attorneys of the Cherokee Nation; treaty of 29 Dec. 1835 at New Echota.

104. Report on Reorganization of Executive Depts. 23 May.
HR 741, 27-2, v4, 240p. [410]
Indian Dept.

105. Report on the Appalachicola Indians. 24 May.
HR 746, 27-2, v4, 7p. [410]
Seminole treaty of 9 May 1832 at Payne's Landing.

106. R-M of J. Delany. 25 May.
HR 752, 27-2, v4, 8p. [410]
Cherokee country.

107. R-M of W. Waller. 25 May.
HR 755, 27-2, v4, 2p. [410]
Alabama Indian lands; removal.

108. R-C of L. Evans. 25 May.
HR 760, 27-2, v4, 3p. [410]
Licensed trader to the Cherokees in 1834.

109. R-P of M. Hallows. 25 May.
HR 762, 27-2, v4, 2p. [410]
Florida Indians; 1836.

110. R-P of W. Cooley. 25 May.
HR 770, 27-2, v4, 1p. [410]
Florida Indian hostilities in 1840.

111. R-M of M. Weedman. 25 May.
HR 771, 27-2, v4, 1p. [410]
Seminole Indians.

112. R-P of G. Walton. 25 May.
HR 772, 27-2, v4, 2p. [410]
Florida Indian hostilities in 1840.

113. Report on Missouri and Iowa Boundary. 26 May.
HR 791, 27-2, v4, 12p. [410]
Indian boundary line.

114. R-P of S. Neely. 26 May.
HR 802, 27-2, v4, 1p. [410]
Indian battle; 1794; Fort Recovery.

115. R-P of F. Griffith. 26 May.
HR 826, 27-2, v4, 2p. [410]
Indian engagement in 1812.

116. Report on Military Posts from Council Bluffs to the Pacific. 27 May.
HR 830, 27-2, v4, 64p. [410]
Control of Indian hostilities.

117. Report on School Lands in Mississippi and Alabama. 28 May.
HR 753, 27-2, v4, 3p. [410]
Chickasaw cession; treaty of 1834.

118. Letter on Cherokee Indians. 4 June.
HD 237, 27-2, v4, 2p. [404]
Report of Lieut.-Col. Hitchcock on their affairs.

119. R-M of J. Roby. 10 June.
SD 316, 27-2, v4, 2p. [398]
Land bought by him from Indian reservation on Kankakee River; Pottawatomie treaty of 20 Oct. 1832.

120. R-P of J. Drysdale. 10 June.
HR 842, 27-2, v4, 4p. [410]
Florida militia; 1835-36; Indian aggressions.

121. R-P of E. Moreland et al. 10 June.
HR 844, 27-2, v4, 3p. [410]
Cherokee treaties of 1817 and 1819; land in Alabama.

122. Report on Settlers on the Fort Snelling Military Reserve. 10 June.
HR 583, 27-2, v4, 4p. [410]
Sioux treaty of Sept. 1837; not ratified until 15 June 1838, creating problems.

123. Report on the Repeal of the 1819 Indian Civilization Act. 10 June.
HR 854, 27-2, v4, 19p. [410]
Expenditures on education, etc.; discontinuing appropriations.

124. Letter on Emigration of Indians. 18 June.
HD 247, 27-2, v5, 15p. [405]
On expenses of delegation of western Indians to Florida Indians; expenditures for Seminoles who surrendered for emigration.

125. Report on School Lands of Sac and Fox Indians. 23 June.
HR 882, 27-2, v4, 2p. [410]
Treaty of 1824; Iowa.

126. Report on Settlers in Iowa. 1 July.
SD 341, 27-2, v5, 4p. [399]
On the Dubuque claim; land from the Fox Indians in 1788.

127. Report on Dubuque Claim. 2 July.
HR 894, 27-2, v4, 1p. [410]
"Black Hawk purchase" (Sac and Fox Indians); treaty of 21 Sept. 1832.

128. Report on Purchase of Lands. 5 July.
HR 902, 27-2, v4, 3p. [410]
Sac and Fox lands in Iowa; Missouri-Iowa boundary dispute.

129. Report on Cost of Military Depots in Florida. 6 July.
HR 903, 27-2, v4, 12p. [410]
Seminole war.

130. Correspondence with Col. Worth. 7 July.
HD 262, 27-2, v5, 27p. [405]
Progress of the Indian war in Florida; Seminoles and Creeks; etc.

131. Report on Organization of the Army. 8 July.
HR 904, 27-2, v4, 4p. [410]
Florida war; Indians on the western frontier.

132. R-P of T. Stone. 14 July.
SD 351, 27-2, v5, 1p. [399]
Choctaw nation; 1814-15.

133. R-P of J. Burcham. 21 July.
HR 914, 27-2, v4, 1p. [410]
Wayne's Indian campaign; Revolutionary War.

134. R-P of J. Peak. 21 July.
HR 922, 27-2, v4, 1p. [410]
Indian hostilities of 1815 in Missouri.

135. Report on Bill to Pay for Soldiers' Horses. 21 July.
HR 929, 27-2, v4, 3p. [410]
Seminole wars of 1818 and 1836; Black Hawk war of 1832.

136. R-P of W. McLane. 21 July.
HR 933, 27-2, v4, 1p. [410]
Seminole war.

137. Message on Relations Between the U.S. and Texas. 22 July.
HD 271, 27-2, v5, 6p. [405]
Indian depredations across the border.

138. R-M of J. Phillips. 27 July.
SD 377, 27-2, v5, 1p. [399]
Creek war of 1814.

139. R-P of R. Poindexter. 27 July.
HR 947, 27-2, v5, 1p. [411]
Indian wars under Wilkinson and Wayne; 1791-94.

140. Report on the Cherokee Indians. 29 July.
HR 960, 27-2, v5, 5p. [411]
On the Sec. of War's refusal to report on the investigation of frauds concerning the Cherokees.

141. R-P of I. Van Camp. 29 July.
HR 980, 27-2, v5, 2p. [411]
Indians at Fort Valverde in 1779 or 1780; New York; Mohawk River.

142. R-M of Stockbridge Indians. 30 July.
HR 961, 27-2, v5, 3p. [411]
Recommends said Indians be admitted to become citizens of the U.S.; Menomonie lands in Wisconsin.

143. R-M of D. Welch. 8 Aug.
SD 399, 27-2, v5, 2p. [399]
A Stockbridge Indian, wounded at Fort George in 1813.

144. Claims of J. Hernandez and Gen. Clinch. 10 Aug.
HD 283, 27-2, v5, 181p. [405]
Property destroyed and impressed by troops in the Florida campaign.

145. Report on the Court of Inquiry into the Case of Lieut. Brant. 15 Aug.

HR 996, 27-2, v5, 214p. [411]
Disbursing agent for the Indian Dept.

146. Petition of Citizens of Pennsylvania. 19 Aug.
SD 427, 27-2, v5, 1p. [399]
Gen. Wayne's campaign against the northwestern Indians.

147. R-P of J. Patrick. 20 Aug.
HR 1016, 27-2, v5, 2p. [411]
Pottawatomie Indians; Michigan; 1832; Sac war of 1832.

148. R-P of W. Pedon. 20 Aug.
HR 1017, 27-2, v5, 4p. [411]
Removal of the Cherokees in 1838; North Carolina militia.

149. R-P of E. Duvall. 20 Aug.
HR 1034, 27-2, v5, 1p. [411]
Agent for the Cherokee removal.

150. Report on Caddo Indian Treaty. 20 Aug.
HR 1035, 27-2, v5, 129p. [411]
On conflicting claims surrounding the treaty of 1 July 1835.

151. R-P of W. Henry. 20 Aug.
HR 1039, 27-2, v5, 1p. [411]
Winnebago depredations of 1827 in Wisconsin.

152. R-P of P. Parsons. 20 Aug.
HR 1062, 27-2, v5, 2p. [411]
Indian campaign of 1779.

153. R-P of J. McKinley. 20 Aug.
HR 1064, 27-2, v5, 1p. [411]
Killed by Indians at Sandusky, Ohio in 1782.

154. Report on Pensions to Soldiers in Wayne's Campaign. 22 Aug.
SD 433, 27-2, v5, 1p. [399]
Against northwestern Indians.

155. R-P of W. Wootten. 22 Aug.
SD 434, 27-2, v5, 2p. [399]
Indian hostilities of 1836 in Alabama.

156. Report on Removal of the Cherokees. 27 Aug.
HR 1098, 27-2, v5, 100p. [411]
On claims surrounding removal; report of General Scott; statement of moneys paid Cherokees since the treaty of 1835; union between Eastern and Western Cherokees; constitution and laws of Cherokee Nation; etc.

157. Statement of Appropriations. 10 Oct.
SD 444, 27-2, v5, 47p. [399] *or* HD 293, 27-2, v5, 37p. [405]
During the 2d session, 27th Congress; Indian expenses.

158. Annual Message to Congress with Documents; Pres. Tyler. 7 Dec.
SD 1, 27-3, v1, 767p. [413] *or* HD 2, 27-3, v1, 767p. [418]
Indian hostilities in Florida; annual report of the Sec. of War; annual report of the CIA, including education, civilization, trust funds, populations, expenditures, and reports of agents and Supts.; etc.

159. Report on Extra Pay to Army Officers. 13 Dec.
HD 6, 27-3, v1, 56p. [418]
Services as treaty com'rs, agents of removal, etc.; list of said services.

160. Estimates of Appropriations. 15 Dec.
HD 16, 27-3, v2, 200p. [419]
For first six months of 1843 and fiscal year ending 30 June 1844; list of Indian appropriations, treaties, etc.

161. Annual Report of the Sec. of the Treasury. 19 Dec.
SD 5, 27-3, v2, 104p. [414] *or* HD 17, 27-3, v2, 104p. [419]
Indian expenses.

162. Annual Report of the Com'r of the General Land Office. 20 Dec.
SD 10, 27-3, v2, 110p. [414]
Indian land cessions.

163. R-P of W. Dwight. 27 Dec.
HR 6, 27-3, v1, 4p. [426]
Obtaining deeds from Indian tribes for land in Michigan.

164. R-P of J. Hunt. 29 Dec.
HR 12, 27-3, v1, 3p. [426]
Ottawa Indians.

165. Report on the Northern Boundary of Missouri. 31 Dec.
HD 38, 27-3, v3, 43p. [420]
Indian boundary line; Sac and Fox treaty of 1824; etc.

1843

1. Explanations of Appropriations to 30 June 1844. 4 Jan.
HD 39, 27-3, v3, 20p. [420]
Indian Office.

2. R-P of C. Waldron. 4 Jan.
HR 20, 27-3, v1, 2p. [426]
Florida Indian war in 1836.

3. R-P of J. White. 4 Jan.
HR 22, 27-3, v1, 3p. [426]
Indian hostilities of 1777 in Pennsylvania.

4. Report on Establishment of Military Posts from Council Bluffs to the Pacific. 4 Jan.
HR 31, 27-3, v1, 78p. [426]
Indian trade; control of hostilities; foreign contact with Indians.

5. R-P of G. Johnston. 5 Jan.
HR 24, 27-3, v1, 2p. [426]
Claim for Indian supplies; trader to Shawnees prior to the 1831 treaty.

6. R-C of D. Hughes et al. 7 Jan.
HD 42, 27-3, v3, 2p. [420]
Emigrating Creek Indians.

7. R-P of S. Grice. 9 Jan.
SD 37, 27-3, v2, 4p. [414]
Florida war of 1836; Indian hostilities.

8. Resol. of the Alabama Legis. 10 Jan.
HD 46, 27-3, v3, 1p. [420]
Creek land cession of 1832.

9. Report on Choctaw and Chickasaw Land Sales. 10 Jan.
HR 36, 27-3, v1, 1p. [426]
Mississippi; Choctaw cession of 1830; Chickasaw cession of 1834.

10. On the Case of J. Peak. 13 Jan.
SD 61, 27-3, v2, 1p. [414]
Indian engagement of 1815 in Missouri.

11. Mem. of the Indiana Gen. Assembly. 16 Jan.
SD 77, 27-3, v3, 2p. [415]
Extend pensions to those who served in Indian campaigns prior to the treaty of Greenville in 1795.

12. Report on Expenditures from the Chickasaw Fund. 17 Jan.
HD 65, 27-3, v3, 83p. [420]
Statement for 1833-43; expense of surveys of ceded lands.

13. Report on Public Land Sales. 18 Jan.
SD 85, 27-3, v3, 2p. [415]
In Ohio and Michigan; proceeds to go to the Indian tribes under treaty stipulations.

14. Employees in Indian Dept. 19 Jan.
HD 76, 27-3, v3, 13p. [420]
During 1842.

15. R-P of J. Haas. 19 Jan.
HR 69, 27-3, v1, 5p. [426]
Indian land title, Pottawatomie treaty of 20 Oct. 1832.

16. R-P of S. Mayfield. 19 Jan.
HR 71, 27-3, v1, 1p. [426]
Indian campaign of 1812.

17. Report on Creek Indian Claims. 21 Jan.
HD 80, 27-3, v3, 52p. [420]
From Quartermaster-Gen. Jesup; copy of treaty of 24 Mar. 1832; correspondence, etc., from the periods of the war of 1836, and of the removal, also in 1836.

18. Report on Boundary Line Between Missouri and Iowa. 21 Jan.
HR 86, 27-3, v1, 11p. [426]
Recommends adoption of Indian boundary line.

19. On the Relief of S. Neely. 23 Jan.
SD 100, 27-3, v3, 1p. [415]
Indian battle at Fort Recovery in 1794.

20. R-P of J. Monroe. 24 Jan.
HR 88, 27-3, v1, 5p. [426]
Florida Indian depredations of 1839.

21. R-P of I. Cormack. 24 Jan.
HR 91, 27-3, v1, 2p. [426]
Indian campaign of 1813 in Illinois.

22. Mem. of D. Taylor, G. Morris, and J. Rogers. 26 Jan.
HD 93, 27-3, v3, 6p. [420]
Cherokee treaty of 1835-36.

23. R-P of J. Hernandez. 26 Jan.
HR 104, 27-3, v1, 56p. [426]
Seminole war of 1835-37.

24. R-P of W. Barnes. 26 Jan.
HR 105, 27-3, v1, 1p. [426]
Indian battle near Fort Washington; 1792; Northwestern territory.

25. Appropriations for Fulfilling Treaty Stipulations. 28 Jan.
HD 99, 27-3, v3, 13p. [420]
Until 1 July 1844; Miami. Comanche, Delaware, Choctaw, Seneca, Cayuga, Onondaga, Oneida, Tuscarora, Munsee, St. Regis, Stockbridge, and Brothertown Indian treaties.

26. Expense of Negotiating Indian Treaties. 28 Jan.
HD 101, 27-3, v3, 8p. [420]
Explains drafts of Governor Doty, treaty com'r; Sioux, Winnebago, Sac, and Fox negotiations.

27. R-P of S. Enocks. 28 Jan.
HR 118, 27-3, v1, 1p. [426]
Sac and Fox war of 1832.

28. Report on Chickasaw Indian Trust Fund. 1 Feb.
HD 107, 27-3, v3, 4p. [420]
For 1842.

29. Message on Cherokee Claims Com'rs. 1 Feb.
HD 110, 27-3, v4, 8p. [421]
Instructions to com'rs; estimates of cost of establishing and maintaining agencies at various points; treaty of 29 Dec. 1835.

30. R-M of M. Murry. 3 Feb.
HR 137, 27-3, v1, 1p. [426]
Secretary to the Cherokee delegation that signed the treaty of 6 May 1828 in Washington.

31. On the Relief of W. Depeyster and H. Cruger. 3 Feb.
HR 146, 27-3, v1, 3p. [426]
Removal of Seminoles to Arkansas; Florida war.

32. Report on Appropriations of War Dept. 4 Feb.
HD 115, 27-3, v4, 19p. [421]
For 1842; Indian expenses.

33. Protection of Western Frontier of Arkansas. 6 Feb.
SD 127, 27-3, v3, 1p. [415]
Asks increased force to control Indian hostilities.

34. R-P of C. Atwater. 6 Feb.
HR 151, 27-3, v2, 2p. [427]
For negotiating Indian treaty at Prairie du Chien in 1829; Winnebago and other tribes.

35. Report on a Site for the Western Armory. 9 Feb.
HD 133, 27-3, v4, 424p. [421]
Summary report (p. 408) indicates that vulnerability to Indian attack was a major criterion in site selection.

36. Report on Settling Oregon. 9 Feb.
HR 157, 27-3, v2, 8p. [427]
Indian trade.

37. R-P of Wyandot Indians in Ohio. 9 Feb.
HR 160, 27-3, v2, 8p. [427]
On change of location of lands granted said Indians; treaty of 17 Mar. 1842.

38. R-P of C. Wallace. 14 Feb.
HR 175, 27-3, v2, 4p. [427]
Indian boundary line established by the treaty of Greenville, Ohio.

39. R-P of J. Bulow, jr. 14 Feb.
HR 176, 27-3, v2, 16p. [427]
Seminole Indian war.

40. R-M of the U.S. Bank. 14 Feb.
HR 177, 27-3, v2, 11p. [427]
On claim for contract to remove Cherokee Indians.

41. On the Cases of E. Dewey et al. 16 Feb.
HR 181, 27-3, v2, 2p. [427]
Burning of Royalton by the Indians in 1780.

42. Report on a Survey of Grand and Spring Rivers. 16 Feb.
HR 186, 27-3, v2, 2p. [427]
Indians inhabiting the country along the rivers; Missouri.

43. R-P of R. Brumfield. 16 Feb.
HR 193, 27-3, v2, 1p. [427]
Indian engagement of 1814 at the rapids of the Mississippi River.

44. Disbursements by Indian Agents. 18 Feb.
HD 162, 27-3, v5, 149p. [422]
From 1 Oct. 1841 to 30 Sept. 1842.

45. R-P of S. Campbell. 21 Feb.
SD 198, 27-3, v4, 1p. [416]
For money and lands under treaty with Sioux Indians in Sept. of 1837.

46. R-P of Administrator of W. Hunter. 21 Feb.
SD 199, 27-3, v4, 2p. [416]
For expenses in negotiating a treaty with Wyandot Indians in 1839.

47. Report on Sac and Fox Indian Reservation. 22 Feb.
HR 198, 27-3, v2, 1p. [427]
Favors survey for establishing boundary; treaty of 4 Aug. 1824; Iowa.

48. R-P of J. Crane. 22 Feb.
HR 200, 27-3, v2, 2p. [427]
Creek Indians; 1794.

49. R-P of G. Carpenter. 22 Feb.
HR 206, 27-3, v2, 2p. [427]
Black Hawk war; 1832; western frontier of Michigan.

50. R-P of Langtry and Jenkins. 22 Feb.
HR 210, 27-3, v2, 1p. [427]
Breach of contract by U.S.; Cherokee removal under the treaty of New Echota.

51. Report on a Reduction of Officers in the Army. 22 Feb.
HR 220, 27-3, v2, 13p. [427]
Black Hawk and Florida wars; Indian hostilities and removal.

52. Report on the State of the Finances. 22 Feb.

HR 227, 27-3, v2, 13p. [427]
Indian Dept., and Indian expenses.

53. R-P of the Reps. of J. Younglove. 22 Feb.
HR 258, 27-3, v2, 1p. [427]
British and Indians; 1775; New York.

54. Report on Public Expenditures, Revenue, and Debt. 25 Feb.
SD 229, 27-3, v4, 9p. [416]
Indian Dept.; Chiecksaw fund.

55. Message on Frauds on Cherokee Indians. 25 Feb.
HD 219, 27-3, v8, 216p. [425]
Report of Major Hitchcock; special Com'r; this report had been withheld by the Executive in 1842; emigrated Indians west of the Mississippi River.

56. Report on Message of the Pres. Regarding Frauds upon Indians. 25 Feb.
HR 271, 27-3, v3, 229p. [428]
Right of Pres. to withhold papers denied; Cherokee Indians.

57. R-P of L. Bingham. 28 Feb.
SD 235, 27-3, v4, 1p. [416]
Property stolen by the Pottawatomie Indians in 1836.

58. Report on Pensioning a Creek Indian Woman. 28 Feb.
HR 274, 27-3, v3, 4p. [428]
Creek war of 1818.

59. R-P of E. Duvall. 1 Mar.
HR 281, 27-3, v3, 4p. [428]
Claim to land of Cherokee Indians; treaty of 6 May 1828.

60. Indian Civilization Fund. 2 Mar.
HD 203, 27-3, v6, 42p. [423]
Disbursements from 3 Mar. 1819 to 8 Feb. 1842.

61. R-C of G. Hinant. 2 Mar.
HR 286, 273, v4, 3p. [429]
Cherokee Indian Claim Commission, treaty of 1835-36.

62. Report on Removal of Cherokees. 2 Mar.
HR 288, 27-3, v4, 70p. [429]
Papers, correspondence, and statements on said removal.

63. Report on Issue of $200,000,000 Stock. 2 Mar.
HR 296, 27-3, v4, 574p. [429]
Includes payments to Indian tribes; Indian trust funds; etc.

64. Fremont's Expedition to the Rocky Mountains. 3 Mar.
SD 243, 27-3, v4, 207p. [416]
Kanza, Pawnee, Cheyenne, Sioux, and other Indian tribes.

65. Report on Chickasaw Ceded Lands. 3 Mar.
HD 213, 27-3, v7, 5p. [424]
Area of cession of 1832; amount of lands sold, reserved, and unsold to 30 June 1842.

66. Appropriations. 3 Mar.
HD 218, 27-3, v8, 40p. [425]
For half year ending 30 June 1843; Indian expenses.

67. Report on Pay to Officers of the Creek and Seminole Wars. 3 Mar.
HR 287, 27-3, v4, 12p. [429]
For fuel and quarters.

68. Report on Sales, etc., of Public Land. 24 Apr.
SD 246, 27-3, v4, 47p. [416]
Indian trust funds, land cessions, etc.

69. Annual Message to Congress with Documents; Pres. Tyler. 5 Dec.
SD 1, 28-1, v1, 703p. [431] *or* HD 2, 28-1, v1, 726p. [439]
Relations with Indian tribes; annual report of the Sec. of War; annual report of the CIA, including conditions of Indians, treaties, use of liquor, education, populations, appropriations, trust funds, school, agent, and Supt. reports; etc.

70. Additional Appropriations. 7 Dec.
HD 5, 28-1, v1, 4p. [439]
For the year ending 30 June 1844; Indian expenses.

71. Estimates of Appropriations. 7 Dec.
HD 6, 28-1, v1, 123p. [439]
For the year ending 30 June 1845; Indian expenses.

72. Annual Report of the Sec. of the Treasury. 11 Dec.
SD 3, 28-1, v2, 50p. [432] *or* HD 7, 28-1, v1, 50p. [439]
Indian expenses.

73. Special Message of Cherokee Awards. 18 Dec.
HD 22, 28-1, v3, 2p. [441]
Reasons for withholding signature to joint resol. directing payment of said awards under treaty stipulations.

74. Mem. of the Missouri Gen. Assembly. 22 Dec.
HD 25, 28-1, v3, 2p. [441]
Against conversion of a regiment of dragoons to a regiment of in-

fantry; mounted force necessary to control Indians.

75. Mem. of the Missouri Gen. Assembly. 22 Dec.
HD 30, 28-1, v3, 2p. [441]
Ask for the establishment of an additional military post on their western frontier to balance the increase of the Indian population due to the government's policy of removal.

76. Annual Report of the Com'r of the General Land Office. 29 Dec.
SD 15, 28-1, v2, 154p. [432] *or* HD 37, 28-1, v3, 158p. [441]
Indian land cessions and treaties.

1844

1. R-P of B. Crawford. 8 Jan.
SD 27, 28-1, v2, 1p. [432]
From the Com. on Indian Affairs.

2. Report on Treaties with Chippewa Indians. 12 Jan.
HR 27, 28-1, v1, 2p. [445]
Provisions for sale of lands; treaties of 14 Jan. 1837, and 23 Jan. 1838.

3. Report on Mineral Lands of the Upper Mississippi River. 13 Jan.
HD 43, 28-1, v3, 52p. [441]
Lands surrounding Lake Superior, etc., occupied by Indians.

4. R-M of J. Crane. 16 Jan.
HR 30, 28-1, v1, 2p. [445]
Creek hostilities of 1793-94.

5. Report on Land Sales at Chocchuma and Columbus, Mississippi. 16 Jan.
HR 34, 28-1, v1, 1p. [445]
Indemnity to Chickasaw Nation for land sold as Choctaw lands; Choctaw and Chickasaw cessions.

6. R-P of W. Browning and J. Skinner. 16 Jan.
HR 36, 28-1, v1, 3p. [445]
Title to land located in name of Alabatcha, a Choctaw woman; treaty of 30 Sept. 1830 at Dancing Rabbit Creek.

7. R-P of A. Read. 16 Jan.
HR 48, 28-1, v1, 1p. [445]
Indian engagement of 1774 at the mouth of the Big Kenhawa.

8. R-P of J. Hernandez. 19 Jan.
HR 58, 28-1, v1, 75p. [445]
Seminole Indians; 1835-37; including a minority report.

9. Report on Employees in Indian Dept. 23 Jan.
HD 69, 28-1, v3, 11p. [441]
During 1843.

10. R-O of C. Bogard. 23 Jan.
HR 64, 28-1, v1, 2p. [445]
Hostile Indians in Indiana; 1813.

11. Report on a Railroad in Florida. 24 Jan.
SD 62, 28-1, v2, 20p. [432]
Experiences in the Seminole war of 1837-38 would indicate the need of this supply route.

12. Message on Florida Indians. 27 Jan.
HD 82, 28-1, v4, 11p. [442]
On the number of Indians remaining in Florida and measures for their removal.

13. Report on Remounting Second Regiment of Dragoons. 27 Jan.
HR 77, 28-1, v1, 11p. [445]
Frontier exposure; superiority of cavalry in Indian warfare; additional force required; military posts; extent of frontier; cost.

14. R-P of Indiana Citizens. 29 Jan.
SD 65, 28-1, v2, 1p. [432]
British and Indian war.

15. R-P of D. Skinner. 29 Jan.
SD 67, 28-1, v2, 3p. [432]
Indian hostilities of 1836 in Alabama.

16. R-P of W. Thompson. 31 Jan.
HR 85, 28-1, v1, 1p. [445]
Horse lost in battle with Indians; 1812; Ohio.

17. R-P of C. Johnson. 31 Jan.
HR 106, 28-1, v1, 1p. [445]
Indian agent in Pennsylvania.

18. R-P of Heirs of J. Jones. 31 Jan.
HR 115, 28-1, v1, 3p. [445]
On land granted in Virginia by Six Nations; treaty of 1768.

19. On the Relief of G. and R. Allen. 31 Jan.
HR 121, 28-1, v1, 2p. [445]
Land reserved under Pottawatomie Indian treaty of 26 Oct. 1832.

20. Resol. of the Ohio Legis. 5 Feb.
SD 86, 28-1, v2, 2p. [432] *or* HD 105, 28-1, v4, 2p. [442]
Wyandot lands; removal.

21. Report on Expenditures of War Dept. 7 Feb.
SD 99, 28-1, v2, 23p. [432] *or* HD 114, 28-1, v4, 20p. [442]
For 1843; Indian expenses.

22. R-C of Heirs of W. Walker. 8 Feb.
SD 109, 28-1, v3, 2p. [433]
For services in connection with Creek Indians; 1827 delegation to Washington.

23. R-P of J. Washington. 9 Feb.
SD 111, 28-1, v3, 1p. [433]
Service against Indians in 1790.

24. R-P of J. Campau. 9 Feb.
SD 113, 28-1, v3, 4p. [433]
Land in Michigan; records destroyed by British and Indians.

25. R-P of J. Campau, Assignee. 9 Feb.
SD 114, 28-1, v3, 4p. [433]
For a section of land in compliance with the treaty of Saginaw; 24 Sept. 1819; Chippewa Indians.

26. Report on the Chickasaw Fund. 9 Feb.
HD 115, 28-1, v4, 5p. [442]
Statement of expenditures and condition of same.

27. R-M of the Kentucky Legis. 15 Feb.
SD 127, 28-1, v3, 4p. [433]
Shawnee hostilities in 1782; Wayne's campaign against the Indians in 1794.

28. R-P of J. Thomas. 15 Feb.
HR 129, 28-1, v1, 3p. [445]
Indian battle ("Dudley's defeat") of 1813.

29. R-P of J. Watson. 15 Feb.
HR 132, 28-1, v1, 4p. [445]
Slaves of Seminole Indians taken by Creek warriors, sold by them to Watson, and then returned to the Seminoles.

30. R-P of C. Gibson. 15 Feb.
HR 133, 28-1, v1, 2p. [445]
Seminole war; 1839; Florida.

31. Report on School Lands in Alabama. 15 Feb.
HR 145, 28-1, v1, 1p. [445]
On reserving lands for education in the Chickasaw cession; treaty of 24 May 1834.

32. Report on Pensioning an Indian Woman. 15 Feb.
HR 149, 28-1, v1, 5p. [445]
Daughter of a celebrated Creek prophet, Francis; saved life of American citizen taken prisoner in 1818; Creek war of 1817-18.

33. R-C of G. Wallis. 15 Feb.
HR 150, 28-1, v1, 1p. [445]
Sac, Fox, Iowa depredations; supply contract for the Sac, Fox, Iowa, and Pottawatomie Indians.

34. R-P of G. Kelly. 16 Feb.
HR 189, 28-1, v1, 1p. [445]
Indian campaigns under Gens. Harmar and Wayne.

35. Mem. of J. Claiborne. 19 Feb.
HD 137, 28-1, v4, 6p. [442]
Action of Choctaw Commission; frauds contemplated; repeal of law creating Choctaw board, provision to satisfy claims, and speedy removal of Indians urged.

36. R-P of J. Bryan and H. and B. Young. 20 Feb.
SD 132, 28-1, v3, 1p. [432]
Lands bought from Creek Indians in 1836.

37. Report on the Evacuation of Fort Wayne. 22 Feb.
SD 136, 28-1, v3, 4p. [433]
The fort was not needed near the Cherokees; troops moved near the Osages.

38. R-P of J. Custer. 28 Feb.
HR 245, 28-1, v1, 2p. [445]
Seminole war; 1837; Florida.

39. R-M of Heirs of J. Forsyth. 7 Mar.
HR 260, 28-1, v1, 2p. [445]
Creek Indian war of 1836 in Georgia.

40. Report on Occupants of Wyandot Indian Lands. 7 Mar.
HR 279, 28-1, v1, 1p. [445]
Land recently ceded to the U.S.

41. Message on Indian Affairs. 8 Mar.
SD 168, 28-1, v3, 224p. [433]
Proceedings of the Choctaw Commission under the Dancing Rabbit Creek treaty of 27 Sept. 1830.

42. R-P of Langtry and Jenkins. 8 Mar.
HR 291, 28-1, v1, 1p. [445]
Supplies to Cherokee Indians; removal; treaty of New Echota.

43. R-P of R. Evans. 8 Mar.
HR 293, 28-1, v1, 1p. [445]
British and Indians; 1813; New York.

44. Report on Claims for Horses Lost in Service. 8 Mar.
HR 295, 28-1, v1, 2p. [445]
Laws passed since the Black Hawk war.

45. On the Relief for B. Murphy. 9 Mar.
HR 307, 28-1, v1, 3p. [445]
Settled on land ceded to the Cherokee Indians; land relinquished; stock detained by Cherokees; recommends payment out of Cherokee annuity.

46. Report on Oregon Territory. 12 Mar.
HR 308, 28-1, v1, 24p. [445]
Control of Indian hostilities and trade; foreign interference with Indians within the U.S.

47. R-P of S. Steele and J. Daniel. 13 Mar.
SD 189, 28-1, v4, 3p. [434]
Land purchased under Creek treaty of 9 Aug. 1814.

48. Report on Cherokee Indians. 16 Mar.
SD 229, 28-1, v4, 11p. [434]
Condition of tribe; schools; funds; evils complained of; expenditure of treaty fund; representation in Congress.

49. On the Case of M. Wilson. 18 Mar.
HR 340, 28-1, v1, 1p. [445]
Indian campaigns 1762-80.

50. R-P of H. Thompson. 19 Mar.
SD 204, 28-1, v4, 1p. [434]
French and Indian war; 1757.

51. Report on Appropriations for Florida War. 19 Mar.
HD 184, 28-1, v5, 3p. [443]
Statement of balances and request for their reappropriation; Seminoles.

52. Report on Division of U.S. into Two Military Districts.
HR 341, 28-1, v1, 29p. [445]
Indians on the western frontier.

53. R-M of H. Barney. 20 Mar.
SD 209, 28-1, v4, 6p. [434]
Sac and Fox half-breed reservation; treaty of 4 Aug. 1824.

54. R-P of N. Egnew. 23 Mar.
HR 345, 28-1, v1, 1p. [445]
Property destroyed by Indians in war of 1812.

55. R-P of J. Bryan. 27 Mar.
HR 359, 28-1, v2, 4p. [446]
Wyandot Indian treaty negotiations in 1836.

56. Report on Removal of Winnebago Indians. 27 Mar.
HR 363, 28-1, v2, 11p. [446]
Includes mem. of Iowa Legis.; the "neutral grounds", claims of Sac, Fox, Sioux, and other Indians; removal from said ground recommended.

57. R-M of Maj. Taliaferro. 27 Mar.
HR 365, 28-1, v2, 2p. [446]
Indian agent at St. Peter's agency; 1818-39.

58. R-P of E. Pickrell. 27 Mar.
HR 369, 28-1, v2, 1p. [446]
Claims for money borrowed by Shawnee chiefs.

59. R-M of T. Talbot. 27 Mar.
HR 370, 28-1, v2, 3p. [446]
Items stolen by Pawnee Indians; 1827.

60. Report on Trade and Commerce on the Upper Mississippi River. 29 Mar.
SD 242, 28-1, v4, 10p. [434]
Supplies to the Winnebago, Sac, Fox, and Sioux Indians.

61. On the Relief for H. Heth. 29 Mar.
HR 388, 28-1, v2, 2p. [446]
Pottawatomie depredations in 1836.

62. Report on Claims Under Cherokee Treaty. 29 Mar.
HR 391, 28-1, v2, 83p. [446]
Treaty stipulations; action of first board of com'rs; second board of com'rs exceeded its authority and violated instructions; immediate payment of claims adjudicated by it not advisable; minority report.

63. R-M of J. Eldred. 1 Apr.
SD 260, 28-1, v4, 27p. [434]
Purchase of the "copper rock of Lake Superior" from the Chippewas.

64. Resol. of the Ohio Legis. 1 Apr.
HD 218, 28-1, v5, 1p. [443]
Appropriations from the proceeds garnered in the sale of Wyandot lands.

65. Mem. of the American Indian Mission Association. 5 Apr.
SD 272, 28-1, v4, 3p. [434]
Ask establishment of boundaries of Indian Territory; providing for general council and representation by agents in Washington.

66. R-P of E. Swan. 9 Apr.
SD 283, 28-1, v4, 1p. [434]
Indian hostilities in 1796.

67. R-P of R. Barclay. 9 Apr.
SD 288, 28-1, v4, 1p. [434]
Indian hostilities of 1814 in Missouri.

68. On the Case of B. Dell. 9 Apr.
HR 410, 28-1, v2, 3p. [446]
Indian war in Florida.

69. Report on School Lands in Ohio. 9 Apr.
HR 412, 28-1, v2, 1p. [446]
Indian treaty.

70. R-P of I. Ketchum. 10 Apr.
HR 421, 28-1, v2, 2p. [446]
Special agent for Chippewa, Ottawa, and Pottawatomie removal; payment from their annuities of expenses incurred by a deputation to Washington.

71. R-C of I. Ketchum. 10 Apr.
HR 422, 28-1, v2, 1p. [446]
For provisions furnished Chippewa, Ottawa, and Pottawatomie Indians while they removed west of the Mississippi River.

72. R-C of H. Commager. 10 Apr.
HR 424, 28-1, v2, 1p. [446]
Ottawa Indians; removal.

73. R-P of J. Nourse. 10 Apr.
HR 425, 28-2, v2, 5p. [446]
Seminole war; 1836; Florida.

74. R-P of D. Robb. 15 Apr.
SD 301, 28-1, v5, 1p. [435]
Subagent for Shawnee and Delaware Indians in Ohio.

75. R-P of Stockbridge Indians. 15 Apr.
SD 302, 28-1, v5, 1p. [435]
Division of trust fund.

76. R-P of F. St. Vrain et al. 16 Apr.
SD 311, 28-1, v5, 2p. [435]
Illinois in 1832; agent for the Winnebagoes; Sac, and Fox (Black Hawk) war.

77. Mem. of the Cherokee Indians. 17 Apr.
HD 234, 28-1, v5, 32p. [443]
Expenditures under treaty of 1835; misappropriation of funds; action of Cherokee council on J. Ross; relations of Eastern and Western Cherokees; payment of money due heads of families and geographcal separation of parties asked.

78. Mem. of Cherokee Chief, J. Rogers, et al. 17 Apr.
HD 235, 28-1, v5, 36p. [443]
Their history; relations to Eastern Cherokees; injustice of treaty of 1835; conduct of Ross party; title of Western Cherokees exclusive; no union with Eastern band; action of Congress protecting their rights asked.

79. R-M of Shawnee Indians. 19 Apr.
SD 319, 28-1, v5, 3p. [435]
Distribution of trust fund.

80. Report on Entry of Lands in Mississippi. 20 Apr.
HR 447, 28-1, v2, 2p. [446]
Choctaw cession of 1830; Chickasaw cession under the treaty of Oct. 1832 at Pontotoc; boundary between cessions confused.

81. Report on Indian Disbursements. 23 Apr.
HD 240, 28-1, v5, 135p. [443]
Moneys paid for Indian service; 1842-43.

82. Report on Pre-emption. 2 May.
HR 456, 28-1, v2, 1p. [446]
Lands acquired by treaty from the Miami Indians; Indiana.

83. Report on the Great Western Railway Company. 2 May.
HR 467, 28-1, v2, 4p. [446]
Defense of the western fontier against Indian hostilities.

84. Report on Settlers. 2 May.
HR 468, 28-1, v2, 2p. [446]
On lands acquired from the Miami and Pottawatomie Indians.

85. Report on Indian School Fund. 4 May.
HD 247, 28-1, v5, 51p. [443]
Amount of expenditure of funds from 1819; amount belonging to each tribe.

86. Report on Persons Employed Without Authority of Law. 9 May.
HD 250, 28-1, v6, 68p. [444]
Office of Indian Affairs since 4 Mar. 1837.

87. Report on Indians Remaining in Florida. 9 May.
HD 253, 28-1, v6, 19p. [444]
Correspondence on their conduct, number, removal, etc.

88. R-P of J. McIntosh. 10 May.
SD 332, 28-1, v5, 2p. [435]
Indian war in Florida.

89. R-P of R. Paris. 15 May.
HR 486, 28-1, v2, 2p. [446]
Miami Indian depredations in 1832-33.

90. R-P of J. Robinson. 24 May.
HR 499, 28-1, v2, 2p. [446]
British and Indians; 1813.

91. R-P of J. Estes. 24 May.
HR 500, 28-1, v2, 9p. [446]
Sac and Fox (Black Hawk) war of 1832 in Illinois.

92. R-M of M. Thompson. 24 May.
HR 511, 28-1, v2, 2p. [446]
Black Hawk war; Florida Indian war in 1837.

93. R-P of S. Neely. 28 May.
HR 517, 28-1, v3, 2p. [447]
Indian battle of 1794 at Fort Recovery.

94. Report on the Removal of the Chippewa, Ottawa, and Pottawatomie Indians. 29 May.
HR 519, 28-1, v3, 8p. [447]
Treaty of Sept. 1833; attacks on said Indians by the Sioux; negotiation of another treaty.

95. R-P of H. Chouteau. 3 June.
SD 350, 28-1, v6, 36p. [436]
"Dubuque Claim"; land on Mississippi River bought from Sac and Fox Indians in 1774; granted to Dubuque by Spanish Governor in 1796; approved by Land Com'r in 1806; recognized in treaties of 1804 and 1832 with the Sacs and Foxes; occupants of said land ejected by military power in 1833.

96. R-P of Heirs of J. Kennedy. 4 June.
SD 360, 28-1, v6, 3p. [436]
Creek Indians; 1813; Alabama.

97. On the Relief of J. McGuire. 4 June.
SD 362, 28-1, v6, 2p. [436]
Indian campaign of 1776 in North Carolina.

98. On the Relief of G. Gaines. 6 June.
SD 366, 28-1, v6, 4p. [436]
Choctaw Indians; treaty of Dancing Rabbit Creek.

99. R-C of Administrator of A. Pacheco. 7 June.
HR 523, 28-1, v3, 5p. [447]
Slave of Pacheco hired as interpreter during Florida war; captured by Seminole Indians; recaptured; return to owner refused by commanding officer; sent west with Seminoles; payment for said slave recommended.

100. R-P of J. and L. Ward. 7 June.
HR 529, 28-1, v3, 2p. [447]
Removal of Pottawatomie Indians from Illinois and Michigan.

101. On the Relief for D. Robb. 7 June.
HR 533, 28-1, v3, 3p. [447]
Indian agent claims pay for expenses in visiting Washington, and for extra services in connection with Seneca and Shawnee treaties; agent for removal.

102. R-M of Shawnee Chiefs. 7 June.
HR 541, 28-1, v3, 13p. [447]
Shawnee trust funds; debt; payment to chiefs of balance due volunteers in Seminole war.

103. On the Relief of Besiah, an Indian. 7 June.
HR 542, 28-1, v3, 2p. [447]
Pottawatomie treaty of 27 Oct. 1832.

104. Report on Georgia Militia Claims. 7 June.
HR 549, 28-1, v3, 1p. [447]
For expenses of Indian wars on the southern frontier.

105. R-P of A. Hunter. 14 June.
HR 569, 28-1, v3, 11p. [447]
Cherokee country; 1836.

106. Report on Appropriations. 25 July.
SD 406, 28-1, v7, 60p. [437] *or* HD 280, 28-1, v6, 63p. [444]
During the 1st session, 28th Congress; Indian expenses.

107. Annual Message to Congress with Documents; Pres. Tyler. 3 Dec.
SD 1, 28-2, v1, 702p. [449] *or* HD 2, 28-2, v1, 698p. [463]
Indian affairs; annual report of the Sec. of War; annual report of the CIA, including removal, land cessions, liquor, education, populations, and reports from schools, agents, and Supts.; etc.

108. Annual Report of the Sec. of the Treasury. 16 Dec.
SD 6, 28-2, v1, 35p. [449] *or* HD 16, 28-2, v1, 34p. [463]
Indian expenses.

109. Annual Report of the Com'r of the General Land Office. 16 Dec.
SD 7, 28-2, v1, 114p. [449] *or* HD 15, 28-2, v1, 118p. [463]
Indian treaties and land cessions.

110. Estimate of Appropriations. 16 Dec.
HD 17, 28-2, v1, 156p. [463]
For the year ending 30 June 1846; Indian expenses.

111. R-P of Langtry and Jenkins. 18 Dec.
HR 1, 28-2, v1, 3p. [468]
Cherokee removal; treaty of Dec. 1835 at New Echota.

1845

1. R-M of P. Chouteau, jr. 6 Jan.
SD 20, 28-2, v2, 36p. [450]
Sac and Fox lands in Iowa; "Dubuque Claim."

2. Report on Employees of the Indian Dept. 7 Jan.
HD 38, 28-2, v2, 9p. [464]
For 1844.

3. Nicollet's Report of the Hydrographical Basin of the Upper Mississippi River. 11 Jan.
HD 52, 28-2, v2, 170p. [464]

4. R-P of Econchatimico. 11 Jan.
HR 33, 28-2, v1, 3p. [468]
Indian chief from Florida; slaves stolen in Florida by Georgia citizens.
5. R-P of J. Fowler. 13 Jan.
SD 35, 28-2, v2, 1p. [450]
Indian expeditions from 1791 to the treaty of Greenville.
6. R-P of J. Grant. 13 Jan.
SD 37, 28-2, v2, 1p. [450]
Pensions for soldiers of Indian wars prior to 1794 (the treaty of Greenville).
7. Report on Chickasaw Trust Fund. 20 Jan.
SD 49, 28-2, v2, 6p. [450]
United States liable for interest on funds; recommends referring claims of mismanagement to Federal Courts; treaties of 1832 and 1834.
8. R-C of R. Gentry. 21 Jan.
SD 51, 28-2, v2, 5p. [450]
Sac and Fox; 1813 removal.
9. Petition of Ohio Citizens. 22 Jan.
SD 56, 28-2, v2, 2p. [450]
On settlement of Oregon to block British trade with Indians.
10. R-P of C. Allen. 28 Jan.
HR 52, 28-2, v1, 3p. [468]
Seneca peace negotiations.
11. On the Relief of the Heirs of J. Kennedy. 28 Jan.
HR 61, 28-2, v1, 9p. [468]
Creeks; Alabama; treaty of 9 Aug. 1814.
12. R-P of D. Farrer. 28 Jan.
HR 66, 28-2, v1, 2p. [468]
New York Indians; 1835.
13. R-P of G. Russell. 28 Jan.
HR 70, 28-2, v1, 1p. [468]
Cherokee in Georgia; 1835; enrollment prior to removal.
14. R-P of Captain Crozier's Tennessee Volunteers. 28 Jan.
HR 72, 28-2, v1, 1p. [468]
Removal of the Cherokees in 1836.
15. R-P of T. Bronough. 28 Jan.
HR 77, 28-2, v1, 2p. [468]
Taken prisoner by the Indians in 1813.
16. Report on Public Buildings. 28 Jan.
HR 89, 28-2, v1, 10p. [468]
Indian Office rooms.
17. Appropriations of the War Dept. 29 Jan.
HD 76, 28-2, v3, 25p. [465]
For 1843-44; Indian expenses.
18. Mem. of the American Indian Mission Association. 30 Jan.
SD 76, 28-2, v3, 3p. [451]
Fix boundaries of emigrated tribes in the west; increase appropriations for their benefit; provide for representation in Washington; etc.
19. Letter on Georgia Claims. 5 Feb.
HD 103, 28-2, v3, 104p. [465]
Militia services in the Seminole and Creek wars, and in Cherokee country.
20. Report on Contracts for Removal of Choctaws. 7 Feb.
SD 86, 28-2, v3, 53p. [451]
Copies of contracts, licenses to traders, etc.
21. Report on the Florida Militia. 7 Feb.
HR 108, 28-2, v1, 4p. [468]
Operations against Indians in 1835, before they were authorized by the United States.
22. Resol. of the North Carolina Legis. 8 Feb.
HD 106, 28-2, v3, 1p. [465]
Urge speedy settlement of Cherokee claims.
23. Report on Removal of Choctaw Indians. 8 Feb.
HD 107, 28-2, v3, 26p. [465]
Reasons for same; population of tribe; correspondence.
24. Mem. of Cherokee Chiefs. 10 Feb.
SD 90, 28-2, v3, 3p. [451]
On the property of Cherokees; treaties of 1817 and 1835.
25. Resol. of the Illinois Legis. 11 Feb.
HD 108, 28-2, v3, 1p. [465]
Militia services in Indian campaigns.
26. Report on Chickasaw Fund. 12 Feb.
HD 122, 28-2, v3, 4p. [465]
For the year 1844; treaties of 20 Oct. 1832 and 24 May 1834.
27. Report of the Mineral Agent on Lake Superior. 13 Feb.
SD 98, 28-2, v7, 5p. [456]
Chippewa treaty of Oct. 1842; cession of land, and removal.
28. Resol. of the Ohio Legis. 13 Feb.
HD 126, 28-2, v3, 1p. [465]
Wyandot land cesson .

29. Resol. of the Wisconsin Legis. 14 Feb.
SD 100, 28-2, v7, 1p. [456]
Urges extinguishment of Indian title to land north of the Fox River; Menomonie tribe.

30. R-P of S. Enochs. 15 Feb.
HR 125, 28-2, v1, 4p. [468]
Sac and Fox (Black Hawk) war; 1832; Illinois.

31. R-P of J. Davidson. 15 Feb.
HR 144, 28-2, v1, 1p. [468]
Chased by Indians in 1814.

32. R-M of T. Wright. 15 Feb.
HR 149, 28-2, v1, 2p. [468]
Seminole; 1840.

33. R-P of J. Francis. 15 Feb.
HR 150, 28-2, v1, 1p. [468]
Indian depredations.

34. Report on M. Bruner. 15 Feb.
HR 153, 28-2, v1, 2p. [468]
Prisoner of Indians.

35. Report on Indian Disbursements. 17 Feb.
HD 139, 28-2, v3, 122p. [465]
Year ending 30 September 1844.

36. R-M of F. Wood. 17 Feb.
HR 120, 28-2, v1, 4p. [468]
Cherokee trader; 1837; Arkansas.

37. R-P of H. Catlin. 18 Feb.
SD 106, 28-2, v7, 1p. [456]
Creek war; 1836.

38. Mem. of the Missouri Gen. Assembly. 19 Feb.
SD 110, 28-2, v7, 2p. [456]
Missouri-Iowa boundary, "Old Indian boundary line."

39. Report on the Lake Superior Mineral Lands. 20 Feb.
SD 117, 28-2, v7, 9p. [456]
Condition of the Indians at missions; discussion of Indian use of the region prior to ceding the land to the U.S.

40. On the Relief of F. Slocum and Children. 21 Feb.
SD 122, 28-2, v7, 4p. [456]
Authority to pay their annuities as Miami Indians in Indiana rather than west of the Mississippi River.

41. Report on Difficulties Among the Cherokees. 24 Feb.
SD 140, 28-2, v8, 143p. [457]
From United States Com'rs sent to investigate conditions in the West; recommend new treaty be made.

42. R-P of J. McClure and Company. 25 Feb.
HR 173, 28-2, v1, 1p. [468]
Loss of supplies for the Indians on the Mississippi River.

43. R-P of the Heirs of J. Gerard. 25 Feb.
HR 174, 28-2, v1, 10p. [468]
1792; Maumee.

44. R-P of R. Graham. 25 Feb.
HR 180, 28-2, v1, 3p. [468]
Indian traders in Kaskaskia.

45. R-P of I. Johnson. 25 Feb.
HR 183, 28-2, v1, 1p. [468]
Pottawatomies; 1833.

46. Report on National Edifices in Washington. 25 Feb.
HR 185, 28-2, v1, 24p. [468]
Indian Bureau rooms in proposed new War Dept. building.

47. Report on Chickasaw and Choctaw Funds. 1 Mar.
SD 160, 28-2, v9, 77p. [458]
Sends disposition of funds; correspondence; Chickasaw treaty of 1834; etc.

48. Report of Fremont's Expedition to the Rocky Mountains and the Pacific Coast. 3 Mar.
SD 174, 28-2, v11, 693p. [461] *or*
HD 166, 28-2, v4 (pt. 2), 583p. [467]
Includes descriptions of encounters with various Indians.

49. R-P of J. Smith and L. Pease. 3 Mar.
HR 191, 28-2, v1, 1p. [468]
Creek and Seminole depredations; Com'rs.

50. Report on the Choctaw Academy in Kentucky. 3 Mar.
HR 193, 28-2, v1, 13p. [468]
Information before the Committee studying alleged abuses.

51. R-P of Bent, St. Vrain and Company. 3 Mar.
HR 194, 28-2, v1, 9p. [468]
Pawnee depredations; 1838.

52. R-P of A. McCulloch. 3 Mar.
HR 196, 28-2, v1, 6p. [468]
Indian wars of 1689.

53. Report on Salaries of Persons Employed in Washington. 3 Mar.
HR 200, 28-2, v1, 21p. [468]
Includes office of CIA.

54. Report on Lake Superior Mineral Lands. 19 Mar.
SD 175, 29-sp, v11, 22p. [461]
Includes some information on Indians of the area.

55. Congressional Appropriations. 31 Mar.
SD 177, 28-2, v11, 54p. [461] *or*

HD 167, 28-2, v4 (pt. 2), 43p. [467]
Indian appropriations; for the 2d session, 28th Congress.

56. Annual Message to Congress with Documents; Pres. Polk. 2 Dec.
SD 1, 29-1, v1, 893p. [470] *or* HD 2, 29-1, v1, 892p. [480]
Indian Affairs; annual report of the Sec. of War; annual report of the CIA, including removal, treaties, expenditures, trust funds, education, populations, hostilities, and reports of schools, agents, and Supts.; etc.

57. Annual Report of the Sec. of the Treasury. 3 Dec.
SD 2, 29-1, v2, 957p. [471] *or* HD 6, 29-1, v2, 957p. [481]
Indian expenses; estimates for 1846-47.

58. Mem. of the Oregon Legis. 8 Dec.
SD 8, 29-1, v3, 3p. [472]
Indian trade; defense against Indian hostilities.

59. Letter on the Chickasaw Fund. 8 Dec.
HD 8, 29-1, v2, 97p. [481]
Report of the Indian Bureau investigation of investment of funds accrued under treaties of 1832 and 1834.

60. Estimates of Appropriations. 8 Dec.
HD 9, 29-1, v2, 181p. [481]
For the year ending 30 June 1847; Indian expenses.

61. Annual Report of the Com'r of the General Land Office. 15 Dec.
SD 16, 29-1, v3, 114p. [472] *or* HD 12, 29-1, v2, 144p. [481]
Indian treaties and land cessions.

62. Contingent Expenditures of the War Dept. 15 Dec.
HD 31, 29-1, v3, 83p. [482]
Indian Office.

63. Mem. of the Florida Legis. 23 Dec.
SD 22, 29-1, v3, 3p. [472] *or* HD 76, 29-1, v4, 3p. [483]
Losses in Seminole war; Seminole removal.

64. R-C of W. Brook et al. 31 Dec.
HR 3, 29-1, v1, 2p. [488]
Sac and Fox war; 1832.

65. Report on Lands Sales in the NW District of Mississippi. 31 Dec.
HR 8, 29-1, v1, 1p. [488]
Recommends sale of Choctaw lands be legalized and that moneys received be placed in Chickasaw fund.

66. R-P of G. Shurtz et al. 31 Dec.
HR 10, 29-1, v1, 1p. [488]
Treaty of 1817 with the Wyandots and others.

67. Report on Military Posts on Route to Oregon. 31 Dec.
HR 13, 29-1, v1, 5p. [488]
Plains Indian Tribes.

68. R-P of J. Davidson. 31 Dec.
HR 16, 29-1, v1, 1p. [488]
Chased by Indians in 1814.

69. R-C of L. Webster. 31 Dec.
HR 23, 29-1, v1, 2p. [488]
Florida; 1836; quartermaster in Army.

1846

1. Appropriations of the War Dept. 2 Jan.
HD 49, 29-1, v3, 18p. [482]
For 1844-45; Indian expenses.

2. R-P of C. Gibson. 2 Jan.
HR 28, 29-1, v1, 1p. [488]
Seminole Indians; 1839.

3. R-P of M. MacRea. 7 Jan.
SD 42, 29-1, v3, 3p. [472]
Indian wars in the northwest; 1791-96.

4. War Dept. Contracts. 8 Jan.
HD 51, 29-1, v3, 64p. [482]
Indian Office for 1845.

5. R-C of Catlin, Peeples and Company. 12 Jan.
SD 49, 29-1, v4, 1p. [473]
Creek depredations; 1836.

6. R-P of E. White. 12 Jan.
SD 54, 29-1, v4, 1p. [473]
Pawnee depredations.

7. R-P of the Sureties of F. St. Vrain. 13 Jan.
SD 56, 29-1, v4, 3p. [473]
Winnebago agent; Sac and Fox (Black Hawk) war; 1832; Illinois.

8. Resol. of the Indiana Legis. 13 Jan.
HD 63, 29-1, v4, 1p. [483]
Settlers on Miami ceded lands.

9. Mem. of the American Indian Mission Association. 13 Jan.
HD 73, 29-1, v4, 6p. [483]
Organization of a new Indian territory in Oregon.

10. Report on Pensions to Indian Fighters and Soldiers. 13 Jan.

HR 87, 29-1, v1, 12p. [488]
1783 to 1795.

11. Resol. of Sen. Jarnagin. 15 Jan.
SD 68, 29-1, v4, 1p. [473]
Ask preparation of a history of U.S.-Indian relations.

12. R-P of L. Pease and J. Smith. 15 Jan.
HR 88, 29-1, v1, 1p. [488]
Seminole; 1837.

13. Report on the Menominee Indians. 15 Jan.
HR 90, 29-1, v1, 4p. [488]
For extinguishing their claims to land in Wisconsin.

14. R-C of W. Stephens. 15 Jan.
HR 102, 29-1, v1, 3p. [488]
Cherokee; 1817 and 1819.

15. R-C of Roby and Utley. 15 Jan.
HR 103, 29-1, v1, 1p. [488]
Ottawa.

16. R-P of S. Jorden. 16 Jan.
HR 109, 29-1, v1, 1p. [488]
On scouting parties against the Indians; 1782-83.

17. R-C of J. Bulow, jr. 20 Jan.
SD 76, 29-1, v4, 6p. [473]
Seminole war; 1836; Florida.

18. R-C of Alabama. 20 Jan.
HR 127, 29-1, v1, 2p. [488]
Creek and Seminole war; 1836-37; supplies for friendly Indians.

19. R-P of W. Duer. 27 Jan.
HR 133, 29-1, v1, 40p. [488]
Supplies furnished troops engaging Indians in 1791; issues to Indians at Venango, and the rapids of the Ohio.

20. Report on Disbursements to Indians. 28 Jan.
HD 91, 29-1, v4, 178p. [483]
Accounts of 1 Oct. 1844 to 30 Sept. 1845.

21. Letter on Cherokee Indians. 28 Jan.
HD 92, 29-1, v4, 69p. [483]
Information on recent outrages in the Cherokee Nation.

22. R-P of S. Enochs. 30 Jan.
HR 161, 29-1, v1, 4p. [488]
Sac and Fox; 1832; Black Hawk war.

23. R-P of E. White. 2 Feb.
SD 105, 29-1, v4, 3p. [473]
Sub-agent of Indian affairs west of the Rocky Mountains; Oregon.

24. R-C of A. Hunter. 3 Feb.
SD 109, 29-1, v4, 1p. [473]
Supplies to Cherokees in 1836; treaty of Dec. 1835.

25. Mem. of the Missouri Convention. 5 Feb.
HD 104, 29-1, v4, 7p. [483]
Missouri-Iowa boundary; Indian boundary line.

26. R-P of J. Ragan. 9 Feb.
SD 120, 29-1, v4, 3p. [473]
Caddo treaty of 1 July 1835; case against Caddo agent.

27. R-C of L. Evans. 9 Feb.
SD 121, 29-1, v4, 3p. [473]
Cherokee lease; 1834.

28. Report on Chickasaw Fund. 10 Feb.
HD 107, 29-1, v4, 8p. [483]
Treaties of 20 Oct. 1834 and 24 May 1834; statement of the fund.

29. R-P of Langtry and Jenkins. 10 Feb.
HR 190, 29-1, v1, 4p. [488]
Supplies furnished during Cherokee removal; 1838.

30. R-C of G. Humphreys. 10 Feb.
HR 203, 29-1, v1, 5p. [488]
Seminole; 1836.

31. R-P of G. Center. 10 Feb.
HR 204, 29-1, v1, 3p. [488]
Florida Indian hostilities; 1836.

32. R-C of H. Disbrow. 10 Feb.
HR 223, 29-1, v2, 3p. [489]
Indians and British; 1812.

33. R-P of P. Prescott. 10 Feb.
HR 229, 29-1, v2, 1p. [489]
Interpreter for Sioux Indians; St. Peter's Agency.

34. R-P of L. Van Dyck et al. 10 Feb.
HR 237, 29-1, v2, 1p. [489]
Shot by Indians in Revolutionary War.

35. R-P of C. Sanders. 11 Feb.
SD 129, 29-1, v4, 1p. [473]
Commanded friendly Indian troops in Florida war of 1836.

36. On the Case of M. Wets. 12 Feb.
SD 134, 29-1, v4, 1p. [473]
Expedition to the Comanches and other roving Indians in 1834.

37. R-M of the Wyandots. 16 Feb.
SD 135, 29-1, v4, 3p. [473]
Payment for improvements on lands in Ohio ceded to the U.S. by the treaty of 17 Mar. 1842.

38. Mem. of Wyandot Chiefs. 16 Feb.
SD 136, 29-1, v4, 9p. [473]
Urge payment of value of improvements ceded to the U.S.; treaty of 17 Mar. 1842.

39. R-P of D. Robb. 16 Feb.
SD 137, 29-1, v4, 2p. [473]
Services in ratification of Shawnee and other treaties; 1831-32.

40. Resol. of Sen. Sevier. 17 Feb.
SD 148, 29-1, v4, 1p. [473]
Removal of the Miamies from Indiana under the treaty of 28 Nov. 1840.

41. Mem. of the Stockbridge Indians. 17 Feb.
HD 128, 29-1, v4, 3p. [483]
For repeal of 1842 law for the relief of said Indians in Wisconsin.

42. R-C Assignee of P. Hambaugh. 17 Feb.
HR 278, 29-1, v2, 1p. [489]
Trader for Seminole and Micasukie Indians; Florida war.

43. R-C of W. Mathis. 17 Feb.
HR 286, 29-1, v2, 1p. [489]
Wife of blacksmith; 1826-31; Cherokees.

44. R-C of A. Mead et al. 17 Feb.
HR 287, 29-1, v2, 3p. [489]
Ottawa; 1837.

45. R-C of B. Crawford. 17 Feb.
HR 297, 29-1, v2, 1p. [489]
Creek.

46. Resol. of the Wisconsin Legis. 19 Feb.
HD 131, 29-1, v4, 1p. [483]
Fox River valley land titles; Menomonee Indians.

47. R-P of W. Stokes. 21 Feb.
HR 315, 29-1, v2, 2p. [489]
Creeks; 1836; Alabama.

48. R-C of J. and L. Ward. 21 Feb.
HR 318, 29-1, v2, 2p. [489]
1838; removal from Illinois and Wisconsin to west of Mississippi River; Pottawatomie.

49. Report on the Winnebagoes. 21 Feb.
HR 324, 29-1, v2, 1p. [489]
From the CIA; removal.

50. Report on the Northern Cross and Central Railroads in Illinois. 24 Feb.
SD 152, 29-1, v4, 16p. [473]
Amount of land to which Indian title has been extinguished.

51. Report on the Lake Superior Mineral Regions. 24 Feb.
SD 160, 29-1, v4, 37p. [473]
Chippewa land cession; treaty of 5 Aug. 1826; treaty of 4 Oct. 1842; potential conflict between whites and Indians.

52. Mem. of A. Whitney. 24 Feb.
SD 161, 29-1, v4, 10p. [473]
Railroad from Lake Michigan to the Pacific; necessity of extinguishing Sioux title to land from the Mississippi River to the Rocky Mountains.

53. R-P of J. Porter. 25 Feb.
HR 329, 29-1, v2, 3p. [489]
Creek war; 1813.

54. R-P of A. Bayard. 25 Feb.
HR 335, 29-1, v2, 2p. [489]
War with Gr. Britain; Indians; Fort Harrison.

55. R-C of C. Sumption. 25 Feb.
HR 346, 29-1, v2, 2p. [489]
Wyandot and Seneca Indians; 1814.

56. Report on the Miami Indians. 26 Feb.
HD 142, 29-1, v5, 6p. [484]
Contracts for removal; expenditures for removal.

57. R-P of M. Williams. 2 Mar.
SD 176, 29-1, v4, 1p. [473]
Seminole war of 1836 in Florida.

58. R-P of J. Erwin. 2 Mar.
SD 177, 29-1, v4, 20p. [473]
Contract relating to Indian removal; Creeks, Cherokees, Seminoles, and other tribes.

59. Report on a Mail Route from Missouri to the Mouth of the Columbia River. 2 Mar.
SD 178, 29-1, v4, 9p. [473]
Potential Indian depredations.

60. R-M of W. Thomas. 2 Mar.
SD 179, 29-1, v4, 3p. [473]
Supplies to Cherokees in 1836; treaty of Dec. 1835.

61. R-M of W. Thomas. 2 Mar.
SD 180, 29-1, v4, 3p. [473]
Supplies to Cherokees; 1838; North Carolina.

62. R-C of Alabama. 4 Mar.
SD 192, 29-1, v4, 4p. [473]
Creek war of 1836-37.

63. R-P of A. Brereton. 5 Mar.
HR 379, 29-1, v2, 8p. [489]
Wife of physician appointed to treat all Indians visiting Washington, D.C.; 1821-29.

64. R-P of G. Carpenter. 5 Mar.
HR 396, 29-1, v2, 2p. [489]
Black Hawk war; 1832; Michigan militia.

65. R-P of W. Marshall. 5 Mar.
HR 400, 29-1, v2, 9p. [489]
Agent for Miami and Pottawatomie Indians; Indiana; 1834.

66. Mem. of the Mississippi Legis. 11 Mar.
SD 221, 29-1, v5, 1p. [474]
Choctaw treaty of 28 Sept. 1830 at Dancing Rabbit Creek.

67. R-C of L. Laing. 14 Mar.
HR 425, 29-1, v2, 1p. [489]
Indian war, 1791.

68. Report on Pre-emption to Actual Settlers. 14 Mar.
HR 427, 29-1, v2, 2p. [489]
On land acquired by treaty from the Miami Indians.

69. R-M of P. Chouteau, jr. 14 Mar.
HR 432, 29-1, v2, 23p. [489]
"Dubuque Claim"; Iowa Territory; Fox Indians, 1788; Sac and Fox treaty, 1804; etc.

70. R-P of Citizens of Missouri. 16 Mar.
SD 223, 29-1, v5, 3p. [474]
Great and Little Osage treaty of 30 Dec. 1825; Cherokee treaty of 23 May 1836.

71. R-M of P. Starritt. 17 Mar.
SD 228, 29-1, v5, 2p. [474]
Cherokee treaty of 1835-36; land cession.

72. Report of Allen's Expedition to Indian Country. 20 Mar.
HD 168, 29-1, v6, 18p. [485]
Northern Iowa Territory; Sioux and Pottawatomie Indians.

73. Letter on Increasing Military Defenses. 25 Mar.
SD 255, 29-1, v5, 3p. [474]
Indian frontier.

74. R-C of Heir of T. Murray. 27 Mar.
HR 446, 29-1, v2, 2p. [489]
Cherokee treaty negotiations; 1828.

75. Report on the Stockbridge Indians. 27 Mar.
HR 447, 29-1, v2, 19p. [489]
History of the Mohicans and their complaint of U.S. treatment.

76. R-C of B. Dell. 27 Mar.
HR 448, 29-1, v2, 1p. [489]
Florida Indian war.

77. R-P of C. Fulton. 27 Mar.
HR 461, 29-1, v2, 2p. [489]
Wife of militiaman; Indian wars on the Susquehannah.

78. R-P of J. Dusseau. 27 Mar.
HR 470, 29-1, v2, 2p. [489]
Expedition against Indians loyal to British; 1813.

79. R-C of G. Kelly. 27 Mar.
HR 472, 29-1, v2, 1p. [489]
Maumee Indians; Indian war; 1790.

80. R-P of A. Goodwin. 27 Mar.
HR 474, 29-1, v2, 1p. [489]
1813; injured en route to an Indian village.

81. R-C of R. Fitzpatrick. 27 Mar.
HR 479, 29-1, v2, 2p. [489]
Seminole; 1836.

82. Report on the Miami Indians. 27 Mar.
HR 480, 29-1, v2, 1p. [489]
On petition of certain Indians not to be removed west.

83. R-C of J. Rawlings. 27 Mar.
HR 481, 29-1, v2, 2p. [489]
Cherokee; 1792.

84. R-P of N. Otman et al. 27 Mar.
HR 488, 29-1, v2, 1p. [489]
Captured by Indians loyal to British.

85. R-C of J. Crane. 27 Mar.
HR 514, 29-1, v3, 3p. [490]
Creek.

86. R-P of Heirs of J. Motlaw. 27 Mar.
HR 547, 29-1, v3, 2p. [490]
Indian hostilities; 1781; Cherokees.

87. R-M of P. Chouteau et al. 30 Mar.
SD 256, 29-1, v5, 26p. [474]
Sac and Fox lands in Iowa; "Dubuque Claim"; etc.

88. R-M of O. Rees. 30 Mar.
SD 261, 29-1, v5, 1p. [474]
Seminole war.

89. Message on Treaties with Certain Indians. 2 Apr.
SD 273, 29-1, v5, 6p. [474]
Transmits petition of Tonawanda band of Senecas that treaties of 1838 and 1842 between the Six Nations and U.S. do not bind them, because they did not sign said treaties.

90. On the Case of J. Watson. 6 Apr.
HR 535, 29-1, v3, 4p. [490]
Creek and Seminole Indians; 1836; slaves.

91. R-C of J. Edwards. 6 Apr.
HR 556, 29-1, v3, 4p. [490]
Seminole.

92. R-C of Heirs of C. Turner. 6 Apr.
HR 557, 29-1, v3, 13p. [490]
Supplies for the Sioux at St. Peter's agency; Sioux depredations in 1844.

93. R-P of M. Moffit. 6 Apr.
HR 560, 29-1, v3, 2p. [490]
Wife of G. Moffit, an adopted Shawnee Indian.

94. R-P of C. Hudspeth. 6 Apr.
HR 563, 29-1, v3, 3p. [490]
Seminole campaign; 1818.

95. Report on Compensation of Officers and Soldiers of Indian Wars. 6 Apr.
HR 566, 29-1, v3, 1p. [490]
Prior to the treaty of Greenville in 1795.

96. Message on Feuds Among the Cherokees. 13 Apr.
SD 298, 29-1, v5, 224p. [474] *or* HD 185, 29-1, v6, 233p. [485]
Report of the CIA; "Western" versus "Eastern" Cherokees who have emigrated west of the Mississippi River; separation of the parties.

97. Report of Feuds Among the Cherokees. 20 Apr.
SD 301, 29-1, v5, 9p. [474]
From Cherokee agent and Gens. Gaines and Arbuckle; emigrated Cherokees.

98. Report on Additional Funds for Indian Service. 20 Apr.
SD 302, 29-1, v5, 2p. [474]
Estimate of amount needed to carry out treaty with the Kansas Indians and to negotiate treaties with the Chippewas, Ottawas, and Pottawatomies.

99. R-P of J. Watson. 23 Apr.
SD 312, 29-1, v7, 2p. [476]
Indian Dept. agent from 1806-12, in Michigan; British and Indians.

100. Message on Choctaw Treaty. 27 Apr.
HD 189, 29-1, v6, 9p. [485]
Claims arising from treaty of 28 Sept. 1830 at Dancing Rabbit Creek.

101. Message on Chickasaw Indians. 27 Apr.
HD 190, 29-1, v6, 127p. [485]
Claims arising from 1834 treaty; papers on matter; list of reservations.

102. Mem. of J. Ross et al. 4 May.
SD 331, 29-1, v7, 59p. [476]
Criticism of the message of the Pres. and the report of the CIA; against extension of U.S. criminal laws over Cherokee Nation; treaty relations with Cherokees.

103. R-M of J. Eldred and Sons. 4 May.
HR 584, 29-1, v3, 3p. [490]
Trader for Ontonagon band of Chippewas of Lake Superior; 1841.

104. Report on Wyandot Lands. 4 May.
HR 587, 29-1, v3, 1p. [490]
Authorizes private sales after they have again been offered at public sale.

105. R-C of G. Russell. 4 May.
HR 589, 29-1, v3, 2p. [490]
Cherokees; 1835; Georgia.

106. R-C of Heirs of Primeau and Chapman. 4 May.
HR 596, 29-1, v3, 2p. [490]
Yankton Sioux; 1835.

107. R-P of W. Stubblefield. 4 May.
HR 608, 29-1, v3, 1p. [490]
Indian campaigns; 1791 and '94.

108. R-P of B. Johnson. 4 May.
HR 615, 29-1, v3, 1p. [490]
Indian wars; 1791 and '94.

109. R-P of J. Robinson. 4 May.
HR 625, 29-1, v3, 1p. [490]
Cherokees; 1835; Georgia.

110. R-C of O. Rees. 4 May.
HR 633, 29-1, v3, 2p. [490]
Seminole war.

111. R-P of D. Rogers. 4 May.
HR 642, 29-1, v3, 2p. [490]
Tennessee Volunteers; 1836, General Wool, commanding officer of the Army in the Cherokee Nation.

112. R-C of T. Hall. 6 May.
SD 335, 29-1, v7, 1p. [476]
Indian hostilities during the Revolutionary War in Pennsylvania.

113. Message on Chickasaw Indians. 6 May.
HD 195, 29-1, v6, 21p. [485]
Claims from the treaty of 1834; papers and correspondence on the matter.

114. R-P of M. Chaudonia. 11 May.
HR 653, 29-1, v3, 2p. [490]
Wife of Pottawatomie half-breed.

115. R-C of D. Turnispeed. 11 May.
HR 672, 29-1, v3, 1p. [490]
Creek; 1836; Alabama.

116. Minority Report on the Dubuque Claim. 11 May.
HR 675, 29-1, v3, 11p. [490]
Sees claim as valid; Sac and Fox lands.

117. R-M of J. Hulbert. 15 May.
SD 346, 29-1, v7, 1p. [476]
Indian sub-agent.

118. Resol. of the Michigan Legis. 20 May.
HD 204, 29-1, v6, 18p. [485]
Indian title to mineral lands.

119. R-M of S. Bell. 25 May.
SD 359, 29-1, v7, 1p. [476]
Cherokee Indian visits Seminoles in 1837 to persuade them to remove west.

120. Report on the Cherokee Indians. 2 June.
HR 683, 29-1, v3, 5p. [490]
Emigration and subsistence of Cherokees now in North Carolina.

121. Report on a Judicial District for Western Arkansas. 4 June.
SD 372, 29-1, v7, 3p. [476]
Jurisdiction over the Osage, Cher-

okee, Creek. Choctaw, and other Indian tribes.

122. Mem. of G. Catlin. 5 June.
SD 374, 29-1, v7, 2p. [476]
Propsing sale of Indian portrait collection to U.S.

123. R-C of J. Cocke. 11 June.
SD 385, 29-1, v8, 1p. [477]
Agent to treat with the Cherokees in 1827.

124. Report on Spoliations Committed by U.S. Troops. 16 June.
SD 391, 29-1, v8, 16p. [477]
Florida; 1814; troops following vagrant Indians.

125. R-M of the Heirs of J. Kennedy. 17 June.
HR 689, 29-1, v4, 3p. [491]
Creek; 1813.

126. R-P of S. Perry. 17 June.
HR 691, 29-1 v4, 1p. [491]
Indian supplies lost on Ohio River; bound for Arkansas.

127. R-P of J. Bryan. 17 June.
HR 700, 29-1, v4, 4p. [491]
Com'r to treat with the Wyandot Indians; 1836.

128. R-C of the Heirs of S. Johnston. 17 June.
HR 716, 29-1, v4, 1p. [491]
Sub-agent, killed by Pottawatomies in 1812; Wyandot Indians donated land to heirs.

129. R-P of L. Cheatham. 17 June.
HR 734, 29-1, v4, 4p. [491]
Contracts with agents for Cherokee removal in 1832; violated.

130. R-P of J. McCutchen.17 June.
HR 749, 29-1, v4, 3p. [491]
Loss, in 1812, to troops in Indiana en route to Indian encounter.

131. R-M of the American Indian Mission Association. 22 June.
HR 751, 29-1, v4, 6p. [491]
On removal, education and another Indian Territory west of the Rocky Mountains.

132. Message on Chippewa Indians. 24 June.
SD 403, 29-1, v8, 3p. [477]
Removal of Chippewa from the Lake Superior mineral lands.

133. Mem. of Cherokees Residing in North Carolina. 25 June.
SD 408, 29-1, v8, 24p. [477]
On payment of money according to the 12th and 8th articles of the 1835 treaty.

134. R-C of heirs of G. Galphin. 7 July.
SD 420, 29-1, v8, 3p. [477]
Trader to the Creeks and Cherokees of Georgia in 1773; treaty of 1773.

135. R-C of S. Enochs. 7 July.
SD 421, 29-1, v8, 1p. [477]
Sac and Fox (Black Hawk) war of 1832.

136. Mem. of A. Durand et al. 9 July.
SD 424, 29-1, v8, 2p. [477]
Purchase of Catlin's collection of Indian portraits.

137. Communication from H. Schoolcraft. 9 July.
SD 425, 29-1, v8, 7p. [477]
Land claims in Michigan; Chippewa Indians; treaty of 1796; land cession of 16 June 1820; etc.

138. R-C of Erskine and Eichelberger. 10 July.
SD 427, 29-1, v8, 2p. [477]
Trade with Cherokees; treaty of 1835-36.

139. Message Transmitting the Report of Abert's Expedition on the Upper Arkansas River in 1845. 11 July.
SD 438, 29-1, v8, 75p. [477]
Through Comanche country; contact with Kiowas, Cheyennes, Sioux, Delawares, and other tribes.

140. R-P of G. Hix. 17 July.
HR 788, 29-1, v4, 6p. [491]
Goods taken by U.S. Army; trespassing on Cherokee lands in 1831.

141. R-P of S. Donthit. 24 July.
HR 803, 29-1, v4, 1p. [491]
Com. on Indian Affairs asks to be discharged from considering petition of representative of M. Motlon.

142. Report of Catlin's Indian Gallery. 24 July.
HR 806, 29-1, v4, 3p. [491]
Recommends purchase for Smithsonian Institution.

143. Report on Indian Territories. 28 July.
SD 461, 29-1, v9, 11p. [478]
Favors extension of criminal laws of U.S. over Indian territories; submits view of the CIA; "Civilized Tribes" of Arkansas.

144. R-M of Indiana Citizens and A. Whitney. 31 July.
SD 466, 29-1, v9, 51p. [478]
Railroad from the Mississippi River to the Pacific; extinguishing Indian title to land.

145. Report on Seminole War of 1836. 3 Aug.
SD 470, 29-1, v9, 1p. [478]
Favors claims cases being sent to Federal Courts.

146. R-C of J. Baldwin. 3 Aug.
SD 471, 29-1, v9, 1p. [478]
Army spoliations during the Seminole war; 1835-36.

147. On the Relief of C. Fulton. 4 Aug.
SD 472, 19-2, v9, 1p. [478]
Indian skirmishes on the Susquehannah River in 1800.

148. R-P of M. Clitz. 7 Aug.
SD 480, 29-1, v9, 1p. [478]
Sac and Fox war of 1832.

149. R-C of Estate of J. Housman. 8 Aug.
SD 484, 29-1, v9, 2p. [478]
Indian hostilities; 1840; Florida.

150. R-P of P. McElvaine. 8 Aug.
HR 822, 29-1, v4, 2p. [491]
Wyandot treaty, 1836; land office registrar.

151. R-M of C. Wallace. 10 Aug.
SD 485, 29-1, v9, 20p. [478]
Virginia military tract in Ohio; Greenville treaty, or Indian boundary line.

152. Statement of Appropriations. 21 Sept.
SD 490, 29-1, v9, 66p. [478] *or* HD 228, 29-1, v7, 57p. [486]
1st session, 29th Congress; Indian expenses.

153. Estimates of Appropriations. 7 Dec.
HD 3, 29-2, v1, 166p. [497]
For the year ending 30 June 1848; Indian expenses.

154. Annual Message to Congress with Documents; Pres. Polk. 8 Dec.
SD 1, 29-2, v1, 704p. [493] *or* HD 4, 29-2, v1, 704p. [497]
Relations with the Indians; annual report of the Sec. of War; annual report of the CIA, including removal, trust funds, and reports of schools, agents, and Supts.; etc.

155. Annual Report of the Sec. of the Treasury. 9 Dec.
SD 2, 29-2, v1, 111p. [493] *or* HD 7, 29-2, v2, 111p. [498]
Indian expenses.

156. Annual Report of the Com'r of the General Land Office. 10 Dec.
HD 9, 29-2, v2, 113p. [498]
Indian treaties and land cessions.

157. Receipts and Expenditures. 10 Dec.
HD 10, 29-2, v2, 380p. [498]
For the year ending 30 June 1846; Indian expenses.

158. R-M of C. Wallace. 28 Dec.
SD 20, 29-2, v2, 40p. [494]
Virginia bounty land in Ohio; Greenville (Indian) treaty line.

159. Resol. of the Florida Legis. 28 Dec.
SD 21, 29-2, v2, 1p. [494]
For removal from the state of the Seminole Indians.

1847

1. Report on a Right of Way through Public Lands in Illinois. 4 Jan.
SD 23, 29-2, v2, 17p. [494]
For a railroad; land to which Indian title has been extinguished.

2. Report on Contingent Expenses of the War Dept. 4 Jan.
SD 24, 29-2, v2, 53p. [494] *or* HD 30, 29-2, v3, 53p. [499]
Office of the CIA for the year ending 30 June 1846.

3. Report on Judicial Districts of Arkansas. 6 Jan.
SD 39, 29-2, v2, 3p. [494]
Extension of jurisdiction over the Indian tribes; Osages, Cherokees, Creeks, Choctaws, and other tribes.

4. R-C of E. White. 7 Jan.
SD 45, 29-2, v2, 1p. [494]
Pawnee depredations.

5. R-C of A. Bills. 9 Jan.
HR 6, 29-2, v1, 1p. [501]
Indian wars; 1791-95.

6. Letter on Seminole Indians. 11 Jan.
SD 51, 29-2, v2, 3p. [494]
Gov. of Florida on their depredations; aks their removal.

7. R-M of H. Wright. 11 Jan.
SD 52, 29-2, v2, 3p. [494]
Seminole war in Florida.

8. R-C of A. Watson. 11 Jan.
SD 55, 29-2, v2, 2p. [494]
Seminole war in Florida.

9. R-P of S. Gordon. 11 Jan.
SD 56, 29-2, v2, 1p. [494]
Creek war of 1813 in Alabama.

10. R-C of J. Baldwin. 14 Jan.
SD 58, 29-2, v2, 2p. [494]
Seminole war; 1835; Florida.

11. R-M of B. Crawford. 14 Jan.
SD 59, 29-2, v2, 5p. [494]
Trader to the Creeks in Arkansas; 1840; liquor.

12. R-M of S. Bell. 14 Jan.
SD 62, 29-2, v2, 1p. [494]
A Cherokee Indian who visited the Seminoles to persuade them to remove from Florida; 1837.

13. R-P of M. Galphin. 14 Jan.
SD 65, 29-2, v2, 3p. [494]
Trader to the Cherokees in Georgia in 1773; treaty of 1773.

14. R-C of Erskine and Eichelberger. 14 Jan.
SD 67, 29-2, v2, 2p. [494]
Cherokee debts; treaty of 1835-36.

15. R-P of C. Gibson. 15 Jan.
SD 69, 29-2, v2, 2p. [494]
Seminole war; 1839; Florida.

16. Clerks Employed in the War Dept. 16 Jan.
HD 40, 29-2, v3, 10p. [499]
Office of the CIA during 1846.

17. On the Relief of F. Fellanny. 18 Jan.
SD 73, 29-2, v2, 1p. [494]
Florida Indian war.

18. R-C of T. Talbot. 18 Jan.
SD 75, 29-2, v2, 2p. [494]
Missouri-Mexico trade; 1826; Pawnee depredations.

19. Contracts of the War Dept. 19 Jan.
HR 46, 29-2, v3, 71p. [499]
Indian office for 1846.

20. R-C of the Heirs of A. Loughrey. 20 Jan.
HR 30, 29-2, v1, 6p. [501]
Expedition of 1781 against the Mohawks and Senecas in Ohio.

21. Report on the Seminoles. 25 Jan.
SD 90, 29-2, v2, 15p. [494]
Condition of Seminoles still in Florida; removal of said Indians to the west.

22. Balances of Appropriations. 27 Jan.
HD 65, 29-2, v4, 18p. [500]
Indian expenses; appropriations for fiscal 1846.

23. R-C of J. Housman. 30 Jan.
SD 101, 29-2, v3, 6p. [495]
Indian hostilities of 1839 in Florida.

24. Report on the Cherokee Commission. 3 Feb.
SD 113, 29-2, v3, 20p. [495]
Instructions to Com'rs under the 17th article of the Cherokee treaty of 1835-36; claims.

25. R-P of Col. Watson. 6 Feb.
SD 124, 29-2, v3, 2p. [495]
Indian Dept. of Michigan; 1812; depredations by the British and Indians.

26. Resol. of the Florida Legis. 8 Feb.
SD 133, 29-2, v3, 1p. [495]
Losses by Indian depredations during the Seminole war.

27. Report on the Texas Indians. 8 Feb.
HD 76, 29-2, v4, 9p. [500]
From the Com'rs to the "wild tribes" of the Southwest; treaty negotiations.

28. R-M of A. Gallatin. 9 Feb.
HR 53, 29-2, v1, 23p. [501]
Appropriation for a taking of a census of Indian tribes.

29. Report on Oregon Territory. 16 Feb.
HR 55, 29-2, v1, 3p. [501]
Cost of extinguishing Indian title to land.

30. Report on the Chickasaw Fund. 17 Feb.
HR 94, 29-2, v4, 4p. [500]
From treaties of 20 Oct. 1832, and 24 May 1834.

31. R-M of New York Citizens. 19 Feb.
SD 156, 29-2, v3, 127p. [495]
Adverse to exempting the Tonawanda band of Senecas from the fulfillment of the treaty of 20 May 1842; calls for removal of Indians.

32. R-M of D. Vann and W. Ross. 19 Feb.
SD 157, 29-2, v3, 5p. [495]
Payments due the Cherokee Nation under the treaties of 25 Oct. 1805, 27 Feb. 1819, and 29 Dec. 1835; concerns costs of removal.

33. R-C of Seminole Warriors. 20 Feb.
SD 166, 29-2, v3, 1p. [495]
For service in the U.S. Army during the Florida Indian war.

34. R-P of D. Smith. 20 Feb.
SD 167, 29-2, v3, 1p. [495]
Indian campaign under Gen. Wayne in Ohio.

35. Resol. of the Illinois Legis. 22 Feb.
SD 174, 29-2, v3, 2p. [495]
On the "Illinois campaign" of 1778-79 against the British and Indians.

36. Report on Comanches and Other Indians. 24 Feb.
HD 100, 29-2, v4, 5p. [500]
Council with "wild tribes" of the Southwest; treaties negotiated with said tribes are not ratified by Congress; Indians must be induced to remain peaceable until treaty stipulations can be carried out.

37. R-C of the Heirs of G. Galphin. 24 Feb.
HR 77, 29-2, v1, 1p. [501]
Cherokee and Creek debts to a trader prior to 1773 in Georgia.

38. R-C of S. Bell. 24 Feb.
HR 80, 29-2, v1, 1p. [501]
Cherokee Indian who visited the Seminoles in 1837 in order to persuade them to remove west.

39. R-P of L. Van Dyck et al. 24 Feb.
HR 84, 29-2, v1, 1p. [501]
Indian battle during the Revolutionary War.

40. R-P of G. Houston. 24 Feb.
HR 85, 29-2, v1, 4p. [501]
Concerning proceeds from the sale of Chickasaw ceded lands; would go to the tribal trust fund.

41. R-M of P. Starrett et al. 25 Feb.
SD 185, 29-2, v3, 1p. [495]
To enlarge the powers of the Cherokee Claims Commission formed under the treaty of 1835-36.

42. Resol. of the Indiana Legis. 25 Feb.
SD 190, 29-2, v3, 1p. [495]
Settlers on Miami ceded lands.

43. Resol. of the Indiana Legis. 25 Feb.
SD 197, 29-2, v3, 1p. [495]
On sale of liquor to the Indians.

44. R-P of J. Baldwin. 2 Mar.
SD 212, 29-2, v3, 1p. [495]
Indian hostilities in Florida.

45. R-M of the Reps. of J. Dubuque. 3 Mar.
SD 218, 29-2, v3, 26p. [495]
"Dubuque claim"; Sac and Fox land cession of 1788 in Iowa; treaties with the Sac and Fox Indians of 3 Nov. 1804, and 21 Sept. 1832; etc.

46. Statement of Appropriations. 1 Apr.
SD 224, 29-2, v3, 67p. [495] *or* HD 124, 29-2, v4, 75p. [500]
For the 2d session, 29th Congress; Indian expenses.

47. Estimates of Appropriations. 6 Dec.
HED 2, 30-1, v1, 196p. [514]
For the year ending 30 June 1849.

48. Annual Message to Congress with Documents; Pres. Polk. 7 Dec.
SED 1, 30-1, v1, 1618p. [503] *or* HED 8, 30-1, v2, 1618p. [515]
Indian removal; Cherokee claims and funds; annual report of the Sec. of War; annual report of the CIA, including annuities, liquor, trust funds, and reports from schools, farms, agents, and Supts.; etc.

49. Report on Disbursements to the Indians. 9 Dec.
HED 5, 30-1, v1, 171p. [514]
From 1 Oct. 1845 to 30 Sept. 1846.

50. Annual Report of the Sec. of the Treasury. 9 Dec.
HED 6, 30-1, v1, 175p. [514]
For fiscal 1847.

51. Annual Report of the Com'r of the Gen. Land Office. 13 Dec.
SED 2, 30-1, v2, 230p. [504]
Indian treaties, land cessions, and reservations.

52. Notes from an Expedition; Fort Leavenworth to San Diego, California. 16 Dec.
SED 7, 30-1, v3, 416p. [505] *or* HED 41, 30-1, v4, 614p. [517]
Encounters with Indian tribes of the Southwest during 1846-47 (House version includes an expedition to New Mexico).

53. R-P of J. Williams. 20 Dec.
HR 5, 30-1, v1, 44p. [524]
Indian hostilities of 1812 near Detroit.

54. R-C of L. Blake. 29 Dec.
SR 7, 30-1, v1, 4p. [512]
Creek removal of 1827-28.

55. R-P of M. Galphin. 29 Dec.
SR 8, 30-1, v1, 3p. [512]
Trader to the Creeks and Cherokees in Georgia prior to 1733; treaty of 1773.

56. R-M of C. Wallace. 30 Dec.
SR 10, 30-1, v1, 45p. [512]
Virginia military tract in Ohio; Indian treaty line part of the boundary of said tract; Indians serving with the U.S. during the Revolutionary War include the Cherokees and Chickasaws.

57. R-P of T. Talbot. 30 Dec.
SR 11, 30-1, v1, 3p. [512]
Pawnee depredations upon the Missouri-Mexico trade route in 1827.

58. R-P of G. Hollenback. 30 Dec.
HR 12, 30-1, v1, 4p. [524]
Sac and Fox (Black Hawk) war of 1832; Illinois.
59. R-P of W. Brook. 30 Dec.
HR 13, 30-1, v1, 4p. [524]
Sac and Fox (Black Hawk) war of 1832; Illinois.
60. R-P of P. Cunningham. 30 Dec.
HR 15, 30-1, v1, 4p. [524]
Sac and Fox (Black Hawk) war of 1832; Illinois.

1848

1. Report on Fort Armstrong in Illinois. 3 Jan.
SED 9, 30-1, v3, 3p. [505]
Used as an arms depot in 1841 when Indian hostilities threatened to break out.
2. Report on Judicial Districts of Arkansas. 3 Jan.
SR 12, 30-1, v1, 3p. [512]
Jurisdiction over Indian tribes, including Osages, Cherokees, Creeks, and Choctaws.
3. Mem. of Cherokee Indians. 4 Jan.
HMD 8, 30-1, v1, 71p. [523]
Wrongs committed by agents of the U.S.; treaties of 1785, 1791, 1798, 1804, 1805, 1806, 1807, 1816, 1817 1817, 1818, 1819, 1828, 1835, etc.
4. Resol. of the Ohio Legis. 4 Jan.
HMD 9, 30-1, v1, 1p. [523]
Delaware Indians.
5. Report of the Regents of the Smithsonian Institution. 6 Jan.
SMD 23, 30-1, v1, 208p. [511]
Ancient mounds of the Mississippi River valley.
6. On the Relief of G. Gaines. 10 Jan.
SR 20, 30-1, v1, 1p. [512]
Report of Com. on Indian Affairs.
7. R-C of J. Watson and C. Coddington. 10 Jan.
SR 21, 30-1, v1, 5p. [512]
Indian Dept. in Michigan; 1806-1812; trade.
8. On the Relief of S. Gordon. 11 Jan.
SR 23, 30-1, v1, 1p. [512]
Indian hostilities of 1812 in Mississippi.
9. On the Relief of F. Fellanny. 12 Jan.
SR 26, 30-1, v1, 1p. [512]
Florida Indian war.
10. Contingent Expenses of the War Dept. 12 Jan.
HED 20, 30-1, v3, 6p. [516]
Including the office of the CIA.
11. R-P of G. Hix. 12 Jan.
HR 46, 30-1, v1, 6p. [524]
Trade in Cherokee country without a license.
12. R-M of the Illinois Legis. 12 Jan.
HR 48, 30-1, v1, 1p. [524]
Black Hawk War claims from 1832.
13. R-P of W. Harriss. 12 Jan.
HR 51, 30-1, v1, 4p. [524]
Sac and Fox (Black Hawk) war; 1832; Illinois.
14. R-P of E. Ackley. 12 Jan.
HR 52, 30-1, v1, 4p. [524]
Sac and Fox (Black Hawk) war; 1832; Illinois.
15. R-P of G. Hollenback. 12 Jan.
HR 53, 30-1, v1, 4p. [524]
Sac and Fox (Black Hawk) war; 1832; Illinois.
16. R-P of A. Hunter. 12 Jan.
HR 61, 30-1, v1, 2p. [524]
U.S. troops stationed in the Cherokee Nation commit depredations in 1836.
17. On the Case of J. and L. Ward. 12 Jan.
HR 73, 30-1, v1, 2p. [524]
Pottawatomie removal; 1838.
18. R-P of J. Bryan. 12 Jan.
HR 93, 30-1, v1, 2p. [524]
Wyandot treaty negotiations; 1836.
19. Memoirs from an Expedition to Northern Mexico. 13 Jan.
SMD 26, 30-1, v1, 141p. [511]
Indian tribes of the Southwest.
20. R-C of D. Robb. 19 Jan.
HR 117, 30-1, v1, 3p. [524]
Emigration of the Senecas and Shawnees in 1832.
21. R-M of S. Bell. 20 Jan.
SR 36, 30-1, v1, 2p. [512]
Cherokee Indian who tried, in 1837, to persuade the Seminoles to remove from Florida to west of the Mississippi River.
22. R-C of J. Lewis. 24 Jan.
SR 40, 30-1, v1, 1p. [512]
Blacksmith to the Cherokees in 1839.
23. Report on a Railroad in Illinois. 24 Jan.

SR 42, 30-1, v1, 15p. [512]
Land to which Indian title has been extinguished.

24. R-P of G. Center. 25 Jan.
SR 45, 30-1, v1, 4p. [512]
Indian war in Florida; 1836.

25. R-P of the Heirs of J. Gerard. 25 Jan.
HR 121, 30-1, v1, 11p. [524]
Messenger to hostile Indians in 1792; Ohio.

26. R-M of L. Benedict. 25 Jan.
HR 127, 30-1, v1, 3p. [524]
Pottawatomie treaty of 20 Oct. 1832.

27. R-P of J. and D. Miller. 25 Jan.
HR 129, 30-1, v1, 3p. [524]
Choctaw treaty of 1830; Chickasaw land cession.

28. Report on Employees in the Indian Dept. 26 Jan.
HED 26, 30-1, v3, 11p. [516]
For the year 1847.

29. Report on War Dept. Contracts. 26 Jan.
HED 29, 30-1, v3, 114p. [516]
For 1847; Indian Dept.

30. Clerks Employed in the War Dept. 26 Jan.
HED 31, 30-1, v3, 12p. [516]
Indian Dept.

31. R-P of M. Caffey. 27 Jan.
HR 153, 30-1, v1, 1p. [524]
Seminole campaign of 1818.

32. Resol. of the Florida Legis. 31 Jan.
HMD 15, 30-1, v1, 4p. [523]
Seminole war in Florida; 1839-40.

33. R-P of the Heirs of J. Kennedy. 3 Feb.
HR 155, 30-1, v1, 19p. [524]
Creek hostilities; 1813.

34. R-P of C. Waldron. 3 Feb.
HR 158, 30-1, v1, 3p. [524]
Seminole war.

35. R-P of M. Hagen. 3 Feb.
HR 160, 30-1, v1, 6p. [524]
Seminole war; 1835-36; Florida.

36. R-C of the Heirs of I. Taulbee. 3 Feb.
HR 161, 30-1, v1, 3p. [524]
Black Hawk war; 1832; Illinois.

37. R-P of J. Elzaurdi. 9 Feb.
HR 187, 30-1, v1, 27p. [524]
Seminole war; 1835-36; Florida.

38. R-P of J. Monroe. 9 Feb.
HR 202, 30-1, v2, 4p. [525]
Indian war; 1813; Indiana.

39. R-M of Col. Vigo. 9 Feb.
HR 216, 30-1, v2, 62p. [525]
Indian trader in 1778; "Illinois campaign" of 1778.

40. Report on an Expedition to New Mexico. 10 Feb.
SED 23, 30-1, v4, 132p. [506] *or* HED 41, 30-1, v4, 614p. [517]
Encounters with Indian tribes of the Southwest; maps and sketches. (House version includes an expedition from Missouri to California.)

41. R-P of D. Smith. 10 Feb.
SR 61, 30-1, v1, 1p. [512]
Indian battle under Gen. Wayne.

42. Resol. of the Illinois Legis. 11 Feb.
SMD 48, 30-1, v1, 1p. [511]
Sac and Fox (Black Hawk) war of 1832.

43. R-P of J. Baldwin. 11 Feb.
SR 62, 30-1, v1, 2p. [512]
Seminole war; 1835-36; Florida.

44. Appropriations of the War Dept. 18 Feb.
SED 27, 30-1, v4, 15p. [506]
From 1 July 1846 to 30 June 1847; Indian expenses.

45. Resol. of the Florida Legis. 29 Feb.
SMD 60, 30-1, v1, 1p. [511]
Removal of Indians from the state.

46. Resol. of the Florida Legis. 29 Feb.
SMD 65, 30-1, v1, 2p. [511]
Seminole depredations; 1842; Florida.

47. Report of an Expedition to Oregon in 1846. 29 Feb.
HMD 29, 30-1, v1, 36p. [523]
Indians of the area around the Columbia River.

48. On the Relief of the Reps. of G. Fisher. 29 Feb.
HR 240, 30-1, v2, 2p. [525]
Indian war; 1812; Mississippi.

49. R-C of H. Andrew. 29 Feb.
HR 244, 30-1, v2, 5p. [525]
Seminole war; 1835; Florida.

50. R-P of J. Fugate. 29 Feb.
HR 284, 30-1, v2, 1p. [525]
British and Indians; 1813; Ohio.

51. R-C of T. Talbot et al. 29 Feb.
HR 299, 30-1, v2, 5p. [525]
Pawnee depredations upon traders in 1827.

52. R-P of L. Wright. 29 Feb.
HR 303, 30-1, v2, 2p. [525]
Indian spies; 1780-81.

53. R-P of A. McDonald. 29 Feb.
HR 305, 30-1, v2, 1p. [525]
Indian campaign; battle of Maumee; 1813.

54. Report on the Chickasaw Fund. 2 Mar.
HED 43, 30-1, v5, 4p. [518]
Treaties of 20 Oct. 1832, and 24 May 1834.

55. R-C of W. and M. Davis. 4 Mar.
SR 81, 30-1, v1, 2p. [512]
Seminole war; 1837-39; Florida.

56. R-C of J. Brown. 7 Mar.
HR 317, 30-1, v2, 6p. [525]
Sisseton Sioux hostilities; council; 1844-46.

57. R-P of G. and H. Bloom. 9 Mar.
HR 323, 30-1, v2, 2p. [525]
Pottawatomie treaty of 20 Oct. 1832.

58. R-P of H. Hall. 9 Mar.
HR 353, 30-1, v2, 6p. [525]
Indian war; 1836; Florida.

59. R-C of H. Genther. 10 Mar.
SR 84, 30-1, v1, 1p. [512]
Payments to the Cherokees in 1841.

60. Resol. of the Indiana Legis. 13 Mar.
HMD 48, 30-1, v1, 2p. [523]
On payment of annuities to Miami Indians still in Indiana.

61. Report on Bonds of the State of Indiana. 14 Mar.
SR 86, 30-1, v1, 50p. [512]
Held as part of the Chickasaw trust fund, and other such funds.

62. R-C of J. Sutherland. 14 Mar.
HR 386, 30-1, v2, 1p. [525]
Indian war under Gen. Wayne; 1794.

63. R-P of Reps. of R. Lassiter. 15 Mar.
SR 89, 30-1, v1, 1p. [512]
Indian war; 1835-36; Florida.

64. R-C of D. Jewell. 15 Mar.
HR 396, 30-1, v2, 3p. [525]
Indian hostilities; 1837; Florida.

65. R-C of J. Yearty. 15 Mar.
HR 397, 30-1, v2, 3p. [525]
Indian hostilities; 1837; Florida.

66. R-P of C. Gibson. 17 Mar.
SR 92, 30-1, v1, 2p. [512]
Seminole war; 1839; Florida.

67. Mem. of the Wisconsin Legis. 22 Mar.
SMD 89, 30-1, v1, 2p. [511]
Propose a treaty with the Menomonees to extinguish their title to land.

68. Mem. of the Alabama Legis. 22 Mar.
HMD 61, 30-1, v1, 2p. [523]
Expenses of the Creek war; 1836-37.

69. Mem. of the Mississippi Legis. 24 Mar.
HMD 64, 30-1, v1, 3p. [523]
Indian reservations embracing school lands.

70. R-P of L. Daily. 28 Mar.
HR 406, 30-1, v2, 5p. [525]
Sac and Fox (Black Hawk) war; 1832; Illinois.

71. R-C of C. Allen. 28 Mar.
HR 410, 30-1, v2, 6p. [525]
Seneca treaty negotiations, 1838.

72. R-P of W. Gibson. 28 Mar.
HR 421, 30-1, v2, 3p. [525]
Indian depredations near Santa Fe in 1846.

73. R-P of the Heirs of M. Hover. 28 Mar.
HR 425, 30-1, v2, 5p. [525]
Indian prisoner; French and Indian war.

74. Report on the Reduction of Price of Miami Lands. 28 Mar.
HR 434, 30-1, v2, 2p. [525]
Miami treaties of 1837, 1839, and 1841; land cessions in Indiana.

75. Report on the Seneca Indians. 29 Mar.
SED 31, 30-1, v4, 77p. [506]
Investigation of money withheld by a U.S. sub-agent.

76. R-C of J. Chapman et al. 30 Mar.
HR 442, 30-1, v2, 11p. [525]
Treaty of 26 Nov. 1833 at Chicago; Chippewas, Ottawas, and Pottawatomies.

77. R-P of J. Bayless. 30 Mar.
HR 451, 30-1, v2, 2p. [525]
Indian force; 1813; Fort Meigs.

78. R-P of B. Perkins. 30 Mar.
HR 453, 30-1, v2, 2p. [525]
Indian depredations in 1819 near Council Bluffs.

79. R-C of the Heirs of R. Laughlin. 30 Mar.
HR 467, 30-1, v2, 2p. [525]
British and Indians; 1791; Pennsylvania.

80. Resol. of the Indiana Legis. 31 Mar.
SMD 101, 30-1, v1, 1p. [511]
Miami reserve lands.

81. Resol. of the Indiana Legis. 31 Mar.
SMD 106, 30-1, v1, 1p. [511]
Miami reserve lands.

82. Resol. of the Indiana Legis. 31 Mar.
SMD 113, 30-1, v1, 1p. [511]
Miami reserve lands.

83. Resol. of the Indiana Legis. 31 Mar.
SMD 114, 30-1, v1, 1p. [511]
Lands ceded by the Miami Indians.

84. Resol. of the Indiana Legis. 31 Mar.
SMD 116, 30-1, v1, 1p. [511]
To pay annuities to Miami Indians in the state who have not removed west.

85. R-C of T. Wendell. 7 Apr.
SR 112, 30-1, v1, 5p. [512]
Chippewa treaty of 14 Jan. 1837, amended 20 Dec. 1837.

86. R-C of S. Hubbard. 7 Apr.
SR 115, 30-1, v1, 2p. [512]
Chippewa depredations; 1812; Detroit.

87. Report on the Fort Snelling Military Reserve. 10 Apr.
SED 34, 30-1, v5, 3p. [507]
Treaty with the Sioux, dated 23 Sept. 1805.

88. R-C of J. Edwards. 11 Apr.
SR 118, 30-1, v1, 2p. [512]
Seminole war; Florida.

89. R-C of S. Findlay. 11 Apr.
SR 119, 30-1, v1, 3p. [512]
Shawnee treaty of 8 Aug. 1831.

90. R-C of J. Bryan. 14 Apr.
SR 125, 30-1, v1, 2p. [512]
Treaty negotiations with the Wyandots; 1836; Ohio.

91. Resol. of the Texas Legis. 17 Apr.
SMD 122, 30-1, v1, 1p. [511]
Preservation of friendly relations with the Indians of Texas.

92. R-C of J. McElrath. 18 Apr.
HR 474, 30-1, v2, 3p. [525]
Seminole campaign of 1818.

93. R-P of the Reps. of W. Freeman. 18 Apr.
HR 476, 30-1, v2, 14p. [525]
Creek campaign; 1836-37.

94. R-P of I. Johnson. 26 Apr.
HR 505, 30-1, v3, 2p. [526]
Council in 1833 with the Miami and Pottawatomie Indians.

95. R-C of H. Clamorgan et al. 26 Apr.
HR 506, 30-1, v3, 4p. [526]
Indian trade; 1797; western Illinois.

96. R-C of C. Findlay. 26 Apr.
HR 507, 30-1, v3, 1p. [526]
Shawnee treaty of 8 Aug. 1831; recruits for the Seminole war.

97. On the Relief of the Heirs of A. Hogeboom. 26 Apr.
HR 523, 30-1, v3, 2p. [526]
Agent of removal for the Seneca Indians; 1845.

98. R-P of L. Van Dyck. 26 Apr.
HR 527, 30-1, v3, 1p. [526]
Indian battle in New York.

99. R-C of D. Bukey. 26 Apr.
HR 528, 30-1, v3, 1p. [526]
Indian wars; Revolutionary War.

100. R-P of A. Dade. 26 Apr.
HR 532, 30-1, v3, 1p. [526]
Indian war; 1835; Florida.

101. R-C of G. McGuire. 26 Apr.
HR 544, 30-1, v3, 6p. [526]
Acting Supt. of Indian Affairs in St. Louis from 2 Sept. 1838 to 29 Mar. 1839.

102. R-P of E. Van Ness et al. 28 Apr.
SR 138, 30-1, v1, 1p. [512]
Indian war; 1836; Florida.

103. R-C of G. Humphreys. 28 Apr.
SR 139, 30-1, v1, 1p. [512]
Indian war; 1836; Florida.

104. R-P of L. Sharpe. 28 Apr.
HR 568, 30-1, v3, 1p. [526]
Indian prisoner; served U.S. 1793-1813.

105. R-C of J. Holland. 28 Apr.
HR 569, 30-1, v3, 1p. [526]
Indian hostilities.

106. Message on Troubles in Yucatan. 29 Apr.
SED 40, 30-1, v5, 19p. [507]
Indians warring on whites.

107. Resol. of the Florida Legis. 3 May.
HMD 82, 30-1, v1, 1p. [523]
Removal of the Seminoles.

108. R-C of H. and J. Gratiot. 4 May.
HR 591, 30-1, v3, 29p. [526]
Mining on Ottawa, Pottawatomie, and Chippewa lands in Wisconsin; treaty of 1829; claim is made that the land belonged to the Winnebagoes.

109. Message on Yucatan. 5 May.
SED 42, 30-1, v6, 17p. [508]
Indian war.

110. R-P of F. Martin. 5 May.
SR 146, 30-1, v1, 1p. [512]
Indian hostilities; Florida.

111. Petition of Oregon Citizens. 8 May.
SMD 136, 30-1, v1, 6p. [511]
Surrounded by Indians; have no power or right to treat with the tribes.

112. Message on Yucatan. 9 May.
SED 43, 30-1, v6, 29p. [508]
Indian war.

113. Message on Protection of Whites. 15 May.
SED 45, 30-1, v6, 4p. [508]
War between the whites and Indians in Yucatan.

114. Letter on Cherokee Claims. 16 May.
HED 63, 30-1, v8, 46p. [521]
Under the treaty of 1835-36.

115. Report on Pay of Tennessee Mounted Volunteers. 16 May.
HR 597, 30-1, v3, 4p. [526]
Cherokee nation; 1836.

116. On the Case of W. Turner. 16 May.
HR 599, 30-1, v3, 5p. [526]
Indian hostilities; Florida.

117. R-C of W. Yonge. 16 May.
HR 600, 30-1, v3, 7p. [526]
Creek and Seminole hostilties; 1836-37.

118. Report on Donation Claims in Arkansas. 16 May.
HR 604, 30-1, v3, 2p. [526]
Treaty of 23 May 1828 with the western Cherokees.

119. R-C of the Heirs of A. Loughery. 16 May.
HR 605, 30-1, v3, 5p. [526]
Indian campaign of 1781 in Ohio.

120. Mem. of B. Marshall et al. 17 May.
HMD 90, 30-1, v1, 5p. [523]
Creek delegates on unsettled business; treaties of 1821, 1826, 1832, and 1838.

121. R-C of E. Cogswell. 17 May.
HR 618, 30-1, v3, 3p. [526]
Texas Indians; treaties with the tribes of the Southwest.

122. R-C of J. Sutton. 17 May.
HR 619, 30-1, v3, 3p. [526]
Texas Indians; treaties.

123. Report on Annuities of the Miami Indians. 17 May.
HR 620, 30-1, v3, 5p. [526]
To be paid those Indians who did not remove from Indiana.

124. R-C of M. Thompson. 18 May.
HR 630, 30-1, v3, 3p. [526]
Black Hawk war; Florida Indian war.

125. Report on Cherokees in North Carolina. 18 May.
HR 632, 30-1, v3, 37p. [526]
Funds for the removal of these Indians.

126. Message on the Cherokee Indians. 20 May.
HED 65, 30-1, v8, 32p. [521]
Claims under treaty of Aug. 1846.

127. R-C of L. Williams. 20 May.
HR 644, 30-1, v3, 6p. [526]
Cherokee treaty of 1835.

128. Mem. of J. Thornton. 25 May.
SMD 143, 30-1, v1, 24p. [511]
Indian hostilities in Oregon; general Indian war on the Columbia River.

129. Message on Indian Difficulties in Oregon. 29 May.
SED 47, 30-1, v6, 8p. [508]
War with the Cayuse Indians on the Columbia River.

130. Report on Indian Disbursements. 30 May.
SED 48, 30-1, v6, 253p. [508]
Period of 1 Oct. 1846 to 9 Sept. 1847.

131. R-P of I. Garrison. 30 May.
HR 645, 30-1, v3, 8p. [526]
Florida Indian war; 1835-36.

132. R-P of W. Snavely. 30 May.
HR 647, 30-1, v3, 24p. [526]
Pottawatomie treaty of 27 Oct. 1832.

133. R-M of A. Rawson. 30 May.
HR 650, 30-1, v3, 2p. [526]
Seneca reservation in Ohio.

134. Report on Virginia Military Land Warrants. 30 May.
HR 663, 30-1, v3, 55p. [526]
Treaty of Hopewell in 1786.

135. Message on Conditions in Yucatan. 31 May.
SED 49, 30-1, v6, 10p. [508]
Indian war.

136. Proceedings of the Senate on the Treaty with Mexico. 31 May.
SED 52, 30-1, v7, 384p. [509]
Treaty of 2 Feb. 1848 at Guadalupe Hidalgo; concerns Indian tribes of the Southwest.

137. Report on Creek Indian Reservations. 1 June.
HED 66, 30-1, v8, 15p. [521]
Lists of reservations unsold and reservations set apart under the treaty of 1832.

138. Fremont's Expedition to Oregon and Upper California. 5 June.
SMD 148, 30-1, v1, 67p. [511]
Indians of the Great Basin, California, and Oregon.

139. Mem. of the Cherokee Delegation. 13 June.
SMD 145, 30-1, v1, 5p. [511]
Treaties of 6 Aug. 1846, and 1835.

140. R-P of the Administrator of the Estate of J. Johnston. 14 June.

HR 677, 30-1, v3, 29p. [526]
Indian trader in Michigan; married the daughter of a Chippewa chief.

141. R-P of W. Russell. 14 June.
HR 678, 30-1, v3, 7p. [526]
Indian disturbances; 1841-43; Missouri.

142. Report on Creek Indians in the Florida War. 15 June.
SED 55, 30-1, v7, 5p. [509]
List of Creek Indians killed or wounded in service of U.S. during the Florida war; 1836-37.

143. Communication on Indians in Texas. 15 June.
SR 171, 30-1, v1, 52p. [512]
Relations with said Indians; depredations by the Comanches, Arapahoes, Kiowas, and other tribes of the Southwest; treaty negotiations.

144. Report on a Canal Connecting Lakes Superior and Huron. 15 June.
SR 174, 30-1, v1, 7p. [512]
Indian situation around the lakes.

145. Mem. of Creek Delegates. 19 June.
SMD 147, 30-1, v1, 5p. [511]
Treaties of 1821, 1826, 1832, and 1838; Osage treaty of 1839; Seminole war.

146. Report on a Railroad in Missouri. 19 June.
SR 178, 30-1, v1, 13p. [512]
Old Indian trading house.

147. R-P of M. Leverett. 20 June.
HR 685, 30-1, v3, 3p. [526]
Indian campaigns; 1779-80; Georgia frontier.

148. R-P of J. Luce. 21 June.
SR 185, 30-1, v1, 1p. [512]
Indian agent in Arkansas.

149. Report of a Geological Reconnaissance. 22 June.
SED 57, 30-1, v7, 134p. [509]
In the Chippewa land district, the Winnebago reserve, Kickapoo country, and a strip of Sioux country in Wisconsin, Iowa, and Minnesota.

150. Report of the Choctaw Com'rs. 23 June.
SMD 149, 30-1, v1, 1p. [511]
Extract of report to Pres.; Choctaw claims.

151. R-P of the Heirs of J. Watson. 23 June.
HR 724, 30-1, v3, 22p. [526]
Creeks fighting in the Seminole war.

152. R-P of T. Judge. 23 June.
HR 726, 30-1, v3, 5p. [526]
Seminole agent; delegations to Washington, D.C. in 1844-45.

153. R-P of the Union Bank of Florida. 23 June.
HR 728, 30-1, v3, 13p. [526]
Florida Indian war.

154. Report on Public Lands. 23 June.
HR 732, 30-1, v3, 18p. [526]
Land to which Indian title has been extinguished.

155. Report on the Emigration of Indians. 24 June.
SR 190, 30-1, v1, 4p. [512]
Expenses incurred by Seneca, Onondaga and Cayuga Indians in an ineffectual attempt to emigrate to territory assigned to them in the Southwest.

156. Report on Organizing Indian Territory. 27 June.
HR 736, 30-1, v3, 14p. [526]
An Indian territory west of the Mississippi River for those Indians who have been removed.

157. R-C of R. Mitchell. 27 June.
HR 737, 30-1, v3, 1p. [526]
Sub-agent for the Pottawatomies.

158. Report on Indian Appropriations. 30 June.
HR 738, 30-1, v3, 2p. [526]
Recommends amendments to appropriations act; Cherokee treaty.

159. R-P of Settlers in Iowa. 3 July.
SR 198, 30-1, v1, 2p. [512]
Sac and Fox half-breed reservation.

160. R-C of Rusk, Taylor, and Gaines. 5 July.
SR 200, 30-1, v1, 1p. [512]
Travel expenses of the Choctaw Com'rs.

161. Message on the Mexican Treaty. 6 July.
SED 60, 30-1, v7, 74p. [509] *or* HED 69, 30-1, v8, 74p. [521]
Treaty of 2 Feb. 1848 at Guadalupe Hidalgo; concerns Indian tribes of the Southwest.

162. R-P of New York Citizens. 7 July.
SR 201, 30-1, v1, 2p. [512]
Seneca treaties of 1832 and 1848 on removal.

163. R-M of I. Bush et al. 7 July.
HR 740, 30-1, v4, 71p. [527]
Florida Indian war; refusal of Indians to remove westwards.

164. R-C of Virginia Officers and Soldiers. 12 July.
SR 204, 30-1, v1, 7p. [512]
Involves Cherokee lands.

165. R-P of the Reps. of J. Piatt. 12 July.
HR 747, 30-1, v4, 41p. [527]
Supplies to troops and Indians in Michigan; 1814.

166. R-C of T. Gammage. 12 July.
HR 750, 30-1, v4, 5p. [527]
Creek war of 1836.

167. R-C of S. Olmstead. 12 July.
JR 754, 30-1, v4, 2p. [527]
Indian depredations in Iowa.

168. R-C of D. Garnsey. 12 July.
HR 759, 30-1, v4, 3p. [527]
Removal of the Cattaraugus Indians from New York.

169. R-M of A. Slaeke and the Heirs of D. Repentigny. 17 July.
SR 209, 30-1, v1, 10p. [512]
Land in Michigan; Indian council in 1664; Hennepin's maps of Indian country, and descriptions of the Chippewas; trade.

170. Mem. of R. Gurley et al. 18 July.
SMD 152, 30-1, v1, 16p. [511]
Purchase of Catlin's Indian portraits.

171. R-P of Sault Ste. Marie Citizens. 19 July.
SR 212, 30-1, v1, 3p. [512]
British and Indian hostilities; War of 1812.

172. On the Relief of W. Stokes. 19 July.
HR 764, 30-1, v4, 11p. [527]
Creek hostilities; 1836.

173. R-C of the Heirs of W. Armstrong. 19 July.
HR 771, 30-1, v4, 29p. [527]
Choctaw Indian agent; removal and treaty negotiations.

174. R-C of A. McKim. 19 July.
HR 781, 30-1, v4, 1p. [527]
Indian wars of 1791-92.

175. R-C of R. Perry. 19 July.
HR 785, 30-1, v4, 1p. [527]
Indian campaign under Gen. Wayne in Ohio.

176. Message on New Mexico and California. 24 July.
HED 70, 30-1, v8, 49p. [521]
Indians in those areas mentioned.

177. R-M of B. Marshall et al. 25 July.
SR 215, 30-1, v1, 70p. [512]
Concerns claims of the Creek Indians under various treaties with the the U.S. and with Georgia; transcript of talks between Com'rs of Georgia and Creek chiefs; etc.

178. R-C of Heirs of J. Houseman. 25 July.
HR 798, 30-1, v4, 11p. [527]
Indian war in Florida.

179. R-P of E. Cobbs. 25 July.
HR 801, 30-1, v4, 2p. [527]
Creek and Seminole war; 1818.

180. R-M of M. McAffee. 28 July.
SR 218, 301, v1, 2p. [512]
Choctaw treaty of Dancing Rabbit Creek; 1830.

181. Message on Indian Populations. 2 Aug.
HED 76, 30-1, v8, 12p. [521]
In Oregon, California, and New Mexico.

182. On the Relief of the Reps. of A. Brereton. 8 Aug.
SR 234, 30-1, v1, 2p. [512]
Medical attention to Indians visiting Washington, D.C.

183. Report on the Purchase of Catlin's Collection. 8 Aug.
HR 820, 30-1, v4, 3p. [527]
Appropriation to purchase said collection of paintings and curiosities illustrative of Indian manners and customs.

184. R-P of the Heirs of Capt. Ransom. 8 Aug.
HR 823, 30-1, v4, 2p. [527]
Service against British and Indians; 1778.

185. R-M of the Creek Indians. 8 Aug.
HR 826, 30-1, v4, 32p. [527]
Claim for funds due under the treaty made at Indian Springs in 1821; relevant documents, etc.

186. Report on Sac and Fox Annuities. 9 Aug.
SED 70, 30-1, v8, 128p. [510]
Report of the Supt. of Indian Affairs in St. Louis on difficulties occurring in payment of annuities; extracts from newspapers showing how Indians were plundered by traders.

187. Mem. of the Oregon Legis. 10 Aug.
HMD 98, 30-1, v1, 26p. [523]
War with the Cayuse Indians.

188. R-P of C. Browne. 11 Aug.
SR 240, 30-1, v1, 2p. [512]
Supplies to troops in Georgia, North and South Carolina, Florida, and the Creek Nation; 1812-14.

189. Report on Draining the Everglades in Florida. 12 Aug.
SR 242, 30-1, v1, 133p. [512]
Seminole lands.

190. Statement of Appropriations. 16 Sept.
SMD 155, 30-1, v1, 76p. [511] *or* HMD 101, 30-1, v1, 84p. [523]
For the 1st session, 30th Congress; Indian expenses.

191. Annual Message to Congress with Documents; Pres. Polk. 5 Dec.
HED 1, 30-2, v1, 1275p. [537]
Indian war in Oregon; annual report of the Sec. of War; annual report of the CIA, including removal, trust funds, Indian debts, and reports of Supts., agents, schools, and farms; etc.

192. Estimates of Appropriations. 5 Dec.
HED 2, 30-2, v2, 186p. [538]
For the year ending 30 June 1850; Indian expenses.

193. Annual Report of the Sec. of the Treasury. 11 Dec.
HED 7, 30-2, v2, 77p. [538]
Fiscal 1848; Indian expenses.

194. Report on a Tract of Land in Illinois. 11 Dec.
HED 8, 30-2, v2, 20p. [538]
Involves questions over Indian land grants.

195. Annual Report of the Com'r of the Gen. Land Office. 14 Dec.
SED 2, 30-2, v2, 264p. [530] *or* HED 12, 30-2, v3, 264p. [539]
Indian treaties, land cessions and reservations.

196. Receipts and Expenditures. 18 Dec.
HED 11, 30-2, v4, 366p. [540]
Includes Indian expenses.

197. Resol. of Rep. Vinton. 18 Dec.
HMD 3, 30-2, v1, 2p. [544]
Refers portion of the annual message of the Pres. dealing with the Indian war in Oregon to the Com. on Military Affairs; that portion dealing with Indian relations sent to the Com. on Indian Affairs.

198. Report on a Railroad in Illinois. 19 Dec.
SR 244, 30-2, v1, 16p. [535]
Amount of land to which Indian title has been extinguished.

199. R-P of G. Farmer. 28 Dec.
HR 9, 30-2, v1, 4p. [545]
Road in Tennessee near the Chickasaw Old Town.

1849

1. Fremont's Memoir of an Expedition to Upper California. 2 Jan.
HMD 5, 30-2, v1, 40p. [544]
Indians of the Great Basin, and California.

2. R-P of P. Knaggs. 3 Jan.
SR 248, 30-2, v1, 2p. [535]
Treaty of 24 Sept. 1819 with the Saginaw Indians; trade among the Chippewas.

3. R-C of P. Godfrey. 3 Jan.
SR 249, 30-2, v1, 2p. [535]
Chippewa treaty of 24 Sept. 1819 at Saginaw.

4. R-P of S. Perry. 3 Jan.
HR 11, 30-2, v1, 2p. [545]
Indian supplies bound for Arkansas sunk on the Mississippi River.

5. Report on the Dismemberment of Texas. 3 Jan.
HR 16, 30-2, v1, 9p. [545]
Hostile Indians of the Southwest.

6. Appropriations and Balances of the War Dept. 6 Jan.
HED 27, 30-2, v4, 33p. [540]
Indian expenses.

7. Contingent Expenses of the War Dept. 6 Jan.
HED 28, 30-2, v4, 83p. [540]
Fiscal 1848; office of the CIA.

8. Report on Employees in the Indian Dept. 8 Jan.
SED 7, 30-2, v1, 10p. [529] *or* HED 31, 30-2, v4, 10p. [540]
During 1848.

9. Motion of Sen. Benton. 12 Jan.
SMD 14, 30-2, v1, 2p. [533]
Land in California; no Pueblo or Rancheria Indians to be disturbed in their possessions.

10. Clerks in the War Dept. 16 Jan.
SED 11, 30-2, v1, 16p. [529] *or* HED 39, 30-2, v4, 16p. [540]
For 1848; office of the CIA.

11. R-C of the Heirs of Semoice. 16 Jan.
HR 28, 30-2, v1, 2p. [545]
Land title belonging to a friendly Creek Indian; Creek treaty of 9 Aug. 1814.

12. Report on Cherokee Claims. 17 Jan.
SED 12, 30-2, v1, 4p. [529]
Statement of claims of the Cherokee Nation according to principles established by the treaty of 6 Aug. 1846.

13. Resol. of the Florida Legis. 17 Jan.
SMD 21, 30-2, v1, 1p. [533] *or* HMD 30,302-, v1, 1p. [544]
Concerns volunteers in the Seminole war.
14. Contracts of the War Dept. 23 Jan.
SED 17, 30-2, v1, 96p. [529] *or* HED 44, 30-2, v5, 96p. [541]
For 1848; Indian Dept.
15. Mem. of Texas Citizens. 24 Jan.
SMD 33, 30-2, v1, 8p. [533]
Railroad to the Pacific; securing the Southwest from Indian encroachments.
16. R-P of S. Bowen. 24 Jan.
HR 40, 30-2, v1, 2p. [545]
Audit of the Chickasaw trust fund.
17. R-P of W. Crews. 24 Jan.
HR 43, 30-2, v1, 5p. [545]
Removal of the Cherokees from North Carolina.
18. R-C of T. Proctor. 25 Jan.
SR 265, 30-2, v1, 1p. [535]
For services as a Seminole interpreter.
19. R-P of J. Watson. 29 Jan.
SR 274, 30-2, v1, 3p. [535]
Sec. of the Indian Dept. office in Michigan from 1806 to 1812.
20. R-C of M. Reneau. 29 Jan.
SR 275, 30-2, v1, 1p. [535]
Osage treaty of 1825; half-breed Indian lands.
21. R-M of the Arkansas Legis. 31 Jan.
SR 276, 30-2, v1, 3p. [535]
Military road from Arkansas to California; regulation of Indians of the Southwest.
22. Resol. of the Florida Legis. 31 Jan.
HMD 21, 30-2, v1, 3p. [544]
Asks Congress to take action to keep Indians within their prescribed boundaries; urges removal of all Indians.
23. Resol. of the Florida Legis. 31 Jan.
HMD 32, 30-2, v1, 1p. [544]
Soldiers in the Florida Indian war.
24. Resol. of the Florida Legis. 31 Jan.
HMD 33, 30-2, v1, 1p. [544]
Concerns soldiers in the Seminole war; 1838-39.
25. Remonstrance of a Choctaw Delegate. 3 Feb .
HMD 35, 30-2, v1, 4p. [544]
P. Pitchlynn speaks against passage of a bill to unite under one government the several Indian tribes west of the Mississippi River.
26. On the Case of the Widow of A. Pacheco. 5 Feb.
SR 282, 30-2, v1, 1p. [535]
Black interpreter captured by Seminoles during the Florida war; he is ordered to remove west with the Indians.
27. Petition of Chippewa Indians on Lake Superior. 7 Feb.
HMD 36, 30-2, v1, 2p. [544]
Asks for a grant of 24 sections of land covering the graves of their fathers, their sugar orchards, rice lakes, etc.; also asks for money to pay the expense of a delegation to Washington, D.C.
28. Message on the Treaty with Mexico. 8 Feb.
HED 50, 30-2, v5, 82p. [541]
Treaty of 2 Feb. 1848 at Guadalupe Hidalgo; affects Indians of the Southwest.
29. Resol. of the Pennsylvania Legis. 8 Feb.
HMD 38, 30-2, v1, 1p. [544]
Asks Congress to grant the Indians a portion of the Northwest Coastal region, and aid in establishing for them a permanent home.
30. Resol. of the North Carolina Legis. 8 Feb.
HMD 39, 30-2, v1, 2p. [544]
Asks Congress to grant the Indians land out West, and aid in establishing for them a permanent home.
31. R-P of N. Egnew. 8 Feb.
HR 59, 30-2, v1, 1p. [545]
Action of the Com. on Indian Affairs.
32. R-M of Sioux Half and Quarter Breeds. 8 Feb.
HR 60, 30-2, v1, 1p. [545]
Distribution of funds paid under the treaty of 29 Sept. 1837.
33. Mem. of Judge Wind et al. 10 Feb.
HMD 40, 30-2, v1, 2p. [544]
Treaty stipulations with the "Old Settler," or Western Cherokees.
34. Mem. of W. Cooley and J. Drew. 10 Feb.
HMD 41, 30-2, v1, 5p. [544]
Payment of sums due the "Old Settler," or Western Cherokees.

35. Report on Claims Against the Cherokees. 12 Feb.
SED 28, 30-2, v3, 189p. [531]
Documentation concerning said claims; being adjusted under the treaty of 6 Aug. 1846.

36. Mem. of Citizens Residing in the Mississippi River Valley. 12 Feb.
SMD 52, 30-2, v1, 3p. [533]
Asks that persons traveling to California to search for gold be protected from hostile Indians.

37. R-M of S. Colt. 12 Feb.
SR 295, 30-2, v1, 18p. [535]
On improved fire arms, deemed best suited for use in Indian country (this document should have been printed as SR 296).

38. R-M of the Arkansas Gen. Assembly. 12 Feb.
SR 297, 30-2, v1, 1p. [535]
Bounty land for those serving in Indian wars.

39. R-C of J. Duval. 12 Feb.
SR 298, 30-2, v1, 4p. [535]
Removal of the Apalachicola Indians from Florida in 1838.

40. R-M of J. Skinner et al. 12 Feb.
HR 66, 30-2, v1, 4p. [545]
On creation of a "home dept.," or a Dept. of the Interior; Indian relations would be handled in this proposed new dept.

41. R-C of Georgia. 13 Feb.
SR 304, 30-2, v1, 2p. [535]
Creek war of 1836.

42. Report on a Cherokee Treaty. 13 Feb.
HMD 43, 30-2, v1, 7p. [544]
Estimate of funds needed to carry out the treaty of 1846.

43. R-P of D. Wilson. 13 Feb.
HR 84, 30-2, v1, 2p. [545]
British and Indians; 1814; New York.

44. R-P of P. Branch. 13 Feb.
HR 85, 30-2, v1, 2p. [545]
British and Indians; 1813; New York.

45. R-M of W. Bradley et al. 17 Feb.
SR 310, 30-2, v1, 6p. [535]
Railroad from Missouri to the Pacific; will speed Indian civilization.

46. Resol. of the Indiana Legis. 17 Feb.
HMD 44, 30-2, v1, 2p. [544]
Grant of land for a university; would be within the Miami land reserve.

47. Resol. of the Indiana Legis. 17 Feb.
HMD 45, 30-2, v1, 1p. [544]
Recommends passage of a bill giving soldiers of the War of 1812 and Indian wars the same bounty land and extra pay as allowed soldiers in the Mexican war.

48. Report on Charges Against W. Medill. 17 Feb.
HR 104, 30-2, v1, 71p. [545]
Select com. has investigated charges of corruption made against the CIA, and fully acquits him; journal of proceedings.

49. Report on Wyandot Reserve Lands. 27 Feb.
HR 116, 30-2, v1, 2p. [545]
Lands ceded under the treaty of 17 Jan. 1842 in Ohio.

50. On the Relief of C. Wallace. 27 Feb.
HR 118, 30-2, v1, 14p. [545]
Virginia military tract in Ohio; bounded by the Greenville, or Indian treaty line.

51. R-P of U. Wilson. 28 Feb.
HR 120, 30-2, v1, 1p. [545]
Indian wars of 1789-90.

52. R-C of R. Mitchell. 28 Feb.
HR 125, 30-2, v1, 3p. [545]
Sac, Fox, and Iowa depredations of 1838-39.

53. R-C of A. Watson. 28 Feb.
HR 135, 30-2, v1, 1p. [545]
Property destroyed by Indians in Florida.

54. Letter on the Chickasaw Fund. 2 Mar.
HED 66, 30-2, v7, 5p. [543]
Statement of the condition of the fund; treaties of 20 Oct. 1832, and 24 May 1834.

55. R-C of the Heirs of Col. Crowell. 3 Mar.
HR 144, 30-2, v1, 1p. [545]
Disbursal of money to the Creeks while an Indian agent in 1826; negotiated the treaty of 1826.

56. Mem. of W. Ross et al. 16 Mar.
SED 3, 31-sp, v1, 5p. [547]
Asks fulfillment of Cherokee treaty stipulations; treaties of 1835 and 1846; "Old Settler," or Western Cherokees.

57. Journal of an Expedition from Santa Fe to San Diego. 19 Mar.
SED 2, 31-sp. v1, 85p. [547]

Encounters with Navaho, Apache, Pimo, and other Indians of the Southwest; talks with some Indians are printed.

58. Statements of Appropriations. 16 Apr.
SMD 65, 30-2, v1, 63p. [533]
During the 2d session, 30th Congress; Indian expenses.

59. List of Private Claims. 16 Apr.
SMD 67, 30-2, v2, 1104p. [534]
From the commencement of the 14th Congress, to the close of the 30th Congress; includes claims involving Indians.

60. Estimates of Appropriations. 3 Dec.
HED 1, 31-1, v1, 288p. [567]
For fiscal 1851; Indian expenses.

61. Annual Message to Congress with Documents; Pres. Taylor. 24 Dec.
SED 1, 31-1, v1-3, 2066p. [549-551] *or* HED 5, 31-1, v3 (pts. 1-3), 2066p. [569-571]
Indian relations; annual report of the Sec. of War (Serials 549 and 569); annual report of the Sec. of Interior (Serials 550 and 570); annual report of the Gen. Land Office (Serials 550-551 and 570-571); annual report of the CIA (Serials 550 and 570), including removal of the Seminoles, Indian affairs in Texas, instructions to Sioux Com'rs, Stockbridge Indian treaty, trust funds, and reports of Supts., agents, and schools, etc.

62. Annual Report of the Sec. of the Treasury. 24 Dec.
SED 2, 31-1, v4, 995p. [552] *or* HED 4, 31-1, v2, 995p. [568]
Indian expenses during fiscal 1849.

63. Report on Cherokee Claims. 31 Dec.
SED 6, 31-1, v6, 4p. [554] *or* HED 29, 31-1, v7, 3p. [576]
Adjustments made under the treaties of 1835-36 and 1846.

64. Letter on Disbursements for Indians. 31 Dec.
HED 11, 31-1, v4, 345p. [572]
Made from 1 Oct. 1847 to 30 Sept. 1848.

1850

1. Expenditures of the War Dept. 10 Jan.
SED 10, 31-1, v6, 11p. [554] *or* HED 25, 31-1, v7, 11p. [576]
For fiscal 1849; includes Seminole hostilities.

2. Report on a Route from Arkansas to Santa Fe. 14 Jan.
SED 12, 31-1, v6, 25p. [554] *or* HED 45, 31-1, v8, 89p. [577]
Encounters with Indians of the Southwest; journal of the expedition (House version includes a report by Capt. Marcy on the same subject).

3. R-P of Citizens of Sault Ste. Marie. 14 Jan.
SR 5, 31-1, v1, 4p. [565]
British and Indians; War of 1812.

4. R-P of J. Downs. 15 Jan.
SR 7, 31-1, v1, 2p. [565]
Creek war; 1813-14.

5. R-P of W. Crews. 22 Jan.
HR 2, 31-1, v1, 4p. [583]
Cherokee removal.

6. Message on California and New Mexico. 24 Jan.
SED 18, 31-1, v9, 952p. [557] *or* HED 17, 31-1, v5, 976p. [573]
Indians of said territories; Indian depredations; treaty of Guadalupe Hidalgo; etc.

7. R-C of L. Thomas and T. Rogers. 28 Jan.
SR 24, 31-1, v1, 1p. [565]
Legal defense of two Sisseton Sioux indicted for murder in 1844.

8. R-C of J. Sutton. 29 Jan.
HR 15, 31-1, v1, 3p. [583]
Blacksmith to the Indians in Texas; 1848.

9. R-M of W. Osborne. 29 Jan.
HR 24, 31-1, v1, 1p. [583]
Property destroyed by Indians in 1849 in the Rio Grande River Valley.

10. Message on the Boundary of Texas. 31 Jan.
SED 24, 31-1, v6, 37p. [554]
Indian depredations in the Southwest.

11. R-P of J. Williams. 31 Jan.
SR 29, 31-1, v1, 2p. [565]
Choctaw and Cherokee land certificates in Arkansas.

12. R-P of O. Dibble and G. Bates. 4 Feb.
SR 38, 31-1, v1, 7p. [565]
Canal to connect Lakes Superior and Huron; Chippewa treaty of 1842 involved; influence of the Hudson Bay Co. over Indian tribes.

13. Resol. of the Indiana Legis. 4 Feb.
HMD 26, 31-1, v1, 2p. [581]
Land in the Miami reserve; ceded lands.

14. R-C of J. Watson. 5 Feb.
SR 43, 31-1, v1, 2p. [565]
Indian Dept. in Michigan; 1806-12.

15. Resol. of the Indiana Legis. 6 Feb.
SMD 40, 31-1, v1, 2p. [563]
Land donation from the Miami reserve.

16. R-M of J. Dickson. 6 Feb.
HR 25, 31-1, v1, 3p. [583]
Provisions furnished Indians at military posts in Indiana in 1817.

17. R-P of S. Dewey. 7 Feb.
HR 45, 31-1, v1, 1p. [583]
Prisoner of Indians; 1780; Canada.

18. R-C of the Heirs of J. Van Valkenburgh. 7 Feb.
HR 66, 31-1, v1, 1p. [583]
Killed by Indians in 1781.

19. R-M of Iowa Citizens. 13 Feb.
SR 47, 31-1; v1, 2p. [565]
Land recently ceded to the U.S. by Indians.

20. R-P of the Heirs of J. Kennedy. 13 Feb.
SR 50, 31-1, v1, 2p. [565]
Indian hostilities.

21. R-C of G. Collier and W. Pettus. 13 Feb.
HR 74, 31-1, v1, 1p. [583]
Salary as a Com'r to the Sioux in 1838.

22. R-P of S. Bowen. 13 Feb.
HR 77, 31-1, v1, 2p. [583]
Accountant for the Chickasaw trust fund.

23. R-C of I. Johnson. 13 Feb.
HR 97, 31-1, v1, 6p. [583]
Supplies furnished the Com'rs to the Miamies in 1833.

24. R-P of the Securities of S. Bunch. 13 Feb.
HR 98, 31-1, v1, 10p. [583]
Sub-agent to the Osage Indians; lost U.S. funds.

25. Memoir of a Military Expedition from San Antonio to Saltillo, Mexico. 18 Feb.
SED 32, 31-1, v10, 67p. [558]
Lipan, Mescalero, and Comanche depredations in Mexico.

26. Mem. of the Wisconsin Legis. 18 Feb.
SMD 47, 31-1, v1, 2p. [563]
Menomonee treaty and cession of land.

27. R-P of the Reps. of W. Slacum. 18 Feb.
SR 61, 31-1, v1, 3p. [565]
Expedition to Oregon in 1836; presents given to Indians.

28. R-C of the Heirs of J. Watson. 20 Feb.
HR 102, 31-1, v1, 20p. [583]
Slaves captured by Creeks in the Seminole war.

29. R-P of M. Hetzel. 25 Feb.
SR 73, 31-1, v1, 4p. [565]
Cherokee removal in 1838.

30. R-C of Soldiers of Virginia. 25 Feb.
SR 76, 31-1, v1, 6p. [565]
Service in Cherokee country in 1779; Chickasaw treaty of 19 Oct. 1818.

31. Mem. of the Missouri Legis. 25 Feb.
HMD 34, 31-1, v1, 2p. [581]
Extension of the southwestern boundary of the state to facilitate trade; extinguishment of Seneca and Quapaw title to land.

32. Resol. of the Tennessee Legis. 25 Feb.
HMD 37, 31-1, v1, 1p. [581]
Soldiers in the Seminole war.

33. Mem. of Directors of the Pacific Railroad Co. 28 Feb.
SMD 59, 31-1, v1, 7p. [563]
Would carry Indian annuity goods.

34. Mem. of the Michigan Legis. 28 Feb.
HMD 45, 31-1, v1, 2p. [581]
Farms designed for defense against Indians.

35. R-C of Capt. McClellan. 4 Mar.
SR 79, 31-1, v1, 1p. [565]
Indian war in Florida; 1840.

36. R-M of Michigan Citizens. 6 Mar.
SR 80, 31-1, v1, 1p. [565]
British and Indians; 1813.

37. R-P of M. Williams. 6 Mar.
HR 127, 31-1, v1, 1p. [583]
British and Indians; 1812.

38. R-P of the Heirs of Lieut. Col. Miller. 6 Mar.
HR 134, 31-1, v1, 4p. [583]
Indian invasion of Pennsylvania in 1794.

39. R-P of T. McQuaide et al. 6 Mar.
HR 138, 31-1, v1, 4p. [583]
Bounty land to rangers who served against the Indians.

40. R-M of T. Allen et al. 13 Mar.
HR 140, 31-1, v1, 117p. [583]
Whitney's railroad to the Pacific; would not think of using Indian lands along the route.

41. On the Case of A. Bayard. 13 Mar.
HR 141, 31-1, v1, 2p. [583]
Indian battle at Fort Harrison.

42. R-M of Citizens. of the U.S. 13 Mar.
HR 171, 31-1, v1, 5p. [583]
Abolition of the office of chaplain in the military and at Indian stations; Indian Bureau indicates that no such office exists.

43. R-M of the Minnesota Legis. 13 Mar.
HR 172, 31-1, v1, 2p. [583]
Appropriation for roads to be used to deliver goods to the Indians.

44. Documents on a Proposed Treaty with Indians. 18 Mar.
SMD 70, 31-1, v1, 5p. [563]
Concerns a treaty to be negotiated with Indians of the Southwest; list of tribes involved.

45. Report on an Expedition to the Pembina Settlement. 19 Mar.
HED 51, 31-1, v8, 55p. [577]
Establishment of a military post on the Red River of the north; description of Sioux, Chippewa, and Winnebago Indians; etc.

46. Report on the Chickasaw Indians. 19 Mar.
HED 58, 31-1, v8, 5p. [577]
Annual statement on the tribal trust fund.

47. Disbursements to the Indians. 21 Mar.
SED 41, 31-1, v10, 134p. [558] *or* HED 61, 31-1, v8, 134p. [577]
From 1 Oct. 1848 to 30 June 1849.

48. Report on an Expedition to Minnesota. 22 Mar.
SED 42, 31-1, v10, 56p. [558]
Description of Sioux, Winnebago, and Chippewa Indians.

49. R-C of H. McClintock et al. 26 Mar.
SR 93, 31-1, v1, 1p. [565]
Employed on the Sac and Fox reservation.

50. Report on California. 27 Mar.
HED 59, 31-1, v8, 32p. [577]
Discusses the number and condition of Indians in said Territory.

51. R-P of G. Ransom et al. 28 Mar.
HR 187, 31-1, v1, 2p. [583]
Service against British and Indians; 1778

52. R-C of the Heirs of Semoice. 28 Mar.
HR 194, 31-1, v1, 2p. [583]
Concerns land title to a Creek Indian in Alabama; treaty of 9 Aug. 1814.

53. R-P of the Heirs of S. Smith. 28 Mar.
HR 195, 31-1, v1, 1p. [583]
A Creek Indian; concerns title to land in Alabama.

54. Report on an Armory at Fort Massac. 28 Mar.
HR 214, 31-1, v2, 5p. [584]
Indians on the western frontier.

55. Message on Indians on the Mexican Frontier. 3 Apr.
SED 44, 31-1, v10, 3p. [558] *or* HED 62, 31-1, v8, 3p. [577]
Indian depredations; matter mentioned in the treaty of Guadalupe Hidalgo with Mexico.

56. R-C of W. Harding. 5 Apr.
SR 98, 31-1, v1, 2p. [565]
Enrolling agent for the U.S. among the Cherokees during their removal westwards.

57. R-C of Menomonee Indians. 8 Apr.
SR 101, 31-1, v1, 1p. [565]
Under the treaty of 3 Sept. 1836 made in Wisconsin.

58. R-M of M. Thompson. 11 Apr.
HR 235, 31-1, v2, 3p. [584]
Black Hawk war of 1832; Florida Indian war of 1837.

59. R-C of M. Robison. 11 Apr.
HR 242, 31-1, v2, 2p. [584]
Creek war of 1836.

60. R-M of J. Stilwell. 11 Ap.
HR 263, 31-1, v2, 2p. [584]
Destruction of Indian towns on the Wabash River during the Indian wars of 1783-95.

61. R-C of Capt. Cicott. 11 Ap.
HR 267, 31-1, v2, 5p. [584]
Property destroyed by Pottawatomies, Ottawas, and Chippewas in Michigan; 1812.

62. Resol. of the Texas Legis. 12 Ap.
SMD 96, 31-1, v1, 3p. [563]
Indian hostilities on the state's western frontier.

63. Mem. of the Texas Legis. 12 Ap.
SMD 97, 31-1, v1, 3p. [563]
Indian hostilities on the state's frontier.

64. R-P of M. Paquette and T. Brisbois. 15 Apr.
SR 105, 31-1, v1, 2p. [565]
Winnebago treaty of 1829 at Prairie du Chien.

65. R-M of J. Marsh. 15 Apr.
SR 106, 31-1, v1, 1p. [565]
Indian depredations.

66. R-P of Citizens of Louisiana. 24 Apr.
HR 276, 31-1, v2, 1p. [584]
For removal of Choctaw Indians from their midst.

67. R-P of the Heirs of Al-lo-lah. 24 Apr.
HR 277, 31-1, v2, 8p. [584]
Title to land in Indiana given to a Miami Indian by the treaty of 6 Nov. 1838.

68. R-P of J. Cruttenden. 24 Apr.
HR 278, 31-1, v2, 1p. [584]
Losses while in the Indian Service.

69. Report on the Winnebago Indians. 24 Apr.
HR 279, 31-1, v2, 2p. [584]
Claim against the tribe; adjustment under the treaty of 1 Nov. 1837.

70. Report on the Treaty of Guadalupe Hidalgo. 24 Apr.
HR 280, 31-1, v2, 3p. [584]
Recommends rigid enforcement of the treaty concerning suppression of Indian incursions into Mexico.

71. Report on Certain Miami Indians. 24 Apr.
HR 281, 31-1, v2, 2p. [584]
Treaty of 6 Nov. 1838; removal; Indians still in Indiana.

72. R-C of M. and R. Bean. 29 Apr.
SR 114, 31-1, v1, 8p. [565]
Property ceded to Cherokee Indians; treaty of 6 May 1828.

73. Report on California. 6 May.
SED 47, 31-1, v10, 164p. [558]
Geological reports; Gen. Smith discusses Indian hostilities; etc.

74. R-M of the Wisconsin Legis. 6 May.
SR 117, 31-1, v1, 1p. [565]
Survey of the Menomonee purchase, and in favor of pre-emption rights to settlers; treaty of 18 Oct. 1848.

75. R-C of Erskine and Eichelburger. 7 May.
SR 120, 31-1, v1, 3p. [565]
Debt contracted by John Gunter, Jr., a Cherokee Indian, prior to the Cherokee treaty of 29 Dec. 1835; removal.

76. R-P of G. Thomas. 9 May.
HR 302, 31-1, v2, 1p. [584]
Creek war; 1836; Georgia and Alabama.

77. R-P of W. Edwards. 9 May.
HR 306, 31-1, v2, 1p. [584]
Escort to Indian traders near Fort Gibson, Arkansas.

78. R-P of J. Woodward. 9 May.
HR 309, 31-1, v2, 1p. [584]
British and Indians; 1778; New York.

79. R-M of the Heirs of S. Riggs. 9 May.
HR 312, 31-1, v2, 2p. [584]
Seminole war; 1818; Florida.

80. R-P of H. Donaldson. 9 May.
HR 316, 31-1, v2, 1p. [584]
Indian hostilities; 1811; Kaskaskia in Illinois.

81. R-P of W. Pierce. 9 May.
HR 318, 31-1, v2, 1p. [584]
Indian war; 1792; on the Miami River.

82. R-P of J. Caldwell. 9 May.
HR 319, 31-1, v2, 1p. [584]
Indian war; 1795.

83. R-P of Citizens of Indiana. 9 May.
HR 320, 31-1, v2, 1p. [584]
Soldiers in Indian wars.

84. R-P of Indiana Citizens. 9 May.
HR 321, 31-1, v2, 1p. [584]
Indian campaign of 1812 under Gen. Wayne.

85. R-M of T. Snodgrass. 13 May.
SR 124, 31-1, v1, 2p. [565]
Agent of Cherokee removal in 1838.

86. R-C of Heirs of N. Brush. 13 May.
SR 125, 31-1, v1, 2p. [565]
Seminole war in Florida; 1836.

87. Routes from Arkansas to the Rio Grande River. 16 May.
HED 67, 31-1, v8, 12p. [577]
Journal of an expedition; Indians of the Southwest.

88. Geological Report on the Copper District of Lake Superior. 16 May.
HED 69, 31-1, v9, 224p. [578]
History of the region; Sioux, Chippewa, Mohawk, and other Indian tribes.

89. R-P of the Reps. of J. Piatt. 16 May.
HR 325, 31-1, v2, 51p. [584]
Supplies to Indians; 1814; Michigan.

90. R-C of the Heirs of G. Galphin. 17 May.
HR 334, 31-1, v2, 114p. [584]
Claim based on indebtedness of Creek and Cherokee Indians; 1773.

91. Message on Seminole Indians in Florida. 21 May.
SED 49, 31-1, v13, 173p. [561]
Relative to hostilities committed by the Seminole Indians in Florida during the past year, their removal, etc.

92. Message on Affairs in California and Oregon. 22 May.
SED 52, 31-1, v13, 180p. [561]
Cayuse war in Oregon; list of Indian tribes in Oregon; etc.

93. R-M of E. Lomax. 24 May.
SR 142, 31-1, v1, 3p. [565]
Florida Indian war; 1836.

94. R-M of Texas Volunteers. 12 June.
HR 352, 31-1, v2, 3p. [584]
Lipan Indian hostilities on the Texas frontier in 1848-49.

95. R-P of J. Rolls. 14 June.
HR 353, 31-1, v2, 1p. [584]
Florida Indian war in 1836.

96. R-P of S. Menifield. 14 June.
HR 365, 31-1, v2, 1p. [584]
Indian ranger; 1794; Ohio River.

97. R-P of W. Quait. 14 June.
HR 366, 31-1, v2, 1p. [584]
Indian hostilities of 1817 in Florida.

98. R-P of W. Denham. 14 June.
HR 398, 31-1, v2, 1p. [584]
Creek war prior to 1820.

99. R-P of F. Dixon. 17 June.
SR 150, 31-1, v1, 1p. [565]
Indian wars of the northwest.

100. R-M of S. Coody. 24 June.
SR 158, 31-1, v1, 2p. [565]
Depredations by U.S. troops in Cherokee country.

101. R-P of J. Goff. 9 July.
SR 163, 31-1, v1, 5p. [565]
Florida Indian war; 1836.

102. R-C of J. Bulow, jr. 23 July.
HR 403, 31-1, v3, 15p. [585]
Creek and Seminole wars of 1836.

103. Reconnaissances of Routes from San Antonio to El Paso, and an Expedition to Navajo Country. 24 July.
SED 64, 31-1, v14, 250p. [562]
Journals of encounters with various tribes of the Southwest; maps, drawings, and paintings.

104. Appropriations of the Interior Dept. 25 July.
HED 77, 31-1, v10, 9p. [579]
Year ending 30 June 1849; Indian expenses.

105. Contingent Expenditures of the Interior Dept. 25 July.
HED 78, 31-1, v10, 67p. [579]
Office of the CIA; year ending 30 June 1849.

106. Clerks in the Interior Dept. 25 July.
HED 79, 31-1, v10, 25p. [579]
For 1849; Office of the CIA.

107. Annual Report of the Smithsonian Institution. 30 July.
SMD 120, 31-1, v2, 207p. [564] *or*
HMD 50, 31-1, v2, 207p. [582]
Ancient mounds on the Mississippi River, etc.

108. R-P of Citizens of Indiana. 31 July.
HR 434, 31-1, v3, 1p. [585]
Land cessions by Miami treaties.

109. R-M of J. Rogers. 2 Aug.
SR 175, 31-1, v1, 2p. [565]
Cherokee treaties of 1817, 1819, and 1835.

110. R-M of Delegates of Cherokee Nation. 8 Aug.
SR 176, 31-1, v1, 10p. [565]
Recommends Cherokee Nation be allowed a certain sum for subsistence; treaties of 1835 and 1846.

111. R-C of A. and J. Kendall, and S. Stambaugh. 10 Aug.
SR 180, 31-1, v1, 3p. [565]
Cherokee treaties of 1817, 1819, 1835, and 1846.

112. R-M of R. Armstrong. 22 Aug.
SR 186, 31-1, v1, 2p. [565]
Creek war of 1814.

113. R-M of J. Tucker. 23 Aug.
SR 188, 31-1, v1, 1p. [565]
Florida Indian war; 1838.

114. R-C of Followers of Gen. McIntosh. 26 Aug.
SR 189, 31-1, v1, 5p. [565]
Treaty of 1826 with the Creeks.

115. R-C of Friendly Creeks. 28 Aug.
SR 190, 31-1, v1, 8p. [565]
Losses sustained in war of 1814.

116. Report on the Ewing Investigation. 6 Sept.
HR 489, 31-1, v3, 276p. [585]
Charges against the Sec. of Interior regarding Indian affairs; decisions on claims against Chickasaw, Pottawatomie, Sac, Fox, and other Indian tribes.

117. Report on the Hot Springs of Arkansas. 9 Sept.
SED 70, 31-1, v14, 116p. [562]
Quapaw treaty of 24 Aug. 1818.

118. R-C of Seneca Indians of New York. 9 Sept.
SR 192, 31-1, v1, 5p. [565]

Money lost through an appointed agent.

119. R-M of the Central Bank of Georgia. 10 Sept.
SR 193, 31-1, v1, 2p. [565]
Creek depredations during 1836-1837.

120. Report on Removal of Winnebago Indians. 17 Sept.
HR 501, 31-1, v3, 64p. [585]
Under various treaties.

121. R-P of G. Burns. 19 Sept.
SR 207, 31-1, v1, 1p. [565]
Indian wars of the northwest; 1790-1794.

122. R-C of W. Hansell et al. 20 Sept.
SR 211, 31-1, v1, 2p. [565]
Legal counsel for the Cherokees in 1835.

123. R-M of E. Tracey et al. 23 Sept.
SR 212, 31-1, v1, 2p. [565]
Lease of lands to which Indian title has not been extinguished; Ottawas, Pottawatomies, and Chippewas.

124. R-C of the Executor of A. Hunter. 24 Sept.
SR 213, 31-1, v1, 2p. [565]
Cherokee treaty negotiations in 1835; supplies.

125. Statements of Appropriations. 12 Nov.
SMD 128, 31-1, v1, 90p. [563] *or* HMD 57, 31-1, v2, 90p. [582]
For the 1st session, 31st Congress; Indian expenses.

126. Annual Message to Congress with Documents; Pres. Fillmore. 2 Dec.
SED 1, 31-2, v1, 932p. [587] *or* HED 1, 31-2, v1, 932p. [595]
Indian incursions into Mexico; annual report of the Sec. of War; annual report of the Sec. of Interior; annual report of the CIA, including trust funds, instructions to Com'rs in Oregon, and reports from Supts., agents, and schools; etc.

127. Annual Report of the Com'r of the Gen. Land Office. 9 Dec.
SED 2, 31-2, v2, 157p. [588] *or* HED 9, 31-2, v3, 157p. [597]
Indian land cessions, reservations, and treaties.

128. Balances and Appropriations of the Interior Dept. 10 Dec.
HED 3, 31-2, v2, 8p. [596]
Indian expenses.

129. Message on Indian Incursions into Mexico. 10 Dec.
HED 4, 31-2, v2, 2p. [596]
Treaty of Guadalupe Hidalgo is violated.

130. Contingent Expenses of the Interior Dept. 16 Dec.
HED 7, 31-2, v3, 95p. [597]
Office of the CIA.

131. Annual Report of the Sec. of the Treasury. 17 Dec.
SED 4, 31-2, v2, 176p. [588] *or* HED 11, 31-2, v3, 176p. [597]
Indian expenses for fiscal 1850.

132. R-P of V. Morass. 30 Dec.
SR 222, 31-2, v1, 2p. [593]
Land bounded by the Chippewa reservation.

1851

1. Mem. of the Oregon Legis. 6 Jan.
SMD 5, 31-2, v1, 6p. [592]
Cayuse war; removal of Indians; etc.

2. Report on Bounty Lands. 6 Jan.
HR 4, 31-2, v1, 29p. [606]
For soldiers in Indian wars.

3. Report on Payment of Troops. 15 Jan.
SR 239, 31-2, v1, 1p. [593]
Bounty land and extra pay to Indian volunteers.

4. R-P of R. Jemison. 20 Jan.
SR 243, 31-2, v1, 1p. [593]
Creek war; 1836; Alabama.

5. Employees of the Indian Dept. 21 Jan.
HED 27, 31-2, v5, 12p. [599]
For 1850.

6. R-C of the Heirs of J. Bulow, jr. 25 Jan.
SR 253, 31-2, v1, 6p. [593]
Seminole depredations; 1836; Florida.

7. R-C of W. Hart. 29 Jan.
SR 256, 31-2, v1, 6p. [593]
Choctaw treaty of 27 Sept. 1830 at Dancing Rabbit Creek; removal.

8. R-M of A. Ray. 29 Jan.
HR 14, 31-2, v1, 2p. [606]
Cherokee treaties of 1817, 1819, and 1835-1836.

9. R-P of the Sureties of S. Bunch. 29 Jan.

HR 15, 31-2, v1, 12p. [606]
Sub-agent for the Osage Indians.

10. R-C of P. Random. 29 Jan.
HR 16, 31-2, v1, 5p. [606]
Friendly Creek Indian during the Creek war of 1813-1814.

11. R-C of the Heirs of W. Armstrong. 29 Jan.
HR 17, 31-2, v1, 6p. [606]
Choctaw agent in 1835.

12. R-C of D. Bread et al., Oneida Indians. 29 Jan.
HR 18, 31-2, v1, 1p. [606]
Interest on indebtedness of U.S.; treaty of 1794 with the Six Nations.

13. R-P of M. Woodbury and E. Odell. 29 Jan.
HR 19, 31-2, v1, 1p. [606]
Sioux treaty of 1837.

14. R-P of J. Snow and A. Bangs. 31 Jan.
SR 265, 31-2, v1, 4p. [593]
Telegraph from the Mississippi River to California; Indian depredations.

15. R-P of S. Floyd. 31 Jan.
SR 268, 31-2, v1, 1p. [593]
Indian campaign; 1811; battle of Tippecanoe.

16. Report on Lieut. Whipple's Expedition. 1 Feb.
SED 19, 31-2, v3, 28p. [589]
From San Diego to the Colorado River.

17. Resol. of the Pennsylvania Legis. 10 Feb.
SMD 16, 31-2, v1, 2p. [592]
Soldiers in Indian wars.

18. Letter on Office of Indian Affairs. 11 Feb.
HED 25, 31-2, v5, 4p. [599]
On reorganization of Office; addition of Pacific Coast and Southwestern Indians.

19. On the Relief of Tennessee Volunteers. 18 Feb.
HR 32, 31-2, v1, 1p. [606]
Cherokee country; 1836.

20. R-P of H. Beetley. 20 Feb.
SR 307, 31-2, v1, 1p. [593]
Choctaw nation; 1815.

21. Mem. of the Oregon Legis. 25 Feb.
SMD 29, 31-2, v1, 11p. [592]
Expenses of the Cayuse war.

22. R-M of J. Irwin. 25 Feb.
SR 315, 31-2, v1, 2p. [593]
Indian depredations; Georgia frontier.

23. R-C of T. Mangham et al. 25 Feb.
HR 37, 31-2, v1, 139p. [606]
Intercourse with Indian tribes; Creek and Cherokee delegations; depredations.

24. Report on Chickasaw Fund. 3 Mar.
HED 41, 31-2, v5, 4p. [599]
Treaties of 30 Oct. 1832, 1 July 1834, and 20 Apr. 1836.

25. Clerks in the Interior Dept. 3 Mar.
HED 54, 31-2, v5, 17p. [599]
Office of the CIA.

26. Resol. of the Florida Gen. Assembly. 3 Mar.
HMD 18, 31-2, v1, 1p. [605]
Losses in the Seminole war of 1849.

27. Resol. of the Florida Gen. Assembly. 3 Mar.
HMD 19, 31-2, v1, 1p. [605]
Volunteers in the Seminole war of 1849.

28. Resol. of the Florida Gen. Assembly. 3 Mar.
HMD 20, 31-2, v1, 1p. [605]
Seminole war in 1839.

29. R-P of D. Troxel. 3 Mar.
HR 53, 31-2, v1, 2p. [606]
Cherokee campaign; 1780; battle at Highwassee River.

30. R-C of the Heirs of R. Baker. 3 Mar.
HR 87, 31-2, v1, 2p. [606]
Supplies to the Choctaw Indians.

31. R-C of F. Wood. 3 Mar.
HR 88, 31-2, v1, 6p. [606]
Cherokee trader; 1837.

32. R-P of M. Williams. 3 Mar.
HR 89, 31-2, v1, 6p. [606]
Iroquois, or St. Regis, Indians.

33. Report on a Post Road from Fort Smith to San Diego. 3 Mar.
HR 95, 31-2, v1, 6p. [606]
Depredations of the Apaches, and other Southwestern Indians.

34. Report on a Military Reserve on the St. Peter's River. 3 Mar.
HR 99, 31-2, v1, 4p. [606]
Minnesota; Indian treaties and land titles.

35. Annual Report of the Smithsonian Institution. 6 Mar.
SMD 1, 32-sp, v1, 325p. [607]
Culbertson's expedition to the Upper Missouri in 1850, including discussion of Sioux, Gros Ventre, Assiniboine, Crow, Blackfeet Sioux, and other tribes; etc.

36. Stansburg's Expedition to the Great Salt Lake of Utah, and through the Rocky Mountains. 12 Mar.
SED 3, 32-sp, v2, 487p. [608]
Encounters with Pawnee, Sioux, Utah, Shoshone, and other Indian tribes; descriptions of Indian life-styles, language, etc.
37. Report on the Geology of the Lake Superior Land District. 13 Mar.
SED 4, 32-sp, v3, 406p. [609]
Discusses early explorations by whites of the area; origin of Indian names; etc.
38. Statements of Appropriations. 2 June.
HMD 21, 31-2, v1, 40p. [605]
Indian expenses.
39. Annual Message to Congress with Documents; Pres. Fillmore. 2 Dec.
SED 1, 32-1, v1-3, 1601p. [611-613] *or* HED 2, 32-1, v2 (pts. 1-3), 1601p. [634-636]
Indian relations; annual report of the Sec. of War (Serials 611 and 634); annual report of the Sec. of Interior (Serials 612-613 and 636-637); annual report of the Com'r of the Gen. Land Office (Serials 613 and 636); annual report of the CIA (Serials 613 and 636), including treaties negotiated, removal, trust funds, hostilities, expenses, and reports of Supts., agents, and schools; etc.
40. Estimates of Appropriations. 2 Dec.
HED 1, 32-1, v1, 218p. [633]
For the year ending 30 June 1853; Indian expenses.
41. Resol. of the California Legis. 8 Dec.
SMD 3, 32-1, v1, 1p. [629]
Erection of forts for protection from Indians.
42. R-P of V. Morass. 16 Dec.
SR 2, 32-1, v1, 3p. [630]
Land bounded by the Chippewa reservation in Michigan.
43. Report on Roads in Minnesota. 23 Dec.
HED 12, 32-1, v3, 12p. [637]
Supplies to Chippewa and Winnebago country.

1852

1. R-C of Virginia Soldiers. 2 Jan.
SR 11, 32-1, v1, 4p. [630]
Cherokee country in 1779.
2. Annual Report of the Sec. of the Treasury. 6 Jan.
SED 11, 32-1, v4, 87p. [614] *or* HED 18, 32-1, v3, 87p. [637]
Indian expenses, fiscal 1851.
3. R-M of D. Cash and G. Ellis. 6 Jan.
HR 4, 32-1, v1, 2p. [656]
Seminole war in Florida.
4. On the Case of P. Miller. 6 Jan.
HR 8, 32-1, v1, 2p. [656]
Spy on Indian frontier in 1792.
5. Report on Interest to New Hampshire. 13 Jan.
HR 26, 32-1, v1, 2p. [656]
Same sort of payment as that made to Georgia for the Cherokee, Creek, and Seminole wars of 1836-1837.
6. Additional Estimates for the Interior Dept. 14 Jan.
HED 30, 32-1, v5, 26p. [640]
To fulfill treaty stipulations with various tribes.
7. Resol. of the Michigan Legis. 15 Jan.
SMD 13, 32-1, v1, 2p. [629]
Ottawa and Chippewa treaty of 28 Mar. 1836; balance due.
8. R-M of M. Thompson. 19 Jan.
SR 34, 32-1, v1, 2p. [630]
Indian war of 1837 in Florida.
9. R-P of F. Gardiner. 26 Jan.
SR 45, 32-1, v1, 1p. [630]
Indian war in Florida.
10. R-P of R. Jemison and B. Williamson. 27 Jan.
SR 51, 32-1, v1, 1p. [630]
Creek war; 1836; Alabama.
11. On the Case of J. Hill and Sons. 27 Jan.
SR 55, 32-1, v1, 1p. [630]
Indian depredations in California.
12. R-C of Reps. of Gen. Watson. 29 Jan.
HR 45, 32-1, v1, 6p. [656]
Creek warriors in the Seminole war.
13. Report on Heirs of Semoice. 29 Jan.
HR 57, 32-1, v1, 2p. [656]
Creek Indian treaty of 9 Aug. 1814, land title.
14. On the Case of J. Newell. 29 Jan.
HR 64, 32-1, v1, 1p. [656]
Wyandot treaty of 1842 in Ohio.
15. On the Case of E. McCallock. 29 Jan.
HR 68, 32-1, v1, 1p. [656]

Wyandot treaty of 1842 in Ohio.

16. R-M of the Heirs of D. Landon. 30 Jan.
HR 69, 32-1, v1, 3p. [656]
Indian treaty; 1795; Greenville.

17. R-M of J. Bush et al. 30 Jan.
HR 70, 32-1, v1, 64p. [656]
Seminole war in Florida.

18. R-P of H. Miller. 30 Jan.
HR 91, 32-1, v1, 4p. [656]
Indian campaign of 1794.

19. Contingent Expenses of the Interior Dept. 4 Feb.
HED 48, 32-1, v5, 129p. [640]
Office of the CIA.

20. Mem. of the Alabama Legis. 9 Feb.
SMD 33, 32-1, v1, 7p. [629]
Losses during the Creek war of 1836; treaties of 22 Apr. 1826 and 12 Apr. 1832.

21. On the Case of L. Thomas and T. Rogers. 9 Feb.
SR 71, 32-1, v1, 1p. [630]
Legal counsel to Sisseton Sioux in 1845.

22. Report on Creditors of the Cherokees. 11 Feb.
SED 32, 32-1, v7, 90p. [618]
Correspondence with persons claiming to be creditors of Western Cherokees who emigrated prior to the treaty of 1835.

23. Report on Arkansas Bonds. 12 Feb.
HED 65, 32-1, v6, 1p. [641]
Held in trust for the Chickasaw Indians.

24. R-M of the Reps. of J. Piatt. 12 Feb.
HR 123, 32-1, v1, 39p. [656]
Supplies to Indians; 1813; Michigan.

25. On the Case of M. and R. Bean. 16 Feb.
SR 77, 32-1, v1, 8p. [630]
Cherokee treaty of 1828; land dispute.

26. R-M of J. Rogers. 18 Feb.
SR 78, 32-1, v1, 2p. [630]
Cherokee treaties of 1817, 1819, and 1835.

27. Mem. of C. Lancaster and W. Matlock. 19 Feb.
HMD 14, 32-1, v1, 5p. [652]
Indian hostilities in Oregon.

28. Report on Omaha Indians. 20 Feb.
HED 76, 32-1, v6, 3p. [641]
Estimates for defraying costs of a delegation in Washington, D.C.

29. Mem. of the Minnesota Legis. 28 Feb.
SMD 47, 32-1, v1, 3p. [629]
For ratification of treaties of 23 July and 5 Aug. 1851 with the Sioux.

30 R-P of the Heirs of J. Kennedy. 1 Mar.
SR 100, 32-1, v1, 2p. [630]
Florida Indian depredations.

31. Appropriations and Balances of the Interior Dept. 8 Mar.
SED 45, 32-1, v8, 13p. [619]
Indian expenses.

32. R-P of J. Bryan. 15 Mar.
SR 117, 32-1, v1, 2p. [630]
Treaty Com'r to the Wyandottes in 1836.

33. On the Case of Survivors of Gen. Belknap. 22 Mar.
SR 139, 32-1, v1, 2p. [630]
Florida Indian war.

34. R-P of H. Miller and P. Thompson. 24 Mar.
SR 145, 32-1, v1, 1p. [630]
Osage depredations of 1847.

35. Report on the Amounts Due the St. Regis Indians. 5 Apr.
SED 54, 32-1, v8, 2p. [619]
Treaty with the New York Indians involved.

36. R-P of J. Tucker. 7 Apr.
SR 171, 32-1, v1, 1p. [630]
Florida Indian war.

37. R-C of the Choctaw Indians. 12 Apr.
SR 181, 32-1, v1, 4p. [630]
Concerns of land sales, removal, and citizenship; treaty of 30 Sept. 1830.

38. Report on Debts of Indian Agents. 15 Apr.
SED 61, 32-1, v9, 26p. [620]
Contracted in California.

39. On the Case of C. Seymour. 19 Apr.
SR 185, 32-1, v1, 1p. [630]
Creek war; 1836; Georgia.

40. On the Case of A. and J. Kendall. 20 Apr.
SR 190, 32-1, v1, 2p. [630]
Money paid to the Western Cherokees.

41. R-M of H. Miller. 22 Apr.
SR 202, 32-1, v1, 2p. [630]
Clerk in the BIA.

42. R-P of C. Wallace. 28 Apr.
SR 205, 32-1, v1, 3p. [630]
Virginia bounty lands in Ohio; Indian lands.

43. Report on Promotion of Clerks. 3 May.
SED 69, 32-1, v9, 18p. [620]
Indian Office.

44. Report on Indian Accounts and Disbursements. 3 May.
HED 103, 32-1, v11, 1021p. [647]
For fiscal years 1850 and 1851.

45. Clerks in the Interior Dept. 3 May.
HED 110, 32-1, v12, 21p. [648]
In the OIA.

46. R-C of Florida Volunteers. 5 May.
SR 212, 32-1, v2, 2p. [631]
Indian hostilities of 1840 in Florida.

47. On the Case of R. Fitzpatrick. 25 May.
SR 234, 32-1, v2, 2p. [631]
Seminole depredations; 1838; Florida.

48. On the Relief of L. Dyson. 25 May.
SR 238, 32-1, v2, 1p. [631]
Claim to land in the Caddo Indian reservation.

49. R-M of W. Money. 27 May.
SR 242, 32-1, v2, 2p. [631]
Indian depredations in California.

50. On the Case of W. Cobb and W. Price. 1 June.
HR 146, 32-1, v1, 3p. [656]
Treaties with Alabama Indians.

51. R-C of Biloxi Bay Indians. 17 June.
SR 247, 32-1, v2, 1p. [631]
Choctaw claims.

52. Derby's Expedition to the Gulf of California and the Colorado River.
SED 81, 32-1, v9, 28p. [620]
Encounters with, and descriptions of, Indians in the Colorado River area, Southwestern Indians.

53. Report on a Liquidated Balance Due the Creeks. 19 June.
SED 82, 32-1, v9, 7p. [620]
For losses by the friendly Creeks; 1813-1814; war with Britain.

54. On the Case of H. Emathla et al. 22 June.
SR 270, 32-1, v2, 2p. [631]
Petition by friendly Seminoles for service in the Florida war.

55. Report on Purchase of Catlin's Indian Collection. 23 June.
SR 271, 32-1, v2, 3p. [631]

56. On the Case of Oneida Indians. 6 July.
SR 286, 32-1, v2, 1p. [631]
Ask compensation for capture of gunboats in war of 1812.

57. R-M of S. Belden et al. 7 July.
SR 289, 32-1, v2, 2p. [631]
Indian hostilities on the Rio Grande frontier.

58. On the Case of G. Stealey. 14 July.
SR 295, 32-1, v2, 1p. [631]
Employed in 1850-1851 by U.S. Com'rs to California; northern tribes.

59. R-C of B. Factor. 19 July.
SR 301, 32-1, v2, 2p. [631]
Blacks raised by the Creeks in Florida; Seminole war.

60. R-P of R. Fuller. 28 July.
SR 314, 32-1, v2, 2p. [631]
Indian campaign; 1851; Oregon.

61. Report on Payments on Account of Cherokees. 2 Aug.
HMD 64, 32-1, v1, 31p. [652]
Cherokee Indians of North Carolina.

62. On the Case of J. Hernandez. 9 Aug.
SR 323, 32-1, v2, 1p. [631]
Seminole war; 1835; Florida.

63. R-M of Georgia. 10 Aug.
SR 329, 32-1, v2, 2p. [631]
Cherokee, Creek, and Seminole hostilities; 1835-1838.

64. R-M of J. Barrell et al. 11 Aug.
SR 335, 32-1, v2, 32p. [631]
Land purchased from Indians in 1791 on the Northwest Coast of America.

65. Report on Debts Contracted by Indian Agents. 12 Aug.
SED 104, 32-1, v10, 15p. [621]
In California.

66. R-M of R. Mills. 18 Aug.
SR 344, 32-1, v2, 17p. [631]
Railroad between the Mississippi River and the Pacific; Indian tribes.

67. Annual Report of the Smithsonian Institution. 20 Aug.
SMD 108, 32-1, v1, 104p. [629]
Linguistic studies of Indian languages, explorations, archaeological studies, etc.

68. Report on the Tulare Valley. 24 Aug.
SED 110, 32-1, v10, 17p. [621]
Expedition of Lieut. Derby; encounters with Indian tribes of the Southwest.

69. R-P of Reps. of J. Clamorgan. 28 Aug.
SR 354, 32-1, v2, 25p. [631]
Explored the Missouri River for Spain, and conciliated the Indians on its banks.

70. Clerks in the Interior Dept. 31 Aug.
SED 128, 32-1, v15, 16p. [627]
Indian Office.

71. Letter on Losses of Creeks. 31 Aug.
HED 128, 32-1, v13, 7p. [649]
For Creek losses sustained during war of 1812.

72. Letter from Stockbridge Indians. 31 Aug.
HMD 69, 32-1, v1, 2p. [652]
Treaties and removal; division of tribe.

73. Statements of Appropriations. 29 Nov.
HMD 71, 32-1, v1, 78p. [652]
Indian expenses, 1st session, 32d Congress.

74. Annual Message to Congress with Documents; Pres. Fillmore. 6 Dec.
SED 1, 32-2, v1 and 2, 1292p. [658-659] *or* HED 1, 32-2, v1, (pts. 1 and 2), 1292p. [673-674]
Indian relations; annual report of the Sec. of War (Serials 659 and 674); annual report of the Sec. of Interior (Serials 658 and 673); annual report of the Com'r of the Gen. Land Office (Serials 658 and 673); annual report of the CIA (Serials 658 and 673), including treaty stipulations, annuities, education, and reports of Supts., agents, and schools; etc.

75. Report on Classification of Clerks in the Interior Dept. 8 Dec.
SED 3, 32-2, v3, 7p. [660]
Indian Office.

76. Estimates of Appropriations. 10 Dec.
HED 2, 32-2, v2, 292p. [675]
For the year ending 30 June 1854; Indian expenses.

77. Mem. of State of Georgia. 20 Dec.
SMD 4, 32-2, v1, 7p. [670]
Creek war; 1836-1837; claims for damages.

78. Report on Estimates for the Indian Service. 23 Dec.
HED 4, 32-2, v2, 20p. [675]
Additional funds needed for the year ending 30 June 1854.

79. Appropriations and Balances of the Interior Dept. 23 Dec.
HED 7, 32-2, v3, 8p. [676]
For the year ending 30 June 1852; Indian expenses.

80. R-P of G. Morris. 30 Dec.
SR 363, 32-2, v1, 1p. [671]
Indian battle at the river Raisin in 1812; taken prisoner.

1853

1. Report of Indians on Mexican Territory. 12 Jan.
SED 14, 32-2, v3, 135p. [660]
Correspondence on encroachment of Indians of U.S. on Mexican territories; depredations.

2. Letter on the Friendly Creeks. 17 Jan.
HMD 10, 32-2, v1, 5p. [685]
On claim for land taken by treaty of 8 Aug. 1814.

3. Annual Report of the Sec. of the Treasury. 20 Jan.
SED 22, 32-2, v5, 493p. [662] *or* HED 23, 32-2, v3, 493p. [676]
Indian expenses, fiscal 1852.

4. Message on the Seminole Indians. 20 Jan.
SED 23, 32-2, v3, 8p. [660] *or* HED 19, 32-2, v3, 8p. [676]
Refusal of the Seminoles to remove from Florida under the treaty of May 1842.

5. R-P of the Administrators of J. Anderson. 20 Jan.
SR 377, 32-2, v1, 2p. [671]
British and Indians; 1812; river Raisin.

6. Report on Arkansas Bands. 24 Jan.
SED 26, 32-2, v3, 2p. [660]
Chickasaw trust fund.

7. Report on Land Claims in Indian Reservations. 24 Jan.
SR 382, 32-2, v1, 2p. [671]
Land claims on Sac and Fox half-breed reservations; treaty of 4 Aug. 1824.

8. Report on Seminole Indians. 24 Jan.
SR 379, 32-2, v1, 3p. [671]
On refusal of Seminoles to migrate west of the Mississippi River.

9. Letter on Military Posts. 26 Jan.
HMD 16, 32-2, v1, 16p. [685]
On the Kansas and Upper Minnesota Rivers; Indian hostilities.

10. Message on Territory of Mosquito Indians. 28 Jan.
SED 28, 32-2, v3, 2p. [660]
Treaty of 1850 with Nicaragua.

11. Report on Disbursements to Sioux Indians. 28 Jan.
SED 29, 32-2, v3, 36p. [660]
On allegations of fraud against Supt. Ramsey in disbursement of money to Sioux under treaties of 1851.

12. Marcy's Expedition on the Red River of Louisiana. 4 Feb.
SED 54, 32-2, v8, 320p. [666]
Journal of the exploring party; encounters and descriptions of Indians of the Southwest; prints.

13. R-M of H. Alden and J. Eddy. 8 Feb.
SR 404, 32-2, v1, 3p. [671]
Telegraph to the Pacific; would help in keeping track of movements of Indian tribes.

14. Resol. of the Iowa Legis. 11 Feb.
SMD 37, 32-2, v1, 2p. [670]
Treaty of 4 Aug. 1824 between the U.S. and the Sac and Fox Indians; half-breed lands.

15. Report on a British Colony in Central America. 11 Feb.
SR 407, 32-2, v1, 17p. [671]
Treaties between the U.S., Spain, and Great Britain; Mosquito Indians.

16. Survey of the U.S.-Mexico Boundary. 12 Feb.
SED 38, 32-2, v3, 4p. [660]
Indian hostilities.

17. Report on Amount Due Menomonee Indians. 14 Feb.
SR 410, 32-2, v1, 9p. [671]
Amount due under treaty of 18 Oct. 1848; manner of its payment; removal.

18. Report on the U.S.-Mexico Boundary. 15 Feb.
SED 41, 32-2, v7, 32p. [665]
Apache depredations; encounters with various tribes.

19. Resol. of the Florida Legis. 17 Feb.
SMD 51, 32-2, v1, 1p. [670]
Treaty of Payne's Landing; removal of the Seminoles.

20. On the Case of H. Rice. 17 Feb.
SR 419, 32-2, v1, 3p. [671]
Contract for the removal of the Winnebagoes from Wisconsin and Iowa.

21. Contingent Expenditures of the Interior Dept. 18 Feb.
HED 53, 32-2, v6, 135p. [679]
Indian Office.

22. Clerks in the Interior Dept. 18 Feb.
HED 54, 32-2, v6, 17p. [679]
Indian Office.

23. Report on Chickasaw Trust Fund. 22 Feb.
HED 57, 32-2, v6, 16p. [679]
Statement of accounts for year 1851-1852.

24. On the Case of the Executor of Col. Fanning. 22 Feb.
SR 422, 32-2, v1, 2p. [671]
Indian agent at Fort Gadsden in Florida.

25. R-P of J. Gusman. 22 Feb.
SR 424, 32-2, v1, 1p. [671]
Land purchased from the Boluxi Indians of Louisiana.

26. Annual Report of the Smithsonian Institution. 1 Mar.
SMD 53, 32-2, v1, 96p. [670]
Explorations of Indian country; publications on Indian languages; etc.

27. Report on Indian Affairs in California. 3 Mar.
SED 57, 32-2, v7, 18p. [665]
Condition of the Indians.

28. Sitgreave's Expedition Down the Zuni and Colorado Rivers. 3 Mar.
SED 59, 32-2, v10, 198p. [668]
Journal of the exploration party; encounters with Indians of the Southwest; prints.

29. Report on the California Indians. 17 Mar.
SED 4, 33-sp, v1, 405p. [688]
Correspondence between the OIA and agents and treaty Com'rs; condition of California tribes; treaty negotiations; etc.

30. Report of the Mexican Boundary Commission. 22 Mar.
SED 6, 33-sp, v1, 173p. [688]
Indian depredations.

31. Statements of Appropriations. 20 May.
HMD 24, 32-2, v1, 72p. [685]
During the 2d session, 32d Congress; Indian expenses.

32. Annual Message to Congress with Documents; Pres. Pierce. 6 Dec.

SED 1, 33-1, v1-3, 1929p. [690-692] *or* HED 1, 33-1, v1 (pts. 1-3), 1929p. [710-712]
Annual report of the Sec. of War (Serials 691 and 711); annual report of the Sec. of Interior (Serials 690 and 710); annual report of the Com'r of the Gen. Land Office (Serials 690 and 710); annual report of the CIA (Serials 690 and 710), including instructions to Com'rs, and reports from Supts., agents, and schools; etc.

33. Estimates of Appropriations. 6 Dec.
HED 2, 33-1, v2, 295p. [714]
For the year ending 30 June 1855; Indian expenses.

34. Annual Report of the Sec. of the Treasury. 7 Dec.
SED 2, 33-1, v4, 384p. [694] *or* HED 3, 33-1, v2, 384p. [714]
Indian expenses, fiscal 1853.

35. Mem. of the Iowa Legis. 12 Dec.
SMD 3, 13-1, v1, 2p. [705]
Railroad from Dubuque to the Missouri River; Pottawatomie country.

36. Appropriations of the Interior Dept. 13 Dec.
SED 6, 33-1, v4, 13p. [694] *or* HED 6, 33-1, v3, 13p. [715]
For the year ending 30 June 1853; Indian expenses.

37. On the Case of the Survivors of E. Beebe. 20 Dec.
HR 2, 33-1, v1, 17p. [742]
Sac and Fox depredations in 1821.

38. On the Case of J. Simonton. 20 Dec.
HR 3, 33-1, v1, 7p. [742]
Treaty of 1837 with the Chippewas of Saginaw.

39. R-P of M. Parton. 20 Dec.
HR 4, 33-1, v1, 4p. [742]
Cherokee country of North Carolina.

1854

1. Message on the Treaty of 1850 with Britain. 3 Jan.
SED 13, 33-1, v4, 19p. [694]
Land of the Mosquito Indians; Nicaragua.

2. On the Case of R. Grignon. 3 Jan.
HR 15, 33-1, v1, 5p. [742]
Menomonee treaty of 3 Sept. 1836.

3. Gunnison's Expedition to the Great Basin. 6 Jan.
HED 18, 33-1, v5, 1p. [717]
Central Pacific Railroad; explorations; Utah Indians.

4. R-P of C. Derbigny et al. 9 Jan.
SR 26, 33-1, v1, 3p. [706]
Land purchased from the Ouacha and Chaouacha Indians in 1744; Louisiana.

5. On the Case of Heirs of J. Gerard. 13 Jan.
HR 32, 33-1, v1, 10p. [742]
Indian hostilities; 1792; on the Maumee.

6. R-P of J. Phagan. 17 Jan.
SR 38, 33-1, v1, 1p. [706]
BIA records substantiate claim.

7. On the Case of R. Fitzpatrick. 18 Jan.
SR 49, 33-1, v1, 2p. [706]
Seminole depredations in Florida; 1836.

8. R-P of H. Mackay. 18 Jan.
HR 40, 33-1, v1, 5p. [742]
Creek and Seminole wars; 1836-1838.

9. On the Case of Cash and Ellis. 18 Jan.
HR 41, 33-1, v1, 3p. [742]
Seminole war.

10. R-P of W. Edwards. 18 Jan.
HR 47, 33-1, v1, 1p. [742]
Traders in Indian country near Fort Gibson in 1834.

11. On the Case of J. Hamilton. 18 Jan.
HR 48, 33-1, v1, 8p. [742]
Taken prisoner in Ohio in 1813; British and Indians.

12. Report on Land Grants to Benefit the Insane. 23 Jan.
SR 57, 33-1, v1, 35p. [706]
Statistics on insanity in areas occupied by Indians; racial explanations.

13. Report on Indiana Bonds. 24 Jan.
SR 64, 33-1, v1, 5p. [706]
Chickasaw trust fund.

14. On the Case of D. Huntington. 24 Jan.
HR 60, 33-1, v1, 1p. [742]
Indians of Utah.

15. R-P of the Oneida Indians. 24 Jan.
HR 61, 33-1, v1, 1p. [742]
Treaty of 1838.

16. Report on Chickasaw Trust Fund. 27 Jan.

Condition of fund, and land sales; treaties of 20 Oct. 1832 and 24 May 1834.

17. Disbursements to the Indians. 30 Jan.
SED 25, 33-1, v5, 550p. [695] *or* HED 37, 33-1, v6, 550p. [718]
Year ending 30 June 1852.

18. On the Case of C. Gunter. 30 Jan.
SR 65, 33-1, v1, 1p. [706]
Indian reserve land near the Alabama River.

19. R-P of D. Campau. 30 Jan.
SR 68, 33-1, v1, 2p. [706]
Chippewa land in Michigan.

20. On the Case of J. Kennedy. 31 Jan.
HR 79, 33-1, v1, 2p. [742]
Creek depredations; 1836; Alabama.

21. Estimates of Appropriations for the Indian Service. 6 Feb.
SED 28, 33-1, v5, 5p. [695] *or* HED 43, 33-1, v8, 5p. [721]
Additional funds for the service in New Mexico.

22. Report on Expeditions Regarding a Railroad to the Pacific. 6 Feb.
SED 29, 33-1, v5, 118p. [695] *or* HED 46, 33-1, v8, 118p. [721]
Encounters with the Indians of the Upper Missouri, the Great Basin, and the Southwest.

23. Report on Expenses of the Cayuse War. 6 Feb.
HED 45, 33-1, v8, 8p. [721]
Oregon; 1847-1848.

24. R-M of H. Read. 13 Feb.
SR 96, 33-1, v1, 3p. [706]
Indian agent in Florida; 1818-1821.

25. On the Case of T. Conner. 13 Feb.
SR 99, 33-1, v1, 1p. [706]
Indian war of 1794.

26. R-P of I. Bowman. 13 Feb.
SR 101, 33-1, v1, 2p. [706]
British and Indians; 1780; Illinois.

27. R-P of I. Bowman. 16 Feb.
HR 106, 33-1, v1, 2p. [742]
Chickasaw engagement in 1779.

28. R-P of J. Lewis. 16 Feb.
HR 109, 33-1, v1, 2p. [742]
Creek war; 1812; Tennessee.

29. R-M of Col. Vigo. 16 Feb.
HR 117, 33-1, v1, 9p. [742]
Indian trader in St. Louis in 1778; fought British and Indians in the "Illinois campaign."

30. On the Case of P. Simonds. 16 Feb.
HR 118, 33-1, v1, 4p. [742]
Indian country *en route* to Santa Fe; depredations.

31. Report on Indian Treaties. 21 Feb.
SED 34, 33-1, v8, 16p. [698] *or* HED 55, 33-1, v8, 4p. [721]
Recommends treaties be made with the Indians of Oregon and Washington (Senate version also recommends treaties be made with Indians of the Southwest).

32. R-C of J. Watson. 21 Feb.
SR 119, 33-1, v1, 2p. [706]
Indian Dept.; 1806-1812; Michigan.

33. On the Relief of J. Hamilton. 23 Feb.
SR 128, 33-1, v1, 1p. [706]
British and Indians; 1813; battle at river Raisin.

34. Report on Charges Against A. Ramsey. 24 Feb.
SR 131, 33-1, v1, 3p. [706]
Supt. of Indian Affairs in Minnesota; Sioux treaties of 1851; payments not made.

35. Report on a Contested Election in New Mexico. 24 Feb.
HR 121, 33-1, v1, 4p. [742]
Votes cast by the Pueblo Indians rejected.

36. Report on Accounts of L. Blake. 3 Mar.
SED 44, 33-1, v8, 2p. [698]
Agent for removal of Seminoles from Florida.

37. Report on Expenses of Cayuse War. 8 Mar.
HR 122, 33-1, v2, 5p. [743]
Indian war in Oregon during 1847-1848.

38. R-P of R. Jemison and B. Williamson. 9 Mar.
SR 152, 33-1, v1, 2p. [706]
Creek war; 1836; Alabama.

39. On the Case of H. Miller. 11 Mar.
SR 164, 33-1, v1, 1p. [706]
Clerk in the BIA; 1828-1833.

40. On the Case of M. and R. Bean. 13 Mar.
SR 158, 33-1, v1, 9p. [706]
Land dispute; Cherokee treaty of 6 May 1828.

41. On the Case of A. and J. Kendall. 14 Mar.
SR 165, 33-1, v1, 3p. [706]
Cherokee emigration in 1820; treaty of 1835.

42. R-M of the Cherokee Indians. 20 Mar.

HR 123, 33-1, v2, 13p. [743]
Money due them under treaties of 29 Dec. 1835 and 1846; those Cherokees residing east of the Mississippi River.

43. Report on Indian Appropriations. 22 Mar.
HMD 38, 33-1, v1, 16p. [741]
Estimates for negotiating treaties with Northwest Coast and Southwestern Indians.

44. Report on Indian Lands. 28 Mar.
HED 84, 33-1, v10, 42p. [723]
Extinguishment of Indian title to lands west of Missouri and Iowa; councils held for said purpose.

45. Mem. of the Alabama Legis. 29 Mar.
SMD 45, 33-1, v1, 1p. [705]
Volunteers in the Creek war of 1836.

46. Report on Appropriations for Cherokees. 29 Mar.
HED 85, 33-1, v10, 2p. [723]
Both east and west of the Mississippi River.

47. R-P of J. Beaubien. 30 Mar.
SR 185, 33-1, v2, 3p. [707]
Land in Chicago; Indian agency.

48. On the Case of Erwin and Greathouse. 3 Apr.
SR 190, 33-1, v2, 2p. [707]
Contract for supplies; Creek removal in 1834.

49. R-M of C. Wallace. 3 Apr.
SR 194, 33-1, v2, 6p. [707]
Virginia bounty land in Ohio; Indian boundary line.

50. Mem. of the New Mexico Legis. 4 Apr.
HMD 45, 33-1, v1, 1p. [741]
Asking removal and care of Jicarilla, Utah, and Navajo Indians.

51. Mem. of the New Mexico Legis. 4 Apr.
HMD 47, 33-1, v1, 2p. [741]
To re-establish Fort Atkinson on the Missouri-Santa Fe Route; Indian hostilities.

52. Mem. of the New Mexico Legis. 4 Apr.
HMD 52, 33-1, v1, 1p. [741]
Land claims; Indian hostilities.

53. Report on Estimates for the Indian Dept. 4 Apr.
HMD 55, 33-1, v1, 5p. [741]
Additional estimates required for Indians in New Mexico and beyond the Rocky Mountains.

54. Report on Blackfeet and Other Indians. 5 Apr.
HMD 59, 33-1, v1, 6p. [741]
Communications showing importance of appropriations for the expenses of a council with the Blackfeet, Gros Ventre, Flathead, Pend d'Oreille, and other Indians.

55. Contingent Expenses of the Interior Dept. 6 Apr.
HED 88, 33-1, v11, 92p. [724]
Indian Office.

56. Report on Terms of Treaties with Indians. 7 Apr.
HR 133, 33-1, v2, 11p. [743]
Defining the terms on which treaties shall hereafter be made with Indian tribes that have been removed west of the Mississippi River; list of tribes and populations.

57. On the Case of T. Snodgrass. 12 Apr.
SR 204, 33-1, v2, 3p. [707]
Cherokee removal in 1838.

58. On the Case of G. Barrell et al. 17 Apr.
SR 211, 33-1, v2, 1p. [707]
Land purchased from Indians on the Northwest Coast.

59. On the Case of H. Conner. 17 Apr.
SR 213, 33-1, v2, 3p. [707]
Treaty of 14 Jan. 1837 with the Saginaw band of Chippewa Indians.

60. Report on Indian War Claims. 20 Apr.
SR 226, 33-1, v2, 5p. [707]
Creek and Seminole wars; 1836-1837.

61. On the Case of C. Seymour. 20 Apr.
SR 227, 33-1, v2, 1p. [707]
Creek war; 1836.

62. R-C of California. 26 Apr.
HR 137, 33-1, v2, 6p. [743]
For suppressing Indian aggressions.

63. Survey of a Road from Mendota to the Big Sioux River. 28 Apr.
HED 97, 33-1, v12, 12p. [725]
Encounters with Sioux Indians.

64. Estimates for Indian Service. 28 Apr.
HMD 63, 33-1, v1, 16p. [741]
Expenses of marking eastern boundary of Creek country; treaty of 14 Jan. 1845.

65. R-M of Sioux Half-Breeds. 28 Apr.
HR 138, 33-1, v2, 13p. [743]

Asking that lands set apart for them in Minnesota may be allotted in severalty; treaty of 15 July 1830.

66. Report on Expenses of the Rogue River War. 1 May.
HED 99, 33-1, v12, 5p. [725]
Indian war; 1836; Oregon.

67. On the Case of D. Carter. 24 May.
SR 284, 33-1, v2, 3p. [707]
Cherokee treaty of 1828; emigration.

68. Mem. of the Alabama Legis. 24 May.
HMD 78, 33-1, v1, 2p. [741]
Creek war of 1836.

69. R-C of O. Love. 30 May.
SR 295, 33-1, v2, 2p. [707]
Depredations committed upon the Chickasaw Indians; 1847-1848; Arkansas.

70. Report on Indian Disbursements. 8 June.
SED 69, 33-1, v11, 520p. [701]
Year ending 30 June 1853.

71. R-C of W. Factor. 10 June.
HR 140, 33-1, v2, 1p. [743]
Seminole war in Florida.

72. R-P of M. Hogan. 10 June.
HR 152, 33-1, v2, 2p. [743]
Sioux depredations of 1842 near Fort Snelling.

73. On the Case of E. Mitchell. 10 June.
HR 155, 33-1, v2, 1p. [743]
Indian battle at Fort Recovery in 1793.

74. R-M of J. Johnson. 10 June.
HR 178, 33-1, v2, 2p. [743]
Agent for the Wyandots during 1841-1842; treaty negotiations.

75. Report on Claims Arising from the Black Hawk War. 10 June.
HR 179, 33-1, v2, 2p. [743]
Depredations committed by the Sac and Fox Indians in 1832.

76. R-P of J. Estes. 10 June.
HR 185, 33-1, v2, 23p. [743]
Sac and Fox (Black Hawk) war of 1832.

77. R-P of C. Grignon. 10 June.
HR 197, 33-1, v2, 1p. [743]
Interpreter during the 1848 treaty negotiations with the Menomonee Indians.

78. R-P of C. Christy. 12 June.
HR 279, 33-1, v3, 1p. [744]
Indian depredations of 1850-1851 in northern California.

79. R-C of J. Vandruff. 13 June.
HR 196, 33-1, v2, 1p. [743]
Sac depredations during 1829-1831.

80. On the Relief of Reps. of J. Watson. 13 June.
HR 198, 33-1, v2, 4p. [743]
Indian Dept. in Michigan during 1806-1812.

81. Fremont's Expedition Across the Rocky Mountains. 15 June.
SMD 67, 33-1, v1, 7p. [705] *or*
HMD 8, 33-2, v1, 7p. [807]
Encounter with the Utahs, and other Indians of the Great Basin.

82. On the Case of L. Blake. 19 June.
SED 71, 33-1, v12, 65p. [702]
Agent for the removal of the Seminoles from Florida.

83. R-M of G. Stealy. 21 June.
SR 313, 33-1, v2, 1p. [707]
Expenses of a mission to the Indians of northern California.

84. Report on Indian Appropriations. 21 June.
HR 201, 33-1, v2, 2p. [743]
On amendments to Senate bill making appropriations for the expenses of the Indian Dept., and for fulfilling treaty stipulations for year ending 30 June 1855.

85. Mem. of J. Fremont. 22 June.
SMD 69, 33-1, v1, 4p. [705]
Contract to provide supplies for California Indians; treaties made in 1851.

86. R-M of the Survivor of S. Buckner. 23 June.
HR 222, 33-1, v2, 1p. [743]
Contract for removal of the Chickasaws in 1837.

87. Receipts and Expenditures. 24 June.
HED 112, 33-1, v14, 601p. [727]
Year ending 30 June 1853; Indian expenses.

88. R-M of the Muscogee, or Creek Indians. 26 June.
SR 323, 33-1, v2, 11p. [707]
Asking compensation for lands forcibly taken from them; history of Southeastern Indians.

89. R-M of Lieut. Evans. 30 June.
HR 245, 33-1, v2, 2p. [743]
Property lost when Indians set fire to the prairie near Santa Fe.

90. R-P of Citizens of Ohio. 30 June.
HR 246, 33-1, v2, 1p. [743]
Indian reservations.

91. R-M of Dr. Wooster. 30 June.
HR 267, 33-1, v3, 1p. [744]
Schools for the education of California Indians.

92. R-P of I. Bowman. 30 June.
HR 275, 33-1, v3, 2p. [744]
Chickasaw battle; 1779; Illinois regiment.

93. Report on Treaty with the Pottawatomies. 6 July.
SED 76, 33-1, v12, 22p. [702]
Fulfillment of stipulations of a treaty made on 26 Oct. 1832.

94. R-C of J. Shaw. 7 July.
SR 341, 33-1, v2, 1p. [707]
Interpreter at a trial of some Winnebago Indians in 1828.

95. On the Relief of Heirs of Col. Morgan. 8 July.
HR 276, 33-1, v3, 3p. [744]
Gathered a force of western Indians to fight in the Florida war in 1837.

96. R-M of Gen Walbach. 13 July.
SR 355, 33-1, v2, 1p. [707]
Treaty negotiations of 1801-1802 with the Cherokees, Chickasaws, Creeks, and Choctaws.

97. R-M of J. Fremont. 14 July.
HR 289, 33-1, v3, 7p. [744]
Treaty Com'r to the California Indians in 1850-1851.

98. R-M of the Minnesota Legis. 14 July.
HR 291, 33-1, v3, 2p.]744]
Military post near the Pembina River; for protection of citizens and Indians from British attack.

99. R-P of J. Pearce. 14 July.
HR 294, 33-1, v3, 1p. [744]
Indian campaign; 1812; Ohio.

100. Report on Estimates for Indian Treaties. 15 July.
HED 122, 33-1, v16, 3p. [734]
Appropriations needed to carry out treaties with the Sac, Fox, Missouri, Delaware, Iowa, and Kickapoo Indians.

101. R-C of J. Bryan. 15 July.
HR 302, 33-1, v3, 2p. [744]
Treaty Com'r to the Wyandots during 1836.

102. R-P of S. Pool. 15 July.
HR 304, 33-1, v3, 1p. [744]
Indian war; 1838; Florida.

103. On the Relief of H. Miller. 22 July.
HR 335, 33-1, v3, 2p. [744]
Clerk in the BIA during 1828-1833.

104. Annual Report of the Smithsonian Institution. 25 July.
SMD 73, 33-1, v1, 269p. [705] *or*
HMD 97, 33-1, v1, 310p. [741]
Research and publications related to the American Indian.

105. On the Relief of T. Elliott. 25 July.
HR 342, 33-1, v3, 2p. [744]
Keel-boat delivered to the Cherokee agent in Arkansas.

106. R-P of Soldiers in Florida. 25 July.
SR 366, 33-1, v2, 5p. [707]
Seminole war, 1836-1839.

107. Message on the Case of A. Ramsay. 28 July.
SED 61, 33-1, v9, 431p. [699]
Misconduct as Supt of Indian Affairs in Minnesota; payments to the Sioux for fulfilling treaty stipulations.

108. Report on Cha-lah-kee, Muscogee, and Cha-ta Territories. 28 July.
SR 379, 33-1, v2, 31p. [707]
Establishing said territories for Indian occupancy; Choctaws and Chickasaws in Cha-ta, Creeks and Seminoles in Muscogee, and Cherokees in Cha-lah-kee; government over the Indians; etc.

109. R-P of G. Humphreys. 28 July.
SR 380, 33-1, v2, 1p. [707]
Indian hostilities of 1836 in Florida.

110. Message on Indian Supplies. 2 Aug.
SED 87, 33-1, v12, 8p. [702]
Claims for services rendered California Indians under contracts with Indian agents in 1851.

111. Report on Pacific Railroad Explorations. 3 Aug.
HED 129, 33-1, v18 (pts. 1-4), 923p. [736-739]
Encounters with, and descriptions of, Indians of the Plains, Southwest, Great Basin, Plateau, Northwest Coast, and California.

112. R-M of J. Randon. 3 Aug.
HR 360, 33-1, v3, 4p. [744]
Creek war during 1813-1814.

113. On the Relief of S. Coody. 3 Aug.
HR 367, 33-1, v3, 2p. [744]
Depredations committed by U.S. soldiers in Cherokee country.

114. Statements of Appropriations. 9 Oct.
SMD 74, 33-1, v1, 91p. [705] *or* HMD 98, 33-1, v1, 91p. [741]
During the 1st session, 33rd Congress; Indian expenses.

115. Annual Message to Congress with Documents. Pres. Pierce. 4 Dec.
SED 1, 33-2, v1-3, 1341p. [746-748] *or* HED 1, 33-2, v1 (pts. 1-3), 1341p. [777-779]
Annual report of the Sec. of War (Serials 747 and 778); annual report of the Sec. of Interior (Serials 746 and 777); annual report of the General Land Office (Serials 746 and 777); annual report of the CIA (Serials 746 and 777), including reports of Supts., agents, missions, and schools; etc.

116. Annual Report of the Sec. of the Treasury. 6 Dec.
SED 2, 33-2, v4, 520p. [749] *or* HED 3, 33-2, v2, 520p. [780]
Indian expenses; fiscal 1854.

117. Estimates of Appropriations. 6 Dec.
HED 6, 33-2, v3, 300p. [781]
For the year ending 30 June 1856; Indian expenses.

118. Receipts and Expenditures. 12 Dec.
HED 10, 33-2, v4, 656p. [782]
Year ending 30 June 1854; Indian expenses.

119. Additional Estimates for the Interior Dept. 15 Dec.
HED 14, 33-2, v4, 10p. [782]
For the Indian Service on the Northwest Coast.

120. R-C of C. Arnold. 18 Dec.
SR 395, 33-2, v1, 4p. [775]
Florida Indian war; 1838.

121. Message on Creek and Seminole Indians. 18 Dec.
HED 15, 33-2, v4, 33p. [782]
Information on difficulties between Creeks and Seminoles since their removal west.

122. Report on the Miami Indians. 22 Dec.
HMD 7, 33-2, v1, 4p. [807]
Treaties of 6 Nov. 1838, 28 Nov. 1840, and 5 June 1854; sales of their lands west of Missouri.

123. R-P of Col. Shaw. 22 Dec.
HR 3, 33-2, v1, 1p. [808]
Menomonee depredations during 1846-1848.

124. R-M of H. Alden and J. Eddy. 27 Dec.
HR 5, 33-2, v1, 11p. [808]
Underground telegraph wires to the Pacific coast; safe from Indian depredations.

125. Report on Indian Statistics. 29 Dec.
SED 13, 33-2, v6, 11p. [751]
H. Schoolcraft on state of Indian statistics; land holdings and populations.

1855

1. Appropriations of the Interior Dept. 2 Jan.
SED 15, 33-2, v6, 8p. [751] *or* HED 26, 33-2, v5, 8p. [783]
Year ending 30 June 1854; Indian expenses.

2. Message on Correspondence with Gen. Wool. 3 Jan.
SED 16, 33-2, v6, 128p. [751]
His operations in California; Indian depredations.

3. R-P of W. Davis. 3 Jan.
SR 402, 33-2, v1, 1p. [775]
Indian hostilities in Florida; 1849.

4. R-P of R. Fitzpatrick. 5 Jan.
HR 7, 33-2, v1, 2p. [808]
Seminole war; 1835-1836; Florida.

5. R-M of J. Walker. 9 Jan.
SR 409, 33-2, v1, 1p. [775]
Seminole war of Florida.

6. R-P of M. Caffey. 11 Jan.
HR 25, 33-2, v1, 1p. [808]
Seminole war of 1818.

7. R-C of Cherokees. 16 Jan.
HMD 16, 33-2, v1, 3p. [807]
Claim of J. Rogers et al. for additional money due under treaties of 1835-36, and 1846.

8. R-P of J. Pool. 17 Jan.
SR 416, 33-2, v1, 2p. [775]
Blacksmith for the Delawares, Shawnees, Senecas during 1823-1838.

9. Message on Indian Hostilities. 18 Jan.
SED 22, 33-2, v6, 7p. [751] *or* HED 36, 33-2, v5, 7p. [783]
Sioux Indians near Fort Laramie; Indians of California and Oregon.

10. Message on Appropriation for the Indian Dept. 19 Jan.
SED 26, 33-2, v6, 9p. [751] *or* HED 34, 33-2, v5, 9p. [783]
For transportation of Sioux annuity goods.
11. R-P of J. McCrabb. 19 Jan.
SR 419, 33-2, v1, 2p. [775]
Creek and Seminole hostilities.
12. R-C of J. Rogers. 22 Jan.
SR 422, 33-2, v1, 1p. [775]
Supplies for the Chickasaws near Fort Smith, Arkansas.
13. R-M of J. Hughes. 24 Jan.
HR 31, 33-2, v1, 1p. [808]
Indian war in Florida; 1836.
14. Message on Interest Due Cherokees. 25 Jan.
SED 29, 33-2, v6, 2p. [751] *or* HED 42, 33-2, v5, 2p. [783]
Under the treaty of 1835.
15. R-M of J. Rutter et al. 26 Jan.
HR 34, 33-2, v1, 1p. [808]
Extinguish Indian title to land along the entire Missouri River.
16. Report on Military Roads in Kansas. 29 Jan.
HR 36, 33-2, v1, 4p. [808]
Indian hostilities.
17. Report on the Fort Scott Reserve in Kansas. 29 Jan.
HR 37, 33-2, v1, 1p. [808]
Held as a part of Indian country.
18. Report on the Militia of New Mexico. 29 Jan.
HR 38, 33-2, v1, 3p. [808]
Apache hostilities of 1854.
19. Report on Suppression of Indian Hostilities. 29 Jan.
HR 39, 33-2, v1, 1p. [808]
In Utah territory during 1853.
20. Report on Increasing and Reorganizing the Army. 29 Jan.
HR 40, 33-2, v1, 59p. [808]
Hostilities of the Indian tribes on the western frontier.
21. Message on Indian Treaties. 30 Jan.
SED 32, 33-2, v6, 6p. [751] *or* HED 45, 33-2, v5, 6p. [783]
Modification of laws to enable execution of treaties with various Indian tribes in Kansas.
22. R-P of A. Bayard. 30 Jan.
HR 51, 33-2, v1, 1p. [808]
Indian wars of the northwest; 1812.
23. Resol. of the New York Legis. 31 Jan.
HMD 24, 33-2, v1, 1p. [807]
Pensions to soldiers in Indian wars during 1791-1792, and 1794-1795.
24. R-P of J. Loranger. 1 Feb.
SR 469, 33-2, v1, 1p. [775]
Indian depredations; 1812; Michigan.
25. Report on Chickasaw Trust Fund. 1 Feb.
HED 48, 33-2, v5, 4p. [783]
Treaties of 20 Oct. 1832 and 24 May 1834.
26. R-P of J. Collins. 2 Feb.
HR 63, 33-2, v1, 1p. [808]
Indian wars prior to 1800.
27. R-M of L. Benedict. 2 Feb.
HR 68, 33-2, v1, 3p. [808]
Pottawatomie treaty of 20 Oct. 1832.
28. On the Relief of R. Fitzpatrick. 2 Feb.
HR 72, 33-2, v1, 2p. [808]
Seminole war; 1836; Florida.
29. On the Relief of J. Shaw. 2 Feb.
HR 74, 33-2, v1, 1p. [808]
Interpreter in the trial of certain Winnebagoes in 1828.
30. On the Case of G. Herrick. 2 Feb.
HR 75, 33-2, v1, 2p. [808]
Clerk in Indian Bureau.
31. R-P of Heirs of F. Schonmaker. 2 Feb.
HR 84, 33-2, v1, 3p. [808]
Indian depredations; Revolutionary War; New York.
32. Report on a Treaty with the Delaware Indians. 3 Feb.
HED 50, 33-2, v5, 110p. [783]
Treaty of 6 May 1854.
33. Message on Appropriations for the Indian Dept. 5 Feb.
SED 35, 33-2, v7, 3p. [752] *or* HED 53, 33-2, v5, 3p. [783]
For colonizing Texas Indians upon reservations, and for opening communication with Texas Comanches and Apaches who have not yet treated with the U.S.
34. Message on Removal of the California Indians. 5 Feb.
SED 36, 33-2, v7, 2p. [752] *or* HED 57, 33-2, v5, 3p. [783]
To reservations in said state.
35. R-C of W. Read. 6 Feb.
SR 476, 33-2, v1, 1p. [775]
Indian hostilities; 1793; Tennessee.

36. Message on the Chippewa Indians. 7 Feb.
SED 40, 33-2, v7, 3p. [752] *or* HED 61, 33-2, v8, 3p. [788]
Treaty of 30 Sept. 1854 with the Lake Superior Chippewa; treaties of 29 July 1837 and 4 Oct. 1842 with the Mississippi Chippewa.

37. Message on California Indians. 7 Feb.
SED 41, 33-2, v7, 3p. [752] *or* HED 60, 33-2, v8, 4p. [788]
Colonization, or removal of Indians to reservations in said state.

38. Report on an Engagement with the Sioux. 9 Feb.
HED 63, 33-2, v8, 27p. [788]
Near Fort Laramie on 19 Aug. 1854.

39. On the Relief of J. Smith and J. McGraw. 9 Feb.
HR 89, 33-2, v1, 1p. [808]
Indian attacks upon territorial legislators.

40. Report on Army Appropriations. 9 Feb.
HR 90, 33-2, v1, 15p. [808]
To control Indian hostilities.

41. R-C of the Brothertown Indians. 10 Feb.
SED 45, 33-2, v7, 28p. [752] *or* HED 66, 33-2, v8, 28p. [788]
Purchase of Menomonee and Winnebago lands by the New York Indians.

42. R-P of J. Schultz. 12 Feb.
SR 501, 33-2, v1, 2p. [775]
British and Indians; 1782; New York.

43. R-P of the Heirs of A. Harper. 12 Feb.
SR 502, 33-2, v1, 2p. [775]
Prisoner of the Indians; 1778; New York.

44. Report on the Fort Leavenworth Military Reservation. 14 Feb.
SED 50, 33-2, v7, 32p. [752]
CIA presents claim to land on behalf of the Delaware Indians.

45. Explorations of Railroad Routes from the Mississippi to the Pacific. 14 Feb.
SED 78, 33-2, v13 (pts. 1-11), 6211p. [758-768] *or* HED 91, 33-2, v11 (pts. 1-11), 6211p. [791-801]
Journals of expeditions, including descriptions of Indians; a northern route from Minnesota, along the Upper Missouri, to Washington; a central route from Missouri, across the Great Basin, to California; a southern route from the Red River, along the Rio Grande and Colorado Rivers, to southern California; a report on Indian tribes of the Southwest is included in pt. 3 (Serials 760 and 793).

46. Reports on Payments to J. Miller and Pym-y-oh-te-mah. 19 Feb.
HED 74, 33-2, v8, 4p. [788]
Stipulations of treaty of 7 Aug. 1854 with Miami Indians.

47. Message on an Appropriation for Indians. 20 Feb.
SED 56, 33-2, v7, 2p. [752] *or* HED 75, 33-2, v8, 2p. [788]
To pay for a deficit in the trust funds held for Indians.

48. Mem. and Resol. of the Iowa Legis. 20 Feb.
HMD 30, 33-2, v1, 2p. [807]
Garrison near the mouth of the Big Sioux River; near lands owned by the Sioux, Omahas, Ottoes, and other tribes; Indian depredations.

49. Resol. of the Iowa Legis. 20 Feb.
HMD 36, 33-2, v1, 3p. [807]
Settlers and emigrants between the Mississippi and Pacific; line of military posts; Indian depredations.

50. Report on Indian Appropriations. 20 Feb.
HR 92, 33-2, v1, 1p. [808]
Amendments; for fulfilling treaty stipulations.

51. Report on the Fort Leavenworth Military Reservation. 21 Feb.
SED 58, 33-2, v7, 9p. [752]
Established in 1829; treaty of Sept. 1829 with the Delawares.

52. On the Relief of G. Humphreys. 23 Feb.
HR 96, 33-2, v1, 3p. [808]
Indian war of 1836 in Florida.

53. R-P of J. Lindsay. 23 Feb.
HR 103, 33-2, v1, 2p. [808]
Creek treaty of 9 Aug. 1814.

54. R-P of Heirs of M. Jemison. 23 Feb.
HR 106, 33-2, v1, 2p. [808]
Annuities wrongly withheld from the Seneca Indians.

55. R-M of the Heirs of Col. Hardin. 23 Feb.
HR 120, 33-2, v1, 4p. [808]
Indian wars in Ohio; 1774-1792; Miami, Delaware, and Shawnee Indians.

56. R-M of A. Butler. 23 Feb.
HR 121, 33-2, v1, 3p. [808]
Indian Dept. of Pennsylvania during 1838-1842.

57. R-P of F. Argenti. 23 Feb.
HR 127, 33-2, v1, 3p. [808]

Supplies for California Indians under treaties negotiated, but not ratified.

58. Report on Payments to Choctaw Indians. 28 Feb.
SED 64, 33-2, v11, 59p. [756]
Annuities and expenditures for education under various treaties.

59. Report on Indian Disbursements. 1 Mar.
SED 69, 33-2, v11, 270p. [756] *or*
HED 87, 33-2, v10, 270p. [790]
For the year ending 30 June 1854.

60. Message on a Land Survey. 1 Mar.
SED 70, 33-2, v11, 1p. [756] *or*
HED 83, 33-2, v8, 1p. [788]
Land acquired from the Lake Superior Chippewas.

61. Message on Appropriations for the Indian Service. 1 Mar.
SED 71, 33-2, v11, 2p. [756] *or*
HED 84, 33-2, v8, 2p. [788]
For survey of the Choctaw-Chickasaw boundary, and negotiating the treaty of 12 May 1854 with the Menomonees.

62. Annual Report of the Smithsonian Institution. 1 Mar.
SMD 24, 33-2, v1, 463p. [772] *or*
HMD 37, 33-2, v1, 463p. [807]
Research related to North American Indians.

63. Message on a Treaty with the Wyandots. 3 Mar.
SED 74, 33-2, v11, 2p. [756] *or*
HED 88, 33-2, v10, 2p. [790]
To fulfill stipulations of the treaty of 31 Jan. 1855.

64. On the Georgia-Florida Boundary. 3 Mar.
SMD 25, 33-2, v2, 396p. [773]
Cherokee, Creek, Choctaw, and Chickasaw land titles, trade, and treaty relations.

65. List of Private Claims. 3 Mar.
SMD 27, 33-2, v3, 870p. [774]
From the 14th to the 33rd Congress.

66. Message on Pay of Indian Agents. 3 Mar.
HED 94, 33-2, v10, 3p. [790]
On increasing the number and compensation of Indian agents; more agents for California.

67. R-P of Dent, Vantine, and Company. 3 Mar.
HR 149, 33-2, v1, 4p. [808]
Supplies to California Indians under treaty of 28 May 1851 which was not ratified.

68. R-P of Texas Citizens. 3 Mar.
HR 151, 33-2, v1, 4p. [808]
Depredations committed by Comanche, Lipan, and other Indian tribes.

69. Statements of Appropriations. 19 Apr.
SMD 26, 33-2, v2, 88p. [773] *or*
HMD 38, 33-2, v1, 88p. [807]
2d session, 33rd Congress; Indian expenses.

70. Annual Message to Congress with Documents; Pres. Pierce. 31 Dec.
SED 1, 34-1, v1-4, 1644p. [810-813] *or* HED 1, 34-1, v1 (pts. 1-4), 1644p. [840-843]
Indian hostilities; annual report of the Sec. of War (Serials 811 and 841); annual report of the Sec. of Interior (Serials 810 and 840); annual report of the Gen. Land Office (Serials 810 and 840); annual report of the CIA (Serials 810 and 840); including instructions to the Com'rs treating with the Blackfeet Indians, powers of attorney obtained by whites from Indians, treaty councils and articles, Sioux hostilities, trust funds, expenditures, annuities from 1851 treaty of Fort Laramie, and reports of Supts., agents, and schools; etc.

1856

1. Annual Report of the Sec. of the Treasury. 3 Jan.
SED 2, 34-1, v5, 683p. [814] *or*
HED 10, 34-1, v4, 683p. [846]
Indian expenses; year ending 30 June 1855.

2. Estimates of Appropriations. 7 Jan.
HED (no number), 34-1, v16, 324p. [865]
Year ending 30 June 1857; Indian expenses.

3. R-P of J. Horne. 5 Feb.
SR 1, 34-1, v1, 2p. [836]
Choctaw treaty of 1830.

4. Report on Indian Disbursements. 12 Feb.
SED 19, 34-1, v6, 427p. [815] *or*

HED 11, 34-1, v5, 427p. [847]
For the year ending 30 June. 1855.

5. Annual Report on the Chickasaw Fund. 14 Feb.
HED 7, 34-1, v2, 3p. [844]
Treaties of 20 Oct. 1832, and 24 May 1834.

6. Expenditures of the War Dept. 14 Feb.
HED 15, 34-1, v7, 15p. [851]
Costs of suppressing Indian hostilities.

7. Message on Affairs in Kansas Territory. 18 Feb.
SED 23, 34-1, v11, 822p. [820]
Sac, Fox, Chippewa, Ottawa, New York, Wea, and other Indian reservations.

8. On the Case of M. Otero. 18 Feb.
HMD 15, 34-1, v1, 271p. [866]
New Mexico contested election; Pueblo Indian votes.

9. Message on the Mosquito Indians. 19 Feb.
SED 25, 34-1, v10, 146p. [819]
Dispute over land between the U.S., Great Britain, Nicaragua, Costa Rica, and said Indians.

10. Message on Indian Disturbances in California. 21 Feb.
SED 26, 34-1, v10, 68p. [819]
Stretching along the entire northwest Pacific coastline, and encompassing California, Oregon, and Washington.

11. Receipts and Expenditures. 28 Feb.
HED 40, 34-1, v8, 1001p. [852]
For the year ending 30 June 1855; Indian expenses.

12. R-M of E. Linn. 4 Mar.
SR 26, 34-1, v1, 2p. [836]
British and Indians; 1776; Illinois.

13. Resol. of the Florida Legis. 7 Mar.
HMD 50, 34-1, v1, 1p. [866]
Indian hostilities of 1840.

14. Message on Indian Disturbances. 11 Mar.
SED 46, 34-1, v12, 10p. [821] *or*
HED 48, 34-1, v9, 10p. [853]
In Oregon and Washington Territories.

15. Mem. of the Washington Legis. 14 Mar.
HMD 58, 34-1, v1, 1p. [866]
Military road; Indian hostilities.

16. Mem. of the Washington Legis. 14 Mar.
Military road; Indian attacks.

17. Mem. of the Washington Legis. 14 Mar.
Military road; Indian hostilities.

18. Mem. of the Washington Legis. 14 Mar.
HMD 61, 34-1, v1, 2p. [866]
Military road; Indian war.

19. Mem. of the Washington Legis. 14 Mar.
HMD 62, 34-1, v1, 2p. [866]
Military road; Indian attacks.

20. Mem. of the Washington Legis. 14 Mar.
HMD 64, 34-1, v1, 2p. [866]
Expenses of Yakima Indian war.

21. Clerks in the Interior Dept. 17 Mar.
HED 55, 34-1, v9, 22p. [853]
Office of the CIA.

22. Message on the Creek and Seminole Indians. 17 Mar.
HED 58, 34-1, v9, 2p. [853]
Difficulties which have arisen since their emigration west of the Mississippi River.

23. Mem. of the Choctaw Indians. 18 Mar.
SMD 31, 34-1, v1, 88p. [835]
Claims under the treaty of 1830 at Dancing Rabbit Creek; treaty of 22 June 1855.

24. On the Relief of A. Dart. 18 Mar.
HR 5, 34-1, v1, 2p. [868]
Supt. of Indian Affairs in Oregon and Washington.

25. R-M of W. Magraw. 20 Mar.
HR 6, 34-1, v1, 10p. [868]
Mail route from Independence to Salt Lake, Utah; Shawnee, Delaware, Sioux, and other Indian tribes; depredations.

26. Message on Indians of the Upper Missouri. 24 Mar.
HED 65, 34-1, v9, 15p. [853]
Supt. Cumming's expedition up the Missouri River; Com'r appointed to treat with the Blackfeet Indians; encounters with various tribes.

27. R-P of C. Wallace. 25 Mar.
SR 51, 34-1, v1, 3p. [836]
Land in Louisiana; Caddo treaty of 1 July 1835.

28. R-P of W. Trotter. 26 Mar.
SR 55, 34-1, v1, 2p. [836]
Choctaw removal in 1830; supply contract.

29. R-C of Capt. McClellan. 27 Mar.
SR 62, 34-1, v1, 1p. [836]
Indian depredations; 1840; Florida.

30. On the Case of C. Babcock. 27 Mar.
HR 7, 34-1, v1, 2p. [868]
Late Indian agent at Detroit.

31. Act of the Oregon Legis. 1 Apr.
HMD 78, 34-1, v1, 2p. [866]
Volunteers in the Indian war.

32. Letter on Florida Volunteers. 2 Apr.
HMD 76, 34-1, v1, 4p. [866]
Lately called into service to suppress Indian hostilities in said state.

33. Mem. of the Oregon Legis. 2 Apr.
HMD 77, 34-1, v1, 3p. [866]
Expenses of war with Yakima, Klickatat, Wallah-Wallah, and Snake Indians.

34. Report on Pension Laws. 3 Apr.
SR 95, 34-1, v1, 2p. [836]
Pensions to Cherokee warriors under the treaty of 1835.

35. Report on Land Donations in Arkansas. 3 Apr.
HR 25, 34-1, v1, 1p. [868]
Cherokee cession under the treaty of 23 May 1828.

36. Report on Accounts Between the U.S. and Mississippi. 4 Apr.
HR 35, 34-1, v1, 4p. [868]
Choctaw treaties of 18 Oct. 1820, and Dancing Rabbit Creek (1830); Chickasaw treaties of 20 Oct. 1832, and 24 May 1834; land reservations in the state.

37. Appropriations of the Interior Dept. 9 Apr.
SED 54, 34-1, v12, 15p. [821] *or*
HED 77, 34-1, v9, 15p. [853]
Indian expenses for the year ending 30 June 1855.

38. Message on the Boundary with Mexico. 15 Apr.
SED 57, 34-1, v12, 76p. [821]
Survey hampered by Indian hostilities.

39. R-M of A. Jackson et al. 15 Apr.
HR 46, 34-1, v1, 3p. [868]
Payments due these Miami Indians under the treaty of 5 June 1854.

40. R-P of R. Jones. 15 Apr.
HR 47, 34-1, v1, 2p. [868]
Contract entered into with the Menomonees; 1854.

41. R-M of J. Price. 15 Apr.
HR 49, 34-1, v1, 2p. [868]
Seminole war; 1836-1837; Florida.

42. On the Relief of the Heirs of J. Levine. 15 Apr.
HR 52, 34-1, v1, 4p. [868]
Indian campaign of 1774 in Virginia.

43. R-P of D. Demoiville. 15 Apr.
HR 53, 34-1, v1, 1p. [868]
Black Hawk war.

44. Message on Indian Hostilities on the Northwest Coast. 17 Apr.
HED 93, 34-1, v11, 144p. [858]
In Oregon and Washington Territories.

45. Report on a Jail in Arkansas. 17 Apr.
HR 64, 34-1, v1, 2p. [868]
Near Indian country; violations committed in said country.

46. Report on Improvements of the Red River. 24 Apr.
HR 85, 34-1, v1, 2p. [868]
Navigation of the river reaches far into the Indian country; raft region.

47. Exploration of the Big Witchita and Brazos Rivers. 29 Apr.
SED 60, 34-1, v12, 48p. [821]
Capt. Marcy's expedition to locate reservation lands for the Texas Indians.

48. R-M of C. Coffin. 5 May.
SR 159, 34-1, v1, 2p. [836]
Mission founded among the Shawnees in Ohio; removal.

49. Report on Indian Disturbances on the Northwest Coast. 12 May.
SED 66, 34-1, v13, 68p. [822]
In Oregon and Washington Territories.

50. R-P of J. Scranton and J. Hunt. 14 May.
SR 169, 34-1, v1, 3p. [836]
Shipwreck on the Northwest Coast; surrounded by Indians.

51. Message on Indian Appropriations. 16 May.
SED 67, 34-1, v13, 25p. [822] *or*
HED 104, 34-1, v12, 25p. [859]
To fulfill treaty stipulations with various tribes.

52. J. Shaw *vs.* the U.S. 16 May.
HRCC 3, 34-1, v1, 7p. [871]
Interpreter during the trial of Winnebago Indians in 1828.

53. J. Hale *vs.* the U.S. 16 May.
HRCC 19, 34-1, v1, 8p. [871]
Land title in Arkansas; treaty of 24 Aug. 1818 with the Quapaws.

54. Message on the Case of R. Thompson. 19 May.
SED 72, 34-1, v13, 319p. [822]
Services performed for the Menomonees.

55. On the Case of J. Kirby et al. 19 May.
SR 179, 34-1, v1, 2p. [836]
Cherokee treaties of 1817 and 1819.

56. Report on the Message of the Pres. Regarding the Claim of R. Thompson. 19 May.
SR 180, 34-1, v1, 1p. [836]
Menomonee Indians; services performed.

57. Explorations in Dakota Country. 22 May.
SED 76, 34-1, v13, 79p. [822]
Report of the "Sioux Expedition"; encounters with, and descriptions of the Sioux between the Missouri and Platte Rivers, and the Rocky Mountains.

58. R-P of B. Maher. 23 May.
HR 128, 34-1, v1, 2p. [868]
Proprietress of the Western Hotel, or Indian House, in Washington, D.C.; Cherokee delegation.

59. R-M of W. Elam. 23 May.
HR 129, 34-1, v1, 1p. [868]
Indian hostilities; 1855; Texas.

60. On the Case of R. Smith. 23 May.
HR 131, 34-1, v1, 2p. [868]
Campaign against the Rickaree Indians in 1823; Sioux warriors aid U.S. soldiers.

61. R-P of G. Schellenger. 23 May.
HR 134, 34-1, v1, 1p. [868]
Black Hawk war; 1832; Illinois.

62. R-M of M. Winship. 23 May.
HR 146, 34-1, v1, 2p. [868]
Indian war in Florida during 1840; Sioux campaign of 1855.

63. R-P of R. Wimberly. 23 May.
HR 156, 34-1, v1, 1p. [868]
Creek war of 1836 in Georgia.

64. R-P of R. Murry. 23 May.
HR 159, 34-1, v1, 1p. [868]
Seminole war of 1818.

65. J. Lindsay *vs.* the U.S. 23 May.
HRCC 10, 34-1, v1, 17p. [871]
Treaty of 9 Aug. 1814 with the hostile Creeks of Alabama.

66. R-P of G. Giddings. 27 May.
HR 170, 34-1, v1, 2p. [868]
Santa Fe-San Antonio mail route; Indian depredations.

67. Report on a Mail Route in Washington Territory. 28 May.
HR 172, 34-1, v1, 2p. [868]
Would serve to keep Indians in subjection.

68. R-P of G. Jemison et al. 28 May.
HR 176, 34-1, v1, 3p. [868]
Money wrongfully withheld from the Senecas.

69. Letter on Arms for California. 19 June.
SMD 67, 34-1, v1, 3p. [835]
Indian hostilities in northern California.

70. Letter on the Florida Volunteers. 21 June.
HMD 123, 34-1, v2, 3p. [867]
Seminole hostilities in 1855.

71. Letter on the Choctaw Claim for Interest. 21 June.
HMD 125, 34-1, v2, 2p. [867]
Under the treaty of 22 June 1855.

72. Letter on an Error in the Chickasaw Estimates. 21 June.
HMD 126, 34-1, v2, 2p. [867]
Expenses of Chickasaw delegation.

73. R-M of J. and P. Faribault. 23 June.
SR 193, 34-1, v1, 4p. [836]
Sioux land cession of 1820; treaty of 1837; "Pike's Treaty" of 1805; Sioux and Chippewa treaty of 1825.

74. Report on Defence of Nebraska Frontier Settlements. 23 June.
HR 193, 34-1, v1, 5p. [868]
Sioux expedition of Gen. Harney.

75. Message on Federal and Cherokee Courts. 24 June.
HED 113, 34-1, v12, 5p. [859]
Conflict of jurisdiction.

76. Message on Sale of Choctaw Orphan Reservations. 24 June.
HED 114, 34-1, v12, 4p. [859]
Balances from sales; treaty of 1830.

77. Report on Expenses of an Indian War. 24 June.
HR 195, 34-1, v1, 1p. [868]
In Oregon and Washington during 1855-1856.

78. Report on the Grattan Massacre. 1 July.
SED 91, 34-1, v14, 27p. [823]
Incident between U.S. troops and the Sioux stimulated by the killing of a Mormon emigrant's cow.

79. Message on Indian Hostilities in Oregon and Washington Territories. 8 July.
HED 118, 34-1, v12, 58p. [859]
Reports on the Indian war in the Northwest.

80. On the Case of J. M. Lindsay. 11 July.
SR 219, 34-1, v2, 4p. [837]
Treaty of 9 Aug. 1814 with the hostile Creeks in Alabama.

81. On the Case of J. Kirby et al. 18 July.
SR 231, 34-1, v2, 2p. [837]
Cherokee treaties of 1817 and 1819.

82. R-P of M. and R. Bean. 19 July.
HR 210, 34-1, v3, 9p. [870]
Property lost due to the Cherokee treaty of 6 May 1828.

83. R-M of J. Sims. 19 July.
HR 223, 34-1, v3, 3p. [870]
Supplies to Fort Arbuckle, Choctaw Nation.

84. R-C of J. Morrison. 19 July.
HR 224, 34-1, v3, 2p. [870]
Damages by U.S. troops during the Black Hawk war of 1832 in Wisconsin.

85. R-P of A. Bayard. 19 July.
HR 239, 34-1, v3, 3p. [870]
Indian battle at Fort Harrison.

86. R-P of H. Stewart. 19 July.
HR 247, 34-1, v3, 1p. [870]
Seminole war of 1818 in Florida.

87. R-M of G. Dousman. 19 July.
HR 256, 34-1, v3, 2p. [870]
Indian sub-agent at Green Bay, Wisconsin.

88. Mem. and Resol. of the Iowa Legis. 22 July.
SMD 69, 34-1, v1, 2p. [835] *or*
HMD 139, 34-1, v2, 2p. [867]
Extension of the boundaries of the state by extinguishing Indian title to land.

89. R-M of the Heirs of R. McConnell. 23 July.
SR 243, 34-1, v2, 1p. [837]
Indian depredations of 1813 in Alabama; treaty of 1814; compensation to whites, friendly Creeks, Cherokees, Chickasaws, and Choctaws.

90. R-C of Georgia and Alabama Citizens. 23 July.
SR 244, 34-1, v2, 5p. [837]
Creek and Seminole depredations of 1836-37; Creek treaty of 1852, ceding all lands east of the Mississippi River; removal.

91. Report on a Pacific Railroad and Telegraph. 24 July.
HR 274, 34-1, v3, 84p. [870] *or*
HR 358, 34-1, v3, 84p. [870]
Indian hostilities on the frontiers; no railroad will pass through an Indian reservation without their prior consent.

92. Annual Report of the Smithsonian Institution. 25 July.
SMD 73, 34-1, v1, 439p. [835] *or*
HMD 113, 34-1, v2, 439p. [867]
Research and publications relating to the American Indian.

93. R-M of Kerr, Beverly, and Company. 25 July.
HR 280, 34-1, v3, 1p. [870]
Gen. Harney's battles with the Sioux.

94. R-M of S. Haight. 25 July.
HR 281, 34-1, v3, 1p. [870]
British and Indians; 1814; New York.

95. Message on a Council Held at Fort Pierre. 28 July.
SED 94, 34-1, v14, 40p. [823] *or*
HED 130, 34-1, v12, 39p. [859]
Proceedings of the council between Gen. Harney and the Sioux; stipulations agreed upon.

96. R-P of J. Hall. 30 July.
SR 252, 34-1, v2, 1p. [837]
Indian depredations on the Independence-Santa Fe mail route.

97. R-P of J. Hardy and A. Long. 2 Aug.
HR 297, 34-1, v3, 7p. [870]
Contract to mine made with the Winnebago, Ottawa, Pottawatomie, and Chippewa Indians prior to 1823.

98. R-P of J. Hall. 2 Aug.
HR 299, 34-1, v3, 4p. [870]
Independence-Santa Fe mail route; Pawnee, Cheyenne, Comanche, Apache, Kiowa, and Arrapahoe hostilities.

99. R-P of the Heirs of Semoice. 2 Aug.
HR 302, 34-1, v3, 2p. [870]
Depredations upon the friendly Creeks during 1813-14.

100. Message on the Boundary of Mexico. 4 Aug.
SED 108, 34-1, v20 (pts. 1-3), 669p. [832-834] *or* HED 135, 34-1, v14, (pts. 1-3), 669p. [861-863]
Under the treaty of Guadalupe Hidalgo; Indians of the Southwest.

101. R-M of Livingston, Kincaid, and Company. 4 Aug.
SR 257, 34-1, v2, 2p. [837]
Sioux depredations in 1854 near Fort Laramie.

102. Message on Martial Law in Washington Territory. 5 Aug.
SED 98, 34-1, v14, 31p. [823]
Due to factors surrounding the Indian war in the Northwest.

103. R-P of G. Chorpenning. 5 Aug.
HR 323, 34-1, v3, 5p. [870]
Mail route from California to Salt Lake; Indian hostilities.

104. R-P of G. Giddings. 6 Aug.
SR 264, 34-1, v2, 2p. [837]
Indian depredations on the Santa Fe-San Antonio mail route.

105. Report on Railroads in the Territories. 6 Aug.
HR 324, 34-1, v3, 26p. [870]
Iowa Indians on the Mississippi River.

106. Report on Reorganization of Kansas. 11 Aug.
SR 282, 34-1, v2, 16p. [837]
Cherokee treaties of 6 May 1828, 12 Apr. 1833, and 23 May 1836; Indian tribes in Kansas.

107. Contingent Expenses of the Interior Dept. 12 Aug.
HED 140, 34-1, v15, 179p. [864]
For the year ending 30 June 1855; Indian Office.

108. R-M of the Iowa Legis. 14 Aug.
HR 347, 34-1, v3, 2p. [870]
Extension of state's boundary by extinguishing Indian title to land.

109. Appropriations Made by the 31st, 32d, and 33rd Congresses. 16 Aug.
HED 145, 34-1, v15, 320p. [864]
Indian expenses.

110. Report on a Military Road. 16 Aug.
HR 355, 34-1, v3, 3p. [870]
From Missouri to California; Indian hostilities in the west.

111. Message on the Claims of J. Fremont. 18 Aug.
SED 109, 34-1, v16, 144p. [825]
Supplies furnished to the California Indians.

112. Message on Army Appropriations. 23 Aug.
SED 2, 34-2, v16, 1p. [825]
Indian hostilities on the frontiers.

113. Statements of Appropriations. 16 Oct.
SMD 2, 34-2, v1, 91p. [835] *or*
HMD 2, 34-2, v2, 91p. [867]
During the 1st and 2d sessions, 34th Congress; Indian expenses.

114. Estimates of Appropriations. 14 Nov.
HED (no number), 34-3, v12, 284p. [909]
Year ending 30 June 1858; Indian expenses.

115. Annual Report of the Sec. of the Treasury. 9 Dec.
SED 3, 34-3, v1, 672p. [874] *or*
HED 2, 34-3, v2, 672p. [896]
Year ending 30 June 1856; Indian expenses.

116. Annual Message to Congress with Documents; Pres. Pierce. 11 Dec.
SED 5, 34-3, v2-4, 1789p. [875-877] *or* HED 1, 34-3, v1 (pts. 1-3), 1789p. [893-895]
Indian relations; annual report of the Sec. of War (Serials 876 and 894); annual report of the Sec. of Interior (Serials 875 and 893); annual report of the Gen. Land Office (Serials 875 and 893); annual report of the CIA (Serials 875 and 893), including negotiations, appropriations, trust funds, annuities, land warrants, and reports of Supts., agents, and schools; etc.

117. R-P of J. Horne. 11 Dec.
HR 1, 34-3, v1, 2p. [912]
Land purchases under the treaty of 1830 with the Choctaws at Dancing Rabbit Creek.

118. R-P of M. Woodbury et al. 12 Dec.
HR 8, 34-3, v1, 2p. [912]
Sioux half-breeds desire payments due them under the treaty of 1837.

119. R-M of E. Ogden. 18 Dec.
SR 293, 34-3, v1, 2p. [891]
Creek and Seminole hostilities during 1840-1843.

120. R-M of S. Rice. 26 Dec.
HR 39, 34-3, v1, 1p. [912]
Indian battle at Fort Recovery in 1792.

121. R-P of G. Wells et al. 26 Dec.
HR 40, 34-3, v1, 3p. [912]
Reservation made under the treaty of 29 July 1829 with the Chippewas, Ottawas, and Pottawatomies; treaty of 26 Sept. 1833.

122. Report on Land Titles in Kansas. 30 Dec.
SED 13, 34-3, v5, 4p. [878]
Lands set apart to the New York Indians; treaty of 15 Jan. 1838 at Buffalo Creek; Osage and Menomonee lands.

1857

1. Contingent Expenses of the Interior Dept. 7 Jan.

HED 29, 34-3, v3, 127p. [897]
Year ending 30 June 1856; Office of Indian Affairs.

2. R-M of J. Shaw. 10 Jan.
HR 53, 34-3, v1, 3p. [912]
British and Indians; 1812; Missouri.

3. R-M of L. Oatman. 10 Jan.
HR 55, 34-3, v1, 1p. [912]
Appropriation to rescue a captive of the Mohave Indians.

4. R-M of J. Bennett. 10 Jan.
HR 57, 34-3, v1, 1p. [921]
Indian hostilities on the Texas frontier.

5. Letter on Indian Disbursements. 16 Jan.
SED 28, 34-3, v7, 366p. [880] *or*
HED 31, 34-3, v5, 366p. [899]
For the year ending 30 June 1856.

6. R-P of G. O'Brien. 16 Jan.
SR 309, 34-3, v1, 1p. [891]
Clerk for the Chickasaw Indians during 1845-1846.

7. Supplemental Estimates for the Indian Service. 16 Jan.
HED 37, 34-3, v5, 147p. [899]
For California, Texas, and the distant Territories.

8. R-M of J. Wood. 16 Jan.
HR 81, 34-3, v1, 2p. [912]
Indian hostilities; 1850; New Mexico.

9. R-M of M. Williams. 16 Jan.
HR 83, 34-3, v1, 7p. [912]
St. Regis (Iroquois) Indian asks payment due for services in war of 1812.

10. R-M of T. Moody. 16 Jan.
HR 87, 34-3, v1, 2p. [912]
Cherokee campaign; 1776; Tennessee.

11. R-P of the Heirs of I. Johnson. 16 Jan.
HR 93, 34-3, v1, 1p. [912]
Indian wars; 1794-1795; Ohio.

12. R-M of Kerr, Brierly, and Company. 16 Jan.
HR 100, 34-3, v1, 1p. [912]
Gen. Harney's battles with the Sioux.

13. R-M of A. Desmake. 16 Jan.
HR 104, 34-3, v1, 1p. [912]
Indian depredations; 1855; Texas.

14. R-M of H. Groomes. 16 Jan.
HR 105, 34-3, v1, 1p. [912]
British and Indians; 1812; Kentucky.

15. R-M of T. Runnells. 16 Jan.
HR 109, 34-3, v1, 1p. [912]
Seminole war of 1818 in Florida.

16. Persons Employed in the Interior Dept. 19 Jan.
HED 39, 34-3, v5, 26p. [899]
Office of the CIA.

17. Report on Fort Ripley, Minnesota. 20 Jan.
HR 118, 34-3, v1, 2p. [912]
Winnebago reservation; Indians removed there in 1848.

18. R-P of J. Shaw. 22 Jan.
SR 318, 34-3, v1, 2p. [891]
Menomonee depredations; 1846; Wisconsin.

19. R-P of G. Phelps. 23 Jan.
SR 321, 34-3, v1, 1p. [891]
Indian hostilities in Florida; 1839.

20. R-M of A. Dart. 24 Jan.
HR 125, 34-3, v1, 2p. [912]
Late Supt. of Indian Affairs in Oregon.

21. R-M of Florida Volunteers. 24 Jan.
HR 133, 34-3, v1, 5p. [912]
Seminole war in 1838.

22. R-P of J. Ryley. 28 Jan.
SR 335, 34-3, v1, 1p. [891]
An Ottawa Indian who served in with the U.S. in the war of 1812.

23. R-P of Ohio Citizens. 28 Jan.
SR 336, 34-3, v1, 1p. [891]
For a Wyandot Indian who served with the U.S. in the war of 1812.

24. Appropriations and Balances of the Interior Dept. 30 Jan.
SED 31, 34-3, v7, 11p. [880] *or*
HED 53, 34-3, v6, 11p. [900]
Year ending 30 June 1856; Indian expenses.

25. R-M of J. Hall. 30 Jan.
HR 154, 34-3, v1, 1p. [912]
Cession of land in Arkansas to the Cherokees.

26. R-M of Reps. of Col. Wilson. 30 Jan.
HR 163, 34-3, v1, 3p. [912]
Indian hostilities; 1774-1795; Virginia; treaty of Greenville in 1795.

27. Report on a Geological Survey of Oregon and Washington Territories. 31 Jan.
HR 171, 34-3, v1, 4p. [912]
Indian trails; Indian war raises cost of survey.

28. Report on a Military Road. 31 Jan.
HR 172, 34-3, v1, 3p. [912]
In Kansas, from Fort Leavenworth to Fort Riley; troop movements against the Indians.

29. R-M of J. Smith. 2 Feb.
SR 346, 34-3, v1, 1p. [891]
Indian reservation in Alabama.
30. R-P of Reps. of C. Porterfield. 4 Feb.
SR 356, 34-3, v1, 3p. [891]
Cherokee lands; 1779; Ohio River Valley.
31. Annual Report on the Chickasaw Trust Fund. 5 Feb.
HED 64, 34-3, v6, 3p. [900]
Under the treaties of 20 Oct. 1832 and 24 May 1834.
32. R-M of Maj. Alvord. 7 Feb.
SR 366, 34-3, v1, 3p. [891]
Shipwreck on the coast of Washington Territory; Indian depredations.
33. Message on Martial Law in Washington Territory. 10 Feb.
SED 41, 34-3, v8, 56p. [881]
Due to individuals protecting hostile Indians after the commencement of the Indian war in said Territory.
34. Letters on Land Laws. 12 Feb.
SMD 28, 34-3, v1, 4p. [890]
Extension of land laws east of the Cascade Mountains in Oregon, where treaties with the Indians for cession of their lands have been negotiated but not ratified; Indian wars in Oregon and Washington.
35. Report on Volunteers in Washington Territory. 12 Feb.
HR 189, 34-3, v3, 1p. [914]
Indian war; restrained the Klickatat Indians from joining the war along with the Yakamas.
36. Message on Martial Law in Washington Territory. 13 Feb.
SED 47, 34-3, v8, 11p. [881]
Suspicions of intercourse with Indians during the Indian war in said Territory.
37. Report on Expenditures for Indian Tribes. 13 Feb.
SED 48, 34-3, v8, 13p. [881]
Amounts appropriated for the year ending 30 June 1857; amounts drawn for the year ending 30 June 1856.
38. R-P of G. Colvin. 13 Feb.
SR 389, 34-3, v1, 1p. [891]
Indian war during 1794-1795 in Ohio and Kentucky.
39. R-M of Tennessee Citizens. 13 Feb.
HR 204, 34-3, v3, 6p. [914]
Cherokee reservations under the treaties of 1817 and 1819.
40. R-M of D. Gordon. 13 Feb.
HR 206, 34-3, v3, 9p. [914]
Creek depredations in Alabama.
41. R-P of the Administrator of J. Wray. 14 Feb.
SR 391, 34-3, v1, 2p. [891]
Land dispute; Chickasaw treaty of 24 May 1834.
42. Message on Indian Affairs on the Pacific. 16 Feb.
HED 76, 34-3, v9, 256p. [906]
Populations and locations of Indians in California, Oregon, and Washington.
43. Estimate of Appropriations for the Sioux. 16 Feb.
HMD 46, 34-3, v1, 1p. [911]
To execute stipulations entered into with the Sioux by Gen. Harney at Fort Pierre.
44. Report on Lieut. Cooke's Action Against the Sioux. 20 Feb.
SED 58, 34-3, v8, 4p. [881]
Attack on a Brule Sioux village; 3 Sept. 1855; Bluewater, Nebraska.
45. Annual Report of the Smithsonian Institution. 28 Feb.
SMD 54, 34-3, v1, 467p. [890]
Research and publications related to American Indians.
46. R-P of G. Vandiver. 2 Mar.
SR 435, 34-3, v1, 2p. [891]
Cherokee removal in 1838.
47. Message on the Case of E. Beale. 3 Mar.
SED 69, 34-3, v8, 7p. [881]
Late Supt. of Indian Affairs in California.
48. R-M of D. Gordon. 3 Mar.
SR 446, 34-3, v1, 12p. [891]
Indian depredations; 1813; Mississippi.
49. Receipts and Expenditures. 3 Mar.
HED 86, 34-3, v11, 645p. [908]
Year ending 30 June 1856; Indian expenses.
50. R-M of N. Evans. 3 Mar.
HR 244, 34-3, v3, 1p. [914]
Indian depredations; 1850; cargo *en route* to Santa Fe.
51. On the Relief of W. Trotter. 3 Mar.
HR 251, 34-3, v3, 4p. [914]
Contracted to supply emigrating Choctaws in 1831.

52. Report on Pensions for Cherokees. 3 Mar.
HR 252, 34-3, v3, 1p. [914]
Under the treaty of 29 Dec. 1835 at New Echota, and the pension law of 14 Apr. 1842.
53. Report on Invalid Pensions. 3 Mar.
HR 259, 34-3, v3, 10p. [914]
Seminole war of 1817-1818; Black Hawk war of 1832; Florida Indian war of 1836-1842; Creek disturbances during 1836-1837; Southwestern frontier disturbances in 1836; Cherokee country in 1836-1837.
54. Report on Techniques of War. 14 Mar.
SED 1, 35-sp, v1, 360p. [916]
U.S. Army officers in Europe; report on the U.S. Cavalry in operation against Indians.
55. Statements of Appropriations. 18 Apr.
SMD 56, 34-3, v1, 86p. [890] *or*
HMD 73, 34-3, v1, 86p. [911]
During the 3rd session; 34th Congress; Indian expenses.
56. Estimates of Appropriations. 23 Nov.
HED 1, 35-1, v1, 256p. [941]
Year ending 30 June 1859; Indian expenses.
57. Contingent Expenses of the Interior Dept. 8 Dec.
HED 6, 35-1, v1, 126p. [941]
Year ending 30 June 1857; office of the CIA.
58. Annual Report of the Sec. of the Treasury. 9 Dec.
SED 1, 35-1, v1, 379p. [918] *or*
HED 3, 35-1, v1, 379p. [941]
Year ending 30 June 1857; Indian expenses.
59. Appropriations of the Interior Dept. 15 Dec.
SED 6, 35-1, v1, 13p. [918] *or*
HED 10, 35-1, v1, 13p. [941]
Year ending 30 June 1857; Indian expenses.
60. C. Scaife *vs.* the U.S. 18 Dec.
SMD 20, 35-1, v1, 13p. [934] *or*
HRCC 143, 35-1, v2, 7p. [971]
Seminole war; 1841; Florida (Senate version includes extra documents on the case).
61. A. Butler *vs.* the U.S. 18 Dec.
SMD 57, 35-1, v1, 4p. [934] *or*
HRCC 136, 35-1, v2, 13p. [971]
Indian treaty Com'r in 1786 on the Pennsylvania frontier; battle of Miami Rapids, Ohio in 1791 (House version includes personal accounts).
62. J. Rogers *vs.* the U.S. 18 Dec.
SMD 94, 35-1, v1, 80p. [934] *or*
HRCC 46, 34-3, v1, 80p. [915]
Cherokees residing east of the Mississippi River (numbering 2133) request payments due under the treaty of 1835.
63. J. Loranger *vs.* the U.S. 18 Dec.
SMD 118, 35-1, v2, 4p. [935] *or*
HRCC 96, 35-1, v1, 4p. [970]
British and Indians; 1813; Michigan; Indian trader in 1812.
64. Receipts and Expenditures. 18 Dec.
HED 13, 35-1, v4, 738p. [947]
Year ending 30 June 1957; Indian expenses.
65. R-P of J. Hamilton. 19 Dec.
HR 1, 35-1, v1, 8p. [964]
Taken prisoner by the Indians at the battle of River Raisin in 1813; Michigan.

1858

1. Annual Message to Congress with Documents; Pres. Buchanan. 4 Jan.
SED 11, 35-1, v2-5, 1895p. [919-922] *or* HED 2, 35-1, v2 (pts. 1-4), 1895p. [942-945]
Indian relations; annual report of the Sec. of War (Serials 920 and 943); annual report of the Sec. of Interior (Serials 919 and 942); annual report of the Gen. Land Office (Serials 919 and 942); annual report of the CIA (Serials 919 and 942); including land cessions, Indians in Kansas and Nebraska, Seminole removal, Cheyenne hostilities, Northwestern Indian hostilities, and reports of Supts., agents, and schools; etc.
2. R-P of J. Hamilton. 6 Jan.
HR 2, 35-1, v1, 1p. [964]
Taken prisoner by Indians at the battle of River Raisin in 1813.
3. R-P of W. Trotter. 11 Jan.
SR 6, 35-1, v1, 2p. [938]
Supplies for the removal of the Choctaws from Mississippi in 1830.

4. Mem. of H. O'Rielly. 12 Jan.
SMD 134, 35-1, v2, 16p. [935]
Military highways and telegraph to the Pacific; extinguishment of Indian title to a strip of land five miles on either side of a telegraph line or railroad; line of forts 20 mies apart; Blackfoot Indians.
5. Mem. of H. O'Rielly et al. 12 Jan.
SMD 135, 35-1, v2, 2p. [935]
Telegraph lines to Fort Laramie and Salt Lake; Seminole war; Mormon alliance with Indians in a possible "war of Utah."
6. Letter on Indian Disbursements. 20 Jan.
SED 20, 35-1, v7, 330p. [924] *or*
HED 22, 35-1, v7, 330p. [950]
Year ending 30 June 1857.
7. R-M of J. Smith. 20 Jan.
SR 16, 35-1, v1, 1p. [938]
Indian reservation in Alabama.
8. Resol. of the Texas Legis. 20 Jan.
HMD 26, 35-1, v1, 2p. [961]
Defense of that state's western frontier against Indian depredations.
9. R-M of C. Coffin. 21 Jan.
SR 17, 35-1, v1, 2p. [938]
Mission founded among the Shawnees by the Society of Friends; removal to Kansas; treaty of 10 May 1854.
10. R-M of J. Hall. 21 Jan.
HR 18, 35-1, v1, 1p. [964]
Land in Arkansas ceded to the Cherokees by the treaty of 23 May 1828.
11. R-P of S. Burnham. 21 Jan.
HR 38-, 35-1, v1, 1p. [964]
Indian campaign in 1792-1795 under General Wayne.
12. R-M of N. Smith. 22 Jan.
HR 46, 35-1, v1, 1p. [964]
Friendly Creek during the Creek war of 1813-1814.
13. Letter on Indian Affairs in Oregon and Washington Territories. 25 Jan.
HED 39, 35-1, v9, 48p. [955]
On the condition of Indian reservations.
14. R-P of G. O'Brien. 26 Jan.
SR 22, 35-1, v1, 2p. [938]
Clerk for the Chickasaws during 1845-1846; Chickasaw fund.
15. R. Heald *vs.* the U.S. 2 Feb.
SMD 146, 35-1, v3, 4p. [936] *or*
HRCC 150, 35-1, v2, 5p. [971]
Destruction of Fort Dearborn near Chicago in 1812 by the Indians; claimant taken prisoner.
16. R-P of G. Jemison et al. 3 Feb.
HR 69, 35-1, v1, 3p. [964]
Defaults on payments to the Seneca Indians.
17. R-M of the Heirs of J. Bulow. 3 Feb.
HR 70, 35-1, v1, 4p. [964]
Seminole war in Florida.
18. R-P of Illinois Volunteers. 3 Feb.
HR 71, 35-1, v1, 1p. [964]
Black Hawk war of 1832.
19. R-P of J. Crinian. 3 Feb.
HR 75, 35-1, v1, 1p. [964]
Indian battle at Rogue River, Oregon in 1856; Indian campaign of 1853 in California.
20. R-P of G. Phelps. 8 Feb.
SR 55, 35-1, v1, 1p. [938]
Indian hostilities in Florida.
21. Report on War Claims. 9 Feb.
SED 24, 35-1, v7, 16p. [924] *or*
HED 45, 35-1, v9, 16p. [955]
Expenses of Indian war in Oregon and Washington Territories.
22. Resol. of the Tennessee Legis. 9 Feb.
SMD 151, 35-1, v3, 2p. [936] *or*
HMD 53, 35-1, v1, 1p. [961]
Pensions to soldiers in various Indian wars.
23. Resol. of the Iowa Legis. 9 Feb.
SMD 152, 35-1, v3, 2p. [936] *or* HMD 46, 35-1, v1, 2p. [961] *or* HMD 86, 35-1, v3, 2p. [963]
Bounty lands to volunteers of the Spirit Lake expedition against the Sioux in 1857.
24. Mem. and Resol. of the Iowa Legis. 9 Feb.
SMD 153, 35-1, v3, 1p. [936] *or* HMD 47, 35-1, v1, 2p. [961] *or* HMD 85, 35-1, v3, 2p. [963]
Expenses of suppressing an invasion of hostile Sioux in 1857 at Spirit Lake.
25. Resol. of the Georgia Legis. 9 Feb.
HMD 48, 35-1, v1, 2p. [961]
Extinguishment of Indian reservations in said state; compact of 1802 between the U.S. and Georgia; Cherokee treaty of 1817.
26. Receipts, Appropriations, and Expenditures. 10 Feb.

HED 60, 35-1, v9, 10p. [955]
From 1789 to 1857; Indian Dept.; Chickasaw fund.

27. R-P of New York Soldiers. 10 Feb.
HR 78, 35-1, v1, 3p. [964]
Pensions to soldiers engaged in Indian wars during the war of 1812.

28. R-P of W. Hansell et al. 15 Feb.
SR 66, 35-1, v1, 3p. [938]
Attorneys to the Cherokees for three years; treaty of 1835.

29. R-P of J. Hand. 15 Feb.
SR 67, 35-1, v1, 3p. [938]
Purchased certain Choctaw reservations in Mississippi under the treaty of Dancing Rabbit Creek.

30. Employees of the Interior Dept. 16 Feb.
HMD 62, 35-1, v9, 24p. [955]
During 1857; office of the CIA.

31. Resol. of the Texas Legis. 16 Feb.
HMD 63, 35-1, v1, 1p. [961]
Protection from Indian depredations.

32. R-P of J. Allen and A. Carter. 19 Feb.
SR 83, 35-1, v1, 1p. [938]
Location of Choctaw scrip and railroad lands.

33. R-P of E. Merchant. 23 Feb.
SR 84, 35-1, v1, 1p. [938]
Indian campaign in Texas during 1850.

34. R-P of J. McCrabb. 23 Feb.
SR 85, 35-1, v1, 2p. [938]
Disbursements for the Creek and Seminole wars.

35. Mem. and Resol. of the Iowa Legis. 24 Feb.
SMD 167, 35-1, v3, 2p. [936] *or*
HMD 93, 35-1, v3, 2p. [963]
On behalf of J. Thomas and family; Sioux hostilities of 1857.

36. R-M of E. Williams. 24 Feb.
SR 86, 35-1, v1, 3p. [938]
Negotiations during 1819-1832 between the New York, Winnebago, and Menomonee Indians; treaties of 1827, 1831, and 1832; treaty of 15 Jan. 1838 at Buffalo Creek with the St. Regis Indians; lands in Wisconsin ceded; removal west of the Mississippi River.

37. Resol. of the Georgia Legis. 25 Feb.
HMD 70, 35-1 , v3, 2p. [963]
Seminole war of 1817-1818; Seminole and Creek wars of 1836; Cherokee, Creek, and Seminole removal during 1836-1838; bounty lands.

38. Report on Raising Additional Mounted Volunteers. 25 Feb.
HR 107, 35-1, v1, 1p. [964]
Indian hostilities in Texas and the Northwest; disturbances in Utah.

39. Practicality of a Railroad Through the South Pass. 26 Feb.
HED 70, 35-1, v9, 20p. [955]
Black Hills to the valley of the Platte River; Indian tribes would protect the railroad.

40. Message on the Utah Expedition. 26 Feb.
HED 71, 35-1, v10, 215p. [956]
Cheyenne depredations upon troops *en route* to confront the Mormons; documents from the CIA regarding Indians of the Territory; wars with Utes, and other Great Basin tribes.

41. Resol. of the Washington Legis. 1 Mar.
SMD 174, 35-1, v3, 2p. [936] *or*
HMD 71, 35-1, v3, 2p. [963]
On martial law being proclaimed during the late Indian war.

42. Mem. of the Iowa Legis. 1 Mar.
SMD 177, 35-1, v3, 2p. [936]
Railroad to Washington Territory; Omaha Indian reservation; through the Black Hills.

43. R-M of A. Dart. 2 Mar.
SR 98, 35-1, v1, 1p. [938]
Late Supt. of Indian Affairs in Oregon.

44. Letter on the Number of Troops in the War of 1812. 4 Mar.
HED 72, 35-1, v10, 6p. [956]
Indian wars during the same period.

45. R-M of W. Greenwood. 5 Mar.
HR 129, 35-1, v1, 1p. [964]
Com. on Indian Affairs reports on a land claim.

46. R-P of Citizens of Maine. 5 Mar.
HR 130, 35-1, v1, 1p. [964]
Com. on Indian Affairs reports.

47. R-P of J. Shaw. 5 Mar.
HR 131, 35-1, v1, 2p. [964]
Depredations by the Menomonees in Wisconsin.

48. R-P of G. Chorpenning. 5 Mar.
HR 132, 35-1, v1, 4p. [964]
Indian depredations in Utah.

49. R-P of Dent, Vantine, and Company. 5 Mar.
HR 133, 35-1, v1, 2p. [964]
Supplies furnished Indians in California; rejection of the treaty of 28 May 1851 by the Senate.

50. R-P of C. Compare. 5 Mar.
HR 134, 35-1, v1, 1p. [964]
Kansas half-breed lands; rights of Indians to sell their lands.

51. R-M of Maj. Dashiell. 5 Mar.
HR 138, 35-1, v1, 2p. [964]
Indian hostilities; 1857; Florida.

52. R-P of M. Blattenberger. 5 Mar.
HR 147, 35-1, v1, 1p. [964]
Indian hostilities in 1820.

53. On the Case of J. Ketchum. 5 Mar.
HR 151, 35-1, v1, 1p. [964]
Indian hostilities; 1813; Indiana.

54. Resol. of the Texas Legis. 11 Mar.
HMD 75, 35-1, v3, 2p. [963]
Military post at the junction of the Wichita and Red Rivers; depredations of the Comanches and other tribes; strict control of supplies at the Texas Indian reserve.

55. Resol. of the Texas Legis. 11 Mar.
HMD 76, 35-1, v3, 2p. [963]
Request an agent and a reservation for Indians west of the Pecos River.

56. Resol. of the California Legis. 12 Mar.
SMD 197, 35-1, v3, 1p. [936]
Against moving the Sebastian Indian reservation.

57. R-M of the Domestic and Foreign Missionary Society. 12 Mar.
SR 115, 35-1, v1, 1p. [938]
Mission among the Menomonees in Wisconsin until the removal of said Indians.

58. Expenditures in the Territories. 12 Mar.
HED 79, 35-1, v10, 4p. [956]
Since 1845; extinguishment of Indian land titles.

59. R-C of Citizens in Georgia and Alabama. 12 Mar.
HR 177, 35-1, v1, 10p. [964]
Creek treaty of 12 Feb. 1825; removal; Seminole and Creek wars of 1836.

60. R-P of J. Hardy and A. Long. 13 Mar.
SR 116, 35-1, v1, 7p. [938]
Arrangement with the Winnebagoes, Ottawas, Pottawatomies, and Chippewas prior to 1823 to work lead mines.

61. Resol. of the New York Legis. 15 Mar.
SMD 199, 35-1, v3, 1p. [936] *or*
HMD 96, 35-1, v3, 1p. [963]
Pensions to soldiers of the Indian wars during 1791-1795 under Gens. Wayne, Harmer and St. Clair.

62. R-M of Maj. Dashiell. 15 Mar.
SR 117, 35-1, v1, 2p. [938]
Indian hostilities; 1857; Florida.

63. R-M of D. Gordon. 15 Mar.
SR 118, 35-1, v1, 19p. [938]
Property destroyed by U.S. troops during 1813 in Alabama; Indian campaign.

64. R-P of the Reps. of C. Porterfield. 17 Mar.
SR 119, 35-1, v1, 3p. [938]
Cherokee land near the Ohio River in 1779.

65. R-M of H. O'Rielly et al. 24 Mar.
SR 128, 35-1, v1, 3p. [938]
Telegraph in the west; Mormon troubles; security from Indian interruptions during construction.

66. Correspondence Between the Late Sec. of War and Gen. Wool. 25 Mar.
HED 88, 35-1, v10, 213p. [956]
Indian hostilities and depredations in California, the Northwest, the Southwest, and the Great Basin; removal of Indians to reservations; Indian war in the Northwest.

67. Supplemental Estimates for the Indian Service. 26 Mar.
HED 93, 35-1, v11, 98p. [957]
On the Pacific coast, and in the remote Territories on either side of the Rocky Mountains.

68. R-M of J. Dickson. 26 Mar.
HR 184, 35-1, v1, 4p. [964]
Rations to Indians at Fort Harrison, Indiana in 1816.

69. R-P of Hardy and Long. 26 Mar.
HR 187, 35-1, v1, 7p. [964]
Agreement prior to 1823 with Winnebagoes, Ottawas, Chippewas, and Pottawatomies to mine lead.

70. R-M of J. Smith. 26 Mar.
HR 196, 35-1, v1, 1p. [964]
Indian reservation in Alabama.

71. R-P of W. Woolsey. 26 Mar.
HR 225, 35-1, v2, 1p. [965]
Seminole war of 1818.

72. Resol. of the New Mexico Legis. 30 Mar.
SMD 208, 35-1, v3, 2p. [936] *or*
HMD 101, 35-1, v3, 2p. [963]
Removal of all wild Indians from said Territory to the proposed Territory of Arizona.

73. R-P of W. Brownlee. 30 Mar.
SR 138, 35-1, v1, 1p. [938]
Indian difficulties on the frontier shortly after 1817.

74. Sale of the Fort Ripley Military Reservation. 30 Mar.
HED 94, 35-1, v11, 3p. [957]
Indian treaties of 22 Feb. 1855 and 29 July 1837 as they relate to a Catholic mission.

75. Report on the Indian Wars in the Northwest. 31 Mar.
SED 40, 35-1, v12, 66p. [929] *or*
HED 38, 35-1, v9, 66p. [955]
War in Oregon and Washington Territories during 1855-1856.

76. J. Guppy *vs.* the U.S. 1 Apr.
SMD 217, 35-1, v3, 30p. [936] *or*
HRCC 166, 35-1, v3, 30p. [972]
Land dispute in Wisconsin; Menomonee land cession under the treaty of 18 Oct. 1848 at Lake Pow-aw-hay-kon-nay; Menomonee removal in 1852.

77. R-P of A. Mathieson. 1 Apr.
SR 148, 35-1, v1, 1p. [938]
Indian hostilities at Spirit Lake, Iowa in 1857.

78. R-P of J. Rumph. 1 Apr.
HR 243, 35-1, v2, 1p. [965]
Creek war of 1837 in Georgia and Alabama.

79. Exploration for a Road from New Mexico to California. 7 Apr.
SED 43, 35-1, v12, 5p. [929]
Beale's expedition; Mohaves and other Indian tribes of the Southwest.

80. Resol. of the Washington Legis. 7 Apr.
HMD 116, 35-1, v3, 2p. [963]
Condemn Gen. Wool's actions in the late Indian war.

81. Message on Citizens in Carson's Valley, Utah. 13 Apr.
HED 102, 35-1, v12, 3p. [958]
Indian hostilities towards all but Mormons; Mormon alliance with Indians.

82. On the Case of the Administrators of R. Rowland. 14 Apr.
SR 188, 35-1, v2, 2p. [939]
Land purchased under the Creek treaty of 24 May 1832; Alabama.

83. On the Relief of A. Dart. 16 Apr.
SR 193, 35-1, v2, 2p. [939]
Late Supt. of Indian Affairs in Oregon.

84. Letter on the Southern Boundary of Kansas. 16 Apr.
HED 103, 35-1, v12, 3p. [958]
Supplies to Creeks and Cherokees.

85. Report on the Northern and Western Boundaries of Creek Country. 16 Apr.
HED 104, 35-1, v12, 32p. [958]
Bordering the Osages, Cherokees, and other tribes.

86. R-M of the Reps. of Col. Wilson. 17 Apr.
HR 279, 35-1, v2, 3p. [965]
Indian campaigns from 1774 to 1795; treaty of Greenville in 1795.

87. R-P of J. Hand. 17 Apr.
HR 286, 35-1, v2, 3p. [965]
Purchased Choctaw lands in Mississippi under the 1830 treaty of Dancing Rabbit Creek.

88. R-C of J. Thompson and E. McBrier. 17 Apr.
HR 289, 35-1, v2, 7p. [965]
Campaign of 1781 against the Mohawks and Senecas in Ohio under Gen. Clark.

89. R-M of Tennessee Citizens. 17 Apr.
HR 290, 35-1, v2, 8p. [965]
Cherokee reservations under the treaties of 1817 and 1819.

90. R-M of T. Alsbury. 17 Apr.
HR 291, 35-1, v2, 1p. [965]
Indian depredations; 1850; California.

91. R-P of J. Morrison. 17 Apr.
HR 292, 35-1, v2, 2p. [965]
Indian depredations.

92. R-M of M. Marmaduke. 17 Apr.
HR 293, 35-1, v2, 2p. [965]
Pawnee depredations in 1828; treaties of 1825 and 1833.

93. R-M of M. Williams. 17 Apr.
HR 303, 35-1, v2, 8p. [965]
Iroquois Indians of Canada; war of 1812.

94. On the Case of W. Howell. 17 Apr.
HR 308, 35-1, v2, 1p. [965]
Indian hostilities; 1812; *en route* from Fort Knox to Fort Harrison.

95. R-P of M. Hamilton. 17 Apr.
HR 313, 35-1, v2, 2p. [965]
Marauding Indians; 1851; Texas frontier.

96. R-M of A. Bayard. 17 Apr.
HR 315, 35-1, v2, 1p. [965]
Indian wars in 1812; battle at Fort Harrison.

97. R-P of B. Byrne. 23 Apr.
SR 199, 35-1, v2, 2p. [939]
Indian hostilities; 1838; Florida.

98. Report on the Fort Snelling Investigation. 27 Apr.
HR 351, 35-1, v2, 456p. [965]
Usefulness of the Minnesota post; actions of the Sioux, Chippewa, and Winnebago Indians.

99. Mem. of the Wisconsin Legis. 10 May.
SMD 254, 35-1, v4, 2p. [937]
Land grant for a railroad; treaties of 1829 with the Chippewas, Ottawas, Pottawatomies, and Winnebagoes.

100. Message on Indian Affairs in Oregon and Washington Territories. 10 May.
HED 112, 35-1, v12, 21p. [958]
Condition of the Indians of the Northwest.

101. Letter on Kansas Half-Breed Reservations. 10 May.
HED 114, 35-1, v12, 2p. [958]
Treaty with the Kansas Nation of Indians.

102. L-C of J. Johnson and F. Wheeling. 10 May.
HED 116, 35-1, v12, 3p. [958]
Transportation and subsistence of a delegation of Omaha Indians to Washington, D.C. in 1851-1852.

103. Report on Military Roads. 10 May.
HR 369, 35-1, v3, 6p. [966]
In Oregon and Washington; Indian tribes in the Yakima River valley; roads over the Cascade Mountains.

104. R-M of J. Pickell. 11 May.
SR 237, 35-1, v2, 1p. [939]
Indian war in Florida during 1836.

105. Report on a Military Road. 11 May.
HR 372, 35-1, v3, 4p. [966]
From Fort Union to Santa Fe in New Mexico; possible war with the Apaches and Kiowas.

106. Report on Indian Depredations in New Mexico. 12 May.
SED 55, 35-1, v12, 62p. [929] *or*
HED 123, 35-1, v13, 62p. [959]
Listing and description of claims.

107. Letter on a Wagon Road from Fort Defiance to the Colorado River. 12 May.
HED 124, 35-1, v13, 87p. [959]
Journal of Beale's expedition; encounters with Indians of the Southwest.

108. Report on the Creation of Nevada Territory. 12 May.
HR 375, 35-1, v3, 5p. [966]
Out of Utah Territory; Mormon hostilities; Indian hostilities instigated by Mormons.

109. On the Relief of G. O'Brien. 14 May.
HR 396, 35-1, v3, 2p. [966]
Clerk for the Chickasaws during 1845-1846; Chickasaw fund.

110. R. Fitzpatrick *vs.* the U.S. 15 May.
SMD 256, 35-1, v4, 6p. [937] *or*
HRCC 175, 35-1, v3, 18p. [972]
Seminole war; 1836-1840; Florida (House version includes accounts).

111. R-P of E. Ogden. 15 May.
SR 254, 35-1, v2, 2p. [939]
Disbursements for the suppression of Creek and Seminole hostilities.

112. R-M of H. Miller. 15 May.
SR 255, 35-1, v2, 2p. [939]
Clerk in the office of the CIA.

113. Resol. of the New York Legis. 17 May.
SMD 260, 35-1, v4, 1p. [937]
Pensions for soldiers in the Indian wars of 1791-1795.

114. R-P of A. Bayard. 17 May.
SR 257, 35-1, v2, 3p. [939]
Indian battles at Fort Harrison in 1812.

115. On the Case of L. Humphreys et al. 17 May.
SR 258, 35-1, v2, 14p. [939]
Treaty of 1819 with Spain, regarding Florida; British and Indian forces.

116. Report on Fort Snelling as a Military Depot. 18 May.
HMD 133, 35-1, v3, 4p. [963]
Forts Ripley and Ridgely on the Minnesota frontier; control of Sioux and Chippewa depredations; Winnebago reservation completely controlled; Fort Snelling not needed.

117. Petition of Minnesota Citizens. 18 May.
HMD 134, 35-1, v3, 8p. [963]
Fort Snelling no longer needed for protection of the frontier.

118. R-M of the Iowa Legis. 20 May.
SR 268, 35-1, v2, 1p. [939]
Indian depredations.

119. R-M of W. Money. 22 May.
SR 272, 35-1, v2, 3p. [939]
Losses sustained at the hands of U.S. troops in California; Indian depredations stimulated by Gen. Kearny.

120. Report on Expenses of a Geological Survey. 22 May.
HR 409, 35-1, v3, 3p. [966]
In Oregon and Washington; railroad route; expense high because of Indian war.

121. R-M of G. Stealey. 24 May.
SR 274, 35-1, v2, 1p. [939]
Services with a mission to the California Indians during 1850-1851.

122. Annual Report of the Smithsonian Institution. 27 May.
SMD 272, 35-1, v4, 438p. [937] *or*
HMD 135, 35-1, v3, 438p. [963]
Research related to American Indians.

123. On the Relief of Purchasers of Public Lands. 27 May.
SR 284, 35-1, v2, 2p. [939]
Within the Winnebago reservation.

124. On the Relief of C. Scaife. 29 May.
HR 423, 35-1, v4, 2p. [967]
Seminole war; 1840; Florida.

125. On the Relief of E. Ogden. 29 May.
HR 425, 35-1, v4, 3p. [967]
Disbursements during Creek and Seminole hostilities.

126. Report on Land Claims in New Mexico. 29 May.
HR 457, 35-1, v4, 326p. [967]
Indian hostilities upon settlers.

127. On the Relief of E. Williams. 29 May.
HR 459, 35-1, v5, 2p. [968]
Money due for the St. Regis tribe under the treaty of 15 Jan. 1838 with the New York Indians.

128. On the Relief of Livingston, Kincaid, and Company. 29 May.
HR 466, 35-1, v5, 2p. [968]
Sioux depredations near Fort Laramie.

129. On the Case of the Reps. of G. Fisher. 29 May.
HR 467, 35-1, v5, 28p. [968]
Indian hostilities; 1813; Alabama.

130. R-P of J. Thomas. 29 May.
HR 470, 35-1, v5, 1p. [968]
Comanche hostilities; 1850; Texas.

131. R-M of Kerr, Brierly, and Company. 29 May.
HR 471, 35-1, v5, 3p. [968]
Gen. Harney's refusal to treat with Sioux, and attack on their villages in 1856 instigates widespread hostilities; Pawnee depredations prior to 1856.

132. On the Relief of L. Fletcher. 29 May.
HR 488, 35-1, v5, 1p. [968]
Seminole war of 1818.

133. R-P of J. Holland. 29 May.
HR 494, 35-1, v5, 1p. [968]
Cherokee war; 1792-1793; Georgia.

134. R-P of E. Merchant. 29 May.
HR 504, 35-1, v5, 2p. [968]
Indian engagement; 1850; Texas.

135. R-P of G. Cummings et al. 29 May.
HR 513, 35-1, v5, 1p. [968]
Land claims arising from the recent treaty with the Winnebago Indians.

136. R-M of Heirs of J. Beaugrand. 29 May.
HR 514, 35-1, v5, 2p. [968]
Wyandot treaty of 17 Mar. 1842.

137. R-C of H. Jackson. 29 May.
HR 515, 35-1, v5, 1p. [968]
Cheyenne depredations; 1856; near Fort Kearney.

138. R-C of the Munsee Indians. 29 May.
HR 524, 35-1, v5, 3p. [968]
Removal of the Stockbridge and Munsee Indians from Wisconsin to Kansas in 1839.

139. R-M of B. Yates. 29 May.
HR 530, 35-1, v5, 1p. [968]
Indian hostilities; 1812; Ohio.

140. Annual Report of the Chickasaw Trust Fund. 1 June.
HED 133, 35-1, v13, 2p. [959]
Treaties of 20 Oct. 1832 and 26 May 1836.

141. Estimates to Fulfill Treaty Stipulations. 3 June.
HED 134, 35-1, v13, 9p. [959]
Pawnee treaty of 24 Sept. 1857.

142. On the Relief of Reps. of J. Donnelson et al. 4 June.
SR 301, 35-1, v2, 2p. [939]
Adjustment of the boundary of the Chickasaw cession in Mississippi.

143. Estimates for Preservation of Peace. 8 June.
HED 135, 35-1, v13, 13p. [959]
Invasion of the Northern Superintendency by Yanktonais Sioux.

144. Estimate for Payment of Indians. 8 June.
HED 136, 35-1, v13, 5p. [959]
To carry out the agreement of 1856 with the Sioux; council at Fort Pierre.

145. Message on Termination of Difficulties in Utah. 10 June.
SED 67, 35-1, v13, 7p. [930] *or* HED 138, 35-1, v13, 7p. [959]
Indian hostilities in the Great Basin.

146. Report on Lands in Kansas. 14 June.
SED 73, 35-1, v13, 2p. [930]
Claim of St. Regis (New York) Indians to land under the treaty of 15 Jan. 1838 at Buffalo Creek.

147. Statements of Appropriations. 12 Aug.
SMD 273, 35-1, v4, 79p. [937] *or* HMD 137, 35-1, v3, 79p. [963]
During the 1st session, 35th Congress; Indian expenses.

148. Estimates of Appropriations. 17 Nov.
HED 1, 35-2, v1, 332p. [996]
Year ending 30 June 1860; Indian expenses.

149. Annual Message to Congress with Documents; Pres. Buchanan. 6 Dec.
SED 1, 35-2, v1-5, 2953p. [974-978] *or* HED 2, 35-2, v2 (pts. 1-5), 2953p. [997-1001]
Annual report of the Sec. of War (Serials 975-976 and 998-999); annual report of the Sec. of Interior (Serials 974 and 997); annual report of the Gen. Land Office (Serials 974 and 997); annual report of the CIA (Serials 974 and 997), including trust funds, Indian hostilities, and reports of Supts., agents, and schools; etc.

150. Annual Report of the Sec. of the Treasury. 6 Dec.
SED 2, 35-2, v6 (pt. 1), 493p. [979] *or* HED 3, 35-2, v1, 493p. [996]
For the year ending 30 June 1858; Indian expenses.

151. Contingent Expenses of the Interior Dept. 7 Dec.
HED 6, 35-2, v3, 123p. [1002]
Year ending 30 June 1858; Indian expenses.

152. I. Bowman et al. *vs.* the U.S. 13 Dec.
SMD 9, 35-2, v1, 30p. [993] *or* HRCC 183, 35-2, v1, 62p. [1021]
Battle with the Chickasaw Indians in 1779; said Indians were allies of the British (House version incorporates related documents).

153. Appropriations of the Interior Dept. 22 Dec.
SED 7, 35-2, v7, 14p. [981] *or* HED 15, 35-2, v4, 14p. [1003]
Year ending 30 June 1858; Indian expenses.

1859

1. Letter on Claimants Under an Indian Treaty. 4 Jan.
HED 18, 35-2, v4, 2p. [1003]
Treaty with the Rogue River Indians on 10 Sept. 1853.

2. On the Relief of W. Money. 4 Jan.
HR 7, 35-2, v1, 3p. [1018]
Indian depredations in California during 1846; instigated by the actions of Gen. Kearney.

3. R-M of T. Bruquier. 4 Jan.
HR 11, 35-2, v1, 1p. [1018]
Sioux depredations in Iowa.

4. R-M of Dr. Work. 4 Jan.
HR 12, 35-2, v1, 5p. [1018]
Engagement with the Comanches on the Texas frontier in 1848.

5. R-M of J. Shaw. 4 Jan.
HR 15, 35-2, v1, 2p. [1018]
Rangers on the Mississippi River during 1812 to control Indian attacks in that region.

6. Resol. of the Georgia Legis. 5 Jan.
SMD 16, 35-2, v1, 2p. [993] *or* HMD 26, 35-2, v1, 2p. [1016]
Refund of sums expended by the state during the Indian wars of 1794-1796, Indian disturbances of 1817-1818, Florida Indian war of 1836-1837, Creek war, and Cherokee removal.

7. Protection of the Texas Frontier. 6 Jan.
HED 27, 35-2, v5, 77p. [1004]
Depredations of the Kiowa, Comanche, and other Indian tribes of the Southwest.

8. Mem. of M. Switser. 7 Jan.
HMD 12, 35-2, v1, 5p. [1016]
Supplies furnished to the Sioux during 1852 in Minnesota.

9. On the Relief of A. Dart. 7 Jan.
HR 52, 35-2, v1, 2p. [1018]
Late Supt. of Indian Affairs in Oregon.

10. On the Relief of J. Donnelson et al. 7 Jan.
HR 83, 35-2, v1, 4p. [1018]
Adjustment of the boundary of the Chickasaw cession.

11. Report on Florida Volunteers. 11 Jan.
HED 38, 35-2, v5, 8p. [1004]
Hostilities of the remnant of Indians residing in southern Florida.

12. Mem. of Minnesota Citizens. 12 Jan.
SMD 18, 35-2, v1, 7p. [993]
Mail route from St. Paul to the Columbia River; extinction of Indian title to land; contracts with the Crow, Blackfeet, Nez Perce, and other tribes for horses; Indian hostilities.

13. R-M of D. Johnson. 13 Jan.
HR 76, 35-2, v1, 3p. [1018]
Census of 1850 in Wisconsin; many inhabitants familiar only with the French and Chippewa languages.

14. R-P of S. Perry. 13 Jan.
HR 77, 35-2, v1, 2p. [1018]
Loss of Indian supplies in transit from Ohio to Fort Coffee, Arkansas.

15. R-P of J. Valdez. 14 Jan.
HR 89, 35-2, v1, 1p. [1018]
Depredations committed in 1847 by Mexicans and Pueblo Indians in Taos, New Mexico; Navajo campaign of 1846.

16. R-P of E. Mullinax. 14 Jan.
HR 111, 35-2, v1, 1p. [1018]
Seminole war.

17. Resol. of the Arkansas Legis. 15 Jan.
HMD 19, 35-2, v1, 1p. [1016]
Transportation of liquor through Indian country.

18. R-P of M. Larnard. 17 Jan.
SR 345, 35-2, v1, 2p. [994]
Indian hostilities in Washington Territory during 1854.

19. Claims Growing Out of Indian Hostilities. 18 Jan.
HED 51, 35-2, v7, 77p. [1006]
In Washington and Oregon during 1855-1856.

20. Letter on Indian Disbursements. 19 Jan.
SED 15, 35-2, v7, 336p. [981] *or*
HED 13, 35-2, v3, 336p. [1002]
Year ending 30 June 1858.

21. R-M of J. Johnson. 21 Jan.
HR 131, 35-2, v1, 1p. [1018]
Indian depredations; Utah.

22. R-P of J. Johnson. 21 Jan.
HR 132, 35-2, v1, 3p. [1018]
Agent to the Shawnee, Delaware, Seneca, and Wyandot Indians during 1818-1829 in Ohio; treaties of 29 Sept. 1817 with the Wyandots, and 3 Oct. 1818 with the Delawares.

23. R-P of I. Johnson. 21 Jan.
HR 133, 35-2, v1, 2p. [1018]
Supplies transported to the Miami treaty council of 1833; Pottawatomie boys transported to the Choctaw Academy in Kentucky.

24. Mem. of the New Mexico Legis. 24 Jan.
HMD 38, 35-2, v1, 3p. [1016]
Indian depredations within the Territory.

25. R-P of E. Spear. 25 Jan.
SR 356, 35-2, v1, 1p. [994]
Creek war; 1836; battle of Ichawanochawa.

26. R-M of D. Barnes. 26 Jan.
HR 140, 35-2, v1, 1p. [1018]
British and Indians; 1812; New York.

27. Receipts and Expenditures. 27 Jan.
HED 20, 35-2, v4, 670p. [1003]
Year ending 30 June 1858; Indian expenses.

28. Report on Texas Volunteers. 28 Jan.
HR 143, 35-2, v1, 2p. [1018]
Protection of the frontier against Indian assaults during 1854-1858.

29. R-C of the Missionary Society of the Methodist Episcopal Church. 28 Jan.
HR 145, 35-2, v1, 3p. [1018]
Missions among the Indians in Oregon.

30. Employees of the Interior Dept. 29 Jan.
HED 73, 35-2, v7, 21p. [1006]
For 1858; office of the CIA.

31. R-M of R. Chenery. 1 Feb.
HR 150, 35-2, v1, 1p. [1018]
Supplies furnished a California Indian agency in 1852.

32. R-P of W. Bent. 1 Feb.
HR 151, 35-2, v1, 1p. [1018]
Kiowa, Cheyenne, Arapahoe, and Apache depredations during 1854-1855.

33. C. Stuart *vs.* the U.S. 3 Feb.
SMD 34, 35-2, v1, 10p. [993] *or*
HRCC 190, 35-2, v1, 36p. [1021]
Supplies to California Indians not paid for by the U.S. (House version includes related documents).

34. M. Lewis *vs.* the U.S. 3 Feb.
SMD 35, 35-2, v1, 26p. [993] *or*
HRCC 191, 35-2, v1, 36p. [1021]
Supplies furnished California Indians in the Fresno Indian Reservation under the 1851 treaties with said Indians; bill not paid by U.S.

since the treaties were not ratified (House version includes related documents).

35. G. McDougal *vs.* the U.S. 3 Feb.
SMD 37, 35-2, v1, 11p. [993] *or*
HRCC 192, 35-2, v1, 16p. [1021]
Supplies to California Indians under 1851 treaties which were not ratified.

36. Protection Afforded Immigrants by Volunteers. 3 Feb.
HMD 47, 35-2, v1, 61p. [1016]
Volunteers from Oregon and Washington; Indian hostilities during 1854.

37. Report on Military Posts. 3 Feb.
HR 154, 35-2, v1, 3p. [1018]
From Missouri to New Mexico; Kiowa and Comanche country.

38. Report on Volunteers in New Mexico. 3 Feb.
HR 155, 35-2, v1, 2p. [1018]
Indian hostilities.

39. R-P of I. Johnson. 5 Feb.
SR 370, 35-2, v1, 2p. [994]
Transported supplies to the treaty council with the Miami Indians in 1833; transported Pottawatomie boys to the Choctaw Academy in Kentucky.

40. R-P of S. Winn. 5 Feb.
HR 171, 35-2, v1, 2p. [1018]
Tories and Indians; 1776; Fort McIntosh.

41. Report on Costs of Transportation and Subsistence. 7 Feb.
SED 23, 35-2, v7, 1p. [981]
For the Army in suppressing Indian hostilities.

42. Indian Appropriation Bill. 9 Feb.
HR 174, 35-2, v1, 1p. [1018]
To fulfill treaty stipulations.

43. R-P of P. Pitchlynn et al. 15 Feb.
SR 274, 35-2, v1, 18p. [994]
Choctaw delegation refers to claims under the treaties of 1820, 1825, 27 Sept. 1830, 22 June 1855, etc.; land cessions and removal of the Choctaw and Chickasaw Indians.

44. Message on a Special Agent Sent to British Columbia. 17 Feb.
SED 29, 35-2, v10, 30p. [984] *or*
HED 111, 35-2, v12, 30p. [1014]
Relations with the British; encounters with Indians; hostilities of Indians of the Northwest.

45. Report on Col. Wright's Campaign. 18 Feb.
SED 32, 35-2, v10, 82p. [984]
Against the hostile Indians in Washington and Oregon.

46. R-P of T. Leak. 18 Feb.
SR 382, 35-2, v1, 2p. [994]
Sale of Creek lands in Alabama under the treaty of 24 Mar. 1832.

47. On Pensions to Soldiers. 19 Feb.
SR 385, 35-2, v1, 7p. [994]
Those engaged in Indian wars during the period of the war of 1812.

48. S. Hensley *vs.* the U.S. 23 Feb.
SMD 39, 35-2, v1, 34p. [993] *or*
HRCC 189, 35-2, v1, 55p. [1021]
Supplies purchased by the California Indian Treaty Com'rs during 1851; bills not paid by the U.S. because the treaties were not ratified (House version incorporates related documents).

49. Annual Report of the Smithsonian Institution. 24 Feb.
SMD 49, 35-2, v1, 448p. [993] *or*
HMD 57, 35-2, v1, 448p. [1016]
Research and publications relating to American Indians.

50. Annual Report of the Chickasaw Fund. 25 Feb.
HED 102, 35-2, v9, 2p. [1008]
Under treaties of 20 Oct. 1832, and 24 May 1834.

51. Report on Pacific Wagon Roads. 26 Feb.
SED 36, 35-2, v10, 125p. [984] *or*
HED 108, 35-2, v9, 125p. [1008]
Exploring expeditions across the Plains and Upper Missouri, Great Basin, and Southwest; encounters with various Indian tribes.

52. Estimates for Fulfilling Treaty Stipulations. 1 Mar.
HED 106, 35-2, v9, 2p. [1008]
Yankton Sioux treaty of 19 Apr. 1858; Tonawanda treaty of 5 Nov. 1858.

53. Report on Wagon Roads in Utah. 2 Mar.
SED 40, 35-2, v10, 84p. [984]
Exploring expeditions in the Great Basin; encounters with, and descriptions of, Indians; Indian vocabulary.

54. Survey and Exploration of a Northern Route for a Railroad to the Pacific. 3 Mar.
SED 46, 35-2, v18, 839p. [992] *or*
HED 56, 36-1, v11 (pts. 1-2), 839p. [1054-1055]
Encounters with various Indian tribes of the northern Plains and Upper Missouri, Rocky Mountain region, and Northwest.

55. Resol. of the California Legis. 3 Mar.
SMD 54, 35-2, v1, 1p. [993]
Payment of debts due citizens for the Indian wars.

56. Topographical Memoir of the War Dept. of the Pacific. 3 Mar.
HED 114, 35-2, v12, 126p. [1014]
Military operations during the Indian war of 1855-1856 in Washington and Oregon; treaties negotiated, and their effects.

57. R-P of J. Davis. 3 Mar.
HR 200, 35-2, v1, 1p. [1018]
Supplies for volunteers in Indian war in Oregon during 1853.

58. R-P of R. Harrison et al. 3 Mar.
HR 216, 35-2, v1, 22p. [1018]
Gen. Jackson's incursions into Florida in 1814 and 1818; violations of Spain's neutrality; pursuit of Indians.

59. R-P of Texas Citizens. 3 Mar.
HR 255, 35-2, v1, 1p. [1018]
Depredations of the Kickapoo, Wichita, and Comanche Indians.

60. R-P of Heirs of Capt. Orr. 9 Mar.
HR 238, 35-2, v1, 6p. [1018]
Campaign of 1781 against the Mohawks and Senecas in Ohio.

61. R-P of M. Meeker. 31 Mar.
HR 235, 35-2, v1, 2p. [1018]
Agreement made prior to 1823 to mine lead; Winnebago, Ottawa, Pottawatomie, and Chippewa Indians.

62. Statements of Appropriations. 19 Apr.
SMD 55, 35-2, v1, 62p. [993] *or*
HMD 61, 35-2, v1, 62p. [1016]
During the 2d session, 35th Congress; Indian expenses.

63. Estimates of Appropriations. 22 Nov.
HED 1, 36-1, v1, 408p. [1043]
Year ending 30 June 1861; Indian expenses.

1860

1. R-P of T. Leak. 11 Jan.
SR 5, 36-1, v1, 2p. [1039]
Sale of Creek land in Alabama under the treaty of 24 Mar. 1832.

2. Annual Message to Congress with Documents; Pres. Buchanan. 19 Jan.
SED 2, 36-1, v1-4, 2417p. [1023-1026]
British control of Indian depredations on Vancouver Island; military posts to control Indian depredations in the Southwest; annual report of the Sec. of War (Serials 1024-1025); annual report of the Sec. of Interior (Serial 1023); annual report of the Gen. Land Office (Serial 1023); annual report of the CIA (Serial 1023), including trust funds and finances, conditions on reservations, civilization, hostilities, and reports of Supts., agents, and schools; etc.

3. Annual Report of the Sec. of the Treasury. 19 Jan.
SED 3, 36-1, v5, 374p. [1027]
Year ending 30 June 1859; Indian expenses.

4. Report of the Court of Claims. 19 Jan.
SMD 4, 36-1, v1, 14p. [1038]
List of cases sent to the House during the 34th and 35th Congresses; descriptions indicate relevance to Indian affairs.

5. Decisions of the Court of Claims. 19 Jan.
SMD 5, 36-1, v1, 4p. [1038]
Made since the 35th Congress; descriptions indicate relevance to Indian affairs.

6. R-M of the Domestic and Foreign Missionary Society of the Protestant Episcopal Church. 26 Jan.
SR 18, 36-1, v1, 1p. [1039]
Mission among the Menomonees in Wisconsin; Indians removed westwards; Society wishes to purchase land.

7. R-P of M. Maltby. 9 Feb.
SR 39, 36-1, v1, 1p. [1039]
Fort Gibson; 1834; Cherokee Nation.

8. Appropriations of the Interior Dept. 10 Feb.
HED 6, 36-1, v1, 14p. [1043]
Year ending 30 June 1859; Indian expenses.

9. Receipts and Expenditures. 10 Feb.
HED 7, 36-1, v3, 658p. [1045]
Year ending 30 June 1859; Indian expenses.

10. Indian Disbursements. 10 Feb.
HED 10, 36-1, v4, 410p. [1046]
Year ending 30 June 1859.

11. Claims Arising Due to an Indian War. 10 Feb.
HED 11, 36-1, v4, 132p. [1046]
Indian war in Washington and Oregon during 1855-1856.

12. Contingent Expenses of the Interior Dept. 10 Feb.
HED 12, 36-1, v4, 119p. [1046]
Year ending 30 June 1859; Indian expenses.

13. Employees of the Interior Dept. 10 Feb.
HED 13, 36-1, v4, 20p. [1046]
For 1859; office of the CIA.

14. Resol. of the Tennessee Legis. 11 Feb.
HMD 9, 36-1, v4, 2p. [1063]
Pensions to soldiers in Indian wars occurring around 1812.

15. M. Williams *vs.* the U.S. 11 Feb.
HRCC 231, 36-1, v4, 16p. [1075]
U.S. decision to remove the Indians from Florida instigated the Seminole war of 1835-1836; property destroyed by Indians because it had been occupied by U.S. troops.

16. R-P of the Oregon Legis. 14 Feb.
SR 46, 36-1, v1, 1p. [1039]
On behalf of a volunteer in the Indian wars of that Territory (now state).

17. Message on Extinguishment of Indian Land Title. 20 Feb.
SED 15, 36-1, v5, 23p. [1027]
In Kansas, Nebraska, and the eastern slopes of the Rocky Mountains; discovery of gold by Cherokees and Georgians in 1858.

18. R-P of A. Gaylord et al. 20 Feb.
SR 66, 36-1, v1, 3p. [1039]
Asks bounty lands for services in Indian wars.

19. Mem. of the Wisconsin Legis. 21 Feb.
SMD 15, 36-1, v1, 1p. [1038] *or*
HMD 13, 36-1, v5, 32p. [1064]
Frauds practiced upon the Menomonees by whites (House version includes a mem. of Menomonees, and sworn statements on the case).

20. R-P of the Reps. of C. Porterfield. 21 Feb.
SR 73, 3601, v1, 4p. [1039]
Bounty lands granted by Virginia in 1782 within Cherokee boundaries; treaties of 1794 and 1795 with the Cherokees and Chickasaws; land ceded by Indians in 1819.

21. R-P of A. Dart. 24 Feb.
HR 1, 36-1, v1, 3p. [1067]
Late Supt. of Indian Affairs in Oregon.

22. R-P of E. Ogden. 28 Feb.
SR 87, 36-1, v1, 1p. [1039]
Disbursement of funds to suppress Indian hostilities.

23. R-M of M. Sweetser. 28 Feb.
SR 90, 36-1, v1, 2p. [1039]
Trader at Traverse des Sioux on the Minnesota River; Sisseton and Wahpeton Sioux debts to the memorialist.

24. On the Cases of L. Humphreys et al. 28 Feb.
SR 93, 36-1, v1, 28p. [1039]
Under the 1819 treaty with Spain; Gen. Jackson's incursions into neutral Florida in 1814 and 1818 to execute campaigns against the Indians there.

25. Explanation of Estimates for the Indian Service. 28 Feb.
HMD 24, 36-1, v5, 6p. [1064]
Removal of Texas Indians to Wichita Indian country; Pawnee, Ponca, and Yankton Sioux agricultural implements; Chippewa expenses; Blackfeet transportation costs; etc.

26. R-C of W. Gorman. 1 Mar.
SR 99, 36-1, v1, 2p. [1039]
Com'r investigating charges of fraud against A. Ramsey, late Supt. of Indian Affairs in Minnesota.

27. W. Geiger *vs.* the U.S. 1 Mar.
HRCC 242, 36-1, v5, 58p. [1076]
Contracted to construct a barrack at Fort Washita in the Choctaw Nation.

28. Message on the Boundary Between the U.S. and Britain. 2 Mar.
SED 16, 36-1, v9, 7p. [1031]
Survey speeded by control of Indian hostilities in Washington Territory.

29. Report on Additional Estimates for the Indian Service. 2 Mar.
SED 17, 36-1, v9, 16p. [1031]
In Oregon and Washington; removal of Indians to reservations, along with costs of subsistence; treaties of 9 June 1855 with the Yakamas, 11 June 1855 with the Nez Percés, and 16 July 1855 with the Flatheads, Kootenays, and Upper Pend d'Oreilles; aid to the Spokanes, Coeur d'Alénes, Lower Pend d'Oreilles, Okinakanes, and Colvilles who are not under any treaty with the U.S.

30. R-P of the Reps. of C. Porterfield. 2 Mar.
HR 23, 36-1, v1, 6p. [1067]
Bounty lands in Cherokee country; treaties of 1794 and 1795 with the Cherokees and Chickasaws.

31. Report on an Invasion of the Osage Indians. 2 Mar.
HR 40, 36-1, v1, 3p. [1067]
Osage incursion into Missouri during 1837.

32. On the Relief of W. Hansell et al. 2 Mar.
HR 42, 36-1, v1, 3p. [1067]
Attorneys for the Cherokees; payment under the treaty of 1835.

33. R-P of J. Johnson. 2 Mar.
HR 45, 36-1, v1, 3p. [1067]
Agent to the Shawnees, Delawares, Senecas, and Wyandots from 1818 to 1829; Wyandot treaty of 29 Sept. 1817.

34. R-P of C. Blackburn. 2 Mar.
HR 64, 36-1, v1 , 1p. [1067]
Indian hostilities during the war of 1812 in New York.

35. Letter on the New York Indian Reserve in Kansas. 5 Mar.
HED 37, 36-1, v6, 7p. [1048]
Condition of the reservation set apart under the treaties of 15 Jan. 1838 with the New York Indians, and 1842 with the Senecas; rapid influx of settlers on said reservation causing difficulties.

36. Message on Hostilities on the Rio Grande. 6 Mar.
SED 21, 36-1, v9, 22p. [1031]
Incursions of Mexicans and Indians on the Texas frontier.

37. R-M of S. Hensley. 6 Mar.
SR 111, 36-1, v1, 16p. [1039]
Supplies furnished to California Indians under treaties which were not ratified by the Senate.

38. R-P of K. Taylor. 6 Mar.
SR 112, 36-1, v1, 1p. [1039]
Indian hostilities; 1858; Washington Territory.

39. R-M of Wetonsaw. 7 Mar.
SR 116, 36-1, v1, 2p. [1039]
Error in payments under the treaty of 14 Jan. 1837 with the Saginaw band of Chippewas.

40. R-P of W. Petchaka. 8 Mar.
SR 122, 36-1, v1, 1p. [1039]
Land grant under the treaty of 3 Oct. 1818 with the Delawares.

41. R-P of J. Campbell. 8 Mar.
HR 67, 36-1, v1, 2p. [1067]
Indian battles in 1778; Mohawk valley of New York.

42. Report on a Wagon Road from Fort Smith, Arkansas, to the Colorado River. 9 Mar.
HED 42, 36-1, v6, 91p. [1048]
Exploring expedition of 1858-1859; Comanches, Navajoes, Mohaves, and other Indians of the Southwest.

43. R-M of A. Bayard. 9 Mar.
HR 73, 36-1, v1, 2p. [1067]
Indian battle at Fort Harrison in 1812.

44. R-M of the Reps. of Col. Wilson. 9 Mar.
HR 78, 36-1, v1, 3p. [1067]
Indian wars on the Virginia frontier from 1774-1795; treaty of Greenville in 1795.

45. R-P of M. Guthrie. 12 Mar.
SR 128, 36-1, v1, 2p. [1039]
March from Fort Steilacoom, Washington Territory, to Indian country in 1856.

46. R-P of S. Krebs et al. 13 Mar.
SR 130, 36-1, v1, 1p. [1039]
Claims against the U.S. under the Choctaw treaty at Dancing Rabbit Creek have been assumed by the latest treaty with said Indians.

47. On the Case of Sour-john. 13 Mar.
SR 132, 36-1, v1, 2p. [1039]
Payment for lands ceded under the Cherokee treaties of 1817 and 1818 in Georgia.

48. Estimates for Indian Service in Utah. 13 Mar.
HMD 32, 36-1, v5, 4p. [1064]
For the years 1858, 1859, and 1861.

49. Appropriations for the Poncas and Other Indians. 13 Mar.
HMD 33, 36-1, v5, 2p. [1064]
To fulfill treaty stipulations; Ponca treaty of 1855; treaties with tribes in Oregon and Washington.

50. R-P of I. Johnson. 19 Mar.
SR 146, 36-1, v1, 2p. [1039]
Transport of supplies to treaty negotiations with the Miami Indians in 1833; transport of Pottawatomie boys to the Choctaw Academy in Kentucky.

51. Charges Against A. Bonesteel. 19 Mar.
HED 47, 36-1, v8, 9p. [1050]
Agent of the Menomonees accused of not disbursing money meant for said Indians.

52. R-P of M. Meeker. 19 Mar.
HR 89, 36-1, v1, 2p. [1067]
Arrangement with the Winnebagoes, Ottawas, Pottawatomies, and Chippewas to mine lead on the Upper Mississippi River prior to 1823.

53. R-M of the Washington Legis. 19 Mar.
HR 115, 36-1, v1, 1p. [1067]
On behalf of M. Simmons, Indian agent in said Territory during 1854-1856.

54 R-P of I. Johnson. 19 Mar.
HR 116, 36-1, v1, 2p. [1067]
Transport of goods to the treaty council of 1833 with the Miamies; transport of Pottawatomie boys to the Choctaw Academy in Kentucky.

55. R-C of the Missionary Society of the Methodist Episcopal Church. 19 Mar.
HR 120, 36-1, v1, 4p. [1067]
Land at the Dalles on the Columbia River in Oregon taken by the military during the Indian war.

56. Report on Indian Depredation Claims. 19 Mar.
HR 122, 36-1, v1, 3p. [1067]
In New Mexico; treaty of Guadalupe Hidalgo.

57. On the Relief of the Reps. of C. Mason. 19 Mar.
HR 124, 36-1, v1, 1p. [1067]
Duties as Supt. of Indian Affairs removes Governor of Washington Territory from the territorial offices.

58. R-P of S. Burnham. 19 Mar.
HR 133, 36-1, v1, 1p. [1067]
Indian war; 1792-1795; under Gen. Wayne.

59. Message on Frontier Hostilities. 21 Mar.
SED 24, 36-1, v9, 3p. [1031]
Indian and Mexican depredations on the Rio Grande, and in Texas.

60. Resol. of the Texas Legis. 22 Mar.
SMD 39, 36-1, v1, 2p. [1038]
Reimbursement for depredations committed by Indians and Mexicans on the Texas frontier near the Rio Grande.

61. R-M of Land-Owners in Louisiana. 23 Mar.
SR 150, 36-1, v1, 98p. [1039]
Land purchased from the Houmas Indians in 1774.

62. R-M of S. Eastman. 23 Mar.
SR 151, 36-1, v1, 2p. [1036]
Illustrations for Schoolcraft's history of the American Indains; copyright problems.

63. Difficulties on the Texas-Mexico Boundary. 23 Mar.
HMD 38, 36-1, v5, 7p. [1064]
Depredations of Mexicans and Indians.

64. R-P of J. Wood. 23 Mar.
HR 173, 36-1, v1, 1p. [1067]
Indian depredations in New Mexico.

65. R-P of the Washington Legis. 23 Mar.
HR 188, 36-1, v1, 1p. [1067]
Steamship wreck on the coast of said Territory; Indians recover mail.

66. R-M of Kerr, Brierly, and Company. 23 Mar.
HR 197, 36-1, v1, 3p. [1067]
Gen. Harney's actions instigate Sioux depredations; Pawnee depredations.

67. Report on Claims Against the Menomonees. 23 Mar.
HR 198, 36-1, v1, 2p. [1067]
Menomonee depredations in Wisconsin during 1846.

68. Expenses of Suppressing Indian Hostilities. 23 Mar.
HR 201, 36-1, v2, 2p. [1068]
In Utah during 1853.

69. R-P of E. Merchant. 23 Mar.
HR 202, 36-1, v2, 2p. [1068]
Indian hostilities of 1850 in Texas.

70. R-M of Hill and McGunnegle. 23 Mar.
HR 204, 36-1, v2, 3p. [1068]
Supplies to Illinois militia in 1832 during the Black Hawk war.

71. On the Case of H. Baker. 23 Mar.
HR 237, 36-1, v2, 1p. [1068]
Cherokee and Creek removal in 1837.

72. R-P of M. Maltby. 26 Mar.
SR 153, 36-1, v1, 2p. [1039]
Fort Gibson, Cherokee Nation, during 1834; march to Kiowa country; volunteers in war against Texas Indians.

73. Letter on Payment of the New Mexico Militia and Volunteers. 28 Mar.
SMD 45, 36-1, v1, 6p. [1038]
To control Apache and Navajo hostilities.

74. Report on Appropriations for an Indian War. 29 Mar.
SR 161, 36-1, v1, 2p. [1039]
War of 1855-1856 in Oregon and Washington.

75. R-P of D. Wilson. 29 Mar.
HR 253, 36-1, v2, 1p. [1068]
Indian war in Washington Territory.

76. R-P of G. Jemison et al. 29 Mar.
HR 254, 36-1, v2, 3p. [1068]
Payments due Seneca Indians.

77. Settlers on the Miami Reserve in Kansas. 29 Mar.

HR 256, 36-1, v2, 6p. [1068]
Land title of the Miamies shown under the treaty of 5 June 1854; removal of settlers recommended.

78. R-P of H. Miller and Company. 30 Mar.
HR 266, 36-1, v2, 1p. [1068]
Rogue River Indian war of 1853 in Oregon.

79. R-M of G. Durham. 30 Mar.
HR 278, 36-1, v2, 1p. [1068]
Clerk in the office of the CIA during 1855-1857.

80. R-P of E. DeMay. 30 Mar.
HR 297, 36-1, v2, 1p. [1068]
War with the Spokane Indians of 1858 in Washington Territory.

81. R-M of the Shawnee Indians. 30 Mar.
HR 300, 36-1, v2, 4p. [1068]
Depredations committed upon the Shawnees of Kansas during 1855-1857.

82. R-P of J. Denny. 30 Mar.
HR 301, 36-1, v2, 1p. [1068]
Creek war of 1814.

83. R-M of W. Walker. 30 Mar.
HR 314, 36-1, v2, 1p. [1068]
Indian battles of 1779-1782 in North Carolina.

84. Message on Difficulties on the Southwestern Frontier. 2 Apr.
HED 52, 36-1, v8, 147p. [1050]
Hostilities of Mexicans, and the Comanche and other Indians of the Southwest.

85. Report on Land Claims in New Mexico. 2 Apr.
HR 321, 36-1, v2, 326p. [1068]
Depredations of the Apaches and other tribes of the Southwest; etc.

86. R-M of C. Horr. 2 Apr.
HR 329, 36-1, v3, 4p. [1069]
Omaha depredations of 1858 in Nebraska.

87. On Relief of the Survivors of the Sublette Cut-Off Massacre. 2 Apr.
HR 330, 36-1, v3, 4p. [1069]
Utah Indian hostilities of 1859 in Utah.

88. R-P of Settlers in Iowa. 5 Apr.
SR 168, 36-1, v1, 2p. [1039]
On the Fort Atkinson military reserve, and the old Indian agency.

89. R-C of E. Ogden. 5 Apr.
SR 170, 36-1, v1, 2p. [1039]
Disbursements to suppress Creek and Seminole hostilities.

90. Mem. of the Minnesota Legis. 6 Apr.
HMD 68, 36-1, v6, 2p. [1065]
Ask removal of Winnebago Indians from lands set aside for them under the treaty of 1855.

91. Mem. of the Minnesota Legis. 6 Apr.
HMD 69, 36-1, v6, 2p. [1065]
Urge construction of a fort on the Pembina River to protect settlers from Sioux aggressions.

92. R-M of J. Hall. 6 Apr.
HR 344, 36-1, v3, 3p. [1069]
Kiowa depredations of 1859 in Kansas; treaty of 27 July 1853.

93. R-C of G. Fisher. 6 Apr.
HR 345, 36-1, v3, 2p. [1069]
Indian depredations of 1813 in Florida.

94. R-M of J. Johnson. 6 Apr.
HR 346, 36-1, v3, 2p. [1069]
Cheyenne hostilities of 1856 near Fort Kearney.

95. R-P of C. Clark. 6 Apr.
HR 358, 36-1, v3, 2p. [1069]
"Dade's Massacre" of 1835; Florida Indian war.

96. R-P of J. Meyer. 7 Apr.
SR 175, 36-1, v1, 2p. [1039]
Threat of Indian hostilities on the Texas frontier in 1850-1851.

97. Message on Affairs in Utah. 9 Apr.
SED 32, 36-1, v9, 64p. [1031]
Mormon troubles; Indian hostilities.

98. Report on Funds Needed to Complete a Survey. 9 Apr.
SR 177, 36-1, v1, 25p. [1039]
For a railroad to the Pacific through Oregon and Washington; settlements needed for protection of such a railroad from wandering Indians.

99. R-C of A. Fridley. 10 Apr.
SR 181, 36-1, v1, 2p. [1039]
Agent for the Winnebagoes; payments for debts incurred during 1850-1851.

100. On the Relief of S. Hensley. 10 Apr.
HR 395, 36-1, v3, 2p. [1069]
Supplies furnished to California Indians during 1852-1853.

101. Letter on Affairs in Oregon. 12 Apr.
HED 65, 36-1, v9, 269p. [1051]
Correspondence of Gen. Harney; war with the Spokane, Coeur d'Aléne, Nez Percé, Walla-Walla, and other Indians of the Northwest; copies of treaties made.

102. Expedition from the Dalles of the Columbia River to the Great Salt Lake. 13 Apr.
SED 34, 36-1, v9, 51p. [1031]

Encounters with Snake Indians, and other tribes of Oregon and the Great Basin.

103. On the Relief of N. Bukey. 13 Apr.
HR 416, 36-1, v3, 1p. [1069]
Indian wars in 1790 or 1792.

104. R-P of E. Joslyn. 13 Apr.
HR 419, 36-1, v3, 2p. [1069]
Owned land in Washington which was included in a reserve for the Clickatat tribe; unratified treaty with the Yakimas of 1855 at Walla-Walla.

105. R-M of M. Marmaduke. 13 Apr.
HR 420, 36-1, v3, 2p. [1069]
Pawnee depredations of 1828 near the Arkansas River; treaties of 1825-1826 with the Pawnee, Osage, and Kansas Indians.

106. Report on a Pacific Railroad. 13 Apr.
HR 428, 36-1, v3, 65p. [1069]
Central. northern, and southern Pacific railroad routes; compelling Indians of the northwest to move from desirable lands while unruly southern Indians continue to commit hostilities (in the minority report on the southern route).

107. Report on Holding Treaty Councils with Indians. 16 Apr.
SED 35, 36-1, v9, 19p. [1031] *or*
HED 61, 36-1, v9, 19p. [1051]
With the Kiowas, Comanches, and others on the Arkansas River; with the Arapahoes and Cheyennes on the Platte River; with the Sioux and others on Deer Creek; with the Red Lake Chippewas and others on the Red River of the north.

108. Message on Indian Hostilities in New Mexico. 16 Apr.
HED 69, 36-1, v9, 65p. [1051]
Campaign against the Navajo, Kiowa, Pinal, and other Indian tribes of the Southwest.

109. Mem. and Resol. of the Minnesota Legis. 17 Apr.
SMD 53, 36-1, v1, 2p. [1038]
On behalf of J. Thomas; depredations of 1857 committed by Sioux under Ink-pa-du-tah.

110. R-M of J. Ely. 17 Apr.
SR 200, 36-1, v1, 1p. [1039]
Employed in the Indian Bureau in 1855.

111. R-P of J. Cradlebaugh. 18 Apr.
SR 202, 36-1, v1, 4p. [1039]
Transport through Indian country in Utah; depredations.

112. Report on a Contested Election in Nebraska. 20 Apr.
HR 446, 36-1, v3, 11p. [1069]
Votes from a precinct within the Pawnee reserve are not valid, as that land is not part of the Territory.

113. R-P of S. Perry. 20 Apr.
HR 461, 36-1, v3, 1p. [1069]
Indian goods destined for Arkansas lost on the Mississippi River.

114. Message on Conditions in Utah. 2 May.
HED 78, 36-1, v12, 51p. [1056]
Indian and Mormon hostilities.

115. N. Garrison *vs.* the U.S. 2 May.
HRCC 252, 36-1, v5, 23p. [1076]
U.S. troops occupy property in Georgia during 1827; troops charged with removal of the Cherokees.

116. Annual Report of the Chickasaw Fund. 3 May.
HED 79, 36-1, v12, 2p. [1056]
Under the treaties of 20 Oct. 1832 and 24 May 1834.

117. Mem. of the State of California. 4 May.
SMD 57, 36-1, v1, 2p. [1038]
Reimbursement for funds expended to suppress Indian hostilities during 1850-1860.

118. On the Relief of Reps. of D. Bates. 4 May.
HR 489, 36-1, v3, 3p. [1069]
Rent paid to Indians for lease of lead mine lands on the upper Mississippi River; treaty of 13 Feb. 1833 with the Sac and Fox Indians; treaties of 1829 and 1832 with the Pottawatomies, Chippewas, Winnebagoes, and Ottawas.

119. R-P of R. Martin. 4 May.
HR 495, 36-1, v3, 1p. [1069]
Supplies to California Indians in 1851.

120. R-P of J. Monroe. 4 May.
HR 498, 36-1, v3, 2p. [1069]
Indian campaigns during the War of 1812; Indiana Rangers.

121. Letter on Troubles on the Texas Frontier. 5 May.
HED 81, 36-1, v12, 105p. [1056]
Incursions of Mexicans, and Mescaleros, Lipans, and other Indians of the Southwest.

122. R-M of C. Emory. 8 May.
SR 216, 36-1, v2, 2p. [1040]
Seminole war; 1836; Florida.

123. Communication from C. Drew. 9 May.
SMD 59, 36-1, v1, 48p. [1038]
Account of the origin and early prosecution of the Indian war in Oregon; hostilities of the Cayuse, Shasta, Coquille, Rogue River, Modoc, and other Indian tribes.

124. Report on a Transfer of the Indian Bureau. 9 May.
SR 223, 36-1, v2, 3p. [1040]
Transfer of the BIA from Interior to War; War Dept. more involved at the frontiers where the Indians are.

125. R-P of M. Alexander. 9 May.
SR 224, 36-1, v2, 2p. [1040]
Indian battles during 1791-1792, and in 1812-1814; Kentucky and Michigan.

126. Letter on Amount Due the Choctaws. 10 May.
HED 82, 36-1, v12, 39p. [1056]
Proceeds of sale of lands ceded to the U.S. under the treaty of 27 Sept. 1830.

127. On the Relief of R. Chenery. 10 May.
HR 510, 36-1, v3, 2p. [1069]
Supplies furnished to California Indians in 1852.

128. Message on the Massacre at Mountain Meadows, and Other Massacres in Utah. 18 May.
SED 42, 36-1, v11, 139p. [1033]
Emigrants killed by a force of Mormons and Indians; Bannock and Shoshone depredations.

129. R-M of H. Eldredge et al. 18 May.
HR 521, 36-1, v4, 5p. [1070]
Jurisdictional matters concerning Indians in Utah.

130. R-M of A. Jones and H. Brown. 18 May.
HR 532, 36-1, v4, 11p. [1070]
Running boundary lines between the Choctaws and Chickasaws, and the Creeks and Seminoles; treaty of 22 June 1855 with the Chickasaws and Choctaws; treaty of 7 Aug. 1856 with the Creeks and Seminoles; Indian hostilities towards the surveyors; Comanche hostilities; French, Spanish, and American treaty relations with the Indians west of the Mississippi.

131. On the Case of G. Parks. 18 May.
HR 553, 36-1, v4, 2p. [1070]
Cherokee land title under the treaties of 8 July 1817 and 1819.

132. Report on Cherokee Treaties of 1817 and 1819. 18 May.
HR 534, 36-1, v4, 13p. [1070]
The status of grants of reserved lands to the Indians; voluntary removal of Indians from reserved lands results in the land reverting to the U.S.; etc.

133. Report on the Resol. of the Texas Legis. 18 May.
HR 535, 36-1, v4, 11p. [1070]
On depredations committed by Indians and Mexicans; Comanche, Kiowa, and Kickapoo hostilities.

134. R-M of G. Dousman. 18 May.
HR 536, 36-1, v4, 2p. [1070]
Surety for an Indian sub-agent in Green Bay, Wisconsin during 1849-1851.

135. R-P of New Mexico Volunteers. 18 May.
HR 537, 36-1, v4, 2p. [1070]
Campaign against the Navajoes in 1848-1849.

136. R-P of R. and C. Orr. 19 May.
SR 229, 36-1, v2, 3p. [1040]
Gen. Clark's campaign against the Indians of Ohio in 1781.

137. Mem. of the New Mexico Railway Company. 21 May.
HMD 85, 36-1, v6, 12p. [1065]
Southern route to the Pacific; arguments that emancipation of blacks should precede funding for a railroad are countered by a description of treatment of Indians by northerners.

138. Report on Indians in California. 22 May.
SED 46, 36-1, v11, 44p. [1033]
From agents and Supts. on the condition of Indian reservations in the state.

139. Mem. of the Principal Chief of the Cherokee Nation, and His Associates. 23 May.
SMD 61, 36-1, v1, 3p. [1038]
Cherokee land wrongly included within the territorial limits of Kansas.

140. R-M of B. Shelley. 25 May.
HR 592, 36-1, v4, 2p. [1070]
Land included in the Omaha reservation in Nebraska; treaty of 17 Apr. 1854; change in the reservation ordered by the CIA on 21 Mar. 1855.

141. R-M of Suter, Lea, and Company. 26 May.
HR 601, 36-1, v4, 1p. [1070]

Expenses of suppression of Indian hostilities in Utah during 1850-1851.

142. R-M of J. Barron et al. 4 June.
HR 608, 36-1, v4, 4p. [1070]
Mail route from Missouri to California; interruptions due to Indian hostilities.

143. Exploration of the Colorado River. 5 June.
HED 90, 36-1, v14, 366p. [1058]
Expedition of Lieut. Ives during 1857-1858; encounters with, and descriptions of Yuma, Navajo, Mojave, Chemehuevis, and other Indian tribes of the Southwest; Mormons among the Indians.

144. On the Relief of A. Dart. 8 June.
SR 264, 36-1, v2, 1p. [1040]
Late Supt. of Indian Affairs in Oregon.

145. Annual Report of the Smithsonian Institution. 11 June.
HMD 90, 36-1, v7, 450p. [1066]
Research and publications relating to the American Indian.

146. Report on the Colorado Desert. 14 June.
SR 276, 36-1, v2, 12p. [1040]
California Legis. asks it be donated to that state; Ca-hui-ua Indians reside near the desert, but avoid it; mineral wealth.

147. Resol. of the California Legis. 14 June.
HMD 94, 36-1, v7, 2p. [1067]
Establishment of an Indian reservation in Round Valley, Mendocino county; ask U.S. to give the state full control over Indian affairs in the state, jurisdiction over Indians, and adequate funding.

148. R-M of W. Latshaw. 15 June.
HR 631, 36-1, v4, 2p. [1070]
Pawnee depredations during a survey of public lands in Kansas.

149. R-M of R. McKee. 19 June.
SR 282, 36-1, v2, 1p. [1040]
Com'r appointed to treat with the California Indians in 1851.

150. Report on Amount Due the Choctaw Indians. 19 June.
SR 283, 36-1, v2, 10p. [1040]
For sale of land under the treaty of 27 Sept. 1830; treaty of 1855.

151. Report on Sioux Treaties. 19 June.
SR 284, 36-1, v2, 6p. [1040]
Right of Indians to hold lands on the Minnesota River; Medawakanton, Wahpakoota, Sisseton, and Wahpeton bands of Sioux; treaty of 19 June 1858; incursions of settlers.

152. Correspondence with Gen. Harney. 20 June.
HED 98, 36-1, v13, 29p. [1057]
Indian hostilities in Oregon and Washington.

153. On the Relief of L. Fletcher. 22 June.
HR 653, 36-1, v4, 1p. [1070]
Seminole war of 1818.

154. R-P of M. Woodbury et al. 22 June.
HR 657, 36-1, v4, 2p. [1070]
Sioux half-breeds request money due them under the treaty of 1837.

155. Report on Expenses of Suppressing Indian Hostilities in California. 22 June.
HR 660, 36-1, v4, 2p. [1070]
Nine campaigns from 1854 to 1859.

156. Statements of Appropriations. 28 July.
HMD 100, 36-1, v7, 94p. [1067]
During the 1st session, 36th Congress; Indian expenses.

157. Estimates of Appropriations. 21 Nov.
HED 1, 36-2, v1, 394p. [1092]
For the year ending 30 June 1862; Indian expenses.

158. Annual Message to Congress with Documents; Pres. Buchanan. 4 Dec.
SED 1, 36-2, v1-3, 2130p. [1078-1080]
Indian hostilities in Utah; annual report of the Sec. of War (Serial 1079); annual report of the Sec. of the Interior (Serial 1078); annual report of the General Land Office (Serial 1078, including intruders on Cherokee lands, commission to the Cheyennes and Arrapahoes, trust funds, and reports of Supts., agents, and schools; etc.

159. Annual Report of the Sec. of the Treasury. 5 Dec.
HED 2, 36-2, v2, 484p. [1093]
Year ending 30 June 1860; Indian expenses.

160. Contingent Expenses of the Interior Dept. 5 Dec.
HED 3, 36-2, v3, 101p. [1094]
Year ending 30 June 1860; Indian Office.

161. On the Case of A. Bonesteel. 6 Dec.
HED 4, 36-2, v3, 137p. [1094]
Indian agent to the Menomonee Indians; misapplication of funds.

162. Receipts and Expenditures. 18 Dec.
HED 12, 36-2, v5, 569p. [1096]

Year ending 30 June 1860; Indian expenses.

163. S. Norris *vs.* the U.S. 18 Dec.
HRCC 257, 36-2, v1, 152p. [1108]
Supplies furnished California Indians; treaty Com'rs of 1851 draw drafts on the CIA, but these were not paid because of a lack of appropriations.

164. J. Baldwin *vs.* the U.S. 18 Dec.
HRCC 259, 36-2, v2, 18p. [1109]
Shipwreck on the Florida coast in 1835; destroyed by U.S. for fear that the cargo would fall into Indian hands; Florida Indian war.

165. R. Coxe *vs.* the U.S. 18 Dec.
HRCC 261, 36-2, v2, 60p. [1109]
Indian campaign under Gen. St. Clair in 1791.

166. J. Knaggs *vs.* the U.S. 18 Dec.
HRCC 267, 36-2, v2, 52p. [1109]
Indian interpreter for the U.S. prior to 1812; Michigan militia during the War of 1812.

167. Report on Arming a Military Company. 20 Dec.
SR 286, 36-2, v1, 1p. [1090]
In Kentucky; company has fought in the Indian wars on the Miami River.

168. Appropriations and Balances of the Interior Dept. 24 Dec.
HED 16, 36-2, v6, 15p. [1097]
Year ending 30 June 1860; Indian expenses.

169. Letter on Frauds Regarding Indian Trust Funds. 24 Dec.
HED 17, 36-2, v6, 1p. [1097]
Bonds held for the Indians converted to private use.

170. R-M of the Chippewas, Ottawas, and Pottawatomies of Michigan. 24 Dec.
HR 8, 36-2, v1, 2p. [1104]
Supplementary articles (to the treaty of 26 Sept. 1833 at Chicago) agreed to by these Indians on 27 Sept. 1833; they have not lost their benefits by not removing west to Kansas.

171. R-C of G. Fisher. 24 Dec.
HR 11, 36-2, v1, 8p. [1104]
Indian depredations in 1813.

1861

1. On the Case of G. Fisher. 2 Jan.
HED 21, 36-2, v6, 5p. [1097]
Florida Indian depredations during 1813-1814.

2. Indian Disturbances in New Mexico. 7 Jan.
HED 24, 36-2, v6, 17p. [1097]
Navajo, Utah, and Comanche hostilities; Pueblo Indians aid U.S. troops.

3. R-P of R. Austin. 11 Jan.
HR 17, 36-2, v1, 1p. [1104]
Settler on New York Indian lands in Kansas.

4. Private Land Claims in New Mexico. 12 Jan.
HED 28, 36-2, v6, 73p. [1097]
Indian hostilities drive off settlers, and complicate resolution of claims.

5. Indian Depredations in Oregon and Washington. 12 Jan.
HED 29, 36-2, v6, 90p. [1097]
Depredations of U.S. troops on property of the Hudson's Bay Company; massacre of emigrants by Snake Indians; depredations of Indians loyal to British; etc.

6. R-P of E. Plympton. 12 Jan.
HR 24, 36-2, v1, 2p. [1104]
Attack on the Seminoles at Dunn's Lake in Florida; 1842.

7. R-P of P. Navarre. 12 Jan.
HR 27, 36-2, v1, 2p. [1104]
Battle of the River Raisin; captured by British and Indians.

8. Mem. of Reps. of the Choctaw Nation. 14 Jan.
SMD 9, 36-2, v1, 2p. [1089]
Ask payment of amounts due under the treaty of June, 1855.

9. Deficiencies of Funds for the Indian Service. 15 Jan.
HED 31, 36-2, v6, 4p. [1097]
In California, New Mexico, and Utah; salaries of agents for the Poncas, Pawnees, and Yankton Sioux; negotiation costs of the treaty of 19 June 1858 with the Sioux.

10. Additional Estimate for Suppression of Indian Hostilities. 17 Jan.
HED 33, 36-2, v6, 3p. [1097]
In New Mexico for the Navajo war; in Kansas for Kiowa and Comanche hostilities; in Carson Valley, California.

11. R-M of Livingston, Kinkead, and Company. 18 Jan.
HR 36, 36-2, v1, 1p. [1104]
Sioux depredations of 1854 near Fort Laramie.

12. R-P of M. Blattenberger. 21 Jan.
HR 46, 36-2, v1, 1p. [1104]
Indian hostilities in 1820.

13. Report on Construction of a Military Road. 25 Jan.
HED 44, 36-2, v8, 171p. [1099]
From Fort Benson to Fort Walla-Walla; Indians still do not want the road to be built; journal of movement across the northern plains, including encounters with various Indian tribes.

14. Employees in the Interior Dept. 28 Jan.
HED 45, 36-2, v8, 19p. [1099]
During 1860; office of the CIA.

15. Letter on the Snake River Massacre. 28 Jan.
HED 46, 36-2, v8, 16p. [1099]
Emigrants killed by Snake Indians; depredations in Oregon and Washington.

16. Gen. Harney's Administration in Oregon. 31 Jan.
HED 51, 36-2, v9, 3p. [1100]
Of the military dept. in said state; protection from incursions of northern Indians.

17. Relief for Destitute Indians. 2 Feb.
HED 52, 36-2, v9, 2p. [1100]
Crop failures in and around Kansas.

18. Report on Use of Pottawatomie Annuities. 6 Feb.
SR 298, 36-2, v1, 1p. [1090]
To pay bills of the Chippewas, Ottawas, and Pottawatomies of Michigan from the annuities of the Kansas Pottawatomies.

19. On the Claims of Heirs of L. DeBaca. 6 Feb.
HED 58, 36-2, v9, 13p. [1100]
Land claim in New Mexico; hostilities of the Quintarsas Indians; driven from land by the Navajoes.

20. Letter on Money Paid to M. Woodbury et al. 7 Feb.
HED 59, 36-2, v9, 3p. [1100]
Sioux half-breeds; treaty of 29 Sept. 1837.

21. R-M of N. McLean et al. 8 Feb.
HR 68, 36-2, v1, 1p. [1104]
Indian agent for the Minnesota Sioux during 1849-1853.

22. R-P of H. Anderson. 9 Feb.
HR 76, 36-2, v1, 1p. [1104]
Volunteer in Creek war of 1813, and the Seminole war in Florida.

23. Additional Estimate for a Wagon Road. 11 Feb.
HED 63, 36-2, v9, 27p. [1100]
From Fort Kearney, through the South Pass, to California and Oregon; goods for the Washikee band of Snake Indians; Paiute Indian war in Utah.

24. Letter on the South Pass Wagon Road. 11 Feb.
HED 64, 36-2, v9, 39p. [1100]
To the Pacific; peaceful arrangements with the Indians; Snake, Shoshonee, Sheepeater, Paiute, and Bannock Indians.

25. Report on Fraud Surrounding Indian Trust Funds. 12 Feb.
HR 78, 36-2, v2, 365p. [1105]
Abstraction of bonds meant for Indian use.

26. Estimate for Compensation of a Supt. of Indian Affairs. 14 Feb.
HED 66, 36-2, v9, 1p. [1100]
In Washington Territory; also, extra Indian agents.

27. R-M of Lieut. Langdon. 18 Feb.
SR 305, 36-2, v1, 1p. [1090]
Property lost as a result of a military move against Texas Indians.

28. Annual Report of the Smithsonian Institution. 26 Feb.
SMD 21, 36-2, v1, 448p. [1089]
Research and publications related to the American Indian; Indian grammars from California; etc.

29. L-C of H. Rice. 1 Mar.
HED 75, 36-2, v10, 15p. [1101]
Payment for subsisting emigrant Winnebagoes in 1850-1851; removal from Iowa and Wisconsin to Minnesota.

30. R-P of Barrow, Porter, and Company. 2 Mar.
HR 106, 36-2, v2, 2p. [1105]
Mail carriers; Navajo, Cosinas, and Mohave depredations during 1859.

31. Report on Overland Movement of Troops. 15 Mar.
SED 2, 37-sp, v4, 6p. [1082]
To the northern portion of the dept. of the Pacific; through Sioux, Blackfoot, Snake, Crow, and Bannock country; control of hostilities.

32. Statements of Appropriations. 15 Apr.
HMD 44, 36-2, v1, 63p. [1103]
During the 2d session, 36th Congress; Indian expenses.

33. Estimates of Appropriations. 2 July.
HED 1, 37-1, v1, 91p. [1114]
Year ending 30 June 1861 and 30 June 1862; Indian expenses.

34. Annual Message to Congress with Documents; Pres. Lincoln. 5 July.
SED 1, 37-1, v1, 110p. [1112]
Annual report of the Sec. of War.

35. An Act of the Kansas Legis. 15 July.
HMD 7, 37-1, v1, 2p. [1115]
Lands ceded by the Wyandottes under the treaty of 31 Jan. 1855 to be taxed.

36. Letter on Indians and Negroes in the Service of the Southern Confederacy. 27 July.
HED 14, 37-1, v1, 1p. [1114]
Number of Indians in the military of the Confederacy unknown.

37. Annual Message to Congress with Documents; Pres. Lincoln. 3 Dec.
SED 1, 37-2, v1-3, 2159p. [1117-1119]
Indian relations with the U.S. disturbed by the Civil War; annual report of the Sec. of War (Serial 1118); annual report of the Sec. of Interior (Serial 1117); annual report of the Gen. Land Office (Serial 1117); annual report of the CIA (Serial 1117), including attempts of Confederacy to alienate Indians from the U.S., report of a visit to the Central Superintendency; British trade; treaty negotiations, agents for new Territories; fear of Indian troubles on the Upper Missouri; hostilities in the Southwest, affairs on the Pacific coast, and reports of Supts. and agents; etc.

38. Estimates of Appropriations. 4 Dec.
HED 1, 37-2, v1, 262p. [1127]
Year ending 30 June 1863; Indian expenses.

39. A. Anderson *vs.* the U.S. 4 Dec.
HRCC 278, 37-2, v1, 91p. [1146]
Indian hostilities during the War of 1812 in Michigan.

40. J. Beck *vs.* the U.S. 4 Dec.
HRCC 282, 37-2, v1, 54p. [1146]
Navajo depredations of 1849 in New Mexico.

41. S. Johnston et al. *vs.* the U.S. 4 Dec.
HRCC 286, 37-2, v1, 54p. [1146]
Land granted to the claimants under the treaty of 16 Oct. 1826 with the Pottawatomies; choice of land left up to the government; selection of poor quality land, etc.

42. Annual Report of the Sec. of the Treasury. 9 Dec.
SED 2, 37-2, v4, 302p. [1121]
Year ending 30 June 1861; Indian expenses.

43. Contingent Expenses of the Interior Dept. 18 Dec.
HED 13, 37-2, v1, 136p. [1127]
Year ending 30 June 1861; office of the CIA.

1862

1. Letter on War Dept. Occupancy of Land. 7 Jan.
HED 26, 37-2, v1, 50p. [1127]
War Dept. confiscates land in Washington Territory in 1856 for protection of the Cascades from Indian hostilities.

2. Appropriations and Balances of the Interior Dept. 13 Jan.
SED 13, 37-2, v4, 15p. [1121]
Year ending 30 June 1861; Indian expenses.

3. Letter on the Accounts of B. Young. 15 Jan.
HED 29, 37-2, v2, 124p. [1128]
Investigation of the disbursements for Indians made by this *ex officio* Supt. of Indian Affairs in Utah.

4. Report on Payment of War Debts. 24 Jan.
SR 8, 37-2, v1, 2p. [1125]
In Oregon and Washington; Indian war of 1855-1856.

5. Report on a Wagon Road. 24 Jan.
HED 35, 37-2, v3, 36p. [1129]
Examination of the accounts of the late Supt. of the Fort Ridgely-South Pass road; property meant for Messrs. Cullen and Mix of the Indian Bureau not delivered.

6. J. Johnson *vs.* the U.S. 24 Jan.
HRCC 290, 37-2, v1, 39p. [1146]
Kiowa depredations of 1857 near Fort Atkinson on the Arkansas River.

7. Receipts and Expenditures. 27 Jan.
HED 36, 37-2, v3, 560p. [1129]
Year ending 30 June 1861; Indian expenses.

8. Report on Loyalty of Government Employees. 28 Jan.
HR 16, 37-2, v3, 92p. [1144]
Employees of the Indian Bureau included.
9. Mem. of the Minnesota Legis. 11 Feb.
SMD 44, 37-2, v1, 3p. [1124]
Defense of the northern frontier; ask treaty be made with the Red Lake band of Chippewas.
10. R-M of B. Shelley. 17 Feb.
HR 26, 37-2, v3, 2p. [1144]
Improvements made included in the Omaha reservation under the treaty of 17 Apr. 1854.
11. R-P of M. Woodbury et al. 17 Feb.
HR 27, 37-2, v3, 2p. [1144]
Sioux half-breeds ask payment of money due them under the treaty of 1837.
12. R-M of N. McLean et al. 17 Feb.
HR 28, 37-2, v3, 1p. [1144]
Indian agent to the Sioux of Minnesota during 1849-1853.
13. Letter on Transportation of Indian Goods. 24 Feb.
SED 21, 37-2, v4, 4p. [1121]
Contracts made; destinations and descriptions of goods.
14. Resol. of the Kansas Legis. 26 Feb.
SMD 57, 37-2, v1, 2p. [1124] *or*
HMD 75, 37-2, v1, 2p. [1141]
Settlers on Cherokee neutral, and Osage lands; ask extinguishment of title to Cherokee, Osage, Pottawatomie, Kickapoo, Sac and Fox, Ottawa, Kansas, Iowa, Sac and Fox of the Missouri, and the absent Shawnee Indian lands.
15. Employees of the Interior Dept. 26 Feb.
HED 57, 37-2, v5 (pt.1), 31p. [1131]
During 1861; office of the CIA.
16. R-P of J. Pool. 4 Mar.
SR 20, 37-2, v1, 2p. [1125]
Blacksmith for the Delawares, Senecas, and Shawnees during 1823-1838.
17. R-P of S. Burnham. 5 Mar.
HR 45, 37-2, v3, 1p. [1144]
Indian wars of 1792-1795 under Gen. Wayne.
18. Disbursements to the Indians. 10 Mar.
SED 31, 37-2, v4, 301p. [1121]
Year ending 30 June 1861.
19. R-M of A. Jones and H. Brown. 11 Mar.
HR 56, 37-2, v3, 4p. [1144]
Surveyed boundaries between the Choctaw and Chickasaw Nations, and between the Creek and Seminole Nations.
20. R-M of C. Horr. 12 Mar.
HR 59, 37-2, v3, 4p. [1144]
Omaha depredations of 1858 on their reserve in Nebraska.
21. Resol. of the Kansas Legis. 17 Mar.
SMD 64, 37-2, v1, 2p. [1124]
Ask railroad to the Pacific, through Kansas, be constructed; treaty lately concluded with the Pottawatomies must be ratified to procure needed lands.
22. R-P of A. DuNord. 20 Mar.
SR 30, 37-2, v1, 1p. [1125]
Scout and Indian interpreter during the War of 1812; interpreter at the making of several treaties.
23. Message on Military and Naval Defenses. 26 Mar.
HED 92, 37-2, v7, 415p. [1135]
Reprint of reports of frontier defenses against hostile Indians.
24. Message on Affairs in Nevada Territory. 27 Mar.
SED 36, 37-2, v5, 5p. [1122]
Proposed constitution forbids Indians to testify against whites in criminal trials; Shoshone hostilities due to death of a friendly chief.
25. Letter on Indian Affairs in Minnesota. 1 Apr.
SMD 77, 37-2, v1, 5p. [1124]
Bishop Whipple writes of the sad state of affairs in Chippewa and Sioux country.
26. Letter on Additional Estimates for the Indian Service. 2 Apr.
SMD 79, 37-2, v1, 46p. [1124]
To fulfill treaty stipulations, make up for crop failures, and appoint more Indian agents in various areas.
27. Report on Surveys of Land in Kansas and Nebraska. 3 Apr.
SR 32, 37-2, v1, 5p. [1125]
Amount of land under Indian title.
28. Indian Dept. Property in Utah. 4 Apr.
HED 97, 37-2, v7, 31p. [1135]
Report goes with the investigation of the accounts of B. Young, *ex officio* Supt. of Indian Affairs in Utah.
29. On the Relief of Sioux Half-Breeds. 18 Apr.
HR 83, 37-2, v3, 4p. [1144]
Lands granted to them under the

treaty of 15 July 1830; relinquished lands to the U.S.; railroad surveys and land requirements.

30. R-M of E. Parker. 18 Apr.
HR 84, 37-2, v3, 1p. [1144]
Seneca Indian asks U.S. citizenship.

31. R-M of J. Hall. 18 Apr.
HR 85, 37-2, v3, 3p. [1144]
Mail carrier through Indian country west of Arkansas; Kiowa depredations of 1859; treaty of 27 July 1853.

32. Report on the Colorado Desert. 23 Apr.
HR 87, 37-2, v4, 26p. [1145]
Its cession to California; Ca-hui-ua Indians' conceptions of the desert.

33. R-M of the Sac and Fox Indians. 24 Apr.
HR 88, 37-2, v4, 7p. [1145]
Ask indemnity for property destroyed by settlers on their reserve in Kansas during 1854-1860.

34. R-P of C. Clark. 28 Apr.
HR 94, 37-2, v4, 1p. [1145]
Florida Indian war of 1835; "Dade's Massacre."

35. Report on a Road in Wisconsin and Michigan. 30 Apr.
SR 40, 37-2, v1, 6p. [1125]
In the lead mine areas of Lake Superior; Indians sometimes entrusted with delivery of mail when weather conditions are poor.

36. Report on Conduct of the War. 30 Apr.
SR 41, 37-2, v1, 40p. [1125]
No information yet as to Indians being employed by the Confederacy.

37. Message on Indian War Claims. 2 May.
SED 46, 37-2, v5, 12p. [1122]
In Oregon and Washington; war of 1855-1856.

38. R-P of Col. Paddock. 2 May.
HR 97, 37-2, v4, 1p. [1145]
Indian war of 1810-1811; Indiana militia.

39. R-P of W. Sawyer et al. 2 May.
HR 98, 37-2, v4, 4p. [1145]
Land titles; treaties of 1818, and 23 Oct. 1826 with the Miamies.

40. Letter on Private Land Claims in New Mexico. 16 May.
HED 112, 37-2, v9, 39p. [1137]
Settlers kept from land due to Indian hostilities.

41. Preliminary Report on the Eighth Census. 21 May.
HED 116, 37-2, v9, 294p. [1137]
Indian populations; slaves held by Indians west of Arkansas.

42. Petition of the Delaware Indians. 2 June.
SMD 100, 37-2, v1, 2p. [1124]
Interest has not been paid on bonds held in trust for said tribe from Kansas; funds have been abstracted by the agent in charge; ask payments due them.

43. Annual Report of the Smithsonian Institution. 5 June.
HMD 77, 37-2, v1, 463p. [1141]
Research and publications related to American Indians; mounds on the Mississippi River; ancient mining operations near Lake Superior; etc.

44. Report on Half-Breed Kaw Lands in Kansas. 11 June.
SED 58, 37-2, v5, 20p. [1122]
Settlers on lands belonging to said Indians under the treaty of 3 June 1825 with the Kansas tribe.

45. On the Relief of the Wyandot Indians. 11 June.
SR 56, 37-2, v1, 4p. [1125]
Trust funds under the treaty of 1 Apr. 1850 and 31 Jan. 1855.

46. Relief to Indian Refugees in Kansas. 16 June.
HED 132, 37-2, v10, 14p. [1138]
Indians residing west of Arkansas who support the Union, are driven north by Indians and Confederate forces.

47. R-P of W. Sawyer et al. 20 June.
HR 124, 37-2, v4, 3p. [1145]
Land title in Ohio; Miami Indian treaties of 1818 and 1826.

48. On the Relief of J. Jones. 10 July.
HR 138, 37-2, v4, 2p. [1145]
Depredations of 1856 by whites on the property of this Ottawa Indian residing in Kansas.

49. R-C of W. Kennedy. 10 July.
HR 139, 37-2, v4, 2p. [1145]
Depredations of 1860, in Utah, by the Go-shute Indians.

50. Relations Between the U.S. and Northwest British America. 11 July.
HED 146, 37-2, v10, 85p. [1138]
British-Indian trade; Indians residing in the area discussed.

51. An Act for the Construction of the Union Pacific Railroad. 14 July.

SMD 108, 37-2, v1, 12p. [1124]
The U.S. will extinguish Indian title to land which lies along this route as quickly as possible.

52. Statements of Appropriations. 21 Aug.
HMD 91, 37-2, v1, 78p. [1141]
During the 2d session, 37th Congress; Indian expenses.

53. Annual Message to Congress with Documents; Pres. Lincoln. 1 Dec.
HED 1, 37-3, v1-4, 2775p. [1156-1159]
Indian treaties with the Confederacy; Sioux uprising in Minnesota; annual report of the Sec. of War (Serial 1159); annual report of the Sec. of Interior (Serial 1157); annual report of the Gen. Land Office (Serial 1157); annual report of the CIA (Serial 1157), including removal of Indians from Kansas, Indian populations, and reports of Supts., agents, and schools; etc.

54. Estimates of Appropriations. 1 Dec.
HED 2, 37-3, v4, 242p. [1159]
Year ending 30 June 1864; Indian expenses.

55. Annual Report of the Sec. of the Treasury. 5 Dec.
SED 1, 37-3, v1, 275p. [1149]
Year ending 30 June 1862; Indian expenses.

56. Message on Indian Barbarities in Minnesota. 11 Dec.
SED 7, 37-3, v1, 9p. [1149]
Sioux outbreak; Pres. sentences 39 to death after reviewing the evidence, and receiving protests against pardoning the Indians.

57. Letter on Miami Indian Annuities. 22 Dec.
HED 18, 37-3, v4, 2p. [1159]
Certain annuities due under the treaty of 5 June 1854 have not been paid.

58. Letter on Sums Due Indians. 23 Dec.
HED 19, 37-3, v4, 9p. [1159]
Chippewas, Ottawas, and Pottawatomies residing in Michigan; treaties of 29 July 1829, 26 Sept. 1833, and 27 Sept. 1833 (supplementary articles); Pottawatomie treaties of 26 Oct. 1832, 5 June 1846, and 19 June 1846.

59. Appropriations and Balances of the Interior Dept. 23 Dec.
HED 20, 37-3, v4, 15p. [1159]
Year ending 30 June 1862; Indian expenses.

1863

1. R-M of R. Chenery. 6 Jan.
HR 3, 37-3, v1, 2p. [1173]
Supplies furnished to California Indians in 1852.

2. Report and Journal of an Expedition to Oregon. 9 Jan.
SED 17, 37-3, v1, 14p. [1149]
Organized to escort and protect emigrants to the Pacific coast region; Indian depredations; aids Sioux Indian agent in recovering a Sioux woman from the Pawnees; Sioux, Pawnee, and Bannock country; gifts to friendly Sioux, Cayuses, Diggers, and Pawnees.

3. Subsisting Indian Tribes. 14 Jan.
HED 30, 37-3, v5, 3p. [1161]
For the Utah Indians, and other Indians of the Great Basin; special agents needed for the Chippewas and the Upper Missouri Indians.

4. On the Case of J. Beck. 16 Jan.
SR 76, 37-3, v1, 4p. [1151]
Navajo depredations of 1849 in New Mexico.

5. Letter on the Ottawa Indians of Kansas. 16 Jan.
HED 34, 37-3, v5, 9p. [1161]
Sums due these Indians under the treaty of 24 June 1862.

6. Report on Miami Indian Annuities. 20 Jan.
HR 10, 37-3, v1, 1p. [1173]
Money due under the treaty of 5 June 1854 not paid; sum reappropriated.

7. Unexpected Funds for the Indian Service. 22 Jan.
HED 39, 37-3, v5, 3p. [1161]
In Oregon and Washington; outstanding liabilities.

8. R-C of G. Johnson. 23 Jan.
HR 12, 37-3, v1, 2p. [1173]
Seizure of land by U.S. troops during Indian war in Washington Territory.

9. Mem. of the Wyandott Indians. 24 Jan.
SMD 15, 37-3, v1, 3p. [1150]
Wyandotts of Kansas ask indemni-

nification for losses sustained at the hands of white settlers; forced to move to Seneca country; treaty of 31 Jan. 1855.

10. Petition of the Wyandott Indians. 24 Jan.
SMD 16, 37-3, v1, 5p. [1150]
Tribe is denationalizing itself; appeals one last time for funds due under the treaty of 31 Jan. 1855.

11. Report on Indian Removal. 26 Jan.
HR 13, 37-3, v1, 4p. [1173]
Removal of all Indians from Minnesota asked; recommends removal of Sioux and Winnebagoes; inexpedient to remove Chippewas.

12. Letter on Accounts. 28 Jan.
HED 47, 37-3, v5, 81p. [1161]
Of the Supt. of Indian Affairs for the Southern Superintendency; disbursements.

13. Report on Amounts Due Michigan Indians. 29 Jan.
HR 18, 37-3, v1, 2p. [1173]
Pottawatomie, Ottawa, and Chippewa treaty stipulations; treaties of 29 July 1829, 26 Sept. 1833, and 27 Sept. 1833 (supplemental); Pottawatomie treaties of 26 Oct. 1832, 5 June 1846, and 19 June 1846.

14. Letter on Indian Reservations in California. 3 Feb.
HED 49, 37-3, v5, 3p. [1161]
Survey and sale of the Mendocino and Nome Lacke reservations; enlargement of the Round Valley reserve.

15. Estimates for the Indian Service. 5 Feb.
HED 50, 37-3, v5, 2p. [1161]
For the northern district of California.

16. Letter on Survey and Sale of Indian Reservations. 5 Feb.
HED 51, 37-3, v5, 2p. [1161]
The Mendocino and Nome Lacke reserves in California; enlargement of the Round Valley reserve.

17. Letter on Indian Goods Lost. 7 Feb.
HED 56, 37-3, v6, 4p. [1162]
Goods bound for the Yancton Sioux lost with the sinking of the steamer *J. G. Morrow*.

18. R-P of M. Stevens. 9 Feb.
HR 34, 37-3, v1, 2p. [1173]
Indian wars and treaties in Washington Territory; Nez Percé, Flathead and Blackfoot Indian treaties.

19. R-P of E. Baxter. 10 Feb.
SR 86, 37-3, v1, 1p. [1151]
Minnesota volunteers in the Sioux outbreak of 1862.

20. Letter on the Condition of the Munsee and Stockbridge Indians. 10 Feb.
HED 61, 37-3, v6, 4p. [1162]
Dissatisfaction of said Indians with their reservation in Wisconsin.

21. L-C of A. Jones and H. Browne. 10 Feb.
HED 62, 37-3, v6, 9p. [1162]
For surveys of the Chickasaw-Choctaw, Creek-Seminole, and Cherokee boundaries.

22. R-M of G. Johnson. 13 Feb.
HR 35, 37-3, v1, 3p. [1173]
Indian trader among the Shawnees of Ohio during 1819-1831; money due him by said tribe.

23. Disbursements to the Indians. 14 Feb.
SED 39, 37-3, v1, 217p. [1149]
Year ending 30 June 1862.

24. Message on Indian Hostilities. 16 Feb.
HED 68, 37-3, v7, 41p. [1163]
Outbreak of hostilities among the Sioux, Chippewa, and other Indian tribes; the Sioux war.

25. Employees of the Interior Dept. 18 Feb.
HED 69, 37-3, v7, 7p. [1163]
During 1862; office of the CIA.

26. Report on a Military Road from Fort Walla-Walla to Fort Benton. 19 Feb.
SED 43, 37-3, v1, 363p. [1149]
Exploring expedition and road construction from the Missouri to the Columbia River; encounters with the Indians of Oregon and Washington, Missouri region, and the Rocky Mountains.

27. R-P of M. Stevens. 19 Feb.
SR 98, 37-3, v1, 1p. [1151]
Indian wars and treaties in Washington territory.

28. Letter on Salaries of Indian Agents. 21 Feb.
HED 74, 37-3, v7, 2p. [1163]
On raising the salaries of two agents in Nevada and Utah to $1500 *per annum.*

29. Mem. of the New Mexico Legis. 25 Feb.
SMD 34, 37-3, v1, 1p. [1150]
Ask funds to be used to release captive Indians, and return them to their respective tribes.

30. Letter on Indian Accounts. 26 Feb.
HED 75, 37-3, v7, 116p. [1163]
Accounts of the Supt. of the South-

ern Superintendency for the Cherokee, Creek, Choctaw, and other Indian tribes.

31. Contingent Expenses of the Interior Dept. 26 Feb.
HED 76, 37-3, v7, 91p. [1163]
Year ending 30 June 1862; Indian expenses.

32. Mem. of the Minnesota Legis. 27 Feb.
HMD 23, 37-3, v1, 2p. [1171]
Ask extension of pension laws to cover those injured in the late Indian raid in that state.

33. Annual Report of the Smithsonian Institution. 27 Feb.
HMD 25, 37-3, v2, 446p. [1172]
Research related to the American Indian; North American archaeology; etc.

34. Message of the Governor of Utah. 28 Feb.
SMD 37, 37-3, v1, 16p. [1150]
Indian depredations upon emigrants; treaty negotiations; extinguishment of Indian title to land.

35. Expedition from Fort Abercrombie to Fort Benton. 2 Mar.
HED 80, 37-3, v8, 36p. [1164]
Escort and protection of emigrants through Dakota Territory; encounters with northern Plains Indians; Sioux troubles; journal of the expedition.

36. Report on Suppression of Indian Hostilities. 3 Mar.
HR 52, 37-3, v1, 3p. [1173]
Pension to volunteers in New Mexico; Navajo campaign.

37. Report on Land Patents in the Fort Leavenworth Military Reserve. 3 Mar.
HR 56, 37-3, v1, 90p. [1173]
Claims of Delaware Indians to lands within said reserve under treaty stipulations.

38. R-P of G. Chorpenning. 3 Mar.
HR 61, 37-3, v1, 4p. [1173]
Indian depredations of 1851 in Utah.

39. Report on the Accounts of B. Young. 3 Mar.
HR 62, 37-3, v1, 2p. [1173]
Ex officio Supt. of Indian Affairs in Utah.

40. Expedition from Arizona to the Gulf of California. 14 Mar.
SED 1, 38-sp, v1, 22p. [1174]
Survey of supply routes to Arizona; Apache hostilities in the region are noted.

41. Statement of Appropriations. 25 May.
HMD 27, 37-3, v1, 79p. [1171]
During the 3rd session, 37th Congress; Indian expenses.

42. Estimates of Appropriations. 7 Dec.
HED 2, 38-1, v6, 260p. [1186]
Year ending 30 June 1865; Indian expenses.

43. Annual Message to Congress with Documents; Pres. Lincoln. 8 Dec.
HED 1, 38-1, v1-5, 4108p. [1180-1184]
Extinguishment of Indian title to valuable lands; civilization of Indians as wards of the government; annual report of the Sec. of War (Serial 1184); annual report of the Sec. of Interior (Serial 1182); annual report of the Gen. Land Office (Serial 1182); annual report of the CIA (Serial 1182), including conditions in Arizona, conditions in Utah, trust funds, J. Doty's expedition to northern Indians, populations, treaties with the Chippewas, and reports of Supts., agents, and schools; etc.

44. Annual Report of the Sec. of the Treasury. 10 Dec.
HED 3, 38-1, v6, 241p. [1186]
Year ending 30 June 1863; Indian expenses.

45. Receipts and Expenditures. 14 Dec.
HED 8, 38-1, v7, 409p. [1187]
Year ending 30 June 1862; Indian expenses.

46. Resol. of the California Legis. 16 Dec.
HMD 9, 38-1, v1, 1p. [1198]
Ask settlement of accounts outstanding for supplies furnished to California Indians.

1864

1. The Eighth Census. 1 Jan.
HMD (no number), 38-1, v1, 694p. [1202]
Populations of Indian tribes; Indian slavery.

2. R-M of N. McLean et al. 22 Jan.
HR 7, 38-1, v1, 1p. [1206]
Sioux agents during 1849-1857 in Minnesota.

3. Message on Correspondence with Great Britain. 1 Feb.
SED 13, 38-1, v1, 3p. [1176]
Relative to pursuit of hostile Sioux into Hudson's Bay territories.
4. R-M of M. Stevens. 1 Feb.
HR 11, 38-1, v1, 1p. [1206]
Flathead, Blackfeet, and Nez Percé treaties in Washington Territory, other Indian treaties and land cessions.
5. Contingent Expenses of the Interior Dept. 8 Feb.
HED 34, 38-1, v9, 67p. [1189]
Year ending 30 June 1863; Indian Office.
6. Employees of the Interior Dept. 8 Feb.
HED 35, 38-1, v9, 13p. [1189]
During 1863; Indian Office.
7. Resol. of the California Legis. 9 Feb.
HMD 29, 38-1, v3, 2p. [1200]
Ask that, due to continuing depredations, Indians should be gathered together on a far distant reservation.
8. Letter on Indian Affairs in New Mexico. 12 Feb.
HED 38, 38-1, v9, 4p. [1189]
Appropriations needed for the Indian service; Navajo supplies; farming equipment; Apache settlement.
9. Mem. of the Minnesota Legis. 19 Feb.
SMD 36, 38-1, v1, 1p. [1177]
Construction of a line of posts from Fort Abercrombie to Bannock City, Idaho Territory; control of Sioux hostilities.
10. Mem. of the Minnesota Legis. 19 Feb.
SMD 37, 38-1, v1, 2p. [1177]
Ask payment for damages sustained in the Sioux war of 1862.
11. R-C of the Michigan Indians. 19 Feb.
HR 19, 38-1, v1, 3p. [1206]
Amounts due the Chippewas, Ottawas, and Pottawatomies under treaties from 1795 to 1846; removal and land cessions.
12. On the Case of B. Young. 19 Feb.
HR 21, 38-1, v1, 2p. [1206]
Accounts of the *ex officio* Supt. of Indian Affairs in Utah.
13. Resol. of the Kansas Legis. 24 Feb.
SMD 42, 38-1, v1, 1p. [1177]
Ask removal from state of all Indians residing therein.
14. Mem. of the Minnesota Legis. 25 Feb.
SMD 41, 38-1, v1, 1p. [1177]
Mail route from Chippewa Agency to Lake Superior.
15. Resol. of the Kansas Legis. 25 Feb.
SMD 43, 38-1, v1, 1p. [1177] *or*
HMD 31, 38-1, v3, 1p. [1200]
Protests sale of public land for the benefit of Indians rather than for the benefit of educational interests.
16. Resol. of the Kansas Legis. 26 Feb.
SMD 44, 38-1, v1, 1p. [1177]
Ask treaties be made with Indians requiring the cession of their lands, and their removal from the state.
17. Appropriations and Balances of the Interior Dept. 1 Mar.
SED 22, 38-1, v1, 14p. [1176]
Year ending 30 June 1863; Indian expenses.
18. Capt. Fisk's Expedition to the Rocky Mountains. 3 Mar.
HED 45, 38-1, v9, 39p. [1189]
Protection of emigrants from Minnesota to Idaho; Sioux troubles; journal of travels; encounters with Chippewas, Sioux, Gros Ventres, Assiniboines, and Blackfeet; council with the Assiniboines; meeting with Pend d'Oreilles; etc.
19. Mem. of the Minnesota Legis. 4 Mar.
SMD 53, 38-1, v1, 1p. [1177]
Ask pension laws be extended to those who served in the Sioux war of 1862.
20. Mem. of the Minnesota Legis. 4 Mar.
SMD 54, 38-1, v1, 2p. [1177]
Mail route from Minnesota to Oregon and Washington; would need protection from hostile Sioux.
21. Letter on Pre-Emptors on the Winnebago Reservation. 9 Mar.
HED 50, 38-1, v9, 66p. [1189]
Relief for said individuals on Winnebago land in southern Minnesota.
22. Message on Proceeds from Sale of Land. 14 Mar.
SED 28, 38-1, v1, 3p. [1176]
Sale of Wea trust lands in Kansas; trust funds of the Weas, Peorias, Piankeshaws, and Kaskaskias.
23. Letter on the Quapaw Indians. 15 Mar.
HED 57, 38-1, v9, 13p. [1189]
Amounts due under the treaties of 1818, 1824, and 1833; funds for their removal from Kansas, where they are refugees in consequence of the rebellion.
24. Letter on Sioux Depredation Claims. 15 Mar.
HED 58, 38-1, v9, 23p. [1189]
For claims arising as a result of

the Sioux outbreak of 1862 in Minnesota.

25. Mem. of the Milwaukee Chamber of Commerce. 17 Mar.
SMD 72, 38-1, v1, 2p. [1177]
Wagon road from Wisconsin to Idaho; protection from hostile Indians.

26. Petition of the Wea, Peoria, Kaskaskia, and Piankeshaw Indians. 17 Mar.
SMD 73, 38-1, v1, 2p. [1177]
Ask money due for sale of land in Kansas under the treaty of 30 May 1854.

27. Report on the "Hopkins Battery." 18 Mar.
SR 32, 38-1, v1, 1p. [1178]
Captured at the battle of Fort Wayne on 22 Oct. 1862 in the Cherokee Nation.

28. Report on Sales of Public Lands. 24 Mar.
SR 33, 38-1, v1, 2p. [1178]
Proceeds of sales going to Indians rather than education in Kansas.

29. Report on the Quapaw Indians. 28 Mar.
SR 37, 38-1, v1, 3p. [1178]
Amounts due under various treaties; Com. on Indian Affairs instructs the CIA not to open such cases again unless instructed to do so by Congress.

30. On the Relief of N. McLean et al. 28 Mar.
SR 38, 38-1, v1, 1p. [1178]
Indian agents for the Sioux of Minnesota during 1849-1857.

31. Resol. of the California Legis. 31 Mar.
SMD 88, 38-1, v1, 1p. [1177] *or*
HMD 67, 38-1, v3, 1p. [1200]
Ask that lands in the Nome Lacke Indian reservation be sold.

32. Report on Sioux Depredation Claims. 4 Apr.
HR 42, 38-1, v1, 13p. [1206]
As a result of the Sioux raid of 1862 in Minnesota; Sioux treaties of 29 Sept. 1837, 23 July 1851, 5 Aug. 1851, and 19 June 1858.

33. Appropriations for the Navajo Indians. 5 Apr.
HED 65, 38-1, v13, 2p. [1193]
For subsistence on the Bosque Redondo reserve in New Mexico.

34. Mem. of the Wisconsin Legis. 8 Apr.
SMD 96, 38-1, v1, 2p. [1177]
Ask sale of lands ceded by the Stockbridge Indians, and for issuance of land patents to purchasers of said land.

35. Letter on Subsistence for the Navajo Indians. 11 Apr.
SMD 97, 38-1, v1, 3p. [1177]
Said Indians will be collected together on a reservation at Bosque Redondo, New Mexico; will hopefully bring hostilities to a close.

36. Mem. of the New Mexico Legis. 11 Apr.
HMD 68, 38-1, v3, 2p. [1200]
Ask funds to defray the costs of suppressing the depredations of Navajo and other Indian tribes.

37. Mem. of the New Mexico Legis. 11 Apr.
HMD 72, 38-1, v3, 2p. [1200]
Road from Santa Fé to the Taos valley; Navajo depredations upon grain shipments.

38. R-P of P. Navarre. 11 Apr.
HR 54, 38-1, v1, 1p. [1206]
British and Indians; 1812; Michigan.

39. R-M of L. Roberts. 14 Apr.
SR 49, 38-1, v1, 2p. [1178]
Supplies being transported to the Sioux of Minnesota in 1855 are burned in a prairie fire.

40. Letter on an Appropriation for Indian Removal. 14 Apr.
HED 72, 38-1, v13, 3p. [1193]
Removal of the Sioux and Winnebagoes from Minnesota to Dakota.

41. Letter on Subsistence for the Navajo Indians. 18 Apr.
SED 36, 38-1, v1, 12p. [1176] *or*
HED 70, 38-1, v13, 11p. [1193]
Funds to provide supplies for Navajo prisoners of war on a reservation at Bosque Redondo in New Mexico.

42. Appropriations for Indian Tribes. 19 Apr.
HED 73, 38-1, v13, 2p. [1193]
Appointment of an agent for the Kiowa, Apache, and Comanche Indians; at present they are under the charge of the Cheyenne-Arapaho agent.

43. Letter on an Indian Agent's Salary. 21 Apr.
SED 38, 38-1, v1, 2p. [1176] *or*
HED 71, 38-1, v13, 2p. [1193]
Increase in salary from $1000 to $1500 *per annum* for the agent at Green Bay, Wisconsin; Oneida, Menomonee, Stockbridge, and Munsee Indians.

44. Estimates for an Indian Treaty. 27 Apr.
HED 76, 38-1, v15, 4p. [1195]
Treaty of 11 Mar. 1863 with the Chippewas of the Mississippi,

and the Lake Winnebagoshish and Pillager bands of Chippewas.

45. Letter on the New York Indians. 28 Apr.
HED 78, 38-1, v15, 3p. [1195]
Sums due under the treaty of 15 Jan. 1838.

46. Message on the Condition of Nevada Territory. 2 May.
SED 41, 38-1, v1, 3p. [1176]
Indians have been quiet and peaceable.

47. R-M of L. Roberts. 2 May.
HR 64, 38-1, v1, 2p. [1206]
Goods bound for the Sioux of Minnesota lost in a prairie fire in 1855.

48. R-P of M. Wacoutah et al. 5 May.
SR 62, 38-1, v1, 2p. [1178]
Lands due Sioux half-breeds under the treaty of 15 July 1830 at Prairie du Chien.

49. R-M of the Minnesota Legis. 7 May.
SR 64, 38-1, v1, 1p. [1178]
Pensions to volunteers, etc., in the Sioux raid of 1862 not recommended.

50. Report on an Appropriation for the New York Indians. 9 May.
SR 66, 38-1, v1, 1p. [1178]
Removal of the Orchard and First Christian parties to Indian territory.

51. Appropriations for Chippewa Indians. 9 May.
HED 81, 38-1, v15, 3p. [1195]
Under the treaty of 1 Oct. 1863, amended 1 Mar. 1864, and the supplementary treaty of 12 Apr. 1864 with the Red Lake Chippewas, and the Pembina band of Chippewas.

52. Receipts and Expenditures. 10 May.
HED 84, 38-1, v15, 345p. [1195]
Year ending 30 June 1863; Indian expenses.

53. Letter on Sale of Stockbridge Indian Lands. 12 May.
SMD 115, 38-1, v1, 4p. [1177]
Issuance of patents to purchasers of said land in Wisconsin; treaty of 5 Feb. 1856 with the Stockbridges and Munsees.

54. R-M of Hooper and Williams et al. 13 May.
HR 77, 38-1, v1, 4p. [1206]
Indian depredations in Utah during 1855-1856.

55. R-P of T. Kirby. 13 May.
HR 85, 38-1, v1, 1p. [1206]
Indian battles on the Indiana and Illinois frontiers.

56. Message on Refugee Indians in Kansas. 16 May.
SED 44, 38-1, v1, 4p. [1176]
They have not been returned to their homes because rebels and hostile Indians still roam that area.

57. Appropriations for Various Indian Tribes. 16 May.
HED 86, 38-1, v15, 3p. [1195]
Treaty of 2 July 1863 with the eastern bands of Shoshonees; treaty of 30 July 1863 with the western bands of Shoshonees; treaty of 12 Oct. 1863 with the Goship bands of Shoshonees; treaty of 3 Sept. 1863 with the Creeks.

58. Appropriation for the Indian Service. 16 May.
HED 87, 38-1, v15, 2p. [1195]
In Dakota Territory.

59. Letter on Indians in Kansas. 23 May.
SMD 117, 38-1, v1, 1p. [1177]
Subsistence for the Wea, Peoria, Kaskaskia, and Pinakeshaw Indians.

60. Report on Refugee Indians. 23 May.
HED 90, 38-1, v15, 1p. [1195]
On subsisting, clothing, and transporting said Indians.

61. R-P of A. Campbell. 31 May.
SR 76, 38-1, v1, 2p. [1178]
Sum due the interpreter who accompanied the Sioux delegation which signed the treaty of 28 Sept. 1837; under article 2, clause 9 of said treaty.

62. R-M of W. Sawyer et al. 3 June.
HR 105, 38-1, v1, 2p. [1206]
Land grants in Ohio under the treaty of 6 Oct. 1818 with the Miami Indians.

63. On the Relief of W. Brindle. 7 June.
SR 78, 38-1, v1, 3p. [1178]
Sold Indian trust lands in Kansas; Wea, Peoria, Kaskasia, Piankeshaw, and Delaware lands.

64. Appropriations for Indian Tribes. 7 June.
HED 96, 38-1, v15, 2p. [1195]
Treaties of 30 May 1854, and 18 Aug. 1860 with the Weas, Peorias, Kaskaskias, and Piankeshaws.

65. Petition of T. Galbraith. 16 June.
SMD 125, 38-1, v1, 2p. [1177]
Sioux agents asks relief from responsibility for goods destroyed at the agency during the Sioux outbreak of 1862.

66. Letter on a Proposed Treaty. 20 June.
SMD 127, 38-1, v1, 2p. [1177]
Proposed treaty would revoke the right of Indians to fish on all streams in middle Oregon (granted under the treaty of 9 June 1855); liquor abuse.

67. Report on Mexican Volunteers. 21 June.
HR 120, 38-1, v2, 1p. [1207]
Serving for the U.S. against Indians in New Mexico.

68. Petition of Miami Indians. 23 June.
SMD 130, 38-1, v1, 5p. [1177]
Money due under the treaty of 5 June 1854; Western Miamies and Indiana Miamies divide the sum.

69. Letter on Indians in Kansas. 24 June.
SMD 133, 38-1, v1, 5p. [1177]
Accounts current between the U.S. and the Weas, Peorias, Kaskaskias, and Piankeshaws.

70. R-P of G. Chorpenning et al. 27 June.
HR 139, 38-1, v2, 3p. [1207]
Indian hostilities in Utah from 1851 to 1862.

71. Annual Report of the Smithsonian Institution. 28 June.
HMD 83, 38-1, v4, 416p. [1201]
Research related to the American Indian; North American archaeology; aboriginal inhabitants of the Californian peninsula.

72. R-P of R. Murphy. 1 July.
SR 101, 38-1, v1, 2p. [1178]
Sioux agent's accounts not closed.

73. R-M of R. Harrison. 1 July.
SR 102, 38-1, v1, 1p. [1178]
Seminole war of 1838 in Florida.

74. L-C of Michigan Indians. 2 July.
SMD 136, 38-1, v1, 4p. [1177]
Sums due the Pottawatomies and other tribes under treaties dated 1795 to 1846.

75. Statements of Appropriations. 5 Oct.
HMD 85, 38-1, v3, 103p. [1200]
During the 1st session, 38th Congress; Indian expenses.

76. Annual Message to Congress with Documents; Pres. Lincoln. 6 Dec.
HED 1, 38-2, v1-6, 5006p. [1216-1221]
Remodelling of the Indian system of the government; Indian hostilities in Idaho and Montana; annual report of the Sec. of Interior (Serial 1220); annual report of the Gen. Land Office (Serial 1220); annual report of the CIA (Serial 1220), including statements of trust funds, education, and reports of Supts., agents, and schools; etc.

77. Estimates of Appropriations. 6 Dec.
HED 2, 38-2, v7, 223p. [1222]
Year ending 30 June 1866; Indian expenses.

78. Annual Report of the Sec. of the Treasury. 6 Dec.
HED 3, 38-2, v7, 350p. [1222]
Year ending 30 June 1864; Indian expenses.

1865

1. Report on the Disposition of Indian Lands. 6 Jan.
SED 4, 38-2, v1, 3p. [1209]
Sale of Sac and Fox lands in Kansas under the treaty of 1 Oct. 1859.

2. Balances and Appropriations of the Interior Dept. 16 Jan.
HED 23, 38-2, v8, 11p. [1223]
Year ending 30 June 1864; Indian expenses.

3. Mining Laws of Arizona Territory. 25 Jan.
HMD 14, 38-2, v1, 12p. [1232]
Sections 30 and 32 of the law deal with the effects of Indian hostilities on claims.

4. Mem. of the Arizona Legis. 25 Jan.
HMD 16, 38-2, v1, 2p. [1232]
Ask funds to place the Yavapai, Mojave, Yuma, and Hualipai Indians on a reservation in that territory.

5. Mem. of the Arizona Legis. 25 Jan.
HMD 18, 38-2, v1, 1p. [1232]
Ask funds to aid in the war against the Apache Indians.

6. Resol. of the Arizona Legis. 25 Jan.
HMD 19, 38-2, v1, 1p. [1232]
Request arms for service against the Apaches and other hostile tribes.

7. Resol. of the Kansas Legis. 30 Jan.
SMD 16, 38-2, v1, 1p. [1210]

Ask military force to control Indian hostilities on the state's frontier, and to protect overland mail.

8. Report on Michigan Indians. 1 Feb.
SR 111, 38-2, v1, 5p. [1211]
Chippewa, Ottawa, and Pottawatomie Indians who remained in Michigan after the majority of the United Nation was removed (under the treaty of 1833) have a right to certain annuities.

9. Letter on Medals for Indian Chiefs. 2 Feb.
HED 47, 38-2, v8, 1p. [1223]
Asks appropriation of $5000 for medals distributed to leading and influential chiefs.

10. Letter on Goods Purchased for Indians. 2 Feb.
HED 48, 38-2, v8, 2p. [1223]
For the Sioux (at Usher's Landing), Winnebagoes, and Yancton Sioux; original goods destroyed by fire.

11. Resol. of the Kansas Legis. 6 Feb.
SMD 25, 38-2, v1, 2p. [1210]
On extinguishment of Cherokee title to land in said state, and the granting of this land for the construction of a railroad.

12. Letter on Indian Claims. 7 Feb.
HED 52, 38-2, v13, 5p. [1229]
Claims against the Rogue River Indians occasioned by the war of 1853; treaty of 10 Sept. 1853 provides for payment of said claims.

13. Purchases Made for Indians in Arizona. 10 Feb.
HED 57, 38-2, v13, 3p. [1229]
Subsistence for said Indians during 1864; supplies for Pimas and Maricopas who were engaged by the U.S. in the campaign against the Apaches.

14. Annuities of the Chippewas of Lake Superior. 10 Feb.
HED 58, 38-2, v13, 2p. [1229]
Under the treaties of 1842 and 1854; they refuse to accept payments in currency, insisting, rather, on coin.

15. Estimates for Indians of the Southern Superintendency. 10 Feb.
HED 62, 38-2, v13, 5p. [1229]
To subsist refugee Indians returned to their homes from Kansas; to promote peace with the Choctaws, Chickasaws, and Seminoles.

16. R-P of S. Norris. 10 Feb.
HR 11, 38-2, v1, 2p. [1235]
Supplies furnished to California Indians during the 1851 treaty negotiations.

17. Resol. of the Minnesota Legis. 11 Feb.
SMD 30, 38-2, v1, 2p. [1210]
Additional relief for sufferers in the Sioux war of 1862.

18. Resol. of the Nebraska Legis. 13 Feb.
SMD 31, 38-2, v1, 4p. [1210]
Payment of the militia for services in an Indian campaign of 1864, in which portions of the Sioux, Cheyennes, Kiowas, Comanches, and Arapahoes confederated to attack frontier settlements.

19. Employees of the Interior Dept. 13 Feb.
HED 65, 38-2, v13, 11p. [1229]
During 1864; Indian Office.

20. R-P of C. Taylor. 17 Feb.
SR 124, 38-2, v1, 2p. [1211]
Supplies advanced to the U.S. during the Black Hawk war of 1832.

21. Report on Conduct of the War. 20 Feb.
SR 142, 38-2, v2-4, 2318p. [1212-1214]
Volume 3 (Serial 1214) contains testimony concerning the massacre of over 100 Cheyenne and Arapahoe Indians at Sand Creek, Colorado Territory, by U.S. troops under Col. Chivington and Maj. Anthony.

22. Appropriations of Certain Indians. 20 Feb.
HED 70, 38-2, v13, 6p. [1229]
To fulfill stipulations of the treaty of 7 May 1864 with the Chippewa of the Mississippi, and the Pillager and Lake Winnebagoshish bands of Chippewas of Minnesota.

23. Mem. of Cherokee Indians. 21 Feb.
HMD 52, 38-2, v1, 3p. [1232]
Loyal Cherokees, driven from their homes by rebels, ask relief; treaties of 28 Nov. 1785, 2 July 1791, 1835, and 1846.

24. R-P of W. Nicholls. 22 Feb.
SR 131, 38-2, v1, 2p. [1211]
Spy during the War of 1812; British and Indian forces.

25. Deficiencies of Appropriations for Certain Indians. 22 Feb.
HED 71, 38-2, v13, 2p. [1229]
Estimates to supply deficiencies for the Chippewas of Pembina and Red Lake under the treaty of 2 Oct. 1863.

26. Indian Trust Bonds. 23 Feb.
HED 72, 38-2, v13, 2p. [1229]
Payment by West Virginia of interest due Indian tribes holding bonds of the State of Virginia.
27. Receipts and Expenditures. 23 Feb.
HED 73, 38-2, v13, 379p. [1229]
Year ending 30 June 1864; Indian expenses.
28. Letter on an Appropriation to Carry Into Effect an Indian Treaty. 24 Feb.
SED 25, 38-2, v1, 2p. [1209]
Treaty of 29 Aug. 1863 (and Senate amendments of 2 July 1864) with the Great and Little Osages of Kansas.
29. Mem. of the Missouri Legis. 25 Feb.
SMD 44, 38-2, v1, 2p. [1210] *or*
HMD 40, 38-2, v1, 2p. [1232]
Establishment of a fort in the southwest corner of that state; rebel incursions into the state through Cherokee, Seneca, Shawnee, and Chippewa country.
30. Payments to Indian Tribes. 25 Feb.
HED 74, 38-2, v13, 1p. [1229]
Balance due the confederated tribes of the Weas, Kaskaskias, Peorias, and Piankeshaws for sale of trust lands.
31. Report on British Policy Towards Indians. 1 Mar.
SR 138, 38-2, v1, 16p. [1211]
Information to be used in reshaping U.S. Indian policy; British reliance on the Hudson's Bay Company to administer Indian affairs; etc.
32. Annual Report of the Smithsonian Institution. 1 Mar.
HMD 55, 38-2, v2, 450p. [1233]
Research related to the American Indian; aboriginal inhabitants of the California peninsula; explorations of upper California and western Missouri; etc.
33. Annual Report of the Sec. of War. 2 Mar.
HED 83, 38-2, v14, 235p. [1230]
During 1864.
34. Protest of the Cherokee Nation. 2 Mar.
HMD 56, 38-2, v1, 4p. [1232]
Against a bill to consolidate Indian tribes and to establish civil government in Indian Territory.
35. Statements of Appropriations. 5 July.
HMD 58, 38-2, v1, 102p. [1232]
During the 2d session, 38th Congress; Indian expenses.
36. Annual Message to Congress with Documents; Pres. Johnson. 4 Dec.
HED 1, 39-1, v1-6, 6827p. [1244-1254]
Annual report of the Sec. of War (Serials 1249-1252); annual report of the Sec. of Interior (Serial 1248); annual report of the Gen. Land Office (Serial 1248); annual report of the CIA (Serial 1248), including trust lands, trust funds, populations, council proceedings with the Arapahoes, Cheyennes, Apaches, Kiowas, and Comanches, and reports of Supts., agents, and schools; etc.
37. Estimates of Appropriations. 4 Dec.
HED 2, 39-1, v6, 271p. [1254]
Year ending 30 June 1867; Indian expenes.
38. Annual Report of the Sec. of the Treasury. 5 Dec.
HED 3, 39-1, v6, 342p. [1254]
Year ending 30 June 1865; Indian expenses.
39. Resol. of Sen. Pomeroy. 6 Dec.
SMD 7, 39-1, v1, 1p. [1239]
The government should stop being conciliatory towards Indians committing hostilities on the western frontier; the Indians should be whipped into submission.

1866

1. Mem. of the Dakota Legis. 8 Jan.
HMD 13, 39-1, v2, 1p. [1270]
Mail route from Fort Sully to Fort Randall; Minnesota Sioux Indian Agency.
2. Mem. of the Dakota Legis. 8 Jan.
HMD 16, 39-1, v2, 3p. [1270]
Ask for a survey of the Black Hills; Indian hostilities have prevented this to date.
3. Petition of R. McKee. 15 Jan.
SMD 37, 39-1, v1, 4p. [1239]
Asks indemnification for expenses incurred while disbursing agent for the California Indian treaty commission of 1851-1853.
4. Resol. of the Missouri Legis. 31 Jan.
SMD 46, 39-1, v1, 2p. [1239]
Land grants for a railroad from Kansas City to Galveston, Texas; through Indian Territory.

5. Communication on the Winnebago Reservation. 8 Feb.
SMD 51, 39-1, v1, 5p. [1239]
Said Indians from Minnesota after the Sioux uprising of 1862; at first removed to an unsuitable location in Dakota Territory; removed, then, to Nebraska, where they purchased a reserve from the Omahas, at their own expense.
6. Resol. of the Kansas Legis. 8 Feb.
SMD 52, 39-1, v1, 1p. [1239]
Lands meant for the benefit of schools located in Indian reservations.
7. Resol. of the Kansas Legis. 13 Feb.
SMD 55, 39-1, v1, 1p. [1239]
Request for land grant to be given to the Leavenworth, Lawrence, and Fort Gibson Railroad referred to the Com. on Indian Affairs.
8. Petition of S. Goodale. 19 Feb.
SMD 59, 39-1, v1, 3p. [1239]
Construction of a railroad (the Leavenworth, Lawrence, and Fort Gibson line) through Indian Territory; will pass through Creek, Cherokee, and Choctaw country.
9. Resol. of the Kansas Legis. 19 Feb.
SMD 60, 39-1, v1, 1p. [1236]
Ask grant of certain Cherokee lands for the support of schools.
10. Exploration of the Route for a Wagon Road. 5 Mar.
HED 58, 39-1, v8, 32p. [1256]
From western Minnesota to Montana; journal of the expedition; encounters with Sioux and Cheyennes.
11. Mem. of the Iowa Legis. 22 Mar.
HMD 74, 39-1, v3, 2p. [1271]
Aid for the Iowa branch of the Union Pacific Railroad; as a frontier state, it has had to expend resources to control Indian hostilities.
12. Report on the Miami Indians of Indiana. 27 Mar.
HR 42, 39-1, v1, 3p. [1272]
Examination of those who constitute said tribe.
13. Disbursements for the Southern Superintendency. 18 Apr.
HED 91, 39-1, v12, 73p. [1263]
Accounts of the Indian service for the 4th quarter of 1865.
14. Resol. of the Texas Convention. 18 Apr.
HMD 88, 39-1, v3, 2p. [1271]
Construction of a southern branch of the Union Pacific railroad through Indian territory.
15. R-P of C. Crowley. 19 Apr.
SR 69, 39-1, v1, 1p. [1240]
Indian war in Florida.
16. R-P of G. Chorpenning. 27 Apr.
HR 55, 39-1, v1, 4p. [1272]
Indian depredations of 1852-1856 in Utah.
17. Letter on the Indian Service. 7 May.
HED 101, 39-1, v12, 2p. [1263]
On a House Resol. requesting a statement of accounts for the Indian service.
18. Annual Report of the Smithsonian Institution. 7 May.
HED 102, 39-1, v14, 496p. [1265]
Research related to American Indians; Indian vocabularies and grammars; physical characteristics; account of Indians of Hudson's Bay territory; paper on Makah Indians; account of the Navajoes.
19. Resol. of Sen. Wade. 10 May.
SMD 105, 39-1, v1, 1p. [1239]
Asks if the removal of the Sioux from Minnesota to Nebraska (contiguous to Dakota) is in the best interest of all parties involved.
20. Wagon Roads in Western Territories. 10 May.
HED 105, 39-1, v12, 3p. [1263]
In Idaho, Montana, Dakota, and Nebraska; treaty com'rs sent to acquire titles to land; road construction through the country of the Teton band of Sioux halted on the suggestion of com'rs Curtis, Taylor, Sibley, and Reed.
21. Expenditures in the Indian Dept. 10 May.
HED 107, 39-1, v12, 2p. [1263]
CIA indicates that extra clerks are needed to provide the House with a statement of expenditures requested.
22. On the Clerical Force of the Interior Dept. 25 May.
SMD 113, 39-1, v1, 3p. [1239]
Employees in the Indian Office; proposed pay increases.
23. Support of Indians in the Southern Superintendency. 31 May.
SMD 116, 39-1, v1, 6p. [1239]
Ravages of war have left them wholly dependent upon the government; loyal Creeks, Seminoles,

Cherokees, and Wichitas; refugee Indians forced from their lands by rebel forces.

24. Message on Lands for Sioux Indians. 11 June.
HED 126, 39-1, v12, 10p. [1263]
On removal of the Santee Sioux from Crow Creek, Minnesota, and Iowa, to a reserve in Nebraska; account of the Sioux outbreak of 1862; etc.

25. On the Relief of G. Johnson. 15 June.
HR 72, 39-1, v1, 2p. [1272]
Indian trader with the Shawnees of Ohio in 1831; said Indians removed to Kansas in 1832 without paying off a debt to the trader.

26. On the Relief of J. Beck. 15 June.
HR 74, 39-1, v1, 2p. [1272]
Navajo depredations of 1849 near Santa Fé, New Mexico.

27. On the Relief of J. Johnson. 15 June.
HR 75, 39-1, v1, 2p. 1272]
Kiowa depredations of 1857 near Fort Atkinson, on the Arkansas River.

28. R-C of S. Norris. 18 June.
SR 117, 39-1, v1, 2p. [1240]
Supplies to California Indians during the treaty negotiations of 1851.

29. Message on Expenditures for the Indian Service. 25 June.
HED 140, 39-1, v16, 8p. [1267]
Partial response to a House Resol. calling for a statement of accounts; additional clerical help not provided by the House; money on hand on 10 July 1865, and amount expended to 20 Apr. 1866.

30. Indian Affairs in Dakota. 19 July.
HED 147, 39-1, v16, 25p. [1267]
Investigation of conduct of affairs; school funds expended under the treaty of 12 Mar. 1858 with the Poncas, and the treaty of 19 Apr. 1858 with the Yankton Sioux; agent pays teachers when there is no school, hires his son as a "laborer," etc.

31. Receipts and Expenditures. 21 July.
HED 150, 39-1, v16, 3p. [1267]
Accounts from 1 July to 31 Mar. 1866; Indian expenses.

32. Report on the Condition of Utah. 23 July.
HR 96, 39-1, v1, 29p. [1272]
Depredations committed by Mormons in the guise of Indians; inciting of Indians by Mormons; Mountain Meadows massacre.

33. On the Relief of J. Jones. 26 July.
HR 102, 39-1, v1, 1p. [1272]
Claim of an Ottawa Indian for depredations committed by whites on his property in 1856.

34. Statements of Appropriations. 5 Oct.
HMD 130, 39-1, v3, 164p. [1271]
During the 1st session, 39th Congress; Indian expenses.

35. Annual Message to Congress with Documents; Pres. Johnson. 3 Dec.
HED 1, 39-2, v1-4, 3701p. [1281-[1286]
Treaties with Indian tribes; annual report of the Sec. of War (Serial 1285); annual report of the Sec. of Interior (Serial 1284); annual report of the Gen. Land Office (Serial 1284); annual report of the CIA (Serial 1284), including taxation of Indian land, trust funds and trust lands, population of tribes, farming statistics, and reports of Supts., agents, and schools; etc.

36. Estimates of Appropriations. 3 Dec.
HED 2, 39-2, v4, 262p. [1286]
Year ending 30 June 1868; Indian expenses.

37. Annual Report of the Sec. of the Treasury. 3 Dec.
HED 4, 39-2, v5, 394p. [1287]
Year ending 30 June 1866; Indian expenses.

38. Expenditures for the Suppression of Indian Hostilities. 4 Dec.
HED 5, 39-2, v5, 17p. [1287]
During 1864-1865, against the Snakes, Apaches, and Kiowas; in the Southwest, Northwest, and Dakota Territory.

39. Receipts and Expenditures. 11 Dec.
HED 12, 39-2, v6, 504p. [1288]
Year ending 30 June 1865; Indian expenses.

1867

1. Letter on Protection Across the Continent. 3 Jan.
HED 23, 39-2, v6, 55p. [1288]
For emigrants, from Indian hostili-

ties; across the central and northern plains; tour of inspection through Dakota, Montana, and Idaho.

2. Mineral Resources West of the Rocky Mountains. 8 Jan.
HED 29, 39-2, v7, 321p. [1289]
Descriptions of Indians in the various states and territories; historical sketches; the Washoes, Paiutes, and Shoshones of Utah; etc.

3. Mem. of the Dakota Legis. 19 Jan.
HMD 22, 39-2, v1, 2p. [1302]
Ask for a geological survey of the Black Hills; road construction halted due to Indian hostilities; northwestern Indian com'rs suggest halt of activities until treaties are made.

4. Resol. of the Kansas Legis. 25 Jan.
HMD 32, 39-2, v1, 1p. [1302]
Ask benefits of Homestead Law for settlers on lands recently purchased from the Osages.

5. Resol. of the Kansas Legis. 25 Jan.
HMD 33, 39-2, v1, 1p. [1302]
Ask right of pre-emption be given settlers on the Cherokee neutral lands.

6. Report on the Condition of Indian Tribes. 26 Jan.
SR 156, 39-2, v1, 532p. [1279]
Testimony covering the entire continent west of the Mississippi River; major findings: (1) population is declining, (2) Indian wars are often caused by lawless whites, (3) wars also caused by loss of hunting grounds, (4) military *vs.* civilian control of the Indian Bureau is a difficult problem to decide, and (5) evils in the Indian system will not be solved until Indians are civilized, or entirely disappear.

7. Report of Col. Parker on Indian Affairs. 30 Jan.
HMD 37, 39-2, v1, 11p. [1302]
Proposed plan to establish peace with all Indian tribes; transfer of BIA from the Interior Dept. to the War Dept.; territorial government for Indians; appointment of an Indian-white commission to oversee Indian affairs.

8. R-P of J. Carter. 31 Jan.
SR 158, 39-2, v1, 1p. [1279]
Indian hostilities in Utah.

9. Report of Gen. Grant on Indian Affairs. 2 Feb.
HMD 40, 39-2, v1, 2p. [1302]
Transfer of BIA to War Dept., and the abolishment of civil Indian agents and licensed traders; opposed to issuance of arms to Indians.

10. Letter on Issue of Arms to Indians. 2 Feb.
HMD 41, 39-2, v1, 4p. [1302]
Sale of arms to Kiowas, Cheyennes, Sioux, Arapahoes, Comanches, and Apaches; possibility of war on the Kansas frontier.

11. Letter on the Fort Phil. Kearney Massacre. 5 Feb.
SED 15, 39-2, v2, 15p. [1277]
Col. Fetterman's engagement with the Sioux in Dakota Territory.

12. Letter on the Fort Phil. Kearney Massacre. 5 Feb.
SED 16, 39-2, v2, 18p. [1277] *or*
HED 71, 39-2, v11, 18p. [1293]
Sioux hostilities in Dakota Territory; Col. Fetterman's party destroyed.

13. Examination of the Acts of the CIA. 5 Feb.
HR 10, 39-2, v1, 10p. [1303]
Awarded contracts for Indian goods in 1866 to high bidders with inferior quality merchandise.

14. Letter on Indians in Dakota Territory. 7 Feb.
SED 22, 39-2, v2, 12p. [1277]
Condition of Sioux near Lake Traverse and Fort Wadsworth in Dakota; the part they played in the Sioux outbreak of 1862 in Minnesota; cause of their being permitted to remain on the Minnesota frontier.

15. R-M of S. Eastman. 7 Feb.
SR 160, 39-2, v1, 3p. [1279]
Asks reimbursement for illustrations drawn for the Indian Dept.'s *History of the American Indians* in 1850.

16. Resol. of the Wisconsin Legis. 8 Feb.
SMD 18, 39-2, v1, 2p. [1278]
Asks new treaty be made with the Stockbridge Indians, entailing their removal from the state to a more genial climate as *per* their wishes.

17. Message on the Hot Springs Reserve in Arkansas. 8 Feb.
HED 82, 39-2, v11, 8p. [1293]
Cherokee pre-emption claims decided to be not valid.

18. Report on the Sand Creek Massacre. 14 Feb.

SED 26, 39-2, v2, 228p. [1277]
Investigation of Col. Chivington's actions against the Cheyennes and Arapahoes in 1864.

19. Letter on Com'rs to Indian Tribes. 14 Feb.
HED 88, 39-2, v11, 5p. [1293]
Funds for a commission to the Southwest, to visit Comanches, Kiowas, Cheyennes, Arapahoes, Lipans, Mescalaros, Kickapoos, and other Indians, in order to establish peaceful relations with said tribes.

20. Resol. of the Kansas Legis. 15 Feb.
SMD 25, 39-2, v1, 1p. [1278]
Asks extinguishment of all Indian titles to land in the state.

21. Gold Mines East of the Rocky Mountains. 15 Feb.
HED 92, 39-2, v11, 28p. [1293]
Indian hostilities in New Mexico and Dakota (Sioux).

22. Resol. of the Minnesota Legis. 18 Feb.
SMD 28, 39-2, v1, 1p. [1278]
Ask treaty be made with the Sioux to secure a route through Dakota to the gold regions of Montana and Idaho.

23. Mem. of the New Mexico Legis. 18 Feb.
HMD 67, 39-2, v1, 2p. [1302]
Losses due to Indian depredations since 1847 should be reimbursed.

24. Resol. of the Kansas Legis. 20 Feb.
SMD 34, 39-2, v1, 1p. [1278]
Ask removal of Col. Leavenworth as agent to hostile Indians on the western and southwestern frontiers of the state.

25. Resol. of the Kansas Legis. 20 Feb.
SMD 37, 39-2, v1, 1p. [1278]
Lands within Indian reservations lost to the public school fund; ask grant of other lands to replace those lost; ask new Indian treaties take school lands into consideration.

26. R-M of D. Allen and Company. 20 Feb.
SR 176, 39-2, v1, 1p. [1279]
Suspension of overland mail during 1864 because of Indian hostilities on the plains.

27. Resol. of Rep. Bidwell. 25 Feb.
HMD 75, 39-2, v1, 5p. [1302]
On having a larger military force in Utah to protect people from Indian hostilities; conduct of Mormons.

28. Annual Report of the Smithsonian Institution. 28 Feb.
HMD 83, 39-2, v1, 469p. [1302]
Research relating to the American Indian; Indian pottery; notes on the Tinneh or Chepewyan Indians of British and Russian America.

29. Message on Removals and Appointments in the Interior Dept. 2 Mar.
HED 113, 39-2, v11, 4p. [1293]
Indian agents removed by the Indian Dept.

30. Testimony in the Case of A. Cumming. 2 Mar.
HMD 81, 39-2, v1, 19p. [1302]
Supt. of Indian Affairs in Colorado; violations while in office; dispute over civil *vs.* military control of Indian affairs.

31. Protection to Wagon Trains on the Overland Route. 8 Mar.
SED 2, 40-1, v1, 4p. [1308]
Through Dakota, along the Platte River, and from Kansas to New Mexico; protection against Indian hostilities.

32. Appropriations for Shawnee Indians. 8 Mar.
HED 3, 40-1, v1, 3p. [1311]
To fulfill the treaty of 2 Mar. 1867; last of a series of treaties undertaken with a view of removal of all Indians from Kansas.

33. Mem. of the New Mexico Legis. 13 Mar.
HMD 13, 40-1, v1, 2p. [1312]
Indemnification for losses due to Indian hostilities.

34. Mem. of the New Mexico Legis. 13 Mar.
HMD 14, 40-1, v1, 2p. [1312]
Establishment of telegraphic communication between military posts in Kansas and New Mexico; would speed military reaction to Indian hostilities.

35. Armed Expeditions Against the Indians. 21 Mar.
SED 7, 40-1, v1, 3p. [1308]
Campaigns against Indians in the military depts. of Dakota, Platte, and Missouri; Cheyennes, Kiowas, and Sioux.

36. Estimate of Appropriations for the Chippewas of the Mississippi River. 21 Mar.
SED 10, 40-1, v1, 1p. [1308] *or*
HED 8, 40-1, v1, 1p. [1311]
To fulfill the treaty of 19 Mar. 1867.

37. Letter on the Pueblo of Santa Ana in New Mexico. 29 Mar.

HED 13, 40-1, v1, 6p. [1311]
Indian title to land not confirmed; ask investigation.

38. Report on the Union Pacific Railroad Company. 2 Apr.
SED 2, 40-sp, v1, 36p. [1308]
Survey from the Black Hills to Salt Lake delayed because of Indian hostilities in 1865.

39. Employment of L. Bogy in the Interior Dept. 8 Apr.
SED 3, 40-sp, v1, 2p. [1308]
Late CIA: serving as a special agent to deliver goods to Indians west of the Mississippi River, and on the Missouri River.

40. Report on Indian Tribes of the U.S. 13 Apr.
SED 4, 40-sp, v1, 50p. [1308]
Includes population, location, and extent of tribes; lists treaty obligations, and money appropriated annually; progress of each tribe in education and civilization; list of Supts. and agents.

41. Message on Absence of Territorial Officers. 15 Apr.
SED 6, 40-sp, v1, 5p. [1308]
Gov. Cumming of Colorado absent over 2 months, the stated purpose being Indian affairs.

42. Message on Gov. Cumming of Colorado. 17 Apr.
SED 8, 40-sp, v1, 2p. [1308]
Absence from his territorial position investigated; extension of a leave of absence to deal with Indian affairs of the Territory in Washington, D.C.

43. On the Relief of the Navajo Indians. 13 July.
SED 12, 40-1, v1, 2p. [1308]
To supply a deficiency in the appropriation for the Navajoes on the Bosque Redondo reservation in New Mexico.

44. Letter on Indian Hostilities. 13 July.
SED 13, 40-1, v1, 128p. [1308]
Reports on conditions on the frontier; Fort Phil. Kearney massacre; sale of arms to Indians; Cheyennes, Arapahoes, and Sioux on the northern Plains; Cheyennes, Arapahoes, Comanches, and Kiowas on the southern plains.

45. Message on a Treaty with Russia. 16 July.
SED 17, 40-1, v1, 4p. [1308]
Treaty of 20 June 1867, involving the cession of Alaska; article 3 states that all residents of the territory, excepting Indians, will receive U.S. citizenship.

46. Judgments in the Court of Claims. 21 Nov.
HMD 50, 40-1, v1, 34p. [1312]
Since 1863; relevance for Indian affairs revealed in short descriptions of cases.

47. Annual Report of the Sec. of the Treasury. 30 Nov.
HED 2, 40-2, v5, 502p. [1328]
Year ending 30 June 1867; Indian expenses.

48. Statements of Appropriations. 30 Nov.
HMD 55, 40-1, v1, 10p. [1312]
During the 1st session, 40th Congress; Indian expenses.

49. Resol. of Sen. Williams. 2 Dec.
SMD 1, 40-2, v1, 1p. [1319]
On future policy of the government towards Indians; recommends: (1) two reservations be established, one east, and one west of the Rocky Mountains, (2) no more treaties, purchases of land, or annuities, (3) Indians must choose civilization or extermination, (4) all Indians shall be on one of the two reservations formed, and (5) existing agencies shall be dispensed with.

50. Estimates of Appropriations. 2 Dec.
HED 3, 40-2, v5, 299p. [1328]
Year ending 30 June 1869; Indian expenses.

51. Annual Message to Congress with Documents; Pres. Johnson. 3 Dec.
HED 1, 40-2, v1-4, 4542p. [1322-1327]
On the Indian Peace Commission sent to treat with Plains Indians in order to avert a possible war which would delay construction of the strategic Pacific railroad; annual report of the Sec. of War (Serials 1324-1325); annual report of the Sec. of Interior (Serial 1326); annual report of the Gen. Land Office (Serial 1326); annual report of the CIA (Serial 1326), including the Peace Commission, Indian hostilities, trust funds and lands, census, and reports of Supts., agents, schools, and farms; etc.

52. Letter on the Otoe Indian Reservation. 12 Dec.
HED 38, 40-2, v7, 3p. [1330]
For sale of a portion of said reservation (also occupied by the Missouri Indians) under the treaty with those tribes of 15 Mar. 1854, with a supplemental of 9 Dec. 1854.

53. Letter on the Miami Indians. 13 Dec.
HED 45, 40-2, v7, 8p. [1330]
Issue of land patents for the Me-shin-go-me-sia band of Miamies, in the tribe's reservation in Indiana; treaties of 6 Nov. 1838, and 28 Nov. 1840.

54. Mem. of the Board of the Northern Pacific Railroad Company. 17 Dec.
SMD 9, 40-2, v1, 39p. [1319]
Seek funds; military transport to engage hostile Indians would be a major benefit of said railroad; British-Indian trade; military forces will be required to control Indian hostilities during construction.

55. Appropriations for Survey of Indian Lands. 17 Dec.
HED 56, 40-2, v7, 4p. [1330]
For surveying Indian reservations during the year ending 30 June 1869.

56. Letter on Indian Trust Funds. 18 Dec.
HED 59, 40-2, v9, 22p. [1332]
Statements of all funds held by the government.

1868

1. Disbursements for the Indian Service. 6 Jan.
HED 71, 40-2, v9, 209p. [1332]
Year ending 30 June 1867.

2. Letter on the Condition of the Sioux. 7 Jan.
HED 76, 40-2, v9, 6p. [1332]
The destitute condition of the Sioux near Devil's Lake, Dakota Territory.

3. Indian Lands in Kansas. 8 Jan.
HED 85, 40-2, v9, 12p. [1332]
Lands remaining to which Indian title has not yet been extinguished.

4. Report of the Indian Peace Commission. 14 Jan.
HED 97, 40-2, v11, 23p. [1337]
Commission sent to treat for peace, secure safe building of Pacific railroads, and inaugurate a plan for Indian civilization; councils with Plains Indians.

5. Appropriations for Expenses of the Osage Indians. 16 Jan.
HED 103, 40-2, v11, 2p. [1337]
To defray expenses of a delagation of Great and Little Osages to Washington, D.C.

6. Survey of Lands for Cheyennes and Arapahoes. 16 Jan.
HED 104, 40-2, v11, 12p. [1337]
Half-breed lands under the treaty of 14 Oct. 1865; trouble may arise, as the Union Pacific Railroad will pass through the reserves.

7. Deficiency in Appropriations for Indian Tribes. 22 Jan.
HED 110, 40-2, v11, 8p. [1337]
For the Sioux, Arikaras, Gros Ventres, Mandans, Crows, Yancton Sioux, and Poncas during fiscal 1868.

8. Letter on the Quapaw Indians. 27 Jan.
HED 122, 40-2, v11, 3p. [1337]
On the suffering condition of said tribe; request for diversion of funds (under the treaty of 13 May 1833) from support of a farmer to subsistence.

9. Appropriations for Indian Treaties. 27 Jan.
HED 124, 40-2, v11, 2p. [1337]
For the Comanches, Kiowas, Chippewas, Pawnees, Poncas, Shoshones, Sioux, Winnebagoes, Ottoes, Missouris, Assiniboines, Arikaras, Gros Ventres, and Mandans.

10. Mem. of the Montana Legis. 27 Jan.
HMD 38, 40-2, v1, 3p. [1349]
Ask treaty be made with the Blackfeet Indians; treaty concluded in 1865, and not ratified, has incited the Indians to war with whites.

11. Mem. and Resol. of the Dakota Legis. 28 Jan.
HMD 52, 40-2, v1, 3p. [1349]
Indian affairs in the Territory; agriculture of the Mandans, Arikaras, and Minetarees; ask transfer of control of Indian affairs to States and Territories.

12. R-P of F. Richardson. 30 Jan.
SR 20, 40-2, v1, 1p. [1320]

Apache depredations of 1852 in New Mexico.

13. R-P of M. Duffield. 30 Jan.
SR 23, 40-2, v1, 3p. [1320]
Indian depredations in Arizona during 1863-1866.

14. Letter on Cherokee Neutral Lands. 30 Jan.
HED 132, 40-2, v11, 2p. [1337]
Information regarding the sale of said land in Kansas.

15. Letter on a Survey of Choctaw Country. 30 Jan.
HED 133, 40-2, v11, 4p. [1337]
Regarding the eastern boundary of said country, under the treaties of 18 Oct. 1820, 20 Jan. 1825, 27 Sept. 1830, 22 June 1855, and 28 Apr. 1866.

16. R-P of Gen. Anderson. 31 Jan.
SR 25, 40-2, v1, 2p. [1320]
Indian attack on Fort Drane in Florida during 1836.

17. Letter on the Sioux Reservation. 1 Feb.
HED 137, 40-2, v11, 2p. [1337]
Sale of the Sioux reservation in Minnesota.

18. Claim of the Choctaw Nation. 1 Feb.
HED 138, 40-2, v11, 3p. [1337]
Against the U.S. under the treaties of 27 Sept. 1830, 22 June 1855, and 28 Apr. 1866.

19. Interest Due the Cherokees. 3 Feb.
HED 141, 40-2, v11, 3p. [1337]
Payment of interest to the Cherokees of North Carolina under the act of 29 July 1848.

20. R-P of M. Mitchell. 5 Feb.
SR 27, 40-2, v1, 1p. [1320]
Loyal Creek arrested by rebels during the Civil War.

21. R-P of G. Lynch. 5 Feb.
SR 32, 40-2, v1, 1p. [1320]
Indian campaign of 1819.

22. Letter on the Iowa Indians. 5 Feb.
HED 152, 40-2, v11, 4p. [1337]
Diversion of funds (under the treaty of 6 Mar. 1861 with the Sacs, Foxes, and Iowas) from bridge construction to agricultural implements.

23. Mem. of the Minnesota Legis. 7 Feb.
SMD 26, 40-2, v1, 2p. [1319]
Ask removal of Indians from the Black Hills.

24. Deficiency of Funds for the Office of the CIA. 7 Feb.
HED 155, 40-2, v11, 2p. [1337]
Estimates of funds needed for miscellaneous items.

25. Subsistence Stores Issued to Indians. 14 Feb.
SED 27, 40-2, v1, 4p. [1316]
From Jan. 1866 to Oct. 1867; for which payment has not been made by the Interior Dept. to the War Dept.

26. Annuities to Cherokees. 18 Feb.
HED 173, 40-2, v13, 2p. [1339]
Annual payment to the Cherokees of North Carolina under the treaty of 23 May 1836 ay New Echota.

27. Creek Indian Refugees. 18 Feb.
HED 175, 40-2, v13, 6p. [1339]
Appropriation needed to remove Creeks from Cherokee country on the Red River to their former home.

28. Transfer of Jurisdiction over Indian Affairs. 19 Feb.
HED 176, 40-2, v13, 7p. [1339]
Jurisdiction over the Chickasaw fund, and interest payments to Cherokees of North Carolina should be shifted from the Treasury Dept. to the Interior Dept.

29. Message on Russian America. 19 Feb.
HED 177, 40-2, v13, 380p. [1339]
Treaty of 30 Mar. 1867 for the cession, by Russia, of Alaska, to the U.S.; Indian inhabitants of the territory.

30. Appropriations for Navajoes. 22 Feb.
HED 185, 40-2, v15, 2p. [1341]
Supplies for Navajoes on the Bosque Redondo reservation in New Mexico.

31. Appropriations for Sioux. 24 Feb.
HED 184, 40-2, v15, 3p. [1341]
For agricultural improvements among the nine bands of Sioux belonging to the Upper Missouri agency; recommended by the Indian Peace Commission.

32. Report on the Union Pacific Railroad. 25 Feb.
HED 253, 40-2, v17, 97p. [1343]
Cutting timber on the Omaha reservation.

33. Resol. of the California Legis. 2 Mar.
SMD 41, 40-2, v1, 1p. [1319]
Ask funds be given for the construction of a southern railroad to the Pacific; area sparsely populated by whites due to Indian hostility.

34. Indian Spoliation Claims. 3 Mar.
HED 194, 40-2, v15, 2p. [1341]
Indian war of 1855-1856 in Oregon and Washington; Indian war of 1865-1867 in Montana, Dakota, and Nebraska.

35. Appropriations for Sioux. 4 Mar.
HED 199, 40-2, v15, 8p. [1341]
Agricultural supplies to the Sisseton and Wahpeton Sioux under the treaty of 19 Feb. 1867.

36. Appropriations for the Indian Service in California. 4 Mar.
HED 200, 40-2, v15, 15p. [1341]
Debts incurred during 1860-1867.

37. Oregon Indian War Claims. 4 Mar.
HMD 88, 40-2, v2, 11p. [1350]
Audit of claims arising from the war of 1855-1856.

38. Mineral Resources West of the Rocky Mountains. 5 Mar.
HED 202, 40-2, v16, 674p. [1342]
Indian diggings; Indians in the various states and territories.

39. Sioux City and Pacific Railroad. 5 Mar.
HED 203, 40-2, v15, 11p. [1341]
Survey through the Omaha reservation necessary.

40. Treaty with the Choctaws and Chickasaws. 6 Mar.
HED 204, 40-2, v15, 28p. [1341]
Claim settlements under the treaty of 28 Apr. 1866.

41. Mem. of the New Mexico Legis. 6 Mar.
HMD 95, 40-2, v2, 2p. [1350]
Ask authorization to raise volunteer troops to battle hostile Indians.

42. Mem. of the Utah Legis. 9 Mar.
HMD 99, 40-2, v2, 2p. [1350]
Ask funds to suppress Indian hostilities.

43. Resol. of the Kansas Legis. 16 Mar.
SMD 51, 40-2, v1, 1p. [1319] *or*
HMD 100, 40-2, v2, 1p. [1350]
Asks land for school purposes to replace lands lost because they were in Indian reservations.

44. Claims Arising from Sioux Depredations. 17 Mar.
SED 43, 40-2, v2, 3p. [1317]
In Minnesota during 1862.

45. Report on Bounty Lands for Soldiers. 18 Mar.
HR 25, 40-2, v1, 3p. [1357]
Millions of acres of Indian lands, through treaty stipulations, are falling into the hands of land speculators.

46. Resol. of the California Legis. 20 Mar.
HMD 105, 40-2, v2, 2p. [1350]
Bounty land for volunteers in suppressing Indian hostilities during 1863-1865.

47. Mem. of the Minnesota Legis. 23 Mar.
SMD 60, 40-2, v1, 2p. [1319]
Mail service between Fort Abercrombie, and Montana Territory; interruption by hostile Indians.

48. Indians of the Aleutian Isles. 24 Mar.
HED 216, 40-2, v15, 3p. [1341]
Appropriation for gifts to the chiefs of the Koloshian Indians.

49. Claims of the State of Iowa. 24 Mar.
HMD 110, 40-2, v2, 5p. [1350]
Expenses of the State's militia; Sioux hostilities.

50. Appropriations for Chippewas. 26 Mar.
HED 228, 40-2, v15, 4p. [1341]
Removal of Pillager band of Chippewas from Otter Tail Lake to the reservation at White Earth Lake; under the treaty of 7 May 1864.

51. Appropriation for Destitute Indians. 28 Mar.
HED 236, 40-2, v15, 4p. [1341]
For removal of Cherokees scattered through Indian Territory to their own homes; pushed out of their country during the Civil War.

52. Resol. of the California Legis. 6 Apr.
SMD 74, 40-2, v1, 2p. [1319] *or*
HMD 150, 40-2, v2, 2p. [1350]
Aid for the Southern Pacific railroad; through lands occupied mainly by Indians.

53. Unexpended Appropriations. 8 Apr.
SED 48, 40-2, v2, 46p. [1317]
Balances as of 31 Dec. 1867; Indian expenses.

54. On the Relief of the Chippewas. 8 Apr.
HED 246, 40-2, v15, 3p. [1341]
Needs of the Chippewas of Lake Superior; treaties of 1842 and 1854.

55. Letter on the Bosque Redondo Reservation. 10 Apr.
HED 248, 40-2, v15, 8p. [1341]
Unsuitableness of the New Mexico reserve for the Navajoes and Apaches.

56. Appropriations for Friendly Indians. 20 Apr.
HED 255, 40-2, v17, 4p. [1343]
Needs of the Indians for subsistence.

57. Boundary of Choctaw and Chickasaw Country. 21 Apr.
HED 259, 40-2, v17, 2p. [1343]
Between Arkansas and Indian lands; treaty of 22 June 1855.
58. Letter on the Sioux. 24 Apr.
HED 262, 40-2, v17, 2p. [1343]
Destitute condition of Sioux near Devil's Lake, Dakota Territory.
59. Indian Tribes in Kansas. 24 Apr.
HED 263, 40-2, v17, 3p. [1343]
Destitute condition of the Kaws, Quapaws, and Osages; these Indians warring with the Cheyennes, Arapahoes, and Apaches.
60. Destitute Friendly Indians. 24 Apr.
HED 264, 40-2, v17, 2p. [1343]
Supplies for Indians in Kansas, Indian Territory, and Nebraska.
61. Mineral Resources East of the Rocky Mountains. 2 May.
HED 273, 40-2, v17, 72p. [1343]
Indians in the various states and territories; struggle with Sioux for control of the Black Hills.
62. Eastern Division of the Union Pacific Railroad. 6 May.
HED 277, 40-2, v17, 10p. [1343]
An end to Indian troubles near Fort Wallace, Kansas, and Fort Lyon, Colorado.
63. Mem. of the Montana Legis. 11 May.
HMD 125, 40-2, v2, 2p. [1350]
Expenses of volunteers raised to combat hostile Indians during 1866-1867.
64. Report on Treaty Stipulations with Indian Tribes. 14 May.
HR 35, 40-2, v1, 2p. [1357]
Proceeds from sales of land under the Choctaw treaties of 27 Sept. 1853, and 22 June 1855; Choctaw and Chickasaw treaty stipulations.
65. Appropriations for Pottawatomies. 15 May.
HED 290, 40-2, v17, 3p. [1343]
To carry out stipulations of the treaties of 15 Nov. 1861, and 29 Mar. 1866.
66. Report on the Treaty with Russia. 18 May.
HR 37, 40-2, v1, 65p. [1357]
Discussion of treaty-making by the U.S.; Creek treaty of 1790; Alaskan tribes; Russian treaty of 30 Mar. 1867 deals with Indians.
67. Report on the Eastern Division of the Union Pacific Railroad. 25 May.
HR 43, 40-2, v1, 2p. [1357]
Transport of Indian supplies to Albuquerque, New Mexico.
68. Letter on Indian Raids. 26 May.
SED 60, 40-2, v2, 3p. [1317]
Depredations in the Chickasaw nation, and upon Texas citizens by Kiowas and Comanches.
69. Subsistence of Indians. 26 May.
HED 239, 40-2, v15, 3p. [1341]
By the War Dept.; treaties signed with the Sioux, Crows, and Arapahoes.
70. Appropriations for Friendly Indians. 29 May.
HED 296, 40-2, v19, 4p. [1345]
Kawas, Osages, Apaches, Arapahoes, and Cheyennes; end of hostilities after the council at Medicine Lodge Creek.
71. Annual Report of the Smithsonian Institution. 30 May.
SMD 86, 40-2, v1, 506p. [1319]
Research related to American Indians; ancient mounds in the U.S.; notes on Indian history; notes on Apaches.
72. Appropriations for the Indian Service. 6 June.
SED 62, 40-2, v2, 18p. [1317]
Omissions and changes in the appropriations bill for the year ending 30 June 1869.
73. Letter on Creek Indian Enrollment. 10 June.
SED 64, 40-2, v2, 1p. [1317]
Confusion over the number of persons enrolled as Creek Indians; related to payment of per captia dividends.
74. Removal of Navajoes and Utes. 10 June.
HED 308, 40-2, v19, 1p. [1345]
To a reservation in the northwest part of New Mexico.
75. Message on the Great and Little Osages. 11 June.
HED 310, 40-2, v19, 42p. [1345]
On a treaty being negotiated with said Indians; council proceedings.
76. Letter on Affairs in Utah and the Territories. 17 June.
HMD 153, 40-2, v2, 36p. [1350]
Expedition from Kansas, through Utah, to California; journal; encounters with Pawnees, Sioux, Utes; treaty council with the Utes; travels to Northwest Coast and Arizona; etc.

77. Claims of the Loyal Choctaws and Chickasaws. 18 June.
SED 66, 40-2, v2, 6p. [1317]
Under the treaty of 28 Apr. 1866; Indians driven from their homes during the Civil War.

78. R-M of the Governor of Minnesota. 18 June.
SR 132, 40-2, v1, 3p. [1320]
Lands to which Indian title has, or will be extinguished is set aside for a university.

79. Report on the Osage Indian Treaty. 18 June.
HR 63, 40-2, v2, 23p. [1358]
Treaty of 27 May 1868 with the Great and Little Osages; transfer of land to the Leavenworth, Lawrence, and Galveston Railroad Company; means used to procure Indian acceptance not satisfactory; asks Senate not to ratify said treaty.

80. Resol. of the House of Reps. 19 June.
SMD 98, 40-2, v1, 1p. [1319]
Treaty of 27 May 1868 with the Great and Little Osages of Kansas grants 8,000,000 acres of land to a single railroad company; this treaty is unauthorized by laws and the Constitution, and is condemned by the House.

81. Resol. of the California Legis. 22 June.
HMD 144, 40-2, v2, 2p. [1350]
The abandoned Mendocino Indian reservation should be opened to settlers.

82. Mem. of the California Legis. 22 June.
HMD 148, 40-2, v2, 2p. [1350]
Asks steps be taken to ascertain the losses suffered during the Indian depredations of 1861-1864.

83. Receipts and Expenditures. 24 June.
HED 315, 40-2, v20, 591p. [1346]
Year ending 30 June 1866; Indian expenses.

84. R-P of J. Getty. 25 June.
SR 138, 40-2, v1, 1p. [1320]
Property destroyed by U.S. troops; vacant during 1864-1865 as a consequence of the Indian outbreak of 1862 in Minnesota.

85. Report on the Employment of L. Bogy. 26 June.
SR 140, 40-2, v1, 4p. [1320]
Late CIA employed as a special agent to purchase goods for the Indians.

86. Letter on the Tabequache Band of Utah Indians. 27 June.
SED 70, 40-2, v2, 4p. [1317]
Treaty of 7 Oct. 1863 has not been carried into effect; treaty of 2 Mar. 1868 with all seven bands of Utahs; removal of tribe to a reservation.

87. Appropriation for a Sioux Treaty. 29 June.
HED 321, 40-2, v20, 4p. [1346]
Concluded between the Sioux and the Indian Peace Com'rs near Fort Laramie; condition of the Osages and Kaws; settlers on Sac and Fox lands.

88. Indian Hostilities in California. 30 June.
HED 322, 40-2, v20, 2p. [1346]
Reimbursement of the State for the cost of suppression of hostilities.

89. Damages to Settlers in Nebraska. 1 July.
HED 325, 40-2, v20, 4p. [1346]
By reason of locating Santee Sioux on their settlements in 1866.

90. Report on the Pueblo of Santa Anna. 1 July.
HR 70, 40-2, v2, 3p. [1358]
Case of land title in New Mexico; Indians occupy the Pueblo.

91. Report on Land Claims in New Mexico. 1 July.
HR 71, 40-2, v2, 6p. [1358]
Settlers driven from land by Navajo Indians.

92. R-P of Black Beaver. 2 July.
SR 150, 40-2, v1, 1p. [1320]
Delaware Indian in the service of the U.S. as an interpreter for the Wichitas and other tribes; property confiscated by rebels during Civil War.

93. Letter on the Oneida Indians. 6 July.
SED 72, 40-2, v2, 3p. [1317]
Prohibiting the Oneidas from cutting and removing timber from the common lands of the tribe.

94. Report on a Treaty with the Choctaw Indians. 6 July.
HR 77, 40-2, v2, 3p. [1358]
Claims to proceeds of sale of lands in Mississippi under the treaties of 27 Sept. 1830, and 22 June 1855; Choctaw and Chickasaw treaty of 28 Apr. 1866.

95. R-P of Dent, Vantine, and Company. 8 July.
HR 78, 40-2, v2, 2p. [1358]
Supplies to California Indians dur-

ing the treaty negotiations of 1851-1852.

96. Report of Gen. Dodge's Survey Expeditions for the Union Pacific Railroad. 10 July.
HED 331, 40-2, v20, 71p. [1346]
In and around the Black Hills; attack on the survey party by the Sioux.

97. Treaty Stipulations with the Senecas et al. 11 July.
HED 332, 40-2, v20, 3p. [1346]
Treaty of 23 Feb. 1867 with the Senecas, Shawnees, Quapaws, Peorias, Kaskaskias, Weas, Piankeshaws, Ottawas, and Wyandotts.

98. Exploration of the Yellowstone River. 17 July.
SED 77, 40-2, v2, 174p. [1317]
Expedition up the Missouri and Yellowstone Rivers; journal of travels, and encounters with Indians; Sioux and Crow Indians are the major tribes of the area; mission of goodwill to the Indians.

99. R-P of M. Doyle. 17 July.
SR 171, 40-2, v1, 1p. [1320]
Compensation asked for cutting timber in Nevada under a contract with the Indian Dept.

100. Letter on the Kickapoos. 20 July.
HED 340, 40-2, v20, 6p. [1346]
Kickapoos in Mexico committing depredations in Texas; removal of said Indians from Mexico to Kansas and Indian Territory.

101. Mem. on Behalf of Indians by the U.S. Indian Commission. 20 July.
HMD 165, 40-2, v2, 3p. [1350]
U.S. stands "uniformly unjust" in its treaty relations with Indians, which is a major cause of hostilities; asks just treatment in the future.

102. Rights of Freedmen Under an Indian Treaty. 24 July.
SED 82, 40-2, v2, 5p. [1317]
Under the 3rd article of the treaty of 28 Apr. 1866 with the Choctaws and Chickasaws.

103. Letter on California Indians. 24 July.
SED 83, 40-2, v2, 2p. [1317]
Removal of 400 Humboldt and Wylackie Indians from the Smith River Farm to the Round Valley reservation.

104. Statements of Appropriations. 10 Nov.
HMD 168, 40-2, v2, 93p. [1350]
During the 2d session, 40th Congress; Indian expenses.

105. Annual Report of the Sec. of the Treasury. 1 Dec.
HED 2, 40-3, v5, 567p. [1370]
Year ending 30 June 1868; Indian expenses.

106. Estimates of Appropriations. 7 Dec.
HED 3, 40-3, v5, 292p. [1370]
Year ending 30 June 1870; Indian expenses.

107. Report on Choctaw and Chickasaw Trust Funds. 8 Dec.
HR 1, 40-3, v1, 2p. [1388]
Sale of stocks held for said Indians.

108. Annual Message to Congress with Documents; Pres. Johnson. 9 Dec.
HED 1, 40-3, v1-4, 5552p. [1364-1369]
Indian treaties; annual report of the Sec. of War (Serials 1367-1368); annual report of the Sec. of Interior (Serial 1366); annual report of the Gen. Land Office (Serial 1366); annual report of the CIA (Serial 1366), including Indians in Alaska, the efforts of the Indian Peace Commission, Indian hostilities, transfer of the Indian Bureau, civilization, the Indian war on the southern plains, statistics on trust funds and populations, and reports of Supts., agents, schools, and farms; etc.

109. Sale of the Fort Snelling Reservation. 10 Dec.
HED 9, 40-3, v7, 107p. [1372]
Treaty of 1804 between the Sioux and the U.S., represented by Gen. Pike.

110. Resol. of the Oregon Legis. 14 Dec.
SMD 7, 40-3, v1, 1p. [1361]
Losses on account of Indian depredations.

1869

1. Troops Employed on the Plains. 5 Jan.
SED 7, 40-3, v1, 10p. [1360]
To protect Missouri River traffic and the Union Pacific Railroad from Indian hostilities; number and location of troops.

2. Alaskan Fur Interests. 6 Jan.
SED 8, 40-3, v1, 10p. [1360]

Journal of Capt. White's expedition to the waters of Alaska; encounters with the Tomgas, Carsan, Kaigan, Stachine, Kake, Adnochton (or Copper River), Chilkaht, Awke, Tako, and Squill-toos-kin Indians; Indian fur trade with Russians and British (Hudson's Bay Company).

3. Indian Supts. and Agents. 6 Jan.
SED 9, 40-3, v1, 4p. [1360]
List giving names, locations, and those absent from their posts.

4. Reports of Pacific Railroad Companies. 7 Jan.
SED 10, 40-3, v1, 47p. [1360]
Attacks of hostile Plains Indians on survey parties.

5. Sioux Indians on the Upper Missouri. 7 Jan.
SED 11, 40-3, v1, 6p. [1360]
Gen. Harney's report of the condition of said Indians, and the state of affairs since the signing of the treaty of 1868 (made by the Indian Peace Commission).

6. Battle of the Washita River. 7 Jan.
SED 13, 40-3, v1, 38p. [1360]
Between U.S. troops under Gen. Custer, and Cheyennes, Arapahoes, Kiowas, and Comanches; events leading up to the battle.

7. Appropriations to the Creeks. 8 Jan.
HED 31, 40-3, v7, 2p. [1372]
To carry into effect the treaty of 14 June 1866.

8. Battle on the Washita River. 11 Jan.
SED 18, 40-3, v1, 51p. [1360]
Between U.S. troops under Gen. Custer, and Cheyennes, Arapahoes, Kiowas, and Comanches; 27 Nov. 1868; Indian war on the southern plains; events surrounding the battle.

9. Appropriations for the Sacs and Foxes. 12 Jan.
HED 38, 40-3, v7, 13p. [1372]
Under the treaty of 18 Feb. 1867.

10. Pay of the Agent for the Crows. 12 Jan.
HED 39, 40-3, v7, 1p. [1372]
Left out of the estimates for the year ending 30 June 1870.

11. Appropriations for Crow Indians. 12 Jan.
HED 42, 40-3, v7, 9p. [1372]
To fulfill the treaty of 7 May 1868.

12. Appropriations for Ute Indians. 13 Jan.
HED 43, 40-3, v7, 11p. [1372]
To fulfill the treaty of 2 Mar. 1868.

13. Mem. of the Eastern Cherokees. 14 Jan.
SMD 23, 40-3, v1, 2p. [1361]
Protest against treaty of 9 July 1868 with the Western Cherokees, as it disregards the rights of these Cherokees residing in North Carolina.

14. Petition of the Cherokees, Creeks, and Choctaws. 14 Jan.
SMD 24, 40-3, v1, 2p. [1361]
Against returning the BIA to the War Dept. from the Interior Dept.: tribes cannot be bayoneted into civilization.

15. Appropriations for Senecas et al. 18 Jan.
HED 47, 40-3, v7, 21p. [1372]
To fulfill the treaty of 23 Feb. 1867 with Senecas, Shawnees, Quapaws, Peorias, Kaskaskias, Weas, Piankeshaws, Ottawas, and Wyandots.

16. Appropriations for the Cheyenne and Arapaho Indians. 19 Jan.
SED 23, 40-3, v1, 8p. [1360]
Under the treaty of 10 May 1868, made with them by the Indian Peace Commission at Fort Laramie, Dakota Territory.

17. Census of the Cherokees of North Carolina. 20 Jan.
SED 25, 40-3, v1, 2p. [1360]
Appropriation to pay expenses of census.

18. Letter on the Indian Service in California. 20 Jan.
SED 26, 40-3, v1, 2p. [1360]
On growing indebtedness.

19. Appropriations for Sioux Indians. 21 Jan.
SED 28, 40-3, v1, 6p. [1360]
For Sisseton and Wahpeton Sioux at Lake Traverse and Devil's Lake, Dakota, under the treaty of 19 Feb. 1867.

20. Appropriations for Indians. 21 Jan.
SED 31, 40-3, v1, 4p. [1360]
To supply deficiencies in appropriations for Sioux, Arikaras, Gros-Ventres, Mandans, and Crows.

21. Resol. of the Kansas Legis. 21 Jan.
SMD 29, 40-3, v1, 1p. [1361]
Asks transfer of Indian Office from the Interior Dept. to the War Dept.

22. Mineral Resources West of the Rocky Mountains. 21 Jan.
HED 54, 40-3, v9, 256p. [1374]
Indians in the various states and territories; effects of Indian hostilities on mining.

23. Mem. of the Yearly Meeting of the Society of Friends. 25 Jan.
HMD 29, 40-3, v1, 4p. [1385]
On treatment of the Indians by whites; best hope for Indians in the U.S. is to break up the tribal relation, and attach Indians permanently to the land.

24. R-M of J. Reeside. 25 Jan.
HR 11, 40-3, v1, 1p. [1388]
Indian hostilities near Fort Riley, Kansas.

25. Letter on the Ottawas and Chippewas. 26 Jan.
SED 33, 40-3, v1, 8p. [1360]
Tracts of land selected by members of the Grand River band of Ottawas and Chippewas under the treaty of 31 July 1855.

26. Letter on Pottawatomie Claims. 28 Jan.
HED 61, 40-3, v9, 31p. [1374]
Investigation of claims of the Indians against the U.S.; treaty of 7 Aug. 1868 calls for said investigation.

27. Report on Choctaw Trust Funds. 30 Jan.
HR 12, 40-3, v1, 9p. [1388]
Sale of securities held for the Choctaws and Chickasaws in order to pay off claims against said Indians under the treaty of 28 Apr. 1866.

28. Report on Indians Killed by Gen. Custer. 1 Feb.
SED 36, 40-3, v1, 3p. [1360]
Whether they were hostile or peaceable; late Indian agent insists that Black Kettle's band of Cheyennes, engaged in the battle of Washita, was peaceable.

29. Resol. of the Kansas Legis. 1 Feb.
SMD 32, 40-3, v1, 1p. [1361]
Ask payment of claims against Arapaho, Cheyenne, Kiowa, and Comanche Indians for depredations during 1863-1864.

30. Resol. of the Kansas Legis. 1 Feb.
SMD 33, 40-3, v1, 2p. [1361]
Protection of settlers on Cherokee neutral lands.

31. Resol. of the Kansas Legis. 1 Feb.
SMD 34, 40-3, v1, 2p. [1361] *or*
HMD 49, 40-3, v1, 2p. [1385]
Against ratification of a recent Osage treaty without certain amendments.

32. Message on Gen. Harney's Report. 2 Feb.
SED 37, 40-3, v1, 1p. [1360]
Report on the Sioux, congregated under treaties made with the Indian Peace Commission, already transmitted to Congress.

33. Report on the International Pacific Railroad. 2 Feb.
HR 14, 40-3, v1, 3p. [1388]
U.S. to retain money arising from transport of Indian supplies.

34. Indian Affairs in the Military Division of Missouri. 4 Feb.
SED 40, 40-3, v1, 17p. [1360]
Kiowa, Cheyenne, Arapaho, and Comanche hostilities; visit to the site of the battle of Washita.

35. Condition of the Osages. 4 Feb.
SED 41, 40-3, v1, 2p. [1360]
Destitute condition of said Indians.

36. List of Private Claims. 4 Feb.
SMD 43, 40-3, v1, 1231p. [1361]
Brought before the Senate from the 14th to the 39th Congresses; some relate to Indian affairs.

37. Mem. of the Montana Legis. 4 Feb.
HMD 41, 40-3, v1, 1p. [1385]
Removal of the Flatheads from the Bitter Root Valley to a reservation in the Jocko Valley.

38. Mem. of the Montana Legis. 4 Feb.
HMD 43, 40-3, v1, 1p. [1385]
Ask revision of Crow treaty, as it makes a reservation out of lands held by settlers.

39. Message on the Hudson's Bay Company. 5 Feb.
SED 42, 40-3, v1, 4p. [1360]
Unauthorized trade with Indians in Alaska.

40. Subsistence of Native Population in Alaska. 5 Feb.
SED 43, 40-3, v1, 3p. [1360]
Supplies to Indians on St. Paul and St. George Islands.

41. Mem. of the Oregon Legis. 8 Feb.
HMD 45, 40-3, v1, 4p. [1385]
Railroad from Oregon to Nevada; history of Indian troubles.

42. Report on Deficiencies for the Indian Service. 9 Feb.
HR 16, 40-3, v1, 1p. [1388]
In New Mexico.

43. R-C of J. Blackburn. 9 Feb.
HR 17, 40-3, v1, 3p. [1388]
Supplies furnished to the Comanche, Kiowa, and Apache Indians in 1868.

44. Petition of F. Hall. 10 Feb.
HMD 46, 40-3, v1, 8p. [1385]
Land title in the reservation of the Swan Creek and Black River Chippewas in Michigan under the treaty of 5 Aug. 1855.

45. Resol. of the Kansas Legis. 11 Feb.
SMD 48, 40-3, v1, 1p. [1361]
Ask payment of claims against various Plains tribes for depredations committed during 1867-1868.

46. Report on a House Resol. 13 Feb.
SR 224, 40-3, v1, 1p. [1362]
Land title problem under the Cherokee treaties of 1866, and 1868 (supplemental).

47. Annual Report of the Smithsonian Institution. 13 Feb.
HED 83, 40-3, v12, 473p. [1380]
Research and publications related to the American Indian; systems of relationship among Indians; etc.

48. Resol. of the Kansas Legis. 17 Feb.
SMD 56, 40-3, v1, 1p. [1361]
Ask removal of Indians (especially Shawnees) from tax exempt status in the State.

49. Report on the Pacific Railroad. 19 Feb.
SR 219, 40-3, v1, 34p. [1362]
Need of government aid; Apache and Comanche hostilities; Indian wars will end; the locomotive is the sole solution to the Indian problem, as it will take the buffalo range from the Indian and replace it with wheat fields.

50. Report on Support of Indians. 22 Feb.
HR 29, 40-3, v1, 8p. [1388]
Report of expenditures under the late Indian Peace Commission for the Sioux, Shoshone, and Snake Indians.

51. Sac and Fox Indian Trust Lands. 24 Feb.
HED 92, 40-3, v13, 2p. [1381]
On sale of the lands in Kansas ceded to the U.S. under the treaty of 14 Oct. 1868.

52. Report on the Central Pacific Railroad of California. 27 Feb.
SED 54, 40-3, v1, 23p. [1360]
Best route across the Great Basin has not been found, as Indian hostilities have delayed surveys.

53. Letter on Seminoles in Florida. 3 Mar.
SED 55, 40-3, v1, 4p. [1360]
On the remnant Seminoles who have not been removed to Indian Territory; concerning their removal.

54. Statements of Appropriations. 3 Mar.
HMD 57, 40-3, v1, 52p. [1385]
During the 3rd session, 40th Congress; Indian expenses.

55. Statement on the Claim of Kansas. 15 Mar.
HMD 6, 41-1, v1, 9p. [1402]
For militia expenses during the rebel invasion, and Indian expedition of 1864.

56. Letter on Money Due the Wyandotts. 19 Mar.
SED 6, 41-1, v1, 4p. [1393]
Under the treaties of 1842, 31 Jan. 1855, and 23 Feb. 1867 (this last treaty was made with the Senecas, Shawnees, and other Indians of Kansas).

57. Mem. of the Utah Legis. 22 Mar.
HMD 19, 41-1, v1, 245p. [1402]
Ask appropriation to cover costs of an Indian war in said Territory during 1865-1867.

58. Mem. of L. Downing. 23 Mar.
SMD 16, 41-1, v1, 3p. [1399]
Principal chief of the Cherokee Nation against the settling of various other Indian tribes on Cherokee land.

59. Report on Appropriations for the Indian Service. 5 Apr.
HR 8, 41-1, v1, 1p. [1403]
Action on Senate amendments to the Indian appropriation bill.

60. Statements of Appropriations. 10 Apr.
HMD 36, 41-1, v1, 42p. [1402]
During the 1st session, 41st Congress; Indian expenses.

61. Judgments in the Court of Claims. 6 Dec.
SMD 2, 41-2, v1, 5p. [1408]
Some cases relevant to Indian affairs.

62. Annual Message to Congress with Documents; Pres. Grant. 6 Dec.
HED 1, 41-2, v1-3, 2771p. [1411-1414]
A new policy towards the Indians (the "Quaker policy") as wards of the U.S., involving placement of all Indians on reservations, and the inducing of Indians to take their lands in severalty; annual report of the Sec. of War (Serials 1412-1413); annual report of the Sec. of Interior

(Serial 1414); annual report of the Gen. Land Office (Serial 1414); annual report of the CIA (Serial 1414), including formation of reservations, trust funds, and reports of Supts., agents, schools, and farms; etc.

63. Annual Report of the Sec. of the Treasury. 6 Dec.
HED 2, 41-2, v4, 533p. [1415]
Year ending 30 June 1869; Indian expenses.

64. Estimates of Appropriations. 6 Dec.
HED 5, 41-2, v5, 305p. [1416]
Year ending 30 June 1871; Indian expenses.

65. Employees in the Interior Dept. 7 Dec.
SED 1, 41-2, v1, 14p. [1405]
Year ending 30 June 1869; OIA.

66. Disbursements for Indian Tribes. 13 Dec.
SED 5, 41-2, v1, 2p. [1405]
For the maintenance of peace; excess expenditures of the Indian Peace Commission; subsistence for Sioux, Kiowas, Comanches, Apaches, Cheyennes, and Arapahoes; supplies for Plains Indians.

67. Indian Disbursements. 13 Dec.
HED 14, 41-2, v5, 187p. [1416]
Year ending 30 June 1869.

68. Letter on St. Paul and St. George Islands, Alaska. 14 Dec.
HMD 11, 41-2, v1, 3p. [1431]
The killing of seals by natives of the islands (Aleuts).

69. Murder of an Indian. 15 Dec.
HED 16, 41-2, v5, 4p. [1416]
Movement of troops to prevent an Indian outbreak caused by the unprovoked killing of an Indian boy by a white settler.

1870

1. Papers on Indian Depredations. 10 Jan.
HMD 20, 41-2, v1, 7p. [1431]
Losses on the frontier during 1867-1868; Sioux, Cheyenne, Arapahoe, Kiowa, Pawnee, Comanche, and Osage depredations in Kansas.

2. Survey of Indian Reservations. 13 Jan.
HED 53, 41-2, v6, 6p. [1417]
Estimate of appropriations needed for the year ending 30 June 1871 for surveys under treaties with a number of tribes.

3. Resol. of Rep. McCormick. 13 Jan.
HMD 21, 41-2, v1, 1p. [1431]
Asks the Com. on Territories to enquire into the establishment of a territorial government over the civilized tribes inhabiting Indian Territory.

4. Estimates of Appropriations for Sioux. 19 Jan.
HED 67, 41-2, v6, 6p. [1417]
For Sisseton, Wahpeton, and Santee Sioux at Lake Traverse and Devil's Lake, Dakota.

5. Report on the Minnesota State University. 19 Jan.
HR 4, 41-2, v1, 3p. [1436]
Supported by sale of lands to which Indian title has, or may be, extinguished.

6. Suppressing Indian Hostilities in Utah. 20 Jan.
HED 44, 41-2, v5, 7p. [1416]
Expenses of suppressing Ute and Navajo hostilities during 1865-1867.

7. R-C of D. McCann. 21 Jan.
HR 5, 41-2, v1, 3p. [1436]
Transport of annuity goods from Omaha to Fort Laramie in 1866.

8. R-M of J. Lane. 21 Jan.
HR 8, 41-2, v1, 1p. [1436]
Depredations by the Arapahoes, Cheyennes, or Sioux in Nebraska during 1865.

9. Treaty with Delaware Indians. 25 Jan.
HED 83, 41-2, v6, 2p. [1417]
On the report of the negotation of the treaty 4 July 1866.

10. Appropriations for Indians. 25 Jan.
HED 84, 41-2, v6, 2p. [1417]
Board of Indian Com'rs recommends liberal expenditures on education.

11. Resol. of the Kansas Legis. 26 Jan.
SMD 30, 41-2, v1, 1p. [1408]
Ask extinguishment of Indian title to the Black Bob Shawnee reservation.

12. Report on Management of Indians in British America. 27 Jan.
HMD 35, 41-2, v3, 38p. [1433]
To discover why there have been no major Indian wars there, and why civilization is proceeding well; the "Six Nations" of Mohawks, Senecas, Cayugas, Oneidas, Onondagas, and Tuscaroras; populations increasing.

13. Paper on the Claims of Kansas. 28 Jan.
HMD 36, 41-2, v3, 16p. [1433]
For expenses of the 1864 Indian expedition.

14. R-P of M. Estill et al. 2 Feb.
SR 20, 41-2, v1, 3p. [1409]
Supplies to California Indians during 1851.

15. R-P of C. Luth. 2 Feb.
SR 22, 41-2, v1, 1p. [1409]
Cheyenne depredations of 1868 in Nebraska.

16. Report on Claims of the Delaware Indians. 2 Feb.
SR 24, 41-2, v1, 1p. [1409]
Stock stolen since 1854; payment under treaty of 4 July 1866.

17. Affairs on the Red River of the North. 3 Feb.
SED 33, 41-2, v1, 52p. [1405]
Transfer of the Northwest Territory from the Hudson's Bay Company to the Dominion of Canada; Canadian governor driven into the U.S. by inhabitants of that territory, including Indian forces and half-breeds.

18. Claims of Delaware Indians. 3 Feb.
HED 108, 41-2, v6, 13p. [1417]
For stock stolen from them since 1854; under the treaty of 4 July 1866.

19. Appropriations for Indian Interpreters. 7 Feb.
HED 117, 41-2, v6, 2p. [1417]
On deficiencies in the appropriation for the year ending 30 June 1871.

20. L-C of Pottawatomie Indians. 8 Feb.
HED 154, 41-2, v7, 1p. [1418]
Examination of claims under the treaty of 7 Aug. 1868.

21. General Council of Certain Indians. 9 Feb.
SED 36, 41-2, v1, 3p. [1405]
Funds required to defray expenses of a general council guaranteed under treaties with the Cherokees, Creeks, Seminoles, Choctaws, and Chickasaws.

22. Report on Expenses for Troops in Montana. 9 Feb.
SR 31, 41-2, v1, 4p. [1409]
Called to fight an Indian war which never occurred.

23. Sale of Shawnee Lands in Kansas. 11 Feb.
SED 40, 41-2, v2, 210p. [1406]
Belonging to the Black Bob band of Shawnees; two problems: (1) claims of illegal settlers on the lands, and (2) whether the sale of lands is binding or not.

24. Mem. of Members of Black Bob's Band of Shawnees. 1 Feb.
SMD 49, 41-2, v1, 17p. [1408]
Against break-up of the tribal organization by division of lands in severalty; sale of said lands to settlers.

25. Establishment of Indian Tribes. 11 Feb.
HED 125, 41-2, v6, 3p. [1417]
Location and establishment of Kiowas, Comanches, Apaches, Arapahoes, Sacs, Foxes, and Cheyennes on lands in Indian Territory.

26. Claims of Kansas Indians. 11 Feb.
HED 127, 41-2, v6, 7p. [1417]
Claims of Senecas, Shawnees, and Quapaws under the treaty of 23 Feb. 1867.

27. Annuities Withheld from Indian Tribes. 11 Feb.
HED 130, 41-2, v6, 2p. [1417]
No annuities are being withheld from Indians during the year ending 30 June 1871.

28. Indian Goods Lost on the Missouri River. 14 Feb.
SED 44, 41-2, v2, 2p. [1406]
Wreck of the steamer *Last Chance* above Omaha in 1867.

29. Fur Seal Fisheries of Alaska. 14 Feb.
HED 136, 41-2, v6, 6p. [1417]
Indians, or "native Aleutians," are allowed to kill seals for subsistence, and to sell their furs.

30. Report on Oregon Volunteers. 15 Feb.
SR 37, 41-2, v1, 2p. [1409]
Protection of emigrant wagon trains in 1854.

31. Resol. of the Kansas Legis. 16 Feb.
SMD 55, 41-2, v1, 2p. [1408]
Removal of all Indians who have not become citizens; grant their lands to railroad companies; grant land for a railroad through Indian Territory.

32. Resol. of the Kansas Legis. 16 Feb.
SMD 56, 41-2, v1, 2p. [1408]
Ask protection of State's frontier from Indian depredations.

33. Appropriations for Indian Service in Montana. 18 Feb.

HED 137, 41-2, v6, 2p. [1417]
For services at the Flathead and Blackfeet agencies.

34. Appropriations for Sioux Indians. 18 Feb.
HED 138, 41-2, v6, 2p. [1417]
Indebtedness incurred by Geb. Harney in the Sioux district of Dakota.

35. Special Agent Colyer's Report on Fur Seal Fisheries in Alaska. 18 Feb.
HED 144, 41-2, v7, 12p. [1418]
Aleut Indians, on islands off Alaska, hunt seals, and sell their furs.

36. Indian Affairs in Oregon. 18 Feb.
HED 146, 41-2, v7, 4p. [1418]
Interviews with Klamath Indians; possible success of Pres. Grant's "Quaker policy" towards the Indians; desire of Indians to become like whites.

37. Appropriation for the Indian Service. 18 Feb.
HED 148, 41-2, v7, 2p. [1418]
For the payment of claims against Kiowas, Comanches, and Blackfeet.

38. Appropriations for the Fort Berthold Agency. 18 Feb.
HED 150, 41-2, v7, 6p. [1418]
To pay outstanding debts; engagements between agency Indians and the Sioux.

39. Letter on Goods Given to the Kiowas. 18 Feb.
HED 151, 41-2, v7, 3p. [1418]
By J. Tappan in 1868 for the release of white captives.

40. Letter on Money Due S. Ward. 18 Feb.
HED 152, 41-2, v7, 7p. [1418]
For supplies issued to Sioux at Fort Laramie in 1868 by order of the Indian Peace Commission.

41. Engagement with the Piegan Indians. 19 Feb.
SED 49, 41-2, v2, 9p. [1406]
Crow, Piegan, Blood, and Blackfoot Indians of Montana disturbed by non-fulfillment of treaty stipulations by the U.S.; situation tense; Piegan depredations.

42. Resol. of the Kansas Legis. 19 Feb.
SMD 58, 41-2, v1, 1p. [1408]
Protest ratification of a treaty for the sale of the Kaw Indian reserve.

43. Resol. of the Kansas Legis. 19 Feb.
SMD 59, 41-2, v1, 1p. [1408]
Commission to investigate claims arising from Indian depredations favored.

44. Resol. of the Kansas Legis. 22 Feb.
SMD 60, 41-2, v1, 2p. [1408]
Ask payment against Osage, Kaw, and other Indians from their moneys.

45. Resol. of the Kansas Legis. 22 Feb.
SMD 61, 41-2, v1, 2p. [1408]
Ask payment of claims arising from the Indian expedition of 1864.

46. Number of Indians in Various Tribes. 22 Feb.
HED 158, 41-2, v7, 5p. [1418]
List of tribes, populations, and treaties requiring annuity payments.

47. Letter on Flathead Indians. 25 Feb.
HED 165, 41-2, v7, 4p. [1418]
Appropriation for reconstruction of buildings destroyed by fire.

48. Payment of Taxes by Cherokee Indians. 28 Feb.
SED 48, 41-2, v2, 2p. [1406]
On products manufactured in the Cherokee Nation and sold within the Indian Territory.

49. Annual Report of the Smithsonian Institution. 1 Mar.
HED 153, 41-3, v12, 430p. [1460]
For 1869; research related to the American Indian; photographic portraits of Indians.

50. Resol. of Rep. Voorhees. 7 Mar.
HMD 79, 41-2, v3, 2p. [1433]
Regarding a court dispute over taxation of goods produced in the Cherokee Nation for sale in Indian Territory; treaty of 19 July 1866.

51. Appropriations for Certain Indian Treaties. 8 Mar.
SED 57, 41-2, v2, 5p. [1406]
To carry out treaties made by the Indian Peace Commission; Indian hostilities arising because of nonfulfillment by U.S.; Piegans, Sioux, Utes, Cheyennes, Arapahoes, and other Plains Indians being forced into hostilities.

52. Encroachments on Osage Lands. 8 Mar.
HED 179, 41-2, v7, 6p. [1418]
By white settlers in Kansas.

53. Expedition Against the Piegan Indians. 8 Mar.
HED 185, 41-2, v7, 9p. [1418]
Campaign, in Montana, against the Piegan tribe of Blackfeet Indians during 1870.

54. Letter from the Principal Chief of the Cherokee Nation. 8 Mar.
HMD 76, 41-2, v3, 15p. [1433]
Against a territorial form of government over Indian Territory.

55. Mem. of Creek Indians. 9 Mar.
SMD 76, 41-2, v1, 4p. [1408]
Against establishment of a territorial government for Indian Territory.

56. Mem. of Cherokee Indians. 14 Mar.
SMD 83, 41-2, v1, 7p. [1408]
Against establishment of a territorial government over Indian Territory; taxation without representation; etc.

57. R-P of F. Kelly. 15 Mar.
SR 68, 41-2, v1, 2p. [1409]
Captive of the Blackfeet band of Sioux in 1864.

58. Expedition Against the Piegan Indians. 15 Mar.
HED 197, 41-2, v7, 3p. [1418]
Campaign during 1870 during Montana.

59. Black Bob Lands in Kansas. 17 Mar.
SED 65, 41-2, v2, 4p. [1406]
Unwarranted settler encroachment on Shawnee lands.

60. Appropriations for Delaware Indians. 17 Mar.
HED 202, 41-2, v7, 4p. [1418]
To fulfill the treaty of 4 July 1866; dissolution of tribal relations, and accepting U.S. citizenship.

61. Statistics of Mining West of the Rocky Mountains. 17 Mar.
HED 207, 41-2, v10, 805p. [1424]
Indians in New Mexico; Indians in Montana; Indian labor in eastern Nevada; etc.

62. Mem. of the Choctaw Nation. 18 Mar.
SMD 90, 41-2, v1, 12p. [1408]
Against territorial government for Indian Territory.

63. Resol. of the House of Reps. 18 Mar.
SMD 91, 41-2, v1, 1p. [1408]
Appointment of a Special Com. to investigate the subject of a change in Indian policy.

64. Bombardment of an Indian Village. 21 Mar.
SED 67, 41-2, v2, 10p. [1406]
At Wrangel, Alaska; refusal of Chiefs of the Stikine Indians to deliver a murderer to authorities of the government.

65. Mem. of Cherokee Indians. 21 Mar.
SMD 92, 41-2, v1, 3p. [1408]
Against carrying out of a bill giving U.S. ownership of Cherokee lands west of the 96th degree of west longitude; conflict with the treaty of 19 July 1866.

66. Letter on a Treaty with the Shawnees, Quapaws, and Other Kansas Tribes. 21 Mar.
HMD 93, 41-2, v3, 2p. [1433]
Land cession under the treaty of 23 Feb. 1867.

67. Wrangel, Alaska, Previous to Bombardment. 22 Mar.
SED 68, 41-2, v2, 23p. [1406]
Description and drawings of the Indian village; abuse of the Indians of the Stikine tribe; village bombarded by U.S. troops when chiefs refuse to deliver an alleged murderer.

68. Stray Bands of Indians. 23 Mar.
HED 216, 41-2, v11, 5p. [1425]
Removal of Pottawatomies and Winnebagoes from Wisconsin to Kansas and Nebraska respectively.

69. Loyal Indians and Freedmen of the Creek Nation. 23 Mar.
HED 217, 41-2, v11, 2p. [1425]
Payment to those who enlisted in the federal army during the Civil War; under the treaty of 16 June 1866.

70. L-C of A. Hotaling. 23 Mar.
HED 218, 41-2, v11, 2p. [1425]
For rent of land for use of the Indian service in California.

71. Mem. of the New Mexico Legis. 23 Mar.
HMD 95, 41-2, v3, 2p. [1433]
Ask authorization to raise two cavalry regiments for defense against Indians.

72. Condition of Freedmen in Indian Territory. 25 Mar.
SED 71, 41-2, v2, 5p. [1406]
In the Choctaw and Chickasaw Nations, which were disloyal during the Civil War.

73. Mem. of the New Mexico Legis. 25 Mar.
SMD 97, 41-2, v1, 2p. [1408]
Favors location of a Utah Indian reservation in the region of the San Juan River, as stipulated by a treaty with said tribe.

74. L-C of Cherokee Indians. 28 Mar.
SMD 98, 41-2, v1, 3p. [1408]
Concerning control of lands west of the 96th degree of west longitude; treaty of 19 July 1866.

75. Mem. of the Minnesota Legis. 28 Mar.
HMD 104, 41-2, v3, 2p. [1433]
Removal of Sioux from the Lake Traverse reservation who are not authorized to be there; treaty of 19 Feb. 1867 with the Sisseton and Wahpeton Sioux.

76. On the Case of E. Boudinot. 30 Mar.
HR 52, 41-2, v2, 8p. [1437]
Conflict between U.S. tax laws and the treaty of 19 July 1866 with the Cherokees; tax on products sold within Indian Territory.

77. Mem. of the Wisconsin Legis. 31 Mar.
SMD 101, 41-2, v1, 1p. [1408]
Removal of bands of Indians from the State.

78. Claims of the Wyandott Indians. 1 Apr.
SED 77, 41-2, v2, 55p. [1406]
Under the treaty of 23 Feb. 1867.

79. Mem. of Colored People of the Choctaw and Chickasaw Tribes. 1 Apr.
SMD 106, 41-2, v1, 7p. [1408]
Still being deprived of rights by their late Indian masters who fought on the side of the rebels in the Civil War.

80. Report on Arguments Concerning Cherokee Neutral Lands of Kansas. 1 Apr.
HR 53, 41-2, v2, 33p. [1437]
On conflicts over land title, and sale of lands; railroad construction.

81. Mem. of the Minnesota Legis. 4 Apr.
HMD 116, 41-2, v3, 2p. [1433]
Ask establishment of a military post at or near Pembina; Sioux hostilities.

82. Mem. of the Minnesota Legis. 4 Apr.
HMD 120, 41-2, v3, 2p. [1433]
Removal of unauthorized Indians from the Lake Traverse reservation; treaty of 19 Feb. 1867 with the Sisseton and Wahpeton Sioux.

83. Difficulties with Indian Tribes. 6 Apr.
HED 240, 41-2, v11, 179p. [1425]
With Cheyennes, Arapahoes, Comanches, Apaches, and Kiowas during 1867; employment of Osages in the military service; attack on the Cheyenne village on the Washita.

84. R-P of Kansas Citizens and Shawnee Indians. 12 Apr.
SR 99, 41-2, v1, 3p. [1409]
Sale of the lands belonging to the Black Bob band of Shawnees.

85. R-M of A. and W. Ross. 20 Apr.
SR 113, 41-2, v1, 8p. [1409]
Losses on their property in Cherokee country during the Civil War.

86. R-P of M. Orme. 27 Apr.
SR 127, 41-2, v1, 1p. [1409]
Auditor connected with the Chickasaw trust fund.

87. Report on Consolidation of Indian Tribes. 27 Apr.
SR 131, 41-2, v1, 5p. [1409]
Consolidation of the Choctaws, Chickasaws, Creeks, Seminoles, and Cherokees under a territorial government with the name Oklahoma, or "the home of the Red Man."

88. Letter on Indian Tribes in the U.S. 29 Apr.
SMD 136, 41-2, v1, 26p. [1408]
List of tribes, their location, their population, and their condition; all tribes peaceable except for Blackfeet, Bloods, Piegans, Sioux, Cheyennes, Arapahoes, Kiowas, and Comanches.

89. Indians of Southeastern Oregon. 3 May.
SED 84, 41-2, v2, 2p. [1406]
Establishment of Modoc, Shoshone, and Bannock Indians on the Klamath Indian reservation which was established under the Modoc-Klamath treaty of 1864.

90. Report on a Treaty with New York Indians. 3 May.
SR 145, 41-2, v1, 5p. [1409]
Concluded 4 Dec. 1868; cedes lands west of Missouri to the U.S.; surrenders Indian right to be removed there; sale of lands in Kansas to settlers.

91. R-C of Kansas. 3 May.
HR 64, 41-2, v2, 4p. [1437]
Indian expedition of 1864.

92. Efforts to Educate and Civilize Indian Tribes. 11 May.
HED 260, 41-2, v12, 2p. [1426]
Annual funds; charitable organizations; etc.

93. Appropriations for Indians. 11 May.
HED 261, 41-2, v12, 2p. [1426]
Subsistence for the Arapahoes, Cheyennes, Apaches, Kiowas, and Comanches; the failure of Congress

to carry out treaty stipulations has prevented the placement of these Indians on reservations where they might grow crops.

94. Expedition Against the Piegan Indians. 11 May.
HED 269, 41-2, v12, 74p. [1426]
The failure of Congress to act on treaties has resulted in a highly unstable situation in Montana, and can be seen as the cause of the late Piegan campaign.

95. Indian Outrages on the Western and Southwestern Frontiers. 16 May.
HMD 139, 41-2, v3, 8p. [1433]
Comanche, Kiowa, and Osage depredations against whites and Indians of the "Civilized Tribes"; list of individuals captured and released by the hostiles.

96. Resol. of Rep. Conner. 19 May.
HMD 137, 41-2, v3, 2p. [1433]
Asks Mexico to fulfill treaty stipulations; Kickapoo and Lipan raids from Mexico into Texas.

97. Education of Indians of the Central Superintendency. 20 May.
HED 284, 41-2, v12, 3p. [1426]
Appropriations required at the Kiowa and Comanche agency, and the Cheyenne and Arapaho agency.

98. Letter on the Fort Ripley Military Reserve. 23 May.
SED 87, 41-2, v2, 1p. [1406]
It still is required for protection of settlers in Minnesota from Indian hostilities.

99. Message on Encroachments Upon Indians in Wyoming Territory. 23 May.
SED 89, 41-2, v2, 18p. [1406]
Party of citizens being formed at Cheyenne to explore the Black Hills to look for mineral deposits; Sioux, Shoshone, and Crow lands; treaty of 29 Apr. 1868 attacked.

100. Mem. of the Cherokee, Creek, and Choctaw Nations. 23 May.
SMD 143, 41-2, v1, 12p. [1408]
Against territorial government over Indian Territory.

101. R-M of P. Pitchlynn. 27 May.
SR 178, 41-2, v1, 2p. [1409]
Payments to the Choctaws under the treaties of 22 June 1855, and 28 Apr. 1866.

102. Mem. of Texas Citizens. 28 May.
HMD 142, 41-2, v3, 7p. [1433]
Indian hostilities; Indians seem to be those located at the Fort Sill Indian reservation.

103. Amendments to the Cherokee Treaty of 19 July 1866. 2 June.
SMD 148, 41-2, v1, 8p. [1408]
Concerning title to lands, land cessions, etc.

104. R-P of the Rep. of A. Campbell. 3 June.
SR 203, 41-2, v1, 2p. [1409]
Payments and land to the interpreter for the Sioux delegation to Washington, D.C.; treaties of 1837, and 1858.

105. R-C of Kansas Legis. 9 June.
HR 77, 41-2, v3, 13p. [1438]
Settlers on Indian lands in the eastern part of Kansas territory (formed in 1854).

106. Resol. of the Texas Legis. 10 June.
SMD 150, 41-2, v1, 2p. [1408]
Ask prevention of Mexico from harboring hostile Kickapoo and Lipan Indians who commit depredations in Texas.

107. L-C of Black Beaver. 11 June.
HED 290, 41-2, v12, 7p. [1426]
A Delaware Indian who served as a guide to U.S. troops in the Civil War.

108. Appropriations for Indian Delegations to Washington, D.C. 11 June.
HED 291, 41-2, v12, 2p. [1426]
Sioux, Pawnee, and Osage delegations.

109. Indian Reservation in San Diego County, California. 11 June.
HED 296, 41-2, v12, 15p. [1426]
Information concerning the establishment of a reservation in southern California.

110. Letter from Cherokee Indians. 14 June.
SMD 154, 41-2, v1, 4p. [1408]
Transmits address made at the Grand or International Council of Tribes residing in Indian Territory; asks observance of treaty stipulations; "territorial government" bills merely for acquisition of Indian lands.

111. Appropriations for Sioux Indians. 16 June.
HED 297, 41-2, v12, 2p. [1426]
Payments due the upper and lower bands of Sioux of Minnesota under the treaty of 19 June 1858.

112. R-P of J. Traynor. 21 June.
SR 219, 41-2, v1, 1p. [1409]
Battle of Infernal Caverns, Oregon, in 1868 with the Indians.

113. R-M of L. Smith. 21 June.
HR 97, 41-2, v3, 2p. [1438]
Cheyenne depredations of 1864 in Nebraska; captive of the Cheyennes for six months.

114. R-P of the Administrator of G. Upson. 21 June.
HR 98, 41-2, v3, 2p. [1438]
Agent for the Blackfeet, and other Montana tribes; treaty negotiations.

115. On the Relief of J. Birckhead. 22 June.
SR 223, 41-2, v1, 8p. [1409]
Seminole war of 1835 in Florida.

116. R-P of Kansas Citizens. 22 June.
SR 225, 41-2, v1, 3p. [1409]
On imposition of a tax on cattle driven through their country by the Cherokees.

117. Right of Kansas to Certain Lands. 24 June.
SED 101, 41-2, v3, 3p. [1407]
Lands sold to the U.S. by the Osages under the treaty of 29 Sept. 1865.

118. Appropriation for Removal of the Kaw Indians. 27 June.
HED 303, 41-2, v12, 1p. [1426]
From Kansas to Indian Territory.

119. L-C of Reps of G. Fisher. 6 July.
SED 106, 41-2, v3, 4p. [1407]
Creek Indian war.

120. Report on Black Bob Indian Lands. 6 July.
HR 118, 41-2, v3, 7p. [1438]
Shawnee lands in Kansas; conflict over land titles.

121. R-P of G. Fisher. 11 July.
SR 252, 41-2, v1, 15p. [1409]
Property destroyed by U.S. troops during 1813-1814 in the Creek war.

122. Appropriation to Pay Certain Indian Depredation Claims. 14 July.
HED 311, 41-2, v13, 2p. [1427]
Claims against the Cheyennes and Arapahoes.

123. Argument of W. Laughlin. 14 July.
HMD 150, 41-2, v3, 20p. [1433]
On title to the Cherokee neutral lands; treaty of 1835; treaty of 7 Oct. 1861 between the Cherokees and the Confederate States of America.

124. Message of Pres. Grant. 15 July.
SED 115, 41-2, v3, 2p. [1407]
Asks appropriations be made to avert Indian hostilities before adjournment of the session.

125. Statements of Appropriations. 15 July.
HMD 153, 41-2, v3, 144p. [1433]
During the 2d session, 41st Congress; Indian expenses.

126. Property in the Interior Dept. 5 Dec.
SED 1, 41-3, v1, 3p. [1440]
Articles in the OIA.

127. Annual Message to Congress with Documents; Pres. Grant. 5 Dec.
HED 1, 41-3, v1-4, 3417p. [1445-1450]
Continued reform of Indian management by making it a missionary work; agencies given over to religious denominations; annual report of the Sec. of War (Serials 1446-1447); annual report of the Sec. of Interior (Serials 1449-1450); annual report of the Gen. Land Office (Serial 1449); annual report of the CIA (Serial 1449), including difficulties with Plains Indians and Indians in Montana (the Piegan band of Blackfeet Indians), trust funds, the government's "Quaker policy," Sioux delegation in Washington, D.C., census, and reports of Supts., agents, and schools; etc.

128. Annual Report of the Sec. of the Treasury. 5 Dec.
HED 2, 41-3, v5, 513p. [1451]
Year ending 30 June 1870; Indian expenses.

129. Estimates of Appropriations. 5 Dec.
HED 5, 41-3, v6, 291p. [1452]
Year ending 30 June 1872; Indian expenses.

130. Judgments of the Court of Claims. 6 Dec.
SMD 6, 41-3, v1, 8p. [1442]
During 1870; some cases related to Indian affairs.

131. Report on the Effect of the 14th Amendment Upon Indian Tribes. 14 Dec.
SR 268, 41-3, v1, 11p. [1443]
The Com. on the Judiciary believes said amendment has no effect whatever on the status of Indians; they are not citizens, and their treaties are not annulled.

132. Communication from Capt. Adams. 19 Dec.
HMD 12, 41-3, v1, 20p. [1462]
Exploration of the Colorado River

area; Indian success at growing crops; journal of the expedition; Cocopah, Yuma, Mojave, Chimawava, Paiute, Utah, Moquis, Pimo, Maricopa, Apache, Cheyenne, Sioux, and Arapaho Indians discussed.

133. Reconnaissance of the Dept. of Dakota. 21 Dec.
SED 8, 41-3, v1, 32p. [1440]
Report on Forts Ellis, Shaw, Benton, Buford, Stevenson, Rice, Sully, Randall, Abercrombie, Wadsworth, Ransom, Totten, Ripley, and Snelling, along with Camp Looke; surrounding Indian reservations; reasons for construction of forts sometimes concerns control of Indians.

134. On the Relief of Jordan and McPike. 21 Dec.
SR 274, 41-3, v1, 4p. [1443]
Supplies to troops in the Paiute campaign of 1860 in Utah.

135. L-C of the Choctaw Indians. 21 Dec.
HED 25, 41-3, v7, 5p. [1453]
Payment of $250,000 to the Choctaws under the treaty of 28 Apr. 1866.

136. Expenses of Indian Delegations to Washington, D.C. 21 Dec.
HED 26, 41-3, v7, 2p. [1453]
Sec. of Interior granted an appropriation to use.

137. Indian Orphan Accounts. 21 Dec.
HED 27, 41-3, v7, 2p. [1453]
Estimate of appropriation to settle the accounts.

138. Appropriation for the Navajo Indians. 21 Dec.
HED 28, 41-3, v7, 2p. [1453]
For subsistence of Navajoes in New Mexico.

1871

1. Preliminary Report of a Geological Survey of Wyoming and Contiguous Territories. 1 Jan.
HED 325, 42-2, v15, 511p. [1515]
Indians of the area; account of the expedition.

2. R-C of the Choctaw Indians. 5 Jan.
SR 278, 41-3, v1, 1p. [1443]
Payment of $250,000 to the Choctaws only awaits action by the Pres.

3. Petition of California Citizens. 6 Jan.
HMD 17, 41-3, v1, 16p. [1462]
Railroad communication with Arizona; would cross area of hostile Indians; this has raised the price of transport and prevented heavy mining operations in the past.

4. Indiana State Bonds. 9 Jan.
SED 12, 41-3, v1, 12p. [1440]
Held in trust for Chickasaws and Pottawatomies by the Sec. of the Interior.

5. Mem. of the Oregon Legis. 9 Jan.
HMD 19, 41-3, v1, 2p. [1462]
Ask removal of Indians from the Siletz reservation, and sale of the land to settlers.

6. Mem. of the Oregon Legis. 9 Jan.
HMD 22, 41-3, v1, 2p. [1462]
Construction of a road from Nevada to Oregon through an area inhabited only by Indians.

7. R-P of J. Getty. 11 Jan.
SR 284, 41-3, v1, 3p. [1443]
Driven from land during the Indian outbreak of 1862 in Minnesota.

8. Report on Cherokee Neutral Lands. 11 Jan.
HR 5, 41-3, v1, 13p. [1464]
History of the title to said lands; originally ceded to the U.S. by the treaty of 2 June 1825 with the Osages; sale of the lands in Kansas; Cherokee treaties.

9. Survey of the Grande Ronde Reservation. 12 Jan.
HED 46, 41-3, v7, 2p. [1453]
Reserve in Oregon; lands to be assigned to family heads and others.

10. Appropriations for Navajo Indians. 12 Jan.
HED 47, 41-3, v7, 2p. [1453]
To subsist Navajoes in New Mexico.

11. Annuities to Winnebago Indians. 12 Jan.
HED 48, 41-3, v7, 3p. [1453]
Under the treaties of 1 Nov. 1837, and 13 Oct. 1846; Winnebagoes still residing in Minnesota.

12. Mem. of the Dakota Legis. 13 Jan.
SMD 24, 41-3, v1, 1p. [1442]
Extension of telegraph from Yankton to Fort Randall; unsettled condition of Indian affairs in the territory.

13. Report on Cherokee Neutral Lands. 13 Jan.
HR 12, 41-3, v1, 51p. [1464]

History of the title to said lands in Kansas; treaty of 2 June 1825 with the Osages; Cherokee treaties (this represents the minority report of the Com. on Indian Affairs).

14. Mem. of Michigan and Indiana Indians. 16 Jan.
HMD 32, 41-3, v1, 8p. [1462]
Amounts due Pottawatomies remaining in said states under treaties dated from 3 Aug. 1795 to 23 Sept. 1836; ask settlements under the treaties of 1861, and 1866.

15. Survey of Indian Reservations. 18 Jan.
HED 51, 41-3, v7, 2p. [1453]
Cherokee reserve; Choctaw and Chickasaw land cession under the treaty of 28 Apr. 1868.

16. Bonds to Indian Tribes. 18 Jan.
HED 58, 41-3, v7, 3p. [1453]
Delivery of $250,000 worth of bonds to the Choctaws.

17. Mem. on Behalf of the Choctaw Nation. 18 Jan.
HMD 37, 41-3, v1, 10p. [1462]
Claim to proceeds of sale of lands east of the Mississippi River under the treaty of 22 June 1855.

18. Report on Payments Due the Pottawatomies. 19 Jan.
SR 299, 41-3, v1, 7p. [1443]
Under 19 treaties commencing 2 Dec. 1795, and ending 23 July 1846.

19. Report on a Railroad from Salt Lake City to the Colorado River. 20 Jan.
SR 302, 41-3, v1, 2p. [1443]
Could provide transport of annuity goods in Indian reserves in the Great Basin.

20. L-C of Wyandott Indians. 21 Jan.
HED 83, 41-3, v8, 7p. [1454]
Settler and emigrant depredations of 1849, 1859, and 1862-1865 in Kansas.

21. L-C of Jordan and McPike et al. 23 Jan.
SED 19, 41-3, v1, 5p. [1440]
Supplies to troops during the Paiute campaign of 1860 in Utah.

22. Resol. of the Kansas Legis. 23 Jan.
SMD 29, 41-3, v1, 1p. [1442]
Settlers on the Osage diminished reserve; amendments to the Indian appropriations act of 15 July 1870.

23. Expenses of the General Council of Indians. 23 Jan.
HED 64, 41-3, v8, 2p. [1454]
Estimate to cover the annual council of tribes within the Indian Territory.

24. Aid to Civilize the Indians. 23 Jan.
HED 65, 41-3, v8, 2p. [1454]
Additional funds needed for the central superintendency; Kickapoos, Ottawas, Peorias, Quapaws, Senecas, Wyandotts, Shawnees, Delawares, Wichitas, Kaws, Pottawatomies, Kiowas, Comanches, Apaches, Cheyennes, and Arapahoes.

25. L-C of C. Hedges. 23 Jan.
HED 66, 41-3, v8, 5p. [1454]
Supplies to Yancton Sioux during 1866-1867.

26. Mem. of the Dakota Legis. 23 Jan.
HMD 47, 41-3, v1, 2p. [1462]
Wagon road construction; transport of Indian supplies.

27. R-P of S. Evans. 24 Jan.
SR 309, 41-3, v1, 1p. [1443]
Indian attack upon Camp Crittenden in Arizona during 1870.

28. Papers on the Confederacy of Indian Tribes. 24 Jan.
HMD 49, 41-3, v1, 6p. [1462]
Government organized by the tribes within the Indian Territory; protection of the area from the encroachment of whites; etc.

29. L-C of B. Wood. 26 Jan.
HED 77, 41-3, v8, 3p. [1454]
Yancton Sioux depredations of 1869 in Dakota.

30. L-C of J. Bourbeau and C. Lamoureaux. 26 Jan.
HED 78, 41-3, v8, 6p. [1454]
Sioux depredations of 1865 near Fort Laramie.

31. L-C of W. Moore and Company. 26 Jan.
HED 79, 41-3, v8, 9p. [1454]
Cheyenne depredations of 1869 in Kansas.

32. L-C of J. Bissonnette. 26 Jan.
HED 80, 41-3, v8, 6p. [1454]
Sioux, Cheyenne, and Arapaho depredations of 1864-1865 in Dakota.

33. L-C of A. Smith. 26 Jan.
HED 81, 41-3, v8, 3p. [1454]
Supplies to the Sheep-Eaters (or northern Shoshones) in Montana during 1870.

34. L-C of B. Marfin. 26 Jan.
HED 82, 41-3, v8, 3p. [1454]
Navajo depredations in New Mexico during 1870.

35. Resol. of the Kansas Legis. 27 Jan.
SMD 38, 41-3, v1, 2p. [1442]
To protect settlers on the Cherokee neutral lands; Cherokee treaty of 11 Aug. 1866.

36. Proceedings of a Council of Indian Tribes. 30 Jan.
SED 26, 41-3, v1, 23p. [1440]
Held during Dec. of 1870 at Ocmulgee in the Creek Nation, Indian Territory; participating tribes included the Creeks, Seminoles, Cherokees, Choctaws, Chickasaws, Osages, Ottawas, Shawnees, Quapaws, Senecas, Sacs, Foxes, Wyandotts, and Peorias; not included were the Wichitas, Comanches, Kiowas, Cheyennes, and Arapahoes.

37. R-C of S. Ward. 30 Jan.
SR 323, 41-3, v1, 1p. [1443]
Supplies to Sioux in 1865.

38. Absentee Shawnee Lands in Kansas. 1 Feb.
SMD 43, 41-3, v1, 3p. [1442]
Sale of lands to settlers; treaty of 30 May 1854 with the Shawnees.

39. Mem. of the New York Legis. 1 Feb.
SMD 44, 41-3, v1, 1p. [1442]
Ask treaty be made with Senecas by which they will cede their title to the Allegany reservation.

40. Report on the Organization of Indian Territory. 1 Feb.
SR 336, 41-3, v1, 11p. [1443]
Two important changes of policy: (1) establishment of a territorial government, and (2) change in the system of land tenure; wishes of Indians will be considered, but the decisions are to be made in Congress.

41. R-C of the Northwest Fur Company. 1 Feb.
SR 337, 41-3, v1, 3p. [1443]
Supplies to Assiniboines who aided whites at Fort Union to repel a Sioux attack during 1866-1867.

42. Treaties and Conventions Concluded by the U.S. with Other Powers Since 4 July 1776. 2 Feb.
SED 36, 41-3, v2, 912p. [1441]
Treaties with Indian tribes not included; treaties with Great Britain, Spain, Mexico, and Russia relevant to Indian affairs.

43. Appropriations for Montana Indian War Claims. 4 Feb.
HED 97, 41-3, v10, 1p. [1458]
For claims arising in 1867.

44. Montana Indian War Claims. 4 Feb.
HED 98, 41-3, v10, 20p. [1458]
Expenses of suppressing Indian hostilities in 1867.

45. Extension of Time of Payment on Indian Lands. 6 Feb.
SED 32, 41-3, v1, 4p. [1440]
To settlers on Osage lands in Kansas.

46. Mem. of the Oregon Legis. 6 Feb.
HMD 77, 41-3, v2, 2p. [1463]
Ask extinguishment of Indian title to the portions of the Siletz and Grande Ronde reservations lying north of the Grande Ronde agency.

47. R-P of F. Kelly. 7 Feb.
SR 348, 41-3, v1, 1p. [1443]
Sioux hostilities of 1864 near Fort Laramie; taken captive by Indians.

48. L-C of B. Montano. 7 Feb.
HED 106, 41-3, v10, 24p. [1458]
Land claim in New Mexico; settlers driven from land by Navajo and Apache depredations.

49. L-C of the Northwest Fur Company. 7 Feb.
HED 107, 41-3, v10, 2p. [1458]
Subsistence to Indians of the Fort Berthold agency; Sioux harrassment.

50. Alaska Seal Fishery Lease. 7 Feb.
HED 108, 41-3, v10, 24p. [1458]
Support and education of natives employed in the fur industry.

51. Sale of Indian Lands. 8 Feb.
SED 35, 41-3, v1, 3p. [1440]
On the desire of Sacs, Foxes, Iowas, and Omahas to sell their lands in the northern superintendency; already done by Otoes and Missouris under the treaty of 1869.

52. Early Labors of Missionaries in Oregon. 9 Feb.
SED 37, 41-3, v1, 81p. [1440]
History of efforts to civilize Indians, commencing in 1836.

53. Mem. of P. Pitchlynn. 9 Feb.
SMD 65, 41-3, v1, 1p. [1442]
Asks payments due the Choctaws under the treaty of 22 June 1855 be made.

54. R-P of the Survivors of C. Collins. 9 Feb.
SR 353, 41-3, v1, 1p. [1443]
Duty at Fort Gibson, Indian Territory.

55. Report of the Board of Indian Com'rs. 10 Feb.
SED 39, 41-3, v1, 149p. [1440]
2nd annual report; Indian wars threatened and averted; events in Indian Territory; missionaries; reports on various tribes.

56. R-M of E. Boudinot. 10 Feb.
HR 30, 41-3, v1, 12p. [1464]
Concerning taxation of manufactures made in the Cherokee Nation and sold in Indian Territory; conflict between tax laws and the Cherokee treaty of 19 July 1866.

57. Appropriations for Various Indian Tribes. 11 Feb.
SED 40, 41-3, v1, 3p. [1440]
Payments to Peorias, Kaskaskias, Weas, and Piankeshaws under the treaty of 23 Feb. 1867.

58. Military Posts and Depot at Fort Leavenworth. 11 Feb.
SED 41, 41-3, v1, 3p. [1440]
On enlargement of the fort; well situated to control Indian hostilities; on railroad lines, including one to Indian Territory.

59. Black Bob Band of Indians in Kansas. 11 Feb.
SMD 61, 41-3, v1, 5p. [1442]
Conflict over land title between this band of Shawnees and settlers; treaty of 1854.

60. Appropriation for the Ponca Indians. 11 Feb.
HED 109, 41-3, v10, 5p. [1458]
For supplies furnished to them in 1870.

61. Depredations by Apache Indians. 11 Feb.
HED 111, 41-3, v12, 6p. [1460]
Appropriation to cover the costs of depredations committed in 1870 on freight wagons bound for the Cheyenne-Arapaho agency.

62. L-C of Durfee and Peck. 11 Feb.
HED 114, 41-3, v12, 3p. [1460]
Supplies to Crows, Gros Ventres, and Assiniboines in Montana during 1869.

63. On the Account of Durfee and Peck. 11 Feb.
HED 115, 41-3, v12, 5p. [1460]
For rent of Indian agency buildings at Fort Berthold.

64. Report on the Seal Fishery on St. Paul Island, Alaska. 11 Feb.
HED 122, 41-3, v12, 7p. [1460]
Supplies to natives employed in the fur industry through their chiefs.

65. Appropriation for Indian Depredations. 11 Feb.
HED 123, 41-3, v12, 8p. [1460]
Apache and Kiowa depredations in 1870 on supplies bound for the Cheyenne-Arapaho agency.

66. On the Relief of the Fourth and Fifth Indian Regiments. 13 Feb.
SR 359, 41-3, v1, 1p. [1443]
Stationed at Fort Gibson, Indian Territory, during the Civil War.

67. Resol. of the Kansas Legis. 15 Feb.
SMD 63, 41-3, v1, 1p. [1442]
Asks Congress to grant the Chicago, Kansas, and Texas Railroad a right of way through Indian Territory.

68. R-C of J. and C. Dailey. 15 Feb.
SR 361, 41-3, v1, 2p. [1443]
Supplies to Sioux in 1862 at Big Stone Lake, Dakota Territory.

69. R-C of R. Wright. 15 Feb.
SR 362, 41-3, v1, 1p. [1443]
Trader in Indian Territory; disloyalty of Chickasaws and Choctaws during the Civil War forces him to leave.

70. L-C of W. Adair. 15 Feb.
HED 129, 41-3, v12, 4p. [1460]
Cherokee delegate asks reimbursement for money advanced to certain Eastern Cherokees.

71. Black Bob's Band of Shawnee Indians. 15 Feb.
HED 130, 41-3, v12, 5p. [1460]
On their present condition; land titles and sale of lands in Kansas.

72. Osage Indians in Kansas. 15 Feb.
HED 131, 41-3, v12, 4p. [1460]
On their removal from Kansas to Indian Territory.

73. Appropriation for the Pottawatomie Indians. 15 Feb.
HED 133, 41-3, v12, 2p. [1460]
Division of tribal funds under the treaty of 15 Nov. 1861.

74. Mem. of A. Davis et al. 16 Feb.
SMD 66, 41-3, v1, 5p. [1442]
Sale of Miami lands in Kansas, and removal of the tribe to Indian Territory.

75. Osage Indian Lands in Kansas. 16 Feb.
HED 132, 41-3, v12, 2p. [1460]
Indians protest that they have not received any money from the sale

of their lands to settlers; also, Congress has extended the payments for the settlers to a still later date.

76. Transportation of the Mails from the Missouri River to the Pacific. 17 Feb.
SED 44, 41-3, v1, 4p. [1440]
Protection needed against Indian depredations.

77. Appropriation for Eastern Cherokees. 17 Feb.
HED 135, 41-3, v12, 2p. [1460]
To cover costs of a special agent to these North Carolina Indians.

78. Appropriation for the Indian Service. 17 Feb.
HED 136, 41-3, v12, 3p. [1460]
In Montana; expenses incurred during 1868-1869.

79. Tulalip Indian Agency in Washington Territory. 17 Feb.
HED 137, 41-3, v12, 4p. [1460]
Appropriation to cover expenses incurred during 1868-1869.

80. Resol. of the Kansas Legis. 18 Feb.
SMD 69, 41-3, v1, 1p. [1442]
Asks extinguishment of all Indian title to land in the State.

81. R-C of the American Board of Foreign Missions. 20 Feb.
SR 371, 41-3, v1, 2p. [1443]
Losses near Fort Gibson, Cherokee Nation, during the Civil War.

82. Agency Buildings in Creek and Seminole Country. 21 Feb.
HED 121, 41-3, v12, 2p. [1460]
Appropriation for the erection of buildings.

83. Survey of the Pima and Maricopa Reservation. 21 Feb.
HED 139, 41-3, v12, 17p. [1460]
In Arizona, for a proposed extension of the reserve.

84. Mem. of the Kansas Legis. 21 Feb.
HMD 99, 41-3, v2, 2p. [1463]
Ask settlers on the Cherokee neutral lands be protected in their rights; land ceded to U.S. by the treaty of 11 Aug. 1866.

85. Resol. of the Kansas Legis. 22 Feb.
SMD 76, 41-3, v1, 2p. [1442]
Asks that Fort Harker not be abandoned; protection from Indian hostilities.

86. Resol. of the Kansas Legis. 22 Feb.
SMD 77, 41-3, v1, 2p. [1442]
Ask issuance of land patents to Delaware Indians under the treaty of 4 Mar. 1866.

87. Report on Freights on the Pacific Railroads. 24 Feb.
SR 374, 41-3, v1, 4p. [1443]
Expenses of the Indian Service; Indian hostilities.

88. Mem. of R. McKee. 25 Feb.
HMD 102, 41-3, v2, 6p. [1463]
Late disbursing agent of the Indian Dept. in California; treaty negotiations of 1851; failure of Congress to appropriate funds to cover expenses.

89. Report on Affairs in the Indian Dept. 25 Feb.
HR 39, 41-3, v1, 289p. [1464]
Investigation of charges of fraud and misconduct against the CIA, and Indian disbursing officers; report says irregularities exist, but no corruption.

90. Letter on a Cherokee Treaty. 27 Feb.
SMD 82, 41-3, v1, 2p. [1442]
Interpretation of articles 15 and 16 of the treaty of 19 July 1867.

91. Mem. of the Council of the Seneca Nation of Indians. 27 Feb.
SMD 83, 41-3, v1, 1p. [1442]
Against the sale of any part of the Allegany reservation in New York.

92. R-M of the Choctaw Nation. 27 Feb.
HR 41, 41-3, v1, 4p. [1464]
On the claim of the Choctaws to $250,000 in bonds under the treaty of 28 Apr. 1866.

93. Matters of Appropriation and Legislation Concerning Indians. 1 Mar.
SMD 85, 41-3, v1, 4p. [1442]
Locating Indians in Indian Territory; sale of Indian lands in the northern superintendency; Yankton Sioux, Crow, Gros Ventre, and Assiniboine supplies; etc.

94. Annual Report of the Smithsonian Institution. 1 Mar.
HED 20, 42-1, v2, 494p. [1471]
For 1870; research related to American Indians; Indian languages; ethnology of Indians of the Red River of the North; mounds in Georgia, Kentucky, and on the Upper Missouri.

95. Mem. of the Chiefs of the Confederated Tribes of the Kaskaskia, Peoria, Piankeshaw, and Wea Indians. 2 Mar.
SMD 90, 41-3, v1, 4p. [1442]
Ask reimbursement for the alleged misapplication of funds belonging to them by the Indian Dept.

96. Expedition to the Yellowstone in 1870. 3 Mar.
SED 51, 41-3, v1, 40p. [1440]
Journal of travels; encounters with Indians.

97. Statements of Appropriations. 4 Mar.
HMD 107, 41-3, v2, 70p. [1463]
During the 3rd session, 41st Congress; Indian expenses.

98. Petition of Ottawa Indians. 7 Mar.
SMD 5, 42-1, v1, 3p. [1467]
Lands in Kansas set aside to be sold for the benefit of education under the treaty of 24 June 1862; removal to Indian Territory under the treaty of 1867; have not received proceeds from sale of lands.

99. Condition of the Black Bob Band of Shawnees in Kansas. 9 Mar.
SMD 8, 42-1, v1, 2p. [1467] *or*
HMD 3, 42-1, v1, 2p. [1470]
Allotment should proceed, in order that said Indians might benefit.

100. Unadjusted Claims of Florida. 13 Mar.
SED 1, 42-1, v1, 2p. [1466]
Arising from the several Indian wars in said State.

101. Mem. of L. Goldstone. 13 Mar.
HMD 5, 42-1, v1, 2p. [1472]
On the Alaskan seal fishery industry; employment of natives in seal-catching.

102. Letter on Alaska. 15 Mar.
HED 5, 42-1, v1, 32p. [1470]
Indian fur trade with the Russians and British (Hudson's Bay Company); description of the Indian population.

103. L-C of Lieut. Pratt. 15 Mar.
HED 7, 42-1, v1, 5p. [1470]
Comanche depredations of 1869 in Indian Territory.

104. Petition of the Heirs of B. Ladd. 17 Mar.
HMD 14, 42-1, v1, 44p. [1472]
Survey of the Virginia military tract in Ohio; interrupted by Indian incursions.

105. Mem. of the Arizona Legis. 20 Mar.
HMD 16, 42-1, v1, 2p. [1472]
Ask protection from hostile Apaches.

106. Mining West of the Rocky Mountains. 21 Mar.
HED 10, 42-1, v1, 566p. [1470]
Indians of Arizona, etc.

107. Appropriation for Indian Tribes. 21 Mar.
HED 11, 42-1, v2, 2p. [1471]
Subsistence for Arapahoes, Cheyennes, Apaches, Kiowas, and Comanches.

108. Resol. of the Texas Legis. 28 Mar.
SMD 37, 42-1, v1, 2p. [1467]
Ask com. be assigned to study outrages committed by Kickapoo and Lipan Indians in Texas; Indians find refuge in Mexico; captives taken.

109. Charges Against the Supt. of Indian Affairs in Montana. 28 Mar.
HED 15, 42-1, v2, 5p. [1471]
Charges made by the agent to the Blackfeet that the Supt. has withheld Indian goods.

110. Act of the Chickasaw Nation's Legis. 10 Apr.
HMD 29, 42-1, v1, 2p. [1472]
Approves allotment of lands in severalty under the treaty of 28 Apr. 1866; asks removal of negroes from Chickasaw country, and approves a grant of $300.000 for them.

111. Mem. of the Dakota Legis. 10 Apr.
HMD 34, 42-1, v1, 2p. [1472]
Construction of wagon roads; transport of Indian supplies.

112. Resol. of the Michigan Legis. 12 Apr.
SMD 50, 42-1, v1, 1p. [1467]
Ask lands be put on the market; reservations under the treaty of 1855 with the Ottawas and Chippewas.

113. Resol. of the Nebraska Legis. 15 Apr.
SMD 52, 42-1, v1, 2p. [1467]
On the relief of Capt. Murrie; commanded Pawnee Scouts against Cheyennes in 1867; exchange of captives.

114. Communication from Capt. Adams. 15 Apr.
HMD 37, 42-1, v1, 20p. [1472]
Exploring expedition to the Colorado River and its tributaries; mention of Indians residing in the area, and encounters with said Indians.

115. Report of a Reconnaissance of the Yukon River. 17 Apr.
SED 12, 42-1, v1, 113p. [1466]
Exploring expedition; Indians of the area; Russian and British (Hudson's Bay Company) trade; etc.

116. Statements of Appropriations. 20 Apr.
HMD 43, 42-1, v1, 8p. [1472]
During the 1st session, 42d Congress; Indian expenses.

117. Statistics of the Ninth Congress. 21 Nov. HMD (no number), 42-1, v1-3, 2327p. [1473-1475]
Indian populations; taxed and non-taxed Indians, and half-breeds (all located in Serial 1473).

118. Claims Incurred in Suppressing Indian Hostilities. 4 Dec.
SED 1, 42-2, v1, 3p. [1478]
In Oregon and Washington; acted upon.

119. Claims Incurred in Suppression of Indian Hostilities. 4 Dec.
SED 2, 42-2, v1, 6p. [1478]
In Oregon and Washington; not acted upon.

120. Annual Message to Congress with Documents; Pres. Grant. 4 Dec.
HED 1, 42-2, v1-4, 4857p. [1502-1507]
On the new Indian policy of turning over control of reservations to Christian sects; on formation of one Indian Territory or State; annual report of the Sec. of War (Serials 1503-1504); annual report of the Sec. of Interior (Serials 1505-1506); annual report of the Gen. Land Office (Serial 1505); annual report of the CIA (Serial 1505), including a report on the new Indian policy, hostilities of the Indians of the Southwest, report of the Board of Indian Com'rs, mission to the Kickapoos in Mexico, conditions at the Sioux agencies, and reports of Supts., agents, schools, and farms; etc.

121. Annual Report of the Sec. of the Treasury. 4 Dec.
HED 2, 42-2, v4, 581p. [1507]
Year ending 30 June 1871; Indian expenses.

122. Estimates of Appropriations. 4 Dec.
HED 5, 42-2, v6, 302p. [1509]
Year ending 30 June 1873; Indian expenses.

123. Inventory of Property in the Interior Dept. 5 Dec.
SED 3, 42-2, v1, 3p. [1478]
Includes the OIA.

124. Letter on Lands of the Kansas Tribe of Indians. 11 Dec.
SMD 10, 42-2, v1, 4p. [1481]
Sale of the tribe's lands in Kansas which were set aside for them under the treaties of 3 June 1825, 14 Jan. 1846, and 5 Oct. 1859.

125. Mem. of E. Boudinot. 11 Dec.
HMD 9, 42-2, v1, 9p. [1524]
Conflict between U.S. tax laws and the Cherokee treaty of 19 July 1866; sale of goods by a Cherokee Indian within Indian Territory.

126. Balances of Appropriations Unexpended. 14 Dec.
HED 19, 42-2, v6, 54p. [1509]
On 30 June 1871; for Indian expenses.

127. Letter on Fur-Seal Fisheries in Alaska. 14 Dec.
HED 20, 42-2, v6, 9p. [1509]
Aleutian native employees.

128. Estimate of Appropriation for Subsistence of Navajoes. 20 Dec.
HED 22, 42-2, v7, 2p. [1510]
In New Mexico; up to 30 June 1873.

129. Appropriation for Supplies to Sioux. 20 Dec.
HED 23, 42-2, v7, 8p. [1510]
At the Milk River agency in Montana.

130. Estimate of Appropriation for Support of Arikaras, Mandans, and Gros Ventres. 20 Dec.
HED 25, 42-2, v7, 3p. [1510]
At the Fort Berthold agency; for fiscal 1872.

131. Appropriation for the Sacs, Foxes, and Iowas. 20 Dec.
HED 26, 42-2, v7, 3p. [1510]
School buildings in Nebraska under the treaty of 6 Mar. 1861.

1872

1. Receipts and Expenditures. 8 Jan.
HED 29, 42-2, v7, 489p. [1510]
Year ending 30 June 1867; Indian expenses.

2. Appropriation for the Apaches. 8 Jan.
HED 33, 42-2, v7, 2p. [1510]
In Arizona and New Mexico for fiscal 1872.

3. Receipts and Expenditures. 8 Jan.
HED 36, 42-2, v7, 427p. [1510]
Year ending 30 June 1868; Indian expenses.

4. Receipts and Expenditures. 8 Jan.
HED 37, 42-2, v7, 464p. [1510]
Year ending 30 June 1869; Indian expenses.

5. Appropriation for a Special Agent. 11 Jan.
HED 46, 42-2, v7, 2p. [1510]
To make payments to the eastern, or North Carolina Cherokees.

6. Appropriation for the Pawnees. 11 Jan.
HED 47, 42-2, v7, 3p. [1510]
For schools under the treaty of 24 Sept. 1857.

7. Estimate of Appropriation for the Indian Service. 11 Jan.
HED 48, 42-2, v7, 2p. [1510]
At the Choctaw and Chickasaw agency, Indian Territory.

8. Estimate of Appropriation to Reimburse the Subsistence Dept. 11 Jan.
HED 49, 42-2, v7, 2p. [1510]
For providing supplies to Indians during fiscal 1871.

9. Appropriation for the Indian Dept. 12 Jan.
HED 50, 42-2, v7, 2p. [1510]
Required to promote education.

10. Letter on Black Bob Indian Lands. 16 Jan.
HED 64, 42-2, v7, 5p. [1510]
Sale of Shawnee lands in Kansas.

11. Land for the Shawnee Indians. 16 Jan.
HED 65, 42-2, v7, 3p. [1510]
Selection of lands in Kansas under the treaty of 10 May 1854; sale of said lands.

12. Appropriation for the Seminoles. 16 Jan.
HED 66, 42-2, v7, 2p. [1510]
For reservation buildings; treaty of 1 Mar. 1866.

13. Letter on the Condition of the Kaw Indians. 16 Jan.
HED 67, 42-2, v7, 5p. [1510]
Need of subsisting these Indians; removal from Kansas to Indian Territory.

14. Estimate of Appropriation for the Winnebagoes. 16 Jan.
HED 68, 42-2, v7, 4p. [1510]
For civilization; refund of moneys used in removing said Indians from Minnesota.

15. Papers on Claims of Kansas. 17 Jan.
HMD 36, 42-2, v2, 18p. [1525]
Civil War expenses, and expenses of suppressing Indian hostilities in 1865.

16. Removal and Subsistence of Chippewas. 22 Jan.
SMD 40, 42-2, v1, 3p. [1481]
Removal of scattered bands of Chippewas in Minnesota to the reservation at White Earth Lake in that State.

17. Indian Reservations in the Northern Superintendency. 22 Jan.
SMD 41, 42-2, v1, 4p. [1481]
Under the care of the Friends; improvements on the Omaha, Pawnee, and Ottoe reserves; sale of parts of the Ottoe and Missouri reserves; sale of the Sac and Fox reserve, and their removal to Indian Territory.

18. L-C of T. Curtis. 23 Jan.
HED 80, 42-2, v7, 3p. [1510]
Cheyenne depredations of 1865.

19. Letter on Charges Against J. Viall. 23 Jan.
HED 81, 42-2, v7, 2p. [1510]
Answers to charges of the Blackfeet agent against the Supt. of Indian Affairs in Montana.

20. Estimate of Appropriations for the Senecas. 23 Jan.
HED 82, 42-2, v7, 2p. [1510]
Interest due under the treaty of 23 Feb. 1867.

21. Letter on Removal of the Chippewas. 23 Jan.
HED 83, 42-2, v7, 4p. [1510]
Removal of scattered bands in Minnesota to their reservation at White Earth Lake under the treaties of 7 May 1864 and 19 Mar. 1867.

22. Indian Reservations in the Northern Superintendency. 23 Jan.
HED 84, 42-2, v7, 6p. [1510]
Papers from the Com. of Friends; improvements for the Pawnees, Ottoes, and Omahas; sale of reservation lands by Pawnees, Omahas, Sacs, and Foxes.

23. Petition of Freedmen. 23 Jan.
HMD 46, 42-2, v2, 16p. [1525]
Of the Choctaw and Chickasaw Nations; ask funds due from Indians under the treaty of 1866.

24. Resol. of the Kansas Legis. 24 Jan.
SMD 43, 42-2, v1, 1p. [1481]
Ask extinguishment of Indian title to land in the "Cherokee Strip."

25. Appropriation for the Kaws. 24 Jan.
HED 87, 42-2, v8, 2p. [1511]
For subsistence needs during fiscal 1872.

26. Appropriation for the Apaches. 24 Jan.
HED 88, 42-2, v8, 2p. [1511]

Subsistence in Arizona and New Mexico for fiscal 1873.

27. Protest of the Creek, Cherokee, and Choctaw Nations. 24 Jan.
HMD 51, 42-2, v2, 3p. [1525]
Against proposals for a territorial government over Indian Territory.

28. Promotion of Education Among Indians. 25 Jan.
SMD 44, 42-2, v1, 2p. [1481]
Authorization to the Sec. of Interior to draw on Indian education funds as it is seen fit.

29. Selection of Lands for the Shawnees. 25 Jan.
SMD 47, 42-2, v1, 3p. [1481]
Land cessions and selections under the treaty of 10 May 1854; sale of said lands, and the questions arising over land title.

30. L-C of H. Hegwer. 25 Jan.
HED 93, 42-2, v8, 5p. [1511]
Cheyenne depredations of 1867 in Kansas.

31. L-C of C. Weidner. 25 Jan.
HED 94, 42-2, v8, 5p. [1511]
Kiowa depredations of 1868 in Kansas.

32. L-C of Curtis and Cole. 25 Jan.
HED 95, 42-2, v8, 14p. [1511]
Cheyenne and Kiowa depredations of 1864.

33. L-C of C. Denton. 25 Jan.
HED 96, 42-2, v8, 11p. [1511]
Depredations of Indians in Oregon during 1854-1860.

34. L-C of Bickford and Stanley. 25 Jan.
HED 97, 42-2, v8, 5p. [1511]
Kiowa depredations of 1864 in Kansas.

35. L-C of T. Hetherington. 25 Jan.
HED 98, 42-2, v8, 4p. [1511]
Cheyenne depredations of 1867 in Kansas.

36. L-C of J. Howsley. 25 Jan.
HED 99, 42-2, v8, 7p. [1511]
Navajo depredations of 1868 in New Mexico.

37. Appropriations for the Sioux. 25 Jan.
HED 102, 42-2, v8, 9p. [1511]
Subsistence for the Teton and other bands of Sioux near Fort Peck, Montana.

38. L-C of L. Krouse et al. 26 Jan.
HED 100, 42-2, v8, 10p. [1511]
Osage depredations during 1865-1866 in Kansas.

39. Estimate of Appropriation for Surveying Indian Reserves. 26 Jan.
HED 101, 42-2, v8, 2p. [1511]
In Washington and Colorado Territories, and the Red Lake and Pembina, and Chippewa of the Mississippi reservations in Minnesota.

40. Resol. of the Kansas Legis. 30 Jan.
SMD 49, 42-2, v1, 1p. [1481]
Ask removal of settlers from Indian Territory; extension of the State's borders by Indian treaty.

41. Resol. of the Kansas Legis. 30 Jan.
SMD 50, 42-2, v1, 1p. [1481]
Secure lands to bona fide settlers on the Cherokee neutral lands.

42. On the Relief of Citizens Expelled from Camp Mohave, Arizona. 30 Jan.
HED 107, 42-2, v9, 46p. [1512]
Removal of persons from the military reserve; employment of Indians on the reserve.

43. On the Case of E. Boudinot. 30 Jan.
HR 6, 42-2, v1, 4p. [1528]
Conflict between U.S. tax laws and the Cherokee treaty of 19 July 1866; sale of goods within Indian Territory.

44. Mem. of the Choctaw Nation. 31 Jan.
SMD 53, 42-2, v1, 6p. [1481]
Against a territorial government (Oklahoma) over their country in Indian Territory; violation of treaties.

45. Survey of the Cherokee Strip Adjoining Kansas. 7 Feb.
HED 115, 42-2, v10, 2p. [1513]
Ceded to the U.S. under the treaty of 19 July 1866.

46. L-C of M. Bellmard et al. 9 Feb.
HED 119, 42-2, v10, 11p. [1513]
Cheyenne depredations of 1868 in Kansas.

47. R-P of E. Gerry. 12 Feb.
SR 38, 42-2, v1, 1p. [1483]
Cheyenne and Sioux depredations of 1864 in Colorado.

48. Letter on Presents and Provisions for Indians. 13 Feb.
HED 125, 42-2, v10, 3p. [1513]
Year ending 30 June 1871; various tribes.

49. Estimate of Appropriation for the Chippewas. 13 Feb.
HED 130, 42-2, v10, 3p. [1513]
Aid to Indians on the White Earth reservation in Minnesota.

50. L-C of W. Daugherty. 13 Feb.
HED 131, 42-2, v10, 6p. [1513]
Alleged Sioux depredations of 1869.

51. Estimate of Appropriations for Removal of the Osages. 16 Feb.
HED 146, 42-2, v10, 2p. [1513]
From Kansas to Indian Territory.

52. Preliminary Report of a Geological Survey of Montana and Adjacent Territories. 20 Feb.
HED 326, 42-2, v15, 538p. [1515]
Account of the expedition; hostile Indians around Fort Ellis; etc.

53. Resol. of the Kansas Legis. 21 Feb.
SMD 85, 42-2, v2, 2p.[1482]
Asks formation of a new judicial district composed of southern Kansas and the Indian Territory; cases between whites and Cherokees.

54. Appropriations for the Pottawatomies. 21 Feb.
HED 151, 42-2, v10, 3p. [1513]
To carry out stipulations of the treaties of 15 Nov. 1861, 29 Mar. 1866, and 27 Feb. 1867.

55. Estimate of Appropriations for the Osages. 21 Feb.
HED 152, 42-2, v10, 3p. [1513]
Subsistence for the coming year, and to allow them to establish themselves in Indian Territory.

56. Letter on the U.S. Court in Arkansas. 21 Feb.
HED 153, 42-2, v10, 2p. [1513]
Recommends holding the court at Okmulgee, Indian Territory, once each year; jurisdiction over Indians.

57. Resol. of the Rhode Island Legis. 23 Feb.
SMD 87, 42-2, v2, 1p. [1482]
Against opening Indian Territory to white settlers.

58. On the Relief of C. Tracy. 23 Feb.
HR 25, 42-2, v1, 1p. [1528]
Apache depredations of 1870 in Indian Territory.

59. Resol. of the Minnesota Legis. 26 Feb.
SMD 93, 42-2, v2, 1p. [1482]
Ask added compensation for a former agent to the Sioux of Minnesota.

60. Estimate of Appropriation for Removal of the Eastern Cherokees. 27 Feb.
HED 156, 42-2, v10, 2p. [1513]
From North Carolina to Indian Territory under the treaty of 23 May 1836.

61. Appropriation for a General Council of Indians. 27 Feb.
HED 157, 42-2, v10, 3p. [1513]
Of Indians in Indian Territory under Cherokee, Creek, Seminole, Choctaw, and Chickasaw treaties.

62. Letter on Sale of Chippewa Reservations. 27 Feb.
HED 162, 42-2, v10, 3p. [1513]
In Minnesota and Wisconsin; Northern Pacific Railroad intersects one reservation in question.

63. Resol. of the Iowa Legis. 29 Feb.
SMD 97, 42-2, v2, 1p. [1482]
Against opening Indian Territory to white settlers; Creek, Cherokee, Choctaw, Chickasaw, and Seminole treaties would be violated.

64. L-C of W. and G. Dyer. 1 Mar.
HED 163, 42-2, v10, 4p. [1513]
For supplies provided to Paiutes in Nevada during 1861-1862.

65. L-C of the Delaware Indians. 5 Mar.
HED 169, 42-2, v10, 2p. [1513]
Stock stolen by whites since the treaty of 1854.

66. Resol. of the Maine Legis. 8 Mar.
SMD 110, 42-2, v2, 1p. [1482]
Ask observance of all Indian treaties; against encroachment of whites into Indian Territory.

67. Appropriation for Various Tribes of Indian Territory. 8 Mar.
HED 182, 42-2, v10, 4p. [1513]
For industrial pursuits of Senecas, Quapaws, Weas, Shawnees, Peorias, Kaskaskias, Piankeshaws, and Ottawas.

68. Letter on a Reservation to Red Bear, Chief of Chippewas. 8 Mar.
HED 183, 42-2, v10, 2p. [1513]
Under the treaty of 2 Oct. 1863 with the Pembina and Red Lake bands of Chippewas.

69. Mem. of the Colorado Legis. 11 Mar.
HMD 124, 42-2, v3, 2p. [1526]
Construction of a wagon road to the White River Ute Indian agency; transport of Indian goods.

70. Occupancy of Indian Territory. 15 Mar.
SED 51, 42-2, v2, 2p. [1479]
White intruders settling in large numbers.

71. Letter on Chippewa Half-Breeds of Lake Superior. 15 Mar.
HED 193, 42-2, v10, 158p. [1513]
On issuance of scrip to said half-

breeds under the treaty of 30 Sept. 1854.

72. Condition of Inhabitants of Alaska. 19 Mar.
HED 197, 42-2, v10, 7p. [1513]
On the natives of Alaska, and whether or not they should be administratively recognized as Indians prior to positive legislation.

73. Letter on the Third Article of the Nez Percé Treaty. 19 Mar.
HED 198, 42-2, v10, 3p. [1513]
Dated 13 Aug. 1868; concerns education.

74. Mem. of Indians in Michigan and Indiana. 19 Mar.
HMD 137, 42-2, v3, 27p. [1526]
Annuities due Pottawatomies still residing in said states under treaties of 29 July 1829, 27 Sept. 1833, and other treaties.

75. Statistics on Mining West of the Rocky Mountains. 20 Mar.
HED 211, 42-2, v10, 566p. [1513]
Hostile Sioux and Blackfeet Indians in Montana; etc.

76. Condition of Certain Pottawatomies. 21 Mar.
HED 203, 42-2, v10, 4p. [1513]
Lands should be provided to them under various treaties.

77. Appropriation for Twelve Winnebagoes. 21 Mar.
HED 204, 42-2, v10, 3p. [1513]
Payments to Indians who have become citizens of the U.S.

78. R-P of F. Kelly. 22 Mar.
SR 79, 42-2, v1, 1p. [1483]
Sioux depredations of 1864 near Fort Laramie; taken captive.

79. Letter on Various Pacific Railroad Companies. 25 Mar.
HED 213, 42-2, v12, 39p. [1515]
Indian depredations upon survey crews.

80. Mem. of the Minnesota Legis. 25 Mar.
HMD 149, 42-2, v3, 1p. [1526]
Asks U.S. to secure the cession of a Chippewa reservation on Lake Superior so that a harbor can be developed.

81. Mem. of the Minnesota Legis. 25 Mar.
HMD 150, 42-2, v3, 1p. [1526]
Ask completion of a wagon road to the Chippewa reservation at Net Lake; transport of annuities under the treaty of 5 May 1866.

82. R-C of J. and C. Dailey. 26 Mar.
SR 81, 42-2, v1, 2p. [1483]
Provisions furnished to Sioux of Minnesota in 1862.

83. Affairs on the Texas Frontier. 28 Mar.
HED 216, 42-2, v12, 3p. [1515]
Indian raids from Mexico.

84. Resol. of the California Legis. 1 Apr.
HMD 161, 42-2, v3, 2p. [1526]
Ask U.S. to aid in the suppression of hostile Apaches in Arizona.

85. Letter on the Round Valley Indian Reservation. 2 Apr.
HED 224, 42-2, v12, 22p. [1515]
Extension of this reserve in California over lands claimed by settlers.

86. L-C of Dakota Territory. 2 Apr.
HED 230, 42-2, v12, 9p. [1515]
During the Sioux war of 1862.

87. Mem. of P. Pitchlynn. 2 Apr.
HMD 164, 42-2, v3, 6p. [1526]
Choctaw delegate asks payment of money due Choctaws from sale of lands ceded in 1830.

88. On the Relief of Red Bear. 4 Apr.
SR 112, 42-2, v1, 1p. [1483]
Chief of the Pembina band of Chippewas; to be given a reserve of land under the treaty of 2 Oct. 1863.

89. Protest of Indian Delegates. 4 Apr.
HMD 166, 42-2, v3, 4p. [1526]
Against a proposed survey of Indian Territory.

90. Preliminary Report of the Survey of the Colorado River. 5 Apr.
HMD 173, 42-2, v3, 12p. [1526]
Journal of the expedition describes dealings with the Indians of the area.

91. Mem. of Chiefs et al. of the Oneida Indians. 8 Apr.
SMD 128, 42-2, v2, 2p. [1482]
Against division of their Wisconsin reservation, lands in severalty, and citizenship.

92. Mem. of the Wisconsin Legis. 8 Apr.
HMD 176, 42-2, v3, 1p. [1526]
Ask removal of roving bands of Winnebagoes and Pottawatomies from the state.

93. Private Land Claims in New Mexico. 8 Apr.
HMD 181, 42-2, v3, 130p. [1526]
Settlers driven from lands by hostile Navajo and Apache Indians.

94. R-P of the Pottawatomies. 9 Apr.
SR 121, 42-2, v1, 6p. [1483]
Payments due Indians remaining

in Michigan and Indiana under treaties from 1795 to 1846.

95. Appropriation for Creek Orphans of 1832. 10 Apr.
HED 246, 42-2, v12, 6p. [1515]
Funds due them under the treaty of 24 Mar. 1832.

96. Reservation for the Osages. 15 Apr.
SMD 137, 42-2, v2, 10p. [1482]
Removal of Great and Little Osages from Kansas; purchase of a reservation from the Cherokees in Indian Territory under the treaty of 19 July 1866.

97. R-C of Heirs of J. Birckhead and V. Campbell. 15 Apr.
HR 45, 42-2, v1, 8p. [1528]
Seminole war caused by the U.S. attempts to force removal of said Indians to Arkansas; depredations by U.S. troops in Florida during the war of 1836.

98. Letter on the 16th Article of the Cherokee Treaty. 17 Apr.
HED 258, 42-2, v12, 1p. [1515]
Dated 1 9 July 1866; concerned with the settlement of friendly Indians on Cherokee lands west of the 96th meridian, west longitude.

99. L-C of the Chickasaw Nation. 17 Apr.
HED 261, 42-2, v12, 3p. [1515]
For interest due on stocks held in their trust fund.

100. Reconnaissance of the Yellowstone River. 18 Apr.
SED 66, 42-2, v2, 43p. [1479]
Exploring expedition; Crows, Nez Percés, and other Indians of the region.

101. An Exploring Expedition in Nevada and Arizona. 20 Apr.
SED 65, 42-2, v2, 94p. [1479]
Numbers, habits, and disposition of the Indians of the Southwest, including Shoshones, Paiutes, Chemehuevis, Utes, Mohaves, Seviches, Hualapais, Cosninas, and Apaches.

102. Appropriation for Quapaw Lands. 25 Apr.
HED 276, 42-2, v12, 4p. [1515]
Ceded to the U.S. under the treaty of 23 Feb. 1867; located in or near Kansas.

103. Annual Report of the Smithsonian Institution. 26 Apr.
SMD 149, 42-2, v2, 473p. [1482]
Research related to the American Indian; mounds in Dakota and Kentucky; the Pima Indians of Arizona; on the language of the Dakota or Sioux Indians.

104. L-C of Texas. 30 Apr.
HED 277, 42-2, v12, 180p. [1515]
For troops required to suppress frontier Indian hostilities from 1854 to 1860.

105. Appropriation for an Investigation. 30 Apr.
HED 279, 42-2, v13, 1p. [1516]
Of Indian bounty frauds; back pay and bounties to Cherokees, Creeks, and Seminoles who served in Regiments of Indian Home Guards during the Civil War.

106. On the Relief of T. Curtis and J. Richmond. 2 May.
HR 60, 42-2, v1, 2p. [1528]
Apache and Kiowa depredations of 1870 in Indian Territory.

107. Report on a Territory of Oklahoma. 2 May.
HR 61, 42-2, v1, 7p. [1528]
Formation of a territorial government over the Indians in Indian Territory; need to civilize the Indians; Congress has the power to violate treaties at any time.

108. On the Relief of E. Joslyn. 2 May.
HR 62, 42-2, v1, 1p. [1528]
Settler has land included in an Indian reservation in Washington Territory.

109. R-M of E. Gerry. 2 May.
HR 63, 42-2, v1, 3p. [1528]
Cheyenne and Sioux depredations of 1864-1865 in Colorado.

110. Recent Affray in the Indian Territory. 7 May.
SED 70, 42-2, v2, 30p. [1479]
At the court house in Going Snake; recommendation of the establishment of a judicial district in Indian Territory.

111. Appropriation for a Military Post. 7 May.
HED 285, 42-2, v15, 3p. [1520]
In Utah; Indian raids.

112. R-C of Messrs. Durfee and Peck. 9 May.
SR 176, 42-2, v1, 3p. [1483]
Buildings lost in Montana during a threatened Sioux outbreak; Sioux and Comanche depredations.

113. Message on Difficulties in Cherokee Country. 11 May.

HED 287, 42-2, v15, 20p. [1520]
Affray at the courthouse in Going Snake; establishment of a judicial district for Indian Territory.

114. On the Case of A. Cooper. 16 May.
SR 190, 42-2, v1, 2p. [1483]
Indian campaign of 1867 in Idaho.

115. On the Relief of W. Langford. 16 May.
SR 196, 42-2, v1, 1p. [1483]
Title to mission lands in Oregon.

116. Report on Removal of Indians from the Bitter Root Valley, Montana. 16 May.
SR 197, 42-2, v1, 2p. [1483]
Removal of Flatheads and other Indians to the Jocko reservation.

117. Testimony on War Claims in Montana. 18 May.
HMD 215, 42-2, v4, 14p. [1527]
Indian war of 1862; Crow and Sioux hostilities.

118. R-C of S. Ward. 22 May.
SR 206, 42-2, v1, 3p. [1483]
Supplies to Sioux in 1865 near Fort Laramie.

119. Letter on the Nez Percé Reservation. 22 May.
HED 307, 42-2, v15, 4p. [1520]
Purchase and improvement of the reserve in Idaho.

120. R-P of L. Rose. 23 May.
SR 207, 42-2, v1, 1p. [1483]
Mohave depredations of 1858 in New Mexico.

121. Report on Montana War Claims. 24 May.
HR 82, 42-2, v3, 50p. [1542]
Indian war of 1867; hostile Crows and Sioux.

122. R-C of D. McCann. 24 May.
HR 84, 42-2, v4, 3p. [1543]
Indian goods transported from Omaha to Fort Laramie, the Winnebago agency, the Omaha agency, and the Pawnee agency.

123. R-C of C. Denton. 24 May.
HR 85, 42-2, v4, 2p. [1543]
Indian depredations during 1854-1860 in Oregon.

124. Letter on Montana War Claims. 27 May.
HED 312, 42-2, v15, 10p. [1515]
Indian war of 1867.

125. Report on the Territory of Oklahoma. 27 May.
HR 89, 42-2, v4, 3p. [1543]
Minority of the Com. on the Territories does not think the Territory should be organized; violates treaties; Indians do not want it; real reason for this push for territorial government is because Congress granted over 23 million acres of land in Indian Territory to railroad companies, contingent upon extinguishment of Indian title to land; Indian rights are secondary to those who support the measure.

126. Mem. of W. Ross et al. 3 June.
SMD 166, 42-2, v2, 1p. [1482]
Establishment of a separate court for the Indian Territory.

127. School Property of the Ottawas. 3 June.
HED 320, 42-2, v15, 3p. [1515]
Disposition of property in Kansas under the treaty of 24 June 1862, said tribe having removed to Indian Territory.

128. L-C of the Choctaw Indians. 7 June.
SED 87, 42-2, v2, 5p. [1479]
Balance due under the treaty of 1855; known as the "net proceeds claim."

129. Report on Alleged Frauds Against Indian Soldiers. 8 June.
HR 96, 42-2, v4, 590p. [1543]
Against Creeks, Cherokees, and Seminoles who served with the U.S. in the Civil War.

130. Statements of Appropriations. 10 June.
HMD 230, 42-2, v4, 82p. [1527]
During the 2d session, 42d Congress; Indian expenses.

131. Property in the Interior Dept. 2 Dec.
SED 3, 42-3, v1, 3p. [1545]
In the OIA.

132. Annual Message to Congress with Documents; Pres. Grant. 2 Dec.
HED 1, 42-3, v1-4, 7713p. [1552-1562]
Indian policy; Indian Territory; annual report of the Sec. of War (Serials 1558-1559); annual report of the Sec. of Interior (Serials 1560-1561); annual report of the Gen. Land Office (Serial 1560); annual report of the CIA (Serial 1560), including the government's Indian policy, suppressing hostile Indians, Indians and the railroads, legislation, and reports of Supts., agents, schools, and farms; etc.

133. Annual Report of the Sec. of the Treasury. 2 Dec.
HED 2, 42-3, v4, 573p. [1562]
For fiscal 1872; Indian expenses.

134. Estimates of Appropriations. 2 Dec.
HED 5, 42-3, v6, 215p. [1564]
Year ending 30 June 1874; Indian expenses.

135. L-C of the Choctaws. 3 Dec.
HED 10, 42-3, v5, 5p. [1563]
Under the treaty of 1855; the "net proceeds claim."

136. Appropriation for Indian Depredation Claims. 3 Dec.
HED 11, 42-3, v5, 3p. [1563]
Against the Cheyennes, Osages, Sioux, Kiowas, Arapahoes, Navajoes, Blackfeet, Comanches, and Oregon Indians; list of claims.

137. Copy of an Agreement with the Sioux. 3 Dec.
HED 12, 42-3, v5, 4p. [1563]
Dated 20 Sept. 1872, with the Sisseton and Wahpeton Sioux; cession of lands.

138. Convention with the Shoshones and Bannocks. 3 Dec.
HED 21, 42-3, v7, 3p. [1565]
For relinquishment of a portion of their reserve in Wyoming; agreement dated 26 Sept. 1872.

139. Animals Stolen by Indians in Texas. 5 Dec.
SED 7, 42-3, v1, 2p. [1545]
By Comanches, from the army, in 1872 near San Antonio.

140. Mem. of the Dakota Legis. 9 Dec.
HMD 9, 42-3, v1, 13p. [1571]
Ask reimbursement for expenses of suppressing the Sioux war of 1862.

141. Appropriation for a Matron at the Pawnee Agency. 10 Dec.
HED 28, 42-3, v7, 1p. [1565]
Salary for a school matron.

142. Appropriation for Removal of Winnebagoes. 11 Dec.
HED 38, 42-3, v7, 2p. [1565]
From Wisconsin to the Winnebago reservation in Nebraska, or to Indian Territory.

143. Telegraphic Communication in Arizona. 13 Dec.
SED 12, 42-3, v1, 2p. [1545]
Between military stations, in order to prosecute a campaign against the Apaches.

144. On the Relief of Settlers in Kansas. 16 Dec.
SR 241, 42-3, v1, 12p. [1548]
On the Cherokee neutral lands, which were granted to said Indians under the treaty of 29 Dec. 1835.

145. Report on Depredations on the Texas Frontier. 16 Dec.
HED 39, 42-3, v7, 63p. [1565]
By Indians on the southern, northern, and northwestern frontiers of the State.

146. Letter on Cherokee Funds. 17 Dec.
SMD 16, 42-3, v1, 3p. [1546]
On application of funds due from sale of certain lands under the treaty of 19 July 1866.

147. Survey and Cession of Creek Lands. 18 Dec.
SMD 17, 42-3, v1, 2p. [1546]
Survey of line dividing the Creek reservation from lands upon which the Sacs, Foxes, and Seminoles reside under the treaty of 14 June 1866; negotiation for more Creek land cessions authorized.

148. Agreement with the Arapahoes. 19 Dec.
HED 43, 42-3, v7, 4p. [1565]
For release of land ceded to them by the treaty of 28 Oct. 1867; negotiations to begin with the Cheyennes for relinquishment of their lands.

149. Survey of Indian Reservations. 19 Dec.
HED 44, 42-3, v7, 3p. [1565]
Survey of the line dividing the Creek ceded lands upon which the Sacs, Foxes, and Seminoles now reside, from the Creek reservation.

150. Sale of Ottawa Indian Trust-Fund Bonds. 19 Dec.
HED 45, 42-3, v7, 2p. [1565]
The Ottawas having become citizens, it is desirable that their tribal accounts should be closed.

151. Appropriation for a General Indian Council. 19 Dec.
HED 53, 42-3, v7, 2p. [1565]
In Indian Territory; under treaties of 1866 with the Cherokees, Creeks, Seminoles, Choctaws, and Chickasaws.

1873

1. Indian Interference with the Northern Pacific Railroad. 6 Jan.
SED 16, 42-3, v1, 19p. [1545]
Journal of a survey expedition down to Yellowstone River and back to Fort Ellis; meeting with Indians at

the Crow agency; Sioux attack on the party.

2. Claims Against the Kiowas and Arapahoes. 7 Jan.
HED 62, 42-3, v7, 16p. [1565]
For depredations of 1864 in Kansas.

3. Retention of Kickapoo Money as a Trust Fund. 7 Jan.
HED 63, 42-3, v7, 3p. [1565]
For sale of lands under the treaty of 28 June 1862.

4. Appropriation for Boundary Surveys. 7 Jan.
HED 64, 42-3, v7, 2p. [1565]
Of Indian reservations in Indian Territory, Oregon, and Washington.

5. Agreement with the Wichitas, Caddoes, Towoccaroes, Wacoes, and Kecchies. 7 Jan.
HED 65, 42-3, v7, 3p. [1565]
Dated 19 Oct. 1872; Indians cede all of their land for a tract in Indian Territory.

6. Condition of the Paiute Indians. 7 Jan.
HED 66, 42-3, v7, 4p. [1565]
Recommends settling the tribe on a reserve in Nevada.

7. Letter on Indians Wishing to Become Citizens. 7 Jan.
HED 67, 42-3, v7, 2p. [1565]
Bill presented to enable the Swan Creek and Black River bands of Chippewas, and the Munsee, or Christian Indians, residing in Kansas, to become citizens.

8. L-C of the Choctaw Indians. 7 Jan.
HED 69, 42-3, v7, 23p. [1565]
History of the claim arising under various treaties; funds due said to have been paid already.

9. R-C of Black Beaver. 8 Jan.
HR 18, 42-3, v1, 2p. [1576]
A Delaware Indian; property lost in Indian Territory while serving the U.S. during the Civil War.

10. Indian Hostilities in Certain Territories. 9 Jan.
SED 24, 42-3, v1, 68p. [1545]
Expenses incurred by Washington and Oregon during 1856 in the suppression of Indian hostilities; some Rogue River war claims fraudulent.

11. On Relief of Indians in the Northern Superintendency. 9 Jan.
HED 73, 42-3, v7, 3p. [1565]
Sale of the whole of the Otoe, Missouri, and Sac and Fox of the Missouri reservations in Kansas and Nebraska.

12. Estimate of Appropriation for the Kansas Indians. 9 Jan.
HED 74, 42-3, v7, 2p. [1565]
For subsistence needs.

13. Petition of B. Colbert. 9 Jan.
HED 75, 42-3, v7, 2p. [1565]
Asks for a charter to construct and operate a tollbridge between Chickasaw country in Indian Territory, and Texas.

14. Appropriation for a Wagon Road. 9 Jan.
HED 76, 42-3, v7, 2p. [1565]
From the Northern Pacific Railroad to the Red Lake agency; transport of goods for the Chippewas.

15. Estimate of Appropriation for Expenses of Sale of Chippewa Lands in Wisconsin. 9 Jan.
HED 77, 42-3, v7, 2p. [1565]
Under the treaty of 30 Sept. 1854, lands set aside for Chippewas; act of 29 May 1872 calls for sale of said lands.

16. Appropriation for Civilization. 9 Jan.
HED 78, 42-3, v7, 2p. [1565]
For Indians of the Central superintendency.

17. Appropriation for Expenses of Sale of Indian Lands. 9 Jan.
HED 79, 42-3, v7, 2p. [1565]
Omaha, Pawnee, Otoe, Missouri, and Sac and Fox of the Missouri lands in Nevada.

18. Appropriation for Removal of Cheyenne River Agency. 9 Jan.
HED 80, 42-3, v7, 3p. [1565]
From the mouth of the Cheyenne River on the Missouri River, to a more suitable location on the Sioux reservation.

19. L-C of H. Wedeles. 9 Jan.
HED 82, 42-3, v7, 4p. [1565]
Arapaho depredations of 1867 in Kansas.

20. Appropriation for Expenses of Sale of Land. 9 Jan.
HED 83, 42-3, v7, 2p. [1565]
Kansas Indian lands in Kansas; removal of said Indians to Indian Territory.

21. R-P of J. Lusky. 10 Jan.
SR 270, 42-3, v1, 1p. [1548]
Sioux war of 1862 in Minnesota.

22. Deficiencies in Appropriations. 10 Jan.
HED 88, 42-3, v7, 25p. [1565]

Appropriation required to complete the service of fiscal 1873; Indian expenses.

23. L-C of C. Autobees. 10 Jan.
HED 89, 42-3, v7, 5p. [1565]
Comanche, Cheyenne, and Arapaho depredations of 1861-1864 in Colorado.

24. Negotiation with Ute Indians. 10 Jan.
HED 90, 42-3, v7, 16p. [1565]
Council proceedings; extinguishment of a portion of their reservation in Colorado; under the treaty of 2 Mar. 1868.

25. On the Relief of Kreel and Miller. 10 Jan.
HR 17, 42-3, v1, 2p. [1576]
Indian depredations of 1871 in New Mexico.

26. On the Case of G. Ames. 10 Jan.
HR 19, 42-3, v1, 1p. [1576]
Served in Indian campaigns.

27. Forts in Texas. 11 Jan.
HR 26, 42-3, v1, 2p. [1576]
Purchase of land for permanent military posts on the Indian frontier.

28. Mem. of the National Commercial Convention. 14 Jan.
HMD 42, 42-3, v2, 2p. [1572]
To establish a government over Indian Territory; to allot lands to individual Indians, and to open the remainder of the territory for white settlement; to establish free schools.

29. L-C of the Walnut Grove Mining Company. 15 Jan.
HED 95, 42-3, v8, 16p. [1566]
Apache depredations of 1865-1869 in Arizona.

30. Letter on the Condition of the Teton Sioux. 15 Jan.
HED 96, 42-3, v8, 16p. [1566]
List of disbursements for their benefit; etc.

31. Receipts and Expenditures. 15 Jan.
HED 100, 42-3, v8, 477p. [1566]
Year ending 30 June 1870; Indian expenses.

32. Answer of P. Pitchlynn to the Sec. of the Treasury. 15 Jan.
HMD 46, 42-3, v2, 10p. [1572]
On the "net proceeds claim" of the Choctaws; money due from sale of lands under the treaty of 1830; review of claim under the treaty of 1855.

33. R-C of Dakota Territory. 15 Jan.
HR 35, 42-3, v1, 2p. [1576]
For expenses of the Sioux war of 1862.

34. Indian Tribes in Northern California. 16 Jan.
SED 29, 42-3, v1, 11p. [1545]
Removal of the Modocs to the Klamath Indian reservation under the treaty of 14 Oct. 1864; anticipated troubles.

35. Appropriation for Removal of Indians. 18 Jan.
HED 102, 42-3, v8, 2p. [1566]
Removal of the Otter Tail band of Pillagers to the Chippewa reservation at White Earth.

36. Appropriation for Purchase of Land. 18 Jan.
HED 103, 42-3, v8, 3p. [1566]
In the White Earth reservation of Minnesota for the Pembina band of Chippewas.

37. Appropriation for the Apaches. 18 Jan.
HED 105, 42-3, v8, 2p. [1566]
Subsistence in New Mexico and Arizona for fiscal 1873.

38. Letter from T. Foster. 21 Jan.
SMD 39, 42-3, v1, 7p. [1546]
On management and civilization of the Indian tribes.

39. Estimate of Appropriation for Cherokee Transportation. 21 Jan.
SMD 40, 42-3, v1, 2p. [1546]
Removal, by railroad, of eastern Cherokees from North Carolina to Indian Territory.

40. Estimate of Appropriation for the Osages. 21 Jan.
SMD 41, 42-3, v1, 3p. [1546] *or*
HED 142, 42-3, v8, 3p. [1566]
Payment of annual interest on the proceeds of sales of Osage trust and diminished reserve lands under the treaty of 29 Sept. 1865; sale of lands in Kansas.

41. Report on Payment to the Choctaws. 22 Jan.
SR 318, 42-3, v1, 10p. [1548]
Money due under the treaty of 27 Sept. 1830, by the treaty of 22 June 1855; proceeds from sale of ceded lands.

42. R-C of the Northwest Fur Company. 23 Jan.
SR 321, 42-3, v1, 2p. [1548]

Supplies to Indians at Fort Union, Dakota, in 1866-1867.

43. Mem. of the Dakota Legis. 24 Jan.
SMD 45, 42-3, v1, 3p. [1546]
Ask for an exploration of the Black Hills and the Bad Lands; previous surveys halted by Indian hostilities.

44. Land Claims in New Mexico. 25 Jan.
HED 128, 42-3, v8, 37p. [1566]
Settlers driven from the land by hostile Indians.

45. Appropriation for Indians in Northwestern Dakota. 25 Jan.
HED 138, 42-3, v8, 3p. [1566]
To cover debts incurred by the agent for the Arikaras, Mandans, and Gros Ventres.

46. Amendment of the Appropriation Bill. 25 Jan.
HED 139, 42-3, v8, 2p. [1566]
So that the War Dept. might provide subsistence to the Indians and be reimbursed by the Indian Dept.

47. Protest of the Chickasaw Nation. 25 Jan.
HED 141, 42-3, v8, 7p. [1566]
Against measures before Congress which would open Indian Territory to white settlement.

48. Mem. of the Dakota Legis. 27 Jan.
HMD 63, 42-3, v2, 1p. [1572]
Removal of Pembina Chippewas from lands in Dakota (which they ceded under the treaty of 1863) to the White Earth agency in Minnesota.

49. Mem. of the Dakota Legis. 27 Jan.
HMD 65, 42-3, v2, 1p. [1572]
Black Hills a retreat for hostile Sioux; ask that Indians be removed, and the area be opened to whites.

50. Mem. of the Dakota Legis. 27 Jan.
HMD 66, 42-3, v2, 2p. [1572]
Division of the Territory; survey of the Sisseton and Wahpeton Sioux reservation.

51. Report on Montana War Claims. 28 Jan.
SR 345, 42-3, v1, 2p. [1548]
Expenses of suppressing the Indian war of 1867.

52. Appropriation for Removal of Indians. 30 Jan.
HED 147, 42-3, v8, 3p. [1566]
Removal of the Snake, or Paiute, Indians to their reservation in Oregon.

53. Persons Appointed to the Interior Dept. 30 Jan.
HED 152, 42-3, v9, 3p. [1567]
During 1872; in the OIA.

54. Unexpended Balances of Appropriations. 30 Jan.
HED 157, 42-3, v9, 51p. [1567]
On 30 June 1872; Indian expenses.

55. Montana Indian War Claims. 31 Jan.
HED 164, 42-3, v9, 32p. [1567]
Suppression of Indian hostilities in 1867.

56. J. Powell's Survey Expedition to the Colorado River. 31 Jan.
HMD 76, 42-3, v2, 16p. [1572]
Use of Indian guides; ethnological studies of the Indians of the area; study of Indian language.

57. Mem. of the Kansas Legis. 3 Feb.
SMD 53, 42-3, v1, 2p. [1546]
Sioux and Arapaho hostilities; captive taken.

58. Resol. of the North Carolina Legis. 5 Feb.
SMD 56, 42-3, v1, 1p. [1546]
Asks adherence by government to treaty stipulations; pledge undisturbed possession of Indian Territory to tribes occupying it.

59. R-C of J. Pendery. 5 Feb.
SR 376, 42-3, v1, 1p. [1548]
Attorneys for the government in suits against settlers on Delaware lands in Kansas.

60. Mem. of the Nebraska Legis. 7 Feb.
SMD 61, 42-3, v1, 2p. [1546]
Ask action on a proposition of the Otoes and Missouris to sell their land and remove to Indian Territory.

61. Utah Indian War Claims. 8 Feb.
HED 175, 42-3, v9, 1p. [1567]
Suppression of hostilities in 1865-1867.

62. Appropriation for the Mississippi Chippewas. 8 Feb.
HED 176, 42-3, v9, 4p. [1567]
Provisions needed on the White Earth reservation.

63. Appropriation for Removal of the Osages. 8 Feb.
HED 183, 42-3, v9, 2p. [1567]
From Kansas to Indian Territory; Great and Little Osages settled on Cherokee ceded lands.

64. Removal of the Pembina Chippewas. 8 Feb.
HED 188, 42-3, v9, 2p. [1567]
From Dakota to the White Earth reservation in Minnesota.

65. Indian Scouts for the Modoc War. 10 Feb.
SED 39, 42-3, v1, 2p. [1545]
To prosecute said war in Oregon.

66. Resol. of the Kansas Legis. 10 Feb.
SMD 62, 42-3, v1, 1p. [1546]
For relief of settlers on Cherokee neutral lands; ceded to the U.S. by the treaty of 10 Aug. 1866.

67. Resol. of the Kansas Legis. 11 Feb.
SMD 64, 42-3, v1, 2p. [1546]
On outrages perpetrated by the Sioux and Arapahoes; captive taken.

68. L-C of Lieut. Pratt. 11 Feb.
HED 195, 42-3, v9, 5p. [1567]
Comanche depredations of 1869 in Indian Territory.

69. Settlers on Miami Lands. 11 Feb.
HED 199, 42-3, v9, 8p. [1567]
Negotiations taking place over title to lands in Kansas.

70. Letter on the Modoc Difficulties. 11 Feb.
HED 201, 42-3, v9, 12p. [1567]
Resistance to being settled on a reservation under the treaty of 14 Oct. 1864; hostilities in California and Oregon.

71. On the Relief of E. Joslyn. 13 Feb.
SR 436, 42-3, v1, 1p. [1548]
Land incorporated into an Indian reservation in Oregon.

72. Appropriation for the Sioux. 13 Feb.
HED 205, 42-3, v9, 3p. [1567]
Subsistence for fiscal 1873.

73. Appropriations for the Indian Service. 13 Feb.
HED 206, 42-3, v9, 2p. [1567]
In California, Dakota, Montana, Nevada, and Utah.

74. Negroes of the Chickasaw Nation. 13 Feb.
HED 207, 42-3, v9, 3p. [1567]
Adoption into the tribe; treaty of 28 Apr. 1866 with the Choctaws and Chickasaws.

75. Restoration of Lands to the Market. 13 Feb.
HED 208, 42-3, v9, 2p. [1567]
Lands withheld for the Ottawas and Chippewas of Michigan under the treaty of 31 July 1855.

76. Statistics of Mining West of the Rocky Mountains. 13 Feb.
HED 210, 42-3, v9, 550p. [1567]
Effects of Indian hostilities in various locations.

77. Private Land Claims in New Mexico. 14 Feb.
SED 45, 42-3, v1, 20p. [1545]
Settlers driven from land by hostile Indians.

78. Resol. of the Kansas Legis. 14 Feb.
SMD 77, 42-3, v1, 2p. [1546]
On sale of Indian lands known as the Cherokee strip.

79. Resol. of the Nebraska Legis. 15 Feb.
SMD 70, 42-3, v1, 2p. [1546]
On construction of a wagon road from North Platte to the White River Indian agency.

80. Report of the Com'r of U.S. Fisheries. 15 Feb.
SMD 74, 42-3, v2, 808p. [1547]
Indian terms for various species of fish.

81. R-P of S. Dick. 15 Feb.
SR 443, 42-3, v1, 1p. [1548]
Sioux war of 1862 in Minnesota.

82. Mem. of the Choctaw Nation. 17 Feb.
HMD 94, 42-3, v2, 31p. [1572]
On the "net proceeds claim"; answer to the Treasury Dept.; treaties of 1830, and 1855.

83. Military Posts on the Northern Pacific Railroad. 19 Feb.
HED 213, 42-3, v11, 2p. [1569]
Protection from hostile Indians.

84. Unexpended Appropriation for Navajoes. 19 Feb.
HED 215, 42-3, v11, 2p. [1569]
Authorized to use said funds for the current fiscal year.

85. Report on the Territory of Oklahoma. 20 Feb.
SR 471, 42-3, v3, 2p. [1550]
Recommends territorial government over Indian Territory; will not affect treaties of 1866 with the Choctaws, Chickasaws, Creeks, Cherokees, and Seminoles; also, the U.S. has not lost jurisdiction by treaties with the Great and Little Osages, Cheyennes, Arapahoes, Pottawatomies, Sacs, Foxes, Kiowas, and Comanches.

86. Annual Report of the Smithsonian Institution. 20 Feb.
HMD 107, 42-3, v3, 456p. [1573]
Research related to American Indians; ancient aboriginal trade; mounds; Mandan ceremonies; etc.

87. Report on Homesteads for Soldiers and Sailors. 21 Feb.

SR 482, 42-3, v3, 17p. [1550]
Disposition of lands, exclusive of Indian Territory and Indian reservations.

88. Report on Treaty Stipulations with the Choctaw Nation. 22 Feb.
HR 80, 42-3, v1, 29p. [1576]
Treaties of 1820, 1825, and 1830; "net proceeds claim."

89. Resol. of the Kansas Legis. 24 Feb.
HMD 104, 42-3, v3, 2p. [1573]
Deficiency of land for school purposes due to Indian reservations; Cherokee neutral lands.

90. Resol. of the Kansas Legis. 24 Feb.
HMD 105, 42-3, v3, 1p. [1573]
Settlers on the Osage Indian lands.

91. Resol. of the Kansas Legis. 25 Feb.
SMD 85, 42-3, v1, 2p. [1546]
Settlers on the Miami diminished reserve in said State.

92. R-M of Wells, Fargo, and Company. 25 Feb.
SR 501, 42-3, v3, 1p. [1550]
Indian depredations of 1864-1868 in Utah.

93. L-C of J. Baca. 25 Feb.
HED 228, 42-3, v11, 3p. [1569]
Kiowa and Comanche depredations of 1868 in New Mexico.

94. L-C of C. Cutler. 25 Feb.
HED 229, 42-3, v11, 3p. [1569]
Kaw depredations of 1867 in Kansas.

95. L-C of M. Desmarais and Company. 25 Feb.
HED 230, 42-3, v11, 5p. [1569]
Cheyenne depredations of 1868 in Kansas.

96. L-C of Probst and Kirchner. 25 Feb.
HED 231, 42-3, v11, 6p. [1569]
Navajo depredations of 1869 in New Mexico.

97. L-C of S. Ward. 25 Feb.
HED 233, 42-3, v11, 16p. [1569]
Sioux depredations of 1865-1866 near Fort Laramie.

98. On the Relief of Texas Indians. 25 Feb.
HED 234, 42-3, v11, 3p. [1569]
For the Alabama, Coushatta, and Muscogee tribes.

99. L-C of C. Weidner. 25 Feb.
HED 235, 42-3, v11, 6p. [1569]
Cheyenne and Arapaho depredations of 1868 in Kansas.

100. Report on a Delay in Adjustment of a Claim. 27 Feb.
SR 518, 42-3, v3, 6p. [1550]
Claim of G. Fisher; Indian depredations of 1813 in Florida.

101. Reply to Repoerts of Lieut. Bradley. 1 Mar.
SED 51, 42-3, v1, 5p. [1545]
On claims arising from the suppression of Indian hostilities in Oregon and Washington during 1854-1856; includes the Rogue River war.

102. Letter on the Choctaw and Chickasaw Treaty of 28 Apr. 1866. 1 Mar.
SMD 95, 42-3, v1, 4p. [1546]
Relating to adoption of negroes into the tribes, and allotment of lands in severalty.

103. Resol. of the Kansas Legis. 1 Mar.
SMD 96, 42-3, v1, 2p. [1546]
Settlers on Osage ceded lands; treaty of 21 Jan. 1867.

104. Alphabetical List of Private Claims. 1 Mar.
HMD 109, 42-3, v4, 526p. [1574]
From the 32d Congress to the 41st Congress, inclusive.

105. Report of Revised Army Regulations. 1 Mar.
HR 85, 42-3, v1, 221p. [1576]
Section included pertaining to Indians.

106. Protest of Creek and Cherokee Delegations. 3 Mar.
HMD 110, 42-3, v3, 3p. [1573]
Against passage of House bill no. 2635 creating the Territory of Oklahoma; government over Indian Territory; railroad company schemes; white settlers.

107. Statements of Appropriations. 3 Mar.
HMD 111, 42-3, v3, 89p. [1573]
During the 3rd session, 42d Congress; Indian expenses.

108. Report on Investigation of Indian Frauds. 3 Mar.
HR 98, 42-3, v3, 793p. [1578]
Wrongs committed against the Indians, touching annuities, pensions, bounties, bounty-lands, money paid under treaties, etc.

109. Report of the U.S. Geological Survey of the Territories. 10 Mar.
HMD 112, 42-3, v3, 844p. [1573]
Exploring expeditions; ancient Indian mounds; hostile Sioux; Bannocks and Flatheads in Montana.

110. Annual Message to Congress with Documents; Pres. Grant. 1 Dec.
HED 1, 43-1, v1-5, 7842p. [1594-1603]

Collection of all Indians east of the Rocky Mountains into Indian Territory; government over Indian Territory; annual report of the Sec. of War (Serials 1597-1599); annual report of the Sec. of Interior (Serials 1601-1602); annual report of the Gen. Land Office (Serial 1601); annual report of the CIA (Serial 1601), including difficulties in the way of Indian civilization, problem of sovereignty *vs.* wardship, legislation, and reports of Supts., agents, schools, and farms; etc.

111. Annual Report of the Sec. of the Treasury. 1 Dec.
HED 2, 43-1, v5, 720p. [1603]
Year ending 30 June 1873; Indian expenses.

112. Estimates of Appropriations. 1 Dec.
HED 5, 43-1, v7, 325p. [1605]
Year ending 30 June 1875; Indian expenses.

113. Public Property in the Interior Dept. 2 Dec.
SED 2, 43-1, v1, 3p. [1580]
In the OIA.

114. Mem. of E. Boudinot. 4 Dec.
HMD 4, 43-1, v1, 5p. [1617]
Cherokee Indian sells tobacco in Indian Territory; conflict between U.S. laws which say he should be taxed, and the treaty of 19 July 1866 which says he should not be taxed; court case.

115. Sale of Indian Lands in Kansas. 8 Dec.
SED 4, 43-1, v1, 2p. [1580]
Sale of Kansas Indian lands; removal to Indian Territory.

116. Mem. of the Walnut Grove Gold-Mining Company. 8 Dec.
HMD 16, 43-1, v1, 24p. [1617]
Apache depredations of 1864-1869 in Arizona.

117. Agreements with the Cheyennes and Arapahoes. 12 Dec.
HED 12, 43-1, v8, 5p. [1606]
Three agreements made 18 Nov. 1873 calling for relinquishment of the reservation belonging to said tribe under the treaty of 28 Oct. 1867.

118. Resol. of the Tennessee Legis. 15 Dec.
HMD 32, 43-1, v1, 1p. [1617]
Pensions to soldiers in the Indian war of 1836.

119. R-P of A. Darling. 17 Dec.
SR 4, 43-1, v1, 2p. [1586]
Sioux depredations of 1862 in Minnesota.

120. R-P of F. Darling. 17 Dec.
SR 5, 43-1, v1, 1p. [1586]
Sioux depredations of 1862 in Minnesota.

121. Letter on Kansas Indian Lands. 18 Dec.
HED 20, 43-1, v8, 2p. [1606]
Sale of lands in Kansas.

122. Letter on Pottawatomie Indian Funds. 18 Dec.
HED 21, 43-1, v8, 3p. [1606]
Investment of trust funds of the Prairie band; agreement of 18 July 1873 with Pottawatomies.

123. Estimate of Appropriation for the Modocs. 18 Dec.
HED 22, 43-1, v8, 2p. [1606]
Subsistence for Modocs in Indian Territory during fiscal 1874.

124. Estimate of Appropriations for Subsistence. 18 Dec.
HED 23, 43-1, v8, 2p. [1606]
For Kiowas, Comanches, Cheyennes, Arapahoes, Apaches, and Wichitas in Indian Territory.

125. Appropriation for Indian Civilization. 18 Dec.
HED 24, 43-1, v8, 3p. [1606]
In the Central Superintendency.

126. Mem. of Indians in Michigan and Indiana. 18 Dec.
HMD 45, 43-1, v1, 17p. [1617]
Funds due the Pottawatomies under various treaties.

1874

1. Revised Estimates of Appropriations. 7 Jan.
HED 36, 43-1, v7, 39p. [1605]
Year ending 30 June 1875; Indian expenses.

2. Estimate of Appropriations for the Sacs and Foxes of the Missouri. 7 Jan.
HED 37, 43-1, v8, 2p. [1606]
For education under the treaty of 6 Mar. 1861.

3. Letter on an Indian Reservation. 7 Jan.
HED 38, 43-1, v8, 2p. [1606]
For the Gros Ventres, Piegans, Bloods, Blackfeet, River Crow, and other Indians; in Montana.

4. Removal of Indians from Texas and Mexico. 7 Jan.

HED 39, 43-1, v8, 3p. [1606]
Estimate of appropriation for removal of the Kickapoos and other roving tribes to Indian Territory.

5. Estimate of Appropriation for Indian Civilization. 7 Jan.
HED 40, 43-1, v8, 4p. [1606]
For Indians in the Northern Superintendency.

6. Estimate of Appropriation for Apaches. 7 Jan.
HED 41, 43-1, v8, 2p. [1606]
To collect and subsist Apaches on reserves in New Mexico and Arizona.

7. Estimate of Appropriation for Pawnees. 7 Jan.
HED 42, 43-1, v8, 3p. [1606]
To indemnify the tribe for land erroneously excluded from their reservation under the treaty of 24 Sept. 1857.

8. On the Relief of Indian Tribes. 7 Jan.
HED 43, 43-1, v8, 2p. [1606]
In the Northern Superintendency; sale of Indian lands.

9. Estimate of Appropriation for the Winnebagoes. 7 Jan.
HED 44, 43-1, v8, 3p. [1606]
Under the treaty of 8 Mar. 1865.

10. Estimate of Appropriation for the Kansas Indians. 7 Jan.
HED 45, 43-1, v8, 2p. [1606]
Removal of tribe to Indian territory; sale of lands in Kansas.

11. R-M of the Walnut Grove Gold-Mining Company. 9 Jan.
SR 12, 43-1, v1, 1p. [1586]
Apache depredations of 1864-1869 in Arizona.

12. Agreement with the Utes. 12 Jan.
HED 53, 43-1, v8, 5p. [1606]
For relinquishment of lands in Colorado; dated 13 Sept. 1873.

13. Unexpended Balances for the Indian Service. 12 Jan.
HED 54, 43-1, v8, 2p. [1606]
Bill to authorize the Sec. of Interior to use unexpended funds from previous appropriations for present needs.

14. Civilization Funds for the Pawnees. 12 Jan.
HED 55, 43-1, v8, 2p. [1606]
Use of unexpended balances under the treaty of 24 Sept. 1857.

15. Letter on Manner of Paying Annuities. 12 Jan.
HED 56, 43-1, v8, 3p. [1606]
Seminole annuities to be paid to tribal authorities rather than *per capita*; treaty of 7 Aug. 1856; bill authorizing CIA to distribute annuities to best promote civilization.

16. Receipts and Expenditures. 12 Jan.
HED 57, 43-1, v8, 560p. [1606]
During 30 June 1871; Indian expenses.

17. Claim of W. Moore and Company. 12 Jan.
HMD 63, 43-1, v2, 9p. [1618]
Cheyenne depredations of 1869 in Kansas.

18. Letter from the Executive Com. of Friends. 12 Jan.
HMD 66, 43-1, v2, 4p. [1618]
Condition and wants of Indians in the Northern Superintendency.

19. On the Relief of the Chickasaws. 19 Jan.
SMD 29, 43-1, v1, 2p. [1584]
Land survey and allotment under the treaty of 28 Apr. 1866 with the Choctaws and Chickasaws; Choctaws do not want allotment, while the Chickasaws do.

20. Message on Encroachment Upon Indian Territory. 20 Jan.
SED 21, 43-1, v1, 1p. [1580]
The CIA indicates that he has no information which would show that any encroachment is taking place.

21. Indebtedness of the Indian Service. 20 Jan.
SMD 31, 43-1, v1, 3p. [1584]
Prior to 1 July 1873; major part comes from collecting Apaches on reservations and subsisting them.

22. Reservation for Indians in Washington Territory. 20 Jan.
SMD 32, 43-1, v1, 11p. [1584] *or*
HED 102, 43-1, v9, 11p. [1607]
For the Coeur d'Alenes, Upper and Lower Spokanes, Lakes, San Poels, Colvilles, Okinakanes, Colespells, Pend d'Oreilles, Kootenays, Methews, and other tribes in Washington and Idaho.

23. Agreement with the Shoshones and Bannocks. 22 Jan.
HED 61, 43-1, v9, 2p. [1607]
Dated 26 Sept. 1872; relinquishment of a portion of their Wyoming reservation.

24. Mem. of the Gen. Indian Council of Indian Territory. 22 Jan.
HMD 85, 43-1, v2, 2p. [1618]
Against railroad land grants in said territory.
25. Statement of Maj. Powell. 22 Jan.
HMD 86, 43-1, v2, 11p. [1618]
On the condition of Indian tribes west of the Rocky Mountains.
26. Protest of Delegates from Indian Territory. 22 Jan.
HMD 87, 43-1, v2, 2p. [1618]
Against the establishment by Congress of a territorial government over the Indians without their consent.
27. Protest of the Gen. Indian Council of Indian Territory. 22 Jan.
HMD 88, 43-1, v2, 3p. [1618]
Against a territorial government being established over the Indians without their consent.
28. On the Relief of the Choctaws and Chickasaws. 23 Jan.
HED 75, 43-1, v9, 2p. [1607]
Survey and allotment of land under the treaty of 28 Apr. 1866.
29. Estimate of Appropriation for Mechanics at the Pawnee Agency. 23 Jan.
HED 79, 43-1, v9, 2p. [1607]
Carpenter and shoemaker salaries for fiscal 1875.
30. Letter on Apaches in New Mexico and Arizona. 23 Jan.
HED 80, 43-1, v9, 3p. [1607]
Indebtedness incurred by collecting and subsisting the tribe on reservations; list of other debts of the Indian Service.
31. Mem. of P. Pitchlynn. 23 Jan.
HMD 89, 43-1, v2, 46p. [1618]
Choctaw delegate asks payment of money due Choctaws under various treaties.
32. Petition of T. Mesplié. 26 Jan.
HMD 97, 43-1, v2, 10p. [1618]
Asks relief for acting as an Indian missionary, agent, negotiator, and peace-maker in Oregon and Idaho; among the Calapooias, Molallas, Tualatims, Chehalis, Clapsacks, Wascoes, Wisrams, Fair Valleys, Timuos, Deschutes, Dog Rivers, Yocamos, Walla-Wallas, Cayuses, Klickitats, Shoshones, Bannocks, Paiutes, and Utes.
33. Report on Printing of Indian Expenditures. 27 Jan.
SR 48, 43-1, v1, 3p. [1586]
Too bulky to print.
34. Agreement with the Crows. 27 Jan.
HED 89, 43-1, v9, 52p. [1607]
Dated 16 Aug. 1873; relinquishment of reservation lands in Montana; council proceedings.
35. Estimate of Appropriation for Indian Removal. 27 Jan.
HED 90, 43-1, v9, 2p. [1607]
Removal of Kickapoos, Lipans, and Mescaleros from Mexico to Indian Territory.
36. Letter on the Mission Indians. 27 Jan.
HED 91, 43-1, v9, 16p. [1607]
Report on the condition of these southern California Indians.
37. Letter on Survey of Indian Reservations. 27 Jan.
HED 92, 43-1, v9, 3p. [1607]
Estimate of appropriation for fiscal 1875; for subdivision of the reserves.
38. Expenses of General Indian Council. 27 Jan.
HED 93, 43-1, v9, 2p. [1607]
Estimate of appropriation for a Creek, Cherokee, Seminole, Choctaw, and Chickasaw council in Indian Territory under treaty stipulations with said tribes.
39. Letter on White Earth Reservation in Minnesota. 27 Jan.
HED 94, 43-1, v9, 2p. [1607]
Bill to secure land in this Chippewa reservation to the Episcopal Board of Missions.
40. R-P of M. Wright. 28 Jan.
SR 50, 43-1, v1, 2p. [1586]
Sioux depredations of 1862 in Minnesota.
41. R-P of R. Greeland. 30 Jan.
SR 58, 43-1, v1, 1p. [1586]
Seminole hostilities in Florida.
42. R-P of S. Brooks. 30 Jan.
SR 59, 43-1, v1, 1p. [1586]
Captive of the Pawnees during 1868-1869.
43. On the Relief of J. Petri. 30 Jan.
HR 49, 43-1, v1, 3p. [1623]
Saves emigrants to California with the aid of 3 Indians.
44. Report on the Protection of the Texas Frontier. 30 Jan.

HR 61, 43-1, v1, 6p. [1623]
Against Indian depredations.

45. Removal of the Flatheads and Other Indians. 2 Feb.
SMD 45, 43-1, v1, 2p. [1584]
From the Bitter Root Valley to Montana.

46. Mem. of the Kansas Legis. 2 Feb.
HMD 110, 43-1, v2, 4p. [1618]
On the title to lands ceded by the Great and Little Osages under the treaty of 29 Dec. 1865.

47. Report on the Nez Percé Indian Reservation in Idaho. 2 Feb.
HR 63, 43-1, v1, 10p. [1623]
On the purchase of 640 acres for an Indian reservation.

48. Letter on the Round Valley Indian Reservation. 4 Feb.
SMD 47, 43-1, v1, 5p. [1584]
Report on establishing a northern boundary to the California reserve; restoration of part of the reserve to public and other uses.

49. Intercourse with Indian Tribes. 4 Feb.
HED 108, 43-1, v9, 3p. [1607]
To prevent the traffic of spirituous liquors.

50. Omaha Indian Lands in Nebraska. 4 Feb.
HED 109, 43-1, v9, 3p. [1607]
Estimate of appropriation for purchase of lands to be used for the Winnebagoes of Wisconsin; Winnebago treaty of 1 Nov. 1837.

51. Letter on the Allegany Reservation, New York. 4 Feb.
HED 110, 43-1, v9, 2p. [1607]
Lease or sale of the Seneca reservation; Indians protest.

52. Report on the Upper and Lower Bands of Sioux. 6 Feb.
HR 75, 43-1, v1, 4p. [1623]
Payment of debts under the treaties of 19 June 1858.

53. Round Valley Indian Reservation, California. 9 Feb.
HED 118, 43-1, v9, 9p. [1607]
Amendment to an act to restore part of the reservation to public lands.

54. Letter on the Makah Indians, Washington Territory. 9 Feb.
HED 119, 43-1, v9, 3p. [1607]
Estimate of appropriation to pay settlers for improvements on lands set aside as a reservation for said tribe under the treaty of 31 Jan. 1855.

55. Report on the Colville Reservation, Washington Territory. 9 Feb.
HMD 122, 43-1, v2, 7p. [1618]
Established in 1872 for non-treaty Indians; reserve moved by the government to a less desirable location; treatment of Indians; councils.

56. On the Relief of J. Spencer and J. Mead. 9 Feb.
HR 93, 43-1, v1, 2p. [1623]
Supplies furnished to the Kansas Indians in 1866-1867.

57. Letter on the Modoc War. 10 Feb.
HED 122, 43-1, v9, 330p. [1607]
Correspondence and papers on the 1872-1873 war in southern Oregon and northern California.

58. Message on Contracts, Purchases, and Expenditures for the Indian Service. 10 Feb.
HED 123, 43-1, v10, 45p. [1608]
Since 1 July 1873; objections of the Board of Indian Com'rs.

59. R-C of J. Johnson. 10 Feb.
HR 94, 43-1, v1, 1p. [1623]
Kiowa depredations of 1867 in Kansas.

60. R-C of J. Beck. 10 Feb.
HR 95, 43-1, v1, 2p. [1623]
Navajo depredations of 1849 in New Mexico.

61. Resol. of the California Legis. 11 Feb.
SMD 58, 43-1, v1, 1p. [1584]
Ask establishment of an Indian reservation in Siskiyan County.

62. R-P of C. Wetle. 11 Feb.
SR 83, 43-1, v1, 2p. [1586]
Sioux depredations of 1861 in Minnesota.

63. On the Relief of S. Deck. 11 Feb.
HR 96, 43-1, v1, 1p. [1623]
Sioux outbreak of 1862 in Minnesota.

64. R-P of F. Crump and W. Williamson. 12 Feb.
SR 90, 43-1, v1, 1p. [1586]
Soldiers with Gen. Atkinson's "Yellowstone expedition" of 1825 to make treaties with Plains Indian tribes.

65. Expenses of the Board of Indian Com'rs. 12 Feb.
HED 125, 43-1, v10, 2p. [1608]
Use of unexpended balance needs Congressional approval.

66. Annual Report of the Smithsonian Institution. 13 Feb.
SMD 130, 43-1, v2, 452p. [1585]

Research related to the American Indian; ancient mounds in America; etc.

67. Agreement with the Bannocks and Shoshones. 13 Feb.
HED 129, 43-1, v10, 7p. [1608]
Dated 7 Nov. 1873; relinquishment of hunting rights and reservation lands in Idaho granted to them under the treaty of 3 July 1868.

68. Agreement with the Jicarilla Apaches and Utes. 13 Feb.
HED 130, 43-1, v10, 7p. [1608]
Dated 10 Dec. 1873; relinquishment of lands, and location upon a reservation in New Mexico.

69. Mem. of the Shawnee Chiefs and Council. 16 Feb.
SMD 64, 43-1, v1, 2p. [1584]
On sale of Black Bob lands in Kansas.

70. Letter on Cherokees East of the Mississippi River. 16 Feb.
HED 135, 43-1, v10, 3p. [1608]
Census of North Carolina Indians, and distribution of a *per capita*.

71. Resol. of the Kansas Legis. 16 Feb.
HMD 133, 43-1, v3, 2p. [1619]
Settlers on the Osage lands.

72. Resol. of the Kansas Legis. 16 Feb.
HMD 134, 43-1, v3, 1p. [1619]
Sale of Kansas Indian lands.

73. Mem. of the Choctaw, Chickasaw, Cherokee, Creek, and Seminole Indians. 16 Feb.
HMD 142, 43-1, v3, 3p. [1619]
On misinterpretations of the treaties of 1866 with said tribes regarding government over Indian Territory.

74. Report on Legislative, Executive, and Judicial Appropriations. 16 Feb.
HR 139, 43-1, v1, 72p. [1623]
Includes the OIA.

75. Indians of the Siletz Agency in Oregon. 17 Feb.
SMD 65, 43-1, v1, 7p. [1584]
Report and proceedings of a council held regarding the needs of said Indians; due to Senate's failure to ratify the treaty of 11 Aug. 1855.

76. R-M of A. Wilson. 18 Feb.
SR 110, 43-1, v1, 3p. [1586]
Cherokee Indian claim against depredations of U.S. troops in Indian Territory during the Civil War.

77. Statistics on Mining West of the Rocky Mountains. 18 Feb.
HED 141, 43-1, v10, 585p. [1608]
Apache hostilities in Arizona; mining done by Indians; etc.

78. Expenses of the Indian Service. 18 Feb.
HED 142, 43-1, v12, 92p. [1610]
Expenditures and debts incurred from 30 June 1873 to 31 Dec. 1873.

79. Report on an Additional Land District in New Mexico. 19 Feb
SR 114, 43-1, v1, 5p. [1586]
Navajo and Apache hostilities upon mining companies.

80. Mem. of New York Indians. 24 Feb.
SMD 71, 43-1, v1, 4p. [1584]
Against a bill allowing for the sale of the Cattaraugus and Allegany reservations in New York; Seneca treaty stipulations.

81. Land Claim of A. Chaves. 24 Feb.
HED 149, 54-1, v12, 12p. [1610]
Navajo hostilities against settler in New Mexico.

82. Mem. of the Montana Legis. 24 Feb.
HMD 15 1, 43-1, v3, 2p. [1619]
Protection for whites in Deer Lodge and Missoula counties; Flatheads, Nez Percés, Cayuses, Coeur d'Alenes, Klikitatas, Yakimas, Walla-Wallas, Spokanes, Colvilles, Pend d'Oreilles, Kootenays, Kettles, and Modocs in the Bitter Root Valley.

83. Resol. of the Kansas Legis. 24 Feb.
HMD 152, 43-1, v3, 1p. [1619]
Ask reappraisement of New York Indian lands.

84. Resol. of the Wisconsin Legis. 24 Feb.
HMD 155, 43-1, v3, 1p. [1619]
Ask removal of all Indians from State.

85. Estimates of Deficiencies in Appropriations. 25 Feb.
HED 150, 43-1, v12, 17p. [1610]
Year ending 30 June 1874; Indian expenses.

86. Letter on the Mission Indians in California. 25 Feb.
HED 156, 43-1, v12, 3p. [1610]
Indian killed by white settlers; wrongs committed upon the Indians.

87. Letter on the Ute, Paiute, Go-Si Ute, and Shoshone Indians. 25 Feb.
HED 157, 43-1, v12, 35p. [1610]
Condition and wants of these tribes located in Utah, Arizona, Nevada, California, and Idaho.

88. Relief of Indians in Shasta County, California. 25 Feb.
HED 158, 43-1, v12, 4p. [1610]

Appropriation for provisioning the Pitt River, Fall River, and Hot Creek tribes.

89. Report on Ottawa and Chippewa Lands in Michigan. 25 Feb.
HR 186, 43-1, v1, 2p. [1623]
Issuance of land patents to Indians not provided for under the treaty of 31 July 1855.

90. Letter on a Treaty with the Chippewas. 27 Feb.
SED 33, 43-1, v1, 75p. [1580]
Question of land purchases by those on ceded lands under the 10th article of the treaty of 30 Sept. 1854, and 6th article of the treaty of 22 Sept. 1855.

91. Resol. of the Kansas Legis. 2 Mar.
SMD 75, 43-1, v1, 1p. [1584]
Ask transfer of BIA to the War Dept.

92. Resol. of the Kansas Legis. 2 Mar.
SMD 76, 43-1, v1, 1p. [1584]
Ask payment of Indian depredation claims.

93. Letter on the Condition of the Kansas Indians. 2 Mar.
SMD 77, 43-1, v1, 2p. [1584]
Recently removed from Kansas to Indian Territory.

94. Mem. of the Kansas Legis. 2 Mar.
HMD 166, 43-1, v3, 1p. [1619]
Ask that the Prairie band of Pottawatomies be removed and their reservation opened to settlement.

95. R-C of Jordan and McPike. 4 Mar.
SR 155, 43-1, v1, 4p. [1586]
Supplies to volunteers fighting the Paiutes in Utah during 1860.

96. Report on Liability of the U.S. Government to Reimburse Losses at the Hands of Indians. 4 Mar.
SR 156, 43-1, v1, 1p. [1586]
U.S. should not be held liable.

97. Letter on the Kansas Indians. 4 Mar.
HED 167, 43-1, v12, 2p. [1610]
Appropriation for settlement and support of said tribe in Indian Territory; removed from Kansas.

98. Letter on the Flathead Indians in Montana. 4 Mar.
HED 168, 43-1, v12, 2p. [1610]
Appropriation for the relief of the tribe.

99. Letter on the Osage Indians. 4 Mar.
HED 169, 43-1, v12, 4p. [1610]
Use of Great and Little Osage funds from the sale of their lands in Kansas for the purpose of their civilization; treaty of 29 Sept. 1865.

100. Resol. of the California Legis. 9 Mar.
HMD 177, 43-1, v3, 1p. [1619]
Ask establishment of an Indian reservation in Siskiyou County.

101. On the Relief of E. Boudinot. 10 Mar.
SR 168, 43-1, v1, 4p. [1586]
Cherokee Indian sells tobacco in Indian Territory; conflict between U.S. tax laws and the treaty of 19 July 1866.

102. Penalty for Selling Liquor to Indians. 11 Mar.
HED 177, 43-1, v12, 2p. [1610]
Amendment to existing laws fixing a minimum penalty for the violation.

103. L-C of J. Watts. 11 Mar.
HED 181, 43-1, v12, 6p. [1610]
Comanche depredations of 1868 in New Mexico.

104. Resol. of the Minnesota Legis. 16 Mar.
HMD 203, 43-1, v3, 2p. [1619]
School lands sold when the government conveyed the Winnebago reservation to private parties.

105. R-P of S. Stapler. 17 Mar.
SR 175, 43-1, v1, 1p. [1856]
Property of the late Cherokee chief, J. Ross, destroyed during the Civil War.

106. On the Relief of C. Denton. 17 Mar.
SR 177, 43-1, v1, 1p. [1586]
Indians placed on a land claim in Oregon by the U.S. Army during 1854-1860.

107. Report on Cultivation of Timber and the Preservation of Forests. 17 Mar.
HR 259, 43-1, v1, 119p. [1623]
Fires set by Indians; Indian cultivation; estimate of timber in Indian Territory.

108. Report on the Mission Indians of California. 18 Mar.
SR 180, 43-1, v1, 3p. [1586]
Concerning their condition, and an appropriation for their relief.

109. Cost to the Quartermaster's Dept. of the Modoc War. 19 Mar.
HED 185, 43-1, v12, 4p. [1610]
War of 1872-1873 in Oregon and California.

110. Letter on Red Cloud and Whetstone Indian Agencies. 19 Mar.
HED 186, 43-1, v12, 3p. [1610]
Appropriation for subsisting the Sioux at these agencies.

111. Reconnaissance in the Ute Country. 19 Mar.
HED 193, 43-1, v12, 101p. [1610]
Journal of the expedition; originated in disputes between Utes and miners; Utes threaten war if miners are not removed; Utes agree to cede certain lands.

112. Mem. of Oneida Indians. 20 Mar.
SMD 85, 43-1, v1, 3p. [1584]
Payment of money claimed to be due the Six Nations under treaties of 1838, and 1842.

113. Mem. of the Montana Legis. 23 Mar.
HMD 218, 43-1, v3, 2p. [1619]
Protection of the Yellowstone Valley, and the road from Fort Ellis to Bismarck, Dakota, from hostile Indians.

114. L-C of F. Gutierres and J. Gallegos. 25 Mar.
SED 38, 43-1, v1, 18p. [1580]
Land claim in New Mexico; several Indian pueblos involved.

115. Report on Osage Indian Lands. 25 Mar.
SR 204, 43-1, v1, 2p. [1586]
Use of funds from the sale of said lands in Kansas for the benefit of the Osages.

116. Report on War Claims and Claims of Aliens. 26 Mar.
HR 262, 43-1, v1, 104p. [1623]
Indicates when government will pay for Indian spoliations.

117. Report on Hot Springs Reservation, Arkansas. 26 Mar.
HR 263, 43-1, v2, 4p. [1624]
Quapaw land title extinguished by the treaty of 24 Aug. 1818.

118. Report on Sale of Kansas Indian Lands. 26 Mar.
HR 267, 43-1, v2, 3p. [1624]
Kansas tribe removed to Indian Territory; appraisement on their lands in Kansas is too high, delaying sale of said lands.

119. Report on the Upper and Lower Bands of Sioux. 27 Mar.
SR 225, 43-1, v1, 4p. [1586]
Payment of Indian debts from proceeds of land sales under the treaty of 19 June 1858.

120. On the Relief of Heirs of G. Fisher. 27 Mar.
HR 330, 43-1, v2, 4p. [1624]
Depredations of U.S. troops during the Creek war of 1813 in Mississippi Territory.

121. On the Relief of J. Dunlap. 30 Mar.
SMD 92, 43-1, v1, 4p. [1584]
Settler on the Kansas Indian diminished reserve lands in Kansas.

122. Mem. of J. Beeson. 1 Apr.
SMD 94, 43-1, v1, 4p. [1584]
Asks appointment of a delegation to visit Indian Territory and devise means to improve the condition of the tribes there.

123. Letter on Punishment of Crimes Committed by and Against Indians. 1 Apr.
SMD 95, 43-1, v1, 2p. [1584] *or*
HED 200, 43-1, v12, 3p. [1610]
Bill conferring exclusive jurisdiction over Indian reservations upon the U.S. courts.

124. Chippewas on the Red Cliff and Bad River Reservations. 1 Apr.
HED 201, 43-1, v12, 2p. [1610]
Appropriation for the relief of said Indians.

125. Restoration of Lands in California to Pre-Emption Settlement. 2 Apr.
HED 205, 43-1, v12, 14p. [1610]
Lands withdrawn as Indian reservations.

126. Private Land Claims in New Mexico. 3 Apr.
HED 206, 43-1, v12, 28p. [1610]
Land grants to Indian pueblos; Apaches residing on claimed lands; Navajo hostilities.

127. Resol. of the California Legis. 6 Apr.
HMD 240, 43-1, v3, 1p. [1619]
On expenses of the Modoc war.

128. Black Bob Indian Lands in Kansas. 8 Apr.
SED 39, 43-1, v1, 2p. [1580]
Protest by the Supt. of the Central Superintendency against a bill providing for the sale of these Shawnee lands.

129. Letter on Freedmen of the Choctaw and Chickasaw Nations. 8 Apr.
SMD 97, 43-1, v1, 2p. [1584]
Their rights under the treaty of 28 Apr. 1866.

130. Report on the Choctaw Award. 9 Apr.
HR 391, 43-1, v2, 17p. [1624]
Payments due under the treaties of 27 Sept. 1830, and 22 June 1855; proceeds from land sales.

131. Report on Land Grants to the St. Paul and Pacific Railroad Company. 10 Apr.
SR 264, 43-1, v1, 4p. [1586]
Railroad will serve as a barrier

against hostile Indians, and aid transport of Indian goods.

132. Report on Depredations on the Texas Frontier. 11 Apr.
HR 395, 43-1, v2, 3p. [1624]
Committed by Indians.

133. Report on the L'Anse and Vieux de Sert Bands of Chippewas. 11 Apr.
HR 396, 43-1, v2, 5p. [1624]
Had lands given them under the treaty of 30 Sept. 1854 wrongfully withheld.

134. On the Case of J. Thomas. 11 Apr.
HR 411, 43-1, v2, 1p. [1624]
Husband killed in Modoc war.

135. Treaty with the Choctaws and Chickasaws. 14 Apr.
HED 212, 43-1, v15, 4p. [1613]
Dated 28 Apr. 1866; inaction of Indians concerning the rights of negroes residing among them.

136. R-P of D. McCann. 15 Apr.
HR 417, 43-1, v2, 7p. [1624]
Teams delayed in Cheyenne, Wyoming while transporting goods to Sioux agencies.

137. On the Relief of J. Fell et al. 17 Apr.
HR 420, 43-1, v2, 8p. [1624]
Walnut Grove Mining Company of Arizona; Apache depredations in 1865-1869.

138. R-C of H. Webster et al. 17 Apr.
HR 439, 43-1, v3, 7p. [1625]
Ask reimbursement for improvements on lands set apart for the Makahs in Washington Territory under the treaty of 31 Jan. 1855.

139. Indian Agencies in Nevada. 20 Apr.
SED 42, 43-1, v1, 44p. [1580]
Report on the Walker River, Pyramid Lake, and Muddy Valley reservations; circumstances surrounding their formation.

140. L-C of the Doña Ana Colony. 20 Apr.
SED 43, 43-1, v2, 87p. [1581]
Land claim in New Mexico; Indian hostilities.

141. Resol. of the Board of Com'rs of Morris County, Kansas. 20 Apr.
SMD 46, 43-1, v1, 1p. [1584]
On taxation of Kansas Indian lands which are sold.

142. Report on the Seneca Indians. 20 Apr.
HR 478, 43-1, v3, 6p. [1625]
Regarding the opening of the Cattaraugus and Allegany reservations, left to the tribe under the treaty of 11 Nov. 1794.

143. Protection of the Texas Frontier. 21 Apr.
HED 222, 43-1, v16, 1p. [1614]
Against Indian and Mexican depredations.

144. R-P of Citizens of New Ulm, Minnesota. 23 Apr.
SR 302, 43-1, v2, 1p. [1587]
Sioux outbreak of 1862.

145. Supt. of Education for Indian Territory. 24 Apr.
HED 227, 43-1, v16, 2p. [1614]
Creation of the office to administer the $120,000 annually disbursed in Indian Territory on education.

146. Letter on Citizenship of Indians. 24 Apr.
HED 228, 43-1, v16, 2p. [1614]
Bill enabling Indians to become U.S. citizens.

147. Protection of Citizens in Montana. 29 Apr.
SED 46, 43-1, v2, 2p. [1581]
In the Bitter Root and Hell-Gate Valleys; claimed by the Flathead Indians; traversed by Nez Percés, Cayuses, Coeur d'Alenes, Klikitats, Yakimas, Walla-Wallas, Spokanes, Colvilles, Pend d'Oreilles, Kootenays, Kettles, and Modocs on their way to the buffalo grounds; Indian depredations.

148. R-P of J. Leflore and J. Harris. 29 Apr.
SR 314, 43-1, v2, 11p. [1587]
Reserve of land in Mississippi given to the chief of the Choctaws under the treaty of 27 Sept. 1830 at Dancing Rabbit Creek.

149. Letter on the Kickapoo Indians. 30 Apr.
HED 236, 43-1, v16, 2p. [1614]
Appropriation to subsist those Indians who have removed from Mexico to Indian Territory.

150. Bids for Indian Goods. 2 May.
HED 238, 43-1, v16, 2p. [1614]
Bill on regulation of bids for contracts to supply and transport goods; past abuses.

151. Message on Geographical and Geological Surveys West of the Mississippi River. 2 May.
HED 240, 43-1, v16, 15p. [1614]
List of expeditions under the various depts.; consolidation of efforts considered; Indian hostilities affect costs.

152. J. Powell's Report on an Exploration of the Colorado River. 2 May.
HMD 265, 43-1, v5, 29p. [1621]
Ethnographic description of the In-

dians of the region, including language, organization, mythology, etc.; includes Utes Paiutes, Shoshones, Navajoes, Mojaves, and other tribes.

153. On the Relief of A. Hine. 2 May.
HR 513, 43-1, v3, 2p. [1625]
Steamer used by Gen. Sully's northwestern Indian expedition in 1864 sunk in the Yellowstone River.

154. R-M of W. Dearing. 2 May.
HR 530, 43-1, v3, 1p. [1625]
Served in Seminole war.

155. R-P of A. Lasley. 4 May.
SR 319, 43-1, v2, 1p. [1587]
Indian engagement at Cow Creek in Kansas.

156. Report on Admission of New Mexico as a State. 5 May.
HR 561, 43-1, v3, 3p. [1625]
Indian war during 1860-1870; Pueblo Indians are U.S. citizens under the treaty of Guadalupe Hidalgo.

157. Letter on the Indian Service in California. 6 May.
HED 243, 43-1, v16, 2p. [1614]
Appropriation to cover debts.

158. Letter on the Stockbridges and Munsees in Wisconsin. 6 May.
HED 244, 43-1, v16, 2p. [1614]
Appropriation for the relief of said Indians; sale of lands.

159. White Earth Reservation in Minnesota. 6 May.
HED 246, 43-1, v16, 2p. [1614]
Appropriation for subdivision of the reservation.

160. Letter on the Osage Indians. 6 May.
HED 247, 43-1, v16, 2p. [1614]
Estimate of appropriation to pay interest on the proceeds of lands sold in Kansas under the treaty of 29 Sept. 1865.

161. Report on Removal of Indians from Wisconsin. 6 May.
HR 562, 43-1, v3, 2p. [1625]
Removal of Pottawatomies, Winnebagoes, and Chippewas.

162. On the Relief of Settlers on the Absentee Shawnee Lands in Kansas. 8 May.
SR 337, 43-1, v2, 3p. [1587]
Land reserved to the Shawnees under the treaty of 1854.

163. On the Relief of B. Hammond. 11 May.
SR 340, 43-1, v1, 2p. [1587]
Agent for the Colorado River reservation in Arizona dies *en route* to the reserve.

164. Resol. on the Statue of the "Dying Indian." 11 May.
HMD 273, 43-1, v5, 1p. [1621]
Ask its removal to the Statuary Hall of the House.

165. Message on the Relief of J. Spencer and J. Mead. 12 May.
HED 249, 43-1, v16, 5p. [1614]
For supplies furnished the Kansas Indians in 1867.

166. R-M of D. and D. Sanford. 13 May .
SR 345, 43-1, v2, 3p. [1587]
Kiowa and Comanche depredations of 1872 in Texas.

167. Report on Allotments of Land to Indians; 13 May.
SR 346, 43-1, v2, 2p. [1587]
Allotments to Shawnees in Indian Territory.

168. On the Relief of Indian Home-Guard Regiments. 14 May.
HMD 276, 43-1, v5, 2p. [1621]
Cherokee, Creek and Seminole soldiers in the Civil War.

169. Report on Jurisdiction Over Indian Reservations. 20 May.
SR 367, 43-1, v2, 2p. [1587]
Amendments to a bill giving U.S. Courts exclusive jurisdiction over Indian reservations.

170. R-M of P. Pitchlynn. 20 May.
HR 599, 43-1, v3, 12p. [1625]
On Choctaw claims against the U.S. under various treaties.

171. Letter on the Sale of Pine Timber. 22 May.
SED 50, 43-1, v2, 1p. [1581]
Belonging to the Chippewas; legality of sale questioned.

172. Transfer of Indian Funds. 25 May.
SMD 112, 43-1, v1, 2p. [1584]
Belonging to the Kaskaskias, Peorias, Weas, and Piankeshaws, to the U.S.

173. Letter for Support of the Osages. 25 May.
SMD 113, 43-1, v1, 1p. [1584]
From proceeds of sale of their lands in Kansas; for civilization expenses in Indian Territory.

174. Message on Depredations on the Frontiers of Texas. 26 May.
HED 257, 43-1, v17, 32p. [1615]
Kickapoo, Lipan, and Mescalero raids from Mexico.

175. Report on Surveys West of the Mississippi River. 26 May.
HR 612, 43-1, v4, 91p. [1626]

List of exploring expeditions, and the purposes for which they were carried out; hostile Indians; description of the Indians.

176. Report on Admission of Colorado as a State. 28 May.
HR 619, 43-1, v4, 6p. [1626]
Early growth stunted by Indian wars.

177. Land Claim in New Mexico. 29 May.
HED 258, 43-1, v17, 13p. [1615]
Involves the Indian pueblo of Nambe.

178. R-P of G. Chorpenning. 29 May.
HR 622, 43-1, v4, 3p. [1626]
Indian depredations in Utah.

179. Mem. of Indian Delegations from Indian Territory. 1 June.
SMD 117, 43-1, v1, 3p. [1584]
Against appointment of a Supt. of schools in that territory.

180. Resol. of the Texas Legis. 1 June.
HMD 286, 43-1, v5, 2p. [1621]
Ask reimbursement of H. Warren for Kiowa, Cheyenne, and Comanche depredations of 1871.

181. Report on the Western Judicial District of Arkansas. 1 June.
HR 626, 43-1, v4, 328p. [1626]
Jurisdiction over cases involving Indians and whites, but not over cases involving Indian and Indian; crime increased in Indian Territory while the railroads were being constructed.

182. On the Relief of Freedmen of the Choctaw and Chickasaw Nations. 2 June.
SMD 118, 43-1, v1, 3p. [1584]
Under the treaty of 28 Apr. 1866.

183. Report on the Mission of St. James, Washington Territory. 3 June.
HR 630, 43-1, v4, 2p. [1626]
Missionary station and lands among the Indians.

184. Report on the Creek Orphan Fund. 4 June.
SR 411, 43-1, v2, 8p. [1587]
Established under the treaty of 24 March 1832.

185. R-C of E. Murphy. 4 June.
HR 632, 43-1, v4, 2p. [1626]
Mescalero Apache depredations of 1870 in Texas.

186. R-C of H. Warren. 4 June.
HR 633, 43-1, v4, 3p. [1626]
Kiowa and Comanche depredations of 1871 in Texas.

187. Report on Sundry Civil Appropriations. 4 June.
HR 636, 43-1, v4, 49p. [1626]
Indian expenses, and trust funds.

188. Report on the Navajo Indian Reservation. 6 June.
HR 638, 43-1, v4, 1p. [1626]
Relinquishment of land under the agreement of 27 Mar. 1874.

189. Report on Indian Appropriations. 6 June.
HR 639, 43-1, v4, 1p. [1626]
Amendments to the Indian appropriations bill.

190. Report on the Creek Orphan Fund. 6 June.
HR 640, 43-1, v4, 6p. [1626]
Originated by the treaty of 24 Mar. 1832.

191. Mem. of P. Pitchlynn. 8 June.
SMD 121, 43-1, v1, 73p. [1584]
On unsettled claims of the Choctaw Nation under various treaties.

192. Protest of Seneca Indians. 8 June.
SMD 122, 43-1, v1, 2p. [1584]
Against a bill providing for sale of lands within the Allegany and Cattaraugus reservations in New York.

193. Reconnaissance of Northwestern Wyoming. 16 June.
HED 285, 43-1, v17, 210p. [1615]
Descriptive journal of the expedition notes encounters with Indians and mentions the tribes of the area; troubles with Indian scouts.

194. Remonstrance of the Choctaw Delegates. 16 June.
HMD 294, 43-1, v5, 11p. [1621]
On the rights of freedmen under the Choctaw and Chickasaw treaty of 28 Apr. 1866.

195. R-P of G. Chorpenning. 16 June.
HR 653, 43-1, v4, 3p. [1626]
Indian depredations in Utah.

196. On the Relief of G. Jocknick. 16 June.
HR 661, 43-1, v4, 3p. [1626]
Clerk in the Interior Dept. involved in payments made to the Cherokees of North Carolina; trials regarding alleged frauds.

197. Report on California Indian-War Bonds. 16 June.
HR 669, 43-1, v4, 1p. [1626]
Issued in 1852.

198. On the Case of A. Brown. 16 June.
HR 728, 43-1, v4, 1p. [1626]
Seminole war of 1818 in Florida.

199. J. Powell's Report of an Exploration of the Colorado River. 18 June.
HMD 300, 43-1, v6, 291p. [1622]

Journal of the expedition; encounters with Utes, Navajoes, and other Indian tribes; descriptions of the Indians.

200. On the Relief of J. Spencer and J. Mead. 18 June.
HR 738, 43-1, v4, 1p. [1626]
Supplies furnished the Kansas Indians.

201. Report on the Delaware Indians. 18 June.
HR 739, 43-1, v4, 2p. [1626]
Payment for depredations committed by whites; provided for under the treaty of 4 July 1866.

202. Resol. of Sen. Patterson. 19 June.
SMD 127, 43-1, v1, 1p. [1584]
On territorial government for Indian Territory.

203. Report on Oklahoma Territory. 19 June.
SR 465, 43-1, v2, 1p. [1587]
Com. on Territories asks authority to visit Indian Territory to inquire into public sentiment regarding the formation of a territorial government over the Indians.

204. Payment of New Mexico Volunteers. 19 June.
HED 272, 43-1, v17, 1p. [1615]
For suppression of Indian hostilities.

205. Letter on the Hot Springs of Arkansas. 19 June.
HED 273, 43-1, v17, 6p. [1615]
Cherokee claims for area rejected.

206. Land Claim in New Mexico. 19 June.
HED 280, 43-1, v17, 10p. [1615]
Involves the Indian town of Sandia.

207. Letter on Military Sites in Texas. 19 June.
HED 282, 43-1, v17, 46p. [1615]
On purchase of said sites; Indian depredations.

208. Dakota War Claims. 19 June.
HED 286, 43-1, v17, 143p. [1615]
Arising from the Sioux war of 1862.

209. Report on the Investigation of the Conduct of Indian Affairs. 22 June.
HR 778, 43-1, v5, 283p. [1627]
Frauds, and irregularity surrounding contracts for Indian supplies and transportation for the fiscal years ending 30 June 1873, and 30 June 1874.

210. R-C of W. Hughes. 22 June.
HR 779, 43-1, v5, 2p. [1627]
To confirm a sale of land in Kansas by a Shawnee Indian.

211. On the Relief of J. Fletcher. 22 June.
HR 780, 43-1, v5, 5p. [1627]
Cheyenne and Arapaho depredations of 1870 in Indian Territory.

212. Report on Indian Hostilities in Washington and Oregon During 1855-1856. 22 June.
HR 837, 43-1, v5, 2p. [1627]
On claims arising from the war.

213. Disbursements of the Indian Dept. 6 Nov.
HED 6, 43-2, v10, 12p. [1643]
Year ending 30 June 1874.

214. Annual Message to Congress with Documents; Pres. Grant. 7 Dec.
HED 1, 43-2, v1-8, 6264p. [1634-1641]
Recommends a territorial government over Indian Territory; annual report of the Sec. of War (Serials 1635-1637); annual report of the Sec. of Interior (Serials 1639-1640); annual report of the Gen. Land Office (Serial 1639); annual report of the CIA (Serial 1639), including populations, the Sioux problem, the Black Hills expedition, the "wild tribes" of the Southwest, Indian Territory, and reports of Supts., agents, schools, and farms; etc.

215. Annual Report of the Sec. of the Treasury. 7 Dec.
HED 2, 43-2, v8, 809p. [1641]
Year ending 30 June 1874; Indian expenses.

216. Estimates of Appropriations. 7 Dec.
HED 5, 43-2, v10, 270p. [1643]
Year ending 30 June 1876; Indian expenses.

217. List of Property in the Interior Dept. 8 Dec.
SED 1, 43-2, v1, 3p. [1629]
Including the OIA.

218. Private Land Claims in New Mexico. 8 Dec.
SED 2, 43-2, v1, 16p. [1629]
Cheyenne hostilities; trade with the Comanches.

219. Mem. of J. Fell et al. 8 Dec.
HMD 3, 43-2, v1, 26p. [1653]
Walnut Grove Gold-Mining Company; Apache depredations of 1864-1869 in Arizona.

220. Mem. of Indians in Michigan and Indiana. 8 Dec.
HMD 5, 43-2, v1, 21p. [1653]
Pottawatomies (exempted from removal under the treaty of 27 Sept.

1833) ask funds due them under various treaties.

221. Mem. of the Texas and Pacific Railway Company, and the Atlantic and Pacific Railroad Company. 8 Dec.
HMD 6, 43-2, v1, 7p. [1653]
Southern railroad to the Pacific would allow for control of Indian hostilities and provide for Indian civilization.

222. Montana Indian War Claims. 9 Dec.
HED 9, 43-2, v11, 5p. [1644]
Payment of claims arising from the 1867 war.

223. Receipts and Expenditures. 9 Dec.
HED 10, 43-2, v11, 657p. [1644]
Year ending 30 June 1873; Indian expenses.

224. Fort Kearney Military Reservation. 10 Dec.
HED 12, 43-2, v11, 1p. [1644]
Land purchased from the Pawnees under the treaty of 6 Aug. 1848.

225. Report on Hot Springs, Arkansas. 10 Dec.
HR 3, 43-2, v1, 5p. [1656]
Establishing title to the land; Quapaw title extinguished under the treaty of 24 Aug. 1818.

226. Survey of Indian Reservations. 15 Dec.
HED 21, 43-2, v11, 2p. [1644]
Estimate of funds required to survey various reservations during the year ending 30 June 1876.

227. Military Wagon Road in Wyoming and Montana. 15 Dec.
HED 22, 43-2, v11, 4p. [1644]
Would pass the Crow agency; transport of Indian supplies.

228. Judgments Rendered by the Court of Claims. 15 Dec.
HMD 17, 43-2, v1, 11p. [1653]
Various cases concern Indians; during 1874.

229. Military Post Near Carlin, Nevada. 16 Dec.
HED 33, 43-2, v11, 2p. [1644]
Changes in the status of Indians has rendered some posts unnecessary.

230. Letter on Sioux Agencies. 16 Dec.
HED 35, 43-2, v11, 2p. [1644]
Appropriation needed for the transport of supplies under the treaty of 29 Apr. 1868.

231. Letter on the Pawnee Indians. 16 Dec.
HED 36, 43-2, v11, 3p. [1644]
Removal of the Pawnees from Nebraska to Indian Territory; sale of their reservation in Nebraska.

232. Letter on the Northern Sioux. 18 Dec.
HED 43, 43-2, v11, 2p. [1644]
Appropriation needed to subsist Sioux at the Red Cloud and Whetstone agencies.

233. Petition of California Citizens. 21 Dec.
SMD 13, 43-2, v1, 2p. [1630]
Ask land grant in Alaska for a shipbuilding company, and that a military post be built to protect the company from hostile Indians; presence of warlike Indians on the Alaskan shores.

234. Modoc War Claims. 22 Dec.
HED 45, 43-2, v12, 119p. [1645]
Claims of Oregon, California, and citizens of those States arising from the 1872-1873 war.

235. Liabilities of Choctaws to Individuals. 23 Dec.
HED 47, 43-2, v12, 29p. [1645]
Choctaw debts to be paid under the treaty of 22 June 1855.

236. Indians of the Central Superintendency. 23 Dec.
HED 49, 43-2, v12, 2p. [1645]
Appropriation needed for education and civilization.

237. Apaches of Arizona. 23 Dec.
HED 50, 43-2, v12, 2p. [1645]
Appropriation for collecting and subsisting the tribe upon reservations.

238. North Carolina Cherokees. 23 Dec.
HED 51, 43-2, v12, 11p. [1645]
On land titles of the eastern Cherokees, and their unsettled accounts.

239. Education of Captives of the Cheyennes. 23 Dec.
HED 52, 43-2, v12, 3p. [1645]
Appropriation for education of two young women who were captured in the Indian Territory.

240. Removal of the Modocs. 23 Dec.
HED 53, 43-2, v12, 3p. [1645]
Appropriation to remove the Modocs from Oregon to Indian Territory; land purchased from the Quapaws.

241. Letter on Absentee Shawnees. 23 Dec.
HED 54, 43-2, v12, 1p. [1645]
Claims for property taken by rebels during the Civil War.

242. Timber for the Use of Indians. 23 Dec.
HED 61, 43-2, v12, 2p. [1645]

Recommends legislation to allow Indians to cut and sell timber; Indians prevented from doing so by a Supreme Court decision.

1875

1. On the Case of J. Brown. 6 Jan.
SR 498, 43-2, v1, 1p. [1632]
Escorted Indian agent to California in 1849.
2. On the Case of W. Mayfield. 8 Jan.
SR 511, 43-2, v1, 1p. [1632]
Injured in Rogue River Indian war of 1855-1856 in Oregon.
3. Private Land Claims in New Mexico. 8 Jan.
HED 62, 43-2, v12, 111p. [1645]
Apache and Navajo rights to land.
4. On the Relief of J. Dunlap. 8 Jan.
HR 52, 43-2, v1, 2p. [1656]
Settler on the Kansas Indian diminished-reserve lands in Kansas.
5. Indian Depredation Claims. 11 Jan.
HED 65, 43-2, v12, 59p. [1645]
List of claims during the period 1864-1874; amount, date committed, place, tribe, and action on the claim.
6. Mem. of the Dakota Legis. 11 Jan.
HMD 31, 43-2, v1, 2p. [1653]
Ask land grant for a railroad from Yankton to the Yellowstone National Park *via* the Black Hills; Indian reservations should be reopened.
7. Mem. of the Dakota Legis. 11 Jan.
HMD 33, 43-2, v1, 2p. [1653]
Asks that Sioux title to the Black Hills be extinguished, and that the same be opened for settlement.
8. Deficiencies in Appropriations. 13 Jan.
HED 69, 43-2, v12, 27p. [1645]
Year ending 30 June 1875; Indian expenses.
9. Contingent Expenses of the Interior Dept. 13 Jan.
HED 84, 43-2, v13, 33p. [1646]
Year ending 30 June 1874; OIA.
10. Geological and Geographical Surveys. 13 Jan.
HED 85, 43-2, v13, 9p. [1646]
Appropriation needed to continue exploring expeditions; distribution and description of Indians in Colorado, Utah, and New Mexico.
11. L-C of W. Lyon and Son. 13 Jan.
HED 86, 43-2, v13, 6p. [1646]
For printing 1000 volumes of Choctaw laws.
12. Indians in Washington Territory. 13 Jan.
HED 87, 43-2, v13, 3p. [1646]
On consolidation of tribes, and sale of reservations not needed; extension of the Skokomish and Lummi reservations.
13. Letter on the Utes of Colorado. 13 Jan.
HED 88, 43-2, v13, 2p. [1646]
Appropriation for subsisting the Utes under the treaty of 2 Mar. 1868.
14. Letter on the Cherokee Indians. 13 Jan.
HED 89, 43-2, v13, 3p. [1646]
Authorization for a loan to be negotiated to purchase supplies.
15. Letter on Creek Annuities. 13 Jan.
HED 90, 43-2, v13, 2p. [1646]
Appropriation necessary under the treaties of 24 Jan. 1826, 14 Feb. 1833, and 7 Aug. 1856.
16. Support of Indians in Indian Territory. 13 Jan.
HED 91, 43-2, v13, 3p. [1646]
Appropriation to subsist the Cheyenne, Apaches, Arapahoes, Kiowas, Comanches, and Wichitas.
17. Indians of the Northern Superintendency. 13 Jan.
HED 92, 43-2, v13, 2p. [1646]
Amendment to an act for the relief of certain tribes; Pawnees stricken from the act.
18. Removal of the Weeminuche Indians. 13 Jan.
HED 97, 43-2, v13, 2p. [1646]
Weeminuche band of Utes removed to the Ute reservation in Colorado under an agreement ratified 29 Apr. 1874.
19. On the Case of J. Terrell. 13 Jan.
HED 98, 43-2, v13, 3p. [1646]
Disbursing agent to the North Carolina Cherokees.
20. Letter on the Malheur Reservation, Oregon. 13 Jan.
HED 99, 43-2, v13, 3p. [1646]
Appropriation for civilization and subsistence.
21. Indian Tribes in Kansas. 13 Jan.
HED 101, 43-2, v15, 24p. [1648]
Examination of the accounts of the

Peorias, Kaskaskias, Weas, and Piankeshaws under the treaty of 23 Feb. 1867.

22. Statements on the Texas and Pacific Railroad. 13 Jan.
HMD 36, 43-2, v1, 19p. [1653]
Control of Indian troubles in the Southwest.

23. Mem. of the Oregon Legis. 14 Jan.
SMD 32, 43-2, v1, 2p. [1630]
Ask compensation for spoliations committed during the Modoc war of 1872.

24. Indian Service in Colorado. 14 Jan.
HED 102, 43-2, v15, 2p. [1648]
Appropriation to cover the expenses of negotiations with the Utes.

25. Letter on the Fond du Lac Reservation. 14 Jan.
HED 103, 43-2, v15, 2p. [1648]
Sale of a portion of this Chippewa reservation in Minnesota.

26. Mem. of Citizens of the Chickasaw Nation. 15 Jan.
SMD 34, 43-2, v1, 2p. [1630]
Against territorial government over Indian Territory; Board of Indian Peace Com'rs, which recommended immediate formation of such a government, is chaired by an executive of a railroad company claiming large tracts of land in Indian Territory.

27. Removal of Pawnee Indians from Nebraska. 15 Jan.
SMD 35, 43-2, v1, 2p. [1630]
Sale of reservation in Nebraska, and removal to Indian Territory.

28. Sale of a Portion of the Fond du Lac Indian Reservation. 15 Jan.
SMD 36, 43-2, v1, 1p. [1630]
Minnesota reserve occupied by the Fond du Lac band of Chippewas.

29. On the Case of Heirs of J. Sinclair. 15 Jan.
SR 528, 43-2, v1, 4p. [1632]
Indian hostilities of 1855 in Washington Territory.

30. Amount Due J. Terrell. 19 Jan.
SMD 41, 43-2, v1, 3p. [1630]
Disbursing agent to the Cherokees of North Carolina during 1853-1861.

31. Indians of the Central Superintendency. 19 Jan.
SMD 42, 43-2, v1, 2p. [1630]
Estimate of appropriation needed for civilization and education.

32. Agreement with the Utes. 19 Jan.
SMD 44, 43-2, v1, 2p. [1630]
Expenses incurred in negotiations with the Utes for extinguishment of their right to a portion of their reservation in Colorado.

33. Military Wagon Road in Nebraska. 19 Jan.
SR 532, 43-2, v1, 2p. [1632]
From Sidney to the Red Cloud and Spotted-Tail agencies.

34. St. James Mission, Washington Territory. 19 Jan.
HED 117, 43-2, v15, 1p. [1648]
Claim for land refused by the War Dept., as it was not a missionary station among Indian tribes.

35. Letter on the Osage Indians. 19 Jan.
HED 119, 43-2, v15, 2p. [1648]
Appropriation to pay the Osages interest on proceeds from land sold in Kansas under the treaty of 29 Sept. 1865.

36. Indian Service in Oregon. 19 Jan.
HED 120, 43-2, v15, 5p. [1648]
Appropriation for a mill at the Siletz agency.

37. Indian Service in California. 19 Jan.
HED 121, 43-2, v15, 2p. [1648]
Appropriation to supply a deficiency in the proceeds of the sale of lands in the Round Valley reservation.

38. Amendment to the Indian Appropriation Bill. 19 Jan.
HED 122, 43-2, v15, 2p. [1648]
To cover the expenses of a Choctaw Indian at the Government Hospital for the Insane, and to defray costs of a Choctaw youth *en route* back to Indian Territory.

39. Indian Service in New Mexico. 19 Jan.
HED 123, 43-2, v15, 2p. [1648]
Appropriation for subsisting the Navajoes.

40. Grande Ronde Indian Agency, Oregon. 19 Jan.
HED 124, 43-2, v15, 2p. [1648]
Appropriation needed for incidental expenses; treaty of 29 Nov. 1854 with the Umpquas and Calapooias; treaty of 22 Jan. 1855 with the Calapooias, Molallas, and Clackamas.

41. Mem. of the Oregon Legis. 25 Jan.
SMD 53, 43-2, v1, 2p. [1630]
Ask extinguishment of Umatilla

title to their reservation, and their removal to the Nez Percé reservation.

42. Mem. of the Oregon Legis. 25 Jan.
SMD 54, 43-2, v1, 2p. [1630]
Ask construction of a wagon road; will serve the Fort Klamath, Yanox, and Klamath Indian agencies.

43. Annual Report of the Smithsonian Institution. 26 Jan.
HMD 56, 43-2, v2, 416p. [1654]
Research related to the American Indian; ancient mounds; Blackfeet, California, Delaware, Go-si-Ute, Gros Ventres, Haidah, Assiniboine, Piegan, Crow, Sac, Fox, Sioux, and Wyandott Indians; vocabularies.

44. Report on the Judicial District of Oklahoma. 26 Jan.
HR 122, 43-2, v2, 1p. [1657]
Creation of a judicial district over Indian Territory, with jurisdiction over Indians.

45. Letter on the Modoc War. 27 Jan.
HED 131, 43-2, v15, 19p. [1648]
Costs incurred by the Army in the 1872-1873 war in Oregon and California.

46. Supplemental Estimate for the Indian Service. 27 Jan.
HED 132, 43-2, v15, 3p. [1648]
Required to meet liabilities contracted during the year ending 30 June 1874.

47. Chippewas of Lake Superior. 27 Jan.
HED 137, 43-2, v15, 4p. [1648]
Appropriation for civilization and support during the year ending 30 June 1876; treaty of 30 Sept. 1854.

48. Jicarilla Apache and Ute Indians. 27 Jan.
HED 138, 43-2, v15, 3p. [1648]
Removal of said Indians to a reservation, and relinquishment of claims to land in New Mexico under the agreement of 10 Dec. 1873.

49. Prairie Band of Pottawatomies. 27 Jan.
HED 139, 43-2, v15, 2p. [1648]
On investment of funds received from land sales under the treaty of 15 Nov. 1861.

50. Letter on the Kaskaskias. 27 Jan.
HED 140, 43-2, v15, 2p. [1648]
Appropriation to make payments due the Kaskaskias, Peorias, Weas, and Piankeshaws arising from sale of trust lands in Kansas under the treaty of 1854.

51. Letter on the Kickapoos. 27 Jan.
HED 141, 43-2, v15, 2p. [1648]
Appropriation to pay Indians who have elected to become U.S. citizens; under treaty of 28 June 1862.

52. Indians Killed by U.S. Troops. 1 Feb.
SED 22, 43-2, v1, 8p. [1629]
Numbers of Indians killed or captured; numbers of civilians and soldiers killed by Indians; list of tribes and circumstances.

53. Mem. of Citizens of the Cherokee Nation. 2 Feb.
SMD 66, 43-2, v1, 13p. [1630]
Against formation of a territorial government over Indian Territory; railroad interests involved.

54. Resol. of the Kansas Legis. 3 Feb.
SMD 69, 43-2, v1, 2p. [1630]
Ask lands for school purposes in lieu of the Cherokee neutral lands.

55. Letter on the Sioux. 3 Feb.
HED 144, 43-2, v15, 2p. [1648]
Appropriation for presents meant to extinguish Sioux rights to hunt in Wyoming which are granted to them under the treaty of 29 Apr. 1868.

56. Resol. of the Nevada Legis. 4 Feb.
HMD 61, 43-2, v2, 2p. [1654]
Ask that an executive order creating the Muddy, or Moapa Indian reservation be rescinded.

57. On the Case of J. Carr. 6 Feb.
SED 24, 43-2, v1, 8p. [1629]
Illegal transport of liquor to Alaska; violation of Indian intercourse laws.

58. Mem. of Citizens of the Creek Nation. 6 Feb.
SMD 71, 43-2, v1, 5p. [1630]
Against formation of a territorial government over Indian Territory; railroad interests.

59. R-P of A. Boone. 6 Feb.
SR 612, 43-2, v1, 1p. [1632]
Agent to negotiate Indian treaties in Colorado in 1861.

60. Report on Oklahoma Territory. 6 Feb.
SR 613, 43-2, v1, 1p. [1632]
On establishing a territorial government over Indian Territory.

61. Resol. of the New York Legis. 8 Feb.
HMD 75, 43-2, v2, 1p. [1654]
Ask leases between Indians and white settlers on the Allegany reservation be confirmed.

62. Protest of the Osage Nation. 9 Feb.
SMD 72, 43-2, v1, 5p. [1630]
Against formation of a territorial government over Indian Territory; railroad interests.

63. Mem. of Cherokee Indians. 10 Feb.
SMD 77, 43-2, v1, 7p. [1630]
Ask investigation of alleged irregularities in the management of Cherokee trust funds.

64. Nez Percé Indian Reservation in Idaho. 10 Feb.
HED 156, 43-2, v15, 1p. [1648]
Appropriation to pay those who lost improvements when they were removed from said reservation; treaty of 11 June 1855.

65. Report on Alien Claims. 10 Feb.
HR 134, 43-2, v3, 432p. [1658]
Includes Choctaw and Cherokee claims, slaves captured from Seminoles, slaves captured by Creeks, indemnification by the U.S. for property taken by Indians, and the rule of interest observed in Indian wars.

66. Mem. of P. Pitchlynn. 11 Feb.
SMD 78, 43-2, v1, 4p. [1630]
Asks payment of money due the Choctaws under various treaties.

67. On the Relief of J. Dorsey and W. Shepard. 11 Feb.
SR 649, 43-2, v1, 5p. [1632]
Supplies to troops engaged in quelling Paiute disturbances in Utah Territory during 1860.

68. Report on Pawnee Lands in Nebraska. 11 Feb.
HR 140, 43-2, v2, 2p. [1657]
A Pawnee council was held in 1874, at which time they agreed to remove to Indian Territory and sell their reservation in Nebraska.

69. On the Case of T. Crook. 12 Feb.
SR 654, 43-2, v1, 4p. [1632]
Default on supply contract due, in part, to Indian troubles near Fort Dodge, Kansas.

70. Resol. of the Tennessee Legis. 15 Feb.
HMD 79, 43-2, v2, 2p. [1654]
On the Texas and Pacific Railroad Company; would solve the Indian difficulties in the Southwest.

71. Eastern Band of Cherokees. 16 Feb.
HED 169, 43-2, v15, 12p. [1648]
Appropriation to pay the costs of suits brought by the Indians against present and former agents among them.

72. Report on Sundry Civil Appropriations. 16 Feb.
HR 149, 43-2, v2, 77p. [1657]
Year ending 30 June 1876; Indian expenses.

73. Report on Oklahoma Territory. 16 Feb.
HR 151, 43-2, v4, 5p. [1659]
Does not recommend the formation of a territorial government over Indian Territory, as this would violate several treaties; the result would be the subversion of Indian nationalities in the Territory.

74. Illicit Traffic in Liquor in Alaska. 17 Feb.
SED 27, 43-2, v1, 3p. [1629]
Distillation and transport of liquor among the Indians; potential hostilities with the Sitkas over the matter.

75. R-C of S. Adams. 17 Feb.
SR 662, 43-2, v1, 3p. [1632]
For exploring the Colorado River; report shows the account of the expedition to be false; ancient pueblos and ruins described by H. Schoolcraft and L. Morgan among others.

76. R-P of R. Grelaud. 18 Feb.
HR 197, 43-2, v4, 2p. [1659]
Seminole hostilities of 1857 in Florida.

77. On the Case of S. Howe and M. Cranston. 18 Feb.
HR 213, 43-2, v4, 1p. [1659]
Soldiers killed in the Modoc war of 1873 in northern California.

78. On the Case of W. Adair and C. Vann. 19 Feb.
SED 29, 43-2, v1, 37p. [1629]
Attorneys for the Osages, hired to try to procure a higher price for Osage lands in Kansas, and to resist ratification of the treaty of 27 May 1868; competition with railroad interest.

79. Report on the Modoc War. 19 Feb.
HR 248, 43-2, v4, 3p. [1659]
Reasons behind the 1872-1873 war in Oregon and California; treaty of 14 Oct. 1864.

80. Resol. of Sen. Ingalls. 20 Feb.
SMD 102, 43-2, v1, 1p. [1630]
That a special com. be authorized to visit Indian Territory and report on conditions there.

81. Part III of the Report of the Com'r of Fish and Fisheries. 20 Feb.
SMD 108, 43-2, v2, 777p. [1631]
Indian words for fish; Indian sentiment on catching salmon; Indian meal of oysters; Indian graveyard.

82. Letter on the Kaskaskia, Peoria, Piankeshaw, and Wea Indians. 20 Feb.
HMD 90, 43-2, v2, 2p. [1654]
Appropriation necessary to indemnify said Indians for lands in Kansas which were erroneously sold.

83. Resol. of the Kansas Legis. 22 Feb.
HMD 91, 43-2, v2, 2p. [1654]
Purchase of Cherokee lands under the treaty of 19 July 1866.

84. Letter on the Western Judicial District of Arkansas. 23 Feb.
HED 175, 43-2, v18, 156p. [1651]
Includes dealings in Indian Territory; claims arising from expenditures of the marshall's office.

85. Statistics on Mining West of the Rocky Mountains. 23 Feb.
HED 177, 43-2, v18, 540p. [1651]
Apache hostilities in Arizona now affecting mining there much less.

86. Receipts and Expenditures. 23 Feb.
HED 179, 43-2, v18, 573p. [1651]
Year ending 30 June 1872; Indian expenses.

87. Resol. of the Kansas Legis. 24 Feb.
SMD 112, 43-2, v1, 2p. [1630]
Asks establishment of a U.S. district court for Indian Territory.

88. Report on Custer's Expedition to the Black Hills. 26 Feb.
SED 32, 43-2, v1, 9p. [1629]
Account of the exploring expedition; Sioux agencies and guides; no encounters with hostile Indians.

89. Indian Appropriation Bill. 27 Feb.
HR 266, 43-2, v7, 1p. [1662]
Amendments to the bill for year ending 30 June 1876.

90. Report on the Texas and Pacific Railroad. 27 Feb.
HR 267, 43-2, v7, 4p. [1662]
Would provide for control of hostile Indians, and reduce the cost of transport of Indian goods.

91. Report on a Bill to Cover Deficiencies in Appropriations. 1 Mar.
HR 270, 43-2, v7, 51p. [1662]
Indian expenses.

92. On the Case of J. Nix. 2 Mar.
SR 692, 43-2, v1, 2p. [1632]
Sioux outbreak of 1862 in Minnesota.

93. Report on the Western Judicial District of North Carolina. 2 Mar.
HR 275. 43-2, v7, 2p. [1662]
Prosecution of parties guilty of frauds upon the Cherokees of North Carolina; Indian civil suits; etc.

94. Mem. of Cherokee Delegates. 3 Mar.
HMD 99, 43-2, v3, 3p. [1655]
An alleged mem. by Cherokee Indians (see 1875:63) is a forgery; they deny the Senate's right to interfere in local affairs of the Cherokee Nation.

95. Report on Indians in Washington Territory. 3 Mar.
HR 296, 43-2, v7, 2p. [1662]
Recommends reducing the number of reservations, and alloting lands in those reservations which shall remain.

96. Report on the Pottawatomies of Kansas. 3 Mar.
HR 319, 43-2, v7, 3p. [1662]
Claims made under various treaties; investigating com'rs appointed under the treaty of 7 Aug. 1868.

97. On the Relief of J. Roane. 3 Mar.
HR 323, 43-2, v7, 1p. [1662]
Supplies to California Indians during 1856-1860.

98. Statements of Appropriations. 4 Mar.
HMD 95, 43-2, v2, 104p. [1654]
During the 2d session, 43rd Congress; Indian expenses.

99. Resol. of Sen. Clayton. 8 Mar.
SMD 3, 44-sp, v1, 1p. [1630]
Ask that a com. be appointed to visit Indian Territory.

100. Message on the Black Hills Country. 17 Mar.
SED 2, 44-sp, v1, 15p. [1629]
Within the Sioux reservation; whites encroaching on the area; treaty violations; Army's attempt to halt the emigrants.

101. Disbursements of the Indian Dept. 28 Oct.
HED 6, 44-1, v8, 13p. [1685]
Year ending 30 June 1875.

102. Annual Report of the Sec. of the Treasury. 6 Dec.
HED 2, 44-1, v6, 907p. [1683]
Year ending 30 June 1875; Indian expenses.

103. Estimates of Appropriations. 6 Dec.
HED 5, 44-1, v8, 318p. [1685]
Year ending 30 June 1877; Indian expenses.
104. Property in the Interior Dept. 7 Dec.
SED 1, 44-1, v1, 3p. [1664]
Includes the OIA.
105. Annual Message to Congress with Documents; Pres. Grant. 7 Dec.
HED 1, 44-1, v1-5, 8364p. [1672-1682]
Conflict between the Sioux Indians and miners entering the Black Hills; annual report of the Sec. of War (Serials 1674-1678); annual report of the Sec. of Interior (Serials 1680-1681); annual report of the Gen. Land Office (Serial 1680); annual report of the CIA (Serial 1680), including issues surrounding the Sioux treaty of 1868, the Sioux problem and the Black Hills, Mission Indians of California, Indian Territory, and reports of Supts., agents, schools, and farms; etc.
106. Contingent Expenses of the Interior Dept. 10 Dec.
HED 13, 44-1, v5, 34p. [1682]
Year ending 30 June 1875; OIA.
107. Mem. of the Pottawatomies. 13 Dec.
SMD 15, 44-1, v1, 6p. [1665]
Claims for depredations committed upon their reservation in Kansas, under the treaty of 27 Feb. 1867.
108. Letter on Indian Agents. 14 Dec.
SMD 17, 44-1, v1, 2p. [1665]
Would be required by law to maintain detailed accounts of their financial operations, and file quarterly statements.
109. Transfer of Indian Trust Funds. 14 Dec.
HED 15, 44-1, v9, 1p. [1686]
From the Interior Dept. to the U.S. Treasurer.
110. Transfer of Indian Trust Funds. 14 Dec.
HED 16, 44-1, v9, 2p. [1686]
From the Interior Dept. to the U.S. Treasurer.
111. Resol. of a Council of the Senecas. 15 Dec.
HMD 22, 44-1, v1, 1p. [1698]
On survey and leasing of lands in the Allegany and Cattaraugus reservations in New York.
112. Investigation of the Osage Indian Agency. 20 Dec.
SED 6, 44-1, v1, 108p. [1664]
Charges of irregularities committed by the agent; proceedings of the investigation.

1876

1. Letter on the Sisseton and Wahpeton Sioux. 5 Jan.
HED 42, 44-1, v10, 30p. [1687]
Concerning land allotments under the treaty of 19 Feb. 1867.
2. Letter on the Alaska Seal Fisheries. 5 Jan.
HED 43, 44-1, v10, 23p. [1687]
Description of the native Aleuts upon the islands off the Alaskan coast; fur trade with the Russians.
3. Letter on Alaska Territory. 6 Jan.
SED 12, 44-1, v1, 33p. [1664]
Effects of liquor on the Indians; council with the Stickeens; visits to other tribes, with councils ensuing; trade situation, particularly with respect to seals; Russian influence.
4. Resol. of Sen. Clayton. 6 Jan.
SMD 23, 44-1, v1, 2p. [1665]
Establishment of inferior courts in Indian Territory to try minor offenses.
5. Mem. of the Choctaw Nation. 10 Jan.
SMD 34, 44-1, v1, 2p. [1665]
Ask investigation and payment of their claims against the U.S. under the treaties of 1830, and 1885; asks jurisdiction be given to the Court of Claims.
6. On the Case of J. Nix. 10 Jan.
SR 10, 44-1, v1, 2p. [1667]
Sioux outbreak of 1862 in Minnesota.
7. Red Cloud and Whetstone Agencies. 12 Jan.
HED 57, 44-1, v10, 7p. [1687]
Appropriation needed to subsist the Sioux at those agencies.
8. Letter on C. and S. Germain. 12 Jan.
HED 59, 44-1, v10, 3p. [1687]
Destitute condition of 2 young women held captive by the Cheyennes, and finally recaptured.
9. Resol. and Mem. of the Constitutional Convention of Texas. 12 Jan.
HMD 37, 44-1, v1, 5p. [1698]

On compensation for losses by Indian depredations on the frontier.

10. Letter on the Cheyennes, Kiowas, Comanches, and Arapahoes. 13 Jan.
SED 15, 44-1, v1, 2p. [1664]
Statement of expenditures for support of captive Indians from said tribes.

11. Mem. of the Choctaw Nation. 13 Jan.
HMD 40, 44-1, v1, 95p. [1698]
On the "net proceeds" claim arising under the treaties of 1830, and 1855.

12. Petition of M. West. 13 Jan.
HMD 44, 44-1, v1, 5p. [1698]
Service in the Kiowa and Cheyenne campaign of 1868-1869; husband dies at Fort Arbuckle, Indian Territory.

13. Letter on Indian Agents. 18 Jan.
SED 17, 44-1, v1, 3p. [1664]
List of those who have sent in abstracts of their quarterly expenditures.

14. Letter on the Pawnees in Nebraska. 18 Jan.
HED 80, 44-1, v10, 11p. [1687]
Sale of their reservation there, and removal to Indian Territory; present needs of the tribe.

15. Letter on Alaska. 20 Jan.
HED 83, 44-1, v10, 478p. [1687]
Seal-fisheries; Indians of Alaska; trade with Russians, Americans, and the British Hudson's Bay Company.

16. Interpreters at the Klamath Agency, Oregon. 20 Jan.
HED 84, 44-1, v12, 2p. [1689]
One required for the Klamaths and Modocs, and the other for the Wolpahpe Snake Indians under treaty stipulations.

17. Pottawatomies and Winnebagoes in Wisconsin. 20 Jan.
HED 85, 44-1, v12, 3p. [1689]
Disposition of funds appropriated for said Indians; their removal from and return to Wisconsin.

18. Letter on the Winnebagoes of Nebraska. 25 Jan.
HED 101, 44-1, v12, 2p. [1689]
On funds for their support taken from the amount due the Winnebagoes of Wisconsin.

19. Mem. of J. Fell et al. 25 Jan.
HMD 83, 44-1, v4, 26p. [1701]
For the Walnut Grove Gold-Mining Company; Apache depredations of 1864-1869 in Arizona.

20. R-P of J. Dorsey. 26 Jan.
SR 25, 44-1, v1, 4p. [1667]
Supplies to troops during the Paiute disturbances of 1860 in Utah Territory.

21. Mem. of Arkansas Citizens. 27 Jan.
SMD 42, 44-1, v1, 3p. [1665]
Against establishment of a U.S. court in Indian Territory; would mean Indians would sit as jurors in cases involving whites.

22. Mem. of the New Mexico Legis. 28 Jan.
HMD 63, 44-1, v2, 2p. [1699]
Admission as a State; effects of Indian hostilities on the Territory's population.

23. Tonkawa Indians at Fort Griffin, Texas. 1 Feb.
HED 102, 44-1, v12, 7p. [1689]
Indians subsisted by the Army; recommends that they be put on a reservation.

24. Supplies for Red Cloud Agency. 1 Feb.
HED 103, 44-1, v12, 2p. [1689]
Shortage exists at this Sioux agency.

25. Ottawa and Chippewa Trust Funds. 1 Feb.
HED 104, 44-1, v12, 6p. [1689]
Transfer of funds from the Interior Dept. to the Treasury Dept.; funds exist by the treaties of 28 Mar. 1836, and 31 July 1855.

26. Consolidation of the Miamies with Other Tribes. 1 Feb.
HED 105, 44-1, v12, 5p. [1689]
With the Piankeshaws, Kaskaskias, Peorias, and Weas in Indian Territory; act to abolish tribal relations with the Miamies.

27. Jurisdiction Over Indians in Certain States. 1 Feb.
HED 106, 44-1, v12, 2p. [1689]
Transfer of control over Indians from the U.S. government to the States of New York (Oneidas, Onondagas, Tuscaroras, Senecas, and Tonawandas), North Carolina (Cherokees), Michigan (Chippewas, Ottawas, and Pottawatomies), Wisconsin (Chippewas, Oneidas, Menomonies, and Stockbridges), Minnesota (Chippewas), and Iowa (Sacs and Foxes).

28. Winnebagoes and Pottawatomies in Wisconsin. 1 Feb.

HED 119, 44-1, v12, 7p. [1684]
Statement of disbursements for the case of stray bands of said tribes in Wisconsin.

29. Transfer of Certain Indian Trust Funds. 3 Feb.
HED 118, 44-1, v12, 2p. [1689]
From the Interior Dept. to the U.S. Treasurer; Sec. of Interior would still distribute interests on those funds, etc.

30. Message on Indian Agents. 4 Feb.
HED 128, 44-1, v12, 8p. [1689]
Numbers of agents in the country, and their salaries.

31. R-P of J. Chapman. 4 Feb.
HR 48, 44-1, v1, 1p. [1708]
Services rendered the Osages in 1861-1862.

32. Report on a Pottawatomie Treaty. 11 Feb.
HR 70, 44-1, v1, 4p. [1708]
Dated 27 Feb. 1867; on claims of the tribe for depredations committed by U.S. citizens during the great emigrations to California, etc.

33. On the Relief of Heirs of W. Stevens. 11 Feb.
HR 71, 44-1, v1, 2p. [1708]
Driven from land during the Sioux outbreak of 1862 in Dakota.

34. R-P of Capt. Spencer. 11 Feb.
HR 73, 44-1, v1, 2p. [1708]
Service during the Sioux troubles of 1857 in Minnesota.

35. Survey of the Black Hills. 14 Feb.
HED 125, 44-1, v12, 5p. [1689]
To verify reports of mineral wealth in the area which is reserved to the Sioux Indians; invasion of miners possible.

36. Mem. of the Colorado Legis. 14 Feb.
HMD 85, 44-1, v4, 3p. [1701]
Establishment of a military post, and a military road to Fort Defiance; hostile Utes, Paiutes, Apaches, and Navajoes in southern Colorado.

37. Mem. of the Colorado Legis. 14 Feb.
HMD 86, 44-1, v4, 2p. [1701]
Present grievances of the Ute Indians; benefits due under the agreement (or "Brunot treaty") of 1873 in which the Utes agreed to cede part of their reservation to the U.S.

38. Mem. of the New Mexico Legis. 14 Feb.
HMD 87, 44-1, v4, 2p. [1701]
Ask settlement of Indian depredation claims.

39. Mem. of the Montana Legis. 14 Feb.
HMD 90, 44-1, v4, 3p. [1701]
Improvement of the Missouri and Yellowstone Rivers; transport of goods to the Crow agency.

40. Report on Admission of New Mexico. 15 Feb.
SR 69, 44-1, v1, 5p. [1667]
Pueblo Indians in the Territory; population was low initially due to Indian hostility.

41. Resol. of the California Legis. 16 Feb.
HMD 92, 44-1, v4, 1p. [1701]
Transfer of the OIA from the Interior Dept. to the War Dept.

42. Resol. of the Minnesota Legis. 21 Feb.
HMD 95, 44-1, v4, 1p. [1701]
Asks a treaty be made with Indians occupying the Black Hills so that the same may be opened for occupation.

43. Mem. of the Chippewa Indians. 23 Feb.
SMD 63, 44-1, v1, 3p. [1665]
Turtle Band of Chippewas asks that a reservation in Dakota be set aside for them in exchange for a cession of the remainder of their lands.

44. R-P of J. Friend. 23 Feb.
SR 92, 44-1, v1, 1p. [1667]
Comanche depredations of 1867-1868 in Texas.

45. Report on Amending Pension Laws. 24 Feb.
HR 117, 44-1, v1, 2p. [1708]
Including soldiers of the Black Hawk and Seminole wars.

46. Letter on W. Ross. 25 Feb.
HED 132, 44-1, v12, 4p. [1689]
Complicity of W. Ross, former Cherokee delegate, in the alleged Indian-bounty frauds of J. Wright.

47. Report on the Klamath Reservation. 25 Feb.
HR 183, 44-1, v1, 7p. [1708]
Set aside under the treaty of 1864; claims of owners of lands within the limits of the reserve.

48. Deficiency of Supplies at Red Cloud Agency. 29 Feb.
SED 30, 44-1, v1, 12p. [1664]
Supplies needed at the agency in Nebraska immediately; Sitting Bull's band of Sioux have come to the agency, and they must be en-

ticed to stay until their unity (and Sitting Bull's authority) has been destroyed.

49. Letter on W. Ross. 29 Feb.
HED 134, 44-1, v12, 49p. [1689]
His complicity in the alleged Indian-bounty frauds of J. Wright; Cherokee delegate who claims to be principal chief of the Cherokee.

50. Jurisdiction of the War Dept. Over Alaska Territory. 29 Feb.
HED 135, 44-1, v12, 56p. [1689]
To regulate trade and intercourse with the Indians; liquor traffic.

51. Texas Frontier Troubles. 29 Feb.
HR 343, 44-1, v2, 201p. [1709]
Indian depredations.

52. Letter on C. Hutchinson. 2 Mar.
HED 139, 44-1, v12, 6p. [1689]
Case against this former agent to the Ottawas related to management of proceeds from sale of lands belonging to the tribe.

53. Private Land Claims in New Mexico. 3 Mar.
SED 31, 44-1, v1, 20p. [1664]
Land occupied by settlers except during Indian troubles.

54. R-P of A. Chapman. 3 Mar.
SR 118, 44-1, v1, 1p. [1667]
Scout for U.S. during 1874 in Indian Territory and Texas.

55. Report on the Mission of St. James, Washington Territory. 3 Mar.
HR 189, 44-1, v1, 2p. [1708]
Land claims of a missionary society there to teach the Indians.

56. On the Relief of J. Sinclair. 3 Mar.
HR 190, 44-1, v1, 3p. [1708]
Service against hostile Snakes in Idaho Territory during 1868.

57. On the Relief of R. McKee. 3 Mar.
HR 202, 44-1, v1, 1p. [1708]
For debts incurred as disbursing agent for the Indian Commission to California in 1851.

58. Message on Military Arrests in Alaska Territory. 6 Mar.
SED 33, 44-1, v1, 25p. [1664]
List of those arrested, giving the cause of arrest; includes selling liquor to Indians.

59. On the Relief of C. Hedges. 6 Mar.
SR 126, 44-1, v1, 8p. [1667]
Supplies for the Yankton Sioux during 1866-1867 in Dakota.

60. Resol. of the Kansas Legis. 6 Mar.
HMD 121, 44-1, v5, 1p. [1702]
Opposes reduction of Army strength on the frontier; cites recent hostilities of the Sioux, Cheyennes, and Arapahoes.

61. Mem. and Resol. of the Wyoming Legis. 6 Mar.
HMD 123, 44-1, v5, 3p. [1702]
Protests against the way Indians are treated by the government, which is swayed by the "Indian-loving fanatic of the East."

62. Letter on Liquor Being Introduced Into Indian Territory. 7 Mar.
SED 34, 44-1, v1, 1p. [1664]
U.S. district court has exempted Indians from the penalty of introducing liquor to said territory.

63. Expenditures for Fulfilling a Treaty with the Sioux. 9 Mar.
HMD 126, 44-1, v5, 4p. [1702]
Year ending 30 June 1876.

64. Transfer of the Indian Bureau. 9 Mar.
HR 354, 44-1, v2, 234p. [1709]
From the Interior Dept. to the War Dept.; would prevent the annihilation of the prairie tribes; Sioux agencies need reorganization; recommend transfer.

65. R-P of H. Sumner. 10 Mar.
HR 233, 44-1, v1, 2p. [1708]
Service in the Black Hawk war of 1832.

66. Report on Transfer of the Indian Bureau. 14 Mar.
HR 240, 44-1, v1, 47p. [1708]
Testimony on the transfer of the bureau from the Interior Dept. to the War Dept.; Army-Indian relations investigated; recommends transfer.

67. Report on the Pawnees. 14 Mar.
HR 241, 44-1, v1, 12p. [1708]
On subsisting the tribe during and after its removal from Nebraska to Indian Territory; sale of the Pawnee reservation in Nebraska.

68. Resol. of the Kansas Legis. 15 Mar.
SMD 78, 44-1, v1, 1p. [1665]
Ask for settlement of Indian depredation claims covering the period 1860-1870.

69. Resol. of the Kansas Legis. 15 Mar.
SMD 79, 44-1, v1, 2p. [1665]
Ask right-of-way through Indian Territory be granted to 2 railroad companies.

70. Report on Mission Lands. 17 Mar.
HR 249, 44-1, v1, 2p. [1708]

Stations among the Indians in Idaho, Oregon, Montana, and Washington.

71. On the Relief of R. Wright. 17 Mar.
HR 256, 44-1, v1, 1p. [1708]
Claim against Chickasaws disallowed under the treaty adopted in 1852, and under the Choctaw and Chickasaw treaty of 28 Apr. 1866.

72. On the Relief of S. Marshall. 17 Mar.
HR 257, 44-1, v1, 1p. [1708]
Purchasing and disbursing agent for the California Indian treaty commission of 1851.

73. Collection of Customs in Alaska Territory. 20 Mar.
SED 37, 44-1, v1, 10p. [1664]
Indians of Alaska; trade; government of the Indians.

74. Report on the Pottawatomies. 21 Mar.
HR 291, 44-1, v1, 4p. [1708]
Claims against the U.S. for failure to pay all of the annuities due under treaties dated 1795 to 1846; claims to be investigated under the treaty of 7 Aug. 1868.

75. Message on the Sioux. 23 Mar.
HED 145, 44-1, v12, 8p. [1689]
Report on causes of the exhaustion of the appropriation for subsistence of the Sioux at Red Cloud, and other agencies.

76. Indian Hostilities in Oregon and California. 23 Mar.
HR 297, 44-1, v1, 1p. [1708]
Payment of claims for suppressing hostilities of 1872-1873.

77. Fees Paid U.S. Attorneys. 24 Mar.
HR 298, 44-1, v1, 18p. [1708]
List of cases, including that of the Eastern, or North Carolina Cherokees, etc.

78. Province of Oklahoma. 24 Mar.
HR 299, 44-1, v1, 8p. [1708]
Establishment of a territorial form of government over Indian Territory.

79. R-P of M. Hance. 24 Mar.
HR 314, 44-1, v1, 2p. [1708]
Sioux depredations of 1867 near Lodge Pole Creek.

80. R-C of W. Morrison. 24 Mar.
HR 315, 44-1, v1, 1p. [1708]
Missouri and Ottoe depredations of 1861.

81. On the Case of L. McLaughlin. 24 Mar.
HR 321, 44-1, v1, 1p. [1708]
Army scout wounded during an Indian battle of 1868 in Kansas.

82. Indian Depredation Claims. 27 Mar.
HED 147, 44-1, v12, 26p. [1689]
List of claims from 1874 to 1876; includes dates, tribe, location, and action on the claim.

83. Expenditures of the Board of Indian Com'rs. 27 Mar.
HED 150, 44-1, v12, 2p. [1689]
Reports clerical error in the statement of the OIA.

84. Deficiencies in Appropriations. 29 Mar.
HED 151, 44-1, v12, 31p. [1689]
Year ending 30 June 1876; Indian expenses.

85. On the Relief of C. Hedges. 30 Mar.
SR 199, 44-1, v1, 1p. [1667]
Supplies to the Yankton Sioux during 1866-1867.

86. R-P of E. Abbott. 31 Mar.
SR 209, 44-1, v1, 2p. [1667]
Land claims in Michigan; shape of claim due to mode of defense used against Indian attack.

87. Message on the Pawnees. 4 Apr.
HED 154, 44-1, v12, 12p. [1689]
Recently removed to Indian Territory, and in need of supplies.

88. Annual Report of the Smithsonian Institution. 7 Apr.
SMD 115, 44-1, v1, 422p. [1665]
Research related to the American Indian; Indian vocabularies; ancient artifacts from Michigan; etc.

89. On the Case of Col. Emory. 7 Apr.
HR 363, 44-1, v2, 2p. [1709]
Service in the Creek country during 1835-1836; scout against the Indians during 1858-1859 at Fort Arbuckle.

90. Reduction of the Fort Laramie Reserve. 10 Apr.
SR 246, 44-1, v1, 1p. [1667]
Red Cloud agency located on said military reserve in Wyoming.

91. R-P of H. Peterson. 10 Apr.
SR 250, 44-1, v1, 4p. [1667]
Sioux outbreak of 1862 in Minnesota.

92. Letter on the Resources of Alaska. 12 Apr.
SED 48, 44-1, v1, 5p. [1664]
Indian trade; Hudson's Bay Company; settlers.

93. Statistics on Mining West of the Rocky Mountains. 13 Apr.
HED 159, 44-1, v14, 519p. [1691]
Apache hostilities in Arizona; Indian troubles likely in the Black Hills; etc.

94. Letter on the Apaches in New Mexico. 18 Apr.
SMD 91, 44-1, v1, 5p. [1665]
Appropriation needed to subsist said tribe, otherwise they will leave their reservation.

95. Report on the Turtle Mountain Band of Chippewas. 18 Apr.
SR 275, 44-1, v1, 2p. [1667]
Recommends establishing a reservation for the band in northern Dakota; Assiniboines, or other tribes may settle there as well.

96. Improvement of the Oconto River. 18 Apr.
SR 276, 44-1, v1, 2p. [1667]
Would require working within the Menomonee reservation in Wisconsin.

97. Testimony on Management of the Indian Dept. 18 Apr.
HMD 167, 44-1, v5, 431p. [1702]
Alleged frauds in the handling of Indian Dept. contracts.

98. Report on the Miami Indians. 19 Apr.
SR 280, 44-1, v1, 2p. [1667]
Payment of funds required to carry out the agreement of 15 Jan. 1872; Miami tribal relations abolished, and they either confederate with the Kaskaskias, Weas, Peorias, and Piankeshaws, or they become citizens.

99. On the Relief of Mrs. Short. 21 Apr.
HR 421, 44-1, v2, 1p. [1709]
Cheyenne hostilities of 1874 in Kansas.

100. R-C of the Administrator of O. Short. 21 Apr.
HR 422, 44-1, v2, 1p. [1709]
Cheyenne depredations in Kansas.

101. R-C of C. Short. 21 Apr.
HR 423, 44-1, v2, 1p. [1709]
Cheyenne hostilities in Kansas.

102. On the Relief of F. Babcock. 21 Apr.
HR 425, 44-1, v2, 2p. [1709]
U.S. marshall for western Arkansas; arrests Indian in the Cherokee Nation, Indian Territory, for murder.

103. Resources of the Black Hills. 25 Apr.
SED 51, 44-1, v1, 71p. [1664]
Survey conducted under the orders of the CIA.

104. Indian Disturbances in the Sioux Reservation. 26 Apr.
SED 52, 44-1, v1, 12p. [1664]
Activities of Sitting Bull's band in western Dakota and eastern Montana; proposed military operations.

105. Report on the Civil Service. 27 Apr.
SR 289, 44-1, v1, 81p. [1667]
Includes operations within the OIA.

106. Letter on Arizona Indians. 28 Apr.
HMD 172, 44-1, v5, 6p. [1702]
Appropriation for the subsistence of Apaches.

107. Brothertown Reservation in Wisconsin. 29 Apr.
HR 445, 44-1, v3, 1p. [1710]
On allotment of the reservation to individual Brothertown Indians under the treaty of 20 Oct. 1832.

108. Expenditures of the Indian Bureau. 3 May.
SED 55, 44-1, v1, 2p. [1664]
Annual expenditures since its organization in 1832, up to 1875.

109. On the Case of E. Fox. 5 May.
HR 487, 44-1, v3, 2p. [1710]
Command of Indian troops loyal to the U.S. in the War of 1812.

110. Report on the Choctaws. 15 May.
HR 499, 44-1, v3, 23p. [1710]
Claim for payments due under the treaty of 27 Sept. 1830; land cession; settlement called for under the treaty of 22 June 1855.

111. On the Relief of Sureties of J. Huntington. 17 May.
SR 319, 44-1, v1, 1p. [1667]
Supt. of Indian Affairs in Oregon during 1865.

112. Report on New Mexico. 19 May.
HR 503, 44-1, v3, 23p. [1710]
Admission as a State; population of the Pueblo Indians; Indian wars of 1860-1870.

113. Mem. of the Creek Delegation. 25 May.
SMD 103, 44-1, v1, 6p. [1665]
On funds due the Creek orphans under the treaty of 24 Mar. 1832.

114. Fish Commission Report. 31 May.
SMD 107, 44-1, v2, 1029p. [1666]
Employment of Indian women in California.

115. Report on a Military Wagon Road. 1 June.
HR 616, 44-1, v3, 3p. [1710]
In Wyoming; Indian supplies to the Shoshone, Blackeet, and Crow agencies.

116. On the Case of G. Armes. 1 June.
HR 620, 44-1, v3, 3p. [1710]
Pursuit of a Sioux war party in 1866 near Fort Sedgwick.

117. Report on the Alaska Commercial Company. 3 June.

HR 623, 44-1, v5, 143p. [1712]
Sale of liquor to the Indians, and inciting them to do violence.

118. Resol. of Sen. Maxey. 6 June.
SMD 110, 44-1, v1, 1p. [1665]
On issuance of bonds by railroad companies predicated upon conditional grants of land in Indian Territory.

119. Accounts of the Treasury Dept. 6 June.
SR 371, 44-1, v2, 37p. [1668]
Indian trust funds, and expenditures for Indians investigated.

120. Letter on the Great and Little Osages. 7 June.
SMD 112, 44-1, v1, 8p. [1665]
Use of funds belonging to the tribes by sale of lands in Kansas under the treaty of 29 Sept. 1865.

121. Communication Between Colorado and New Mexico. 8 June.
HED 172, 44-1, v14, 34p. [1691]
Roads between the areas; good communication needed to Fort Wingate, as it is near the Navajo reservation in New Mexico.

122. R-M of F. Culver. 9 June.
HR 642, 44-1, v5, 2p. [1712]
Service in negotiating the treaty of 18 Feb. 1861 with the Cheyennes and Arapahoes.

123. R-C of J. Phillips. 9 June.
HR 643, 44-1, v5, 2p. [1712]
Sioux and Cheyenne depredations of 1872 near Fort Fetterman, Wyoming.

124. On the Relief of B. Beveridge. 9 June.
HR 644, 44-1, v5, 1p. [1712]
Com. of Indian Affairs reports negatively.

125. On the Relief of J. Jackson. 9 June.
HR 645, 44-1, v5, 5p. [1712]
Kiowa depredations of 1871-1872 in Texas.

126. R-P of M. Ladd and J. Williams. 9 June.
HR 646, 44-1, v5, 1p. [1712]
Payments due these Menomonee half-breeds in Wisconsin under the treaty of 3 Sept. 1836.

127. Report on the Eastern Band of Cherokees. 9 June.
HR 647, 44-1, v5, 1p. [1712]
Suit regarding the right of these North Carolina Cherokees to participate in funds of the Cherokee Nation, now removed to Indian Territory; recommends jurisdiction be given to the Court of Claims.

128. R-C of M. Trisarre. 9 June.
HR 649, 44-1, v5, 1p. [1712]
Mescalero Apache depredations of 1854 in New Mexico.

129. R-C of J. Gonzalez. 9 June.
HR 650, 44-1, v5, 1p. [1712]
Apache depredations of 1849 in New Mexico.

130. Letter on Matters at Fort Sill. 12 June.
HED 175, 44-1, v14, 4p. [1691]
Treatment of Kiowas and Comanches by the military is said to be wretched; remonstrance against transfer of the Indian Bureau to the War Dept.

131. Report on Sioux Lands. 15 June.
HR 674, 44-1, v5, 1p. [1712]
Amendment to a bill providing for an agreement to be made with the Sioux for cession of a part of their reservation; requires that they not be removed from their present reservation.

132. Mem. of Wyandott Delegates. 16 June.
SMD 116, 44-1, v1, 4p. [1665]
Ask payment of money due the tribe under the treaty of 23 Feb. 1867.

133. Letter from the Osages. 17 June.
SED 76, 44-1, v1, 4p. [1664]
Against the establishment of a territorial government over Indian Territory.

134. Report on the Signal-Service. 26 June.
SR 429, 44-1, v2, 4p. [1668]
Telegraphs connecting military posts on the Indian frontier to aid in control of depredations.

135. Receipts and Disbursements. 27 June.
SMD 118, 44-1, v1, 4p. [1665]
From 1834 to 1875; disbursements on the Indians.

136. On the Relief of Heirs of W. Stevens. 1 July.
SR 440, 44-1, v2, 2p. [1668]
Land claim in Dakota; settlers driven off by Sioux during 1862-1867.

137. Settlers in Wind River Valley. 7 July.
HR 740, 44-1, v5, 3p. [1712]
Settler lands incorporated into a Shoshone and Bannock reservation in Wyoming; under the treaty of 3 July 1868.

138. R-C of Spencer and Mead. 7 July.
HR 741, 44-1, v5, 6p. [1712]
Supplies to the Kansas Indians during 1866-1867; Cheyenne hostilities.

139. Message on a Hostile Demonstration by the Sioux Indians. 13 July.
SED 81, 44-1, v1, 6p. [1664]
First news of the disaster regarding Gen. Custer's forces; observance of the treaty of 1868 by nearly all Sioux, save Sitting Bull's band.

140. On the Relief of S. Crawford. 14 July.
HR 759, 44-1, v5, 3p. [1712]
Contract to provide hay for Camp Supply, Indian Territory, in 1873.

141. Resol. of the Texas Legis. 17 July.
HMD 185, 44-1, v9, 2p. [1706]
Frontier protection against hostile Indians.

142. Military Expedition Against the Sioux. 18 July.
HED 184, 44-1, v14, 63p. [1691]
Operations of Generals Crook, Terry, and Gibbon; Sitting Bull's band leads the hostile segment of the Sioux Nation; report of the disaster which overtook Gen. Custer and troops of the Seventh Cavalry.

143. Lands Located Under Military Warrants in Certain States. 19 July.
HR 766, 44-1, v5, 5p. [1712]
Includes an act of 1857 concerned with Indian reservations in Mississippi.

144. On the Relief of A. Greenwood. 27 July.
HR 785, 44-1, v6, 2p. [1713]
CIA from 1859 to 1861; expenses of expedition to the Arkansas River in 1860 to make a treaty with the Cheyennes and Arapahoes.

145. Employees of the Interior Dept. 3 Aug.
SED 87, 44-1, v1, 4p. [1664]
Numbers employed during 1859-1875; includes the OIA.

146. Management of the War Dept. 5 Aug.
HR 799, 44-1, v8, 577p. [1715]
Correspondence on enlargement of the Sioux reservation; charges against the late Sec. of War (W. Belknap) regarding sale of post and Indian traderships.

147. Resol. of the Texas Legis. 7 Aug.
SMD 130, 44-1, v1, 1p. [1665]
Condolences to the family of Gen. Custer who was killed during a frontier operation against the Indians.

148. On the Relief of E. and S. Clark. 8 Aug.
SR 528, 44-1, v2, 6p. [1668]
Land claim in Florida; Indian depredations of 1812.

149. R-P of E. Gurley. 8 Aug.
HR 804, 44-1, v7, 3p. [1714]
Prosecuting attorney in a case where 19 Texans were charged with murdering 7 Caddo Indians.

150. Report on the Stockbridge and Munsee Indians. 8 Aug.
HR 813, 44-1, v7, 2p. [1714]
Problems surrounding the tribal enrollment of 1871; a number of Indians denied tribal status.

151. Message on an Increase of the Army. 11 Aug.
SED 90, 44-1, v1, 3p. [1664]
For contingencies which may arise in Indian country; campaign of Generals Crook and Terry against the Sioux; Indians with the U.S. troops as scouts.

152. Statements of Appropriations. 15 Aug.
HMD 192, 44-1, v10, 92p. [1707]
During the 1st session, 44th Congress; Indian expenses.

153. Disbursements of the Indian Dept. 14 Nov.
HED 6, 44-2, v8, 12p. [1754]
Year ending 30 June 1876.

154. Judgments Rendered by the Court of Claims. 4 Dec.
SMD 4, 44-2, v1, 28p. [1722]
Year ending 4 Dec. 1876; cases involving Indian goods, and Indian depredations.

155. Annual Report of the Sec. of the Treasury. 4 Dec.
HED 2, 44-2, v6, 1020p. [1752]
Year ending 30 June 1876; Indian expenses.

156. Estimates of Appropriations. 4 Dec.
HED 5, 44-2, v8, 272p. [1754]
Year ending 30 June 1878; Indian expenses.

157. Property of the Interior Dept. 5 Dec.
SED 1, 44-2, v1, 3p. [1718]
Includes the OIA.

158. Annual Message to Congress with Documents; Pres. Grant. 5 Dec.
HED 1, 44-2, v1-5, 7574p. [1741-1751]
Hostilities in the Black Hills caused by the avarice of the white man in his search for gold; cession of the Black Hills; annual report of the Sec. of War (Serials 1742-1747); annual report of the Sec. of Interior (Serials 1749-1750); annual report

of the Gen. Land Office (Serial 1749); annual report of the CIA (Serial 1749), including allotments of reservations, Indian Territory, the Sioux Commission of 1876, the Sioux war, the Nez Percé Commission, and reports of Supts., agents, schools, and farms; etc.

159. On the Relief of J. Fletcher. 8 Dec.
HR 9, 44-2, v1, 3p. [1769]
Cheyenne and Arapahoe depredations of 1870 between Fort Dodge, Kansas, and Camp Supply, Indian Territory.

160. R-P of J. Porter. 13 Dec.
SR 538, 44-2, v1, 3p. [1732]
Indian depredations upon a supply train *en route* from Fort Laramie to Fort Phil. Kearney in Dakota.

161. Removal of the Sioux. 14 Dec.
SED 4, 44-2, v1, 3p. [1718] *or*
HED 10, 44-2, v5, 3p. [1751]
On removal of the Sioux from their 1868 treaty reservation to Indian Territory; actions of the 1876 Sioux Commission seeking land cessions, rights-of-way, etc., through agreements.

162. Indian Depredations in New Mexico. 19 Dec.
HR 30, 44-2, v1, 1p. [1769]
Claimants supply no proof of losses.

163. Sioux or Dakota Indians in Minnesota. 19 Dec.
HR 31, 44-2, v1, 2p. [1769]
Claims for supplies furnished the Sioux prior to the 1862 outbreak.

164. On the Relief of J. Pickering. 19 Dec.
HR 32, 44-2, v1, 1p. [1769]
Debts incurred in building a school house for the Pottawatomies.

165. Message on Concessions from the Sioux. 26 Dec.
SED 9, 44-2, v1, 90p. [1718]
Report and journal of proceedings of the 1876 Sioux Commission appointed to obtain land cessions, rights-of-way, etc., from the Sioux; removal of the Sioux to Indian Territory is recommended; the cession of the Black Hills; failure of the 1875 commission sent to obtain the Black Hills; etc.

166. Mem. of the Oregon Legis. 29 Dec.
HMD 22, 44-2, v1, 1p. [1762]
Ask extinguishment of Indian title to the Siletz reservation; settle Indians on the Salmon River agency lands.

1877

1. Balances of Appropriations. 6 Jan.
HED 18, 44-2, v5, 8p. [1751]
Year ending 30 June 1875; Indian expenses.

2. Estimates of Appropriations. 6 Jan.
HED 19, 44-2, v5, 9p. [1751]
Year ending 30 June 1877; Indian expenses.

3. On the Case of L. McLaughlin. 8 Jan.
SR 557, 44-2, v1, 1p. [1732]
Injured in the 1868 battle of Rickaree Fork, against the Cheyennes.

4. Report on Oklahoma Territory. 10 Jan.
HR 82, 44-2, v1, 13p. [1769]
Government over the 31 tribes in Indian Territory; railroad construction; would not require Indians to surrender their lands; minority report says the act would violate treaties.

5. Courts of Justice in Alaska. 12 Jan.
SED 14, 44-2, v1, 5p. [1718]
Indian trade at Fort Wrangel, which is located at the mouth of the Stickeen River; influx of miners.

6. On the Case of J. Fenscke. 12 Jan.
HR 87, 44-2, v1, 1p. [1769]
Sioux hostilities of 1862 at the Lower Sioux agency in Minnesota.

7. R-P of Kaskaskia, Peoria, Piankeshaw, and Wea Indians. 17 Jan.
SR 582, 44-2, v1, 3p. [1732]
Proceeds of sale of their lands in Kansas (under the treaty of 1854) wrongfully diverted from their trust funds.

8. R-M of B. Holladay. 17 Jan.
SR 583, 44-2, v1, 7p. [1732]
Indian depredations upon mail carriers between the Missouri River and Salt Lake City, Utah, during 1860-1866.

9. R-C of C. Hedges. 19 Jan.
HR 112, 44-2, v1, 1p. [1769]
The Com. of Indian Affairs reports favorably.

10. On the Case of Lieut. Hill. 19 Jan.
HR 114, 44-2, v1, 1p. [1769]
Indian agent in Wyoming during 1870-1871.

11. On the Relief of S. Hanway. 19 Jan.
HR 127, 44-2, v1, 1p. [1769]
Service in the Indian Home Guards.

12. On the Relief of J. Theiren. 22 Jan.
SR 603, 44-2, v1, 1p. [1732]
Liquor seized by troops at Mann's Fort in Indian Territory in 1847.

13. On the Relief of J. Pearman. 23 Jan.
SR 607, 44-2, v1, 2p. [1732]
Services during 1861-1862 on the Nebraska frontier against Indians.

14. Texas and Pacific Railroad. 24 Jan.
HR 139, 44-2, v1, 16p. [1769]
Connection between Vinita, Indian Territory and this line is authorized.

15. Resol. of the Kansas Legis. 26 Jan.
SMD 30, 44-2, v1, 2p. [1722]
Ask money be appropriated from the Indian civilization fund to pay attorney's fees for settlers defending titles to the Osage ceded lands; unlawful issuance of patents by railroad companies.

16. Increase of the Cavalry Force on the Texas Frontier. 30 Jan.
HED 33, 44-2, v9, 3p. [1755]
To control Indian depredations; no Kiowa, Comanche, Cheyenne, or Arapahoe raids in the area of Fort Sill; no troops sent to the Sioux war.

17. On the Relief of Capt. Adams. 31 Jan.
SR 624, 44-2, v1, 7p. [1732]
Exploration of the Colorado River proves to be partially fallacious; ancient dwellings along the river in New Mexico and Arizona.

18. Government Exhibits at the Centennial. 1 Feb.
HR 144, 44-2, v1, 25p. [1769]
Display on the Indians jointly sponsored by the Indian Bureau and the Smithsonian Institution.

19. Mem. of the Choctaw Nation. 2 Feb.
SMD 34, 44-2, v1, 2p. [1722]
Ask settlement of the "net proceeds claim" arising under the treaty of 1830; settlement called for under the Choctaw and Chickasaw treaty of 1855.

20. Explorations in the Black Hills. 6 Feb.
SMD 41, 44-2, v1, 2p. [1722]
Cost of printing illustrations of Prof. Jenney's expedition under the direction of the CIA.

21. War Claims of Montana and Dakota. 8 Feb.
SED 34, 44-2, v2, 2p. [1719]
Appropriation required.

22. Petition of Chickasaw Indians. 8 Feb.
SMD 42, 44-2, v1, 2p. [1722]
Ask equitable division of school funds under the treaty of 22 June 1855.

23. Osage Ceded Lands. 13 Feb.
SED 35, 44-2, v2, 3p. [1719]
Ceded lands sold by the Leavenworth, Lawrence, and Galveston Railroad Company prior to 25 Feb. 1874.

24. R-P of N. Johnson. 13 Feb.
HR 166, 44-2, v2, 1p. [1770]
Service in the War of 1812; Gen. Winchester taken prisoner by the Indians.

25. R-P of W. Foulk. 14 Feb.
SR 656, 44-2, v1, 10p. [1732]
Court-martialed; violation of the Army regulations at Camp Supply, Indian Territory, in 1871.

26. Annual Report of the Smithsonian Institution. 16 Feb.
SMD 46, 44-2, v3, 488p. [1724]
Research related to the American Indian; account of the Sioux or Dakota Indians; Indian dwellings and vocabularies; mission to the western Nevada and California Indians.

27. Sale of Lands in Alaska Territory. 16 Feb.
HR 174, 44-2, v2, 4p. [1770]
Declining population in Alaska; conduct of the Indians there.

28. R-P of T. Walker. 21 Feb.
SR 685, 44-2, v1, 3p. [1732]
Land offices in Kansas allowed clerks because of the magnitude of sales of Osage, and other Indian lands.

29. Petition on Behalf of the Chickasaw Nation. 21 Feb.
HMD 41, 44-2, v1, 5p. [1762]
Ask payment of interest due under the treaties of 1832, 1834, 1852, and 1866.

30. Northern Boundary Survey. 23 Feb.
SED 41, 44-2, v2, 49p. [1719]
Between the U.S. and possessions of Great Britain under the treaty of Ghent; report of the Northern Boundary Commission; the Chippewas near Lake of the Woods; Assiniboine myth for the name given the "Hill of the Murdered Scout;" Sioux, Blackfeet, and Gros Ventre hunters.

31. Removal of Fort Garland. 23 Feb.
SED 42, 44-2, v2, 2p. [1719]
Too near the Ute reservation in Colorado.

32. Report on the Osages. 2 Mar.
HR 186, 44-2, v2, 4p. [1770]
Treaty of 1865 provides for sale of lands in Kansas at $1.25 per acre; treaty of 1868 would have sold the same land to a railroad company for $.20 per acre; attorneys hired by the Osages see that the 1868 treaty is not ratified.

33. R-M of R. Buchanan. 2 Mar.
HR 187, 44-2, v2, 9p. [1770]
U.S. government has used his patented portable boat, without a license, in the Rogue River, Coeur d'Alene, Spokane, and other Indian wars; invented during the Indian war of 1856 in Oregon and California.

34. Statements of Appropriations. 3 Mar.
HMD 44, 44-2, v1, 74p. [1762]
During the 2d session, 44th Congress; Indian expenses.

35. Indian Lands in Kansas. 3 Mar.
HR 188, 44-2, v2, 4p. [1770]
Question of title to the Black Bob Shawnee lands; settlers have moved onto the lands.

36. Military Post in Colorado. 3 Mar.
HR 199, 44-2, v2, 1p. [1770]
Reports adversely to the removal of Fort Garland to a location near the Ute reservation.

37. On the Relief of the Heirs of G. Fisher. 3 Mar.
HR 212, 44-2, v2, 1p. [1770]
U.S. military spoliations during the Creek war.

38. Report on the Creek Orphan Fund. 3 Mar.
HR 214, 44-2, v2, 7p. [1770]
Creek claims regarding the fund established by the treaty of 24 Mar. 1832.

39. Operations of Troops in Modoc Country. 10 Mar.
SED 1, 45-sp, v2, 18p. [1719]
During the 1873 war in California and Oregon.

40. Estimates of Appropriations. 15 Oct.
HED 5, 45-2, v13, 302p. [1805]
Year ending 30 June 1878; Indian expenses.

41. Interior Dept. Fire. 17 Oct.
HED 2, 45-1, v1, 15p. [1773]
Loss of records in the OIA.

42. Report of the Union Pacific Railroad. 25 Oct.
SED 2, 45-1, v1, 17p. [1780]
Proposed construction of a railroad through the Black Hills; would have a positive effect in settling the Indian troubles there.

43. Condition of C. and S. German. 25 Oct.
HED 4, 45-1, v1, 2p. [1773]
Two young women held captive by the Cheyennes during 1874; two of their sisters were previously recaptured from the Cheyennes.

44. Buildings at the Lower Brulé Agency in Dakota. 25 Oct.
HED 6, 45-1, v1, 2p. [1773]
Appropriation for construction at this Sioux agency (formerly the White River Agency).

45. Disbursements of the Indian Dept. 30 Oct.
HED 6, 45-2, v13, 10p. [1805]
Year ending 30 June 1877.

46. Resol. of Sen. Davis. 9 Nov.
SMD 9, 45-1, v1, 1p. [1785]
Asks preparation of a list of tribes, their populations and locations, and treaty obligations of the U.S.

47. Mem. of the Choctaw Nation. 10 Nov.
HMD 14, 45-1, v1, 4p. [1774]
Ask settlement (under the treaty of 1855) of the "net proceeds claim" arising from the treaty of 27 Sept. 1830.

48. Mexican Border Troubles. 13 Nov.
HED 13, 45-1, v1, 244p. [1773]
Incursions of marauding Indians and Mexicans into Texas; Kickapoo, Lipan, and other tribes.

49. Letter on War Survivors. 26 Nov.
SMD 13, 45-1, v1, 6p. [1785]
Number of survivors of the Seminole, Black Hawk, Florida, and other wars; claims arising from said wars.

50. R-M of B. Holladay. 26 Nov.
SR 18, 45-1, v1, 5p. [1789]
Indian depredations while carrying mail from the Missouri River to Salt Lake City, Utah, during 1860-1866.

51. Organization of Indian Territory. 27 Nov.
HMD 18, 45-1, v1, 3p. [1774]
Recommend territorial form of government be established, along with allotment of land, etc.

52. Statements of Appropriations. 1 Dec.
HMD 20, 45-1, v1, 6p. [1774]
During the 1st session, 45th Congress; Indian expenses.

53. Judgments of the Court of Claims. 3 Dec.
SMD 4, 45-2, v1, 11p. [1785]
Cases involving Indians.

54. Annual Message to Congress with Documents; Pres. Hayes. 3 Dec.
HED 1, 45-2, v1-10, 7184p. [1793-1802]
Nez Percé campaign; recommends abolishment of tribal relations, and citizenship for Indians; annual report of the Sec. of War (Serials 1794-1978); annual report of the Sec. of Interior (Serials 1800-1801); annual report of the Gen. Land Office (Serial 1800); annual report of the CIA (Serial 1800), including the Nez Percé and Sioux wars, removals to Indian Territory, the Sioux Commission, the Sitting Bull Commission, Alaska Indians, and reports of Supts., agents, schools, and farms; etc.

55. Annual Report of the Sec. of the Treasury. 3 Dec.
HED 2, 45-2, v11, 632p. [1803]
Year ending 30 June 1877; Indian expenses.

56. Resol. of Sen. Teller. 7 Dec.
SMD 6, 45-2, v1, 1p. [1785]
Asks for information on payments made to the Utes for land cessions under the agreement of 13 Sept. 1873.

57. Mem. of Delegates of the Choctaw and Chickasaw Nations. 10 Dec.
SMD 8, 45-2, v1, 3p. [1785]
Against a bill allowing Indians to become citizens; would violate the treaties of 1832, 1855, and 1866.

58. Brothertown Indian Reservation. 14 Dec.
HR 37, 45-2, v1, 1p. [1822]
Allotment in severalty of land in Wisconsin under the treaty of 20 Oct. 1832 was not completed.

1878

1. Estimates for Payment of Claims. 11 Jan.
HED 27, 45-2, v10, 190p. [1802]
Claims under special statutes include the Seminole war.

2. Testimony on Texas Border Troubles. 12 Jan.
HMD 64, 45-2, v6, 313p. [1820]
Indian raids from Mexico. Gen. Jackson's pursuit of Seminoles into Spanish territory in 1818 is mentioned as a precedent for incursions into Mexico.

3. Letter on the Apaches and Utes. 14 Jan.
SED 8, 45-2, v1, 10p. [1780]
On their removal from the Cimarron Valley, New Mexico, to the Rio de los Pinos agency (for the Utes) and the Mescalero Apache agency.

4. Resol. of Sen. Mitchell. 14 Jan.
SMD 16, 45-2, v1, 2p. [1785]
Establishment of four Indian Territories for all reservation Indians.

5. Remonstrance of Creek and Seminole Delegates. 14 Jan.
SMD 18, 45-2, v1, 3p. [1785]
Against the bill allowing Indians to become citizens; violates numerous treaties; would lead to tribal disintegration.

6. Mem. of Michigan and Indiana Indians. 15 Jan.
HMD 8, 45-2, v1, 39p. [1815]
Pottawatomies exempted from removal under the treaty of 27 Sept. 1833; ask for funds due under various treaties.

7. On the Relief of A. Call. 15 Jan.
HR 58, 45-2, v1, 1p. [1822]
Escort services through hostile Indian country in Utah during 1853-1855.

8. On the Relief of J. Brice. 15 Jan.
HR 61, 45-2, v1, 2p. [1822]
Arapahoe depredations of 1868 near Fort Lyon.

9. Property in the Interior Dept. 17 Jan.
SED 11, 45-2, v1, 3p. [1780]
Including the OIA.

10. Report on Pensions. 17 Jan.
HR 64, 45-2, v1, 12p. [1822]
Services in the Creek war of 1835-1836, the Seminole war in Florida of 1835-1842, and the Black Hawk war of 1832.

11. On the Relief of E. Murphy. 17 Jan.
HR 65, 45-2, v1, 2p. [1822]
Mescalero Apache depredations of 1861 and 1870 in Texas.

12. On the Relief of R. Buchanan. 17 Jan.
HR 73, 45-2, v1, 2p. [1822]

Invention of a portable boat during the Rogue River Indian war of 1856-1857 in Oregon and California; U.S. uses boat even after it has been patented.

13. Message on the Nez Percé War. 18 Jan.
SED 14, 45-2, v1, 10p. [1780]
Causes and history of the war, along with its probable cost; pursuit of Chief Joseph's band for refusal to go onto a reservation.

14. Claims of Texas. 22 Jan.
SED 19, 45-2, v1, 195p. [1780]
In repelling Indian invasions from 1854 to 1877; Kickapoos, Comanches, and other Indian tribes involved.

15. Election of a Delegate from Indian Territory. 22 Jan.
HR 95, 45-2, v1, 8p. [1822]
Representation in Congress for the Cherokees, Creeks, Seminoles, Choctaws, and Chickasaws.

16. Consolidation of Indian Agencies. 24 Jan.
SED 20, 45-2, v1, 8p. [1780]
Establishment of a large reservation in the Colville country for Indians on reservations in Washington and Oregon.

17. Removal of the Kickapoo Indians. 28 Jan.
SMD 23, 45-2, v1, 5p. [1785]
From Mexico and Texas to Indian Territory.

18. Receipts and Expenditures. 28 Jan.
HED 39, 45-2, v15, 681p. [1807]
Year ending 30 June 1874; Indian expenses.

19. Lands Ceded to the U.S. by the Utes. 29 Jan.
SED 21, 45-2, v1, 4p. [1780]
Under the agreement of 13 Sept. 1873; payments to the Utes.

20. Receipts and Expenditures. 31 Jan.
HED 35, 45-2, v15, 686p. [1807]
Year ending 30 June 1873; Indian expenses.

21. On the Relief of G. Hesselberger. 4 Feb.
SR 49, 45-2, v1, 4p. [1789]
Attended treaty com'rs during the negotiations at Medicine Lodge Creek in 1867; rescued 2 young women who had been captives of the Kiowas.

22. Resol. of the California Legis. 4 Feb.
HMD 19, 45-2, v1, 1p. [1815]
Favors transfer of the Indian Bureau from the Interior Dept. to the War Dept.

23. On the Case of P. Loose. 5 Feb.
SR 62, 45-2, v1, 1p. [1789]
Killed in the Nez Percé campaign in 1877.

24. Contingent Expenses of the Interior Dept. 5 Feb.
HED 42, 45-2, v14, 23p. [1806]
Year ending 30 June 1877; OIA.

25. Estimates of Deficiencies in Appropriations. 8 Feb.
HED 45, 45-2, v14, 71p. [1806]
For fiscal 1878; Indian expenses.

26. Balances to be Reappropriated. 8 Feb.
HED 46, 45-2, v14, 43p. [1806]
For fiscal 1875, and prior years; Indian expenses.

27. On the Case of J. Thomas. 8 Feb.
HR 180, 45-2, v1, 1p. [1822]
Modoc war death; 1873; Oregon.

28. On the Relief of E. Leitensdorfer. 8 Feb.
HR 189, 45-2, v1, 1p. [1822]
Induced the Pueblo Indians of New Mexico to remain peaceful during the U.S. invasion of Mexico in 1846-1847.

29. R-C of E. Gurley. 8 Feb.
HR 192, 45-2, v1, 3p. [1822]
Prosecuting attorney in a case in which whites murdered 7 Caddo Indians in Texas during 1858.

30. Resol. and Amendment of Sen Voorhees and Sen. Dorsey. 14 Feb.
SMD 30 (pts. 1 and 2), 45-2, v1, 2p. [1785]
Ask investigations of railroad activities regarding issuance of bonds on contingent land-grants, and of establishment of government over Indian Territory.

31. Annual Report of the Smithsonian Institution. 15 Feb.
SMD 35, 45-2, v1, 500p. [1785]
Research related to the American Indian.

32. Report on Salmon-Fisheries. 15 Feb.
SR 98, 45-2, v1, 6p. [1789]
Located upon a supposed Indian reservation situated on the Columbia River in Washington Territory.

33. On the Relief of J. McGregor. 15 Feb.
HR 226, 45-2, v1, 1p. [1822]
Services at the Malheur Indian agency in Oregon during 1874.

34. On the Relief of H. Warren. 15 Feb.
HR 227, 45-2, v1 , 1p. [1822]

Favorable report by the Com. on Indian Affairs.

35. R-C of F. Culver. 15 Feb.
HR 228, 45-2, v1, 2p. [1822]
Services in effecting the treaty of 18 Feb. 1861 with the Cheyennes and Arapahoes; treaty of 1851 with the Cheyennes, Arapahoes, Kiowas, Comanches, and Apaches, and why it failed.

36. Report on the Western Cherokees. 15 Feb.
HR 230, 45-2, v1, 10p. [1822]
Claims of the "Old Settlers" against the U.S.; history of the tribe's relations with the government.

37. Distribution of U.S. Troops. 19 Feb.
HED 55, 45-2, v14, 35p. [1806]
Lists duties of officers; officers acting as Indian agents at Spotted Tail and Red Cloud agencies in Dakota.

38. Survey of Land in Indian Territory. 21 Feb.
SED 32, 45-2, v1, 5p. [1780]
Purpose was to ascertain the locations and quantities of reserved land, with the aim being to allot these lands to individuals; list of treaties calling for the surveys.

39. Cost of the Sioux War. 21 Feb.
SED 33 (pts. 1 and 2), 45-2, v1, 9p. [1780]
Funds expended, and casualties of the 1876-1877 war in Dakota.

40. The Texas Pacific Railroad. 21 Feb.
HR 238 (pts. 1-4), 45-2, v1, 35p. [1822]
Solution to the Indian problem of the Southwest.

41. Objections of Indian Delegations. 25 Feb.
HMD 32, 45-2, v1, 5p. [1815]
Against bills providing for the election of a delegate from Indian Territory to Congress.

42. Mem. of Indian Delegates. 25 Feb.
HMD 33, 45-2, v1, 10p. [1815]
From the Cherokees, Creeks, Seminoles, Choctaws, and Chickasaws of Indian Territory; opposed to transfer of the Indian Bureau from the Interior Dept. to the War Dept.

43. Transfer of the Indian Bureau. 25 Feb.
HR 241, 45-2, v1, 20p. [1822]
From the Interior Dept. to the War Dept.; description of management of Indian affairs.

44. On the Case of W. Brindle. 25 Feb.
HR 242, 45-2, v1, 3p. [1822]
Disbursing agent in the Pawnee land district of Kansas in 1857-1861.

45. Building for a National Museum. 25 Feb.
HR 244, 45-2, v1, 19p. [1822]
Would house a display on Indians co-sponsored by the Indian Bureau and the Smithsonian Institution, and Indian materials from explorations.

46. Persons on the Pension-Rolls. 26 Feb.
SED 27, 45-2, v1, 2p. [1780]
Number residing in Indian Territory.

47. Report on the Choctaw Nation. 26 Feb.
HR 251, 45-2, v2, 39p. [1823]
Settlement of the claim arising under the treaty of 27 Sept. 1830, as called for in the Choctaw and Chickasaw treaty of 22 June 1855.

48. Report on the Territory of Lincoln. 28 Feb.
SR 110, 45-2, v1, 4p. [1789]
To be created from parts of Montana, Wyoming, and Dakota; would embrace the Black Hills, which was ceded to the U.S. by the Sioux in 1876; separated from the populous, southeastern Dakota by the Sioux reservation.

49. R-C of Montana Citizens. 1 Mar.
HR 285, 45-2, v2, 1p. [1823]
For service in Nez Percé war of 1877.

50. On the Case of J. Thomas. 1 Mar.
HR 330, 45-2, v2, 1 p. [1823]
Service in the Modoc war.

51. On the Relief of G. Hesselberger. 1 Mar.
HR 348, 45-2, v2, 4p. [1823]
Stationed at Fort Dodge, Kansas; treaty negotiations at Medicine Lodge Creek in 1867; rescued 2 women who had been captives of the Kiowas.

52. Railroad and Telegraph to the Pacific. 4 Mar.
SR 111, 45-2, v1, 12p. [1789]
Effects of Indian removal on the government's transportation account.

53. On the Relief of Capt. Foulk. 5 Mar.
SR 117, 45-2, v1, 5p. [1789]
Court-martial stemming from misconduct in Indian Territory.

54. Report on the Pottawatomies. 6 Mar.
SR 123, 45-2, v1, 1p. [1789]

To legalize land patents under the treaties of 1861, and 1867.

55. Arrears Due the Chickasaw Nation. 8 Mar.
HMD 39, 45-2, v3, 6p. [1817]
Congress failed to appropriate funds due the Chickasaws under several treaties with the U.S.

56. Arrears Due the Chickasaw Nation. 8 Mar.
HR 354, 45-2, v2, 3p. [1823]
Amounts due for land cessions in Mississippi under treaties of 1832, and 1834; settlement under the treaties of 1852, and 1866.

57. Lines of Communication Between Colorado and New Mexico. 9 Mar.
HED 66, 45-2, v14, 38p. [1806]
Survey expeditions; Ute reservation under the treaty of 2 Mar. 1868 is ceded to the U.S. under the agreement of 13 Sept. 1873; Indian depredations.

58. On the Case of Maj. Haller. 11 Mar.
HR 375, 45-2, v2, 5p. [1823]
At Fort Dalles during the Oregon Indian war of 1855-1856.

59. R-C of J. Spencer and J. Mead. 12 Mar.
HR 376, 45-2, v2, 5p. [1823]
Supplies furnished the Kansas Indians during 1866-1867.

60. Counsel Fees in Osage Land Suits. 12 Mar.
HR 377 (pts. 1 and 2), 45-2, v2, 5p. [1823]
Sale of lands under the treaty of 21 Jan. 1867; land claims, in Kansas, of railroad companies.

61. On the Relief of S. Marble et al. 12 Mar.
HR 378, 45-2, v2, 2p. [1823]
Kiowa hostilities of 1872 in Texas; 3 children held captive.

62. Fresh Water on the Fort Yuma Desert. 14 Mar.
HR 380, 45-2, v2, 10p. [1823]
Indian beliefs about the "Desert of Death" in California.

63. Petition of Creek Delegates. 16 Mar.
HMD 38, 45-2, v3, 5p. [1817]
Ask awards be made to those Creeks who enlisted in the Federal Army during the Civil War.

64. On the Relief of Mrs. Short. 16 Mar.
HR 404, 45-2, v2, 1p. [1823]
Cheyenne hostilities of 1874 in Kansas.

65. R-C of C. Dahler. 16 Mar.
HR 410, 45-2, v2, 1p. [1823]
Contract not fulfilled due to Indian hostilities of 1867 in Montana.

66. R-P of T. Walker. 20 Mar.
SR 176, 45-2, v1, 5p. [1789]
Hired clerk for land-office in Iowa; only Kansas land-offices, selling Osage and other Indian lands, were authorized to hire clerks.

67. Pottawatomie Indian Treaty. 29 Mar.
HR 433, 45-2, v2, 4p. [1823]
White emigrant depredations upon Indian lands in Kansas; claims under the treaty 27 Feb. 1867.

68. On the Case of G. Smith. 2 Apr.
SR 214, 45-2, v2, 4p. [1790]
Commanded Indian troops against hostile Indians in New Mexico, Indian Territory, and Texas.

69. R-P of C. Whiting. 2 Apr.
SR 220, 45-2, v2, 5p. [1790]
In charge of removing the Navajoes from Fort Sumner back to their own country in New Mexico.

70. Report on the Brothertown Indians. 2 Apr.
SR 224, 45-2, v2, 1p. [1790]
Allotment in severalty of a tract of land in Wisconsin under the treaty of 27 Oct. 1832 was not completed.

71. On the Relief of M. Spencer. 3 Apr.
SR 225, 45-2, v2, 2p. [1790]
Depredations during the Creek war of 1813 in Alabama.

72. Report on the Arid Region of the U.S. 3 Apr.
HED 73, 45-2, v13, 195p. [1805]
The region of the Rocky Mountains; timber-lands suffer most from fires set by Indians, and removal of the Indians would be the first step necessary for their protection.

73. Officers Dismissed from the Tenth Cavalry. 4 Apr.
SED 52 (pts. 1 and 2), 45-2, v2, 14p. [1781]
Affairs in Indian Territory.

74. R-P of J. Turner et al. 4 Apr.
SR 241, 45-2, v2, 2p. [1790]
Indian agent in Kansas defaults on his bond.

75. R-P of M. Duffield. 4 Apr.
HR 459, 45-2, v2, 3p. [1823]
Hostile Indians of Arizona in 1864-1866.

76. On the Relief of J. Richard and J. Brown. 5 Apr.
SR 242, 45-2, v2, 2p. [1790]
Contract for supplies to the Los

Pinos agency in Colorado during 1875.

77. Private Land-Claim in New Mexico. 5 Apr.
HR 463, 45-2, v2, 3p. [1823]
Occupancy prevented by hostile Indians during 1838-1861.

78. R-P of D. and D. Sanford. 5 Apr.
HR 465, 45-2, v2, 6p. [1823]
Comanche and Kiowa depredations of 1872 in Texas.

79. Eastern Band of Cherokees. 5 Apr.
HR 466 (pts. 1 and 2), 45-2, v2, 5p. [1823]
Claim of North Carolina Cherokees against the Cherokee Nation based on the treaty of 29 Dec. 1835.

80. On the Relief of S. Marshall. 5 Apr.
HR 467, 45-2, v2, 1p. [1823]
Disbursing agent of the California Indian treaty commission of 1850.

81. Military Telegraph in Dakota and Montana. 9 Apr.
SR 243, 45-2, v2, 3p. [1790]
From Deadwood City, Dakota, to Forts Keogh, Custer, and Ellis; area of Indian hostilities.

82. Letter on Campaigns in Dakota. 15 Apr.
SED 63, 45-2, v2, 9p. [1781]
During the 3rd quarter of 1877; against the Sioux and Nez Percé.

83. Salt Spring Lands in Minnesota. 16 Apr.
SR 259, 45-2, v2, 6p. [1790]
Land cessions by the Chippewas under the treaties of 22 Feb. 1855, 20 Mar. 1865, and 18 Apr. 1867; lands in the White Earth reservation.

84. Military Post in the Black Hills. 16 Apr.
SR 261, 45-2, v2, 1p. [1790]
Appropriation for construction of a post to protect citizens from Indian hostilities.

85. On the Case of A. O'Brien. 16 Apr.
HR 517, 45-2, v2, 3p. [1823]
Service in the Seminole war of 1836 in Florida.

86. On the Case of E. Roberts. 16 Apr.
HR 591, 45-2, v3, 2p. [1824]
Military expedition against the Chippewas in 1862.

87. R-P of C. Hawley. 16 Apr.
HR 592, 45-2, v3, 1p. [1824]
Frontier service against Indians after the Civil War.

88. The Texas Pacific Railroad. 17 Apr.
HR 619 (pts. 1 and 2), 45-2, v3, 13p. [1824]
Transport of Indian supplies.

89. Geological and Geographical Surveys. 19 Apr.
HED 81, 45-2, v17, 22p. [1809]
Information on all expeditions conducted under the supervision of the Interior Dept.; report of Prof. Hayden; ethnographic material collected during the past 10 years.

90. Abandonment of Military Posts. 20 Apr.
HED 79, 45-2, v17, 16p. [1809]
Recommendations to give up Forts Rice and Sully near the new Red Cloud and Spotted Tail Sioux agencies; elimination of all but Forts Sill, Reno, Elliot, Leavenworth, Riley, and Camp Supply surrounding Indian Territory; Forts Klamath, Bidwell, Boisé, and Halleck to be maintained in the Dept. of California; control of Indians in the Southwest.

91. On the Relief of J. McGregor. 24 Apr.
SR 281, 45-2, v2, 1p. [1790]
Services at the Malheur Indian agency in Oregon during 1874.

92. Claims of Kansas. 24 Apr.
SR 283, 45-2, v2, 9p. [1790]
For suppression of Cheyenne, Arapahoe, Comanche, Kiowa, and Sioux hostilities during 1862-1869.

93. R-C of J. Dorsey and W. Shepard. 24 Apr.
HR 665, 45-2, v3, 4p. [1824]
Supplies to troops engaging the Paiutes during 1860 in Utah Territory.

94. R-C of N. Garrison. 24 Apr.
HR 672, 45-2, v3, 2p. [1824]
Destruction of property by troops and captive Indians during 1838 in Georgia.

95. R-C of T. Walker. 24 Apr.
HR 673, 45-2, v3, 5p. [1824]
Authorization for extra clerks at land-offices in Kansas engaged in selling Osage and other Indian lands.

96. Relations Between the U.S. and Mexico. 25 Apr.
HR 701, 45-2, v3, 678p. [1824]
Apache, Lipan, Mescalero, and Kickapoo raids from Mexico into Texas.

97. Protection of the Northern Frontier of Montana. 29 Apr.
SR 286, 45-2, v2, 5p. [1790]
Appropriation for a military post; Crows, Assiniboines, Gros Ventres, Bloods, Piegans, Nez Percé, and

various bands of Sioux near the British American border.

98. Additional Clerical Services. 30 Apr.
SR 300, 45-2, v2, 1p. [1790]
In the Pawnee land district of Kansas.

99. Geological and Geographical Surveys. 30 Apr.
HED 80, 45-2, v17, 19p. [1809]
Information on all expeditions conducted under the supervision of the Interior Dept. during the past 10 years; report of Prof. Powell; ethnographic material collected.

100. Lands Located on Military Warrants. 30 Apr.
HR 707 (pts. 1 and 2), 45-2, v4, 14p. [1825]
Choctaw, Chickasaw, and Creek lands in Alabama and Mississippi in 1855-1857.

101. Boundary Line Between Colorado and Utah. 30 Apr.
HR 708, 45-2, v4, 2p. [1825]
Problems with the location of the Ute reservation.

102. Land Entries by Indians in Michigan. 1 May.
HED 82, 45-2, v17, 5p. [1809]
Investigation of frauds practiced upon Indians endeavoring to take advantage of homestead laws; treaty of 31 July 1855 with the Ottawas and Chippewas.

103. Mem. of the Choctaw Nation. 2 May.
SMD 59, 45-2, v2, 4p. [1786]
Asks settlement of the claim arising under the treaty of 27 Sept. 1830, and investigated under the treaty of 1855.

104. Baptist Domestic and Indian Missions. 8 May.
SR 358, 45-2, v2, 2p. [1790]
Payments for a school in the Pottawatomie country of Kansas.

105. Rights of Indians to Impose Taxes. 10 May.
SED 74, 45-2, v2, 55p. [1781]
In Indian Territory; cattle tax imposed by the Cherokees; taxation of the Missouri, Kansas, and Texas Railroad by the Choctaws.

106. Geological and Geographical Surveys. 10 May.
HED 88, 45-2, v17, 8p. [1809]
Information on all expeditions conducted under the supervision of the War Dept. during the past 10 years; ethnographic information.

107. R-C of M. Lockwood. 11 May.
HR 804, 45-2, v4, 5p. [1825]
Losses in the Nez Percé war of 1877 in Montana.

108. Appraisal of Lands in Indian Territory. 15 May.
SMD 69, 45-2, v2, 21p. [1786]
Lands west of the 96th degree of west longitude ceded by the Cherokees under the treaty of 19 July 1866.

109. R-P of T. Mesplie. 15 May.
SR 380, 45-2, v2, 2p. [1790]
Missionary to Indians in Oregon, Idaho, and Montana.

110. Election of a Delegate from Indian Territory. 18 May.
HR 807 (pts. 1 and 2), 45-2, v4, 5p. [1825]
Recommends adoption of a substitute bill proposed by the Choctaw, Chickasaw, Creek, Cherokee, and Seminole delegates which would authorize the Indian Council of the Territory to appoint the delegate to Congress.

111. Arrears Due the Chickasaw Nation. 18 May.
HR 808, 45-2, v4, 8p. [1825]
Funds due for sale of tribal land in Mississippi under the treaties of 1832 and 1834; settlement under the treaties of 1852 and 1866.

112. Suit Against the Cherokee Nation. 21 May.
SR 406, 45-2, v2, 2p. [1790]
By the Eastern Band of Cherokees, residing in North Carolina for a share of the proceeds arising from the sale of land by the Cherokee Nation of Indian Territory.

113. Protection of Colorado Citizens from Indians. 23 May.
HED 91, 45-2, v17, 4p. [1809]
Anticipated outbreak of the Utes due to the failure of Congress to meet stipulations of the agreements of 1873; location of Fort Garland.

114. On the Case of W. Langford. 23 May.
HR 830, 45-2, v4, 7p. [1825]
Mission lands in Nez Percé country, Idaho, during 1836-1846; hostilities of other tribes during 1848.

115. Supplies Furnished the Sioux of Minnesota. 23 May.

HR 833, 45-2, v4, 2p. [1825]
Subsequent to 1860, and prior to the Sioux outbreak of 1862.

116. Settlers in Wind River Valley, Wyoming. 24 May.
HR 835, 45-2, v5, 3p. [1826]
Relief for settlers whose lands were incorporated into the Shoshone and Bannock reservation under the treaty of 3 July 1868.

117. Removal of Indian Tribes. 27 May.
HMD 27, 45-2, v6, 5p. [1820]
Removal and consolidation of Indians in Oregon, Washington, Colorado, Kansas, Nebraska, Iowa, Wisconsin, Minnesota, and Dakota; reduction of agencies, and sale of vacated lands.

118. Letter on the Mem. of B. Overton. 28 May.
SED 87, 45-2, v2, 12p. [1781]
Governor of the Chickasaw Nation on the "permit law" of that nation; regarding powers of taxation, etc.

119. Employees of the Interior Dept. 28 May.
HED 94, 45-2, v17, 9p. [1809]
List of those who have served in the Army or Navy; OIA.

120. R-C of Heirs of J. Beaubien. 31 May.
SR 454, 45-2, v2, 4p. [1790]
Claim to a part of Fort Dearborn in Chicago, Illinois; treaty of Greenville, dated 30 Aug. 1795, with the Indians.

121. Creek Orphan Claim. 1 June.
HR 905, 45-2, v5, 2p. [1826]
Amounts due under the treaty of 24 Mar. 1832.

122. Letter on a Wisconsin Land-Claim. 3 June.
HMD 60, 45-2, v6, 4p. [1820]
For lands included in the Lac de Flambeau reservation, created under the treaty of 30 Sept. 1854 with the Chippewas of Lake Superior and the Mississippi.

123. Resol. of Sen. Patterson. 6 June.
SMD 77, 45-2, v2, 1p. [1786]
Asks authority for subcommittee to take testimony in Indian Territory during the recess regarding issuance of bonds by railroads, and establishment of a territorial government.

124. R-P of B. Overton. 6 June.
SR 476, 45-2, v2, 7p. [1790]
On arrears of interest due on trust funds of the Chickasaw Nation held by the U.S. under various treaties.

125. Payments from the Sale of Osage Lands. 7 June.
HR 914, 45-2, v5, 9p. [1826]
Sale of Kansas lands under the treaty of 1868; attorneys hired to protect the Osages from railroad company frauds.

126. R-M of E. Boudinot. 10 June.
HR 920, 45-2, v5, 3p. [1826]
Sale of tobacco by a Cherokee Indian within Indian Territory; conflict between the treaty of 1866 and internal revenue laws.

127. On the Relief of Montana Citizens. 11 June.
SR 497, 45-2, v2, 2p. [1790]
Volunteers in the Nez Percé war of 1877.

128. Mem. of Delegates from Indian Territory. 12 June.
SMD 82, 45-2, v2, 5p. [1786]
Against opening the Territory to white settlers, establishment of the Oklahoma Territory, abolishment of tribal relations, and allotment of land in severalty.

129. R-M of B. Holladay. 13 June.
SR 513, 45-2, v3, 16p. [1791]
Indian depredations on his property while carrying the U.S. mails during 1861-1866; Colorado.

130. On the Relief of J. Fletcher. 14 June.
SR 521, 45-2, v3, 3p. [1791]
Cheyenne and Arapahoe depredations of 1870 *en route* from Fort Dodge, Kansas, to Camp Supply, Indian Territory.

131. Equalization of Bounties. 17 June.
HR 1000, 45-2, v5, 3p. [1826]
Benefits to soldiers in Indian wars.

132. Extending the Jurisdiction of the Court of Claims. 17 June.
HR 1001, 45-2, v5, 2p. [1826]
To cover claims arising under Indian treaties.

133. Election of a Delegate from Indian Territory. 17 June.
HR 1002, 45-2, v5, 12p. [1826]
Representation of the Creeks, Seminoles, Cherokees, Chickasaws, and Choctaws in Congress.

134. R-C of F. Plummer. 19 June.
HR 1015, 45-2, v5, 2p. [1826]
Evacuation of Fort Cobb, Indian

Territory, in 1861 during the Civil War.

135. Statements of Appropriations. 20 June.
HMD 66, 45-2, v6, 103p. [1820]
During the 2d session, 45th Congress; Indian expenses.

136. Disbursements of the Indian Dept. 31 Oct.
HED 6, 45-3, v14, 12p. [1855]
Year ending 30 June 1878.

137. Judgments of the Court of Claims. 2 Dec.
SMD 7, 45-3, v1, 36p. [1833]
Year ending 2 Dec. 1878; cases related to Indian affairs.

138. Annual Message to Congress with Documents; Pres. Hayes. 2 Dec.
HED 1, 45-3, v1-11, 7968p. [1842-1852]
Bannock hostilities; march of the Northern Cheyennes from Indian Territory to Dakota where they are turned over to the U.S. by Sioux at the Red Cloud agency; Indian cavalry; transfer of the Indian Bureau; annual report of the Sec. of War (Serials 1843-1848); annual report of the Sec. of Interior (Serials 1850-1851); annual report of the Gen. Land Office (Serial 1850); annual report of the CIA (Serial 1850), including statistics on Indians, trust funds, legislation, and reports on Supts., agents, schools, and farms; etc.

139. Annual Report of the Sec. of the Treasury. 2 Dec.
HED 2, 45-3, v12, 667p. [1853]
Year ending 30 June 1878; Indian expenses.

140. Estimates of Appropriations. 2 Dec.
HED 5, 45-3, v14, 326p. [1855]
Year ending 30 June 1880; Indian expenses.

141. Surveys of the Territories. 3 Dec.
HMD 5, 45-3, v1, 27p. [1861]
Ethnological materials collected on the North American Indians.

142. Property in the Interior Dept. 12 Dec.
SED 5, 45-3, v1, 3p. [1828]
Including the OIA.

143. Confirmation of Land Conveyances. 13 Dec.
HR 5, 45-3, v1, 2p. [1866]
Made by guardians for incompetent members of the Shawnee tribe, when the guardian was appointed by the courts of the territory or State of Kansas.

144. On the Relief of A. Fisher. 13 Dec.
HR 6, 45-3, v1, 2p. [1866]
Land incorporated into the Skokomish reservation in Washington Territory.

145. On the Relief of C. Wilder. 13 Dec.
HR 19, 45-3, v1, 2p. [1866]
Lands in Kansas ceded to the Shawnees under the treaty of 10 May 1854.

146. R-C of Col. Meacham. 20 Dec.
HR 51, 45-3, v1, 2p. [1866]
Member of the Modoc treaty commission of 1873 in California; Com'rs attacked at a council, with some killed, and all left for dead.

1879

1. Report of the Com'r of Fish and Fisheries. 13 Jan.
SMD 31, 45-3, v2, 988p. [1834]
Potential Indian hostilities in California; Indian employees at the fishery on the McCloud River in California.

2. Purchase of Fort Clark, Texas. 16 Jan.
SR 579, 45-3, v1, 4p. [1837]
Fort needed to restrain Indian hostilities on the north and western frontiers of Texas.

3. On the Case of H. Gates. 16 Jan.
SR 586, 45-3, v1, 1p. [1837]
Service in the Seminole war in Florida.

4. R-P of H. Read. 20 Jan.
SR 604, 45-3, v1, 6p. [1837]
Indian hostilities in New Mexico during 1863.

5. Estimates of Deficiencies in Appropriations. 20 Jan.
HED 31, 45-3, v11, 43p. [1852]
Year ending 30 June 1879; Indian expenses.

6. Military Post at El Paso, Texas. 21 Jan.
SR 606, 45-3, v1, 3p. [1837]
Necessary for protection of mails against Indian depredations.

7. On the Relief of J. Fitzgerald. 21 Jan.
SR 609, 45-3, v1, 2p. [1837]
Physician to the Cheyennes and Arapahoes in 1869-1870 near Camp Supply, Indian Territory.

8. Education of Indian Children. 22 Jan.
SED 39, 45-3, v1, 9p. [1828]
On an arrangement between Lawrence University of Appleton, Wisconsin, and the CIA for the education of youths from the Oneida tribe.

9. On the Relief of H. Jones. 22 Jan.
SR 617, 45-3, v1, 1p. [1837]
Indian agent in Wisconsin sells timber on a reservation during 1872; contract disallowed.

10. Message on the Choctaw Claim. 24 Jan.
HED 34, 45-3, v16, 49p. [1858]
On the "net proceeds" claim arising under the treaty of 27 Sept. 1830; settlement under the treaty of 22 June 1855.

11. Petition of B. Overton. 27 Jan.
SMD 46, 45-3, v1, 4p. [1833]
Chickasaw delegate on handling of trust funds by the Sec. of Interior; funds arose under various treaties.

12. On the Relief of Kansas. 28 Jan.
SR 640, 45-3, v1, 4p. [1837]
Expenses of suppressing Indian hostilities in 1861.

13. On the Relief of J. Chickering. 28 Jan.
SR 644, 45-3, v1, 12p. [1837]
Expedition of 1874 against hostile Indians in Texas.

14. On the Relief of Montana Citizens. 28 Jan.
SR 646, 45-3, v1, 1p. [1837]
Volunteers in the 1877 Nez Percé war.

15. Klamath Indian Reservation Lands. 28 Jan.
HR 75, 45-3, v1, 12p. [1866]
Claims of land owners within the reservation established by the Klamath, Modoc, and Snake treaty of 4 Oct. 1864.

16. Mem. of the Western Cherokees. 29 Jan.
SMD 51, 45-3, v1, 4p. [1833]
Ask a settlement of claims of the Western, or "Old Settler" Cherokees which arose under the treaties of 1835-1836, and 1846.

17. Mem. of I. Garvin. 29 Jan.
SMD 52, 45-3, v1, 3p. [1833]
Principal chief of the Choctaws against the establishment of a territorial government over Indian Territory.

18. R-P of H. de Ahna. 30 Jan.
HR 82, 45-3, v1, 2p. [1866]
Collector of customs in Alaska; no defense from the wild Indians.

19. R-P of E. Benham and F. Potter. 31 Jan.
SR 692, 45-3, v1, 2p. [1837]
Service of 1824 on the Indian frontier.

20. Transfer of the Indian Bureau. 31 Jan.
SR 693 (pts. 1 and 2), 45-3, v1, 40p. [1837]
From the Interior Dept. to the War Dept.; history of control of Indian affairs within government.

21. On the Relief of J. Robertson. 31 Jan.
HR 84, 45-3, v1, 1p. [1866]
Attorney for the North Carolina, or Eastern Cherokees in 1871.

22. On the Relief of R. Reeves. 31 Jan.
HR 85, 45-3, v1, 2p. [1866]
Appointed to survey the boundary between Wyoming and Dakota in 1877; passed through the Black Hills; Sioux hostilities.

23. California Indian War Bonds. 31 Jan.
HR 86, 45-3, v1, 2p. [1866]
Payment of bonds issued in 1852.

24. R-C of L. Brown. 31 Jan.
HR 87, 45-3, v1, 4p. [1866]
Payment for improvements made on the Nez Percé reservation in Idaho; treaty of 11 June 1855 covers reimbursement of the U.S. government.

25. On the Relief of Capt. Campbell. 31 Jan.
HR 91, 45-3, v1, 10p. [1866]
Arrests made in Alaska during 1874 for sale of liquor in Indian country.

26. Transfer of the Indian Bureau. 31 Jan.
HR 92, 45-3, v1, 20p. [1866]
From the Interior Dept. to the War Dept.

27. Transfer of the Indian Bureau. 31 Jan.
HR 93, 45-3, v1, 20p. [1866]
From the Interior Dept. to the War Dept.

28. Testimony on Transfer of the Indian Bureau. 1 Feb.
SMD 53, 45-3, v3, 406p. [1835]
From the Interior Dept. to the War Dept.; Indians testify on the transfer, and on Indian relations with the military.

29. Remonstrance of the Chief and Delegates to the Eastern Cherokees. 1 Feb.
HMD 17, 45-3, v1, 4p. [1861]
Against passage of any bill allowing the Eastern Cherokees to sue the Cherokee Nation.

30. Permit Law of the Chickasaw Nation. 3 Feb.
SR 698, 45-3, v2, 4p. [1838]

Validity of law requiring all persons who are not Chickasaws to register and pay a fee in order to work or reside in Chickasaw country.

31. Public Service and Resources of Alaska. 4 Feb.
SED 59, 45-3, v4, 163p. [1831]
List of Indian tribes in Alaska, along with their condition; Indian trade; liquor traffic.

32. On the Relief of Oregon. 4 Feb.
SR 701, 45-3, v2, 2p. [1838]
Expenses of suppressing the Modoc war in 1872-1873.

33. Survey of the Western Boundary of Arkansas. 4 Feb.
SR 714, 45-3, v2, 5p. [1838]
Between Arkansas and Indian country; conflict over lines set up under the Choctaw treaty of 20 Jan. 1825, and the Cherokee treaty of 6 May 1828.

34. On the Relief of Officers of the Fifth Infantry. 5 Feb.
SR 715, 45-3, v2, 7p. [1838]
Called from Fort Leavenworth, Kansas, following the Custer massacre to serve in the campaign of 1876-1877 against the Sioux bands under Sitting Bull and Crazy Horse; belongings lost when the steamboat *J. Donald Cameron* sinks on the Missouri River.

35. Clerical Force in the Indian Office. 6 Feb.
SED 6, 45-3, v1, 3p. [1828]
Increase in number and salary.

36. Klamath Indian Reservation. 6 Feb.
SR 731, 45-3, v2, 20p. [1838]
Claims of settlers on reservation lands prior to the Klamath, Modoc, and Snake treaty of 14 Oct. 1864 which established said reserve.

37. Ute Indians in Colorado. 8 Feb.
SED 62 (pts. 1 and 2), 45-3, v4, 63p. [1831]
Negotiations with the Utes for extinguishment of their title to lands in Colorado; agreement of 9 Nov. 1878 involving land cessions.

38. Annual Report of the Smithsonian Institution. 8 Feb.
SMD 59, 45-3, v3, 575p. [1835]
Research related to the American Indian.

39. On the Case of Col. Collins. 8 Feb.
SR 736, 45-3, v2, 6p. [1838]
Indian campaign of 1859 in California.

40. Negotiations with the Indians of Colorado. 8 Feb.
HED 84, 45-3, v16, 9p. [1858]
Negotiations with the Utes for a cession of land; agreement made 9 Nov. 1878.

41. Great and Little Osages. 10 Feb.
HR 106, 45-3, v1, 1p. [1866]
Proceeds due them for lands sold in Kansas under the treaty of 21 Jan. 1867.

42. Report on the Poncas. 10 Feb.
HR 107, 45-3, v1, 2p. [1866]
Shameful treatment of the tribe by the government; reservation in Dakota granted under the treaties of 12 Mar. 1858, and 10 Mar. 1865, is ceded to the Sioux without consultation with them; removed to Indian Territory.

43. Affairs in Indian Territory. 11 Feb.
SR 744, 45-3, v3, 1140p. [1839]
Protests of the various Indian councils and delegates against the formation of a territorial government; Indian citizenship; lands claimed by railroads; establishment of a U.S. court with jurisdiction over the territory; representation in Congress.

44. Exploration Near Pagosa Springs, Colorado. 12 Feb.
SED 65, 45-3, v4, 27p. [1831]
Plans for a fort to be located there; near the proposed consolidated Ute reservation; Ute beliefs regarding geological phenomena.

45. Escape of Cheyennes from Fort Robinson. 12 Feb.
SMD 64, 45-3, v1, 49p. [1833]
During Jan. of 1879 in Nebraska; Indians subsequently slaughtered by U.S. forces.

46. Resol. of Sen. Allison. 12 Feb.
SMD 65, 45-3, v1, 1p. [1833]
Asks examination be made of the removal of Northern Cheyennes from the Sioux reservation to Indian Territory, their return to Sioux country, their capture, escape, slaughter, and recapture.

47. On the Relief of the Winnebagoes. 12 Feb.
SR 747, 45-3, v2, 3p. [1838]
Removal of the tribe from Wiscon-

sin under the treaty of 16 June 1838; removal from Minnesota under a Congressional act of 1863; removal of scattered bands to Nebraska under the treaty of 1866; condition of those Winnebagoes who returned to Wisconsin.

48. On the Relief of J. Spencer and J. Mead. 12 Feb.
SR 749, 45-3, v2, 1p. [1838]
Supplies furnished the Kansas Indians.

49. Homesteads on Public Lands. 12 Feb.
SR 750, 45-3, v2, 2p. [1838]
Establishment of a colony in northwestern Kansas; would check Indian hostilities.

50. R-P of A. Dart. 12 Feb.
SR 754, 45-3, v2, 2p. [1838]
Former Supt. of Indian Affairs in Oregon.

51. Mem. of the State Grange of Texas. 13 Feb.
SMD 70, 45-3, v1, 2p. [1833]
That treaty stipulations with tribes in Indian Territory be observed by the U.S.

52. On the Relief of H. Fuller et al. 15 Feb.
SR 768, 45-3, v2, 4p. [1838]
Sureties for the late Supt. of Indian Affairs in Washington Territory.

53. Mem. of Cherokee, Creek, Chickasaw, Seminole, and Choctaw Delegates. 19 Feb.
SMD 73, 45-3, v1, 2p. [1833]
Against establishment of a U.S. court in Indian Territory, the bill which will destroy tribal relations, etc.

54. Survey of the Rogue River, Oregon. 22 Feb.
HED 97, 45-3, v16, 9p. [1858]
Indian half-breed settlers in the river valley.

55. On the Case of M. Harris. 26 Feb.
SR 847, 45-3, v2, 1p. [1838]
Service in the Creek war of 1836.

56. On the Relief of J. Dorsey and W. Shepard. 27 Feb.
SR 853, 45-3, v2, 4p. [1838]
Supplies to troops engaged in the Paiute war of 1860 in Utah Territory.

57. Resol. of the Nebraska Legis. 28 Feb.
SMD 79, 45-3, v1, 10p. [1833]
Removal of the Santee Sioux from Knox county to the old Ponca reservation which was vacated by the Spotted Tail band of Sioux.

58. On the Case of Maj. Haller. 28 Feb.
SR 860, 45-3, v2, 4p. [1838]
Oregon Indian war of 1855-1856.

59. Statements of Appropriations. 3 Mar.
HMD 34, 45-3, v3, 89p. [1863]
During the 3rd session, 45th Congress; Indian expenses.

60. Lands to Indians in Severalty. 3 Mar.
HR 165, 45-3, v1, 3p. [1866]
Allotment of lands in severalty on all reservations outside of Indian Territory; legislation proposed; aid to civilization; break-up of tribal relations.

61. Bands of Chippewas in Wisconsin. 3 Mar.
HR 166, 45-3, v1, 2p. [1866]
Consolidation of the Lac de Flambeau, Bad River, and Lec Court Oreilles bands, and allotment of lands in severalty.

62. Equal Rights to All Religious Denominations Among Indians. 3 Mar.
HR 167, 45-3, v1, 2p. [1866]
Denominations should have equal access to Indian reservations.

63. Organization of Oklahoma Territory. 3 Mar.
HR 188, 45-3, v2, 38p. [1867]
To provide a territorial form of government for Indian Territory; treaty relations with tribes in Indian Territory.

64. R-P of A. Heinrici. 3 Mar.
HR 247, 45-3, v2, 1p. [1867]
Service in Black Hawk war of 1832, and in the Florida wars.

65. On the Case of M. Spencer. 3 Mar.
HR 253, 45-3, v2, 2p. [1867]
Daughter of Capt. Dunn who was killed at Fort Mims in the Creek war of 1812-1813.

66. On the Relief of M. Kirby. 3 Mar.
HR 263, 45-3, v2, 4p. [1867]
Service in the Seminole war of 1836-1838 in Florida; took part in Cherokee removal of 1838.

67. Pensions to Teamsters and Indians. 3 Mar.
HR 264, 45-3, v2, 2p. [1867]
Loyal Indians who served in the War of 1812.

68. Pensions to Teamsters and Expressmen. 3 Mar.

HR 268, 45-3, v2, 2p. [1867]
Service in the War of 1812; had to cross lands occupied by hostile Indians who were loyal to Great Britain.

69. Resol. of Rep. Springer. 18 Mar.
HMD 3, 46-1, v1, 3p. [1876]
The Com. on Indian Affairs shall report matters relating to the expenses of the Indian Dept.

70. Estimates of Appropriations. 19 Mar.
SED 1, 46-1, v1, 106p. [1869]
To complete the fiscal year ending 30 June 1880; Indian expenses.

71. Resol. of Sen. Rollins. 1 Apr.
SMD 18, 46-1, v1, 1p. [1873]
Com. on Indian Affairs shall receive the estimates of the Indian Dept., and report the annual appropriation bill.

72. Surveys West of the 100th Meridian. 7 Apr.
SED 11, 46-1, v1, 3p. [1869]
Sec. of War asks appropriation to continue said surveys; important in establishing posts for controlling Indians.

73. Protest of Cherokee, Creek, and Choctaw Delegates. 8 May.
HMD 13, 46-1, v1, 7p. [1876]
Against organization of a territorial government over Indian Territory.

74. Resol. of Sen. Vest. 13 May.
SMD 33, 46-1, v1, 1p. [1873]
Asks information on lands within Indian Territory which were ceded to the U.S., and whether these lands are now occupied.

75. Message on Occupation of Indian Territory by White Settlers. 16 May.
SED 20, 46-1, v1, 34p. [1869]
Information on settlers, and what has been done to prevent them from entering the Territory.

76. Amount Due the Choctaw Nation. 16 May.
HR 4, 46-1, v1, 4p. [1934]
Claim arising from land sales under the treaty of 27 Sept. 1830; settlement under the treaty of 1855.

77. Message on Lands in Indian Territory. 26 May.
SED 26, 46-1, v1, 6p. [1869]
On lands ceded to the U.S. by the treaties of 1866 with the Cherokees, Creeks, and Seminoles; what tribes are being settled on those lands; etc.

78. R-P of Persons in Baxter Springs, Kansas. 11 June.
HR 13, 46-1, v1, 2p. [1934]
Rejects their request to settle on Quapaw lands in Indian Territory.

79. Industrial Training Schools for Indian Youths. 14 June.
HR 29, 46-1, v1, 3p. [1934]
Under treaties with the Cheyennes, Arapahoes, Kiowas, Comanches, Crows, Navajoes, Sioux, Utes, Northern Cheyennes, and Northern Arapahoes; establish schools in vacant military posts.

80. Resol. of Sen. Walker. 16 June.
SMD 41, 46-1, v1, 1p. [1873]
Asks information on the following Indian wars: the war in Oregon, Idaho, California, and Nevada in 1865-1868; the Cheyenne, Arapaho, Kiowa, and Comanche war of 1868-1869 in Kansas, Colorado, and Indian Territory; the Modoc war of 1872-1873; the Apache war of 1873 in Arizona; the Kiowa, Comanche, and Cheyenne war of 1874-1875 in Kansas, Colorado, Texas, Indian Territory, and New Mexico; the Northern Cheyenne and Sioux war of 1876-1877; the Nez Percé war of 1877; the Bannock war of 1878; and the Northern Cheyenne war of 1878-1879.

81. Removal of J. Bell et al. from the Cherokee Nation. 20 June.
SED 29, 46-1, v1, 5p. [1869]
Cherokees removed from lands not considered open to settlement.

82. Equal Rights to Religious Denominations. 25 June.
HR 32, 46-1, v1, 1p. [1934]
On Indian reservations.

83. Statements of Appropriations. 1 July.
HMD 22, 46-1, v1, 18p. [1876]
During the 1st session, 46th Congress; Indian expenses.

84. Disbursements of the Indian Dept. 25 Oct.
HED 6, 46-2, v15, 10p. [1916]
Year ending 30 June 1879.

85. Judgments of the Court of Claims. 1 Dec.
SMD 4, 46-2, v1, 8p. [1890]
Year ending 29 Nov. 1879; cases relevant to Indian affairs.

86. Annual Message to Congress with Documents; Pres. Hayes. 1 Dec.

HED 1, 46-2, v1-12, 9328p. [1902-1913]
Regulation of uncivilized tribes in Alaska; Ute and Apache hostilities; the "Indian policy" of the government, involving education, allotment, and disposal of unused reservation lands; suggests that Indian Territory may be opened to settlers; annual report of the Sec. of War (Serials 1903-1908); annual report of the Sec. of Interior (Serials 1910-1912); annual report of the Gen. Land Office (Serial 1910); annual report of the CIA (Serial 1910), including reports of Supts., agents, and schools; etc.

87. Annual Report of the Sec. of the Treasury. 1 Dec.
HED 2, 46-2, v13, 628p. [1914]
Year ending 30 June 1879; Indian expenses.

88. Estimates of Appropriations. 1 Dec.
HED 5, 46-2, v15, 267p. [1916]
Year ending 30 June 1881; Indian expenses.

89. Compensation of Citizen Volunteers. 4 Dec.
SED 2, 46-2, v1, 4p. [1882]
Those who participated during 1877 in the battle of Big Hole, Montana, against the Nez Percés.

90. R-P of M. Cahill. 4 Dec.
SR 17, 46-2, v1, 1p. [1893]
Indian battles in 1859.

91. Removal of Certain Cherokees. 8 Dec.
SED 6, 46-2, v1, 7p. [1882]
Arrest and removal of J. Bell et al. for settling on unauthorized lands in Indian Territory.

92. Squatters in Indian Territory. 9 Dec.
SED 10, 46-2, v1, 2p. [1882]
On operations to control their emigration into Indian Territory.

93. Protection of the Rio Grande Frontier. 9 Dec.
SR 40, 46-2, v1, 4p. [1893]
Depredations of Apaches and other tribes in Texas.

94. R-P of Officers of the Fifth Cavalry. 9 Dec.
SR 43, 46-2, v1, 7p. [1893]
Cavalry sent to fight the Sioux under Sitting Bull and Crazy Horse after Custer's death in 1876; possessions lost when steamer *J. Donald Cameron* sinks in the Missouri River.

95. Lands of Indian Tribes. 10 Dec.
HR 2, 46-2, v1, 3p. [1934]
Calls for a change in Indian policy; collect tribes on fewer reservations, and open freed lands for settlement.

96. Property in the Interior Dept. 15 Dec.
SED 15, 46-2, v1, 3p. [1882]
Including the OIA.

97. R-M of the Montana Legis. 16 Dec.
SR 57, 46-2, v1, 1p. [1893]
Establishment of a post near Henry's Lake to protect settlers from hostile Indians.

98. Mem. and Testimony on the Claim of B. Holladay. 17 Dec.
SMD 19, 46-2, v1, 89p. [1890]
Overland stage line from Kansas to Utah during 1862-1866 subject to Indian depredations.

1880

1. Petition of the St. Regis Indians. 6 Jan.
SMD 20, 46-2, v1, 4p. [1890]
Ask to be allowed to remain on their reservation in New York.

2. Payments Made to the Utes. 7 Jan.
SED 27, 46-2, v1, 6p. [1882]
For cession of lands in Colorado under the agreement of 13 Sept. 1873.

3. Mining Camps on Ute Reservations. 7 Jan.
SED 29, 46-2, v1, 98p. [1882]
On the location, and number of camps; efforts made to remove the miners from the Colorado reservations; etc.

4. Ute Indians in Colorado. 7 Jan.
SED 31, 46-2, v1, 274p. [1882]
Correspondence on the Utes concerning such items as their hostilities towards whites, encroachments on their reservations, etc.

5. R-C of J. Dorsey and W. Shepard. 7 Jan.
SR 63, 46-2, v1, 4p. [1893]
Supplies to troops during Paiute outbreak of 1860 in Utah.

6. On the Relief of Capt. Campbell. 9 Jan.
HR 31, 46-2, v1, 10p. [1934]
Arrests in Alaska for selling liquor in Indian country.

7. On the Case of M. West. 9 Jan.
HR 73, 46-2, v1, 1p. [1934]
Service in Indian campaign of 1868.
8. R-M of S. Buchanan. 9 Jan.
HR 75, 46-2, v1, 2p. [1934]
Service in Black Hawk war, Cherokee removal, Rogue River war in Oregon, and other campaigns against the Indians.
9. R-C of F. Rinquet. 12 Jan.
SR 70, 46-2, v1, 1p. [1893]
Indian hostilities of 1878 in Oregon.
10. On the Relief of Capt. Campbell. 12 Jan.
SR 72, 46-2, v1, 16p. [1893]
Arrests made for sale of liquor in Indian country of Alaska.
11. On the Relief of Settlers in Kansas. 13 Jan.
SR 89, 46-2, v1, 2p. [1893]
On the Kansas Indian trust and diminished reserve lands.
12. Military Posts on the Rio Grande Frontier. 14 Jan.
HR 88, 46-2, v1, 6p. [1934]
To stop Indian incursions into Texas.
13. Estimates of Deficiencies. 15 Jan.
HED 24, 46-2, v21, 38p. [1922]
Appropriations for the year ending 30 June 1880; expenses of a special session of the Montana Legis. due to Indian depredations.
14. On the Case of E. Boudinot. 16 Jan.
HR 120, 46-2, v1, 6p. [1934]
Cherokee Indian sells tobacco in Indian Territory; conflict between internal revenue laws and the treaty of 19 July 1866.
15. California War Bonds. 16 Jan.
HR 123, 46-2, v1, 2p. [1934]
Issued in 1852 to cover expenses of suppressing Indian hostilities.
16. On the Case of J. Nix. 19 Jan.
SR 109, 46-2, v1, 1p. [1893]
Service in Sioux outbreak of 1862 in Minnesota.
17. Pensions to Soldiers. 19 Jan.
HR 127, 46-2, v1, 7p. [1934]
In the Creek, Black Hawk, and Florida wars.
18. R-C of J. Hunt. 21 Jan.
SR 131, 46-2, v1, 1p. [1893]
Indian depredations in Oregon.
19. Report on a Wagon Road. 21 Jan.
SR 133, 46-2, v1, 1p. [1893]
From Sidney, Nebraska, via Forts Robinson and Sheridan, to the Rosebud agency on the Sioux reservation.
20. On the Case of J. Dolan. 21 Jan.
SR 138, 46-2, v1, 2p. [1893]
Service in the Apache, Comanche, and Kiowa campaigns of 1855-1861 in Arizona and Indian Territory.
21. R-C of Kansas. 21 Jan.
SR 139, 46-2, v1, 3p. [1893]
Suppression of Indian hostilities in 1861.
22. On the Relief of J. Chickering. 21 Jan.
SR 148, 46-2, v1, 12p. [1893]
Court-martialed for drunkenness while on an Indian campaign in Texas during 1874.
23. R-C of Montana Citizens. 23 Jan.
HR 134, 46-2, v1, 2p. [1934]
For service in the Nez Percé war of 1877.
24. Completion of Fort Assiniboine, Montana. 27 Jan.
SED 57, 46-2, v3, 2p. [1884]
Part of the northern chain of military posts, which includes Forts Pembina, Totten, Buford, and Assiniboine; new post needed near Wood Mountain, Montana; route used by hostile Indians coming from Canada to the Missouri and Yellowstone Rivers, and Indian agencies in Dakota.
25. San Antonio and Mexican Border Railway Company. 28 Jan.
HR 165, 46-2, v1, 9p. [1934]
Would connect forts on the Texas frontier, and aid in the control of hostile Indians.
26. R-P of Wolff and Brown. 29 Jan.
SR 166, 46-2, v1, 5p. [1893]
Horses taken by troops during 1865 in Colorado; Indians were threatening.
27. On the Case of the Widow of Maj. Thornburgh. 2 Feb.
SR 173, 46-2, v1, 1p. [1893]
Battle against the Utes in Colorado.
28. Indian Trust Funds. 2 Feb.
SR 186, 46-2, v1, 12p. [1893]
Bill authorizing the Sec. of Interior to deposit said funds in the treasury in lieu of investment.
29. On the Case of W. Gaines. 3 Feb.
SR 202, 46-2, v1, 1p. [1893]
Service in the Creek war of 1813.

30. Bands of Chippewas in Wisconsin. 4 Feb.
HR 175, 46-2, v1, 2p. [1934]
Bill to consolidate the Indians, allot lands in severalty, and sell unalloted lands.

31. Contingent Expenses of the Interior Dept. 5 Feb.
HED 38, 46-2, v21, 22p. [1922]
Year ending 30 June 1879; OIA.

32. Title to Lands in Ohio. 5 Feb.
HR 178, 46-2, v1, 2p. [1934]
Land grant to a Shawnee chief under the treaty of 29 Sept. 1817, and the supplemented treaty of 17 Sept. 1818.

33. Titles at Hot Springs, Arkansas. 5 Feb.
HR 179, 46-2, v1, 8p. [1934]
Quapaw title extinguished by the treaty of 1818.

34. Frontier Defense Expenses of Texas. 6 Feb.
HR 184, 46-2, v1, 4p. [1934]
In controlling hostile Indians.

35. Claims of States Against the U S. 9 Feb.
SED 74, 46-2, v3, 199p. [1884]
Claims of the "second grand class" are those arising from the suppression of Indian wars and hostilities; the claims of Texas arising from Indian depredations on the frontiers of that State.

36. R-P of B. Holladay. 9 Feb.
SR 216, 46-2, v1, 18p. [1893]
Indian depredations of 1860-1866 while carrying the mail between the Missouri River and Salt Lake City, Utah.

37. On the Relief of the Winnebagoes. 11 Feb.
SR 253, 46-2, v1, 5p. [1893]
Land cessions and removals under the treaties of 1838, 1846, 1855, and 1866; division of annuities between Nebraska and Wisconsin Winnebagoes.

38. R-M of J. Beeson. 11 Feb.
SR 254, 46-2, v1, 1p. [1893]
Services against hostile Indians.

39. R-P of E. Gurley. 11 Feb.
HR 201, 46-2, v2, 3p. [1935]
Attorney in the trial of 19 whites for the murder of seven Caddo Indians in Texas during 1858.

40. Mission of St. James. 13 Feb.
HR 254, 46-2, v2, 2p. [1935]
Among the Indians of Oregon.

41. R-P of W. Redus. 13 Feb.
HR 255, 46-2, v2, 2p. [1935]
Osage depredations of 1872 in Indian Territory.

42. R-C of H. Warren. 13 Feb.
HR 256, 46-2, v2, 3p. [1935]
Kiowa depredations of 1871 in Texas.

43. Mem. of Indian Delegates. 16 Feb.
SMD 41, 46-2, v1, 9p. [1890]
Against organization of a territorial government over Indian Territory.

44. On the Case of Dr. Appel. 17 Feb.
SR 271, 46-2, v1, 2p. [1893]
Physician during 1877-1879 at the Mescalero Apache agency, New Mexico.

45. Settlers on Osage Lands. 17 Feb.
SR 274, 46-2, v1, 3p. [1893]
On Osage trust and diminished reserve lands in Kansas; open for settlement under the treaty of 20 Sept. 1865.

46. Contracts for Indian Supplies. 18 Feb.
SED 87, 46-2, v3, 5p. [1884]
Information as to interests of members of the Board of Indian Com'rs being involved in particular contracts.

47. On the Case of A. McFadden. 20 Feb.
HR 309, 46-2, v2, 2p. [1935]
Service in Black Hawk war of 1832 in Illinois.

48. On the Relief of Lieut. Farrow. 24 Feb.
SR 297, 46-2, v1, 1p. [1893]
Service in the Bannock war of 1878 in Oregon.

49. Report of the Public Lands Commission. 25 Feb.
HED 46, 46-2, v22, 790p. [1923]
Codification of laws, and recommendations for legislation; Indian reservations in Utah; etc.

50. Resol. of Sen. Carpenter. 3 Mar.
SMD 46, 46-2, v1, 1p. [1890]
Asks investigation as to whether or not the Congress, under existing treaties, has a right to make Indian Territory a separate judicial district; if so what would be the jurisdiction of the courts established.

51. Report on a Court in Texas. 2 Mar.
SR 332, 46-2, v1, 1p. [1893]
Bill to establish a court in Texas which would have jurisdiction over that part of Indian Territory occupied by the Choctaws and Chickasaws.

52. R-C of A. Dart. 3 Mar.
SR 333, 46-2, v1, 2p. [1893]

Late Supt. of Indian Affairs in Oregon Territory.

53. Condition of Affairs in Alaska. 5 Mar.
SED 105, 46-2, v4, 34p. [1885]
Relations with Indians; Indian trade; employed Indians; effect of liquor traffic.

54. Permanent and Indefinite Appropriations. 5 Mar.
SR 334, 46-2, v1, 10p. [1893]
Indian expenditures during 1877-1879.

55. Police for Indian Reservations. 9 Mar.
HR 430, 46-2, v2, 2p. [1935]
Extension of criminal laws of the U.S. to Indian reservations.

56. Creek Orphan Fund. 9 Mar.
HR 431, 46-2, v2, 2p. [1935]
Fund, arising from the treaty of 24 Mar. 1832, needs to be reimbursed by the U.S.

57. Exclusion of Reservation Indians from Texas. 9 Mar.
HR 432, 46-2, v2, 1p. [1935]
Said Indians were in the habit of hunting in Texas; led to depredations.

58. Absentee Shawnee Lands. 9 Mar.
HR 433, 46-2, v2, 2p. [1935]
Sale of lands in Kansas to settlers.

59. Indian War Expenses of Kansas. 9 Mar.
HR 440, 46-2, v2, 1p. [1935]
Expenses of the State in suppressing Indian hostilities during 1865-1870.

60. On the Relief of T. Little. 9 Mar.
HR 450, 46-2, v2, 2p. [1935]
Service in campaigns against the Sioux in 1867-1868, against the Kiowas and Comanches, and against the Kiowas in 1872.

61. Message on an Agreement with the Utes. 10 Mar.
SED 114 (pts. 1 and 2), 46-2, v4, 5p. [1885]
Dated 3 Mar. 1880; cession of their reservation in Colorado; allotments of land in severalty (part 2, dated 26 May 1880, urges ratification of the agreement to avoid open hostilities).

62. Annual Report of the Smithsonian Institution. 10 Mar.
SMD 54, 46-2, v2, 631p. [1891]
Research related to the American Indian; Indian mounds in Indiana and Florida; Indian shell-heaps and relics.

63. Judicial System of Montana. 10 Mar.
HR 470, 46-2, v2, 4p. [1935]
Establishment of a judicial district in eastern Montana; cases arising on the Indian reservations located there; raids from Canada by Sitting Bull's band of Sioux.

64. Removal of Indians to Indian Territory. 10 Mar.
HR 474, 46-2, v2, 2p. [1935]
Settlement of tribes in said territory should receive Congressional approval; for the safety of whites and civilized Indians, no wild tribes should be settled there.

65. R-P of L. Mitchell. 10 Mar.
HR 481, 46-2, v2, 3p. [1935]
Service against Utes and Bannocks in 1860.

66. Report of the Com'r of Fish and Fisheries. 15 Mar.
SMD 59, 46-2, v3, 897p. [1892]
Indians on the fishery reservation at McCloud River, California.

67. Accounts Between the U.S. and Florida. 17 Mar.
SR 378, 46-2, v3, 3p. [1895]
Claims arising from the Seminole war of 1855-1857.

68. Land Patents in Indian Territory. 19 Mar.
SED 124, 46-2, v4, 12p. [1885]
Issued to the Cherokees, Choctaws, and Creeks; maps of tract locations filed by railroad companies, but not acted upon.

69. On the Relief of J. Hensley et al. 23 Mar.
SR 398, 46-2, v3, 1p. [1895]
Com. on Indian Affairs reports.

70. Surveys West of the Mississippi River. 25 Mar.
SED 118, 46-2, v4, 2p. [1885]
Appropriations needed; important in locating posts to control the Indians.

71. Condition of Affairs in Alaska. 31 Mar.
SED 132 (pts. 1 and 2), 46-2, v4, 49p. [1885]
Indian relations; Indian trade; effects of liquor traffic.

72. Pacific Railway System. 1 Apr.
HR 691, 46-2, v3, 6p. [1936]
Land grants in Indian Territory.

73. Military Post in Montana. 2 Apr.
SED 134, 46-2, v4, 3p. [1885]
Protection of settlements of Judith Basin and the Muscleshell from hostile Indians; between Forts Custer and Assiniboine.

74. On the Relief of J. Dolan. 6 Apr.
HR 696, 46-2, v3, 1p. [1936]
Killed by Utes in 1879; Colorado.

75. On the Relief of W. Helm. 6 Apr.
HR 697, 46-2, v3, 1p. [1936]
Service in Nez Percé war of 1878 in Montana.

76. School Lands to Kansas. 6 Apr.
HR 721, 46-2, v3, 2p. [1936]
Lands to State for educational purposes in lieu of those situated in Indian reservations.

77. Osage Trust Lands. 6 Apr.
HR 722, 46-2, v3, 1p. [1936]
Sale of said lands at auction.

78. On the Relief of H. Taylor. 6 Apr.
HR 728, 46-2, v3, 2p. [1936]
Sale of Osage trust lands and Cherokee strip lands in Kansas.

79. Indemnity Lands to Wisconsin. 6 Apr.
HR 736, 46-2, v3, 4p. [1936]
To replace lands within the Chippewa reservations established under the treaty of 13 Sept. 1854.

80. On the Relief of A. Graham. 6 Apr.
HR 748, 46-2, v3, 1p. [1936]
Kiowa and Comanche depredations.

81. R-P of A. Sharp. 6 Apr.
HR 749, 46-2, v3, 1p. [1936]
Taken captive by the Sioux in 1857 near Spirit Lake, Iowa.

82. On the Relief of S. McDougall and C. Wilder. 6 Apr.
HR 750, 46-2, v3, 2p. [1936]
On title to Shawnee lands in Kansas, under the treaty of 10 May 1854.

83. New York Indian Lands in Kansas. 6 Apr.
HR 751 (pts. 1 and 2), 46-2, v3, 10p. [1936]
Sale of said lands.

84. Industrial Training Schools for Indians. 6 Apr.
HR 752, 46-2, v3, 4p. [1936]
Under treaties with, notably, the Cheyennes, Arapahoes, Kiowas, Comanches, Crows, Navajoes, Sioux, Utes, Northern Cheyennes, and Northern Arapahoes.

85. Unpaid Accounts of the Indian Bureau. 6 Apr.
HR 753, 46-2, v3, 2p. [1936]
Claims for services rendered, and supplies furnished for the Indian service.

86. Courts of Justice in Alaska. 6 Apr.
HR 754, 46-2, v3, 6p. [1936]
Indian population; rights of all but the uncivilized tribes are stated in the U.S.-Russian treaty of 3 Mar. 1867.

87. Territory of Oklahoma. 6 Apr.
HR 755 (pts. 1 and 2), 46-2, v3, 12p. [1936]
Establishment of a court in Indian Territory with jurisdiction over Indians; recommends allotment of land in severalty, and citizenship.

88. San Antonio and Mexican Border Railway Company. 7 Apr.
HR 756 (pts. 1 and 2), 46-2, v3, 13p. [1936]
Protection of the Texas frontier from Indian raids.

89. On the Relief of M. Kahn. 7 Apr.
HR 832, 46-2, v3, 2p. [1936]
Native of Afghanistan enrolled in U.S. Army as a Blackfoot Indian.

90. Completion of a Road from Fort Bridge to the Uintah Agency. 8 Apr.
SED 143, 46-2, v4, 1p. [1885]
Because of the Ute Indians.

91. On the Case of M. Spencer. 8 Apr.
HR 859, 46-2, v3, 2p. [1936]
Father served in Creek Indian war.

92. R-C of J. Dorsey and W. Shepard. 8 Apr.
HR 864, 46-2, v3, 4p. [1936]
Paiute depredations of 1860 in Utah Territory.

93. R-C of J. Dorsey and W. Shepard. 8 Apr.
HR 865, 46-2, v3, 4p. [1936]
Paiute depredations of 1860 in Utah Territory.

94. R-M of J. Sutter. 8 Apr.
HR 867, 46-2, v3, 4p. [1936]
Land-claim; active in controlling the Indians of southern California beginning in 1838.

95. R-C of S. Yeomans and A. Leech. 8 Apr.
HR 872, 46-2, v3, 5p. [1936]
Expenses at Iowa land-office; extra clerks authorized for Kansas offices to handle sales of Osage and other lands.

96. R-M of A. Meacham. 8 Apr.
HR 899, 46-2, v3, 2p. [1936]

Appointed to a peace commission sent to the Modocs of California; attacked at a council in 1873 with the Modocs.

97. R-P of L. Volin. 8 Apr.
HR 905, 46-2, v3, 3p. [1936]
Attempt to cut timber on the Sioux reservation in Dakota during 1872 is stopped by Yanktonais Sioux.

98. R-P of M. Kirby. 8 Apr.
HR 926, 46-2, v3, 4p. [1936]
Service in Seminole war of 1836-1838 in Florida.

99. R-C of Capt. Weston. 8 Apr.
HR 946, 46-2, v3, 1p. [1936]
Nez Percé depredations in Montana.

100. R-C of I. Slocum. 8 Apr.
HR 999, 46-2, v4, 2p. [1937]
Sioux war of 1857.

101. R-C of E. Lieburg. 8 Apr.
HR 1000, 46-2, v4, 1p. [1937]
Spoliations of U.S. troops during Indian raid.

102. Chippewas in Minnesota and Dakota. 14 Apr.
SMD 71, 46-2, v2, 2p. [1891]
On their condition; recommends consolidation of all Chippewas on the White Earth reservation, along with the sale of all other reserves.

103. Sale of Bonds Held in Trust for Shawnees. 14 Apr.
SMD 72, 46-2, v2, 2p. [1891]
From sale of lands in Kansas; for distribution *per capita* through the CIA.

104. R-C of C. Denton. 14 Apr.
SR 475, 46-2, v3, 11p. [1895]
Indians settled on his land in Oregon by the U.S. Army during 1854-1860.

105. Ethnology of North American Indians. 17 Apr.
HMD 35, 46-2, v4, 3p. [1931]
Bureau of Ethnology, Smithsonian Institution, requests appropriation to continue work.

106. Sioux Reservation. 19 Apr.
SED 151, 46-2, v4, 2p. [1885]
On erroneous surveys of the reserve west of Big Stone Lake, in Dakota; estimate for re-survey.

107. R-M of H. Wilson. 21 Apr.
SR 510, 46-2, v5, 1p. [1897]
Service in the Black Hawk war.

108. Letter on the Cherokee Nation. 23 Apr.
SMD 76, 46-2, v2, 5p. [1891]
Payments for the relief of the Cherokees out of funds arising from sale of their lands in Indian Territory.

109. Letter from the Cherokee Delegation. 23 Apr.
SMD 77, 46-2, v2, 3p. [1891]
On the appropriation for the relief of the Cherokees to be deducted from funds due the tribe for sale of lands in Indian Territory.

110. On the Relief of L. Morris. 24 Apr.
HR 1131, 46-2, v4, 2p. [1937]
Bonded Indian traders in the Choctaw Nation.

111. On the Case of W, Barnhard. 24 Apr.
HR 1204, 46-2, v4, 2p. [1937]
Indian campaign of 1863 in Dakota.

112. On the Case of G. Hord. 24 Apr.
HR 1207, 46-2, v4, 1p. [1937]
Indian campaign of 1862 in Minnesota.

113. R-P of F. Cornell. 24 Apr.
HR 1222, 46-2, v4, 1p. [1937]
Service in Montana Indian war of 1867.

114. R-C of Florida. 24 Apr.
HR 1230, 46-2, v4, 3p. [1937]
Surrounding the Seminole war of 1855-1857.

115. Sale of Fort Logan, Montana. 27 Apr.
SR 520, 46-2, v5, 1p. [1897]
Now 100 miles from the scene of Indian raids.

116. R-M of the Minnesota Legis. 27 Apr.
SR 523, 46-2, v5, 1p. [1897]
Service in Sioux outbreak of 1862 in Minnesota.

117. On the Relief of J. Bacon. 27 Apr.
SR 524, 46-2, v5, 2p. [1897]
Service in Gen. Sully's campaign of 1864 against the Sioux of the Upper Missouri.

118. Employees of the Interior Dept. 28 Apr.
SED 162, 46-2, v4, 23p. [1885]
During 1879 in the OIA.

119. Investigation of the Treasury Dept. 28 Apr.
SR 539, 46-2, v5, 316p. [1897]
Accounts of the Indian Dept.; Indian expenditures.

120. Lands in Severalty to Peorias and Miamies. 28 Apr.
HR 1319, 46-2, v4, 2p. [1937]
Allotment of lands in Indian Territory; sale of Miami lands in Kansas; distribution of trust funds; steps toward citizenship.

121. On the Relief of H. Warren. 30 Apr.
SR 551 (pts. 1 and 2), 46-2, v5, 20p. [1897]
Kiowa depredations of 1871 in Texas.

122. On the Case of A. McAuley. 30 Apr.
SR 557, 46-2, v5, 1p. [1897]
Service in the Seminole and Creek wars.

123. Ute Indian Outbreak. 1 May.
HMD 38, 46-2, v4, 205p. [1931]
Testimony taken from whites and Indians on the outbreak in Colorado.

124. Settlers on the Uncompahgre Park in Colorado. 4 May.
SED 169, 46-2, v4, 3p. [1885]
Indian claims to land questioned.

125. R-C of Capt. Campbell. 5 May.
SR 573, 46-2, v6, 11p. [1898]
Arrests made for sale of liquor in Indian country of Alaska.

126. On the Relief of B. Moreland. 6 May.
SR 575, 46-2, v6, 2p. [1898]
Land in Minnesota encorporated into the Winnebago reservation during 1856-1861, under the treaty of 27 Feb. 1855.

127. Klamath River Reservation. 7 May.
HR 1354, 46-2, v4, 5p. [1937]
Restoration of the California reservation to the public domain; Indians removed to the Hoopah reservation in 1862.

128. R-P of T. Allcock. 8 May.
HR 1359, 46-2, v4, 1p. [1937]
Service in the Seminole war during 1837-1839 in Florida.

129. Transfer of the BIA. 8 May.
HR 1393, 46-2, v4, 2p. [1937]
From the Interior Dept. to the War Dept.

130. Great and Little Osages. 8 May.
HR 1395, 46-2, v4, 2p. [1937]
Sale of lands in Kansas under the treaty of 21 Jan. 1861.

131. Legislative, Executive, and Judicial Appropriation Bill. 10 May.
HR 1397, 46-2, v4, 2p. [1937]
Estimates and recommendations for 1880-1881; OIA.

132. Agreement with the Utes of Colorado. 11 May.
HR 1401, 46-2, v4, 8p. [1937]
Sale of their reservation; settlement in New Mexico and Utah.

133. On the Case of J. Black. 12 May.
HR 1419, 46-2, v4, 1p. [1937]
Forgery concerning a draft issued by the Indian Dept.

134. Claims for Supplies Furnished the Sioux of Minnesota. 12 May.
HR 1420, 46-2, v4, 2p. [1937]
During 1860-1862.

135. Cherokee and Arkansas River Railroad. 12 May.
HR 1422, 46-2, v4, 3p. [1937]
Through Indian Territory; right of way granted in the Cherokee treaty of 9 July 1866, the Creek treaty of 14 June 1866, the Kansas treaty of 5 Oct. 1859, and the Osage treaty of 29 Sept. 1865.

136. On the Case of J. Luskey. 12 May.
HR 1427, 46-2, v4, 1p. [1937]
Service in the Seminole war.

137. Creek Orphan Fund. 13 May.
SR 599, 46-2, v6, 3p. [1898]
Unwarranted handling of funds arising from the treaty of 24 Mar. 1832; bill to reimburse the fund.

138. White River Ute Commission Investigation. 14 May.
HED 83, 46-2, v24, 84p. [1925]
Testimony on the Ute outbreak in Colorado.

139. Alaska Territory. 17 May.
SED 179, 46-2, v4, 23p. [1885]
Conditions there, and transfer of jurisdiction from the War Dept. to the Treasury Dept.; Indian affairs; Indian trade; liquor traffic; fears of an uprising of the Sitkas.

140. On the Relief of Lieut. Payne. 18 May.
SR 624, 46-2, v6, 2p. [1898]
Property lost at Camp Supply, Indian Territory.

141. On the Relief of E. Byrne. 18 May.
SR 629, 46-2, v6, 1p. [1898]
Service with the Tenth Cavalry in Indian Territory.

142. On the Relief of W. Spencer. 21 May.
SR 654, 46-2, v6, 5p. [1898]
Service during the Sioux troubles of 1857 in Minnesota.

143. On the Case of A. Luettiwitz. 21 May.
HR 1502, 46-2, v4, 2p. [1937]
Injured in a Sioux attack on 9 Sept. 1876.

144. On the Case of Capt. Payne. 21 May.
HR 1503, 46-2, v4, 2p. [1937]
Service in White River Ute campaign of 1879.

145. Citizen Volunteers of Idaho and Washington. 21 May.

HR 1505, 46-2, v4, 2p. [1937]
Service in the Nez Percé war of 1877.

146. R-C of Heirs of R. Hurley. 21 May.
HR 1514, 46-2, v4, 7p. [1937]
Supplies to volunteers in the Paiute war of 1860 in Utah Territory.

147. R-C of Bowers and Richards. 21 May.
HR 1515, 46-2, v4, 2p. [1937]
Supplies to the Rio Verde reservation in Arizona during 1874.

148. R-C of W. Hooper and Company. 21 May.
HR 1516, 46-2, v4, 1p. [1937]
Supplies to the Rio Verde reservation in Arizona during 1874.

149. On the Case of E. Fish and Company. 21 May.
HR 1517, 46-2, v4, 1p. [1937]
Supplies to the San Carlos agency in 1873; Arizona.

150. On the Case of W. Hugus et al. 21 May.
HR 1518, 46-2, v4, 1p. [1937]
Supplies at the San Carlos reservation in Arizona; 1873.

151. Debt Due the Osages. 21 May.
HR 1519, 46-2, v4, 2p. [1937]
Frauds surrounding sale of lands in Kansas to railroads, under the Drum Creek treaty of 1868.

152. Duluth and Winnipeg Railroad Company. 21 May.
HR 1520, 46-2, v4, 1p. [1937]
Right of way through the Red Lake and Pembina reservations in Minnesota.

153. R-P of H. Wright. 21 May.
HR 1529, 46-2, v5, 2p. [1938]
Service in Seminole war in Florida.

154. Resources of Alaska. 27 May.
SED 192, 46-2, v5, 6p. [1886]
Indian affairs near Sitka; liquor production by Indians; Indian depredations when vessels arrive; Sitka and Chilcat hostilities.

155. Lands in Severalty to Indians. 28 May.
HR 1576, 46-2, v5, 10p. [1938]
An act of Congress, to allot lands in severalty, can legally alter provisions of treaties; this step is necessary in order for Indians to survive.

156. Removal of the Ponca Indians. 31 May.
SR 670, 46-2, v6, 534p. [1898]
From Dakota to Indian Territory in 1877; by a blunder in making the Sioux treaty of 1868, the Ponca reserve in Dakota was ceded to the Sioux; Poncas removed illegally; whole proceedings condemned in the report.

157. R-P on Behalf of A. Chapman. 1 June.
SR 691, 46-2, v7, 1p. [1899]
Scout during a campaign of 1874 against the Kiowas and Comanches in Indian Territory.

158. Timber Depredations. 2 June.
SMD 100, 46-2, v2, 3p. [1891]
Protection of Indian reservations from squatters and from those who would cut and remove timber is needed; depredations in Indian Territory.

159. R-C of J. Devine. 4 June.
HR 1587, 46-2, v5, 2p. [1938]
Spoliations by U.S. troops during the Sioux outbreak of 1862 in Minnesota.

160. R-C of A. Freitag. 4 June.
HR 1597, 46-2, v5, 1p. [1938]
Property taken by troops during Sioux outbreak of 1862 in Minnesota.

161. On the Relief of G. Smith. 4 June.
HR 1624, 46-2, v5, 2p. [1938]
Supt. of Indian Affairs in Montana; defaults on accounts.

162. On the Relief of F. Yates et al. 4 June.
HR 1637, 46-2, v5, 4p. [1938]
Transportation of property; removal of Whetstone agency from White River, Dakota, to the new Sioux reservation in 1872-1873.

163. R-P of M. Heintzelman. 4 June.
HR 1645, 46-2, v5, 1p. [1938]
Service in the Florida, California, and Oregon Indian wars.

164. R-P of S. Hathaway. 4 June.
HR 1649, 46-2, v5, 1p. [1938]
Killed by Indians in Kansas; 1865.

165. Amendment of Revised Statutes. 4 June.
HR 1657, 46-2, v5, 2p. [1938]
To allow pensions for volunteers in the Sioux outbreak of 1862 in Minnesota.

166. R-P of M. Heintzelman. 5 June.
SR 699, 46-2, v7, 1p. [1899]
Service in campaigns against Indians in California and Oregon.

167. Removal of the Northern Cheyennes. 8 June.
SR 708, 46-2, v7, 353p. [1899]
From the Sioux reservation in Dakota to Indian Territory in 1877;

return of some bands to Dakota; recommendations made.

168. Letter on a Private Land Claim in Arizona. 9 June.
SED 207, 46-2, v5, 43p. [1886]
Land originally granted to the Indian pueblo of Tumacacori.

169. Title to Lands for Cemetery Purposes. 9 June.
HR 1709, 46-2, v5, 1p. [1938]
To the Senecas on the Allegany reservation in New York.

170. R-C of T. McCormick. 9 June.
HR 1721, 46-2, v5, 2p. [1938]
Cheyenne attack on Union Pacific railroad workers in 1867.

171. R-C of H. Buggert. 9 June.
HR 1725, 46-2, v5, 3p. [1938]
Sioux war of 1862 in Minnesota.

172. Wagons for the Indian Service. 11 June.
SED 210, 46-2, v5, 30p. [1886]
On rejection of bids alleged to be lower than those finally accepted.

173. R-C of Dodd, Brown, and Company. 12 June.
SR 714, 46-2, v7, 1p. [1899]
Depredations by various Indian tribes.

174. R-P of R. Hall. 12 June.
HR 1755, 46-2, v5, 2p. [1938]
Disease contracted in the Cherokee Nation.

175. R-P of H. Hoffman. 12 June.
HR 1770, 46-2, v5, 2p. [1938]
Indian hostilities of 1863 in Minnesota.

176. R-C of J. Bridger. 12 June.
HR 1771, 46-2, v5, 2p. [1938]
Trade with Indians during 1843-1857 in Utah.

177. San Antonio and Mexican Railway Company. 14 June.
SR 716, 46-2, v7, 9p. [1899]
Would connect forts on the Texas frontier; control of Indian raids.

178. Kansas City, Fort Scott, and Gulf Railroad Company. 14 June.
SR 717, 46-2, v7, 2p. [1899]
Constructed through the New York Indian and Cherokee neutral lands in Kansas.

179. Statements of Appropriations. 16 June.
HMD 47, 46-2, v4, 110p. [1931]
During the 2d session, 46th Congress; Indian expenses.

180. Disbursements of the Indian Dept. 29 Oct.
HED 6, 46-3, v15, 10p. [1965]
Year ending 30 June 1880.

181. Judgments of the Court of Claims. 6 Dec.
SMD 5, 46-3, v1, 13p. [1944]
Cases relevant to Indian affairs.

182. Annual Message to Congress with Documents; Pres. Hayes. 6 Dec.
HED 1, 46-3, v1-12, 10,587p. [1951-1962]
Indian education; Ute agreement; end of hostilities of the Apaches, and Sitting Bull's band of Sioux; allotment; annual report of the Sec. of War (Serials 1952-1957); annual report of the Sec. of Interior (Serials 1959-1961); annual report of the Gen. Land Office (Serial 1959); annual report of the CIA (Serial 1959), including Indian police, railroads through Indian lands, invasion of Indian Territory, and reports of Supts. and agents; etc.

183. Annual Report of the Sec. of the Treasury. 6 Dec.
HED 2, 46-3, v13, 598p. [1963]
Year ending 30 June 1880; Indian expenses.

184. Estimates of Appropriations. 6 Dec.
HED 5, 46-3, v15, 275p. [1965]
Year ending 30 June 1882; Indian expenses.

185. Permanent Annual Appropriations. 8 Dec.
SED 3, 46-3, v1, 43p. [1941]
Amounts paid from 1865 to 1879; Indian expenses.

186. R-C of Powers and Newman, and D. and B. Powers. 10 Dec.
HR 7, 46-3, v1, 2p. [1982]
Cheyenne and Arapaho depredations of 1867 between Forts Harker and Wallace.

187. Mem. of G. Jackson et al. 20 Dec.
SMD 13, 46-3, v1, 2p. [1944]
Ask permission to settle on public lands in Indian Territory.

188. List of Private Claims. 21 Dec.
SMD 14, 46-3, v2 (pts. 1 and 2), 2056p. [1945-1946]
From the 14th to the 46th Congress; object of claims listed, revealing relevance of particular claims for Indian affairs.

189. Confederated Otoe-Missouria Reservation. 21 Dec.
HR 31, 46-3, v1, 2p. [1982]

Indians, in council, agree to sell reserves in Nebraska and Kansas, and to remove to Indian Territory.

1881

1. Killing of a Ponca Chief by Soldiers. 5 Jan.
SED 14, 46-3, v1, 15p. [1941]
Big Snake killed in the office of the agent of the Poncas in Indian Territory.
2. Expenses of Certain Indian Wars. 5 Jan.
SED 15, 46-3, v1, 20p. [1941]
Bannock war of 1878; Nez Percé war of 1877; Sioux and Northern Cheyenne war of 1876-1877; Kiowa, Comanche, and Cheyenne war of 1874-1875; Apache war of 1873; Modoc war of 1872-1873; Cheyenne, Kiowa, Arapaho, and Comanche war of 1868-1869; Oregon, California, and Idaho war of 1865-1868.
3. Wind River Valley Settlers. 7 Jan.
HR 38, 46-3, v1, 1p. [1982]
Lands encorporated into the Shoshone and Bannock reservation under the treaty of 3 July 1868; Wyoming.
4. R-M of S. Merchant. 7 Jan.
HR 41, 46-3, v1, 2p. [1982]
Service of 1835-1837 in the Seminole war; Florida.
5. Petaca Land Grant in New Mexico. 7 Jan.
HR 45, 46-3, v1, 2p. [1982]
Settlers driven off by hostile Indians.
6. Lake Superior and Mississippi Chippewas. 8 Jan.
HR 50, 46-3, v1, 2p. [1982]
Appropriation to fulfill stipulations of various treaties; investigated under the treaty of 30 Sept. 1854.
7. Indian Appropriation Bill. 8 Jan.
HR 55, 46-3, v1, 1p. [1982]
Year ending 30 June 1882.
8. Property in the Interior Dept. 11 Jan.
SED 18, 46-3, v1, 4p. [1941]
Including the OIA.
9. On the Relief of Gen. Ord. 11 Jan.
SR 740, 46-3, v1, 5p. [1948]
Service in the Seminole war in Florida during 1839-1842, the Yakima expedition of 1855, and the Rogue River expedition of 1856.
10. Accounts of D. Clapp. 12 Jan.
SED 19, 46-3, v1, 26p. [1941]
Late agent of the Crow Indians in Montana.
11. Population and Resources of Alaska. 15 Jan.
HED 40, 46-3, v18, 86p. [1968]
Description of Alaskan Indians; Indian trade.
12. R-C of J. Spencer and J. Mead. 15 Jan.
HR 72, 46-3, v1, 5p. [1982]
Supplies to the Kansas Indians in 1866-1867; Cheyenne hostilities.
13. R-C of Dodd, Brown, and Company. 15 Jan.
HR 73, 46-3, v1, 1p. [1982]
Depredations upon traders by various Indian tribes.
14. Act to Confirm Title to Land in Ohio. 17 Jan.
SR 760, 46-3, v1, 1p. [1948]
Title granted under the Wyandott, Seneca, Shawnee, and Ottawa treaties of 29 Sept. 1817, and 17 Sept. 1818.
15. Report of the Public Land Commission. 18 Jan.
HED 47 (pts. 1-4), 46-3, v25-26, 2106p. [1975-1976]
Indian reservations; cost of quitting Indian titles to public lands; pueblos in New Mexico; lands in Indian Territory; laws and legislative acts affecting Indians; digest of Indian treaties affecting titles to public lands.
16. R-P of Gen. Averell. 18 Jan.
HR 91, 46-3, v1, 5p. [1982]
Service against the Navajoes during 1858 in New Mexico.
17. Annuities of Certain Sioux. 18 Jan.
HR 95, 46-3, v1, 4p. [1982]
Bill to restore money and annuities to Sioux who served in the U.S. Army during 1862-1863 against hostile Sioux.
18. Petition of A. Carrier. 19 Jan.
SMD 20, 46-3, v1, 3p. [1944]
Indian agent for the Poncas in Dakota during 1875-1876 asks relief.
19. Annual Report of the Smithsonian Institution. 19 Jan.
SMD 31, 46-3, v1, 772p. [1944]
Research relevant to the American Indian; census of Indians.
20. R-M of S. Buchanan. 21 Jan.
SR 777, 46-3, v1, 2p. [1948]
Service in the Black Hawk war of

1832, in the Cherokee removal of 1838, in the Florida war until 1844, and in the Rogue River war of 1856.

21. Estimates of Deficiencies for the Indian Service. 21 Jan.
HED 56, 46-3, v18, 7p. [1968]
Deficiencies in appropriations for 1881.

22. Title to Certain Public Grounds. 25 Jan.
SR 795 (pts. 1 and 2), 46-3, v1, 6p. [1948]
The Fort Dearborn addition in Chicago, Illinois; occupied as an Indian agency.

23. U.S. District Court at Wichita, Kansas. 25 Jan.
HR 122, 46-3, v1, 2p. [1982]
Jurisdiction would extend over certain areas of Indian Territory.

24. R-C of W. Langford. 1 Feb.
SR 816, 46-3, v1, 4p. [1948]
Land claim in Flathead and Nez Percé country of Idaho.

25. Removal of the Poncas. 2 Feb.
SED 30, 46-3, v1, 63p. [1941]
Report of commission appointed to study the removal of Poncas from Dakota to Indian Territory; injustice suffered by the tribe regarding incorporation of their reservation into that of the Sioux.

26. Report of the Ute Commission. 2 Feb.
SED 31, 46-3, v3, 54p. [1943]
Appointed to carry out the agreement made with Utes for the sale of their reservation in Colorado.

27. On the Relief of Montana Citizens. 2 Feb.
SR 827, 46-3, v1, 2p. [1948]
Service in the Nez Percé war of 1877.

28. R-C of Georgia. 2 Feb.
SR 828, 46-3, v1, 2p. [1948]
For defense of her frontiers against Indians during 1795-1818.

29. Legislative, Executive, and Judicial Appropriation Bill. 2 Feb.
HR 148, 46-3, v1, 2p. [1982]
Year ending 30 June 1882; Indian expenses.

30. Abandonment of Camp Sheridan, Nebraska. 4 Feb.
SED 33, 46-3, v3, 6p. [1943]
Need of camp questioned because of the 1877 removal of the Red Cloud (Pine Ridge) and Spotted Tail (Rosebud) agencies to Dakota.

31. Deficiency for Indian Supplies. 4 Feb.
SED 34, 46-3, v3, 5p. [1943]
At the Cheyenne and Arapaho, and Kiowa, Comanche, and Wichita agencies in Indian Territory.

32. R-P of P. Grattan. 4 Feb.
HR 162, 46-3, v1, 1p. [1982]
"Grattan massacre" of 1854 near Fort Laramie, Nebraska Territory.

33. R-P of J. Chambers. 4 Feb.
HR 173, 46-3, v1, 1p. [1982]
Wounded in Indian battle.

34. Land Grants to Railroads. 7 Feb.
HMD 10, 46-3, v1, 28p. [1981]
Pacific railroads include the Northern, Union, Central, New Mexico Southern, and Texas Southern; New Mexico Southern route passes through Indian Territory.

35. Mem. of J. McCurtain. 8 Feb.
SMD 32, 46-3, v1, 2p. [1944]
Principal chief of the Choctaw Nation on treaty violations; asks payments due under the treaty of 1830 be paid.

36. R-M of the Western Cherokees. 9 Feb.
SR 849, 46-3, v1, 8p. [1948]
Claim based on stipulations of the treaties of 1835, 1836, and 1846.

37. Money Due for Indian Supplies. 9 Feb.
SR 852, 46-3, v1, 3p. [1948]
Supplies furnished the Sioux in Minnesota during 1860-1862.

38. Territory of Pembina. 14 Feb.
SR 864, 46-3, v1, 2p. [1948]
Agreements between the Sioux and the Chicago and Northwestern, and Chicago, Milwaukee, and St. Paul Railway Companies, for right of ways through the Sioux reservation.

39. Crow Indian Treaty. 14 Feb.
HR 216, 46-3, v1, 2p. [1982]
Crows desire to sell part of the reservation set aside for them under the treaty of 1868; agreements calling for such a sale made 14 May 1880, and 12 June 1880.

40. R-P of D. Swanger. 14 Feb.
HR 229, 46-3, v1, 1p. [1982]
Sioux depredations of 1857 in Minnesota.

41. R-C of Georgia. 14 Feb.
HR 230, 46-3, v1, 2p. [1982]
For military operations against Indians during 1795-1818.

42. R-P of A. Carrier. 14 Feb.
HR 231, 46-3, v1, 3p. [1982]
Late agent to the Poncas in Dakota.

43. R-C of F. Yates. 16 Feb.
SR 875, 46-3, v1, 4p. [1948]
Moved property from the Whetstone Sioux agency at White River to the new reservation in Dakota in 1872-1873.

44. Indian War Bonds. 17 Feb.
SR 878, 46-3, v1, 2p. [1948]
Issued by California in 1852 for expenses incurred in suppressing Indian hostilities.

45. Abandoned Military Reservations. 17 Feb.
HED 90, 46-3, v28, 19p. [1978]
List of forts and camps no longer needed, including the reasons for abandonment; reasons include cessation of Indian hostilities, and removal of Indians, agencies, and reservations.

46. Resol. of the Texas Legis. 21 Feb.
SMD 46, 46-3, v1, 1p. [1944]
Asks that the St. Louis and San Francisco Railway Company be granted a right of way through the Choctaw Nation in Indian Territory.

47. R-P of J. Conrad. 22 Feb.
SR 896, 46-3, v1, 6p. [1948]
Service in Indian wars in Texas, Dakota, and Montana.

48. Stockbridge and Munsee Indians of Wisconsin. 22 Feb.
HMD 14, 46-3, v1, 30p. [1981]
On who is to be allowed tribal funds and reservation lands under the treaty of 5 Feb. 1856.

49. Military Road in Oregon. 22 Feb.
HR 332, 46-3, v1, 41p. [1982]
Area near the Cascade Mountains inhabited by hostile Indians; Indian outbreak of 1878 in eastern Oregon.

50. On the Relief of Idaho Citizens. 22 Feb.
HR 333, 46-3, v1, 1p. [1982]
Volunteers in the Bannock war of 1878.

51. R-C of S. McDonald. 25 Feb.
SR 906, 46-3, v1, 3p. [1948]
Right of way through the Osage reservation in Kansas granted to a railroad company.

52. Testimony on the Removal of the Poncas. 28 Feb.
SMD 49, 46-3, v1, 102p. [1944]
From Dakota to Indian Territory; disposal of their reservation in Dakota.

53. R-P of C. Thompson. 28 Feb.
HR 345, 46-3, v2, 1p. [1983]
Service against Indians at Fort Mohave, Arizona.

54. Gen. Deficiency Bill. 1 Mar.
HR 381, 46-3, v2, 2p. [1983]
Year ending 30 June 1881; Indian appropriations.

55. Private Land-Claims in New Mexico. 2 Mar.
SED 63, 46-3, v3, 87p. [1943]
Pueblo Indian lands.

56. R-P of P. Grattan. 3 Mar.
SR 931, 46-3, v1, 1p. [1948]
"Grattan massacre" near Fort Laramie, Nebraska Territory, in 1854; hostile Indians.

57. Statements of Appropriations. 4 Mar.
HMD 17, 46-3, v1, 101p. [1981]
During the 3rd session, 46th Congress; Indian expenses.

58. Disbursements of the Indian Dept. 20 Oct.
HED 6, 47-1, v16, 10p. [2024]
Year ending 30 June 1881.

59. Annual Message to Congress with Documents; Pres. Arthur. 5 Dec.
HED 1, 47-1, v1-13, 12,666p. [2009-2021]
Surrender of Sitting Bull; intruders into Indian Territory; the new Indian policy, including extension of laws and jurisdiction over Indians, allotment of land in severalty, and education; annual report of the Sec. of War (Serials 2010-2015); annual report of the Sec. of Interior (Serials 2017-2020); annual report of the Gen. Land Office (Serial 2017); annual report of the CIA (Serial 2018), including removal of the Mescalero Apaches, general statistics, allotment, railroads, and reports of Supts. and agents; etc.

60. Annual Report of the Sec. of the Treasury. 5 Dec.
HED 2, 47-1, v14, 706p. [2022]
Year ending 30 June 1881; Indian expenses.

61. Estimates of Appropriations. 5 Dec.
HED 5, 47-1, v16, 319p. [2024]
Year ending 30 June 1883; Indian expenses.

62. Military Post in Washington Territory. 7 Dec.
SED 1, 47-1, v1, 5p. [1986]
Recommends construction of a post in northern Washington to counter possible Indian hostilities; movements of the Colvilles.

63. Employees of the Interior Dept. 8 Dec.
SED 5, 47-1, v1, 45p. [1986]
In the Indian service.

64. Right of Way Across Choctaw Lands. 15 Dec.
SED 15, 47-1, v1, 22p. [1986]
Applications of the Chicago, Texas, and Mexican Central, and the St. Louis, and San Francisco Railway Companies to cross Choctaw lands in Indian Territory; meets approval of the Choctaws.

65. Letter on the Crow Indians. 16 Dec.
SED 19, 47-1, v1, 5p. [1986]
Bill to ratify the agreement of 12 June 1880 for sale of the western portion of the Crow reservation in Montana.

66. Mem. of the Mayor and City Council of Paris, Texas. 16 Dec.
SMD 18, 47-1, v1, 1p. [1993]
Ratification of an act of the Choctaw council granting a right of way through their lands to the St. Louis and San Francisco Railway Co.

67. Disposition of Certain Clothing. 20 Dec.
SED 28, 47-1, v1, 2p. [1986]
Purchased for Paiutes, Shoshones, Modocs, Quapaws, Chippewas, Bannocks, Apaches, Nez Percés, Wichitas, and Sheepeaters.

68. Education in Alaska. 20 Dec.
SED 30, 47-1, v1, 28p. [1986]
Education of Indians and half-breeds in Alaska by the Russian and U.S. governments.

69. Sale of Miami Lands. 20 Dec.
SR 11, 47-1, v1, 3p. [2004]
Sale of lands in Kansas under the treaty of 5 June 1854; allotment; dissolution of tribal relations by the act of 3 Mar. 1873.

70. Supplies to the Sioux. 21 Dec.
SR 14, 47-1, v1, 3p. [2004]
Claims for supplies furnished the Sioux of Minnesota during 1860-1862.

71. R-C of F. Yates. 21 Dec.
SR 16, 47-1, v1, 4p. [2004]
Transport of property of Whetstone agency from White River to the new Sioux reservation in Dakota.

1882

1. Right of Way Through the Choctaw Nation. 9 Jan.
SED 44, 47-1, v2, 14p. [1987]
On a bill passed by the Choctaw council granting a right of way to the St. Louis and San Francisco Railway Co.

2. Resol. of Sen. Teller. 9 Jan.
SMD 24, 47-1, v1, 1p. [1993]
On opening of the Ute reservation in Colorado for settlement.

3. R-P of Dr. Appel. 10 Jan.
SR 24, 47-1, v1, 2p. [2004]
Physician at the Mescalero Apache agency, New Mexico, during 1877-1879.

4. Creek Orphan Fund. 10 Jan.
SR 25, 47-1, v1, 3p. [2004]
Claim for reimbursement of the fund; treaty of 24 Mar. 1832.

5. Mem. of the Omaha Indians. 11 Jan.
SMD 31, 47-1, v1, 14p. [1993]
Title to lands alloted in severalty to members of the tribe.

6. R-P of J. Hertford. 11 Jan.
SR 33, 47-1, v1, 3p. [2004]
Clerk at the Sac and Fox agency, Indian Territory; 1879.

7. R-P of J. Bacon. 11 Jan.
SR 39, 47-1, v1, 2p. [2004]
Gen. Sully's 1864 campaign against the Sioux of the Upper Missouri.

8. Agreement with the Shoshones and Bannocks. 11 Jan.
HED 18, 47-1, v18, 16p. [2026]
Made 18 July 1881; cession of lands in the Fort Hall Indian reservation in Idaho for the use of the Utah and Northern railway.

9. R-C of E. Gurley. 11 Jan.
HR 3, 47-1, v1, 2p. [2065]
Attorney in case involving the murder of 7 Caddo Indians in Texas; 1858.

10. Publications of the War Dept. 12 Jan.
SED 47, 47-1, v2, 19p. [1987]
From 4 Mar. 1789 to 4 Mar. 1881; reports of survey and explorations through Indian country.

11. Condition of Indians Occupying Reservations. 18 Jan.
SED 54, 47-1, v2, 5p. [1987]
A bill proposing to improve the condition of reservation Indians by reduction of reservation sizes, and allotment of lands in severalty.

12. Message on the Kickapoo Indians 18 Jan.
SED 55, 47-1, v2, 3p. [1987]
On settlement of the estates of deceased Kickapoos in Kansas; allotment; treaty of 28 June 1862.

13. Otoe and Missouria Reservation. 18 Jan.
SED 56, 47-1, v2, 3p. [1987]
For the sale of reservation lands in Nebraska and Kansas.

14. Deficiency in the Indian Service. 18 Jan.
SED 57, 47-1, v2, 4p. [1987]
Appropriation for a deficiency for the year ending 30 June 1882.

15. Appropriation for the Indian Com'rs. 18 Jan.
SED 58, 47-1, v2, 2p. [1987]
Defraying expenses of the Board of Indian Com'rs.

16. Medical Inspector for the Indian Service. 18 Jan.
SED 59, 47-1, v2, 2p. [1987]
Bill to create said position; supervision for agency physicians; health inspections at all Indian reservations.

17. Crow Indian Reservation. 18 Jan.
SED 61, 47-1, v2, 22p. [1987]
Bill to ratify the agreement of 23 Aug. 1881; sale of reservation lands in Montana which are needed by the Northern Pacific Railroad.

18. Miami Lands in Kansas. 18 Jan.
HR 22, 47-1, v1, 3p. [2065]
Bill providing for the sale of said lands.

19. R-P of T. Little. 19 Jan.
HR 29, 47-1, v1, 2p. [2065]
Service in the Florida Indian war in 1856-1857, in Sioux engagements of 1867-1868, and in battles against Comanches and Kiowas in Texas and Indian Territory.

20. R-P of J. Taggert. 19 Jan.
HR 33, 47-1, v1, 1p. [2065]
Homestead on a location of Sioux half-breed scrip.

21. Sale of Timber on the Menomonee Reservation. 19 Jan.
HR 34, 47-1, v1, 1p. [2065]
Authorizes sale of timber cut in 1876-1877; Wisconsin.

22. Posts on the Rio Grande Frontier. 20 Jan.
HED 20, 47-1, v19, 17p. [2027]
Indian depredations.

23. U.S.-Texas Boundary. 24 Jan.
SED 70, 47-1, v2, 309p. [1987]
Involves surveys of Creek, Choctaw, Chickasaw, and other Indian lands in Indian Territory.

24. Affairs in Alaska. 24 Jan.
SED 71, 47-1, v4, 198p. [1989]
Relations between the Indians and whites residing in Alaska.

25. Eastern Shawnee Indians. 24 Jan.
SED 72, 47-1, v4, 3p. [1989]
Per capita distribution of $2000 to the Eastern Shawnees at the Quapaw agency, Indian Territory.

26. Sale of Timber Cut on the Menomonee Reservation. 24 Jan.
SED 74, 47-1, v4, 2p. [1989]
Bill authorizing the sale of lumber cut by the Menomonees during 1876-1877.

27. Cession of Lands in Indian Territory. 24 Jan.
SED 75, 47-1, v4, 9p. [1989]
Proposition of the Creeks for the cession of their lands occupied by the Seminoles.

28. R-P of J. Spencer and J. Mead. 24 Jan.
SR 58, 47-1, v1, 5p. [2004]
Supplies to the Kansas Indians in 1866-1867.

29. R-P of A. McAuley. 24 Jan.
SR 81, 47-1, v1, 1p. [2004]
Service in Creek and Seminole war.

30. Salary of the CIA. 25 Jan.
HED 29, 47-1, v19, 2p. [2027]
To increase the salary to $5000 per year.

31. Estimates of Deficiencies. 25 Jan.
HED 33, 47-1, v19, 78p. [2027]
Appropriations for fiscal 1882; Indian expenses.

32. Western Miamies at the Quapaw Agency. 26 Jan.
HED 36, 47-1, v19, 3p. [2027]
Distribution of proceeds from the sale of their lands in Kansas.

33. Abandoned Military Reservations. 26 Jan.
HED 39, 47-1, v19, 42p. [2027]
Disposal of reservations; the rea-

sons for abandonment are sometimes relevant to Indian affairs.

34. Funds of the Miamies in Kansas. 26 Jan.
HED 40, 47-1, v19, 4p. [2027]
Consolidation of funds under the treaties of 6 Oct. 1818, 23 Oct. 1834, and 5 June 1854.

35. Funds of the Chippewas and Ottawas. 26 Jan.
HED 47, 47-1, v19, 3p. [2027]
Disposal of bonds and funds held by the Treasurer of the U.S.

36. R-C of J. Fletcher. 26 Jan.
HR 87, 47-1, v1, 3p. [2065]
Cheyenne and Arapaho depredations of 1870 in Indian Territory.

37. R-C of F. Yates et al. 27 Jan.
HR 99, 47-1, v1, 4p. [2065]
Transportation in removal of the Whetstone agency from White River to the new Sioux reservation in Dakota; 1872-1873.

38. Private Land Claims in Arizona. 30 Jan.
SED 81, 47-1, v4, 14p. [1989]
Claim abandoned periodically due to Indian hostilities.

39. A Certain Land Claim in New Mexico. 30 Jan.
HR 131, 47-1, v1, 2p. [2065]
Settler periodically driven off by hostile Indians.

40. R-P of Fifth Infantry Officers. 31 Jan.
SR 100, 47-1, v1, 7p. [2004]
Property lost; Sioux campaign of 1876-1877; Custer's death.

41. R-C of Kansas, Nevada, Oregon, Texas, Idaho, and Washington. 31 Jan.
HR 141 (pts. 1 and 2), 47-1, v1, 6p. [2065]
For suppressing Indian hostilities.

42. R-P of A. Lempp. 31 Jan.
HR 148, 47-1, v1, 2p. [2065]
Service in Indian wars of 1833-1836 in Florida, Texas, and Wisconsin.

43. R-C of S. Yeomans and A. Leech. 1 Feb.
HR 176, 47-1, v1, 4p. [2065]
Hire of clerks in land offices; sale of Osage and other Indian lands in Kansas.

44. R-C of Oregon. 2 Feb.
SR 114, 47-1, v1, 2p. [2004]
Costs of the Modoc war; 1872-1873.

45. Sale of Dead and Damaged Timber on Indian Reservations. 2 Feb.
HED 56, 47-1, v19, 2p. [2027]
Bill authorizing Indians to sell such timber.

46. Advertising the Sale of Kansas Indian Lands. 2 Feb.
HED 60, 47-1, v19, 3p. [2027]
Payment of newspaper accounts for advertising done in 1874-1875.

47. Shoshone Lands in Duck Valley, Nevada. 2 Feb.
HED 61, 47-1, v19, 12p. [2027]
Payment of settlers for improvements on lands taken for the use of the Shoshones.

48. R-P of A. McFadden. 2 Feb.
HR 199, 47-1, v1, 2p. [2065]
Service in Black Hawk war of 1832.

49. Homestead Entries in Michigan. 3 Feb.
SED 88, 47-1, v4, 5p. [1989]
Settlement upon an Indian reservation.

50. Timber Depredations on Indian Reservations. 3 Feb.
SED 89, 47-1, v5, 2p. [1990]
Bill to prevent such depredations.

51. R-P of E. Finley. 3 Feb.
HR 214, 47-1, v1, 2p. [2065]
Service in Black Hawk war of 1832.

52. School for Indian Children in Alaska. 4 Feb.
HR 236, 47-1, v1, 3p. [2065]
Transfer of the title to a building from the U.S. to a mission society.

53. R-P of L. Hentig. 7 Feb.
SR 130, 47-1, v1, 1p. [2004]
Serviceman killed by Indians in Arizona; 1881.

54. R-C of Kansas. 7 Feb.
SR 133, 47-1, v1, 4p. [2004]
Suppression of Indian hostilities.

55. Mormon Connection with a Paiute and Navajo Outbreak. 7 Feb.
HED 65, 47-1, v19, 2p. [2027]
Mormons alleged to be inciting Indians of Arizona to commit hostilities.

56. R-P of S. Merchant. 7 Feb.
HR 286, 47-1, v1, 2p. [2065]
Service in Seminole war; 1835-1837; Florida.

57. Indian Apporpriation Bill. 7 Feb.
HR 304, 47-1, v1, 1p. [2065]
Year ending 30 June 1883.

58. Barracks and Quarters. 8 Feb.
SED 95, 47-1, v5, 4p. [1990]
Including Forts Coeur d'Alene and Lapwai, and Boise Barracks in Indian country.

59. R-C of E. Gurley. 8 Feb.
SR 141, 47-1, v1, 2p. [2004]
Attorney in case involving the murder of 7 Caddo Indians in Texas; 1858.

60. R-C of Georgia. 8 Feb.
SR 148, 47-1, v1, 2p. [2004]
Costs of frontier defense against Indians during 1795-1818.

61. R-P of J. Spencer and J. Mead. 8 Feb.
HR 309, 47-1, v1, 5p. [2065]
Supplies to Kansas Indians in 1866-1867.

62. Creek Orphan Fund. 8 Feb.
HR 310, 47-1, v1, 3p. [2065]
Bill to reimburse the fund (established under the treaty of 24 Mar. 1832); unauthorized expenditures.

63. Agreement with the Crows of Montana. 8 Feb.
HR 311, 47-1, v1, 5p. [2065]
Made 12 June 1880; cession of a portion of their reservation; mineral lands.

64. Unpaid Accounts in the Indian Bureau. 8 Feb.
HR 312, 47-1, v1, 3p. [2065]
For services and supplies furnished at various agencies.

65. Letter on the Northern Cheyenne Raid. 9 Feb.
SED 100, 47-1, v5, 2p. [1990]
Damages of 1878 in Indian Territory, Kansas, and Nebraska.

66. R-C of J. Dorsey and J. Shepard. 9 Feb.
SR 144, 47-1, v1, 5p. [2004]
Supplies to troops in Paiute campaign of 1860 in Utah Territory.

67. Lands Located with Military Land Warrants. 9 Feb.
HR 345 (pts. 1 and 2), 47-1, v1, 8p. [2065]
Acts involving Chickasaw, Creek, and Choctaw lands in Alabama and Mississippi.

68. Seneca Indians of New York. 9 Feb.
HR 347, 47-1, v1, 1p. [2065]
Ask grant of land in the Allegany reservation for a cemetery.

69. R-P of D. Swanger. 9 Feb.
HR 348, 47-1, v1, 1p. [2065]
Injured in Sioux outbreak of 1862 in Minnesota.

70. Urgent Deficiencies in Appropriations. 10 Feb.
HR 378, 47-1, v1, 1p. [2065]
For the year ending 30 June 1882; for the Indian service, and principally for the Sioux.

71. Green Bay Indian Agency. 14 Feb.
SR 172, 47-1, v1, 2p. [2004]
The sale of dead and down timber in Wisconsin.

72. Sale of Logs Cut by Indians. 14 Feb.
SR 173, 47-1, v1, 2p. [2004]
On the Menomonee reservation in Wisconsin; cut in 1876-1877.

73. Claim of C. Ewing Against the Osages. 14 Feb.
HED 73, 47-1, v19, 52p. [2027]
All papers and payments surrounding this claim; attorney hired by the Osages to secure funds due them.

74. R-P of O. Love and W. Gilschrist. 14 Feb.
HR 405, 47-1, v2, 2p. [2066]
Chickasaw Indians suffer from Comanche depredations of 1866-1867 in Indian Territory.

75. Claims for Supplies to Sioux. 14 Feb.
HR 406, 47-1, v2, 3p. [2066]
Between 1860 and 1862 in Minnesota; cause of Sioux outbreak in 1862 a delay in arrival of annuity supplies.

76. R-P of Powers and Newman, and D. and B. Powers. 14 Feb.
SR 407, 47-1, v2, 2p. [2066]
Cheyenne and Arapaho depredations of 1867 between Forts Harker and Wallace.

77. R-P of J. Fletcher. 14 Feb.
HR 408, 47-1, v2, 2p. [2066]
Cheyenne and Arapaho depredations of 1870 in Indian Territory.

78. Disbursement of Money by Indian Agents. 14 Feb.
HR 409, 47-1, v2, 3p. [2066]
Conflict between Interior and Treasury Depts. over control of disbursements for the Indians.

79. Bounty Land for Florida Indian Wars. 14 Feb.
HR 422, 47-1, v2, 1p. [2066]
For persons who served during 1854-1860.

80. Ute Reservation in Colorado. 15 Feb.
SED 108, 47-1, v5, 8p. [1990]
On settlement of the reserve which was ceded to the U.S. by agreement with the Utes.

81. R-P of I. Walker. 16 Feb.
SR 183, 47-1, v1, 8p. [2004]
Purchase of a ferry franchise under the Wyandott treaty of 31 Jan. 1855.

82. Education in Alaska. 16 Feb.
HED 78, 47-1, v19, 2p. [2027]
Appropriation needed for teachers; education would help native Alaskans throw off tribal relations.

83. Annual Report of the Board of Indian Com'rs. 16 Feb.
HED 79, 47-1, v19, 97p. [2027]
On allotment, missions, law for Indians, schools, etc.

84. Training Schools for Indian Youths. 16 Feb.
HR 446, 47-1, v2, 4p. [2066]
Bill providing for establishment of industrial schools in unoccupied military barracks.

85. Umatilla Lands in Oregon. 16 Feb.
HR 447, 47-1, v2, 1p. [2066]
Disposal of reservation lands adjacent to the town of Pendleton.

86. Indian Agent at Green Bay, Wisconsin. 16 Feb.
HR 448, 47-1, v2, 1p. [2066]
Sale of fallen timber on reservations.

87. New York Indian Lands in Kansas. 16 Feb.
HR 449 (pts. 1 and 2), 47-1, v2, 17p. [2066]
Sale of lands to settlers.

88. Publications of the Justice Dept. 17 Feb.
SED 109, 47-1, v5, 12p. [1990]
Opinions of the Attorney-Gen. on Choctaw, and Eastern Cherokee cases.

89. Occupation by Settlers of a Portion of Indian Territory. 17 Feb.
SED 111, 47-1, v5, 4p. [1990]
On the rights of settlers to occupy any lands in Indian Territory.

90. Lands in Colorado. 20 Feb.
SR 186, 47-1, v1, 3p. [2004]
On opening lands lately occupied by the Uncompahgre and White River Ute Indians for settlement.

91. Education of Indian Children. 21 Feb.
SED 113, 47-1, v5, 10p. [1990]
Expenditures for education under treaty stipulations; student population.

92. Public Lands. 21 Feb.
SR 193, 47-1, v1, 9p. [2004]
Proceeds of the sale of Choctaw, Chickasaw, and Creek lands in Mississippi and Alabama.

93. Report of U.S. Naval Officers Cruising in Alaskan Waters. 24 Feb.
HED 81, 47-1, v19, 52p. [2027]
Indian-white relations in Alaska; trade; liquor.

94. Steamer *J. Don Cameron.* 24 Feb.
HR 476, 47-1, v2, 7p. [2066]
Sinks in the Upper Missouri with property of the soldiers in the Fifth Infantry; 1877; regiment in Dakota in a campaign against the Sioux; Custer's massacre.

95. R-P of S. McDonald. 24 Feb.
HR 486, 47-1, v2, 2p. [2066]
Land claim; railroad through the Osage reservation in Kansas.

96. R-P of A. Sharp. 24 Feb.
HR 487, 47-1, v2, 1p. [2066]
Captive of the Sioux; 1857; Spirit Lake, Iowa.

97. R-P of Evans, Nichols, and Co. 24 Feb.
HR 488, 47-1, v2, 1p. [2066]
Osage depredations of 1866 in Missouri.

98. R-P of T. Brooks and Co. 24 Feb.
HR 489, 47-1, v2, 1p. [2066]
Osage depredations of 1866 in Missouri.

99. R-P of E. Allen. 24 Feb.
HR 490, 47-1, v2, 3p. [2066]
Contract for supplies to the Red Cloud and Spotted Tail Sioux agencies in Dakota; 1878.

100. R-P of J. Black. 24 Feb.
HR 491, 47-1, v2, 6p. [2066]
Services rendered in the Indian Dept.

101. R-P of L. Hentig. 24 Feb.
HR 507, 47-1, v2, 1p. [2066]
Apache hostilities of 1881 near Fort Apache, Arizona.

102. R-P of H. Wright. 24 Feb.
HR 512, 47-1, v2, 2p. [2066]
Service in the Seminole war; 1841-1843; Florida.

103. U.S. Courts at Wichita, Kansas. 25 Feb.
HR 545, 47-1, v2, 1p. [2066]
Jurisdiction over Indian Territory.

104. Delaware Indians. 25 Feb.
HR 557, 47-1, v2, 2p. [2066]
Amount due for sale of lands in Kansas under the treaties of 1854, 1860, and 1866; removal to Cherokee country, Indian Territory.

105. Malheur Reservation. 28 Feb.
SED 121, 47-1, v5, 4p. [1990]
Recommends sale of the reservation; Oregon.

106. On Seating a Delegate from Alaska. 28 Feb.
HR 560 (pts. 1 and 2), 47-1, v2, 13p. [2066]
Indian population discussed.

107. Indian Lands in Colorado. 28 Feb.
HR 561, 47-1, v2, 3p. [2066]
Lately occupied by the Uncompahgre and White River Utes; ceded to U.S. by agreement; opening of lands for settlement.

108. Indian Prisoners. 1 Mar.
SED 120, 47-1, v5, 10p. [1990]
Held at Forts Randall, Keogh, Union, Lowell, Leavenworth, and Davis by order of the War Dept.; Sioux, Mescalero Apaches, Paiutes, Apaches, Siletz, Nez Percés, and Cheyennes confined; reasons why they are being held.

109. Seneca Nation of New York Indians. 1 Mar.
HED 83, 47-1, v19, 12p. [2027]
Their remonstrance against Senate bill No. 19, "to provide for allotment of lands in severalty to Indians upon various reservations."

110. Railroad Right of Way. 1 Mar.
HR 579, 47-1, v2, 1p. [2066]
Through an Indian reservation in Michigan; Saginaw and Mount Pleasant Railroad Co.

111. Delaware Indians. 1 Mar.
HR 580, 47-1, v2, 13p. [2066]
Payment of claims for depredations committed by whites in Kansas as stipulated in the treaty of 4 July 1866.

112. Sioux Reservation West of Big Stone Lake. 1 Mar.
HR 581, 47-1, v2, 1p. [2066]
Erroneous survey of the reservation in Dakota.

113. Crow Reservation in Montana. 1 Mar.
HR 582, 47-1, v2, 1p. [2066]
Sale of part of the reservation for the use of the Northern Pacific Railroad as stipulated in an agreement.

114. R-C of M. Duffield. 1 Mar.
HR 598, 47-1, v2, 2p. [2066]
Indian depredations of 1864 in Arizona.

115. Creek and Seminole Indians. 1 Mar.
HR 609, 47-1, v2, 1p. [2066]
Amount due Creeks for lands purchased for the Seminoles.

116. Claim of the Cherokee Indians. 2 Mar.
HED 89, 47-1, v20, 37p. [2028]
Money due for lands ceded to the U.S. in Indian Territory by the treaty of 19 July 1866.

117. Fort Thornburgh, Utah. 2 Mar.
HED 90, 47-1, v20, 3p. [2028]
Necessity of post due to removal of Utes from Colorado to Utah.

118. Military Post at Fort Selden, New Mexico. 3 Mar.
SED 125, 47-1, v5, 8p. [1990]
Control of the Indians.

119. R-P of J. Conrad. 3 Mar.
HR 616, 47-1, v2, 6p. [2066]
Service in Indian wars on the frontiers of Texas, Dakota, and Montana.

120. Military Post at Fort Selden, New Mexico. 4 Mar.
HED 92, 47-1, v20, 8p. [2028]
Estimates for construction; control of Indians.

121. Removal of the Eastern Cherokees. 4 Mar.
HED 96, 47-1, v20, 6p. [2028]
Appropriation for costs of removal of certain Cherokees from North Carolina to Indian Territory.

122. R-P of W. Grounds. 4 Mar.
HR 633, 47-1, v2, 5p. [2066]
Hualapai depredations of 1874 in Arizona.

123. Cost to the U.S. of Indian Wars. 6 Mar.
SED 123, 47-1, v5, 9p. [1990]
Modoc, Texas, Sioux, Nez Percé, Bannock, Northern Cheyenne, Ute, Sheepeater, and Apache wars since 1872.

124. Receipts and Expenditures. 6 Mar.
HED 117, 47-1, v21, 417p. [2029]
Year ending 30 June 1876; Indian expenses.

125. Mem. of Citizens of Gunnison, Colorado. 7 Mar.
SMD 63, 47-1, v1, 3p. [1993]
To open the Ute reservation for settlement.

126. Sale of Kickapoo Lands. 8 Mar.
SR 233, 47-1, v1, 3p. [2004]
Reserved in Kansas under the treaty of 28 June 1862.

127. Contingent Expenses of the Interior Dept. 8 Mar.
HED 105, 47-1, v20, 35p. [2028]
Year ending 30 June 1881; OIA.

128. Accounts for Advertising Kansas Indian Lands. 8 Mar.
HR 657, 47-1, v3, 2p. [2067]
Sale of lands in Kansas; 1874-1875.

129. Fort Hall and Lemhi Reservations. 8 Mar.
HR 658, 47-1, v3, 2p. [2067]
Sale of lands by the agreement of 14 May 1880 with the Shoshones, Bannocks, and Sheepeaters; Idaho.

130. Sale of a Portion of the Shoshone and Bannock Reservation. 8 Mar.
HR 659, 47-1, v3, 2p. [2067]
Right of way for the Utah and Northern Railway Co.; Fort Hall reservation in Idaho.

131. Amendment of Revised Statutes. 9 Mar.
SED 128, 47-1, v5, 3p. [1990] *or*
HED 101, 47-1, v20, 3p. [2028]
Sale of annuity goods to whites by Lower Brulé Sioux in Dakota; bill to prevent this.

132. Allotment of Certain Indian Lands. 9 Mar.
SR 243, 47-1, v1, 3p. [2004]
On the Umatilla reservation in Oregon; created by treaty with the Walla-Wallas, Cayuses, and Umatillas.

133. Salary of the CIA. 9 Mar.
HR 688, 47-1, v3, 1p. [2067]
Increase to $5000 per year.

134. R-P of G. Storrs. 9 Mar.
HR 689, 47-1, v3, 3p. [2007]
Sioux depredations of 1862 in Minnesota; service in Sioux outbreak.

135. Expenses of the Ute Commission. 10 Mar.
HED 111, 47-1, v20, 2p. [2028]
Appropriation needed; sale of Colorado lands by agreement wtih the Utes.

136. Receipts and Expenditures. 10 Mar.
HED 121, 47-1, v21, 412p. [2029]
Year ending 30 June 1877; Indian expenses.

137. Sale of Dead Timber. 13 Mar.
HR 748, 47-1, v3, 2p. [2067]
Bill authorizing such sales on Indian reservations.

138. Letter on the Kansas Indians. 14 Mar.
SED 136, 47-1, v5, 9p. [1990]
Indebtedness of the tribe to individuals; sale of their lands; classes of scrip under the treaties of 5 Oct. 1859, and 13 Mar. 1862.

139. R-P of M. Lee. 14 Mar.
SR 256, 47-1, v1, 2p. [2004]
Service in the Seminole war in Florida; 1840-1845.

140. Receipts and Expenditures. 14 Mar.
HED 97, 47-1, v20, 570p. [2028]
For fiscal 1874-1875; Indian expenses.

141. Departmental Expenses Investigation. 15 Mar.
SR 265 (pts. 1 and 2), 47-1, v2, 1561p. [2005]
Regarding contingent expenses; includes OIA.

142. R-P of J. Luskey. 16 Mar.
HR 787, 47-1, v3, 1p. [2067]
Service in Seminole war.

143. Price of Osage Lands in Kansas. 17 Mar.
HED 124, 47-1, v22, 6p. [2030]
Osages decline to accede to the terms of the act of 3 Mar. 1881 reducing the price of their lands in Kansas.

144. R-P of Gen. Hatch. 17 Mar.
HR 796, 47-1, v3, 1p. [2067]
Disbursing agent for the Ute Commission.

145. R-P of Dr. Appel. 17 Mar.
HR 797, 47-1, v3, 2p. [2067]
Physician at the Mescalero Apache agency during 1877-1879 in New Mexico.

146. R-C of Dr. Tonner. 17 Mar.
HR 809, 47-1, v3, 1p. [2067]
Agent at the Colorado River reservation in Arizona; 1871-1873.

147. R-P of G. Quick. 21 Mar.
SR 286, 47-1, v1, 1p. [2004]
Service in the Black Hawk war of 1832.

148. R-C of H. Hobson. 22 Mar.
SR 294, 47-1, v1, 1p. [2004]
Supplies to troops in Oregon Indian war; 1856.

149. R-C of California. 22 Mar.
SR 306, 47-1, v1, 2p. [2004]
Suppression of Indian hostilities; 1872-1873.

150. Property in the Interior Dept. 23 Mar.
SED 140, 47-1, v5, 4p. [1990]
In the OIA.

151. Indian Depredation Claims. 24 Mar.
HED 135, 47-1, v22, 37p. [2030]
Continuation of list made in 1875; claims prior to 15 Mar. 1882; lists date, location, tribe involved, and action on the claim.

152. Reimbursement of Certain States. 24 Mar.
HR 843, 47-1, v3, 3p. [2067]
Expenses incurred by Oregon and California in the Modoc war of 1872-1873.

153. R-P of A. McFadden. 27 Mar.
SR 327, 47-1, v1, 2p. [2004]
Service in the Black Hawk war of 1832.

154. Estimated Costs of Pensions. 27 Mar.
HED 137, 47-1, v22, 5p. [2030]
Indian wars prior to 1846, including the Seminole war of 1818, the Black Hawk war of 1832, the Creek war of 1837, the Cherokee war of 1837, the Florida Indian war of 1839, and the New York frontier disturbance of 1839.

155. R-P of L. Prine. 28 Mar.
SR 333, 47-1, v1, 1p. [2004]
Casualty in Florida Indian war; 1856.

156. R-C of the Western Cherokees. 29 Mar.
SR 353, 47-1, v3, 6p. [2006]
Based on stipulations of the treaties of 1835, 1836, and 1846; referral to the Court of Claims.

157. Lands Granted to Railroads. 29 Mar.
HED 144, 47-1, v22, 45p. [2030]
Lands in Indian Territory granted to the Atlantic and Pacific Railroad Co.

158. Prevention of Trespass on Indian Lands. 29 Mar.
HED 145, 47-1, v22, 3p. [2030]
Bill to increase protection of Indian lands; intruders into Indian Territory.

159. Completion of Fort Lewis, Colorado. 29 Mar.
HED 146, 47-1, v22, 3p. [2030]
Located between the Navajoes and Utes, where both tribes can be controlled.

160. R-C of J. Hertford. 29 Mar.
HR 894, 47-1, v3, 3p. [2067]
Clerk at the Sac and Fox agency; 1879.

161. Indian Inspectors and Agents. 30 Mar.
HED 149, 47-1, v22, 2p. [2020]
On their terms of office.

162. Condition of the Gen. Land Office. 3 Apr.
SR 362, 47-1, v3, 159p. [2006]
Concerned with a conflict over jurisdiction between the BIA and Gen. Land Office regarding disposal or occupancy of public lands.

163. Mem. of Omaha Indians. 4 Apr.
SMD 78, 47-1, v1, 4p. [1993]
Allotment of lands within that portion of the Omaha reservation which was sold to the Winnebagoes.

164. R-P of Powers and Newman, and D. and B. Powers. 4 Apr.
SR 375, 47-1, v3, 2p. [2006]
Cheyenne and Arapaho depredations of 1867 between Forts Harker and Wallace.

165. R-P of W. Lockhart. 4 Apr.
SR 376, 47-1, v3, 2p. [2006]
Service in the Black Hawk war of 1832.

166. R-P of A. McAuley. 4 Apr.
SR 379, 47-1, v3, 2p. [2006]
Service in Creek and Seminole war.

167. R-C of O. Love and W. Gilschrist. 5 Apr.
SR 386, 47-1, v3, 2p. [2006]
Comanche depredations upon Chickasaw Indians; 1866-1867; Indian Territory.

168. Depredations on Indian Reservations. 5 Apr.
SR 392, 47-1, v3, 2p. [2006]
Protection of reservations from timber depredations.

169. Message on the Claim of P. Garreaux. 5 Apr.
HED 159, 47-1, v22, 3p. [2030]
Formerly interpreter at the Fort Berthold agency in Dakota; depredation committed by Sioux of the Grand River agency upon his property (being used by Gros Ventres).

170. Fort McKinney, Wyoming. 6 Apr.
HED 160, 47-1, v22, 10p. [2030]
Appropriation for construction; located in buffalo region resorted to by the Sioux, Northern Cheyennes, and Arapahoes.

171. Right of Way Through Indian Territory. 6 Apr.
HR 934, 47-1, v3, 5p. [2067]
To the St. Louis and San Francisco Railroad; act of the general council of the Choctaw Nation.

172. R-C of I. Chaves et al. 6 Apr.
HR 935, 47-1, v3, 10p. [2067]
Navajo and Apache lands in New Mexico; land claims.

173. R-P of J. Sturtevant. 10 Apr.
HR 995, 47-1, v4, 2p. [2068]
Service against Indians in Washington Territory; 1855.

174. R-P of Z. Shepherd. 10 Apr.
HR 996, 47-1, v4, 1p. [2068]
Service as an Indian spy.

175. R-M of B. Holladay. 11 Apr.
SR 403, 47-1, v3, 11p. [2006]

Indian depredations of 1860-1866 upon a mail contractor; between Salt Lake City and the Missouri River.

176. Hot Springs Reservation in Arkansas. 11 Apr.
HR 1001, 47-1, v4, 3p. [2068]
Extinguishment of Quapaw title to the area in 1818.

177. Delaware Indians. 12 Apr.
SR 405, 47-1, v3, 12p. [2006]
Claims for stock stolen by whites in Kansas; payment under the treaty of 3 July 1866.

178. Transportation of Indian Supplies. 12 Apr.
HED 167, 47-1, v22, 2p. [2030]
Increased appropriation for fiscal 1882.

179. Confirmation of Land in Indian Territory. 12 Apr.
HED 169, 47-1, v22, 4p. [2030]
To the Cheyennes and Arapahoes; set apart by an Executive Order of 10 Aug. 1869 in lieu of land set apart by the treaty of 28 Oct. 1867.

180. Right of Way for Railroad Purposes. 14 Apr.
HED 171, 47-1, v22, 5p. [2030]
Through the Otoe and Missouria reservation in Kansas and Nebraska.

181. Coal Lands Upon the San Carlos Division of the White Mountain Reservation. 18 Apr.
HED 173, 47-1, v22, 4p. [2030]
Lease of lands to mining interests; Arizona; reserve occupied by bands of Apaches, Apache Mohaves, and Apache Yumas.

182. Indian Training School. 18 Apr.
HED 175, 47-1, v22, 4p. [2030]
To be constructed on the site of old Fort Ripley in Minnesota.

183. Troops on Indian Reservations. 19 Apr.
SED 161, 47-1, v6, 9p. [1991]
List of forts and military reservations within Indian reservations; inordinate consumption of timber on said reservations.

184. R-C of W. Beddo et al. 19 Apr.
SR 446, 47-1, v3, 8p. [2006]
Kiowa and Comanche depredations in Texas.

185. R-P of T. Butler. 20 Apr.
HR 1080, 47-1, v4, 1p. [2068]
Payment of annuities to the Miamies of Indiana in 1880-1881.

186. R-P of F. Phillips. 20 Apr.
HR 1081, 47-1, v4, 3p. [2068]
Nez Percé depredations of 1877 in Idaho.

187. Settlers in Wyoming. 20 Apr.
HR 1101, 47-1, v4, 1p. [2068]
Improvements made in the Wind River Valley encorporated into the Shoshone and Bannock reservation (treaty of 1868).

188. Civil Government for Alaska. 20 Apr.
HR 1106 (pts. 1 and 2), 47-1, v4, 7p. [2068]
Indian population discussed.

189. Government for Southeastern Alaska. 21 Apr.
SR 457, 47-1, v3, 45p. [2006]
Indian population discussed.

190. Boundary Between the U.S. and Mexico. 21 Apr.
HED 180, 47-1, v22, 5p. [2030]
Protection of survey parties from hostile Indians needed.

191. Relief of Volunteers. 21 Apr.
HR 1114, 47-1, v4, 4p. [2068]
In Oregon, Idaho, Washington, and Montana; Nez Percé war of 1877; Bannock war of 1878.

192. Personal Assaults in Indian Territory. 22 Apr.
HED 181, 47-1, v22, 4p. [2030]
Cheyenne Indian attempts to kill the U.S. agent at the Cheyenne and Arapaho Agency; jurisdictional concerns.

193. Letter on the Columbia River. 24 Apr.
SED 186, 47-1, v6, 135p. [1991]
Colville Indian reservation; Sans Poil Indian settlement; Okinakane, and Chelan Indians; origin of names of geographical features in Indian languages; etc.

194. R-P of P. Twiggs. 24 Apr.
HR 1130, 47-1, v4, 3p. [2068]
Service in the Seminole war; 1836-1837; Florida.

195. R-P of R. Ross. 25 Apr.
SR 491, 47-1, v3, 2p. [2006]
Service in the Indian Home Guards; composed of loyal Osages and Cherokees during the Civil War.

196. Resol. of Sen. Call. 27 Apr.
SMD 86, 47-1, v1, 1p. [1993]
Use of the military against Apaches in Arizona.

197. Cherokee Lands. 27 Apr.
HR 1146, 47-1, v4, 4p. [2068]

Title to land; fulfillment of treaty stipulations (treaties of 1828, 1833, and 1866).

198. Oregon Short-Line Railroad Co. 28 Apr.
SR 498, 47-1, v3, 2p. [2006]
Would cross the Fort Hall Indian reservation; agreement made with Indians.

199. Turtle Mountain Band of Chippewas. 28 Apr.
HR 1144, 47-1, v4, 6p. [2068]
On extinguishing their title to lands in Dakota; treaty of 1863 with the Pembina Chippewas; removal to the White Earth reservation in Minnesota.

200. Klamath Reservation in California. 28 Apr.
HR 1148, 47-1, v4, 3p. [2068]
Restoration of said reserve to the public domain.

201. Mexican Pottawatomies. 28 Apr.
HR 1149, 47-1, v4, 2p. [2068]
Funds due said Indians under the treaty of 27 Feb. 1867.

202. R-P of J. Burchard. 28 Apr.
HR 1150, 47-1, v4, 2p. [2068]
Indian agent at the Round Valley reservation in California.

203. Cherokee Central Railroad and Telegraph Co. 1 May.
SR 502, 47-1, v3, 2p. [2006]
Establishment of a railway through Indian Territory.

204. R-P of Dr. Price. 2 May.
SR 506, 47-1, v3, 1p. [2006]
Physician at the Hoopa Valley Indian reservation.

205. R-P of Dr. Reed. 2 May.
SR 507, 47-1, v3, 1p. [2006]
Physician to the White Mountain Apaches on the San Carlos reservation, Arizona.

206. R-P of J. Bacon. 3 May.
HR 1162, 47-1, v4, 2p. [2068]
Service in Sioux campaign of 1864.

207. Relief of the Estate of J. Riley. 3 May.
HR 1180, 47-1, v4, 2p. [2068]
Choctaw Indian makes contact with soldier.

208. R-C of B. Holladay. 3 May.
HR 1182, 47-1, v4, 11p. [2068]
Indian depredations between the Missouri River and Salt Lake City; mail carrier.

209. Little Rock and Fort Smith Railroad Lands. 3 May.
HR 1205, 47-1, v4, 1p. [2068]
Track laid in Indian Territory removed.

210. R-C of the First Minnesota Mounted Rangers. 4 May.
SR 534, 47-1, v3, 2p. [2006]
Indian war of 1862.

211. Troops in Arizona. 4 May.
HED 193, 47-1, v23, 3p. [2031]
Protection of citizens from hostile Apaches.

212. Fort Dodge Military Reservation, Kansas. 6 May.
HED 195, 47-1, v23, 4p. [2031]
On disposal of lands; treaty of 1865 with the Osages.

213. R-P of J. Nix. 8 May.
SR 539, 47-1, v3, 1p. [2006]
Service in the Sioux outbreak of 1862 in Minnesota.

214. R-P of J. Sturtevant. 9 May.
SR 551, 47-1, v3, 2p. [2006]
Service against hostile Indians; 1855; Washington Territory.

215. R-P of Capt. Lyster. 9 May.
SR 554, 47-1, v3, 4p. [2006]
Loss of property at Camp Supply, Indian Territory in 1877.

216. Eastern Cherokees in North Carolina. 11 May.
HED 196, 47-1, v23, 68p. [2031]
Their lands and trust funds; trespasses on their lands by white settlers.

217. R-C of Kansas, Nevada, Oregon, Texas, Idaho, and Washington. 12 May.
SR 575, 47-1, v3, 3p. [2006]
Suppression of Indian hostilities; Bannock and Umatillas in 1877-1878; White River and Elko Indian wars in 1875 and 1878; etc.

218. R-P of A. McAuley. 12 May.
HR 1252, 47-1, v4, 2p. [2068]
Creek and Seminole war in Florida.

219. R-P of L. Morris. 12 May.
HR 1261, 47-1 , v4, 2p. [2068]
Traders to the Choctaws sued for failure to obtain proper authorization from the Choctaw Nation.

220. Interest Due the Osages. 15 May.
HED 200, 47-1, v23, 4p. [2031]
On the proceeds of land sales under the treaty of 29 Sept. 1865.

221. Annual Report of the Smithsonian Institution. 16 May.
SMD 109, 47-1, v2, 839p. [1994]
Research related to the American

Indian; Indian bread; Indian remains in Georgia and Illinois.

222. Resol. of Sen. Call. 17 May.
SMD 94, 47-1, v1, 1p. [1993]
Pensions to survivors of the Indian wars prior to 1848.

223. On the Relief of the Delawares. 17 May.
SR 589, 47-1, v4, 2p. [2007]
Land cessions and allotments under the treaties of 1829, 1854, 1860, and 1866; removal to Cherokee lands in Indian Territory; funds due the Delawares.

224. R-P of W. McNamara. 17 May.
SR 591, 47-1, v4, 2p. [2007]
Service in several Indian campaigns in Texas, Kansas, Wyoming, and Indian Territory.

225. R-P of L. Hentig. 19 May.
SR 597, 47-1, v4, 2p. [2007]
Apache hostilities; 1881; near Fort Apache, Arizona.

226. Gen. Deficiency Bill. 20 May.
HR 1274, 47-1, v4, 44p. [2068]
Year ending 30 June 1882; Indian appropriations.

227. Disposition of Lands in Military Reserves. 23 May.
SR 628, 47-1, v4, 4p. [2007]
Forts Rice and Randall in Dakota; portions in the Sioux reservation.

228. R-P of J. Stranch. 23 May.
SR 635, 47-1, v4, 3p. [2007]
Horse lost to Indians during Mexican War; 1847.

229. Indian War Claim of Florida. 23 May.
HED 203, 47-1, v23, 97p. [2031]
For suppression of Seminole hostilities during 1855-1860.

230. Settlers on the Round Valley Reservation. 23 May.
HED 205, 47-1, v23, 4p. [2031]
Payments for improvements made on the California Indian reservation.

231. Apaches at the Mescalero and Jicarilla Agencies. 23 May.
HED 207, 47-1, v23, 3p. [2031]
Appropriation for their consolidation and support.

232. R-P of L. Boddy. 24 May.
SR 650, 47-1, v4, 4p. [2007]
Modoc hostilities of 1872 in Oregon; treaty of 14 Oct. 1864 with the Modocs, Klamaths, and other tribes.

233. R-C of J. Riley. 31 May.
SR 658, 47-1, v4, 1p. [2007]
Choctaw Indian enters contract with U.S. soldier in 1868.

234. R-C of E. Baldwin. 31 May.
SR 661, 47-1, v4, 2p. [2007]
Services on the Colorado Indian reservation in Arizona.

235. R-C of L. Wilson. 31 May.
SR 669, 47-1, v4, 1p. [2007]
Contract for Indian supplies in 1877.

236. R–C of J. Leathers. 1 June.
SR 676, 47-1, v4, 2p. [2007]
Fined for fishing in Pyramid Lake, Nevada, within an Indian reservation.

237. Legislative, Executive, and Judicial Appropriation Bill. 2 June.
HR 1276, 47-1, v4, 164p. [2068]
Year ending 30 June 1883; Indian expenses.

238. R-P of A. Chapman. 5 June.
SR 691, 47-1, v4, 1p. [2007]
Service in the Indian Territory campaign of 1874 against the Kiowas and Comanches.

239. Message on the Cherokees. 6 June.
SED 179, 47-1, v6, 3p. [1991]
Appropriation to pay for legal services rendered the Cherokees of North Carolina.

240. Boundary Between Texas and Indian Territory. 6 June.
HR 1282, 47-1, v5, 6p. [2069]
Dispute over claim to land.

241. Brevet Commissions for Service in Indian Wars. 6 June.
HR 1290, 47-1, v5, 3p. [2069]
House Com. on Military Affairs defines Indian wars as "wars" in all senses of the word; disputes the Senate's view on the matter, which is that Indian wars are not really wars.

242. Sale of Kickapoo Lands in Kansas. 6 June.
HR 1303, 47-1, v5, 4p. [2069]
Lands reserved by the treaty of 28 June 1868.

243. White River and Uncompahgre Utes. 6 June.
HR 1304, 47-1, v5, 8p. [2069]
On title to lands in the Colorado reservation lately occupied by the Utes; settlement on the lands.

244. Sale of the Otoe and Missouria Reservation. 6 June.
HR 1305, 47-1, v5, 6p. [2069]

In Kansas and Nebraska; right of way of the Republican Valley Railroad.

245. R-P of H. Kelley. 6 June.
HR 1326, 47-1, v5, 1p. [2069]
Indian battle of 1858; death at the Shoshone and Bannock agency in 1879.

246. R-P of Col. Meacham. 6 June.
HR 1346, 47-1, v5, 2p. [2069]
Negotiating party attacked by Modocs in California; 1873; Modoc war.

247. R-P of G. Quick. 6 June.
HR 1348, 47-1, v5, 1p. [2069]
Service in Black Hawk war of 1832.

248. Monument at the Wyandot Mission. 6 June.
HR 1376, 47-1, v5, 2p. [2069]
Founded among the Wyandots of Ohio in 1816.

249. Oregon Short Line Railroad Co. 8 June.
HR 1384, 47-1, v5, 2p. [2069]
Agreement made for a right of way through the Fort Hall Indian reservation in Idaho.

250. Settlement with Pottawatomies. 12 June.
HR 1404, 47-1, v5, 5p. [2069]
Funds due said Indians of Michigan and Indiana under various treaties.

251. Publications of the Interior Dept. 14 June.
SED 182, 47-1, v6, 76p. [1991]
From 1789 to 1881; list of OIA publications; numerous circulars, etc., related to Indian affairs.

252. R-P of A. Larkin. 15 June.
SR 733, 47-1, v4, 4p. [2007]
Cherokee depredations of 1874 in Indian Territory.

253. Right of Way Through the Papago Reservation. 16 June.
HR 1424, 47-1, v5, 1p. [2069]
To the Arizona Southern Railroad Co.; Arizona.

254. Pawnee Reservation in Indian Territory. 20 June.
HED 218, 47-1, v23, 3p. [2031]
On enlargement of the reservation.

255. Settlers in the Duck Valley Reservation. 20 June.
HR 1460, 47-1, v5, 1p. [2069]
Payment for improvements made on lands encorporated into this Shoshone reservation in Nevada.

256. R-C of F. Plummer. 20 June.
HR 1495, 47-1, v5, 2p. [2069]
Fort Cobb, Indian Territory, evacuated due to a Confederate attack; Civil War.

257. Private Land Claim in New Mexico. 20 June.
HR 1500, 47-1, v5, 6p. [2069]
Settler driven from land during the Indian insurrection of 1860.

258. R-C of Reps. of A. Chaves. 20 June.
HR 1501, 47-1, v5, 10p. [2069]
Settler periodically driven from land by hostile Indians.

259. Sale of Timber on the Menomonee Reservation. 21 June.
SR 744, 47-1, v4, 2p. [2007]
For the benefit of the tribe; Wisconsin.

260. Right of Way in Arizona. 21 June.
SR 746, 47-1, v4, 2p. [2007]
Grant of right of way to the Arizona Southern Railroad Co. through the Papago Indian reservation.

261. R-P of E. Porter. 23 June.
HR 1511, 47-1, v5, 1p. [2069]
Battle at the Little Big Horn (Custer massacre) with the Sioux; 1876; Montana.

262. Construction of Military Quarters. 26 June.
SED 187, 47-1, v6, 2p. [1991]
In Arizona; control of Indian hostilities.

263. Mem. of Sen. Allison. 26 June.
SMD 112, 47-1, v2, 3p. [1994]
Legislative appropriations bill; OIA.

264. Sundry Civil Appropriation Bill. 26 June.
HR 1520, 47-1, v5, 149p. [2069]
Year ending 30 June 1883; includes Sioux reservation, Crow reservation boundary survey, Ute Commission, etc.

265. R-P of E. Custer. 27 June.
SR 751, 47-1, v4, 1p. [2007]
Widow of G. Custer asks for increase in pension; battle of 1876 on the Little Big Horn River, Montana.

266. R-P of L. Mitchell. 27 June.
SR 758, 47-1, v4, 3p. [2007]
Service against the Gosh Utes and Bannocks in Utah Territory; 1860.

267. R-P of C. French. 27 June.
SR 759, 47-1, v4, 2p. [2007]
Service in Florida Indian war; 1837-1838.

268. Definition of the Words "Indian Country." 28 June.

SR 773, 47-1, v4, 4p. [2007]
As used in the Revised Statutes and other laws of the U.S.

269. Jicarilla Apache Reservation. 28 June.
HED 220, 47-1, v23, 6p. [2031]
Payments to settlers who made improvements on reservation lands.

270. Sale of a Portion of the Omaha Reservation. 1 July.
HR 1530, 47-1, v5, 12p. [2069]
In Nebraska; allotment of the remaining lands in severalty.

271. Agreement with the Sioux. 1 July.
HR 1536, 47-1, v5, 2p. [2069]
Bill authorizes the making of an agreement which would entail cession of a portion of the Sioux reservation in Dakota to the U.S.

272. Manufacture of Salt in Indian Territory. 1 July.
HR 1545, 47-1, v5, 2p. [2069]
Bill authorizing the Cherokees to lease salt deposits on unassigned lands belonging to the tribe.

273. R-C of J. Bridger. 6 July.
SR 790, 47-1, v4, 2p. [2007]
Indian trader in Utah, beginning in 1843.

274. R-P of E. Merchant. 7 July.
HR 1579, 47-1, v5, 1p. [2069]
Indian battle on the Mexican frontier.

275. Alleged Excess in Certification of Lands to Railroad Companies. 10 July.
HED 223, 47-1, v23, 14p. [2031]
Lands within the former Winnebago reservation to the St. Paul and Sioux City Railroad.

276. R-P of R. Marshall. 14 July.
HR 1625, 47-1, v6, 1p. [2070]
Service against Indians in Kansas; 1875.

277. R-P of J. Nix. 14 July.
HR 1630, 47-1, v6, 1p. [2070]
Service in Sioux outbreak of 1862 in Minnesota.

278. R-P of M. Clements. 14 July.
HR 1631, 47-1, v6, 1p. [2070]
Service against Indians in Kansas; 1875.

279. Lands Available for Settlement by Colored People. 15 July.
SMD 117, 47-1, v4, 5p. [1996]
Within Indian Territory.

280. Umatilla Reservation Lands. 15 July.
HR 1654, 47-1, v6, 1p. [2070]
Allotment of lands in severalty; Oregon.

281. Indian Traders. 15 July.
HR 1655, 47-1, v6, 2p. [2070]
Amendment to the Revised Statutes concerning who is or is not to be considered a legitimate trader.

282. R-C of H. Buggert. 15 July.
HR 1677, 47-1, v6, 3p. [2070]
Service in Sioux outbreak of 1862 in Minnesota.

283. R-C of Georgia. 15 July.
HR 1684, 47-1, v6, 3p. [2070]
For frontier defense against Indians; 1795-1818.

284. R-C of the Western Cherokees. 15 July.
HR 1693, 47-1, v6, 7p. [2070]
Based on errors made in relation to interest due them on the proceeds of sale of Cherokee lands east of the Mississippi under the treaty of 1835.

285. Fishery Industry of the U.S. 18 July.
SMD 124 (pts. 1-7), 47-1, v6-11, 3569p. [1998-2003]
Indian porpoise, sea-otter, and whale hunting; Indian shell middens; use of mussels, shell-fish, clams, and oysters; sealing by Makah Indians.

286. Forts Dodge and Wallace, Kansas. 21 July.
HED 225, 47-1, v23, 7p. [2031]
Disposal of the posts; portion of Fort Dodge military reservation is within area of the Osage trust lands (treaty of 1865).

287. On the Case of Gen. Pleasonton. 24 July.
HR 1704, 47-1, v6, 5p. [2070]
Service against Apaches, Navajoes, Utah Indians, Seminoles, Sioux, and Oregon Indians; 1850-1859.

288. R-P of J. Fenscke. 24 July.
HR 1705, 47-1, v6, 1p. [2070]
Employed at the Lower Sioux agency, Minnesota, at the time of the Sioux outbreak in 1862.

289. List of Private Claims. 25 July.
HMD 53, 47-1, v2, 744p. [2036]
From the 42d to the 46th Congress; includes Indian depredation claims, etc.

290. Army Record of Certain Officers. 26 July.
SR 855, 47-1, v4, 3p. [2007]

In the Indian Home Guard; Cherokee delegates to Washington.

291. R-P of C. French. 26 July.
HR 1714, 47-1, v6, 2p. [2070]
Service in Florida Indian war; 1837-1838.

292. R-C of C. Dahler. 26 July.
HR 1717, 47-1, v6, 3p. [2070]
Service as acting governor of Montana in 1867; suppression of Indian hostilities.

293. Letter on the Poncas. 29 July.
SED 192, 47-1, v6, 2p. [1991]
Money paid to the Poncas since 1871 under the treaty of 2 Mar. 1858, and numerous acts of Congress.

294. R-P of E. Porter. 29 July.
SR 865, 47-1, v4, 1p. [2007]
Casualty at the battle of the Little Big Horn in 1876; Custer massacre; Sioux war.

295. R-C of Dr. Reed. 31 July.
HR 1788, 47-1, v6, 1p. [2070]
Physician to the White Mountain Apaches on the San Carlos reservation, Arizona.

296. R-P of F. Plummer. 1 Aug.
SR 871, 47-1, v4, 2p. [2007]
Service in Florida Indian war, and in Indian Territory.

297. Statements of Appropriations. 8 Aug.
HMD 58, 47-1, v13, 152p. [2047]
During the 1st session, 47th Congress; Indian expenses.

298. Annual Report of the Bureau of Ethnology. 9 Sept.
HMD 61, 47-1, v20, 514p. [2055]
Including studies of Indian languages, mortuary customs, houses and houselife, Zuni fetishes, Iroquois myths, Navajo silversmiths, shell art, animal carvings, etc.

299. Contributions to North American Ethnology. (no date)
HMD 66, 47-1, v26, 418p. [2062]
Cup-shaped sculptures of aboriginal Americans, etc.

300. Disbursements of the Indian Dept. 26 Oct.
HED 6, 47-2, v17, 10p. [2106]
Year ending 30 June 1882; Indian expenses.

301. Annual Message to Congress with Documents; Pres. Arthur. 4 Dec.
HED 1, 47-2, v1-14, 11,112p. [2090-2103]
The Indian policy of allotment, education, and extending jurisdiction over tribes; annual report of the Sec. of War (Serials 2091-2096); annual report of the Sec. of Interior (Serials 2099-2102); annual report of the Gen. Land Office (Serial 2099); annual report of the CIA (Serial 2100), including railroad rights of way through Indian reservations, appropriations needed, education, annuities, Sioux commission appointed in 1882, and reports of agents; etc.

302. Annual Report of the Sec. of the Treasury. 4 Dec.
HED 2, 47-2, v15, 638p. [2104]
Year ending 30 June 1882; Indian expenses.

303. Estimates of Appropriations. 4 Dec.
HED 5, 47-2, v17, 316p. [2106]
Year ending 30 June 1884; Indian expenses.

304. Judgments of the Court of Claims. 4 Dec.
HMD 5, 47-2, v1, 6p. [2115]
Year ending 3 Dec. 1881; cases relevant to Indian affairs.

305. Indian Appropriation Bill. 4 Dec.
HR 1812, 47-2, v1, 1p. [2159]
Year ending 30 June 1884.

306. Alleged Shelling of Alaskan Villages. 6 Dec.
HED 9 (pts. 1-4), 47-2, v14, 11p. [2103]
Indian village shelled to teach them a lesson; Hoochenoo Indians were becoming troublesome after one of their number was accidentally killed on a whaling boat.

307. Abstract of Indian Depredation Claims. 7 Dec.
HED 10, 47-2, v14, 2p. [2103]
Acted upon since 8 Apr. 1882; lists location, date, tribe involved, and action on claim.

308. Agreement Made by the Paiutes. 8 Dec.
SED 7, 47-2, v1, 5p. [2073]
Dated 9 Aug. 1882; provides for granting a right of way through the Walker River reservation, Nevada, to the Carson and Colorado Railroad Co.

309. Correspondence with Naval Officers in Alaska. 13 Dec.
HED 17, 47-2, v14, 6p. [2103]

Threatened aggressions of Indians; Indian education.

310. Resol. of Sen. Voorhees. 14 Dec.
SMD 11, 47-2, v1, 1p. [2083]
Asks for report on disputes between the Cherokees and the U.S.

311. "Old Settler" Cherokees. 16 Dec.
SED 17, 47-2, v1, 17p. [2073]
Claims of the Western Cherokees for funds due them under the treaties of 1835, and 1846.

312. Abandoned Military Reservations. 19 Dec.
SED 20, 47-2, v1, 56p. [2073]
Camp Independence, California, broken up at the beginning of the Nez Percé war; portion of Fort Dodge reservation in the Osage trust lands; etc.

313. Message on the Nez Percé and Other Indians. 21 Dec.
HED 24, 47-2, v14, 4p. [2103]
Allotment on the Nez Percé reservation in Idaho; allotment on the Grande Ronde reservation in Oregon; Nez Percé treaty of 9 June 1863; Willamette treaty of 22 Jan. 1855.

314. Publication and Distribution of Public Documents. 22 Dec.
HMD 12, 47-2, v1, 66p. [2115]
Binding of copies of Durant's collection of revised Indian treaties (act of 20 June 1874).

315. Postal Routes in Dakota. 27 Dec.
SED 28, 47-2, v2, 5p. [2075]
Would cross the Sioux reservation.

316. Surplus Subsistence Funds. 27 Dec.
HED 25, 47-2, v14, 2p. [2103]
Appropriated for 1882; funds diverted to other tribes; list of tribes involved.

1883

1. Land Patents to Railroad Companies. 2 Jan.
HED 29, 47-2, v14, 39p. [2103]
Atlantic and Pacific Railroad located in Indian Territory; Leavenworth, Lawrence, and Galveston Railroad on Osage lands in Kansas.

2. Cherokee Indian Lands. 4 Jan.
SR 908, 47-2, v1, 3p. [2087]
On title to a tract of land situated along the Arkansas River; treaties of 1828, 1833, and 1866.

3. Indian Civilization Fund. 9 Jan.
SED 35, 47-2, v3, 30p. [2076]
Statement of receipts and expenditures from the fund; originally established in 1819.

4. Right of Way for Railroad Purposes. 9 Jan.
SR 916, 47-2, v1, 2p. [2087]
Through the Fort Smith military reservation in Arkansas, and the Choctaw Nation.

5. R-P of H. Kelley. 9 Jan.
SR 917, 47-2, v1, 1p. [2087]
Service against Indians in 1858; soldier dies at the Shoshone and Bannock agency in 1879.

6. Date of Entry Into Military Service. 9 Jan.
SR 920, 47-2, v1, 5p. [2087]
Case of Capt. Miles, commander of troops in the Nez Percé and Bannock wars in Washington and Idaho.

7. Claims Allowed for Supplies. 10 Jan.
HED 42, 47-2, v19, 9p. [2108]
On account of the Indian service.

8. Claims Allowed Under Exhausted Appropriations. 11 Jan.
HED 45, 47-2, v19, 63p. [2108]
For expenses of the Indian service.

9. R-C of California. 11 Jan.
HR 1847, 47-2, v1, 25p. [2159]
Indian war bonds issued during the hostilities of 1851-1852.

10. Consolidation of Certain Railroads. 12 Jan.
HR 1856, 47-2, v1, 3p. [2159]
To connect the Gulf region with the Pacific; forming a southern railroad network; would run a great distance through Indian country.

11. Contingent Expenses of the Interior Dept. 13 Jan.
HED 47, 47-2, v19, 27p. [2108]
Year ending 30 June 1882; OIA.

12. On the Case of Maj. Reno. 16 Jan.
SR 926, 47-2, v1, 5p. [2087]
Dismissed from the Army on various charges; record shows valuable service in Indian wars.

13. R-P of J. Blazer. 16 Jan.
SR 928, 47-2, v1, 3p. [2087]
Mescalero Apache depredations of 1879 in New Mexico.

14. R-P of E. Chirouse. 16 Jan.
SR 929, 47-2, v1, 2p. [2087]
Accounts of this former Indian agent.

15. Agreement with Several Indian Tribes. 19 Jan.
SED 44, 47-2, v3, 28p. [2076]
Dated 2 Sept. 1882, with the confederated Flathead, Kootenay, and Upper Pend d'Oreilles Indians on the Jocko (Flathead) reserve in Montana; sale of land needed by the Northern Pacific Railroad.

16. Cherokee Lands in Indian Territory. 20 Jan.
HED 54, 47-2, v19, 39p. [2108]
Payment for lands ceded to the U.S. under the treaty of 19 July 1866.

17. Annual Report of the Smithsonian Institution. 22 Jan.
HMD 26, 47-2, v5, 873p. [2121]
Research related to the American Indian; Indian deities and mythology; language; industries.

18. Appropriation for the 10th Census. 26 Jan.
SR 941, 47-2, v1, 9p. [2087]
Needed to continue work; Indian statistics.

19. Estimates of Deficiencies. 26 Jan.
HED 60, 47-2, v19, 32p. [2108]
In appropriations for fiscal 1882-1883; Indian expenses.

20. Buildings at Certain Military Posts. 26 Jan.
HED 61, 47-2, v19, 53p. [2108]
Completion of Fort Custer, Montana, necessary in order to control the Sioux; etc.

21. Right of Way Through the Fort Smith Military Reserve. 26 Jan.
HR 1889, 47-2, v1, 2p. [2159]
Railroad already has a right of way through the Choctaw Nation to said reserve.

22. Creation of Additional Land Districts in Dakota. 29 Jan.
HR 1894, 47-2, v1, 2p. [2159]
To handle lands to be ceded to the U.S. by the Sioux; reduction of the Great Sioux reservation; also, the Turtle Mountain region.

23. Sale of Timber on Menomonee Lands. 29 Jan.
HR 1895 , 47-2, v1, 2p. [2159]
Bill authorizing sale of said timber; Wisconsin.

24. R-P of L. Boddy. 29 Jan.
HR 1896, 47-2, v1, 4p. [2159]
Settlement on lands ceded under the treaty of 14 Oct. 1864 with the Klamaths, Modocs, and other tribes; Modoc war of 1872-1873 in Oregon.

25. Legislative, Executive, and Judicial Appropriation Bill. 2 Feb.
HR 1923, 47-2, v1, 192p. [2159]
Year ending 30 June 1884; Indian expenses.

26. Letter on the Sioux. 3 Feb.
SED 55, 47-2, v3, 2p. [2076]
Deficiency in appropriation for fulfilling treaty stipulations; supplies needed at Standing Rock Agency; agreement of 28 Feb. 1877.

27. Sioux Indian Treaties. 3 Feb.
HED 68, 47-2, v19, 14p. [2108]
Report of the Sioux Commission; agreement made 7 Aug. 1882 with the Sioux for the breaking up of the Great Sioux reservation in Dakota into separate reserves, with the sale of surplus lands created.

28. Mem. of the Creek Nation. 3 Feb.
HMD 18, 47-2, v1, 60p. [2115]
On the subject of allotment of lands in severalty; cases of actual allotments to various tribes looked at; the policy of allotment is opposed.

29. Population Statistics at the 10th Census. 3 Feb.
HMD 42 (pt. 1), 47-2, v13, 1038p. [2129]
Indian populations (other census vols. contain scattered information on Indians and Indian Territory; see Serials 2129-2152 for the 10th Census).

30. R-P of E. Smith. 3 Feb.
HR 1925, 47-2, v1, 1p. [2159]
Senate Com. on Indian Affairs passed a similar bill the previous year.

31. R-P of E. Conner. 3 Feb.
HR 1926, 47-2, v1, 4p. [2159]
Service against Indians loyal to Great Britain in the War of 1812 in Indiana; trader to the Delawares and other tribes in 1821; interpreter at the treaty of Greenville in 1795.

32. Invasion of Indian Territory. 5 Feb.
SED 58, 47-2, v3, 2p. [2076]
Amendment to Revised Statutes recommended which would impose a penalty of imprisonment for unlawful entry on Indian lands.

33. Cherokee Indian Matters. 8 Feb.
SED 60, 47-2, v3, 29p. [2076]
Reports on claims of the Eastern and Western Cherokees; funds due under the treaties of 1835, and 1846.

34. R-P of J. Little and H. Williams. 8 Feb.
SR 965, 47-2, v1, 2p. [2087]
Lease of mining lands from the Iowa Indians; Kansas and Nebraska.

35. R-P of L. Tatum. 9 Feb.
HR 1932, 47-2, v1, 6p. [2159]
Agent to the Kiowas and Comanches in Indian Territory; 1869-1873.

36. Mississippi, Albuquerque, and Inter-Ocean Railway Co. 9 Feb.
HR 1933, 47-2, v1, 1p. [2159]
Bill to construct a rail line through the Choctaw and Chickasaw Nations is rejected.

37. On the Case of Gen. Anderson. 9 Feb.
HR 1934, 47-2, v1, 2p. [2159]
Service in the Navajo campaign of 1861-1862.

38. R-P of O. Meacham. 10 Feb.
SR 976, 47-2, v1, 1p. [2087]
Treaty com'r to the Modocs attacked in 1873 at a negotiating council in California; Modoc war.

39. Violation of Internal Revenue Laws in Alaska. 10 Feb.
HED 75, 47-2, v21, 4p. [2110]
Sale of liquor is illegal, as Alaska is to be regarded as Indian country.

40. Report of the Board of Indian Com'rs. 10 Feb.
HED 77, 47-2, v21, 67p. [2110]
Education, Indian land, missions, etc.

41. Eastern and Western Cherokees. 12 Feb.
HED 79, 47-2, v21, 13p. [2110]
Differences between the two groups regarding distribution of interest on proceeds from the sale of common property.

42. R-P of S. Darley. 12 Feb.
HR 1947, 47-2, v1, 1p. [2159]
Service against Apaches in 1852.

43. Stockbridges and Munsees in Wisconsin. 12 Feb.
HR 1950, 47-2, v1, 2p. [2159]
Tribal dispute over rights of occupancy within the reservation established by the treaty of 1856; allotments.

44. Public Timber in Montana. 13 Feb.
SED 66, 47-2, v3, 2p. [2073]
Timber depredations reported on the Crow reservation.

45. Property in the Interior Dept. 13 Feb.
SED 67, 47-2, v3, 4p. [2073]
Including the OIA.

46. Letter on the Sioux. 14 Feb.
SED 68, 47-2, v3, 2p. [2073]
Appropriation to fulfill article 10 of the treaty of 29 Apr. 1868; delivery of cows and oxen to Sioux who engage in farming.

47. Petition of the Six Nations of New York Indians. 16 Feb.
SMD 38, 47-2, v1, 7p. [2083]
Ask compensation for lands belonging to them in Kansas.

48. R-C of Florida. 16 Feb.
SR 995, 47-2, v2, 3p. [2088]
For expenses of the Seminole war of 1855-1857.

49. Stock Cattle for the Sioux. 19 Feb.
SED 70, 47-2, v3, 8p. [2073]
Appropriation for purchase of cattle for the Red Cloud and Red Leaf bands of Sioux; reimbursal for ponies taken in 1876.

50. Sums Expended for Attorney's Fees. 19 Feb.
SED 71, 47-2, v3, 2p. [2073]
By Indian tribes trying to collect funds due them by the U.S.

51. Sundry Civil Appropriation Bill. 19 Feb.
HR 1960, 47-2, v2, 83p. [2160]
Year ending 30 June 1884; expense of a census of the Winnebagoes in Wisconsin, etc.

52. Judgments of the Court of Claims. 2 Mar.
HMD 25, 47-2, v4 (pt. 1), 5p. [2118]
Year ending 3 Dec. 1882; cases relevant to Indian affairs.

53. Indian Treaty of Buffalo Creek, New York. 2 Mar.
HR 2001, 47-2, v2, 4p. [2160]
Dated 15 Jan. 1838; history of the treaty relations between the U.S. and New York Indians; removal from New York, cession of lands in Wisconsin acquired from the Menomonees, and acquisition of lands in what was to be Kansas.

54. Cruise of the Steamer *Corwin* in the Arctic Ocean. 3 Mar.
HED 105, 47-2, v23, 120p. [2112]
Medical and anthropological notes on the Eskimo Indians of northern Alaska.

55. Statements of Appropriations. 3 Mar.
HMD 36, 47-2, v4 (pt. 1), 102p. [2118]
During the 2d session, 47th Congress; Indian expenses.

56. Report of the Telegraph Commission. 3 Mar.
HR 2004, 47-2, v2, 12p. [2160]
Lines in Indian Territory, and on the frontiers.

57. Indiana Methodist Church of Norfolk County, Virginia. 3 Mar.
HR 2013, 47-2, v2, 1p. [2160]
Organized from persons of Indian descent.

58. Mineral Resources of the U.S. 30 June.
HMD 75, 48-1, v40, 828p. [2252]
Minerals located in Indian Territory.

59. Register of Officers and Employees of the U.S. 1 July.
HMD 4 (pt. 1 and 2), 48-1, v2-3, 1843p. [2214-2215]
Including Indian Com'rs, Indian agents, employees in the OIA, etc.

60. Disbursements of the Indian Dept. 27 Oct.
HED 6, 48-1, v13, 21p. [2193]
Year ending 30 June 1883.

61. Report on the Public Domain. 1 Dec.
HMD 45 (pts. 1-4), 47-2, v16-19, 3083p. [2155-2158]
Land laws, and land statistics; Indian reservations and Indian Territory; digest of relevant Indian treaties (Serial 2157).

62. Annual Report of the Sec. of the Treasury. 3 Dec.
HED 2, 48-1, v14, 825p. [2194]
Year ending 30 June 1883; Indian expenses.

63. Estimates of Appropriations. 3 Dec.
HED 5, 48-1, v16, 337p. [2196]
Year ending 30 June 1885; Indian expenses.

64. Judgments of the Court of Claims. 4 Dec.
SMD 5, 48-1, v1, 6p. [2170]
Cases related to Indian affairs.

65. Mem. of the Montana Legis. 4 Dec.
SMD 7, 48-1, v1, 2p. [2170]
Depredations of the Piegan tribe of the Blackfoot Nation.

66. Annual Message to Congress with Documents; Pres. Arthur. 4 Dec.
HED 1, 48-1, v1-13, 9914p. [2181-2193]
Indian hostilities on the Mexican border; lands for public use near the Blackfoot and Flathead reservations in Montana; annual report of the Sec. of War (Serials 2182-2187); annual report of the Sec. of Interior (Serials 2190-2192); annual report of the Gen. Land Office (Serial 2190); annual report of the CIA (Serial 2191), including appropriations, Indian agents, laws for the government of Indians, allotment of lands in severalty, railroads, intrusions on Indian lands, etc.

67. Right of Way Through the Sioux Reservation. 11 Dec.
HED 11, 48-1, v13, 11p. [2193]
Agreements of 12 June, 23 Dec., and 31 Dec. 1880 granting a right of way to the Dakota Central Railway Co.

68. Lands to Chippewa Indians. 11 Dec.
HED 12, 48-1, v13, 8p. [2193]
Allotment of lands in severalty to Chippewas of Lake Superior residing in Wisconsin.

69. Lands in Duck Valley, Nevada. 11 Dec.
HED 13, 48-1, v13, 13p. [2193]
Payments to settlers for improvements made on lands taken for the Shoshones.

70. Timber Depredations on Indian Reservations. 11 Dec.
HED 14, 48-1, v13, 3p. [2193]
Legislation to stop said depredations.

71. Right of Way for Railroad Purposes. 11 Dec.
HED 15, 48-1, v13, 7p. [2193]
Agreement of 9 Aug. 1882 with the Paiutes granting the Carson and Colorado Railway Co. a right of way through the Walker River reservation in Nevada.

72. Estates of Deceased Kickapoo Indians. 11 Dec.
HED 16, 48-1, v13, 4p. [2193]
Concerns land titles and allotment in Kansas.

73. Trespasses on Indian Lands. 11 Dec.
HED 17, 48-1, v13, 5p. [2193]
Legislation to stop settler encroachments on Indian lands.

74. Deficiency for the Indian Bureau. 11 Dec.
HED 18, 48-1, v13, 3p. [2193]
Appropriation to meet the needs of fiscal 1884.

75. Indian Depredation Claims. 14 Dec.
HED 23, 48-1, v18, 4p. [2198]
Committed since 6 Dec. 1882; includes date, location, and tribe involved in the depredation.

76. Civil Government for Alaska. 18 Dec.
SR 3, 48-1, v1, 3p. [2173]
Indian population; Indian land title; liquor production by Indians.

77. Land in Indian Territory. 19 Dec.
SED 13, 48-1, v1, 82p. [2162]
Confirmation of land title to the Cheyennes and Arapahoes, and the Wichitas, Caddoes, and affiliated bands.

78. Message on the Old Settler or Western Cherokees. 19 Dec.
SED 14, 48-1, v1, 10p. [2162]
Claim involving proceeds of the sale of lands under the treaty of 1835.

79. Sale of Indian Lands in Montana. 19 Dec.
SED 15, 48-1, v1, 33p. [2162]
Under the agreement of 2 Sept. 1882 with the confederated tribes of Flatheads, Kootenays, and Upper Pend d'Oreilles; reservation lands to be used by the Northern Pacific Railroad.

80. Indian Lands in Washington Territory. 19 Dec.
SED 16, 48-1, v1, 6p. [2162]
Land cessions under the agreements of 18 Apr. 1879 and 7 July 1883 with Chief Moses and other Indians on the Columbia and Colville reservations.

81. Supplies for the Crow Indians. 19 Dec.
SED 17, 48-1, v1, 3p. [2162]
Appropriation required for fiscal 1884.

82. Land Patents in Indian Territory. 19 Dec.
SED 18, 48-1, v1, 4p. [2162]
To the Kickapoo and Iowa Indians.

83. Fort Hall and Lemhi Reservations in Idaho. 19 Dec.
SED 19, 48-1, v1, 6p. [2162]
Land cessions and allotment under the agreement of 14 May 1880 with the Shoshones, Bannocks, and Sheepeaters.

84. Chicago, Milwaukee, and St. Paul Railway Co. 19 Dec.
SED 20, 48-1, v1, 12p. [2162]
Agreements of 2 Nov., 10 Nov., and 13 Nov. 1880 with the Sioux, granting a right of way to said railroad through their reservation in Dakota.

85. Message on the Relief of Certain Indians. 19 Dec.
SED 21, 48-1, v1, 4p. [2162]
Allotments on the Nez Percé reservation in Idaho (treaty of 9 June 1863), and on the Grande Ronde reservation in Oregon (Willamette treaty of 22 Jan. 1855).

86. Round Valley Indian Reservation. 19 Dec.
SED 22, 48-1, v1, 5p. [2162]
Payments to settlers for improvements made on said reservation.

87. Allotment of Land to Certain Indians. 19 Dec.
SED 23, 48-1, v1, 2p. [2162]
To the Chehalis Indians on their reservation in Oregon.

88. Abandoned Military Reservations. 19 Dec.
SED 25, 48-1, v1, 63p. [2162]
Military post at White River, Colorado, is abandoned due to the removal of the Utes; etc.

1884

1. Indian Homestead Entries. 8 Jan.
SED 35, 48-1, v1, 3p. [2162]
Bill allowing Indians to make entries without payment of the required fees.

2. Allotment of Lands to Certain Indians. 8 Jan.
SED 36, 48-1, v1, 6p. [2162]
To the Arikara, Gros Ventre, and Mandan Indians on the Fort Berthold reservation in Dakota.

3. Condition of the Crow Indians. 9 Jan.
SED 42, 48-1, v1 , 5p. [2162]
Increased appropriation for supplies is needed.

4. L-C of F. Sandoval. 9 Jan.
SED 43, 48-1, v1, 13p. [2162]
Indian land title in New Mexico.
5. R-C of J. Bridger. 9 Jan.
SR 21, 48-1, v1, 2p. [2173]
Indian trade in Utah.
6. Petaca Land Grant. 10 Jan.
SED 45, 48-1, v1, 4p. [2162]
Indians involved in New Mexico land claim.
7. Mission Indians in California. 14 Jan.
SED 49, 48-1, v1, 37p. [2162]
Rights guaranteed under the treaty of Guadalupe Hidalgo; U.S. citizens; land title issues involved; allotment of lands in severalty on defined reservations.
8. Oklahoma District, Indian Territory. 14 Jan.
SED 51, 48-1, v4, 3p. [2165]
Appropriation for settlement of freedmen in Indian Territory under the Seminole, Creek, Cherokee, Choctaw, and Chickasaw treaties of 1866.
9. Location of Certain Indian Lands. 14 Jan.
SED 52, 48-1, v4, 2p. [2165]
Appropriation for survey of lands purchased from the Creeks for the use of the Seminoles in Indian Territory.
10. L-C of T. Calabazas et al. 14 Jan.
SED 53, 48-1, v4, 14p. [2165]
Private land claim in Arizona; land title issues involving the Pimas and Papagos.
11. Leases of Lands for Cattle Grazing. 14 Jan.
SED 54, 48-1, v4, 160p. [2165]
Within Indian Territory, to U.S. citizens.
12. R-P of M. Jones. 14 Jan.
SR 25, 48-1, v1, 3p. [2173]
Land title issues; Klamath reservation in Oregon.
13. L-C of Albuquerque, New Mexico. 15 Jan.
SED 56, 48-1, v4, 24p. [2165]
Private land claim; Pueblo Indian insurrection of 1860.
14. R-P of L. Boddy. 15 Jan.
SR 32, 48-1, v1, 4p. [2173]
Modoc war of 1872-1873 in Oregon; land title issues under the treaty of 14 Oct. 1864 with the Modocs, and other tribes.
15. Ute Agreement. 15 Jan.
SR 33, 48-1, v1, 1p. [2173]
Sale of reservation in Colorado.
16. Supplies Furnished the Sioux. 15 Jan.
SR 35, 48-1, v1, 3p. [2173]
Amounts due for supplies delivered during 1860-1862 in Minnesota.
17. R-P of A. Pleasonton. 15 Jan.
HR 7, 48-1, v1, 4p. [2253]
Military service against the Apaches, Navajoes, Utes, Sioux, Seminoles, and Oregon Indians.
18. R-P of L. Boddy. 15 Jan.
HR 9, 48-1, v1, 4p. [2253]
Modoc war of 1872-1873 in Oregon; treaty of 14 Oct. 1864 with the Modocs, Klamaths, and other tribes.
19. On the Case of J. Monteith. 15 Jan.
HR 10, 48-1, v1, 3p. [2253]
Agent to the Nez Percés at the Lapwai agency in Idaho; accounts.
20. R-C of J. Leathers. 16 Jan.
SR 47, 48-1, v1, 2p. [2173]
Fishing within an Indian reservation in Nevada.
21. Contingent Expenses of the Interior Dept. 18 Jan.
HED 59, 48-1, v20, 58p. [2200]
Year ending 30 June 1883; OIA.
22. Sale of Timber. 22 Jan.
SR 60, 48-1, v1, 2p. [2173]
On the Menomonee reservation in Wisconsin.
23. "Oklahoma Lands" in Indian Territory. 22 Jan.
SR 64, 48-1, v1, 2p. [2173]
On opening said lands for settlement; lands were ceded to the U.S. by the Creeks and Seminoles under treaties of 1866; reserved for settlement of freedmen and Indians.
24. R-P of Brevet Maj. Gen. Averell. 22 Jan.
HR 56, 48-1, v1, 5p. [2253]
Service against the Navajoes; 1858; New Mexico.
25. Boundary Between Indian Territory and Texas. 22 Jan.
HR 63, 48-1, v1, 4p. [2253]
Dispute over the line.
26. Sioux Nation of Indians. 23 Jan.
SED 70 (pts. 1 and 2), 48-1, v4, 71p. [2165]
Cessions to the U.S. of parts of the Great Sioux reservation; reports of the Sioux Commission of 1882, etc.; railway rights of way; agree-

ments of 1882-1883; irregularities surrounding said agreements.

27. R-C of G. Carlyle. 23 Jan.
SR 70, 48-1, v1, 1p. [2173]
Sioux depredations of 1866 near Fort Sedgwick, Nebraska.

28. Gulf, Colorado, and Santa Fé Railway Co. 24 Jan.
HR 110, 48-1, v1, 2p. [2253]
Right of way through Indian Territory.

29. Mexican and Other War Pensions. 24 Jan.
HR 115, 48-1, v1, 16p. [2253]
Seminole of 1817, Cherokee, Black Hawk of 1832, Creek of 1835-1836, and Seminole of 1836-1842.

30. Indebtedness Incurred by California in Indian Wars. 25 Jan.
SMD 40, 48-1, v2, 3p. [2171]
Bonds issued during 1851-1852.

31. Claims Under the Act of 7 August 1882. 30 Jan.
HED 72, 48-1, v20, 9p. [2200]
For services rendered, and supplies furnished on account of the Indian service.

32. Land Claim in New Mexico. 30 Jan.
HR 133, 48-1, v1, 7p. [2253]
Indian insurrection of 1860.

33. R-C of I. Minor. 31 Jan.
SR 96, 48-1, v1, 3p. [2173]
Supplies to the Hoopa Valley reservation in California; 1874.

34. Lake Traverse Indian Reservation. 31 Jan.
HED 71, 48-1, v20, 42p. [2200]
Right of way for the Chicago, Milwaukee, and St. Paul Railway Co. under the treaty of 19 Feb. 1867 with the Sisseton and Wahpeton Sioux.

35. Pensions for Mexican and Other Wars. 31 Jan.
HR 151, 48-1, v1, 2p. [2253]
Creek, Florida, and Black Hawk wars; Cherokee removal.

36. R-C of A. Chaves. 31 Jan.
HR 173, 48-1, v1, 10p. [2253]
Navajo depredations; New Mexico.

37. R-C of I. Chaves et al. 31 Jan.
HR 175, 48-1, v1, 9p. [2253]
Navajo and Apache depredations in New Mexico.

38. Red Lake Reservation, Minnesota. 31 Jan.
HR 183, 48-1, v1, 3p. [2253]
Allotment of lands in severalty to the Chippewas; sale of the remainder of the reservation.

39. Cherokee Nation of Indians. 4 Feb.
SED 86, 48-1, v5, 25p. [2166]
Distribution of appropriated funds by the tribe's national authorities; protection of people adopted into said Nation.

40. Lands Certified to Railroad Companies. 4 Feb.
SED 88, 48-1, v5, 10p. [2166]
Case involving the Leavenworth, Lawrence, and Galveston Railroad Co., and Osage lands in Kansas.

41. Damage to Chippewa Indians. 4 Feb.
HED 76, 48-1, v20, 37p. [2200]
On the Lake Winnibigoshish and Leech Lake reservations in Minnesota due to construction of reservoirs.

42. R-C of Florida. 5 Feb.
SR 109, 48-1, v1, 3p. [2173]
Expenses of suppressing Indian hostilities; 1855-1860.

43. Payments for Supplies Furnished to the Sioux. 5 Feb.
HR 209, 48-1, v1, 3p. [2253]
During 1860-1862 in Minnesota.

44. Mexican Pottawatomies of Kansas. 5 Feb.
HR 210, 48-1, v1, 3p. [2253]
Final settlements with said Indians under the treaty of 27 Feb. 1867.

45. Southern Kansas Railway Co. 5 Feb.
HR 211, 48-1, v1, 2p. [2253]
Right of way through Indian Territory.

46. R-C of J. Dorsey and W. Shepard. 5 Feb.
HR 219, 48-1, v1, 2p. [2253]
Supplies to troops during the Paiute disturbances of 1860 in Utah Territory.

47. R-P of Gen. Burnett. 5 Feb.
HR 228, 48-1, v1, 10p. [2253]
Service in Black Hawk war of 1832, and in Florida Indian war of 1836.

48. Estimates of Deficiencies in Appropriations. 6 Feb.
HED 82, 48-1, v16, 31p. [2196]
Year ending 30 June 1884; Indian expenses.

49. R-P of W. Grounds. 7 Feb.
HR 253, 48-1, v1, 5p. [2253]
Hualapai depredations of 1874 near their reservation in Arizona.

50. R-P of H. Van Trees. 7 Feb.
HR 271, 48-1, v1, 1p. [2253]
Service in Indian invasion of Kansas; 1874.

51. R-P of M. Clements. 7 Feb.
HR 273, 48-1, v1, 1p. [2253]
Service in Indian invasion of Kansas; 1874.

52. R-P of R. Marshall. 7 Feb.
HR 274, 48-1, v1, 1p. [2253]
Service in Indian invasion of Kansas; 1874.

53. El Sopori Land Claim in Arizona. 8 Feb.
SED 93, 48-1, v5, 183p. [2166]
Apache hostilities in 1861.

54. R-P of M. Barnes. 8 Feb.
HR 295, 48-1, v1, 2p. [2253]
Service in the Seminole war in Florida.

55. To Indemnify California. 12 Feb.
SR 158, 48-1, v2, 3p. [2174]
For debts incurred in Indian wars.

56. R-P of W. Allen. 12 Feb.
SR 164, 48-1, v2, 1p. [2174]
Oregon Indian war; 1855.

57. R-C of T. Brooks and Co. 12 Feb.
HR 352, 48-1, v2, 1p. [2254]
Indian depredations.

58. R-C of Evans, Nichols, and Co. 12 Feb.
HR 353, 48-1, v2, 1p. [2254]
Indian depredations.

59. Boundary Between the U.S. and Texas. 13 Feb.
SED 99, 48-1, v5, 6p. [2166]
Survey of line between Texas and Choctaw and Chickasaw countries.

60. Receipts and Expenditures. 13 Feb.
HED 93, 48-1, v24, 265p. [2204]
Year ending 30 June 1878; Indian expenses.

61. Compensation to the Sioux. 14 Feb.
SED 103, 48-1, v6, 3p. [2167]
Appropriation to compensate for ponies taken from the Sioux.

62. On the Case of J. Foster. 15 Feb.
SED 105, 48-1, v6, 15p. [2167]
Jurisdictional matters involving the case of the murder of an Arapaho by a Creek Indian in Indian Territory.

63. R-P of J. Dear. 15 Feb.
SR 180, 48-1, v2, 3p. [2174]
Indian trader; Fort Robinson, Nebraska.

64. Lands in Indian Territory. 18 Feb.
SED 109, 48-1, v6, 18p. [2167]
Status of lands other than those claimed by the five Civilized Tribes.

65. Expenditures for the Indian Service. 18 Feb.
HED 95, 48-1, v24, 5p. [2204]
Open-market expenditures of the Indian Dept. to 31 Jan. 1884.

66. R-P of W. Byers and Co. 20 Feb.
SR 208, 48-1, v2, 2p. [2174]
Water-rights on the Umatilla reservation in Oregon.

67. Nez Percé and Bannock Wars. 20 Feb.
HR 386, 48-1, v2, 4p. [2254]
Pensions for volunteers in said wars; Montana, Idaho, Oregon, and Washington.

68. Umatilla Lands in Oregon. 20 Feb.
HR 387, 48-1, v2, 4p. [2254]
Allotment of reservation lands in severalty; treaty of 11 Apr. 1859 with the Walla Wallas, Cayuses, and Umatillas; agreement of 1879.

69. Receipts and Expenditures. 21 Feb.
HED 98, 48-1, v24, 456p. [2204]
Year ending 30 June 1879; Indian expenses.

70. Indian Depredation Claims. 21 Feb.
HED 102, 48-1, v25, 3p. [2205]
Committed since 5 Dec. 1883; lists date, location, and tribe involved.

71. R-P of E. Dobbs et al. 23 Feb.
HR 439, 48-1, v2, 1p. [2254]
Chiracahua Apache depredations of 1881 in Arizona.

72. R-P of H. Kelley. 23 Feb.
HR 458, 48-1, v2, 1p. [2254]
Death at the Shoshone and Bannock agency.

73. Resol. of Sen. Voorhees. 25 Feb.
SMD 56, 48-1, v2, 1p. [2171]
On leases of lands in Indian Territory for cattle grazing.

74. Mexican Claims. 25 Feb.
HED 103, 48-1, v25, 788p. [2205]
Indian depredation claims founded on the treaty of Guadalupe Hidalgo included.

75. Fort Worth and Denver Railway Co. 25 Feb.
HR 475, 48-1, v2, 2p. [2254]
Right of way through Indian Territory.

76. Civil Government for Alaska. 25 Feb.
HR 476, 48-1, v2, 2p. [2254]
Indian population; control of Indian affairs.

77. R-P of F. Nelson et al. 25 Feb.
HR 482, 48-1, v2, 2p. [2254]
Service in Ute hostilities of 1879 in Colorado.

78. White Mountain Reservation, Arizona. 25 Feb.
HR 496, 48-1, v2, 2p. [2254]
To correct the boundaries of the reservation, and segregate the Deer Creek coal fields.

79. Property in the Interior Dept. 26 Feb.
SED 116, 48-1, v6, 5p. [2167]
Including the OIA.

80. R-P of Maj. Walker. 26 Feb.
SR 226, 48-1, v2, 2p. [2174]
Property loss at Camp Smith, located in the Indian country of Oregon.

81. Sale of the Iowa Indian Reservation. 26 Feb.
SR 232, 48-1, v2, 3p. [2174]
In Kansas and Nebraska; issuance of a patent for a reservation in Indian Territory.

82. Resol. of the New York Legis. 26 Feb.
HMD 39, 48-1, v19, 2p. [2231]
On Indian education, allotment, etc.

83. R-P of H. Leach. 26 Feb.
HR 507, 48-1, v2, 2p. [2254]
Sioux and Cheyenne depredations of 1871.

84. Allotment of Certain Indian Lands. 27 Feb.
SR 234, 48-1, v2, 3p. [2174]
Within the Umatilla reservation in Oregon; treaty of 11 Apr. 1859 with the Walla Wallas, Cayuses, and Umatillas; agreement of 1879.

85. R-C of M. Thompson. 27 Feb.
SR 235, 48-1, v2, 7p. [2174]
Cherokee Indian; depredations of U.S. troops during the Civil War; treaty of 7 Oct. 1861 between the Cherokees and the Confederate States.

86. R-P of A. Durrant. 29 Feb.
HR 567, 48-1, v2, 2p. [2254]
Service in Modoc war in Oregon.

87. R-C of J. Payne. 29 Feb.
HR 577, 48-1, v2, 1p. [2254]
Property loss at Camp Supply, Indian Territory.

88. R-C of J. Bacon. 29 Feb.
HR 581, 48-1, v2, 2p. [2254]
Service against the Sioux on the Missouri River in 1864.

89. Sale of Indian Lands in Montana. 4 Mar.
SR 252, 48-1, v2, 2p. [2174]
Agreement with the Flatheads, Kootenays, and Upper Pend d'Oreilles; land in the Flathead reservation required by the Northern Pacific Railroad.

90. R-P of J. Monteith. 4 Mar.
SR 263, 48-1, v2, 3p. [2174]
Indian agent to the Nez Percés at the Lapwai Agency in Idaho.

91. R-P of F. Plummer. 4 Mar.
SR 264, 48-1, v2, 2p. [2174]
Military actions in Indian Territory during the Civil War.

92. R-P of Officers of the Fifth Infantry. 4 Mar.
SR 266, 48-1, v2, 7p. [2174]
Loss of the steamer *J. Don Cameron;* Sioux war of 1876-1877; Custer massacre.

93. R-P of L. Morris. 4 Mar.
HR 610, 48-1, v2, 2p. [2254]
Traders in the Choctaw Nation.

94. On the Case of J. Macklin. 4 Mar.
HR 621, 48-1, v2, 5p. [2254]
Service against the Sioux in 1876.

95. R-P of Officers of the Fifth Infantry. 4 Mar.
HR 622, 48-1, v2, 7p. [2254]
Sinking of the steamer *J. Don Cameron;* Sioux war of 1876; Custer's massacre.

96. Brevet Commissions for Indian Campaigns. 4 Mar.
HR 623, 48-1, v2, 3p. [2254]
Commissions withheld in the past because of doubt as to whether Indian wars are "wars."

97. North Carolina Bonds. 5 Mar.
HR 672 (pts. 1 and 2), 48-1, v3, 5p. [2255]
Bonds held as a trust fund for the Cherokees; were issued to aid the North Carolina Railroad Co.

98. New York Indian Lands in Kansas. 5 Mar.
HR 673, 48-1, v3, 7p. [2255]
Land title issues; lands allotted to Indians under the treaty of 1838; settlers on lands.

99. Protest of D. Bushyhead et al. 7 Mar.
SMD 62, 48-1, v2, 4p. [2171]
Cherokee chief and delegation, and Creek delegates on another railroad through Indian Territory.

100. Condition of Certain Indians. 7 Mar.
SR 283, 48-1, v2, 449p. [2174]
Condition of the Sioux Indians; issues surrounding the reduction in

size of the Great Sioux Reservation; condition of the Crow Indians; agreements; treaties; agents and agencies; annuities; appropriations; railroads.

101. R-P of W. Spencer. 7 Mar.
HR 689, 48-1, v3, 1p. [2255]
Obtains murderer from armed Indians in Minnesota; 1857.

102. Claims for Depredations. 7 Mar.
HR 693, 48-1, v3, 4p. [2255]
Committed by the Utes at the White River agency, Colorado; 1879.

103. R-P of H. Frazier. 7 Mar.
HR 694, 48-1, v3, 1p. [2255]
Chiracahua Apache depredations of 1881 in Arizona.

104. R-P of G. Storrs. 7 Mar.
HR 695, 48-1, v3, 3p. [2255]
Sioux outbreak of 1862 in Minnesota.

105. Cherokee Lands. 10 Mar.
SR 287, 48-1, v2, 3p. [2174]
Cherokee reservation; treaties of 1828, 1833, and 1866.

106. R-P of J. Jones. 11 Mar.
SR 296, 48-1, v2, 4p. [2174]
Service in the Sioux war of 1862; Minnesota.

107. R-P of M. Moss. 11 Mar.
SR 297, 48-1, v2, 1p. [2174]
Scout in Indian country.

108. R-P of C. McCay. 11 Mar.
SR 300, 48-1, v2, 1p. [2174]
Service in Cherokee removal; 1837-1838.

109. Justices of the Supreme Court of Dakota. 11 Mar.
HR 753, 48-1, v3, 2p. [2255]
Devil's Lake, Fort Berthold, and Standing Rock Indian agencies located in the judicial district.

110. Kickapoo Lands in Kansas. 11 Mar.
HR 765, 48-1, v2, 5p. [2255]
Bill authorizes sale of their reservation in Kansas, land allotments in Indian Territory, etc.

111. R-C of S. Wood. 11 Mar.
HR 766, 48-1, v3, 2p. [2255]
Kiowa depredations of 1870 in Texas.

112. R-C of O. Streeter. 12 Mar.
SR 314, 48-1, v2, 2p. [2174]
Census of 1860 in Dakota; population of whites, half-breeds, and Indians.

113. Northern Pacific Railroad. 12 Mar.
HED 114, 48-1, v26, 4p. [2206]
Location of the railway through the Crow and Flathead reservations in Montana.

114. R-C of J. Fletcher. 17 Mar.
SR 329, 48-1, v2, 1p. [2174]
Indian depredations of 1870 between Fort Dodge, Kansas, and Camp Supply, Indian Territory.

115. R-C of Volunteers in Indian Wars. 18 Mar.
SR 337, 48-1, v2, 1p. [2174]
Nez Percé war; citizens of Oregon, Washington, Idaho, and Montana.

116. Eastern and Northern Judicial Districts of Texas. 18 Mar.
HR 797, 48-1, v3, 6p. [2255]
Jurisdiction over Choctaw and Chickasaw country in Indian Territory.

117. Steam Vessel for Service in Alaska. 18 Mar.
HR 802, 48-1, v3, 4p. [2255]
Indian affairs in Alaska; Indian subsistence depends on the sea-otter.

118. Claims of Certain States and Territories. 18 Mar.
HR 807, 48-1, v3, 4p. [2255]
Mariposa war of 1851 in California.

119. Eastern Band of Cherokees. 18 Mar.
HR 827, 48-1, v3, 2p. [2255]
Appropriation to cover attorney fees and expenses of delegations to Washington from North Carolina.

120. Sale of the Iowa Indian Reservation. 18 Mar.
HR 828, 48-1, v3, 4p. [2255]
In Kansas and Nebraska; removal to Indian Territory.

121. Agreements with Sioux Indians. 18 Mar.
HR 829, 48-1, v3, 4p. [2255]
Dated 2 Nov., 10 Nov., and 13 Nov. 1880; right of way through the Sioux reservation in Dakota to the Chicago, Milwaukee, and St. Paul Railway Co.

122. Agreements with Sioux Indians; 18 Mar.
HR 830, 48-1, v3, 4p. [2255]
Dated 12 June, 23 Dec., and 31 Dec. 1880; right of way through the Sioux reservation in Dakota to the Dakota Central Railway Co.

123. R-P of F. Potter. 18 Mar.
HR 899, 48-1, v3, 2p. [2255]
Service on the Indian frontier in 1824.

124. R-C of T. English. 19 Mar.
SR 347, 48-1, v3, 3p. [2175]
Seminole war of 1836 in Florida.

125. Military Academy West of the Mississippi River. 19 Mar.
SR 348, 48-1, v3, 2p. [2175]
For the training of Indian youths.

126. Indian Appropriation Bill. 19 Mar.
HR 953, 48-1, v3, 2p. [2255]
Year ending 30 June 1855; Indian Dept.

127. Cherokees East of the Mississippi River. 21 Mar.
SED 135, 48-1, v6, 2p. [2167]
Concerning the roll of said Indians.

128. Annual Report of the Bureau of Ethnology. 21 Mar.
HR 964, 48-1, v3, 1p. [2255]
Printing of additional copies.

129. R-P of the Estate of G. Maxwell. 22 Mar.
HR 971, 48-1, v3, 3p. [2255]
Cheyenne depredations of 1868 on the Arkansas River.

130. Allotment of Lands in Severalty. 25 Mar.
SR 380, 48-1, v3, 1p. [2175]
To Chippewas of Lake Superior near the Red Cliff reservation in Wisconsin.

131. Crow Reservation in Montana. 26 Mar.
SED 139, 48-1, v6, 20p. [2167]
On the leasing of lands in said reservation.

132. Settlement with Certain Indians. 28 Mar.
HR 1006, 48-1, v4, 2p. [2256]
Distribution of a portion of the tribal funds of the Confederated Peorias, Weas, Kaskaskias, and Piankeshaws to those electing to become U.S. citizens under the treaty of 23 Feb. 1867.

133. R-P of Nevada. 1 Apr.
SR 406, 48-1, v3, 1p. [2175]
Expenses of suppressing Indian hostilities; White Pine war of 1875; Elks war of 1878.

134. R-P of Idaho. 1 Apr.
SR 407, 48-1, v3, 2p. [2175]
Expenses of suppressing the Bannock and Nez Percé wars of 1878-1879.

135. R-P of Capt. Northup. 1 Apr.
SR 410, 48-1, v3, 4p. [2175]
Service in Sioux war of 1862 in Minnesota; Fort Ridgely.

136. Civil and Criminal Process of Territorial Courts. 1 Apr.
HR 1034, 48-1, v4, 1p. [2256]
Jurisdiction within Indian reservations.

137. Stockbridge and Munsee Indians. 1 Apr.
HR 1054, 48-1, v4, 2p. [2256]
Dispute over enrollment and distribution of tribal funds; treaty of 1856; allotment of reservation lands in Wisconsin.

138. R-P of J. Burchard. 1 Apr.
HR 1055, 48-1, v4, 2p. [2256]
Indian agent at Round Valley, California.

139. R-C of Heirs of Black Beaver. 1 Apr.
HR 1103, 48-1, v4, 2p. [2256]
Delaware Indian in the U.S. Army; service in the Mexican and Civil Wars, and at Forts Cobb and Arbuckle.

140. Land Grants in Kansas. 4 Apr.
HR 1113 (pts. 1 and 2), 48-1, v4, 15p. [2256]
For railroad construction; within the Kickapoo, Delaware, Pottawatomie, Sac, Fox, and Kansas Indian reservations, and the Osage trust lands.

141. R-C of S. Wood. 8 Apr.
SR 423, 48-1, v3, 2p. [2175]
Kiowa depredations of 1870 in Texas.

142. Steamer for Duty in Alaskan Waters. 10 Apr.
SED 149, 48-1, v6, 4p. [2167] *or*
HED 60, 48-1, v20, 4p. [2200]
Maintenance of order among the natives.

143. Indian Depredation Claims. 10 Apr.
HED 132, 48-1, v27, 13p. [2207]
List of all claims allowed for depredations committed by tribes having annuities or other funds due them from the U.S.

144. R-P of T. Rhoades. 11 Apr.
HR 1131, 48-1, v4, 1p. [2256]
Apache depredations of 1871 in Texas.

145. R-P of J. Kaula. 11 Apr.
HR 1132, 48-1, v4, 2p. [2256]
Sioux outbreak of 1862 in Minnesota.

146. R-P of J. Cook. 11 Apr.
HR 1133, 48-1, v4, 2p. [2256]
Chippewa hostilities of 1872 in Minnesota.

147. R-P of T. McCormick. 11 Apr.
HR 1134, 48-1, v4, 1p. [2256]

Cheyenne depredations of 1867 in Kansas.

148. R-P of W. Beddo et al. 11 Apr.
HR 1135, 48-1, v4, 8p. [2256]
Kiowa and Comanche depredations in Texas 1866-1873.

149. R-P of H. Dougherty. 11 Apr.
HR 1199, 48-1, v5, 2p. [2257]
Military operations within the Cherokee country of Indian Territory during the Civil War.

150. R-C of L. and A. Lee. 11 Apr.
HR 1247, 48-1, v5, 1p. [2257]
Property taken by U.S. Army in Indian Territory; 1863.

151. Forfeiture of the Land Grant to the Northern Pacific Railroad Co. 11 Apr.
HR 1256, 48-1, v5, 32p. [2257]
Affecting the Sioux (Dakota), Crow (Montana), Coeur d'Alene (Idaho), Yakima (Washington), and Puyallup (Washington) reservations.

152. Settlers on a Certain Indian Reservation. 12 Apr.
HR 1295, 48-1, v5, 1p. [2257]
Claims for improvements encorporated into the Duck Valley reservation, Nevada, occupied by the Shoshones.

153. R-P of F. Bulkley. 12 Apr.
HR 1296, 48-1, v5, 3p. [2257]
Kiowa depredations of 1870 in Indian Territory.

154. Sale of the Sac and Fox Reservation. 15 Apr.
HR 1306, 48-1, v5, 2p. [2257]
In Kansas and Nebraska; removal to Indian Territory.

155. Citizenship in the Indian Nations. 15 Apr.
HR 1307, 48-1, v5, 3p. [2257]
Cherokees, Choctaws, Seminoles, Chickasaws, and Creeks; commission proposed to handle claims; conflict with treaties.

156. Payment of Kaw or Kansas Indian Scrip. 15 Apr.
HR 1308, 48-1, v5, 3p. [2257]
Sale of reservation lands in Kansas under the treaty of 17 Nov. 1860.

157. R-C of F. Plummer. 15 Apr.
HR 1312, 48-1, v5, 2p. [2257]
Military operations in Indian Territory; Civil War.

158. Execution of the Treaty of 1819 with Spain. 21 Apr.
SED 158, 48-1, v6, 20p. [2167]
Involves Florida Indian hostilities of 1818.

159. R-P of J. Chesum. 24 Apr.
HR 1343, 48-1, v5, 2p. [2257]
Comanche depredations of 1868 near Fort Sumner, New Mexico.

160. R-P of J. Fletcher. 24 Apr.
HR 1344, 48-1, v5, 3p. [2257]
Cheyenne and Arapaho depredations of 1870 in Indian Territory.

161. Leasing Indian Lands to U.S. Citizens. 24 Apr.
HR 1345, 48-1, v5, 1p. [2257]
Within Indian Territory; distribution of funds appropriated to the Cherokees.

162. R-P of C. Beers et al. 24 Apr.
HR 1346, 48-1, v5, 2p. [2257]
Sioux depredations of 1866 on the Big Horn River.

163. R-P of J. Fell et al. 24 Apr.
HR 1347, 48-1, v5, 4p. [2257]
Apache depredations of 1865-1869 in Arizona.

164. R-C of the Delaware Indians. 24 Apr.
HR 1348, 48-1, v5, 13p. [2257]
Depredations committed by whites in Kansas; treaty of 4 July 1866.

165. Delaware Indians. 24 Apr.
HR 1349, 48-1, v5, 3p. [2257]
Payment to tribe of proceeds from sale of lands ceded to the U.S. under the treaty of 4 July 1866; Kansas.

166. Supplies Furnished to the Sioux. 24 Apr.
HR 1350, 48-1, v5, 1p. [2257]
In Minnesota.

167. R-P of S. Crane. 24 Apr.
HR 1411, 48-1, v5, 2p. [2257]
Service in California Indian wars of 1852; service in Rogue River war of 1856 in Oregon.

168. R-C of J. Shirley and F. DeLong. 24 Apr.
HR 1417, 48-1, v5, 1p. [2257]
Settlers on lands near Fort Hall Station, Idaho, which were set apart for an Indian reservation.

169. Supplemental List of Claims Allowed. 26 Apr.
HED 144, 48-1, v27, 31p. [2207]
Rogue River Indian war.

170. Supplemental Estimates for the Indian Service. 26 Apr.
HED 145, 48-1, v27, 16p. [2207]
Appropriation required to pay

claims for services rendered and supplies furnished.

171. R-P of R. Marshall. 28 Apr.
SR 474, 48-1, v3, 1p. [2175]
Indian invasion of 1874 in Kansas.

172. R-P of M. Clements. 28 Apr.
SR 475, 48-1, v3, 1p. [2175]
Indian invasion of 1874 in Kansas.

173. R-P of H. Van Trees. 28 Apr.
SR 476, 48-1, v3, 1p. [2175]
Indian invasion of 1874 in Kansas.

174. R-P of Wolff and Brown. 29 Apr.
SR 481, 48-1, v3, 9p. [2175]
Indian hostilities of 1865 in Colorado.

175. Massacre of Dr. Whitman et al. 29 Apr.
HED 147, 48-1, v27, 2p. [2207]
Missionary near the Columbia River in Oregon; 1847.

176. Mille Lac Indian Reservation. 29 Apr.
HED 148, 48-1, v27, 18p. [2207]
History of this Chippewa reservation in Minnesota; treaties of 22 Feb. 1855, and 7 May 1864.

177. R-P of F. McKittrick. 7 May.
HR 1449, 48-1, v5, 3p. [2257]
Mescalero Apache depredations of 1873 in New Mexico.

178. R-P of F. Phillips. 7 May.
HR 1450, 48-1, v5, 3p. [2257]
Nez Percé depredations of 1877 in Idaho.

179. Southern Kansas Railway Co. 7 May.
HR 1451, 48-1, v5, 1p. [2257]
Right of way through Indian Territory.

180. R-P of O. Love and W. Gilschrist. 7 May.
HR 1452, 48-1, v5, 2p. [2257]
Comanche depredations upon Chickasaws in Indian Territory; Choctaw and Chickasaw treaty of 22 June 1855.

181. R-P of J. Cook. 13 May.
SR 537, 48-1, v4, 3p. [2176]
Chippewa (Pillager band) depredations of 1872 in Minnesota.

182. R-P of M. Barnes. 15 May.
SR 533, 48-1, v5, 2p. [2177]
Service in the Seminole war in Florida; 1840-1843.

183. Legislative, Executive, and Judicial Appropriation Bill. 19 May.
HR 1557, 48-1, v6, 5p. [2258]
Year ending 30 June 1855; OIA.

184. Public Grounds in Chicago. 20 May.
HR 1561, 48-1, v6, 4p. [2258]
Fort Dearborn reservation; Indian agency location, 1803-1839.

185. R-P of G. Comstock. 20 May.
HR 1574, 48-1, v6, 3p. [2258]
Cheyenne and Sioux hostilities of 1864.

186. R-C of O. Love and W. Gilschrist. 22 May.
SR 569, 48-1, v5, 2p. [2177]
Chickasaw Indians; depredations committed by Comanches during 1866-1867 in Indian Territory; Choctaw and Chickasaw treaty of 22 June 1855.

187. R-C of W. Beddo et al. 22 May.
SR 570, 48-1, v5, 8p. [2177]
Kiowa and Comanche depredations in Texas.

188. R-P of E. Connor. 22 May.
HR 1660, 48-1, v6, 4p. [2258]
British and Indians, 1812; trader to the Delawares in Indiana, 1821.

189. Eastern and Northern Judicial Districts of Texas. 26 May.
SR 575, 48-1, v5, 3p. [2177]
Parts of Indian Territory occupied by Choctaws and Chickasaws to be attached to said districts; jurisdiction over the Indians.

190. Boundary Between Texas and Indian Territory. 26 May.
SR 576, 48-1, v5, 1p. [2177]
Dispute over the boundary line.

191. Shooting of Black Wolf in Montana. 27 May.
SED 176, 48-1, v6, 3p. [2167]
Cheyenne Indian shot; perpetrator of crime not brought to justice.

192. R-C of J. Burchard. 28 May.
SR 583, 48-1, v7, 2p. [2179]
Indian agent at Round Valley, California.

193. R-C of G. Brott. 28 May.
SR 588, 48-1, v7, 1p. [2179]
Supposed Sioux depredations of 1862; Fort Abercrombie, Dakota.

194. Forfeiture of Land Grant to the Atlantic and Pacific Railroad Co. 28 May.
HR 1663, 48-1, v6, 16p. [2258]
Land title issues in Indian Territory; Cherokees, Creeks, Choctaws, and Chickasaws.

195. Kansas City, Fort Scott, and Gulf Railroad Co. 31 May.
HR 1723, 48-1, v6, 2p. [2258]
Right of way through Indian Territory.

196. Division of the Sioux Reservation. 31 May.
HR 1724, 48-1, v6, 7p. [2258]
Bill to reduce the reservation in Dakota by about 1/3, and open land for settlement; treaty of 29 Apr. 1868, agreement of 1877, and agreement submitted to Congress in 1883.

197. Indian School at Yuma, Arizona. 4 June.
HR 1731, 48-1, v6, 1p. [2258]
Appropriation for the Yuma Indians.

198. R-P of J. Fenske. 4 June.
HR 1738, 48-1, v6, 2p. [2258]
Service in Sioux outbreak of 1862 in Minnesota.

199. Affairs of Certain Indians. 6 June.
SED 180, 48-1, v6, 3p. [2167]
Damages to Chippewa lands within the Lake Winnibigoshish and Leech Lake reservations due to construction of reservoirs by the U.S.

200. Report of the Com'r of Fish and Fisheries. 6 June.
HMD 67, 48-1, v32, 1301p. [2244]
For 1883; distribution of fish to Indian Territory.

201. R-P of A. Pleasonton. 7 June.
HR 1789, 48-1, v6, 5p. [2258]
Service against the Sioux, Seminoles, Apaches, Navajoes, Utah, and Oregon Indians.

202. Resol. of Sen. Voorhees. 10 June.
SMD 104, 48-1, v2, 1p. [2171]
On contracts to supply beef to Indians.

203. R-P of A. Durrant. 12 June.
SR 674, 48-1, v7, 2p. [2179]
Service in the Modoc war.

204. R-C of H. Hobson. 16 June.
SR 677, 48-1, v7, 2p. [2179]
Supplies to the army in the Rogue River war of 1856; Oregon.

205. R-C of Rev. Willey. 16 June.
SR 683, 48-1, v7, 2p. [2179]
Missionary activities among the Cherokees.

206. R-P of M. Haeberle. 19 June.
SR 723, 48-1, v7, 1p. [2179]
Indian hostilities of 1862 in Minnesota.

207. Northern Pacific Railroad. 20 June.
SED 187. 48-1, v6, 5p. [2167]
Examination of the railway; Flathead reservation in Montana.

208. Pottawatomies of Kansas and Indian Territory. 20 June.
HR 1956, 48-1, v7, 4p. [2259]
Settlement of claims; treaty of 7 Aug. 1868; reservation purchased from the Creeks and Seminoles.

209. Legislative, Executive, and Judicial Appropriations. 21 June.
SR 760, 48-1, v7, 21p. [2179]
Year ending 30 June 1885; OIA.

210. Settlement of an Indian Treaty. 21 June.
SR 761, 48-1, v7, 1p. [2179]
Concluded 15 Jan. 1838 at Buffalo Creek, New York.

211. R-P of O. Streeter. 21 June.
HR 1964, 48-1, v7, 2p. [2259]
Census in Dakota; 1860; hostile Indians.

212. Sundry Civil Appropriations Bill. 21 June.
HR 1968, 48-1, v7, 28p. [2259]
Public land service; amounts of Indian land sold during 1880-1883.

213. R-P of N. Myrick et al. 24 June.
SR 771, 48-1, v7, 3p. [2179]
Supplies furnished the Sioux of Minnesota during 1860-1862.

214. R-P of M. Ord. 24 June.
SR 787, 48-1, v7, 2p. [2179]
Service in Seminole war of 1836 in Florida.

215. Annual Report of the Smithsonian Institution. 24 June.
HMD 69, 48-1, v34, 996p. [2246]
Research related to the North American Indians; Indian mounds; Siouan phonology; etc.

216. Pensions to Soldiers. 26 June.
HR 2007, 48-1, v7, 2p. [2259]
In the battle of Tippecanoe against the Indians; 1811.

217. Disposal of Cherokee Reservation in Arkansas. 26 June.
HR 2021, 48-1, v7, 3p. [2259]
Land not a proper Indian reservation.

218. Contracts for Beef Cattle. 27 June.
SED 200, 48-1, v7, 120p. [2168]
Furnished to the Indians in 1883-1884.

219. Deficiency Appropriation Bill. 27 June.
SR 807, 48-1, v7, 20p. [2179]
Including the Indian service.

220. R-M of the Old Settler or Western Cherokees. 28 June.
HR 2023, 48-1, v7, 2p. [2259]
Funds withheld from Cherokees by a Supt. of Indian Affairs.

221. Protest of a Stockbridge Delegate. 1 July.
SMD 119, 48-1, v2, 12p. [2171]
Enrollment and land allotment disputes stemming from the treaty of 1856.

222. P-P of H. Kelley. 1 July.
SR 832, 48-1, v7, 1p. [2179]
Service against Indians in 1858; death at Shoshone and Bannock agency.

223. U.S. Law over Unorganized Territory. 2 July.
HR 2030, 48-1, v7, 1p. [2259]
Adjacent to Indian Territory.

224. R-P of L. Huggins. 2 July.
HR 2101, 48-1, v7, 1p. [2259]
Indian outbreak of 1862 in Minnesota.

225. R-P of D. Webber. 2 July.
HR 2105, 48-1, v7, 1p. [2259]
Modoc war of 1873.

226. Klamath Indian Reservation. 2 July.
HR 2124, 48-1, v7, 1p. [2259]
In California; recommends opening reservation for settlement.

227. R-P of J. Waide. 2 July.
HR 2125, 48-1, v7, 2p. [2259]
Kiowa and Comanche depredations of 1871 in Texas.

228. R-C of B. Lockwood. 2 July.
HR 2127, 48-1, v7, 1p. [2259]
Services provided to the Eastern Cherokees.

229. R-P of W. Houghton. 2 July.
HR 2128, 48-1, v7, 1p. [2259]
Service in Black Hawk war.

230. R-P of R. Adams. 2 July.
HR 2129, 48-1, v7, 2p. [2259]
Sioux and Cheyenne depredations of 1864 in Nebraska.

231. R-C of W. Midkiff. 2 July.
HR 2132, 48-1, v7, 2p. [2259]
Comanche and Kiowa depredations of 1868 in Texas.

232. Resol. of Sen. Miller. 3 July.
SMD 124, 48-1, v2, 1p. [2171]
On the condition of Indian tribes in California and Indian Territory.

233. R-P of J. Fenscke. 3 July.
SR 864, 48-1, v7, 2p. [2179]
Sioux war of 1862 in Minnesota.

234. Report of the Com'r of Fish and Fisheries. 3 July.
HMD 68, 48-1, v33, 1275p. [2245]
For 1884; carp reports for Indian Territory.

235. R-P of S. Ripley. 5 July.
SR 892, 48-1, v7, 1p. [2179]
Service in Indian campaigns.

236. Sale of Pottawatomie Lands. 5 July.
HR 2139, 48-1, v7, 4p. [2259]
Belonging to the Prairie band residing in Kansas; removal.

237. R-P of A. Holburn. 5 July.
HR 2162, 48-1, v7, 2p. [2259]
Cheyenne depredations of 1867 in Colorado.

238. Northern Cheyenne Indians. 7 July.
SED 208, 48-1, v7, 2p. [2168]
Condition of the tribe located on the Tongue and Rosebud Rivers.

239. Statements of Appropriations. 7 July.
HMD 64, 48-1, v25, 122p. [2237]
During the 1st session, 48th Congress; Indian expenses.

240. Disbursements of the Indian Dept. 25 Oct.
HED 6, 48-2, v15, 19p. [2290]
Year ending 30 June 1884.

241. Annual Message to Congress with Documents; Pres. Arthur. 1 Dec.
HED 1, 48-2, v1-15, 11071p. [2276-2290]
Jurisdiction over Indian reservations; purchase of the Sioux reservation; annual report of the Sec. of War (Serials 2277-2283); annual report of the Sec. of Interior (Serials 2286-2289); annual report of the Gen. Land Office (Serial 2286); annual report of the CIA (Serial 2287), including removals, allotment of land in severalty, jurisdiction, Indian police, education, railroad operations, and reports of agents; etc.

242. Annual Report of the Sec. of the Treasury. 1 Dec.
HED 2, 48-2, v16, 683p. [2291]
Year ending 30 June 1884; Indian expenses.

243. Estimates of Appropriations. 1 Dec.
HED 5, 48-2, v18, 323p. [2293]
Year ending 30 June 1886; Indian expenses.

244. Resol. of Sen. Vest. 2 Dec.
SMD 5 (pts. 1 and 2), 48-2, v1, 2p. [2265]
On leases of land in Indian Territory or on any Indian reservation.

245. Military Reconnaissance in Alaska. 3 Dec.
SED 2, 48-2, v1 (pt. 1), 121p. [2261]
Detailed description of the Indian tribes of Alaska; accounts of the expedition.

246. Zuni Reservation. 3 Dec.
HED 11, 48-2, v21, 29p. [2296]

Claims to portions of said reservation in Arizona and New Mexico.

247. R-C of A. Salazar. 8 Dec.
HED 15, 48-2, v21, 8p. [2296]
Land claim in New Mexico; Indian pueblo at Santa Clara.

248. Contingent Fund of the Interior Dept. 8 Dec.
HED 17, 48-2, v21, 19p. [2296]
Expenditures during fiscal 1884; OIA.

249. Purchases for the Interior Dept. 8 Dec.
HED 18, 48-2, v21, 4p. [2296]
Made on the open market for the Indian Service.

250. Utah and Northern Railway Co. 9 Dec.
SED 6, 48-2, v1 (pt. 1), 6p. [2261]
Report on failure of the company to compensate the Shoshone and Bannock Indians for a right of way through the Fort Hall reservation in Idaho; agreement of 18 July 1881.

251. Congressional Directory. 10 Dec.
SMD 14 (pts. 1 and 2), 48-2, v1, 412p. [2265]
Description of duties of the CIA.

252. Indian Depredations. 11 Dec.
HED 20, 48-2, v21, 4p. [2296]
Claims since 20 Feb. 1884; includes date, tribe, place, etc.

253. Appropriation for the Indian Service. 11 Dec.
HED 26, 48-2, v21, 2p. [2296]
Year ending 30 June 1886; court expenses for Indian offenses; fulfilling treaties with the Pottawatomies, Columbias, and Colvilles.

254. Bureau of Catholic Missions. 12 Dec.
HED 29, 48-2, v21, 4p. [2296]
Appropriation for the support and education of Indian pupils on the Flathead reservation in Montana.

255. Jamestown and Northern Railway Co. 15 Dec.
HED 31, 48-2, v21, 10p. [2296]
Right of way through the Devil's Lake reservation of the Sioux Indians; Dakota; treaty of 19 Feb. 1867, and agreement of 28 July 1883; branch of Northern Pacific Railroad.

256. Funds for the Support of Indian Schools. 16 Dec.
HED 38, 48-2, v21, 3p. [2296]
Removal of restrictions upon expenditures from said fund.

257. Expedition to Alaska. 16 Dec.
HED 44, 48-2, v23, 695p. [2298]
Ethnological sketch of the Indians of Point Barrow.

258. R-C of C. Cochiti. 17 Dec.
HED 42, 48-2, v21, 26p. [2296]
Land claim in New Mexico; Navajo hostilities; Indian land title.

259. Appropriation for Certain Agencies. 17 Dec.
HED 45, 48-2, v21, 2p. [2296]
Deficiencies at the Blackfeet, Crow, Fort Belknap, and Fort Peck agencies.

260. R-P of E. Harris. 17 Dec.
HR 2171, 48-2, v1, 1p. [2328]
Service against Modocs in California; 1873.

261. R-C of the Administrator of the Estate of R. Fitzpatrick. 17 Dec.
HR 2176, 48-2, v1, 5p. [2328]
Seminole war of 1836 in Florida.

262. Annual Report of the Bureau of Ethnology. (no date)
HMD 32, 48-2, v8, 680p. [2317]
Research related to the American Indian; third annual report.

1885

1. Opinions of the Attorney-General. (no date)
HMD 15, 48-2, v3, 510p. [2312]
Decisions related to the American Indian from 1789 to 1881.

2. Annual Report of the Bureau of Ethnology. (no date)
HMD 42, 48-2, v17, 595p. [2327]
Research related to the American Indian; fourth annual report.

3. Appropriation for Lawrence School. 5 Jan.
SED 14, 48-2, v1 (pt. 1), 2p. [2261]
Indian industrial school in Lawrence, Kansas.

4. Cheyenne and Arapaho Indians. 5 Jan.
SED 16, 48-2, v1 (pt. 1), 27 p. [2261]
On the condition of said Indians in Indian Territory; disarming the Indians to promote civilization.

5. Leases of Lands in Indian Territory. 6 Jan.
SED 17, 48-2, v1 (pt. 1), 220p. [2261]

Report of leases made for grazing and other purposes; Sec. of Interior recommends lands not used by Indians be opened for settlement.

6. Price Paid for Certain Cherokee Lands. 6 Jan.
SED 19, 48-2, v1 (pt. 1), 2p. [2261]
Lands west of the Arkansas River purchased for the Pawnees, Nez Percés, Poncas, Otoes, Missourias, and Osages.

7. Coal on White Mountain Reservation. 6 Jan.
SED 20, 48-2, v1 (pt. 1), 7p. [2261]
Report of deposits within this Indian reservation in Arizona.

8. Leases of Land on the Crow Reservation. 6 Jan.
SED 22, 48-2, v1 (pt. 1), 45p. [2261]
For grazing and other purposes in Montana; agreement of 12 June 1880.

9. Flathead Indian Pupils. 7 Jan.
HED 69, 48-2, v27, 1p. [2302]
Appropriation for support and education.

10. Allotment of Lands in Severalty. 9 Jan.
HR 2247, 48-2, v1, 2p. [2328]
Bill to provide for allotment of reservation lands in severalty to the Indians; U.S. would acquire title to all lands not allotted.

11. St. Louis and San Francisco Railroad Co. 10 Jan.
HR 2260, 48-2, v1, 1p. [2328]
Right of way through Choctaw and Chickasaw lands in Indian Territory.

12. R-C of Captain and Co. 12 Jan.
HED 77, 48-2, v27, 6p. [2302]
Supplies furnished the Osages in Kansas; 1871-1872.

13. Relief of Certain States and Territories. 13 Jan.
SR 984, 48-2, v1, 2p. [2273]
Expenses of suppressing Indian hostilities; Texas, Colorado, Oregon, Nebraska, California, Nevada, Washington Territory, and Idaho Territory.

14. Indian Depredations. 14 Jan.
HED 86, 48-2, v27, 2p. [2302]
Claims since 10 Dec. 1884; includes dates, tribes, places, etc.

15. Nez Percé Indians. 15 Jan.
HED 88, 48-2, v27, 2p. [2302]
Removal from Indian Territory; return to Idaho of all except certain members of Chief Joseph's band.

16. R-M of G. Getty. 16 Jan.
SR 1003, 48-2, v1, 5p. [2273]
Service in Pottawatomie removal, and Seminole hostilities.

17. R-P of E. Alvord. 16 Jan.
HR 2299, 48-2, v1, 2p. [2328]
Service in Seminole war in Florida.

18. Indian Appropriation Bill. 16 Jan.
HR 2306, 48-2, v1, 2p. [2328]
Year ending 30 June 1886.

19. Property for Indian School Purposes. 17 Jan.
HED 100, 48-2, v27, 6p. [2302]
Appropriation to purchase land in the Moquis reservation in Arizona; for education of Moqui and Navajo Indians.

20. Resol. of Sen. Plumb. 20 Jan.
SMD 25, 48-2, v1, 1p. [2265]
Unoccupied lands in Indian Territory acquired from the Creeks and Seminoles under treaties of 1866.

21. Confirming Land Titles in Certain Cases. 20 Jan.
SR 1026, 48-2, v1, 7p. [2273] *or*
HR 2454, 48-2, v1, 6p. [2328]
Lands in Michigan temporarily withdrawn for Indian purposes.

22. Amendment to Resol. of Sen. Plumb. 21 Jan.
SMD 27, 48-2, v1, 1p. [2265]
On relinquishment of Creek and Seminole lands under the treaties of 1866; unoccupied land in Indian Territory.

23. R-C of J. Leathers. 23 Jan.
HR 2363, 48-2, v1, 2p. [2328]
Tried for fishing within an Indian reservation in Nevada.

24. Claims of the Omaha Indians. 24 Jan.
SED 46, 48-2, v1 (pt. 1), 5p. [2261]
Against the Winnebagoes for horses stolen in Nebraska.

25. Treaties and Conventions. 24 Jan.
SED 47, 48-2, v1 (pt. 2), 1434p. [2262]
Concluded since 4 July 1776 with foreign powers; those concerning Indians include treaties with France (1803), Spain (1795), Mexico (1831), and Great Britain (1794, 1796, and 1814).

26. Estimates for Deficiencies in Appropriations. 24 Jan.
HED 115, 48-2, v18, 55p. [2293]
For fiscal 1885; Indian expenses.

27. Mescalero Indian Reservation. 24 Jan.
HED 124, 48-2, v27, 6p. [2302]
Appropriation to pay for improvements on said reservation in New Mexico.

28. Arrears of Pensions in Certain Cases. 24 Jan.
HR 2382, 48-2, v1, 2p. [2328]
Service in Indian wars.

29. Indian Industrial School. 26 Jan.
HED 127, 48-2, v27, 2p. [2302]
Appropriation for equipment needed by a school in Oregon.

30. Omaha Lands in Nebraska. 26 Jan.
HED 129, 48-2, v27, 3p. [2302]
Appropriation to cover expenses of sale of said lands.

31. Annual Report of the Smithsonian Intitution and National Museum. 27 Jan.
SMD 33 (pts. 1 and 2), 48-2, v2, 1408p. [2266]
Research related to the American Indians.

32. R-P of V. Calloway. 27 Jan.
SR 1079, 48-2, v1, 1p. [2273]
Indian wars of 1810-1811.

33. R-P of J. Babb et al. 27 Jan.
SR 1095, 48-2, v1, 1p. [2273]
Settlers lose improvements when Nevada lands are set aside as a Shoshone reservation.

34. Certain Lands in Indian Territory. 28 Jan.
SED 50, 48-2, v2 (pt. 1), 71p. [2263]
Unoccupied lands acquired by the U.S. from the Creeks and Seminoles under treaties of 1866 with each tribe.

35. Claims Allowed by the Interior Dept. 29 Jan.
HED 153, 48-2, v27, 164p. [2302]
Under exhausted appropriations; claims involving the Indians.

36. Lands in Indian Territory. 30 Jan.
SED 54, 48-2, v2 (pt. 1), 7p. [2263]
On legislation to open for settlement those lands acquired from the Creeks and Seminoles by treaties of 1866; objections of Creek delegation.

37. Affairs at a Certain Indian Agency. 2 Feb.
SED 58, 48-2, v2 (pt. 1), 1p. [2263]
Transmittal letter for report of affairs at the Kiowa, Comanche, and Wichita Indian agency.

38. R-C of Dorsey and Shepard. 4 Feb.
SR 1147, 48-2, v1, 5p. [2273]
Paiute depredation of 1860 in Utah Territory.

39. Indian Depredation Claims. 4 Feb.
HED 182, 48-2, v28, 22p. [2303]
Since 13 Jan. 1885; lists date, tribe, place, etc.

40. R-P of F. Thomas. 6 Feb.
SR 1169, 48-2, v1, 2p. [2273]
Service against Indians.

41. R-P of E. Alvord. 6 Feb.
SR 1172, 48-2, v1, 2p. [2273]
Service in Seminole war of 1836 in Florida.

42. R-P of W. Lockhart. 6 Feb.
SR 1178, 48-2, v1, 1p. [2273]
Service in Black Hawk war of 1832.

43. R-P of H. Dougherty. 6 Feb.
SR 1179, 48-2, v1, 2p. [2273]
Military activities in the Cherokee Nation, Indian Territory, during the Civil War.

44. Receipts and Expenditures. 6 Feb.
HED 203, 48-2, v28, 386p. [2303]
Year ending 30 June 1880; Indian expenses.

45. R-P of D. McKinney. 6 Feb.
HR 2506, 48-2, v1, 1p. [2328]
Taken captive by Indians in 1833 in the area of Fort Gibson.

46. Supplemental Deficiency Estimates. 7 Feb.
HED 196, 48-2, v18, 12p. [2293]
Appropriations for fiscal 1885; Indian expenses.

47. Indian Depredation Claims. 7 Feb.
HED 197, 48-2, v28, 21p. [2303]
Claims not heretofore reported; lists date, tribe, place, etc.

48. Thanks of Congress to the Crew of the Steamer *Corwin*. 7 Feb.
HR 2507, 48-2, v1, 5p. [2328]
Revenue cutter in the waters of Alaska; control over Eskimos and other Indian tribes.

49. R-P of E. Thornburgh. 7 Feb.
HR 2508, 48-2, v1, 2p. [2328]
Service against the Utes in 1878.

50. Exploring Expeditions in Alaska. 10 Feb.
SED 65, 48-2, v2 (pt. 1), 1p. [2263]
Transmittal letter for report of expedition to northern Alaska; description of Indians.

51. R-P of F. Nelson et al. 10 Feb.
SR 1207, 48-2, v1, 2p. [2273]
Service against the Utes in Colorado; 1879.

52. R-P of H. Cook. 10 Feb.
SR 1214, 48-2, v1, 1p. [2273]
Service in Indian country.

53. Cherokee Indians. 11 Feb.
HED 208, 48-2, v28, 3p. [2303]
Estimate of expenditures for the removal of certain Eastern Cherokees to Indian Territory.

54. R-P of J. Brent. 12 Feb.
HR 2513, 48-2, v1, 2p. [2328]
Service in Creek removal, and the Seminole war.

55. R-P of J. Chambers. 13 Feb.
SR 1272, 48-2, v1, 1p. [2273]
Wounds inflicted by Indians.

56. Indian Appropriations Bill. 13 Feb.
SR 1283, 48-2, v1, 4p. [2273]
Appropriations for 1885; estimates for 1886.

57. R-P of G. Bean. 13 Feb.
HR 2527, 48-2, v1, 2p. [2328]
Battle with Indians at Fort Provo, Utah, in 1849.

58. Civil Government of Alaska. 16 Feb.
HED 227, 48-2, v29, 4p. [2304]
Appropriation needed; funds for commission to look into the condition of the Indians.

59. R-P of J. and C. Hulett. 17 Feb.
HR 2548, 48-2, v1, 1p. [2328]
Ute depredations of 1879 in Colorado.

60. R-C of W. Morrison. 17 Feb.
HR 2589, 48-2, v1, 2p. [2328]
Former trader at the Otoe and Missouria agency; depredations by Indians from said tribes.

61. R-P of E. Thornburg. 18 Feb.
SR 1335, 48-2, v2, 2p. [2274]
Service against Utes in Colorado; 1879.

62. R-P of W. Lockhart. 18 Feb.
HR 2607, 48-2, v2, 1p. [2329]
Black Hawk war of 1832.

63. Leasing Lands on the Crow Reservation. 19 Feb.
SED 80 (pts. 1 and 2), 48-2, v2 (pt. 1), 13p. [2263]
For grazing purposes in Montana; report on leases made.

64. Indians in Washington Territory. 19 Feb.
SED 82, 48-2, v2 (pt. 1), 11p. [2263]
Agreement made 13 Jan. 1885 with the confederated Yakimas; grants right of way through their reservation to the Northern Pacific Railroad.

65. R-P of C. Thomas. 20 Feb.
SR 1362, 48-2, v2, 3p. [2274]
Attack upon treaty Com'rs by the Modocs; 1873; Oregon.

66. On the Case of G. Newman. 21 Feb.
SED 91, 48-2, v2 (pt. 1), 4p. [2263]
Payment for supplies delivered to the Blackfeet agency in 1883.

67. Indian Education and Civilization. 23 Feb.
SED 95, 48-2, v2 (pt. 2), 693p. [2264]
History of American Indians, and relations between Indians and whites; report on Indian reservations, education, and missionary activities.

68. R-C of the Western Cherokees. 23 Feb.
SR 1392, 48-2, v2, 2p. [2274]
Amounts due under treaty stipulations.

69. Sundry Civil Appropriation Bill. 23 Feb.
HR 2627, 48-2, v2, 4p. [2329]
North American ethnology, etc.

70. Mem. of the Loyal Creeks. 24 Feb.
SMD 54, 48-2, v1, 7p. [2265]
Claims of Creeks who enlisted in the Federal army, loyal refugees, and freedmen; Civil War.

71. Revenue Marine Service. 25 Feb.
HED 252, 48-2, v29, 2p. [2304]
Appropriation needed; control of liquor traffic involving Indians; control of Indians in the northwest of Alaska.

72. Right of Way in Pennsylvania. 26 Feb.
SR 1440, 48-2, v2, 2p. [2274]
Railroad to cross Carlisle military reservation, site of an Indian school.

73. R-M of J. Fell et al. 26 Feb.
SR 1441, 48-2, v2, 4p. [2274]
Apache depredations of 1865-1869 in Arizona.

74. R-P of G. Bean. 27 Feb.
SR 1477, 48-2, v2, 2p. [2274]
Indian battle at Fort Provo, Utah, in 1849.

75. R-P of L. Huggins. 27 Feb.
SR 1499, 48-2, v2, 1p. [2274]
Indian outbreak of 1862 in Minnesota.

76. R-C of B. Reinhart and Co. 27 Feb.
SR 1517, 48-2, v2, 1p. [2274]

Indian agent at the Western Shoshone agency in Nevada.

77. Condition of Certain Indians in California. 27 Feb.
SR 1522, 48-2, v2, 197p. [2274]
Testimony on the handling of affairs at the Round Valley reservation, on the condition of the Mission Indians, and on various other issues.

78. Mem. of J. Adams. 28 Feb.
SMD 61, 48-2, v1, 13p. [2265]
On behalf of the Stockbridge and Munsee Indians; claims arising from the treaty of 1856.

79. R-P of E. Connor. 28 Feb.
SR 1523, 48-2, v2, 4p. [2274]
Trader to Delawares and other tribes in Indiana prior to, and after the War of 1812; British and Indians.

80. Land Claim in Mississippi. 28 Feb.
SR 1555, 48-2, v2, 1p. [2274]
Land cessions by the Chickasaws under the treaties of 20 Oct. 1832, and 24 May 1834.

81. R-C of S. Marston. 28 Feb.
HR 2647, 48-2, v2, 1p. [2329]
Accounts of this former agent at the Union agency, Indian Territory; during fiscal 1877 and 1878.

82. Reservations for Certain Indians. 28 Feb.
HR 2648, 48-2, v2, 5p. [2329]
Bill to provide separate reservations in northern Montana for the Piegan, Assiniboine, Gros Ventre and Blackfeet tribes, along with the bands of Sioux at the Fort Peck agency.

83. R-C of the Western Cherokees. 28 Feb.
HR 2651, 48-2, v2, 26p. [2329]
Alleged errors committed by accounting officers of the government; under the treaties of 1835-1836, and 1846.

84. Range and Ranch Cattle Traffic. 2 Mar.
HED 267, 48-2, v29, 200p. [2304]
Relation of cattle business to the interests of the Indians; cattle grazing in Indian Territory, and on Indian reservations.

85. Amendment of Bounty Laws. 3 Mar.
SR 1566, 48-2, v2, 7p. [2274]
Claims against Indians, accounts of Indian agents, etc.

86. R-P of A. Dickerman et al. 3 Mar.
HR 2688, 48-2, v3, 1p. [2330]
Indian depredations during 1860-1871 in Kansas.

87. Statements of Appropriations. 4 Mar.
HMD 38, 48-2, v2, 107p. [2311]
During the 2d session, 84th Congress; Indian expenses.

88. Resol. of Sen. Ingalls. 13 Mar.
SMD 7, 49-sp, v1, 1p. [2265]
Occupation of the Oklahoma lands in Indian Territory by settlers.

89. Resol. of Sen. Manderson. 19 Mar.
SMD 14, 49-sp, v1, 1p. [2265]
Condition of Indians in Alaska.

90. Resol. of Sen. Morgan. 2 Apr.
SMD 25, 49-sp, v1, 1p. [2265]
Appropriations to the Cherokees; mishandling of funds.

91. Bulletins of the U.S. Geological Survey. 5 May.
HMD 33, 49-1, v1, 498p. [2406]
Volume 3; Bulletin No. 21 deals with lignites on the Great Sioux reservation in Dakota.

92. A Descriptive Catalogue of the Government Publications of the U.S. 1 June.
SMD 67, 48-2, v4, 1396p. [2268]
Compiled by Ben. Perley Poore; lists documents, some of which concern Indian affairs.

93. Official Register. 1 July.
HMD 27 (pts. 1 and 2), 49-1, v5-6, 1859p. [2410-2411]
List of all agents and officers in the service of the U.S.

94. Mineral Resources of the U.S. 1 Sept.
HMD 36, 49-1, v9, 1030p. [2414]
Minerals in Indian Territory.

95. Annual Report of the Sec. of the Treasury. 7 Dec.
HED 2, 49-1, v17-18, 1814p. [2384-2385]
Year ending 30 June 1885; Indian expenses.

96. Estimates of Appropriations. 7 Dec.
HED 5, 49-1, v21, 344p. [2388]
Year ending 30 June 1887; Indian expenses.

97. Judgments of the Court of Claims. 8 Dec.
SMD 6, 49-1, v1, 12p. [2342]
Cases involving Indians.

98. Annual Message to Congress with Documents; Pres. Cleveland. 8 Dec.
HED 1, 49-1, v1-16, 13659p. [2368-2383]
Indians as wards of the government; search for an Indian policy; appoint-

ment of a commission to investigate the Indian problem; Apache and Cheyenne depredations; Sioux claims; annual report of the Sec. of War (Serials 2369-2375); annual report of the Sec. of Interior (Serials 2378-2381); annual report of the Gen. Land Office (Serial 2378); annual report of the CIA (Serial 2379); etc.

99. Disbursements of the Indian Dept. 9 Dec.
HED 6, 49-1, v20, 19p. [2387]
Year ending 30 June 1885.

100. Boundary of the Crow Creek Agency. 10 Dec.
SED 1, 49-1, v1, 120p. [2333]
Sioux reservation in Dakota; parts opened for settlement without consent being given by Indians; violates treaty of 1868.

101. Contingent Expenditures of the Interior Dept. 12 Dec.
HED 15, 49-1, v20, 20p. [2387]
Year ending 30 June 1885; OIA.

102. Northern Cheyenne Indians. 15 Dec.
HED 17, 49-1, v20, 3p. [2387]
Condition of said tribe in Montana; appropriation recommended.

103. Petition of Santee Sioux Indians. 16 Dec.
SMD 14, 49-1, v1, 4p. [2342]
Ask that they be secured patents to their lands; and the rights of citizenship.

104. Congressional Directory. 17 Dec.
SMD 15 (pts. 1-3), 49-1, v1, 610p. [2342]
Duties of the CIA listed.

105. Timber Depredations on Public Reserves. 21 Dec.
SED 13, 49-1, v1, 5p. [2333]
Proposed legislation concerning Indian reservations.

106. Trespasses Upon Indian Lands. 21 Dec.
SED 14, 49-1, v1, 6p. [2333]
Legislation concerning Indian Territory and other Indian lands; encroachments by whites.

107. Mission Indians in California. 21 Dec.
SED 15, 49-1, v1, 33p. [2333]
Condition of Indians; bill for their relief.

108. Jamestown and Northern Railroad Co. 21 Dec.
SED 16, 49-1, v1, 10p. [2333]
Right of way through the Devil's Lake reservation in Dakota; agreement of 28 July 1883 with the Sioux.

109. Carson and Colorado Railroad Co. 21 Dec.
SED 17, 49-1, v1, 9p. [2333]
Right of way through the Walker River reservation in Nevada; agreement of 9 Aug. 1882 with the Paiutes.

110. Kickapoo Lands in Kansas. 21 Dec.
SED 19, 49-1, v1, 5p. [2333]
Settlement of estates of deceased Kickapoo Indians.

111. Utah and Northern Railroad. 21 Dec.
SED 20, 49-1, v1, 7p. [2333]
Failure to compensate Shoshone and Bannock Indians for lands used in the Fort Hall reservation of Idaho.

112. Agreement with Certain Indians. 21 Dec.
SED 21, 49-1, v1, 12p. [2333]
Dated 13 Jan. 1885 with confederated tribes on the Yakima reservation, Washington; right of way granted the Northern Pacific Railroad.

113. Sisseton and Wahpeton Sioux. 21 Dec.
SED 22, 49-1, v1, 51p. [2333]
Agreement of 8 Dec. 1884 granting a right of way through the Lake Traverse reservation, Dakota, to the Chicago, Milwaukee, and St. Paul Railway Co.

1886

1. Monographs of the U.S. Geological Survey. (no date)
HMD 305, 49-1, v2, 243p. [2407]
Volume 10: hostilities of 1870 by the Uinta Utes upon an exploring expedition.

2. Monographs of the U.S. Geological Survey. (no date)
HMD 397, 49-1, v27, 770p. [2433]
Volume 12; mining in Colorado; area often warred over by the Arapahoes and Utes.

3. Lands in Severalty to Certain Indians. 5 Jan.
HED 21, 49-1, v25, 9p. [2392]
Allotment of lands to California Indians on the Round Valley reservation.

4. Resol. of the Maine Legis. 5 Jan.
HMD 48, 49-1, v10, 2p. [2415]
Appropriations for Indian education; allotment; citizenship; etc.

5. R-C of J. Leathers. 6 Jan.
SR 3, 49-1, v1, 3p. [2355] *or*
HR 479, 49-1, v2, 3p. [2436]
Trade without a license, and sale of liquor on the Pyramid Lake Indian reservation, Nevada.

6. Miami Indians. 6 Jan.
HED 23, 49-1, v25, 27p. [2392]
On money taken from the funds of said tribe in Indiana and Kansas, and given to other Indians; violations of the treaties of 1854, and 1858.

7. Receipts and Expenditures. 7 Jan.
HED 29, 49-1, v27, 462p. [2394]
For 1881; Indian expenses.

8. Resol. of Rep. Joseph. 7 Jan.
HMD 57, 49-1, v10, 1p. [2415]
Asks investigation of the handling of the campaign now going on against the Chiricahua Apaches in New Mexico and Arizona.

9. Trial of Indians Committing Certain Crimes. 12 Jan.
SED 33, 49-1, v1, 7p. [2333]
Legislation extending jurisdiction over Indians for specific crimes.

10. Receipts and Expenditures. 12 Jan.
HED 31, 49-1, v27, 414p. [2394]
For 1882; Indian expenses.

11. Resol. of Sen. Bowen. 13 Jan.
SMD 32, 49-1, v1, 1p. [2342]
Removal of all Indians in the U.S. to Indian Territory.

12. R-P of G. Getty. 13 Jan.
SR 31, 49-1, v1, 5p. [2355] *or*
HR 3176, 49-1, v11, 5p. [2445]
Service in the Seminole war (1849), in the Pottawatomie removal (1840), etc.

13. Red Cloud and Red Leaf Bands of Sioux. 20 Jan.
HED 35, 49-1, v25, 4p. [2392]
Appropriation for ponies taken in 1876.

14. Chippewa Indians in Minnesota. 25 Jan.
SED 44, 49-1, v1, 7p. [2333]
Negotiations proposed to bring about consolidation of all Chippewas upon the White Earth reservation.

15. Red Lake Indian Reservation. 26 Jan.
HR 176, 49-1, v1, 3p. [2435]
Occupied by Chippewas in Minnesota; bill calls for cession of land, and allotment of lands in severalty.

16. St. Louis and San Francisco Railway Co. 27 Jan.
HR 182, 49-1, v1, 1p. [2435]
Right of way through Choctaw and Chickasaw lands in Indian Territory.

17. R-C of I. Chaves et al. 27 Jan.
HR 186, 49-1, v1, 10p. [2435]
Apache and Navajo land title; New Mexico.

18. Agreement with the Crows. 28 Jan.
SED 49, 49-1, v1, 6p. [2333]
Dated 26 Feb. 1885; amendment to the Act of 11 Apr. 1882 calling for land cessions in Montana.

19. Repeal of Laws Relating to Public Lands. 1 Feb.
SR 69, 49-1, v1, 12p. [2355]
Repeals will not affect disposal of abandoned Indian reservations, which is done in accordance with treaty stipulations; Ute and Osage reservations.

20. Resol. of Sen. Dawes. 3 Feb.
SMD 60, 49-1, v2, 1p. [2343]
Asks for papers of H. Ward, Indian inspector.

21. Lands in Severalty to the Crows. 3 Feb.
HED 53, 49-1, v30, 3p. [2398]
Allotment under the agreement of 12 June 1880; Montana; appropriation needed.

22. Forfeit of Lands Granted to a Certain Railroad. 3 Feb.
HR 193, 49-1, v1, 17p. [2435]
Land grants in Indian Territory to the Atlantic and Pacific Railroad Co.; land title issues (Choctaws, Chickasaws, Creeks, and Cherokees).

23. Punishment for Larceny. 3 Feb.
HR 196, 49-1, v1, 1p. [2435]
In Indian Territory; horse-stealing.

24. R-P of G. Roberts. 3 Feb.
HR 249, 49-1, v1, 1p. [2435]
Sioux outbreak; 1862; Minnesota.

25. R-C of Florida. 3 Feb.
HR 303, 49-1, v1, 3p. [2435]
Expenditures in the Seminole war; 1855-1857.

26. R-C of J. Bacon. 3 Feb.
HR 308, 49-1, v1, 2p. [2435]
Sioux campaign of 1864; Missouri River.

27. Report of the Directors of the Union Pacific Railroad. 4 Feb.

SED 69, 49-1, v4, 252p. [2336]
Indian depredations in the Black Hills during 1866, etc.

28. Funds of the Miami Indians. 4 Feb.
HED 57, 49-1, v30, 3p. [2398]
Bill authorizing use of funds belonging to the Miamies residing in Indian Territory.

29. Robbery in Indian Territory. 4 Feb.
HR 314, 49-1, v1, 1p. [2435]
Increase in punishment for said crime.

30. Accounts of A. Meacham. 9 Feb.
SED 65 (pts. 1 and 2), 49-1, v1, 5p. [2333]
Late Supt. of Indian Affairs in Oregon.

31. Agent for the Winnebagoes. 9 Feb.
SED 66, 49-1, v1, 2p. [2333]
Appropriation for an agent to be in Wisconsin.

32. Estimates for Deficiencies in Appropriations. 9 Feb.
HED 62, 49-1, v21, 49p. [2388]
Year ending 30 June 1886; Indian expenses.

33. Infantry Branch of the Army. 10 Feb.
SR 103, 49-1, v4, 5p. [2358]
Reduction not advised because of "savage Sioux" still in the U.S., etc.

34. R-P of A. Luettwitz. 10 Feb.
SR 104, 49-1, v4, 2p. [2358] *or*
HR 3178, 49-1, v11, 2p. [2445]
Attack on a Sioux village; 1876.

35. R-C of S. Marston. 11 Feb.
SR 106, 49-1, v4, 1p. [2358] *or*
HR 3897, 49-1, v2, 1p. [2501]
Agent at the Union agency, Indian Territory.

36. Indian Appropriation Bill. 11 Feb.
HR 386, 49-1, v2, 1p. [2436]
Year ending 30 June 1887.

37. U.S. Courts in Indian Territory. 11 Feb.
HR 388, 49-1, v2, 1p. [2436]
Bill recommended for passage.

38. Extension of U.S. Laws. 11 Feb.
HR 389, 49-1, v2, 2p. [2436]
Jurisdiction over the unorganized territory adjacent to Indian Territory; Cherokee treaty of 6 May 1828.

39. R-P of M. Blake. 11 Feb.
HR 447, 49-1, v2, 2p. [2436]
Service against the Seminoles, Apaches, and Navajoes during 1836-1861.

40. Claims Allowed by Accounting Officers. 12 Feb.
HED 70, 49-1, v30, 276p. [2398]
Under exhausted funds; claims involving Indians.

41. R-C of R. Fitzpatrick. 12 Feb.
HR 470, 49-1, v2, 5p. [2436]
Seminole war; 1836; Florida.

42. Sac, Fox, and Iowa Reservations. 15 Feb.
SED 70, 49-1, v4, 11p. [2336]
Sale of reservations in Kansas and Nebraska; problems regarding allotment

43. On the Case of H. Ward. 15 Feb.
SED 71, 49-1, v4, 2p. [2336]
Indian inspector suspended.

44. Kansas and Arkansas Valley Railway Co. 15 Feb.
SR 107, 49-1, v4, 2p. [2358]
Right of way through Indian Territory.

45. Resol. of Rep. Gifford. 15 Feb.
HMD 121, 49-1, v10, 1p. [2415]
School facilities for the Sioux in Dakota.

46. St. Louis and San Francisco Railway Co. 16 Feb.
SR 110, 49-1, v4, 2p. [2358]
Right of way through the Choctaw and Chickasaw nations of Indian Territory.

47. R-P of M. Hewston. 16 Feb.
SR 118, 49-1, v4, 1p. [2358]
Service against Indians in New Mexico; 1860.

48. R-P of W. Spencer. 16 Feb.
SR 122, 49-1, v4, 8p. [2358]
Service against Sioux; 1857; Minnesota.

49. Cavalry in New Mexico and Arizona. 16 Feb.
HR 531 (pts. 1 and 2), 49-1, v2, 8p. [2436]
Hostilities of the Chiricahua Apaches under the leadership of Geronimo.

50. Eastern and Western Bands of Cherokees. 16 Feb.
HR 539, 49-1, v2, 3p. [2436]
Referral of claims to the Court of Claims; funds due under treaty stipulations.

51. Amending the Revised Statutes. 16 Feb.
HR 550, 49-1, v2, 2p. [2436]

Extension of pension laws to include service in State militias against Indians; Sioux outbreak of 1862 in Minnesota.

52. R-P of J. Bainter. 18 Feb.
SR 129, 49-1, v4, 1p. [2358] *or*
HR 3193, 49-1, v11, 2p. [2445]
Cheyenne and Sioux depredations of 1864.

53. R-P of G. Comstock. 18 Feb.
SR 130, 49-1, v4, 1p. [2358] *or*
HR 3194, 49-1, v11, 3p. [2445]
Cheyenne and Sioux depredations of 1864.

54. R-C of the American Board of Com'rs for Foreign Missions. 18 Feb.
SR 132, 49-1, v4, 2p. [2358]
Mission land in the Cherokee Nation of Indian Territory; treaty of 19 July 1866.

55. Census of the Indians. 18 Feb.
HED 79, 49-1, v30, 2p. [2398]
Appropriation for taking census.

56. R-P of F. Potter. 23 Feb.
SR 145, 49-1, v4, 2p. [2358]
Service on the Indian frontier in 1824.

57. Judicial Districts in Texas. 23 Feb.
HR 633, 49-1, v2, 5p. [2436]
Jurisdiction over the Chickasaw and Choctaw Nations in Indian Territory.

58. Sale of the Kickapoo Diminished Reservation. 23 Feb.
HR 642, 49-1, v2, 4p. [2436]
Set aside for the tribe in Kansas under the treaty of 28 June 1862; allotment of lands in severalty.

59. Deceased Kickapoo Indians in Kansas. 24 Feb.
HR 673, 49-1, v2, 5p. [2436]
Settlement of estates; land title issues; allotment of lands.

60. Lands Granted to a Certain Railroad. 24 Feb.
HR 706, 49-1, v2, 18p. [2436]
To the Southern Pacific Railroad Co.; consolidated to the Atlantic and Pacific Railroad Co. running through Indian Territory.

61. Land Districts in Dakota. 24 Feb.
HR 707, 49-1, v2, 2p. [2436]
Creation of additional land districts to handle business concerning lands ceded to the U.S. by the Sioux Indians; lands presently part of the great Sioux reservation.

62. Permanent and Indefinite Appropriations. 25 Feb.
HMD 128, 49-1, v10, 20p. [2415]
Appropriations for the Indians; includes annuities, etc.

63. Clerical Force in the OIA. 26 Feb.
HED 89, 49-1, v30, 3p. [2398]
Appropriation for fiscal 1887.

64. Disallowed Accounts. 1 Mar.
SED 78, 49-1, v6, 448p. [2339]
Claims, accounts, and vouchers against the U.S. paid by disbursing officers in the Indian service.

65. Railway Through Indian Territory. 2 Mar.
HR 768, 49-1, v3, 2p. [2437]
Right of way for the Kansas and Arkansas Valley Railway Co.

66. Railway Through Indian Territory. 2 Mar.
HR 769, 49-1, v3, 2p. [2437]
Right of way for the Denison and Washita Valley Railway Co.

67. R-C of Maj. Candee. 2 Mar.
HR 827, 49-1, v3, 3p. [2437]
Disbursing agent at Fort Arbuckle, Indian Territory.

68. Kansas City, Fort Scott, and Gulf Railroad Co. 2 Mar.
HR 840, 49-1, v3, 1p. [2437]
Right of way through the Cherokee country of Indian Territory.

69. Cherokee Indians. 3 Mar.
SED 82, 49-1, v6, 11p. [2339]
Distribution of proceeds from sale of lands in Indian Territory to freedmen, and other citizens of the Cherokee Nation.

70. Sac and Fox Lands in Nebraska. 3 Mar.
SED 83, 49-1, v6, 3p. [2339]
Reappraisement and sale of said lands.

71. Eastern Cherokee Indians. 3 Mar.
SED 84, 49-1, v6, 3p. [2339]
Claims for payments to be made under treaty stipulations; removal.

72. Natural History Collections Made in Alaska. 3 Mar.
SMD 156, 49-1, v8, 337p. [2349]
Narrative of expedition deals with contract with Indians.

73. R-C of Florida. 3 Mar.
SR 183, 49-1, v4, 2p. [2358]
Suppression of Indian hostilities; 1855-1860.

74. Right of Way Through Indian Territory. 3 Mar.

HR 849, 49-1, v3, 2p. [2437]
To the Fort Worth and Denver City Railway Co.

75. Sac, Fox, and Iowa Reservations. 3 Mar.
HR 850, 49-1, v3, 1p. [2437]
Sale of the reservations in Nebraska and Kansas; allotment.

76. R-C of A. Sharp. 3 Mar.
HR 858, 49-1, v3, 3p. [2437]
Sioux hostilities of 1857 in Iowa; captive of the Indians.

77. Education in Alaska. 4 Mar.
SED 85, 49-1, v6, 93p. [2339]
Including the Indians; classification of Indians and non-Indians.

78. 17th Annual Report of the Board of Indian Com'rs. 4 Mar.
HED 109, 49-1, v30, 140p. [2398]
For 1885; allotment; inspection of the Indian service; etc.

79. Receipts and Expenditures. 9 Mar.
HED 116, 49-1, v21, 109p. [2388]
During 1855-1885; Indian expenses.

80. Omaha Indians. 10 Mar.
SED 90, 49-1, v6, 4p. [2339]
For relief of the tribe; funds for improvements on allocated lands.

81. Cherokee Reservation in Arkansas. 11 Mar.
HR 1004, 49-1, v3, 3p. [2437]
Sale of said reservation; treaty stipulations concerned with the lands.

82. R-P of A. Hancock. 12 Mar.
HR 1023, 49-1, v3, 4p. [2437]
Service against the Seminoles, and in Indian Territory.

83. R-P of J. Shawbell. 12 Mar.
HR 1048, 49-1, v4, 2p. [2438]
Service in Indian Territory during the Civil War.

84. R-C of M. Casey. 12 Mar.
HR 1075, 49-1, v4, 1p. [2438]
Settlement on Sac and Fox ceded lands in Nebraska.

85. Transfers of Abandoned Military Reservations. 16 Mar.
SED 98, 49-1, v6, 3p. [2339]
Some to be used as Indian schools; Cantonment (Indian Territory), Fort Hall (Idaho), Fort Lapwai (Idaho), and Fort Stevenson (Dakota).

86. Indian Depredation Claims. 16 Mar.
HED 125, 49-1, v31, 290p. [2399]
Claims against Indians, and by Indians; claims filed and unpaid; lists dates, tribes, places, etc.

87. Indians and Yellowstone Park. 16 Mar.
HR 1076, 49-1, v4, 346p. [2438]
Report of a commission appointed to investigate expenditures for Indians, and management of Indian affairs; Sioux, Crow, Flathead, Coeur d'Alene, Colville, Yakima, Puyallup, Umatilla, Navajo, Pueblo, Apache, and other Indian agencies in Indian Territory and elsewhere.

88. Survey for a Railroad. 17 Mar.
SMD 84, 49-1, v2, 3p. [2343]
Through British Columbia to Alaska; settlements of Indians.

89. R-C of Colorado. 17 Mar.
SR 228, 49-1, v4, 2p. [2358]
Suppression of Indian hostilities; 1868.

90. R-C of W. Shimmins and G. McPherson. 17 Mar.
SR 232, 49-1, v4, 2p. [2358]
Contract made by Supt. of Indian Affairs in Nevada; 1863.

91. Right of Way Through Indian Territory. 17 Mar.
HR 1091, 49-1, v4, 1p. [2438]
Granted to the St. Louis and San Francisco Railway Co.; through the Choctaw and Chickasaw Nations.

92. R-P of J. Thomas. 17 Mar.
HR 1121, 49-1, v4, 2p. [2438]
Service in the Modoc war of 1873 in California.

93. Indian Training School in Oregon. 18 Mar.
SED 106, 49-1, v7, 4p. [2340]
Purchase of a tract of land.

94. Use of Funds for the Benefit of Indians. 18 Mar.
SED 107, 49-1, v7, 2p. [2340]
Indians dissatisfied at not being able to use the funds.

95. Oregon Military Wagon Road. 18 Mar.
HED 131, 49-1, v31, 27p. [2399]
History of road; control of Klamath, and other warlike tribes.

96. R-C of S. Marshall. 18 Mar.
HR 1159, 49-1, v4, 1p. [2438]
Supplies to California Indians in 1850.

97. R-C of F. Fulsom. 19 Mar.
HR 1218, 49-1, v4, 1p. [2438]

Choctaw Indian in Indian Territory seeks reimbursement for losses at the hands of whites; treaty of 22 June 1855.

98. Forfeited Land Grants of the Northern Pacific Railroad Co. 22 Mar.
HR 1226, 49-1, v4, 21p. [2438]
Land title issues involving the Sioux, Crows, Coeur d'Alenes, Yakimas, and Puyallups.

99. Sioux Reservation in Dakota. 22 Mar.
HR 1227, 49-1, v4, 6p. [2438]
Bill to divide the reservation into smaller portions, and to sell the remainder; history of the Sioux and Chippewas in the region, including treaties made.

100. R-P of M. Hardie. 23 Mar.
SR 252, 49-1, v4, 2p. [2358]
Investigated the Modoc war claims, and Indian war claims in Montana and Dakota; 1867-1874; etc.

101. R-P of T. Allcock. 23 Mar.
HR 1287, 49-1, v5, 3p. [2439]
Service in the Seminole war; 1836-1839; Florida.

102. R-C of California. 23 Mar.
HR 1298, 49-1, v5, 2p. [2439]
Expenses of Indian wars.

103. Haskell Institute, Lawrence, Kansas. 24 Mar.
HR 1315, 49-1, v5, 4p. [2439]
Appropriation needed to complete this school for Indian youths.

104. Organization of Oklahoma Territory. 25 Mar.
HR 1322, 49-1, v5, 1p. [2439]
Bill (not printed here) proposed.

105. Annual Bulletins of the Bureau of Ethnology. 25 Mar.
HR 1330, 49-1, v5, 1p. [2439]
On the printing of said bulletins.

106. Resol. of Rep. Wellborn. 29 Mar.
HMD 188, 49-1, v13, 1p. [2418]
On Cherokee claims under the treaty of 1835.

107. Resol. of Rep. Springer. 29 Mar.
HMD 190, 49-1, v13, 1p. [2418]
Asks a census be taken of the Indian tribes in the U.S., listing population, lands held, etc.

108. Railroads Across Indian Territory. 29 Mar.
HR 1356, 49-1, v5, 2p. [2439]
Bill allowing all companies to secure a right of way through Indian Territory by means other than a special Act of Congress.

109. R-P of S. Messer. 29 Mar.
HR 1374, 49-1, v5, 1p. [2439]
Service during the removal of the Cherokees from North Carolina in 1837.

110. Cruise of the Revenue Steamer *Corwin*. 30 Mar.
HED 153, 49-1, v32, 102p. [2400]
In the Arctic Ocean; Indians of Alaska.

111. Civil and Criminal Process. 30 Mar.
HR 1390, 49-1, v5, 1p. [2439]
Jurisdiction over Indian reservations given to Territorial courts.

112. R-P of J. Jones. 30 Mar.
HR 1406, 49-1, v5, 4p. [2439]
Engagement at Fort Ridgely, Minnesota, with the Sioux; 1862.

113. Current and Contingent Expenses of the Indian Dept. 30 Mar.
HR 1411, 49-1, v5, 2p. [2439]
Act giving Territorial courts jurisdiction over Indians; expenses will still be covered by the U.S., and not the Territories.

114. R-P of F. Murry. 30 Mar.
HR 1422, 49-1, v5, 2p. [2439]
Service in the Seminole war; 1839-1841; Florida.

115. Delaware Indians. 1 Apr.
SR 380, 49-1, v4, 4p. [2358]
Payments due for lands ceded under the treaties of 1818, 1829, 1860, and 1866; etc.

116. Chippewa Indians. 6 Apr.
SED 117, 49-1, v7, 3p. [2340]
Appropriation to said tribe for damages due to construction of reservoirs in Minnesota.

117. R-P of E. Barker. 6 Apr.
SR 401, 49-1, v5, 1p. [2359] *or*
HR 2050, 49-1, v7, 1p. [2441]
Service against British and Indians, 1812; Indiana.

118. Sale of the Site of Fort Omaha, Nebraska. 6 Apr.
SR 417, 49-1, v5, 3p. [2359]
Sioux, and other hostile Indians still in the area.

119. Wichita and Arkansas Valley Railroad Co. 6 Apr.
HR 1473, 49-1, v5, 2p. [2439]
Right of way through Indian Territory.

120. Pacific and Great Eastern Railway Co. 6 Apr.
HR 1474, 49-1, v5, 1p. [2439]
Right of way through Indian Territory.

121. Prairie Band of Pottawatomies. 6 Apr.
HR 1476, 49-1, v5, 2p. [2439]
Allotment of lands in severalty in Kansas; sale of remaining land.

122. R-C of S. Larimer. 6 Apr.
HR 1546, 49-1, v6, 3p. [2440]
Captured by the Sioux; 1864; Wyoming.

123. Reimbursing Interest on War Loans. 6 Apr.
HR 1560, 49-1, v6, 6p. [2440]
To States and Territories; incurred during Indian wars; Seminole war in Florida, etc.

124. Indian Appropriations. 8 Apr.
SR 428, 49-1, v5, 5p. [2359]
For fiscal 1887.

125. Indian Depredations. 9 Apr.
SED 121, 49-1, v7, 2p. [2340]
Appropriation for the investigation of claims.

126. Claims of Certain Indians. 9 Apr.
SED 122, 49-1, v7, 21p. [2340]
Compensation for lands ceded; Spokane, Pend d'Oreille, and Coeur d'Alene Indians; removal of said tribes.

127. R-C of the Estate of J. How. 9 Apr.
HR 1610, 49-1, v6, 6p. [2440]
Late agent at the Western Shoshone agency in Nevada; 1878-1880.

128. Resol. of Sen. Maxey. 12 Apr.
SMD 98, 49-1, v2, 1p. [2343]
On property moved into Indian Territory for sale, etc.

129. R-C of J. Fletcher. 13 Apr.
SR 502, 49-1, v5, 3p. [2359] *or*
HR 3624, 49-1, v1, 3p. [2500]
Cheyenne and Arapaho depredations; 1870.

130. R-P of the Heirs of Lieut. Stewart. 13 Apr.
SR 504, 49-1, v5, 3p. [2359]
Northwest Indian military expedition; 1865.

131. Supplemental Deficiency Estimates. 13 Apr.
HED 176, 49-1, v21, 27p. [2388]
Appropriations for fiscal 1886; Indian expenses.

132. R-C of J. English. 14 Apr.
SR 539, 49-1, v5, 3p. [2359]
Seminole war; 1836; Florida.

133. Pottawatomie Indians. 15 Apr.
SED 124, 49-1, v7, 3p. [2340]
Claims of members of that tribe residing in Indiana and Michigan to funds due them under various treaties.

134. Repealing Revised Statutes. 15 Apr.
HR 1641, 49-1, v6, 1p. [2440]
Pensions for service in Indian wars to those who were resident in Confederate States during the Civil War.

135. Allotment of Lands to United Peorias and Miamies. 15 Apr.
HR 1682, 49-1, v6, 1p. [2440]
In Indian Territory.

136. Sale of the Otoe and Missouria Reservation. 15 Apr.
HR 1683, 49-1, v6, 1p. [2440]
In Kansas and Nebraska; extension of the time that settlers have to pay for the land.

137. Organization of Oklahoma Territory. 15 Apr.
HR 1684, 49-1, v6, 26p. [2440]
Composed of that part of the U.S. known as Indian Territory; shall not interfere with Indian rights under treaties and agreements; five civilized tribes not under Territorial jurisdiction.

138. R-P of J. Waters. 20 Apr.
SR 574, 49-1, v5, 1p. [2359]
Indian war; 1847; Oregon.

139. R-P of F. Korth. 20 Apr.
SR 577, 49-1, v5, 1p. [2359] *or*
HR 1520, 49-1, v5, 1p. [2439]
Service at Lower Sioux agency in Minnesota; Sioux outbreak of 1862.

140. R-P of R. Montgomery. 20 Apr.
SR 650, 49-1, v5, 3p. [2359] *or*
HR 3334, 49-1, v11, 2p. [2445]
Service against hostile Indians.

141. Creation of the Office of Assistant CIA. 20 Apr.
HR 1763, 49-1, v6, 2p. [2440]
Does not create a new office, just a new title for the chief clerk.

142. R-P of L. Scanland. 20 Apr.
HR 1808, 49-1, v6, 2p. [2440]
Service in the Black Hawk war.

143. Allotment of Lands in Severalty to Indians. 20 Apr.
HR 1835, 49-1, v6, 2p. [2440]
Amendments to a bill providing for allotment on Indian reservations.

144. R-C of C. Cochiti. 21 Apr.
SED 128, 49-1, v7, 5p. [2340]

Land claim in New Mexico; Indian land title.

145. Army Record of Officers. 21 Apr.
HR 1847, 49-1, v6, 3p. [2440]
In the Indian Home Guards.

146. R-C of Certain Settlers. 22 Apr.
HR 1884, 49-1, v6, 1p. [2440]
In the Wind River Valley of Wyoming Territory; improvements included in the Bannock and Shoshone reservation under the treaty of 1868.

147. R-C of H. DeAhna. 23 Apr.
HR 1902, 49-1, v7, 2p. [2441]
Collector of customs in Alaska; protection from, and education of the Indians.

148. School of Military Instruction. 26 Apr.
HR 1948, 49-1, v7, 4p. [2441]
For cavalry and light artillery to be located at Fort Riley; pursuit of bands of Indians; completion of Fort Robinson near the Sioux and Cheyenne reservation; Custer's massacre.

149. R-P of A. French. 27 Apr.
SR 767, 49-1, v5, 2p. [2359]
Service in Seminole war; 1836; Florida.

150. R-P of B. Thebant. 27 Apr.
SR 775, 49-1, v5, 1p. [2359] *or*
HR 3523, 49-2, v1, 1p. [2500]
Seminole war in Florida; 1849.

151. R-C of E. Sinclair. 27 Apr.
SR 796, 49-1, v6, 2p. [2360]
U.S. Army depredations of 1833 in the Creek Nation, Alabama.

152. Army Officers in Indian Campaigns. 27 Apr.
HR 1967, 49-1, v7, 2p. [2441]
On conferring brevet rank on said officers; Modoc and Arizona wars; no Senate confirmations.

153. Estates of Dead Kickapoos. 27 Apr.
HR 1992, 49-1, v7, 1p. [2441]
Settlement of said estates; Kansas.

154. Post 157, Grand Army of the Republic. 28 Apr.
HR 2029, 49-1, v7, 1p. [2441]
Gen Wayne's headquarters in Greenville, Ohio; campaign against the Indians; treaty of 1795.

155. R-C of J. Hiatt and Co. 22 June.
SR 828, 49-1, v6, 3p. [2360] *or*
HR 1475, 49-1, v5, 3p. [2439] *or*
HR 2916, 49-1, v10, 3p. [2444]
Osage debts; licensed traders in 1878.

156. R-P of E. Chirouse. 29 Apr.
SR 829, 49-1, v6, 2p. [2360]
Accounts of the late Indian agent.

157. R-P of J. Malo. 29 Apr.
SR 830, 49-1, v6, 2p. [2360]
Service at a school among the Turtle Mountain Chippewas of Dakota.

158. Property in the Interior Dept. 30 Apr.
SED 132, 49-1, v7, 6p. [2340]
In the OIA.

159. Removal of the Southern Utes. 30 Apr.
SR 836, 49-1, v6, 6p. [2360]
From Colorado to Utah; change in site of reservation requested by Indians.

160. Sale of the Cherokee Reservation. 30 Apr.
SR 838, 49-1, v6, 3p. [2360]
In Arkansas; not, in the proper sense, an Indian reservation.

161. Settlement of Cherokee Claims. 30 Apr.
SR 839, 49-1, v6, 4p. [2360]
Western, or "Old Settler" Cherokees; fulfillment of treaty stipulations.

162. R-P of J. Nix. 1 May.
HR 2140, 49-1, v7, 1p. [2441]
Sioux outbreak of 1862 in Minnesota.

163. R-P of H. Burnett. 1 May.
HR 2151, 49-1, v7, 5p. [2441]
Service in Seminole, Creek, and Black Hawk wars.

164. R-P of J. Brice. 1 May.
HR 2173, 49-1, v7, 1p. [2441]
Arapaho depredations of 1868 in Missouri.

165. R-C of B. Pacheco and P. Padilla. 3 May.
SED 137, 49-1, v7, 4p. [2340]
Land claim in New Mexico; Apaches residing in the area.

166. R-P of M. Worth. 4 May.
SR 922, 49-1, v6, 5p. [2360] *or*
HR 2759, 49-1, v9, 5p. [2443]
Service in the Seminole war; 1841-1845 in Florida; Seminole removal; Black Hawk war.

167. Repair of Military Quarters. 5 May.
SR 930, 49-1, v6, 5p. [2360]
At Forts Robinson, Niobrara, and Russell in Nebraska and Wyoming; control of the Sioux in Dakota and Nebraska.

168. Ordnance Account of Kansas. 5 May.
HR 2235, 49-1, v7, 2p. [2441]
Issued to protect the State from Indian invasions during 1868-1874.

169. Chicago, Kansas, and Nebraska Railway Co. 5 May.
SR 2247, 49-1, v7, 1p. [2441]
Right of way through Indian Territory.

170. Mescalero Indian Reservation. 6 May.
HED 221, 49-1, v33, 7p. [2401]
Claims involving settlers' improvements on the reservation in New Mexico.

171. Ordnance Account with Dakota Territory. 6 May.
HR 2291, 49-1, v8, 2p. [2442]
For defense against hostile Indians.

172. Kansas City, Fort Scott, and Gulf Railroad Co. 6 May.
HR 2302, 49-1, v8, 2p. [2442]
Right of way through Indian Territory.

173. Supplemental List of Claims Allowed. 8 May.
HED 225, 49-1, v33, 94p. [2401]
Claims involving Indians.

174. Cree Indians in Montana. 10 May.
HED 231, 49-1, v33, 4p. [2401]
Appropriation for relief of renegade British Crees on the Blackfeet reservation in Montana.

175. Resol. of Rep. Henley. 10 May.
HMD 282, 49-1, v13, 1p. [2418]
California Indian war claims.

176. Indian Reservations in Northern Montana. 10 May.
HR 2336, 49-1, v8, 1p. [2442]
Right of way for railroads through Indian country; U.S. holds all title to land, and Indians are merely tenants.

177. Kansas and Arkansas Valley Railway Co. 11 May.
HR 2343, 49-1, v8, 2p. [2442]
Right of way through Indian Territory.

178. Seneca Lands in New York. 11 May.
HR 2344, 49-1, v8, 4p. [2442]
Allotment of lands in severalty on the Cattaraugus and Allegany reservations.

179. Indian Agent in Michigan. 12 May.
HED 234, 49-1, v33, 2p. [2401]
Salary increase; at the Mackinac agency.

180. Frontier Line Between Alaska and British Columbia. 17 May.
SED 143, 49-1, v7, 20p. [2340]
Treaty of 1867 with Russia, concerning Indian affairs in Alaska.

181. R-P of F. Evans. 18 May.
SR 1122, 49-1, v7, 1p. [2361] *or*
HR 585, 49-1, v2, 2p. [2436]
Indian military campaigns in California during 1862.

182. Receipts and Expenditures. 19 May.
HED 365, 49-1, v35, 513p. [2403]
During 1883; Indian expenses.

183. Denison and Washita Railway Co. 19 May.
HR 2488, 49-1, v8, 2p. [2442]
Right of way through Indian Territory.

184. Legislative, Executive, and Judicial Appropriations. 20 May.
HR 2495, 49-1, v8, 11p. [2442]
Year ending 30 June 1887; OIA.

185. Mission Indians of California. 24 May.
HR 2556, 49-1, v8, 4p. [2442]
U.S. failed to protect the rights of these Indians under the treaty of Guadalupe Hidalgo; settler encroachments on their land; bill provides for the creation of reservations.

186. Credit for Ordnance Stores Issued to Dakota. 25 May.
SR 1199, 49-1, v7, 2p. [2361]
Defense against hostile Indians.

187. Credit for Ordnance Stores to Oregon. 25 May.
SR 1212, 49-1, v7, 2p. [2361]
Nez Percé war of 1877-1878.

188. R-P of W. Forman. 25 May.
SR 1217, 49-1, v7, 2p. [2361]
Citizen of the Cherokee Nation, Indian Territory; U.S. Army depredations during Civil War.

189. Arkansas, New Mexico, and Pacific Railroad Co. 25 May.
HR 2582, 49-1, v9, 3p. [2443]
Right of way through Indian Territory.

190. R-C of the American Board of Com'rs of Foreign Missions. 25 May.
HR 2612, 49-1, v9, 2p. [2443]
Property in the Cherokee Nation destroyed by U.S. Army during the Civil War.

191. R-C of Freedmen. 25 May.
HR 2614, 49-1, v9, 11p. [2443]
Rights, under treaties, of freedmen adopted into the Delaware and Shawnee tribes within the Cherokee Nation; distribution of Cherokee funds.

192. Mexican Treaty of 20 Jan. 1883. 25 May.

HR 2615, 49-1, v9, 52p. [2443]
Indian population of Mexico.

193. Resol. of Sen. Wilson. 27 May.
SMD 116, 49-1, v5, 1p. [2346]
Asks investigation of Indian trade licenses.

194. R-P of I. Fossett. 27 May.
SR 1241, 49-1, v7, 2p. [2361] *or*
HR 2084, 49-1, v7, 2p. [2441]
Service against the Sioux; 1863; Dakota.

195. R-P of L. Paul. 1 June.
SR 1262, 49-1, v7, 3p. [2361] *or*
HR 2773, 49-1, v9, 3p. [2443]
Seminole war during 1842; Utah military expeditions against the Indians during 1858-1860.

196. Kansas City, Fort Scott, and Gulf Railway Co. 2 June.
HED 255, 49-1, v33, 2p. [2401]
Act authorizing construction and operation of a railroad through Indian Territory.

197. R-C of S. Larimer. 2 June.
HR 2700, 49-1, v9, 4p. [2443]
Captured by hostile Sioux in 1864 near Deer Creek Station, Wyoming Territory.

198. R-P of G. Newman. 3 June.
SR 1275, 49-1, v7, 4p. [2361] *or*
HR 1812, 49-1, v6, 4p. [2440] *or*
HR 3127, 49-1, v10, 4p. [2444]
Supplies to the Blackfeet agency, Montana, during 1883-1884.

199. Condition of the Indian Tribes. 4 June.
SR 1278 (pts. 1-3), 49-1, v8-9, 2116p. [2362-2363]
Testimony on conditions in Indian Territory, and in other Indian reservations; leases of lands in Indian Territory.

200. R-C of Dr. Price. 9 June.
SR 1301, 49-1, v7, 1p. [2361]
Physician at the Hoopa Valley Indian reservation.

201. R-C of P. Sinnott. 9 June.
SR 1302, 49-1, v7, 5p. [2361]
Indian agent at the Grande Ronde agency in Oregon; 1872-1874; allotment of land in severalty to the Rogue River, Caw Creek, Shasta, and Umpqua Indians.

202. Navajo Indian Reservation. 9 June.
HED 263, 49-1, v33, 19p. [2401]
Appropriation for sinking wells and constructing irrigation dams, etc., on the reservation in Arizona and New Mexico.

203. R-C of E. Northcutt and Brothers. 10 June.
SR 1303, 49-1, v7, 4p. [2361]
Rogue River war of 1855 in Oregon.

204. R-P of H. Harrell. 10 June.
SR 1309, 49-1, v7, 2p. [2361]
Seminole war in Florida.

205. Shoshone and Bannock Indians. 12 June.
SR 2767, 49-1, v9, 1p. [2443]
Bill authorizing negotiations to take place with said tribes concerning a right of way through the Fort Hall reservation to the Utah and Northern Railway Co.

206. Western Yearly Meeting of Friends. 15 June.
HR 2839, 49-1, v9, 1p. [2443]
Money expended to purchase land for a school in North Carolina for the Eastern Cherokees.

207. R-C of G. Pettigrew. 15 June.
HR 2844, 49-1, v9, 1p. [2443]
Cherokee depredations in Indian Territory.

208. R-C of G. Maxwell et al. 17 June.
HR 2885, 49-1, v10, 3p. [2444]
Cheyenne, Arapaho, Kiowa, and Comanche depredations of 1865-1870 in Kansas, and Indian Territory.

209. R-C of J. Little and H. Williams. 21 June.
SR 1355, 49-1, v10, 4p. [2364]
Lease for mining operations on Iowa Indian lands in Kansas and Nebraska.

210. R-P of F. Plummer. 22 June.
SR 1370, 49-1, v10, 2p. [2364] *or*
HR 619, 49-1, v2, 2p. [2436]
Military activities during the Civil War at Fort Cobb, Indian Territory.

211. Trust Funds and Unexpected Balances. 22 June.
HED 293, 49-1, v35, 9p. [2403]
Indian trust funds in the custody of the Treasurer of the U.S.; list of tribes, and amounts in their accounts.

212. R-C of G. Fell et al. 22 June.
HR 2917, 49-1, v10, 5p. [2444]
Apache depredations of 1865-1869 in Arizona Territory.

213. R-C of F. Skinner. 22 June.
HR 3026, 49-1, v10, 2p. [2444]
Indian service at Fort Peck agency, Montana.

214. R-C of W. Morrison. 22 June.
HR 3031, 49-1, v10, 2p. [2444]
Otoe and Missouria depredations upon the licensed trader among them.

215. Indian Traders. 23 June.
SED 174, 49-1, v8, 3p. [2341]
On renewal and non-renewal of licenses.

216. Round Valley Agency in California. 23 June.
HED 295, 49-1, v35, 2p. [2403]
Appropriation for indebtedness incurred.

217. R-C of W. Martin. 24 June.
SED 187, 49-1, v8, 18p. [2341]
Indian depredations of 1849 in Oregon Territory.

218. R-P of R. Barnes. 24 June.
SR 1384, 49-1, v10, 3p. [2364] *or*
HR 2572, 49-1, v8, 4p. [2442]
Service against Seminole Indians in Florida; 1840-1841.

219. Legislative, Executive, and Judicial Appropriations. 28 June.
SR 1387, 49-1, v10, 35p. [2364]
For fiscal 1887; OIA.

220. Indian Industrial School. 29 June.
SED 192, 49-1, v8, 3p. [2341]
Appropriation to improve the school at Carlisle, Pennsylvania.

221. R-C of H. Shipley. 30 June.
SR 1416, 49-1, v10, 3p. [2364]
Contract for services at the Nez Percé agency, Idaho; 1880.

222. Military Quarters in Wyoming and Nebraska. 30 June.
HR 3112, 49-1, v10, 4p. [2444]
Forts Russell, Robinson, and Niobrara; close to the Sioux and Cheyenne reservation.

223. Claims Arising Out of Indian Treaties. 30 June.
HR 3117, 49-1, v10, 28p. [2444]
Bill establishing a board of com'rs to examine all claims involving Indians.

224. Annual Report of the Smithsonian Institution. 1 July.
HMD 170 (pts. 1 and 2), 49-2, v11-12, 1749p. [2498-2499]
Year ending 30 June 1886; research related to the American Indian.

225. R-P of S. O'Connor. 1 July.
HR 3162, 49-1, v11, 8p. [2445]
Service in Indian Territory.

226. R-P of O. Burke. 1 July.
HR 3165, 49-1, v11, 2p. [2445]
Service in Indian Territory.

227. R-P of W. Spencer. 1 July.
HR 3169, 49-1, v11, 2p. [2445]
Demands murderer from Indian warriors at the Yellow Medicine agency in Minnesota; 1857.

228. R-P of T. Little. 1 July.
HR 3173, 49-1, v11, 4p. [2445]
Service against Seminoles, Sioux, Comanches, and Kiowas.

229. R-P of C. Whiting. 1 July.
HR 3181, 49-1, v11, 5p. [2445]
Service in Navajo removal; New Mexico.

230. R-P of D. Rousseau. 1 July.
HR 3182, 49-1, v11, 4p. [2445]
Service in the Sioux and Cheyenne war of 1876-1878.

231. R-P of C. Campbell. 1 July.
HR 3183, 49-1, v11, 27p. [2445]
Service against hostile Indians in Arizona, Texas, New Mexico, and Indian Territory; Kiowas, Cheyennes, etc.

232. R-P of J. Chickering. 1 July.
HR 3184, 49-1, v11, 7p. [2445]
Service against Indians in Texas and Indian Territory.

233. R-P of W. Webb. 1 July.
HR 3185, 49-1, v11, 4p. [2445]
Service in Indian Territory.

234. R-P of T. Riley. 1 July.
HR 3187, 49-1, v11, 7p. [2445]
Service in the Nez Percé war; 1877.

235. Maricopa and Phoenix Railroad Co. 1 July.
HR 3192, 49-1, v11, 1p. [2445]
Right of way through the Gila River Indian reservation in Arizona.

236. R-C of Len-ne-pi-ze-qua. 2 July.
SR 1430, 49-1, v10, 2p. [2364]
Per capita share of the final payment to the Miamies of Indiana; treaty of 5 June 1854.

237. Navajo Agency. 6 July.
SED 202, 49-1, v8, 2p. [2341]
Appropriation to pay employees at the agency in New Mexico.

238. R-P of L. Owen. 6 July.
SR 1437, 49-1, v10, 4p. [2364] *or*
HR 4164, 49-2, v2, 3p. [2501]
Service against Seminole, Spokane, and Coeur d'Alene Indians.

239. R-P of J. Armstrong. 6 July.
SR 1442, 49-1, v10, 1p. [2364]
Battle of the Little Big Horn; 1876; Montana.

240. R-C of Certain Soldiers. 6 July.
SR 1445, 49-1, v10, 2p. [2364]
Service in the several Florida Indian wars.

241. Right of Way Through an Indian Reservation. 7 July.
SED 204, 49-1, v8, 4p. [2341]
Pres. vetoes bill granting a right of way to a railroad through a reservation in northern Montana; Piegan, Gros Ventre, Blood, Blackfeet, and other tribes.

242. Northern Cheyenne Indians. 12 July.
SED 212, 49-1, v8, 3p. [2341]
Funds to subsist Cheyennes going from the Sioux reservation (Dakota) to the Tongue River agency (Montana).

243. Surrender of Sitting Bull. 12 July.
HED 356, 49-1, v35, 5p. [2403]
Bill to pay J. Legaré for services in procuring said surrender in 1881.

244. On the Case of A. Pleasonton. 15 July.
SR 1489, 49-1, v11, 5p. [2365]
Service against Canadian half-breeds, Apaches, Sioux, Seminoles, etc.

245. Right of Way to Certain Railroads. 17 July.
SR 1494, 49-1, v11, 7p. [2365]
Through the reservation of the Gros Ventres, Piegans, Bloods, Blackfeet, and other tribes, in Montana; response to the President's veto of the bill.

246. Annual Report of the Smithsonian Institution. 17 July.
HMD 15 (pts. 1 and 2), 49-1, v25-26, 2235p. [2431-2432]
Research related to the American Indian.

247. Ordnance Account of Colorado. 17 July.
HR 3230, 49-1, v11, 2p. [2445]
Incurred because of Indian hostilities.

248. R-C of L. Pearlman. 17 July.
HR 3349, 49-1, v11, 6p. [2445]
Supplies to troops during Paiute war of 1860 in Utah Territory.

249. Trust Funds in the Interior Dept. 20 July.
HED 379, 49-1, v35, 10p. [2403]
Report on trust funds held for the Indians.

250. R-P of V. Randall. 23 July.
SR 1556, 49-1, v11, 2p. [2365] *or*
HR 2561, 49-1, v8, 2p. [2442]
Seminole war in Florida.

251. Veto Messages of Presidents of the U.S. 24 July.
SMD 53, 49-2, v2, 549p. [2451]
Tyler on Cherokee certificates in 1843; Grant on Indian trust funds, and sale of Indian lands in 1876.

252. R-C of F. and C. Huning et al. 27 July.
HR 3438, 49-1, v11, 4p. [2445]
Navajo, Kiowa, Cheyenne, and Apache depredations in New Mexico.

253. Appointments in Executive Depts. 29 July.
SED 219, 49-1, v8, 22p. [2341]
During 1883-1886; OIA.

254. Statements of Appropriations. 5 Aug.
HMD 394, 49-1, v17, 162p. [2422]
During the 1st session, 49th Congress; Indian expenses.

255. Mineral Resources of the U.S. 15 Sept.
HMD 146, 49-2, v6, 583p. [2493]
Summary of 1885; coal, coke, and mineral waters in Indian Territory.

256. Disbursements Made by the Indian Dept. 23 Oct.
HED 6, 49-2, v18, 21p. [2477]
Year ending 30 June 1886.

257. Wharton's Digest of International Law. 20 Nov.
SMD 162 (pts. 1-3), 49-1, v9-11, 2693p. [2350-2352]
Indian land titles, warfare, citizenship, etc.

258. Annual Message to Congress with Documents; Pres. Cleveland. 6 Dec.
HED 1, 49-2, v1-12, 11440p. [2460-2471]
Surrender of hostile Apaches under the leadership of Geronimo; recommends general legislation calling for allotment of Indian lands in severalty; land title issues involving railroads and settler encroachment need legislative action; annual report of the Sec. of War (Serials 2461-2465); annual report of the Sec. of Interior (Serials 2467-2470); annual report of the Gen. Land Office (Serial 2468); annual report of the CIA (Serial 2467).

259. Annual Report of the Sec. of the Treasury. 6 Dec.

HED 2 (pts. 1 and 2), 49-2, v13, 1349p. [2472]
Year ending 30 June 1886; Indian expenses.

260. Estimates of Appropriations. 6 Dec.
HED 5, 49-2, v15, 350p. [2474]
Year ending 30 June 1888; Indian expenses.

261. Congressional Directory. 11 Dec.
SMD 11, 49-2, v1, 430p. [2450]
Duties of the CIA listed.

262. Kansas Indians. 11 Dec.
HED 29, 49-2, v20, 3p. [2479]
Appropriation needed to fulfill the treaty of 14 Jan. 1846.

263. Miami Indians. 13 Dec.
SED 5, 49-2, v1, 3p. [2448]
Appropriation to pay the Eel River band a principal sum in lieu of all annuities received under various treaties.

264. Resol. of Rep. Holman. 13 Dec.
HMD 31, 49-2, v1, 1p. [2488]
Expenditures for Indians and Yellowstone Park.

265. Additional Land District in Oregon. 14 Dec.
HR 3478, 49-2, v1, 2p. [2500]
Area would embrace the Fort Klamath Indian reservation.

266. St. Paul, Minneapolis, and Manitoba Railroad Co. 16 Dec.
HR 3487, 49-2, v1, 3p. [2500]
Right of way through Indian reservations in northwestern Dakota and northern Montana.

267. Seal Islands of Alaska. 20 Dec.
SED 7, 49-2, v1, 4p. [2448]
Natives employed in hunting.

268. Indian Appropriation Bill. 21 Dec.
HR 3490, 49-2, v1, 1p. [2500]
Year ending 30 June 1888.

269. R-C of A. Carrier. 21 Dec.
HR 3498, 49-2, v1, 1p. [2500]
Services rendered to the U.S., and to Indians residing on the old Winnebago reservation in Dakota.

270. Military Instruction. 22 Dec.
SR 1630, 49-2, v1, 4p. [2456]
For the cavalry; pursuit of marauding Indians.

271. Claims Allowed by Accounting Officers. 22 Dec.
HED 49, 49-2, v20, 106p. [2479]
Under exhausted appropriations; claims involving the Indians.

1887

1. Account of P. Winston, Jr. 6 Jan.
HED 61, 49-2, v20, 4p. [2479]
For legal services in defense of T. Hill, captain of police on the Nez Percé agency.

2. R-P of Z. Shepherd. 7 Jan.
HR 3529, 49-2, v1, 1p. [2500]
Service in the Black Hawk war.

3. Indian Depredation Claims. 8 Jan.
HED 77, 49-2, v20, 25p. [2479]
Examined prior to 1 Jan. 1887; lists date, tribe, and location.

4. Land for Indian Training School. 8 Jan.
HR 3534, 49-2, v1, 2p. [2500]
Purchase of land in Oregon.

5. Payment of Trust Fund to Delawares. 10 Jan.
SED 21, 49-2, v1, 5p. [2448]
Per capita payment to Delawares resident in the Cherokee Nation, Indian Territory.

6. Resol. of Rep. James. 10 Jan.
HMD 65, 49-2, v1, 1p. [2488]
Public exhibitions by wild Indians.

7. R-P of W. Meagher. 14 Jan.
HR 3571, 49-2, v1, 3p. [2500]
Indian disturbance in Montana.

8. Mission Indians of California. 17 Jan.
SED 28, 49-2, v1, 2p. [2448]
Appropriation to pay S. Ward, special counsel to said Indians.

9. Indians of Fort Berthold Reservation. 17 Jan.
SED 30, 49-2, v1, 10p. [2448]
Agreement of 14 Dec. 1886 for cession of part of the reservation, and allotments of land in severalty on the diminished reservation; Arikara, Mandan, and Gros Ventre tribes; Dakota.

10. Estimates of Deficiencies in Appropriations. 17 Jan.
HED 89, 49-2, v15, 46p. [2474]
Year ending 30 June 1887; Indian expenses.

11. Physicians in Attendance Upon Indians. 18 Jan.
SED 31, 49-2, v1, 2p. [2448]
Appropriation to pay said physicians.

12. Eastern and Western Cherokees. 18 Jan.
SR 1680, 49-2, v1, 8p. [2456]
Referral of claims under various treaties to the Court of Claims.

13. Expenses of the Indian Dept. 18 Jan.
HR 3622, 49-2, v1, 2p. [2500]
Section of bill gives territorial courts jurisdiction over Indians; U.S. to reimburse said courts.

14. Jamestown and Northern Railroad Co. 18 Jan.
HR 3623, 49-2, v1, 1p. [2500]
Right of way through the Sisseton and Wahpeton Sioux reservation in Dakota; treaty of 19 Feb. 1867.

15. R-C of the Cherokees. 18 Jan.
HR 3644, 49-2, v1, 1p. [2500]
Under the treaty of 14 Feb. 1833.

16. On the Relief of Hiatt and Co. 19 Jan.
SED 35, 49-2, v1, 29p. [2448]
Credit extended by these licensed traders to the Osages in 1878.

17. R-C of G. Ortiz. 19 Jan.
SED 37, 49-2, v1, 5p. [2448]
Land title issues involving the Indians of Nambe pueblo, New Mexico.

18. Resol. of Rep. Peters. 19 Jan.
HMD 87, 49-2, v1, 1p. [2488]
Residents of Kansas fired upon by U.S. troops in Indian Territory.

19. R-C of R. Newell. 19 Jan.
HR 3678, 49-2, v1, 2p. [2500]
Captured by hostile Pawnees in Nebraska Territory; 1858.

20. R-C of R. Adams. 19 Jan.
HR 3679, 49-2, v1, 2p. [2500]
Sioux and Cheyenne depredations of 1864 in Nebraska.

21. R-C of B. Moreland. 20 Jan.
SR 1692, 49-2, v1, 2p. [2456]
Settler's land in Minnesota encorporated into the Winnebago reservation; treaty of 27 Feb. 1855.

22. Washington, Idaho, and Montana Territories. 20 Jan.
HR 3689, 49-2, v1, 10p. [2500]
Acreage of Indian and military reservations in Montana.

23. Supplies Furnished the Interior Dept. 25 Jan.
SED 49, 49-2, v1, 1p. [2448]
Year ending 30 June 1886; OIA.

24. Petaca Grant, No. 105. 25 Jan.
SED 52, 49-2, v1, 6p. [2448]
Land title in New Mexico; Indian hostilities.

25. Private Land Claim No. 138. 27 Jan.
SED 56, 49-2, v1, 34p. [2448]
Land title issues involving the Indians of the pueblo of Santa Clara; New Mexico.

26. R-C of S. Barclay et al. 27 Jan.
SR 1738, 49-2, v1, 17p. [2456] *or*
HR 3925, 49-2, v2, 17p. [2501]
Sureties on the bond of the late Indian agent at the Wichita agency, Indian Territory.

27. R-M of the Walnut Grove Gold-Mining Co. 27 Jan.
SR 1741, 49-2, v1, 23p. [2456]
Apache depredations of 1864-1869 in Arizona.

28. Receipts and Expenditures. 27 Jan.
HED 110, 49-2, v23, 428p. [2482]
Year ending 30 June 1884; Indian expenses.

29. Location of Certain U.S. Courts in Texas. 27 Jan.
HR 3774, 49-2, v1, 1p. [2500]
Bill pending to establish courts in Indian Territory.

30. Alleged Violations of House Rule 34. 27 Jan.
HR 3798, 49-2, v1, 25p. [2500]
Ex-members of the House working for the railroads; right of way through an Indian reservation in northern Montana.

31. Lands in Oregon. 29 Jan.
SED 60, 49-2, v1, 6p. [2448]
Withdrawn from settlement and attached to the Warm Springs Indian reservation; treaty of 25 June 1855 with the Warm Springs Indians.

32. Judgments of the Court of Claims. 1 Feb.
HED 120, 49-2, v23, 3p. [2482]
Includes case involving Choctaw Nation.

33. Spokane and Palouse Railway Co. 1 Feb.
HR 3836, 49-2, v2, 1p. [2501]
Right of way through the Coeur d'Alene Indian reservation in Idaho.

34. R-P of M. Hunter. 2 Feb.
SR 1778, 49-2, v2, 2p. [2457] *or*
HR 3214, 49-1, v11, 3p. [2445]
Service in Indian Territory; 1836.

35. R-C of W. Martin. 2 Feb.
SR 1780, 49-2, v2, 3p. [2457]
Indian hostilities of 1849 in Oregon.

36. Indian Appropriations. 2 Feb.
SR 1781, 49-2, v2, 4p. [2457]
Year ending 30 June 1888.

37. Education of Apaches in Florida. 3 Feb.
SED 73, 49-2, v1, 17p. [2448]
Confined at Fort Marion; older

children sent to Carlisle Indian Training School in Pennsylvania.

38. Legislative, Executive, and Judicial Appropriations. 3 Feb.
HR 3916 (pts. 1-3), 49-2, v2, 59p. [2501]
Salaries in the OIA.

39. Prosecutions Against Indians. 3 Feb.
HR 3922, 49-2, v2, 1p. [2501]
Adverse report on House bill 10695.

40. Allotments of Indian Lands in Severalty. 4 Feb.
SED 76, 49-2, v1, 2p. [2448]
Appropriation needed for special agents to carry out allotment.

41. Utah Midland Railway Co. 8 Feb.
HR 3977, 49-2, v2, 2p. [2501]
Right of way through the Uintah and Uncompahgre Indian reservations.

42. Northern District of Iowa. 8 Feb.
HR 3999, 49-2, v2, 1p. [2501]
Action of the House Com. on Indian Affairs.

43. Rocky Fort and Cooke City Railway Co. 10 Feb.
HR 4008, 49-2, v2, 1p. [2501]
Right of way through the Crow reservation in Montana.

44. Account of S. Ward. 12 Feb.
HED 161, 49-2, v24, 4p. [2483]
Special attorney for the Mission Indians of California.

45. R-P of L. Paul. 15 Feb.
SR 1868, 49-2, v2, 3p. [2457] *or*
HR 1405, 50-1, v5, 3p. [2602]
Service in Indian Territory, and against hostile Indians in Utah; Seminole war in 1842.

46. Resolution of Inquiry. 15 Feb.
HR 4050, 49-2, v2, 7p. [2501]
Report concerning U.S. troops firing upon residents of Kansas in Indian Territory.

47. Mem. of the Arizona Legis. 16 Feb.
SMD 63, 49-2, v2, 2p. [2451]
On Navajoes roaming outside of their reservation.

48. Organization of Alaska Territory. 16 Feb.
HR 4088, 49-2, v2, 3p. [2501]
Indian population statistics.

49. Hampton and Old Point Railroad Co. 16 Feb.
HR 4093, 49-2, v2, 1p. [2501]
Right of way for a street-railway in Virginia; inmates of the Indian school inconvenienced.

50. Lands for Mining Purposes. 17 Feb.
SR 1898, 49-2, v2, 2p. [2457]
Coal in Indian Territory; leases in the Choctaw, Chickasaw, Cherokee, Creek, and Seminole Nations.

51. Contingent Expenditures of the Interior Dept. 17 Feb.
HED 177, 49-2, v24, 20p. [2483]
Year ending 30 June 1886; Indian expenses.

52. Miami Indians of Indiana. 17 Feb.
HR 4109, 49-2, v2, 5p. [2501]
Funds due under various treaties.

53. R-P of Reps. A. Gibbs and B. Dowell. 18 Feb.
SR 1902, 49-2, v2, 3p. [2457]
Attorneys defending an officer at Fort Klamath, Oregon, against charges of introducing liquor onto the Fort Klamath Indian reservation.

54. Claims Allowed by Accounting Officers. 19 Feb.
HED 180, 49-2, v24, 75p. [2483]
Under exhausted appropriations; claims involving Indians.

55. Dependent Pension Bill. 19 Feb.
HR 4126, 49-2, v2, 16p. [2501]
Vetoed by the Pres.; service in Indian wars.

56. Shoshone and Bannock Indians. 19 Feb.
HR 4131, 49-2, v2, 1p. [2501]
Bill authorizes negotiations to take place concerning a right of way through the Fort Hall reservation to be given the Utah and Northern Railway Co.

57. Billings, Clark's Fort, and Cooke City Railroad Co. 19 Feb.
HR 4132, 49-2, v2, 2p. [2501]
Right of way through the Crow reservation in Montana.

58. Washington and Idaho Railroad Co. 19 Feb.
HR 4133, 49-2, v2, 2p. [2501]
Right of way through the Coeur d'Alene reservation in Idaho.

59. Spokane and Palouse Railway Co. 19 Feb.
HR 4134, 49-2, v2, 2p. [2501]
Right of way through the Coeur d'Alene reservation in Idaho.

60. Utah Midland Railway Co. 19 Feb.
HR 4135, 49-2, v2, 2p. [2501]
Right of way through the Uintah and Uncompahgre Indian reservations in Utah.

61. Indian School Building. 19 Feb.
HR 4136, 49-2, v2, 1p. [2501]
Agreement of 17 July 1883 with the Tonasket Indians; school on the Colville reservation in Washington Territory.

62. Yankton and Missouri Valley Railway Co. 19 Feb.
HR 4137, 49-2, v2, 1p. [2501]
Right of way through the Yankton Indian reservation in Dakota.

63. Northern Pacific Railroad. 19 Feb.
HR 4138, 49-2, v2, 5p. [2501]
Agreement of 9 June 1885 with the Yakimas; right of way through the Yakima reservation in Washington Territory.

64. Massacre Near Fort Philip Kearny. 21 Feb.
SED 97, 49-2, v1, 6p. [2448]
Col. Carrington's report of the 1866 massacre in Dakota.

65. Resol. of Sen. Platt. 21 Feb.
SMD 73, 49-2, v2, 1p. [2451]
Investigation of Indian trade licenses.

66. Creditors of Pottawatomies. 21 Feb.
SR 1912, 49-2, v2, 3p. [2457] *or*
HR 3978, 49-2, v2, 3p. [2501]
Lawyer seeks payment for services rendered the Pottawatomies.

67. Brevet Rank of Certain Officers. 23 Feb.
SR 1943, 49-2, v2, 3p. [2457]
For service in Indian campaigns.

68. R-C of C. Beers et al. 23 Feb.
HR 4152, 49-2, v2, 3p. [2501]
Sioux depredations of 1866.

69. Dearborn Park in Chicago, Illinois. 23 Feb.
HR 4162, 49-2, v2, 4p. [2501]
Initially the site of an Indian agency; Indians removed in 1839.

70. Brevet Rank. 24 Feb.
SR 1950, 49-2, v2, 1p. [2457]
Service in Indian campaigns.

71. R-C of J. English. 25 Feb.
SR 1960 (pts. 1 and 2), 49-2, v2, 8p. [2457]
Losses by the Seminole war; Florida.

72. Veto of House Bill No. 7648. 25 Feb.
HED 194, 49-2, v25, 3p. [2484]
Involving J. How, Indian agent.

73. Arizona Narrow-Gauge Railroad Co. 25 Feb.
HR 4170, 49-2, v2, 1p. [2501]
Right of way through the White Mountain Indian reservation; control of troublesome Apaches.

74. R-C of Florida. 26 Feb.
SR 1962, 49-2, v3, 108p. [2458] *or*
HR 367, 50-1, v2, 94p. [2599]
Suppression of Indian hostilities.

75. Shawnee Indian Lands. 28 Feb.
SED 111, 49-2, v2, 254p. [2449]
Sale of land allotted and patented to members of Black Bob's band in Kansas.

76. R-C of J. Hobbs. 28 Feb.
SR 1970, 49-2, v3, 1p. [2458] *or*
HR 2713, 49-1, v9, 2p. [2443]
Supplies furnished during negotiations with Cheyennes and Arapahoes; 1860.

77. R-C of A. Culver. 28 Feb.
SR 1972, 49-2, v3, 3p. [2458]
Supplies furnished during negotiations with Cheyennes and Arapahoes; 1860.

78. Claims Against the Choctaw Nation. 28 Feb.
SR 1978, 49-2, v3, 129p. [2458]
For professional and other services on account of judgments rendered against the U.S.

79. Sitting Bull's Band. 28 Feb.
HED 197, 49-2, v25, 3p. [2484]
Appropriation to subsist the remainder of the band (in Canada) if they return to the Sioux reservation.

80. Chippewa Indians in Minnesota. 1 Mar.
SED 115, 49-2, v2, 133p. [2449]
Agreements of 11 Aug. 1886 (also 7 Sept. 1886), and 23 Aug. 1886 with Red Lake, White Earth, Pillager, and Lake Winnebagoshish Chippewas; land cessions, consolidations of bands, and allotment of lands in severalty; proceedings of councils.

81. Surrender of Geronimo. 2 Mar.
SED 117, 49-2, v2, 77p. [2449]
Correspondence with Gen. Miles on the surrender of this leader of hostile Apaches; Arizona.

82. Statements of Appropriations. 3 Mar.
HMD 166, 49-2, v6, 111p. [2493]
During the 2d session, 49th Congress; Indian expenses.

83. New York Indian Lands in Kansas. 3 Mar.
HR 4179, 49-2, v2, 3p. [2501]
Bill giving settlers on these lands the right to purchase them.

84. Indian Traders. 3 Mar.
HR 4180, 49-2, v2, 1p. [2501]
Right of Indians to trade among themselves without restraint or need of license.

85. H. Allen's Expedition to Alaska. (no date)
SED 125, 49-2, v2, 172p. [2449]
Historical discussion of the area; encounters with, and descriptions of the Indians.

86. Greely Relief Expedition. (no date)
HMD 157, 49-2, 75p. (*in* v22 [pt. 2], 49-1.) [2428]
Eskimos serve as interpreters, and informants as to the location of the lost exploring party.

87. Bulletins of the U.S. Geological Survey. (no date)
HMD 164, 49-2, v8, 558p. [2495]
Volume 5: contains bulletin no. 32 on mineral springs, including those in Indian Territory.

88. Bulletins of the U.S. Fish Commission. (no date)
HMD 165, 49-2, v9, 495p. [2496]
Volume 6; introduction of carp into Indian Territory.

89. Fifth Annual Report of the Bureau of Ethnology. (no date)
HMD 167, 49-2, v10, 617p. [2497]
Includes a report on mounds in the northern U.S., a history of Cherokee-U.S. treaty relations, a description of a Navajo ceremony, a report on the Seminoles, and a report on Zuni religious life.

90. Official Register. 1 July.
HMD 87 (pts. 1 and 2), 50-1, v3-4, 2045p. [2567-2568]
List of all agents employed by the U.S.

91. Annual Report of the Smithsonian Institution. 1 July.
HMD 600 (pts. 1 and 2), 50-1, v17-18, 1544p. [2581-2582]
Research related to the American Indian.

92. Mineral Resources of the U.S. 13 Aug.
HMD 42, 50-1, v2, 821p. [2566]
Coal and coke in Indian Territory.

93. Disbursements for the Indian Dept. 8 Nov.
HED 8, 50-1, v18, 25p. [2550]
Year ending 30 June 1887.

94. Congressional Directory. 3 Dec.
SMD 1 (pts. 1-3), 50-1, v1, 692p. [2516]
Responsibilities of the CIA are listed.

95. Annual Report of the Sec. of the Treasury. 5 Dec.
HED 2, 50-1, v16, 1020p. [2548]
Year ending 30 June 1887; Indian expenses.

96. Estimates of Appropriations. 5 Dec.
HED 5, 50-1, v19, 368p. [2551]
Year ending 30 June 1889; Indian expenses.

97. Annual Message to Congress with Documents; Pres. Cleveland. 6 Dec.
HED 1, 50-1, v1-15, 14260p. [2532-2547]
Annual report of the Sec. of War (Serials 2533-2538); annual report of the Sec. of Interior (Serials 2541-2546); annual report of the Gen. Land Office (Serial 2541); annual report of the CIA (Serial 2542); etc.

98. Private Land Claim, No. 62. 7 Dec.
SED 4, 50-1, v1, 12p. [2504]
Land title issues in New Mexico involving the Jicarilla Apaches.

99. Judgments of the Court of Claims. 7 Dec.
SMD 4, 50-1, v1, 6p [2516]
Case of the Choctaw Indians.

100. Private Land Claim, No. 76. 8 Dec.
SED 7, 50-1, v1, 5p. [2504]
Residence pattern caused by Indian hostilities; New Mexico.

101. Powers and Duties of Committees. 8 Dec.
HMD 28, 50-1, v1, 2p. [2565]
Includes Com. on Indian Affairs.

102. Private Land Claim, No. 66. 12 Dec.
SED 13, 50-1, v1, 32p. [2504]
Land title issues in New Mexico involving the Navajoes and Utes.

103. Private Land Claim, No. 75. 12 Dec.
SED 14, 50-1, v1, 26p. [2504]
Land title issues in New Mexico involving the Indians of the pueblo of Nambé.

104. Private Land Claim, No. 126. 12 Dec.
SED 15, 50-1, v1, 28p. [2504]
Navajo hostilities in New Mexico.

105. Private Land Claim, No. 71. 12 Dec.
SED 21, 50-1, v1, 7p. [2504]
Indian depredations in New Mexico.

106. Private Land Claim, No. 132. 12 Dec.
SED 23, 50-1, v1, 4p. [2504]
Land title issues in New Mexico involving the Indians of the pueblo of Santa Clara.

107. Accounts of the Treasurer of the U.S. 12 Dec.
HED 15, 50-1, v22, 1162p. [2554]
Year ending 30 June 1887; Indians.

108. Resol. of Rep. Lanham. 12 Dec.
HMD 32, 50-1, v1, 1p. [2565]
On establishment of a Com. on Indian Depredation Claims.

109. Claims Allowed by Accounting Officers. 16 Dec.
HED 19, 50-1, v18, 154p. [2550]
Reported to the 49th Congress, 2d session; includes claims related to Indians.

110. Report of the Texas Boundary Commission. 16 Dec.
HED 21, 50-1, v18, 170p. [2550]
Dispute over boundary between Texas and Indian Territory.

111. Private Land Claim, No. 17. 19 Dec.
SED 29, 50-1, v1, 32p. [2504]
Apache hostilities in Arizona.

112. Conduct of Affairs in the Seal Islands. 19 Dec.
SED 31, 50-1, v1, 12p. [2504]
Employment of natives in Alaska; Aleuts.

113. Indian Operations on the Plains. 20 Dec.
SED 33, 50-1, v1, 55p. [2504]
History of military operations provided by Col. Carrington; Fort. Phil. Kearney massacre; Sioux and Cheyenne hostilities; etc.

114. Resol. of Sen. Butler. 20 Dec.
SMD 16, 50-1, v1, 1p. [2516]
Recommends com. be formed to ascertain the condition of the Five Civilized Tribes; citizenship question.

115. Rules of the House. 21 Dec.
HR 1, 50-1, v1, 2p. [2598]
Establishment of a Com. on Indian Depredation Claims.

116. Revised Estimates of Deficiencies. 22 Dec.
HED 29, 50-1, v19, 43p. [2551]
Appropriations for year ending 30 June 1887; Indian expenses.

117. Urgent Deficiencies. 22 Dec.
HED 30, 50-1, v19, 25p. [2551]
Appropriations for year ending 30 June 1888, Indian expenses.

118. Bulletins of the U.S. Geological Survey, Vol. 6. (no date)
HMD 375, 50-1, v2, 602p. [2566]
Bulletin No. 40 deals with aboriginal mounds on glacial Lake Agassiz.

1888

1. Capt. Hall's Co. of Oregon Volunteers. 4 Jan.
SED 36, 50-1, v1, 2p. [2504]
Cayuse war of 1847-1848.

2. Private Land Claim, No. 146. 4 Jan.
SED 38, 50-1, v1, 52p. [2504]
Land title issues in New Mexico involving the Isleta Pueblo Indians.

3. Right of Way Through Indian Reservations. 5 Jan.
SED 40, 50-1, v1, 4p. [2504]
Bill authorizing the Sec. of Interior to fix the amount of compensation to be paid to Indians for railroad rights of way; case of the Chippewas (treaty of 30 Sept. 1854) versus the Duluth, Superior, and Michigan Railway Co.

4. Trespasses on Indian Lands. 5 Jan.
SED 41, 50-1, v1, 8p. [2504]
Legislation calling for prosecution of trespassers; Oklahoma district of Indian Territory.

5. Timber Depredations on Public Lands. 5 Jan.
SED 42, 50-1, v1, 6p. [2504]
Bill to amend the Revised Statutes relating to timber depredations so as to include Indian lands.

6. Jamestown and Northern Railroad Co. 5 Jan.
SED 43, 50-1, v1, 12p. [2504]
Right of way through the Devil's Lake reservation in Dakota; Sioux Indians; branch of the Northern Pacific Railroad.

7. Carson and Colorado River Railroad Co. 5 Jan.
SED 44, 50-1, v1, 12p. [2504]
Right of way through the Walker River reservation in Nevada; Paiute Indians; agreement of 9 Aug. 1882.

8. Northern Pacific Railroad. 5 Jan.
SED 45, 50-1, v1, 24p. [2504]
Right of way through the Yakima reservation in Washington Territory; confederated Yakimas; agreement of 13 Jan. 1885.

9. Chicago, Milwaukee, and St. Paul Railway Co. 5 Jan.
SED 46, 50-1, v1, 54p. [2504]
Right of way through the Lake Traverse reservation in Dakota; Sisseton and Wahpeton Sioux; agreement of 8 Dec. 1884.

10. Reduction of Round Valley Reservation. 5 Jan.
HED 33, 50-1, v24, 23p. [2557]
Settler encroachments; lands to be allotted in severalty, with excess to be sold; California.

11. Petition of Omaha Indians. 9 Jan.
SMD 26, 50-1, v1, 6p. [2516]
On citizenship, taxation, and annuities.

12. Indian Depredation Claims. 9 Jan.
HED 34, 50-1, v25, 31p. [2557]
During 1887; lists tribe involved, when committed, etc.

13. Chickasaw Treaty Stipulations. 9 Jan.
HED 42, 50-1, v25, 34p. [2557]
Appropriation to fulfill said stipulations under the treaty of 22 June 1854; findings of the Court of Claims.

14. Cattle for Northern Cheyennes. 9 Jan.
HED 43, 50-1, v25, 2p. [2557]
Appropriation to purchase said cattle for the Tongue River agency, Montana.

15. Hoopa Valley Wagon Road, California. 9 Jan.
HED 44, 50-1, v25, 4p. [2557]
Appropriation to construct a road from the Hoopa Valley Indian agency to the southern edge of the reservation.

16. Mission Indians of California. 9 Jan.
HED 45, 50-1, v25, 3p. [2557]
Appropriation to provide irrigation ditches, etc., for said Indians.

17. Osage Indian Agent. 9 Jan.
HED 46, 50-1, v25, 2p. [2557]
Appropriation to increase the salary of the agent in Indian Territory.

18. Reduction of Indian Reservations. 9 Jan.
HED 63, 50-1, v25, 77p. [2557]
Report of the Northwest Indian Commission; agreements with the Arikara, Gros Ventre, Mandan, Chippewa, Piegan, Blood, Blackfeet, River Crow, Spokane, Coeur d'Alene, Pend d'Oreille or Calispel, and Jocko reservation Indians; Minnesota, Dakota, Montana, Idaho, and Washington negotiations.

19. R-P of M. Graziani. 10 Jan.
SR 17, 50-1, v1, 2p. [2519]
Service against Indians; 1876; Wyoming.

20. Punishment of Crime in Indian Territory. 10 Jan.
HR 7, 50-1, v1, 2p. [2598]
Legislation calling for punishment of burglary and larceny.

21. R-C of P. Sinnott. 11 Jan.
SR 30, 50-1, v1, 5p. [2519]
Late Indian agent at the Grande Ronde agency in Oregon; 1872-1885.

22. Ute Indian Losses. 11 Jan.
HED 68, 50-1, v25, 11p. [2557]
Sustained at the hands of civil authorities and militia from Colorado; 1887.

23. Efficiency of the Infantry. 12 Jan.
SR 36, 50-1, v1, 5p. [2519]
Needed to cope with the Sioux and other Indian tribes.

24. Inspection of Indian Schools. 16 Jan.
SED 50, 50-1, v1, 17p. [2504]
By special agent C. Clark; Carlisle school in Pennsylvania; Chippewa schools in Minnesota and elsewhere.

25. Coal Deposits on the Crow Reservation. 16 Jan.
HED 81, 50-1, v25, 6p. [2557]
Appropriation to open and develop said deposits in Montana; near Fort Custer.

26. Resol. of Rep. Cutcheon. 16 Jan.
HMD 113, 50-1, v1, 1p. [2565]
Asks investigation of disturbances in Colorado between whites and the Colorow band of Utes; 1887.

27. Table of Cases Argued in the Supreme Court. 17 Jan.
HED 91, 50-1, v26, 92p. [2558]
Cherokee and Choctaw cases.

28. Duluth, Rainy Lake River, and Southwestern Railway Co. 17 Jan.
HR 32, 50-1, v1, 2p. [2598]
Right of way through the Boisé Fort reservation in Minnesota.

29. Purchase of Supplies from Indians. 18 Jan.
SED 53, 50-1, v7, 4p. [2510]
Army purchase of supplies from the Utes at the Uintah and Ouray agency, Utah.

30. Claims Allowed by Accounting Officers. 18 Jan.
HED 90, 50-1, v26, 167p. [2558]
Including those involving Indians.

31. Punishment for Crimes Committed. 19 Jan.
SR 71, 50-1, v1, 1p. [2519]
For larceny in Indian Territory.

32. Jurisdiction of Courts. 19 Jan.
HR 57, 50-1, v1, 1p. [2598]
Within Indian Territory.

33. Chippewas of Minnnesota. 20 Jan.
HED 110, 50-1, v26, 32p. [2558]
Ratification of the agreements of 23 Aug. 1886 (Red Lake bands), and 11 Aug. and 7 Sept. 1886 (White Earth bands); Northwest Indian Commission; allotment and reduction of reservations.

34. Sioux Indians. 21 Jan.
HED 102, 50-1, v26, 4p. [2558]
Appropriation for the Red Cloud and Red Leaf bands for ponies taken from them.

35. Indian Reservations. 21 Jan.
HED 105, 50-1, v26, 2p. [2558]
Appropriation for survey and allotment of lands in severalty.

36. Kickapoo Indians. 21 Jan.
HED 106, 50-1, v26, 2p. [2558]
Appropriation to fulfill treaty stipulations; treaties of 18 May 1854, and 28 June 1862.

37. Arickaree, Gros Ventre, and Mandan Indians. 21 Jan.
HED 107, 50-1, v26, 13p. [2558]
Ratification of the agreement of 14 Dec. 1886 with said tribes; Northwest Indian Commission; reduction of the Fort Berthold reservation in Dakota.

38. Resol. of Sen. Mitchell. 23 Jan.
SMD 36, 50-1, v1, 1p. [2516]
Asks information on the Coeur d'Alene reservation in Idaho Territory.

39. Mission Indians in California. 23 Jan.
SR 74, 50-1, v1, 33p. [2519] *or*
HR 3282, 50-1, v10, 37p. [2607]
On the condition of said Indians, and measures to be adopted for their relief.

40. Resol. of Rep. Woodburn. 23 Jan.
HMD 138, 50-1, v1, 3p. [2565]
Investigation of the Alaska Commercial Co.; virtual enslavement of the natives on the Aleutian Islands.

41. Private Land Claim, No. 146. 24 Jan.
SED 60, 50-1, v7, 6p. [2510]
Land title issues in New Mexico involving the Isleta Pueblo Indians.

42. Agreement with Certain Indians. 24 Jan.
HR 104, 50-1, v1, 5p. [2598]
With the Gros Ventres, Piegans, Bloods, Blackfeet, and River Crows, in Montana; land cessions to the U.S.

43. R-C of W. Martin. 25 Jan.
SR 84, 50-1, v1, 3p. [2519] *or*
HR 3375, 50-1, v10, 3p. [2607]
Indian depredations in 1849 near Fort Hall, Utah Territory.

44. R-C of C. Ruffee. 25 Jan.
HR 116, 50-1, v1, 2p. [2598]
Indian agent at the White Earth agency in Minnesota.

45. Receipts and Expenditures. 26 Jan.
HED 124, 50-1, v27, 556p. [2559]
Year ending 30 June 1885; Indian expenses.

46. Ejectment of Persons from Public Lands. 30 Jan.
SED 65, 50-1, v7, 6p. [2510]
Lands purchased of the Chippewas and Muncies in Kansas; removal of Indians to Indian Territory prevented due to lands having been allotted in severalty; Indians are U.S. citizens.

47. Indian Agent at Mackinac, Michigan. 31 Jan.
HED 130, 50-1, v26, 2p. [2558]
Increase in salary.

48. Additional Land District in Oregon. 31 Jan.
HR 180, 50-1, v1, 2p. [2598]
Area lately occupied by Indians.

49. Choctaw Coal and Railway Co. 31 Jan.
HR 182, 50-1, v1, 1p. [2598]
Construction of a railroad through Indian Territory.

50. R-C of S. Barclay et al. 1 Feb.
SR 159, 50-1, v1, 17p. [2519]
Sureties on the bond of the late Indian agent at the Wichita agency.

51. R-P of M. Pierce. 1 Feb.
SR 180, 50-1, v1, 3p. [2519]
Service in the Nez Percé war; 1877.

52. Amendment of the Revised Statutes. 1 Feb.
HR 212, 50-1, v1, 2p. [2598]
Allowing Indians, other than fullbloods, to trade without a license; bill not recommended.

53. Claims for Cattle Stolen. 6 Feb.
SED 66, 50-1, v7, 4p. [2510]
Osage depredations of 1866 in Indian Territory.

54. Resol. of Rep. Morrill. 6 Feb.
HMD 173, 50-1, v1, 1p. [2565]
On claim involving legal services provided for the Pottawatomies.

55. Warm Springs Indian Reservation. 7 Feb.
SED 70, 50-1, v7, 3p. [2510]
Survey of the boundary of the reservation; Oregon.

56. R-C of the Western Cherokees. 7 Feb.
SR 217, 50-1, v1, 15p. [2519] *or*
HR 342, 50-1, v2, 24p. [2599]
Funds due under various treaty stipulations; bill authorizes case to be heard by the Court of Claims.

57. Agreement with the Shoshones and Bannocks. 7 Feb.
HED 140, 50-1, v26, 31p. [2558]
Dated 27 May 1887; surrender of a portion of the Fort Hall reservation in Idaho; right of way to the Utah and Northern Railway Co.

58. Marriage Between White Men and Indian Women. 7 Feb.
HR 250, 50-1, v1, 1p. [2598]
Legislation concerning said marriages.

59. Organization of Oklahoma Territory. 7 Feb.
HR 263 (pts. 1 and 2), 50-1, v2, 30p. [2599]
Encompassing Indian Territory; list of tribes, populations, acreage in reservations, etc.; treaty stipulations.

60. Western Yearly Meeting of Friends. 7 Feb.
HR 291, 50-1, v2, 1p. [2599]
Claim for money expended on an Indian training school in North Carolina.

61. R-C of P. Winston. 8 Feb.
SR 219, 50-1, v1, 2p. [2519] *or*
SR 2094, 50-1, v8, 2p. [2526] *or*
HR 1141, 50-1, v4, 2p. [2601]
Attorney for the capt. of Indian police at the Nez Percé agency, Idaho.

62. Creditors of the Pottawatomies. 9 Feb.
SR 223, 50-1, v1, 3p. [2519] *or*
HR 160, 50-1, v1, 3p. [2598]
Legal services provided for the tribe in their claim against the U.S.

63. Indian Agents. 9 Feb.
HED 143, 50-1, v26, 3p. [2558]
Accounts of the agents at the Mackinac agency in Michigan, and at the Umatilla agency in Oregon.

64. Miami and Pottawatomie Treaties. 9 Feb.
HED 146, 50-1, v26, 2p. [2558]
Appropriation to fulfill Miami treaties of 1795, 1805, and 1809, and the Pottawatomie treaty of 1807.

65. R-C of Texas. 10 Feb.
HR 370, 50-1, v2, 3p. [2599]
Boundary between Texas and Indian Territory.

66. Coeur d'Alene Indian Reservation. 13 Feb.
SED 76, 50-1, v7, 7p. [2510]
Information on the area and boundaries of the reservation in Idaho; Indian population; opening of lands to occupation under mineral laws.

67. Omaha Indian Reservation. 14 Feb.
SED 77, 50-1, v7, 2p. [2510]
Sale of lands (in Nebraska); payments due, etc.

68. Public Lands in Nebraska. 14 Feb.
SED 78, 50-1, v7, 2p. [2510]
Original acreage included in Indian reservations; proceeds from sale of Pawnee lands.

69. R-P of F. Ricketts. 14 Feb.
SR 265, 50-1, v1, 6p. [2519] *or*
HR 759, 50-1, v3, 7p. [2600] *or*
HR 1406, 50-1, v5, 3p. [2602
Seminole war; 1852; Florida.

70. R-P of V. Grier. 14 Feb.
SR 270, 50-1, v1, 2p. [2519]
Service against the Apaches, Spokanes, and other hostile Indians.

71. Southwestern, Arkansas, and Indian Territory Railroad Co. 15 Feb.
HR 495, 50-1, v2, 1p. [2599]
Bridge to be built in Arkansas.

72. Kansas City and Pacific Railroad Co. 15 Feb.
HR 499, 50-1, v2, 1p. [2599]
Right of way through Indian Territory.

73. Moorhead, Leech Lake, and Northern Railway Co. 15 Feb.
HR 500, 50-1, v2, 2p. [2599]
Right of way through the White Earth reservation in Minnesota.

74. Great Sioux Reservation in Dakota. 16 Feb.
HR 533, 50-1, v2, 4p. [2599]
Divison and reduction of the reser-

vation; treaty of 1868; agreements of 1876, and 1882.

75. U.S. Officials in Indian Territory. 17 Feb.
HR 544, 50-1, v2, 1p. [2599]
Extends protection of U.S. laws over Indians employed as guard, etc., by U.S. marshalls.

76. Yankton and Missouri River Railway Co. 21 Feb.
HR 563, 50-1, v2, 1p. [2599]
Right of way through the Yankton reservation in Dakota.

77. Omaha Reservation in Nebraska. 21 Feb.
HR 564, 50-1, v2, 1p. [2599]
Reservation sold in 1884-1885; proceeds and interest not available to Indians as yet.

78. R-C of F. Skinner. 21 Feb.
HR 613, 50-1, v3, 3p. [2600]
Physician at the Fort Peck Indian agency.

79. R-C of L. Pearlman. 21 Feb.
HR 638, 50-1, v3, 4p. [2600]
Indian hostilities of 1860 in what is now Nevada.

80. Surveys in Indian Reservations. 23 Feb.
SED 90, 50-1, v7, 4p. [2510]
Appropriation needed to enable the "speedy execution" of the allotment act.

81. R-C of the Reps. of S. Marston. 23 Feb.
SR 352, 50-1, v2, 1p. [2520]
Late Indian agency at Union agency, Indian Territory.

82. Southern and Western Boundaries of Kansas. 23 Feb.
SR 353, 50-1, v2, 3p. [2520]
Involves the borders of Indian Territory; Cherokee treaties of 1828, 1833, and 1835.

83. R-P of Maj. Averell. 23 Feb.
SR 355, 50-1, v2, 9p. [2520] *or*
HR 335, 50-1, v2, 5p. [2599] *or*
HR 2766, 50-1, v8, 5p. [2605]
Navajo campaign; 1858; New Mexico.

84. R-C of E. Leib. 23 Feb.
SR 357, 50-1, v2, 6p. [2520] *or*
HR 1987, 50-1, v6, 5p. [2603]
Service against hostile Indians; 1868-1877; in Kansas, Nebraska, Wyoming, and Arizona.

85. R-P of A. Pleasonton. 23 Feb.
SR 361, 50-1, v2, 5p. [2520] *or*
SR 1189, 50-1, v5, 5p. [2523] *or*
HR 340, 50-1, v2, 5p. [2599]
Service against the Sioux, Apaches, Navajoes, Utah Indians, and other tribes.

86. R-C of P. Sinnott. 23 Feb.
SR 365, 50-1, v2, 5p. [2520]
Late Indian agent at the Grande Ronde agency in Oregon.

87. Admission of South Dakota. 24 Feb.
HR 709, 50-1, v3, 92p. [2600]
Area of land included within Indian reservations; 21 million acres in the great Sioux reservation.

88. Resol. of Rep. Bayne. 27 Feb.
HMD 281, 50-1, v6, 1p. [2570]
Concerning an order issued by the CIA prohibiting missionaries from teaching the scriptures in government schools.

89. Resol. of Rep. Peel. 27 Feb.
HMD 284, 50-1, v6, 1p. [2570]
On funds belonging to the Ottawas for land sales in Kansas.

90. R-P of A. Yates. 28 Feb.
SR 394, 50-1, v2, 2p. [2520] *or*
HR 1637, 50-1, v5, 2p. [2602]
Service against the Sioux in 1876; Custer's massacre; Little Big Horn River.

91. Indian Fishing Privileges. 28 Feb.
HED 183, 50-1, v26, 11p. [2558]
Appropriation to purchase land on the Columbia River in Oregon for use by the Indians on the Warm Springs reservation; treaties of 25 June 1855, and 15 Nov. 1865.

92. Claims Allowed by Accounting Officers. 1 Mar.
SED 101, 50-1, v7, 29p. [2510]
Under exhausted appropriations; claims involving Indians.

93. Red Lake Chippewas in Minnesota. 1 Mar.
HR 789, 50-1, v3, 17p. [2600]
Recent agreement not approved, as it leaves too much land to the Red Lake Chippewas as a band; bill substituted calling for allotment, and sale of surplus lands.

94. Billings, Clark's Fort, and Cooke City Railroad Co. 1 Mar.
HR 790, 50-1, v3, 3p. [2600]
Right of way through the Crow reservation in Montana.

95. R-C of Wind River Valley Settlers. 1 Mar.
HR 792, 50-1, v3, 3p. [2600]

Land and improvements encorporated into an Indian reservation; treaty of 1868 with the Shoshones and Bannocks; Wyoming.

96. R-C of D. Whitfield. 2 Mar.
HR 816, 50-1, v3, 2p. [2600]
Surety on the bond of an Indian agent in Kansas.

97. Aberdeen, Bismarck, and Northwestern Railway Co. 2 Mar.
HR 817, 50-1, v3, 2p. [2600]
Right of way through the Sioux reservation in Dakota.

98. R-C of E. Moore and D. Woodson. 2 Mar.
HR 819, 50-1, v3, 3p. [2600]
Sale of Indian trust lands in Kansas; Delaware and Wea treaties of 1854.

99. R-C of J. Beck. 2 Mar.
HR 830, 50-1, v3, 3p. [2600]
Navajo depredations of 1849 in New Mexico.

100. Trespassers on Indian Lands. 3 Mar.
HR 839, 50-1, v3, 1p. [2600]
Legislation proposed.

101. Amendment of the Revised Statutes. 3 Mar.
HR 840, 50-1, v3, 1p. [2600]
Timber depredations on Indian lands.

102. Completion of Certain Forts. 5 Mar.
SR 441, 50-1, v2, 1p. [2520]
Forts Robinson and Niobrara in Nebraska; close to the great Sioux reservation.

103. Lands in Severalty to Certain Indians. 5 Mar.
HR 843, 50-1, v3, 1p. [2600]
Allotments for the United Peorias and Weas in Indian Territory.

104. R-C of Cherokee Freedmen et al. 5 Mar.
HR 844, 50-1, v3, 11p. [2600]
Freedmen, and adopted Shawnees and Delawares ask for their share of the funds of the Cherokee Nation.

105. Indian Commission. 5 Mar.
HR 845, 50-1, v3, 3p. [2600]
Bill creating a commission to look into the condition of Indian affairs; allotment and citizenship.

106. New York Indian Lands. 7 Mar.
SMD 76, 50-1, v1, 4p. [2516]
On the relief of settlers on these lands in Kansas; Indians to whom the lands were allotted in 1860, were never in possession of said lands.

107. R-C of the American Board of Com'rs for Foreign Missions et al. 7 Mar.
SR 486, 50-1, v2, 4p. [2520]
Property destroyed by U.S. troops in Indian Territory during the Civil War.

108. R-C of Oregon. 7 Mar.
SR 488, 50-1, v2, 2p. [2520]
Nez Percé war of 1877.

109. R-P of M. Kirby. 7 Mar.
SR 493, 50-1, v2, 3p. [2520] *or*
HR 609, 50-1, v3, 4p. [2600]
Service in the Seminole war during 1836-1838 in Florida; Cherokee removal.

110. Settlers on the Winnebago and Crow Creek Reservations. 7 Mar.
HR 859, 50-1, v3, 2p. [2600]
Lands in said reservations opened for settlement on 27 Feb. 1885, and then closed again on 17 Apr. 1885; Dakota.

111. Southern Ute Indians. 7 Mar.
HR 861, 50-1, v3, 10p. [2600]
Ute delegation asks that the tribe be removed from Colorado to a reservation in Utah.

112. R-C of J. and C. Hulett. 8 Mar.
SR 506, 50-1, v2, 2p. [2520] *or*
HR 2878, 50-1, v8, 2p. [2605]
White River Ute depredations of 1879 in Colorado.

113. Methods of Transacting Business in the Executive Depts. 8 Mar.
SR 507 (pts. 1-3), 50-1, v3-4, 2229p. [2521-2522]
Including the OIA.

114. Sale of New York Indian Lands. 8 Mar.
SR 508, 50-1, v2, 8p. [2520] *or*
HR 15, 50-1, v1, 7p. [2598]
History of the tribe's acquisition of land title; allotments in Kansas never occupied by Indians.

115. R-C of H. Shipley. 8 Mar.
SR 510, 50-1, v2, 3p. [2520]
Services performed at the Nez Percé agency in Idaho.

116. Contingent Expenses of the Indian Dept. 8 Mar.
HR 957, 50-1, v3, 2p. [2600]
Expense of punishing Indians who have committed crimes to be borne by the U.S. government, not territories.

117. Judicial Districts of Texas. 10 Mar.
HR 1007, 50-1, v4, 3p. [2601]
Jurisdiction over parts of Choctaw and Chickasaw Nations in Indian Territory.

118. The Five Civilized Tribes. 10 Mar.
HR 1010, 50-1, v4, 4p. [2601]
Control of Indian commerce under various treaties; leases of land; Creeks, Cherokees, Choctaws, Seminoles, and Chickasaws.

119. R-C of L. Morris. 12 Mar.
SR 514, 50-1, v2, 2p. [2520] *or*
HR 10, 50-1, v1, 2p. [2598]
Licensed traders fail to obtain permission to trade from the Choctaws.

120. Unlawful Grazing on Indian Lands. 12 Mar.
HR 1015, 50-1, v4, 1p. [2601]
Bill imposing penalties on trespassers.

121. Offenders to be Arrested in Indian Territory. 12 Mar.
HR 1016, 50-1, v4, 1p. [2601]
U.S. marshals will be allowed to pursue criminals into said Territory.

122. R-P of H. Burnett. 13 Mar.
SR 519, 50-1, v2, 4p. [2520] *or*
HR 2247, 50-1, v6, 4p. [2603]
Service in the Seminole, Creek, and Black Hawk wars.

123. Pension Laws. 13 Mar.
SR 546, 50-1, v2, 2p. [2520]
Bill to include service against Indians by those not in the U.S. Army.

124. R-P of M. Worth. 13 Mar.
SR 557, 50-1, v2, 5p. [2520] *or*
HR 2292, 50-1, v7, 5p. [2604]
Service in the Black Hawk and Seminole wars, as well as in the Cherokee removal.

125. Admission of Territories. 13 Mar.
HR 1025, 50-1, v4, 145p. [2601]
Dakota, Washington, New Mexico, and Montana; Indian populations and reservations.

126. Amending the Revised Statutes. 13 Mar.
HR 1039, 50-1, v4, 2p. [2601]
Pensions for service against Indians.

127. R-P of L. Owen. 13 Mar.
HR 1065, 50-1, v4, 4p. [2601]
Service against Seminoles, Spokanes, and Coeur d'Alenes.

128. R-P of W. Compton. 13 Mar.
HR 1102, 50-1, v4, 1p. [2601]
Service in the Creek Nation; 1814.

129. Miami Indians. 13 Mar.
HR 1133 (pts. 1 and 2), 50-1, v4, 8p. [2601]
Funds improperly taken from the tribe; treaty of 1854.

130. R-C of A. Sharp. 14 Mar.
HR 1149, 50-1, v4, 3p. [2601]
Taken captive by Sioux; 1857; Iowa.

131. Letter from J. Swan. 15 Mar.
SMD 78, 50-1, v1, 3p. [2516]
Includes enforcement of laws regarding introduction of liquor to Indians in Alaska.

132. Admission of Washington Territory. 15 Mar.
SR 585 (pts. 1 and 2), 50-1, v2, 48p. [2520]
Northern Idaho should be attached to the new State, as it can be reached from southern Idaho only by a circuitous route through the Umatilla Indian reservation.

133. Appropriation for Texas. 15 Mar.
HED 219, 50-1, v28, 1p. [2560]
Reimbursement for suppressing Indian hostilities.

134. Sisseton and Wahpeton Sioux. 16 Mar.
HR 1164, 50-1, v4, 1p. [2601]
Agreement between the Indians and the Chicago, Milwaukee, and St. Paul Railway Co.; right of way through the Lake Traverse reservation.

135. Territory of Idaho. 16 Mar.
HR 1182, 50-1, v4, 8p. [2601]
Allotment of the Nez Percé reservation suggested.

136. Indian Appropriation Bill. 16 Mar.
HR 1185, 50-1, v4, 2p. [2601]
Year ending 30 June 1889.

137. Survivors of the Indian Wars of 1832-1842. 17 Mar.
HR 1194, 50-1, v4, 4p. [2601]
Black Hawk, Creek, and Seminole wars; Cherokee disturbances.

138. Carson City Indian School. 17 Mar.
HR 1195, 50-1, v4, 3p. [2601]
Education of Shoshone youths in Nevada; appropriation needed to establish the school.

139. Medawakanton Band of Sioux. 20 Mar.
HED 228, 50-1, v28, 3p. [2560]
Appropriation for the support of said band in Minnesota.

140. R-C of C. Beers et al. 20 Mar.
HR 1201, 50-1, v4, 4p. [2601]
Sioux depredations of 1866.

141. R-C of E. Jones. 20 Mar.
HR 1203, 50-1, v4, 1p. [2601]
Cheyenne hostilities of 1874 in Kansas.

142. R-C of F. and C. Huning et al. 20 Mar.
HR 1204, 50-1, v4, 4p. [2601]
Navajo, Kiowa, Cheyenne, and Apache depredations in New Mexico.

143. Admission of Montana. 26 Mar.
SR 733, 50-1, v5, 2p. [2523]
Acreage included in Indian reservations.

144. Organization of Alaska Territory. 26 Mar.
HR 1318, 50-1, v4, 5p. [2601]
Population of the uncivilized natives.

145. Otoe and Missouria Indians. 27 Mar.
SED 131, 50-1, v10, 19p. [2513]
Number of acres, and sale of their reservation in Kansas and Nebraska.

146. R-C of H. Wood. 27 Mar.
HR 1423, 50-1, v5, 4p. [2602]
Fort Cobb, Indian Territory, evacuated during the Civil War.

147. R-C of R. Montgomery. 27 Mar.
HR 1429, 50-1, v5, 2p. [2602]
Service against Indians in the West since 1865.

148. R-C of the Heirs of R. Hurley. 27 Mar.
HR 1436, 50-1, v5, 5p. [2602]
Service in Paiute war of 1860 in Utah Territory.

149. R-C of G. Maxwell. 27 Mar.
HR 1459, 50-1, v5, 2p. [2602]
Cheyenne depredations of 1868 on the Arkansas River.

150. R-C of J. Jackson. 27 Mar.
HR 1460, 50-1, v5, 3p. [2602]
Kiowa depredations of 1871-1872 in Texas.

151. R-C of J. Kaula. 27 Mar.
HR 1461, 50-1, v5, 2p. [2602]
Sioux hostilities of 1862 in Minnesota.

152. R-P of S. O'Connor. 29 Mar.
SR 776, 50-1, v5, 8p. [2523]
Service against Indians in New Mexico; 1881.

153. R-C of A. Leschinsky. 29 Mar.
HR 1477, 50-1, v5, 3p. [2602]
Danger of Indian incursions on the McLeod River in California; 1870.

154. R-C of H. Wedeles. 29 Mar.
HR 1482, 50-1, v5, 4p. [2602]
Arapaho depredations of 1867 in Kansas.

155. R-C of the Reps. of G. McDougall. 31 Mar.
SR 786, 50-1, v5, 3p. [2523]
Supplies to California Indians; 1851.

156. Brevet Promotions of Army Officers. 31 Mar.
SR 790, 50-1, v5, 3p. [2523]
Service in Indian wars.

157. Brevet Rank in the Army. 31 Mar.
SR 792, 50-1, v5, 1p. [2523] *or*
HR 1225, 50-1, v4, 2p. [2601] *or*
HR 2858, 50-1, v8, 2p. [2605]
Service in Indian campaigns.

158. R-P of G. Dillman. 3 Apr.
SR 810, 50-1, v5, 1p. [2523]
Service in Black Hawk and Florida Indian wars.

159. R-P of P. Thompson. 3 Apr.
SR 849, 50-1, v5, 2p. [2523] *or*
HR 1892, 50-1, v6, 2p. [2603]
Service in the Black Hawk war; 1832.

160. Forfeiture of Land Grants. 3 Apr.
HR 1498, 50-1, v5, 16p. [2602]
By the Northern Pacific Railroad Co.; lands in the Sioux, Crow, Coeur d'Alene, Yakima, and Puyallup reservations existing under various treaties.

161. Railroad Indemnity Withdrawals. 5 Apr.
HED 246, 50-1, v28, 117p. [2560]
Lands in Indian Territory, etc.

162. Seminole Indians. 9 Apr.
SED 139, 50-1, v10, 15p. [2513]
Condition of Seminoles in Florida; removal to Indian Territory.

163. R-P of W. Madden. 10 Apr.
SR 886, 50-1, v5, 2p. [2523]
Service at Fort Kearny, Indian Territory.

164. R-P of J. Hancock. 10 Apr.
SR 903, 50-1, v5, 1p. [2523]
Service in the Seminole war; 1836-1837.

165. Resol. of Sen. Mitchell. 11 Apr.
SMD 95, 50-1, v1, 1p. [2516]
Investigation of Indian depredation claims.

166. R-P of D. McKibbin. 13 Apr.
HR 1510, 50-1, v5, 2p. [2602]
Service against hostile Indians; 1856-1857.

167. Billings, Clark's Fort, and Cooke City Railroad Co. 13 Apr.
HR 1528, 50-1, v5, 1p. [2602]
Right of way through the Crow reservation.

168. R-C of J. Little and H. Williams. 13 Apr.
HR 1529, 50-1, v5, 4p. [2602]
Mineral rights on Iowa Indian land in Kansas and Nebraska.

169. Montana, Kansas, and Texas Railroad Co. 13 Apr.
HR 1530, 50-1, v5, 1p. [2602]
Right of way through Indian Territory.

170. R-C of W. Midkiff. 13 Apr.
HR 1665, 50-1, v5, 4p. [2602]
Comanche and Kiowa depredations of 1868 in Texas.

171. Legislative, Executive, and Judicial Appropriation Bill. 14 Apr.
HR 1667, 50-1, v5, 34p. [2602]
Year ending 30 June 1889; Indian expenses.

172. Indian Depredation Claims. 14 Apr.
HR 1696, 50-1, v5, 15p. [2602]
Legislation to speed adjudication of claims; list of liabilities of the U.S. to Indian tribes in annuities, etc.

173. R-C of J. Fell et al. 14 Apr.
HR 1701, 50-1, v5, 26p. [2602]
Apache depredations of 1865-1869 in Arizona.

174. R-C of E. Ellis. 14 Apr.
HR 1702, 50-1, v5, 3p. [2602]
Legal services for the Pottawatomies.

175. Reimbursement for Moneys Expended. 16 Apr.
SR 952, 50-1, v5, 11p. [2523]
During the Paiute war of 1860 in Utah Territory, and other Indian wars.

176. Resol. of Rep. Barry. 16 Apr.
HMD 362, 50-1, v6, 1p. [2570]
On pensions to survivors of Indian wars.

177. Sums Due Indian Agents. 17 Apr.
SED 146, 50-1, v10, 4p. [2513]
Salaries withheld from certain agents.

178. R-P of P. Bottineau. 17 Apr.
SR 1008, 50-1, v5, 2p. [2523] *or*
HR 3127, 50-1, v8, 3p. [2605]
Service as a guide, scout, and interpreter; 1857-1872; Sioux and Chippewas.

179. R-P of E. Anderson. 17 Apr.
SR 1015, 50-1, v5, 2p. [2523] *or*
HR 2159, 50-1, v6, 2p. [2603]
Service in Sioux war of 1862-1863 in Minnesota.

180. Washington and Idaho Railroad Co. 17 Apr.
HR 1713, 50-1, v5, 1p. [2602]
Right of way through the Coeur d'Alene reservation.

181. R-C of H. Newman. 17 Apr.
HR 1787, 50-1, v6, 3p. [2603]
Kiowa, Cheyenne, Arapaho, and Comanche depredations.

182. R-P of E. Wilkins. 17 Apr.
HR 1800, 50-1, v6, 1p. [2603]
Service in the Creek war; 1836.

183. Fort Smith and El Paso Railway Co. 20 Apr.
HR 1867, 50-1, v6, 1p. [2603]
Right of way through Indian Territory; Choctaw, Chickasaw, Kiowa, Comanche, and Apache lands.

184. R-P of D. Seely. 24 Apr.
SR 1084, 50-1, v5, 1p. [2523] *or*
HR 892, 50-1, v3, 1p. [2600]
Service against Indians in Minnesota; 1865.

185. R-P of W. Riddell. 24 Apr.
SR 1095, 50-1, v5, 7p. [2523] *or*
HR 1413, 50-1, v5, 6p. [2602] *or*
HR 3064, 50-1, v8, 7p. [2605]
Modoc Peace Commission; 1873.

186. R-P of R. Barnes. 24 Apr.
HR 1915, 50-1, v6, 3p. [2603]
Service in the Seminole war; 1840-1841; Florida.

187. Pima County, Arizona. 24 Apr.
HR 1926, 50-1, v6, 2p. [2602]
Business depression due to Indian hostilities in 1886.

188. Improvements at Forts Robinson and Niobrara. 24 Apr.
HR 1948, 50-1, v6, 1p. [2603]
Located in Nebraska near the great Sioux reservation.

189. Fort Smith and Choctaw Bridge Co. 24 Apr.
HR 1950, 50-1, v6, 2p. [2603]
Construction of a bridge in the Choctaw Nation near Fort Smith, Arkansas.

190. Indians Who Served in the U.S. Army. 24 Apr.
HR 1953, 50-1, v6, 6p. [2603]
Payments to Sisseton and Wahpeton Sioux who served in the Sioux outbreak of 1862.

191. Permanent and Indefinite Appropriations. 26 Apr.
HMD 389, 50-1, v6, 16p. [2570]
Proposed repeal of certain Indian appropriations.

192. R-C of A. McCreary. 27 Apr.
HR 1981, 50-1, v6, 22p. [2603]
Licensed traders to the Osages in Indian Territory; 1873.

193. R-C of the Tillamook Indians. 30 Apr.
SED 154, 50-1, v10, 3p. [2513]
Claim to lands in Oregon never extinguished; treaties of 1851 and 11 Aug. 1855 go unratified.

194. R-P of B. Thebant. 1 May.
SR 1161, 50-1, v5, 1p. [2523] *or*
HR 2289, 50-1, v7, 1p. [2604]
Service in Seminole war; 1849-1850; Florida.

195. R-C of D. Boutwell. 1 May.
HR 1996, 50-1, v6, 1p. [2603]
Second Indian Home Guards; Civil War.

196. Winnebago Reservation in Nebraska. 1 May.
HR 2013, 50-1, v6, 1p. [2603]
Sale of land to provide funds for improving their allotment acreage.

197. Umatilla Reservation in Oregon. 1 May.
HR 2014, 50-1, v6, 1p. [2603]
Sale of surplus land following allotment to the Indians.

198. R-C of Rollins and Presbrey. 3 May.
SED 158, 50-1, v10, 25p. [2513]
For legal services rendered to the Eastern Cherokees.

199. R-P of the Widow of Lieut. Stewart. 3 May.
SR 1190, 50-1, v5, 3p. [2523]
Service against Indians on the upper Missouri River; 1865-1866.

200. R-C of Pottawatomies of Indiana and Michigan. 3 May.
SR 1194, 50-1, v6, 42p. [2524] *or*
HR 3281, 50-1, v10, 42p. [2607] *or*
HR 3502, 50-1, v10, 43p. [2607]
Funds due under various treaties.

201. Uintah Valley Indian Reservation. 3 May.
SR 1198, 50-1, v6, 2p. [2524] *or*
HR 791, 50-1, v3, 3p. [2600]
Restoration of part of the Ute reservation to the public lands; minerals found.

202. Fur Bearing Animals in Alaska. 4 May.
HED 296, 50-1, v29, 5p. [2561]
Education of the natives; elimination of liquor traffic.

203. Alaska Seal and Fur Co. 4 May.
HED 297, 50-1, v29, 8p. [2561]
Virtual enslavement of the natives.

204. Employment of Matrons at Agencies. 7 May.
SED 160, 50-1, v10, 3p. [2513]
Appropriation for matrons to instruct Indian women in domestic affairs.

205. R-C of J. Fenimore. 7 May.
SR 1201, 50-1, v6, 1p. [2524]
Cayuse war; 1847; Oregon.

206. R-C of D. Meriwether. 7 May.
SR 1207, 50-1, v6, 6p. [2524] *or*
HR 307, 50-1, v2, 7p. [2599]
Supt. of Indian Affairs in New Mexico.

207. R-P of J. Gallagher. 8 May.
SR 1238, 50-1, v6, 1p. [2524] *or*
HR 3553, 50-2, v1, 1p. [2673]
Seminole war; 1836; Florida.

208. R-P of B. Clements. 8 May.
SR 1252, 50-1, v6, 2p. [2524]
Service in the Seminole war in Florida; 1856-1857.

209. New York Indian Lands in Kansas. 8 May.
HED 298, 50-1, v29, 7p. [2561]
Sale of said lands; Indians forced off lands by armed settlers.

210. R-P of W. Spencer. 8 May.
HR 2059, 50-1, v6, 3p. [2603]
Service against Sioux; 1857; Minnesota.

211. Indian Upon the Oneida Reservation. 8 May.
HR 2079, 50-1, v6, 2p. [2603]
Allotment of lands in severalty in Wisconsin; U.S. trusteeship reduced from 25 to 5 years.

212. R-P of M. Tilley. 9 May.
SR 1263, 50-1, v6, 1p. [2524]
Indian massacre of 1849 in Florida.

213. R-C of A. Mueller. 10 May.
SR 1282, 50-1, v6, 2p. [2524]
Confederate troop depredations of 1864 in the Cherokee Nation.

214. R-C of Nevada. 14 May.
SR 1286, 50-1, v6, 153p. [2524]
Suppression of Indian hostilities.

215. R-P of S. Alexander. 14 May.
HR 2179, 50-1, v6, 3p. [2603]
Service in Black Hawk (Sac and Fox), and Seminole wars; supervised Seminole removal from Florida.

216. Freedmen in the Chickasaw Nation. 15 May.
SED 166, 50-1, v10, 18p. [2513]

Status and condition of the freedmen; stipulations of the treaty of 28 Apr. 1866 with the Choctaws and Chickasaws.

217. Tillamook Lands in Oregon. 15 May.
SED 168, 50-1, v10, 3p. [2513]
Unratified treaties of 6 Aug. 1851 with the Naalem band, and 7 Aug. 1851 with the Tillamook tribe; title to land ceded in the treaties.

218. R-P of W. Lemons. 15 May.
SR 1342, 50-1, v6, 1p. [2524]
Service against Indians in Tennessee; battles of Talladega, Horse Shoe, and Hickory Flats.

219. Milwaukee, West Shore, and Western Railway Co. 15 May.
HR 2200, 50-1, v6, 6p. [2603]
Construction through the Lac de Flambeau reservation in Wisconsin; Chippewa treaty of 30 Sept. 1854.

220. Printing of the Act of 8 Feb. 1887. 16 May.
SR 1343, 50-1, v6, 1p. [2524]
To provide for allotment of lands in severalty to Indians in the U.S.

221. Claims for Indian Supplies. 21 May.
SR 1353, 50-1, v6, 7p. [2524]
Furnished to Sioux in Minnesota prior to the outbreak of 1862.

222. R-C of a U.S. District Attorney. 22 May.
HED 327, 50-1, v29, 3p. [2561]
Services performed for Pueblo Indians in New Mexico.

223. Sale of Flathead Lands. 22 May.
HR 2249, 50-1, v6, 4p. [2603]
Sale of lands in the Bitter Root Valley of Montana; removal of Indians to the Jocko reservation.

224. Puyallup Valley Railway Co. 23 May.
HR 2269, 50-1, v7, 1p. [2604]
Right of way through the Puyallup Indian reservation, Washington.

225. R-P of N. Cook. 23 May.
HR 2273, 50-1, v7, 1p. [2604]
Service in the Cherokee war of 1838 in Georgia.

226. R-P of C. Whittlesey. 23 May.
HR 2296, 50-1, v7, 2p. [2604]
In numerous Indian engagements.

227. Indian Appropriations Bill. 24 May.
SR 1375, 50-1, v6, 5p. [2524]
Year ending 30 June 1889.

228. Leavenworth and Rio Grande Railway Co. 24 May.
HR 2335, 50-1, v7, 1p. [2604]
Right of way through Indian Territory.

229. R-P of E. Sexton. 25 May.
SR 1383, 50-1, v6, 1p. [2524]
Service against Indians; 1862-1863; Minnesota.

230. Amending the Revised Statutes. 26 May.
HR 2342, 50-1, v7, 2p. [2604]
Pension laws for service in Indian wars while not in U.S. Army.

231. R-P of B. Henderson. 28 May.
SR 2355, 50-1, v7, 1p. [2604]
Service in Black Hawk war.

232. R-P of W. Thompson. 28 May.
HR 2356, 50-1, v7, 1p. [2604]
Service in Black Hawk war; 1832; Illinois.

233. Pensions for Service in the Mexican War. 28 May.
HR 2358, 50-1, v7, 6p. [2604]
Indian hostilities occur simultaneously in the Southwest.

234. Duluth and Winnipeg Railway Co. 29 May.
HR 2394, 50-1, v7, 1p. [2604]
Right of way through the Fond du Lac reservation in Minnesota.

235. Right of Way Through Indian Territory. 29 May.
HR 2396, 50-1, v7, 1p. [2604]
Action of the Com. on Indian Affairs regarding House bill no. 10062.

236. R-C of the Heirs of J. West. 29 May.
HR 2397, 50-1, v7, 7p. [2604]
Cherokees take possession of saline lands in Indian Territory; treaty of 6 Aug. 1846.

237. R-C of D. Hedges and E. Spaulding. 29 May.
HR 2400, 50-1, v7, 2p. [2604]
Licensed trader to the Sioux during 1866-1867 at the Yankton agency in Dakota; debts incurred by Indians.

238. Military Stores for the Montana Militia. 29 May.
HR 2402, 50-1, v7, 1p. [2604]
For Indian outbreaks.

239. R-P of O. Farrand. 31 May.
HR 2405, 50-1, v7, 1p. [2604]
Payment of annuities to a Miami Indian.

240. Cree Indians of Montana. 2 June.
HED 341, 50-1, v29, 6p. [2561]
On the relief of said Indians near

Fort Assiniboine; removal to the Fort Belknap agency; driven south from Canada.

241. R-P of M. Heintzelman. 5 June.
SR 1475, 50-1, v6, 2p. [2524] *or*
HR 2791, 50-1, v8, 2p. [2605]
Service against Indians in Florida, Oregon, California, and Arizona (Yuma Indians).

242. R-P of J. Dickey. 5 June.
SR 1480, 50-1, v6, 1p. [2524] *or*
HR 2248, 50-1, v6, 1p. [2603]
Service in Black Hawk war; 1832.

243. Shoshone and Bannock Indians. 5 June.
HR 2431, 50-1, v7, 3p. [2604]
Agreement made surrendering a portion of the Fort Hall reservation, Idaho, to the U.S.; right of way granted to the Utah and Northern Railway Co. also.

244. R-P of M. Emory. 6 June.
HR 2447, 50-1, v7, 3p. [2604]
Service against hostile Indians.

245. R-P of V. Grier. 6 June.
HR 2451, 50-1, v7, 2p. [2604]
Service against hostile Apaches and Spokanes.

246. R-P of A. Yates. 8 June.
HR 2520, 50-1, v7, 1p. [2604]
Service in the Sioux war; 1876; Custer's massacre.

247. Mem. in Behalf of Certain Cherokees. 11 June.
SMD 129, 50-1, v2, 5p. [2517]
North Carolina Cherokees recently removed to Indian Territory ask reimbursement for the expense of said removal.

248. Sisseton and Wahpeton Sioux. 12 June.
SED 188, 50-1, v10, 3p. [2514]
Patents issued to certain Indians under the treaty of 19 Feb. 1867 are surrendered so that said Indians might take allotments on the Lake Traverse reservation, Dakota.

249. Fire-Proof Building for the National Museum. 12 June.
SR 1539, 50-1, v6, 4p. [2524]
To house Indian artifacts.

250. Methodist College Association of Southwestern Kansas. 12 June.
HR 2583, 50-1, v7, 1p. [2604]
Sale of Osage trust lands.

251. Railroad Land Grants in Kansas. 14 June.
SED 194, 50-1, v11, 177p. [2514]
Osage ceded lands under the treaty of 2 June 1825; location of the New York Indian reservation under the treaty of 15 Jan. 1838.

252. R-C of S. Larimer. 14 June.
SR 1591, 50-1, v6, 4p. [2524] *or*
HR 1131, 50-1, v4, 4p. [2601] *or*
HR 3072, 50-1, v8, 4p. [2605]
Taken captive by Sioux in 1864; Wyoming Territory.

253. R-C of T. Lord. 14 June.
SR 1593, 50-1, v6, 3p. [2524]
On duty at the Yankton Sioux agency, Dakota; 1869-1870.

254. R-P of M. Ord. 14 June.
SR 2596, 50-1, v7, 2p. [2604]
Service in Seminole and Northwest Coast Indian wars.

255. Permanent Exposition of the Three Americas. 16 June.
HR 2601, 50-1, v7, 57p. [2604]
North American Indian exhibits.

256. St. Louis and San Francisco Railroad Co. 16 June.
HR 2606, 50-1, v7, 1p. [2604]
Right of way through Indian Territory.

257. R-P of M. King. 19 June.
SR 1607, 50-1, v6, 1p. [2524]
Service on the Indian frontier.

258. R-P of J. Magher. 19 June.
SR 1621, 50-1, v6, 2p. [2524] *or*
HR 1758, 50-1, v5, 2p. [2602]
Service against Indians in 1856; Spirit Lake, Iowa.

259. R-P of V. Smith. 20 June.
SED 197, 50-1, v11, 2p. [2514]
Pres. vetoes pension; service in Sioux outbreak of 1862 in Minnesota.

260. R-P of J. Turner. 20 June.
SR 1633, 50-1, v7, 2p. [2525] *or*
HR 1756, 50-1, v5, 2p. [2602]
Battle with Indians at Apache Pass, Arizona; 1869.

261. Creek Claims. 21 June.
SED 198, 50-1, v11, 22p. [2514]
Creeks ask reimbursement for the expenses incurred during their removal westwards.

262. R-P of C. Campbell. 21 June.
HR 2705, 50-1, v8, 3p. [2605]
Service in Indian Territory.

263. Claims Allowed by Accounting Officers. 22 June.
HED 377, 50-1, v29, 37p. [2561]
Including those involving Indians.

264. Supplemental Deficiencies. 23 June.
HED 376, 50-1, v19, 33p. [2551]
Appropriations for year ending 30 June 1888; Indian expenses.

265. Resol. of Sen. Jones. 25 June.
SMD 150, 50-1, v2, 1p. [2517]
Pres. asked to return bill granting a right of way through Indian Territory to the Paris, Choctaw, and Little Rock Railway Co.

266. R-P of E. Warren. 25 June.
SR 1649, 50-1, v7, 4p. [2525]
Topographical engineer on the 1855 Sioux expedition.

267. Shoshones, Bannocks, and Sheepeaters. 25 June.
HR 2754, 50-1, v8, 3p. [2605]
Bill to ratify the agreement of 14 May 1880; surrender of the Lemhi reservation in Idaho; removal to the Fort Hall reservation; land cessions and allotments; etc.

268. R-C of the Presbyterian Mission Board. 26 June.
SED 204, 50-1, v11, 5p. [2514]
Ask reimbursement for improvements made on an Indian school in New Mexico.

269. Employees Below the Classified Service. 26 June.
SED 205, 50-1, v11, 29p. [2514]
Including the OIA.

270. R-P of J. Wagoner. 27 June.
SR 1651, 50-1, v7, 1p. [2525] *or*
HR 2049, 50-1, v6, 2p. [2603]
Battle of the Little Big Horn in 1876; Custer's expedition against the Sioux.

271. R-C of J. Campbell. 29 June.
HED 379, 50-1, v29, 3p. [2561]
Assistant to U.S. attorney in Arizona; trial of Apaches.

272. R-C of H. Alexander and L. Chalmers. 29 June.
HED 381, 50-1, v29, 2p. [2561]
Legal services to Apache and Maricopa Indians in Arizona.

273. Receipts and Expenditures. 29 June.
HED 382, 50-1, v27, 468p. [2559]
Year ending 30 June 1886; Indian expenses.

274. Annual Report of the Smithsonian Institution. 1 July.
HMD 142 (pts. 1 and 2), 50-2, v14-15, 1778p. [2668-2669]
Research related to the North American Indian.

275. Settlement of Certain Accounts. 2 July.
SR 1680, 50-1, v7, 3p. [2525]
Between the U.S. and several States; sale of Choctaw, Chickasaw, Creek, Ute, and other Indian reservations.

276. R-P of J. Morton. 5 July.
SED 209, 50-1, v11, 2p. [2514] *or*
SR 403, 50-1, v2, 2p. [2520] *or*
HR 1831, 50-1, v6, 2p. [2603]
Battle at the Little Big Horn; Custer's campaign against the Sioux (executive document is a presidential veto).

277. Wyoming Midland Railway Co. 6 July.
HR 2809, 50-1, v8, 2p. [2605]
Right of way through the Wind River or Shoshone reservation.

278. Mem. of C. Brownell. 9 July.
SMD 153, 50-1, v2, 16p. [2517]
On U.S. Courts in Indian Territory; treaty stipulations violated.

279. R-P of A. Hopper. 10 July.
SR 1744, 50-1, v7, 1p. [2525]
Sioux raid of 1862.

280. R-C of J. Hogan. 10 July.
HR 2811, 50-1, v8, 1p. [2605]
Snake and Shoshone depredations of 1860 in Utah Territory.

281. R-P of F. Plummer. 10 July.
HR 2815, 50-1, v8, 2p. [2605]
Service in Indian Territory (Fort Cobb) during the Civil War.

282. R-C of C. Edson et al. 10 July.
HR 2836, 50-1, v8, 3p. [2605]
Taken captive by Rogue River Indians in 1856; Oregon.

283. R-P of E. Russell. 11 July.
SR 1773, 50-1, v7, 1p. [2525] *or*
HR 2048, 50-1, v6, 1p. [2603]
Service in Seminole war; 1836; Florida.

284. R-P of F. Travis. 11 July.
SR 1777, 50-1, v7, 2p. [2525] *or*
HR 1761, 50-1, v5, 2p. [2502]
Florida Indian war; 1841.

285. Organization of Oklahoma Territory. 11 July.
HR 2857, 50-1, v8, 33p. [2605]
Out of what is now Indian Territory; tribal populations, etc.

286. Mining Lands to the Five Nations. 12 July.
HR 2860, 50-1, v8, 1p. [2605]
Bill authorizing land leases in Indian Territory for mining purposes.

287. Cedar Rapids, Iowa Falls, and Northwestern Railway Co. 12 July.
HR 2862, 50-1, v8, 2p. [2605]
Right of way through the Pipe Stone Indian reservation; Yankton Sioux treaty of 19 Apr. 1858.

288. Rio Grande Pacific Railway Co. 12 July.
HR 2867, 50-1, v8, 2p. [2605]
Right of way through the Uintah and Uncompahgre reservations in Utah.

289. R-C of I. Fieldhouse. 14 July.
HR 2876, 50-1, v8, 2p. [2605]
Sioux, Northern Cheyenne, and Northern Arapaho depredations of 1874 in Wyoming.

290. R-C of M. Desmaris and Co. 14 July.
HR 2877, 50-1, v8, 2p. [2605]
Cheyenne depredations of 1868 in Kansas.

291. R-C of R. Romero. 14 July.
HR 2879, 50-1, v8, 2p. [2605]
Cheyenne and Sioux depredations of 1870 in Colorado.

292. R-C of M. Silva. 14 July.
HR 2880, 50-1, v8, 1p. [2605]
Mescalero Apache depredations of 1869 in New Mexico.

293. R-P of A. Deck. 16 July.
SED 216, 50-1, v11, 2p. [2514] *or*
SR 328, 50-1, v2, 1p. [2520]
Indian camapign of 1864 in Colorado (executive document is a presidential veto).

294. Sundry Civil Appropriations Bill. 17 July.
SR 1814, 50-1, v7, 146p. [2525]
Year ending 30 June 1889; for the Indian school in Albuquerque, New Mexico, etc.

295. R-P of S. Fowler. 17 July.
SR 1821, 50-1, v7, 1p. [2525] *or*
HR 3900, 50-2, v2, 1p. [2674]
Sioux war of 1862 in Minnesota.

296. R-P of F. Field. 17 July.
HR 2918, 50-1, v8, 2p. [2605]
Creek agent during 1869-1870 in Indian Territory.

297. R-C of F. Bulkley. 18 July.
HR 2951, 50-1, v8, 2p. [2605]
Kiowa depredations of 1870.

298. R-C of E. Dobbs et al. 18 July.
HR 2955, 50-1, v8, 1p. [2605]
Chiracahua Apache depredations of 1881 in Arizona.

299. R-C of J. Luff. 18 July.
HR 2956, 50-1, v8, 2p. [2605]
Paiute depredations of 1865 in Nevada.

300. R-P of Muck-a-pec-wak-keu-zah. 19 July.
SR 1859, 50-1, v7, 2p. [2525] *or*
HR 2856, 50-1, v8, 2p. [2605]
Sioux Indian; service in troops against hostile Sioux in Minnesota; 1862-1863.

301. Printing of Matter from the Bureau of Ethnology. 20 July.
SR 1875, 50-1, v8, 1p. [2526]
Related to American Indians.

302. R-P of S. Slayton. 25 July.
HR 3031, 50-1, v8, 2p. [2605]
Service in Florida Indian war; 1837-1838.

303. R-P of M. Boyle. 25 July.
HR 3037, 50-1, v8, 1p. [2605]
Service in Seminole war; 1836.

304. R-P of R. Franklin. 25 July.
HR 3039, 50-1, v8, 1p. [2605]
Service in Black Hawk war; 1832.

305. R-P of E. Horton. 25 July.
HR 3042, 50-1, v8, 1p. [2605]
Indian hostilities of 1867 on the Platte River.

306. R-P of L. Pugh. 25 July.
HR 3044, 50-1, v8, 1p. [2605]
Service in Indian war; 1836.

307. R-P of M. Lemon. 25 July.
HR 3049, 50-1, v8, 1p. [2605]
Northwest Indian war of 1811 in Indiana; battle of Tippecanoe.

308. R-P of E. Rawlings. 25 July.
HR 3051, 50-1, v8, 1p. [2605]
Black Hawk war; 1832.

309. R-P of J. Ward. 25 July.
HR 3053, 50-1, v8, 1p. [2605]
Florida Indian war; 1837-1840.

310. R-P of G. Harlan. 25 July.
HR 3054, 50-1, v8, 2p. [2605]
Creek war of 1836.

311. R-P of N. Murphy. 25 July.
HR 3055, 50-1, v8, 1p. [2605]
Black Hawk war; 1832.

312. R-P of W. Thompson. 25 July.
HR 3056, 50-1, v8, 1p. [2605]
Florida Indian war; 1836.

313. R-P of J. Dill. 25 July.
HR 3057, 50-1, v8, 1p. [2605]
Black Hawk war; 1832.

314. R-P of J. Miner. 25 July.
HR 3058, 50-1, v8, 1p. [2605]
Florida Indian war; 1838-1840.

315. R-P of H. Youngblood. 25 July.
HR 3061, 50-1, v8, 1p. [2605]
Service in Indian wars; 1836.

316. R-P of J. Bush. 25 July.
HR 3063, 50-1, v8, 1p. [2605]
Black Hawk war.

317. Fort Smith, Paris, and Dardanelle Railway Co. 26 July.
SED 225, 50-1, v11, 6p. [2514]
Pres. vetoes bill granting a right of way through Indian Territory; Cherokee treaty of 1866.

318. R-P of W. Ryan. 30 July.
HR 3122, 50-1, v8, 1p. [2605]
Service in Indian wars.

319. Statue of Z. Taylor. 31 July.
HR 3135, 50-1, v8, 1p. [2605]
Service in Indian wars.

320. R-P of E. Custer. 1 Aug.
SR 1956, 50-1, v8, 1p. [2526] *or*
HR 2004, 50-1, v6, 1p. [2603]
Battle with Sioux at the Little Big Horn; 1876.

321. R-C of C. Denton. 1 Aug.
SR 1963, 50-1, v8, 3p. [2526]
Indian depredations in Oregon.

322. Lands for Cemetery Purposes. 2 Aug.
HR 3143, 50-1, v8, 1p. [2605]
Indian hostilities near Moscow, Idaho.

323. R-P of M. Lee. 8 Aug.
SR 2000, 50-1, v8, 1p. [2526] *or*
HR 3062, 50-1, v8, 1p. [2605]
Cherokee removal from Georgia in 1838.

324. Pottawatomie Indians. 8 Aug.
HR 3210, 50-1, v10, 34p. [2607]
Claims against the U.S. under various treaty stipulations.

325. Pipestone Reservation. 8 Aug.
HR 3228, 50-1, v10, 3p. [2607]
Sale of Yankton Sioux lands in Minnesota; treaty of 1858.

326. R-C of California, Oregon, and Nevada. 10 Aug.
SR 2014, 50-1, v8, 2p. [2526] *or*
HR 3396, 50-1, v10, 2p. [2607]
Suppression of Indian hostilities during the Civil War; transportation routes.

327. Right of Way Through Indian Reservations. 15 Aug.
SED 237, 50-1, v11, 91p. [2514]
List of rights of way granted to railroads, and similar bills pending; etc.

328. Resol. of Sen. Mitchell. 15 Aug.
SMD 177, 50-1, v2, 1p. [2517]
Asks information on allotments of land in severalty to the Puyallup Indians in Washington Territory.

329. R-P of D. Myers. 15 Aug.
SR 2037, 50-1, v8, 2p. [2526]
Seminole wars; 1836; Florida.

330. Fort Smith and Choctaw Bridge Co. 15 Aug.
HR 3266, 50-1, v10, 1p. [2607]
Construction of a bridge in Choctaw country; jurisdiction over disputes arising.

331. R-P of G. Quick. 15 Aug.
HR 3268, 50-1, v10, 1p. [2607]
Black Hawk war; 1832.

332. R-P of J. Copes. 17 Aug.
SR 2059, 50-1, v8, 1p. [2526] *or*
HR 2874, 50-1, v8, 1p. [2605]
Service in the Black Hawk war.

333. R-P of J. Garrett. 17 Aug.
SR 2064, 50-1, v8, 1p. [2526] *or*
HR 3124, 50-1, v8, 1p. [2605]
Service in the Black Hawk war.

334. R-P of M. Hargain. 17 Aug.
SR 2065, 50-1, v8, 1p. [2526] *or*
HR 3052, 50-1, v8, 1p. [2605]
Florida Indian war; 1840-41.

335. R-P of J. Chase. 17 Aug.
HR 3277, 50-1, v10, 1p. [2607]
Licensed Indian trader in New Mexico; 1876-1877.

336. Sundry Civil Appropriation Bill. 27 Aug.
SMD 189, 50-1, v2, 7p. [2517]
Year ending 30 June 1889; payments for the Peoria, Piankeshaw, Wea, and Kaskaskia Indians.

337. R-C of S. Marshall. 27 Aug.
SR 2102, 50-1, v8, 4p. [2526] *or*
HR 921, 50-1, v3, 3p. [2600]
Supplies to California Indians in 1850.

338. Sundry Civil Appropriation Bill. 27 Aug.
HR 3354, 50-1, v10, 14p. [2607]
Year ending 30 June 1889; amendments concerning Indian expenses.

339. Claims Allowed by Accounting Officers. 4 Sept.
SED 255, 50-1, v11, 42p. [2514]
Includes claims involving Indians.

340. R-P of M. Vanbuskirk. 4 Sept.
SR 2153, 50-1, v8, 1p. [2526] *or*
HR 3134, 50-1, v8, 1p. [2605]
Service in Florida Indian war; 1836-1839.

341. Mineral Resources of the U.S. 10 Sept.
HMD 4, 50-2, v2, 832p. [2655]
Coal, coke, and minerals in Indian Territory.

342. Unpaid Accounts of U.S. Attorneys. 13 Sept.
SED 266, 50-1, v11, 20p. [2514]
Case involving land title within the Papago reservation, Arizona.

343. R-P of C. Junot. 13 Sept.
SR 2217, 50-1, v8, 1p. [2526] *or*
HR 2976, 50-1, v8, 1p. [2605]
Service in Florida Indian war; 1840.

344. R-P of Lieut. Powell. 13 Sept.
SR 2231, 50-1, v8, 1p. [2526] *or*
HR 3223, 50-1, v10, 1p. [2607]
Black Hawk war; 1832.

345. R-C of H. Elliff. 13 Sept.
HR 3450, 50-1, v10, 1p. [2607]
Rogue River and Cow Creek Indian depredations of 1855 in Oregon.

346. R-C of P. Davis. 14 Sept.
HR 3451, 50-1, v10, 1p. [2607]
Paiute and Bannock depredations of 1878 in Oregon.

347. R-C of I. Nichols. 14 Sept.
HR 3452, 50-1, v10, 1p. [2607]
Rogue River Indian depredations of 1855-1856.

348. R-C of G. Comstock. 14 Sept.
HR 3452, 50-1, v10, 2p. [2607]
Cheyenne and Sioux depredations of 1864.

349. R-C of J. Bainter. 14 Sept.
HR 3454, 50-1, v10, 2p. [2607]
Cheyenne and Sioux depredations of 1864 in Nebraska.

350. R-C of G. Engle. 14 Sept.
HR 3455, 50-1, v10, 1p. [2607]
Bannock and Paiute depredations of 1878 in Oregon.

351. R-C of J. Miller. 14 Sept.
HR 3456, 50-1, v10, 1p. [2607]
Rogue River Indian depredations of 1855 in Oregon.

352. R-C of M. Riley. 14 Sept.
HR 3457, 50-1, v10, 1p. [2607]
Rogue River Indian depredations of 1856 in Oregon.

353. R-C of the Heirs of G. Harris. 14 Sept.
HR 3458, 50-1, v10, 1p. [2607]
Rogue River Indian depredations of 1855 in Oregon.

354. R-C of J. Walker. 14 Sept.
HR 3459, 50-1, v10, 1p. [2607]
Rogue River war; 1855-1856; Oregon.

355. R-C of V. Schutz. 14 Sept.
HR 3460, 50-1, v10, 1p. [2607]
Rogue River war; 1855-1856; Oregon.

356. R-C of B. Bishop. 14 Sept.
HR 3461, 50-1, v10, 1p. [2607]
Indian war; 1855-1856; Oregon and Washington.

357. R-C of W. McKay. 14 Sept.
HR 3462, 50-1, v10, 1p. [2607]
Umatilla, Walla Walla, and Cayuse hostilities of 1855.

358. R-C of B. Dowell. 14 Sept.
HR 3463, 50-1, v10, 1p. [2607]
Rogue River war; 1855; Oregon.

359. R-C of I. Bailey. 14 Sept.
HR 3464, 50-1, v10, 1p. [2607]
Pitt River, Modoc, Hot Creek, and Paiute hostilities of 1862 in California.

360. R-C of K. Hatton. 14 Sept.
HR 3465, 50-1, v10, 1p. [2607]
Modoc depredations of 1872 in Oregon.

361. R-C of A. Morrison. 14 Sept.
HR 3466, 50-1, v10, 1p. [2607]
Puyallup depredations of 1855 in Washington.

362. R-C of E. Northcutt and Brothers. 14 Sept.
HR 3467, 50-1, v10, 1p. [2607]
Rogue River Indian depredations of 1855 in Oregon.

363. R-C of J. Russell. 14 Sept.
HR 3468, 50-1, v10, 1p. [2607]
Cow Creek and Umpqua Indian hostilities of 1855-1856 in Oregon.

364. R-C of G. Arnold. 14 Sept.
HR 3469, 50-1, v10, 1p. [2607]
Indian hostilities of 1855-1856 in Oregon and Washington.

365. R-C of California. 17 Sept.
SR 2246, 50-1, v8, 2p. [2526]
Suppression of Indian hostilities.

366. Resol. of Rep. Morrill. 17 Sept.
HMD 576, 50-1, v6, 3p. [2570]
Asks investigation of charges that the Sioux Commission used undue influence to secure Indian signatures to a recent agreement made.

367. General Deficiency Appropriations. 18 Sept.
SR 2257, 50-1, v8, 25p. [2526]
Year ending 30 June 1888; Indian expenses.

368. Stockbridges and Munsees in Wisconsin. 20 Sept.
SR 2261, 50-1, v8, 1p. [2526] *or*
SR 2262, 50-1, v8, 2p. [2526] *or*
HR 1339, 50-1, v4, 2p. [2601]

Dispute over enrollment in the tribe, and allotments of land.

369. Black Bob Lands in Kansas. 20 Sept.
SR 2265, 50-1, v8, 5p. [2526] *or*
HR 181, 50-1, v1, 4p. [2598]
Sale of these lands which have been allotted and patented to Black Bob Shawnees; treaty of 10 May 1854.

370. Persons Reimbursed for Moneys Expended. 21 Sept.
HR 3491, 50-1, v10, 12p. [2607]
As a result of Indian hostilities.

371. R-P of Capt. Duley. 25 Sept.
SR 2282, 50-1, v8, 2p. [2526] *or*
HR 3118, 50-1, v8, 3p. [2605]
Service in Sioux outbreak of 1862 in Minnesota.

372. Claims Allowed by Accounting Officers. 28 Sept.
HED 455, 50-1, v29, 12p. [2561]
Including those involving Indians.

373. R-C of D. Boutwell. 28 Sept.
HR 3520, 50-1, v10, 1p. [2607]
Second Indian Home Guards; Civil War.

374. R-P of J. Ellis. 1 Oct.
SR 2308, 50-1, v8, 1p. [2526] *or*
HR 3317, 50-1, v10, 1p. [2607]
Service against the Navajoes and Apaches in New Mexico.

375. Puyallup Indian Lands. 2 Oct.
SED 274, 50-1, v11, 15p. [2514]
Allotments made on their reservation in Washington Territory.

376. R-P of L. Wallen. 2 Oct.
SR 2319, 50-1, v8, 1p. [2526] *or*
HR 1228, 50-1, v4, 1p. [2601]
Dealt with Navajoes and Apaches in New Mexico.

377. Issue of Military Stores. 3 Oct.
SR 2333, 50-1, v8, 3p. [2526]
To Montana; suppression of Indian hostilities.

378. R-P of J. Rosier. 4 Oct.
SR 2356, 50-1, v8, 1p. [2526]
Service in Seminole war; 1836; Florida.

379. Absentee Shawnee Lands in Kansas. 4 Oct.
SR 2357, 50-1, v8, 4p. [2526] *or*
HR 4160, 50-2, v3, 4p. [2675]
Sale of these lands; treaty of 2 Nov. 1854.

380. R-C of A. McCreary. 8 Oct.
SR 2367, 50-1, v8, 23p. [2526]
Licensed traders to Osages; 1873; Indian Territory.

381. R-P of M. Myers. 9 Oct.
HR 3527, 50-1, v10, 1p. [2607]
Seminole war; 1836; Florida.

382. Resol. of Sen. Teller. 18 Oct.
SMD 210, 50-1, v2, 1p. [2517]
Purchase of wagons for the Indian service; prison labor used.

383. Statement of Appropriations. 20 Oct.
SMD 212, 50-1, v3, 486p. [2518]
During the 1st session, 50th Congress; Indian expenses.

384. Annual Report of the Bureau of Ethnology. (no date)
HMD 571, 50-1, v14, 733p. [2578]
Research related to the American Indian.

385. Cruise of the Revenue Steamer *Corwin*. (no date)
HMD 602, 50-1, v19, 128p. [2583]
In the Arctic Ocean; contacts with the Indians of Alaska.

386. Disbursements of the Indian Dept. 3 Nov.
HED 8, 50-2, v19, 23p. [2645]
Year ending 30 June 1888.

387. Annual Message to Congress with Documents; Pres. Cleveland. 3 Dec.
HED 1, 50-2, v1-16, 14426p. [2626-2633]
Indian management; railroads through reservations; Apaches held as prisoners; allotments of land in severalty; education; reduction of the Sioux reservation; annual report of the Sec. of War (Serials 2628-2633); annual report of the Sec. of Interior (Serials 2636-2641); annual report of the Gen. Land Office (Serial 2636); annual report of the CIA (Serial 2637); etc.

388. Annual Report of the Sec. of the Treasury. 3 Dec.
HED 2, 50-2, v17, 1003p. [2643]
Year ending 30 June 1888; Indian expenses.

389. Estimates of Appropriations. 3 Dec.
HED 5, 50-2, v20, 359p. [2646]
Year ending 30 June 1890; Indian expenses.

390. Mem. of W. Bryant. 6 Dec.
SMD 11, 50-2, v1, 3p. [2614]
On the case of L. Riel, a Canadian half-breed; question arises as to the legal definition of an Indian, i.e., how much Indian blood makes one an Indian.

391. Congressional Directory. 7 Dec.
SMD (pts. 1 and 2), 50-2, v1, 506p. [2614]
Lists duties of the CIA.

392. Outrages in Alaska. 10 Dec.
SED 13, 50-2, v1, 2p. [2610]
Dept. of Interior has no information concerning alleged outrages committed upon Indian females.

393. Indian Trust Bonds. 11 Dec.
HED 13, 50-2, v19, 10p. [2645]
Overpayment of interest on Louisiana bonds held as Indian trust funds.

394. Account of W. Pinney. 11 Dec.
HED 16, 50-2, v19, 2p. [2645]
Court stenographer in case involving Apaches; 1888; Arizona.

395. On the Case of J. Shirley. 11 Dec.
HMD 31, 50-2, v1, 5p. [2654]
Claim involving lands encorporated into the Fort Hall Indian reservation; Idaho.

396. Bridge Across the Poteau River. 12 Dec.
HR 3560, 50-2, v1, 1p. [2673]
In the Choctaw Nation, Indian Territory.

397. Survey of Historic Grounds. 13 Dec.
HED 28, 50-2, v19, 6p. [2645]
In the Maumee Valley in Ohio; battle of Fallen Timbers in 1794, when Gen. Wayne defeats allied Indian tribes under Turkey Foot.

398. Legislative, Executive, and Judicial Appropriation Bill. 14 Dec.
HR 3608, 50-2, v1, 14p. [2673]
Salaries in the OIA.

399. Sioux Reservation. 17 Dec.
SED 17, 50-2, v1, 293p. [2610]
Council proceedings of the Sioux Commission's negotiations regarding an opening of part of the Sioux reservation in Dakota; sent to obtain the consent of the Indians.

400. Settlements on Account of Modoc Hostilities. 17 Dec.
SED 18, 50-2, v1, 6p. [2610]
Reimbursement of Oregon for expenses of suppressing Modoc hostilities in 1872-1873.

401. Arms for the Oregon Militia. 17 Dec.
SR 2408; 50-2, v1, 1p. [2618] *or*
HR 1193, 50-2, v4, 1p. [2601]
For home defense because of five Indian reservations located within the State.

402. Indian School in Lawrence, Kansas. 18 Dec.
HED 32, 50-2, v25, 3p. [2651]
Appropriation for the construction of a chapel and gymnasium.

403. Indian School in Albuquerque, New Mexico. 18 Dec.
HED 33, 50-2, v25, 4p. [2651]
Appropriation to pay the Presbyterian Board of Home Missions for improvements made at said school.

404. Eastern Band of Cherokees. 18 Dec.
HED 36, 50-2, v25, 3p. [2651]
Appropriation for legal proceedings in behalf of said Indians; North Carolina; concerns land matters.

405. Allotment of Lands in Severalty. 18 Dec.
HR 3615, 50-2, v1, 1p. [2673]
To United Peoria and Miami Indians; Indian Territory.

406. Expenditures for North American Ethnology. 19 Dec.
HMD 55, 50-2, v1, 19p. [2654]
Funding for research related to the American Indian.

407. Indians in Alaska. 21 Dec.
SED 30, 50-2, v1, 6p. [2610]
Condition of Indian population; information on the treatment of Indian women by whites is requested, but not furnished.

408. Leases of Land in Indian Territory. 27 Dec.
SED 22, 50-2, v1, 7p. [2610]
Schedules of contracts for mining coal, and for grazing purposes.

409. Bulletins of the U.S. Geological Survey, Volume 7. (no date)
HMD 137, 50-2, v11 (pt. 1), 617p. [2664]
Bulletin No. 45 deals with the geology of Texas; information on explorations into Indian Territory.

1889

1. Polvareda Land Grant No. 131. 4 Jan.
SED 49, 50-2, v1, 9p. [2610]
Land title issues involving Indians in New Mexico; Navajo depredations.

2. Sioux Reservation in Dakota. 5 Jan.
HR 3645, 50-2, v1, 5p. [2673]
Bill to reduce said reservation, and open the remaining lands to settlement.

3. Claims Allowed by Accounting Officers. 8 Jan.
HED 59, 50-2, v25, 68p. [2651]
Includes claims involving Indians.

4. Support of Sioux Indians. 8 Jan.
HED 61, 50-2, v25 , 5p. [2651]
Appropriation to support the Medawakanton band in Minnesota.

5. Sundry Civil Appropriations Bill. 8 Jan.
HR 3646, 50-2, v1, 78p. [2673]
Payments to Western Miamies; claims of Indian soldiers; etc.

6. Stallions for Northern Cheyennes. 9 Jan.
HED 62, 50-2, v25, 3p. [2651]
Appropriation to purchase horses for Cheyennes at the Tongue River agency in Montana.

7. Seed for Turtle Mountain Chippewas. 9 Jan.
HED 63, 50-2, v25, 5p. [2651]
Appropriation for purchase of seed; Dakota.

8. Indian School in Genoa, Nebraska. 9 Jan.
HED 65, 50-2, v25, 4p. [2651]
Appropriation needed in order to expand the school.

9. Estimates of Deficiencies. 12 Jan.
HED 71, 50-2, v20, 40p. [2646]
Appropriations for the year ending 30 June 1889; Indian expenses.

10. R-C of D. Mitchell. 12 Jan.
HR 3685, 50-2, v1, 86p. [2673]
Supplies to troops engaged in Indian campaigns; Kansas.

11. Ute Indian Commission. 14 Jan.
SED 67, 50-2, v2, 84p. [2611]
Council proceedings of the Commission's negotiations regarding land cessions in Colorado, and removal of Utes to Utah; agreement of 13 Nov. 1888.

12. R-P of D. Alvord. 15 Jan.
HR 3737, 50-2, v1, 1p. [2673]
Indian war of 1836 in Georgia.

13. R-P of W. Wilson. 15 Jan.
HR 3744, 50-2, v1, 1p. [2673]
Black Hawk war; 1832; Illinois.

14. Ordnance Issued to Washington Territory. 15 Jan.
HR 3750, 50-2, v1, 2p. [2673]
Borrowed during the Nez Percé war; 1877-1878.

15 . Refuge Stations in Alaska. 15 Jan.
HR 3751, 50-2, v1, 4p. [2673]
Near Points Barrow and Hope; civilization of the Eskimos.

16. R-C of J. Dorsey. 15 Jan.
HR 3757, 50-2, v1, 2p. [2673]
Paiute, Shoshone, and Bannock depredations of 1864-1865 in Nevada.

17. Volunteer Troops Guarding Mail Routes. 16 Jan.
SED 70, 50-2, v2, 366p. [2611]
Overland routes to the Pacific during 1861-1866; Indian hostilities in California, Oregon, Washington, Nevada, Arizona, New Mexico, Utah, Wyoming, and Idaho.

18. R-P of M. Personeus. 18 Jan.
HR 3774, 50-2, v1, 1p. [2673]
Battle against Sioux at the Little Big Horn River; 1876; Custer's massacre.

19. Alaska Seal and Fur Co. 19 Jan.
SED 74, 50-2, v2, 13p. [2611]
Report of the governor of Alaska; condition and treatment of the Indians.

20. Volunteers in the Nez Percé War. 22 Jan.
SED 82, 50-2, v3, 27p. [2612]
Records on file in the War Dept. regarding volunteers from Washington and Idaho who participated in the 1877 war.

21. R-P of J. Boyd. 22 Jan.
SR 2451, 50-2, v1, 1p. [2618] *or*
HR 3965, 50-2, v2, 1p. [2674]
Service against Indians in Minnesota; 1861-1863.

22. Cherokee Freedmen. 23 Jan.
SED 83, 50-2, v3, 6p. [2612]
On an appropriation for their benefit.

23. Big Horn Southern Railroad Co. 23 Jan.
HR 3825, 50-2, v1, 1p. [2673]
Right of way through the Crow reservation in Montana.

24. Ordnance for Washington Territory. 23 Jan.
HR 3827, 50-2, v1, 2p. [2673]
For the Nez Percé war; 1877-78.

25. Volunteers in the Nez Percé War. 25 Jan.
SED 85, 50-2, v3, 1p. [2612]
No records on file in the Interior Dept.

26. R-C of J. Bridger. 25 Jan.
SED 86, 50-2, v3, 23p. [2612]

For improvements made at Fort Bridger, Utah; formerly an Indian trading post.

27. R-C of Florida. 25 Jan.
SR 2482, 50-2, v1, 11p. [2618]
Expenses of the Seminole war; 1856-1857.

28. Indian Depredation Claims. 25 Jan.
HED 103, 50-2, v25, 23p. [2651]
Claims presented during 1888; lists tribe involved, date, etc.

29. Fort Smith, Paris, and Dardanelle Railway Co. 25 Jan.
HR 3848, 50-2, v1, 2p. [2673]
Right of way through Indian Territory.

30. Seal Fisheries of Alaska. 28 Jan.
SED 90, 50-2, v3, 5p. [2612]
Condition of the natives.

31. R-P of N. Smith. 29 Jan.
SR 2493, 50-2, v1, 1p. [2618]
Service against Indians in 1812; battles of the Thames and Tippecanoe.

32. Cherokee Central Railway Co. 29 Jan.
HR 3877, 50-2, v2, 1p. [2674]
Right of way through Indian Territory.

33. Fur-Seal Fisheries in Alaska. 29 Jan.
HR 3883, 50-2, v2, 465p. [2674]
Natives employed in the industry; Aleuts.

34. R-P of E. Paschal. 31 Jan.
SR 2501, 50-2, v1, 1p. [2618] *or*
HR 3531, 50-1, v10, 1p. [2607]
Service in Florida Indian war; 1836.

35. R-P of J. Brown. 31 Jan.
SR 2503, 50-2, v1, 1p. [2618] *or*
HR 3740, 50-2, v1, 1p. [2673]
Service in Black Hawk war; Illinois.

36. R-P of M. Allen. 31 Jan.
SR 2520, 50-2, v1, 1p. [2618]
Service against Indians in Washington Territory; 1858.

37. Oregon Volunteers. 4 Feb.
SED 96, 50-2, v3, 3p. [2612]
Capt. Hall's co. which served in the Cayuse war of 1848.

38. Mem. of O. Ames et al. 4 Feb.
SMD 60, 50-2, v2, 1p. [2615]
Protection of the ancient ruins of Casa Grande in Arizona; of the greatest ethnological interest.

39. Observance of Treaty Stipulations. 4 Feb.
SMD 61, 50-2, v2, 12p. [2615]
Regarding the "net proceeds claim" of the Choctaw Nation.

40. Forest City and Watertown Railroad Co. 4 Feb.
HR 3923, 50-2, v2, 1p. [2674]
Right of way through the great Sioux reservation in Dakota.

41. Yankton and Missouri Valley Railway Co. 4 Feb.
HR 3924, 50-2, v2, 1p. [2674]
Right of way through the Yankton Sioux reservation; Dakota.

42. Denison and Washita Valley Railway Co. 5 Feb.
HR 3940, 50-2, v2, 1p. [2674]
Right of way through Indian Territory.

43. St. Paul, Minneapolis, and Manitoba Railway Co. 5 Feb.
HR 3941, 50-2, v2, 1p. [2674]
Right of way through the White Earth Chippewa reservation; Minnesota.

44. Suits Against the U.S. 5 Feb.
HR 3945, 50-2, v2, 3p. [2674]
Chickasaw, Creek, and Choctaw treaties; land cessions in Alabama and Mississippi.

45. Shoshones, Bannocks, and Sheepeaters. 5 Feb.
HR 3956, 50-2, v2, 1p. [2674]
Bill to ratify the agreement of 14 May 1880; Fort Hall and Lemhi reservations in Idaho.

46. Agreement with the Creeks. 6 Feb.
SED 98, 50-2, v3, 8p. [2612]
Dated 19 Jan. 1889; cession of land in Indian Territory to the U.S.; paves the way for settlement of unassigned Indian lands.

47. R-P of I. Howze. 6 Feb.
SR 2536, 50-2, v1, 1p. [2618] *or*
HR 3529, 50-1, v10, 1p. [2607]
Florida Indian war; 1836.

48. Mem. of the Nevada Legis. 7 Feb.
SMD 67, 50-2, v2, 1p. [2615]
Final settlement of all Indian depredation claims.

49. R-P of R. Andrews. 7 Feb.
HR 3972, 50-2, v2, 1p. [2674]
Florida Indian war; 1836.

50. R-P of B. Cooper. 7 Feb.
HR 3973, 50-2, v2, 1p. [2674]
Florida Indian war; 1836.

51. R-P of J. Mann. 7 Feb.
HR 3975, 50-2, v2, 1p. [2674]

Stationed at Fort Snelling, Indian Territory; 1841-1846.

52. Mem. of the Dakota Legis. 8 Feb.
SMD 69, 50-2, v2, 1p. [2615]
Urge passage of the pending bill for the opening to settlement of a portion of the Sioux reservation.

53. R-P of J. Starr. 8 Feb.
SR 2557, 50-2, v1, 1p. [2618] *or*
HR 3743, 50-2, v1, 1p. [2673]
Service in Black Hawk war; 1832.

54. R-P of M. Stacey. 8 Feb.
SR 2560, 50-2, v1, 2p. [2618] *or*
HR 3822, 50-2, v1, 2p. [2673]
Service against Apaches in 1881.

55. Seal Fisheries in the Bering Sea. 12 Feb.
SED 106, 50-2, v3, 281p. [2612]
Seizure of British ships; regulations concerning native Alaskans are printed.

56. Settlement of Debt Due U.S. by Arkansas. 12 Feb.
HR 3998 (pts. 1 and 2), 50-2, v2, 46p. [2674]
Involves Indian trust funds.

57. R-P of A. Boatright. 13 Feb.
SR 2584, 50-2, v1, 1p. [2618] *or*
HR 3974, 50-2, v2, 1p. [2674]
Black Hawk war; 1832; Illinois.

58. Indian Appropriation Bill. 13 Feb.
HR 4028, 50-2, v2, 2p. [2674]
Year ending 30 June 1890.

59. R-P of M. Hanie. 13 Feb.
HR 4041, 50-2, v2, 1p. [2674]
Service in Creek war of 1837-1838.

60. R-P of J. Hayes. 13 Feb.
HR 4043, 50-2, v2, 1p. [2674]
Black Hawk war; 1832; Illinois.

61. R-P of S. McClenachan. 13 Feb.
HR 4046, 50-2, v2, 1p. [2674]
Florida Indian war; 1837-1839.

62. R-P of W. Schaffer. 13 Feb.
HR 4048, 50-2, v2, 2p. [2674]
Service against Indians at Fort McPherson, Nebraska; 1872.

63. R-P of Powell's Battalion of Missouri Volunteers. 13 Feb.
HR 4049, 50-2, v2, 3p. [2674]
Service against Pawnees, Sioux, Arapahoes, and Cheyennes in Indian Territory during the Mexican war; protection of supply routes.

64. R-P of J. Hollen et al. 13 Feb.
HR 4050, 50-2, v2, 3p. [2674]
Employees at the Sac and Fox agency in Iowa; 1886-87.

65. Admission of Arizona, Idaho, and Wyoming. 13 Feb.
HR 4053, 50-2, v2, 57p. [2674]
Indian reservations in those Territories.

66. R-P of G. Hunter. 15 Feb.
SR 2603, 50-2, v1, 1p. [2618] *or*
SR 2631, 50-2, v2, 1p. [2619] *or*
HR 4044, 50-2, v2, 1p. [2674]
Service in the Nez Percé war of 1877; Washington Territory volunteers.

67. Admission of New Mexico. 16 Feb.
HR 4090, 50-2, v3, 29p. [2675]
Land title issues involving Indians; Indian reservations occupied by Mescalero Apaches, Navajoes, Zunis, and Pueblos.

68. Seminole Lands in Indian Territory. 19 Feb.
SED 122, 50-2, v3, 5p. [2612]
Proposition made by the Seminole delegation entrusted with the task of relinquishing certain lands to the U.S.

69. Hearings Before the Com. of Territories. 19 Feb.
SMD 80, 50-2, v2, 56p. [2615]
On the organization of Oklahoma Territory; Indian objections based on various treaties.

70. R-P of M. Barnes. 19 Feb.
SR 2616, 50-2, v2, 2p. [2619]
Service in the Seminole war; Florida.

71. R-P of A. Barker. 19 Feb.
HR 4105, 50-2, v3, 1p. [2675]
Florida Indian war; 1832-1839.

72. R-C of J. Devine. 20 Feb.
SR 2636, 50-2, v2, 2p. [2619] *or*
HR 975, 50-1, v4, 2p. [2601]
Sioux outbreak of 1862 in Minnesota; depredations of troops.

73. R-P of C. Zentmeyer. 21 Feb.
HR 4118, 50-2, v3, 1p. [2675]
Sioux hostilities of 1862 at the Lower Sioux agency in Minnesota.

74. Private Land Claim No. 158. 22 Feb.
SED 125, 50-2, v3, 24p. [2612]
Land title issues involving Indians in New Mexico.

75. Private Land Claim No. 159. 22 Feb.
SED 126, 50-2, v3, 13p. [2612]
Land title issues involving Indians in New Mexico.

76. Timber-Cutting on the Chippewa Reservation. 23 Feb.

SED 128, 50-2, v3, 20p. [2612]
La Pointe agency in Wisconsin; correspondence on allotment and timber contracts.

77. St. Louis and San Francisco Railway Co. 23 Feb.
HR 4127, 50-2, v3, 1p. [2675]
Right of way through Indian Territory.

78. Mem. of the National Council of Congregational Churches. 26 Feb.
SMD 88, 50-2, v2, 3p. [2615]
On the suppression of the traffic of liquors on Indian reservations.

79. R-P of W. Hawkins. 26 Feb.
SR 2662, 50-2, v2, 1p. [2619] *or*
HR 3899, 50-2, v2, 1p. [2674]
Service in Black Hawk war; 1832; Illinois.

80. R-P of Lucy. 26 Feb.
SR 2663, 50-2, v2, 2p. [2619] *or*
HR 3976, 50-2, v2, 2p. [2674]
Sioux Indian serves with U.S. during the Sioux outbreak; 1862; Minnesota.

81. R-P of W. Martin. 26 Feb.
SR 2668, 50-2, v2, 1p. [2619] *or*
HR 4114, 50-2, v3, 1p. [2675]
Florida, Oregon, and Washington Indian wars; 1837-56.

82. R-P of L. Baker. 26 Feb.
SR 2670, 50-2, v2, 1p. [2619] *or*
HR 4113, 50-2, v3, 1p. [2675]
Service in Florida Indian war; 1836.

83. R-P of I. Wells. 26 Feb.
SR 2678, 50-2, v2, 1p. [2619] *or*
HR 4116, 50-2, v3, 1p. [2675]
Service in Black Hawk war; 1832; Illinois.

84. Claims Allowed by Accounting Officers. 27 Feb.
SED 132, 50-2, v4, 52p. [2613]
Including claims involving Indians.

85. Supplemental Estimate of Deficiencies. 27 Feb.
SED 134, 50-2, v4, 9p. [2613]
In connection with U.S. courts; case of the Northern Pacific Express Co. involves a piece of the Sioux half-breed scrip.

86. Alleged Bribery of the Cherokee Council. 27 Feb.
SED 136, 50-2, v4, 6p. [2613]
By cattlemen, for the purpose of obtaining leases of land for grazing purposes in Indian Territory.

87. R-P of M. Hunt. 27 Feb.
SR 2688, 50-2, v2, 2p. [2619]
Service on Indian frontier; 1848-1856.

88. R-C of J. Whitfield. 28 Feb.
SR 2694, 50-2, v2, 2p. [2619]
Surety on the bond of an Indian agent in Nebraska Territory.

89. On the Case of J. Hassler. 28 Feb.
HR 4154, 50-2, v3, 4p. [2675]
Chippewa agent in Minnesota during 1869-1870; service against the Sioux in Dakota during 1867-69.

90. Klamath Reservation. 1 Mar.
SED 140, 50-2, v4, 23p. [2613]
Report on the survey of said reservation in California; question arises as to whether or not the reservation is to be sold.

91. Alleged Outrages in Alaska. 1 Mar.
SED 141, 50-2, v4, 24p. [2613]
Report of governor of Alaska concerning alleged outrages committed upon Indian females and other persons.

92. R-C of the Heirs of P. Beck, Jr. 1 Mar.
SR 2702, 50-2, v2, 4p. [2619]
Navajo depredations of 1849 in New Mexico.

93. Boundary Between Alaska and British Columbia. 2 Mar.
SED 146, 50-2, v4, 40p. [2613]
U.S.-Russian treaty of 30 Mar. 1867 on the uncivilized tribes of Alaska.

94. Statements of Appropriations. 2 Mar.
SMD 94, 50-2, v4, 364p. [2617]
During the 2d session, 50th Congress; Indian expenses.

95. Report on Indian Traders. 2 Mar.
SR 2707, 50-2, v5, 635p. [2623]
Investigation of the issuance of trading licenses by the CIA.

96. Chippewa Allotments and Timber Contracts. 2 Mar.
SR 2710, 50-2, v6, 1392p. [2624]
Investigation of misconduct regarding administration of Indian affairs in Wisconsin and Minnesota.

97. Proceedings Upon the Acceptance of the Statue of L. Cass. 2 Mar.
HMD 145, 50-2, v16, 106p. [2670]
Intimately involved with Indian policy as a soldier, territorial governor, Sec. of War, and U.S. Senator.

98. On the Case of L. Riel. 19 Mar.
SED 1, 51-sp, v4, 12p. [2613]
Participation of American Indian in the insurrection of 1885 in Canada.

99. Printing of Certain Acts. 20 Mar.
SR 1, 51-sp, v2, 2p. [2619]
Act No. 155 concerning Indian appropriations.

100. Methods of Business in Executive Depts. 28 Mar.
SR 3, 51-sp, v2, 220p. [2619]
Indian claims in the Treasury Dept.; Indian accounts with the Office of the Second Comptroller.

101. Resol. of Sen. Dawes. 29 Mar.
SMD 12, 51-sp, v2, 1p. [2615]
On the "Langford claim"; land title within the Lapwai Indian reservation in Idaho.

102. Official Register. 1 July.
HMD 41 (pts. 1 and 2), 51-1, v5-6, 2292p. [2764-2765]
List of agents and employees of the U.S. government.

103. Annual Report of the Smithsonian Institution. 1 July.
HMD 224 (pts. 1 and 2), 51-1, v20-21, 1811p. [2779-2780]
Research related to the American Indian.

104. Disbursements of the Interior Dept. 22 Nov.
HED 8, 51-1, v24, 25p. [2739]
Year ending 30 June 1889.

105. Annual Report of the Sec. of the Treasury. 2 Dec.
HED 2, 51-1, v19, 1125p. [2734]
Year ending 30 June 1889; Indian expenses.

106. Estimates of Appropriations. 2 Dec.
HED 5, 51-1, v21, 368p. [2736]
Year ending 30 June 1891; Indian expenses.

107. List of Reports to be Made to Congress. 2 Dec.
HMD 115, 51-1, v9, 23p. [2768]
By the Sec. of Interior and the CIA on Indian affairs.

108. Annual Message to Congress with Documents; Pres. Harrison. 3 Dec.
HED 1, 51-1, v1-18, 15546p. [2714-2733]
Division and reduction of the Sioux reservation in Dakota; the opening of portions of Indian Territory for settlement; no policy for the establishment of Indian reservations in Alaska; annual report of the Sec. of War (Serials 2715-2720); annual report of the Sec. of Interior (Serials 2724-2730); annual report of the Gen. Land Office (Serial 2724); annual report of the CIA (Serial 2725); etc.

109. Private Land Claim No. 160. 4 Dec.
SED 2, 51-1, v1, 49p. [2678]
Land title issues in New Mexico involving the Navajo Apaches.

110. Congressional Directory. 5 Dec.
SMD 13 (pts. 1-3), 51-1, v1, 765p. [2697]
Duties of the CIA listed.

111. Resol. of Sen. Stanford. 5 Dec.
SMD 16, 51-1, v2, 1p. [2698]
On the Indian war claims of California.

112. Capt. Hall's Co. of Volunteers. 9 Dec.
SED 6, 51-1, v1, 20p. [2678]
Service in the Cayuse war; 1848; Oregon.

113. Treaties with the Kickapoos. 9 Dec.
HED 15, 51-1, v24, 2p. [2739]
Appropriation for fulfilling the treaties of 28 June 1862, and 18 May 1854.

114. Exigency Purchases of Indian Goods. 9 Dec.
HED 18, 51-1, v24, 2p. [2739]
Statement of open-market purchases during fiscal 1889.

115. Receipts and Expenditures. 9 Dec.
HED 294, 51-1, v34, 572p. [2749]
For year ending 30 June 1887; Indian expenses.

116. Judgments Rendered by the Court of Claims. 9 Dec.
HMD 9, 51-1, v1, 5p. [2760]
Includes cases of several Indian agents.

117. Petition of A. Spalter. 11 Dec.
SMD 20, 51-1, v2, 2p. [2698]
Service in the French and Indian war.

118. R-P of E. Leib. 12 Dec.
SR 5, 51-1, v1, 4p. [2703]
Service against Indians on the Plains; 1866-67.

119. Nevada Rebellion War Claims. 16 Dec.
SED 10, 51-1, v1, 696p. [2678]
Expenditures on control of Indian hostilities (report includes documents from the 50th Congress, 1st and 2d sessions).

120. California Rebellion War Claims. 16 Dec.
SED 11, 51-1, v2, 759p. [2679]

Expenditures on control of Indian hostilities (report includes documents from the 50th Congress, 1st and 2d sessions).

121. Langford Land Claim. 16 Dec.
SED 12, 51-1, v2, 155p. [2679]
Land title on the Lapwai Indian reservation in Idaho; Nez Percé agency.

122. Stock Cattle for Poncas. 16 Dec.
HED 45, 51-1, v26, 2p. [2741]
Application of subsistence funds to the purchase of cattle and horses in South Dakota and Indian Territory.

123. Property Transfer on Indian Reservations. 16 Dec.
HED 48, 51-1, v26, 3p. [2741]
Items transferred between agencies, and items sold.

124. Subsistence and Civilization Funds. 16 Dec.
HED 52, 51-1, v26, 2p. [2741]
Diversion of funds from the Arapahoes, Cheyennes, Kiowas, Comanches, Wichitas, and affiliated bands, to the Northern Cheyennes in Montana.

125. Coeur d'Alene Reservation. 18 Dec.
SED 14, 51-1, v2, 91p. [2679]
Council proceedings of negotiations with the Coeur d'Alenes; agreement of 9 Sept. 1889; cession of a part of the reservation; agreement of 26 Mar. 1887.

126. Right of Way Through the Puyallup Indian Reservation. 18 Dec.
SED 15, 51-1, v2, 2p. [2679]
Indians, in council, vote to refuse a right of way to the Puyallup Valley Railway Co.

127. Account Between the U.S. and Florida. 18 Dec.
HED 68, 51-1, v26, 10p. [2741]
Expenses incurred in suppressing Indian hostilities.

128. Oregon Rebellion War Claims. 19 Dec.
SED 17, 51-1, v3, 699p. [2680]
Expenditures on control of hostile Indians (includes documents from the 50th Congress).

129. R-P of W. Madden. 19 Dec.
SR 22, 51-1, v1, 1p. [2703] *or*
HR 1893, 51-1, v6, 2p. [2812]
Service at Fort Kearny, Indian Territory, in 1854.

130. R-C of the Reps. of S. Marston. 19 Dec.
SR 32, 51-1, v1, 2p. [2703]
Indian agent at the Union agency in Indian Territory.

131. Round Valley Indian Reservation. 20 Dec.
HED 72, 51-1, v26, 3p. [2741]
Allotment of lands in severalty, and reduction of the reservation; California.

132. Expenditures on North American Ethnology, etc. 21 Dec.
HMD 43, 51-1, v1, 20p. [2760]
Research related to the American Indian.

1890

1. Legal Status of Indians and Land. 6 Jan.
SED 21, 51-1, v5, 1p. [2682]
Within Indian Territory; information not made public because of pending negotiations with these tribes.

2. Resol. of Sen. Plumb. 6 Jan.
SMD 40, 51-1, v2, 1p. [2698]
Oppressive treatment of Alaskan natives in the seal industry.

3. Town-Site Entries in Oklahoma. 6 Jan.
HR 4, 51-1, v1, 4p. [2807]
Congressional act of 2 Mar. 1889 opens lands in Indian Territory to white settlement.

4. R-P of B. Thebant. 9 Jan.
SR 71, 51-1, v1, 1p. [2703] *or*
HR 1076, 51-1, v4, 1p. [2810]
Seminole war in Florida; 1849-50.

5. R-P of J. Gallagher. 9 Jan.
SR 74, 51-1, v1, 1p. [2703] *or*
HR 1073, 51-1, v4, 1p. [2810]
Seminole war in Florida; 1836.

6. On the Case of J. Sechler. 13 Jan.
SR 76, 51-1, v1, 1p. [2703] *or*
HR 584, 51-1, v2, 1p. [2808]
Land title in Colorado; Cheyenne and Arapaho treaty of 14 Oct. 1865.

7. Steam Vessel for Alaska. 13 Jan.
HED 93, 51-1, v26, 11p. [2741]
To be used by civil authorities; control of Indian hostilities.

8. Private Land Claim, No. 134. 13 Jan.
HED 96, 51-1, v26, 5p. [2741]
Land title issues involving Indians in New Mexico.

9. Relief of the Chippewas of Lake Superior. 13 Jan.
HED 99, 51-1, v26, 4p. [2741]
Appropriation for subsistence and clothing at the La Pointe agency in Wisconsin.
10. California Indian War Claims. 15 Jan.
SED 26, 51-1, v5, 4p. [2682]
Expenses incurred during 1854-73; Humbolt Indian expedition of 1861; Modoc war of 1872-73.
11. R-P of G. Fitzclarence. 16 Jan.
SR 103, 51-1, v1, 1p. [2703] *or*
HR 517, 51-1, v2, 1p. [2808]
Transport of Indian prisoners in California.
12. R-P of J. Hayes. 16 Jan.
SR 105, 51-1, v1, 1p. [2703] *or*
HR 1058, 51-1, v4, 1p. [2810]
Black Hawk war of 1832 in Illinois.
13. Contingent Expenses of the Interior Dept. 16 Jan.
HED 117, 51-1, v28, 19p. [2743]
Year ending 30 June 1889; OIA.
14. Indian Depredation Claims. 18 Jan.
HED 122, 51-1, v28, 15p. [2743]
During 1889; list of tribes involved, dates, etc.
15. L-C of J. Taylor. 18 Jan.
HED 123, 51-1, v28, 4p. [2743]
Indian depredations of 1856 in Oregon.
16. L-C of H. Shepard. 18 Jan.
HED 124, 51-1, v28, 3p. [2743]
Yakama depredations of 1856 in Washington.
17. L-C of Raymond Brothers. 18 Jan.
HED 125, 51-1, v28, 6p. [2743]
Bannock depredations of 1878 in Montana.
18. L-C of E. Montoya and Sons. 18 Jan.
HED 127, 51-1, v28, 4p. [2743]
Apache depredations of 1880 in New Mexico.
19. Apache Indians. 20 Jan.
SED 35, 51-1, v5, 12p. [2682]
Report on Apaches held as prisoners at Mount Vernon Barracks, Alabama; removal of some Indians to Indian Territory recommended.
20. Admission of Wyoming. 20 Jan.
SR 115, 51-1, v1, 35p. [2703]
The Indian population is not warlike, and is being educated in farming.
21. Brevet Rank in the Army. 20 Jan.
SR 123, 51-1, v1, 3p. [2703]
For service in Indian campaigns.
22. Pottawatomies of Indiana and Michigan. 20 Jan.
SR 129, 51-1, v1, 42p. [2703]
Amounts due under various treaties.
23. L-C of A. Whitcomb. 20 Jan.
HED 129, 51-1, v28, 3p. [2743]
Sioux depredations of 1856-59 in Nebraska.
24. L-C of R. Blinn. 20 Jan.
HED 130, 51-1, v28, 3p. [2743]
Cheyenne depredations of 1871.
25. Sioux in North Dakota. 20 Jan.
HED 131, 51-1, v28, 6p. [2743]
Appropriation for subsistence at the Devil's Lake agency.
26. L-C of E. Montoya and Sons. 20 Jan.
HED 132, 51-1, v28, 4p. [2743]
Mescalero Apache depredations of 1879-80 in New Mexico.
27. Chippewas of Lake Superior. 21 Jan.
HR 15, 51-1, v1, 3p. [2807]
Appropriation for subsisting Indians at the La Pointe agency in Wisconsin.
28. Withdrawal of Troops from Fort Klamath, Oregon. 23 Jan.
SED 37, 51-1, v5, 17p. [2682]
Information concerning potential Indian hostilities if troops are removed; Modoc, Klamath, and Pitt River Indians located on a nearby reservation.
29. Claims Allowed by Accounting Officers. 23 Jan.
HED 144, 51-1, v31, 152p. [2746]
Including those involving Indians.
30. L-C of J. and J. McVay. 24 Jan.
HED 150, 51-1, v31, 5p. [2746]
Indian depredations of 1856 and 1858 in Oregon.
31. L-C of T. Van Pelt. 24 Jan.
HED 151, 51-1, v31, 3p. [2746]
Indian depredations of 1856 in Oregon.
32. La Pointe Agency in Wisconsin. 27 Jan.
SED 39, 51-1, v5, 3p. [2682]
Condition of Chippewas at said agency.
33. Mem. of the Legis. of Washington. 28 Jan.
SMD 60, 51-1, v2, 2p. [2698]
Investigation of losses suffered during the Indian war of 1855-56; caused by treaties being made with the Yakimas, Walla Wallas, Cayuses, and Umatillas.

34. Mem. of the Washington Legis. 28 Jan.
SMD 66, 51-1, v2, 2p. [2698]
Construction of a railroad through the Puyallup reservation; asks Congress to overrule a decision against said construction made by the tribe.

35. R-P of J. Wash. 28 Jan.
SR 194, 51-1, v1, 1p. [2703]
Seminole war in Florida; 1836.

36. Miami Indians of Indiana. 28 Jan.
HR 22, 51-1, v1, 6p. [2807]
Bill to reimburse the Indians for moneys improperly withheld; due under various treaties.

37. Mem. of a Convention at Oklahoma City. 30 Jan.
SMD 74, 51-1, v2, 2p. [2698]
Settlers on town sites in the Oklahoma country of Indian Territory.

38. Absentee Shawnee Lands. 30 Jan.
SR 200, 51-1, v1, 4p. [2703]
Sale of said lands in Kansas; treaty of 2 Nov. 1854.

39. Estimates of Deficiencies. 30 Jan.
HED 174, 51-1, v21, 52p. [2736]
Appropriations for year ending 30 June 1890; Indian expenses.

40. R-C of J. Little and H. Williams. 4 Feb.
SR 218, 51-1, v1, 4p. [2703]
Mining lease made with the Iowa Indians in Nebraska.

41. R-P of E. Warren. 6 Feb.
SR 231, 51-1, v1, 3p. [2703] *or*
HR 1385, 51-1, v5, 4p. [2811] *or*
HR 1452, 51-1, v5, 3p. [2811]
Service in Sioux expedition of 1855.

42. R-P of M. Worth. 6 Feb.
SR 233, 51-1, v1, 5p. [2703] *or*
HR 1892, 51-1, v6, 6p. [2812]
Service in the Black Hawk and Seminole wars, and the Cherokee removal.

43. New York Indian Lands in Kansas. 6 Feb.
HR 26, 51-1, v1, 8p. [2807]
Questions of land title, and sale of lands to settlers; original bill vetoed by Pres.

44. Sale and Removal of Fort Bliss, Texas. 6 Feb.
HR 28, 51-1, v1, 5p. [2807]
Located so that troops could be transported quickly to counteract Indian hostilities.

45. Indian Trust Funds. 10 Feb.
SED 50, 51-1, v5, 5p. [2682]
Amount of funds invested in State bonds which have not been paid at maturity.

46. Sioux Reservation. 10 Feb.
SED 51, 51-1, v5, 308p. [2682]
Report and council proceedings of the Sioux Commission sent to obtain consent from the Indians for a division and reduction of the Great Sioux reservation; consent obtained.

47. R-P of A. Babcock. 11 Feb.
SR 236, 51-1, v1, 2p. [2703]
Land and improvements located within the Grande Ronde Indian reservation in Oregon.

48. R-P of J. White. 11 Feb.
SR 254, 51-1, v1, 1p. [2703] *or*
HR 1894, 51-1, v6, 1p. [2812]
Service in Black Hawk war; 1832.

49. R-C of C. Adams. 12 Feb.
SR 271, 51-1, v1, 1p. [2703]
Indian agent at Los Pinos agency in Colorado; 1872-74.

50. Fur Seals on St. Paul and St. George Islands. 13 Feb.
SMD 86, 51-1, v2, 5p. [2698]
Fund to be set up for the education of the natives.

51. Steam Vessel for Civil Government. 13 Feb.
SR 287, 51-1, v1, 2p. [2703]
Patrol of native villages in Alaska.

52. Office of Chief Clerk in the OIA. 14 Feb.
HED 196, 51-1, v31, 2p. [2746]
On re-establishment of said office.

53. Northern Boundary of Nebraska. 14 Feb.
HED 201, 51-1, v31, 2p. [2746]
Involves a reduction of the Sioux reservation, with lands being ceded to Nebraska.

54. Amended Estimates for the Indian Service. 14 Feb.
HED 205, 51-1, v31, 3p. [2746]
Year ending 30 June 1891; support of non-reservation training schools.

55. R-P of M. Personeus. 15 Feb.
HR 61, 51-1, v1, 1p. [2807]
Battle of the Little Big Horn River; Custer's campaign.

56. Organization of Oklahoma Territory. 15 Feb.
HR 66, 51-1, v1, 12p. [2807]
Proposed legislation would exclude the lands of the Five Civilized

Tribes from the Territory, but would create courts in those Nations; population figures given for Indian Territory.

57. Brevet Rank in the Army. 15 Feb.
HR 79, 51-1, v1, 7p. [2807]
For service in Indian campaigns.

58. Crow Indian Reservation. 15 Feb.
HR 80, 51-1, v1, 2p. [2807]
Bill authorizing negotiations with Indians for cession of a portion of their reserve.

59. Chicago, Milwaukee, and St. Paul Railway Co. 15 Feb.
HR 81, 51-1, v1, 1p. [2807]
Railway has been constructed through the Lake Traverse reservation of the Sisseton and Wahpeton Sioux, but agreement on this has not been ratified yet.

60. Fort Berthold Agency, North Dakota. 15 Feb.
HR 82, 51-1, v1, 9p. [2807]
Agreement of 14 Dec. 1866 with the Arickarees, Gros Ventres, and Mandans yet to be ratified; land cessions and allotment.

61. R-P of H. Burton. 15 Feb.
HR 166, 51-1, v1, 1p. [2807]
Black Hawk war; 1832; Illinois.

62. R-P of S. Cooper. 15 Feb.
HR 167, 51-1, v1, 1p. [2807]
Black Hawk war; 1832.

63. R-P of W. Scurlock. 15 Feb.
HR 177, 51-1, v1, 1p. [2807]
Creek war; 1837-38; Alabama.

64. Section 4693 of the Revised Statutes. 15 Feb.
HR 186, 51-1, v1, 2p. [2807]
On disabilities received by State militiamen in service against Indians; Sioux outbreak of 1862 in Minnesota.

65. Legislation in Behalf of Indians. 17 Feb.
SED 64, 51-1, v9, 5p. [2686]
Bill to amend the act which provides for allotment of lands in severalty.

66. R-C of H. Wood. 17 Feb.
HR 201, 51-1, v1, 4p. [2807]
Civil War action at Fort Cobb, Indian Territory; 1861.

67. Oklahoma Territory. 17 Feb.
HR 205, 51-1, v1, 12p. [2807]
Territorial government over Indian Territory, except for the lands of the Five Civilized Tribes, and the Quapaw agency.

68. R-C of Cherokee Indians. 17 Feb.
HR 224, 51-1, v1, 5p. [2807]
Expenses of removal from North Carolina to Indian Territory; moneys due under the treaty of 29 Dec. 1835.

69. R-C of A. McCreary. 17 Feb.
HR 225, 51-1, v1, 23p. [2807]
Debts of Osage Indians; traders in Indian Territory.

70. Denison and Washita Railway Co. 17 Feb.
HR 232, 51-1, v1, 2p. [2807]
Construction within Indian Territory.

71. R-P of M. Harney. 18 Feb.
SR 295, 51-1, v1, 2p. [2703] *or*
HR 1695, 51-1, v6, 2p. [2812]
Service in the Black Hawk, Seminole, Sioux, and other Indian hostilities; treaty com'r after 1868.

72. Bridge Over the Arkansas River. 18 Feb.
HR 276, 51-1, v1, 1p. [2807]
Within Indian Territory.

73. R-C of J. Legare. 18 Feb.
HR 277, 51-1, v1, 7p. [2807]
Services in securing the surrender of Sitting Bull and his band of Sioux Indians.

74. Lake Traverse Indian Reservation. 19 Feb.
SED 66, 51-1, v9, 29p. [2686]
Agreement of 12 Dec. 1889 with the Sisseton and Wahpeton Sioux in North and South Dakota; cession of all unallotted lands to the U.S.

75. Warm Springs Indian Reservation. 19 Feb.
SED 67, 51-1, v9, 16p. [2686]
Report on disputed northern boundary of said reservation in Oregon.

76. R-C of the Reps. of G. McDougall. 19 Feb.
SR 319, 51-1, v2, 10p. [2704] *or*
HR 1143, 51-1, v4, 9p. [2810] *or*
HR 2126, 51-1, v7, 10p. [2813]
Furnished supplies to California Indians in 1850; treaties remain unratified, leaving debts unpaid.

77. R-C of the Pottawatomie Indians. 19 Feb.
HR 324, 51-1, v2, 42p. [2808]
Funds due under various treaties; referred to the Court of Claims.

78. Kansas City and Pacific Railroad Co. 20 Feb.

SR 341, 51-1, v2, 1p. [2704]
Right of way through Indian Territory.

79. Indian School Transportation. 20 Feb.
HED 219, 51-1, v32, 2p. [2747]
Appropriation for transporting Indian children to and from schools.

80. L-C of Jones, Russell, and Co. 20 Feb.
HED 220, 51-1, v32, 2p. [2747]
Cheyenne and Arapaho depredations.

81. Indian School in Carlisle, Pennsylvania. 20 Feb.
HED 221, 51-1, v32, 2p. [2747]
Appropriation for buildings, walks, and fences.

82. Compensation for H. Carrington. 24 Feb.
SED 70, 51-1, v9, 32p. [2686]
Special agent of the OIA; sale of Flathead lands in Montana; removal of tribe to the Jocko reservation.

83. Removal of Indians. 24 Feb.
SED 71, 51-1, v9, 8p. [2686]
Papago and other Indians to be transferred from the Papago reservation in Maricopa county to other Papago, Pima, or Maricopa reservations in Arizona Territory; etc.

84. Agreements with the Coeur d'Alenes. 24 Feb.
SMD 95, 51-1, v2, 4p. [2698]
On ratification of agreements made under Indian appropriation acts of 30 June 1887, and 2 Mar. 1889.

85. R-P of N. Smith. 25 Feb.
SR 351, 51-1, v2, 1p. [2704] *or*
HR 576, 51-1, v2, 1p. [2808]
Service in Indian wars prior to 1812; battle of Tippecanoe.

86. Southern Utes of Colorado. 25 Feb.
HR 408, 51-1, v2, 4p. [2808]
Agreement calling for surrender of their reservation in Colorado, and acceptance of a reserve in Utah Territory; would be adjacent to the Navajo reservation.

87. Monument to W. Harrison. 25 Feb.
HR 427, 51-1, v2, 1p. [2808]
Served as governor over the great Indian Territory, etc.

88. Affairs in Indian Territory. 26 Feb.
SED 72, 51-1, v9, 61p. [2686]
Affairs at Guthrie and Oklahoma City from the opening to settlement of said Territory to the present date.

89. Galena, Guthrie, and Western Railway Co. 26 Feb.
HR 449, 51-1, v2, 1p. [2808]
Right of way through Indian Territory.

90. Abandonment of Military Reservations. 28 Feb.
SED 73, 51-1, v9, 8p. [2686]
Fort Yuma (California), and Fort Klamath (Oregon) revert to Indian reservations; etc.

91. Relief of Destitute Indians. 28 Feb.
HED 241, 51-1, v32, 2p. [2747]
Appropriation for Indians not having treaty funds; notably the Chippewas of Wisconsin, and the Sioux of North Dakota.

92. Quapaw Indians. 1 Mar.
HR 559, 51-1, v2, 2p. [2808]
Bill providing for allotment of lands in severalty, and sale of surplus land.

93. On the Case of W. Bennett. 3 Mar.
SR 380, 51-1, v2, 3p. [2704]
Misconduct of an Army officer in the Osage Nation, Indian Territory.

94. Little Falls, Mille Lacs, and Lake Superior Railway Co. 4 Mar.
HR 631, 51-1, v2, 1p. [2808]
Right of way through lands occupied by the Mille Lacs Indians; Minnesota.

95. Reservation of the Turtle Mountain Chippewas. 4 Mar.
HR 632, 51-1, v2, 3p. [2808]
Bill authorizing negotiations for the surrender of said reservation in North Dakota; consolidation with Minnesota Chippewas.

96. Palouse and Spokane Railway Co. 5 Mar.
HR 645, 51-1, v2, 1p. [2808]
Right of way through the Nez Percé reservation in Idaho.

97. R-C of H. Shipley. 6 Mar.
SR 400, 51-1, v2, 3p. [2704]
Services at the Nez Percé agency in Idaho; 1880.

98. Chippewas in Minnesota. 6 Mar.
HED 247, 51-1, v32, 193p. [2747]
Report of the Chippewa Commission; council proceedings; agreement for relinquishment of land title by the Chippewas; etc.

99. Forfeiture of Lands. 7 Mar.
SR 421, 51-1, v2, 2p. [2704]
Pawnee reservation lands in Nebras-

ka not paid for by settlers residing on them.

100. Survey of a Railroad Land Grant. 7 Mar.
HED 250, 51-1, v32, 3p. [2741]
To the Atlantic and Pacific Railroad Co. in Arizona and New Mexico; through Indian reservations.

101. Indians in Florida. 7 Mar.
HR 675, 51-1, v3, 1p. [2809]
To be located on lands in severalty.

102. Lands in Ormsby County, Nevada. 7 Mar.
HR 676, 51-1, v3, 1p. [2809]
Com. on Indian Affairs reconveys land to the county.

103. Omaha Lands in Nebraska. 8 Mar.
HR 721, 51-1, v3, 1p. [2809]
Bill extending time of payment to purchases of said lands.

104. Buildings for the Chilocco School. 11 Mar.
SED 77, 51-1, v9, 3p. [2686]
Industrial school for Indians in Indian Territory.

105. R-P of J. Tribble. 11 Mar.
SR 424, 51-1, v2, 1p. [2704] *or*
HR 208, 51-1, v1, 1p. [2807]
Florida Indian war; 1836-37.

106. R-P of J. Prator. 11 Mar.
SR 425, 51-1, v2, 1p. [2704] *or*
HR 257, 51-1, v1, 1p. [2807]
Service in Indian war; 1836; Georgia Volunteers.

107. R-P of H. Morgan. 11 Mar.
SR 426, 51-1, v2, 1p. [2704] *or*
HR 169, 51-1, v1, 1p. [2807]
Creek war; 1836; Georgia Volunteers.

108. R-P of G. Lee. 11 Mar.
SR 427, 51-1, v2, 1p. [2704] *or*
HR 170, 51-1, v1, 1p. [2807]
Florida Indian war; 1838.

109. Salaries in the OIA. 11 Mar.
HED 265, 51-1, v34, 5p. [2749]
Increase of salary for the CIA, assistant CIA, and financial clerk.

110. Legal Status of Indians in Indian Territory. 12 Mar.
SED 78, 51-1, v9, 31p. [2686]
Report on Indian land titles obtained by treaty stipulation.

111. Telegraphing, and Purchase of Indian Supplies. 13 Mar.
HED 269, 51-1, v34, 2p. [2749]
Increased estimate of appropriations for fiscal 1891.

112. Sac and Fox Indians. 14 Mar.
SED 82 (pts. 1 and 2), 51-1, v9, 89p. [2686]
Report on persons added to the membership or roll of the Sac and Fox Indians.

113. Fort Walla Walla, Washington. 14 Mar.
SR 461, 51-1, v2, 2p. [2704]
Appropriation for improvements; control of Indians on the Umatilla, Warm Springs, Yakima, Nez Percé, Coeur d'Alene, Colville, and Moses reservations.

114. Permanent and Indefinite Appropriations. 14 Mar.
HED 274, 51-1, v34, 22p. [2749]
Repeal of certain appropriations; Indian expenses.

115. Spokane Falls and Northern Railway Co. 14 Mar.
HR 846, 51-1, v3, 1p. [2809]
Right of way through the Colville Indian reservation in Washington.

116. World's Exposition. 15 Mar.
HR 890, 51-1, v3, 21p. [2809]
World's Fair of 1892 in Chicago; exhibits on American Indians.

117. Treatment of Certain Apaches. 17 Mar.
SED 83, 51-1, v9, 53p. [2686]
On the seizure and imprisonment of Chatto and other Apaches who had been assured of safe conduct to Washington, D.C. to discuss certain affairs as delegates of the tribe.

118. Authorizing a Lottery Co. 18 Mar.
SED 84, 51-1, v9, 3p. [2686]
By the Indian territorial government of the Creek Nation.

119. R-C of the Estate of J. Whitfield. 18 Mar.
HR 868, 51-1, v3, 2p. [2809]
Surety on the bond of an Indian agent in Nebraska.

120. Mem. of the Chickasaw Indians. 19 Mar.
SMD 107, 51-1, v2, 26p. [2698]
Favor relinquishment of Choctaw and Chickasaw lands west of the 98th meridian of west longitude; rights to lands obtained under various treaties.

121. R-C of P. Sinnott. 19 Mar.
SR 490, 51-1, v2, 6p. [2704] *or*
HR 1202, 51-1, v4, 6p. [2810]
Indian agent at the Grande Ronde agency, Oregon.

122. Southern Ute Commission. 19 Mar.
HED 283, 51-1, v34, 3p. [2749]
Appropriation to cover expenses.

123. Sioux Reservations. 19 Mar.
HED 284, 51-1, v34, 2p. [2749]
Appropriation for surveys and allotment.

124. Indian School in Carlisle, Pennsylvania. 19 Mar.
HED 285, 51-1, v34, 3p. [2749]
Appropriation for buildings.

125. Zuni Agency in New Mexico. 19 Mar.
HED 287, 51-1, v34, 5p. [2749]
Appropriation for support of Indians, and salary for an agent.

126. Issue of Ordnance to Washington. 19 Mar.
HR 888, 51-1, v3, 3p. [2809]
During the Nez Percé war of 1877-78.

127. R-C of R. Woodbridge. 19 Mar.
HR 894, 51-1, v3, 2p. [2809]
Clerk at the Fort Peck Indian agency in Montana; 1883.

128. Apache Indians. 20 Mar.
SED 88, 51-1, v9, 18p. [2686]
Correspondence concerning events which occurred in 1886; council proceedings regarding cessation of hostilities.

129. Mem. of Cherokee Chiefs and Delegates. 20 Mar.
SMD 109, 51-1, v2, 4p. [2698]
Against amendments to the bill creating Oklahoma Territory which would encorporate the Cherokee strip, or "outlet" into said Territory; treaty and agreement stipulations cited.

130. Pittsburgh, Columbus, and Fort Smith Railway Co. 21 Mar.
HR 901, 51-1, v3, 1p. [2809]
Right of way through Indian Territory.

131. Relief of Certain Indian Agents. 25 Mar.
HED 298, 51-1, v35, 4p. [2750]
Claims for payments due; settlement of accounts.

132. Employment of Indian Scouts. 25 Mar.
HED 299, 51-1, v35, 9p. [2750]
By the U.S. Army in pursuing hostile Indians in the U.S. and Mexico; transfer of Chiricahua Apaches from Mount Vernon Barracks, Alabama, to Fort Sill, Indian Territory.

133. Expenses of the Indian Dept. 25 Mar.
HR 1046, 51-1, v4, 1p. [2810]
Jurisdiction over Indian tribes conferred on territorial courts in 1885; expense must be handled by the U.S.

134. Pensions to Survivors of Indian Wars. 25 Mar.
HR 1049, 51-1, v4, 4p. [2810]
Embracing the Black Hawk, Creek, Seminole, and Cherokee wars during 1832-42.

135. Indian Depredation Claims. 26 Mar.
HR 1079, 51-1, v4, 8p. [2810]
Select Com. on Indian Depredation Claims reports a bill creating a special tribunal to adjust said claims.

136. R-C of J. Fell et al. 26 Mar.
HR 1083, 51-1, v4, 26p. [2810]
Apache depredations of 1865-69 in Arizona.

137. Proposed Military Post in Alaska. 28 Mar.
SR 557, 51-1, v2, 2p. [2704]
Control of Indians; Yukon River site questioned.

138. Education of Children. 28 Mar.
HED 303, 51-1, v35, 2p. [2750]
Indian tribes of Alaska.

139. Coeur d'Alene Indians of Idaho. 28 Mar.
HR 1109, 51-1, v4, 46p. [2810]
Bill to ratify and confirm two agreements made with said tribe; land cessions.

140. Abandoned Military Reservations. 28 Mar.
HR 1116, 51-1, v4, 1p. [2810]
No longer needed to control Indian hostilities; Wyoming.

141. Mineral Resources of the U.S. 29 Mar.
HMD 230, 51-1, v16, 652p. [2775]
Coal, coke, and mineral springs in Indian Territory.

142. Duluth and Winnipeg Railroad Co. 31 Mar.
HR 1165, 51-1, v4, 1p. [2810]
Construction through the Winibigoshish, Cass Lake, White Oak Point, and Red Lake Indian reservations in Minnesota.

143. Patents Issued to Indians. 1 Apr.
SED 92, 51-1, v9, 2p. [2686]
Number of patents issued under the allotment or severalty act; list of allotments awaiting patents.

144. R-P of J. Russell. 1 Apr.
SR 586, 51-1, v2, 1p. [2704] *or*

HR 1668, 51-1, v6, 1p. [2812]
Service in Black Hawk war; 1832; Illinois.

145. Pawnee Reservation in Nebraska. 1 Apr.
HR 1175, 51-1, v4, 2p. [2810]
Bill seeking payments for lands purchased within said reservation.

146. Klamath River Reservation. 1 Apr.
HR 1176, 51-1, v4, 2p. [2810]
Bill provides for sale of this California reservation, and removal of Klamaths resident there to the Hoopa Valley reservation.

147. R-C of D. Boutwell. 2 Apr.
HR 1183, 51-1, v4, 1p. [2810]
Service in Indian Home Guards during Civil War.

148. Steam-Vessel for Civil Government in Alaska. 2 Apr.
HR 1203, 51-1, v4, 5p. [2810]
Control of Indian population.

149. Sale of Timber Reserved for Menomonees. 2 Apr.
HR 1206, 51-1, v4, 1p. [2810]
From their reservation in Wisconsin.

150. Pottawatomie Treaty Obligations. 4 Apr.
HR 1230, 51-1, v5, 5p. [2811]
Claims of tribe for depredations committed by whites.

151. R-C of D. Hedges and E. Spalding. 4 Apr.
HR 1231, 51-1, v5, 2p. [2811]
Supplies to Yankton Sioux during 1866-67.

152. R-P of W. Short. 7 Apr.
HR 1290, 51-1, v5, 1p. [2811]
Florida Indian war; 1836-37.

153. Legislative, Executive, and Judicial Appropriation Bill. 7 Apr.
HR 1307, 51-1, v5, 18p. [2811]
Year ending 30 June 1891; salaries in the OIA.

154. R-P of M. Mann. 8 Apr.
SR 614, 51-1, v2, 1p. [2704] *or*
HR 260, 51-1, v1, 1p. [2807]
Creek war; 1836; Alabama.

155. R-P of W. Dunn. 8 Apr.
SR 615, 51-1, v2, 1p. [2704] *or*
HR 192, 51-1, v1, 1p. [2807]
Florida Indian war; 1836.

156. R-P of T. Edwards. 8 Apr.
SR 616, 51-1, v2, 1p. [2704] *or*
HR 258, 51-1, v1, 1p. [2807]
Florida Indian war; 1836.

157. R-P of S. Wyrick. 8 Apr.
SR 617, 51-1, v2, 1p. [2704] *or*
HR 259, 51-1, v1, 1p. [2807]
Indian war; 1836; Georgia Volunteers.

158. R-P of W. Carter. 8 Apr.
SR 620, 51-1, v2, 1p. [2704]
Florida Indian war; 1836.

159. R-P of A. Hopper. 8 Apr.
SR 632, 51-1, v2, 1p. [2704] *or*
HR 2353, 51-1, v7, 1p. [2813]
Service against Indians in Minnesota; 1862.

160. R-C of S. Duvall. 8 Apr.
HR 1333, 51-1, v5, 3p. [2811]
Missionary among the Sac and Fox Indians in Kansas; school established, but not supported under treaties of 1859, and 1862 (unratified).

161. Sisseton and Wahpeton Sioux. 9 Apr.
HR 1356, 51-1, v5, 9p. [2811]
Agreement of 12 Dec. 1889; allotment, and surrender of surplus-lands on the Lake Traverse reservation in South Dakota.

162. War Claims of California, Oregon, and Nevada. 10 Apr.
SR 644, 51-1, v3, 44p. [2705]
Suppression of Indian hostilities.

163. On the Case of R. Harris. 10 Apr.
SR 646, 51-1, v3, 2p. [2705]
Civil War service at Fort Blunt, Cherokee Nation.

164. Agreement with the Sisseton and Wahpeton Sioux. 11 Apr.
SR 661, 51-1, v3, 4p. [2705]
Relinquishment of unallotted lands on the Lake Traverse reservation; payment of moneys due under various treaties.

165. Compulsory School Attendance in Alaska. 12 Apr.
HED 321, 51-1, v35, 3p. [2750]
In order to civilize the natives.

166. Salaries in the OIA. 12 Apr.
HR 1411, 51-1, v5, 1p. [2811]
Salary increases for the CIA, assistant CIA, and financial clerk.

167. Fort Abraham Lincoln. 12 Apr.
HR 1428, 51-1, v5, 1p. [2811]
Not to be expanded, because Fort Yates is adequate for control of Indians in that region of North Dakota.

168. R-P of A. Macomb. 15 Apr.
SR 686, 51-1, v3, 1p. [2705] *or*
HR 2270, 51-1, v7, 1p. [2813]
Black Hawk war of 1832.

169. R-P of R. Spain. 16 Apr.
SR 702, 51-1, v3, 1p. [2705]
Service in the Seminole war; Florida.

170. Education of Sioux Indians. 17 Apr.
HED 333, 51-1, v35, 6p. [2750]
Appropriations under the treaty of 29 Apr. 1868, and the agreement of 1876.

171. Supplemental Estimates for Indian Schools. 17 Apr.
HED 334, 51-1, v35, 9p. [2750]
For enlargement and support of schools upon reservations.

172. Cemetery in Moscow, Idaho. 18 Apr.
HR 1506, 51-1, v5, 1p. [2811]
Those killed in Indian outbreak buried there.

173. Money Due the Creek Nation. 18 Apr.
HR 1507, 51-1, v5, 3p. [2811]
Under article 3 of the treaty of 1866.

174. Sale of Intoxicants to Canadian Indians. 19 Apr.
SED 105, 51-1, v9, 4p. [2686]
On legislation which would prohibit said sales.

175. L-C of the Seneca Indians. 19 Apr.
HED 340, 51-1, v35, 2p. [2750]
For lands taken by the U.S. in Indian Territory.

176. Land Leases by Indians. 19 Apr.
HR 1588, 51-1, v5, 1p. [2811]
To the railroads having rights of way through lands of the Five Civilized Tribes.

177. Ute Indian Reservation. 21 Apr.
HR 1605, 51-1, v5, 4p. [2811]
Bill to restore part of the Uncompahgre reservation to the public domain.

178. R-P of M. Boyle. 21 Apr.
HR 1619, 51-1, v5, 1p. [2811]
Seminole war; 1836.

179. R-P of J. Furlow. 21 Apr.
HR 1620, 51-1, v5, 1p. [2811]
Indian war of 1836; Georgia.

180. Federal Courts in Kansas. 22 Apr.
HR 1631, 51-1, v5, 1p. [2811]
Court in Wichita has jurisdiction over offenses committed in Indian Territory.

181. Portland and Puget Sound Railroad Co. 23 Apr.
HR 1674, 51-1, v6, 2p. [2812]
Right of way through the Puyallup reservation in Washington.

182. Crow Indian Reservation. 24 Apr.
SED 110, 51-1, v9, 4p. [2686]
Illegal occupation of a portion of the reservation by settlers; boundaries unsettled.

183. Allotment of Lands in Severalty to Indians. 24 Apr.
HR 1700, 51-1, v6, 2p. [2812]
Amendment of the act of 1887; would allot an equal amount of land, per capita, without regard to age, sex, or conjugal relations.

184. Grave of Maj. Gen. St. Clair. 25 Apr.
HR 1738, 51-1, v6, 2p. [2812]
Governor of the Northwest Territory in 1787; battle with the Miami Indians in 1788.

185. R-P of C. Edson. 29 Apr.
SR 775, 51-1, v3, 2p. [2705] *or*
HR 315, 51-1, v2, 2p. [2808]
Services rendered during the Rogue River war in Oregon; 1856.

186. R-P of W. Hill. 29 Apr.
SR 778, 51-1, v3, 1p. [2705] *or*
HR 441, 51-1, v2, 1p. [2808]
Service in Oregon Indian war, and against the Paiutes; 1854.

187. R-P of W. Yohe. 29 Apr.
SR 784, 51-1, v3, 1p. [2705] *or*
HR 175, 51-1, v1, 1p. [2807]
Seminole war in Florida; 1837-40; battle of Lake Okeechobee.

188. R-P of J. Reed. 29 Apr.
SR 793, 51-1, v3, 1p. [2705] *or*
HR 209, 51-1, v1, 1p. [2807]
Black Hawk war; 1832; Illinois.

189. Allotment of Lands in Severalty to Indians. 29 Apr.
HR 1809, 51-1, v6, 2p. [2812]
Amendments to the act of 1887; section 4 allows for the leasing of allotted lands if it is deemed that the Indians are incapable of improving the land; etc.

190. Absentee Shawnee Lands. 29 Apr.
HR 1810, 51-1, v6, 5p. [2812]
Bill providing for the sale of said lands to settlers; Kansas.

191. R-P of G. Chapman. 29 Apr.
HR 1814, 51-1, v6, 1p. [2812]
Indian inspector of the U.S.; work at the Mille Lacs, Leech Lake, Winnebago, and White Earth reservations in Minnesota.

192. Stockbridge and Munsee Indians. 2 May.
HR 1856, 51-1, v6, 2p. [2812]
Bill provides for sale of reservation in Wisconsin; terminates tribal relations, and questions of annuities and supervision.

193. Protection of the American Bison. 3 May.
HR 1876, 51-1, v6, 2p. [2812]
Preservation of buffalo from extinction likened to the preservation of the American Indian; civilization compared to domestication.

194. Western Miami Indians. 5 May.
HR 1901, 51-1, v6, 1p. [2812]
Bill calling for allotment of their remaining lands, distribution of their tribal funds, and citizenship.

195. Pottawatomie Indians. 7 May.
SED 112, 51-1, v9, 5p. [2686]
Report on tribal membership and tribal funds; treaties of 1861, and 1868.

196. R-P of J. Reddick. 7 May.
SR 890, 51-1, v4, 1p. [2706] *or*
HR 1304, 51-1, v5, 1p. [2811]
Black Hawk war; 1832.

197. R-P of S. Dark. 7 May.
SR 919, 51-1, v4, 1p. [2706] *or*
HR 174, 51-1, v1, 1p. [2807]
Black Hawk war; 1832; Illinois.

198. R-C of the Pottawatomies. 8 May.
HR 1926, 51-1, v6, 5p. [2812]
Amounts due the tribe under various treaties.

199. L-C of A. Dickerman. 9 May.
HED 371, 51-1, v35, 3p. [2750]
Osage depredations of 1864-65 in Kansas.

200. R-P of C. Johnson. 9 May.
HR 1968, 51-1, v6, 1p. [2812]
Black Hawk war of 1832; Sac and Fox war of 1831 in Illinois.

201. Oklahoma Territory. 13 May.
SED 117, 51-1, v9, 2p. [2686]
Appropriation for courts to have jurisdiction over Indian Territory.

202. Capitan Grande and La Jolla Reservations. 13 May.
SED 118, 51-1, v9, 16p. [2686]
Illegal occupation of said reservations of the Mission Indian agency in California.

203. R-P of G. Vogdes. 13 May.
SR 946, 51-1, v7, 2p. [2709]
Service in Seminole war; Florida; 1849-50, and 1856.

204. R-P of E. Garrett. 13 May.
SR 985, 51-1, v7, 1p. [2709] *or*
HR 439, 51-1, v2, 1p. [2808]
Black Hawk war; 1832; Illinois.

205. Office of the Surveyor General. 14 May.
SED 120, 51-1, v9, 2p. [2686]
In South Dakota; appropriation needed for survey of the lands relinquished by the Sioux from their reservation.

206. Northern Cheyennes. 14 May.
SED 121, 51-1, v9, 18p. [2686]
Condition of members of said tribe residing at the Pine Ridge agency, South Dakota; abused by the Sioux; ask removal to the Tongue River reservation in Montana.

207. Indian Depredation Claims. 16 May.
SR 1016, 51-1, v7, 19p. [2709]
Bill giving U.S. district and circuit courts jurisdiction over said claims.

208. California Indian War Claims. 17 May.
SED 122, 51-1, v9, 190p. [2686]
Suppression of hostile Indians; 1854-73.

209. California Indian War Claims. 17 May.
SR 1026, 51-1, v7, 2p. [2709]
Expenses of suppressing Indian hostilities.

210. R-P of G. Quick. 20 May.
SR 1036, 51-1, v7, 1p. [2709] *or*
HR 1103, 51-1, v4, 1p. [2810]
Black Hawk war; 1832; Illinois.

211. R-P of H. McMann. 20 May.
SR 1037, 51-1, v7, 1p. [2709]
Service against Indians on the Plains.

212. R-P of M. Blake. 20 May.
SR 1044, 51-1, v7, 2p. [2709] *or*
HR 681, 51-1, v3, 2p. [2809]
Seminole war in Florida; service against Apaches and Navajoes.

213. R-P of I. Hensley. 20 May.
SR 1054, 51-1, v7, 1p. [2709] *or*
HR 760, 51-1, v3, 1p. [2809]
Sioux outbreak of 1862 in Minnesota.

214. R-P of W. Crawford. 20 May.
SR 1065, 51-1, v7, 1p. [2709] *or*
HR 1291, 51-1, v5, 1p. [2811]
Creek war; 1836; Georgia.

215. R-P of W. Chapman. 20 May.
SR 1066, 51-1, v7, 1p. [2709] *or*
HR 862, 51-1, v3, 1p. [2809]
Florida Indian war; 1836.

216. R-P of L. Owen. 20 May.
SR 1067, 51-1, v7, 4p. [2709]
Service against Seminoles, Coeur d'Alenes, Spokanes, and Modocs.

217. Seminole Indians. 22 May.
SED 126, 51-1, v11, 11p. [2688]
Request for negotiations concerning purchase by Seminoles of Creek lands in Indian Territory.

218. Settlers on Indian Reservations. 23 May.
HR 2085 , 51-1, v7, 2p. [2813]
Winnebago and Crow Creek reservations in Dakota Territory were opened in Feb. of 1885, and closed in Apr. of 1855; bill covers losses of settlers required to vacate lands; Sioux treaties violated.

219. R-P of A. Seiter. 24 May.
SR 1130, 51-1, v7, 1p. [2709] *or*
HR 1366, 51-1, v5, 1p. [2811]
Sioux outbreak of 1862 in Minnesota.

220. Eastern Shawnee Indians. 24 May.
HR 2145, 51-1, v7, 2p. [2813]
Bill on allotment of lands in severalty in Indian Territory, and on distribution of tribal funds.

221. R-P of G. Pease. 26 May.
HR 2155, 51-1, v7, 1p. [2813]
Black Hawk war; 1832; Illinois.

222. R-C of L. and A. Lee. 26 May.
HR 2164, 51-1, v7, 1p. [2813]
U.S. Army depredations in Indian Territory during the Civil War.

223. R-P of J. Morris. 27 May.
SR 1183, 51-1, v7, 1p. [2709] *or*
HR 1292, 51-1, v5, 1p. [2811]
Service in Creek war; 1838; Georgia.

224. Delaware Indians of Indian Territory. 27 May.
HR 2168, 51-1, v7, 6p. [2813]
Funds due under the treaties of 1829, 1854, 1860, and 1866.

225. R-C of J. Dunlap. 27 May.
HR 2177, 51-1, v7, 6p. [2813]
Resident on the Kansas Indian diminished reservation in Kansas; land title.

226. R-P of L. Wallen. 28 May.
SR 1211, 51-1, v7, 2p. [2709] *or*
HR 652, 51-1, v2, 2p. [2808]
Control of Apache and Navajo hostilities in New Mexico during the Civil War.

227. Negotiations with the Cherokees. 28 May.
HED 400, 51-1, v37, 2p. [2752]
Appropriation to continue negotiations concerned with getting Indians to cede their lands to the U.S.

228. Chippewa Indians of Minnesota. 28 May.
HR 2197, 51-1, v7, 1p. [2813]
Amendments to the act of 1889 which calls for land cessions, land sales, removal, and allotments on the White Earth and Red Lake reservations.

229. Salaries in the OIA. 29 May.
SED 130, 51-1, v11, 2p. [2688]
Salary increases proposed.

230. Chippewa Treaty Stipulations. 29 May.
SED 133, 51-1, v11, 14p. [2688]
Non-fulfillment of the treaty of 30 Sept. 1854; inaccurate land surveys.

231. Resol. of Sen. Spooner. 29 May.
SMD 154, 51-1, v2, 1p. [2698]
Investigation of the practices of certain courts in Arkansas and Texas regarding crimes committed in Indian Territory.

232. R-P of J. McCrabb. 29 May.
SR 1227, 51-1, v7, 1p. [2709] *or*
HR 1027, 51-1, v3, 1p. [2809]
Service in Creek and Seminole wars; 1837-39; Florida, Georgia, and Alabama.

233. R-P of M. Greening. 3 June.
SR 1251, 51-1, v7, 1p. [2709] *or*
HR 2993, 51-1, v9, 1p. [2815]
Service in Creek war; 1836; Alabama.

234. R-P of T. Statham. 3 June.
SR 1255, 51-1, v7, 1p. [2709] *or*
HR 1289, 51-1, v5, 1p. [2811]
Service in Florida Indian war; 1836.

235. Indian Appropriation Bill. 3 June.
HED 405, 51-1, v37, 2p. [2752]
CIA on the necessity for the early passage of said bill.

236. Agreement with the Sisseton and Wahpeton Sioux. 3 June.
HR 2271, 51-1, v7, 1p. [2813]
Amendments to ratification bill.

237. Pillager Band of Chippewas. 4 June.
SED 137, 51-1, v11, 6p. [2688]
Non-fulfillment of the treaty of 21 Aug. 1847; also involves Menomonees and Sioux.

238. R-C of Certain Persons. 4 June.
SR 1285, 51-1, v7, 12p. [2709]
Expenditures in suppressing Paiute hostilities of 1860 in Utah Territory.

239. Land Title in Albuquerque, New Mexico. 4 June.
HR 2324, 51-1, v7, 3p. [2813]
Papers lost in Indian hostilities of 1860.

240. Indian Appropriation Bill. 4 June.
HR 2325, 51-1, v7, 2p. [2813]
Year ending 30 June 1891.

241. R-P of O. Collinsworth. 5 June.
SR 1290, 51-1, v7, 1p. [2709] *or*
HR 2052, 51-1, v6, 1p. [2812]

Service in Creek war; 1836; Alabama.

242. R-P of C. Zentmeyer. 5 June.
SR 1292, 51-1, v7, 1p. [2709] *or*
HR 1416, 51-1, v5, 1p. [2811]
Employee at Lower Sioux agency at the time of the 1862 outbreak in Minnesota.

243. R-C of D. Mitchell. 6 June.
SR 1310, 51-1, v8, 88p. [2710] *or*
HR 121, 51-1, v1, 88p. [2807]
Supplies furnished to troops engaged in an Indian campaign in Kansas; 1868-69; Fort Harker.

244. Cherokee Indians. 7 June.
SED 145, 51-1, v11, 4p. [2688]
Money appropriated by the Cherokee Nation in violation of treaties; Cherokee freedmen.

245. Salmon Fisheries of Alaska. 9 June.
HMD 211, 51-1, v18, 50p. [2777]
Natives employed in industry; effects of industry on natives; etc.

246. R-P of J. Mann. 9 June.
HR 2377, 51-1, v7, 1p. [2813]
Service at Fort Snelling in Indian country; 1841-46.

247. Land Title in Sault Ste. Marie, Michigan. 9 June.
HR 2383, 51-1, v7, 5p. [2813]
Indian title extinguished by the treaty of 16 June 1820.

248. Selection of Indemnity Lands. 9 June.
HR 2384, 51-1, v7, 4p. [2813]
By States and Territories in lieu of lands falling within Indian reservations.

249. Monument at the Tippecanoe Battle-Field. 9 June.
HR 2387, 51-1, v7, 1p. [2813]
Battle between Indians and U.S. forces under Gen. Harrison; Indiana.

250. R-P of F. Myrick. 11 June.
SR 1343, 51-1, v8, 1p. [2710] *or*
HR3572, 51-2, v3, 1p. [2887]
Sioux outbreak of 1862 in Minnesota.

251. R-C of Texas. 12 June.
HED 413, 51-1, v37, 2p. [2752]
Expenses of suppressing Indian hostilities during fiscal years 1865-82.

252. Omaha Lands in Nebraska. 13 June.
SR 1357, 51-1, v8, 1p. [2710]
Bill extending the time of payment to purchasers of said lands; lands sold in 1883.

253. Red Lake and Western Railway and Navigation Co. 13 June.
HR 2444, 51-1, v7, 1p. [2813]
Right of way through the Red Lake Indian reservation; Minnesota.

254. Disbursing Officers of the Interior Dept. 14 June.
HED 417, 51-1, v37, 4p. [2752]
Accounts of the Indian Service to be submitted quarterly, not monthly.

255. Town Sites in Alaska. 14 June.
HR 2450, 51-1, v8, 7p. [2814]
Missionary activities among the natives; recommends that Dahl and Long Islands be reserved for the Hydah tribe of natives.

256. On the Case of E. Fish and Co. et al. 16 June.
SMD 165, 51-1, v4, 6p. [2700]
Supplies furnished to Indians on reservations in Arizona to avoid an outbreak of hostilities; 1873-74.

257. Purchase of Lands in Indian Territory. 18 June.
SED 155, 51-1, v11, 1p. [2688]
Agreement of 20 May 1890 with the Iowa Indians; agreement of 12 June 1890 with the Sac and Fox Indians.

258. Boundaries of the Uncompahgre Reservations. 19 June.
SED 157, 51-1, v11, 2p. [2688]
Pres. vetoes bill changing the boundaries of this Ute reservation in Utah.

259. Postmasters in Guthrie, Oklahoma City, and Kingfisher. 19 June.
HR 2490, 51-1, v8, 2p. [2814]
In Indian Territory.

260. New York Indian Lands in Kansas. 20 June.
SR 1393, 51-1, v8, 10p. [2710]
Sale of said lands to settlers.

261. R-C of the Estate of B. West. 21 June.
SR 1394, 51-1, v8, 9p. [2710] *or*
HR 1205, 51-1, v4, 8p. [2810]
Cherokee Indian loses salt-works to the Cherokee Nation; Indian Territory.

262. U.S. Courts at Fort Smith, Arkansas, and Paris, Texas. 23 June.
SED 164, 51-1, v11, 5p. [2688]
Appointment of com'rs to investigate crimes in Indian Territory questioned.

263. Chickasaw Indians. 23 June.
SED 165, 51-1, v11, 6p. [2688]
Appropriation to reimburse the Chickasaw general fund under the treaty of 22 June 1852.

264. Indian Depredation Claims. 24 June.
SED 167, 51-1, v11, 2p. [2688]
Amounts paid out by the government because of said claims.

265. Establishment of an Indian School. 24 June.
SMD 172, 51-1, v4, 3p. [2700]
In Flandreau, South Dakota; would serve the Sioux reservations west of the Missouri River, and the Sisseton and Wahpeton Sioux reservation at Lake Traverse.

266. R-P of A. Reeves. 24 June.
SR 1400, 51-1, v8, 1p. [2710] *or*
HR 1611, 51-1, v5, 1p. [2811]
Service in Creek war; 1838; Georgia.

267. R-P of M. Grant. 24 June.
SR 1402, 51-1, v8, 1p. [2710] *or*
HR 2042, 51-1, v6, 1p. [2812]
Service in Creek war; 1836; Georgia.

268. Establishment of an Indian School. 24 June.
SR 1407, 51-1, v8, 2p. [2710]
At Flandreau, South Dakota; would service Sioux from various reservations in that State.

269. R-P of M. Smith. 24 June.
HR 2536, 51-1, v8, 1p. [2814]
Seminole war; 1835.

270. R-C of W. Martin. 25 June.
SR 1410, 51-1, v8, 3p. [2710] *or*
HR 118, 51-1, v1, 3p. [2807]
Supplies furnished to troops engaged against hostile Indians; 1849; Fort Hall, Utah Territory.

271. Contributions to North American Ethnology, Volume 2. 25 June.
HMD 272 (pts. 1 and 2), 51-1, v44-45, 1528p. [2803-2804]
The Klamath Indians of southwestern Oregon; ethnographic sketch, language, and dictionary; A. Gatschet.

272. War Claims of California, Oregon, and Nevada. 25 June.
HR 2553, 51-1, v8, 45p. [2814]
Suppression of Indian hostilities; Bannock and Umatilla hostilities of 1877-78; Modoc war; etc.

273. Lands for Schools in New Mexico. 27 June.
SR 1421, 51-1, v8, 2p. [2710]
U.S. failed to provide protection from Indian hostilities.

274. R-P of M. Crook. 28 June.
SR 1422, 51-1, v8, 6p. [2710] *or*
HR 2580, 51-1, v8, 2p. [2814] *or*
HR 2906, 51-1, v9, 6p. [2815]
Rogue River, Yakima, Snake, Sioux, Apache, and other campaigns; negotiations to open the Great Sioux reservation for settlement.

275. R-P of M. Pierce. 28 June.
SR 1423, 51-1, v8, 3p. [2710] *or*
HR 2938, 51-1, v9, 3p. [2815]
Service in Nez Percé war; 1877.

276. Annual Report of the Smithsonian Institution. 1 July.
HMD 129 (pts. 1 and 2), 51-2, v10-11, 1678p. [2878-2879]
Research related to the American Indian.

277. Sherman and Northwestern Railway Co. 1 July.
HR 2602, 51-1, v8, 1p. [2814]
Right of way through the Chickasaw Nation in Indian Territory.

278. R-P of M. McIntosh. 2 July.
SR 1439, 51-1, v8, 1p. [2710] *or*
HR 3453, 51-2, v1, 1p. [2885]
Battle at the Little Big Horn River in 1876; Custer's massacre; Sioux.

279. Sioux Indians in Dakota. 2 July.
HR 2616, 51-1, v8, 3p. [2814]
Bill carrying out the act of 1889 for the division and reduction of the great Sioux reservation; agreement of 1889; appropriation needed.

280. Agreement with the Iowa Indians. 3 July.
SED 171, 51-1, v11, 23p. [2688]
Dated 20 May 1890; cession of lands in Indian Territory; made by the Cherokee Commission.

281. Sac and Fox Agreement. 3 July.
SED 172, 51-1, v11, 21p. [2688]
Dated 12 June 1890; land cessions in Indian Territory; made by the Cherokee Commission.

282. Rio Grande Junction Railway Co. 7 July.
SR 1454, 51-1, v8, 3p. [2710]
To cross lands on which the Grand Junction Indian school (in Colorado) is located.

283. Northern Pacific and Yakima Irrigation Co. 7 July.
HR 2624, 51-1, v8, 1p. [2814]
Right of way through the Yakima reservation.

284. Puyallup Indian Reservation. 8 July.
HR 2631, 51-1, v8, 1p. [2814]
Bill authorizing an investigation of said reservation in Washington, and authorizing negotiations for a reduction of the Colville reservation.

285. R-P of P. Adams. 9 July.
SR 1464, 51-1, v8, 1p. [2710] *or*
HR 2180, 51-1, v7, 1p. [2813]
Service in Black Hawk war; 1832; Illinois.

286. Sundry Civil Appropriation Bill. 9 July.
SR 1466, 51-1, v8, 136p. [2710]
Education of Eskimos and other Indians in Alaska; etc.

287. R-P of J. Dill. 12 July.
SR 1485, 51-1, v9, 1p. [2711] *or*
HR 1032, 51-1, v3, 1p. [2809]
Service in Black Hawk war; 1832; Illinois.

288. Omaha Lands in Nebraska. 12 July.
SR 1491, 51-1, v9, 2p. [2711] *or*
HR 2684, 51-1, v8, 1p. [2814]
Bill extending the time of payment to purchasers of said lands.

289. Indian Industrial Schools. 14 July.
HR 2711, 51-1, v8, 2p. [2814]
Bill to establish schools in Wisconsin, Michigan, Minnesota, Montana, and South Dakota.

290. Resol. of Sen. Daniel. 15 July.
SMD 182, 51-1, v4, 1p. [2700]
Amounts due certain States to be encorporated into the Indian appropriation bill.

291. R-C of N. Butler. 15 July.
HR 2726, 51-1, v8, 2p. [2814]
Made timber survey on the Red Lake Indian reservation in Minnesota.

292. Cession of Certain Lands. 16 July.
SED 186, 51-1, v11, 12p. [2688]
Agreements of 25 June 1890 with the Citizen band of Pottawatomies, and 26 June 1890 with the Absentee Shawnees; made by the Cherokee Commission; lands in Indian Territory.

293. R-P of M. Brachall. 16 July.
SR 1509, 51-1, v9, 1p. [2711] *or*
HR 2518, 51-1, v8, 1p. [2814]
Service in Black Hawk war; 1832; Illinois.

294. Appropriations for the Indian Dept. 16 July.
SR 1510, 51-1, v9, 17p. [2711]
Year ending 30 June 1891.

295. Sisseton and Wahpeton Indians. 17 July.
HED 443, 51-1, v37, 2p. [2752]
On the destitute condition of these Indians in South Dakota (Lake Traverse reservation); urgent need to ratify the agreement with these bands of Sioux.

296. Railroad Crossings in Indian Territory. 18 July.
HR 2764, 51-1, v8, 1p. [2814]
Bill regarding payment of damages for one railroad being crossed by another.

297. Seneca Nation of New York Indians. 22 July.
HR 2786, 51-1, v9, 4p. [2815]
Bill authorizing Indians to lease lands on the Cattaraugus and Allegany reservations in New York.

298. Seal Fisheries of the Bering Sea. 23 July.
HED 450, 51-1, v37, 96p. [2752]
Dispute between the U.S. and Great Britain involves Indians of Alaska.

299. Lands in Colorado. 23 July.
HR 2811, 51-1, v9, 1p. [2815]
Relief of settlers on lands lately occupied by the Uncompahgre and White River Utes.

300. Rio Grande Junction Railway Co. 23 July.
HR 2812, 51-1, v9, 4p. [2815]
Construction across lands of the Grand Junction Indian School; Colorado.

301. R-C of Florida. 24 July.
SR 1539, 51-1, v9, 15p. [2711]
Expenses of the Seminole war in 1856-57.

302. Intruders Upon Indian Reservations. 25 July.
SED 192, 51-1, v11, 3p. [2688]
Legislation to strengthen penalties against violators; intruders on Indian lands in Indian Territory.

303. Montana and Wyoming Railroad Co. 25 July.
HR 2832, 51-1, v9, 2p. [2815]
Right of way through the Crow reservation.

304. Various Tribes in Indian Territory. 26 July.
HR 2837, 51-1, v9, 4p. [2815]
Claims of Shawnees, Delawares, and Cherokee freedmen against the Cherokee Nation referred to

the Court of Claims; treaty of 19 July 1866.

305. Accounts of Disbursing Agents. 4 Aug.
SED 201, 51-1, v11, 1p. [2688]
To be rendered quarterly; Indian service included.

306. Kansas Trust and Diminished Reserve Lands. 5 Aug.
HR 2914, 51-1, v9, 1p. [2815]
Sale of Kansas Indian lands in Kansas.

307. Enrollment of Cherokee Freedmen, Delawares, and Shawnees. 9 Aug.
HED 456, 51-1, v37, 4p. [2752]
Appropriation to complete the work of enrollment.

308. R-C of E. Ayres. 12 Aug.
HR 2959, 51-1, v9, 6p. [2815]
Land title issues involving the Chickasaws; Mississippi; treaties of 1832, and 1834.

309. Boundaries of the Uncompahgre Reservation. 14 Aug.
HR 2967, 51-1, v9, 4p. [2815]
Bill to change said boundaries, and restore lands to the public domain; Ute agreement of 1880.

310. Claims Allowed by Accounting Officers. 15 Aug.
SED 211, 51-1, v11, 51p. [2688]
Includes claims involving Indians.

311. Private Land Claim No. 133. 15 Aug.
SED 212, 51-1, v11, 19p. [2688]
Navajo hostilities in New Mexico.

312. Deficiency Appropriation Bill. 15 Aug.
SR 1589, 51-1, v9, 13p. [2711]
Year ending 30 June 1890; Indian artifacts at the Smithsonian Institution.

313. R-P of M. Lambert. 16 Aug.
SR 1592, 51-1, v9, 1p. [2711] *or*
HR 1863, 51-1, v6, 1p. [2812]
Service in Creek war; 1836; Alabama.

314. R-P of G. Stephens. 16 Aug.
SR 1594, 51-1, v9, 1p. [2711] *or*
HR 2136, 51-1, v7, 1p. [2813]
Service in Cherokee war; 1838.

315. Choctaw and Chickasaw Nations. 18 Aug.
SED 219, 51-1, v12, 119p. [2689]
Report on intruders in their nations; treaty of 22 June 1855 being violated; etc.

316. Ratification of Coeur d'Alene Agreements. 19 Aug.
HR 2988, 51-1, v9, 47p. [2815]
Land cessions in Washington and Idaho.

317. R-C of R. Newell. 19 Aug.
HR 2989, 51-1, v9, 2p. [2815]
Pawnee depredations of 1858.

318. R-P of J. Featherstone. 20 Aug.
SR 1604, 51-1, v9, 1p. [2711] *or*
HR 1992, 51-1, v6, 1p. [2812]
Service in Creek and Seminole wars in 1836-37.

319. R-P of L. Rawlingson. 21 Aug.
SR 1609, 51-1, v9, 1p. [2711] *or*
HR 2643, 51-1, v8, 1p. [2814]
Service in Black Hawk war; 1832; Illinois.

320. R-P of W. Parish. 21 Aug.
SR 1611, 51-1, v9, 1p. [2711] *or*
HR 2519, 51-1, v8, 1p. [2814]
Service in Black Hawk war; 1832; Illinois.

321. Flathead Indian Lands. 22 Aug.
SED 221, 51-1, v12, 35p. [2689]
Sale of lands in the Bitter Root Valley of Montana; removal of tribe to the Jocko reservation.

322. Coal Leases in Indian Territory. 25 Aug.
SMD 223, 51-1, v4, 36p. [2700]
Legality of leases questioned; would create a monopoly.

323. R-P of S. Keener. 25 Aug.
SR 1625, 51-1, v9, 1p. [2711] *or*
HR 1615, 51-1, v5, 1p. [2811]
Service in Indian wars; 1836; Alabama Volunteers.

324. R-P of E. Lockett. 25 Aug.
SR 1626, 51-1, v9, 1p. [2711] *or*
HR 2713, 51-1, v8, 1p. [2814]
Service in Florida Indian war; 1836.

325. R-P of R. Barnes. 26 Aug.
SR 1637, 51-1, v9, 1p. [2711] *or*
HR 1866, 51-1, v6, 1p. [2812]
Service in Florida Indian war; 1836.

326. Report of the Com'r of Fish and Fisheries for 1888. 27 Aug.
HMD 274, 51-1, v47, 1030p. [2806]
Native Aleuts employed in sea-otter hunting; etc.

327. Cherokee and Shawnee Claims. 28 Aug.
SR 1661, 51-1 , v9, 8p. [2711]
Under various treaties; bill refers claims to the Court of Claims.

328. R-P of J. Robertson. 28 Aug.
SR 1662, 51-1, v9, 1p. [2711] *or*
HR 2526, 51-1, v8, 1p. [2814]
Service in Indian war; 1836; Georgia Volunteers.

329. R-P of J. Knetsar. 29 Aug.
SR 1665, 51-1, v9, 1p. [2711] *or*
HR 2033, 51-1, v6, 1p. [2812]
Black Hawk war; 1832; Illinois.

330. Transfer of Appropriations. 30 Aug.
SED 223, 51-1, v12, 2p. [2689]
Within the Indian service.

331. R-P of M. Cushing. 30 Aug.
SR 1667, 51-1, v9, 1p. [2711]
Service against Indians; 1871; Arizona.

332. Choctaw Coal and Railway Co. 30 Aug.
HR 3034, 51-1, v10, 3p. [2816]
On leases made by individuals of the Choctaw Nation to said company; coal mining.

333. Seneca Nation of New York Indians. 4 Sept.
SR 1680, 51-1, v9, 4p. [2711]
Bill authorizing leases made on the Cattaraugus and Allegany reservations in New York.

334. Contributions to North American Ethnology, Volume 6. 4 Sept.
HMD 273, 51-1, v46, 812p. [2805]
The Cegiha language; speech of the Omaha and Ponka tribes of the Siouan linguistic family; J. Dorsey.

335. Blankets for the Indian Service. 5 Sept.
SED 225, 51-1, v12, 17p. [2689]
On the contract awarded for 1889.

336. Gross Amount Appropriated. 6 Sept.
SR 1690, 51-1, v9, 5p. [2711]
During the present session; Indian expenses.

337. R-P of U. Bryant. 9 Sept.
SR 1700, 51-1, v9, 2p. [2711] *or*
HR 3052, 51-1, v10, 2p. [2816]
Service in Florida Indian war.

338. R-P of S. Beezley. 10 Sept.
SR 1707, 51-1, v9, 1p. [2711] *or*
HR 1623, 51-1, v5, 2p. [2811]
Service in Black Hawk war; 1832.

339. Relief of the Stockbridge Indians. 12 Sept.
SR 1718, 51-1, v9, 2p. [2711]
Allotment of lands in severalty; Wisconsin; sale of unallotted lands.

340. Newport and Kings Valley Railroad Co. 12 Sept.
HR 3081, 51-1, v10, 1p. [2816]
Right of way through the Siletz Indian reservation.

341. R-P of C. Gunn. 15 Sept.
SR 1723, 51-1, v9, 1p. [2711] *or*
HR 1622, 51-1, v5, 1p. [2811]
Service in California Indian war; 1858-59.

342. R-P of T. Riley. 15 Sept.
SR 1741, 51-1, v9, 1p. [2711] *or*
HR 1864, 51-1, v6, 1p. [2812]
Service in Black Hawk war; 1832.

343. R-P of M. Hargain. 15 Sept.
SR 1743, 51-1, v9, 1p. [2711] *or*
HR 2517, 51-1, v8, 1p. [2814]
Service in Florida Indian war; 1840-41.

344. R-M of the Choctaws and Chickasaws. 22 Sept.
HR 3147, 51-1, v10, 35p. [2816]
Land title issues in Indian Territory; treaties of 27 Sept. 1850, 22 June 1855, and 1866.

345. Miami Indians of Indiana. 24 Sept.
SR 1798, 51-1, v9, 5p. [2711]
Bill to reimburse the tribe for moneys improperly withheld from them under various treaties.

346. R-P of M. Dewees. 25 Sept.
SR 1802, 51-1, v9, 2p. [2711] *or*
HR 3120, 51-1, v10, 2p. [2816]
Service against the Sioux; service in Indian Territory.

347. Bill to Reimburse Certain Persons. 25 Sept.
HR 3185, 51-1, v10, 12p. [2816]
Those who expended moneys to suppress the Paiute hostilities of 1860 in Utah Territory.

348. L-C of W. Slusher. 26 Sept.
HED 468, 51-1, v37, 2p. [2752]
Sioux depredations of 1865 in Nebraska.

349. L-C of T. Owen. 26 Sept.
HED 469, 51-1, v37, 3p. [2752]
Arapaho depredations of 1872 in New Mexico.

350. R-P of A. Joiner. 27 Sept.
SR 1816, 51-1, v9, 1p. [2711] *or*
HR 2513, 51-1, v8, 1p. [2814]
Service in Indian wars of 1836; Georgia Volunteers.

351. R-P of S. Humphreys. 27 Sept.
SR 1817, 51-1, v9, 1p. [2711] *or*
HR 2515, 51-1, v8, 1p. [2814]
Service in Florida Indian war; 1838-39.

352. Fort Worth and Denver City Railway Co. 29 Sept.
HR 3227, 51-1, v10, 1p. [2816]
Amendment to act granting said company a right of way through Indian Territory.

353. Resol. of Sen. Jones. 30 Sept.
SMD 243, 51-1, v4, 1p. [2700]
Investigation of negotiations with the Cherokees relative to a tract of land known as the "Cherokee outlet."

354. R-C of Certain Settlers. 1 Oct.
SED 239, 51-1, v12, 9p. [2689]
Antagonized by the Northern Pacific Railroad Co., and other railroads; lines through the Crow, and Flathead reservations.

355. Statement of Appropriations. 1 Oct.
SMD 246, 51-1, v6, 613p. [2702]
During the 51st Congress, 1st session; Indian expenses.

356. R-P of J. Bagby. 1 Oct.
SR 1831, 51-1, v9, 1p. [2711] *or*
HR 3137, 51-1, v10, 1p. [2816]
Service in Black Hawk war; 1832; Illinois Volunteers.

357. Opinions of the Attorney-General, Volume 17. (no date)
HMD 237, 51-1, v27, 753p. [2786]
Including Indian schools, reservations, and trust funds; etc.

358. Opinions of the Attorney-General, Volume 18. (no date)
HMD 238, 51-1, v28, 676p. [2787]
Includes Indian contracts, leases, immigration, police, and trust funds; internal revenue in Indian Territory; etc.

359. Opinions of the Attorney-General, Volume 19. (no date)
HMD 239, 51-1, v29, 788p. [2788]
Includes Indian allottees, citizenship, and schools; leases of Indian land; etc.

360. Bulletin of the U.S. Fish Commission, Volume 8, for 1888. (no date)
HMD 261, 51-1, v18, 503p. [2777]
Fishing methods of Indians in Alaska.

361. Disbursements of the Indian Dept. 11 Nov.
HED 8, 51-2, v25, 27p. [2855]
Year ending 30 June 1890.

362. Annual Message to Congress with Documents; Pres. Harrison. 1 Dec.
HED 1, 51-2, v1-18 and 21, 16489p. [2830-2848 and 2851]
Policies of reducing large reservations, allotting lands in severalty, and restoring excess lands to the public domain are being carried out; annual report of the Sec. of War (Serials 2831-2837); annual report of the Sec. of Interior (Serials 2840-2846); annual report of the Gen. Land Office (Serial 2840); annual report of the CIA (Serial 2841); etc.

363. Annual Report of the Sec. of the Treasury. 1 Dec.
HED 2, 51-2, v19, 1015p. [2849]
Year ending 30 June 1890; Indian expenses.

364. Estimates of Appropriations. 1 Dec.
HED 5, 51-2, v22, 373p. [2852]
Year ending 30 June 1892; Indian expenses.

365. Congressional Directory. 3 Dec.
SMD 9 (pts. 1 and 2), 51-2, v1, 552p. [2819]
Lists duties of the CIA.

366. Cession of Certain Indian Lands. 4 Dec.
SED 1, 51-2, v1, 24p. [2818]
Agreement of 1890 with the Cheyenne and Arapaho Indians for cession of their lands in Indian Territory; belong to them under the treaty of 28 Oct. 1867; allotments to be made.

367. Additional Provisions for the Sioux. 4 Dec.
HED 36, 51-2, v25, 6p. [2855]
Appropriation for subsistence goods is required; Indians unhappy at the sharp reduction of their annuities under the agreement of 28 Feb. 1877, and other treaties.

368. Sioux Indian Appropriations. 4 Dec.
HED 37, 51-2, v25, 4p. [2855]
To fulfill assurances made to the Indians by the Sioux Commission of 1889.

369. Appropriation for the Apaches. 4 Dec.
HED 41, 51-2, v25, 10p. [2855]
For support of Apache prisoners at Mount Vernon, Alabama, and at Fort Union, New Mexico.

370. Receipts and Expenditures. 4 Dec.
HED 47, 51-2, v25, 527p. [2855]
For the year ending 30 June 1888; Indian expenses.

371. R-C of A. McCreary. 5 Dec.
HR 3248, 51-2, v1, 23p. [2885]
Indebtedness of Osages to licensed traders.

372. Possession of Arms by Certain Indians. 6 Dec.
SED 2, 51-2, v1, 23p. [2818]
In Nebraska, North Dakota, and

South Dakota; potential exists for a Sioux outbreak; Ghost Dance movement.

373. Support of Sioux of Different Tribes. 6 Dec.
HED 52, 51-2, v28, 5p. [2858]
Appropriation necessary for rations due under the agreement of 28 Feb. 1877.

374. Mission Indians of California. 6 Dec.
HR 3251, 51-2, v1, 4p. [2885]
Bill for their protection and relief; involves the Serranos, Dieguenos, Coahuila, and San Luis Rey or San Luisenos tribes or bands.

375. Arms and Ordnance for South Dakota. 6 Dec.
HR 3252, 51-2, v1, 1p. [2885]
For protection from Indian depredations.

376. Salaries of Employees in the Interior Dept. 8 Dec.
HED 58, 51-2, v28, 4p. [2858]
None below a fair standard within the OIA.

377. P. Turnley *vs.* the U.S. 9 Dec.
HMD 19, 51-2, v1, 10p. [2869]
Court of Claims action; service on the Upper Missouri River in Sioux country during 1854-57.

378. Miami Indians of Indiana. 9 Dec.
HR 3259, 51-2, v1, 1p. [2885]
Bill to reimburse Miamies for moneys improperly withheld; treaty of 5 June 1854.

379. Salary Due Com'r J. Wallace. 10 Dec.
HED 75, 51-2, v28, 3p. [2858]
Expenses of work in the Cherokee Nation; collected information on claims of the Delawares, Shawnees, and freedmen of said Nation.

380. Armament of Certain Indians. 11 Dec.
SED 9, 51-2, v1, 51p. [2818]
In Nebraska, and North and South Dakota; potential Sioux outbreak; Sitting Bull's influence; Ghost Dance movement.

381. R-P of B. Roan. 11 Dec.
SR 1852, 51-2, v1, 1p. [2826] *or*
HR 3136, 51-1, v10, 1p. [2816]
Florida Indian war; 1836.

382. R-P of R. England. 11 Dec.
SR 1853, 51-2, v1, 1p. [2826] *or*
HR 2261, 51-1, v7, 1p. [2813]
Creek war; 1836; Georgia.

383. R-P of J. Guthrie. 11 Dec.
SR 1855, 51-2, v1, 1p. [2826] *or*
HR 3058, 51-1, v10, 1p. [2816]
Florida Indian war; 1836.

384. Army Appropriations. 11 Dec.
HR 3274, 51-2, v1, 10p. [2885]
For fiscal 1892; payment of Indian scouts; subsistence for Indian prisoners, etc.

385. Choctaw Coal and Railway Co. 11 Dec.
HR 3279, 51-2, v1, 2p. [2885]
Has been granted a right of way through Indian Territory.

386. Expenditures of the Smithsonian Institution. 12 Dec.
HMD 39, 51-2, v1, 29p. [2869]
During fiscal 1890; expense of research related to the American Indian.

387. Condition of the Natives of Alaska. 16 Dec.
SED 14, 51-2, v1, 5p. [2818]
On the impoverished and destitute condition of Eskimos and other natives of Alaska; introduction of reindeer proposed.

388. R-P of L. Danley. 16 Dec.
SR 1862, 51-2, v1, 1p. [2826] *or*
HR 3575, 51-2, v3, 1p. [2887]
Black Hawk war; 1832; Illinois.

389. Changing the Boundary of the Uncompahgre Reservation. 16 Dec.
HR 3305, 51-2, v1, 5p. [2885]
Restoration of mineral lands within this Ute reservation to the public domain.

390. R-P of J. West. 17 Dec.
SR 1866, 51-2, v1, 1p. [2826] *or*
HR 3576, 51-2, v3, 1p. [2887]
Black Hawk war; 1832; Illinois.

391. R-P of N. Moore. 17 Dec.
SR 1867, 51-2, v1, 1p. [2826] *or*
HR 3577, 51-2, v3, 1p. [2887]
Seminole war; 1837-38.

392. Sisseton and Wahpeton Sioux. 17 Dec.
HED 100, 51-2, v28, 2p. [2858]
Destitute condition of Indians on the Lake Traverse reservation requires ratification of the agreement with said Indians which is before Congress; sale of surplus lands.

393. Arkansas State Bonds Held by the U.S. 17 Dec.
HR 3314, 51-2, v1, 13p. [2885]
Involves Indian trust funds.

394. R-P of W. Brooks. 18 Dec.
SR 1875, 51-2, v1, 1p. [2826]
Creek war; 1836; Alabama.

395. Buildings for the Cheyenne River Agency. 18 Dec.
HED 104, 51-2, v28, 4p. [2858]
Appropriation for this Sioux agency in South Dakota which is being relocated on the Missouri River.

396. Lower Brulé Agency. 18 Dec.
HED 105, 51-2, v28, 18p. [2858]
Appropriation for relocating this Sioux agency, and for constructing new buildings.

397. Missoula and Northern Railroad Co. 18 Dec.
HR 3317, 51-2, v1, 2p. [2885]
Right of way through the Flathead reservation in Montana.

398. Resol. of Sen. Manderson. 19 Dec.
SMD 28, 51-2, v3, 1p. [2821]
Asks inquiry into the condition of Indians in North and South Dakota, the occupation of reservations by U.S. troops, and arms in the hands of Indians.

399. R-P of C. Renfo. 19 Dec.
SR 1879, 51-2, v1, 1p. [2826] *or*
HR 3114, 51-1, v10, 1p. [2816]
Creek war; 1838; Alabama.

400. Indian Depredation Claims. 20 Dec.
SR 1886, 51-2, v1, 1p. [2826]
Act concerning adjudication and payment of said claims.

401. Disposition of Timber on Indian Reservations. 22 Dec.
SED 23, 51-2, v1, 18p. [2818]
On Chippewa reservations in Wisconsin.

402. R-P of E. Baldy. 23 Dec.
SR 1892, 51-2, v1, 1p. [2826] *or*
HR 3266, 51-2, v1, 1p. [2885]
Creek war; 1836; Georgia.

403. Military Post at Plattsburgh, New York. 29 Dec.
SR 1900, 51-2, v1, 2p. [2826]
Scene of wars between the French inhabitants of Canada and the Iroquois Indians.

404. Building at Cheyenne River Agency. 30 Dec.
HED 122, 51-2, v28, 2p. [2858]
Appropriation to construct a boarding-school building.

405. Distribution of Public Documents. 30 Dec.
HED 128, 51-2, v28, 94p. [2858]
Lists documents, including some related to Indian affairs.

1891

1. Contingent Expenses of the Interior Dept. 2 Jan.
HED 130, 51-2, v33, 18p. [2863]
Year ending 30 June 1890; OIA, and Indian related expenses.

2. Supplemental Estimates for the Indian Service. 2 Jan.
HED 131, 51-2, v33, 4p. [2863]
Year ending 30 June 1892.

3. Choctaw Coal and Railway Co. 5 Jan.
SR 1902, 51-2, v1, 2p. [2826]
Possesses a right of way through Indian Territory.

4. Additional Subsistence for Indians. 5 Jan.
HED 139, 51-2, v33, 3p. [2863]
Appropriation for principally the Yankton Sioux, Arickarees, Mandans, Gros Ventres, Northern Arapahoes, Sisseton Sioux, and Devil's Lake Sioux.

5. Mem. of Creek Delegates. 6 Jan.
SMD 38, 51-2, v3, 6p. [2821]
Ask payment of claims against the U.S. made by Creeks who enlisted in the Federal Army, loyal refugees, and freedmen; Civil War.

6. R-P of N. Hartley. 6 Jan.
SR 1907, 51-2, v1, 1p. [2826] *or*
HR 1294, 51-1, v5, 1p. [2811]
Black Hawk war; 1832.

7. Seal Fisheries of the Bering Sea. 6 Jan.
HED 144, 51-2, v33, 54p. [2863]
Dealings between the U.S., Russia, and Britain affect Indians in Alaska, and on the Northwest Coast; Russian-U.S. treaty of 17 Apr. 1824; etc.

8. Resol. of Rep. McAdoo. 6 Jan.
HMD 80, 51-2, v1, 1p. [2869]
Requests all information surrounding the arrest and killing of Sitting Bull, one of the chiefs of the Sioux Indians.

9. Chief Sitting Bull. 6 Jan.
HR 3375, 51-2, v1, 1p. [2885]
Request for information concerning his arrest and death.

10. Umatilla Irrigation Co. 6 Jan.
HR 3379, 51-2; v1, 1p. [2885]
Right of way through the Umatilla reservation in Oregon.

11. R-C of D. Mitchell. 7 Jan.
SR 1908, 51-2, v1. 88p. [2826] *or*
HR 3532, 51-2, v3, 90p. [2887]
Supplies to Fort Harker, Kansas, in 1868-69; Indian campaign.

12. Claims Against Fond du Lac Indians. 7 Jan.
HR 3382, 51-2, v1, 2p. [2885]
Concerns contracts for timber.

13. Communication of S. Jackson. 8 Jan.
SMD 39, 51-2, v3, 8p. [2821]
Destitute condition of natives in Alaska; need to import reindeer from Siberia.

14. R-P of E. Gordon. 8 Jan.
SR 1922, 51-2, v1, 2p. [2826] *or*
SR 2290, 51-2, v2, 1p. [2827] *or*
HR 3589, 51-2, v3, 2p. [2887]
Powder River expedition of 1876 against the Sioux.

15. R-P of G. Hume. 9 Jan.
SR 1938, 51-2, v1, 32p. [2826]
Kansas Home Guard; suppression of Indian hostilities.

16. Fireproof Building for the National Museum. 9 Jan.
HR 3399, 51-2, v1, 2p. [2885]
Protection of collections of Indian artifacts, etc.

17. Experiment Station in Alaska. 9 Jan.
HR 3414, 51-2, v1, 22p. [2885]
Education of Eskimos and other natives in Alaska; debate over whether Alaskan natives are Indians or not.

18. R-P of M. Hogan. 10 Jan.
SR 1945, 51-2, v1, 1p. [2826] *or*
HR 2378, 51-1, v7, 1p. [2813]
Seminole war; 1840-42; Florida.

19. The Western Miami Indians *vs.* the U.S. 10 Jan.
HMD 83, 51-2, v1, 4p. [2869]
Court of Claims action; conflict over enrollment in the tribe, allotments, and distribution of tribal funds; treaties of 6 Nov. 1838, 28 Nov. 1840, and 5 June 1854.

20. Legislative, Executive, and Judicial Appropriation Bill. 10 Jan.
HR 3407, 51-2, v1, 21p. [2885]
Salaries and additional employee for the OIA; fiscal 1892.

21. Estimates of Deficiencies. 12 Jan.
HED 167, 51-2, v22, 43p. [2852]
Appropriations for the year ending 30 June 1891; Indian expenses.

22. Proceedings of a Convention in Alaska. 13 Jan.
SED 39, 51-2, v1, 3p. [2818]
Legislative needs, including control of sale of liquor to Indians; etc.

23. R-P of E. Pelouze. 13 Jan.
SR 1958, 51-2, v1, 2p. [2826] *or*
HR 3793, 51-2, v4, 2p. [2888]
Seminole hostilities; 1856-57; Florida.

24. R-P of O. Day. 13 Jan.
SR 1960, 51-2, v1, 1p. [2826] *or*
HR 3099, 51-1, v10, 1p. [2816]
Florida Indian war; 1836-37.

25. Claims Allowed by Accounting Officers. 13 Jan.
HED 171, 51-2, v33, 25p. [2863]
Includes claims involving Indians.

26. Agreement with Cheyennes and Arapahoes. 13 Jan.
HR 3441, 51-2, v1, 5p. [2885]
Made in Oct. of 1890; calls for allotment, and cession of lands in that part of Indian Territory known as the "Cherokee outlet"; treaty of 28 Oct. 1867.

27. R-P of E. Lee. 15 Jan.
SR 1966, 51-2, v1, 2p. [2826] *or*
HR 3781, 51-2, v4, 2p. [2888]
Acting commissary of subsistence for Indians at Fort Sill, Indian Territory; 1869-70.

28. R-P of W. Todd. 15 Jan.
SR 1970, 51-2, v1, 1p. [2826] *or*
HR 3268, 51-2, v1, 1p. [2885]
Creek war; 1836; Georgia.

29. R-P of T. Gorham. 15 Jan.
SR 1972, 51-2, v1, 1p. [2826] *or*
HR 3269, 51-2, v1, 1p. [2885]
Service in Florida Indian war, and Cherokee war; 1837-38.

30. R-P of W. Fornby. 15 Jan.
SR 1973, 51-2, v1, 1p. [2826] *or*
HR 3270, 51-2, v1, 1p. [2885]
Creek war; 1836; Georgia.

31. Pottawatomie and Absentee Shawnee Indians. 16 Jan.
HR 3481, 51-2, v3, 3p. [2887]
Agreements of 25 June 1890 (Pottawatomie) and 26 June 1890 (Shawnee) calling for relinquishment of reservations' lands in Oklahoma Territory.

32. Buildings Rented by the Government. 17 Jan.
SMD 44, 51-2, v3, 3p. [2821]
OIA located in the Atlantic Building, Washington, D.C.

33. Fort Gibson, Tahlequah, and Great Northeastern Railway Co. 17 Jan.
HR 3489, 51-2, v3, 1p. [2887]
Right of way through the Cherokee Nation, Indian Territory.

34. R-C of B. Moreland. 17 Jan.
HR 3494, 51-2, v3, 2p. [2887]
Land in Minnesota incorporated into the Winnebago reservation; treaty of 27 Feb. 1855.

35. Crow Indian Reservation. 19 Jan.
SED 43, 51-2, v1, 26p. [2818]
Agreement of 8 Dec. 1890 for the sale of the western portion of the reservation; council proceedings.

36. R-P of D. Porter. 20 Jan.
SR 2002, 51-2, v1, 1p. [2826] *or*
HR 3140, 51-1, v10, 1p. [2816]
Indian war of 1836; Georgia.

37. R-P of S. Phillips. 20 Jan.
SR 2011, 51-2, v1, 1p. [2826] *or*
HR 1627, 51-1, v5, 1p. [2811]
Seminole war; 1818.

38. R-P of J. Murphy. 22 Jan.
SR 2033, 51-2, v1, 1p. [2826] *or*
HR 3119, 51-1, v10, 1p. [2816]
Black Hawk war; 1832.

39. R-P of S. Wenzel. 22 Jan.
SR 2045, 51-2, v1, 1p. [2826] *or*
HR 3216, 51-1, v10, 1p. [2816]
Florida Indian war.

40. R-P of M. Hoffman. 22 Jan.
SR 2050, 51-2, v1, 2p. [2826] *or*
HR 3333, 51-2, v1, 2p. [2885]
Service in Black Hawk and Florida Indian wars.

41. R-P of J. Gallagher. 22 Jan.
SR 2052, 51-2, v1, 1p. [2826] *or*
HR 2703, 51-1, v8, 1p. [2814]
Florida Indian war; 1839-44.

42. R-P of E. Johnston. 22 Jan.
SR 2063, 51-2, v1, 1p. [2826] *or*
HR 3459, 51-2, v1, 1p. [2885]
Black Hawk war; 1832.

43. R-P of M. Williams. 22 Jan.
SR 2064, 51-2, v1, 1p. [2826] *or*
HR 3458, 51-2, v1, 1p. [2885]
Black Hawk war; 1832.

44. R-P of M. Kent. 22 Jan.
SR 2068, 51-2, v1, 1p. [2826] *or*
HR 3265, 51-2, v1, 1p. [2885]
Florida Indian war; 1818.

45. R-P of M. Floyd. 22 Jan.
SR 2069, 51-2, v1, 1p. [2826]
Creek war; 1836; Georgia.

46. R-P of G. Griffith. 22 Jan.
SR 2070, 51-2, v1, 1p. [2826] *or*
HR 3117, 51-1, v10, 1p. [2816]
Creek war; 1836; Georgia.

47. R-P of L. Atkinson. 22 Jan.
SR 2071, 51-2, v1, 1p. [2826] *or*
HR 2709, 51-1, v8, 1p. [2814]
Creek war; Georgia.

48. R-P of C. McKelvey. 22 Jan.
SR 2072, 51-2, v1, 1p. [2826] *or*
HR 1628, 51-1, v5, 1p. [2811]
Florida Indian war; 1837-38.

49. Cherokee Outlet. 23 Jan.
HR 3584, 51-2, v3, 9p. [2887]
Bill to open this portion of Indian Territory to homestead settlement; located between Oklahoma Territory and Kansas; land title at issue under various treaties; cattle interests involved.

50. Brevet Rank in the Army. 24 Jan.
HED 206, 51-2, v33, 2p. [2863]
For service in Indian campaigns.

51. R-P of J. Davis. 24 Jan.
HR 3597, 51-2, v3, 1p. [2887]
Indian war of 1836.

52. Compensating Sioux Indians. 26 Jan.
SED 45, 51-2, v1, 4p. [2818]
Those Sioux residing on the Crow Creek reservation received less land per capita on their diminished reserve; reduction of the great Sioux reservation.

53. Claims of the Umatilla Commission. 27 Jan.
HED 210, 51-2, v36, 2p. [2866]
Expenses incurred in carrying out an act providing for allotment of land in severalty on the Umatilla reservation in Oregon.

54. Indian Appropriation Bill. 27 Jan.
HR 3615, 51-2, v3, 2p. [2887]
For fiscal 1892.

55. R-P of S. Thomasson. 28 Jan.
SR 2085, 51-2, v1, 1p. [2826] *or*
HR 3409, 51-2, v1, 1p. [2885]
Creek war of 1836; Georgia; Cherokee disturbances of 1838.

56. R-P of W. Riddell. 29 Jan.
SR 2091, 51-2, v1, 7p. [2826] *or*
HR 2147, 51-1, v7, 7p. [2813]
Modoc Peace Commission; 1873.

57. Indian School Land in Arizona. 29 Jan.
HED 216, 51-2, v36, 3p. [2866]
Bill setting apart land near Phoenix for said purpose.

58. Indian School at Phoenix, Arizona. 30 Jan.
HED 218, 51-2, v36, 4p. [2866]

Appropriation to establish said school; proposal for a school at Fort McDowell is eliminated.

59. Traveling Expenses of the Indian School Superintendent. 30 Jan.
HED 219, 51-2, v36, 2p. [2866]
Deficiency in the appropriation for 1890.

60. Indian School at Carlisle, Pennsylvania. 30 Jan.
HED 220, 51-2, v36, 2p. [2866]
Additional appropriation requested.

61. Treaties with the Kickapoos. 30 Jan.
HED 221, 51-2, v36, 2p. [2866]
Amended estimate of appropriation needed to fulfill said treaties; allotments made under the treaty of 28 June 1862.

62. Indian Schools. 30 Jan.
HED 222, 51-2, v36, 8p. [2866]
Estimate of appropriations needed to support certain schools for fiscal 1892.

63. R-C of C. Adams. 30 Jan.
HR 3636, 51-2, v3, 1p. [2887]
Indian agent at Los Pinos agency, Colorado.

64. R-P of I. Agan. 31 Jan.
SR 2115, 51-2, v1, 1p. [2826] *or*
HR 2865, 51-1, v9, 1p. [2815]
Florida Indian war; 1837-40.

65. Fort Brown Military Reserve in Texas. 31 Jan.
HR 3650, 51-2, v3, 8p. [2887]
Report includes information on disease at Forts Sill, Reno, and Gibson, in Indian Territory.

66. R-P of M. Hawkins. 3 Feb.
SR 2128, 51-2, v1, 1p. [2826] *or*
HR 2133, 51-1, v7, 1p. [2813]
Black Hawk war; 1832; Illinois.

67. Sundry Civil Appropriations Bill. 3 Feb.
HR 3662, 51-2, v3, 55p. [2887]
Support of Indians on military reservations, etc.

68. R-P of M. Martin. 4 Feb.
SR 2138, 51-2, v2, 1p. [2827] *or*
HR 2516, 51-1, v8, 1p. [2814]
Seminole war; 1818; Florida.

69. R-P of M. McKibben. 5 Feb.
SR 2140, 51-2, v2, 2p. [2827] *or*
HR 3925, 51-2, v5, 2p. [2889]
Service in Indian Territory; 1871-72.

70. R-P of E. Custer. 5 Feb.
SR 2141, 51-2, v2, 4p. [2827] *or*
HR 3328, 51-2, v1, 4p. [2885]
Battle at the Little Big Horn River in 1876; Sioux Indians; Custer campaign.

71. Choctaw Coal and Railway Co. 5 Feb.
HR 3699, 51-2, v3, 1p. [2887]
Right of way through Indian Territory; time limits for construction are extended.

72. Agreement with the Crow Indians. 5 Feb.
HR 3700, 51-2, v3, 4p. [2887]
Dated 8 Dec. 1890; relinquishment of a portion of their reservation in Montana.

73. Kansas and Arkansas Valley Railway Co. 5 Feb.
HR 3715, 51-2, v3, 1p. [2887]
Right of way through Indian Territory; company seeks additional lines.

74. R-P of N. Knetsar. 6 Feb.
SR 2146, 51-2, v2, 1p. [2827] *or*
HR 3457, 51-2, v1, 1p. [2885]
Black Hawk war; 1832; Illinois.

75. Protest of Creek Delegates. 6 Feb.
HMD 104, 51-2, v1, 2p. [2869]
Against extension of the jurisdiction of the U.S. Court in Indian Territory; violates the treaties of 4 Apr. 1832, 28 Aug. 1856, and 11 Aug. 1866.

76. R-P of J. Hendricks. 7 Feb.
SR 2151, 51-2, v2, 1p. [2827] *or*
HR 1621, 51-1, v5, 1p. [2811]
Black Hawk war; 1832.

77. Fulfilling Treaties with the Creeks. 7 Feb.
HED 238, 51-2, v36, 4p. [2866]
Appropriation to cover the expense of removal of 129 Indians from Alabama to Indian Territory; treaty of 4 Apr. 1832.

78. Administration of Justice in Alaska. 9 Feb.
SMD 65, 51-2, v3, 4p. [2821]
Appropriation needed; protection of the natives from whites; natives violate laws when following tribal customs, and under the influence of liquor.

79. On the Case of W. Spencer. 9 Feb.
SR 2170, 51-2, v2, 4p. [2827] *or*
HR 3197, 51-1, v10, 4p. [2816]
Service against the Sioux; 1857; Minnesota.

80. Seal Islands of Alaska. 10 Feb.
SED 49, 51-2, v1, 35p. [2818]
Condition of the Alaskan natives.

81. Ceding Arid Lands to the States and Territories. 11 Feb.
HR 3767, 51-2, v4, 202p. [2888]
Report includes table showing U.S. expenditures on extinguishing Indian land title; etc.

82. Cherokee Outlet. 11 Feb.
HR 3768, 51-2, v4, 27p. [2888]
Dispute over land title under various treaties; U.S. wants land opened for settlement, while the Cherokee Nation and cattle interests are opposed to this.

83. Negotiations with the Navajo Indians. 12 Feb.
SED 52, 51-2, v1, 4p. [2818]
Located in Utah, New Mexico, and Arizona; reduction of their reservation due to alleged mineral discoveries.

84. R-P of H. Hasson. 12 Feb.
SR 2202, 51-2, v2, 1p. [2827] *or*
HR 3676, 51-2, v3, 1p. [2887]
Service against hostile Indians.

85. R-P of M. Swift. 12 Feb.
SR 2207, 51-2, v2, 1p. [2827] *or*
HR 3673, 51-2, v3, 1p. [2887]
Black Hawk war; 1832.

86. R-P of M. Ellis. 12 Feb.
SR 2218, 51-2, v2, 1p. [2827] *or*
HR 3580, 51-2, v3, 1p. [2887]
Florida Indian war; 1838.

87. R-P of W. Scott. 12 Feb.
SR 2223, 51-2, v2, 1p. [2827] *or*
HR 3677, 51-2, v3, 1p. [2887]
Creek war; 1836; Alabama.

88. R-P of I. Stout. 12 Feb.
SR 2224, 51-2, v2, 1p. [2827] *or*
HR 3582, 51-2, v3, 1p. [2887]
Florida Indian war; 1836-37.

89. Investigation of Irrigation. 13 Feb.
SED 53 (pts. 1 and 2), 51-2, v1, 351p. [2818]
Irrigation systems of the Indians.

90. Quapaw Indians. 13 Feb.
HR 3805, 51-2, v4, 1p. [2888]
Bill for allotment of land in severalty within Indian Territory.

91. Treaty with the Rogue River Indians. 14 Feb.
SED 54, 51-2, v1, 2p. [2818]
Dated 14 July 1851, and unratified; does not contain any cession of land.

92. R-P of M. Dubridge. 14 Feb.
SR 2243, 51-2, v2, 1p. [2827] *or*
HR 3674, 51-2, v3, 1p. [2887]
Florida Indian war; 1836-40.

93. R-P of N. Glenn. 16 Feb.
SR 2248, 51-2, v2, 1p. [2827] *or*
HR 3565, 51-2, v3, 1p. [2887]
Black Hawk war; 1832; Illinois.

94. R-P of C. McRoberts. 16 Feb.
SR 2250, 51-2, v2, 1p. [2827] *or*
HR 3680, 51-2, v3, 1p. [2887]
Black Hawk war; 1832.

95. Probate Court in Oklahoma Territory. 16 Feb.
HR 3819, 51-2, v4, 3p. [2888]
Courts in Oklahoma are overloaded due to extension of their jurisdiction over parts of Indian Territory.

96. R-P of E. Satterfield. 17 Feb.
SR 2253, 51-2, v2, 1p. [2827] *or*
HR 3118, 51-1, v10, 1p. [2816]
Black Hawk war; 1832; Illinois.

97. R-P of A. Wallace. 17 Feb.
SR 2254, 51-2, v2, 1p. [2827] *or*
HR 2710, 51-1, v8, 1p. [2814]
Florida Indian war; 1837.

98. R-P of E. Mounts. 17 Feb.
SR 2255, 51-2, v2, 1p. [2827] *or*
HR 3691, 51-2, v3, 1p. [2887]
Black Hawk war; 1832; Illinois.

99. R-P of H. Allhorn. 17 Feb.
SR 2256, 51-2, v2, 1p. [2827] *or*
HR 3681, 51-2, v3, 1p. [2887]
Florida Indian war; 1838-43.

100. R-P of M. Tennery. 17 Feb.
SR 2257, 51-2, v2, 1p. [2827] *or*
HR 3566, 51-2, v3, 1p. [2887]
Black Hawk war; 1832; Illinois.

101. R-P of B. Jones. 17 Feb.
SR 2259, 51-2, v2, 1p. [2827] *or*
HR 3135, 51-1, v10, 1p. [2816]
Florida Indian war; 1836.

102. R-P of J. Walton. 17 Feb.
SR 2262, 51-2, v2, 1p. [2827] *or*
HR 3536, 51-2, v3, 1p. [2887]
Florida Indian war; 1836-37.

103. Claims of Pacific Railroads. 17 Feb.
HED 264, 51-2, v36, 18p. [2866]
For services performed for the U.S.; includes transport of goods and personnel for the Indian service.

104. Reimbursing the Western Miamies. 17 Feb.
HR 3852, 51-2, v4, 4p. [2888]
For money and lands improperly taken from them; treaties of 1840, and 1854 are violated.

105. Yuma Pumping Irrigation Co. 17 Feb.
HR 3854, 51-2, v4, 1p. [2888]
Right of way in Arizona; favorable recommendations of the CIA.

106. Indian School at Carson City, Nevada. 18 Feb.
SMD 73, 51-2, v3, 2p. [2821]
Appropriation for maintenance.

107. R-P of J. Smith. 18 Feb.
SR 2291, 51-2, v2, 1p. [2827] *or*
HR 3690, 51-2, v3, 1p. [2887]
Florida Indian war; 1836-37.

108. R-P of M. Stovall. 18 Feb.
SR 2292, 51-2, v2, 1p. [2827] *or*
HR 3581, 51-2, v3, 1p. [2887]
Florida Indian war; 1836.

109. R-P of W. Young. 18 Feb.
SR 2293, 51-2, v2, 1p. [2827] *or*
HR 3579, 51-2, v3, 1p. [2887]
Cherokee war; 1838.

110. R-P of N. Springer. 18 Feb.
SR 2294, 51-2, v2, 1p. [2827] *or*
HR 3679, 51-2, v3, 1p. [2887]
Creek war; 1836; Georgia.

111. R-P of F. Lambert. 18 Feb.
SR 2306, 51-2, v2, 1p. [2827] *or*
HR 3139, 51-1, v10, 1p. [2816]
Creek war; 1836.

112. Fort Abraham Lincoln. 18 Feb.
SR 2313, 51-2, v2, 2p. [2827]
In North Dakota, near the Sioux reservations.

113. On the Case of W. Hall. 18 Feb.
SR 2319, 51-2, v2, 7p. [2827]
Operations against the Indians in Oregon.

114. Sale of Firearms and Ammunition to Indians. 18 Feb.
HR 3861, 51-2, v4, 1p. [2888]
Bill to strictly control said sales.

115. R-P of R. Moore. 19 Feb.
SR 2321, 51-2, v2, 1p. [2827] *or*
HR 3567, 51-2, v3, 1p. [2887]
Black Hawk war; 1832.

116. R-C of the Estate of R. Crooks. 19 Feb.
SR 2329, 51-2, v2, 3p. [2827] *or*
HR 1702, 51-1, v6, 3p. [2812]
Chippewa indebtedness to this licensed trader; 1842-48.

117. R-C of the Estate of R. Crooks. 19 Feb.
SR 2330, 51-2, v2, 2p. [2827] *or*
HR 1634, 51-1, v5, 2p. [2811]
Licensed trader; indebtedness of the Menomonees, Chippewas, and Winnebagoes.

118. Sale of Timber Reserved for Chippewas. 21 Feb.
HR 3963, 51-2, v5, 2p. [2889]
Bill proposes to allow Chippewas to log and sell their own timber; Wisconsin; Menomonees already doing this.

119. R-P of E. Spalding. 23 Feb.
SR 2382, 51-2, v3, 1p. [2828] *or*
HR 3607, 51-2, v3, 1p. [2887]
Seminole war; 1836-37; Florida.

120. Issue of Arms to Certain States. 23 Feb.
HR 3968, 51-2, v5, 1p. [2889]
To North and South Dakota, Wyoming, Montana, and Nebraska; protection from Indian depredations.

121. Topeka, Okmulgee, and Gulf Railway Co. 23 Feb.
HR 3969, 51-2, v5, 1p. [2889]
Right of way through Indian Territory.

122. R-P of D. Sanders. 24 Feb.
SR 2419, 51-2, v3, 1p. [2828] *or*
HR 3886, 51-2, v5, 1p. [2889]
Indian war of 1836-37; Arkansas Volunteers.

123. R-C of P. Sinnott. 24 Feb.
HR 3985, 51-2, v5, 1p. [2889]
Indian agent at Grande Ronde agency in Oregon.

124. Indian Depredation Claims. 25 Feb.
HED 277, 51-2, v36, 27p. [2866]
Claims investigated for fiscal 1890; lists tribes involved, dates, etc.

125. Mission Indian Commission. 26 Feb.
SED 59, 51-2, v1, 2p. [2818]
Appropriation to cover expenses; California.

126. Carlisle Indian Training School. 26 Feb.
SED 61, 51-2, v1, 2p. [2818]
School does not have the staff to answer a Senate resol. requesting information.

127. R-P of M. Lemmon. 26 Feb.
SR 2432, 51-2, v3, 1p. [2828] *or*
HR 1858, 51-1, v6, 1p. [2812]
Service against Indians prior to 1812.

128. R-P of A. Junot. 26 Feb.
SR 2441, 51-2, v3, 1p. [2828] *or*
HR 3883, 51-2, v5, 1p. [2889]
Florida Indian war; 1840.

129. R-P of M. Brooks. 26 Feb.
SR 2443, 51-2, v3, 1p. [2828] *or*
HR 3885, 51-2, v5, 1p. [2889]
Creek war; 1838; Georgia.

130. R-P of S. Malone. 26 Feb.
SR 2444, 51-2, v3, 1p. [2828] *or*
HR 3868, 51-2, v4, 1p. [2888]
Indian war of 1836; Georgia Volunteers.

131. Brevet Rank in the Army. 26 Feb.
SR 2450, 51-2, v3, 2p. [2828]
For service in Indian campaigns.

132. R-P of R. Ware. 26 Feb.
SR 2474, 51-2, v3, 1p. [2828] *or*
HR 3869, 51-2, v4, 1p. [2888]
Florida Indian war; 1836.

133. R-P of C. McClelland. 26 Feb.
SR 2477, 51-2, v3, 1p. [2828] *or*
HR 3741, 51-2, v4, 1p. [2888]
Service in Indian campaigns.

134. Payment of Awards to Creek Indians. 26 Feb.
HR 4010, 51-2, v6, 6p. [2890]
For service in the Federal Army during the Civil War; treaties of 7 Aug. 1856, and 14 June 1866.

135. Allotments of Land on the Pottawatomie Reservation. 27 Feb.
SED 64, 51-2, v1, 21p. [2818]
Information on instructions governing said allotments; Indian Territory.

136. Claims Allowed by Accounting Officers. 27 Feb.
SED 67, 51-2, v1, 12p. [2818]
Includes claims involving Indians.

137. Annual Report of the American Historical Association. 27 Feb.
SMD 83, 51-2, v5, 310p. [2823]
Research relating to the American Indian.

138. R-P of N. Moon. 27 Feb.
SR 2522, 51-2, v3, 1p. [2828] *or*
HR 3882, 51-2, v5, 1p. [2889]
Creek war; 1837-38; Alabama.

139. Indian Depredation Claims. 28 Feb.
SMD 86, 51-2, v3, 4p. [2821]
Jurisdiction over said claims is conferred upon the Court of Claims.

140. R-P of G. Harlan. 28 Feb.
SR 2561, 51-2, v3, 1p. [2828] *or*
HR 3742, 51-2, v4, 1p. [2888]
Creek war; 1836; Georgia.

141. R-P of P. Frederick. 28 Feb.
SR 2568, 51-2, v3, 2p. [2828] *or*
HR 3875, 51-2, v4, 2p. [2888]
Service against Seminoles; Florida.

142. R-P of W. Hale. 28 Feb.
SR 2569, 51-2, v3, 1p. [2828] *or*
HR 3873, 51-2, v4, 1p. [2888]
Klamath River Indian war; 1855; California.

143. R-P of J. Brownlee. 28 Feb.
SR 2570, 51-2, v3, 1p. [2828] *or*
HR 3945, 51-2, v5, 1p. [2889]
Oregon Indian war; 1855-56.

144. Amendment of the Revised Statutes. 28 Feb.
HR 4027, 51-2, v6, 2p. [2890]
Pensions for service in State militias against Indians; Sioux outbreak of 1862 in Minnesota.

145. Omaha and Winnebago Reservations. 3 Mar.
SED 73, 51-2, v1, 10p. [2818]
Indians are leasing to whites the lands which have been allotted to them in severalty.

146. Statements of Appropriations. 3 Mar.
SMD 95, 51-2, v7, 270p. [2825]
Made during the 51st Congress, 2d session; Indian expenses.

147. Bulletin of the U.S. Fish Commission, Volume 9 for 1889. (no date)
HMD 131, 51-2, v13, 515p. [2881]
Includes report of use of natives in the salmon industry of Alaska.

148. Official Register of the U.S. 1 July.
HMD 50 (pts. 1 and 2), 52-1, v27-28, 2616p. [2985-2986]
List of persons employed by the U.S. government; Indian service.

149. Annual Report of the Smithsonian Institution. 1 July.
HMD 334 (pts. 1 and 2), 52-1, v43-44, 1644p. [3001-3002]
Research concerned with the American Indian.

150. Disbursements of the Indian Dept. 4 Dec.
HED 8, 52-1, v29, 25p. [2949]
Year ending 30 June 1891.

151. Congressional Directory. 5 Dec.
SMD 1 (pts. 1-3), 52-1, v1, 1000p. [2903]
Duties of the CIA.

152. Annual Report of the Sec. of the Treasury. 7 Dec.
HED 2, 52-1, v23, 1004p. [2943]
Year ending 30 June 1891; Indian expenses.

153. Estimates of Appropriations. 7 Dec.
HED 5, 52-1, v26, 402p. [2946]
Year ending 30 June 1893; Indian expenses.

154. Annual Message to Congress with Documents; Pres. Harrison. 9 Dec.
HED 1, 52-1, v1-22, 17201p. [2920-2942]
Negotiations with Indians for reduction of their reservations; education of the Indians; Sioux outbreak of 1890; land cessions in Oklahoma Territory; annual report of the Sec. of War (Serials 2921-2930); annual

report of the Sec. of Interior (Serials 2933-2939); annual report of the Gen. Land Office (Serial 2933); annual report of the CIA (Serial 2934); etc.

155. Survey of Lands in Arizona. 22 Dec.
SED 10, 52-1, v1, 3p. [2892]
Granted to the Atlantic and Pacific Railroad Co.; through the Navajo, Moqui, Hualipai, and Zuni reservations.

156. Umatilla Indian Reservation, Oregon. 22 Dec.
SMD 27, 52-1, v2, 2p. [2904]
On sale of lands in said reservation.

157. Annual Report of the Bureau of Ethnology, 1885-86. (no date)
HMD 107, 52-1, v31, 452p. [2989]
Research related to the American Indian; includes Indian linguistic families, Ojibwa and Cherokee ceremonial, etc.

158. Annual Report of the Bureau of Ethnology, 1886-87. (no date)
HMD 295, 52-1, v41, 334p. [2999]
Research related to the American Indian; includes Pueblo architecture, Navajo ceremonial practices, etc.

1892

1. Cheyenne and Arapaho Lands. 5 Jan.
HED 10, 52-1, v29, 1p. [2949]
Appropriation for allotments to be made in Oklahoma Territory; agreement of Oct., 1890, calling for land cessions.

2. U.S. Board on Geographic Names. 5 Jan.
HED 16, 52-1, v29, 56p. [2949]
Standardization of spellings; many derived from Indian names.

3. Contingent Expenses of the Interior Dept. 5 Jan.
HED 47, 52-1, v33, 18p. [2953]
For fiscal 1891; OIA.

4. Expenditures pf the Smithsonian Institution. 5 Jan.
HMD 28, 52-1, v1, 28p. [2959]
Expenses of ethnographic and archaeological research related to the American Indian.

5. Cession of Tonkawa Indian Lands. 6 Jan.
SED 13, 52-1, v1, 15p. [2892]
Agreement of 21 Oct. 1891; cession of lands in that portion of Oklahoma Territory known as the "Cherokee Outlet."

6. Cession of Lands in Oklahoma Territory. 6 Jan.
SED 14, 52-1, v1, 18p. [2892]
Under the agreement of 4 June 1891 with the Wichita and affiliated bands of Indians.

7. Cession of Lands in Washington. 6 Jan.
SED 15, 52-1, v1, 29p. [2892]
Cession of a portion of the Colville reservation; agreement of 9 May 1891 with the Colvilles, Nez Percés, and other tribes residing on the reservation.

8. Disposition of Timber on Indian Reservations. 7 Jan.
SED 16, 52-1, v1, 21p. [2892]
Marketing of timber on Chippewa reservations in Wisconsin.

9. Subsistence of the Sioux. 11 Jan.
HED 64, 52-1, v33, 2p. [2953]
Appropriation needed to off-set an urgent deficiency; discontent growing.

10. Expenditures for Indian Supplies. 11 Jan.
HED 66, 52-1, v33, 9p. [2953]
Statements for fiscal 1891; relief for destitute Indians.

11. Warm Springs Indian Reservation, Oregon. 11 Jan.
HED 69, 52-1, v33, 78p. [2953]
Report and testimony concerning the location of the northern boundary of the reservation.

12. Shoshone and Arapaho Indians. 11 Jan.
HED 70, 52-1, v33, 61p. [2953]
Cession and relinquishment of part of the Wind River reservation in Wyoming; agreement of 2 Oct. 1891.

13. Pah-Ute Indians. 11 Jan.
HED 71, 52-1, v33, 26p. [2953]
Cession and relinquishment of part of the Pyramid Lake reservation in Nevada; agreement of 17 Oct. 1891.

14. Kickapoo Indians. 11 Jan.
HED 72, 52-1, v33, 18p. [2953]
Cession of the Kickapoo reservation in Oklahoma Territory; agreement of 21 June 1891.

15. Legalizing the Records of the Indian Office. 12 Jan.
HED 73, 52-1, v33, 5p. [2953]
Bill legalizing all deed to land, etc.,

made in the Indian Office; land grants to Indians, etc.

16. Distribution of Public Documents. 12 Jan.
HED 74, 52-1, v33, 138p. [2953]
During fiscal 1891; including annual reports of the CIA, and Board of Indian Com'rs.

17. The Public Printing. 13 Jan.
SR 18, 52-1, v1, 483p. [2911]
Includes publication of reports from the Indian Office.

18. R-C of Persons Residing in Nevada. 13 Jan.
SR 21, 52-1, v1, 12p. [2911] *or*
HR 117, 52-1, v1, 12p. [3042]
For expenditures made during the Pah-Ute war of 1860 in Utah Territory.

19. Agreements with Certain Indians. 18 Jan.
SED 17, 52-1, v1, 11p. [2892]
On ratification of agreements made with several tribes in Montana; agreements of 18 Mar. 1887 (Upper and Middle bands of Spokanes), 21 Apr. 1887 (Lower Pend d'Oreilles or Calispels), and 27 Apr. 1887 (Flatheads, Pend d'Oreilles, and Kootenais).

20. New York Indians *vs.* the U.S. 18 Jan.
SMD 46, 52-1, v2, 7p. [2904]
Findings of the Court of Claims; concerning an unexecuted stipulation of the treaty of 15 Jan. 1838.

21. R-C of J. Little and H. Williams. 19 Jan.
SR 41, 52-1, v1, 4p. [2911] *or*
HR 786, 52-1, v3, 5p. [3044]
Lease of mineral lands in Kansas and Nebraska from the Iowa Indians; 1870.

22. R-C of the Reps. of S. Marston. 19 Jan.
SR 47, 52-1, v1, 2p. [2911]
Late Indian agent at the Union agency in Indian Territory; 1876-78.

23. Hutchison and Southern Railroad Co. 19 Jan.
HR 3, 52-1, v1, 3p. [3042]
Amendment to the act granting said company a right of way through Indian Territory.

24. Fond du Lac Chippewa Indians. 20 Jan.
HED 80, 52-1, v34, 3p. [2954]
Appropriation for said tribe in Minnesota; timber depredations upon their lands.

25. Umatilla Indian Reservation, Oregon. 20 Jan.
HED 82, 52-1, v34, 2p. [2954]
Appropriation for allotment of lands in severalty; sale of lands.

26. Legal Costs Incurred by Indians. 20 Jan.
HED 83, 52-1, v34, 4p. [2954]
Appropriation to pay said costs incurred in contests relating to public lands.

27. L-C of J. Gilman. 20 Jan.
HED 86, 52-1, v34, 12p. [2954]
Services performed at the San Carlos Indian agency, Arizona.

28. R-C of P. Sinnott. 21 Jan.
SR 78, 52-1, v1, 5p. [2911] *or*
HR 685, 52-1, v2, 5p. [3043]
Late Indian agent at the Grande Ronde agency in Oregon; 1872-1885.

29. R-C of H. Shipley. 21 Jan.
SR 80, 52-1, v1, 3p. [2911] *or*
HR 2215, 52-2, v1, 1p. [3140]
Services performed at the Nez Percé agency in Idaho; 1880.

30. Mineral Resources of the U.S. 23 Jan.
HMD 296, 52-1, v42, 679p. [3000]
Coal in Indian Territory.

31. Estimates of Deficiencies. 26 Jan.
HED 94, 52-1, v26, 26p. [2946]
Appropriations for fiscal 1892; Indian expenses.

32. Mission Indians in California. 26 Jan.
HED 96, 52-1, v34, 18p. [2954]
Report of the Mission Indian Commission; recommendations for the relief of said tribe.

33. Attorney for the Mission Indians, California. 26 Jan.
HED 97, 52-1, v34, 3p. [2954]
Appropriation to continue the employment of a special attorney.

34. R-P of E. Starr. 28 Jan.
SR 135, 52-1, v1, 1p. [2911]
Service in Creek and Seminole wars.

35. Chippewa Indians in Minnesota. 29 Jan.
HED 104, 52-1, v34, 2p. [2954]
Appropriation for relief of Indians; fiscal 1893.

36. Resol. of Sen. Perkins. 1 Feb.
SMD 56, 52-1, v2, 1p. [2904]
Payments to be made to the Citizen band of Pottawatomies residing in Oklahoma and Kansas; agreement ratified in 1891.

37. Boundary Between Nebraska and South Dakota. 3 Feb.
SR 152, 52-1, v2, 2p. [2912]
Involves the Pine Ridge and Rosebud reservations; Sioux.

38. Mem. of County Com'rs in Washington State. 4 Feb.
SMD 62, 52-1, v2, 2p. [2904]
Ask removal of all restrictions under which lands within the Puyallup Indian reservation are held.

39. Fort Walla Walla Military Reservation. 4 Feb.
SR 167, 52-1, v2, 2p. [2912]
Appropriation for improvements; serves as a menace to Indians on the Nez Percé, Yakima, Umatilla, Warm Springs, Coeur d'Alene, Colville, and Moses reservations; Oregon, Idaho, and Washington.

40. Payments to Delaware Indians. 5 Feb.
HR 122, 52-1, v1, 2p. [3042]
For loss of improvements on lands over which the Leavenworth, Pawnee, and Western Railroad Co. was granted a right of way.

41. Klamath River Reservation. 5 Feb.
HR 161, 52-1, v1, 2p. [3042]
Bill providing for sale of this reservation; not used by Indians since 1861-62.

42. Mines and Mining in Indian Territory. 5 Feb.
HR 162, 52-1, v1, 8p. [3042]
Bill to regulate the mines; safety of miners, etc.

43. R-C of the Estate of B. West. 6 Feb.
HR 182, 52-1, v1, 9p. [3042]
Saline deposits appropriated for the use of the Cherokee Nation by the Cherokee council in 1843.

44. Indian Students at the Hampton Institute. 9 Feb.
SED 31, 52-1, v1, 87p. [2892]
Résumé and history of each student who has attended this school in Virginia; follow-up reports on activities after leaving the school.

45. Northern Pacific Railroad Co. 9 Feb.
SED 32, 52-1, v1, 27p. [2892]
On ratification of an agreement made 13 Jan. 1885 with Indians of the Yakima reservation in Washington; grants right of way across said reservation.

46. R-P of T. Chill. 9 Feb.
SR 185, 52-1, v2, 1p. [2912] *or*
HR 2352, 52-2, v2, 1p. [3141]
Black Hawk war; 1832.

47. R-C of Inhabitants of Chelan, Washington. 9 Feb.
HR 237, 52-1, v1, 2p. [3042]
Town located on lands released from the Columbia Indian reservation.

48. R-C of Florida. 10 Feb.
SR 198, 52-1, v2, 15p. [2912]
Expenses of the Seminole war; 1856-57.

49. R-C of A. Babcock. 10 Feb.
SR 199, 52-1, v2, 2p. [2912]
Settler makes improvements on lands located within the Grande Ronde Indian reservation; Oregon.

50. War Claims of California, Nevada, and Oregon. 10 Feb.
HR 254, 52-1, v1, 45p. [3042]
Suppression of hostile Indians during the Civil War period; etc.

51. Report of the Puyallup Indian Commission. 11 Feb.
SED 34, 52-1, v1, 90p. [2892]
Investigation of sales made of lands allotted to Indians in severalty; Washington State.

52. R-C of Florida. 11 Feb.
HR 273, 52-1, v1, 104p. [3042]
For expenditures in the suppression of Indian hostilities, and for purchase of State bonds by the Indian trust fund.

53. On the Case of W. Spencer. 12 Feb.
HR 299, 52-1, v1, 5p. [3042] *or*
HR 1665, 52-1, v7, 6p. [3048]
Service in Sioux troubles of 1857; Minnesota.

54. U.S. Courts in Idaho. 13 Feb.
HR 309, 52-1, v1, 2p. [3042]
Numerous cases concern sale of liquor to Indians within the State's two northern Indian reservations, etc.

55. Indian Appropriation Bill. 13 Feb.
HR 325, 52-1, v2, 3p. [3043]
Year ending 30 June 1893.

56. Mem. of the Mayor and City Council of Tacoma, Washington. 15 Feb.
SMD 73, 52-1, v2, 2p. [2904]
Removal of restrictions concerning land in the Puyallup Indian reservation.

57. Marinette and Western Railroad Co. 15 Feb.
HR 347, 52-1, v2, 1p. [3043] *or*
HR 692, 52-1, v3, 3p. [3044]
Right of way through the Menomonee reservation in Wisconsin; title to timber remains with Indians.

58. R-C of Rev. Travis. 15 Feb.
HR 348, 52-1, v2, 1p. [3043]

Adverse report of Com. on Indian Affairs.

59. Uncompahgre Indian Reservation. 16 Feb.
SR 240, 52-1, v2, 3p. [2912]
Portion of the reserve to be returned to the public domain because of the discovery of minerals; Ute Indians.

60. Appointment of an Inspector of Mines. 17 Feb.
HED 132, 52-1, v34, 3p. [2954]
For Indian Territory; disaster at Krebs.

61. Payment of Certain Per Diem Clerks. 17 Feb.
HED 133, 52-1, v34, 3p. [2954]
In the Indian Office.

62. Gainsville, McCallister, and St. Louis Railway Co. 17 Feb.
HR 386, 52-1, v2, 1p. [3043]
Right of way through Indian Territory.

63. Gainsville, Oklahoma, and Gulf Railway Co. 17 Feb.
HR 387, 52-1, v2, 1p. [3043]
Right of way through Indian Territory.

64. An Act to Pay Choctaws and Chickasaws. 18 Feb.
SED 42, 52-1, v5, 41p. [2900]
For lands in Oklahoma Territory now occupied by Cheyennes and Arapahoes.

65. Reports on Indian Schools. 18 Feb.
SED 43, 52-1, v5, 1p. [2900]
Transmittal letter for reports on the Santee Normal, Lincoln, Wabash, Rensselaer, and St. Ignatius schools.

66. Mem. of North Dakota Citizens. 18 Feb.
SMD 75, 52-1, v2, 3p. [2904]
Ask removal of the Chippewas from the Turtle Mountain region; settlement of land title disputes there.

67. Indian Schools in South Dakota. 18 Feb.
SR 260, 52-1, v2, 3p. [2912]
To be established near Chamberlain and Rapid City; Sioux Indians.

68. Military Posts in Alaska. 19 Feb.
SR 262, 52-1, v2, 2p. [2912]
Few Indians in the Yukon River valley; post there would be useless.

69. Exploration of the Interior of Alaska. 19 Feb.
SR 264, 52-1, v2, 2p. [2912]
Fur trade with the natives residing in the interior.

70. Mem. of Citizens of Tacoma, Washington. 23 Feb.
SMD 78, 52-1, v2, 2p. [2904]
Removal of restrictions concerning lands within the Puyallup Indian reservation.

71. On the Case of R. Carrick. 25 Feb.
SR 279, 52-1, v2, 6p. [2912]
Service in Indian campaigns in the West; 1867-70.

72. Jurisdiction of the Supreme Court. 25 Feb.
SR 281, 52-1, v2, 66p. [2912]
Extended over tribal courts of the Five Civilized Tribes; etc.

73. R-C of D. Boutwell. 25 Feb.
HR 433, 52-1, v2, 1p. [3043]
Indian Home Guards; Civil War.

74. Mem. of Wichitas, Caddoes, and Affiliated Tribes. 26 Feb.
SED 46, 52-1, v5, 25p. [2900]
On their claims to the lands they occupy in Oklahoma Territory; agreement of 4 June 1891 for cession of said lands.

75. Mem. of the Chickasaw Indians. 26 Feb.
SMD 82, 52-1, v2, 13p. [2904]
On whether lands ceded by the treaty of 28 Apr. 1866 were ceded "in trust," or were ceded "absolutely" to the U.S.; lands occupied by the Cheyenne and Arapaho Indians only temporarily to be opened for settlement.

76. Claims of Deputy Marshals, Oklahoma. 26 Feb.
HED 144, 52-1, v35, 36p. [2955]
Many appointed by the U.S. marshal in Indian Territory.

77. Deficiencies for the Indian Service. 26 Feb.
HED 145, 52-1, v35, 9p. [2955]
Appropriations needed for removal of certain Flatheads to the Jocko reservation, and for support of the Indian school in Carson City, Nevada.

78. Opening Lands to Settlement. 27 Feb.
HR 478, 52-1, v2, 1p. [3043]
Acquired under an agreement with the Cheyenne and Arapaho Indians.

79. Resol. of Sen. Morgan. 29 Feb.
SMD 83, 52-1, v2, 1p. [2904]
On establishment of a military school for Indians west of the Mississippi River.

80. Sale of Stone and Timber Lands. 29 Feb.
HR 482, 52-1, v2, 3p. [3043]
Lands within Indian reservations are exempted.

81. R-P of E. Boatright. 29 Feb.
HR 490, 52-1, v2, 1p. [3043]
Black Hawk war; 1832.

82. Payments to Yankton Sioux Indians. 2 Mar.
SR 302, 52-1, v2, 16p. [2912]
Those Sioux who served Gen. Sully in his 1864 campaign against hostile Sioux who had taken part in the 1862 war in Minnesota.

83. Permanent and Indefinite Appropriations. 4 Mar.
HED 152, 52-1, v35, 7p. [2955]
Includes Indian appropriations.

84. Supplies for Natives on the Seal Islands. 5 Mar.
HED 154, 52-1, v35, 2p. [2955]
Appropriation for fiscal 1893; Alaska.

85. Stockbridge and Munsee Indians. 7 Mar.
HR 558, 52-1, v2, 20p. [3043]
Dispute between tribal members over tribal membership.

86. Canal Across an Indian Reservation. 9 Mar.
SED 54, 52-1, v5, 5p. [2900]
Construction of an irrigation canal across the Colorado River reservation; Ute Indians; California; treaty and agreement stipulations.

87. Jurisdiction over the Bering Sea. 9 Mar.
SED 55, 52-1, v5, 102p. [2900]
Arbitration between Britain and the U.S.; involves natives of the seal islands of Alaska.

88. Government Post in Minnesota. 9 Mar.
HED 158, 52-1, v35, 6p. [2955]
Appropriation to establish a post on the Rainy Lake River; timber depredations on the Red Lake Indian reservation.

89. Arid Lands of the U.S. 9 Mar.
HR 569, 52-1, v2, 12p. [3043]
Bill providing for the disposal of said lands; the Cherokee Strip (or Outlet) and other Indian lands are exempted.

90. Creation of a Judicial District. 9 Mar.
HR 571, 52-1, v2, 1p. [3043]
In Kansas; extends jurisdiction over the Quapaw reservation in Indian Territory.

91. Cherokee Indian Land Cession. 10 Mar.
SED 56, 52-1, v5, 39p. [2900]
Agreement of 4 Jan. 1892 providing for the cession of the "Cherokee outlet"; report of the Cherokee Commission.

92. R-C of Nebraska. 10 Mar.
SR 352, 52-1, v2, 3p. [2912] *or*
HR 1541, 52-1, v5, 2p. [3046]
Expenses of repelling a threatened invasion by the Sioux in 1890-91; battle of Wounded Knee.

93. R-C of G. Jocknick. 10 Mar.
HR 612, 52-1, v2, 2p. [3043]
Witness to payments made to the Eastern Cherokees of North Carolina; arrested for attempted fraud.

94. Revision of Pension Laws. 10 Mar.
HR 614, 52-1, v2, 2p. [3043]
Soldiers from seceding States who served in Indian wars relieved of necessity of proving their loyalty.

95. Establishment of a Government Post. 14 Mar.
SMD 94, 52-1, v2, 13p. [2904]
On the Rainy Lake River in Minnesota; timber depredations on the Red Lake Indian reservation.

96. Mem. of the Choctaw Nation. 14 Mar.
SMD 95, 52-1, v2, 25p. [2904]
Agreement between the U.S. and the Cheyennes and Arapahoes to open land up for settlement; Choctaws insist that these lands belong to them, as they were merely held in trust by the U.S.

97. Mission Indian Commission. 14 Mar.
HR 691, 52-1, v3, 1p. [3044]
Bill to carry out certain of their recommendations; establishment of a reservation; claims of settlers and the Southern Pacific Railroad Co. are satisfied.

98. Arkansas State Bonds. 14 Mar.
HR 693, 52-1, v3, 13p. [3044]
Held by the U.S. for the Indian trust fund.

99. R-P of O. Goodwin. 15 Mar.
SR 384, 52-1, v2, 1p. [2912] *or*
HR 2209, 52-2, v1, 1p. [3140]
Service in Modoc war; Oregon.

100. Affairs at Rosebud and Pine Ridge Reservations. 16 Mar.
SED 58, 52-1, v5, 185p. [2900]
Adjustment of differences between the Sioux of said reservations in South Dakota; boundary dispute, etc.; council proceedings.

101. Admission of New Mexico. 16 Mar.
HR 736, 52-1, v3, 45p. [3044]
Indian title to land not affected; acreage of the Mescalero Apache, Navajo, Zuni, and Pueblo reservations.

102. Admission of Arizona. 16 Mar.
HR 737, 52-1, v3, 30p. [3044]
Dread of the Apache has disappeared; Indian reservations.

103. Indian Appropriation Bill. 17 Mar.
SR 400, 52-1, v2, 6p. [2912]
Year ending 30 June 1893.

104. On the Case of D. Ransom. 18 Mar.
SR 408, 52-1, v2, 4p. [2912] *or*
HR 950, 52-1, v4, 4p. [3045] *or*
HR 1766, 52-1, v7, 4p. [3048]
Service against hostile Indians in Washington Territory; 1858.

105. Report on the Cherokee Outlet. 21 Mar.
SED 63, 52-1, v5, 28p. [2900]
Investigation of Cherokee title to these lands under various treaties and agreements; legality of the agreement made concerning cession of said lands.

106. Protection of Miners in the Territories. 21 Mar.
HED 169, 52-1, v35, 2p. [2955]
Includes Indian Territory.

107. R-C of C. Relf. 22 Mar.
SR 417, 52-1, v2, 2p. [2912]
Seminole depredations; 1836; Florida.

108. Military Post Near Helena, Montana. 22 Mar.
SR 421, 52-1, v2, 3p. [2912] *or*
HR 623, 52-1, v2, 3p. [3043]
Bill to establish such a post; railroads there would permit rapid movement of troops to Indian assemblages.

109. R-C of M. Thierer. 23 Mar.
SR 429, 52-1, v2, 1p. [2912]
Alcohol seized in Indian country by troops from Fort Man.

110. Survivors of Indian Wars. 23 Mar.
HR 818, 52-1, v3, 3p. [3044]
During 1832-42; Black Hawk, Creek, and Seminole wars; Cherokee disturbances and removal.

111. R-C of Rep. of G. McDougall. 23 Mar.
HR 839, 52-1, v3, 8p. [3044]
Supplies to California Indians in 1850.

112. Sundry Civil Appropriation Bill. 24 Mar.
HR 847, 52-1, v3, 45p. [3044]
For fiscal 1893; defense costs in Indian depredation claims, etc.

113. Adjustment of Certain Sales of Land. 25 Mar.
SR 445, 52-1, v2, 11p. [2912] *or*
SR 653, 52-1, v3, 11p. [2913] *or*
HR 1793, 52-1, v7, 15p. [3048]
Lands in the late Otoe and Missouria reservation in Nebraska and Kansas; lands sold above appraised value.

114. Citizen Band of Pottawatomies. 25 Mar.
HR 851, 52-1, v3, 1p. [3044]
Action of the Com. on Indian Affairs.

115. On the Case of W. Hugo. 26 Mar.
HR 873, 52-1, v3, 10p. [3044]
Service against Apaches in New Mexico.

116. Employment of Attorneys by Indians. 28 Mar.
SED 65, 52-1, v5, 4p. [2900]
To look after their interests in adjudication of depredation claims.

117. Resol. of Sen. Wolcott. 28 Mar.
SMD 108, 52-1, v5, 1p. [2907]
Asks Pres. to refrain from allotting lands in severalty to the Southern Utes at their present locale due to a pending removal of the tribe.

118. R-C of the Estate of J. Whitfield. 28 Mar.
SR 451, 52-1, v2, 2p. [2912] *or*
HR 1407, 52-1, v5, 2p. [3046]
Surety on the bond of an Indian agent in Nebraska Territory in 1857; land office register in Kansas; sale of Delaware and other Indian trust lands.

119. R-C of D. Woodson. 28 Mar.
HR 880, 52-1, v3, 4p. [3044]
Special agent for the sale of Delaware and Wea trust lands in Kansas.

120. R-P of D. Land. 28 Mar.
HR 899, 52-1, v3, 1p. [3044]
Florida Indian war; 1839-40.

121. R-P of A. Landes. 28 Mar.
HR 901, 52-1, v3, 1p. [3044]
Black Hawk war; 1832.

122. R-C of I. Owen. 30 Mar.
SR 464, 52-1, v3, 3p. [2913] *or*
HR 1496, 52-1, v5, 2p. [3046]
Service against hostile Indians in California; 1851.

123. R-C of G. Ihrie. 31 Mar.
SR 476, 52-1, v3, 3p. [2913]
Rogue River Indian war; 1856; California.

124. R-P of H. Bethards. 4 Apr.
HR 975, 52-1, v4, 1p. [3045]
Florida Indian war; 1856-57.

125. R-P of J. Meigs. 5 Apr.
SR 493, 52-1, v3, 1p. [2913] *or*
HR 2444, 52-2, v2, 1p. [3141]
Seminole war; 1835-36; Florida.

126. R-P of A. Northrup. 5 Apr.
SR 495, 52-1, v3, 3p. [2913] *or*
HR 2066 (pts. 1 and 2), 52-1, v10, 3p. [3051]
Service in Sioux outbreak of 1862 in Minnesota.

127. R-P of J. Offley. 5 Apr.
SR 508, 52-1, v3, 2p. [2913]
Service in Indian Territory, and in South Dakota in 1890-91.

128. R-P of J. Dean. 5 Apr.
SR 509, 52-1, v3, 1p. [2913] *or*
HR 1863, 52-1, v7, 1p. [3048]
Florida Indian war; 1840-41.

129. Agreement with Certain Indians. 9 Apr.
HR 1035, 52-1, v4, 5p. [3045]
At the Colville reservation in Washington; cession of lands to the U.S.

130. Indian Appropriation Bill. 11 Apr.
HR 1052, 52-1, v4, 1p. [3045]
For fiscal 1893; Com. on Indian Affairs does not concur with Senate amendments, and recommends a conference.

131. R-P of M. Turner. 12 Apr.
SR 535, 52-1, v3, 1p. [2913] *or*
HR 56, 52-1, v1, 1p. [3042]
Florida Indian war; 1836.

132. R-P of L. Lane. 12 Apr.
SR 536, 52-1, v3, 1p. [2913] *or*
HR 221, 52-1, v1, 1p. [3042]
Indian war of 1836; Georgia militia.

133. R-P of Tendoy. 12 Apr.
SR 537, 52-1, v3, 2p. [2913] *or*
HR 1830, 52-1, v7, 2p. [3048]
Chief of the Bannock, Shoshone, and Sheepeater tribes of Indians; pension recommended for service against the Nez Percés in 1877, etc.

134. Denison and Northern Railway Co. 12 Apr.
HR 1060, 52-1, v4, 1p. [3045]
Right of way through Indian Territory.

135. Resol. of Sen. Jones. 13 Apr.
SMD 126, 52-1, v5, 1p. [2907]
Payments to the Choctaw and Chickasaw Nations for their interest in the Cheyenne and Arapaho reservation of Indian Territory.

136. Choctaw and Chickasaw Indians. 13 Apr.
SR 552, 52-1, v3, 35p. [2913] *or*
HR 1661, 52-1, v7, 35p. [3048]
On the proposed act to pay said Indians for lands now occupied by the Cheyenne and Arapaho Indians; land title at issue, with various treaty stipulations involved; lands are being ceded to the government, and will be part of Oklahoma.

137. Chief Clerk for the Indian Bureau. 13 Apr.
HED 193, 52-1, v35, 2p. [2955]
CIA explains need for a chief clerk.

138. R-C of Citizens of Oregon, Idaho, and Washington. 14 Apr.
SR 559, 52-1, v3, 6p. [2913]
Service in the Nez Percé, Bannock, and Shoshone wars; 1877-78.

139. R-C of N. Gonzales. 14 Apr.
HR 1073, 52-1, v4, 2p. [3045]
Navajo depredations of 1863 in New Mexico.

140. Changing the Boundary of the Uncompahgre Reservation. 14 Apr.
HR 1076, 52-1, v4, 4p. [3045]
Restoration of a portion of this Ute reservation to the public domain; Utah Territory.

141. Sale of Timber in Wisconsin. 14 Apr.
HR 1077, 52-1, v4, 1p. [3045]
From Chippewa reservations (Lac du Flambeau, La Pointe, and Lac Court Oreilles).

142. On the Case of A. Anderson. 15 Apr.
HR 1082, 52-1, v4, 2p. [3045]
Service in Navajo campaign of 1861-62.

143. Domesticated Reindeer in Alaska. 15 Apr.
HR 1093, 52-1, v4, 1p. [3045]
Would permit natives there to be self-supporting.

144. Reserving Lands in Oklahoma. 15 Apr.
HR 1095, 52-1, v4, 2p. [3045]
To be sold after Oklahoma becomes a State in order to support education, etc.; list of Indian reservations, and their surplus acreage after allotment; these lands "may yet become" a part of Oklahoma out of which this reserve may be made.

145. Support of the Cheyennes and Arapahoes. 16 Apr.
HED 198, 52-1, v35, 4p. [2955]
Appropriation for fiscal 1893; Oklahoma Territory.

146. Citizenship of Indians. 16 Apr.
HR 1130, 52-1, v4, 1p. [3045]
Bill granting citizenship to Indians when they reach the age of 21, provided that they have had schooling.

147. Agreement with the Cherokees. 18 Apr.
SR 570, 52-1, v3, 1p. [2913]
Com. on Printing recommends additional copies be made.

148. Claims Allowed by Accounting Officers. 18 Apr.
HED 199, 52-1, v35, 58p. [2955]
Includes claims involving Indians.

149. Chippewa Indians. 19 Apr.
SR 571, 52-1, v3, 7p. [2913]
On fulfillment of the treaties of 1837, 1842, 1854, and 1855; payments for land cessions.

150. Sale of Timber. 19 Apr.
SR 573, 52-1, v3, 1p. [2913]
From the Menomonee reservation in Wisconsin.

151. On the Case of J. Long. 19 Apr.
HR 1140, 52-1, v4, 11p. [3045]
Indian agent at Detroit, Michigan; 1869-70.

152. Oregon and Washington War Claims. 20 Apr.
HED 203, 52-1, v37, 1p. [2957]
Indian war of 1855-56.

153. Deficiency Estimates. 21 Apr.
HED 205, 52-1, v26, 21p. [2946]
Appropriations for fiscal 1892; Indian expenses.

154. Indians of the Standing Rock Agency. 22 Apr.
SED 84, 52-1, v6, 12p. [2901]
Granting pensions and medals to families of Indian policemen; service in the engagement at Sitting Bull's camp in 1890; Sioux Indians of North Dakota.

155. Schools Within the Chickasaw Cession. 25 Apr.
SR 600, 52-1, v3, 3p. [2913]
Bill authorizing Mississippi to sell lands heretofore appropriated to the use of schools in the Chickasaw cession.

156. Deputy Marshals in Oklahoma. 25 Apr.
HED 210, 52-1, v37, 6p. [2957]
Appointments of the U.S. marshal in Indian Territory; service on the Iowa, Sac, and Fox lands.

157. L-C of A. English. 26 Apr.
HED 215, 52-1, v37, 4p. [2957]
Legal defense of Apache Indians accused of various crimes in Arizona.

158. Southern Ute Indians, Colorado. 26 Apr.
HR 1205 (pts. 1 and 2), 52-1, v4, 5p. [3045]
Agreement calling for their removal to a new reservation in Utah Territory.

159. R-C of W. Shimmins and G. McPherson. 28 Apr.
HR 1226, 52-1, v4, 4p. [3045]
Contract for timber made with the Indian Dept.; Nevada.

160. On the Case of W. Fletcher. 29 Apr.
HR 1244, 52-1, v4, 2p. [3045]
Service against hostile Indians in Texas.

161. On the Case of D. Stanley. 29 Apr.
HR 1245, 52-1, v4, 7p. [3045]
Service against Cheyennes in 1857, and in Indian Territory.

162. Allotments of Lands to Certain Indian Tribes. 2 May.
SR 615, 52-1, v3, 53p. [2913]
Sec. of Interior is enforcing the allotment, or "Dawes" act at the Quapaw agency in Indian Territory; involves the Western Miamies, Weas, Kaskaskias, Piankeshaws, Peorias, Ottawas, Modocs, Eastern Shawnees, Senecas, Wyandottes, and Quapaws; citizenship for tribes is recommended.

163. R-P of W. Harllee. 3 May.
SR 617, 52-1, v3, 1p. [2913]
Florida Indian war; 1837.

164. Lands of the Otoes and Missourias. 5 May.
SED 93, 52-1, v6, 5p. [2901]
Amendment to the act providing for the sale of said lands in Kansas and Nebraska; reduction of the time period during which lands allotted to Indians are not subject to alienation by sale or lease.

165. R-C of J. Bridger. 5 May.
SR 625, 52-1, v3, 23p. [2913] *or*
HR 1576, 52-1, v5, 24p. [3046]
Trade with the Indians during 1843-57 in Utah Territory; Fort Bridger.

166. Sale of Indian Lands in Kansas. 6 May.
SED 94, 52-1, v6, 6p. [2901]
Belonging to the Swan Creek and

Black River Chippewas, and the Munsee or Christian Indians.

167. Records of the OIA. 7 May.
HR 1316, 52-1, v5, 1p. [3046]
Act legalizing deed, land grants, etc., made in the OIA.

168. Settlement of Accounts with Certain States. 9 May.
SR 775, 52-1, v4, 6p. [2914]
Proceeds from sales of public lands; Choctaw, Chickasaw, and Creek cessions in Mississippi and Alabama; Indian reservation lands in North and South Dakota, Wyoming, and Montana.

169. Spokane and Pelouse Railway Co. 10 May.
SR 641, 52-1, v3, 2p. [2913]
Construction deadline extended; being built through the Nez Percé reservation in Idaho.

170. 11th and 12th Annual Reports of the Bureau of Ethnology. 10 May.
HR 1338, 52-1, v5, 1p. [3046]
Bill on printing the reports.

171. Students at the Hampton Institute. 11 May.
SR 655, 52-1, v3, 1p. [2913]
Com. on Printing recommends additional copies of this report on Indian students be printed.

172. R-C of W. Hall. 11 May.
HR 1361, 52-1, v5, 2p. [3046]
Son of an Indian woman sold into slavery.

173. Indians on the Colville Reservation. 12 May.
SR 664, 52-1, v3, 5p. [2913]
Bill to ratify an agreement with said Indians; Sen. Com. on Indian Affairs does not recommend ratification, as the Indians never had title to these lands, and the U.S. should not pay for what already belongs to it.

174. Miami Indians. 12 May.
HR 1380, 52-1, v5, 9p. [3046]
Bill to reimburse the Miamies of Indiana for moneys improperly withheld from them; treaty of 1854.

175. Indians of the White Earth Agency. 13 May.
SED 99, 52-1, v6, 15p. [2901]
On allotments to these Chippewas in Minnesota; treaty of 18 Apr. 1867.

176. Sale of the Klamath Indian Reservation. 13 May.
SMD 153, 52-1, v5, 1p. [2907]
House and Senate disagreement concerning said sale, and allotments of land to be made.

177. Land Patents to Indians. 17 May.
SED 101, 52-1, v6, 1p. [2901]
On the surrender of, and cancellation of patents in certain cases.

178. Additional Justices for the Supreme Court of Oklahoma. 17 May.
HR 1413, 52-1, v5, 3p. [3046]
Seven new counties to be formed out of the Cheyenne and Arapaho reservation; increased population and case load.

179. R-C of the Mo-kaw-ho-ko Band of Sac and Fox Indians. 18 May.
SR 690, 52-1, v4, 4p. [2914]
Claim for annuities due under the treaties of 1804, 1837, and 1842; payment not recommended because the band violated a treaty of 1868.

180. R-P of G. Jones. 20 May.
SR 698, 52-1, v4, 1p. [2914]
Black Hawk war; 1832.

181. Jurisdiction of the Supreme Court of the U.S. 20 May.
HR 1437, 52-1, v5, 2p. [3046]
Reports adversely on bill to extend jurisdiction over the high courts of the Cherokees, Choctaws, Chickasaws, Creeks, and Seminoles; violation of Cherokee treaties of 29 Dec. 1835, and 31 July 1866.

182. Railroad Passenger Service. 21 May.
HR 1460, 52-1, v5, 1p. [3046]
Regulation of rates in Indian Territory and Oklahoma.

183. R-P of N. Renfro. 24 May.
SR 719, 52-1, v4, 1p. [2914] *or*
HR 224, 52-1, v1, 1p. [3042]
Creek war; 1838; Alabama Volunteers.

184. R-P of M. Gatlin. 24 May.
SR 720, 52-1, v4, 1p. [2914] *or*
HR 491, 52-1, v2, 1p. [3043]
Indian war of 1836; Georgia Volunteers.

185. R-P of D. Barrow. 24 May.
SR 722, 52-1, v4, 1p. [2914] *or*
HR 492, 52-1, v2, 1p. [3043]
Indian war of 1836; Georgia Volunteers.

186. R-P of A. Jones. 24 May.
SR 733, 52-1, v4, 2p. [2914] *or*
HR 338, 52-1, v2, 2p. [3043]
Rogue River war; 1855-56; Oregon.

187. R-P of J. Davis. 24 May.
SR 734, 52-1, v4, 1p. [2914] *or*
HR 339, 52-1, v2, 1p. [3043]
Black Hawk war; 1832.

188. Colville Indian Reservation. 27 May.
HR 1525, 52-1, v5, 1p. [3046]
Action of the Com. on Indian Affairs.

189. Legislative, Executive, and Judicial Appropriation Bill. 28 May.
HR 1526, 52-1, v5, 22p. [3046]
For fiscal 1893; OIA.

190. Watertown, Sioux City, and Duluth Railway Co. 31 May.
SR 765, 52-1, v4, 1p. [2914]
Right of way through lands formerly known as the Sisseton and Wahpeton Sioux reservation.

191. Midland Pacific Railroad Co. 31 May.
SR 766, 52-1, v4, 4p. [2914]
Right of way through the Crow Creek Sioux reservation in South Dakota.

192. Protection of Indian Tribes. 31 May.
HR 1530, 52-1, v5, 1p. [3046]
Removal of trespassers from their lands; several thousand trespassers on land of the Chickasaw Nation defy removal.

193. R-C of the First National Bank of Newton, Massachusetts. 1 June.
SR 770, 52-1, v4, 15p. [2914]
Payment of interest on an award to the Choctaw Nation under the treaty of 27 Sept. 1830.

194. Brevet Rank in the Army. 1 June.
HED 249, 52-1, v37, 2p. [2957]
For service in Indian campaigns.

195. Indian Depredation Cases. 2 June.
SED 107, 52-1, v6, 3p. [2901]
Judgments of the Court of Claims.

196. R-C of the Shawnees and Delawares. 3 June.
HR 1554, 52-1, v5, 1p. [3046]
Money due from sale of lands.

197. Coahuilla Mission Indians. 6 June.
SED 108, 52-1, v6, 15p. [2901]
Information on the removal and replacement of the tribal chief; California.

198. Abandoned Military Reserves. 6 June.
SMD 172, 52-1, v5, 11p. [2907]
Fort Yuma, California, to be reserved for Indian uses; etc.

199. An Indian Depredation Case. 7 June.
SED 109, 52-1, v6, 1p. [2901]
Case of E. Babcock erroneously included in the list of judgments of the Court of Claims.

200. Annual Report of the American Historical Association for 1891. 7 June.
SMD 173, 52-1, v5, 508p. [2907]
Early Indians of Texas, the Indian service, Indian attack on Deerfield, Massachusetts, and other research touching on the American Indian.

201. Amendments to the Revised Statutes. 8 June.
HR 1598, 52-1, v5, 3p. [3046]
On punishment of crimes, and judicial procedures in Indian Territory and Oklahoma.

202. Stenographers and Typewriters. 10 June.
HMD 270, 52-1, v1, 8p. [2959]
Dates and locations of examinations for the above positions in the Indian service.

203. Cherokee Outlet. 13 June.
HR 1631, 52-1, v5, 5p. [3046]
Ratification of the agreement of 19 Dec. 1891 with the Cherokees, in which the Cherokee Outlet is ceded to the U.S.; treaties of 1828, 1835, and 1866 regarding land title.

204. R-P of H. Heinze. 15 June.
SR 811, 52-1, v4, 1p. [2914] *or*
HR 1625, 52-1, v5, 1p. [3046]
Sioux war; 1862; Minnesota.

205. R-P of F. Meredith. 15 June.
SR 813, 52-1, v4, 1p. [2914] *or*
HR 494, 52-1, v2, 1p. [3043]
Black Hawk war; 1832.

206. R-P of T. Williams. 15 June.
SR 816, 52-1, v4, 1p. [2914]
Black Hawk war; 1832; Illinois.

207. Mission Indian Commission. 15 June.
HR 1633, 52-1, v5, 1p. [3046]
Bill (see 1892:97) must be passed or a recent agreement with these Indians will fail.

208. Resol. of Rep. Peel. 17 June.
HMD 275, 52-1, v1, 1p. [2959]
On payments to the Choctaw and Chickasaw Nations for their interest in the Cheyenne and Arapaho reservation.

209. R-C of H. Jones. 17 June.
HR 1659, 52-1, v7, 2p. [3048]
Logging contract on the Keshena reservation in Wisconsin; 1872.

210. Kickapoo Indians in Oklahoma. 17 June.
HR 1662, 52-1, v7, 2p. [3048]
Agreement calling for cession of land.

211. General Deficiency Bill. 18 June.
HR 1666, 52-1, v7, 3p. [3048]
Appropriations for fiscal 1892; Indian expenses.

212. Indian Lands in Oklahoma and Indian Territory. 22 June.
HED 265, 52-1, v37, 17p. [2957]
Information as to what Indian lands are now occupied for grazing purposes; legal rights of persons holding leases in the Cherokee Outlet (ceded to U.S. under the Cherokee agreement of 19 Dec. 1891).

213. Claims Arising from Indian Depredations. 27 June.
SED 117, 52-1, v6, 4p. [2901]
On how payments shall be made when judgments are rendered against tribes; list of tribal debts and funds.

214. Legislative, Executive, and Judicial Appropriations Bill. 27 June.
SR 839, 52-1, v4, 5p. [2914]
Year ending 30 June 1893; OIA.

215. Pensions for Survivors of Indian Wars. 29 June.
SR 857, 52-1, v5, 2p. [2915]
Wars of 1832-62; Black Hawk, Creek, Cherokee, Seminole, Cayuse, Rogue River, and Sioux wars.

216. On the Case of D. Callinan. 30 June.
SR 861, 52-1, v5, 3p. [2915]
Sioux troubles in Dakota; 1890-91.

217. R-P of M. Calhoun. 30 June.
HR 1715, 52-1, v7, 1p. [3048]
Battle of the Little Big Horn River (1876) against the Sioux; Montana.

218. R-P of E. Luke. 30 June.
HR 1718, 52-1, v7, 1p. [3048]
Black Hawk war; 1832.

219. Claims Allowed by Accounting Officers. 1 July.
SED 123, 52-1, v6, 27p. [2901]
Supplemental list; includes claims involving Indians.

220. Annual Report of the Smithsonian Institution. 1 July.
HMD 114 (pts. 1 and 2), 52-2, v22-23, 1495p. [3131-3132]
Research related to the American Indian.

221. R-C of Grubb and Robinson. 1 July.
HR 1751, 52-1, v7, 1p. [3048]
Materials sold to the Prairie band of Pottawatomies.

222. R-P of S. Kingsley. 2 July.
HR 1775, 52-1, v7, 1p. [3048]
Florida Indian war; 1839.

223. Sundry Civil Appropriation Bill. 6 July.
SR 883, 52-1, v5, 33p. [3915]
For fiscal 1893; survey of the Crow Indian reservation, and other Indian expenses.

224. R-P of J. Hall. 7 July.
HR 1834, 52-1, v7, 1p. [3048]
Black Hawk war; 1832.

225. Indian Depredation Cases. 8 July.
SED 134, 52-1, v6, 5p. [2901]
Judgments of the Court of Claims since 1 June 1892.

226. On the Relief of the Eastern Cherokees. 8 July.
SED 135, 52-1, v6, 2p. [2901]
Use of trust funds to pay taxes; North Carolina.

227. On the Case of F. Fields. 8 July.
HR 1814, 52-1, v7, 4p. [3048]
Creek agent in Indian Territory; 1869-70.

228. Indian Depredation Claims. 9 July.
SR 903, 52-1, v5, 13p. [2915]
Appropriation required for the payment of judgments of the Court of Claims.

229. R-C of N. Smith. 9 July.
HR 1827, 52-1, v7, 1p. [3048]
Ex-chief of the Eastern Cherokees of North Carolina; asks payments due from tribe.

230. R-P of W. Russell. 9 July.
HR 1833, 52-1, v7, 1p. [3048]
Indian war; 1855-56; Oregon.

231. New York Indians *vs.* the U.S. 12 July.
SR 910, 52-1, v5, 7p. [2915]
Findings of the Court of Claims; funds due under the treaty of 15 Jan. 1838; history of treaty relations between these Indians and the U.S.

232. Blue Mountain Irrigation and Improvement Co. 12 July.
SR 911, 52-1, v5, 6p. [2915]

Right of way for reservoir and canals through the Umatilla Indian reservation, Oregon.

233. Yuma Pumping Irrigation Co. 12 July.
HR 1856, 52-1, v7, 2p. [3048]
Right of way for ditches across the Yuma reservation in Arizona.

234. Judgments of the Court of Claims. 13 July.
SED 138, 52-1, v6, 4p. [2901]
Case of a blacksmith at the Klamath agency in Oregon.

235. Claims Allowed by Accounting Officers. 13 July.
SED 140, 52-1, v6, 6p. [2901]
Includes those involving Indians.

236. Fort Randall Military Reservation. 13 July.
SR 912, 52-1, v5, 4p. [2915]
In South Dakota and Nebraska, near the Rosebud Sioux reservation; use of buildings for Indian school.

237. White Mountain Apache Reservation. 13 July.
HR 1857, 52-1, v7, 2p. [3048]
Portion of reservation restored to the public domain.

238. New York Indian Treaty. 13 July.
HR 1858, 52-1, v7, 8p. [3048]
Settlement with Indians under the treaty of 15 Jan. 1838 for unexecuted stipulations of that treaty.

239. Exclusion of Intoxicants from Indian Territory. 14 July.
HR 1866, 52-1, v7, 1p. [3048]
Amends law so that beer and other malt liquors are excluded; these liquors are sold there because of an ambiguity in the law.

240. Enforcement of Certain Laws. 14 July.
HR 1893, 52-1, v7, 1p. [3048]
Bill to enforce laws of Arkansas concerning railroad employees, etc., within Indian Territory and Oklahoma.

241. Appropriation for the Sioux Indians. 16 July.
SED 143, 52-1, v6, 2p. [2901]
On the distribution of moneys meant to pay Indian scouts and soldiers.

242. Resol. of Rep. Breckinridge. 16 July.
HMD 325, 52-1, v1, 1p. [2959]
On admission of Indian Territory into the Union as a State.

243. Admission of Indian Territory. 16 July.
HR 1927, 52-1, v7, 2p. [3048]
Resol. calling for an inquiry into the possible admission of Indian Territory into the Union as a State.

244. Fort Randall Military Reservation. 18 July.
SR 950, 52-1, v5, 2p. [2915]
Use of lands by Nebraska for school purposes; Indian school proposed, to serve Sioux reservations in South Dakota.

245. Circuit Courts of Appeal. 19 July.
SED 145, 52-1, v6, 3p. [2901]
Pres. vetoes a bill which would have made it impossible to appeal a decision of the Court of Claims on any Indian depredation case.

246. Agreement with the Pah-Utes. 19 July.
SMD 203, 52-1, v5, 2p. [2907]
On the Pyramid Lake and Walker River reservations in Nevada; 17 Oct. 1891; land cessions.

247. R-P of J. Granberry. 19 July.
SR 967, 52-1, v5, 1p. [2915] *or*
HR 1765, 52-1, v7, 1p. [3048]
Creek war; 1836; Georgia Volunteers.

248. R-P of J. White. 19 July.
SR 979, 52-1, v5, 1p. [2915] *or*
HR 1764, 52-1, v7, 1p. [3048]
Black Hawk war; 1832; Illinois Volunteers.

249. Northern Pacific Railroad Co. 19 July.
HR 1945, 52-1, v7, 4p. [3048]
Right of way through the Puyallup Indian reservation in Washington; agreement of 21 Nov. 1876 with the Puyallups.

250. R-P of S. Briggs. 19 July.
HR 1949, 52-1, v7, 1p. [3048]
Creek war; 1836; Alabama Volunteers.

251. R-P of J. Prator. 20 July.
SR 992, 52-1, v5, 1p. [2915] *or*
HR 1776, 52-1, v7, 1p. [3048]
Indian war of 1836; Georgia Volunteers.

252. R-P of M. Hitchcock. 20 July.
SR 1000, 52-1, v5, 2p. [2915] *or*
HR 2159, 52-2, v1, 2p. [3140]
Service against Creek, Florida, and Northwestern Indians.

253. Taxation of Indian Citizens. 20 July.
SR 1003, 52-1, v5, 8p. [2915]
Bill providing that lands allotted to Indians in severalty should be taxed; these Indians have dissolved their tribal relations and taken U.S. citizenship; they must not be immune from taxation.

254. Pensions to Survivors of Indian Wars. 20 July.
SR 1006, 52-1, v5, 1p. [2915]
Black Hawk, Creek, Cherokee, and Seminole wars; 1832-42.

255. Blue Mountain Irrigation and Improvement Co. 20 July.
HR 1963, 52-1, v10, 1p. [3051]
Right of way for canals, etc., through the Umatilla Indian reservation in Oregon.

256. R-P of J. Smith. 21 July.
SR 1009, 52-1, v5, 2p. [2915] *or*
HR 1781, 52-1, v7, 2p. [3048]
Seminole war; 1938-41; Florida.

257. R-P of S. Davis. 21 July.
SR 1012, 52-1, v5, 1p. [2915] *or*
HR 1838, 52-1, v7, 1p. [3048]
Florida Indian war; 1836-46.

258. R-P of T. Ellis. 21 July.
SR 1015, 52-1, v5, 1p. [2915]
Florida Indian war; 1837.

259. R-P of J. Kirtley. 21 July.
SR 1021, 52-1, v5, 1p. [2915] *or*
HR 1716, 52-1, v7, 1p. [3048]
Black Hawk war; 1832.

260. R-P of B. Morgan. 21 July.
HR 1977, 52-1, v10, 1p. [3051]
Black Hawk war; 1832; Illinois Volunteers.

261. R-P of A. Absher. 21 July.
HR 1980, 52-1, v10, 1p. [3051]
Black Hawk war; 1832; Illinois Volunteers.

262. R-P of R. Bridges. 21 July.
HR 1982, 52-1, v10, 1p. [3051]
Black Hawk war; 1832.

263. Supplemental Judgment of the Court of Claims. 22 July.
SED 146, 52-1, v6, 1p. [2901]
Case involving money spent by an Indian agent.

264. Indian Land Patents. 22 July.
SED 147, 52-1, v6, 1p. [2901]
Bill on the surrender of, and cancellation of, said patents in certain cases.

265. On the Relief of the Eastern Cherokees. 23 July.
SR 1064, 52-1, v5, 3p. [2915] *or*
HR 1871, 52-1, v7, 2p. [3048]
Bill authorizing use of their trust funds to pay taxes on their lands in North Carolina.

266. Indian Land Patents. 23 July.
HED 273, 52-1, v37, 1p. [2957]
Amendment to act concerning the surrender and cancellation of certain patents.

267. Allotments of Land Among Certain Indians. 23 July.
HR 2040, 52-1, v10, 2p. [3051]
At the Quapaw agency in Indian Territory; involves the western Miamies, Weas, Piankeshaws, Kaskaskias, Peorias, Ottawas, Modocs, Eastern Shawnees, Senecas, Wyandottes, and Quapaws.

268. R-P of H. Alvis. 25 July.
SR 1070, 52-1, v5, 1p. [2915] *or*
HR 1354, 52-1, v5, 1p. [3046]
Florida Indian war; Louisiana Volunteers.

269. Fort Brown Military Reservation. 25 July.
HR 2050, 52-1, v10, 8p. [3051]
Report includes information on malaria at Fort Sill, Reno, and Gibson in Indian Territory.

270. Temporary Government for Oklahoma. 25 July.
HR 2054, 52-1, v10, 1p. [3051]
Enlargement of the jurisdiction of the U.S. Court in Indian Territory.

271. Agreement with the Cherokees. 26 July.
SR 1079, 52-1, v5, 15p. [2915]
For cession of lands in the "Cherokee Outlet"; history of treaty relations concerning title to these lands; amendments suggested.

272. Resol. of Rep. Simpson. 27 July.
HMD 331, 52-1, v1, 1p. [2959]
Authorizes an investigation of cattle-grazing on Cherokee lands (ceded to the U.S. by the agreement of 19 Dec. 1891).

273. Cattle on Cherokee Lands. 27 July.
HR 2085, 52-1, v10, 1p. [3051]
Investigation of violations of law.

274. R-P of E. Carpenter. 29 July.
SR 1095, 52-1, v5, 1p. [2915] *or*
HR 2047, 52-1, v10, 1p. [3051]
Florida Indian war; 1839-44.

275. R-C of the Reps. of E. Ayres. 29 July.
HR 2113, 52-1, v10, 2p. [3051]
Purchase of lands granted to Chickasaw Indians under the treaty of 24 May 1834; Mississippi.

276. Resol. of Sen. Perkins. 2 Aug.
SMD 221, 52-1, v5, 1p. [2907]
Investigation of charges made by the Cherokees that intruders have settled on their lands.

277. Stockbridge and Munsee Indians. 2 Aug.
SMD 226, 52-1, v5, 71p. [2907]
Testimony taken concerning a dis-

pute between tribal members over who should be enrolled; Wisconsin; various treaties concerned.

278. Stockbridge and Munsee Indians. 2 Aug.
SR 1108, 52-1, v5, 58p. [2915]
Dispute over tribal membership and rights to lands in Wisconsin; treaty of 1856.

279. Report on the Navajo Indians. 4 Aug.
SED 156, 52-1, v6, 16p. [2901]
Navajoes moving off their reservation in New Mexico and Arizona, and are committing depredations; solutions to the problem are studied.

280. Statements of Appropriations. 5 Aug.
SMD 227, 52-1, v7, 381p. [2909]
During the 1st session, 52d Congress; Indian expenses.

281. Contributions to North American Ethnology, Volume 7. (no date)
HMD 26, 52-1, v21, 675p. [2979]
A Dakota-English Dictionary by S. Riggs; Siouan linguistic family.

282. Bulletins of the U.S. Geological Survey, Numbers 84-86. (no date)
HMD 337, 52-1, v45, 1242p. [3003]
Number 84 includes neocene geology of Indian Territory.

283. Population and Resources of Alaska. (no date)
HMD 340 (pt. 7), 52-1, v50 (pt. 9), 293p. [3020]
Statistics of the Eleventh Census; population, and other information concerning the Indians of Alaska; etc.

284. Report on Indians in the U.S. (no date)
HMD 340 (pt. 15), 52-1, v50 (pt. 6), 690p. [3016]
Statistics from the Eleventh Census; Indian populations, 1822-1890; history of Indians, Indian policy, and Indian administration in the U.S.; condition of Indian tribes; locations of various tribes; Indian wars and depredation claims; legal status of Indians; Indians of Canada; etc.

285. Population of the U.S. (no date)
HMD 340 (pt. 18), 52-1, v50 (pt. 8), 2321p. [3018-3019]
Statistics of the Eleventh Census; population of Indian tribes in the U.S.; etc.

286. Annual Report of the Sec. of the Treasury. 5 Dec.
HED 2, 52-2, v23, 1156p. [3098]
Year ending 30 June 1892; Indian expenses.

287. Estimates of Appropriations. 5 Dec.
HED 5, 52-2, v26, 407p. [3101]
Year ending 30 June 1894; Indian expenses.

288. Expenditures of the Smithsonian Institution. 5 Dec.
HMD 5, 52-2, v1, 36p. [3110]
For fiscal 1892; including expense of ethnological researches among American Indians.

289. Annual Message to Congress with Documents; Pres. Harrison. 6 Dec.
HED 1, 52-2, v1-22, 16378p. [3076-3097]
Cession of the Cherokee Strip and other Indian lands to the U.S.; policy of allotment and education; Choctaw and Chickasaw title to lands occupied by other tribes; annual report of the Sec. of War (Serials 3077-3084); annual report of the Sec. of Interior (Serials 3087-3094); annual report of the Gen. Land Office (Serial 3087); annual report of the CIA (Serial 3088); etc.

290. List of Reports to be Made to Congress. 6 Dec.
HMD 8, 52-2, v1, 27p. [3110]
Includes reports concerning Indian affairs.

291. Judgments of the Court of Claims. 6 Dec.
HMD 13, 52-2, v1, 6p. [3110]
For the year ending 3 Dec. 1892; cases involving Indians included.

292. Public Documents. 7 Dec.
HED 14, 52-2, v28, 60p. [3103]
"Finding list" includes annual reports of the CIA, etc.

293. Deficiency Estimates. 9 Dec.
HED 72, 52-2, v26, 17p. [3101]
Appropriations for fiscal 1893; cost of defense in Indian depredation cases; etc.

294. Congressional Directory. 12 Dec.
SMD 1 (pts. 1 and 2), 52-2, v1, 592p. [3064]
Duties of the CIA.

295. R-C of E. Ayres. 12 Dec.
HR 2149, 52-2, v1, 1p. [3140]
Land title issues involving Indians in Mississippi.

296. Chicago, Rock Island, and Pacific Railway Co. 12 Dec.
HR 2152, 52-2, v1, 1p. [3140]
Right of way through Indian Territory.

297. Mo-Ka-Ho-Ko Band of Sac and Fox Indians. 12 Dec.
HR 2153, 52-2, v1, 2p. [3140]
Funds claimed due under the treaty of 14 Oct. 1868.

298. Relief of Chippewas in Minnesota. 13 Dec.
HED 124, 52-2, v28, 8p. [3103]
On liability of U.S. for damages caused by the construction of dams and reservoirs.

299. Resol. of Sen. Platt. 15 Dec.
SMD 12, 52-2, v1, 1p. [3064]
Requests information on Indian trust funds, and depredation claims.

300. Appropriation for Fulfilling Treaties. 20 Dec.
HED 141, 52-2, v30, 2p. [3105]
Choctaw treaties of 18 Oct. 1820, and 22 June 1855.

301. Contingent Expenditures of the Interior Dept. 20 Dec.
HED 142, 52-2, v30, 21p. [3105]
For fiscal 1892; OIA.

302. R-C of H. Lee. 22 Dec.
HR 2194, 52-2, v1, 4p. [3140]
Attorney employed by Winnebago Indians in Wisconsin.

303. Ninth Annual Report of the Bureau of Ethnology; 1887-88. (no date)
HMD 11, 52-2, v2, 663p. [3111]
Research related to American Indians; Apache medicine-men; ethnological researches at Point Barrow, Alaska (Eskimos); etc.

1893

1. Indian Trust Funds. 4 Jan.
SED 15, 52-2, v1, 6p. [3055]
List of tribal funds, and various claims made upon them for depredations.

2. Agreement with the Pawnee Indians. 4 Jan.
SED 16, 52-2, v1, 14p. [3055]
Dated 23 Nov. 1892; cession of land in Oklahoma Territory.

3. Agreement with Various Indian Tribes. 4 Jan.
SED 17, 52-2, v1, 24p. [3055]
Made with the Kiowas, Apaches, and Comanches; 21 Oct. 1892; cession of land in Oklahoma Territory.

4. Expenses of Timber Experts. 4 Jan.
HED 151, 52-2, v30, 7p. [3105]
Incurred in connection with the sale of the lands of the Eastern band of Cherokees in North Carolina.

5. Contracts Made with Indians. 5 Jan.
SED 18, 52-2, v1, 786p. [3055]
Concerning compensations made to attorneys representing various tribes in claims cases.

6. Indian Depredation Claims. 5 Jan.
SED 21, 52-2, v2, 12p. [3056]
Number of claims filed in the Court of Claims, and judgments rendered.

7. Money Paid to Attorneys on Behalf of Indian Tribes. 6 Jan.
SED 23, 52-2, v2, 4p. [3056]
Out of appropriations made during the 51st Congress; lists tribe, attorneys, and services performed.

8. Big Horn Southern Railroad Co. 6 Jan.
HR 2201, 52-2, v1, 4p. [3140]
Construction through the Crow reservation in Montana.

9. Resol. of Sen. Mitchell. 7 Jan.
SMD 19, 52-2, v1, 1p. [3064]
Asks information on a treaty made 11 Aug. 1855 with various tribes inhabiting the coast of Oregon.

10. Introduction of Domestic Reindeer into Alaska. 10 Jan.
SMD 22, 52-2, v1, 39p. [3064]
Plan to civilize and make the Eskimos and other natives of Alaska self-sufficient.

11. Chicago, Rock Island, and Pacific Railway Co. 11 Jan.
HR 2217, 52-2, v1, 1p. [3140]
Use of lands in the Chickasaw Nation, Indian Territory.

12. Oklahoma Midland Railway Co. 11 Jan.
HR 2222, 52-2, v1, 1p. [3140]
Right of way through Indian Territory.

13. Applicants for Indian War Pensions. 11 Jan.
HR 2224, 52-2, v1, 1p. [3140]
Must have proof of citizenship.

14. R-P of E. Brown. 13 Jan.
SR 1159, 52-2, v1, 1p. [3072] *or*
HR 1861, 52-1, v7, 1p. [3048]
Service in Black Hawk war; 1832.

15. Navajo Indian Reservation. 13 Jan.
HR 2237, 52-2, v1, 1p. [3140]
Amendment to a resol. on said reservation.

16. Support of the Native Inhabitants of Alaska. 14 Jan.
HED 180, 52-2, v30, 1p. [3105]
Appropriation for fiscal 1894.

17. Claims Allowed by Accounting Officers. 17 Jan.
HED 191, 52-2, v30, 37p. [3105]
Includes claims involving Indians.

18. Allotment of Lands to Indians. 17 Jan.
HR 2256, 52-2, v1, 2p. [3140]
To those tribes at the Quapaw agency in Indian Territory; sale of surplus lands.

19. Sale of Indian Lands. 17 Jan.
HR 2257, 52-2, v1, 1p. [3140]
Unallotted lands at the Quapaw agency, Indian Territory; Western Miamies, Ottawas, Wyandottes, Eastern Shawnees, Senecas, and Confederated Peorias.

20. Claims of Certain Legal Counsel. 18 Jan.
HED 193, 52-2, v30, 15p. [3105]
Cost of defending Apaches in Arizona.

21. Sundry Civil Appropriation Bill. 18 Jan.
HR 2281, 52-2, v1, 7p. [3140]
Relief of Alaskan natives; etc.

22. Fort Randall Military Reservation. 18 Jan.
HR 2283, 52-2, v1, 2p. [3140]
School lands; land title of the Sioux and Ponca Indians; Nebraska.

23. Lease of Indian Reservations. 19 Jan.
HR 2293, 52-2, v1, 2p. [3140]
Oil Springs, Cattaraugus, and Allegany reservations in New York; Seneca Indians; oil and gas fields.

24. General Deficiency Bill. 20 Jan.
HR 2300, 52-2, v1, 10p. [3140]
For fiscal 1893; Indian war pensions.

25. R-C of J. Wheeler. 21 Jan.
SR 1186, 52-2, v1, 2p. [3072]
Accounts of this late Indian agent at the Warm Springs agency in Oregon.

26. Mille Lacs Reservation, Minnesota. 21 Jan.
HR 2321, 52-2, v2, 2p. [3141]
Disposal of this late Indian reserve.

27. Supplies for the Indian Service. 23 Jan.
SED 33, 52-2, v2, 5p. [3056]
Statement of open-market purchases which exceeded $500 during fiscal 1892.

28. Salmon Fisheries of Alaska. 24 Jan.
SED 31, 52-2, v2, 13p. [3056]
Indian labor; difficulties between native fishermen and fishermen from British Columbia.

29. Indian Depredation Cases. 24 Jan.
SED 32, 52-2, v2, 5p. [3056]
Court of Claims decisions in cases against the Sioux and Rogue River Indians.

30. R-P of J. Fortier. 24 Jan.
SR 1200, 52-2, v1, 1p. [3072] *or*
HR 1806, 52-1, v7, 1p. [3048]
Sioux outbreak of 1862 in Minnesota.

31. Treaty with Indians in Oregon. 25 Jan.
SED 34, 52-2, v2, 5p. [3056]
Information regarding a treaty made on 11 Aug. 1855 with tribes inhabiting the coast of Oregon; treaty stipulations, Senate action, fulfillment of treaty, etc.

32. Amendment to Indian Appropriation Bill. 25 Jan.
SED 204, 52-2, v30, 2p. [3105]
For fiscal 1894; provision of funds to the Indian school in Genoa, Nebraska.

33. R-C of J. Palmer. 25 Jan.
SR 1204, 52-2, v1, 3p. [3072] *or*
HR 2226, 52-2, v1, 4p. [3140]
Lands incorporated into the Pine Ridge reservation; Sioux Indians.

34. R-P of S. Murphy. 25 Jan.
SR 1212, 52-2, v1, 1p. [3072] *or*
HR 1979, 52-1, v10, 1p. [3051]
Creek war; 1836; Alabama Volunteers.

35. Navajo Indian Reservation. 25 Jan.
HED 201, 52-2, v30, 14p. [3105]
Regarding an Executive order to restore that part of said reservation lying in Utah to the public domain.

36. Sale of Property at Indian Agencies. 25 Jan.
HED 203, 52-2, v30, 2p. [3105]
Property sale and transfer during fiscal 1892.

37. Legislative, Executive, and Judicial Appropriation Bill. 26 Jan.
HR 2359, 52-2, v2, 18p. [3141]
For fiscal 1894; OIA.

38. Case of E. Wells. 28 Jan.
SR 1225, 52-2, v1, 4p. [3072] *or*
HR 856, 52-1, v3, 4p. [3044]
Service in Indian country during 1866-70 as a result of the Fetterman massacre at Fort Phil Kearney, Wyoming.

39. Big Horn Southern Railroad Co. 28 Jan.
HR 2374, 52-2, v2, 1p. [3141]
Construction through the Crow reservation; Montana.

40. R-C of R. McGee. 30 Jan.
SR 1230, 52-2, v1, 2p. [3072]
Brulé Sioux depredations of 1864 in Kansas.

41. Receipts and Expenditures of the U.S. 30 Jan.
HED 256, 52-2, v33, 501p. [3108]
For fiscal 1890; Indian expenses.

42. Case of Maj. Gen. Robinson. 30 Jan.
HR 2383, 52-2, v2, 4p. [3141]
Florida Indian war; 1857.

43. Removal of Suits from Courts of Indian Tribes. 30 Jan.
HR 2384, 52-2, v2, 9p. [3141]
Changes of venue from Indian to U.S. courts for Indians who have become U.S. citizens.

44. Agreement with Indians on the Siletz Reservation. 1 Feb.
SED 39, 52-2, v2, 13p. [3056]
Dated 31 Oct. 1892; cession of lands in Oregon.

45. Permanent Census Bureau. 1 Feb.
HR 2393 (pts. 1 and 2), 52-2, v2, 113p. [3141]
Would include a division of Indian statistics.

46. R-P of F. Gardiner. 3 Feb.
SR 1251, 52-2, v1, 2p. [3072] *or*
HR 1055, 52-1, v4, 2p. [3045]
Seminole war; 1835; Florida.

47. Appropriation for Fulfilling Treaty Stipulations. 3 Feb.
HR 2419, 52-2, v2, 1p. [3141]
For fiscal 1894; various tribes.

48. R-P of J. Cleveland. 6 Feb.
SR 1266, 52-2, v1, 1p. [3072] *or*
HR 1836, 52-1, v7, 1p. [3048]
Black Hawk war; 1832; Illinois Volunteers.

49. Resol. of Businessmen's Meeting in Oklahoma. 7 Feb.
SMD 43, 52-2, v1, 5p. [3064]
Asks ratification of the agreement which provides for the opening of the Cherokee Outlet for settlement, etc.

50. Turtle Mountain Indians. 7 Feb.
HED 229, 52-2, v30, 77p. [3105]
Agreement of 22 Oct. 1892 with this band of Chippewas; cession of land in North Dakota.

51. Building Construction at the Shoshone Agency. 7 Feb.
HED 233, 52-2, v32, 3p. [3107]
Estimate for substation and bridge; Wyoming.

52. Colorado River Irrigation Co. 7 Feb.
HR 2440, 52-2, v2, 1p. [3141]
Right of way through the Yuma Indian reservation.

53. R-P of M. Doubleday. 8 Feb.
SR 1270, 52-2, v1, 7p. [3072]
Service against Apaches in Texas (1854-55), and against Florida Indians (1856-58).

54. Disbursements of the Indian Dept. 8 Feb.
HED 239, 52-2, v32, 27p. [3107]
For fiscal 1892.

55. Agreement Made Between Various Sioux. 9 Feb.
SR 1275 (pts. 1 and 2), 52-2, v1, 40p. [3072]
Between Rosebud and Lower Brulé Sioux; would encorporate Lower Brulés into the Rosebud tribe; made in Mar. of 1892; council proceedings.

56. Timber Culture Laws. 9 Feb.
HR 2450, 52-2, v3, 1p. [3142-pt. 1]
Portions of the Great Sioux reservation in Nebraska and South Dakota which were opened to settlement.

57. Cherokee Outlet. 9 Feb.
HR 2455, 52-2, v3, 1p. [3142-pt. 1]
House rejects Senate amendments to bill on ratification of an agreement with the Cherokees; cession of the Cherokee Outlet.

58. Indian Depredation Claims. 11 Feb.
SED 60, 52-2, v2, 3p. [3056]
List of judgments in favor of claimants since 30 June 1891, and not paid.

59. Publication of the Eleventh Census. 11 Feb.
SR 1281, 52-2, v1, 5p. [3072]
Includes volume on Indian statistics.

60. Sundry Civil Appropriation Bill. 13 Feb.
SR 1287, 52-2, v2, 15p. [3073]
Includes appropriation for relief of Alaskan natives; for fiscal 1894.

61. Agreement with the Utes. 13 Feb.
HR 2487, 52-2, v3, 2p. [3142-pt. 1]
Removal of Confederated Utes from Colorado to Utah; claims against the tribe.

62. Condition of Navajo Indian Country. 14 Feb.
SED 68, 52-2, v2, 50p. [3056]
Inspection of the country in Arizona and New Mexico; plan to restrict the Navajoes to their reservation, and furnish irrigation and water.

63. Relief of the Stockbridge and Munsee Indians. 15 Feb.
SMD 54, 52-2, v1, 2p. [3064]
On allotments of land to tribal members in Wisconsin.

64. Relief to Indian Citizens. 15 Feb.
HR 2509, 52-2, v3, 2p. [3142-pt. 1]
On taxation of the lands of Indian citizens.

65. Chicago, Rock Island, and Pacific Railway Co. 16 Feb.
HR 2516, 52-2, v3, 1p. [3142-pt. 1]
Right of way through the Chickasaw Nation, Indian Territory.

66. Kansas City, Pittsburg, and Gulf Railroad Co. 17 Feb.
HR 2522, 52-2, v3, 1p. [3142-pt. 1]
Right of way through Indian Territory.

67. R-P of S. Kagwaich. 18 Feb.
SR 1306, 52-2, v2, 1p. [3073]
Indian serves in First Michigan Sharpshooters during Civil War.

68. R-P of S. Anderson. 21 Feb.
SR 1325, 52-2, v2, 2p. [3073]
Seminole war; 1850; Florida.

69. Contracts with Indian Tribes. 21 Feb.
SR 1328, 52-2, v2, 7p. [3073]
Printing of exhibits relating to contracts between various Indian tribes and attorneys.

70. Reimbursing the Western Miami Indians. 21 Feb.
HR 2544, 52-2, v3, 13p. [3142-pt. 1]
Funds due under the treaties of 1840, and 1854.

71. Interoceanic Railway Co. 23 Feb.
HR 2548, 52-2, v3, 1p. [3142-pt. 1]
Right of way through Indian Territory.

72. Gulf, Colorado, and Santa Fe Railway Co. 23 Feb.
HR 2551, 52-2, v3, 1p. [3142-pt. 1]
Right of way through the Chickasaw Nation, Indian Territory.

73. Indian Depredation Cases. 27 Feb.
SED 92, 52-2, v8, 3p. [3062]
Judgments of the Court of Claims since 6 Feb. 1893.

74. Claims of Friendly Indians. 27 Feb.
SED 93, 52-2, v8, 14p. [3062]
For depredations committed by hostile Indians during the disturbances at Pine Ridge, South Dakota; 1890-91; Pine Ridge, Rosebud, Cheyenne River, Standing Rock, and Tongue River agencies.

75. Midland Pacific Railway Co. 27 Feb.
HR 2585, 52-2, v3, 1p. [3142-pt. 1]
Right of way through an Indian reservation in South Dakota.

76. Reports on the Seal Islands. 28 Feb.
SED 107, 52-2, v8, 140p. [3062]
Actions of Alaskan natives included.

77. Southern Kansas Railway Co. 28 Feb.
HR 2593, 52-2, v3, 1p. [3142-pt. 1]
Right of way through Indian Territory.

78. Claims Allowed by Accounting Officers. 1 Mar.
SED 98, 52-2, v8, 17p. [3062]
Includes claims involving Indians.

79. Indian Appropriations. 1 Mar.
SR 1357, 52-2, v2, 2p. [3073]
For fiscal 1894.

80. Annual Report of the American Historical Association; 1892. 2 Mar.
SMD 57, 52-2, v4, 705p. [3067]
Historical research related to the American Indian.

81. U.S. Civil Service. 2 Mar.
SMD 61, 52-2, v1, 174p. [3064]
Includes requirements for entering the Indian Service.

82. R-P of M. Hardaway. 2 Mar.
HR 2607, 52-2, v3, 1p. [3142-pt. 1]
Creek war; 1836; Alabama Volunteers.

83. Permanent and Indefinite Appropriations. 2 Mar.
HR 2610, 52-2, v3, 37p. [3142-pt. 1]
Repeal of certain Indian appropriations.

84. Northern Pacific Railroad Co. 3 Mar.
SED 106, 52-2, v8, 2p. [3062]
On land grants to the company; land title issues involving Indians.

85. Statements of Appropriations. 3 Mar.
SMD 70, 52-2, v8, 343p. [3071]
Made during the 2d session, 52d Congress; Indian expenses.

86. Condition of the Treasury. 3 Mar.
HR 2621, 52-2, v3, 84p. [3142-pt. 1]
Expenditures on the Indian service; Indian war pensions; etc.

87. Receipts and Expenditures of the U.S. (no date)
HED 228, 52-2, v31, 527p. [3106]
For fiscal 1889; Indian expenses.

88. Statistical Abstract of the U.S. for 1892. (no date)
HED 255, 52-2, v32, 364p. [3107]
Includes Indian populations, schools, and reservations.

89. Index of U.S. Government Publications; 1889-93. (no date)
HMD 95, 52-2, v9, 487p. [3118]
Compiled by J. Ames; primarily Congressional documents.

90. Tenth Annual Report of the Bureau of Ethnology; 1888-89. (no date)
HMD 116, 52-2, v25, 852p. [3134]
Research related to the American Indian; picture-writing by American Indians; etc.

91. Amendment to the Senate Rules. 20 Mar.
SMD 11, 53-sp, v1, 1p. [3142-pt. 2]
Indian appropriation bill to be referred to the Com. on Indian Affairs.

92. Congressional Directory. 20 Apr.
SMD 46, 53-sp, v1, 308p. [3142-pt. 2]
Duties of the CIA listed.

93. Resol. of Sen. Jones. 20 Apr.
SMD 40, 53-sp, v1, 1p. [3142-pt. 2]
Investigations of the Com. on Indian Affairs on Indian reservations, and at Indian schools.

94. Official Register of the U.S. 1 July.
HMD 29 (pts. 1 and 2), 53-2, v2-3, 2779p. [3230-3231]
Lists all employees of the Indian service.

95. Annual Report of the Smithsonian Institution. 1 July.
HMD 184 (pts. 1 and 2), 53-2, v29-30, 1622p. [3257-3258]
Research related to the American Indian.

96. Congressional Directory. 7 Aug.
SMD 8, 53-1, v1, 309p. [3145]
Duties of the CIA listed.

97. Mem. of C. Mousso. 14 Aug.
SMD 14, 53-1, v1, 4p. [3145]
On title to land in Minnesota; set apart for half-breed Sioux or Dakotas under the treaty of 15 July 1830.

98. List of Reports to be Made to Congress. 15 Aug.
HMD 8, 53-1, v1, 23p. [3151]
Includes reports related to Indian affairs.

99. Fort Totten Military Reservation. 4 Sept.
SR 16, 53-1, v1, 2p. [3147] *or*
HR 1113, 53-2, v3, 3p. [3271]
Lands set aside for an Indian school in North Dakota are transferred to that State.

100. Choctaw and Chickasaw Nations. 8 Sept.
SED 8, 53-1, v1, 14p. [3144]
Statement of the amounts paid out to said Nations under the appropriations of 3 Mar. 1891.

101. R-C of Florida. 11 Sept.
HR 4 (pts. 1 and 2), 53-1, v1, 115p. [3157]
For suppression of Indian hostilities.

102. L-C of C. Costello. 12 Sept.
SED 12, 53-1, v1, 3p. [3144]
Lands and improvements on the Round Valley Indian reservation in California are lost to the claimant.

103. Judgments Against the U.S. 15 Sept.
SED 15, 53-1, v1, 2p. [3144]
For which no appropriations have been made; cases involving the Western Cherokees and Shawnees; Indian depredation cases.

104. Receipts and Expenditures of the U.S. 16 Sept.
SMD 55, 53-1, v1, 6p. [3145]
For fiscal 1893; Indian expenses.

105. Pension Laws. 23 Sept.
HR 26, 53-1, v1, 2p. [3157]
Suspension of statutes requiring proof of loyalty to the Union; affects soldiers in Indian wars.

106. R-P of M. Hitchcock. 26 Sept.
SR 34, 53-1, v1, 2p. [3147] *or*
HR 279 (pts. 1 and 2), 53-2, v1, 3p. [3269]
Service against the Creeks, in the Florida war, and with the Northwestern Indians.

107. R-P of T. Chill. 26 Sept.
SR 38, 53-1, v1, 1p. [3147] *or*
HR 1446, 53-2, v4, 1p. [3272]
Black Hawk war; 1832.

108. Action of Troops in the Cherokee Strip. 28 Sept.
HR 47, 53-1, v1, 1p. [3157]
Investigation of alleged outrages committed upon settlers; Cherokee Strip opened 16 Sept. 1893.

109. Laws Organizing Executive Depts. 30 Sept.
SR 41, 53-1, v2, 175p. [3148] *or*
HR 49, 53-1, v2, 175p. [3158]
References to statutes creating the office of CIA, the OIA, etc.

110. Mineral Resources of the U.S. 30 Sept.
HMD 38, 53-2, v4, 857p. [3232]
Coal in Indian Territory.

111. Land Offices Abolished or Consolidated. 3 Oct.
SED 22, 53-1, v1, 30p. [3144]
Includes offices for Indian lands in Kansas and Nebraska.

112. Rights to Settlers in Oklahoma. 4 Oct.
HR 73, 53-1, v1, 3p. [3157]
Located on Absentee Shawnee, Pottawatomie, Cheyenne, Arapaho, Iowa, Sac, and Fox lands in Oklahoma Territory.

113. Railroad Stations in the Territories. 4 Oct.
HR 74, 53-1, v1, 2p. [3157]
Certain companies not building depots in Indian Territory and the Cherokee Outlet in violation of their land grants.

114. Reimbursal of Nebraska. 5 Oct.
SR 45, 53-1, v1, 2p. [3147] *or*
HR 485, 53-2, v2, 1p. [3270]
For expenses incurred in repelling a threatened invasion by the Sioux in 1890-91.

115. Organization of Executive Depts. 9 Oct.
SR 47, 53-1, v2, 207p. [3148] *or*
HR 88, 53-1, v2, 207p. [3158]
Information concerning persons employed in the OIA, etc.

116. Offenses Committed on Fort Logan Military Reservation. 9 Oct.
HED 14, 53-1, v1, 8p. [3150]
Bill to allow prosecution of crimes committed on military reserves; based on similar bill regarding Indian reservations.

117. Treaties with Certain Indians in Oregon. 10 Oct.
SED 25, 53-1, v1, 58p. [3144]
Treaties of 20 Sept. 1851 with bands of Tootoonas and Coquille Indians; treaties made between 11 Aug. and 8 Sept. 1855 with bands of Tillamook, Siuslaw, Umpqua, Kowes Bay, Coquille, Tootooteney, and Chitco, or Illinois River Indians; etc.

118. Voting Regulations in the Cherokee Outlet. 10 Oct.
HR 91, 53-1, v1, 1p. [3157]
Voter qualifications; Oklahoma Territory.

119. Amendment to Timber-Culture Laws. 10 Oct.
HR 93, 53-1, v1, 1p. [3157]
Lands from the Great Sioux reservation which were opened to settlement.

120. R-P of F. Norman. 11 Oct.
HR 95, 53-1, v1, 1p. [3157]
Florida Indian war; 1836.

121. Special Judge for Indian Territory. 13 Oct.
HR 105, 53-1, v1, 1p. [3157]
To be in the Federal court there.

122. R-C of J. Little and H. Williams. 17 Oct.
SR 55, 53-1, v1, 4p. [3147] *or*
HR 439, 53-2, v1, 4p. [3269]
Leases of mineral lands from the Iowa Indians in Nebraska and Kansas.

123. R-C of J. Palmier. 17 Oct.
SR 56, 53-1, v1, 3p. [3147]
Lands and improvements lost to the Pine Ridge reservation; Sioux Indians.

124. Extending Relief to Indian Citizens. 17 Oct.
SR 57, 53-1, v1, 9p. [3147]
On taxation of lands allotted to Indian citizens.

125. R-C of Certain Cherokees. 17 Oct.
HR 116, 53-1, v1, 1p. [3157]
Ask allotments of land due them in the Cherokee Outlet under the Cherokee agreement ratified in 1893.

126. Fees for a Clerk of the U.S. Court. 24 Oct.
HR 138, 53-1, v1, 1p. [3157]
Located in Indian Territory.

127. Amending the Revised Statutes. 24 Oct.
HR 141, 53-1, v1, 9p. [3157]
Punishment of crimes on military reservations; based on laws dealing with Indian reservations.

128. Appropriation for the Justice Dept. 27 Oct.
HED 24, 53-1, v1, 5p. [3150]
Expenses of case involving Eastern Cherokees.

129. Mille Lacs Indian Reservation. 30 Oct.
HR 149, 53-1, v1, 2p. [3157]

Protection of settlers on lands formerly a Chippewa reservation; Minnesota.

130. Fort Meade, South Dakota. 2 Nov.
SR 64, 53-1, v1, 2p. [3147]
Bill to enlarge Fort Meade is rejected on the grounds that Indian wars are about at an end.

131. Opening of the Cherokee Strip. 2 Nov.
HED 27, 53-1, v1, 86p. [3150]
Investigation into the conduct of U.S. troops engaged in the opening of the Cherokee Strip on 16 Sept. 1893.

132. Admission of Utah. 2 Nov.
HR 162 (pts. 1 and 2), 53-1, v1, 39p. [3157]
Constitution deals with Indian land titles, and jurisdiction over Indians.

133. Choctaw Coal and Railway Co. 2 Nov.
HR 166, 53-1, v1, 1p. [3157]
Action of the Com. on Indian Affairs.

134. Congressional Directory. 1 Dec.
SMD 12 (pts. 1-3), 53-2, v3, 891p. [3169]
Duties of the CIA.

135. Judgments of the Court of Claims. 4 Dec.
SMD 5, 53-2, v1, 5p. [3167]
Cases on Cherokee, Delaware, and Shawnee treaty relations.

136. Annual Message to Congress wtih Documents; Pres. Cleveland. 4 Dec.
HED 1, 53-2, v1-21, 16692p. [3197-3218]
Pres. discusses Indian policy; annual report of the Sec. of War (Serials 3198-3206); annual report of the Sec. of Interior (Serials 3209-3215); annual report of the Gen. Land Office (Serial 3209); annual report of the CIA (Serial 3210); etc.

137. Estimates of Appropriations. 4 Dec.
HED 5, 53-2, v24, 397p. [3221]
Year ending 30 June 1895; Indian expenses.

138. Expenditures of the Smithsonian Institution. 4 Dec.
HMD 8, 53-2, v1, 39p. [3229]
Including ethnological research among American Indians.

139. Military Post Near Reno, Nevada. 7 Dec.
SR 75, 53-2, v1, 2p. [3179]
Pi-Ute Indians on the Walker Lake and Pyramid Lake reservations have not been hostile for years past.

140. Intruders in the Cherokee Nation. 7 Dec.
HED 26, 53-2, v26, 6p. [3223]
Appropriation for their removal.

141. Disbursements Made for the Indian Dept. 9 Dec.
HED 36, 53-2, v26, 25p. [3223]
Year ending 30 June 1893.

142. The Discovery of Nebraska. 11 Dec.
SMD 14, 53-2, v1, 60p. [3167]
Account of early explorations of that region; Indians encountered there, including Pawnees, Omahas, and Otoes.

143. Indian Depredation Claims. 12 Dec.
SED 7 (pts. 1 and 2), 53-2, v1, 6p. [3160]
Judgments made up to 4 Dec. 1893.

144. R-C of I. Owen. 13 Dec.
SR 92, 53-2, v1, 2p. [3179] *or*
HR 1027, 53-2, v3, 2p. [3271]
California Indian war; 1851.

145. Deficiency Estimates for the Interior Dept. 13 Dec.
HED 37, 53-2, v26, 3p. [3223]
Cost of advertising Cheyenne and Arapaho lands open for settlement.

146. R-C of Certain Citizens. 14 Dec.
SR 110, 53-2, v1, 7p. [3179]
Services in the war against the Nez Percés, Bannocks, and Shoshones; 1877-78; Oregon, Idaho, and Washington.

147. Selections of Public Land in Montana. 14 Dec.
HR 214, 53-2, v1, 2p. [3269]
From lands in the Bitter Root Valley, ceded to the U.S. in 1872 by the Flatheads and other tribes.

148. Urgent Deficiency Appropriation Bill. 15 Dec.
HR 215, 53-2, v1, 72p. [3269]
Pensions for Indian wars.

149. Annual Report of the Sec. of the Treasury. 19 Dec.
HED 2, 53-2, v22, 1259p. [3219]
Year ending 30 June 1893; Indian expenses.

150. Opening Abandoned Military Reservations. 19 Dec.
HR 232, 53-2, v1, 2p. [3269]
To be handled in the same manner as the opening of Indian lands in Dakota, Montana, and Oklahoma.

151. Judgments of the Court of Claims. 20 Dec.
SED 11, 53-2, v1, 3p. [3160]
Since 4 Mar. 1893; case of Pottawatomies of Michigan and Indiana on amounts due under treaties.

152. Contingent Expenses of the Interior Dept. 20 Dec.
HED 50, 53-2, v26, 21p. [3223]
For fiscal 1893; OIA.

153. Arkansas State Bonds. 20 Dec.
HR 239, 53-2, v1, 5p. [3269]
Held for the Indian trust fund.

154. Admission of Oklahoma. 20 Dec.
HR 242, 53-2, v1, 6p. [3269]
Land leases in the Cherokee Strip.

155. Resol. of Sen. Kyle. 21 Dec.
SMD 21, 53-2, v1, 1p. [3167]
Asks information related to Sioux half-breeds.

1894

1. Negotiations with Shoshones and Arapahoes. 3 Jan.
HED 51, 53-2, v26, 19p. [3223]
Agreement of 2 Oct. 1891 for land cessions in Wyoming not ratified; negotiations reopened, but no new agreement is made; council proceedings.

2. R-C of E. Fish et al. 4 Jan.
SR 134, 53-2, v1, 6p. [3179] *or*
HR 729, 53-2, v2, 7p. [3270]
Supplies for the Indian service in Arizona; 1873-74.

3. L-C of J. White. 4 Jan.
HED 53, 53-2, v26, 6p. [3233]
For drawings of proposed buildings at the Lower Brulé agency, South Dakota.

4. Fond du Lac Band of Chippewas. 4 Jan.
HED 55, 53-2, v26, 3p. [3223]
Timber depredations on their lands in Minnesota.

5. L-C of J. Heard. 8 Jan.
SED 20, 53-2, v1, 11p. [3160] *or*
HR 1354, 53-2, v4, 7p. [3272]
For legal services rendered to the Western Cherokees.

6. Presbyterian Board of Home Missions. 8 Jan.
SR 135, 53-2, v1, 3p. [3179] *or*
HR 360, 53-2, v1, 1p. [3269] *or*
HR 1371, 53-2, v4, 1p. [3272]
Title to land on the Omaha reservation in Nebraska.

7. Relief of Settlers in Oklahoma. 8 Jan.
SR 137, 53-2, v1, 1p. [3179] *or*
HR 224, 53-2, v1, 1p. [3269]
Opening of the Iowa and Kickapoo reservations.

8. Land Leases in Oklahoma. 8 Jan.
HR 251, 53-2, v1, 1p. [3269]
Proclamation opening the Cherokee Outlet.

9. Misdemeanors in Indian Territory. 10 Jan.
HED 67, 53-2, v26, 4p. [3223]
On the present method of trying misdemeanors.

10. Choctaw Coal and Railway Co. 11 Jan.
SR 142, 53-2, v1, 2p. [3179] *or*
HR 1344, 53-2, v4, 2p. [3272]
Construction in Indian Territory.

11. Settlers on Public Lands in Oklahoma. 17 Jan.
HR 263, 53-2, v1, 3p. [3269]
Lands ceded by the Sacs, Foxes, Iowas, Citizen band of Pottawatomies, Absentee Shawnees, Cheyennes, and Arapahoes.

12. Agreement with the Yankton Sioux or Dakota Indians. 18 Jan.
SED 27, 53-2, v1, 101p. [3160]
Made 31 Dec. 1892; investigation of the manner in which the agreement was negotiated and concluded; council proceedings.

13. Damages Sustained by Settlers. 18 Jan.
SMD 42, 53-2, v1, 2p. [3167]
On the Crow Creek and Winnebago reservations in South Dakota.

14. R-C of the Reps. of S. Marston. 18 Jan.
SR 169, 53-2, v1, 2p. [3179]
Late Indian agent at the Union agency in Indian Territory.

15. Repeal of Section 4716, Revised Statutes. 18 Jan.
HR 266, 53-2, v1, 1p. [3269]
Pensions for service in Indian wars by those who subsequently aided the South in the Civil War.

16. Building Construction at the Shoshone Agency. 20 Jan.
HED 77, 53-2, v26, 4p. [3223]
Appropriation required; Wyoming.

17. Agreement with the Yankton Sioux. 22 Jan.
HED 80, 53-2, v26, 3p. [3223]

Made 31 Dec. 1892; Indians petition for ratification.

18. Pah-Ute Reservations in Nevada. 24 Jan.
SR 177, 53-2, v1, 4p. [3179]
Bill to secure relinquishment of Indian title to all of the Walker River, and a portion of the Pyramid Lake reservations.

19. Case of D. Ransom. 25 Jan.
SR 180, 53-2, v1, 4p. [3179] *or*
HR 518, 53-2, v2, 4p. [3270] *or*
HR 951, 53-2, v3, 4p. [3271]
Service against hostile Indians in Washington Territory; 1858.

20. Bridge Across the Niobrara River. 26 Jan.
SR 182, 53-2, v1, 2p. [3179]
Transportation to the Ponca, and Yankton Sioux reservations; Nebraska.

21. Amendment to Indian Appropriation Bill. 27 Jan.
HED 87, 53-2, v26, 2p. [3223]
Payments to Iowa Indians for lands ceded in Oklahoma.

22. Pension Appropriation Bill. 27 Jan.
HR 291, 53-2, v1, 23p. [3269]
Service in Indian wars.

23. Agreement with the Nez Percé Indians. 29 Jan.
SED 31, 53-2, v1, 68p. [3160]
Made 1 May 1893; land cessions in Idaho; council proceedings.

24. Settlers on Indian Reservations. 29 Jan.
SED 32, 53-2, v1, 117p. [3160]
On the Crow Creek and Winnebago reservations in South Dakota; damages sustained in 1885 when the reservations were opened, and then closed for settlement.

25. Sale of Indian Lands. 29 Jan.
SR 184, 53-2, v1, 4p. [3179]
The remainder of the confederated Otoe and Missouria reservation in Kansas and Nebraska.

26. L-C of J. Hitt et al. 30 Jan.
HED 92, 53-2, v26, 12p. [3223]
Cases involving Puyallup Indians in Washington, and Indian police at the Flathead agency in Montana.

27. R-P of A. Potter. 31 Jan.
SR 189, 53-2, v1, 2p. [3179]
Service at Fort Gibson, Indian Territory.

28. Agreement Between Sioux Indians. 1 Feb.
SMD 70, 53-2, v1, 7p. [3167]
Between Indians of the Rosebud and Lower Brulé agencies in 1892; settlement of Lower Brulés on the Rosebud reservation.

29. Agreement with the Yankton Sioux. 1 Feb.
SR 196, 53-2, v1, 10p. [3179]
Made 31 Dec. 1892; cession of land in South Dakota.

30. R-C of Certain People. 1 Feb.
SR 197, 53-2, v1, 13p. [3179] *or*
SR 232, 53-2, v1, 13p. [3179]
Expense of suppressing Indian hostilities in Nevada; Pah-Ute war of 1860.

31. Claims Allowed by Accounting Officers. 1 Feb.
HED 93, 53-2, v26, 46p. [3223]
Cases involving Indians.

32. Property Returns by U.S. Officers. 2 Feb.
SR 201, 53-2, v2, 6p. [3148] *or*
HR 392, 53-2, v2, 6p. [3158]
Includes returns made by Indian agents.

33. Sundry Civil Appropriation Bill. 3 Feb.
HR 348, 53-2, v1, 8p. [3269]
For fiscal 1895; Alaskan natives, Eastern Cherokees, judges for Indian Territory, etc.

34. Umatilla Irrigation Co. 3 Feb.
HR 355, 53-2, v1, 1p. [3269]
Extension of time for construction across the Umatilla Indian reservation in Oregon.

35. Reservations of Lands in the Cherokee Outlet. 7 Feb.
SED 37, 53-2, v1, 9p. [3160]
Town site selections made prior to the opening of the Outlet; these selections followed allotments being made to Indians.

36. Deficiency Estimates. 8 Feb.
HED 103, 53-2, v24, 73p. [3221]
Appropriations for fiscal 1894; Indian expenses.

37. Assistant to the Supt. of Indian Schools. 8 Feb.
HED 105, 53-2, v29, 2p. [3226]
Appropriation to create the office.

38. Repeal of Certain Permanent and Indefinite Appropriations. 8 Feb.
HMD 86, 53-2, v1, 49p. [3229]
Includes those related to certain Indians.

39. Leases on Indian Reservations. 8 Feb.
HMD 87, 53-2, v1, 1p. [3229]

Would delay the opening of Wichita, Comanche, Kiowa, and Apache lands in Oklahoma; agreement of 4 June 1891.

40. Leases on Indian Reservations. 8 Feb.
HR 386, 53-2, v1, 1p. [3269]
On Wichita, Iowa, and Apache lands; might prevent disposal of surplus lands ceded to the U.S. in a recent agreement.

41. L-C of Various Deputy Marshals. 9 Feb.
HED 107, 53-2, v29, 2p. [3226]
Services at the opening of Iowa, Sac, and Fox lands in Oklahoma.

42. Purchase of Textile Fabrics. 12 Feb.
SED 39, 53-2, v1, 5p. [3160]
During fiscal 1893 by the Indian Service.

43. Pensions for Service in the Arkansas Volunteers. 12 Feb.
SED 40, 53-2, v1, 6p. [3160]
Stationed at Fort Gibson, Cherokee Nation, Indian Territory; 1846-47.

44. Duluth and Winnipeg Railroad Co. 13 Feb.
SR 206, 53-2, v1, 3p. [3179] *or*
HR 920, 53-2, v3, 3p. [3271]
Right of way through the White Earth reservation in Minnesota; Chippewa Indians.

45. Construction of a Wagon Road. 15 Feb.
SED 41, 53-2, v1, 4p. [3160]
In the Hoopa Valley Indian reservation; California.

46. Survey and Allotment of Indian Reservations. 15 Feb.
SED 42, 53-2, v1, 2p. [3160]
At the Pine Ridge, Rosebud, Lower Brulé, and Standing Rock reservations; North and South Dakota.

47. Grant of Public Lands to Mississippi. 15 Feb.
HR 436, 53-2, v1, 5p. [3269]
For education; Indian land title (Creek) involved as early as 1812.

48. R-C of A. Gray. 16 Feb.
HR 452, 53-2, v1, 3p. [3269]
Title to land in the Round Valley Indian reservation; California.

49. Indians of the Crow Creek Reservation. 17 Feb.
HED 121, 53-2, v29, 4p. [3226]
Appropriation for these Sioux Indians of South Dakota; unfairly treated in the division of the Great Sioux reservation.

50. Chippewas of Minnesota. 17 Feb.
HR 459, 53-2, v1, 4p. [3269]
Allotments, and sale of timber lands on the Red Lake and White Earth reservations.

51. R-C of the Shawnee Indians. 19 Feb.
SR 214, 53-2, v1, 1p. [3179]
Appropriation to take testimony.

52. Amount Paid to the Chickasaws; 20 Feb.
SED 45, 53-2, v1, 1p. [3160]
As interest on their trust funds.

53. Relief of Settlers in South Dakota. 20 Feb.
HR 470, 53-2, v1, 3p. [3269]
Settled on the Crow Creek and Winnebago reservations, and then were removed; Sioux lands.

54. R-C of J. O'Keane. 22 Feb.
SR 225, 53-2, v1, 1p. [3179]
Services at the Tulalip Indian agency in Washington; 1882.

55. Sioux Reservation. 22 Feb.
SR 226, 53-2, v1, 3p. [3179]
Carrying out of the act of 1889 which calls for division of the reservation, and sale of surplus lands.

56. Making of Property Returns. 27 Feb.
SR 229, 53-2, v1, 5p. [3179]
By Indian agents.

57. Eastern Cherokees *vs.* W. Thomas et al. 27 Feb.
HED 128, 53-2, v29, 147p. [3226]
Land title case in North Carolina.

58. R-P of C. Black. 27 Feb.
HR 492 (pts. 1 and 2), 53-2, v2, 3p. [3270]
Seminole and Black Hawk wars.

59. R-C of E. Moore and D. Woodson. 28 Feb.
HR 509, 53-2, v2, 3p. [3270]
Special agents in charge of sale of Delaware (treaty of 6 May 1854), and united Wea, etc., (treaty of 30 May 1854) lands in Kansas.

60. Alleged Violations of the Civil-Service Law. 1 Mar.
SMD 101, 53-2, v1, 67p. [3167]
Within the Indian school service.

61. Mem. of Kiowas, Apaches, and Comanches. 1 Mar.
SMD 102, 53-2, v1, 15p. [3167]
Insist that the agreement of 6 Oct. 1892 which calls for cession of their lands in Oklahoma is a fraud.

62. R-C of P. Corbett. 1 Mar.
SR 233, 53-2, v1, 4p. [3179]

U.S. marshal stops liquor sales to Indians in Nevada.

63. Agreement with Indians on the Siletz Reservation. 2 Mar.
HR 527, 53-2, v2, 2p. [3270]
Made 31 Oct. 1892; cession of unallotted lands in Oregon.

64. Annual Report of the American Historical Association; 1893. 5 Mar.
SMD 104, 53-2, v4, 615p. [3170]
Research related to the American Indian.

65. Choctaw Tribe of Indians. 5 Mar.
SMD 109, 53-2, v5, 6p. [3171]
Statement concerning their title to land, and desire to maintain tribal relations.

66. R-C of H. Shipley. 6 Mar.
SR 241. 53-2, v1, 3p. [3179]
Services at the Nez Percé agency in Idaho.

67. Administration of Justice. 7 Mar.
SMD 114, 53-2, v5, 4p. [3171]
Report on law enforcement in the territory of the Five Civilized Tribes.

68. War Claims of California, Nevada, and Oregon. 8 Mar.
HR 558, 53-2, v2, 4p. [3270]
Protection of transportation routes against hostile Indians during the Civil War.

69. R-C of Chadwick, Wilson, and Co. 10 Mar.
HR 567, 53-2, v2, 1p. [3270]
Contract with the Cherokee Nation; legal status of said Nation.

70. Agreement with the Yankton Sioux. 10 Mar.
HR 570, 53-2, v2, 1p. [3270]
Made 31 Dec. 1892; cession of lands in South Dakota.

71. Sioux Mixed-Blood Indians. 12 Mar.
SED 59, 53-2, v1, 160p. [3160]
Orders, opinions, and directives concerning Sioux mixed-bloods; allotment of land involved.

72. Chickasaw Trust Funds. 12 Mar.
SED 60, 53-2, v1, 2p. [3160]
Interest account of non-paying bonds.

73. Indian School at Cherokee, North Carolina. 12 Mar.
HED 142, 53-2, v29, 4p. [3226]
Appropriation for fiscal 1895.

74. Army Appropriations. 19 Mar.
HR 604, 53-2, v2, 12p. [3270]
Fiscal 1895; Indian prisoners at Mount Vernon Barracks, Alabama.

75. Agreement with the Yakima Indians. 21 Mar.
SED 67, 53-2, v1, 41p. [3160]
Made 8 Jan. 1894; land cessions in Washington; council proceedings.

76. Agreement with the Yuma Indians. 21 Mar.
SED 68, 53-2, v1, 32p. [3160]
Made 4 Dec. 1893; land cessions in California; report on councils held.

77. R-C of E. Van Antwerp and C. Bates. 22 Mar.
SMD 126, 53-2, v5, 16p. [3171]
Survey of the Pine Ridge reservation in South Dakota; Sioux Indians.

78. Agreement with the Southern Utes. 22 Mar.
SR 279, 53-2, v1, 5p. [3179] *or*
HR 799, 53-2, v2, 3p. [3270]
Made in 1880; allotments at a reservation near the Navajoes.

79. Agreement with the Coeur d'Alenes. 23 Mar.
HED 158, 53-2, v29, 18p. [3226]
Made 7 Feb. 1894; land cession in Idaho; council proceedings.

80. Survey of Fort Hall Indian Reservation. 27 Mar.
HED 161, 53-2, v29, 2p. [3226]
Appropriation for the survey made under the agreement of 14 May 1890 with the Shoshones and Bannocks is not sufficient; Idaho.

81. Indian School at Phoenix, Arizona. 27 Mar.
HED 163, 53-2, v29, 3p. [3226]
Appropriation for fiscal 1895.

82. Introduction of Reindeer Into Alaska. 28 Mar.
SED 70, 53-2, v1, 187p. [3160]
For the benefit of Eskimos and other Alaskan natives.

83. International Council of the Five Nations. 28 Mar.
SMD 129, 53-2, v5, 2p. [3171]
Act of Council protesting dissolution of tribal relations, and relinquishment of land title.

84. R-C of A. Babcock. 28 Mar.
SR 280, 53-2, v1, 2p. [3179]
Lands within the Grande Ronde Indian reservation, Oregon.

85. War Claims of California, Nevada, and Oregon. 29 Mar.
SR 287, 53-2, v1, 45p. [3179]
Suppression of hostile Indians.

86. L-C of A. Winston. 31 Mar.
HED 171, 53-2, v29, 3p. [3226]
Defends persons charged with selling liquor to Indians.

87. Methods of Accounting in the Treasury; 2 Apr.
SR 293, 53-2, v2, 35p. [3148] *or*
HR 409, 53-2, v2, 35p. [3158]
Accounts for the Indian Service.

88. Moore's History and Digest of International Arbitrations to which the U.S. has been a Party. 2 Apr.
HMD 212 (pts. 1-6), 53-2, v39 (pts. 1-6), 5337p. [3267 (pts. 1-6)]
Arbitrations with Spain, Russia, Great Britain, etc., sometimes are concerned with American Indians.

89. Petition of Yankton Sioux. 3 Apr.
SMD 134, 53-2, v5, 3p. [3171]
Ask ratification of the agreement of 1892.

90. R-C of E. Douglass. 4 Apr.
SR 303, 53-2, v1, 8p. [3179] *or*
HR 1227, 53-2, v4, 9p. [3272]
Late agent at the White Earth agency in Minnesota; Chippewa Indians.

91. Bridge Across the Niobrara River, Nebraska. 4 Apr.
HR 655, 53-2, v2, 3p. [3270]
Supplies to the Ponca and Yankton Sioux reservations.

92. Indians in Utah. 4 Apr.
HR 660, 53-2, v2, 4p. [3270]
Land allotments on the Uncompahgre reservation; land cessions on the Uintah reservation; Ute treaty of 1868, and agreement of 1880.

93. Confederated Otoe and Missouria Reservation. 4 Apr.
HR 661, 53-2, v2, 6p. [3270]
Sale of remaining lands in Kansas and Nebraska.

94. Indian School at Cherokee, North Carolina. 5 Apr.
HED 175, 53-2, v29, 3p. [3226]
Appropriation for fiscal 1895.

95. Indian School at Fort Shaw, Montana. 5 Apr.
HED 176, 53-2, v29, 5p. [3226]
Appropriation for fiscal 1895.

96. Indian Agencies of the U.S. 9 Apr.
SED 75, 53-2, v4, 6p. [3163]
List of agencies, agents, tribes, annuities, and allotment statistics.

97. Tsimpsheean Indians. 10 Apr.
SMD 144, 53-2, v5, 4p. [3171]
Missionary work among these Indians of British Columbia and Alaska; citizenship.

98. R-C of Florida. 13 Apr.
SR 326, 53-2, v1, 4p. [3179]
Expense of Seminole wars.

99. St. Paul, Minneapolis, and Manitoba Railway Co. 13 Apr.
SR 328, 53-2, v1, 3p. [3179] *or*
HR 1128, 53-2, v3, 3p. [3271]
Right of way through the White Earth, Leech Lake, Chippewa, and Fond du Lac reservations in Minnesota.

100. R-C of the Heirs of J. Bridger. 14 Apr.
SR 329, 53-2, v1, 24p. [3179]
Trader to the Indians in Utah Territory.

101. Annual Settlement of Public Accounts. 17 Apr.
SMD 153, 53-2, v5, 8p. [3171]
Accounts of the Indian Dept.

102. Reserving Lands in Oklahoma. 17 Apr.
SR 333, 53-2, v5, 2p. [3183]
For school purposes; Cherokee Outlet lands.

103. Right of Way for Irrigation Purposes. 17 Apr.
HR 714, 53-2, v2, 1p. [3270]
Through the Yakima reservation, Washington.

104. Indian Depredation Claims. 20 Apr.
SED 82, 53-2, v4, 5p. [3163]
Judgments rendered by the Court of Claims since 1 July 1892.

105. Legal Defense in Indian Depredation Cases. 20 Apr.
SED 83, 53-2, v4, 3p. [3163]
Persons employed in said defense.

106. Indian War Claims of California. 20 Apr.
SED 84, 53-2, v4, 106p. [3163]
Indian hostilities of 1851-59.

107. California, Oregon, and Nevada War Claims. 23 Apr.
SMD 162, 53-2, v5, 70p. [3171]
Suppression of Indian hostilities.

108. R-C of W. Hurt. 26 Apr.
SR 361, 53-2, v5, 3p. [3183]
Improvements in the Round Valley Indian reservation; California.

109. R-C of J. Morrison. 26 Apr.
SR 367, 53-2, v5, 3p. [3183] *or*
HR 564, 53-2, v2, 3p. [3270]
Land title issue in Oklahoma; Arapaho and Cheyenne agreement of 1890, calling for allotments, and land cessions.

110. Mem. of Members of the Bar in Indian Territory. 27 Apr.
SMD 166, 53-2, v5, 4p. [3171]
Defects in the judicial system there.

111. Indian Appropriation Bill. 30 Apr.
HR 802, 53-2, v2, 5p. [3270]
For fiscal 1895.

112. Case of J. Abert. 30 Apr.
HR 803, 53-2, v2, 5p. [3270]
Seminole war; 1856-57; Florida.

113. Additional Ground for Railroad Stations. 2 May.
HR 827, 53-2, v3, 2p. [3271]
Within Indian Territory.

114. Seal Islands in Alaska. 3 May.
HED 207, 53-2, v29, 4p. [3226]
Appropriation for the natives.

115. Report on the Five Civilized Tribes. 7 May.
SR 377, 53-2, v15, 13p. [3183]
Present condition of tribes, and whites dwelling among them.

116. R-C of J. Legare. 7 May.
HR 841, 53-2, v3, 2p. [3271]
Expenses of securing the surrender of Sitting Bull and his Sioux followers in 1881.

117. Wahpaykootey and Medawakantan Bands of Sioux. 10 May.
SED 94, 53-2, v4, 3p. [3163]
Money paid, and due said bands under the treaties of 1836, 1851, and 1858; also concerns the Santee Sioux of Nebraska.

118. R-P of S. Burns. 11 May.
HR 871, 53-2, v3, 1p. [3271]
Florida Indian war; 1836.

119. R-P of G. Harrington. 11 May.
HR 888, 53-2, v3, 1p. [3271]
Custer's battle on the Little Big Horn River; 1876; Montana.

120. Indian Depredation Claims. 14 May.
SED 96, 53-2, v4, 9p. [3163]
Judgments up to 1 Aug. 1893.

121. R-P of H. Dent. 14 May.
SR 403, 53-2, v5, 1p. [3183]
Service in numerous Indian wars.

122. R-P of M. Doubleday. 14 May.
SR 405, 53-2, v5, 2p. [3183] *or*
HR 1224, 53-2, v4, 5p. [3272]
Service against Apaches (1854-55), and Florida Indians (1856-58).

123. L-C of E. Moore and D. Woodson. 14 May.
HED 221, 53-2, v29, 5p. [3226]
Agents in charge of sale of Delaware, Kaskaskia, Peoria, Wea, Piankeshaw, and Iowa trust lands.

124. Legislative, Executive, and Judicial Appropriation Bill. 15 May.
HR 904, 53-2, v3, 16p. [3271]
Fiscal 1895; Indian Office.

125. Wagon Road in California. 18 May.
SR 416, 53-2, v5, 3p. [3183]
On the Hoopa Valley Indian Reservation.

126. Albany and Astoria Railway Co. 18 May.
HR 921, 53-2, v3, 2p. [3271]
Right of way through the Grande Ronde reservation in Oregon.

127. Calvary Cathedral, Sioux Falls, South Dakota. 19 May.
SR 420, 53-2, v5, 8p. [3183]
Embezzlement of funds at this Indian boarding school.

128. Kansas and Arkansas Valley Railway Co. 24 May.
HR 956, 53-2, v3, 1p. [3271] *or*
HR 976, 53-2, v3, 1p. [3271]
Right of way through Indian Territory.

129. Warm Springs Indian Reservation. 24 May.
HR 957, 53-2, v3, 1p. [3271]
Investigation of boundaries; Oregon.

130. Payment for Omaha Indian Lands. 24 May.
HR 958, 53-2, v3, 3p. [3271]
Deadline for payments extended; Nebraska.

131. Eastern Nebraska and Gulf Railway Co. 25 May.
SR 434, 53-2, v5, 1p. [3183] *or*
HR 1100, 53-2, v3, 1p. [3271]
Right of way through the Omaha and Winnebago reservations.

132. Mill at Pima Agency, Arizona. 28 May.
HED 227, 53-2, v29, 2p. [3226]
Appropriation for fiscal 1895.

133. Uncompahgre and Uintah Reservations. 29 May.
SR 450, 53-2, v5, 5p. [3183]
Allotment of reservation lands, and sale of surplus lands; Ute agreement of 1880; Utah.

134. Employees of the Interior Dept. 31 May.
SED 105, 53-2, v4, 47p. [3163]
List of appointments, promotions, dismissals, and resignations; Indian Office.

135. Army Appropriation Bill. 31 May.
SR 458, 53-2, v5, 16p. [3183]
Expenses of moving Apache prisoners from Mount Vernon Barracks, Alabama, to Fort Sill, Indian Territory.

136. Mineral Resources of the U.S. 1 June.
HMD 181, 53-2, v28, 818p. [3256]
Coal and manganese in Indian Territory.

137. Opening of Indian Reservations. 2 June.
HR 1017, 53-2, v3, 22p. [3271]
List of Indian reservations, tribes on them, and dates and treaties under which they were established; procedures for opening reservations for settlement.

138. Brainerd and Northern Minnesota Railway Co. 5 June.
SMD 202, 53-2, v5, 2p. [3171]
Right of way through the Leech Lake Indian reservation.

139. Petition of E. White. 6 June.
SMD 203, 53-2, v5, 4p. [3171]
Indian agent for the Kiowas, Comanches, and Wichitas in Indian Territory during 1885-89.

140. Agreement with the Nez Percés. 8 June.
HR 1050, 53-2, v3, 2p. [3271]
Made 1 May 1893; cession of land in Idaho.

141. R-P of M. Lafferty. 8 June.
HR 1054, 53-2, v3, 1p. [3271]
Seminole war; 1818.

142. Reports Made by Army Officers. 13 June.
SED 113, 53-2, v4, 6p. [3163]
From Fort Lane, Oregon, during 1855; Rogue River Indian war.

143. Colville Reservation, Washington. 15 June.
HED 238, 53-2, v29, 4p. [3226]
Appropriation for surveys, allotments, and opening surplus lands for settlement.

144. Abstract of the Eleventh Census; 1890. 15 June.
HMD 185, 53-2, v1, 263p. [3229]
Indian population.

145. R-C of H. Lee. 21 June.
HR 1124, 53-2, v3, 4p. [3271]
Attorney for Winnebagoes in Wisconsin.

146. R-C of P. Mitchell et al. 21 June.
HR 1125, 53-2, v3, 1p. [3271]
Survey of Eastern Cherokee timber lands in North Carolina.

147. Brainerd and Northern Minnesota Railway Co. 21 June.
HR 1129, 53-2, v3, 2p. [3271]
Right of war through the Leech Lake reservation; Minnesota.

148. Increase of Pensions. 22 June.
HR 1142, 53-2, v3, 3p. [3271]
Service in Indian wars.

149. Agreement with Yuma Indians in California. 22 June.
HR 1145, 53-2, v3, 2p. [3271]
Made 4 Dec. 1893; allotment.

150. Annual Report of the Smithsonian Institution. 1 July.
HMD 90 (pts. 1 and 2), 53-3, v15-16, 1866p. [3341-3342]
Research related to the American Indian.

151. Resol. of Sen. Lindsay. 2 July.
SMD 220, 53-2, v5, 1p. [3171]
Asks information on Indian campaigns during 1850-91.

152. Indian Depredation Claims. 3 July.
SED 128, 53-2, v4, 2p. [3163]
Judgments of the Court of Claims.

153. Survey of the Klamath Reservation. 9 July.
SED 129, 53-2, v4, 29p. [3163]
Alleged erroneous survey; settlers on lands excluded by the survey; reservation in Oregon made by the treaty of 14 Oct. 1864 with the Klamath, Modoc, and Snake Indians.

154. Expenses of a Judge. 9 July.
SED 131, 53-2, v4, 2p. [3163]
At the U.S. court in Indian Territory.

155. Indian Appropriation Bill. 10 July.
SR 510, 53-2, v5, 2p. [3183]
Year ending 30 June 1895.

156. Rogue River Indians. 11 July.
SED 135, 53-2, v4, 4p. [3163]
Reports on the loyalty of said Indians during the Indian wars of 1855-56 in Washington and Oregon.

157. Case of W. Hugo. 12 July.
SR 526, 53-2, v14, 11p. [3192]
Late Indian agent at the Ponca agency in Dakota Territory; 1870.

158. Red Cliff Indian Reservation, Wisconsin. 12 July.
SR 527, 53-2, v14, 3p. [3192] *or*
HR 977, 53-2, v3, 3p. [3271]
Enlargement of the reservation; allotments to the Chippewas residing there; treaty of 1854.

159. Winnebago Indians, Minnesota. 12 July.
SR 529, 53-2, v14, 4p. [3192]
Land title issue under the treaty of 15 Apr. 1859.

160. Kansas City, Oklahoma, and Pacific Railway Co. 12 July.
HR 1232, 53-2, v4, 2p. [3272]
Right of way through Cheyenne and Arapaho lands in Oklahoma and Indian Territory.

161. R-C of Minnesota. 12 July.
HR 1234, 53-2, v4, 3p. [3272]
Sioux raid of 1857 in Iowa and Minnesota; captives retaken from Ink-pa-du-ta's band.

162. Indian Appropriation Bill. 13 July.
SED 136, 53-2, v4, 3p. [3163]
Estimates to be included in the bill for fiscal 1895.

163. Resol. of Sen. Pettigrew. 13 July.
SMD 227 (pts. 1 and 2), 53-2, v5, 2p. [3171]
Investigation of arrest, and removal of Lower Brulé Indians to their new reservation.

164. R-C of B. Poteet. 13 July.
SR 532, 53-2, v14, 2p. [3192]
Settler on Sac and Fox lands in Nebraska.

165. Resol. of Sen. Jones. 14 July.
SMD 228, 53-2, v5, 1p. [3171]
Investigations in Indian reservations, and at Indian schools.

166. L-C of Wyandotte Indians. 19 July.
SMD 223, 53-2, v5, 3p. [3171]
Payments due under the treaty of 23 Feb. 1867.

167. Claims Allowed by Accounting Officers. 20 July.
SED 152, 53-2, v4, 30p. [3163]
Includes claims involving Indians.

168. Arkansas, Texas, and Mexican Central Railway Co. 20 July.
SR 562, 53-2, v14, 1p. [3192] *or*
HR 1078, 53-2, v3, 1p. [3271]
Right of way through Indian Territory.

169. R-P of W. Hugo. 24 July.
HR 1307, 53-2, v4, 6p. [3272]
Service against Indians in New Mexico.

170. Agreements with the Wichitas, Comanches, Kiowas, and Apaches. 26 July.
HR 1321, 53-2, v4, 2p. [3272]
Cession of lands in Oklahoma which were originally leased from the Choctaws and Chickasaws; title to land at issue.

171. Amendment to Indian Appropriation Bill. 27 July.
HED 255, 53-2, v29, 1p. [3226]
Sale of bonds for several Indian tribes.

172. R-C of Heirs of D. Filhiol. 27 July.
HR 1294 (pts. 1 and 2), 53-2, v4, 34p. [3272]
Land title issues involving the Quapaws; Hot Springs, Arkansas.

173. Claims Allowed by Accounting Officers. 30 July.
SED 164, 53-2, v4, 6p. [3163]
Includes claims involving Indians.

174. Payment of Judgments of the Court of Claims. 31 July.
SMD 249, 53-2, v5, 1p. [3171]
Indian depredation claims.

175. Deficiencies in Appropriations. 31 July.
SR 597, 53-2, v14, 1p. [3192]
For fiscal 1894; Indian depredation claims.

176. R-P of Sharp Nose. 1 Aug.
HR 1352, 53-2, v4, 3p. [3272]
War chief of the Northern Arapahoes serves U.S. as an Indian scout.

177. Appropriation for the Navajoes. 2 Aug.
SED 170, 53-2, v4, 2p. [3163]
For subsisting the New Mexico tribe.

178. R-P of E. Luke. 3 Aug.
SR 625, 53-2, v14, 1p. [3192] *or*
HR 877, 53-2, v3, 1p. [3271]
Black Hawk war; 1832.

179. R-P of A. Schwatka. 3 Aug.
SR 626, 53-2, v14, 2p. [3192] *or*
HR 1448, 53-2, v4, 2p. [3272]
Service at the Spotted Tail Indian agency, Dakota Territory; explorations in Alaska; research on the Eskimos.

180. Admission of New Mexico. 3 Aug.
SR 628, 53-2, v14, 38p. [3192] *or*
HR 155, 53-1, v1, 37p. [3157]
Populations of the Mescalero Apaches, Navajoes, Zunis, and Pueblos; reservation lands.

181. R-C of W. McLeod. 3 Aug.
SR 631, 53-2, v14, 1p. [3192] *or*
HR 1277, 53-2, v4, 1p. [3272]
Disbursing agent to the Medwakanton band of Sioux in Minnesota; 1886-87.

182. R-C of G. Johnson. 6 Aug.
HR 1372, 53-2, v4, 2p. [3272]
Mohave hostilities on the Colorado River.

183. R-C of F. Murphy et al. 6 Aug.
HR 1373, 53-2, v4, 4p. [3272]
Bill to enroll the claimants as members of the Sac and Fox of the Missouri tribe of Indians.

184. Town-site Entries in Oklahoma. 7 Aug.
HR 1379, 53-2, v4, 5p. [3272]

Legal issues surrounding entries; Sac, Fox, Iowa, Pottawatomie, Shawnee, Cheyenne, Arapaho, and Cherokee land cessions.

185. University of Oklahoma. 7 Aug.
HR 1380, 53-2, v4, 2p. [3272]
Lands set aside under the proclamation opening the Cherokee Outlet for settlement.

186. Settlers on the Cherokee Outlet. 7 Aug.
HR 1382, 53-2, v4, 1p. [3272]
Commutation of homestead entries.

187. Indian Depredation Claims. 7 Aug.
HR 1390, 53-2, v4, 1p. [3272]
Action of the Com. on the Judiciary.

188. R-C of K. Eberle. 9 Aug.
HR 1395, 53-2, v4, 2p. [3272]
Sac Indian woman to receive annuities of the Sac and Fox tribe; Black Hawk war of 1832.

189. Towns in Oklahoma. 9 Aug.
HR 1401, 53-2, v4, 1p. [3272]
Organized in the Cherokee Strip.

190. Irrigation System. 9 Aug.
HR 1402, 53-2, v4, 1p. [3272]
Through the Yakima reservation, Washington.

191. R-P of M. Wyse. 10 Aug.
HR 1410, 53-2, v4, 2p. [3272]
Service in an Indian war.

192. L-C of Minnesota. 13 Aug.
SED 174, 53-2, v4, 9p. [3163]
School lands located within Chippewa reservations.

193. R-P of A. Props. 13 Aug.
SR 675, 53-2, v14, 1p. [3192] *or*
HR 872, 53-2, v3, 1p. [3271]
Sabine Indian war; 1836-37; Arkansas Volunteers.

194. R-P of M. Frank. 13 Aug.
HR 1415, 53-2, v4, 1p. [3272]
Florida Indian war; 1818.

195. R-P of W. Shipp. 13 Aug.
HR 1416, 53-2, v4, 1p. [3272]
Creek war; 1836.

196. Allotment of Lands to Indians. 13 Aug.
HR 1422, 53-2, v4, 1p. [3272]
Correction of errors made.

197. Missouri, Oklahoma, and Texas Railway Co. 13 Aug.
HR 1423, 53-2, v4, 1p. [3272]
Right of way through Indian Territory.

198. Oklahoma Central Railway Co. 13 Aug.
HR 1424, 53-2, v4, 1p. [3272]
Right of way through Indian Territory.

199. Northern Mississippi Railway Co. 13 Aug.
HR 1425, 53-2, v4, 1p. [3272]
Right of way through the Leech Lake, Chippewa, and Winnebagoshish reservations in Minnesota.

200. Altamonte Water Co. 13 Aug.
HR 1426, 53-2, v4, 8p. [3272]
Dam would affect the Fond du Lac reservation in Minnesota.

201. Bridge Across the South Canadian River. 13 Aug.
HR 1437, 53-2, v4, 2p. [3272]
To the Wichita Indian agency.

202. List of Private Claims. 14 Aug.
SMD 266 (pts. 1-3), 53-2, v9 (pts. 1-3), 3139p. [3175 (pts. 1-3)]
From the 47th to the 51st Congress; claims involving Indians included.

203. R-P of J. Davenport. 15 Aug.
SR 685, 53-2, v14, 1p. [3192] *or*
HR 289, 53-2, v1, 1p. [3269]
Oregon Indian war; 1856.

204. R-P of W. Armstrong. 15 Aug.
HR 1438, 53-2, v4, 1p. [3272]
Service at Fort Gibson in the Cherokee Nation.

205. Winnebagoes of Minnesota. 15 Aug.
HR 1450, 53-2, v4, 5p. [3272]
Allotment and land patents.

206. Sale of Timber. 18 Aug.
SR 696, 53-2, v14, 1p. [3192]
On the Jicarilla Apache reservation.

207. Richardson's Compilation of the Messages and Papers of the Presidents; 1789-1897. 20 Aug.
HMD 210 (pts. 1-10), 53-2, v37 (pts. 1-10), 7052p. [3265 (pts. 1-10)]
Numerous references to Indians spread throughout the compilation.

208. R-P of Arkansas Volunteers. 21 Aug.
HR 1463, 53-2, v4, 2p. [3272]
Service at Fort Gibson, Cherokee Nation.

209. Private Claims. 24 Aug.
HMD 213, 53-2, v40, 749p. [3268]
From the 47th to the 51st Congress; includes claims involving Indians.

210. R-P of C. Dyall. 24 Aug.
HR 1472, 53-2, v4, 2p. [3272]
Florida Indian war; 1836.

211. Statements of Appropriations. 28 Aug.
SMD 277, 53-2, v11, 589p. [3177]
During the 1st and 2d sessions, 53rd Congress; Indian expenses.

212. Fur Seal Arbitration in Paris. (no date)
SED 177 (pts. 1-16), 53-2, v7 (pts. 1-16), 8246p. [3166 (pts. 1-16)]
Negotiations between the U.S. and Great Britain over seal hunting in the Bering Sea; Alaskan natives, or Indians are brought into the discussion at various points.

213. Eleventh Annual Report of the Bureau of Ethnology; 1889-90. (no date)
HMD 81, 53-2, v9, 600p. [3237]
Research related to the American Indian; the Sia Indians (M. Stevenson); Eskimos and other Indians of the Hudson's Bay Territory (L. Turner); Siouan cults (J. Dorsey).

214. Twelfth Annual Report of the Bureau of Ethnology; 1890-91. (no date)
HMD 82, 53-2, v10, 790p. [3238]
Research related to the American Indian; report on explorations of Indian mounds (C. Thomas).

215. Contributions to North American Ethnology, Volume 9. (no date)
HMD 173, 53-2, v21, 271p. [3249]
Dakota Grammar, Texts, and Ethnography by S. Riggs.

216. Bulletins of the Geological Survey. (no date)
HMD 178, 53-2, v25, 728p. [3253]
No. 99 lists work done in Indian Territory; No. 100 indexes publications on the geology of Indian Territory.

217. Bulletins of the Geological Survey. (no date)
HMD 180, 53-2, v27, 814p. [3255]
No. 108, a reconnaissance in central Washington, discusses artesian water supplies on the Yakima Indian reservation.

218. Congressional Directory. 1 Dec.
SMD 19 (pts. 1 and 2), 53-3, v2, 609p. [3282]
Duties of the CIA.

219. Annual Message to Congress with Documents; Pres. Cleveland. 3 Dec.
HED 1, 53-3, v1-20, 14954p. [3292-3311]
Revolution in the Mosquito Indian region of Nicaragua; transfer of Apache prisoners; success of the allotment policy; annual report of the Sec. of War (Serials 3295-3302); annual report of the Sec. of Interior (Serials 3305-3309); annual report of the Gen. Land Office (Serial 3305); annual report of the CIA (Serial 3306); etc.

220. Annual Report of the Sec. of the Treasury. 3 Dec.
HED 2, 53-3, v21 1134p. [3312]
Year ending 30 June 1894; Indian expenses.

221. Estimates of Appropriations. 3 Dec.
HED 5, 53-3, v25, 386p. [3316]
Year ending 30 June 1896; Indian expenses.

222. Judgments Rendered by the Court of Claims. 4 Dec.
SMD 14, 53-3, v1, 20p. [3281]
Case on contract to educate Indian pupils.

223. Contingent Expenses of the Interior Dept. 4 Dec.
HED 10, 53-3, v28, 24p. [3319]
For fiscal 1894; Indian Office.

224. Opening of Indian Reservations. 4 Dec.
HR 1478, 53-3, v1, 22p. [3345]
Bill proposing to open reservations to settlers; lists reservations, tribes, acreages, and treaties or laws that established these reserves.

225. List of Reports to be Made to Congress. 6 Dec.
HMD 20, 53-3, v1, 23p. [3327]
Includes those to be made by the CIA.

226. Pension Appropriation Bill. 6 Dec.
HR 1479, 53-3, v1, 10p. [3345]
Indian wars.

227. Report of the Dawes Commission. 10 Dec.
SMD 24, 53-3, v1, 43p. [3281]
Commission to the Five Civilized Tribes, appointed in 1893; negotiations for allotment, and substitution of a territorial government for tribal governments.

228. R-P of J. Meigs. 11 Dec.
SR 713, 53-3, v1, 1p. [3288] *or*
HR 1768, 53-3, v2, 1p. [3346]
Seminole war of 1835 in Florida.

229. R-P of K. Crittenden. 11 Dec.
SR 716, 53-3, v1, 1p. [3288] *or*
HR 1541, 53-3, v1, 2p. [3345]
Killed in 1876; Custer's battle with Indians at the Little Big Horn River.

230. R-P of Gen. McClernard. 11 Dec.
SR 717, 53-3, v1, 1p. [3288] *or*
HR 1555, 53-3, v1, 1p. [3345]
Black Hawk war; 1832.

231. Resol. of Sen. Mitchell. 12 Dec.
SMD 26, 53-3, v1, 1p. [3281]

Survey of the Klamath reservation boundaries; Oregon.

232. Contract Schools for Indians. 13 Dec.
HED 107, 53-3, v28, 3p. [3319]
On discontinuing said schools, and replacing them with government schools.

233. Salary of the Clerk to the Supt. of Indian Schools. 13 Dec.
HED 109, 53-3, v28, 2p. [3319]
To be provided for in the urgent deficiency bill pending in Congress.

234. Receipts and Expenditures of the U.S. 13 Dec.
HED 110, 53-3, v25, 60p. [3316]
Year ending 30 June 1894; Indian expenses.

235. R-P of T. Smith. 13 Dec.
HR 1498, 53-3, v1, 1p. [3345]
Creek war; 1836; Georgia Volunteers.

236. R-P of C. Perkins. 13 Dec.
HR 1499, 53-3, v1, 1p. [3345]
Black Hawk war; 1832; Illinois Volunteers.

237. Salaries in the Office of the CIA. 17 Dec.
HED 119, 53-3, v28, 4p. [3319]
For fiscal 1896.

238. R-P of E. Beall. 17 Dec.
HR 1504, 53-3, v1, 2p. [3345]
Florida Indian war; 1836.

239. R-P of P. Reynolds. 18 Dec.
SR 732, 53-3, v1, 1p. [3288] *or*
HR 560, 53-2, v2, 1p. [3270]
Cherokee disturbances; 1836-37.

240. R-P of M. Levans. 18 Dec.
SR 733, 53-3, v1, 1p. [3288] *or*
HR 636, 53-2, v2, 1p. [3270]
Seminole war; 1818; Florida.

241. L-C of Winston and Winston. 18 Dec.
HED 122, 53-3, v28, 5p. [3319]
Legal defense for an Indian charged with murder; Washington.

242. Winnebago Indians in Minnesota. 20 Dec.
SR 738, 53-3, v1, 2p. [3288]
Concerning land patents.

243. R-P of S. Briggs. 20 Dec.
HR 1532, 53-3, v1, 1p. [3345]
Creek war; 1836; Alabama Volunteers.

244. Kansas City, Oklahoma, and Pacific Railway Co. 21 Dec.
HR 1535, 53-3, v1, 1p. [3345]
Action of the Com. on Indian Affairs.

245. Gainesville, McAlister, and St. Louis Railway Co. 21 Dec.
HR 1536, 53-3, v1, 1p. [3345]
Right of way through Indian Territory.

246. R-C of Citizens of Oregon, Washington, and Idaho. 21 Dec.
HR 1538, 53-3, v1, 7p. [3345]
Nez Percé, Bannock, and Shoshone wars of 1877-78.

247. Interest on Certain State Bonds. 22 Dec.
HED 138, 53-3, v28, 2p. [3319]
Held in trust funds for Indians.

248. L-C of J. Friend. 22 Dec.
HED 143, 53-3, v28, 1p. [3319]
Indian depredation claim.

249. Expenditures of the Smithsonian Institution. 22 Dec.
HMD 40, 53-3, v1, 35p. [3327]
For fiscal 1894; research related to American Indians.

1895

1. Affairs at Bluefields. 3 Jan.
SED 20, 53-3, v1, 207p. [3275]
Political affairs in the Central American country of Nicaragua involving the Mosquito Indians, and their sovereignty.

2. Compensation for Land Surveys. 3 Jan.
HED 144, 53-3, v28, 2p. [3319]
Lands of the Five Civilized Tribes in Indian Territory.

3. Appropriation for Indian Police Service. 3 Jan.
HED 147, 53-3, v28, 3p. [3319]
Deficiency exists for fiscal 1895.

4. Puyallup Indian Commission. 4 Jan.
HED 166, 53-3, v32, 4p. [3323]
Appropriation to defray the expense involved in making allotments and land sales in Washington.

5. Expenses of U.S. Courts. 4 Jan.
HED 168, 53-3, v32, 1p. [3323]
Located in Indian Territory.

6. Counsel for the Mission Indians. 4 Jan.
HED 169, 53-3, v32, 2p. [3323]
Appropriation for the employment of an attorney; California.

7. Correction of Errors in Allotment. 4 Jan.
HR 1544, 53-3, v1, 1p. [3345]
Bill enabling the Sec. of Interior to

correct errors surrounding the issuance of land patents to Indians.

8. Resol. of Rep. Flynn. 8 Jan.
HMD 45, 53-3, v1, 1p. [3327]
Asks about the delay in opening the lands ceded by the Kickapoos under the agreement of 21 June 1891; Oklahoma.

9. U.S. Court in Indian Territory. 8 Jan.
HR 1547, 53-3, v1, 1p. [3345]
Action of the Com. on Judiciary.

10. Delay in Opening the Kickapoo Reservation. 8 Jan.
HR 1553, 53-3, v1, 1p. [3345]
Resol. asking for information is amended.

11. L-C of W. Munson. 9 Jan.
SED 29, 53-3, v1, 4p. [3275]
Claim against the Chickasaw Nation.

12. Moneys Due the Cherokee Nation. 9 Jan.
HED 182, 53-3, v32, 32p. [3323]
Under the treaties of 1817, 1819, 1825, 1833, 1835-36, 1846, 1866, and 1868; in compliance with article 2 of the agreement of 19 Dec. 1891.

13. R-C of S. Keller. 10 Jan.
HR 752, 53-3, v1, 3p. [3288] *or*
HR 1927, 53-3, v2, 3p. [3346]
Licensed trader to the Pottawatomies in Kansas.

14. R-C of Northrup and Chick. 10 Jan.
SR 753, 53-3, v1, 1p. [3288]
Trade with the Pottawatomies of Kansas.

15. Judgments of the Court of Claims. 11 Jan.
SED 32, 53-3, v1, 10p. [3275]
Indian depredation cases to 1 Jan. 1895.

16. R-C of the Estate of E. Crawford. 11 Jan.
SR 756, 53-3, v1, 3p. [3288]
Led U.S. troops and Indian scouts into Mexico in pursuit of hostile Apaches; 1886.

17. Navajo Indians in New Mexico. 11 Jan.
HED 192, 53-3, v32, 4p. [3323]
Appropriation for their immediate relief.

18. Indian Appropriation Bill. 12 Jan.
HR 1575, 53-3, v1, 8p. [3345]
For fiscal 1896.

19. Mem. on Behalf of the Sac and Fox Indians of the Mississippi. 14 Jan.
SMD 48, 53-3, v1, 27p. [3281]
Claims for annuities due under various treaties; made by that portion of the tribe residing in Iowa.

20. Sundry Civil Appropriation Bill. 15 Jan.
HR 1582, 53-3, v1, 10p. [3345]
Subsistence for Alaskan natives; North American ethnology; etc.

21. Agreement with the Wichitas and Affiliated Bands. 15 Jan.
HR 1585, 53-3, v1, 2p. [3345]
Land cession in Oklahoma; Choctaws and Chickasaws claim title to the land.

22. R-P of W. Monasco. 16 Jan.
SR 776, 53-3, v1, 1p. [3288] *or*
HR 875, 53-2, v3, 1p. [3271]
Creek war; 1836; Alabama Volunteers.

23. Pay of Indian Agents. 16 Jan.
HED 207, 53-3, v32, 3p. [3323]
Amended estimates of appropriations for fiscal 1896.

24. Sioux Indians of Devil's Lake, North Dakota. 16 Jan.
HED 208, 53-3, v32, 2p. [3323]
Amended appropriation for support for fiscal 1896.

25. Appropriation for Salaries in the Indian Office. 16 Jan.
HED 209, 53-3, v32, 2p. [3323]
Amended estimate for fiscal 1896.

26. Gila Valley, Globe, and Northern Railway Co. 16 Jan.
HR 1597, 53-3, v1, 1p. [3345]
Through Indian country.

27. Sioux Annuities. 19 Jan.
SED 39, 53-3, v1, 2p. [3275]
Appropriations necessary for the fiscal years 1895-1902 under the treaty of 1851, and the agreement of 1889.

28. Civil Government for Alaska. 19 Jan.
HR 1616, 53-3, v1, 2p. [3345]
Laws regarding liquor; effects on Indians.

29. Lands in Oklahoma. 21 Jan.
SR 795, 53-3, v1, 12p. [3288]
Claims of newspapers for the expenses of advertising the opening of Cheyenne and Arapaho lands.

30. Choctaw and Chickasaw Freedmen. 21 Jan.
SR 796, 53-3, v1, 1p. [3288]
Action of the Com. on Printing; statements to the Dawes Commission.

31. Sale of Kickapoo and Pottawatomie Lands. 21 Jan.
HR 1624, 53-3, v1, 1p. [3345]
Surplus, or unallotted lands in Kansas.

32. Survey of Indian Lands. 21 Jan.
HR 1627, 53-3, v1, 1p. [3345]
Estimate of cost of surveying Creek, Cherokee, Seminole, Choctaw, and Chickasaw lands in Indian Territory.

33. R-P of J. Patman. 22 Jan.
SR 805, 53-3, v1, 1p. [3288] *or*
HR 475, 53-2, v2, 1p. [3270]
Creek war; 1836; Georgia Volunteers.

34. R-P of R. Cobb. 22 Jan.
SR 806, 53-3, v1, 1p. [3288] *or*
HR 984, 53-2, v3, 1p. [3271]
Sac and Fox war of 1831.

35. Delay in Opening Lands in Oklahoma. 22 Jan.
HED 222, 53-3, v32, 2p. [3323]
Lands ceded to the U.S. by the Kickapoos under the agreement of 21 June 1891; difficulties of making allotments.

36. Claims Allowed by Accounting Officers. 22 Jan.
HED 234, 53-3, v32, 27p. [3323]
Including Indian accounts.

37. Engrossing and Recording Land Patents. 23 Jan.
SR 808, 53-3, v2, 12p. [3148] *or*
HR 1652, 53-3, v2, 12p. [3158]
Issuance of patents by the Gen. Land Office for lands allotted to Indians.

38. Bering Sea Tribunal. 23 Jan.
HED 243, 53-3, v32, 4p. [3323]
Numbers of fur seals killed; Indian canoe catch.

39. Indian Depredation Claims. 23 Jan.
HED 245, 53-3, v32, 16p. [3323]
Judgments of the Court of Claims.

40. R-P of A. Rawlings. 23 Jan.
HR 1653, 53-3, v1, 1p. [3345]
Sabine Indian war; 1836-37; Arkansas Volunteers.

41. Address from Sac and Fox Delegates. 24 Jan.
SMD 72, 53-3, v1, 5p. [3281]
That portion of the tribe residing in Oklahoma protests over the claim of the Iowa segment of the tribe which is asking for a share of the Sac and Fox annuities.

42. R-P of C. Wessels. 24 Jan.
SR 816, 53-3, v1, 2p. [3288] *or*
HR 1773, 53-3, v2, 2p. [3346]
Seminole war in Florida.

43. Appropriation for Judges in Oklahoma. 24 Jan.
HED 247, 53-3, v32, 3p. [3323]
Expenses compared with those of judges in Indian Territory.

44. Cost of Land Surveys. 25 Jan.
HED 252, 53-3, v32, 3p. [3323]
Choctaw, Chickasaw, Seminole, Cherokee, and Creek lands in Indian Territory.

45. Division of the Sioux Reservation. 28 Jan.
HR 1686, 53-3, v1, 2p. [3345]
Indians on the Crow Creek reservation received a smaller *per capita* acreage than the Indians on other diminished reserves; bill compensates for this by appropriating money to said Indians.

46. R-P of W. Holman. 29 Jan.
SR 833, 53-3, v2, 1p. [3289] *or*
HR 1405, 53-2, v4, 1p. [3272]
Sabine Indian war; 1836; Arkansas Volunteers.

47. R-P of M. Williams. 29 Jan.
SR 840, 53-3, v2, 1p. [3289] *or*
HR 1614, 53-3, v1, 1p. [3345]
Seminole war; 1838-40; Florida.

48. Disbursements for the Indian Dept. 29 Jan.
HED 262, 53-3, v33, 27p. [3324]
Year ending 30 June 1894.

49. R-C of G. Ball. 29 Jan.
HR 1699, 53-3, v1, 1p. [3345]
Land warrant for service in the Black Hawk war.

50. Resol. of Sen. Platt. 30 Jan.
SMD 80, 53-3, v1, 1p. [3281]
Asks information on enrollment and allotment questions among the Stockbridges and Munsees in Wisconsin.

51. Veto Message of Pres. Cleveland. 1 Feb.
SED 49, 53-3, v1, 3p. [3275]
Bill granting the Gila Valley, Globe, and Northern Railway Co. a right of way through the San Carlos Indian reservation in Arizona; Indians too hostile.

52. Arkansas Northwestern Railway Co. 1 Feb.
HR 1751, 53-3, v2, 1p. [3346]

Right of way through Indian Territory.

53. Census of the Western Cherokees. 2 Feb.
SED 50, 53-3, v1, 4p. [3275]
Appropriation to complete census.

54. L-C of the Ogden Land Co. 2 Feb.
SED 52, 53-3, v1, 40p. [3275]
Company's claim to Seneca lands in New York.

55. R-C of the Peoria, Piankeshaw, Wea, and Kaskaskia Indians. 2 Feb.
SR 868, 53-3, v2, 4p. [3289]
Funds due under the treaties of 1854 and 1867.

56. Case of J. Williams. 2 Feb.
HR 1755, 53-3, v2, 1p. [3346]
Did not strictly follow Indian Dept. rules while running the Fort Hall School.

57. Legislative, Executive, and Judicial Appropriation Bill. 4 Feb.
HR 1758, 53-3, v2, 16p. [3346]
For fiscal 1896; Indian Office.

58. Salaries of Certain Postmasters. 5 Feb.
SR 880, 53-3, v2, 3p. [3289]
On lands in Indian Territory which were opened for settlement.

59. R-C of B. Richards. 5 Feb.
SR 884, 53-3, v2, 9p. [3289]
Supplies delivered for Sioux at the Pine Ridge agency, South Dakota.

60. R-P of M. Nale. 5 Feb.
HR 1767, 53-3, v2, 1p. [3346]
Sabine Indian war; 1836; Mississippi Volunteers.

61. R-P of E. Granger. 6 Feb.
SR 888, 53-3, v2, 2p. [3289]
Seminole war; 1836; Florida.

62. Agreement with the Kiowas, Apaches, and Comanches. 6 Feb.
HR 1775, 53-3, v2, 3p. [3346]
Land cessions in Oklahoma opposed by the Indians who thought the lands were not to be opened until 1898 (the expiration date of the 1868 treaty at Medicine Lodge); Choctaws and Chickasaws claim title to the land.

63. Indian Appropriation Bill. 7 Feb.
SR 900, 53-3, v2, 2p. [3289]
For fiscal 1896.

64. Sale of Intoxicants to Indians. 7 Feb.
HR 1781, 53-3, v2, 4p. [3346]
Bill to prohibit sales of liquor.

65. R-C of G. Brott. 8 Feb.
SR 909, 53-3, v2, 2p. [3289]
U.S. Army depredations during the Sioux outbreak of 1862 in Minnesota.

66. Klamath Indian Reservation. 9 Feb.
SED 62, 53-3, v5, 21p. [3279]
On the accuracy of the survey of boundary lines of the reservation; Oregon.

67. Regulations Regarding Fur Seals. 11 Feb.
SED 67, 53-3, v5, 438p. [3279]
Arbitration between the U.S. and Great Britain; involves natives of Alaska, etc.; Makah Indian fishing in the Bering Sea.

68. Resol. of Sen. Pettigrew. 11 Feb.
SMD 100, 53-3, v1, 1p. [3281]
Authority to investigate conditions on Indian reservations, at Indian schools, and in Indian Territory.

69. Fur Seal Hunting in the Bering Sea. 11 Feb.
HED 306, 53-3, v33, 5p. [3324]
The taking of 7,500 seals per year is allowed for the subsistence of the Alaskan natives.

70. Chippewa Indians in Minnesota. 11 Feb.
HED 307, 53-3, v33, 10p. [3324]
Appropriation to pay for lands lost due to the construction of reservoirs on the Mississippi River.

71. R-P of M. Hamilton. 12 Feb.
SR 918, 53-3, v2, 1p. [3289] *or*
HR 1042, 53-2, v3, 1p. [3271]
Seminole war; 1818; Florida.

72. R-C of C. Baronett. 13 Feb.
SR 925, 53-3, v2, 2p. [3289]
Nez Percé depredations of 1877.

73. R-P of R. Gamble. 13 Feb.
SR 926, 53-3, v2, 2p. [3289]
Seminole war; 1836 and 1842; Florida.

74. Miami Indians of Indiana. 13 Feb.
HMD 69, 53-3, v1, 2p. [3327]
Findings of the Court of Claims in their case against the U.S.; funds due under various treaties.

75. R-P of J. Jones. 13 Feb.
HR 1828, 53-3, v2, 1p. [3346]
Florida Indian war; 1836.

76. R-P of W. Russell. 13 Feb.
HR 1829, 53-3, v2, 1p. [3346]
Oregon Indian war; 1855-56.

77. R-P of J. Morris. 13 Feb.
HR 1830, 53-3, v2, 1p. [3346]
Comanche and Pawnee campaigns; 1834-37.

78. R-P of J. Bunker. 13 Feb.
HR 1831, 53-3, v1, 1p. [3346]
Sabine Indian war; 1836-37; Arkansas Volunteers.

79. Condition of U.S. Finances. 14 Feb.
SED 73, 53-3, v6, 5p. [3280]
Expenditures on Indians in 1894.

80. Removal of the Eastern Band of Cherokees. 14 Feb.
HED 312, 53-3, v33, 2p. [3324]
Appropriation to pay those Cherokees who have removed to Indian Territory under the treaty of 29 Dec. 1835.

81. Fort Totten, North Dakota. 15 Feb.
SED 79, 53-3, v6, 10p. [3280]
Maintenance of the fort on the Cut Head or Devil's Lake Sioux Indian reservation; Indian school.

82. Agreements with Certain Indians. 15 Feb.
SR 940, 53-3, v2, 3p. [3289]
Made 21 Apr. 1887 with Lower Pend d'Oreilles or Calispels; made 27 Apr. 1887 with the Confederated Flatheads, Pend d'Oreilles, and Kootenais; made 18 Mar. 1887 with the Upper and Middle Spokanes; land cessions in Washington and Idaho.

83. R-P of S. Brady. 16 Feb.
HR 1845, 53-3, v2, 1p. [3346]
Creek war; 1836; Georgia Volunteers.

84. Judgments of the Court of Claims. 18 Feb.
SED 86, 53-3, v6, 2p. [3280]
Indian depredation cases.

85. Sundry Civil Appropriations for 1896. 18 Feb.
SR 950, 53-3, v2, 2p. [3289]
For survey of the San Carlos Indian reservation, Arizona.

86. Condition of Business in the Executive Depts. 18 Feb.
SR 952, 53-3, v2, 41p. [3148] *or*
HR 1851, 53-3, v2, 41p. [3158]
Includes the Indian division of the Interior Dept., and the OIA; accounts.

87. R-P of J. Jones. 19 Feb.
SR 963, 53-3, v2, 1p. [3289] *or*
HR 1827, 53-3, v2, 1p. [3346]
Creek war; 1836; Georgia Volunteers.

88. Legislative, Executive, and Judicial Appropriations. 20 Feb.
SR 965, 53-3, v2, 2p. [3289]
Fiscal 1896; Indian Office.

89. R-P of J. Laughlin. 20 Feb.
HR 1885, 53-3, v2, 1p. [3346]
Black Hawk war; 1832.

90. R-P of C. Leeper. 20 Feb.
HR 1886, 53-3, v2, 1p. [3346]
Black Hawk war; 1832.

91. Mount Vernon Military Reservation. 21 Feb.
SR 971, 53-3, v2, 2p. [3289] *or*
HR 1819, 53-3, v2, 2p. [3346]
Apache prisoners of war removed in the fall of 1894; Alabama.

92. R-C of L. Noyes. 21 Feb.
HR 1897, 53-3, v2, 5p. [3346]
Native dissension on the Alaskan fur seal islands.

93. Amending the U.S. Pension Laws. 21 Feb.
HR 1899, 53-3, v2, 4p. [3346]
Pensions are now granted for the Black Hawk, Cherokee, and Seminole wars of 1832-42; the amendment would include the Seminole war of 1818, the "La Fevre" or Winnebago war of 1827, the Sabine war of 1836, the Cayuse war of 1847-48, the Texas and New Mexico wars of 1849-55, the California wars of 1850-56, the Utah war of 1850-53, and the Oregon and Washington wars prior to 1856.

94. R-C of E. Ayres. 21 Feb.
HR 1900, 53-3, v2, 6p. [3346]
Land purchased from Chickasaws in Mississippi; 1839.

95. Kansas City, Pittsburg, and Gulf Railroad Co. 21 Feb.
HR 1905, 53-3, v2, 1p. [3346]
Right of way through Indian Territory.

96. Coal Fields on the San Carlos Reservation. 22 Feb.
SMD 125, 53-3, v1, 2p. [3281]
On survey and segregation of these fields in Arizona; consent of Indians should be obtained.

97. R-P of A. Morris. 22 Feb.
SR 978, 53-3, v2, 2p. [3289]
Modoc war of 1873; Nez Percé war of 1877.

98. R-P of C. Reed. 22 Feb.
SR 980, 53-3, v2, 1p. [3289]
Seminole war; 1836 and 1842; Florida.

99. Arkansas State Bonds. 23 Feb.
SED 91, 53-3, v6, 8p. [3280]
Held for the Chickasaw orphans, and national trust funds.

100. Domestic Reindeer in Alaska. 23 Feb.
SED 92, 53-3, v6, 100p. [3280]
To benefit the Eskimos and other Alaskan Indians.

101. L-C of Capt. Bullis. 23 Feb.
SMD 127, 53-3, v1, 2p. [3281]
Late Indian agent at the San Carlos agency in Arizona.

102. Mem. of the Seneca Nation of New York Indians. 23 Feb.
SMD 129, 53-3, v1, 4p. [3281]
On the claim of the Ogden Land Co. to title to land within Seneca reservations in New York.

103. Miami Indians *vs.* the U.S. 23 Feb.
SMD 131, 53-3, v1, 3p. [3281]
Findings of the Court of Claims; funds due under various treaties; Indiana branch of the tribe.

104. Indians on the Crow Creek Reservation. 23 Feb.
SMD 132, 53-3, v1, 1p. [3281]
Compensation for having received less land *per capita* than Indians on other diminished reserves; division of the Great Sioux reservation.

105. New Mexico Volunteers. 23 Feb.
SR 983, 53-3, v2, 8p. [3289] *or*
HR 675, 53-2, v2, 7p. [3270]
Service against Pueblo Indians; 1847.

106. R-P of A. Laughlin. 26 Feb.
SR 995, 53-3, v2, 1p. [3289] *or*
HR 1887, 53-3, v2, 1p. [3346]
Black Hawk war; 1832.

107. R-P of M. Button. 26 Feb.
SR 1002, 53-3, v2, 1p. [3289] *or*
HR 1447, 53-2, v4, 1p. [3272]
Sabine Indian war; 1837; Arkansas Volunteers.

108. Establishment of a U.S. Court in Indian Territory. 27 Feb.
SMD 137, 53-3, v1, 7p. [3281]
Senate-House conference on amendments to an act creating said court.

109. R-P of Kansas Cavalry Volunteers. 27 Feb.
HR 1945, 53-3, v2, 4p. [3346]
Service against Cheyennes, Kiowas, Comanches, and Apaches in 1867-68; Custer's battle on the Washita River.

110. Claims Allowed by Accounting Officers. 28 Feb.
SED 102, 53-3, v6, 11p. [3280]
Some related to the Indian Service.

111. Bonds of Officers of the U.S. 28 Feb.
SR 1022, 53-3, v2, 12p. [3148] *or*
HR 1910, 53-3, v2, 12p. [3158]
Indian agents, Supts., inspectors, and supervisors.

112. War Claims Against the U.S. 28 Feb.
HR 1957, 53-3, v2, 37p. [3346]
By various States; suppression of Indian hostilities during the Civil War.

113. Arkansas State Bonds. 28 Feb.
HR 1959, 53-3, v2, 16p. [3346]
In the Chickasaw trust fund.

114. R-P of D. Sexton. 1 Mar.
SR 1031, 53-3, v2, 1p. [3289] *or*
HR 1452, 53-2, v4, 1p. [3272]
Rogue River war; 1853; Oregon Volunteers.

115. R-P of W. Durley. 1 Mar.
SR 1041, 53-3, v2, 1p. [3289] *or*
HR 1884, 53-3, v2, 1p. [3346]
Black Hawk war; 1832; Illinois Volunteers.

116. Statements of Appropriations. 2 Mar.
SMD 150, 53-3, v6, 432p. [3286]
During the 3rd session, 53rd Congress; Indian expenses.

117. R-P of C. Greene. 2 Mar.
SR 1036, 53-3, v2, 1p. [3289] *or*
HR 1739, 53-3, v1, 1p. [3345]
Creek war; 1836; Georgia Volunteers.

118. R-P of A. Abercrombie. 2 Mar.
SR 1040, 53-3, v2, 1p. [3289] *or*
HR 1457, 53-2, v4, 1p. [3272]
Creek war; 1836; Alabama Volunteers.

119. R-C of B. Moreland. 2 Mar.
SR 1042, 53-3, v2, 2p. [3289] *or*
HR 1533, 53-3, v1, 2p. [3345]
Land encorporated into the Winnebago reservation in Minnesota; 1856.

120. Net Proceeds from the Sale of Public Lands. 2 Mar.
SR 1043, 53-3, v2, 56p. [3289] *or*
HR 1552, 53-3, v1, 25p. [3345]
Sale of Indian lands under various treaties (Senate version includes extra exhibits).

121. Laws and Decision Regarding U.S. Court Officials. 2 Mar.

HMD 87, 53-3, v1, 300p. [3327]
Includes Indian Territory and Indian country.

122. Annual Report of the American Historical Association for 1894. 2 Mar.
HMD 91, 53-3, v17, 614p. [3343]
Research related to the American Indians.

123. Opinions of the Attorneys-General of the U.S., Volume 20. (no date)
HMD 44, 53-3, v5, 852p. [3331]
Decisions concerning the Cherokee, Crow, Pueblo, and Sioux mixed-blood Indians; etc.

124. Eleventh Report of the U.S. Civil Service Commission. (no date)
HMD 79, 53-3, v10, 424p. [3336]
Information on the Indian Service.

125. Annual Report of the Smithsonian Institution. 1 July.
HD 425 (pts. 1 and 2), 54-1, v81-82, 1980p. [3448-3449]
Research related to the American Indian.

126. Annual Report of the Sec. of War. 26 Nov.
HD 2, 54-1, v3-11, 5829p. [3370-3378]
Conflict between whites and Bannock Indians in Wyoming; etc.

127. Annual Report of the Sec. of Interior. 27 Nov.
HD 5, 54-1, v14-22, 7924p. [3381-3389]
Indian affairs in the U.S.; annual report of the Gen. Land Office (Serial 3381); annual report of the CIA (Serial 3382); etc.

128. Annual Report of the Attorney-General of the U.S. 30 Nov.
HD 9, 54-1, v23, 247p. [3390]
Legal issues involving the Eastern Cherokee, Mission, and Black Bob Shawnee Indians; etc.

129. Annual Message to Congress with Documents; Pres. Cleveland. 2 Dec.
HD 1, 54-1, v1-2, 1563p. [3368-3369]
Jurisdiction over the Mosquito Indians of Nicaragua.

130. Estimates of Appropriations. 2 Dec.
HD 12, 54-1, v29, 402p. [3396]
Year ending 30 June 1897; Indian expenses.

131. Reports to be Made to Congress. 2 Dec.
HD 15, 54-1, v32, 25p. [3399]
The CIA on Indian affairs.

132. Judgments Rendered by the Court of Claims. 3 Dec.
SD 8, 54-1, v1, 44p. [3347]
Includes judgments against the Cherokee Nation, and the New York Indians; etc.

133. Statistical Abstract of the U.S. 3 Dec.
HD 100, 54-1, v51, 424p. [3418]
For 1895; Indian population, etc.

134. Report of the Dawes Commission. 5 Dec.
SD 12, 54-1, v1, 21p. [3347]
Appointed to negotiate with the Five Civilized Tribes; recommends U.S. assume political control over Indian Territory.

135. Contingent Expenses of the Interior Dept. 6 Dec.
HD 23, 54-1, v32, 22p. [3399]
Fiscal 1895; Indian Office.

136. Congressional Directory. 7 Dec.
SD 14 (pts. 1-3), 54-1, v15, 1085p. [3361]
Duties of the CIA.

137. Moneys Due the Cherokee Nation. 9 Dec.
SD 16, 54-1, v1, 4p. [3347]
Under various treaties.

138. Receipts and Disbursements. 9 Dec.
HD 41, 54-1, v29, 64p. [3396]
For fiscal 1895; Indian Service.

139. Annual Report of the Sec. of the Treasury. 10 Dec.
HD 8, 54-1, v25, 944p. [3392]
Year ending 30 June 1895; Indian expenses.

140. Prohibition of Liquor Sales to Indians. 11 Dec.
SD 21, 54-1, v1, 6p. [3347]
Bill to prohibit said sales, and the reasons for it.

141. Agreement with the Turtle Mountain Indians. 12 Dec.
SD 23, 54-1, v1, 4p. [3347]
Made 22 Oct. 1892; land cessions in North Dakota by this band of Chippewas.

142. Disbursements for the Indian Dept. 20 Dec.
HD 89, 54-1, v47, 29p. [3414]
For fiscal 1895.

143. Allotment of Wichita Lands. 24 Dec.
HD 97, 54-1, v47, 13p. [3414]
Allotment of lands in Oklahoma under the agreement of 1891 is delayed due to the claim of the Choctaws and Chickasaws to the lands in question.

144. Indian Depredation Claims. 30 Dec.
SD 50, 54-1, v3, 2p. [3349]
Judgments in favor of claimants.

145. Mem. of the Arizona Legis. 31 Dec.
HD 104, 54-1, v47, 2p. [3414]
On depredations of the Papago Indians, and kindred tribes.

1896

1. Improvements of Intruders in the Cherokee Nation. 6 Jan.
HD 116, 54-1, v47, 46p. [3414]
Appraisal of said improvements.
2. Delinquent Accounting Officers. 7 Jan.
HD 119, 54-1, v47, 3p. [3414]
Includes officers in the Indian Service.
3. Exploration of the Olympic Mountains, Washington. 8 Jan.
SD 59, 54-1, v3, 20p. [3349]
Indians on the Quinaiult reservation are encountered.
4. R-P of Northrup and Chick. 9 Jan.
SR 31, 54-1, v1, 1p. [3362]
Action of the Com. on Indian Affairs.
5. R-P of S. Keller. 9 Jan.
SR 32, 54-1, v1, 3p. [3362] *or*
SR 1450, 54-1, v6, 3p. [3462]
Licensed trader to the Pottawatomies.
6. R-C of S. Marston. 9 Jan.
SR 37, 54-1, v1, 2p. [3362] *or*
HR 1206, 54-1, v5, 2p. [3461]
Late Indian agent at the Union agency, Indian Territory.
7. Estimates of Deficiencies. 9 Jan.
HD 128, 54-1, v29, 33p. [3396]
Appropriations for fiscal 1896; Indian Service.
8. Condition of Business in the Executive Depts. 9 Jan.
HD 129, 54-1, v47, 32p. [3414]
Includes the OIA.
9. Atchison and Nebraska Railroad Co. 10 Jan.
SR 39, 54-1, v1, 2p. [3362] *or*
HR 258, 54-1, v1, 2p. [3457]
Right of way across Sac, Fox, and Iowa allotted lands; leased to the Chicago, Burlington, and Quincy Railroad Co.
10. Expenditures of the Smithsonian Institution. 10 Jan.
HD 133, 54-1, v47, 35p. [3414]
On North American ethnology, and other research on the American Indian.
11. Fort Hays Military Reserve. 11 Jan.
HR 27, 54-1, v1, 3p. [3457]
Established in Kansas as a base for operations against Indians.
12. Columbia and Red Mountain Railway Co. 14 Jan.
SR 44, 54-1, v1, 1p. [3362] *or*
HR 420, 54-1, v2, 1p. [3458]
Right of way through the Colville reservation, Washington.
13. R-P of R. Gamble. 14 Jan.
SR 50, 54-1, v1, 2p. [3362]
Seminole war; 1836; Florida.
14. R-P of A. Schwatka. 14 Jan.
SR 55, 54-1, v1, 2p. [3362] *or*
HR 486, 54-1, v2, 2p. [3458]
Publications on the Alaskan Eskimo.
15. R-P of M. Hitchcock. 14 Jan.
SR 59, 54-1, v1, 2p. [3362]
Service in the Florida Indian war, and the Creek war, etc.
16. R-P of H. Dent. 14 Jan.
SR 70, 54-1, v1, 1p. [3362] *or*
HR 2911, 54-2, v3, 1p. [3556]
Service in Indian wars on the frontier.
17. R-P of M. Doubleday. 14 Jan.
SR 71, 54-1, v1, 2p. [3362]
Service against Apaches (1854-55), and against Florida Indians (1856-58).
18. Arkansas State Bonds. 16 Jan.
SR 76, 54-1, v1, 9p. [3362]
Held in the Chickasaw trust fund.
19. R-C of J. Bridger. 16 Jan.
SR 80, 54-1, v1, 23p. [3362] *or*
HR 468, 54-1, v2, 23p. [3458]
Trader to Indians in Utah; 1843-57.
20. Allotment of Certain Indian Lands. 17 Jan.
HR 66, 54-1, v1, 1p. [3457]
To the Uncompahgre and Uintah Indians in Utah.
21. Duluth and North Dakota Railroad Co. 17 Jan.
HR 71, 54-1, v1, 1p. [3457]
Action of the Com. on Indian Affairs.
22. Kansas Cavalry Volunteers. 17 Jan.
HR 72, 54-1, v1, 3p. [3457]
Campaign of 1867-69 against the Cheyennes, Kiowas, Comanches, and Apaches.

23. Old Settler, or Western Cherokees. 20 Jan.
SD 77, 54-1, v3, 35p. [3349]
Information on payments made for legal and other services rendered these Indians in their prosecution of a claim against the U.S.

24. Omaha and Winnebago Reservations. 21 Jan.
SD 79, 54-1, v3, 175p. [3349]
Testimony concerning the condition of affairs on said reservations.

25. Fort Assiniboine Military Reserve. 21 Jan.
SR 94, 54-1, v1, 2p. [3362] *or*
HR 400, 54-1, v2, 2p. [3458]
Located on an Indian reservation in Montana; Indian land title extinguished in 1888.

26. Reimbursal of Rev. Ashley. 21 Jan.
HD 161, 54-1, v53, 8p. [3420]
For moneys expended on the legal defense of Sioux policemen at the Cheyenne River agency, South Dakota.

27. Homestead Settlers on the Yankton Reservation. 21 Jan.
HR 100, 54-1, v1, 2p. [3457]
Lands opened to settlement in 1895; South Dakota.

28. R-P of A. Morris. 22 Jan.
SR 92, 54-1, v1, 3p. [3362] *or*
HR 869, 54-1, v4, 2p. [3460]
Modoc war of 1873, and Nez Percé war of 1877.

29. Punishment for Capital Crimes. 22 Jan.
HR 108, 54-1, v1, 22p. [3457]
Lists homicides brought to trial in Indian Territory during 1890-92.

30. Annuities of the Santee Sioux. 23 Jan.
SD 85, 54-1, v3, 15p. [3349]
Petitions ask for payment of annuities withheld since the Sioux outbreak of 1862.

31. R-C of J. O'Keane. 23 Jan.
SR 111, 54-1, v1, 1p. [3362]
Services at the Tulalip Indian agency, Washington, in 1882.

32. R-C of Grubb and Robinson. 23 Jan.
SR 113, 54-1, v1, 1p. [3457]
Lumber sold to the Prairie band of Pottawatomies in Kansas; 1881-83.

33. Payment for Legal Services Rendered to Certain Indians. 23 Jan.
HR 114, 54-1, v1, 2p. [3457]
Services rendered to the "Old Settler," or Western Cherokees.

34. Brainerd and Northern Minnesota Railway Co. 23 Jan.
HR 116, 54-1, v1, 2p. [3457]
Right of way through the Leech Lake and Chippewa Indian Reservations.

35. Chippewas in Minnesota. 23 Jan.
HR 119, 54-1, v1, 2p. [3457]
Amendments to an act calling for land cessions.

36. Suits Against the U.S. 24 Jan.
SD 92, 54-1, v3, 3p. [3349]
Includes Indian depredation claims.

37. Land Title of W. Morgan. 27 Jan.
SR 125, 54-1, v1, 3p. [3362]
Kansas Indian trust lands in Kansas.

38. Fur-Seal Fisheries of Alaska. 27 Jan.
HD 175, 54-1, v54, 240p. [3421]
Includes a report on natives resident upon islands off Alaska.

39. Free Homesteads on Lands Purchased from Indians. 27 Jan.
HR 147, 54-1, v1, 12p. [3457]
Reservation lands ceded to the U.S. under various agreements.

40. Appropriations for Cavalry Horses. 28 Jan.
HD 178, 54-1, v53, 2p. [3420]
To go to Indian scouts and others.

41. Persons Reimbursed for Moneys Expended. 29 Jan.
SR 144, 54-1, v1, 13p. [3362]
Suppression of Pah-Ute hostilities of 1860 in Utah Territory.

42. War Claims of Certain States. 29 Jan.
SR 145, 54-1, v1, 81p. [3362] *or*
HR 1648, 54-1, v7, 53p. [3463]
Expenditures during the Civil War; includes protection of transportation routes from hostile Indians in California, Oregon, and Nevada; etc.

43. Urgent Deficiency Appropriation Bill. 30 Jan.
SR 150, 54-1, v1, 8p. [3362]
U.S. Courts in Indian Territory.

44. R-C of J. Schwarz. 30 Jan.
SR 151, 54-1, v1, 3p. [3362]
Made the plans for an Indian school in Flandreau, South Dakota.

45. St. Louis, Oklahoma, and Southern Railway Co. 30 Jan.
HR 188, 54-1, v1, 1p. [3457]
Right of way through Indian Territory.

46. Kansas City, Pittsburg, and Gulf Railroad Co. 30 Jan.

HR 189, 54-1, v1, 1p. [3457]
Right of way through Indian Territory.

47. R-C of Minnesota. 31 Jan.
HR 205, 54-1, v1, 3p. [3457]
Expense of rescuing captives held by Ink-pa-du-kah's band of Sioux in 1857; Sioux outbreak of 1857.

48. Rights of Indians to Hunt on Unoccupied Public Domain. 31 Jan.
HR 206, 54-1, v1, 3p. [3457]
Bill calling for the surrender or modification of Shoshone, Bannock, and Arapaho hunting privileges in Wyoming and Idaho.

49. St. Louis and Oklahoma City Railroad Co. 31 Jan.
HR 207, 54-1, v1, 2p. [3457]
Right of way through Indian Territory.

50. Uncompahgre Indian Reservation. 1 Feb.
HD 191, 54-1, v53, 18p. [3420]
On land allotments to the Utes, and restoration of certain lands to the public domain.

51. Jurisdiction of the 8th U.S. Circuit Court. 1 Feb.
HR 217, 54-1, v1, 1p. [3457]
Over Indian Territory.

52. Arkansas and Choctaw Railroad Co. 1 Feb.
HR 218, 54-1, v1, 1p. [3457]
Right of way through the Choctaw Nation, Indian Territory.

53. Army Appropriation Bill. 3 Feb.
HR 223, 54-1, v1, 10p. [3457]
Subsistence for Apache prisoners; fiscal 1897.

54. Protection of Railway Cars. 3 Feb.
HR 225, 54-1, v1, 1p. [3457]
Bill making it unlawful to shoot at cars in Indian Territory.

55. Gainesville, McAlester, and St. Louis Railway Co. 3 Feb.
HR 227, 54-1, v1, 1p. [3457]
Right of way through Indian Territory.

56. Fort Smith and Western Coal Railroad Co. 3 Feb.
HR 228, 54-1, v1, 2p. [3457]
Right of way through Indian Territory.

57. Case of Brevet Maj. Gen. Webb. 4 Feb.
SR 158, 54-1, v1, 4p. [3362] *or*
HR 380 (pts. 1 and 2), 54-1, v2, 10p. [3458]
Seminole war; 1855; Florida (House report looks at the case in greater detail).

58. Senate Bill 1704. 4 Feb.
SR 162, 54-1, v1, 1p. [3362]
Action of the Com. on Indian Affairs.

59. Mineral Land Laws. 4 Feb.
SR 163, 54-1, v1, 2p. [3362]
Extended to lands in the Colville reservation, Washington; school lands exempted.

60. R-P of E. Filgate. 4 Feb.
SR 164, 54-1, v1, 2p. [3362]
Service at Fort Gibson, Cherokee Nation, during 1846-48.

61. R-P of E. Sutherland. 4 Feb.
SR 172, 54-1, v1, 4p. [3362] *or*
HR 524, 54-1, v2, 4p. [3458]
Service against Apaches and Comanches in New Mexico.

62. Lease of Alaska Seal Islands. 4 Feb.
HD 197, 54-1, v53, 3p. [3420]
Includes amounts expended on Alaskan natives.

63. R-C of D. Boutwell. 4 Feb.
HR 234, 54-1, v1, 1p. [3457]
Indian Home Guards during the Civil War.

64. Reimbursal of Capt. Bullis. 5 Feb.
HD 202, 54-1, v53, 2p. [3420]
Expenses incurred in a suit brought against him by a former Indian trader at the San Carlos agency, Arizona.

65. Railroad Passenger Rates in Indian Territory. 5 Feb.
HR 257, 54-1, v1, 1p. [3457]
Bill to regulate said rates.

66. R-C of H. Shipley. 6 Feb.
SR 216, 54-1, v1, 3p. [3362] *or*
HR 1855, 54-1, v8, 3p. [3464]
Services at the Nez Percé agency, Idaho, in 1880.

67. Additional Ground for Railroad Stations. 6 Feb.
HR 267, 54-1, v1, 2p. [3457]
In Indian Territory.

68. R-C of the Fond du Lac Band of Chippewas. 6 Feb.
HR 268, 54-1, v1, 13p. [3457]
Failure of the U.S. to carry out stipulations of the treaty of 30 Sept. 1854.

69. R-P of C. Reed. 7 Feb.
SR 223, 54-1, v1, 1p. [3362]
Seminole war; 1836 and 1842; Florida.

70. Proceeds from Sale of Public Lands. 7 Feb.
SR 226, 54-1, v1, 75p. [3362]
Includes distribution of proceeds from the sale of Indian lands.

71. R-C of E. Fish et al. 7 Feb.
SR 229, 54-1, v1, 6p. [3362] *or*
SR 1180, 54-2, v1, 7p. [3474] *or*
HR 1459, 54-1, v6, 6p. [3462]
Supplies to various Indian reservations in Arizona; 1873-74.

72. Purchase of Reindeer for Alaska. 7 Feb.
HD 211, 54-1, v53, 2p. [3420]
Food for Alaskan natives.

73. Case of F. Field. 8 Feb.
HR 301, 54-1, v2, 2p. [3458]
Indian agent in the Creek Nation, Indian Territory; 1869-70.

74. Domestic Reindeer in Alaska. 10 Feb.
SD 111, 54-1, v4, 136p. [3350]
For the benefit of Eskimos and other Alaskan natives.

75. Relief to Indian Citizens. 10 Feb.
SR 235, 54-1, v1, 10p. [3362] *or*
HR 749, 54-1, v3, 11p. [3459]
On taxation of lands allotted to Indians; hereafter, agreements made to purchase unallotted lands will provide for a fund to pay said taxes.

76. Intoxicating Liquors in Alaska. 11 Feb.
SD 113, 54-1, v4, 32p. [3350]
Laws regarding liquor difficult to enforce; effects on natives.

77. R-P of I. Morrow. 11 Feb.
SR 240, 54-1, v1, 3p. [3362] *or*
HR 1012, 54-1, v4, 3p. [3460]
Ute campaign; 1872; Utah.

78. Land District in Montana. 11 Feb.
SR 247, 54-1, v1, 1p. [3362]
Includes condition of roads through the Flathead reservation.

79. Grand Lodge of Masons, Indian Territory. 11 Feb.
HR 320, 54-1, v2, 1p. [3458]
Bill incorporating said organization.

80. Agreement with the Fort Belknap Reservation Indians. 12 Feb.
SD 117, 54-1, v4, 32p. [3350]
Made 9 Oct. 1895; lands ceded in Montana by the Gros Ventres and Assiniboines; council proceedings.

81. Agreement with the Blackfeet Indians. 12 Feb.
SD 118, 54-1, v4, 36p. [3350]
Made 26 Sept. 1895; land cessions in Montana; council proceedings.

82. R-C of the Reps. of G. McDougall. 13 Feb.
SR 275, 54-1, v2, 8p. [3363] *or*
HR 204, 54-1, v1, 9p. [3457]
Supplies to California Indians; 1850.

83. Annual Report of the American Historical Association, 1895. 13 Feb.
HD 291, 54-1, v62, 1257p. [3429]
Research related to the American Indian.

84. R-C of Nebraska. 13 Feb.
HR 344, 54-1, v2, 2p. [3458]
Expenses incurred suppressing Sioux hostilities during 1890-91; massacre at Wounded Knee.

85. R-P of S. Hyams. 13 Feb.
HR 347, 54-1, v2, 1p. [3458]
Seminole war; 1836; Florida.

86. R-C of K. Eberle. 13 Feb.
HR 356, 54-1, v2, 2p. [3458]
Woman of the Sac tribe claims moneys are due her out of Sac and Fox annuities.

87. Kansas City, Fort Scott, and Memphis Railroad Co. 14 Feb.
HR 376, 54-1, v2, 2p. [3458]
Right of way through Indian Territory.

88. Surveying Lands in Indian Territory. 15 Feb.
HD 243, 54-1, v58, 4p. [3425]
Appropriation needed to survey the lands of the Five Civilized Tribes.

89. Negotiations with the Crows and Flatheads. 17 Feb.
SR 285, 54-1, v2, 1p. [3363]
For land cessions in Montana; fund created to cover taxes upon lands which might be allotted to Indians.

90. R-C of G. Simpson and L. Shaw. 17 Feb.
HR 402, 54-1, v2, 2p. [3458]
Survey of the Grand Portage Indian reservation in Minnesota; 1892.

91. R-C of the Heirs of W. Dougherty. 17 Feb.
HR 405, 54-1, v2, 1p. [3458]
Former Indian agent in Missouri.

92. R-P of J. Meigs. 18 Feb.
SR 294, 54-1, v2, 1p. [3363] *or*
HR 1564, 54-1, v6, 1p. [3462]
Seminole war; 1835; Florida.

93. Appropriation to Conduct Negotiations with Indians. 18 Feb.
HD 248, 54-1, v58, 5p. [3425]

With Ute Indians on the Uintah and Uncompahgre reservations in Utah for modification of treaties and agreements.

94. Northern Cheyenne and Arapaho Indians. 18 Feb.
HD 249, 54-1, v58, 4p. [3425]
Use of unexpended appropriations to purchase cattle for the Tongue River reservation, Montana.

95. Indian Appropriation Bill. 18 Feb.
HR 407, 54-1, v2, 4p. [3458]
For fiscal 1897.

96. Legislative, Executive, and Judicial Appropriation Bill. 18 Feb.
HR 415, 54-1, v2, 16p. [3458]
For fiscal 1897; OIA.

97. R-P of P. Daly. 19 Feb.
SR 312, 54-1, v2, 2p. [3363] *or*
HR 1776, 54-1, v7, 2p. [3463]
Service among Comanches; 1857-61; Texas.

98. Protection of Salmon Fisheries in Alaska. 19 Feb.
HD 251, 54-1, v58, 3p. [3425]
To protect the food supply of Alaskan Indians.

99. Amending the Statutes at Large. 19 Feb.
HR 440, 54-1, v2, 2p. [3458]
Pension laws; for service in the Civil War, followed by service in Indian campaigns.

100. Mem. on Behalf of the Modocs, Klamaths, and Snakes. 20 Feb.
SD 131, 54-1, v4, 29p. [3350]
Claim for land excluded from the Klamath reservation, Oregon, due to an erroneous survey under the treaty of 14 Oct. 1864.

101. Payment of Volunteer Soldiers. 20 Feb.
SR 323, 54-1, v2, 1p. [3363]
Seminole war; Florida.

102. Choctaw, Oklahoma, and Gulf Railway Co. 20 Feb.
HR 450, 54-1, v2, 2p. [3458]
Right of way through Indian Territory.

103. Arkansas Northwestern Railway Co. 20 Feb.
HR 452, 54-1, v2, 1p. [3458]
Right of way through Indian Territory.

104. Additional Clerical Force for the Interior Dept. 21 Feb.
HD 255, 54-1, v58, 3p. [3425]
Including the Indian Division.

105. Town Sites in Oklahoma. 21 Feb.
HR 478, 54-1, v2, 2p. [3458]
Attached as a substitute bill to the act enlarging the jurisdiction of the U.S. Court in Indian Territory.

106. Sale of Indian Lands. 24 Feb.
HD 258, 54-1, v58, 3p. [3425]
Removal of restrictions upon the sale of the allotted lands of the Puyallup Indians in Washington.

107. Case of D. Gordon. 24 Feb.
HR 492 (pts. 1 and 2), 54-1, v2, 9p. [3458]
Campaigns against the Sioux (1867 and 1879) and Bannocks (1877); etc.

108. Decisions of Courts Relating to War Claims. 24 Feb.
HR 501, 54-1, v2, 2p. [3458]
On the printing of said decisions; includes Indian depredation claims, etc.

109. R-P of A. Nolan. 25 Feb.
SR 345, 54-1, v2, 2p. [3363] *or*
HR 1008, 54-1, v4, 2p. [3460]
Military service in Indian Territory.

110. R-C of S. Peel. 25 Feb.
HR 507, 54-1, v2, 3p. [3458]
Legal services performed for the "Old Settler" or Western Cherokees.

111. Statistics from the Pension Office. 26 Feb.
SD 134, 54-1, v4, 5p. [3350]
For service in Indian wars.

112. Army Appropriation Bill. 26 Feb.
SR 361, 54-1, v2, 2p. [3363]
Includes support of Apache prisoners at Fort Sill, Oklahoma.

113. Seal Life on the Pribilof Islands. 27 Feb.
SD 137 (pts. 1 and 2), 54-1, v5-6, 529p. [3351-3352]
Report deals with the condition of the Alaskan natives, or Indians; liquor traffic, schools, etc.

114. Mem. of the Eastern Cherokees. 2 Mar.
SD 143, 54-1, v4, 9p. [3350]
On moneys due under various treaties.

115. Expenses of the Indian Depts. 3 Mar.
HD 269, 54-1, v58, 5p. [3425]
Appropriation bill amended because of events at the White Mountain Apache reservation, Arizona.

116. Bulletin of the U.S. Fish Commission. 6 Mar.
HD 79, 54-1, v49, 486p. [3416]

Fish and mollusks of Indian Territory; etc.

117. Legislation in Behalf of Certain Chippewas. 6 Mar.
HD 283, 54-1, v61, 4p. [3428]
Permits certain Chippewas to remain on lands which they have improved, rather than remove to the Red Lake reservation, Minnesota.

118. Criminal Jurisdiction of the Supreme Court. 6 Mar.
HR 666, 54-1, v3, 4p. [3459]
Removal of all but capital cases from the docket; previous noncapital cases sometimes involved Indians.

119. Amendments to the Indian Appropriation Bill. 9 Mar.
SR 427, 54-1, v2, 1p. [3363]
Increased appropriation for the Poncas of Nebraska.

120. Payments for Indian Supplies. 9 Mar.
SR 428, 54-1, v2, 2p. [3363] *or*
HR 737, 54-1, v3, 2p. [3459]
For the Indian industrial school at Genoa, Nebraska.

121. Sac and Fox Lands in Iowa. 11 Mar.
SD 160, 54-1, v7, 3p. [3353]
Title transferred to the Sec. of Interior.

122. Lands in the Uncompahgre Reservation. 11 Mar.
SD 161, 54-1, v7, 3p. [3353]
Reasons why mineral lands have not been returned to the public domain, and opened to entry.

123. R-P of J. Matchett. 11 Mar.
SR 451, 54-1, v2, 1p. [3363]
Seminole war; 1856-57; Florida.

124. Appropriation for Cavalry Horses. 11 Mar.
HD 299, 54-1, v61, 2p. [3428]
For Indian scouts and others.

125. Appropriation for the Nez Percé Reservation. 12 Mar.
SD 163, 54-1, v7, 2p. [3353]
For sawmills under the agreement of 1 May 1893.

126. Amendment to the Indian Appropriation Bill. 12 Mar.
SR 466, 54-1, v2, 1p. [3363]
Action of the Com. on Indian Affairs.

127. Gulf, Colorado, and Santa Fe Railroad Co. 12 Mar.
HR 738, 54-1, v3, 1p. [3459]
Depot grounds in the Chickasaw Nation.

128. Interoceanic Railway Co. 12 Mar.
HR 750, 54-1, v3, 1p. [3459]
Construction in Indian Territory delayed.

129. Delegate from Alaska. 12 Mar.
HR 751, 54-1, v3, 5p. [3459]
Report includes Indian population of Alaska.

130. L-C of the Sac and Fox Indians of the Mississippi. 13 Mar.
SD 167, 54-1, v7, 27p. [3353]
Moneys due that portion of the tribe residing in Iowa under various treaties.

131. Settlement of the Accounts of E. Chirouse. 13 Mar.
SR 471, 54-1, v2, 1p. [3363] *or*
HR 1823, 54-1, v8, 1p. [3464]
Indian agent at the Tulalip agency, Washington.

132. Amending the Indian Appropriation Bill. 13 Mar.
SR 473, 54-1, v2, 2p. [3363]
Increase for the Indian industrial school at Genoa, Nebraska.

133. Muskogee, Oklahoma, and Western Railroad Co. 13 Mar.
SR 474, 54-1, v2, 1p. [3363] *or*
HR 1453, 54-1, v6, 2p. [3462] *or*
HR 1811, 54-1, v7, 1p. [3463]
Right of way through Indian Territory.

134. R-P of Gen. Thayer. 13 Mar.
HR 761, 54-1, v3, 2p. [3459]
Service of Nebraska Volunteers against hostile Indians; 1855-61.

135. Public Land Surveys. 16 Mar.
SD 169, 54-1, v7, 4p. [3353]
In Indian Territory.

136. Petition of the Ardmore Bar Association. 16 Mar.
SD 173, 54-1, v7, 7p. [3353]
On jurisdiction over criminal prosecutions in Indian Territory.

137. R-P of L. Mason. 17 Mar.
SR 493, 54-1, v2, 2p. [3363] *or*
HR 1966, 54-1, v8, 2p. [3464]
Sioux campaign; 1890-91; South Dakota.

138. R-P of B. Dowell. 17 Mar.
SR 496, 54-1, v2, 2p. [3363]
Rogue River and Modoc wars in Oregon.

139. R-P of P. Castleman. 17 Mar.
SR 498, 54-1, v2, 2p. [3363] *or*
HR 1558, 54-1, v6, 2p. [3462]

Service in the Washington and Oregon Indian war; 1855-56.

140. Indian Trust Funds. 18 Mar.
SD 176, 54-1, v7, 2p. [3353]
Condition of the Cherokee, Creek, Choctaw, Chickasaw, and Seminole funds.

141. Monument at Fort Recovery, Ohio. 18 Mar.
HR 855, 54-1, v4, 2p. [3460]
Site of a battle with Indians; 1791.

142. Compensation of Judges, Court of Claims. 19 Mar.
SR 518, 54-1, v3, 4p. [3364]
Extra-ordinary cases heard, involving the Shawnees, Delawares, Cherokees, Cherokee freedmen, etc.

143. Admission of New Mexico as a State. 19 Mar.
SR 520, 54-1, v3, 11p. [3364] *or*
HR 2259, 54-1, v9, 20p. [3465]
Indian population given (House version includes minority report, etc.).

144. Legislative, Executive, and Judicial Appropriation Bill. 20 Mar.
SR 532, 54-1, v3, 11p. [3364]
U.S. Courts in Indian Territory.

145. Monument at Greenville, Ohio. 20 Mar.
HR 873, 54-1, v4, 2p. [3460]
To commemorate the treaty made 3 Aug. 1795 between Gen. Wayne and Wyandots, Delawares, Shawnees, Ottawas, Chippewas, Pottawatomies, Miamies, Weas, Piankeshaws, Kickapoos, and Kaskaskias.

146. Restoring Rights of Certain Sioux Indians. 23 Mar.
SR 553, 54-1, v3, 15p. [3364]
Santee and Flandreau Sioux have the benefits of the treaties of 1837 and 1851 restored to them; several amendments to the bill are proposed.

147. Settlers on Public Lands. 23 Mar.
SR 539, 54-1, v3, 1p. [3364]
Bill involves ceded portions of Indian reservations.

148. Fire Proof Building for the National Museum. 23 Mar.
SR 540, 54-1, v3, 8p. [3364]
To house Indian artifacts, etc.

149. Affairs in Indian Territory. 24 Mar.
SD 182, 54-1, v7, 123p. [3353]
Papers relative to conditions in said Territory; reprints of reports of the Dawes Commission to the Five Civilized Tribes.

150. Pensions to Survivors of Indian Wars. 24 Mar.
SR 542, 54-1, v3, 5p. [3364] *or*
HR 145, 54-1, v1, 4p. [3457]
Black Hawk (1832), Creek (1836), Cherokee (1838), Seminole (1818, 1836), Winnebago (1827), Texas and New Mexico (1849-55), Sabine (1836), Utah (1850-53), Cayuse (1847-48), California (1851-52), and Oregon and Washington (1851-56) Indian wars.

151. R-P of T. Routon. 24 Mar.
SR 554, 54-1, v3, 2p. [3364]
Creek war; 1836.

152. Arrests of Indians Upon Indian Reservations. 24 Mar.
HD 319, 54-1, v61, 1p. [3428]
Bill permitting U.S. officers to arrest Indians.

153. R-C of the Estate of R. Crooks. 25 Mar.
SR 570, 54-1, v3, 3p. [3364] *or*
HR 1313, 54-1, v5, 3p. [3461]
Chippewas indebted to this trader.

154. R-C of R. McGee. 25 Mar.
SR 572, 54-1, v3, 2p. [3364] *or*
HR 1810, 54-1, v7, 2p. [3463]
Brulé Sioux hostilities of 1864 in Kansas.

155. San Carlos Reservation Indians. 25 Mar.
HD 320, 54-1, v61, 18p. [3428]
Agreement made 25 Feb. 1896 for cession of lands in Arizona; council proceedings.

156. Claims Allowed by Accounting Officers. 25 Mar.
HD 322, 54-1, v61, 35p. [3428]
Includes claims involving the Indian Service.

157. Homesteaders on Indian Lands in Montana. 25 Mar.
HR 935, 54-1, v4, 2p. [3460]
Bill to relieve settlers on Crow ceded land from paying $1.50 per acre.

158. Petition of the Creek and Seminole Nations. 26 Mar.
SD 190, 54-1, v7, 2p. [3353]
Protest measures pending which would deprive them of the right of self-government; protest recommendations of the Dawes Commission.

159. Property Tax on Indian Reservations in Oklahoma. 26 Mar.

HR 947, 54-1, v4, 1p. [3460]
Bill not recommended, as it would violate treaty stipulations.

160. Sundry Civil Appropriation Bill. 26 Mar.
HR 966, 54-1, v4, 7p. [3460]
For fiscal 1897; includes support of Alaskan natives, etc.

161. Indians of Nebraska and South Dakota. 27 Mar.
SD 192, 54-1, v7, 5p. [3353]
History of the Santee Sioux, and the Flandreau Sioux (formerly the Medawakanton and Wahpakoota Sioux).

162. Estimates of Deficiencies. 27 Mar.
HD 324, 54-1, v29, 48p. [3396]
Appropriations for fiscal 1896; Indian Service.

163. Proceeds from Sale of Public Lands. 30 Mar.
HR 996, 54-1, v4, 48p. [3460]
Includes sale of ceded Indian lands, and distribution of the proceeds.

164. Fort Lewis Military Reserve. 30 Mar.
HR 1013, 54-1, v4, 2p. [3460]
Premises turned over to the Sec. of Interior for Indian school purposes; Colorado; remainder returned to the public domain.

165. Rent of a Warehouse at Rushville, Nebraska. 1 Apr.
HD 335, 54-1, v61, 2p. [3428]
Storage of supplies for the Sioux.

166. Free Homes on Lands Purchased from Indians. 1 Apr.
HR 1039, 54-1, v4, 13p. [3460]
Homesteaders would not pay for lands ceded by Indians under this bill.

167. Additional Judges for the U.S. Court in Indian Territory. 1 Apr.
HR 1063, 54-1, v4, 6p. [3460]
Jurisdiction over the Territory.

168. Sac and Fox Indians. 2 Apr.
SD 196, 54-1, v7, 3p. [3353]
Dispute over tribal funds between the Oklahoma and Iowa branches of the tribe.

169. Indian Appropriation Bill. 2 Apr.
SR 608, 54-1, v3, 5p. [3364]
For the year ending 30 June 1897.

170. Payments by the Cherokee Nation. 3 Apr.
HD 340, 54-1, v61, 4p. [3428]
To intruders, for improvements which they made on Indian lands.

171. Protection of the People of Indian Territory. 3 Apr.
HR 1102, 54-1, v4, 4p. [3460]
Bill changing the government of the Territory; jurisdiction over the area to go to U.S. Courts; etc.

172. Public Lands in Greer County, Oklahoma. 4 Apr.
HR 1113 (pts. 1 and 2), 54-1, v4, 4p. [3460]
Choctaw and Chickasaw claims to land title involved.

173. Claims Against the Fond du Lac Indians. 4 Apr.
HR 1115, 54-1, v4, 1p. [3460]
Illegal contracts for sale of reservation timber; Minnesota.

174. Indian Reservation Lands. 6 Apr.
SD 197, 54-1, v7, 9p. [3353] *or*
SD 204, 54-1, v7, 10p. [3353]
On the existing policy regarding the disposal of said lands.

175. Indian Depredation Claims. 7 Apr.
HD 348, 54-1, v61, 1p. [3428]
Judgments of the Court of Claims.

176. Appropriation for Contingencies of the Indian Dept. 8 Apr.
HD 350, 54-1, v61, 2p. [3428]
For fiscal 1896.

177. Jails in Indian Territory. 9 Apr.
SD 202, 54-1, v7, 4p. [3353]
Conditions at said jails.

178. R-P of W. Tumblin. 9 Apr.
SR 655, 54-1, v3, 1p. [3364] *or*
HR 1554, 54-1, v6, 1p. [3462]
Florida Indian war; 1835-36.

179. R-C of J. Williams. 9 Apr.
HR 1179, 54-1, v5, 1p. [3461]
Supt. of the Fort Hall Indian school.

180. Sale of Liquor to Indians. 10 Apr.
HR 1209, 54-1, v5, 13p. [3461]
Bill to prohibit said sale.

181. Fort Bidwell, California. 11 Apr.
HR 1217, 54-1, v5, 2p. [3461]
Abandoned reserve to be used as an Indian training school.

182. R-C of the Heirs of J. West. 11 Apr.
HR 1224, 54-1, v5, 2p. [3461]
Saline property taken by the Cherokee National council, Indian Territory.

183. Bridge Across the Arkansas River. 11 Apr.
HR 1226, 54-1, v5, 1p. [3461]
Between Oklahoma and the Osage reservation.

184. R-P of S. Stilwell. 14 Apr.
SR 677, 54-1, v3, 8p. [3364] *or*
HR 1960, 54-1, v8, 9p. [3464]
Cheyenne and Sioux outbreak of 1868 in Kansas.

185. R-P of E. Gilbert. 14 Apr.
SR 699 (pts. 1 and 2), 54-1, v3, 3p. [3364]
Battle of Richaree Fork against the Cheyennes; 1868; Kansas.

186. R-P of J. Bunker. 14 Apr.
HR 1244, 54-1, v5, 1p. [3461]
Sabine war; 1836-37; Arkansas Volunteers.

187. Mem. of the Choctaws and Chickasaws. 15 Apr.
SD 214, 54-1, v8, 21p. [3354]
Claim to land title in Oklahoma.

188. Forts and Battlefields in the Maumee Valley, Ohio. 15 Apr.
SR 709, 54-1, v4, 3p. [3365] *or*
HR 1344, 54-1, v5, 6p. [3461]
Preservation of Forts Industry, Meigs, Miami, Defiance, and Wayne; commemoration of numerous battles with Indians in that area (House version includes graveyards of soldiers).

189. Red Lake Chippewas of Minnesota. 15 Apr.
HR 1306, 54-1, v5, 3p. [3461]
Bill allowing some Indians to remain on ceded lands because of improvements they have made.

190. R-C of D. McKnight. 16 Apr.
HR 1311, 54-1, v5, 3p. [3461]
Attorney for the "Old Settler," or Western Cherokees.

191. R-P of W. Quinn. 16 Apr.
HR 1319, 54-1, v5, 5p. [3461]
Sioux mixed-blood serves in Minnesota Volunteers in the 1862 Sioux outbreak.

192. R-C of Florida. 17 Apr.
HR 1351, 54-1, v5, 4p. [3461]
Seminole war of 1855-57.

193. General Deficiency Bill. 18 Apr.
HR 1361, 54-1, v5, 8p. [3461]
Appropriations for fiscal 1896; Indian depredation claims, etc.

194. Rights of Land Purchasers. 20 Apr.
SR 737, 54-1, v4, 4p. [3365] *or*
HR 2264, 54-1, v9, 3p. [3465]
Purchase of lands granted by the U.S. to railroads; Atlantic and Pacific Railroad Co. through Indian Territory.

195. Title to Certain Lands. 20 Apr.
HR 1375, 54-1, v5, 3p. [3461]
Bill to quit title to land; includes lands ceded by Cherokees, Cheyennes, Arapahoes, Absentee Shawnees, and Pottawatomies.

196. R-C of A. Babcock. 21 Apr.
SR 748, 54-1, v4, 2p. [3365] *or*
SR 1486, 54-2, v3, 6p. [3476]
Land inside the Grande Ronde Indian reservation, Oregon.

197. R-P of M. Wyse. 21 Apr.
SR 751, 54-1, v4, 2p. [3365] *or*
SR 1570, 54-2, v3, 21p. [3476] *or*
HR 443, 54-1, v2, 2p. [3458]
Seminole war in Florida; Cherokee removal in 1838.

198. R-P of M. McKay. 21 Apr.
SR 755, 54-1, v4, 2p. [3365]
Interpreter for Indian scouts during the Oregon Indian war.

199. R-P of F. Kautz. 21 Apr.
SR 773, 54-1, v4, 3p. [3365] *or*
HR 2617, 54-2, v2, 3p. [3555]
Rogue River war of 1855 in Oregon; Apache campaign of 1875-78 in Arizona.

200. Petition of North Dakota Citizens. 22 Apr.
SD 229, 54-1, v8, 2p. [3354]
Asks that the agreement of 1892 with the Turtle Mountain band of Chippewas be ratified; land cessions.

201. R-C of S. Dresser. 23 Apr.
SR 786, 54-1, v4, 4p. [3365] *or*
HR 2666, 54-2, v2, 4p. [3555]
Ute outbreak of 1878 in Colorado.

202. Allotted Lands in Oklahoma. 23 Apr.
HR 1457, 54-1, v6, 1p. [3462]
Com. on Indian Affairs amends a bill concerned with said lands.

203. R-C of J. Friend. 24 Apr.
HR 1475, 54-1, v6, 1p. [3462]
Comanche hostilities of 1868 in Texas; Indians take captives.

204. Preservation of Burial Places. 24 Apr.
HR 1489, 54-1, v6, 3p. [3462]
In the Maumee Valley of Ohio; casualties of Indian wars.

205. Construction of a Government Road. 27 Apr.
SR 798, 54-1, v4, 3p. [3365]
Between Fort Washakie on the Shoshone reservation, and Yellowstone Park; through Shoshone, Bannock, and Arapaho hunting grounds.

206. Reimbursing Settlers for Certain Improvements. 28 Apr.
SR 810, 54-1, v4, 14p. [3365]
Encorporated into Yellowstone Park; Sioux, Crow, Blackfeet, Blood, and Piegan hostilities during 1867-75.

207. R-P of R. Brasie. 28 Apr.
HR 1499, 54-1, v6, 1p. [3462]
Florida Indian war; 1840-45.

208. R-P of L. Dodge. 28 Apr.
HR 1521, 54-1, v6, 2p. [3462]
Powder River expedition against hostile Indians in Wyoming; 1877-79.

209. R-P of W. Russell. 28 Apr.
HR 1524, 54-1, v6, 1p. [3462]
Oregon Indian war; 1855-56.

210. R-P of M. Calhoun. 29 Apr.
SR 813, 54-1, v4, 2p. [3365] *or*
HR 2677, 54-2, v2, 2p. [3555]
Custer's expedition against the Sioux in 1876; battle of the Little Big Horn River, Montana.

211. Canadian Cree Indians. 29 Apr.
SR 821, 54-1, v4, 7p. [3365]
Appropriation to remove said Indians from Montana back to Canada.

212. Amounts Allowed the Southern Pacific Railroad Co. 30 Apr.
SD 236, 54-1, v8, 22p. [3354]
Includes Indian accounts.

213. Denison and Northern Railroad Co. 20 Apr.
HR 1540, 54-1, v6, 1p. [3462]
Construction in Indian Territory delayed.

214. Kaw or Kansas Indian Scrip. 1 May.
HR 1580, 54-1, v6, 12p. [3462]
Bill to pay the balance due on said scrip is rejected, as the scrip was issued without authority.

215. Settlers in Oklahoma. 1 May.
HR 1581, 54-1, v6, 2p. [3462]
Bill affecting settlers whose entries on Cheyenne, Arapaho, or Cherokee lands were less than 160 acres.

216. Mem. of the Turtle Mountain Chippewas. 2 May.
SD 239, 54-1, v8, 4p. [3354]
Asks that the agreement of 22 Oct. 1892 be ratified; land cessions in North Dakota.

217. R-P of J. Jones. 5 May.
SR 862, 54-1, v4, 1p. [3365] *or*
HR 334, 54-1, v2, 1p. [3458]
Florida Indian war; 1836.

218. Settlement Between the U.S. and Arkansas. 5 May.
HR 1634, 54-1, v7, 372p. [3463]
Concerns State bonds held in the Chickasaw Trust fund, etc.

219. R-P of H. Andrews. 7 May.
SR 887, 54-1, v5, 1p. [3366] *or*
HR 271, 54-1, v1, 1p. [3457]
Black Hawk war; 1832; Illinois Volunteers.

220. R-P of W. Durley. 7 May.
SR 889, 54-1, v5, 1p. [3366] *or*
HR 135, 54-1, v1, 1p. [3457]
Black Hawk war; 1832; Illinois Volunteers.

221. Military Road in Wyoming. 7 May.
HR 1659, 54-1, v7, 2p. [3463]
Would traverse the hunting grounds of Indians from the Shoshone reservation.

222. Agreement with the Shoshones and Arapahoes. 8 May.
SD 247, 54-1, v8, 17p. [3354]
Made 21 Apr. 1896; land cessions in Wyoming; council proceedings.

223. U.S. Court in Indian Territory. 8 May.
SR 898, 54-1, v5, 2p. [3366]
Amendments to bill concerning said court.

224. Deputy U.S. Marshalls, Indian Territory. 11 May.
SR 909, 54-1, v5, 2p. [3366]
Bill to validate appointments made to said office.

225. R-P of J. Gullett. 13 May.
HR 1782, 54-1, v7, 1p. [3463]
Creek war; 1836; Alabama Volunteers.

226. Free Homesteads in Oklahoma. 16 May.
SR 964, 54-1, v5, 22p. [3366]
On Indian reservation lands opened to settlers under agreements with the U.S.; list of lands which have been ceded (includes lands outside of Oklahoma as well).

227. Mixed-Blood Indians. 18 May.
SR 969, 54-1, v5, 2p. [3366]
Bill defining the rights and privileges of said Indians under various treaties.

228. Fort Dodge, Kansas. 18 May.
HR 1869, 54-1, v8, 3p. [3464]
Part of this abandoned military reserve lies within the limits of Osage trust lands.

229. California War Claims. 19 May.
SD 265, 54-1, v8, 5p. [3354]
For Indian wars; 1850-59.

230. R-P of C. Barry. 19 May.
SR 977, 54-1, v5, 1p. [3366] *or*
HR 555, 54-1, v2, 1p. [3458]
Indian hostilities of 1848 on the Texas frontier.

231. R-P of E. Beall. 19 May.
SR 979, 54-1, v5, 2p. [3366] *or*
HR 484, 54-1, v2, 2p. [3458]
Florida Indian war; 1837.

232. R-P of E. Williams. 19 May.
SR 990, 54-1, v5, 1p. [3366] *or*
HR 506, 54-1, v2, 1p. [3458]
Florida Indian war; 1836.

233. R-P of N. Gentry. 19 May.
SR 991, 54-1, v5, 1p. [3366] *or*
HR 483, 54-1, v2, 1p. [3458]
Cherokee war; 1836; Tennessee Volunteers.

234. Issuance of Land Patents, and Sale of Lands. 19 May.
HR 1892, 54-1, v8, 1p. [3464]
Involves the Swan Creek and Black River Chippewas, and the Munsee, or Christian Indians of Kansas.

235. Chickasaw Trust Funds. 20 May.
SR 1002, 54-1, v5, 8p. [3366]
History of the fund; bill for payment of arrears of interest on said funds.

236. R-C of H. Phillips. 20 May.
HR 1913, 54-1, v8, 4p. [3464]
Carried word of the Fetterman massacre from Fort Phil. Kearny to Fort Laramie in 1866; Sioux hostilities.

237. R-P of E. Shriver. 20 May.
HR 1917, 54-1, v8, 1p. [3464]
Service in Indian Territory during the Civil War.

238. R-P of B. Shriver. 20 May.
HR 1918, 54-1, v8, 1p. [3464]
Service in Indian Territory during the Civil War.

239. Deficiency Estimates. 21 May.
SD 268, 54-1, v29 (House Documents), 16p. [3396]
Appropriations for fiscal 1896; Indian Service.

240. Amending the Indian Appropriation Bill. 21 May.
SD 272, 54-1, v11, 3p. [3357]
For fiscal 1897.

241. R-C of Little and Williams. 21 May.
SR 1016, 54-1, v5, 4p. [3366] *or*
HR 482, 54-1, v2, 4p. [3458]
Mineral lands leased from Iowa Indians in Nebraska and Kansas.

242. R-C of A. Farnsworth. 21 May.
HR 1922, 54-1, v8, 1p. [3464]
Sioux and Cheyenne depredations.

243. Agreement with Certain Indians. 21 May.
HR 1932, 54-1, v8, 2p. [3464]
Made 22 Apr. 1896 with Indians on the Shoshone, or Wind River reservation in Wyoming; land cessions.

244. Claims Allowed by Accounting Officers. 22 May.
SD 274, 54-1, v11, 14p. [3357]
Including those for Indian service.

245. Indian Depredation Claims. 22 May.
SD 275, 54-1, v11, 1p. [3357]
Judgments of the Court of Claims.

246. R-P of C. Greene. 22 May.
SR 1018, 54-1, v5, 1p. [3366] *or*
HR 752, 54-1, v3, 1p. [3459]
Creek war; 1836; Georgia Volunteers.

247. R-P of E. Brown. 22 May.
SR 1020, 54-1, v5, 1p. [3366] *or*
HR 631, 54-1, v3, 1p. [3459]
Florida Indian war; 1839-44.

248. Railroad Depots in Indian Territory. 22 May.
HR 1965, 54-1, v8, 1p. [3464]
Amendment to act calling for more depots; would prevent the elimination of any already existing depots.

249. Deficiency Appropriations. 23 May.
SR 1032, 54-1, v5, 8p. [3366]
Fiscal 1896; for the Indian Service, Indian depredation claims, and settlement with the Eastern Cherokees.

250. R-P of H. Prince. 23 May.
SR 1035, 54-1, v5, 1p. [3366] *or*
HR 559, 54-1, v2, 1p. [3458]
Creek war; 1836; Georgia Volunteers.

251. R-P of N. Prince. 23 May.
SR 1036, 54-1, v5, 1p. [3366] *or*
HR 558, 54-1, v2, 1p. [3458]
Creek war; 1836; Georgia Volunteers.

252. R-C of H. Corum and S. Davis. 23 May.
HR 1982, 54-1, v8, 2p. [3464]
Supplies furnished the Warm Springs Indian agency in Oregon; 1888.

253. Admission of Oklahoma as a State. 23 May.
HR 1988, 54-1, v8, 12p. [3464]
Including Indian reservations in the Territory, and their size.

254. R-P of A. Phillips. 23 May.
HR 1991, 54-1, v8, 6p. [3464]
Service in the Indian Home Guards during the Civil War.

255. Amending the Indian Appropriation Bill. 26 May.
SD 290, 54-1, v11, 2p. [3357]
For fiscal 1897.

256. R-P of C. O'Brien. 26 May.
SR 1059, 54-1, v5, 1p. [3366] *or*
HR 2601, 54-2, v2, 1p. [3555]
Indian warfare near Fort Kearney.

257. R-P of M. Prince. 26 May.
SR 1070, 54-1, v5, 1p. [3366] *or*
HR 567, 54-1, v2, 1p. [3458]
Indian war of 1836; Georgia Volunteers.

258. R-P of A. Rawlings. 27 May.
SR 1076, 54-1, v5, 1p. [3366] *or*
HR 472, 54-1, v2, 1p. [3458]
Sabine war; 1836; Arkansas Volunteers.

259. R-P of J. Sturgis. 27 May.
HR 2027, 54-1, v8, 1p. [3464]
Son killed at the battle of Little Big Horn River; Custer's campaign.

260. Hudson Reservoir and Canal Co. 28 May.
HR 2049, 54-1, v8, 3p. [3464]
Right of way through the Gila River Indian reservation, Arizona; occupied by Pimas, Maricopas, and Sacatons.

261. R-P of N. McNeil. 2 June.
SR 1101, 54-1, v5, 1p. [3366] *or*
HR 601, 54-1, v3, 1p. [3459]
Indian campaign of 1862; Minnesota Volunteers.

262. R-P of F. Stay. 2 June.
HR 2156, 54-1, v9, 2p. [3465]
Sioux war; 1865; Minnesota Mounted Rangers.

263. Judgments of the Court of Claims. 3 June.
SD 300, 54-1, v11, 1p. [3357]
Indian depredation cases.

264. Judgments of the Court of Claims. 3 June.
SD 301, 54-1, v11, 1p. [3357]
Indian depredation cases.

265. R-P of C. Capron. 4 June.
HR 2190, 54-1, v9, 1p. [3465]
Service in the Indian campaign on the Big Horn River.

266. R-P of L. Sugs. 4 June.
HR 2205, 54-1, v9, 1p. [3465]
Cherokee disturbances; 1838; Georgia Volunteers.

267. Otoe and Missouria Reservation. 5 June.
HR 2237, 54-1, v9, 5p. [3465]
Adjustment and revision of sales of reservation lands in Kansas and Nebraska, and confirmation of land titles.

268. R-P of H. Tucker. 5 June.
HR 2239, 54-1, v9, 2p. [3465]
Service in the great Indian raid of 1868 in Kansas.

269. R-P of H. Farmer. 6 June.
SR 1129, 54-1, v5, 1p. [3366] *or*
HR 2455, 54-2, v2, 1p. [3555]
Cherokee war; Tennessee Volunteers.

270. Indian Depredation Claims. 6 June.
SR 1133, 54-1, v5, 12p. [3366]
Bill amending an act to provide for adjudication and payment of said claims.

271. Indian Trust Funds. 6 June.
HR 2271, 54-1, v9, 1p. [3465]
Funds invested in Virginia State bonds have not borne interest; dispute exists over whether the liability is Virginia's, or West Virginia's.

272. Mixed-Blood Indians. 6 June.
HR 2276, 54-1, v9, 2p. [3465]
Bill confirming the title of mixed-bloods to their lands; question arises as to the proper definition of an Indian.

273. Chickasaw Trust Funds. 8 June.
SD 309, 54-1, v11, 12p. [3357]
Indians apply for a withdrawal of $100,000.

274. Statements of Appropriations. 11 June.
SD 316, 54-1, v14, 503p. [3360]
During the 1st session, 54th Congress; Indian expenses.

275. Catalogue of Public Documents. 16 June.
HD 410, 54-1, v75, 638p. [3442]
From the 1st, 2d, and 3rd sessions, 53rd Congress; documents of the Congress and Executive Depts. arranged by title; documents on Indian affairs included.

276. 13th Annual Report of the Bureau of Ethnology. (no date)
HD 266, 54-1, v61, 500p. [3427]
Research related to North American Indians.

277. Report of the Com'r of Fish and Fisheries. (no date)
HD 424, 54-1, v80, 723p. [3447]

Investigation of the waters of Indian Territory.

278. Annual Report of the Smithsonian Institution. 1 July.
HD 352 (pts. 1 and 2), 54-2, v72-73, 1909p. [3548-3549]
Research related to the American Indian.

279. Annual Report of the Sec. of War. 24 Nov.
HD 2, 54-2, v2-9, 5975p. [3478-3485]
Pursuit of renegade Apaches; deportation of Canadian Crees; etc.

280. Annual Report of the Attorney-General of the U.S. 30 Nov.
HD 9, 54-2, v23, 294p. [3499]
Courts in Indian Territory; etc.

281. Annual Report of the Sec. of Interior. 3 Dec.
HD 5, 54-2, v12-19, 7567p. [3488-3495]
Indian Affairs; annual report of the Gen. Land Office (Serial 3488); annual report of the CIA (Serial 3489); etc.

282. Annual Message to Congress; Pres. Cleveland. 7 Dec.
HD 1, 54-2, v1, 1046p. [3477]
Negotiations with the Five Civilized Tribes in Indian Territory; minerals on the Ute reservation; allotment; etc.

283. Estimates of Appropriations. 7 Dec.
HD 12, 54-2, v26, 413p. [3502]
Year ending 30 June 1898; Indian expenses.

284. Indian Depredation Claims. 8 Dec.
SD 10, 54-2, v1, 2p. [3467]
Judgments rendered.

285. Judgments Rendered by the Court of Claims. 8 Dec.
SD 11, 54-2, v1, 65p. [3467]
Includes a claim of the New York Indians, etc.

286. Document Index. 10 Dec.
HD 430, 54-1, v88, 236p. [3455]
For the 1st session, 54th Congress.

287. Congressional Directory. 12 Dec.
SD 16 (pts. 1 and 2), 54-2, v7, 660p. [3473]
Duties of the CIA.

288. Urgent Deficiency Estimates. 14 Dec.
HD 70, 54-2, v26, 12p. [3502]
Fiscal 1897; expense of U.S. courts in Indian Territory, etc.

289. Receipts and Expenditures. 14 Dec.
HD 75, 54-2, v26, 62p. [3502]
Fiscal 1896; Indian expenses.

290. Leases Made by the Senecas. 15 Dec.
SD 23, 54-2, v1, 5p. [3467]
Concerns lands in the Allegany reservation, New York.

291. Legislative, Executive, and Judicial Appropriation Bill. 15 Dec.
HR 2331, 54-2, v1, 17p. [3554]
For year ending 30 June 1898; Indian Service.

292. Annual Report of the Sec. of the Treasury. 15 Dec.
HD 8, 54-2, v22, 981p. [3498]
Year ending 30 June 1896; Indian expenses.

293. Irrigation Investigation. 16 Dec.
SD 27, 54-2, v1, 58p. [3467]
To benefit the Pimas, Maricopas, and Papagoes on the Gila River reservation, Arizona.

294. Expenditures of the Smithsonian Institution. 16 Dec.
HD 98, 54-2, v29, 40p. [3505]
Fiscal 1896; on ethnology of North American Indians, etc.

295. Mem. of the "Old Settler" or Western Cherokees. 17 Dec.
HD 103, 54-2, v29, 6p. [3505]
Asks that the balance of an appropriation for legal services rendered to the tribe be paid to the Indians.

296. Bonds of the Original State of Virginia. 19 Dec.
HD 127, 54-2, v29, 1p. [3505]
Held in certain Indian trust funds.

297. R-C of C. Hazelwood. 19 Dec.
HR 2356, 54-2, v1, 2p. [3554] *or*
HR 2469, 54-2, v2, 2p. [3555]
Kiowa and Comanche depredations of 1866-71 in Texas.

298. Chippewas of Minnesota. 22 Dec.
HD 133, 54-2, v29, 12p. [3505]
Concerns lands subject to overflow as a result of the construction of reservoirs.

299. Statistical Abstract of the U.S. 31 Dec.
HD 158, 54-2, v29, 412p. [3525]
Indian population, etc.

300. 14th Annual Report of the Bureau of Ethnology. (no date)
HD 230 (pts. 1 and 2), 54-2, v55 (pts. 1 and 2), 1197p. [3531 (pts. 1 and 2)]
Research related to the American Indian; reports on the Menomonees (Hoffman), Coronado expedition (Winship), and Ghost-Dance religion and Sioux outbreak of 1890 (Mooney).

1897

1. Receipt and Distribution of Public Documents. 5 Jan.
SD 42, 54-2, v3, 10p. [3469]
Includes documents from the OIA, etc.
2. R-P of E. Holman. 5 Jan.
SR 1171, 54-2, v1, 2p. [3474] *or*
HR 907, 54-1, v4, 2p. [3460]
Sabine Indian war; 1836-37; Arkansas Volunteers.
3. Appropriation for a Boarding School. 5 Jan.
HD 138, 54-2, v29, 3p. [3505]
For Chippewas at the White Earth reservation, Minnesota.
4. Board of Indian Com'rs. 5 Jan.
HR 2383, 54-2, v1, 4p. [3554]
Bill to abolish the office of the CIA, and to create in lieu thereof a board of Indian com'rs; report gives a short history of the Indian service.
5. Introduction of Domestic Reindeer Into Alaska. 6 Jan.
SD 49, 54-2, v3, 144p. [3469]
To benefit Eskimos, and other Alaskan natives.
6. Condition of the Work of the Depts. 6 Jan.
HD 152, 54-2, v48, 14p. [3524]
Including the OIA.
7. Amendment to the General Deficiency Bill. 7 Jan.
SR 1178, 54-2, v1, 1p. [3474]
Payment of J. O'Keane for services at the Tulalip agency, Washington, during 1882.
8. Kansas, Oklahoma Central, and Southwestern Railway Co. 7 Jan.
HR 2400, 54-2, v1, 1p. [3554]
Construction through Indian Territory is delayed.
9. R-P of L. Payne. 7 Jan.
HR 2454, 54-2, v2, 1p. [3555]
Ute campaign; battle at Milk River.
10. Buildings at Navajo Springs, Colorado. 9 Jan.
HD 168, 54-2, v48, 3p. [3524]
For the use of the Southern Utes.
11. R-C of the Turtle Mountain Band of Pembina Chippewas. 9 Jan.
HR 2473, 54-2, v2, 4p. [3555]
Agreement of 22 Oct. 1892 remains unratified; land cessions in North Dakota.
12. R-P of J. McGrath. 12 Jan.
SR 1186, 54-2, v1, 2p. [3474]
Service in Custer's campaign against Black Kettle's band of Indians in Kansas; 1869.
13. L-C of D. Day. 12 Jan.
HD 174, 54-2, v48, 5p. [3524]
U.S. Indian agent at the Southern Ute agency, Colorado.
14. Digest of Decisions Relating to Indian Affairs. 12 Jan.
HD 175, 54-2, v48, 3p. [3524]
Appropriation to cover the cost of compiling such a digest.
15. Certain Deputy Marshals in Indian Territory. 12 Jan.
HR 2489, 54-2, v2, 1p. [3555]
Action of the Com. on the Judiciary.
16. R-P of M. Hess. 12 Jan.
HR 2497, 54-2, v2, 2p. [3555]
Sioux outbreak; 1862; Minnesota Volunteers.
17. R-P of A. King. 13 Jan.
SR 1209, 54-2, v1, 1p. [3474] *or*
HR 2804, 54-2, v3, 2p. [3556]
Black Hawk war; 1832; Missouri Militia.
18. Army Appropriation Bill. 14 Jan.
SR 1212, 54-2, v1, 2p. [3474]
Support of Apache prisoners of war.
19. Indian Appropriation Bill. 14 Jan.
HR 2517 (pts. 1 and 2), 54-2, v2, 7p. [3555]
Year ending 30 June 1898; Indian Service.
20. Amounts Due the Union and Kansas Pacific Railroad Companies. 16 Jan.
HD 188, 54-2, v48, 10p. [3524]
Transport of Indian goods, etc.
21. Delinquent Accounts of U.S. Officers. 16 Jan.
HD 189, 54-2, v48, 22p. [3524]
Includes persons in the Indian Service.
22. Act to Repeal Timber-Culture Laws. 18 Jan.
HR 2540, 54-2, v2, 2p. [3555] *or*
HR 2963, 54-2, v3, 2p. [3556]
Concerns payments by settlers for lands in South Dakota, North Dakota, and Nebraska which were formerly part of the Sioux reservation.
23. Galveston and Great Northern Railway Co. 18 Jan.
HR 2541, 54-2, v2, 1p. [3555]

Construction through Indian Territory.

24. Reorganization of the Line of the Army. 19 Jan.
HR 2548, 54-2, v2, 12p. [3555]
Report takes into consideration the diminished use of the Army against Indians.

25. R-P of B. Reeder. 20 Jan.
SR 1266, 54-2, v1, 1p. [3474] *or*
HR 936, 54-1, v4, 1p. [3460]
Service against Indians during the war with Mexico.

26. R-P of M. Lafferty. 20 Jan.
SR 1268, 54-2, v1, 1p. [3474] *or*
HR 754, 54-1, v3, 1p. [3459]
Seminole war; 1818; Florida.

27. R-P of M. Peck. 20 Jan.
SR 1269, 54-2, v1, 1p. [3474] *or*
SR 1321, 54-2, v2, 1p. [3475] *or*
HR 2505, 54-2, v2, 1p. [3555]
Engagement with hostile Comanches and Osages during the war with Mexico; 1848.

28. Commission to Negotiate with Crow, Flathead, and Other Indians. 20 Jan.
HD 198, 54-2, v48, 2p. [3524]
Appropriation for continued service.

29. Eastern Judicial District of Texas. 20 Jan.
HR 2587, 54-2, v2, 3p. [3555]
Report on a Presidential veto of a bill to establish a new judicial division; includes mention of jurisdiction by the Paris court over parts of Indian Territory.

30. Sale of Intoxicating Liquors to Indians. 21 Jan.
SR 1294, 54-2, v1, 13p. [3474]
Bill prohibiting such sale.

31. R-P of H. Hutter. 21 Jan.
HR 2589, 54-2, v2, 2p. [3555]
Service in the Black Hawk and Seminole wars.

32. Survey of the Blackfeet Reservation in Montana. 22 Jan.
HD 203, 54-2, v48, 4p. [3524]
Appropriation to continue the survey under the agreement of 26 Sept. 1895.

33. Eastern Nebraska and Gulf Railway Co. 22 Jan.
HR 2598, 54-2, v2, 1p. [3555]
Construction through the Omaha and Winnebago reservations in Nebraska is delayed.

34. Rental of the Seal Islands of Alaska. 23 Jan.
SD 81, 54-2, v3, 12p. [3469]
Report includes information on the Alaskan natives.

35. Irrigation Papers No. 2. 25 Jan.
HD 342, 54-2, v70, 98p. [3546]
On the Gila Basin, Arizona; area includes the Pima reservation.

36. Free Homesteads on Public Lands. 25 Jan.
HR 2614, 54-2, v2, 5p. [3555]
Concerned with entries on lands ceded to the U.S. by Indians.

37. R-P of R. Selden. 25 Jan.
HR 2616, 54-2, v2, 1p. [3555]
Seminole war; 1841-42; Florida.

38. R-P of J. McKinney. 26 Jan.
SR 1324, 54-2, v2, 1p. [3475] *or*
HR 1083, 54-1, v4, 1p. [3460]
Rogue River war; 1855-56; Oregon.

39. R-P of D. Giles. 26 Jan.
SR 1325, 54-2, v2, 1p. [3475] *or*
HR 1084, 54-1, v4, 1p. [3460]
Rogue River war; 1855-56; Oregon.

40. Osage Indian Funds. 26 Jan.
SR 1336, 54-2, v2, 153p. [3475]
Investigation of fraud concerning said funds.

41. Pensions to Survivors of Indian Wars, and Their Dependents. 26 Jan.
HR 2635, 54-2, v2, 2p. [3555]
Bill to increase the size of pensions.

42. R-P of S. Daub. 26 Jan.
HR 2636, 54-2, v2, 2p. [3555]
Husband killed in battle with Indians; 1866.

43. Klamath Boundary Commission. 27 Jan.
SD 93, 54-2, v3, 19p. [3469]
Investigation of erroneous surveys made of this reservation in Oregon; report includes Indian testimony.

44. Disposition of Lands Belonging to the Choctaws. 27 Jan.
SD 94, 54-2, v3, 10p. [3469]
Agreement made 18 Dec. 1896; land allotments and cessions in Indian Territory; Dawes Commission.

45. R-P of M. Frank. 29 Jan.
SR 1351, 54-2, v2, 1p. [3475] *or*
HR 2805, 54-2, v3, 1p. [3556]
Florida Indian war; 1818.

46. Survey of the Lands of the Chickasaw Nation. 29 Jan.
HD 226, 54-2, v48, 4p. [3524]
Appropriation required.

47. Serial Documents Published by the U.S. 1 Feb.
SD 103, 54-2, v4, 91p. [3470]
Includes lists of Indian depredation claims, and reports of the Bureau of Ethnology, CIA, Smithsonian Institution, etc.

48. Amendment to the Indian Appropriation Bill. 1 Feb.
SR 1362, 54-2, v2, 23p. [3475]
Funds due the Medawakanton and Wahpakoota bands of Sioux (Santee and Flandreau Sioux) under the treaties of 1837 and 1851.

49. R-P of Arkansas Volunteers. 2 Feb.
SR 1370, 54-2, v2, 2p. [3475] *or*
HR 865, 54-1, v4, 2p. [3460]
Service against hostile Indians while at Fort Gibson, Cherokee Nation, during the Mexican war.

50. Sisseton and Wahpeton Sioux. 2 Feb.
SR 1384, 54-2, v2, 5p. [3475]
Restoration of lands and annuities (under the treaty of 1851) which had been lost to the U.S. after the Sioux outbreak of 1862.

51. Deficiency Estimates. 2 Feb.
HD 250, 54-2, v26, 49p. [3502]
Appropriations for fiscal 1897; Indian Service.

52. Amounts Due Certain Indians. 4 Feb.
SR 1390, 54-2, v2, 5p. [3475]
Amounts due various bands of Chippewas in Minnesota under various treaties, etc.

53. Appropriation for the Genoa Indian School. 4 Feb.
SR 1400, 54-2, v2, 3p. [3475]
For fiscal 1897 in Nebraska.

54. St. Paul, Minneapolis, and Manitoba Railway Co. 4 Feb.
HR 2787, 54-2, v3, 1p. [3556]
Construction through the White Earth, Leech Lake, Chippewa, and Fond du Lac reservations is delayed.

55. Treaty with the Navajoes. 4 Feb.
HR 2803, 54-2, v3, 1p. [3556]
Action of the Com. on Indian Affairs.

56. R-P of I. Whitenberg. 4 Feb.
HR 2806, 54-2, v3, 1p. [3556]
Sabine war; 1836; Tennessee Volunteers.

57. R-P of S. Blazer. 4 Feb.
HR 2807, 54-2, v3, 1p. [3556]
Indian war of 1836; Tennessee Volunteers.

58. Mem. of the Creek Indians. 6 Feb.
SD 111, 54-2, v4, 10p. [3470]
Concerning their rejection of an agreement submitted to them by the Dawes Commission; land allotment and a change in the government of Indian Territory.

59. Correspondence Between the Cherokees and the Dawes Commission. 6 Feb.
SD 112, 54-2, v4, 6p. [3470]
Concerning a proposed change in their tribal government, and their method of land tenure.

60. Claims Allowed by Accounting Officers. 6 Feb.
HD 260, 54-2, v58, 24p. [3534]
Includes claims involving the Indian Service.

61. Transportation for Indian Pupils. 6 Feb.
HD 261, 54-2, v58, 2p. [3534]
Appropriation to pay the Chesapeake and Ohio Railroad Co.; transported students to and from the Hampton Normal and Agricultural Institute.

62. State Bonds Belonging to the U.S. 6 Feb.
HD 263, 54-2, v58, 19p. [3534]
Bonds in the Indian trust funds.

63. Indian Depredation Claims. 8 Feb.
HD 265, 54-2, v58, 1p. [3534]
Judgments of the Court of Claims.

64. R-P of T. Joyce. 8 Feb.
HR 2839, 54-2, v3, 1p. [3556]
Florida Indian war; 1837-40.

65. R-P of D. Tollett. 9 Feb.
SR 1420, 54-2, v2, 1p. [3475] *or*
HR 1304, 54-1, v5, 1p. [3461] *or*
HR 2929, 54-2, v3, 1p. [3556]
Sabine Indian war; 1836-37; Arkansas Volunteers.

66. R-P of E. Anderson. 9 Feb.
SR 1421, 54-2, v2, 2p. [3475] *or*
HR 1151, 54-1, v5, 1p. [3461]
Creek war; 1836; Georgia Volunteers.

67. R-P of E. Roberts. 9 Feb.
SR 1432, 54-2, v2, 2p. [3475] *or*
HR 3008, 54-2, v3, 2p. [3556]
Expedition against Chippewas in 1862.

68. Reorganizing the Judicial District of Arkansas. 9 Feb.
HR 2842, 54-2, v3, 1p. [3556]
Western district formerly had jurisdiction over parts of Indian Territory.

69. R-C of B. Moreland. 10 Feb.
SR 1443, 54-2, v2, 2p. [3475] *or*
HR 1170, 54-1, v5, 2p. [3461]
Settler's improvements encorporated into the Winnebago reservation in Minnesota; 1856.

70. Sundry Civil Appropriation Bill. 11 Feb.
HR 2891, 54-2, v3, 13p. [3556]
Includes support of Alaskan natives for fiscal 1898.

71. Duluth and Winnipeg Railroad Co. 11 Feb.
HR 2893, 54-2, v3, 1p. [3556]
Construction through the White Earth and Chippewa reservations is delayed.

72. Division of San Carlos Reservation. 12 Feb.
SD 121, 54-2, v4, 2p. [3470]
Creation of a new reservation to be known as the Fort Apache reservation; Arizona.

73. Indian Appropriation Bill. 12 Feb.
SR 1455, 54-2, v3, 5p. [3476]
For fiscal 1898.

74. Accounts of the Central Pacific Railroad Co. 12 Feb.
HD 284, 54-2, v58, 11p. [3534]
Transport of Indian supplies, etc.

75. Claim of the Sisseton and Wahpeton Bands of Sioux. 13 Feb.
SD 126, 54-2, v4, 17p. [3470]
For annuities due under the treaty of 23 July 1851; history of the claim.

76. Mem. of the Chickasaw Nation. 13 Feb.
SD 127, 54-2, v4, 4p. [3470]
On their rejection of an agreement submitted to them by the Dawes Commission; concerns tribal government, and land tenure.

77. R-C of Reps. of E. Ayres. 13 Feb.
SR 1457, 54-2, v3, 9p. [3476]
Purchased Chickasaw lands in Mississippi; 1839; title dispute.

78. R-P of J. Porterfield. 15 Feb.
HR 2944, 54-2, v3, 1p. [3556]
Creek war; 1836; Alabama Volunteers.

79. Mississippi Choctaws. 16 Feb.
SD 129, 54-2, v4, 6p. [3470]
Concerns their rights to citizenship in the Choctaw Nation.

80. Protest of Cherokee Delegates. 16 Feb.
SD 130, 54-2, v4, 6p. [3470]
On claims against the "Old Settler," or Western Cherokees.

81. Lower Brulé Sioux. 16 Feb.
SD 132, 54-2, v4, 15p. [3470]
Hearings before the Com. on Indian Affairs regarding the removal of said Indians from their lands in South Dakota; includes Indian testimony.

82. General Deficiency Bill. 18 Feb.
HR 2977, 54-2, v3, 1p. [3556]
Fiscal 1897; includes Indian depredation claims.

83. Disposition of Certain Lands in Minnesota. 18 Feb.
HR 2984, 54-2, v3, 3p. [3556]
Chippewa lands damaged by the construction of dams and reservoirs.

84. Payment of Bonds and Stocks Owned by the U.S. 18 Feb.
HR 2986, 54-2, v3, 2p. [3556]
Payments due from various States; Indian trust funds.

85. R-P of A. Augustine. 19 Feb.
SR 1504, 54-2, v3, 1p. [3476] *or*
HR 1069, 54-1, v4, 1p. [3460]
Cayuse war; 1847-48; Oregon.

86. R-C of the Naalem Band of Tillamooks. 19 Feb.
SR 1505, 54-2, v3, 3p. [3476] *or*
HR 2588, 54-2, v2, 2p. [3555]
Treaty of 6 Aug. 1851 was not ratified, and still the U.S. took possession of their lands in Oregon; Indians received no money.

87. Red Lake Reservation. 19 Feb.
HR 2995, 54-2, v3, 1p. [2995]
Action of the Com. on Indian Affairs.

88. Mem. on Behalf of Catawba Indians. 23 Feb.
SD 144, 54-2, v5, 12p. [3471]
As to the status of tribal lands in the Carolinas, and possible funds due from sale of said lands; ask for lands in Indian Territory.

89. Ogden Land Co. 23 Feb.
HD 309, 54-2, v58, 6p. [3534]
On title to lands in the Allegany and Cattaraugus reservations in New York; Senecas.

90. Treaty with the Navajoes. 23 Feb.
HD 310, 54-2, v58, 17p. [3534]
Made 1 June 1868; concerning removal of non-reservation Navajoes to the reservation set up under said treaty.

91. R-P of A. Abercrombie. 24 Feb.
SR 1530, 54-2, v3, 1p. [3476] *or*

HR 1232, 54-1, v5, 1p. [3461]
Creek war of 1836; Alabama Volunteers.

92. Mem. of the Seneca Nation. 25 Feb.
SD 154, 54-2, v5, 10p. [3471]
Protesting the proposed purchase by the U.S. of title to lands within the Allegany and Cattaraugus reservations, New York; this title is in the hands of the Ogden Land Co.

93. R-P of S. Spyker. 26 Feb.
SR 1554, 54-2, v3, 1p. [3476] *or*
HR 1534, 54-1, v6, 1p. [3462]
Creek war; 1836; Alabama Volunteers.

94. Claims Allowed by Accounting Officers. 27 Feb.
SD 162, 54-2, v5, 7p. [3471]
Includes claims related to the Indian Service.

95. Mem. of Members of the Bar of Indian Territory. 27 Feb.
SD 164, 54-2, v5, 20p. [3471]
Ask for an additional judge to be appointed to the U.S. court in Indian Territory.

96. Indian Depredation Claims. 27 Feb.
SD 165, 54-2, v5, 2p. [3471]
Judgments rendered by the Court of Claims.

97. Deficiency Appropriations. 1 Mar.
SR 1559, 54-2, v3, 1p. [3476]
For fiscal 1897; Indian depredation claims.

98. Perrine Grant, Florida. 3 Mar.
SR 1574 (pts. 1 and 2), 54-2, v3, 51p. [3476]
Seminole hostilities of 1848 interfere with legal matters surrounding title to the land.

99. Mississippi Choctaws. 3 Mar.
HR 3080, 54-2, v3, 6p. [3556]
On their right to citizenship in the Choctaw Nation, which is guaranteed by various treaties.

100. Congressional Directory. 12 Mar.
SD 1 (pts. 1 and 2), 55-1, v1, 605p. [3558]
Duties of the CIA.

101. Surveys of the Indian Territory. 19 Mar.
SD 4, 55-1, v2, 4p. [3559]
Appropriation to continue the survey is requested.

102. Mem. of S. Parker. 19 Mar.
SD 5, 55-1, v2, 7p. [3559]
Attorney for the Western Cherokees asks for moneys due him; Sec. of the Interior had refused to pay him.

103. Survey of Townships in Nebraska. 19 Mar.
SR 1, 55-1, v1, 2p. [3569]
Action of the Com. on Indian Affairs.

104. Consideration of House Bill. No. 16. 19 Mar.
HR 3, 55-1, v1, 1p. [3588]
Debate on Indian appropriation bill is limited to 40 minutes.

105. Compromise Between the U.S. and Arkansas. 22 Mar.
SR 2, 55-1, v1, 10p. [3569] *or*
HR 251, 55-2, v2, 6p. [3718]
On State bonds held for the benefit of Indian trust funds.

106. Homesteaders on the Sioux Reservation. 22 Mar.
SR 3, 55-1, v1, 6p. [3569]
Bill relieving them of the necessity of paying $1.25 per acre for their homesteads in Nebraska, South Dakota, and North Dakota.

107. Santee Sioux of Nebraska, and Flandreau Sioux of South Dakota. 22 Mar.
SR 4, 55-1, v1, 23p. [3569]
Bill restoring to these Indians all the rights and privileges enjoyed by them prior to 1862 under the treaties of 1837 and 1851; proposed amendment to the Indian Appropriation Bill.

108. Free Homesteads for Bona Fide Settlers. 22 Mar.
SR 5, 55-1, v1, 12p. [3569] *or*
HR 349, 55-2, v2, 12p. [3718]
On lands ceded to the U.S. by Indians; list of recent cessions.

109. Mixed-Blood Indians. 22 Mar.
SR 6, 55-1, v1, 2p. [3569]
Bill confirming the title of mixed-bloods to their lands under various treaties; defining the term "Indian."

110. Indian Citizens. 22 Mar.
SR 7, 55-1, v1, 11p. [3569]
Regarding taxation of lands allotted to Indians; establishment of "tax funds."

111. Chippewas in Minnesota. 22 Mar.
SR 8, 55-1, v1, 5p. [3569]
Bill calling for the payment of sums due said Indians under various treaties, etc.

112. Sisseton and Wahpeton Sioux. 23 Mar.
SR 9, 55-1, v1, 27p. [3569]
Bill to restore annuities to these Indians (lost after the outbreak of 1862); due under the treaty of 1851.

113. Repeal of Timber Culture Laws. 23 Mar.
SR 10, 55-1, v1, 2p. [3569]
Concerning lands formerly a part of the Sioux reservation in North Dakota, South Dakota, and Nebraska.

114. Proceeds from the Sale of Public Lands. 23 Mar.
SR 12, 55-1, v1, 75p. [3569]
Concerned with Indian lands.

115. R-C of G. Anderson. 30 Mar.
SR 21, 55-1, v1, 2p. [3569] *or*
HR 801, 55-2, v3, 2p. [3719]
Improvements made on lands within the Rosebud reservation; Sioux Indian lands.

116. Settlement of the Account Between the U.S. and Florida. 30 Mar.
SR 23, 55-1, v1, 14p. [3569] *or*
HR 1120, 55-2, v4, 4p. [3720]
Expenses of the Seminole war; 1855-57 (Senate version includes relevant documentation).

117. Amendment to the Indian Appropriation Bill. 5 Apr.
SR 47, 55-1, v1, 5p. [3569]
Concerns payments to Sioux who served in armies of the U.S. against their own people in the outbreak of 1862.

118. Appeal of Cherokee Delegates. 6 Apr.
SD 24, 55-1, v2, 5p. [3559]
Against pending legislation which would extend the jurisdiction of U.S. courts over Indian Territory, destroy Cherokee courts, and effectively remove self-government by the Indians; violates treaties.

119. Amending the Indian Appropriation Bill. 6 Apr.
SR 52, 55-1, v1, 1p. [3569]
Concerning the establishment of a warehouse for Indian goods in Omaha, Nebraska.

120. R-C of J. Bridger. 8 Apr.
SR 66, 55-1, v1, 23p. [3569]
Establishment of Fort Bridger, Utah, for protection from hostile Indians, and Mormons.

121. Uintah Reservation, Utah. 13 Apr.
SD 32, 55-1, v2, 19p. [3559]
Concerning negotiations with the Ute Indians on this reservation for cession of lands.

122. Investigation of Affairs at the Kiowa, Comanche, and Apache Reservation. 13 Apr.
SD 34, 55-1, v2, 388p. [3559]
Concerning conditions there, and charges made against the acting Indian agent; testimony from the Indians, and others.

123. Deficiency Estimates. 19 Apr.
SD 41, 55-1, v4, 2p. [3561]
For the contingent expense appropriation of the Interior Dept.; phone service to the Indian Office.

124. L-C of R. De Graffenreid and G. Turner. 19 Apr.
SD 43, 55-1, v4, 3p. [3561]
Legal services performed in Indian Territory.

125. Council with the Wichitas, Caddoes, and Delawares. 29 Apr.
SD 53, 55-1, v4, 14p. [3561]
Proceedings of a council held on the 23rd and 24th of Mar., 1897; on the opening of their reservation, allotment, and the "Jerome treaty."

126. Statements of an Ogalalla Sioux Delegation. 4 May.
SD 61, 55-1, v4, 33p. [3561]
Affairs at Pine Ridge Agency, South Dakota.

127. Mem. of the Principal Chief of the Creek Nation. 6 May.
SD 67, 55-1, v5, 6p. [3562]
For the payment of awards to Creeks who enlisted in the Federal Army during the Civil War, etc.

128. Oil Leases of the Seneca Indians. 11 May.
SD 76, 55-1, v5, 150p. [3562]
Investigation (with testimony) of the events surrounding a lease made to the Seneca Oil Co.

129. Pine Lands and Timber on the Red Lake Reservation. 13 May.
SD 85, 55-1, v5, 142p. [3562]
Regarding examinations and estimates of these lands on this Chippewa reservation in Minnesota.

130. Mem. of Sioux Indians. 17 May.
SD 90, 55-1, v5, 4p. [3562]
On Indians employed and taken from the Pine Ridge reservation, South Dakota, to accompany Buffalo Bill's Wild West Show.

131. Agreement with the Choctaws and Chickasaws. 19 May.
SD 93, 55-1, v5, 11p. [3562]
Made 23 Apr. 1897; calls for allotment of land in severalty, revision of the present system of legislative authority and legal jurisdiction, etc.

132. Indian Depredation Claims. 26 May.
SD 110, 55-1, v5, 2p. [3562]
Judgments of the Court of Claims.

133. Claims Allowed by Accounting Officers. 27 May.
SD 121, 55-1, v5, 13p. [3562]
Includes some involving the Indian Service.

134. Appropriation for an Indian School. 28 May.
SD 125, 55-1, v5, 3p. [3562]
Support of the school at Carlisle, Pennsylvania.

135. R-C of Reps. of G. McDougall. 28 May.
SR 141, 55-1, v2, 8p. [3570] *or*
HR 458, 55-2, v2, 8p. [3718]
Claimant never reimbursed for supplies given to California Indians in 1852.

136. Amounts Found Due by Accounting Officers. 1 June.
SD 132, 55-1, v5, 2p. [3562]
Some debts incurred by the Indian Service.

137. Second Homestead Entries. 3 June.
SR 145, 55-1, v2, 3p. [3570]
Bill allowing individuals to make a second entry; disposal of Seminole, Sac and Fox, Crow, and Kickapoo lands is involved.

138. Payment to Cherokee Freedmen. 4 June.
SD 136, 55-1, v6, 29p. [3563]
Concerning the reason why said payment was suspended, and why it is to be resumed.

139. California Indian War Bonds. 4 June.
SD 137, 55-1, v6, 2p. [3563]
Concerning interest payments on said bonds, etc.

140. Allotments to Wichita Indians. 7 June.
SD 143, 55-1, v6, 1p. [3563]
Pres. suspends allotment of lands; Choctaws and Chickasaws have claimed title to the lands involved.

141. R-C of A. Babcock. 11 June.
SR 150, 55-1, v2, 3p. [3570]
Lands settled upon which were inside the Grande Ronde Indian reservation, Oregon.

142. R-M of Choctaw Freedmen. 15 June.
SD 149, 55-1, v6, 2p. [3563]
Agreement of 23 Apr. 1897 between the Dawes Commission and the Choctaws and Chickasaws ignores the rights of the freedmen.

143. Pensions to Survivors of Indian Wars. 15 June.
SR 152, 55-1, v2, 5p. [3570]
Pension laws amended to admit survivors of the Sac and Fox war of 1831; etc.

144. Deficiency Appropriation Bill. 22 June.
SR 159, 55-1, v2, 11p. [3570]
For fiscal 1897; increases for the Indian Service.

145. Chickasaw Freedmen. 23 June.
SD 157, 55-1, v6, 59p. [3563]
Their rights under the Choctaw and Chickasaw treaty of 1866, etc.

146. R-P of M. Frank. 29 June.
SR 180, 55-1, v2, 1p. [3570] *or*
HR 424, 55-2, v2, 1p. [3718]
Florida Indian war; 1818.

147. R-P of S. Stilwell. 29 June.
SR 184, 55-1, v2, 8p. [3570] *or*
HR 981, 55-2, v4, 8p. [3720]
Indian camapign of 1867 in Kansas; Cheyennes, Arapahoes, Kiowas, and Comanches; Custer's expedition.

148. R-P of M. Calhoun. 29 June.
SR 185, 55-1, v2, 2p. [3570] *or*
HR 422, 55-2, v2, 2p. [3718]
Sioux expedition of 1876; battle at the Little Big Horn River.

149. R-P of E. Roberts. 29 June.
SR 225, 55-1, v2, 2p. [3570]
Chippewa campaign of 1862.

150. R-P of A. King. 29 June.
SR 251, 55-1, v2, 1p. [3569]
Black Hawk war; 1832; Missouri militia.

151. R-P of G. McGrath. 29 June.
SR 260, 55-1, v2, 1p. [3570]
Service in Custer's campaign against Black Kettle's band in 1869; Kansas.

152. R-P of A. Abercrombie. 29 June.
SR 280, 55-1, v2, 1p. [3570] *or*
HR 1217, 55-2, v5, 1p. [3721]
Creek war; 1836; Alabama Volunteers.

153. R-P of J. Sturgis. 29 June.
SR 283, 55-1, v2, 1p. [3570]
Battle with Sioux at the Little Big Horn River.

154. R-P of S. Spyker. 29 June.
SR 295, 55-1, v2, 1p. [3570] *or*
HR 803, 55-2, v3, 1p. [3719]
Creek war; 1836; Alabama Volunteers.

155. R-P of M. McKay. 29 June.
SR 312, 55-1, v2, 2p. [3570]
Service in Oregon Indian wars.

156. R-P of P. Castleman. 29 June.
SR 327, 55-1, v2, 2p. [3570] *or*
HR 1012, 55-2, v4, 2p. [3720]
Oregon and Washington Indian war; 1855-56; Oregon Volunteers.

157. R-P of P. Daly. 29 June.
SR 341, 55-1, v2, 2p. [3570] *or*
HR 1024, 55-2, v4, 3p. [3720]
Frontier duty among the Comanches during 1857-61.

158. R-P of W. Tumblin. 29 June.
SR 344, 55-1, v2, 2p. [3570]
Florida Indian war; 1836.

159. R-P of S. McKay. 29 June.
SR 347, 55-1, v2, 2p. [3570]
Troops called into service in Florida during 1846; Indian hostilities.

160. R-P of F. Kautz. 30 June.
SR 352, 55-1, v2, 3p. [3570]
Rogue River war of 1855; Apache hostilities during 1875-78.

161. Mem. of the Wichitas, Caddoes, and Delawares. 1 July.
HD 74, 55-1, v1, 10p. [3571]
Asks that allotment of land not take place until certain matters are resolved; Choctaw and Chickasaw claim to lands involved; etc.

162. Jurisdiction of the U.S. Court in Western Arkansas. 12 July.
HD 83, 55-1, v1, 2p. [3571]
Jurisdiction of this court over Indian Territory is repealed, as U.S. courts are being established there.

163. Annual Report of the American Historical Association for 1896. 15 July.
HD 353 (v1), 54-2, v74, 1313p. [3550 (pt. 1)]
Research related to the North American Indians.

164. Allotment of Land to Choctaw and Chickasaw Freedmen. 17 July.
SD 183, 55-1, v6, 12p. [3563]
Protest against ratification of any agreement which does not provide for allotment of land to freedmen; agreement made 23 Apr. 1897 does not contain such a provision.

165. Reports to be Made to Congress. 27 July.
HD 90, 55-1, v1, 24p. [3571]
Includes those to be made by the CIA.

166. Statements of Appropriations. 24 July.
SD 191, 55-1, v10, 479p. [3567]
For the 2d session, 54th Congress, and the 1st session, 55th Congress; Indian expenses.

167. Index to Congressional Documents and Reports. 1 Aug.
HD 356, 54-2, v77, 131p. [3553]
For the 54th Congress, 2d session.

168. Catalogue of Public Documents. 1 Nov.
HD 355, 54-2, v76, 692p. [3552]
For the 54th Congress, 1st session; U.S. publications on Indians are listed.

169. 12th Report of the Civil Service Commission. (no date)
HD 318, 54-2, v63, 123p. [3539]
Affairs in the Indian Service.

170. 13th Report of the Civil Service Commission. (no date)
HD 321, 54-2, v63, 315p. [3539]
Affairs in the Indian Service.

171. 15th Annual Report of the Bureau of Ethnology. (no date)
HD 339, 54-2, v68, 487p. [3544]
Research related to the American Indian; reports on stone implements (Holmes), Siouan Indians (McGee), Siouan sociology (Dorsey), Tusayan Katcinas (Fewkes), and the Casa Grande ruins in Arizona (Mindeleff).

172. 16th Annual Report of the Bureau of Ethnology. (no date)
HD 93, 55-1, v10, 445p. [3580]
Research related to the American Indian; including cliff ruins in Arizona (Mindeleff), Tusayan snake ceremonies (Fewkes), etc.

173. Index to Documents and Reports. (no date)
HD 96, 55-1, v17, 54p. [3587]
For the 1st session, 55th Congress.

174. Annual Report of the Sec. of War. 10 Nov.
HD 2, 55-2, v2-9, 5415p. [3630-3637]
Potential Indian hostilities in Alaska; no serious Indian disturbances during the past year.

175. Seal and Salmon Fisheries, and General Resources of Alaska. 15 Nov.
HD 92 (pts. 1-4), 55-1, v6-9, 2494p. [3576-3579]
References to Alaskan Indians and their affairs.

176. Annual Report of the Sec. of Interior. 16 Nov.
HD 5, 55-2, v12-22, 8978p. [3640-3650]
Indian affairs; annual report of the

Gen. Land Office (Serial 3640); annual report of the CIA (Serial 3641); etc.

177. Annual Report of the Attorney-General of the U.S. 30 Nov.
HD 9, 55-2, v27, 339p. [3655]
Includes Indian depredation claims, attorneys for the Mission Indians, etc.

178. Annual Message to Congress; Pres. McKinley. 6 Dec.
HD 1, 55-2, v1, 644p. [3629]
On the Dawes Commission to the Five Civilized Tribes; negotiations aimed at extinguishing tribal title to lands by either cession of the same to the U.S., or by allotment of land in severalty; agreements with the Creeks, Choctaws, and Chickasaws.

179. Annual Report of the Sec. of the Treasury. 6 Dec.
HD 8, 55-2, v26, 934p. [3654]
Year ending 30 June 1897; Indian expenses.

180. Estimates of Appropriations. 6 Dec.
HD 12, 55-2, v31, 448p. [3659]
For fiscal 1899; Indian expenses.

181. Contingent Expenses of the Interior Dept. 6 Dec.
HD 16, 55-2, v34, 23p. [3662]
Fiscal 1897; Indian Office.

182. Indian Depredation Claims. 7 Dec.
HD 92, 55-2, v34, 2p. [3662]
Judgments of the Court of Claims.

183. Expenditures of the Smithsonian Institution. 7 Dec.
HD 93, 55-2, v34, 42p. [3662]
On North American ethnology concerned with the American Indian, etc.

184. Receipts and Expenditures. 7 Dec.
HD 94, 55-2, v31, 64p. [3659]
For fiscal 1897; Indian Service.

185. Agreements with Certain Sioux. 8 Dec.
SD 9, 55-2, v1, 1p. [3590]
Concerning transmittal of copies of all treaties and agreements made with the Sisseton, Wahpeton, Santee of Nebraska, and Flandreau bands of Sioux.

186. Alaska Gold Fields. 13 Dec.
SD 14, 55-2, v1, 14p. [3590]
Conditions in the Klondike region of Alaska; a detachment of Indian scouts is needed to help control lawlessness in the region.

187. Congressional Directory. 13 Dec.
SD 22 (pts. 1 and 2), 55-2, v2, 662p. [3591]
Duties of the CIA.

188. Congress of the Indian Tribes of the U.S. 13 Dec.
SR 397, 55-2, v1, 5p. [3620]
Amendments to a bill providing for the holding of such a Congress in Omaha, Nebraska, during 1898; reasons behind the Congress.

189. Omaha Northern Railway Co. 13 Dec.
SR 398, 55-2, v1, 1p. [3620] *or*
HR 300, 55-2, v2, 3p. [3718]
Construction across the Omaha and Winnebago reservations in Nebraska.

190. Spokane Falls and Northern Railway Co. 13 Dec.
SR 399, 55-2, v1, 1p. [3620] *or*
HR 560, 55-2, v3, 1p. [3719]
Right of way through the Colville reservation, Washington.

191. Legislative, Executive, and Judicial Appropriation Bill. 13 Dec.
HR 32, 55-2, v1, 42p. [3717]
Fiscal 1899; OIA.

192. R-C of H. Phillips. 15 Dec.
SR 401, 55-2, v1, 4p. [3620] *or*
HR 1900, 55-3, v1, 4p. [3840]
Service during the Sioux hostilities of 1866 near Fort Phil. Kearny.

193. Survey of Lands in Indian Territory. 15 Dec.
HD 149, 55-2, v39, 4p. [3667]
Appropriation needed to complete the survey.

194. Statistical Abstract of the U.S. 15 Dec.
HD 259, 55-2, v53, 424p. [3681]
Indian populations, etc.; 1897.

195. Case of E. Chirouse. 16 Dec.
SR 407, 55-2, v1, 1p. [3620]
Accounts of this Indian agent at the Tulalip agency, Washington.

196. Water for the Southern Ute Reservation. 16 Dec.
HD 152, 55-2, v39, 6p. [3667]
Report on irrigating the reservation in Colorado.

197. Urgent Deficiency Estimates. 16 Dec.
HD 156, 55-2, v31, 12p. [3659]
For fiscal 1898; expenses of the Commission to the Crows, Flatheads, and other Indians, etc.

198. Gila Valley, Globe, and Northern Railway Co. 16 Dec.
HR 63, 55-2, v1 , 1p. [3717]
Indians on the San Carlos reserva-

tion have not consented to construction of this railroad through their lands; time limit extended.

199. Choctaw-Chickasaw Union Party. 17 Dec.
SD 25, 55-2, v1, 2p. [3590]
Party objects to the agreement recently made between the Dawes Commission and the Choctaw and Chickasaw Nations.

200. Report on Domestic Reindeer in Alaska. 17 Dec.
SD 30, 55-2, v1, 124p. [3590]
Introduced to benefit Eskimos and other Alaskan natives.

201. Agreement with the Creek Nation. 18 Dec.
SD 34, 55-2, v1, 14p. [3590]
Made 27 Sept. 1897; would have provided for allotment of lands, restructuring of tribal government, etc.; the agreement is rejected by the Creek council, and negotiations begin again; Dawes Commission.

202. Agriculture in Alaska. 18 Dec.
HD 160, 55-2, v39, 36p. [3667]
Discusses animals and plants used by Alaskan natives for food.

1898

1. Civil Service Rules. 5 Jan.
SD 41 (pts. 1-3), 55-2, v3, 9p. [3592]
Includes list of officers in the Indian Service who would be exempt from following said rules.

2. Deficiency Appropriation for the Indian Service. 5 Jan.
HD 177, 55-2, v39, 3p. [3667]
Fiscal 1898; surveying and alloting reservations, etc.

3. Increased Appropriation for the Dawes Commission. 5 Jan.
HD 181, 55-2, v39, 4p. [3667]
For fiscal 1899; negotiations with the Five Civilized Tribes.

4. Delinquent Accounts of Officers of the U.S. 5 Jan.
HD 189, 55-2, v39, 20p. [3667]
Including persons in the Indian Service.

5. Claims Allowed by Accounting Officers. 6 Jan.
HD 194, 55-2, v39, 19p. [3667]
Including those related to the Indian Service.

6. Amendment to Section 2234, Revised Statutes. 7 Jan.
SR 415, 55-2, v1, 1p. [3620] *or*
HR 132, 55-2, v1, 2p. [3717]
Concerns sureties on the bonds of registers and receivers who sell Indian lands.

7. Deficiency Estimates. 8 Jan.
HD 203, 55-2, v31, 16p. [3659]
For fiscal 1898; Indian Service.

8. Liabilities of Registers and Receivers. 10 Jan.
SD 52, 55-2, v3, 2p. [3592]
Arising from sales of Indian lands.

9. Railroad Passenger Rates Through Indian Territory. 10 Jan.
SR 418, 55-2, v1, 1p. [3620]
Bill to prevent railroads from charging more than 3 cents per mile.

10. Confirming Cash Entries of Public Lands. 10 Jan.
SR 419, 55-2, v1, 3p. [3620]
Action of the Com. on Indian Affairs.

11. Payments to Klamaths, Modocs, and Snakes. 10 Jan.
SR 420, 55-2, v1, 6p. [3620]
For lands excluded from the Klamath reservation, Oregon, due to faulty surveys; treaty of 1864.

12. R-C of the Estate of R. Crooks. 10 Jan.
SR 421, 55-2, v1, 2p. [3620] *or*
SR 830, 55-2, v3, 3p. [3622]
Concerns depts of the Menomonees, Chippewas, and Winnebagoes.

13. State Bonds Belonging to the U.S. 10 Jan.
HD 207, 55-2, v51, 2p. [3679]
Held in Indian trust funds.

14. Mission Indians of California. 11 Jan.
SD 54, 55-2, v3, 7p. [3592]
Amendments to an act for the relief of said Indians; would include in the several Mission Indian reservations certain lands cultivated by the Indians.

15. Agreement with the Seminole Nation. 13 Jan.
SD 56, 55-2, v3, 4p. [3592]
Made 16 Dec. 1897; provides for allotment, a restructuring of tribal government, etc.; Dawes Commission.

16. Criminal and Penal Laws Relating to Alaska. 14 Jan.
SD 60, 55-2, v3, 144p. [3592]

Includes laws concerning sale of liquor and firearms to Indians, etc.

17. Offered and Unoffered Public Lands. 14 Jan.
HR 130, 55-2, v1, 2p. [3717]
Procedures which follow extinguishment of Indian title to land.

18. Nebraska, Kansas, and Gulf Railway Co. 14 Jan.
HR 134, 55-2, v1, 1p. [3717]
Right of way through Indian Territory.

19. Railroad Rights of Way in Alaska. 14 Jan.
HR 137, 55-2, v1, 3p. [3717]
Act to regulate railroad construction said not to apply to Indian reservation lands (section 7); act also concerns homestead entries.

20. Agreement with the Choctaws and Chickasaws. 17 Jan.
SD 65, 55-2, v3, 11p. [3592]
Made 23 Apr. 1897; provides for allotment of lands, for a restructuring of tribal government, etc.; Dawes Commission.

21. Report on the Santee and Flandreau Sioux. 17 Jan.
SD 67, 55-2, v3, 77p. [3592]
Formerly the Medawakanton-Wahpakoota Confederacy; copies of treaties and agreements dated 1825, 1830, 1836, 1837, 1851, 1858, 1868, and 1876.

22. Report on the Sisseton and Wahpeton Sioux. 17 Jan.
SD 68, 55-2, v4, 59p. [3593]
Copies of treaties and agreements dated 1830, 1836, 1851, 1858, 1867, and 1889.

23. Dealings with Certain Sioux Indians. 17 Jan.
HD 228, 55-2, v51, 3p. [3679]
Concerning funds due the Sisseton, Wahpeton, Medawakanton, and Wahpakoota bands of Sioux.

24. Fort Meade, South Dakota. 20 Jan.
SD 76, 55-2, v4, 8p. [3593]
On maintenance of the fort; located near the Pine Ridge and Rosebud reservations of Sioux Indians; it should be made a permanent post.

25. Otoe and Missouria Reservation Lands. 20 Jan.
SR 474, 55-2, v1, 4p. [3620] *or*
HR 2198, 55-3, v2, 6p. [3841]
Revision and adjustment of sales of these lands in Kansas; confirmation of land titles.

26. Amending Section 2139, Revised Statutes. 20 Jan.
HR 201, 55-2, v1, 2p. [3717]
Concerning sale of liquor to Indians on the six Indian reservations in New York.

27. Agreements with the Creeks and Seminoles. 21 Jan.
SD 78, 55-2, v4, 10p. [3593]
Creek agreement made 27 Sept. 1897; Seminole agreement made 16 Dec. 1897; both provide for allotment of land, for a restructuring of tribal government, etc.; Dawes Commission.

28. R-P of C. Moore. 21 Jan.
SR 481, 55-2, v1, 2p. [3620]
Service in the Black Hawk and Seminole wars; Cass's treaty expedition of 1826.

29. Gulf, Colorado, and Santa Fe Railway Co. 21 Jan.
HR 219, 55-2, v1, 1p. [3717]
Construction within Indian Territory.

30. Agreement with the Uintah and White River Ute Indians. 22 Jan.
SD 80, 55-2, v4, 5p. [3593]
Made 8 Jan. 1898; lands ceded to the U.S. for the use of the Uncompahgre Utes who wish to remove to the Uintah reservation; Utah.

31. Muscogee Coal and Railway Co. 22 Jan.
HR 229, 55-2, v1, 2p. [3717]
Right of way through Indian Territory.

32. Choctaw and Chickasaw Freedmen. 24 Jan.
SD 84, 55-2, v4, 23p. [3593]
Report on their status under various treaties; claims under the treaty of 1866.

33. Case of Maj. Gen. Webb. 25 Jan.
SR 495, 55-2, v1, 4p. [3620]
Seminole war; 1856; Florida.

34. R-C of J. Shirley. 26 Jan.
SR 501, 55-2, v1, 1p. [3620]
Lands incorporated into an Indian reservation in Idaho.

35. Violence in Oklahoma. 27 Jan.
SD 98, 55-2, v4, 4p. [3593]
Woman killed by Seminole Indians; two Seminoles killed by a mob.

36. Soldier's Home at Hot Springs, South Dakota. 27 Jan.
SR 513, 55-2, v1, 11p. [3620]
The Springs were used as a resort by the Indians in the Black Hills.

37. Violence in Oklahoma. 28 Jan.
SD 99 (pts. 1-3), 55-2, v4, 12p. [3593]
Woman killed by Seminole Indians; two Seminole men killed by a mob of whites.

38. Remonstrance Against Ratification of the Seminole Agreement. 31 Jan.
SD 105, 55-2, v4, 4p. [3593]
Adopted at a mass convention of Seminoles; agreement dated 16 Dec. 1897.

39. Argument for Free Homes. 31 Jan.
SD 106, 55-2, v4, 11p. [3593]
Free homesteads on lands ceded to the U.S. by Indians; focus is on Sioux lands.

40. Increase of Minimum Pensions. 31 Jan.
SR 520, 55-2, v1, 2p. [3620]
For service in Indian wars during 1832-42.

41. R-P of C. Abney. 1 Feb.
SR 528, 55-2, v1, 1p. [3620] *or*
HR 536, 55-2, v2, 1p. [3718]
Indian war of 1836; South Carolina Volunteers.

42. R-P of Itewayaka, or "One-Armed Jim." 1 Feb.
SR 530, 55-2, v1, 4p. [3620] *or*
HR 913, 55-2, v4, 4p. [3720]
Sisseton Sioux Indian serves as a scout for the U.S. during 1863-66.

43. Kaskaskia, Peoria, Piankeshaw, and Wea Indians. 1 Feb.
SR 532, 55-2, v1, 3p. [3620] *or*
HR 1279, 55-2, v5, 3p. [3721]
Funds due from sales of lands ceded to the U.S. under the treaty of 1854; treaty of 1867 said to be unfair to them.

44. Support of Indian Contract Schools. 2 Feb.
SD 112, 55-2, v10, 6p. [3599]
Concerning appropriations for fiscal 1899; contract schools listed.

45. Map of Alaska with Descriptive Text. 2 Feb.
SD 195, 55-2, v11, 44p. [3600]
Includes descriptions of routes to the gold deposits in the Klondike which have been used in the past by Indians.

46. Indian Depredation Claims. 2 Feb.
HD 272, 55-2, v51, 2p. [3679]
Judgments of the Court of Claims.

47. Collated Claims. 3 Feb.
SR 544 (pts. 1 and 2), 55-2, v1, 219p. [3620]
Bill providing for the settlement of claims; Piute Indian claims; etc.

48. Sioux Indians on the Crow Creek Reservation. 3 Feb.
SR 546, 55-2, v1, 1p. [3620]
These Indians have moneys due them because they received less land per capita than Indians on other Sioux reservations; U.S. has not paid the money.

49. Report on the Dawes Commission. 3 Feb.
HD 274, 55-2, v51, 7p. [3679]
Concerning the status of the Mississippi Choctaws; they did not remove to Indian Territory with the rest of the tribe under the treaty of 1830.

50. R-C of S. Dresser. 3 Feb.
HR 343, 55-2, v2, 5p. [3718]
Ute hostilities of 1878 in Colorado; "White River," or "Meeker" Massacre.

51. Payment of Certain Bonds and Stocks Owned by the U.S. 5 Feb.
HR 352, 55-2, v2, 2p. [3718]
Held in Indian trust funds.

52. Irrigation in the Montezuma Valley, Colorado. 7 Feb.
SD 124, 55-2, v10, 5p. [3599]
Within the boundaries of the Southern Ute reservation.

53. Fort Meade, South Dakota. 7 Feb.
SR 552, 55-2, v1, 2p. [3620]
The fort should be maintained, as the threat of Sioux hostilities still exists.

54. Indian Appropriation Bill. 9 Feb.
SR 556, 55-2, v1, 5p. [3620] *or*
HR 189, 55-2, v1, 5p. [3717]
For fiscal 1899.

55. Site of the Fort Phil. Kearny Massacre. 10 Feb.
SR 563, 55-2, v1, 5p. [3620] *or*
HR 1648, 55-2, v6, 5p. [3722]
Monument should be erected; Fetterman's command is overwhelmed by Sioux Indians in 1866.

56. Case of Gen. Grigg. 10 Feb.
SR 564, 55-2, v1, 5p. [3620] *or*

HR 1326 (pts. 1 and 2), 55-2, v5, 6p. [3721]
Service against Indians on the Northwest Coast; 1858.

57. Agreement with the Comanche, Kiowa, and Apache Indians. 10 Feb.
HR 431, 55-2, v2, 3p. [3718] *or*
HR 1281, 55-2, v5, 2p. [3721]
Ratification delayed; Choctaw and Chickasaw claim to the lands involved must be settled; would open lands in Oklahoma for settlement.

58. Confederated Otoe and Missouria Indians. 11 Feb.
SD 132, 55-2, v10, 31p. [3599]
Issues surrounding sale of their lands in Kansas and Nebraska.

59. Asylum for Insane Indians. 11 Feb.
SR 567, 55-2, v1, 18p. [3620]
Bill to establish such an asylum; statistics on insanity given.

60. Education of Indian Children. 14 Feb.
SD 136, 55-2, v10, 4p. [3599]
Information on costs of educating Indian students at particular schools, on transportation costs, on the value of the education, and on the permanency of the experience.

61. R-P of E. Houghton. 14 Feb.
HR 445, 55-2, v2, 2p. [3718]
Sioux outbreak; 1862; Minnesota.

62. Education in Alaska. 15 Feb.
SD 137, 55-2, v10, 186p. [3599]
Detailed report on all aspects of education; educating Alaskan Indians.

63. Education of White and Negro Children in Indian Territory. 16 Feb.
HD 310, 55-2, v51, 8p. [3679]
Concerning a lack of facilities and funds for said purposes.

64. Fort Shaw Military Reservation, Montana. 17 Feb.
SR 602, 55-2, v1, 5p. [3620]
Bill to open for settlement those lands not used for the Indian Industrial School; fort abandoned.

65. 14th Report of the Civil Service Commission. 17 Feb.
HD 314, 55-2, v61, 562p. [3689]
Includes information on the Indian Service.

66. Petition of M. Hamilton. 18 Feb.
SD 143, 55-2, v11, 5p. [3600]
Operations in Indian country between Santa Fe and Fort Leavenworth during the Mexican war.

67. Leases of the Seneca Nation of New York Indians. 18 Feb.
SD 145, 55-2, v11, 15p. [3600]
On regulation of leases of land within the Cattaraugus, Allegany, and Oil Spring reservations; New York.

68. Restoration of Annuities to Certain Indians. 18 Feb.
SR 605, 55-2, v1, 5p. [3620]
To the Sisseton and Wahpeton bands of Dakota or Sioux Indians; these were lost after the outbreak of 1862.

69. R-P of L. Thomasson. 19 Feb.
HR 482, 55-2, v2, 1p. [3718]
Creek and Cherokee wars; 1836-38; Georgia Volunteers.

70. Denison and Northern Railway Co. 21 Feb.
HR 502, 55-2, v2, 1p. [3718]
Time extended for construction through Indian Territory.

71. Sundry Civil Appropriation Bill. 21 Feb.
HR 504, 55-2, v2, 10p. [3718]
Fiscal 1899; counsel for Mission Indians, American ethnology, etc.

72. Appropriation for the Justice Dept. 22 Feb.
HD 318, 55-2, v51, 4p. [3679]
Includes expense of legal dealings involving Indians.

73. Petition and Mem. of the Turtle Mountain Band of Chippewas. 23 Feb.
SD 154, 55-2, v11, 26p. [3600]
Concerns claims and disputes over certain lands in North Dakota; issues surrounding cession, or relinquishment of said lands.

74. R-C of V. Mullan. 23 Feb.
SR 609, 55-2, v1, 5p. [3620] *or*
HR 2110, 55-3, v2, 5p. [3841]
Concerns California Indian war bonds.

75. Federal Jail at Fort Smith, Arkansas. 23 Feb.
HR 529, 55-2, v2, 1p. [3718]
For persons convicted in U.S. courts in Indian Territory.

76. R-C of D. Randall. 24 Feb.
SR 611, 55-2, v1, 4p. [3620]
Improvements relinquished to the U.S. for the use of the Nez Percés in Idaho.

77. Supplemental Deficiency Estimates. 24 Feb.
HD 319, 55-2, v31, 23p. [3659]

Fiscal 1898; includes a census of the Navajoes, etc.

78. U.S. Courts in Indian Territory. 26 Feb.
HD 322, 55-2, v51, 1p. [3679]
Estimate to cover salaries and expenses.

79. R-C of J. Tousaint. 28 Feb.
SR 621, 55-2, v3, 1p. [3622] *or*
HR 1517, 55-2, v6, 2p. [3722]
Indian depredation claims.

80. R-P of M. Huddleston. 1 Mar.
SR 628, 55-2, v3, 1p. [3622] *or*
HR 1855, 55-3, v1, 1p. [3840]
Sabine war; 1836-37; Arkansas Mounted Gunmen.

81. R-P of T. Lane. 1 Mar.
SR 630, 55-2, v3, 1p. [3622] *or*
HR 476, 55-2, v2, 1p. [3718]
Sac and Fox war; 1831; Illinois Volunteers.

82. R-P of P. Breen. 1 Mar.
SR 643, 55-2, v3, 2p. [3622]
Service against Indians in Arizona; 1892.

83. Laws for Indian Territory. 1 Mar.
HR 593, 55-2, v3, 4p. [3719]
Answers remaining questions regarding the jurisdiction of the U.S. in said Territory.

84. Free Homesteads. 2 Mar.
SD 168, 55-2, v11, 15p. [3600]
Concerns homestead entries on Indian lands; various Indian lands are involved.

85. Agreement with Indians at the Fort Hall Reservation, Idaho. 3 Mar.
SD 169, 55-2, v11, 16p. [3600]
Made 5 Feb. 1898 with the Shoshones and Bannocks; provides for cessions of lands to the U.S.

86. Certain Lands Acquired from Indians. 7 Mar.
HD 332, 55-2, v51, 12p. [3679]
Concerning free homesteads on these lands; list of ceded lands involved.

87. Claims Allowed by Accounting Officers. 7 Mar.
HD 333, 55-2, v51, 10p..[3679]
Includes some related to the Indian Service.

88. Uncompahgre Reservation, Utah. 7 Mar.
HD 335, 55-2, v51, 3p. [3679]
Resol. to postpone the opening of this reservation.

89. Examination of the Civil Service. 9 Mar.
SR 659, 55-2, v4, 1163p. [3623]
Letters and testimony on the Indian Service.

90. Graves of Soldiers in the Maumee Valley, Ohio. 9 Mar.
HR 672, 55-2, v3, 5p. [3719]
Report gives an account of battles with Indians in the area during 1794-1813.

91. R-P of E. Kolb. 10 Mar.
SR 664, 55-2, v3, 1p. [3622]
Action of the Com. on Indian Affairs.

92. St. Louis, Oklahoma, and Southern Railway Co. 10 Mar.
SR 665, 55-2, v3, 1p. [3622] *or*
HR 646, 55-2, v3, 1p. [3719] *or*
HR 1280, 55-2, v5, 1p. [3721] *or*
HR 1818, 55-3, v1, 1p. [3840]
Right of way through Indian Territory.

93. Chicago, Rock Island, and Pacific Railway Co. 10 Mar.
SR 666, 55-2, v3, 2p. [3622] *or*
HR 644, 55-2, v3, 2p. [3719]
Bill to extend the time for construction through Indian Territory.

94. Bridge Across the Arkansas River. 11 Mar.
HR 709, 55-2, v3, 2p. [3719]
To be built by Cherokees in Indian Territory.

95. Denison, Bonham, and New Orleans Railway Co. 14 Mar.
HR 716, 55-2, v3, 2p. [3719]
Right of way through Indian Territory.

96. Petition of Seneca Indians. 15 Mar.
SD 190, 55-2, v11, 29p. [3600]
On regulation of leases made within their reservations in New York; distribution of proceeds from oil wells.

97. Gainesville, McAlester, and St. Louis Railway Co. 17 Mar.
HR 748, 55-2, v3, 1p. [3719] *or*
HR 1745, 55-3, v1, 1p. [3840]
Amendment to the act granting a right of way through Indian Territory.

98. Lands Necessary for Public Improvements. 21 Mar.
SR 696, 55-2, v3, 1p. [3622] *or*
HR 1278, 55-2, v5, 1p. [3721]
For cities and towns in Indian Territory.

99. Commutation of Certain Homesteaders in Oklahoma. 21 Mar.

SR 699, 55-2, v3, 1p. [3622] *or*
HR 348, 55-2, v2, 1p. [3718]
Agreement with the Kickapoos is involved.

100. R-P of D. Smith. 22 Mar.
SR 705, 55-2, v3, 1p. [3622] *or*
HR 606, 55-2, v3, 1p. [3719]
Florida Indian war; 1836; Alabama Volunteers.

101. R-P of M. Vockey. 22 Mar.
SR 708, 55-2, v3, 1p. [3622] *or*
HR 625, 55-2, v3, 1p. [3719]
Service at Fort Gibson, Cherokee Nation.

102. R-P of S. Fowler. 22 Mar.
SR 716, 55-2, v3, 1p. [3622] *or*
HR 605, 55-2, v3, 1p. [3719]
Seminole war; 1837-40; Florida.

103. R-P of J. Preston. 22 Mar.
SR 729, 55-2, v3, 1p. [3622] *or*
HR 2179, 55-3, v2, 1p. [3841]
Service against Comanches between Fort Leavenworth and Sante Fé.

104. R-P of R. English. 23 Mar.
SR 761, 55-2, v3, 1p. [3622] *or*
HR 484, 55-2, v2, 1p. [3718]
Sabine war; 1836; Kentucky Volunteers.

105. R-P of J. Wagoner. 23 Mar.
SR 762, 55-2, v3, 1p. [3622] *or*
HR 622, 55-2, v3, 1p. [3719]
Battle of the Little Big Horn River.

106. Turtle Mountain Band of Chippewas. 24 Mar.
HR 820, 55-2, v3, 20p. [3719]
Bill to transfer the claim of said band to the Court of Claims; dispute exists over title to certain lands in North Dakota; agreement now before Congress does not represent the desires of the Indians.

107. Railroad Companies in Indian Territory. 25 Mar.
HR 826, 55-2, v3, 1p. [3719]
Bill authorizing said companies to lease the property and facilities of other railroads within the Territory.

108. Deficiency Estimate for Army and Navy Pensions. 26 Mar.
HD 381, 55-2, v51, 4p. [3679]
Fiscal 1898; for service in Indian wars, 1832-42.

109. R-P of M. Nale. 29 Mar.
SR 790, 55-2, v3, 1p. [3622] *or*
HR 469, 55-2, v2, 1p. [3718]
Sabine war; 1836; Mississippi Volunteers.

110. R-P of W. Russell. 29 Mar.
SR 796, 55-2, v3, 1p. [3622] *or*
HR 1856, 55-3, v1, 2p. [3840]
Oregon Indian war; 1855-56.

111. Uncompahgre Reservation. 29 Mar.
HR 846, 55-2, v3, 1p. [3719]
Extension for 6 months from 1 Apr. 1898 of the time of opening said reservation for settlement.

112. Sundry Civil Appropriation Bill. 30 Mar.
SR 813, 55-2, v3, 4p. [3622]
Fiscal 1899; American ethnology, payments to Seminoles, attorneys for the Mission Indians, etc.

113. Missouri, Oklahoma, and Texas Railway Co. 1 Apr.
HR 917, 55-2, v4, 1p. [3720]
Right of way through Indian Territory.

114. L-C of H. Stroup and H. Smith. 6 Apr.
HD 402, 55-2, v64, 2p. [3692]
Services performed for the Dawes Commission to the Five Civilized Tribes.

115. R-P of S. Fielder. 7 Apr.
HR 1011, 55-2, v4, 1p. [3720]
Creek war; 1836; Alabama Volunteers.

116. Sale of Liquor in Alaska. 12 Apr.
SD 234, 55-2, v21, 6p. [3610]
Prohibitions which apply to the whole population are unenforceable; just limited to Indians in other areas.

117. R-P of L. Mason. 12 Apr.
SR 855, 55-2, v3, 2p. [3622] *or*
HR 807, 55-2, v3, 2p. [3719]
Sioux campaign of 1890-91; South Dakota.

118. R-P of S. Blazer. 12 Apr.
SR 861, 55-2, v3, 1p. [3622]
Indian war of 1836; Tennessee Volunteers.

119. R-P of D. Melvin. 12 Apr.
SR 870, 55-2, v3, 1p. [3622] *or*
HR 808, 55-2, v3, 1p. [3719]
Creek war; 1836; Alabama Volunteers.

120. R-P of E. Rogers. 12 Apr.
SR 872, 55-2, v3, 1p. [3622] *or*
HR 722, 55-2, v3, 1p. [3719]
Cherokee wars; 1836-38; Tennessee Volunteers.

121. R-P of M. Hess. 12 Apr.
SR 877, 55-2, v3, 2p. [3622] *or*

HR 725, 55-2, v3, 2p. [3719]
Sioux outbreak; 1862; Minnesota.

122. Annual Report of the Smithsonian Institution. 14 Apr.
HD 575 (pts. 1-3), 55-2, v78-79 (pts. 1 and 2), 2308p. [3706-3708]
Research related to the American Indian.

123. Fort Smith and Western Coal Railroad Co. 15 Apr.
HR 1096, 55-2, v4, 1p. [3720]
Time needed to complete construction is extended; action by Com. on Indian Affairs.

124. Indians of Fort Hall Reservation. 19 Apr.
SR 925, 55-2, v6, 1p. [3625]
Amendments to a bill to ratify an agreement made with these Indians; Idaho.

125. Fort Dodge Military Reservation. 19 Apr.
HR 1115, 55-2, v4, 3p. [3720]
Abandoned reserve, when established, was partially located on the Osage trust lands in Kansas.

126. Washington Improvement and Development Co. 20 Apr.
HR 1117, 55-2, v4, 1p. [3720]
Railroad through the Colville reservation, Washington.

127. Determination of Rights of Certain Indians. 20 Apr.
HR 1118, 55-2, v4, 2p. [3720]
Bill authorizes Delawares, Peorias, Seminoles, loyal Seminoles, loyal Creeks, and Chickasaw freedmen to bring suit against the U.S. in the Court of Claims; etc.

128. R-C of W. Clark and W. Bill. 20 Apr.
HR 1121, 55-2, v4, 2p. [3720]
Liquor seized by the Army during 1873 in Dakota Territory; problem arose as to whether the liquor was in Indian country.

129. Arkansas, Texas, and Mexican Central Railway Co. 21 Apr.
SR 938, 55-2, v6, 1p. [3625] *or*
HR 660, 55-2, v3, 1p. [3719]
Action of the Com. on Indian Affairs; right of way through Indian Territory.

130. R-P of F. Shetais. 21 Apr.
SR 944, 55-2, v6, 1p. [3625] *or*
HR 601, 55-2, v3, 1p. [3719]
Sioux war; 1865; Minnesota Mounted Rangers.

131. Pottawatomie and Kickapoo Reservations. 21 Apr.
HR 1134, 55-2, v4, 2p. [3720]
Amendments to a bill providing for allotment of lands in severalty, and sale of surplus lands; Kansas.

132. Annuities to Certain Indians. 25 Apr.
SD 251, 55-2, v22, 3p. [3611]
Restoration of annuities (under the treaty of 1851) to the Sisseton, Wahpeton, Medawakanton, and Wahpakoota Sioux; these bands remained loyal during the 1862 outbreak.

133. Ute Indian Commission. 25 Apr.
HR 1172, 55-2, v4, 2p. [3720]
Charged with making allotments on the Uintah reservation in Utah, and obtaining the cession to the U.S. of all lands not allotted.

134. Case of M. Campbell. 26 Apr.
SR 955, 55-2, v6, 2p. [3625]
Issuance of a land patent to this Nez Percé allottee; Nez Percé reservation, Idaho.

135. Persons Reimbursed for Moneys Expended. 26 Apr.
HR 1195, 55-2, v5, 13p. [3721]
During the Pah-Ute war of 1860 in Nevada.

136. R-C of H. Jones. 2 May.
SR 989, 55-2, v6, 2p. [3625] *or*
HR 527, 55-2, v2, 8p. [3718]
Contract made with the Indian agent on the Menomonee reservation, Wisconsin (House version includes relevant documents).

137. Agreements with Certain Sioux Indians. 3 May.
HD 447, 55-2, v64, 55p. [3692]
Settlement of differences between the Rosebud and Lower Brulé Indians in South Dakota; Rosebud agreement made 10 Mar. 1898; Lower Brulé agreement made 1 Mar. 1898; also involves land cessions, modification of existing treaties, etc.; council proceedings.

138. Chippewa Indians, Minnesota. 5 May.
SR 998, 55-2, v6, 3p. [3625] *or*
HR 1660, 55-3, v1, 3p. [3840]
Amendments to a bill providing for allotments to be made on the White Earth reservation.

139. Mille Lacs Indian Reservation. 9 May.
SR 1007, 55-2, v6, 4p. [3625] *or*
HR 1174, 55-2, v4, 4p. [3720]
Reservation to be subject to entry under U.S. land laws; ceded to the

U.S. by the Chippewa treaties of 1863, 1864, and 1867.

140. R-P of J. Augur. 10 May.
SR 1020, 55-2, v6, 4p. [3625]
Rogue River war; 1856; Oregon and Washington.

141. R-P of M. Taylor. 10 May.
SR 1032, 55-2, v6, 1p. [3625] *or*
HR 979, 55-2, v4, 1p. [3720]
Creek war; 1836; Alabama Volunteers.

142. R-P of B. Gresham. 10 May.
SR 1036, 55-2, v6, 2p. [3625] *or*
HR 1130, 55-2, v4, 2p. [3720]
Creek war; 1836; Georgia Volunteers.

143. R-P of J. Wheeler. 10 May.
SR 1045, 55-2, v6, 1p. [3625]
Bannock outbreak; 1878; Oregon.

144. R-P of G. Gamache. 10 May.
SR 1054, 55-2, v6, 1p. [3625]
Battle of Acton in 1862; against the Indians.

145. Right of Way to the Village of Flandreau, South Dakota. 19 May.
SR 1120, 55-2, v6, 2p. [3625] *or*
HR 938, 55-2, v4, 2p. [3720]
Road over lands formerly owned by the Sioux Indians.

146. Chicago, Milwaukee, and St. Paul Railway Co. 20 May.
SR 1125, 55-2, v6, 19p. [3625] *or*
HR 1316, 55-2, v5, 18p. [3721]
Return of funds to the company which were given to the Interior Dept. for a right of way through the Sioux reservation in Dakota; agreements made 2 Nov. 1880, 10 Nov. 1880, and 13 Nov. 1880.

147. R-P of E. Brannan. 24 May.
SR 1132, 55-2, v6, 2p. [3625] *or*
HR 1789, 55-3, v1, 3p. [3840]
Seminole war; 1856-58; Florida.

148. Petition of Choctaw Indians. 25 May.
SD 274, 55-2, v22, 6p. [3611]
Against the actions of the Dawes Commission, and the "Curtis bill"; the sentiment is that the U.S. is moving too quickly on the matter of allotment, etc.

149. Disbursements from the Creek Trust Fund. 25 May.
HD 499, 55-2, v64, 67p. [3692]
To pay debts of the government of the Creek Nation.

150. Colony of Natives on Annette Island, Alaska. 26 May.
SD 275, 55-2, v22, 28p. [3611]
On conditions among the Indians; missionary activities; attempts to remove the colony.

151. Telegraph and Telephone Lines in Indian Territory. 3 June.
HR 1503, 55-2, v6, 1p. [3722]
Bill authorizes construction of said lines, and provides for payments to tribes through whose territory the lines run.

152. Agreement with the Seminoles. 3 June.
HR 1504, 55-2, v6, 1p. [3722]
Made 16 Dec. 1897; calls for allotment of lands in severalty, abandonment of their tribal government, and acceptance of a more suitable government.

153. Agreement with the Shoshones and Bannocks. 4 June.
HR 1507, 55-2, v6, 4p. [3722]
At the Fort Hall reservation, Idaho; lands ceded to the U.S.

154. Kettle River Valley Railway Co. 4 June.
HR 1508, 55-2, v6, 1p. [3722]
Right of way through a portion of the Colville reservation which has been returned to public domain.

155. Kansas, Oklahoma, and Gulf Railway Co. 9 June.
SR 1209, 55-2, v8, 1p. [3627] *or*
HR 1530, 55-2, v6, 1p. [3722]
Construction through the Chilocco Indian reservation, Oklahoma.

156. Annual Report of the American Historical Association, 1897. 9 June.
HD 577, 55-2, v81, 1281p. [3710]
Research related to the American Indian.

157. Land Leases in the Uncompahgre Reservation. 13 June.
HR 1548, 55-2, v6, 11p. [3722]
Mineral lands within this Ute reservation; Utah.

158. R-P of W. Christenberry. 17 June.
SR 1250, 55-2, v8, 1p. [3627] *or*
HR 1136, 55-2, v4, 1p. [3720]
Cherokee disturbances; 1838; Tennessee Volunteers.

159. Missouri, Kansas, and Texas Railway Co. 17 June.
HR 1588, 55-2, v6, 2p. [3722]
Bill authorizes the company to restore the channel of the South Canadian River in Indian Territory.

160. Town-Site Entries in Oklahoma. 18 June.
HD 544, 55-2, v64, 3p. [3692]
Involves an act providing for said entries in the Cherokee Outlet.

161. Agreements with Certain Sioux Indians. 20 June.
SR 1266, 55-2, v8, 4p. [3627]
Agreements with Sioux on the Rosebud and Lower Brulé reservations; some Lower Brulé improvements are included within the boundaries of the Rosebud reservation.

162. Missouri and Kansas Telephone Co. 21 June.
HR 1598, 55-2, v6, 1p. [3722]
Bill authorizes construction in the Ponca, Otoe, and Missouria reservations; Oklahoma.

163. Indian Depredation Claims. 22 June.
SD 301, 55-2, v26, 4p. [3615]
Judgments of the Court of Claims.

164. Supplemental Deficiency Estimates. 22 June.
SD 302, 55-2, v31 (House volume), 16p. [3659]
Fiscal 1898; Indian Service.

165. Judgments Rendered by the Court of Claims. 22 June.
SD 303, 55-2, v26, 38p. [3615]
Includes cases involving the Indian Service.

166. Indian Appropriation Bill. 22 June.
SD 304, 55-2, v26, 6p. [3615]
Amendments concerning the bill for fiscal 1899.

167. Claims Allowed by Accounting Officers. 23 June.
SD 311, 55-2, v26, 14p. [3615]
Includes claims involving the Indian Service.

168. Attendance of Certain Indians at the Trans-Mississippi and International Exposition. 23 June.
SD 312, 55-2, v26, 4p. [3615]
Arrangements to secure the attendance of Iroquois, Delawares, Abenakis, Pottawatomies, Wyandottes, and other tribes who have moved from the U.S. to Canada.

169. R-P of W. Morgan. 23 June.
SR 1286, 55-2, v8, 1p. [3627] *or*
HR 977, 55-2, v4, 1p. [3720]
Florida Indian war; 1838-43.

170. Sundry Civil Appropriation Bill. 24 June.
SD 313, 55-2, v26, 4p. [3615]
Amendment concerning cost of investigating the violence between Seminoles and whites in Oklahoma.

171. Deficiency Appropriation Bill. 24 June.
SR 1338, 55-2, v8, 2p. [3627] *or*
HR 1574, 55-2, v6, 2p. [3722]
For fiscal 1898; judgments in Indian depredation cases, jails in Indian Territory, etc.

172. R-P of O. Sparks. 28 June.
SR 1352, 55-2, v8, 1p. [3627]
Florida Indian war; 1836.

173. R-P of E. Miller. 29 June.
SR 1359, 55-2, v8, 2p. [3627] *or*
HR 2242, 55-3, v2, 2p. [3841]
Indian agent to the Navajoes is murdered by them in 1872.

174. Indian Depredation Claims. 29 June.
HR 1632, 55-2, v6, 3p. [3722]
Sioux depredations of 1862 in Minnesota.

175. R-P of A. Pinkston. 1 July.
SR 1375, 55-2, v8, 1p. [3627] *or*
HR 1234, 55-2, v5, 1p. [3721]
Creek war; 1836; Alabama Volunteers.

176. R-P of T. Cobia. 1 July.
SR 1376, 55-2, v8, 2p. [3627]
Florida Indian war; 1836.

177. R-P of H. Fowler. 5 July.
SR 1400, 55-2, v8, 1p. [3627] *or*
HR 1233, 55-2, v5, 1p. [3721]
Creek war; 1836; Georgia Volunteers.

178. Appropriations, 55th Congress, 2d Session. 8 July.
SD 339, 55-2, v26, 2p. [3615]
Indian Service.

179. Statements of Appropriations. 8 July.
SD 342, 55-2, v27, 532p. [3616]
For the 2d session, 55th Congress; Indian expenses.

180. Official Opinions of the Attorneys-General of the U.S. (no date)
HD 554, 55-2, v69, 725p. [3697]
Includes opinions on Indian depredations, use of the military in Indian Territory, etc.

181. Bulletin of the U.S. Fish Commission. (no date)
HD 561, 55-2, v71, 442p. [3699]
Includes Indians fishing for salmon, Indian Territory pearls, etc.

182. Catalogue of Public Documents. (no date)
HD 585, 55-2, v86, 418p. [3715]
Of the 55th Congress, 2d session.

183. Index of Documents and Reports. (no date)
HD 586, 55-2, v87, 364p. [3716]
For the 55th Congress, 2d session.

184. Annual Report of the Sec. of Interior. 22 Nov.
HD 5, 55-3, v14-25, 9995p. [3756-3767]
Report on Indian Affairs; annual report of the Gen. Land Office (Serial 3756); annual report of the CIA (Serial 3757); etc.

185. Annual Report of the Sec. of War. 29 Nov.
HD 2, 55-3, v2-10, 6118p. [3744-3752]
For year ending 30 June 1898.

186. Annual Report of the Attorney-General. 30 Nov.
HD 9, 55-3, v30, 384p. [3772]
Indian depredation claims, jails in Indian Territory, attorneys for the Mission Indians, etc.

187. Statistical Abstract of the U.S. 2 Dec.
HD 162, 55-3, v69, 446p. [3811]
Indian populations, etc.

188. Congressional Directory. 5 Dec.
SD 4 (pts. 1 and 2), 55-3, v2, 663p. [3726]
Duties of the CIA.

189. Annual Message to Congress; Pres. McKinley. 5 Dec.
HD 1, 55-3, v1, 1286p. [3743]
Dawes Commission to the Five Civilized Tribes; Chippewa outbreak in Minnesota; etc.

190. Estimates of Appropriations. 5 Dec.
HD 12, 55-3, v34, 444p. [3776]
Year ending 30 June 1900; Indian expenses.

191. Urgent Deficiency Estimates. 5 Dec.
HD 15, 55-3, v34, 16p. [3776]
For fiscal 1899; subsistence of Indians held as prisoners by the Army, etc.

192. Expenditures of the Smithsonian Institution. 5 Dec.
HD 22, 55-3, v36, 47p. [3778]
Fiscal 1898; expense of research related to the American Indian.

193. Payments to Certain Alsea Indians. 5 Dec.
HD 25, 55-3, v36, 2p. [3778]
Made from the permanent fund of the tribe; residents of the Siletz reservation, Oregon.

194. Claim of the Sisseton and Wahpeton Bands of Sioux. 6 Dec.
SD 10, 55-3, v1, 18p. [3725]
For annuities due under the treaty of 1851; these were wrongly withheld after the outbreak of 1862.

195. Judgments Rendered by the Court of Claims. 6 Dec.
SD 15, 55-3, v1, 56p. [3725]
Includes claims involving the Indian Service, the New York Indians, etc.

196. Annual Report of the Sec. of the Treasury. 6 Dec.
HD 8, 55-3, v29, 1043p. [3771]
Year ending 30 June 1898; Indian expenses.

197. Indian Depredation Claims. 6 Dec.
HD 43, 55-3, v36, 2p. [3778]
Judgments rendered against the U.S. and Indian tribes.

198. Receipts and Expenditures. 6 Dec.
HD 44, 55-3, v34, 59p. [3776]
For fiscal 1898; Indian expenses.

199. Contingent Expenses of the Interior Dept. 6 Dec.
HD 58, 55-3, v44, 19p. [3786]
Fiscal 1898; Indian Office.

200. Claim of the Medawakanton and Wahpakoota Bands of Sioux. 12 Dec.
SD 30, 55-3, v1, 10p. [3725]
Funds due under the treaties of 1837, and 1851; wrongly withheld after the outbreak of 1862.

201. L-C of J. Koogler. 12 Dec.
HD 68, 55-3, v44, 2p. [3786]
Legal services performed in Indian Territory.

202. Account of F. Lewis. 12 Dec.
HD 70, 55-3, v44, 4p. [3786]
Counsel for the Mission Indians of California.

203. Introduction of Reindeer Into Alaska. 13 Dec.
SD 34, 55-3, v4, 149p. [3728]
Introduced for the benefit of Eskimos and other Alaskan natives.

204. Supplemental Appropriation for the Dawes Commission. 13 Dec.
HD 75, 55-3, v44, 3p. [3786]
Expenses of negotiations with the Five Civilized Tribes.

205. An Act for the Protection of the People of Indian Territory. 14 Dec.
SD 33, 55-3, v4, 6p. [3728]
Appropriation to carry out this act (the "Curtis Act"); calls for the Dawes Commission to proceed with the allotment of land in severalty, etc.

206. Appropriation for the Commission to the Crows, Flatheads, Etc. 14 Dec.
HD 76, 55-3, v44, 2p. [3786]
To continue negotiations with said tribes.

207. Salaries in the Indian Territory Division. 15 Dec.
HD 81, 55-3, v44, 3p. [3786]
For employees in the Interior Dept.

208. Salaries, Etc., in the Indian Office. 16 Dec.
HD 84, 55-3, v44, 2p. [3786]
Appropriation for fiscal 1900.

209. An Act for the Protection of the People of Indian Territory. 16 Dec.
HD 89, 55-3, v44, 3p. [3786]
Appropriation to carry out this act (the "Curtis Bill"); provides for allotment, etc.

210. Stenographer for the Supt. of Indian Schools. 21 Dec.
HD 96, 55-3, v44, 2p. [3786]
Estimate for fiscal 1900.

1899

1. School at the Leech Lake Reservation. 4 Jan.
HD 106, 55-3, v44, 2p. [3786]
Appropriation for a building; Minnesota.

2. Annuities of Certain Sioux Indians. 5 Jan.
SR 1441, 55-3, v1, 22p. [3739]
Restoration of annuities to the Sisseton and Wahpeton Sioux; taken away after the outbreak of 1862.

3. Legislative, Executive, and Judicial Appropriation Bill. 5 Jan.
HR 1717, 55-3, v1, 19p. [3840]
Fiscal 1900; Indian Service.

4. Kansas, Oklahoma Central, and Southwestern Railway Co. 5 Jan.
HR 1718, 55-3, v1, 1p. [3840]
Right of way through Indian Territory.

5. Mem. of the Indian Rights Association. 6 Jan.
SD 49, 55-3, v4, 7p. [3728]
Concerning timber lands within the Chippewa reservation of Minnesota; logging contracts, appraisal of the lands, etc.

6. Little River Valley Railway Co. 7 Jan.
HR 1722, 55-3, v1, 1p. [3840]
Right of way through the Choctaw Nation of Indian Territory.

7. Delinquent Accounts. 9 Jan.
HD 130, 55-3, v65, 19p. [3807]
Of U.S. Indian agents, etc.

8. R-P of T. Chill. 10 Jan.
SR 1455, 55-3, v1, 1p. [3739]
Black Hawk war; 1832; Indiana Militia.

9. R-P of I. Gibson. 10 Jan.
SR 1457, 55-3, v1, 1p. [3739] *or*
HR 1891, 55-3, v1, 1p. [3840]
Sabine war; 1836-37; Arkansas Volunteers.

10. Protection of Timber in Indian Territory. 10 Jan.
HR 1726, 55-3, v1, 1p. [3840]
Bill to regulate the lumber industry there.

11. Indian Appropriation Bill. 12 Jan.
SR 1469, 55-3, v1, 2p. [3739] *or*
HR 1684, 55-3, v1, 2p. [3840]
For fiscal 1900.

12. Case of Brig. Gen. Stanton. 12 Jan.
SR 1476, 55-3, v1, 2p. [3739]
Service in the Sioux war of 1876.

13. Arkansas and Choctaw Railway Co. 12 Jan.
HR 1734, 55-3, v1, 1p. [3840]
Construction through the Choctaw and Chickasaw Nations.

14. Indian Industrial School, Fort Keogh, Montana. 13 Jan.
HD 139, 55-3, v65, 3p. [3807]
Cost of establishing such a school.

15. Indebtedness of the Choctaw Nation. 13 Jan.
HD 140, 55-3, v65, 3p. [3807]
Use of tribal funds to discharge outstanding debts.

16. Proposed Removal of the Northern Cheyennes. 17 Jan.
HD 153, 55-3, v65, 146p. [3807]
Removal from the Cheyenne to the Crow reservation in Montana; both tribes reject the proposal.

17. Sale of Lands by Certain Indians. 18 Jan.
HD 158, 55-3, v65, 5p. [3807]
Sale of lands allotted to Pottawatomies, Pawnees, Peorias, and Miamies; Oklahoma.

18. R-P of N. Dowell. 19 Jan.
SR 1494, 55-3, v1, 2p. [3739]
Modoc war; 1854; Oregon and Washington.

19. Clearwater Valley Railroad Co. 19 Jan.
SR 1495, 55-3, v1, 1p. [3739] *or*
HR 2095, 55-3, v2, 2p. [3841]
Right of way through Nez Percé lands in Idaho.

20. Muskogee, Oklahoma, and Western Railroad Co. 20 Jan.
HR 1804, 55-3, v1, 1p. [3840]
Construction through Indian Territory.

21. Buildings for Schools. 21 Jan.
SD 68, 55-3, v7, 3p. [3731]
Additional appropriation needed for schools on the Chippewa reservations in Minnesota.

22. Timber on the Chippewa Reservations. 21 Jan.
SD 70, 55-3, v7, 253p. [3731]
Concerning the appraisal of timber, and the cutting of dead and fallen timber in Minnesota; history of laws related to this subject.

23. Petition of C. Manderson. 23 Jan.
SD 71, 55-3, v7, 8p. [3731]
On the establishment of a fort near Sheridan, Wyoming; would be strategically located near Sioux, Blackfeet, Flathead, Crow, Northern Cheyenne, Ute, Shoshone, and Bannock reservations.

24. Loyal Seminole Rolls and Losses. 23 Jan.
SD 72, 55-3, v7, 8p. [3731]
Investigation of claims arising from service in the Civil War; settlement called for in the treaty of 1866, and the agreement of 1897.

25. R-C of E. Hill. 23 Jan.
HR 1814, 55-3, v1, 2p. [3840]
Wyandotte Indian asks authorization to sell allotted land in Indian Territory.

26. St. Louis, Tecumseh, and Lexington Railway Co. 24 Jan.
HR 1817, 55-3, v1, 1p. [3840]
Action of the Com. on Indian Affairs.

27. Big Three Railroad Co. 24 Jan.
HR 1819, 55-3, v1, 2p. [3840]
Construction through Indian Territory.

28. Railroad Rights of Way. 24 Jan.
HR 1822, 55-3, v1, 1p. [3840]
Through the Nez Percé reservation; Idaho.

29. Legislative, Executive, and Judicial Appropriation Bill. 25 Jan.
SR 1525, 55-3, v1, 2p. [3739]
Fiscal 1900; Indian Office.

30. Kiowa, Comanche, and Apache Reservation. 26 Jan.
SD 77, 55-3, v7, 64p. [3731]
Concerning the quality of lands in said reservation, and on the assent of the Indians to the agreement of 6 Oct. 1892, which calls for allotment of lands in severalty, and the ceding of unallotted lands to the U.S. (Jerome agreement); council proceedings.

31. Indian Depredation Claims. 26 Jan.
SR 1531, 55-3, v1, 8p. [3739]
Report is concerned with depredations committed by the Sioux and Cheyennes during 1890-91; discussion of the effects of the "messiah craze," or "ghost dance religion" on Indians; account of the Wounded Knee massacre.

32. R-P of H. Farmer. 26 Jan.
HR 1859, 55-3, v1, 2p. [3840]
Cherokee war; Tennessee Mounted Infantry.

33. Agriculture in Alaska. 27 Jan.
HD 169, 55-3, v26, 58p. [3768]
Farming would aid the Alaskan natives.

34. R-P of G. Brown. 27 Jan.
HR 1863, 55-3, v1, 2p. [3840]
Indian engagement in 1882.

35. Number of Adult Males in Certain Tribes. 28 Jan.
SD 84, 55-3, v7, 2p. [3731]
Total number of adult males for the Kiowa, Comanche, and Apache tribes is given in order to ascertain whether 3/4 of said males attached their names to the agreement of 1892.

36. Agreement with the Cherokee Nation. 28 Jan.
SD 88, 55-3, v7, 16p. [3731]
Made 14 Jan. 1899; provides for allotment of lands, for restructuring of the tribal government, etc.; Dawes Commission.

37. Indian Depredation Claims. 28 Jan.
HD 183, 55-3, v70, 3p. [3812]
Judgments of the Court of Claims.

38. Petitions on the "W. Whitaker Home." 30 Jan.
SD 90, 55-3, v7, 7p. [3731]
Ask U.S. to support this home for white orphans in Indian Territory.

39. Military Post Near Sheridan, Wyoming. 30 Jan.
SR 1556, 55-3, v1, 9p. [3739]
Post should be established, as it would be in the midst of Indian country; Crow, Cheyenne, Sioux, Blackfeet, Ute, Flathead, Shoshone, and other reservations are all close to the site.

40. Deficiency Estimates. 30 Jan.
HD 185, 55-3, v34, 46p. [3776]
For fiscal 1899; Indian expenses.

41. R-P of E. McLain. 30 Jan.
HR 1872, 55-3, v1, 1p. [3840]
Sabine war; 1836; Arkansas Mounted Gunmen.

42. R-P of W. Quinn. 31 Jan.
SR 1560, 55-3, v1, 5p. [3739] *or*
HR 1685, 55-3, v1, 5p. [3840]
Sioux Indian serves as a scout for the U.S.

43. Claims Allowed by Accounting Officers. 31 Jan.
HD 191, 55-3, v70, 17p. [3812]
Claims involving the Indian Service.

44. Judgments of the Court of Claims. 1 Feb.
HD 197, 55-3, v70, 10p. [3812]
Case involving the Indian Service.

45. Chippewas of the Mississippi and of Lake Superior. 2 Feb.
SD 97, 55-3, v7, 2p. [3731]
Bill authorizing the Sec. of the Interior to fulfill certain treaty stipulations.

46. Fort Smith and Western Railroad Co. 2 Feb.
HR 1890, 55-3, v1, 1p. [3840]
Construction through the Choctaw and Creek Nations, Indian Territory.

47. Railroad Rights of Way. 2 Feb.
HR 1896, 55-3, v1, 2p. [3840]
Through Indian reservations, lands, and allotments; general bill to inject uniformity into the granting of rights of way.

48. Payment of the Cherokee Nation to the Cherokee Freedmen. 3 Feb.
SD 101, 55-3, v7, 47p. [3731]
Investigation of the enrollment and payment of the Cherokee Freedmen under a decree of the Court of Claims.

49. Certain Laws for Indian Territory. 3 Feb.
HR 1901, 55-3, v1, 1p. [3840]
Arkansas laws regarding corporations to be put into effect in Indian Territory.

50. R-C of Reps. of E. Ayres. 4 Feb.
SR 1599, 55-3, v1, 43p. [3739]
Concerns title to lands purchased from the Chickasaw Indians in 1839; Mississippi.

51. Sundry Civil Appropriation Bill. 6 Feb.
HR 1940, 55-3, v1, 10p. [3840]
Fiscal 1900; legal counsel for the Mission Indians, supplies to Alaskan natives, American ethnology, etc.

52. R-P of B. Lowe. 7 Feb.
SR 1620, 55-3, v1, 2p. [3739] *or*
HR 1478, 55-2, v6, 2p. [3722]
Service against Indians on the Texas frontier.

53. Choctaw, Oklahoma, and Gulf Railroad Co. 8 Feb.
HR 2058, 55-3, v2, 1p. [3841]
Right of way through Indian reservations.

54. Appropriation to Purchase Reindeer. 9 Feb.
HD 216, 55-3, v70, 3p. [3812]
For the benefit of Alaskan natives.

55. R-P of I. Stephans. 10 Feb.
SR 1645, 55-3, v1, 2p. [3739]
Black Hawk war; 1832.

56. Improvements on Certain Lands. 14 Feb.
HD 228, 55-3, v70, 34p. [3812]
Within the Wind River or Shoshone reservation, Wyoming; settlers lose improvements after the treaty of 1868, and settlements have to be made.

57. Ohio Centennial and Northwest Territory Exposition. 14 Feb.
HR 2108, 55-3, v2, 4p. [3841]
Battles with Indians on the Maumee River an important part of the area's history.

58. Relief of Certain Settlers on Public Lands. 14 Feb.
HR 2111, 55-3, v2, 2p. [3841]
Contested or cancelled entries the subject of the bill; involves Kansas Indian trust lands.

59. Clearwater Short Line Railway Co. 16 Feb.
HR 2144, 55-3, v2, 1p. [3841]
Right of way through the Nez Percé reservation; Idaho.

60. R-P of J. Doherty. 17 Feb.
SR 1675, 55-3, v1, 1p. [3739] *or*
HR 1884, 55-3, v1, 1p. [3840]
Seminole war; 1818; Florida.

61. Sioux City and Omaha Railway Co. 17 Feb.
HR 2172, 55-3, v2, 1p. [3841]
Construction through the Omaha and Winnebago reservations; Nebraska.

62. Gulf and Northern Railroad Co. 18 Feb.
HR 2181, 55-3, v2, 2p. [3841]
Right of way through Indian Territory, the Ponca reservation, and the Osage Nation.

63. Case of I. Smith. 20 Feb.
SD 126, 55-3, v11, 3p. [3735]
Homesteader on ceded Sioux lands is unable to pay for said lands.

64. Rifles for Use in Indian Schools. 20 Feb.
HD 239, 55-3, v70, 2p. [3812]
Worn-out rifles transferred from the War Dept. to the Interior Dept.

65. Mem. of the Indianola Public Free School Society. 20 Feb.
HD 242, 55-3, v70, 2p. [3812]
Concerning schools for whites in Indian Territory.

66. Relief of People in the Yukon River Country. 20 Feb.
HD 244, 55-3, v70, 123p. [3812]
Routes to area used by Alaskan Indians when engaging in trade.

67. Military Road in Wyoming. 20 Feb.
HD 245, 55-3, v70, 19p. [3812]
Would cross the former hunting grounds of Indians from the Wind River and Fort Hall reservations.

68. Support of Certain Indians. 21 Feb.
HD 247, 55-3, v70, 3p. [3812]
Appropriation for the Sioux of Devil's Lake, and the Turtle Mountain Chippewas.

69. Denison, Bonham, and Gulf Railway Co. 23 Feb.
HR 2254, 55-3, v2, 1p. [3841]
Right of way through Indian Territory.

70. Arkansas Northwestern Railway Co. 23 Feb.
HR 2282, 55-3, v2, 1p. [3841]
Construction in Indian Territory.

71. Agreement with the Creek Nation. 24 Feb.
HD 252, 55-3, v70, 13p. [3812]
Made 1 Feb. 1899; provides for allotment, etc.; Dawes Commission.

72. Deficiency Appropriation for U.S. Courts. 25 Feb.
SD 136, 55-3, v11, 1p. [3735]
Those courts located in Indian Territory.

73. R-P of B. Randall. 25 Feb.
SR 1807, 55-3, v3, 1p. [3741]
Sioux outbreak; 1862; Minnesota.

74. Mem. of the Oklahoma Legis. 27 Feb.
SD 140, 55-3, v11, 2p. [3735]
Asks that lands allotted to Indians be subject to taxation.

75. Indian Depredation Claims. 27 Feb.
SD 143, 55-3, v11, 4p. [3735]
Judgments of the Court of Claims.

76. Claims Allowed by Accounting Officers. 28 Feb.
SD 149, 55-3, v11, 7p. [3735]
Includes claims related to the Indian Service.

77. Deficiencies in Appropriations. 28 Feb.
SD 150, 55-3, v11, 2p. [3735]
For the purchase of Indian supplies during fiscal 1898.

78. R-P of A. Taylor. 28 Feb.
SR 1826, 55-3, v3, 1p. [3741] *or*
HR 2203, 55-3, v2, 1p. [3841]
Cherokee war; 1837-38; Tennessee Volunteers.

79. R-P of J. Gullett. 28 Feb.
SR 1846, 55-3, v3, 1p. [3741] *or*
HR 1886, 55-3, v1, 1p. [3840]
Creek war; 1836; Alabama Volunteers.

80. Case of J. Wood. 28 Feb.
HR 2316, 55-3, v2, 2p. [3841]
Service in the Sioux campaign.

81. General Deficiency Bill. 28 Feb.
HR 2317, 55-3, v2, 4p. [3841]
Fiscal 1899; appropriations for settlement of Indian depredation claims, etc.

82. Judgments of the Court of Claims. 1 Mar.
SD 153, 55-3, v11, 26p. [3735]
Includes cases involving the Indian Service, the Pottawatomies, etc.

83. "Old Settler" or Western Cherokees. 1 Mar.
SD 160, 55-3, v11, 8p. [3735]
Claim for moneys due them under the treaty of 1846.

84. Payments to Osage Indians. 1 Mar.
SD 162, 55-3, v11, 65p. [3735]
On payments to individual Osages

out of the Osage trust fund to pay debts owed to licensed traders.

85. Explorations in Alaska During 1898. 1 Mar.
SD 172, 55-3, v13, 138p. [3737]
Descriptions of the Indian tribes of Alaska.

86. Loyal Seminoles. 1 Mar.
SR 1875, 55-3, v3, 11p. [3741]
Claims for losses incurred during the Civil War.

87. Pensions to Soldiers and Sailors. 1 Mar.
HR 2327, 55-3, v2, 2p. [3841]
Persons serving in Confederate Army are sent west to fight Indians.

88. Indian Reservations in Nevada. 3 Mar.
SD 166, 55-3, v11, 51p. [3735]
Information on the Pyramid Lake, Walker River, Duck Valley, and Moapa River reservations occupied by Pah-Ute, Washoe, and Digger Indians; information on allotments.

89. Statements of Appropriations. 3 Mar.
SD 173, 55-3, v14, 583p. [3738]
During the 3rd session, 55th Congress; Indian expenses.

90. Annual Report of the Smithsonian Institution. 4 Mar.
HD 309 (pts. 1 and 2), 55-3, v91-92, 2042p. [3833–3834]
Research related to the American Indian.

91. Compilation of Treaties. 11 Apr.
HD 276, 55-3, v80, 797p. [3822]
Indians are involved in the treaties of 1814, and 1796 with Great Britain; etc.

92. Annual Report of the American Historical Association. 21 Apr.
HD 295, 55-3, v83, 754p. [3825]
Research related to the American Indian.

93. Bulletin for the U.S. Fish Commission. 1 May.
HD 308, 55-3, v90, 585p. [3822]
Indians of the Northwest Coast involved in salmon fishing.

94. Index to Documents and Reports. 2 Nov.
HD 318, 55-3, v97, 136p. [3839]
For the 3rd session, 55th Congress.

95. 15th Report of the Civil Service Commission. (no date)
HD 296, 55-3, v84, 736p. [3826]
Includes the Indian Service.

96. 17th Annual Report of the Bureau of American Ethnology. (no date)
HD 316 (pts. 1 and 2), 55-3, v94-95, 845p. [3836-3837]
Research related to the American Indian; including the Seri Indians (McGee), the calendar history of the Kiowas (Mooney), Navajo houses (Mindeleff), and archaeology of Arizona (Fewkes); etc.

97. Document Catalogue. (no date)
HD 317, 55-3, v96, 1069p. [3838]
For the 55th Congress.

Appendixes

APPENDIX I: ENTRIES FROM POORE'S *CATALOGUE* NOT IN THE SERIAL SET

Poore's *Catalogue* of government publications lists a number of documents on Indian affairs from the period 1817-1881 which were not published in the Serial Set. These are primarily publications of the Interior Department and the Bureau of Indian Affairs. Because Poore's *Catalogue* has an inadequate index and is very time-consuming to use, these documents are relatively inaccessible. Therefore, Appendix I lists, in chronological order, those documents from the *Catalogue* that are relevant to Indian affairs, but which were not published in the Serial Set. The titles, reference information and abstracts are all taken from the *Catalogue*. No attempt has been made to verify these citations or to supplement the list with other non-Congressional documents from the same period. These entries are not included in the Subject Index.

1818

a. Biennial Register. Sec. of State.
Compiled by order of Congress.
Register of all officers and agents, civil and military, in the service of the U.S.

1820

a. Biennial Register. Sec. of State.
Compiled by order of Congress.
Register of all officers and agents, civil and military, in the service of the U.S.

1821

a. Expedition Through the Great Lakes. H. Schoolcraft. Albany.
Library of Congress. 8 volumes.
Journals of travels from Detroit, through the great chain of lakes, to the sources of the Mississippi River.

b. Annual Report of the Adjutant-General.
Library of the Adjutant-General's Office. 49p.

1822

a. Biennial Register. Sec. of State.
Compiled by order of Congress. 141p.
Register of all officers and agents, civil and military, in the service of the U.S.

b. Report on Indian Affairs. J. Morse. New Haven.
Library of B. P. Poore. Map and portrait. 496p.
State of the Indian tribes; condition, numbers, names, territory, and general affairs of the Indians.

1824

a. Biennial Register. Sec. of State.
Compiled by order of Congress. 140p.
Register of all officers and agents, civil and military, in the service of the U.S.

1825

a. Report of the Expedition up the Missouri River.
General Atkinson.
b. Report of Indian Affairs. 1825-1837.
Published by the BIA. 722p.

1826

a. Biennial Register. Sec. of State.
Compiled by order of Congress. 152p.
Register of all officers and agents, civil and military, in the service of the U.S.
b. Indian Treaties. S. S. Hamilton. Washington.
Library of Congress. 8vo.
With laws and regulations relating to Indian affairs.
c. Letter on the Seminole Indians. Sec. of War. Washington.
Library of B. P. Poore. 109p.
Letter transmitting information in relation to the instructions given to the Com'rs for negotiation with the Florida Indians.

1828

a. Biennial Register. Sec. of State.
Compiled by order of Congress. 180p.
Register of all officers and agents, civil and military, in the service of the U.S.
b. Speech on the Emigration of Indians. Rep. Vinton. 29 Feb.
Political Pamphlets, Vol. CXLII, Library of Congress. 28p.
Review of the legislation concerning the Indians; proposed plan of emigration.

1829

a. Remarks on Indian Reform. I. McCoy. New York.
Library of Congress: Miscellaneous Pamphlets, v. 18.
The condition and prospects of the American Indians.
b. Remarks on the Seminole War. G. Owen. Washington.
Library of P. Force. 31p.
The claim of Goergia for indemnity for property lost and destroyed, as provided for in the treaty of 1821 at Indian Springs with the Creek Indians.

1830

a. Biennial Register. Sec. of State.
Compiled by order of Congress. 224p.
Register of all officers and agents, civil and military, in the service of the U.S.
b. Speeches in Congress on the Removal of the Indians. Boston.
Library of Congress. 120p.
Delivered in April and May of 1830.
c. History of the Indian Tribes of North America.
An act, approved 3 March 1837, appropriated \$3,000 to pay for a subscription made in 1830 for this work, to be composed of twenty numbers each.

1831

a. Correspondence on the Florida Matter. A. Jackson and J. Calhoun. Washington.
Library of B. Poore. 52p.
Occurrences in the Seminole war.

1832

a. Laws Relating to Indians.
Law Library of Congress. Published by Thompson and Homans. 72p.
Laws of the colonial and state governments on Indians and Indian affairs from 1633 to 1831, inclusive, with laws from the U.S. Congress during 1800-1830.
b. Biennial Register. Sec. of State.
Compiled by order of Congress. 407p.
Register of all officers and agents, civil and military, in the service of the U.S.
c. Laws on Indian Affairs. By Authority. Washington.

Library of Congress.
Laws of the colonial and state governments from 1633 to 1831, inclusive.

1833

a. Biennial Register. Sec. of State.
Compiled by order of Congress. 267p.
Register of all officers and agents, civil and military, in the service of the U.S.

b. Laws Relating to Indian Affairs.
Law Library of Congress. Printed by F. Blair. 98p.
Laws passed since 1826, and treaties with Indian tribes concluded since 1830.

1834

a. Report of an Expedition from Fort Gibson to the Shawnee Villages, Colonel Dodge.

b. Suspended Lands. 15 Nov.
Library of the Interior Dept.
Circular suspending certain lands from public sale proposed to be selected by Indian chiefs under treaty stipulations.

1835

a. Biennial Register. Sec. of State.
Compiled by order of Congress. 297p.
Register of all officers and agents, civil and military, in the service of the U.S.

1837

a. Indian Treaties, 1778-1837. By authority. Washington.
Library of Congress.

1838

a. Biennial Register. Sec. of State.
Compiled by order of Congress. 325p.
Register of all officers and agents, civil and military, in the service of the U.S.

b. Mississippi and Alabama Lands. Sec. Woodbury. 4 Aug.
Library of the Interior Dept. 1p.
Embracing country ceded by the Choctaws under the treaty of 1830 at Dancing Rabbit Creek.

1839

a. Biennial Register. Sec. of State.
Compiled by order of Congress. 311p.
Register of all officers and agents, civil and military, in the service of the U.S.

1840

a. Report on Indian Affairs.
Published by the BIA. 168p.

1841

a. Report on Indian Affairs.
Published by the BIA. 110p.

b. Biennial Register. Sec. of State.
Compiled by order of Congress. 422p.
Register of all officers and agents, civil and military, in the service of the U.S.

c. Report on the Upper Mississippi River.
I. Nicollet. 18 Feb.
Published by order of the Sec. of War. 170p. and map.
Between the Falls of St. Anthony and the sources of the Mississippi River.

1842

a. Report on Indian Affairs.
Published by the BIA. 160p.

b. Report of the Exploring Expedition to the Rocky Mountains. Capt. Fremont.
Under the direction of the Topographical Bureau. 583p.
During 1843 and 1844.

1843

a. Report on Indian Affairs.
Published by the BIA. 198p.

b. Biennial Register. Sec. of State.
Compiled by order of Congress. 803p.
Register of all officers and agents, civil and military, in the service of the U.S.

1844

a. Report on Indian Affairs.
Published by the BIA. 205p.

1845

a. Report on Indian Affairs.
Published by the BIA. 142p.
b. Biennial Register.
Compiled by order of Congress. 568p.
Register of all officers and agents, civil and military, in the service of the U.S.

1846

a. Report on Indian Affairs.
Published by the BIA. 163p.

1847

a. Report on Indian Affairs.
Published by the BIA. 221p.
b. Choctaw Land Claims. 7 June.
Library of the Interior Dept. 1p.
Circular relating to certificates of Choctaw claims.
c. Excessive Locations with Choctaw Certificates. 19 Aug.
Library of the Interior Dept.
Circular sent to offices in Mississippi, Louisiana, Alabama, and Arkansas.

1848

a. Report on Indian Affairs.
Published by the BIA. 221p.
b. Pre-emption Claims of Volunteers (Miami Indians). 11 April.
Library of the Interior Dept.
c. Sales of Improved Lands in Ohio. 23 Sept.
Library of the Interior Dept.
Notice of sale of lands ceded by the Wyandot Indians in 1812.

1849

a. Report on Indian Affairs.
Published by the BIA. 230p.

1850

a. Regulations of the Indian Bureau.
Interior Dept. Pamphlet.
Digest of the laws relating to Indian affairs and the regulations of the BIA.
b. Laws, Regulations, Etc.
Published by the BIA. 113p.
c. Report on Indian Affairs.
Published by the BIA. 85p.
d. Opinions of the Attorney-General. Attorney-General J. Crittenden.
Published by the Justice Dept., Vol. 5, 1852. pp. 245-685.
Duties of Supts. of Indian Affairs, etc.
e. History of the Indian Tribes. H. Schoolcraft. 10 Aug.
Published in Philadelphia by authority of Congress. 6 vols.

1851

a. Report on Indian Affairs.
Published by the BIA. 318p.
b. Sale of Improved Lands in Ohio. 17 July.
Library of the Interior Dept.
Lands ceded by the Wyandot Indians.

1852

a. Smithsonian Contributions to Knowledge, Vol. IV.
Published by the Smithsonian Institution. 426p.
Dakota grammar and dictionary by Riggs.
b. Report on Indian Affairs.
Published by the BIA. 176p.
c. History of the Indian Tribes.
Published by the BIA. Pt. 2, 560p.
Historical and statistical information.
d. Land Assignment by a Creek Indian. 4 Aug.
Library of the Interior Dept. 1p.
On assignment of land warrants under the act of 1850.

1853

a. Report on Indian Affairs.
Published by the BIA. 240p.
b. History of the Indian Tribes.
Published by the BIA. Pt. 3, 582p.

c. Indian Bibliography. H. Schoolcraft. 1 Oct. History of the Indian Tribes. Vol. IV, pp. 522-551.
   Publications in the Indian tongues of the U.S.

1854

a. Report on Indian Affairs. Published by the BIA. 336p.
b. History of the Indian Tribes. Published by the BIA. Pt. 4, 667p.
c. Separate Indian Treaties. 1854-1868. Published by the BIA. 1075p.

1855

a. Report on Indian Affairs. Published by the BIA. 256p.
b. History of the Indian Tribes. Published by the BIA. Pt. 5, 712p.

1856

a. Report on Indian Affairs. Published by the BIA. 282p.

1857

a. Report on Indian Affairs. Published by the BIA. 414p.
b. History of the Indian Tribes. Published by the BIA. Pt. 6, 756p.
c. Dakota or Sioux Scrip. 21 Mar. Library of the Interior Dept. 4p.
   Circular on the location of half-breed Dakota or Sioux scrip issued under the act of 17 July 1874, with forms, etc.
d. Settlers in the Choctaw Cession. 14 May. Library of the Interior Dept. 2p.
   Circular on settlers within the limits of the Choctaw cession of 1830.
e. Land Certificates to Mixed Bloods. 24 Nov. Library of the Interior Dept. 3p.
   Circular on certificates issued by Indian agents to mixed-bloods of the Chippewas of Lake Superior, under the 7th section, 2d article of the treaty concluded 30 Sept. 1854.

1858

a. Report on Indian Affairs. Published by the BIA. 317p.

1859

a. Report on Indian Affairs. Published by the BIA. 452p.

1860

a. Report on Indian Affairs. Published by the BIA. 242p.

1861

a. Opinions of the Attorney-General. Acting Attorney-General Coffey. Published by the Justice Dept., Vol. 10, pp. 107-116 and 501-517.
   Patents for lands reserved to the half-breeds of the Kansas Indians, etc.
b. Report on Indian Affairs. Published by the BIA. 221p.

1862

a. Smithsonian Miscellaneous Collections. Vol. 2. Published by the Smithsonian Institution. 714p.
   North American Indian portraits; L. Morgan on "relationship."
b. Report on Indian Affairs. Published by the BIA. 432p.

1863

a. Report on Indian Affairs. Published by the BIA. 513p.
b. Smithsonian Contributions to Knowledge. Vol. 8. Published by the Smithsonian Institution. 558p.
   Ancient mining operations on Lake Superior.

1864

a. Report on Indian Affairs. Published by the BIA. 506p.

b. Location of the Sioux Land Scrip. 22 Feb. Library of the Interior Dept. 2p.
   Location of half-breed Dakota or Sioux scrip under the act of 17 July 1854.

1865

a. Report on Indian Affairs. Published by the BIA. 590p.
b. Certificates Under the Treaty with the Chippewas. 13 Mar. Library of the Interior Dept.
   On certificates issued under the 7th section, 2d article of the treaty of 30 Sept. 1854 with the Chippewas of Lake Superior.

1866

a. Report on the Cherokee Question. Interior Dept. Pamphlet.
   Made by direction of the President.
b. Report on Indian Affairs. Published by the BIA. 372p.
c. Cherokee Question. Published by the BIA. 58p.
   Report to the President.

1867

a. Agreement Between the Cherokees and Delawares. Interior Dept. Pamphlet.
   Adjustment of disputes on boundaries, etc.
b. Report on the Phil. Kearney Massacre. Interior Dept. Pamphlet.
   Report on the massacre; declaration of future government policy on the Indian question.
c. Report on Indian Affairs. Published by the BIA. 397p.

1868

a. Report on Indian Affairs. Published by the BIA. 380p.

1869

a. Report on Indian Affairs. Published by the BIA. 616p.
b. Smithsonian Miscellaneous Collections. Vol. 8. Library of the Smithsonian Institution. 921p.
   Circular on archaeology and ethnology.

1870

a. Report on Indian Affairs. Published by the BIA. 395p.
b. Smithsonian Contributions to Knowledge. Library of the Smithsonian Institution. Vol. 16. 498p.
   J. Swan on the Indians of Cape Flattery.
c. Report on the Piegan Indians. 7 Mar. Interior Dept. Pamphlet.
   Letter and documents from the Sec. of the Interior in response to a House resolution.
d. Right of Indians to Homesteads. 4 April. Library of the Interior Dept. 1p.
   On Indian rights.

1871

a. Smithsonian Contributions to Knowledge. Vol. 17. Library of the Smithsonian Institution. 616p.
   L. Morgan: Systems of consanguinity and affinity of the human family.
b. Report on Indian Affairs. Published by the BIA. 706p.
c. Suspension of Land Laws Relative to the Chippewa Indians. 21 Apr. Library of the Interior Dept. 1p.
   On suspending action on all applications of Chippewa or mixed-bloods to enter lands under treaties with the Chippewas of Pembina and Red Lake.
d. Osage Indian Lands in Kansas. 26 Apr. Library of the Interior Dept. Circular.

1872

a. Report on Indian Affairs. Published by the BIA. 471p.
b. Location of Sioux Half-Breed Scrip. 27 Jan. Library of the Interior Dept. 1p.
   Requirements in application to locate said scrip on unsurveyed lands.
c. Lands Within Limits of Indian Reservations. 5 July.

Library of the Interior Dept. 2p.
Action taken by local officers on lands within the limits of the Ottawa and Chippewa reservation in Michigan.

d. Disposal of the Cherokee Strip. 7 Aug.
Library of the Interior Dept. 3p.

1873

a. Report on Indian Affairs.
Published by the BIA. 388p.
b. Report on the Mission Indians.
Published by the BIA. 15p.
c. Report on Crow Negotiations.
Published by the BIA. 49p.
Com'rs' report.
d. Report on Shoshone Negotiations.
Published by the BIA. 30p.
Com'rs' report.
e. Report on Ute Negotiations.
Published by the BIA. 48p.
Com'rs' report.
f. Settlement of Indians.
Published by the BIA. 8p.
Between the trustees of Ottawa University, the Ottawa Indians of Blanchard's Fork and Roche de Boeuf, and the Baptist Home Missionary Society.
g. Notes Upon the Treaties of the U.S. J. Davis.
Library of the State Dept. 245p.
h. Opinions of the Attorney-General. Acting Attorney-General Phillips.
Published by the Justice Dept. Vol. 14.
Indian reservation in Nebraska, etc.
i. Claims of Sioux Half-Breeds. 15 Mar.
Library of the Interior Dept. 2p.
On the approval of claims of Sioux half-breeds or mixed-bloods of the Lake Superior band of Chippewas.

1874

a. Investigation of Indian Affairs.
Published by the Interior Dept. Pamphlet.
Report of the Com'r appointed to investigate charges against CIA Smith.
b. Report on Half-Breed Chippewa Scrip.
Published by the Interior Dept. Pamphlet.
Correspondence.
c. Report on Indian Affairs.
Published by the BIA. 364p.
d. Report of the CIA.
Published by the BIA. 50p.
On the Red Cloud and Whetstone agencies.
e. Pamphlet on Indian Tribes.
Published by the BIA. 36p.
Report on Indians in Arizona, California, Nevada, and Utah.
f. Half-Breed Chippewa Scrip.
Published by the BIA. 331p.
Correspondence.
g. Pre-Emptors on Offered and Unoffered Lands. 10 June.
Library of the Interior Dept. 1p.
Circular relating to lands in Fort Ridgely and Sioux Indian reservations in Minnesota; claims initiated prior to 3 June 1874.
h. Bitter Root Valley Indian Lands. 18 July.
Library of the Interior Dept.
Instructions in relation to sale of said lands.
i. Sale of Kansas Indian Lands. 3 Oct.
Library of the Interior Dept.
j. Location of Sioux Scrip. 12 Nov.
Library of the Interior Dept.
Notice on the location of Sioux half-breed scrip by heirs of deceased scrip-ees.

1875

a. Report on Indian Affairs.
Published by the BIA. 377p.
b. Easy Reading Lessons for Indians.
Published by the BIA. 80p.
c. Compilation of Revised Statutes.
Published by the BIA. 192p.
On Indian affairs.
d. Pawnee Removal and Necessities.
Published by the BIA. 16p.
e. Investigation of the Red Cloud Agency.
Published by the BIA. 852p.
f. Letter on the Claim of North Carolina Cherokees.
Published by the BIA. 9p.
g. Report of the CIA.
Published by the BIA. 77p.
On the Red Cloud agency.
h. Report of the CIA.
Published by the BIA. 20p.
On the Black Hills relinquishment.
i. Report of the CIA.
Published by the BIA. 8p.
On the Mission Indians of California.
j. Ethnological Directions.
Published by the BIA. 22p.
On Indian tribes.

k. Revised Statutes on Indian Affairs.
Interior Dept. Pamphlet.

l. Easy Reading Lessons for Indians.
Interior Dept. Pamphlet.
For distribution among the agencies.

m. Ethnological Directions.
Interior Dept. Pamphlet.
For the preservation of ethnological remains.

n. Report on North Carolina Cherokees.
Interior Dept. Pamphlet.
On their claim.

o. Investigation of the Red Cloud Agency.
Interior Dept. Pamphlet.
Charges of Professor Marsh on possible fraud and mismanagement at the agency.

p. Biennial Register. Sec. of the Interior.
Compiled by order of Congress. 1211p.
Register of all civil and military agents in the service of the U.S.

q. Geological and Geographical Survey.
F. Hayden.
Bulletins, Vol. 1, No. 1.
Includes ruins in southwestern Colorado.

r. Restoration of Homestead Entry. 18 Mar.
Library of the Interior Dept. 3p.
Includes the market of certain Indian lands in Michigan.

s. Proof of Abandonment and Entry by Indians. 25 Mar.
Library of the Interior Dept. 1p.
Under the 1st section of the act of 3 Mar. 1875.

1876

a. The Black Hills.
Interior Dept. Pamphlet.
Minerals, climate, etc.

b. List of Indian Reservations.
Interior Dept. Pamphlet.
Also Superintendents, agents, and regulations on trade.

c. Revised Statutes on Indian Affairs.
Law Library of Congress. 192p.
Acts of Congress since 22 June 1874.

d. Smithsonian Contributions to Knowledge. Vol. 21.
Library of the Smithsonian Institution.
Includes the Haidah Indians.

e. Geological and Geographical Surveys.
Prof. Hayden.
Eighth Annual Report. 526p.
Includes ancient ruins in southwestern Colorado.

f. Geological and Geographical Survey. F. Hayden.
Bulletins, Vol. 2, No. 1.
Includes ancient ruins in Arizona and Utah; human remains in Colorado; ancient art in Colorado; ornaments employed by the ancient tribes of Utah and Arizona; language and utensils of the modern Utes.

g. Report on the Mission Indians in California.
Published by the BIA. 17p.

h. Trade with Indian Tribes.
Published by the BIA. 13p.
Laws and regulations.

i. Book of Instructions.
Published by the BIA. 106p.
To Superintendents and Indian agents.

j. Compilation of Revised Statutes.
Publihsed by the BIA. 192p.
On Indian affairs.

k. Supreme Court Decisions. No. 61.
Published by the BIA. 5p.

l. List of Indian Reservations.
Published by the BIA. 10p.

m. Natural Resources of the Black Hills of Dakota.
Published by the BIA. 71p.

n. Report on Agencies.
Published by the BIA. 12p.
Red Cloud and Spotted Tail.

o. Report on Indian Affairs.
Published by the BIA. 357p.

1877

a. Study of Indian Languages. Prof. Powell.
Published by the Interior Dept. First Edition. 104p.
Introduction to the study of Indian languages, with words, phrases, and sentences to be collected.

b. Contributions to North American Ethnology.
Vol. 1. 375p.
W. Dall: Tribes of the extreme Northwest; G. Gibbs: Tribes of western Washington and northwestern Oregon.

c. Contributions to North American Ethnology.
Vol. 3. 638p.
S. Powers: Tribes of California.

d. Report on Indian Affairs.
Published by the BIA. 520p.
e. Report on Agencies.
Published by the BIA. 41p.
In the Indian Territory.
f. Instruction Book.
Published by the BIA. 108p.
For Superintendents and Indian agents.
g. Supreme Court Decisions Affecting Indians.
Interior Dept. Pamphlet.
On questions of law, concerning which differences of opinion had arisen.
h. Biennial Register. Sec. of the Interior.
Compiled by order of Congress. 971p.
Register of all civil and military agents in the service of the U.S.

1878

a. Smithsonian Miscellaneous Collections. Vol. 14.
Library of the Smithsonian Institution. 911p.
Includes catalogue of photograph portraits of American Indians.
b. Smithsonian Miscellaneous Collections. Vol. 15.
Library of the Smithsonian Institution.
Includes American archaeology.
c. Report on Indian Affairs.
Published by the BIA. 411p.
d. Rules and Regulations.
Published by the BIA. 10p.
For government of U.S. Indian police service.
e. Dacotah or Sioux Half-Breed Scrip. 28 May.
Library of the Interior Dept. 3p.

1879

a. Report on Indian Affairs.
Published by the BIA. 375p.
b. Laws and Regulations.
Published by the BIA. 13p.
Relating to trade with Indian tribes.
c. Monographs of the Geological Survey. Vol. 12. Prof. Hayden.
Contributions to the ethnography and philology of the Indian tribes of the valley of the Missouri River and its tributaries.
d. Records of Recent Progress in Science.
Library of the Smithsonian Institution.
Includes O. Mason on Anthropology.
e. Biennial Register. Sec. of the Interior.
Compiled by order of Congress. Vol. 1, 530p.; Vol. 2, 629p.
Register of all civil and military agents of the U.S.
f. Oddities of Colonial Legislation. J. Dillon.
Law Library of Congress. 784p.
Includes a history of legislation in America related to Indians.
g. Register of the Interior Dept. Sec. Schurz. 1 Jan.
Published by the Interior Dept. 102p.

1880

a. Report on the Ute Outbreak.
Published by the Interior Dept. Pamphlet.
b. Report on the Black Hills. H. Newton and W. Jenney.
Interior Dept. 584p.
Resources, etc., of this region in Dakota.
c. Smithsonian Contributions to Knowledge, Vol. 20.
Library of the Smithsonian Institution. 537p.
Includes mounds in Tennessee; prehistoric man in Alabama; etc.
d. Report of the Bureau of Ethnology.
Smithsonian Institution. 131p.
Mortuary customs of the American Indians.
e. Report of the Bureau of Ethnology.
Smithsonian Institution. 76p.
Sign language among the American Indians.
f. Report of the Bureau of Ethnology.
Smithsonian Institution. 329p.
Gesture signs and signals of American Indians.
g. Report of the Bureau of Ethnology.
Smithsonian Institution. 239p.
Introduction to the study of Indian languages.
h. Instruction Book.
Published by the BIA. 231p.
To Indian agents.
i. Report on Indian Affairs.
Published by the BIA. 385p.
j. Bulletins.
Published by the Bureau of Education.
Includes Indian schools at Carlisle Barracks.

1881

a. Contributions to North American Ethnology. L. Morgan.
Vol. 4. 281p.
Houses and house life of American aborigines.

b. Report of the Bureau of Ethnology. J. Powell.
Published by the Smithsonian Institution.
For the year 1879-1880.

c. Report of the Bureau of Ethnology, 1879-1880. J. Powell.
Library of the Smithsonian Institution. 638p.
Includes mythology of American Indians; Wyandot government; cessions of land by Indian tribes to the U.S.; sign language of American Indians; etc.

d. Report on Indian Affairs.
Published by the BIA. 204p.

e. Biennial Register. Sec. of the Interior.
Compiled by order of Congress. Vol. 1, 876p.; Vol. 2, 892p.
Register of all civil and military agents in the service of the U.S.

APPENDIX II: THE AMERICAN STATE PAPERS ON INDIAN AFFAIRS

The American State Papers on Indian Affairs consist of documents selected from papers of the 1st through the 19th Congresses (1789-1827) and published in two volumes by Gales and Seaton. These documents are arranged chronologically and are numbered sequentially (hereafter referred to as the *ASPIA* numbers). During the period from 1817 to 1827 there was some overlap in the publication of the ASPIA and the Congressional Set. To a great extent the documents on Indian affairs in both collections are the same, however many documents published in the ASPIA were not included in the Serial Set.

Appendix II is composed of two lists which are arranged sequentially by ASPIA numbers. The first indicates documents published in both the ASPIA and the Serial Set while the second lists documents published only in the ASPIA. Those entries not printed in the Serial Set are not indexed in the Subject Index.

It should be noted that other documents relating to Indian affairs were published in other classes of the American State Papers; however, no attempt has been made to compare the contents of these other classes (e.g., Military Affairs and Public Lands) with the Listing of Documents from the Serial Set.

A. Congressional Documents Printed in Both *American State Papers: Indian Affairs* and in the U.S. Serial Set

ASPIA Document Number	Reference Number in Chronological Section	ASPIA Document Number	Reference Number in Chronological Section
151	1818:6	156	1818:23
153	1818:17	157	1818:27
154	1818:18	158	1819:7

ASPIA Document Number	Reference Number in Chronological Section
159	1819:8
162	1820:6
163	1820:13
164	1820:22
165	1820:29
166	1820:31
167	1820:30
168	1820:40
169	1820:39
170	1820:44
173	1821:9
177	1822:3
178	1822:4
179	1822:6
180	1822:10
182	1822:21
183	1822:19
184	1822:25
185	1822:27
186	1822:24
187	1822:10
188	1822:33
189	1822:44
190	1823:2
194	1823:17
195	1823:18
196	1823:19
199	1824:8
203	1824:22
204	1824:24
205	1824:26
206	1824:27
207	1824:29
208	1824:31
209	1824:32
211	1824:35
212	1824:36
213	1824:37
215	1825:5
217	1825:8
218	1825:12
220	1825:20
221	1825:22
223	1825:26
225	1825:29
229	1826:12
230	1826:15
231	1826:13
232	1826:25
233	1826:27
234	1826:32
237	1826:39
238	1826:42
239	1826:47
240	1826:50
241	1826:53
242	1826:54
244	1826:62
245	1827:1
246	1827:4
247	1827:6
248	1827:10
249	1827:5

B. Congressional Documents Printed in *American State Papers: Indian Affairs* But *Not* Printed in the U.S. Serial Set

ASPIA Document Number	
149	Pres. transmits treaties. 10 Dec. 1817. 15th C., 1st sess.
150	Report on amendments to treaties. 29 Dec. 1817. 15th C., 1st sess.
152	Pres. on Creek treaty. 6 Mar. 1818. 15th C., 1st sess.
155	Pres. transmits treaties. 30 Nov. 1818. 15th C., 2nd sess.
160	Pres. on Cherokee treaty. 2 Mar. 1819. 15th C., 2nd sess.
161	Pres. on Chippewa and Kickapoo treaties. 4 Jan. 1820. 16th C., 1st sess.
171	Pres. on treaties with several tribes. 14 Dec. 1820. 16th C., 2nd sess.
175	Pres. on Georgia claims. 10 Feb. 1821. 16th C., 2nd sess.
176	Pres. on Chicago treaty. 24 Dec. 1821. 17th C., 1st sess.
181	Mem. on Indian civilization. 28 Jan. 1822. 17th C., 1st sess.
191	Pres. on treaties with Osage and Sac and Fox. 6 Jan. 1823. 17th C., 2nd sess.
192	Pres. on Choctaw treaty. 6 Feb. 1823. 17th C., 2nd sess.

ASPIA Document Number	
193	Extinguishment of Indian title. 13 Feb. 1823. 17th C., 2nd sess.
197	Expenditures of Indian Dept. 2 Dec. 1823. 18th C., 1st sess.
198	Pres. on treaty with Florida Indians. 15 Dec. 1823. 18th C., 1st sess.
200	Disbursements of Indian Dept. 23 Feb. 1824. 18th C., 1st sess.
210	Pres. transmits treaty with Cherokees. 30 Apr. 1824. 18th C., 1st sess.
216	Treaty with Quapaws. 19 Jan. 1825. 18th C., 2nd sess.
219	Treaty with Choctaws. 27 Jan. 1825. 18th C., 2nd sess.
222	Treaty with Creeks. 28 Feb. 1825. 18th C., 2nd sess.
224	Treaties with Osage, Kanzas, and Shawnees. 14 Dec. 1825. 19th C., 1st sess.
226	Pres. transmits treaties with Sioux et al. 11 Jan. 1826. 19th C., 1st sess.
227	Pres. transmits treaties with Osage et al. 30 Jan. 1826. 19th C., 1st sess.
228	Pres. transmits treaties with Creeks. 31 Jan. 1826. 19th C., 1st sess.
235	Com. on Indian Affairs–Creek treaty. 17 Mar. 1826. 19th C., 1st sess.
236	Pres. transmits supplemental article to Creek treaty. 31 Mar. 1826. 19th C., 1st sess.
243	Pres. transmits treaties with Chippewas et al. 12 Dec. 1826. 19th C., 2nd sess.

APPENDIX III: RECORDS OF THE WAR OF THE REBELLION

Beginning in 1882, and continuing through 1899, documents of both the Confederate and Union Armies from the Civil War period were printed in the Serial Set. Issued in two series with a total of 61 volumes (119 separately-bound parts), these records contain numerous references to military operations in Indian country, to treaties made with Indian tribes and to other events important for the study of Indian affairs.

Appendix III lists all the volumes published in the two Rebellion Records series, together with their Congressional document numbers, designation of the Congress and session of each volume and Serial Set numbers. No attempt has been made to abstract the contents of these volumes nor to incorporate them in the *Guide*, since a comprehensive index to these volumes was published as House Document 558, 56th Congress, 2nd session, volume 135, Serial Set volume number 4209.

Rebellion Record Series	Volume	Congressional Document No.	Congress-Session	Serial Set No.
1	1	HMD 40	52-2	3112
1	2	HMD 41	52-2	3113
1	3	HMD 42	52-2	3114
1	4	HMD 43	52-2	3115
1	5	HMD 54	47-1	2053
1	6	HMD 63	47-1	2058
1	7	HMD 67	47-1	2063
1	8	HMD 27	47-2	2122
1	9	HMD 41	47-2	2128
1	10 pt. 1	HMD 26	48-1	2225

Rebellion Record Series	Volume	Congressional Document No.	Congress-Session	Serial Set No.
1	10 pt. 2	HMD 32	48-1	2229
1	11 pt. 1	HMD 65 pt. 1	48-1	2240
1	11 pt. 2	HMD 65 pt. 2	48-1	2241
1	11 pt. 3	HMD 65 pt. 3	48-1	2242
1	12 pt. 1	HMD 37 pt. 1	48-2	2322
1	12 pt. 2	HMD 37 pt. 2	48-2	2323
1	12 pt. 2 (suppl.)	HMD 54	49-2	2490
1	12 pt. 3	HMD 37 pt. 3	48-2	2324
1	13	HMD 21	49-1	2408
1	14	HMD 22	49-1	2409
1	15	HMD 164	49-1	2416
1	16 pt. 1	HMD 273	49-1	2419
1	16 pt. 2	HMD 338	49-1	2421
1	17 pt. 1	HMD 371	49-1	2425
1	17 pt. 2	HMD 53	49-2	2489
1	18	HMD 325	50-1	2571
1	19 pt. 1	HMD 338	50-1	2572
1	19 pt. 2	HMD 339	50-1	2573
1	20 pt. 1	HMD 341	50-1	2574
1	20 pt. 2	HMD 342	50-1	2575
1	21	HMD 387	50-1	2577
1	22 pt. 1	HMD 585	50-1	2580
1	22 pt. 2	HMD 60	50-2	2656
1	23 pt. 1	HMD 113	50-2	2659
1	23 pt. 2	HMD 129	50-2	2660
1	24 pt. 1	HMD 4	51-1	2761
1	24 pt. 2	HMD 5	51-1	2762
1	24 pt. 3	HMD 6	51-1	2763
1	25 pt. 1	HMD 44	51-1	2766
1	25 pt. 2	HMD 45	51-1	2767
1	26 pt. 1	HMD 105	51-1	2769
1	26 pt. 2	HMD 106	51-1	2770
1	27 pt. 1	HMD 146	51-1	2771
1	27 pt. 2	HMD 147	51-1	2772
1	27 pt. 3	HMD 148	51-1	2773
1	28 pt. 1	HMD 223	51-1	2778
1	28 pt. 2	HMD 228	51-1	2781
1	29 pt. 1	HMD 240	51-1	2789
1	29 pt. 2	HMD 241	51-1	2790
1	30 pt. 1	HMD 245	51-1	2792
1	30 pt. 2	HMD 246	51-1	2793
1	30 pt. 3	HMD 247	51-1	2794
1	30 pt. 4	HMD 248	51-1	2795
1	31 pt. 1	HMD 12	51-2	2870
1	31 pt. 2	HMD 13	51-2	2871
1	31 pt. 3	HMD 14	51-2	2872
1	32 pt. 1	HMD 76	51-2	2873
1	32 pt. 2	HMD 77	51-2	2874
1	32 pt. 3	HMD 78	51-2	2875
1	33	HMD 12	52-1	2961
1	34 pt. 1	HMD 13 pt. 1	52-1	2962
1	34 pt. 2	HMD 13 pt. 2	52-1	2963
1	34 pt. 3	HMD 13 pt. 3	52-1	2964
1	34 pt. 4	HMD 13 pt. 4	52-1	2965

Rebellion Record Series	Volume	Congressional Document No.	Congress-Session	Serial Set No.
1	35 pt. 1	HMD 14 pt. 1	52-1	2966
1	35 pt. 2	HMD 14 pt. 2	52-1	2967
1	36 pt. 1	HMD 15 pt. 1	52-1	2968
1	36 pt. 2	HMD 15 pt. 2	52-1	2969
1	36 pt. 3	HMD 15 pt. 3	52-1	2970
1	37 pt. 1	HMD 16 pt. 1	52-1	2971
1	37 pt. 2	HMD 16 pt. 2	52-1	2972
1	38 pt. 1	HMD 48 pt. 1	52-1	2980
1	38 pt. 2	HMD 48 pt. 2	52-1	2981
1	38 pt. 3	HMD 48 pt. 3	52-1	2982
1	38 pt. 4	HMD 48 pt. 4	52-1	2983
1	38 pt. 5	HMD 48 pt. 5	52-1	2984
1	39 pt. 1	HMD 233 pt. 1	52-1	2993
1	39 pt. 2	HMD 233 pt. 2	52-1	2994
1	39 pt. 3	HMD 233 pt. 3	52-1	2995
1	40 pt. 1	HMD 338 pt. 1	52-1	3004
1	40 pt. 2	HMD 338 pt. 2	52-1	3005
1	40 pt. 3	HMD 338 pt. 3	52-1	3006
1	41 pt. 1	HMD 96 pt. 1	52-2	3119
1	41 pt. 2	HMD 96 pt. 2	52-2	3120
1	41 pt. 3	HMD 96 pt. 3	52-2	3121
1	41 pt. 4	HMD 96 pt. 4	52-2	3122
1	42 pt. 1	HMD 9 pt. 1	53-1	3152
1	42 pt. 2	HMD 9 pt. 2	53-1	3153
1	42 pt. 3	HMD 9 pt. 3	53-1	3154
1	43 pt. 1	HMD 55 pt. 1	53-2	3235
1	43 pt. 2	HMD 55 pt. 2	53-2	3236
1	44	HMD 97	53-2	3240
1	45 pt. 1	HMD 121 pt. 1	53-2	3244
1	45 pt. 2	HMD 121 pt. 2	53-2	3245
1	46 pt. 1	HMD 208 pt. 1	53-2	3261
1	46 pt. 2	HMD 208 pt. 2	53-2	3262
1	46 pt. 3	HMD 208 pt. 3	53-2	3263
1	47 pt. 1	HD 37 pt. 1	54-1	3409
1	47 pt. 2	HD 37 pt. 2	54-1	3410
1	47 pt. 3	HD 37 pt. 3	54-1	3411
1	48 pt. 1	HD 369 pt. 1	54-1	3436
1	48 pt. 2	HD 369 pt. 2	54-1	3437
1	49 pt. 1	HD 251 pt. 1	54-2	3532
1	49 pt. 2	HD 251 pt. 2	54-2	3533
1	50 pt. 1	HD 59 pt. 1	55-1	3583
1	50 pt. 2	HD 59 pt. 2	55-1	3584
1	51 pt. 1	HD 95 pt. 1	55-1	3585
1	51 pt. 2	HD 95 pt. 2	55-1	3586
1	52 pt. 1	HD 288 pt. 1	55-2	3684
1	52 pt. 2	HD 288 pt. 2	55-2	3685
1	53	HD 476	55-2	3686
2	1	HD 65	55-3	3787
2	2	HD 66	55-3	3788
2	3	HD 67	55-3	3789
2	4	HD 284	55-3	3790
2	5	HD 311	55-3	3791
2	6	HD 312	55-3	3792
2	7	HD 313	55-3	3793
2	8	HD 314	55-3	3794

Subject Index

A

B

C

D

E

G

H

I

J

K

L

M

N

O

P

Q

R

S

T

U

V

W

Y